Contents

Terms and Conditions

This document is prepared strictly for the confidential use of our customer(s). It has been provided to you at your specific request. It is not directed to, or intended for distribution to or use by, any person or entity who is a citizen or resident of or located in any locality, state, country or other jurisdiction where such distribution, publication, availability or use would be contrary to law or regulation or which would subject Weiss Ratings or its affiliates to any registration or licensing requirement within such jurisdiction.

No part of the analysts' compensation was, is, or will be, directly or indirectly, related to the specific recommendations or views expressed in this research report.

This document is not intended for the direct or indirect solicitation of business. Weiss Ratings, LLC and its affiliates disclaims any and all liability to any person or entity for any loss or damage caused, in whole or in part, by any error (negligent or otherwise) or other circumstances involved in, resulting from or relating to the procurement, compilation, analysis, interpretation, editing, transcribing, publishing and/or dissemination or transmittal of any information contained herein.

Weiss Ratings has not taken any steps to ensure that the securities or investment vehicle referred to in this report are suitable for any particular investor. The investment or services contained or referred to in this report may not be suitable for you and it is recommended that you consult an independent investment advisor if you are in doubt about such investments or investment services. Nothing in this report constitutes investment, legal, accounting or tax advice or a representation that any investment or strategy is suitable or appropriate to your individual circumstances or otherwise constitutes a personal recommendation to you.

The ratings and other opinions contained in this document must be construed solely as statements of opinion from Weiss Ratings, LLC., and not statements of fact. Each rating or opinion must be weighed solely as a factor in your choice of an institution and should not be construed as a recommendation to buy, sell or otherwise act with respect to the particular product or company involved.

Past performance should not be taken as an indication or guarantee of future performance, and no representation or warranty, expressed or implied, is made regarding future performance. Information, opinions and estimates contained in this report reflect a judgment at its original date of publication and are subject to change without notice. Weiss Ratings offers a notification service for rating changes on companies you specify. For more information visit WeissRatings.com or call 1-877-934-7778. The price, value and income from any of the securities or financial instruments mentioned in this report can fall as well as rise.

Date of Data Analyzed: June 30, 2021

Data Source: Call Report data provided by SNL Financial.

Welcome to Weiss Ratings'
Guide to Banks

Most people automatically assume their bank will survive, year after year. However, prudent consumers and professionals realize that in this world of shifting risks, the solvency of financial institutions can't be taken for granted. After all, your bank's failure could have a heavy impact on you in terms of lost time, lost money (in cases of deposits exceeding the federal insurance limit), tied-up deposits, lost credit lines, and the possibility of being shifted to another institution under not-so-friendly terms.

If you are looking for accurate, unbiased ratings and data to help you choose a commercial bank, savings bank, or savings and loan for yourself, your family, your company or your clients, Weiss Ratings' Guide to Banks gives you precisely what you need.

Weiss Ratings' Mission Statement

Weiss Ratings' mission is to empower consumers, professionals, and institutions with high quality advisory information for selecting or monitoring a financial services company or financial investment.

In doing so, Weiss Ratings will adhere to the highest ethical standards by maintaining our independent, unbiased outlook and approach to advising our customers.

Why rely on Weiss Ratings?

Weiss Ratings provides fair, objective ratings to help professionals and consumers alike make educated financial decisions.

At Weiss Ratings, integrity is number one. Weiss Ratings never takes a penny from rated companies for issuing its ratings. And, we publish Weiss Safety Ratings without regard for institutions' preferences. Our analysts review and update Weiss ratings each and every quarter, so you can be sure that the information you receive is accurate and current – providing you with advance warning of financial vulnerability early enough to do something about it.

Other rating agencies focus primarily on a company's current financial solvency and consider only mild economic adversity. Weiss Ratings also considers these issues, but in addition, our analysis covers a company's ability to deal with severe economic adversity in terms of a sharp decline in the value of its investments and a drop in the collectability of its loans.

Our use of more rigorous standards stems from the viewpoint that a financial institution's obligations to its customers should not depend on favorable business conditions. A bank must be able to honor its loan and deposit commitments in bad times as well as good.

Weiss's rating scale, from A to F, is easy to understand. Only a few outstanding companies receive an A (Excellent) rating, although there are many to choose from within the B (Good) category. A large group falls into the broad average range which receives C (Fair) ratings. Companies that demonstrate marked vulnerabilities receive either D (Weak) or E (Very Weak) ratings. So, there's no numbering system, star counting, or color-coding to keep track of.

Weiss Ratings' Guide to Banks

A Quarterly Compilation of Financial Institutions Ratings and Analyses

Winter 2021-22

GREY HOUSE PUBLISHING

Weiss Ratings
4400 Northcorp Parkway
Palm Beach Gardens, FL 33410
561-627-3300

weiss ratings

Published by Grey House Publishing, Inc., located at 4919 Route 22, Amenia, NY 12501; telephone 518-789-8700. Grey House Publishing neither guarantees the accuracy of the data contained herein nor assumes any responsibility for errors, omissions or discrepancies. Grey House Publishing accepts no payment for listing; inclusion in the publication of any organization, agency, institution, publication, service or individual does not imply endorsement of the publisher.

Grey House Publishing
4919 Route 22
PO Box 56
Amenia, NY 12501-0056

Edition No. 124, Winter 2021-22

ISBN: 978-1-63700-168-4
ISSN: 2158-5962

How to Use This Guide

The purpose of the *Guide to Banks* is to provide consumers, businesses, financial institutions, and municipalities with a reliable source of banking industry ratings and analysis on a timely basis. We realize that the financial safety of a bank is an important factor to consider when establishing a relationship. The ratings and analysis in this Guide can make that evaluation easier when you are considering:

- A checking, merchant banking, or other transaction account
- An investment in a certificate of deposit or savings account
- A line of credit or commercial loan
- Counterparty risk

The rating for a particular company indicates our opinion regarding that company's ability to meet its obligations – not only under current economic conditions, but also during a declining economy or in an environment of increased liquidity demands.

To use this Guide most effectively, we recommend you follow the steps outlined below:

Step 1 To ensure you evaluate the correct company, verify the company's exact name as it was given to you. It is also helpful to ascertain the city and state of the company's main office or headquarters since no two banks with the same name can be headquartered in the same city. Many companies have similar names but are not related to one another, so you will want to make sure the company you look up is really the one you are interested in evaluating.

Step 2 Turn to Section I, the Index of Banks, and locate the company you are evaluating. This section contains all federally-insured commercial banks and savings banks. It is sorted alphabetically by the name of the company and shows the main office city and state following the name for additional verification.
If you have trouble finding a particular institution or determining which is the right one, consider these possible reasons:

- You may have an incorrect or incomplete institution name. There are often several institutions with the same or very similar names. So, make sure you have the exact name and proper spelling, as well as the city in which it is headquartered.
- You may be looking for a *bank holding company*. If so, try to find the exact name of the main bank in the group and look it up under that name.

Step 3 Once you have located your specific company, the first column after the state shows its current Weiss Safety Rating. Turn to *About Weiss Safety Ratings* for information about what this rating means. If the rating has changed since the last edition of this Guide, a downgrade will be indicated with a down triangle ▼ to the left of the company name; an upgrade will be indicated with an up triangle ▲.

Step 4 Following the current Weiss Safety Rating are two prior ratings for the company based on year-end data from the two previous years. Use this to discern the longer-term direction of the company's overall financial condition.

Step 5 The remainder of Section I; provides insight into the areas our analysts reviewed as the basis for assigning the company's rating. These areas include size, capital adequacy, asset quality, profitability, liquidity, and stability. An index within each of these categories represents a composite evaluation of that particular facet of the company's financial condition. Refer to the Critical Ranges In Our Indexes table for an interpretation of which index values are considered strong, good, fair, or weak. In most cases, lower-rated companies will have a low index value in one or more of the indexes shown. Bear in mind, however, that Weiss Safety Rating is the result of a complex qualitative and quantitative analysis which cannot be reproduced using only the data provided here.

Step 6 If the company you are evaluating is not highly rated and you want to find a bank with a higher rating, turn to the page in Section II that has your state's name at the top. This section contains Weiss Recommended Banks by State (rating of A+, A, A- or B+) that have a branch office in your state. If the main office telephone number provided is not a local telephone call or to determine if a branch of the bank is near you, consult your local telephone Yellow Pages Directory under "Banks," "Savings Banks," or "Savings and Loan Associations." Here you will find a complete list of the institution's branch locations along with their telephone numbers.

Step 7 Once you've identified a Weiss Recommended Company in your local area, you can then refer back to Section I to analyze it.

Step 8 In order to use Weiss Safety Ratings most effectively, we strongly recommend you consult the *Important Warnings and Cautions* listed. These are more than just "standard disclaimers." They are very important factors you should be aware of before using this Guide. If you have any questions regarding the precise meaning of specific terms used in the Guide, refer to the Glossary.

Step 9 Make sure you stay up to date with the latest information available since the publication of this Guide. For information on how to set up a rating change notification service, acquire follow-up reports, check ratings online or receive a more in-depth analysis of an individual company, call 1-877-934-7778 or visit www.weissratings.com.

About Weiss Safety Ratings

The Weiss Ratings are calculated based on a complex analysis of hundreds of factors that are synthesized into five indexes: capitalization, asset quality, profitability, liquidity and stability. Each index is then used to arrive at a letter grade rating. A weak score on any one index can result in a low rating, as financial problems can be caused by any one of a number of factors, such as inadequate capital, non-performing loans and poor asset quality, operating losses, poor liquidity, or the failure of an affiliated company.

Our **Capitalization Index** gauges the institution's capital adequacy in terms of its cushion to absorb future operating losses under adverse business and economic scenarios that may impact the company's net interest margin, securities' values, and the collectability of its loans.

Our **Asset Quality Index** measures the quality of the company's past underwriting and investment practices based on the estimated liquidation value of the company's loan and securities portfolios.

Our **Profitability Index** measures the soundness of the company's operations and the contribution of profits to the company's financial strength. The index is a composite of five sub-factors: 1) gain or loss on operations; 2) rates of return on assets and equity; 3) management of net interest margin; 4) generation of noninterest-based revenues; and 5) overhead expense management.

Our **Liquidity Index** evaluates a company's ability to raise the necessary cash to satisfy creditors and honor depositor withdrawals.

Finally, our **Stability Index** integrates a number of sub-factors that affect consistency (or lack thereof) in maintaining financial strength over time. These include 1) risk diversification in terms of company size and loan diversification; 2) deterioration of operations as reported in critical asset, liability, income and expense items, such as an increase in loan delinquency rates or a sharp increase in loan originations; 3) years in operation; 4) former problem areas where, despite recent improvement, the company has yet to establish a record of stable performance over a suitable period of time; and 5) relationships with holding companies and affiliates.

In order to help guarantee our objectivity, we reserve the right to publish ratings expressing our opinion of a company's financial stability based exclusively on publicly available data and our own proprietary standards for safety.

Each of these indexes is measured according to the following range of values.

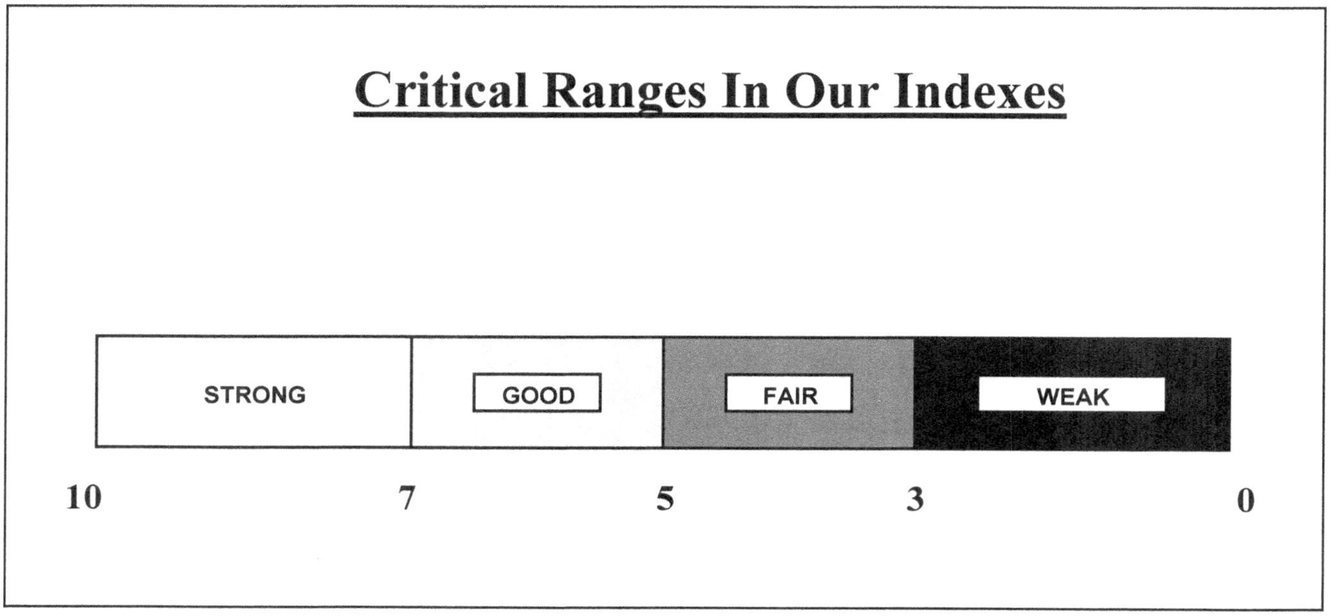

Finally, the indexes are combined to form a composite company rating which is then verified by one of our analysts. The resulting distribution of ratings assigned to all banks looks like this:

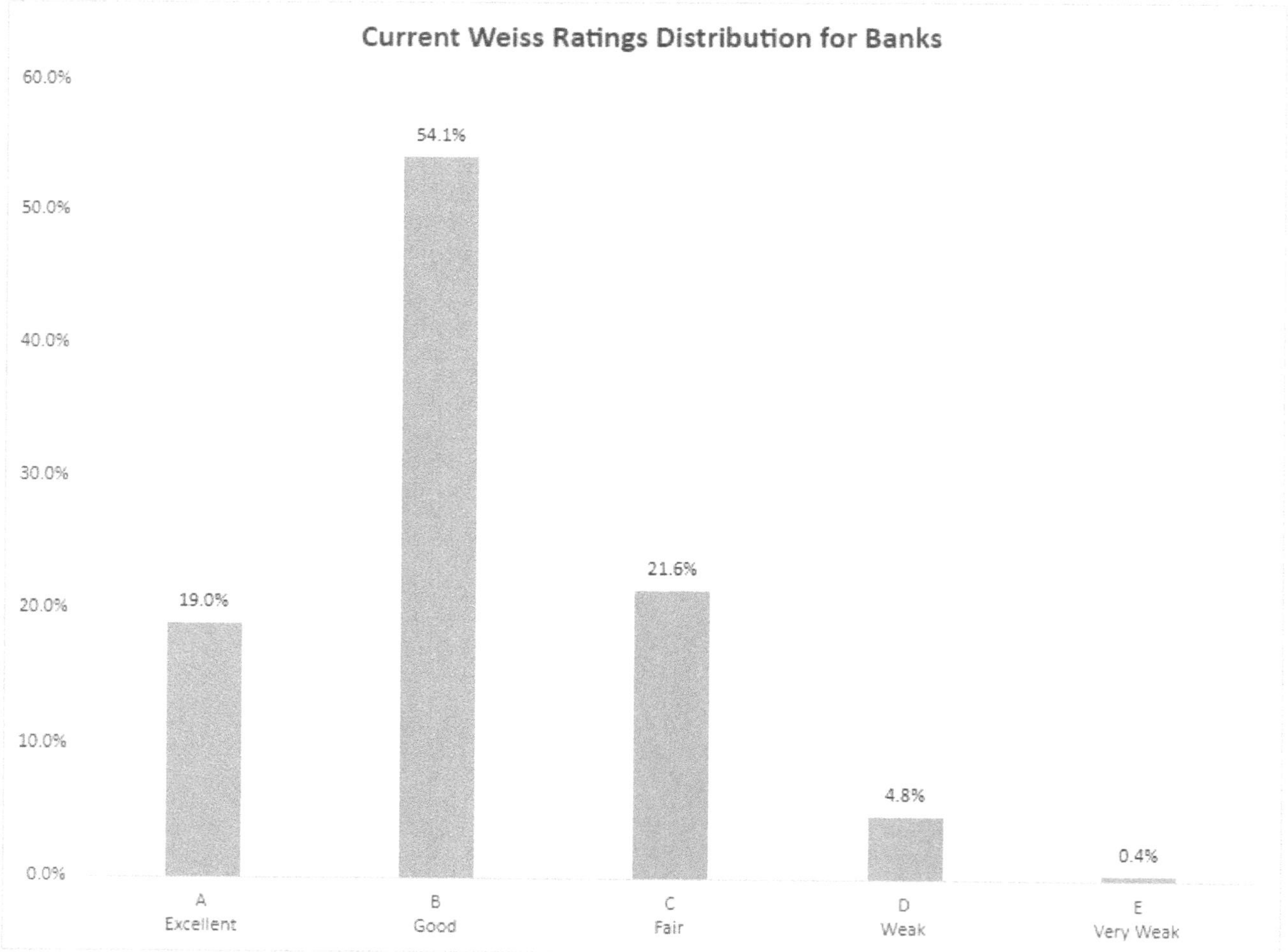

What Our Ratings Mean

A **Excellent.** The institution offers excellent financial security. It has maintained a conservative stance in its business operations and underwriting practices as evidenced by its strong equity base, high asset quality, steady earnings, and high liquidity. While the financial position of any company is subject to change, we believe that this institution has the resources necessary to deal with severe economic conditions.

B **Good.** The institution offers good financial security and has the resources to deal with a variety of adverse economic conditions. It comfortably exceeds the minimum levels for all of our rating criteria, and is likely to remain healthy for the near future. Nevertheless, in the event of a severe recession or major financial crisis, we feel that this assessment should be reviewed to make sure that the company is still maintaining adequate financial strength.

C **Fair.** The institution offers fair financial security, is currently stable, and will likely remain relatively healthy as long as the economic environment remains relatively stable. In the event of a severe recession or major financial crisis, however, we feel this company may encounter difficulties in maintaining its financial stability.

D **Weak.** The institution currently demonstrates what, in our opinion, we consider to be significant weaknesses which could negatively impact depositors or creditors. In the event of a severe recession or major financial crisis, these weaknesses could be magnified.

E **Very Weak.** The institution currently demonstrates what we consider to be significant weaknesses and has also failed some of the basic tests that we use to identify fiscal stability. Therefore, even in a favorable economic environment, it is our opinion that depositors or creditors could incur significant risks.

F **Failed.** The institution has been placed under the custodianship of regulatory authorities. This implies that it will be either liquidated or taken over by another financial institution.

\+ The **plus sign** is an indication that the institution is in the upper third of the letter grade.

\- The **minus sign** is an indication that the institution is in the lower third of the letter grade.

U **Unrated.** The institution is unrated due to the absence of sufficient data for our ratings.

Peer Comparison of Bank Safety Ratings

Weiss Ratings	Veribanc	Bauer Financial	IDC Financial	Bankrate.com	Lace Financial
A+, A, A-	Green, Three Stars w/ Blue Ribbon recognition	5 stars, 4 stars	201-300	1, Five stars	A+, A
B+, B, B-	Green, Three Stars w/out Blue Ribbon recognition	3 ½ stars	166-200	2, Four stars	B+
C+, C, C-	Green Two Stars, Yellow Two Stars	3 stars	126-165	3, Three stars	B, C+
D+, D, D-	Green one star, Yellow one star, Green no stars	2 stars	76-125	4, Two stars	C, D
E+, E, E-	Yellow no stars, Red no stars	1 star	1-75	5, One star	E

Important Warnings and Cautions

1. **A rating alone cannot tell the whole story.** Please read the explanatory information contained here, in the section introductions and in the appendix. It is provided in order to give you an understanding of our rating philosophy as well as to paint a more complete picture of how we arrive at our opinion of a company's strengths and weaknesses. In addition, please remember that our safety rating is not an end-all measure of an institution's safety. Rather, it should be used as a "flag" of possible troubles, suggesting a need for further research.

2. **Safety ratings shown in this directory were current as of the publication date.** In the meantime, the rating may have been updated based on more recent data. Weiss Ratings offers a notification service for ratings changes on companies that you specifiy. For more information call 1-877-934-7778 or visit www.weissratings.com.

3. **When deciding to do business with a financial institution, your decision should be based on a wide variety of factors in addition to Weiss Safety Rating**. These include the institution's pricing of its deposit instruments and loans, the fees you will be charged, the degree to which it can help you meet your long-term planning needs, how these costs/benefits may change over the years, and what other choices are available to you given your current location and financial circumstances.

4. **Weiss Safety Ratings represent our opinion of a company's insolvency risk.** As such, a high rating means we feel that the company has less chance of running into financial difficulties. A high rating is not a guarantee of solvency nor is a low rating a prediction of insolvency. Weiss Safety Ratings are not deemed to be a recommendation concerning the purchase or sale of the securities of any bank that is publicly owned.

5. **All firms that have the same Weiss Safety Rating should be considered to be essentially equal in safety.** This is true regardless of any differences in the underlying numbers which might appear to indicate greater strengths. Weiss Safety Rating already takes into account a number of lesser factors which, due to space limitations, cannot be included in this publication.

6. **A good rating requires consistency.** If a company is excellent on four indicators and fair on one, the company may receive a fair rating. This requirement is necessary due to the fact that fiscal problems can arise from any *one* of several causes including poor underwriting, inadequate capital resources, or operating losses.

7. **Our rating standards are more conservative than those used by other agencies.** We believe that no one can predict with certainty the economic environment of the near or long-term future. Rather, we assume that various scenarios – from the extremes of double-digit inflation to a severe recession – are within the range of reasonable possibilities over the next one or two decades. To achieve a top rating according to our standards, a company must be adequately prepared for the worst-case reasonable scenario, without impairing its current operations.

8. **We are an independent rating agency and do not depend on the cooperation of the companies we rate**. Our data are derived, from quarterly financial statements filed with federal regulators. Although we seek to maintain an open line of communication with the companies being rated, we do not grant them the right to influence the ratings or stop their publication. This policy stems from the fact that this Guide is designed for the protection of our customers.

9. **Inaccuracies in the data issued by the federal regulators could negatively impact the quality of a company's Safety Rating.** While we attempt to find and correct as many data errors as possible, some data errors inevitably slip through. We have no method of intercepting fraudulent or falsified data and must take for granted that all information is reported honestly to the federal regulatory agencies.

10. **Institutions that operate exclusively or primarily as a trust company may have skewed financial information.** Due to the nature of their business, these companies often record high profit levels compared to other more "traditional" banks. Trust companies can usually be recognized by the initials "TC" or "& TC" in their names.

11. **This Guide does not cover nonbank affiliates of banking companies.** Although some nonbank companies may be affiliated with the banks cited in this Guide, the firms are separate corporations whose financial strength is only partially dependent on the strength of their affiliates.

12. **There are many companies with the same or similar sounding names, despite no affiliation whatsoever.** Therefore, it is important that you have the exact name, city, and state of the institution's headquarters before you begin to research the company in this Guide.

13. **Affiliated companies do not automatically receive the same rating.** We recognize that a troubled institution may expect financial support from its parent or affiliates. Weiss Safety Ratings reflect our opinion of the measure of support that may become available to a subsidiary bank, if the subsidiary were to experience serious financial difficulties. In the case of a strong parent and a weaker subsidiary, the affiliate relationship will generally result in a higher rating for the subsidiary than it would have on a stand-alone basis. Seldom, however, would the rating be brought up to the level of the parent.

    This treatment is appropriate because we do not assume the parent would have either the resources or the will to "bail out" a troubled subsidiary during a severe economic crisis. Even when there is a binding legal obligation for a parent corporation to honor the obligations of its subsidiary banks, the possibility exists that the subsidiary could be sold and lose its parental support. Therefore, it is quite common for one affiliate to have a higher rating than another. This is another reason why it is especially important that you have the precise name of the company you are evaluating.

14. **This publication does not include foreign banking companies, or their U.S. branches.** Therefore, our evaluation of foreign banking companies is limited to those U.S. chartered domestic banks owned by foreign banking companies. In most cases, the U.S. operations of a foreign banking company are relatively small in relation to the overall size of the company, so you may want to consult other sources as well. In any case, do not be confused by a domestic bank with a name which is the same as – or similar to – that of a foreign banking company. Even if there is an affiliation between the two, we have evaluated the U.S. institution based on its own merits.

Section I

Index of Banks

An analysis of all rated

U.S. Commercial Banks and Savings Banks

Institutions are listed in alphabetical order.

Section I Contents

This section contains Weiss Safety Ratings, key rating factors, and summary financial data for all U.S. federally-insured commercial banks and savings banks. Companies are sorted in alphabetical order, first by company name, then by city and state.

<u>*Left Pages*</u>

1. **Institution Name** — The name under which the institution was chartered. If you cannot find the institution you are interested in, or if you have any doubts regarding the precise name, verify the information with the bank itself before proceeding. Also, determine the city and state in which the institution is headquartered for confirmation. (See columns 2 and 3.)

2. **City** — The city in which the institution's headquarters or main office is located. With the adoption of intrastate and interstate branching laws, many institutions operating in your area may actually be headquartered elsewhere. So, don't be surprised if the location cited is not in your particular city.

   Also use this column to confirm that you have located the correct institution. It is possible for two unrelated companies to have the same name if they are headquartered in different cities.

3. **State** — The state in which the institution's headquarters or main office is located. With the adoption of interstate branching laws, some institutions operating in your area may actually be headquartered in another state.

4. **Safety Rating** — Weiss rating assigned to the institution at the time of publication. Our ratings are designed to distinguish levels of insolvency risk and are measured on a scale from A to F based upon a wide range of factors. See *About Weiss Safety Ratings* for specific descriptions of each letter grade.

   Highly rated companies are, in our opinion, less likely to experience financial difficulties than lower rated firms. See *About Weiss Safety Ratings* for more information. Also, please be sure to consider the warnings regarding the ratings' limitations and the underlying assumptions.

5. **Prior Year Safety Rating** — Weiss rating assigned to the institution based on data from December 31 of the previous year. Compare this rating to the company's current rating to identify any recent changes.

6. **Safety Rating Two Years Prior** — Weiss rating assigned to the institution based on data from December 31 two years ago. Compare this rating to the ratings in the prior columns to identify longer term trends in the company's financial condition.

7. Total Assets	The total of all assets listed on the institution's balance sheet, in millions of dollars. This figure primarily consists of loans, investments (such as municipal and treasury bonds), and fixed assets (such as buildings and other real estate). Overall size is an important factor which affects the company's ability to diversify risk and avoid vulnerability to a single borrower, industry, or geographic area. Larger institutions are usually, although not always, more diversified and thus less susceptible to a downturn in a particular area. Nevertheless, do not be misled by the general public perception that "bigger is better." Larger institutions are known for their inability to quickly adapt to changes in the marketplace and typically underperform their smaller brethren.
8. One Year Asset Growth	The percentage change in total assets over the previous 12 months. Moderate growth is generally a positive since it can reflect the maintenance or expansion of the company's market share, leading to the generation of additional revenues. Excessive growth, however, is generally a sign of trouble as it can indicate a loosening of underwriting practices in order to attract new business.
9. Commercial Loans/ Total Assets	The percentage of the institution's asset base invested in loans to businesses. Commercial loans are the traditional bread and butter of commercial banks, although many have increased their business lending in recent years.
10. Consumer Loans/ Total Assets	The percentage of the institution's asset base invested in loans to consumers, primarily credit cards. Consumer lending has grown rapidly in recent years due to the high interest rates and fees institutions are able to charge. On the down side, consumer loans usually experience higher delinquency and default rates than other loans, negatively impacting earnings down the road.
11. Home Mortgage Loans/ Total Assets	The percentage of the institution's asset base invested in residential mortgage loans to consumers, excluding home equity loans. Savings banks have traditionally dominated mortgage lending. This type of loan typically experiences lower default rates. However, the length of the loan's term can be a subject for concern during periods of rising interest rates.

12. Securities/ Total Assets

The percentage of the institution's asset base invested in securities, including U.S. Treasury securities, mortgage-backed securities, and municipal bonds. This does not include securities the institution may be holding on behalf of individual customers.

Although securities are similar to loans in that they represent obligations to pay a debt at some point in the future, they are a more liquid investment than loans and usually present less risk of default. In addition, mortgage-backed securities can present less credit risk than holding mortgage loans themselves due to the diversification of the underlying mortgages.

13. Capitalization Index

An index that measures the adequacy of the institution's capital resources to deal with potentially adverse business and economic situations that could arise. It is based on an evaluation of the company's degree of leverage compared to total assets as well as risk-adjusted assets. See the Critical Ranges In Our Indexes for a description of the different critical levels presented in this index.

14. Leverage Ratio

A regulatory ratio defined by the federal banking regulators as core (tier 1) capital divided by tangible assets. This ratio answers the question: How much does the institution have in stockholders' equity for every dollar of assets? Thus, the Leverage Ratio represents the amount of actual "capital cushion" the institution has to fall back on in times of trouble. We feel that this is the single most important ratio in determining financial strength because it provides the best measure of an institution's ability to withstand losses.

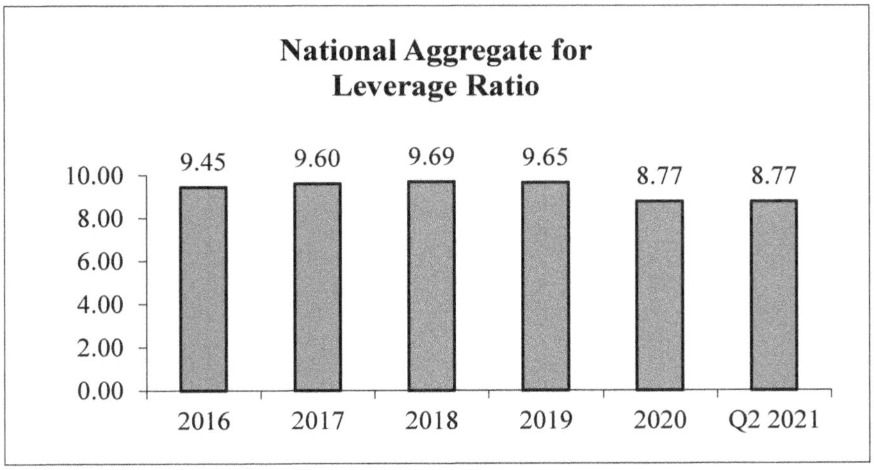

15. Risk-Based Capital Ratio

A regulatory ratio defined by the federal banking regulators as total (tier 1 + tier 2) capital divided by risk-weighted assets. This ratio addresses the issue that not all assets present the same level of credit risk to an institution. As such, all assets and certain off-balance sheet commitments are assigned to risk categories based on the level of credit risk they pose and then weighted accordingly to arrive at risk-weighted assets.

For instance, assets with virtually no risk, such as cash and U.S. Treasury securities, are risk-weighted at 0% and therefore, not included in the calculation. Assets with low risk, for example, high quality mortgage-backed securities and state and municipal bonds, are partially weighted at 20%.

Those assets possessing moderate risk, such as residential mortgages and state and local revenue bonds are partially weighted at 50%. And finally, assets considered to possess "normal" or "high" risk, including certain off-balance sheet commitments such as unfunded loans, are risk-weighted at 100%. The summation of these categories of risk-weighted assets results in the figure used in the denominator of this ratio.

Please be aware that not all banks and savings banks are required to report risk-weighted assets as defined by the federal regulators. Consequently, we have estimated this figure when necessary based on estimates used by the regulators themselves.

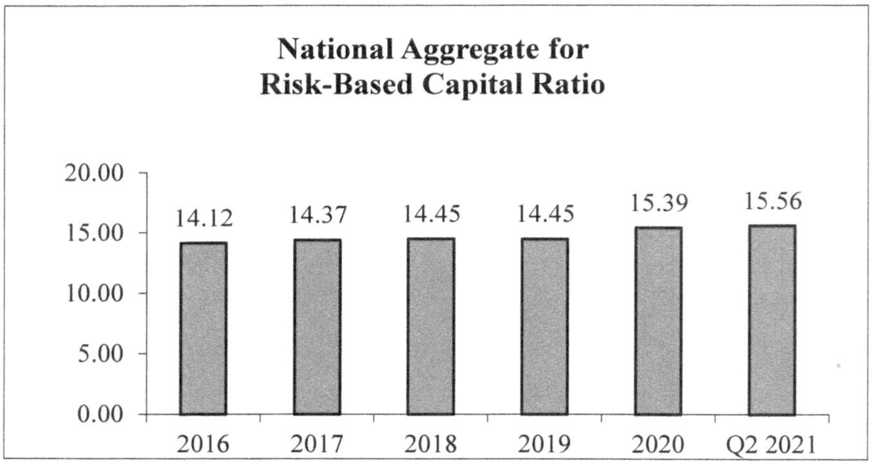

Right Pages

1. **Asset Quality Index** An index that measures the quality of the institution's past underwriting and investment practices, as well as its loss reserve coverage. See the Critical Ranges In Our Indexes for a description of the different critical levels presented in this index.

2. **Adjusted Nonperforming Loans/ Total Loans** The percentage of the institution's loan portfolio which is either past due on its payments by 90 days or more, or no longer accruing interest due to doubtful collectability plus a portion of all restructured loans, less government guaranteed GNMA loans and those loans protected by the FDIC. This ratio is affected primarily by the quality of the institution's underwriting practices and the prosperity of the local economies where it is doing business. While only a portion of these loans will actually end up in default, a high ratio here will have several negative consequences including increased loan loss provisions, increased loan collection expenses, and decreased interest revenues.

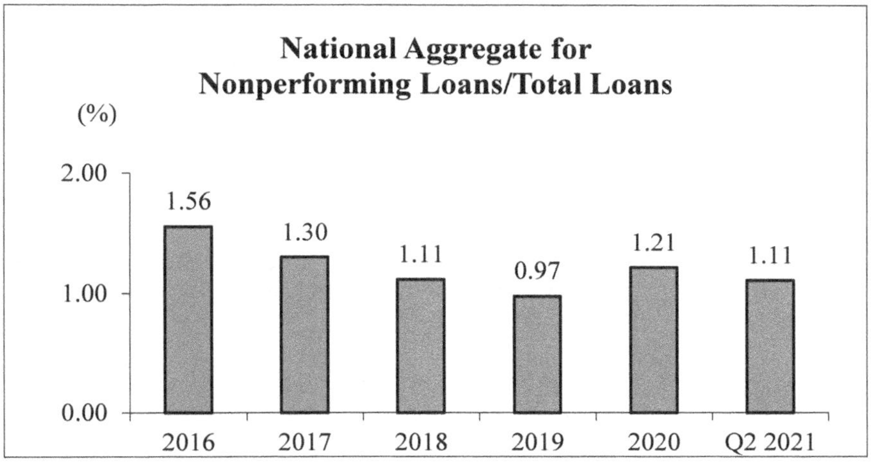

[1]Nonperforming loans were adjusted in 2011 to include a portion of all restructured loans, less government guaranteed GNMA loans and those loans protected by the FDIC.

3. **Adjusted Nonperforming Loans/ Capital**

The percentage of past due 90 days and nonaccruing loans plus a portion of all restructured loans, less government guaranteed GNMA loans and those loans protected by the FDIC to the company's core (tier 1) capital plus reserve for loan losses. This ratio answers the question: If all of the bank's significantly past due and nonaccruing loans were to go into default, how much would that eat into capital? A large percentage of nonperforming loans signal imprudent lending practices which are a direct threat to the equity of the institution.

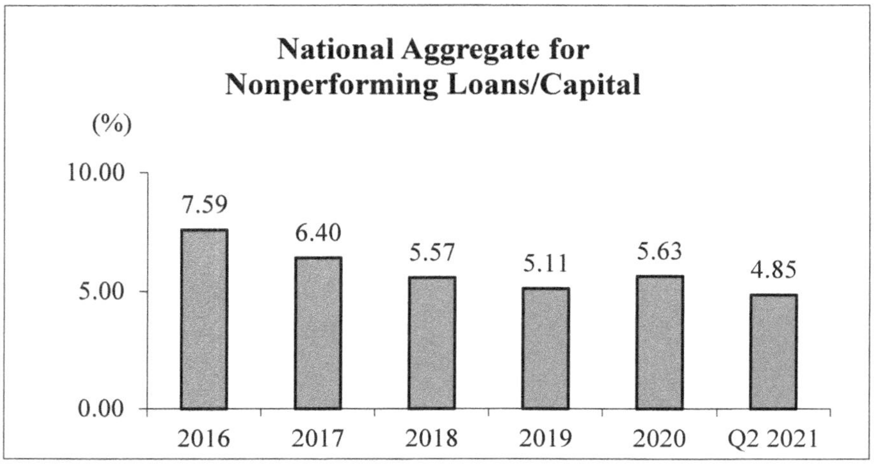

[1] Nonperforming loans were adjusted in 2011 to include a portion of all restructured loans, less government guaranteed GNMA loans and those loans protected by the FDIC.

4. **Net Charge-offs/ Average Loans**

The ratio of foreclosed loans written off the institution's books since the beginning of the year (less previous write-offs that were recovered) as a percentage of average loans for the year. This ratio answers the question: What percentage of the bank's past loans have actually become uncollectible? Past loan charge-off experience is often a very good indication of what can be expected in the future, and high loan charge-off levels are usually an indication of poor underwriting practices.

5. **Profitability Index**

An index that measures the soundness of the institution's operations and the contribution of profits to the company's financial strength. It is based on five sub-factors: 1) gain or loss on operations; 2) rates of return on assets and equity; 3) management of net interest margin; 4) generation of noninterest-based revenues; and 5) overhead expense management. See the Critical Ranges In Our Indexes for a description of the different critical levels presented in this index.

6. **Net Income**

The year-to-date net profit or loss recorded by the institution, in millions of dollars. This figure includes the company's operating profit (income from lending, investing, and fees less interest and overhead expenses) as well as nonoperating items such as capital gains on the sale of securities, income taxes, and extraordinary items.

7. Return on Assets The ratio of net income for the year (year-to-date quarterly figures are converted to a 12-month equivalent) as a percentage of average assets for the year. This ratio, known as ROA, is the most commonly used benchmark for bank profitability since it measures the company's return on investment in a format that is easily comparable with other companies.

Historically speaking, a ratio of 1.0% or greater has been considered good performance. However, this ratio will fluctuate with the prevailing economic times. Also, larger banks tend to have a lower ratio.

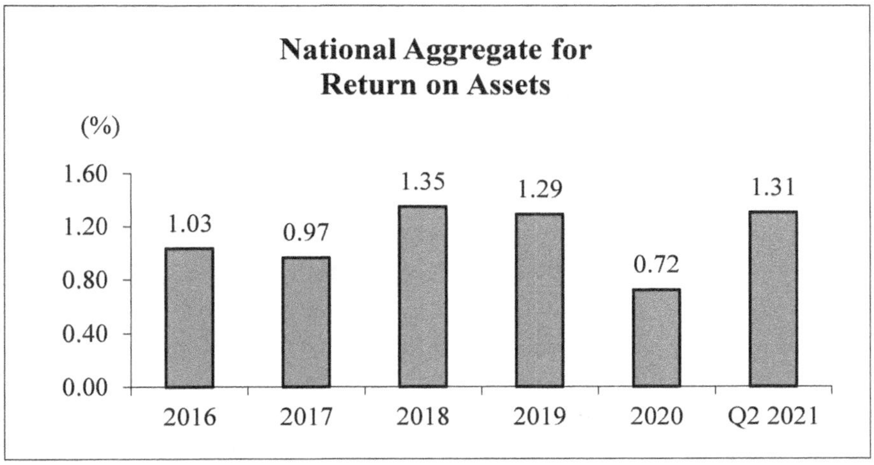

8. Return on Equity The ratio of net income for the year (year-to-date quarterly figures are converted to a 12-month equivalent) as a percentage of average equity for the year. This ratio, known as ROE, is commonly used by a company's shareholders as a measure of their return on investment. It is not always a good measure of profitability, however, because inadequate equity levels at some institutions can result in unjustly high ROE's.

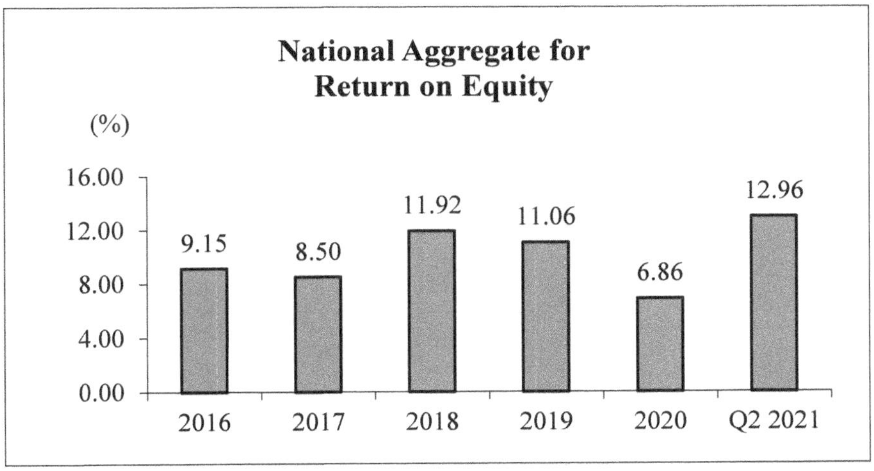

9. Net Interest Spread

The difference between the institution's interest income and interest expense for the year (year-to-date quarterly figures are converted to a 12-month equivalent) as a percentage of its average revenue-generating assets. Since the margin between interest earned and interest paid is generally where the company generates the majority of its income, this figure provides insight into the company's ability to effectively manage interest spreads.

A low Net Interest Spread can be the result of poor loan and deposit pricing, high levels of non-accruing loans, or poor asset/liability management.

10. Overhead Efficiency Ratio

Total overhead expenses as a percentage of total revenues net of interest expense. This is a common measure for evaluating an institution's ability to operate efficiently while keeping a handle on overhead expenses like salaries, rent, and other office expenses. A high ratio suggests that the company's overhead expenses are too high in relation to the amount of revenue they are generating and/or supporting. Conversely, a low ratio means good management of overhead expenses which usually results in a strong Return on Assets as well.

11. Liquidity Index

An index that measures the institution's ability to raise the necessary cash to satisfy creditors and honor depositor withdrawals. It is based on an evaluation of the company's short-term liquidity position, including its existing reliance on less stable deposit sources. See the Critical Ranges In Our Indexes for a description of the different critical levels presented in this index.

12. Liquidity Ratio

The ratio of short-term liquid assets to deposits and short-term borrowings. This ratio answers the question: How many cents can the institution easily raise in cash to cover each dollar on deposit plus pay off its short-term debts? Due to the nature of the business, it is rare (and not expected) for an established bank to achieve 100% on this ratio. Nevertheless, it serves as a good measure of an institution's liquidity in relation to the rest of the banking industry.

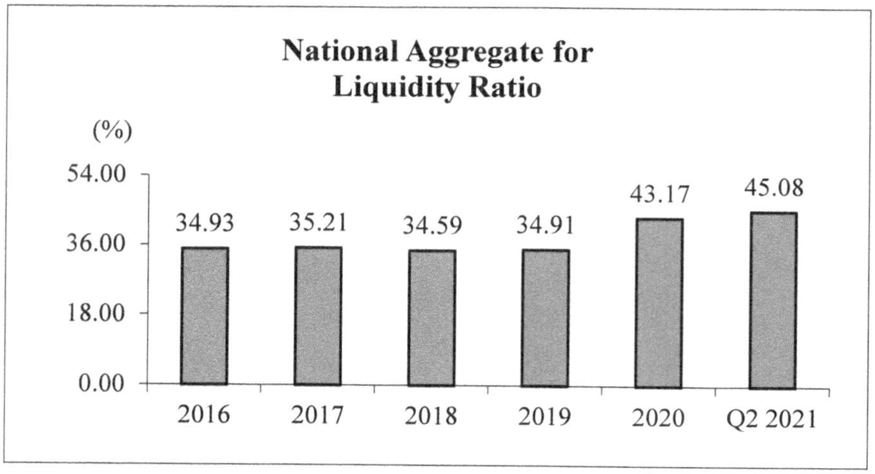

13. Hot Money Ratio

The percentage of the institution's deposit base that is being funded by jumbo CDs and brokered deposits. Jumbo CDs (high-yield certificates of deposit with principal amounts of at least $100,000) and brokered deposits (pooled funds sold by brokers seeking the highest interest rate available) are generally considered less stable (and more costly) and thus less desirable as a source of funds.

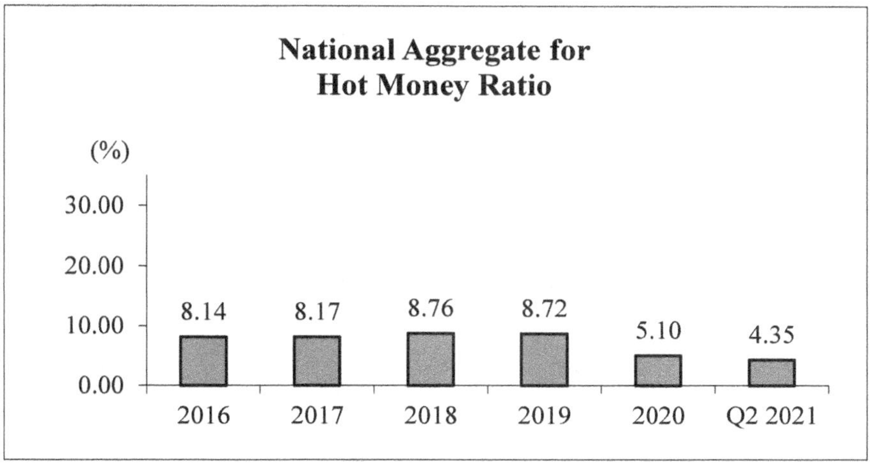

14. Stability Index

An index that integrates a number of factors such as 1) risk diversification in terms of company size and loan diversification; 2) deterioration of operations as reported in critical asset, liability, income and expense items, such as an increase in loan delinquency rates or a sharp increase in loan originations; 3) years in operation; 4) former problem areas where, despite recent improvement, the company has yet to establish a record of stable performance over a suitable period of time; and 5) relationships with holding companies and affiliates. See the Critical Ranges In Our Indexes for a description of the different critical levels presented in this index.

							One	Asset Mix (As a % of Total Assets)						Risk-
Name	City	State	Rating	2020 Rating	2019 Rating	Total Assets ($Mil)	Year Asset Growth	Comm-ercial Loans	Cons-umer Loans	Mort-gage Loans	Secur-ities	Capital-ization Index	Lever-age Ratio	Based Capital Ratio
1st Advantage Bank	Saint Peters	MO	C+	C+	C	133.0	3.66	14.1	0.5	6.9	1.4	7.9	9.7	13.2
1st Bank	Broadus	MT	A-	A-	A-	59.7	15.50	3.8	1.3	0.4	0.0	6.8	8.8	27.2
▲ 1st Bank in Hominy	Hominy	OK	C-	D+	C-	45.9	8.01	9.4	5.8	8.3	39.1	6.5	8.5	0.0
1st Bank of Sea Isle City	Sea Isle City	NJ	C-	C-	C+	308.4	17.76	0.6	0.1	39.8	7.9	7.5	9.4	22.0
1st Bank Yuma	Yuma	AZ	B+	B+	B+	562.8	15.62	7.6	0.1	1.6	28.8	5.9	7.9	16.1
▼ 1st Cameron State Bank	Cameron	MO	C-	C	C	69.8	6.41	0.5	1.5	19.5	40.2	5.9	7.9	26.7
1st Capital Bank	Salinas	CA	B	B	B+	950.7	29.04	14.1	2.5	8.0	27.8	6.6	8.6	14.2
1st Colonial Community Bank	Cherry Hill	NJ	B-	B-	C+	684.9	14.93	11.7	0.3	31.9	18.0	7.8	9.5	16.3
1st Community Bank	Sherrard	IL	C+	C	C	67.9	-2.42	5.6	1.9	9.4	6.8	8.9	10.4	0.0
1st Constitution Bank	Cranbury	NJ	B	B	B	1788.7	2.77	19.9	0.1	7.0	13.0	8.4	10.0	14.0
1st Equity Bank	Skokie	IL	C	C	C-	138.3	-8.18	16.6	0.1	16.0	0.1	10.0	15.7	26.3
1st Federal Savings Bank of SC, Inc.	Walterboro	SC	B-	B-	B-	130.4	15.36	0.1	1.0	46.8	14.0	6.5	8.5	21.0
▲ 1st Financial Bank USA	Dakota Dunes	SD	B-	C	C	886.3	40.49	0.4	40.5	2.9	4.6	10.0	22.5	24.0
1st National Bank	Lebanon	OH	B-	B-	C	244.4	0.25	5.1	0.8	17.4	12.8	6.1	8.1	15.1
1st Security Bank of Washington	Mountlake Terrace	WA	A-	A-	A	2221.5	10.63	8.9	17.9	21.3	10.8	9.3	11.9	0.0
1st Source Bank	South Bend	IN	A-	A-	A-	7720.9	4.78	46.7	1.7	4.9	18.3	10.0	11.1	15.4
1st State Bank	Saginaw	MI	B-	B-	B-	450.4	8.86	30.2	0.1	4.1	7.1	5.6	7.6	14.1
▼ 1st State Bank of Mason City	Mason City	IL	C-	C+	C+	29.7	-7.95	0.4	4.1	10.2	47.7	9.9	11.0	0.0
1st Summit Bank	Johnstown	PA	B-	B-	B	1306.9	11.00	9.9	2.3	23.1	45.7	7.0	9.0	17.9
1st Trust Bank, Inc.	Hazard	KY	C	C	C-	262.4	-0.93	11.4	2.0	18.1	4.4	8.1	9.7	0.0
1st United Bank	Faribault	MN	A-	A-	A-	191.3	13.63	8.6	1.2	4.7	48.0	7.7	9.5	19.0
21st Century Bank	Loretto	MN	A-	A-	B+	607.1	0.60	26.4	0.1	8.0	9.3	10.0	11.9	19.7
▲ 22nd State Bank	Louisville	AL	D	D-	D-	200.3	20.06	9.2	1.5	20.6	11.6	9.3	10.6	15.7
▲ 5Star Bank	Colorado Springs	CO	A-	B+	A-	381.8	4.02	10.7	0.1	6.3	3.7	10.0	11.5	0.0
AB&T	Albany	GA	B	B	B	256.1	12.21	16.1	1.4	15.8	1.2	6.1	8.1	13.7
▲ Abacus Federal Savings Bank	New York	NY	B	B-	B-	354.1	-3.11	0.9	0.0	50.5	0.0	10.0	12.3	28.0
▲ Abbeville Building and Loan, A State Chart	Abbeville	LA	B	B-	B-	61.9	4.91	0.0	0.0	32.5	2.0	10.0	28.8	32.7
▲ Abbeville First Bank, SSB	Abbeville	SC	C+	C-	C	99.2	7.81	5.0	1.3	39.5	31.2	6.7	8.7	0.0
AbbyBank	Abbotsford	WI	C+	C+	B-	640.6	4.07	4.9	0.3	10.2	27.8	6.0	8.0	12.7
▲ Abington Bank	Abington	MA	B	B-	B-	593.0	0.10	3.4	0.0	30.0	7.8	10.0	12.5	0.0
Academy Bank, N.A.	Kansas City	MO	A-	A-	A-	2232.7	-3.82	20.9	0.7	8.7	18.5	10.0	15.8	21.1
ACB Bank	Cherokee	OK	D	D+	D+	122.3	-6.17	9.6	1.7	8.5	18.3	8.8	12.1	0.0
▲ Access Bank	Omaha	NE	B+	B	B	857.3	23.59	15.4	0.3	7.2	8.9	7.6	9.6	13.0
▲ AccessBank Texas	Denton	TX	C+	C	B-	561.3	11.96	13.6	1.2	10.0	5.6	7.6	9.4	13.3
ACNB Bank	Gettysburg	PA	B+	B+	A-	2694.3	12.33	7.4	0.5	13.2	14.6	7.1	9.0	16.4
Adams Bank & Trust	Ogallala	NE	B+	B+	B+	1104.7	16.39	9.5	1.2	9.4	11.4	6.7	9.3	0.0
Adams Community Bank	Adams	MA	C	C	C	839.0	22.17	2.6	0.9	60.8	11.2	5.3	7.3	14.3
Adams County Bank	Kenesaw	NE	B	B	B	216.0	9.81	5.3	0.7	3.2	33.4	6.5	8.5	14.2
▲ Adams State Bank	Adams	NE	A-	B+	B+	60.8	7.57	6.7	4.1	12.4	20.5	10.0	17.0	0.0
Adirondack Bank	Utica	NY	C	C	C	1053.7	10.89	14.4	0.8	19.1	25.5	4.8	6.8	18.0
ADP Trust Co. N.A.	Wilmington	DE	U	U		37.6	17.42	0.0	0.0	0.0	18.6	10.0	93.4	408.6
Adrian Bank	Adrian	MO	A	A	A-	175.2	12.45	7.1	4.2	6.9	38.6	9.5	10.6	24.1
Adrian State Bank	Adrian	MN	C	C	C+	60.0	8.27	3.0	1.1	2.3	11.3	6.9	8.9	0.0
Affinity Bank	Covington	GA	C+	C	C+	786.7	-13.54	29.3	7.5	9.8	4.7	9.1	10.4	15.8
AIG Federal Savings Bank	Wilmington	DE	U	U	U	38.2	1.84	0.0	0.0	0.0	55.6	10.0	97.8	0.0
Alamerica Bank	Birmingham	AL	D	D	D	15.1	-17.83	11.3	2.0	6.8	13.5	10.0	12.3	20.3
Alamosa State Bank	Alamosa	CO	A-	A-	A-	341.5	11.20	4.3	2.7	4.6	29.3	6.6	8.6	0.0
Albany Bank & Trust Co., N.A.	Chicago	IL	B+	B+	A-	686.2	2.11	6.8	0.0	3.4	7.4	10.0	14.9	0.0
▼ Alden State Bank	Alden	MI	B+	A-	A-	272.8	19.98	5.5	2.2	12.1	9.8	9.4	10.6	0.0
Alden State Bank	Alden	NY	B	B-	B-	499.9	28.57	7.3	0.5	34.2	17.0	9.9	10.9	18.4
Alerus Financial, N.A.	Grand Forks	ND	A-	A-	A-	3155.5	9.80	17.0	1.8	17.5	25.4	7.0	9.0	14.8
Algonquin State Bank	Algonquin	IL	C	C	C	156.2	6.14	7.1	19.1	9.9	34.9	9.1	10.4	0.0
All America Bank	Oklahoma City	OK	B-	B-	B-	476.4	0.88	6.5	2.3	15.5	6.4	7.7	9.5	13.1
Allegiance Bank	Houston	TX	B	B	C+	6500.8	11.43	17.7	0.6	9.8	15.0	7.0	9.0	15.2
Alliance Bank	Francesville	IN	A	A	A-	386.7	13.78	9.2	0.3	3.5	40.5	10.0	11.3	18.9
Alliance Bank	Topeka	KS	B+	B+	B+	142.6	11.44	20.9	1.9	15.1	5.8	8.4	9.9	0.0
Alliance Bank	Saint Paul	MN	B+	B	B	763.7	4.94	17.6	0.7	3.4	12.1	7.8	9.5	13.4
Alliance Bank	Cape Girardeau	MO	B+	B+	B+	314.7	11.45	7.7	2.0	17.1	6.7	9.0	12.3	0.0
Alliance Bank	Sulphur Springs	TX	B-	B-	B-	1293.9	22.00	6.5	0.8	10.4	45.4	6.3	8.3	15.2
Alliance Bank	Mondovi	WI	B+	B	B	220.4	12.20	2.4	2.5	13.6	34.8	7.5	9.4	0.0

Arrows denote recent upgrades ▲ or downgrades ▼

Asset Quality Index	Adjusted Non-Performing Loans as a % of Total Loans	Adjusted Non-Performing Loans as a % of Capital	Net Charge-Offs Avg Loans	Profitability Index	Net Income ($Mil)	Return on Assets (R.O.A.)	Return on Equity (R.O.E.)	Net Interest Spread	Overhead Efficiency Ratio	Liquidity Index	Liquidity Ratio	Hot Money Ratio	Stability Index
7.3	0.00	0.0	0.00	**3.8**	0.6	0.82	8.67	4.10	72.7	**1.9**	12.7	19.2	**5.8**
9.3	0.00	0.0	0.00	**9.2**	0.5	1.75	20.24	4.79	48.3	**6.3**	75.0	8.7	**7.6**
4.7	1.99	8.7	-0.06	**4.5**	0.2	1.08	12.87	3.80	69.4	**3.8**	53.1	18.4	**3.2**
8.7	0.14	2.0	0.00	**1.8**	0.1	0.04	0.37	2.72	99.3	**5.2**	40.7	9.2	**4.3**
8.7	0.29	0.8	0.01	**6.3**	3.4	1.25	15.28	3.46	57.2	**6.2**	47.6	4.7	**6.5**
7.8	0.90	3.1	-0.02	**1.7**	0.0	0.04	0.51	2.18	100.9	**6.1**	58.2	6.5	**3.8**
7.5	0.36	2.4	-0.01	**5.0**	3.6	0.85	9.57	3.53	66.2	**6.0**	35.6	1.3	**5.6**
5.5	1.01	7.0	-0.08	**5.2**	3.8	1.17	12.19	3.24	62.6	**1.4**	12.1	19.8	**5.1**
6.0	0.31	1.9	0.00	**4.7**	0.5	1.42	13.68	4.29	65.9	**3.3**	30.0	15.2	**5.5**
4.7	1.40	6.6	0.11	**5.9**	10.2	1.13	9.76	3.56	57.2	**4.9**	24.2	6.9	**9.3**
4.2	3.44	12.6	-0.04	**4.5**	0.8	1.09	6.76	3.07	61.8	**1.3**	30.2	40.8	**8.1**
9.5	0.16	1.0	0.01	**3.5**	0.7	1.09	12.93	2.63	85.0	**5.3**	43.3	8.9	**5.3**
4.0	2.42	7.2	1.46	**9.1**	5.4	1.54	5.91	15.46	88.0	**0.3**	10.7	19.4	**8.2**
4.4	1.76	11.4	0.00	**3.7**	-0.2	-0.18	-2.17	2.67	100.3	**2.0**	25.4	20.1	**6.0**
6.6	0.35	2.1	0.05	**9.1**	21.1	1.97	16.75	4.09	56.1	**1.8**	16.7	10.8	**10.0**
5.5	1.02	5.4	0.13	**8.0**	60.5	1.61	13.92	3.26	53.2	**4.5**	23.6	6.3	**10.0**
4.3	1.23	8.4	0.10	**5.3**	2.6	1.13	15.04	3.36	58.5	**5.6**	30.4	1.6	**4.7**
5.9	3.03	5.8	0.14	**1.3**	0.0	0.07	0.64	1.54	95.5	**6.0**	84.5	11.7	**5.4**
9.2	0.41	2.1	0.05	**4.3**	5.8	0.91	9.54	2.69	63.2	**3.7**	28.1	15.3	**7.2**
4.6	1.52	10.1	0.18	**3.0**	0.6	0.51	5.32	2.78	74.6	**1.0**	26.3	38.4	**4.4**
6.8	1.03	3.6	0.00	**5.7**	1.0	1.06	8.94	2.79	53.9	**7.2**	63.2	2.9	**7.6**
7.1	0.17	0.3	0.01	**8.1**	5.0	1.60	13.77	4.30	46.9	**4.1**	12.2	2.8	**7.6**
1.8	5.67	23.0	0.03	**1.0**	0.3	0.30	2.77	3.60	92.2	**3.3**	28.2	14.8	**4.2**
7.4	0.10	0.6	0.00	**5.4**	2.3	1.11	10.17	3.37	59.3	**2.9**	25.7	15.9	**7.9**
8.7	0.10	0.6	0.00	**4.7**	1.2	0.88	10.58	3.86	63.8	**5.9**	37.6	3.1	**5.6**
9.2	0.38	1.4	0.00	**4.0**	1.4	0.76	5.48	2.94	75.9	**1.2**	30.3	29.6	**7.7**
4.2	2.60	6.4	0.02	**7.9**	0.9	2.98	10.47	3.37	55.3	**2.7**	34.7	19.8	**8.5**
6.2	2.19	5.8	-0.03	**3.8**	0.6	1.19	11.57	3.53	66.8	**3.5**	32.3	15.0	**6.4**
4.0	1.00	6.3	0.00	**4.3**	2.9	0.92	11.46	3.02	63.9	**3.5**	33.8	14.1	**4.8**
7.7	0.28	1.1	0.00	**4.0**	2.8	0.95	5.90	3.11	71.6	**3.3**	31.9	15.7	**7.3**
5.7	1.32	5.4	0.12	**6.0**	17.7	1.55	9.77	3.32	63.5	**1.9**	23.0	23.5	**7.5**
0.7	5.89	39.3	0.58	**6.8**	1.5	2.44	19.83	4.82	46.3	**0.8**	16.5	37.4	**5.3**
5.6	0.53	3.3	0.00	**6.6**	6.0	1.46	14.06	3.40	60.2	**4.9**	28.6	4.3	**7.8**
4.1	1.20	5.4	0.27	**3.6**	1.8	0.67	7.05	3.71	68.2	**2.9**	25.3	15.8	**5.5**
7.2	0.69	3.4	0.01	**6.0**	15.7	1.21	12.40	3.02	55.3	**5.0**	29.9	9.7	**7.9**
8.1	0.30	1.7	0.00	**6.1**	6.5	1.20	12.93	3.82	65.3	**4.0**	32.4	15.8	**8.6**
5.4	0.63	5.1	0.28	**3.1**	1.7	0.44	5.51	2.80	77.7	**4.5**	22.8	5.7	**4.8**
7.4	0.07	0.5	0.00	**5.6**	1.5	1.42	15.87	2.67	42.2	**1.8**	25.3	20.7	**5.9**
8.5	0.00	0.0	-0.02	**6.8**	0.7	2.24	13.03	2.56	44.0	**4.6**	47.4	12.9	**7.9**
4.8	2.08	14.3	0.22	**2.5**	1.7	0.33	4.64	2.54	86.9	**4.8**	24.7	6.2	**5.4**
10.0	na	0.0	na	**7.9**	10.3	63.58	73.71	0.12	17.8	**4.0**	na	0.0	**6.7**
7.4	0.41	1.8	0.07	**9.0**	2.0	2.30	20.56	3.25	43.4	**4.8**	42.3	11.4	**7.8**
2.4	2.44	11.0	0.16	**4.8**	0.3	0.96	10.76	3.16	64.1	**3.8**	31.8	13.5	**6.8**
3.7	1.24	5.6	-0.08	**4.4**	4.6	1.17	9.73	3.09	61.0	**3.8**	21.9	10.5	**7.1**
10.0	na	0.0	na	**9.5**	1.2	6.54	6.74	0.30	39.5	**4.0**	na	100.0	**7.0**
2.8	0.01	27.3	-0.07	**0.0**	-0.5	-6.29	-46.15	2.55	244.3	**1.6**	44.5	53.2	**4.3**
9.0	0.05	0.1	-0.04	**6.0**	2.1	1.26	13.74	2.76	53.0	**4.6**	39.2	11.8	**7.1**
6.7	0.46	4.3	0.00	**4.5**	2.2	0.65	4.28	2.63	64.6	**2.2**	32.0	24.2	**9.1**
5.1	3.37	8.2	-0.16	**5.8**	1.6	1.20	11.14	3.43	56.1	**5.3**	48.7	10.7	**7.5**
3.7	2.82	17.0	0.10	**5.7**	2.5	1.12	10.20	3.30	53.5	**5.2**	35.6	6.5	**5.9**
7.7	0.54	2.4	0.05	**9.3**	28.9	1.87	18.13	3.03	69.0	**6.0**	33.4	4.6	**9.9**
7.6	0.42	0.9	-0.01	**2.6**	0.4	0.52	4.89	2.82	86.7	**5.7**	33.8	2.7	**6.2**
4.1	0.95	8.1	0.02	**7.1**	4.0	1.71	17.07	4.55	58.5	**3.4**	12.4	11.8	**7.4**
5.1	1.10	4.5	0.02	**6.2**	42.9	1.37	10.49	4.05	57.4	**2.7**	29.4	21.0	**9.4**
8.5	0.71	1.6	0.00	**6.1**	2.7	1.43	11.24	3.17	58.2	**5.9**	42.4	5.2	**8.5**
6.7	0.83	2.9	0.00	**4.7**	0.6	0.87	8.67	3.44	62.0	**3.6**	37.6	16.2	**5.6**
5.8	0.94	4.2	-0.03	**7.8**	5.7	1.48	15.21	3.64	53.7	**3.5**	26.4	13.0	**8.1**
7.7	0.27	1.5	0.00	**6.1**	2.0	1.29	10.57	4.07	62.4	**3.4**	18.8	12.4	**7.7**
7.7	0.69	2.3	0.00	**4.1**	6.5	1.05	10.51	2.60	67.9	**5.8**	36.5	6.6	**8.4**
5.6	1.13	5.2	0.05	**7.4**	2.0	1.92	19.57	3.12	50.2	**5.2**	43.7	9.9	**6.7**

Name	City	State	Rating	2020 Rating	2019 Rating	Total Assets ($Mil)	One Year Asset Growth	Asset Mix (As a % of Total Assets): Commercial Loans	Consumer Loans	Mortgage Loans	Securities	Capitalization Index	Leverage Ratio	Risk-Based Capital Ratio
Alliance Bank & Trust Co.	Gastonia	NC	C+	C+	C+	215.5	20.94	17.2	0.5	3.7	7.6	5.2	7.5	11.1
Alliance Bank Central Texas	Woodway	TX	C+	C+	C+	432.8	23.44	13.7	2.0	22.8	13.0	6.9	8.9	13.1
Alliance Community Bank	Petersburg	IL	B-	C+	C+	336.2	12.86	5.3	3.9	12.0	34.4	6.8	8.8	17.6
▲ Alliant Bank	Madison	MO	A-	B+	B+	202.1	16.99	5.8	0.6	20.6	5.4	7.7	9.5	18.0
Allied First Bank, SB	Oswego	IL	B	B-	C	161.9	18.14	12.1	1.2	30.9	4.9	10.0	13.8	0.0
▼ AllNations Bank	Calumet	OK	D-	D	D	48.3	3.55	2.1	0.9	1.9	29.0	8.3	9.8	0.0
Ally Bank	Sandy	UT	B-	B	B+	170075.0	-1.64	13.6	39.7	8.2	18.3	9.4	10.6	15.2
Alma Bank	Astoria	NY	D+	D+	D	1308.2	2.66	13.6	0.1	2.6	2.3	8.4	9.9	14.4
Alpine Bank	Glenwood Springs	CO	A-	A-	A-	5787.7	24.52	6.2	0.7	17.4	18.4	6.3	8.3	14.3
▼ Alpine Capital Bank	New York	NY	B+	A-	A	267.6	5.51	5.4	1.6	0.8	19.4	10.0	20.5	34.5
Altabank	American Fork	UT	A	A	A	3541.2	15.51	5.8	0.3	5.6	42.1	8.0	9.6	17.8
Altamaha Bank and Trust Co.	Vidalia	GA	B	B	B	250.6	22.37	12.2	2.7	12.6	23.0	7.0	9.0	15.6
Alton Bank	Alton	MO	B	B	B+	94.9	19.89	3.9	5.4	13.3	30.7	7.8	11.5	13.2
▲ Altoona First Savings Bank	Altoona	PA	B	B-	B	313.4	21.98	4.9	2.9	20.8	19.8	10.0	11.3	0.0
Alva State Bank & Trust Co.	Alva	OK	C	C+	C	431.2	2.75	10.2	1.2	2.0	21.1	10.0	14.2	20.0
Amalgamated Bank	New York	NY	B	B	B	6561.9	1.25	8.9	3.4	16.5	37.3	5.9	7.9	15.0
Amalgamated Bank of Chicago	Chicago	IL	B-	B-	B	950.1	2.79	2.5	3.1	3.4	18.3	8.4	10.0	18.0
Amarillo National Bank	Amarillo	TX	B+	B+	B+	7506.1	12.05	25.3	12.2	3.8	5.0	6.9	8.9	12.5
Ambler Savings Bank	Ambler	PA	B	B	B	475.8	10.52	6.3	0.0	42.0	18.5	10.0	12.6	26.0
Amboy Bank	Old Bridge	NJ	B	B	B-	2621.2	4.98	3.9	0.0	10.2	11.2	10.0	14.0	19.6
▲ Amerant Bank, N.A.	Coral Gables	FL	C	D+	C+	7521.1	-7.40	13.3	4.1	5.2	17.1	9.2	10.9	14.3
Amerasia Bank	Flushing	NY	A	A	A-	824.8	15.63	3.1	0.1	16.2	0.5	10.0	12.6	18.0
America's Community Bank	Blue Springs	MO	B-	B-	C+	37.2	11.24	3.4	1.6	28.0	0.7	9.3	10.5	14.5
American B&T of the Cumberlands	Livingston	TN	B+	B+	B	335.6	17.18	6.8	2.8	22.2	0.5	6.5	8.5	14.5
American Bank	Bozeman	MT	B+	B+	A-	608.6	22.54	10.7	0.2	7.3	13.9	6.2	8.2	0.0
American Bank	Allentown	PA	B+	B+	B+	796.2	11.80	12.0	0.1	9.3	7.4	8.1	9.8	13.4
American Bank & Trust	Huron	SD	A-	A-	B	1225.6	14.80	14.7	1.3	2.8	24.3	6.9	8.9	13.0
▼ American Bank & Trust Co.	Opelousas	LA	B+	A-	A-	231.3	10.69	8.6	2.6	24.8	14.2	9.3	10.6	0.0
American Bank & Trust Co. Inc.	Bowling Green	KY	B	B	B	585.2	16.10	10.5	0.8	14.5	10.7	4.8	7.3	10.9
American Bank & Trust Co., Inc.	Covington	LA	C+	C	C	211.1	-3.79	8.8	1.2	21.9	0.1	6.1	8.7	0.0
▲ American Bank and Trust Co.	Tulsa	OK	A-	B+	A-	294.0	0.60	18.2	0.3	2.5	21.8	9.3	10.6	0.0
American Bank and Trust Co., N.A.	Davenport	IA	C	C+	C+	485.5	12.13	5.9	1.6	10.9	30.5	6.8	8.8	14.9
American Bank Center	Dickinson	ND	B-	B-	B-	1997.4	10.75	8.3	14.2	5.5	26.7	6.5	8.5	12.5
American Bank N.A.	Waco	TX	B-	B-	B	570.9	12.68	13.2	1.0	20.6	14.0	7.1	9.1	14.6
American Bank of Baxter Springs	Baxter Springs	KS	C+	C+	B-	137.8	10.87	8.2	0.5	8.5	32.3	8.8	10.2	0.0
American Bank of Beaver Dam	Beaver Dam	WI	B	B	B-	184.6	9.17	2.7	0.9	12.8	19.4	8.1	9.7	0.0
American Bank of Commerce	Wolfforth	TX	B	B	B	1398.7	18.78	10.5	0.3	8.7	38.9	5.9	7.9	13.2
American Bank of Missouri	Wellsville	MO	C+	B-	B	526.4	14.38	14.2	0.0	21.2	4.5	6.6	9.2	12.2
American Bank of Oklahoma	Collinsville	OK	C+	C	C	377.5	3.66	19.1	7.0	11.0	3.4	6.2	8.2	11.9
American Bank of the Carolinas	Monroe	NC	D-	D-		85.8	47.33	10.4	1.5	7.0	18.4	9.8	21.8	0.0
American Bank, N.A.	Le Mars	IA	B	B-	C+	372.9	-3.19	9.1	1.3	3.6	2.2	9.5	10.6	15.1
American Bank, N.A.	Corpus Christi	TX	C+	C	B-	1982.6	4.58	21.0	0.8	5.6	22.7	5.9	7.9	14.4
American Bank, N.A.	Dallas	TX	B+	B+	B	206.1	83.53	21.0	23.1	2.9	10.7	6.8	10.6	0.0
American Business Bank	Los Angeles	CA	B	B	B	3732.3	13.26	19.2	0.3	0.9	34.2	5.0	7.0	14.3
American Commerce Bank, N.A.	Bremen	GA	B+	B	B-	422.0	7.00	4.1	0.8	14.1	0.0	10.0	11.7	16.2
▲ American Community Bank	Glen Cove	NY	B+	B-	B	243.5	-0.19	10.6	0.0	14.3	6.1	10.0	12.5	0.0
American Community Bank & Trust	Woodstock	IL	B+	B+	B+	854.3	11.22	22.3	0.1	5.8	17.7	8.0	9.9	0.0
American Community Bank of Indiana	Saint John	IN	B	B-	B-	271.6	7.15	16.6	0.4	21.7	2.2	7.7	9.5	14.3
American Continental Bank	City of Industry	CA	A-	B+	A-	331.3	13.66	3.4	0.0	27.6	0.9	10.0	11.7	0.0
American Eagle Bank	South Elgin	IL	B-	B-	C-	356.9	33.88	2.2	39.8	8.9	7.5	6.9	8.9	13.0
▲ American Equity Bank	Minnetonka	MN	C	D+	D+	94.7	60.29	36.0	0.4	9.6	1.9	10.0	12.6	26.9
▼ American Exchange Bank	Elmwood	NE	B	B+	B	57.7	2.45	13.0	1.3	8.1	28.7	8.2	9.8	0.0
American Exchange Bank	Henryetta	OK	B	B	B-	79.4	4.15	5.8	7.2	36.8	9.2	9.5	10.7	0.0
American Exchange Bank	Lindsay	OK	A-	A-	B+	81.9	-0.24	7.0	3.8	4.5	60.3	10.0	11.2	0.0
American Express National Bank	Sandy	UT	C	C	B-	126565.8	-8.70	21.9	51.8	0.0	6.1	8.9	10.2	16.2
American Federal Bank	Fargo	ND	B+	B	B	669.3	-1.37	5.5	0.9	16.3	7.9	8.1	9.7	15.3
American First National Bank	Houston	TX	A-	A-	A-	2140.1	9.22	6.9	0.2	2.6	2.6	7.7	11.4	13.1
American Heritage Bank	Clovis	NM	B+	B+	B+	118.9	12.98	8.4	0.3	8.1	44.4	8.4	9.9	16.5
American Heritage Bank	Sapulpa	OK	B	B	B-	1524.0	16.61	5.7	1.7	11.5	61.2	6.3	8.3	21.4
American Heritage National Bank	Long Prairie	MN	A-	A-	A-	493.1	14.20	11.4	0.3	6.7	8.9	7.7	9.4	16.8

Asset Quality Index	Adjusted Non-Performing Loans as a % of Total Loans	Adjusted Non-Performing Loans as a % of Capital	Net Charge-Offs Avg Loans	Profitability Index	Net Income ($Mil)	Return on Assets (R.O.A.)	Return on Equity (R.O.E.)	Net Interest Spread	Overhead Efficiency Ratio	Liquidity Index	Liquidity Ratio	Hot Money Ratio	Stability Index
3.9	0.71	6.4	0.00	**4.5**	0.9	0.90	11.91	3.88	70.4	**5.2**	30.6	4.5	**4.2**
7.2	0.77	3.1	0.00	**3.8**	1.4	0.69	7.97	3.54	65.5	**1.8**	20.3	21.0	**5.0**
4.6	1.33	4.6	-0.04	**4.3**	1.8	1.07	9.10	3.01	68.1	**5.7**	49.5	8.8	**6.8**
8.2	0.23	1.4	-0.01	**7.4**	2.0	2.03	21.28	4.12	62.5	**4.4**	34.1	10.6	**7.0**
6.3	3.52	7.8	-0.04	**9.5**	3.3	4.23	32.97	3.01	92.8	**3.7**	46.3	18.1	**9.0**
4.5	8.86	12.5	1.19	**0.0**	-0.1	-0.47	-4.50	3.32	122.9	**5.2**	23.0	1.9	**3.7**
3.7	2.41	9.5	0.30	**8.0**	1874.0	2.20	21.90	3.63	41.7	**2.8**	29.0	16.1	**9.7**
1.3	5.96	27.1	0.19	**2.6**	2.5	0.38	3.84	3.20	74.4	**0.8**	16.4	32.4	**7.8**
9.0	0.43	2.1	0.00	**6.1**	31.8	1.16	13.44	3.43	59.8	**6.4**	33.0	1.4	**8.0**
6.5	3.23	6.0	0.00	**4.9**	1.1	0.84	4.02	2.60	67.3	**5.7**	75.8	10.9	**8.4**
8.5	0.40	1.6	-0.01	**7.9**	23.4	1.35	13.21	2.89	57.9	**4.8**	8.9	2.7	**10.0**
5.9	0.87	3.7	0.08	**5.1**	1.8	1.46	15.23	4.23	65.6	**3.3**	29.6	15.0	**5.9**
5.7	0.67	3.3	0.31	**4.7**	0.5	0.96	8.36	3.57	69.4	**2.5**	28.3	18.5	**6.8**
8.5	0.54	2.2	0.09	**4.0**	1.2	0.76	6.71	3.07	62.0	**3.0**	43.5	22.7	**5.8**
2.1	7.51	22.4	-0.41	**6.3**	3.8	1.77	12.45	3.52	42.6	**2.8**	39.5	22.1	**7.3**
5.1	2.22	10.5	0.12	**4.2**	22.6	0.72	8.37	2.81	69.1	**6.3**	36.6	2.9	**6.4**
8.7	0.19	1.1	0.17	**3.4**	1.7	0.36	3.86	2.92	85.9	**5.2**	27.4	2.7	**5.3**
6.1	0.45	3.0	0.06	**6.8**	61.6	1.72	17.68	3.14	54.4	**4.2**	27.1	12.4	**8.7**
8.0	0.93	4.3	-0.02	**3.9**	1.9	0.82	6.32	2.91	64.7	**3.3**	13.3	12.6	**7.0**
4.3	4.53	10.4	-0.01	**8.3**	29.0	2.18	15.67	2.98	38.4	**4.6**	30.2	12.2	**10.0**
3.5	2.15	12.3	0.06	**3.3**	34.8	0.88	7.98	2.77	73.0	**1.7**	21.1	17.3	**6.9**
7.3	0.56	2.6	0.00	**10.0**	8.0	2.03	16.40	3.84	35.5	**0.8**	19.0	41.4	**9.3**
8.4	0.00	0.0	0.01	**4.0**	0.2	0.94	8.91	4.08	75.8	**1.7**	19.6	22.3	**6.4**
7.7	0.07	0.4	-0.01	**6.5**	3.0	1.79	15.43	3.72	44.2	**2.4**	43.0	31.2	**8.0**
8.0	0.43	1.9	0.01	**5.6**	3.8	1.31	16.08	3.60	62.7	**6.3**	42.9	2.2	**6.4**
5.3	0.84	3.3	0.00	**6.3**	4.9	1.26	12.61	2.95	45.9	**3.2**	12.8	13.0	**7.2**
8.1	0.01	0.6	-0.01	**8.5**	13.1	2.18	23.23	3.87	50.1	**4.0**	14.8	9.4	**9.3**
8.9	0.00	0.4	0.05	**5.2**	1.5	1.30	11.76	3.27	62.9	**5.0**	33.9	7.3	**7.1**
6.5	0.54	3.4	0.08	**3.9**	1.6	0.56	7.61	2.48	71.0	**3.8**	35.6	14.4	**5.8**
5.1	0.80	6.2	-0.01	**4.8**	1.1	1.06	12.30	5.54	70.3	**1.8**	20.2	17.2	**4.8**
8.9	0.00	0.0	0.00	**6.9**	2.3	1.48	14.65	3.67	47.0	**2.2**	31.7	23.5	**6.6**
6.0	1.05	6.1	0.00	**2.8**	1.6	0.73	7.91	2.64	80.5	**4.9**	29.8	6.3	**5.4**
3.8	1.41	8.7	-0.04	**7.5**	15.2	1.55	16.06	3.91	59.7	**3.7**	12.5	9.7	**7.6**
8.7	0.01	0.1	0.00	**4.1**	2.8	1.03	11.17	3.45	70.8	**3.8**	27.6	11.8	**6.5**
9.5	0.43	0.9	0.00	**2.8**	0.5	0.72	6.78	2.30	87.0	**3.3**	33.8	16.6	**6.9**
4.5	0.99	5.7	0.00	**4.5**	1.0	1.06	11.27	3.18	71.6	**5.3**	28.1	2.5	**6.3**
7.9	0.53	2.5	0.03	**4.3**	6.2	0.92	10.94	3.13	68.2	**5.0**	37.2	11.6	**7.2**
3.3	1.21	8.6	0.02	**6.1**	3.5	1.37	13.79	3.89	54.1	**1.4**	9.7	24.8	**7.0**
4.8	0.70	5.4	0.26	**4.6**	2.2	1.21	14.92	4.24	76.6	**1.8**	28.1	26.9	**4.9**
8.8	0.00	0.0	0.00	**0.0**	-0.6	-1.43	-6.23	3.45	133.7	**6.1**	52.5	5.4	**0.6**
5.4	0.23	1.8	0.01	**7.4**	3.6	1.91	17.89	3.31	47.4	**3.1**	20.4	12.6	**8.3**
7.7	0.23	1.5	-0.03	**3.8**	9.2	0.97	11.40	2.85	73.8	**6.4**	38.9	3.5	**6.1**
6.4	0.23	1.3	0.26	**5.0**	0.9	1.04	9.33	5.95	64.7	**1.6**	33.2	34.8	**5.8**
8.7	0.01	0.0	-0.04	**4.9**	18.0	0.99	14.29	2.97	55.7	**6.9**	40.7	1.0	**6.1**
4.8	1.57	6.7	0.00	**7.8**	3.2	1.57	13.49	3.97	47.6	**0.8**	19.1	29.0	**7.4**
6.7	0.00	0.0	0.00	**5.2**	1.7	1.37	11.27	4.06	63.2	**4.0**	18.3	9.4	**7.6**
8.5	0.06	0.4	0.05	**5.5**	5.2	1.23	12.58	3.23	45.2	**4.7**	37.6	10.7	**6.8**
6.9	0.40	2.2	-0.02	**7.2**	2.1	1.59	17.31	3.57	55.9	**3.1**	17.3	13.5	**6.1**
8.9	0.03	0.1	0.00	**7.2**	2.6	1.62	13.73	3.08	47.2	**1.5**	33.7	45.1	**7.7**
6.8	0.15	0.7	0.21	**5.0**	1.7	0.96	10.70	3.20	56.4	**1.0**	27.6	44.6	**4.6**
7.8	0.47	2.1	-0.01	**2.7**	0.3	0.67	6.97	3.68	83.6	**2.6**	42.6	16.2	**5.4**
3.7	6.33	28.2	-0.01	**4.5**	0.4	1.19	12.23	3.41	59.3	**4.7**	43.9	12.0	**7.0**
4.2	1.40	12.8	0.04	**4.9**	0.4	1.14	10.41	5.85	71.7	**3.9**	22.3	10.2	**6.3**
9.3	0.00	0.0	-0.14	**6.5**	0.7	1.84	14.99	4.26	49.5	**6.7**	77.8	6.3	**7.3**
2.4	3.29	10.8	1.05	**10.0**	3753.9	5.62	58.50	5.31	68.3	**2.7**	28.1	1.7	**9.7**
8.1	0.09	0.5	0.00	**7.0**	6.2	1.87	19.93	4.22	63.6	**3.6**	6.7	6.9	**7.6**
7.1	0.14	0.7	0.00	**8.3**	19.5	1.86	16.66	3.99	39.3	**0.7**	11.0	46.7	**9.6**
6.3	1.08	3.4	-0.05	**5.9**	0.7	1.18	10.62	3.57	60.3	**4.3**	54.1	17.0	**7.7**
9.0	0.30	1.1	0.02	**4.3**	8.3	1.11	11.74	2.67	67.6	**3.7**	22.8	13.1	**8.1**
8.4	0.18	0.7	0.00	**5.7**	2.4	0.99	9.67	2.70	55.5	**5.5**	35.3	4.6	**7.3**

Name	City	State	Rating	2020 Rating	2019 Rating	Total Assets ($Mil)	One Year Asset Growth	Asset Mix (As a % of Total Assets): Comm-ercial Loans	Cons-umer Loans	Mort-gage Loans	Secur-ities	Capital-ization Index	Lever-age Ratio	Risk-Based Capital Ratio
American Interstate Bank	Elkhorn	NE	**A**	A	A	128.8	15.96	6.5	0.6	15.2	0.0	**10.0**	16.9	0.0
American Investors Bank and Mortgage	Eden Prairie	MN	**B-**	B-	B-	91.2	7.02	0.4	0.1	15.3	14.6	**9.5**	11.0	14.6
American Metro Bank	Chicago	IL	**B-**	C+	C+	89.7	6.11	5.1	0.0	16.1	0.0	**10.0**	11.1	21.7
▼ American Momentum Bank	College Station	TX	**B**	B+	B+	2660.4	-5.75	19.8	0.2	9.4	4.7	**9.8**	10.9	16.3
American Nation Bank	Ardmore	OK	**B**	B	B	561.4	12.72	3.2	3.2	14.9	29.8	**7.2**	9.1	0.0
American National Bank	Oakland Park	FL	**A-**	A-	A-	479.2	19.37	11.2	0.0	2.0	12.2	**9.2**	10.5	18.1
American National Bank	Omaha	NE	**B+**	B+	B	4473.1	0.43	20.0	18.4	4.0	20.8	**6.7**	8.9	12.3
American National Bank & Trust	Wichita Falls	TX	**B+**	B+	B	1241.5	20.97	5.5	1.7	6.6	8.0	**9.3**	10.9	14.4
American National Bank and Trust Co.	Danville	VA	**B+**	B+	B+	3189.1	11.97	10.1	0.2	8.7	17.2	**6.9**	9.0	14.5
American National Bank of Minnesota	Brainerd	MN	**B+**	B+	B-	362.0	5.83	5.3	2.6	34.9	4.4	**7.8**	9.6	13.9
American National Bank-Fox Cities	Appleton	WI	**A-**	A	A-	360.6	3.71	24.7	0.2	4.7	19.6	**8.9**	12.9	0.0
American Plus Bank, N.A.	Arcadia	CA	**A**	A-	A-	582.8	1.40	10.4	1.1	10.6	3.1	**10.0**	16.0	0.0
American Pride Bank	Macon	GA	**B+**	B+	A-	212.9	0.35	2.8	0.1	4.4	4.1	**10.0**	14.0	17.7
American Riviera Bank	Santa Barbara	CA	**B**	B	B	1150.4	27.46	14.0	0.1	9.6	9.6	**5.9**	7.9	12.4
American Savings Bank	Tripoli	IA	**A-**	B+	B+	56.8	6.26	5.1	1.5	12.3	36.0	**10.0**	18.7	0.0
American Savings Bank, F.S.B.	Honolulu	HI	**B**	B	B+	8909.9	11.10	9.1	1.5	26.7	32.4	**6.0**	8.0	0.0
American State Bank	Osceola	IA	**B+**	B+	B+	268.9	8.28	10.4	3.7	9.8	24.8	**7.8**	9.5	0.0
American State Bank	Sioux Center	IA	**B-**	C+	C	1099.9	1.11	17.8	1.5	3.6	1.1	**9.6**	10.7	14.9
American State Bank	Arp	TX	**C**	C	C+	542.2	5.85	20.3	2.5	17.6	3.8	**2.9**	8.1	0.0
American State Bank & Trust Co	Williston	ND	**A-**	B+	B+	649.9	1.90	10.2	3.0	4.1	54.9	**10.0**	11.5	25.7
American State Bank & Trust Co.	Wichita	KS	**B-**	B-	B	786.1	3.91	9.9	2.0	5.2	24.9	**7.3**	10.1	0.0
American State Bank of Grygla	Grygla	MN	**B-**	B-	B-	73.9	22.18	8.8	5.1	9.1	21.8	**6.8**	8.8	19.8
American Trust & Savings Bank	Lowden	IA	**C**	C	B-	37.9	12.00	2.2	1.5	0.2	44.7	**10.0**	16.0	53.1
Americana Community Bank	Sleepy Eye	MN	**C+**	C+	C+	153.1	10.25	12.8	0.5	4.3	19.8	**5.5**	7.5	12.6
AmeriFirst Bank	Montgomery	AL	**C+**	C+	C+	301.1	47.04	13.8	2.1	14.0	15.3	**5.7**	7.7	11.9
Ameriprise Bank, FSB	Minneapolis	MN	**U**	U	U	9652.5	60.51	1.0	3.6	0.3	86.8	**5.5**	7.5	29.5
Ameris Bank	Atlanta	GA	**B+**	B+	B+	21791.5	10.14	9.6	2.9	18.0	3.7	**9.4**	10.7	14.5
AmeriServ Financial Bank	Johnstown	PA	**C+**	C+	C+	1346.8	9.73	13.2	1.2	14.0	16.0	**6.2**	8.6	11.9
▼ AmeriState Bank	Atoka	OK	**C**	C+	C+	384.6	20.99	10.7	5.6	15.4	4.0	**6.9**	8.9	0.0
AMG National Trust Bank	Greenwood Village	CO	**A**	A	A-	533.0	-5.26	3.2	4.9	2.7	25.4	**10.0**	11.2	16.7
Amistad Bank	Del Rio	TX	**A-**	A-	A-	44.9	7.67	3.6	0.9	4.3	6.7	**10.0**	11.4	0.0
Amory Federal S&L Assn.	Amory	MS	**D**	D+	D+	78.9	-2.08	0.0	0.7	55.3	4.3	**10.0**	13.4	33.7
▼ Anahuac National Bank	Anahuac	TX	**B**	B+	B+	289.2	23.11	4.4	2.4	6.0	52.2	**6.2**	8.2	19.3
ANB Bank	Denver	CO	**B+**	B+	B+	3414.8	12.94	8.1	0.3	12.6	43.2	**6.1**	8.1	16.7
▼ Anchor Bank	Juno Beach	FL	**C-**	C	C	169.8	0.74	11.7	4.9	11.4	10.0	**3.9**	8.7	0.0
Anchor D Bank	Texhoma	OK	**A-**	B+	B+	246.8	6.39	7.5	3.8	7.4	35.4	**10.0**	11.4	18.6
Anchor State Bank	Anchor	IL	**B-**	B-	C+	35.4	36.34	43.3	0.9	0.8	3.3	**10.0**	18.3	26.2
Anchorage Digital Bank N.A.	Sioux Falls	SD	**U**			17.4	na	0.0	0.0	0.0	0.0	**10.0**	92.3	270.6
Anderson Brothers Bank	Mullins	SC	**B**	B-	C+	1275.5	14.13	8.0	26.8	13.0	6.9	**6.7**	8.7	12.8
Anderson State Bank	Oneida	IL	**B**	B	B	105.2	11.38	2.7	1.3	4.2	46.2	**10.0**	14.0	42.0
Andes State Bank	Lake Andes	SD	**C**	C-	D+	25.0	0.26	3.8	4.5	4.4	17.0	**10.0**	11.0	0.0
▲ Andover State Bank	Andover	KS	**B-**	C+	C+	147.9	11.30	18.7	1.0	11.8	1.9	**7.3**	9.2	0.0
Andrew Johnson Bank	Greeneville	TN	**A-**	A-	A-	482.9	14.11	5.9	0.6	22.5	20.1	**7.7**	9.5	16.5
Androscoggin Savings Bank	Lewiston	ME	**C+**	C+	C+	1320.3	4.25	10.9	0.1	24.3	10.6	**7.9**	9.6	14.4
Angelina Savings Bank, SSB	Lufkin	TX	**C**	C	C+	76.1	4.94	12.0	16.8	17.8	0.0	**5.8**	7.8	17.7
Anna State Bank	Anna	IL	**B+**	B+	B+	107.6	15.33	1.6	1.4	17.5	58.0	**10.0**	12.7	0.0
Anna-Jonesboro National Bank	Anna	IL	**B+**	B+	B+	268.1	12.69	3.3	2.6	21.9	50.1	**10.0**	12.3	29.3
Anstaff Bank	Green Forest	AR	**B-**	B-	B	933.3	11.60	8.2	3.0	14.8	23.3	**6.4**	8.4	13.1
Anthem Bank & Trust	Plaquemine	LA	**C+**	C	C	167.3	5.50	23.0	1.6	15.2	16.4	**8.2**	9.8	16.8
ANZ Guam, Inc.	Hagatna	GU	**C**	C	B-	421.3	13.42	6.3	0.1	3.3	0.0	**10.0**	11.1	0.0
Apex Bank	Camden	TN	**B**	B	B-	934.6	6.96	3.0	1.0	49.7	0.2	**10.0**	13.1	0.0
Apollo Bank	Miami	FL	**B-**	B-	B-	946.2	16.36	7.0	1.5	10.4	30.1	**8.5**	10.0	15.4
Apollo Trust Co.	Apollo	PA	**A-**	A-	B+	178.6	8.79	2.7	1.5	47.7	14.3	**9.4**	10.6	18.8
Apple Bank for Savings	New York	NY	**C**	C	B-	16037.8	0.35	28.6	0.2	0.5	23.7	**5.2**	7.2	13.8
Apple River State Bank	Apple River	IL	**A-**	A-	A-	503.1	20.92	8.4	2.3	9.9	35.9	**7.0**	9.0	16.5
▼ Applied Bank	Wilmington	DE	**A-**	A	A	210.8	17.09	5.8	0.0	1.8	0.0	**10.0**	20.7	66.4
▲ Aquesta Bank	Cornelius	NC	**B**	B-	B	739.0	8.99	21.1	0.0	4.3	8.8	**6.8**	8.8	14.4
▲ Arbor Bank	Nebraska City	NE	**B-**	C+	C	519.3	15.71	20.6	1.2	7.5	6.5	**6.0**	8.1	13.6
Arcadian Bank	Hartland	MN	**A-**	A-	B+	177.0	-3.10	17.9	0.7	2.1	14.6	**10.0**	11.7	0.0
Arcola First Bank	Arcola	IL	**C+**	C+	B-	136.1	13.70	2.2	0.3	1.9	77.2	**10.0**	13.1	22.0

Asset Quality Index	Adjusted Non-Performing Loans as a % of Total Loans	Adjusted Non-Performing Loans as a % of Capital	Net Charge-Offs Avg Loans	Profitability Index	Net Income ($Mil)	Return on Assets (R.O.A.)	Return on Equity (R.O.E.)	Net Interest Spread	Overhead Efficiency Ratio	Liquidity Index	Liquidity Ratio	Hot Money Ratio	Stability Index
8.9	0.00	0.0	0.00	**9.0**	1.1	1.74	10.08	3.72	49.3	**5.7**	46.3	7.3	**9.7**
9.7	0.00	0.0	-0.02	**4.4**	0.4	0.88	7.98	3.81	68.9	**2.5**	17.5	16.9	**6.9**
3.1	6.32	25.3	0.08	**3.9**	0.4	0.98	8.85	4.19	73.0	**1.7**	35.6	39.4	**6.6**
4.0	0.97	5.4	0.04	**6.2**	14.5	1.08	7.25	3.86	62.9	**5.3**	29.0	7.1	**9.1**
8.2	0.01	1.6	0.01	**5.7**	4.3	1.59	16.33	3.43	52.5	**1.6**	34.4	36.3	**6.6**
7.5	0.00	0.0	0.00	**6.2**	2.9	1.24	11.75	3.35	48.8	**5.9**	42.4	4.7	**7.2**
5.4	0.65	3.3	-0.08	**7.4**	42.9	1.89	19.32	3.82	52.1	**3.5**	17.8	6.7	**9.7**
5.8	0.41	2.8	0.08	**5.9**	7.4	1.27	11.92	3.48	63.1	**2.7**	19.6	7.8	**9.3**
7.8	0.14	0.7	0.00	**6.7**	23.2	1.52	13.06	3.16	49.9	**5.2**	32.5	9.7	**9.9**
6.1	0.72	5.0	-0.01	**5.5**	2.6	1.48	15.34	4.77	66.7	**1.5**	14.7	16.8	**6.5**
4.1	2.60	10.5	-0.10	**6.9**	2.5	1.49	10.89	3.13	53.2	**0.8**	21.4	13.2	**9.4**
7.2	0.00	0.0	0.00	**9.7**	5.4	1.83	11.77	3.83	32.5	**0.6**	12.7	49.3	**10.0**
7.2	0.76	2.1	0.00	**5.3**	1.4	1.35	9.72	4.36	67.9	**1.2**	18.2	27.3	**7.8**
7.2	0.44	3.4	-0.15	**6.0**	6.1	1.17	14.07	3.91	58.0	**6.2**	32.2	2.7	**7.5**
9.0	0.00	0.0	0.00	**7.3**	0.5	1.81	9.39	3.81	45.1	**4.7**	59.0	14.6	**8.9**
5.9	1.49	8.0	0.11	**6.0**	59.8	1.39	16.46	2.94	63.1	**6.1**	30.9	3.0	**6.4**
5.9	0.39	2.6	-0.01	**9.0**	3.4	2.59	26.29	4.89	46.3	**3.4**	29.6	14.4	**7.9**
4.2	1.48	13.6	0.11	**7.1**	9.8	1.76	16.09	3.03	49.4	**2.3**	17.2	14.1	**8.7**
4.5	0.77	5.4	0.05	**5.0**	3.5	1.33	14.76	4.25	67.9	**3.1**	13.7	13.4	**6.0**
5.4	3.46	10.7	-0.02	**9.0**	6.8	2.14	16.47	3.44	44.8	**6.4**	50.4	4.1	**9.6**
5.1	0.88	3.8	-0.01	**3.7**	2.4	0.60	4.86	3.00	74.2	**4.2**	25.2	8.7	**7.6**
7.4	0.73	2.0	0.00	**4.9**	0.4	1.19	13.16	3.53	67.9	**6.3**	49.1	3.2	**4.6**
9.6	1.62	1.7	-0.85	**2.6**	0.1	0.61	3.87	2.51	80.9	**7.1**	95.6	7.0	**5.4**
4.5	1.26	7.9	-0.01	**3.7**	0.4	0.60	7.93	3.31	76.8	**5.3**	36.0	6.0	**4.5**
4.5	1.44	6.7	-0.04	**3.8**	1.0	0.67	7.81	3.66	75.5	**3.2**	31.2	16.1	**4.7**
9.9	0.06	0.1	0.38	**4.0**	29.8	0.67	8.46	1.25	40.4	**8.6**	95.2	0.0	**8.5**
5.4	0.87	2.8	0.09	**8.8**	225.9	2.15	15.31	3.54	51.0	**4.1**	19.9	6.7	**10.0**
7.8	0.38	2.9	0.02	**3.3**	4.1	0.63	7.21	3.34	76.7	**3.2**	12.4	13.1	**7.1**
1.7	2.72	34.3	-0.04	**6.0**	2.6	1.43	15.34	4.61	62.1	**2.6**	34.9	21.2	**6.4**
8.0	0.00	0.0	0.00	**10.0**	7.6	2.63	21.26	1.95	61.0	**7.5**	60.3	0.2	**7.9**
7.8	0.00	0.0	0.00	**7.9**	0.3	1.58	13.83	4.10	65.7	**4.8**	43.1	11.5	**7.0**
9.8	0.65	2.6	0.41	**0.7**	-0.1	-0.15	-1.16	2.35	96.1	**2.2**	49.1	43.7	**6.0**
9.2	0.13	0.5	-0.02	**4.1**	1.4	0.99	12.16	2.92	70.7	**2.9**	33.5	18.4	**6.2**
9.1	0.21	1.2	-0.03	**4.9**	20.8	1.22	15.70	3.11	62.7	**6.6**	39.3	2.5	**7.6**
7.2	0.02	0.8	-0.01	**1.9**	0.1	0.09	1.11	3.80	96.7	**2.7**	20.6	16.0	**5.0**
8.4	0.05	0.2	-0.68	**6.3**	3.2	2.68	21.46	3.19	62.0	**1.8**	31.1	28.1	**8.0**
8.1	0.00	0.0	0.00	**3.4**	0.1	0.43	2.99	3.70	78.2	**1.4**	21.7	28.2	**6.5**
10.0	na	0.0	na	**9.5**	6.3	75.61	77.05	0.65	48.8	**4.0**	na	0.0	**3.2**
5.1	0.60	4.2	0.51	**9.4**	12.6	2.11	24.23	7.02	56.7	**2.8**	22.9	17.1	**7.5**
9.5	0.00	0.0	0.00	**4.5**	0.6	1.13	7.80	3.15	61.4	**6.6**	71.8	8.0	**8.1**
2.5	7.70	22.5	-0.02	**3.8**	0.1	0.95	8.70	3.11	67.4	**3.2**	56.5	20.2	**4.6**
5.2	0.02	2.5	0.00	**4.8**	0.7	0.93	12.12	4.18	69.5	**4.0**	11.6	8.0	**4.9**
7.2	0.52	2.0	-0.02	**5.6**	2.5	1.04	10.72	3.88	63.3	**4.6**	26.0	6.6	**6.3**
6.8	0.78	4.2	0.00	**3.4**	3.6	0.57	5.89	2.90	76.1	**1.9**	21.7	8.4	**7.9**
3.9	2.77	11.6	0.04	**3.2**	0.1	0.32	4.00	3.33	86.2	**5.7**	47.7	7.1	**4.3**
9.1	1.11	2.5	-0.01	**3.8**	0.4	0.67	5.22	2.46	67.6	**3.6**	55.6	22.0	**7.9**
5.3	5.12	13.9	1.16	**4.3**	1.0	0.80	6.16	3.08	60.9	**4.6**	45.8	13.6	**6.3**
6.2	0.55	2.5	0.00	**5.4**	6.3	1.40	15.31	3.39	60.0	**2.3**	23.3	18.5	**6.7**
5.4	1.18	5.5	0.00	**3.4**	0.6	0.73	7.08	3.41	83.1	**2.4**	21.2	17.4	**6.3**
8.2	2.85	4.0	-0.62	**0.7**	-1.5	-0.73	-6.34	1.04	132.3	**7.5**	92.8	5.5	**5.2**
4.6	1.27	11.5	0.01	**10.0**	19.6	4.24	33.28	6.29	26.8	**1.4**	31.9	19.4	**9.8**
5.3	0.86	4.6	0.00	**4.7**	4.6	1.01	9.82	2.97	64.4	**5.1**	43.7	8.8	**6.8**
9.1	0.00	0.0	-0.01	**5.6**	1.0	1.10	10.47	4.01	68.1	**5.1**	15.5	1.7	**6.9**
6.5	0.61	5.3	0.13	**2.5**	23.3	0.29	3.37	1.83	82.2	**1.8**	20.8	24.2	**6.0**
8.9	0.12	0.5	0.00	**6.1**	3.7	1.53	16.08	2.95	54.5	**4.5**	34.1	10.3	**6.3**
9.4	0.00	0.0	0.01	**5.4**	1.0	1.01	4.85	2.30	78.3	**8.0**	82.0	0.1	**8.4**
6.4	0.19	1.4	0.08	**5.4**	4.5	1.22	14.66	3.43	57.6	**4.5**	19.0	6.1	**5.4**
5.8	0.38	2.3	0.02	**7.0**	5.0	1.92	25.27	4.30	63.5	**4.5**	20.7	5.8	**6.0**
5.1	1.72	4.6	0.00	**9.1**	2.0	2.26	17.64	4.55	58.3	**3.5**	23.7	4.4	**9.1**
10.0	0.00	0.0	0.00	**3.2**	0.4	0.80	5.80	2.69	75.0	**6.3**	63.9	8.7	**5.8**

Name	City	State	Rating	2020 Rating	2019 Rating	Total Assets ($Mil)	One Year Asset Growth	Asset Mix (As a % of Total Assets) Comm-ercial Loans	Cons-umer Loans	Mort-gage Loans	Secur-ities	Capital-ization Index	Lever-age Ratio	Risk-Based Capital Ratio
Argentine Federal Savings	Kansas City	KS	**C**	C	C	60.2	8.14	0.0	0.3	51.3	32.9	**10.0**	13.1	0.0
Arizona Bank & Trust	Phoenix	AZ	**B+**	B+	B+	1645.8	69.54	17.3	0.7	3.9	40.6	**5.5**	7.5	11.7
Arlington State Bank	Arlington	MN	**B-**	B	B+	68.7	17.88	2.5	1.6	1.9	48.0	**6.3**	8.3	23.4
Armed Forces Bank, N.A.	Fort Leavenworth	KS	**A-**	A-	A-	1225.2	4.59	9.4	1.1	5.4	36.4	**10.0**	14.5	25.4
▼ Armor Bank	Forrest City	AR	**C-**	C	C	310.7	71.70	9.2	0.8	8.3	14.1	**6.9**	8.9	0.0
Armstrong Bank	Muskogee	OK	**B**	B-	B-	2394.8	21.97	6.4	3.3	13.9	27.0	**6.4**	8.4	16.0
Armstrong County Building and Loan Assn.	Ford City	PA	**C-**	C	C	94.6	5.47	0.0	0.7	48.4	37.2	**10.0**	13.9	34.8
Aroostook County Federal S&L Assn.	Caribou	ME	**B-**	B-	C+	165.1	11.48	13.8	10.5	43.1	17.3	**8.5**	10.0	16.9
Arrowhead Bank	Llano	TX	**B+**	A-	A-	257.0	24.19	4.2	3.1	22.2	19.8	**6.8**	8.8	16.5
Arthur State Bank	Union	SC	**B**	B+	B+	680.4	14.88	4.7	0.9	28.8	16.3	**5.7**	7.7	14.2
▲ Artisans' Bank	Wilmington	DE	**C+**	C	C	641.0	5.31	5.1	0.1	17.1	22.0	**6.6**	8.6	12.7
Arundel Federal Savings Bank	Glen Burnie	MD	**C-**	C-	C	451.3	3.91	0.3	0.1	58.5	17.3	**10.0**	14.9	0.0
▲ Arvest Bank	Fayetteville	AR	**B**	C+	B-	26237.7	13.01	10.5	6.6	14.7	28.5	**6.2**	8.2	14.3
Ascent Bank	Helena	MT	**B**	B	B	83.0	7.09	22.7	1.1	15.4	7.2	**9.2**	10.5	18.0
Ashton State Bank	Ashton	IA	**B+**	B	B	55.5	9.90	5.8	2.9	8.5	28.4	**10.0**	11.9	0.0
Ashton State Bank	Ashton	NE	**E+**	D-	D-	20.3	2.01	1.4	1.0	0.2	5.9	**6.9**	8.9	16.1
▲ Asian Bank	Philadelphia	PA	**B+**	B	B-	293.6	16.51	7.5	0.0	14.3	4.6	**10.0**	12.0	17.1
▲ Asian Pacific National Bank	San Gabriel	CA	**C+**	C	C	56.3	-1.53	0.0	0.0	6.5	10.6	**10.0**	18.0	0.0
▲ Aspire Bank	Fargo	ND	**C+**	C	D+	55.0	8.27	24.3	0.6	7.4	0.1	**5.3**	8.9	11.2
Associated Bank, N.A.	Green Bay	WI	**B**	B-	B	34102.8	-3.81	15.5	0.9	22.9	15.4	**6.9**	8.9	12.7
Associated Trust Co., N.A.	Milwaukee	WI	**U**	U	U	74.0	7.89	0.0	0.0	0.0	1.4	**10.0**	94.5	166.4
Astra Bank	Scandia	KS	**B-**	B-	B-	382.5	9.40	8.2	0.7	6.2	47.9	**5.9**	7.9	14.1
Atascosa Bank	Pleasanton	TX	**B-**	B-	B	98.0	4.48	4.2	2.3	2.4	56.2	**8.5**	10.0	0.0
Athol Savings Bank	Athol	MA	**B-**	C+	B-	534.5	7.14	2.6	1.9	37.8	23.8	**10.0**	12.5	20.5
▼ Atkins Savings Bank & Trust	Atkins	IA	**B+**	A-	B+	122.6	16.27	7.2	3.0	11.5	40.5	**10.0**	12.3	0.0
▲ Atlantic Capital Bank, N.A.	Atlanta	GA	**A-**	B+	B+	3779.1	30.74	23.1	4.9	1.0	19.2	**8.7**	10.1	15.6
Atlantic Community Bankers Bank	Camp Hill	PA	**C+**	C+	B-	766.6	-10.55	1.7	0.1	2.7	24.6	**10.0**	13.7	25.7
▲ Atlantic Union Bank	Richmond	VA	**B+**	B	B+	19953.9	1.25	15.0	3.0	7.5	17.5	**8.3**	10.4	13.6
Auburn Banking Co.	Auburn	KY	**B-**	B-	B	107.8	17.87	8.3	2.7	19.5	21.1	**6.0**	8.0	12.8
▼ Auburn Savings Bank, FSB	Auburn	ME	**C-**	C	C	100.4	13.15	7.4	0.6	49.6	9.2	**6.2**	8.2	14.8
Auburn State Bank	Auburn	NE	**B+**	A-	A-	219.7	11.63	2.5	1.0	8.7	44.4	**10.0**	15.3	0.0
AuburnBank	Auburn	AL	**B**	B	A-	1035.7	9.82	5.2	0.8	7.6	37.2	**8.2**	9.8	17.9
Audubon State Bank	Audubon	IA	**A-**	A-	B+	135.4	8.97	9.7	2.6	13.1	12.6	**6.9**	8.9	15.3
Austin Bank, Texas N.A.	Jacksonville	TX	**A**	A	A	2479.2	13.19	8.6	4.5	18.7	12.8	**10.0**	12.4	0.0
Austin Capital Bank SSB	Austin	TX	**B+**	B+	B+	383.4	96.86	0.9	75.0	8.7	0.3	**5.0**	7.0	73.6
Austin County State Bank	Bellville	TX	**B+**	B+	B+	277.5	15.01	23.4	0.9	21.5	8.1	**7.0**	9.0	13.3
Auto Club Trust, FSB	Dearborn	MI	**D-**	D-	D-	588.2	3.60	0.0	26.2	17.3	41.0	**7.4**	9.3	15.4
Availa Bank	Carroll	IA	**B**	B	B+	1384.0	10.86	9.9	0.4	8.4	26.3	**5.2**	8.0	0.0
AVB Bank	Broken Arrow	OK	**B-**	B-	B	454.9	3.06	11.2	0.4	19.8	10.9	**8.4**	9.9	15.4
Avidbank	San Jose	CA	**B+**	B+	B+	1601.2	13.50	25.1	0.1	0.3	13.0	**7.3**	9.6	12.8
Avidia Bank	Hudson	MA	**B-**	C+	B	2238.4	11.15	30.8	0.5	15.4	12.8	**6.4**	8.4	13.0
Axiom Bank, N.A.	Maitland	FL	**D+**	C-	C+	635.8	-5.40	14.7	15.0	13.4	0.5	**10.0**	13.1	18.8
Axos Bank	San Diego	CA	**B+**	B+	A-	12745.0	-2.10	8.5	2.9	33.2	1.7	**7.7**	9.5	13.2
▲ b1Bank	Baton Rouge	LA	**B**	C+	B	4328.5	9.17	13.7	1.0	9.0	20.4	**7.5**	9.8	12.9
BAC Community Bank	Stockton	CA	**B**	B	B	801.1	1.67	9.6	0.9	3.8	33.2	**7.4**	9.3	0.0
Badger Bank	Fort Atkinson	WI	**A**	A	A-	186.0	19.70	6.7	1.0	23.8	29.8	**10.0**	11.9	0.0
▼ Baker Boyer National Bank	Walla Walla	WA	**B-**	B+	B+	774.8	13.72	10.3	0.3	16.3	31.9	**5.6**	7.6	16.3
▲ Balboa Thrift and Loan Assn.	Chula Vista	CA	**B+**	B	B-	323.7	-1.21	0.0	71.0	0.9	0.0	**10.0**	14.0	0.0
Ballston Spa National Bank	Ballston Spa	NY	**B-**	B-	B-	696.8	9.12	6.8	4.1	31.0	10.4	**6.4**	8.4	13.4
▲ Banc of California, N.A.	Santa Ana	CA	**B-**	C	C	8023.5	3.48	7.4	0.0	16.0	16.9	**10.0**	12.5	17.3
▼ BancCentral, N.A.	Alva	OK	**D+**	C-	C	558.7	2.65	16.6	1.0	2.6	27.2	**2.6**	6.4	9.6
BancFirst	Oklahoma City	OK	**A-**	A-	A-	9958.6	13.95	14.2	3.7	9.7	5.3	**7.2**	9.1	16.2
Banco Do Brasil Americas	Miami	FL	**C+**	C+	C+	812.3	17.27	1.6	0.7	35.8	5.3	**6.9**	8.9	0.0
Banco Popular de Puerto Rico	San Juan	PR	**C**	C-	C-	61966.0	19.57	4.8	8.8	10.7	34.6	**4.3**	6.4	18.0
BancorpSouth Bank	Tupelo	MS	**B+**	B+	B+	27616.7	18.96	7.0	0.9	16.0	32.9	**6.4**	8.4	14.6
▼ Bandera Bank	Bandera	TX	**B**	B+	B+	84.7	10.91	3.3	3.1	25.9	16.4	**7.7**	9.5	0.0
Banesco USA	Coral Gables	FL	**C+**	C	B-	2054.9	1.61	10.4	0.0	14.8	18.3	**6.6**	8.6	13.7
Bangor Savings Bank	Bangor	ME	**B-**	B-	B-	6415.6	16.92	6.2	0.4	24.9	30.7	**5.4**	7.4	13.3
BANK	Wapello	IA	**A-**	B+	C+	113.1	5.46	17.9	4.4	13.1	0.0	**10.0**	13.1	0.0
Bank & Trust Co.	Litchfield	IL	**B-**	B-	B	419.2	6.33	7.4	6.9	10.7	29.8	**7.6**	9.4	16.8

Asset Quality Index	Adjusted Non-Performing Loans as a % of Total Loans	Adjusted Non-Performing Loans as a % of Capital	Net Charge-Offs Avg Loans	Profitability Index	Net Income ($Mil)	Return on Assets (R.O.A.)	Return on Equity (R.O.E.)	Net Interest Spread	Overhead Efficiency Ratio	Liquidity Index	Liquidity Ratio	Hot Money Ratio	Stability Index
9.6	0.77	3.2	0.00	2.3	0.1	0.27	1.99	3.38	85.7	2.0	40.2	39.9	7.2
7.9	0.08	0.4	0.01	6.6	10.4	1.31	13.51	3.25	57.2	6.8	40.4	1.8	7.9
3.1	0.61	24.3	0.01	2.9	0.1	0.26	2.90	2.34	88.4	6.4	74.5	7.9	4.6
8.5	0.56	1.6	0.12	6.5	6.9	1.17	7.50	2.54	74.9	7.0	55.0	4.2	9.0
8.3	0.04	0.5	0.01	1.5	0.1	0.08	0.75	2.97	85.2	1.9	22.9	20.7	5.0
5.1	1.64	8.2	-0.02	6.1	14.9	1.29	13.27	3.52	60.7	4.3	42.4	16.5	8.2
7.9	0.81	6.3	0.00	1.4	0.0	0.00	0.02	1.16	87.7	2.3	50.1	38.3	6.9
5.3	0.71	4.7	0.00	3.6	0.7	0.82	8.08	2.96	65.7	2.7	33.4	19.3	5.4
7.8	0.29	3.1	0.04	5.1	1.3	1.09	12.23	3.12	64.1	6.0	42.2	4.3	5.2
6.3	1.16	5.0	0.01	4.7	2.9	0.86	10.86	3.72	73.3	5.5	31.7	2.7	5.7
5.6	0.74	5.5	-0.04	3.3	1.7	0.54	5.88	3.02	77.8	4.3	34.5	11.8	6.0
6.6	1.43	6.5	0.00	1.9	0.5	0.24	1.57	2.33	86.4	2.0	30.4	24.9	7.4
5.1	1.08	4.6	0.17	6.4	219.9	1.72	17.72	2.76	69.5	6.5	37.2	2.5	7.8
5.2	1.05	4.9	0.13	4.6	0.3	0.82	7.83	3.88	71.7	4.0	34.7	13.1	6.8
8.7	0.00	1.0	0.00	6.0	0.4	1.48	11.90	3.95	50.5	3.9	47.4	16.9	6.6
0.0	14.76	87.4	0.00	1.2	0.1	0.48	5.65	4.30	91.3	2.2	29.3	18.2	3.3
7.1	0.38	1.9	-0.01	5.2	1.5	1.06	9.63	3.39	55.1	0.9	18.9	37.5	6.1
9.3	0.00	0.0	0.00	2.7	0.2	0.58	3.25	3.13	80.6	2.3	53.3	53.2	7.7
7.9	0.00	0.0	-0.01	6.9	0.6	2.34	26.89	5.01	50.6	4.4	16.5	6.1	4.8
5.4	0.78	3.9	0.08	5.3	190.6	1.12	9.52	2.38	65.7	4.6	15.8	1.9	9.7
8.8	na	0.0	na	10.0	15.3	43.99	50.65	0.64	59.3	4.0	432.8	0.0	7.0
7.0	0.46	2.3	-0.03	3.5	1.6	0.84	9.94	3.17	79.7	5.8	39.2	4.3	5.4
9.8	0.00	0.0	-0.03	3.2	0.2	0.38	3.53	1.71	78.0	6.7	94.8	9.8	5.5
9.0	0.51	2.5	0.01	4.2	2.7	1.03	8.56	2.55	84.0	4.1	39.6	12.8	7.9
4.8	0.40	12.6	0.49	8.3	1.7	2.71	22.30	3.91	33.6	3.8	50.7	18.8	7.6
8.1	0.75	1.8	0.07	6.3	27.4	1.49	13.56	2.96	51.5	6.9	38.5	0.1	9.0
9.2	0.05	0.1	0.00	2.8	1.9	0.50	3.64	1.71	86.3	3.6	45.1	18.3	8.1
6.6	0.35	1.7	0.02	6.3	148.2	1.50	10.27	3.22	59.8	4.3	18.9	7.6	9.7
6.6	0.67	3.4	-0.01	6.6	0.8	1.58	19.63	3.66	62.2	2.7	19.5	15.7	6.0
4.4	1.95	13.6	-0.02	2.4	0.1	0.30	3.67	3.26	88.4	1.3	19.8	29.4	4.2
9.2	0.40	0.5	0.00	5.2	1.3	1.17	7.25	3.19	50.6	3.3	31.4	15.4	8.4
9.0	0.14	0.6	-0.04	4.4	4.0	0.82	7.97	2.71	69.5	5.1	38.3	11.4	7.3
7.0	0.44	1.3	0.00	7.9	1.3	1.92	17.51	3.86	45.3	3.5	23.3	10.2	8.6
7.2	0.77	3.2	0.06	7.9	18.0	1.53	11.69	3.91	57.2	5.1	28.3	8.5	10.0
5.6	0.06	0.8	0.03	7.9	2.5	1.47	21.46	6.60	86.1	4.8	11.6	2.7	5.8
7.7	0.04	2.1	-0.02	6.0	2.0	1.49	16.55	4.58	57.3	0.9	19.1	27.9	6.5
5.3	0.75	2.7	0.18	0.0	-3.1	-1.03	-9.88	2.20	117.0	0.9	27.5	43.2	4.7
8.1	0.24	1.4	0.00	4.3	6.7	0.98	9.88	3.06	67.6	4.5	25.1	10.1	8.2
8.8	0.00	0.0	-0.10	4.2	1.6	0.71	7.16	3.77	69.5	3.2	19.2	13.5	6.3
8.3	0.33	2.1	0.02	5.2	6.6	0.87	9.16	3.94	67.3	5.6	37.5	8.7	7.4
6.4	0.82	3.9	0.07	4.2	10.1	0.93	10.37	3.36	76.5	5.2	25.7	5.7	7.0
4.7	1.20	4.8	0.02	1.3	0.5	0.14	0.92	3.51	95.2	0.8	18.6	43.6	6.4
4.6	1.22	9.9	0.13	9.7	114.3	1.73	18.21	4.33	43.8	2.8	7.9	8.7	9.4
6.9	0.38	2.6	0.06	7.0	32.9	1.52	13.86	4.17	54.0	3.3	23.4	15.0	8.6
6.1	0.48	2.7	-0.01	4.8	4.2	1.06	10.82	3.37	67.7	6.2	40.0	2.3	7.7
8.7	0.50	1.6	0.12	8.7	1.2	1.43	11.65	3.35	56.1	5.6	40.2	6.2	8.1
6.4	0.66	3.2	0.06	3.8	2.3	0.60	7.63	2.89	83.9	6.6	45.9	1.5	5.4
5.6	0.35	1.4	0.47	7.2	2.5	1.49	10.92	6.86	49.6	0.5	11.5	62.8	6.8
6.3	0.41	3.4	0.01	3.7	2.4	0.67	8.21	3.17	72.5	4.2	12.1	6.7	6.1
6.6	0.97	4.9	0.04	4.0	39.5	1.01	7.84	3.39	64.0	4.4	21.3	7.8	8.3
1.5	6.36	42.0	3.06	0.0	-5.0	-1.75	-20.63	3.16	86.9	1.3	26.3	28.8	5.3
7.0	0.64	3.0	0.16	8.3	84.5	1.79	17.94	3.40	54.9	6.3	37.1	3.7	8.2
7.3	0.35	1.9	0.01	3.3	1.7	0.46	4.45	2.91	80.7	3.9	44.8	16.0	6.2
2.3	9.14	30.6	0.18	6.7	404.0	1.41	19.51	3.00	57.6	5.6	31.5	6.0	6.5
6.7	0.45	1.9	0.02	5.8	157.1	1.23	10.89	3.05	60.7	5.0	26.4	7.4	10.0
8.4	0.00	0.0	0.12	4.2	0.3	0.72	7.46	2.81	77.1	5.8	57.9	8.6	5.7
6.3	1.23	7.0	-0.01	4.0	8.3	0.82	9.89	3.20	71.0	2.0	22.6	15.0	6.5
8.0	0.39	2.2	-0.06	3.8	21.3	0.69	8.04	2.99	76.5	4.9	23.4	4.0	7.1
7.2	0.93	2.9	-0.18	7.9	1.3	2.43	18.42	3.61	58.2	5.1	28.3	4.3	7.7
4.7	1.82	7.7	0.08	4.6	1.8	0.85	8.81	2.86	63.0	3.4	36.3	17.0	6.7

Name	City	State	Rating	2020 Rating	2019 Rating	Total Assets ($Mil)	One Year Asset Growth	Asset Mix (As a % of Total Assets) Comm-ercial Loans	Cons-umer Loans	Mort-gage Loans	Secur-ities	Capital-ization Index	Lever-age Ratio	Risk-Based Capital Ratio
Bank 1st	West Union	IA	**A**	A	A	160.2	13.88	3.7	1.6	12.9	44.3	**10.0**	12.6	0.0
Bank 21	Carrollton	MO	**B**	B	C+	159.2	2.82	11.3	1.1	28.8	3.0	**6.5**	8.5	12.2
▲ BANK 34	Alamogordo	NM	**B**	C+	C+	488.0	6.68	11.7	0.1	8.2	12.0	**10.0**	11.9	16.2
Bank First, N.A.	Manitowoc	WI	**B+**	B+	B	2819.0	6.07	13.1	1.2	19.0	5.6	**6.5**	9.5	12.2
Bank Five Nine	Oconomowoc	WI	**B-**	C+	C+	1537.0	15.62	9.1	0.1	8.9	10.5	**8.8**	10.2	16.0
Bank Forward	Hannaford	ND	**B+**	B+	B	847.6	0.57	6.8	2.4	7.7	5.6	**5.6**	8.9	0.0
Bank Independent	Sheffield	AL	**B**	B	B	2114.6	10.46	16.2	0.9	10.6	10.3	**6.5**	8.5	14.0
▲ Bank Iowa	West Des Moines	IA	**B**	B-	B	1709.2	8.54	7.6	0.7	6.8	27.0	**6.7**	8.7	12.8
▲ Bank Leumi USA	New York	NY	**B**	B-	B	8350.8	14.72	21.5	0.0	0.2	22.3	**9.2**	10.5	15.3
▲ Bank Michigan	Brooklyn	MI	**C-**	D+	C-	119.1	-7.94	25.9	0.1	11.1	4.2	**6.7**	8.7	14.1
Bank Midwest	Spirit Lake	IA	**B+**	B+	B-	1162.2	10.54	25.7	0.4	4.9	22.3	**6.6**	8.6	12.8
Bank Northwest	Hamilton	MO	**A-**	A-	A-	196.0	9.66	14.2	1.8	10.2	8.5	**6.4**	8.4	0.0
Bank of Abbeville & Trust Co.	Abbeville	LA	**B**	B	B-	209.1	8.58	8.4	1.6	15.9	30.3	**10.0**	14.6	0.0
Bank of Alapaha	Alapaha	GA	**C+**	C+	B+	225.2	14.14	16.7	5.4	15.0	21.6	**6.9**	8.9	17.0
Bank of Alma	Alma	WI	**A+**	A+	A	277.3	-6.28	4.2	0.6	5.6	25.7	**10.0**	43.6	0.0
Bank of America California, N.A.	San Francisco	CA	**B+**	B+	A-	25697.0	23.90	0.0	0.0	38.8	0.0	**6.5**	8.5	38.7
Bank of America, N.A.	Charlotte	NC	**B+**	B+	B+	2350294.0	8.73	12.0	6.5	8.8	38.3	**5.5**	7.5	14.5
Bank of Anguilla	Anguilla	MS	**C-**	C	C-	165.0	2.72	7.0	3.6	6.7	20.0	**8.0**	9.7	0.0
Bank of Ann Arbor	Ann Arbor	MI	**A-**	A-	A-	2561.3	20.15	16.5	0.4	4.7	5.4	**6.5**	8.5	14.8
Bank of Bartlett	Bartlett	TN	**C+**	C+	C+	472.0	8.61	11.5	2.0	25.6	20.2	**5.8**	7.8	16.6
▼ Bank of Bearden	Bearden	AR	**C+**	B	B+	91.7	47.28	4.6	2.0	4.1	17.9	**4.9**	6.9	25.1
Bank of Belle Glade	Belle Glade	FL	**C**	C+	B-	139.0	-0.82	5.2	0.2	9.4	30.5	**5.7**	7.7	27.6
Bank of Belleville	Belleville	IL	**B-**	C+	C+	335.5	17.42	16.0	0.6	13.9	14.8	**6.7**	8.7	12.6
Bank of Billings	Billings	MO	**B-**	B-	B-	74.6	15.60	17.0	2.8	32.6	0.0	**6.9**	8.9	0.0
Bank of Bird-in-Hand	Bird in Hand	PA	**B**	B	B	665.2	26.10	5.9	0.1	24.3	0.2	**9.0**	12.7	14.2
Bank of Blue Valley	Overland Park	KS	**B+**	B+	B+	1419.4	2.84	14.9	1.1	2.0	39.9	**9.9**	10.9	18.0
Bank of Bluffs	Bluffs	IL	**C+**	C+	B-	61.8	1.70	7.8	4.1	12.0	24.8	**10.0**	12.2	0.0
Bank of Botetourt	Buchanan	VA	**B-**	B-	B	645.3	11.90	7.8	2.9	22.5	5.9	**7.0**	9.0	0.0
Bank of Bourbonnais	Bourbonnais	IL	**B+**	B+	A-	87.1	7.51	2.9	0.2	8.4	0.7	**7.3**	9.2	18.9
Bank of Bozeman	Bozeman	MT	**C+**	C+	C+	108.4	11.76	14.7	2.3	9.1	10.5	**6.3**	8.3	12.0
Bank of Brenham, N.A.	Brenham	TX	**B+**	B+	B	603.0	14.00	2.8	0.6	5.8	81.0	**9.4**	10.6	29.6
Bank of Brewton	Brewton	AL	**B-**	B-	C+	56.2	11.41	11.1	3.6	5.6	55.2	**10.0**	20.9	0.0
Bank of Bridger, N.A.	Bridger	MT	**B**	B	B	719.8	4.44	6.7	1.9	7.5	51.9	**6.9**	8.9	19.8
Bank of Brookfield-Purdin N.A.	Brookfield	MO	**B-**	B-	B-	105.3	13.70	2.6	1.5	3.6	53.5	**9.7**	10.8	35.0
Bank of Brookhaven	Brookhaven	MS	**B**	B	B+	210.7	10.64	8.2	2.0	11.3	35.8	**8.0**	9.6	17.6
Bank of Buffalo	Buffalo	KY	**B**	B	B	74.4	0.93	2.9	5.4	23.3	41.7	**10.0**	11.3	20.1
Bank of Burlington	Burlington	CO	**A-**	B+	B+	80.8	9.54	18.1	0.5	1.4	9.2	**10.0**	11.8	0.0
Bank of Cadiz and Trust Co.	Cadiz	KY	**C**	C+	B-	141.2	10.55	2.5	1.9	17.2	40.8	**5.5**	7.5	16.4
Bank of Calhoun County	Hardin	IL	**C+**	C+	C+	78.5	11.15	1.5	2.3	29.6	7.1	**6.6**	8.6	17.4
Bank of Camilla	Camilla	GA	**B+**	B+	B+	132.2	16.82	6.9	1.1	12.0	28.0	**10.0**	13.2	0.0
Bank of Cashton	Cashton	WI	**A-**	B+	A-	121.4	4.32	18.7	2.0	7.8	14.8	**9.0**	10.3	15.8
Bank of Cattaraugus	Cattaraugus	NY	**C**	C	D+	28.5	20.85	6.1	7.1	14.1	31.7	**5.5**	7.5	20.9
Bank of Cave City	Cave City	AR	**B-**	B-	B-	157.0	12.14	6.3	3.1	13.7	23.6	**6.5**	8.5	17.2
Bank of Central Florida	Lakeland	FL	**B**	B	B+	882.1	18.30	12.0	1.8	8.2	13.7	**6.0**	8.0	18.3
▲ Bank of Charles Town	Charles Town	WV	**B**	B-	B-	671.7	10.69	8.1	0.8	26.5	12.0	**8.8**	10.2	15.9
Bank of Cherokee County	Hulbert	OK	**C+**	C+	C+	162.6	20.46	6.5	7.7	18.8	3.5	**6.4**	8.4	14.6
▼ Bank of Chestnut	Chestnut	IL	**D-**	D	D	20.7	12.38	4.2	8.3	30.2	33.8	**6.5**	8.5	0.0
Bank of Clarke County	Berryville	VA	**B+**	B+	B+	1216.4	19.89	10.3	3.6	17.9	14.5	**6.6**	8.6	12.4
Bank of Clarks	Clarks	NE	**C+**	C+	C+	45.4	8.98	4.4	8.6	2.8	8.8	**8.3**	9.9	17.8
Bank of Clarkson	Clarkson	KY	**B+**	B+	B+	148.3	15.21	0.6	4.7	23.1	35.3	**10.0**	12.2	23.7
Bank of Cleveland	Cleveland	TN	**A**	A	A-	321.4	-1.90	5.6	0.5	16.7	0.6	**10.0**	15.9	25.2
Bank of Colorado	Fort Collins	CO	**A-**	A-	A-	6245.8	18.93	5.7	0.6	10.4	30.4	**6.4**	8.4	15.1
Bank of Columbia	Columbia	KY	**B-**	B-	B	179.9	5.71	10.1	4.4	17.1	15.7	**6.7**	9.2	0.0
Bank of Commerce	Chanute	KS	**B+**	B	B-	395.6	8.23	8.9	3.1	14.7	28.3	**6.9**	8.9	15.1
Bank of Commerce	Greenwood	MS	**A-**	A-	A-	728.3	15.43	9.4	2.1	14.8	41.0	**8.7**	10.3	0.0
Bank of Commerce	Chelsea	OK	**B+**	B+	B+	195.7	7.61	10.8	7.2	13.7	9.3	**9.0**	10.3	18.5
Bank of Commerce	Chouteau	OK	**C**	C	C+	44.4	8.98	7.0	3.0	12.4	22.4	**5.9**	7.9	21.8
Bank of Commerce	Duncan	OK	**D+**	D+	C-	380.2	7.15	20.7	0.9	5.8	7.6	**4.5**	9.9	0.0
Bank of Commerce	Rawlins	WY	**A-**	A-	A-	167.4	6.49	9.1	1.3	12.3	42.3	**10.0**	11.0	21.2
Bank of Commerce & Trust Co.	Crowley	LA	**C**	C	B-	387.2	8.58	4.0	1.4	4.7	75.6	**9.0**	10.4	0.0

Asset Quality Index	Adjusted Non-Performing Loans as a % of Total Loans	Adjusted Non-Performing Loans as a % of Capital	Net Charge-Offs Avg Loans	Profitability Index	Net Income ($Mil)	Return on Assets (R.O.A.)	Return on Equity (R.O.E.)	Net Interest Spread	Overhead Efficiency Ratio	Liquidity Index	Liquidity Ratio	Hot Money Ratio	Stability Index
8.9	0.00	1.4	-0.01	**6.9**	1.3	1.58	12.29	3.51	53.6	**5.3**	53.4	11.8	**8.8**
8.6	0.13	1.2	0.00	**4.9**	0.9	1.16	13.35	3.77	68.6	**3.9**	14.5	9.6	**6.3**
7.5	0.78	0.6	0.00	**4.7**	2.5	1.08	10.52	4.12	67.1	**3.8**	20.2	10.5	**6.3**
6.1	0.59	3.7	0.00	**8.5**	23.9	1.72	14.86	3.48	41.8	**4.5**	12.4	5.1	**9.7**
7.2	0.87	1.5	0.11	**8.1**	13.4	1.80	17.51	3.66	58.9	**2.7**	21.9	14.8	**8.5**
6.1	0.34	2.3	-0.01	**7.3**	7.9	1.84	19.46	3.65	64.6	**2.9**	21.7	10.3	**7.9**
4.9	0.85	9.7	0.13	**5.2**	9.9	0.96	11.27	4.11	74.6	**4.4**	33.0	12.1	**7.4**
6.1	1.05	5.8	0.01	**4.9**	10.8	1.28	13.93	3.44	61.3	**3.4**	21.2	13.3	**8.7**
5.7	0.94	5.4	0.35	**5.0**	42.2	1.04	9.85	3.07	62.7	**5.5**	35.8	6.2	**7.7**
4.7	0.93	6.8	-0.03	**2.8**	0.5	0.75	8.89	4.40	88.2	**1.9**	21.9	18.4	**3.1**
8.1	0.17	1.0	0.04	**6.2**	6.9	1.21	13.22	3.53	67.4	**4.2**	24.7	8.3	**8.5**
7.7	0.23	2.0	0.11	**10.0**	3.4	3.32	37.89	5.29	34.5	**4.0**	24.4	9.8	**7.0**
5.9	2.83	8.3	0.00	**3.7**	0.8	0.80	5.39	2.99	69.2	**3.5**	41.5	17.9	**7.8**
7.6	0.15	0.8	0.01	**3.3**	0.5	0.48	5.38	2.76	70.0	**2.3**	33.1	24.0	**4.0**
8.9	1.83	1.6	-0.01	**10.0**	5.3	3.65	8.50	4.69	10.1	**6.8**	66.5	5.7	**9.7**
6.7	2.83	9.6	-0.02	**4.8**	63.0	0.49	5.85	0.93	32.8	**7.9**	66.5	0.0	**8.2**
6.4	1.00	3.3	0.31	**5.7**	12420.0	1.09	11.23	1.93	63.0	**7.5**	56.2	1.3	**7.9**
4.7	1.58	9.1	0.41	**2.5**	0.4	0.49	5.75	3.08	81.2	**1.5**	22.9	27.5	**4.0**
7.3	0.52	3.0	0.02	**8.0**	19.7	1.62	18.07	3.00	47.4	**6.1**	39.1	5.9	**8.3**
5.6	0.70	4.2	0.10	**3.1**	0.9	0.40	4.91	3.30	90.9	**5.5**	31.9	3.0	**4.3**
9.5	0.01	0.0	0.06	**3.2**	0.1	0.32	4.36	1.67	79.5	**6.2**	72.7	9.4	**5.3**
9.0	1.12	1.9	0.00	**2.3**	0.1	0.15	1.87	1.60	93.1	**6.7**	68.5	6.9	**4.3**
8.5	0.00	0.0	0.00	**4.6**	1.9	1.15	14.77	3.42	60.6	**1.6**	12.9	20.4	**4.2**
3.8	0.76	4.6	-0.04	**5.5**	0.4	1.05	8.59	5.61	69.7	**4.3**	19.5	7.2	**6.3**
8.7	0.02	0.1	0.00	**4.2**	2.6	0.85	6.55	2.82	54.5	**4.3**	10.8	6.3	**7.5**
6.7	1.02	3.5	0.21	**5.5**	8.0	1.15	7.92	3.37	61.6	**6.4**	37.7	3.0	**8.7**
7.6	0.43	1.9	0.56	**3.0**	0.2	0.67	5.36	3.02	79.2	**3.7**	32.1	12.8	**5.9**
6.2	0.44	4.3	0.01	**5.1**	3.6	1.13	12.85	3.27	61.8	**2.0**	28.4	23.8	**6.0**
9.0	0.00	0.0	-0.01	**2.4**	0.1	0.13	1.38	2.38	91.6	**3.0**	50.7	25.2	**6.3**
4.6	1.74	9.7	0.00	**3.9**	0.4	0.67	7.36	3.99	77.8	**3.6**	29.9	13.8	**5.1**
8.3	0.76	0.7	0.00	**5.7**	4.8	1.69	12.46	2.92	36.9	**2.9**	58.7	42.2	**8.2**
7.6	3.69	5.2	0.70	**2.7**	0.2	0.59	2.76	3.43	83.7	**6.4**	72.0	7.6	**6.8**
8.4	0.76	1.1	0.01	**4.7**	3.5	0.98	9.75	3.09	59.7	**5.8**	43.5	5.8	**6.7**
9.7	0.09	0.2	0.00	**3.5**	0.4	0.75	6.49	2.55	70.3	**6.7**	71.1	7.0	**6.9**
8.9	0.00	0.0	0.01	**4.2**	1.0	0.94	9.32	2.98	65.6	**4.1**	41.6	15.1	**6.6**
6.7	0.91	5.5	-0.01	**5.9**	0.6	1.53	12.88	3.06	53.4	**2.4**	45.0	26.6	**7.6**
8.7	0.00	0.0	0.00	**6.2**	0.7	1.69	13.84	2.91	53.7	**3.0**	44.7	22.8	**8.4**
7.5	0.52	2.9	-0.01	**2.9**	0.3	0.36	4.66	2.42	83.8	**4.6**	53.4	15.2	**3.8**
8.1	0.72	2.2	0.00	**3.2**	0.2	0.42	4.68	2.50	79.4	**5.1**	41.5	10.0	**4.5**
6.2	2.57	6.9	-0.01	**4.0**	0.5	0.74	5.30	3.24	74.3	**1.8**	23.9	23.3	**8.0**
8.7	0.15	0.6	-0.01	**5.3**	0.7	1.12	10.75	3.61	64.3	**4.3**	38.0	13.0	**8.2**
9.3	0.15	1.2	0.24	**2.9**	0.1	0.36	4.57	3.94	90.5	**6.0**	33.8	0.9	**3.2**
5.4	0.96	6.4	0.00	**4.9**	0.9	1.19	14.18	3.66	68.5	**2.2**	28.1	16.8	**5.2**
8.8	0.02	0.1	-0.01	**4.7**	4.0	0.98	13.32	2.55	60.9	**6.7**	52.0	2.8	**5.5**
8.7	0.18	0.8	-0.02	**5.0**	3.8	1.16	11.86	3.25	64.0	**3.5**	21.4	11.9	**6.3**
5.6	0.53	3.1	0.10	**3.9**	0.7	0.91	11.64	4.26	77.4	**3.3**	33.9	16.6	**4.1**
4.0	3.02	13.2	-0.08	**2.1**	0.0	0.18	2.22	3.12	90.3	**3.0**	35.6	16.2	**1.7**
6.3	0.73	5.3	-0.03	**5.2**	5.9	1.02	11.73	3.56	67.1	**4.7**	25.0	8.4	**8.0**
3.2	5.53	31.0	0.10	**5.0**	0.2	1.03	10.39	4.10	66.3	**5.6**	48.5	8.0	**6.0**
7.7	0.09	1.2	0.01	**6.4**	0.9	1.20	9.68	3.48	59.4	**4.2**	45.2	15.4	**8.3**
7.7	0.63	2.0	-0.01	**9.8**	3.1	2.01	12.77	4.24	50.4	**4.7**	26.0	5.7	**9.3**
7.5	0.44	2.5	0.00	**7.2**	42.2	1.44	15.68	3.29	51.1	**5.8**	33.4	6.0	**8.1**
3.9	1.70	10.9	0.00	**9.2**	2.2	2.55	26.93	5.06	47.8	**2.8**	26.1	16.2	**8.0**
8.7	0.00	0.0	0.00	**6.8**	3.7	1.90	21.38	3.85	51.6	**3.4**	16.9	12.0	**5.7**
6.9	0.24	2.7	0.08	**7.1**	5.1	1.61	14.91	2.94	46.0	**3.4**	29.7	14.6	**6.9**
4.7	0.18	13.2	0.18	**6.4**	1.3	1.35	13.08	4.47	60.1	**3.9**	34.8	13.6	**6.6**
5.6	2.61	5.9	-0.05	**3.8**	0.2	0.71	9.06	3.59	80.4	**5.4**	40.9	7.5	**3.7**
0.9	3.69	47.7	1.44	**3.9**	1.1	0.56	5.44	3.94	58.3	**1.7**	18.1	22.6	**7.5**
9.1	0.00	0.1	0.00	**5.8**	1.0	1.21	10.53	3.67	61.1	**2.2**	27.2	19.6	**8.0**
6.0	3.67	7.8	0.06	**2.3**	0.2	0.12	1.31	1.51	90.7	**5.5**	46.7	9.0	**4.6**

	Name	City	State	Rating	2020 Rating	2019 Rating	Total Assets ($Mil)	One Year Asset Growth	Comm-ercial Loans	Cons-umer Loans	Mort-gage Loans	Secur-ities	Capital-ization Index	Lever-age Ratio	Risk-Based Capital Ratio
	Bank of Cordell	Cordell	OK	**B+**	B+	B+	43.9	8.59	11.5	0.5	35.2	0.0	**9.1**	10.4	0.0
	Bank of Coushatta	Coushatta	LA	**B-**	B	B	269.2	7.58	4.3	0.9	12.8	50.7	**7.1**	9.1	0.0
▼	Bank of Crocker	Waynesville	MO	**C**	C+	C+	146.4	9.20	3.3	1.5	10.4	39.4	**9.1**	10.4	30.7
	Bank of Crockett	Bells	TN	**B+**	B+	B+	213.5	7.81	9.2	3.5	6.4	48.7	**8.2**	9.8	16.1
	Bank of Dade	Trenton	GA	**A-**	A-	A-	136.6	9.35	1.2	3.9	22.2	52.6	**7.9**	9.6	21.1
	Bank of Dawson	Dawson	GA	**B+**	B+	A-	147.3	12.58	6.5	2.6	13.0	20.2	**10.0**	16.6	27.4
	Bank of Delight	Delight	AR	**A-**	A-	A-	160.4	2.80	8.4	2.3	15.2	9.2	**10.0**	12.3	0.0
	Bank of Delmarva	Salisbury	MD	**C+**	C+	C	1013.9	10.69	6.7	0.1	12.9	5.8	**5.9**	7.9	12.8
	Bank of DeSoto, N.A.	Desoto	TX	**A-**	A-	A-	245.0	8.95	10.6	10.4	18.1	0.9	**6.5**	8.5	0.0
	Bank of Dickson	Dickson	TN	**B-**	B-	B	287.7	9.14	2.7	1.6	34.5	43.3	**9.4**	10.6	0.0
	Bank of Dixon County	Ponca	NE	**A-**	A-	B+	116.9	15.60	11.2	4.9	12.7	16.8	**10.0**	11.3	19.5
	Bank of Doniphan	Doniphan	NE	**B**	B	B	138.5	6.92	8.7	2.2	6.0	40.3	**6.5**	8.9	12.1
	Bank of Dudley	Dublin	GA	**B+**	B+	A-	301.8	20.44	8.9	3.8	11.8	10.3	**9.6**	10.7	0.0
▲	Bank of Eastern Oregon	Heppner	OR	**C-**	D	D+	722.5	10.87	13.6	0.5	2.9	2.9	**2.2**	8.3	0.0
	Bank of Easton	North Easton	MA	**B-**	B-	B-	184.1	5.20	0.0	0.3	40.3	26.6	**9.3**	10.5	0.0
	Bank of Edmonson County	Brownsville	KY	**A-**	B+	B	252.8	9.49	1.8	2.4	22.3	29.5	**9.8**	10.9	19.3
	Bank of Elgin	Elgin	NE	**A-**	A-	B+	66.2	6.20	8.6	1.2	0.4	11.7	**10.0**	13.4	0.0
	Bank of England	England	AR	**A**	A	B+	576.2	5.97	4.3	0.6	55.2	6.8	**10.0**	16.5	19.1
▲	Bank of Erath	Erath	LA	**B-**	C+	B	115.0	8.07	8.5	2.3	16.8	24.0	**10.0**	12.1	0.0
	Bank of Estes Park	Estes Park	CO	**B+**	B+	A-	160.6	13.32	0.6	0.0	9.3	24.4	**7.9**	9.6	0.0
	Bank of Eufaula	Eufaula	OK	**C-**	C	C+	111.6	8.82	2.0	4.6	10.6	44.3	**10.0**	11.7	0.0
	Bank of Evergreen	Evergreen	AL	**B-**	B-	B-	72.0	11.68	10.3	2.3	15.3	48.7	**10.0**	12.3	0.0
	Bank of Farmington	Farmington	IL	**B-**	B-	B-	211.9	7.94	13.7	2.9	11.1	21.6	**9.2**	10.5	15.7
	Bank of Forest	Forest	MS	**B+**	B+	B+	236.2	4.31	5.8	3.1	7.8	42.1	**10.0**	11.9	0.0
	Bank of Frankewing	Frankewing	TN	**B+**	B+	B+	390.9	13.89	11.2	3.7	16.0	7.8	**7.8**	10.0	0.0
	Bank of Franklin	Meadville	MS	**B+**	B+	A-	189.7	9.39	9.8	3.4	16.6	28.9	**8.1**	9.8	0.0
	Bank of Franklin County	Washington	MO	**C+**	C+	C+	322.3	8.35	16.3	1.7	14.4	18.7	**5.3**	8.9	0.0
	Bank of George	Las Vegas	NV	**A**	A	A	543.7	32.71	8.2	0.0	1.2	0.5	**10.0**	11.9	0.0
	Bank of Gibson City	Gibson City	IL	**B-**	B-	C+	121.0	18.30	3.5	3.1	8.4	17.6	**5.9**	7.9	14.3
	Bank of Gleason	Gleason	TN	**B+**	B+	B+	126.9	7.59	8.1	6.7	12.0	47.6	**10.0**	21.7	39.0
	Bank of Grand Lake	Grove	OK	**B-**	B-	B-	211.7	-0.11	5.2	2.5	23.3	21.4	**5.2**	7.2	13.5
▲	Bank of Grandin	Grandin	MO	**B**	C+	B-	194.7	6.11	12.5	7.6	10.1	29.2	**10.0**	14.8	0.0
	Bank of Greeley	Greeley	KS	**B**	B	B	43.9	9.67	5.5	3.6	14.4	14.5	**10.0**	12.3	0.0
	Bank of Greeleyville	Greeleyville	SC	**B+**	B+	B+	118.1	16.89	15.2	6.1	10.6	17.8	**9.0**	10.3	0.0
▼	Bank of Guam	Hagatna	GU	**C-**	C+	C+	2921.5	27.52	9.5	6.0	5.2	22.6	**4.4**	6.4	14.0
	Bank of Gueydan	Gueydan	LA	**B-**	B-	B	81.3	4.06	4.4	6.0	0.7	64.3	**10.0**	19.2	0.0
	Bank of Halls	Halls	TN	**B**	B	B	109.5	7.51	8.6	2.6	6.1	44.3	**6.4**	8.4	14.9
	Bank of Hancock County	Sparta	GA	**B-**	B	B+	88.7	9.51	4.8	5.2	10.0	62.4	**10.0**	18.4	0.0
	Bank of Hartington	Hartington	NE	**B+**	B	B-	120.0	7.28	9.4	1.5	3.4	27.6	**6.9**	8.9	14.8
	Bank of Hawaii	Honolulu	HI	**B**	B	B	22642.1	14.69	5.3	4.4	22.0	37.5	**4.3**	6.3	13.2
▲	Bank of Hays	Hays	KS	**B+**	B	B	327.0	8.61	14.7	1.7	7.6	37.8	**7.4**	9.2	0.0
	Bank of Hazelton	Hazelton	ND	**B-**	B	B	57.2	9.85	6.0	0.7	1.5	24.2	**8.0**	9.7	0.0
▼	Bank of Hazlehurst	Hazlehurst	GA	**C-**	C	D+	133.9	3.58	8.2	1.9	7.7	30.7	**10.0**	11.2	24.7
	Bank of Hillsboro, N.A.	Hillsboro	IL	**B-**	B	B	505.9	19.68	7.3	0.8	7.3	34.0	**7.4**	9.3	0.0
	Bank of Hindman	Hindman	KY	**C+**	C+	C+	280.7	1.76	5.9	1.0	9.6	56.3	**5.9**	7.9	16.1
	Bank of Holland	Holland	NY	**B-**	B-	B-	190.3	19.24	3.8	1.7	40.0	25.2	**5.6**	7.6	13.5
	Bank of Hope	Los Angeles	CA	**B**	B	B	17464.0	1.73	18.8	0.2	3.6	13.0	**9.4**	11.6	14.5
	Bank of Houston, N.A.	Houston	TX	**C**	C-	D+	370.4	52.10	19.2	0.3	11.1	2.9	**8.2**	11.1	0.0
	Bank of Hydro	Hydro	OK	**A-**	A-	A	141.4	3.76	7.7	2.1	30.5	0.6	**8.4**	11.2	0.0
	Bank of Iberia	Iberia	MO	**C-**	C-	C	65.0	9.79	2.4	4.4	20.8	23.5	**6.2**	8.2	17.3
	Bank of Idaho	Idaho Falls	ID	**B**	B-	B-	661.1	19.97	12.4	1.2	5.2	18.5	**7.8**	9.6	15.5
	Bank of Jackson Hole	Jackson	WY	**B+**	B+	B	1355.5	26.45	9.4	0.3	15.8	12.9	**6.6**	8.6	13.4
	Bank of Jamestown	Jamestown	KY	**B-**	B-	B-	237.5	11.06	4.3	0.8	8.2	24.4	**9.1**	11.0	14.2
	Bank of Kampsville	Kampsville	IL	**B**	B	B	127.7	9.69	2.3	6.4	14.5	29.8	**10.0**	15.8	0.0
	Bank of Kilmichael	Kilmichael	MS	**B+**	B+	B+	228.9	8.45	10.2	4.1	11.4	36.7	**6.9**	8.9	0.0
	Bank of Kirksville	Kirksville	MO	**B-**	B-	B+	464.0	2.15	3.1	0.4	12.9	45.8	**10.0**	11.9	40.1
▲	Bank of Labor	Kansas City	KS	**C-**	D+	C	866.4	14.24	17.5	0.1	2.2	53.4	**4.8**	6.8	13.5
	Bank of Lake Mills	Lake Mills	WI	**A**	A-	A-	259.3	2.12	2.4	10.3	26.9	12.9	**10.0**	13.5	21.1
	Bank of Lake Village	Lake Village	AR	**A-**	A-	A-	76.1	7.11	3.7	1.2	3.5	29.3	**10.0**	12.3	20.9
▲	Bank of Lewellen	Lewellen	NE	**B**	B-	C+	22.7	-8.91	5.0	0.9	0.0	31.5	**10.0**	18.6	0.0

Asset Mix columns (Comm-ercial Loans, Cons-umer Loans, Mort-gage Loans, Secur-ities) are As a % of Total Assets.

Arrows denote recent upgrades ▲ or downgrades ▼

Asset Quality Index	Adjusted Non-Performing Loans as a % of Total Loans	Adjusted Non-Performing Loans as a % of Capital	Net Charge-Offs Avg Loans	Profitability Index	Net Income ($Mil)	Return on Assets (R.O.A.)	Return on Equity (R.O.E.)	Net Interest Spread	Overhead Efficiency Ratio	Liquidity Index	Liquidity Ratio	Hot Money Ratio	Stability Index
8.8	0.00	0.0	-0.44	**8.0**	0.3	1.48	14.11	4.40	66.1	**0.9**	21.2	28.2	**6.3**
4.5	3.73	13.7	-0.26	**3.6**	0.9	0.66	6.58	2.62	78.5	**1.9**	15.6	19.6	**6.9**
5.4	2.90	7.9	-0.08	**2.6**	0.3	0.47	4.29	2.75	87.6	**4.4**	54.9	16.7	**6.3**
8.9	0.00	0.0	0.03	**7.8**	1.7	1.71	14.95	3.82	42.8	**2.7**	32.0	19.0	**7.0**
5.9	1.45	5.2	-0.34	**6.8**	1.1	1.65	15.65	3.66	58.0	**5.6**	45.8	8.1	**8.0**
6.0	1.61	4.4	0.05	**5.5**	0.9	1.19	7.09	3.44	61.7	**2.0**	30.8	25.4	**8.4**
8.4	0.27	1.5	0.00	**5.1**	0.9	1.15	9.41	2.69	56.1	**1.2**	25.5	32.1	**8.0**
5.6	1.51	8.3	0.13	**3.7**	2.7	0.55	6.36	3.35	68.7	**3.6**	32.4	16.1	**6.1**
6.2	0.31	4.6	0.34	**8.8**	2.6	2.15	24.27	6.57	54.1	**2.8**	43.7	26.1	**6.9**
4.7	3.00	13.2	0.00	**3.7**	0.9	0.62	5.43	2.78	73.7	**4.9**	46.4	11.9	**7.4**
8.3	0.28	1.5	0.60	**6.6**	0.7	1.31	11.52	4.21	50.8	**2.5**	24.2	17.3	**6.9**
7.1	0.00	3.0	0.00	**4.1**	0.6	0.84	8.24	3.39	71.1	**5.5**	38.7	6.2	**6.5**
6.8	0.48	2.5	0.01	**5.2**	1.3	0.97	8.65	3.70	66.8	**4.7**	32.2	8.5	**6.8**
3.8	1.42	10.7	0.20	**5.6**	3.5	1.06	12.75	4.53	68.6	**5.3**	29.4	3.2	**5.6**
9.1	0.41	1.8	0.00	**3.5**	0.5	0.58	5.42	1.98	63.9	**3.5**	51.4	21.6	**6.6**
6.5	0.95	2.9	-0.03	**5.7**	1.8	1.46	13.55	3.20	59.9	**1.8**	30.7	29.1	**7.7**
7.0	0.00	0.0	0.00	**9.7**	0.9	2.66	18.92	2.33	42.8	**5.0**	28.3	4.8	**9.5**
5.9	0.91	3.1	0.00	**9.5**	18.9	6.45	42.09	2.29	82.3	**0.8**	13.0	32.5	**10.0**
6.5	1.46	5.2	-0.12	**3.3**	0.3	0.53	4.39	3.84	83.6	**3.6**	38.0	16.4	**6.7**
9.5	0.00	0.0	0.00	**3.7**	0.5	0.59	5.79	2.78	80.1	**7.1**	59.7	2.8	**6.7**
8.7	0.73	2.0	0.02	**2.2**	0.2	0.36	2.90	2.51	85.9	**4.2**	47.6	15.8	**5.5**
6.7	2.69	5.3	0.48	**3.9**	0.3	0.83	6.49	3.12	73.0	**3.4**	54.5	21.0	**4.8**
5.2	1.75	5.4	-0.03	**4.0**	0.9	0.86	8.01	3.43	64.3	**3.3**	19.4	12.8	**6.5**
6.6	1.29	4.9	0.38	**4.9**	1.4	1.17	9.24	3.67	67.4	**3.2**	44.2	19.9	**7.9**
6.6	0.41	2.6	-0.04	**4.9**	1.5	0.78	7.74	3.56	71.2	**1.4**	27.8	29.7	**6.8**
7.3	0.30	1.7	0.15	**5.0**	0.8	0.82	8.02	3.87	73.7	**3.4**	29.1	14.2	**6.2**
5.1	1.66	6.4	0.03	**4.1**	1.4	0.91	10.49	3.49	69.6	**3.6**	24.2	11.9	**5.2**
7.2	0.35	0.2	0.00	**9.5**	4.8	1.87	15.38	3.31	57.9	**5.2**	47.8	10.9	**9.9**
5.3	0.82	3.3	0.00	**5.2**	0.6	1.01	9.60	2.84	53.6	**4.4**	30.4	9.8	**5.9**
8.7	0.50	0.8	0.07	**5.6**	0.8	1.27	5.70	3.50	54.6	**4.9**	70.9	16.7	**8.2**
9.2	0.00	0.0	0.08	**4.6**	1.5	1.41	19.77	3.37	66.3	**2.8**	31.0	12.8	**5.0**
4.2	3.23	9.1	0.31	**6.8**	1.8	1.88	12.80	4.17	50.9	**2.5**	34.4	22.3	**8.1**
8.8	0.00	0.0	0.00	**6.0**	0.3	1.52	12.45	3.11	51.7	**4.8**	47.1	12.3	**7.3**
5.1	1.53	5.1	-0.07	**4.4**	0.5	0.82	7.40	3.69	79.4	**4.4**	36.9	12.1	**6.7**
2.8	4.43	27.2	0.23	**3.6**	8.5	0.65	10.06	3.20	77.1	**4.4**	33.4	14.1	**4.2**
8.9	1.15	1.2	-0.12	**3.5**	0.2	0.56	2.92	2.20	69.7	**4.3**	87.8	22.9	**7.0**
4.4	3.51	12.3	-0.08	**4.8**	0.6	1.14	12.49	3.13	58.5	**3.5**	40.0	17.6	**6.7**
9.4	0.32	0.8	-0.01	**2.7**	0.2	0.37	1.90	3.07	90.7	**5.7**	67.9	11.0	**7.6**
8.3	0.00	0.0	0.00	**7.7**	1.4	2.42	26.98	5.23	53.0	**3.9**	18.0	10.0	**6.4**
7.8	0.73	4.0	0.07	**5.8**	128.4	1.19	19.66	2.41	59.2	**5.6**	29.2	5.8	**5.3**
8.6	0.15	0.7	-0.01	**6.0**	2.2	1.38	14.47	3.47	47.4	**3.3**	31.6	15.5	**6.0**
9.0	0.00	0.0	0.00	**3.7**	0.2	0.55	5.54	2.50	76.5	**4.8**	57.4	13.9	**5.8**
4.8	4.07	7.5	1.18	**1.1**	-0.2	-0.32	-2.36	3.10	93.1	**6.1**	44.8	4.0	**5.8**
2.5	7.16	23.4	-0.05	**5.1**	2.3	0.95	9.92	2.88	57.5	**3.1**	25.5	14.7	**6.1**
3.7	2.62	11.2	0.10	**3.4**	0.8	0.57	6.04	2.08	65.3	**2.8**	47.5	29.3	**5.7**
6.7	0.66	5.1	0.00	**4.7**	0.9	1.03	12.86	3.65	66.5	**5.0**	28.8	4.8	**4.3**
4.5	1.38	5.0	0.20	**5.8**	102.9	1.20	8.77	3.14	50.8	**1.9**	19.0	17.8	**9.1**
8.4	0.00	0.0	0.00	**3.4**	1.5	0.88	7.48	3.87	65.8	**3.0**	25.1	15.1	**7.0**
7.1	0.00	0.0	0.00	**8.9**	1.4	2.04	18.10	4.44	56.0	**1.5**	13.9	24.2	**8.8**
5.2	1.90	8.7	-0.33	**3.0**	0.2	0.54	6.45	3.39	84.8	**4.5**	51.1	14.3	**3.6**
5.3	0.97	4.3	0.06	**5.7**	4.3	1.38	13.94	4.15	67.2	**5.7**	30.0	1.1	**6.3**
7.0	2.09	7.7	0.00	**4.9**	6.0	0.93	11.56	2.96	64.2	**5.7**	31.3	5.9	**7.8**
7.7	0.66	2.2	0.00	**4.5**	1.1	0.96	8.61	3.11	60.4	**2.0**	19.8	19.5	**6.4**
8.8	0.58	1.3	0.07	**3.4**	0.3	0.53	3.22	2.32	73.7	**5.3**	61.6	13.5	**8.1**
6.2	1.26	3.3	0.00	**6.4**	1.8	1.65	17.67	4.11	60.2	**3.1**	36.8	18.5	**7.0**
6.7	3.45	8.4	-0.02	**3.5**	1.7	0.71	5.95	1.93	67.4	**6.2**	43.9	3.1	**6.6**
8.7	0.35	1.6	0.04	**2.5**	1.5	0.39	5.71	2.73	87.8	**6.7**	54.0	3.2	**2.7**
8.0	0.13	0.6	0.00	**9.5**	4.6	3.54	27.05	3.29	43.6	**3.5**	24.4	11.5	**9.1**
7.8	0.49	0.7	0.00	**6.3**	0.5	1.30	10.59	4.19	59.1	**3.3**	25.5	11.1	**7.2**
8.9	0.00	0.0	0.00	**5.3**	0.2	1.34	6.91	3.64	59.1	**4.9**	54.8	11.3	**5.8**

	Name	City	State	Rating	2020 Rating	2019 Rating	Total Assets ($Mil)	One Year Asset Growth	Asset Mix (As a % of Total Assets) Comm-ercial Loans	Cons-umer Loans	Mort-gage Loans	Secur-ities	Capital-ization Index	Lever-age Ratio	Risk-Based Capital Ratio
	Bank of Lexington, Inc.	Lexington	KY	**B**	B	B	310.1	10.32	0.9	0.1	34.3	3.9	**9.1**	10.4	19.3
	Bank of Lincoln County	Fayetteville	TN	**A-**	A-	A-	188.0	11.24	8.6	1.2	10.3	9.0	**10.0**	11.3	0.0
▲	Bank of Lindsay	Lindsay	NE	**C+**	C	C+	71.7	-4.04	6.1	1.6	0.8	2.1	**9.6**	12.1	14.7
▲	Bank of Little Rock	Little Rock	AR	**B**	B-	B-	265.7	16.40	10.1	1.5	17.1	45.2	**7.9**	9.6	0.0
	Bank of Locust Grove	Locust Grove	OK	**B**	B	B	50.0	9.66	26.9	35.9	4.4	9.2	**8.3**	11.5	0.0
	Bank of Louisiana	New Orleans	LA	**C-**	D+	C-	92.2	7.87	0.3	3.1	29.3	1.6	**5.2**	7.2	13.9
▲	Bank of Louisiana	Louisiana	MO	**B**	B-	B-	58.1	0.13	8.0	1.6	11.0	22.9	**8.4**	10.0	16.9
▲	Bank of Lumber City	Lumber City	GA	**B-**	C+	C	25.3	-0.25	13.9	9.2	13.2	23.1	**10.0**	15.9	0.0
	Bank of Luxemburg	Luxemburg	WI	**B**	B-	C+	508.7	13.43	14.2	1.2	11.3	21.8	**7.3**	9.2	13.3
	Bank of Madison	Madison	GA	**B+**	A-	A-	361.0	32.14	6.3	0.5	12.0	18.3	**7.4**	9.3	15.5
	Bank of Maple Plain	Maple Plain	MN	**B+**	B+	A-	110.1	13.16	9.6	0.9	12.0	35.0	**10.0**	11.5	23.5
	Bank of Marin	Novato	CA	**A-**	A-	A-	3073.4	-3.40	9.7	0.7	4.9	22.5	**8.3**	9.9	15.3
	Bank of Mauston	Mauston	WI	**A**	A	A	396.8	18.88	4.2	1.4	6.2	43.8	**10.0**	12.0	19.7
	Bank of Maysville	Maysville	KY	**B+**	B+	B+	155.2	9.89	1.5	0.9	24.6	39.9	**10.0**	15.2	29.4
	Bank of Mead	Mead	NE	**B**	B	B	30.0	5.03	10.3	4.1	15.7	40.8	**10.0**	11.3	0.0
	Bank of Millbrook	Millbrook	NY	**C+**	C+	B	287.6	16.25	3.5	0.9	18.2	50.7	**6.6**	8.6	26.6
	Bank of Milton	Milton	WI	**B+**	B+	B	185.8	23.92	6.5	1.2	15.5	25.8	**6.4**	8.4	12.3
	Bank of Mingo	Williamson	WV	**C-**	C-	C-	124.0	33.14	13.7	4.7	23.5	6.4	**7.5**	9.3	14.8
	Bank of Monroe	Union	WV	**A-**	A-	A-	184.5	9.93	8.1	2.8	25.6	26.8	**10.0**	12.8	23.4
	Bank of Montana	Missoula	MT	**A-**	A-	A-	161.9	19.73	29.6	1.1	5.2	0.0	**7.7**	9.5	21.3
	Bank of Montgomery	Montgomery	IL	**D+**	C-	D	47.4	11.17	6.0	1.5	8.7	52.7	**6.4**	8.5	31.7
	Bank of Monticello	Monticello	GA	**B+**	B+	B+	150.4	18.59	7.1	5.0	20.4	15.9	**6.9**	8.9	0.0
	Bank of Monticello	Monticello	MO	**A-**	A-	A-	140.7	17.01	5.9	2.8	8.1	24.4	**9.5**	10.7	0.0
	Bank of Morton	Morton	MS	**B**	B-	B+	81.4	9.00	3.5	5.7	29.7	24.7	**10.0**	12.5	0.0
▲	Bank of Moundville	Moundville	AL	**C**	C-	C-	105.8	9.67	8.6	2.2	11.6	61.0	**6.9**	8.9	20.5
	Bank of New Cambria	New Cambria	MO	**C**	C+	B	37.1	13.44	1.2	0.7	3.4	39.3	**10.0**	11.7	0.0
▲	Bank of New England	Salem	NH	**A**	A-	B	1177.1	15.20	6.0	0.0	0.2	1.0	**10.0**	14.9	0.0
	Bank of New Hampshire	Laconia	NH	**B**	B	B-	2174.4	8.80	6.9	1.8	23.7	17.0	**7.1**	9.1	12.8
	Bank of New Madrid	New Madrid	MO	**A-**	A-	A-	123.7	18.03	2.7	2.3	18.1	31.5	**8.8**	10.2	0.0
	Bank of Newington	Newington	GA	**B-**	B-	C+	167.7	12.18	5.6	1.7	25.0	0.8	**6.6**	8.6	12.7
▼	Bank of Newman Grove	Newman Grove	NE	**D+**	C	C	35.2	-2.06	1.3	3.2	0.0	40.6	**9.8**	10.9	19.8
	Bank of O'Fallon	O'Fallon	IL	**B+**	A-	A-	370.0	10.43	4.5	4.7	37.0	6.6	**10.0**	13.1	25.2
	Bank of Oak Ridge	Oak Ridge	LA	**C+**	C	B-	65.3	-3.80	17.9	0.4	11.3	4.7	**7.7**	9.5	13.1
	Bank of Oak Ridge	Oak Ridge	NC	**B-**	C+	B-	565.2	3.89	18.4	0.7	13.4	8.4	**6.2**	9.5	0.0
	Bank of Ocean City	Ocean City	MD	**A-**	A-	A-	582.3	29.48	7.0	0.2	11.2	17.9	**6.6**	8.6	15.9
	Bank of Odessa	Odessa	MO	**B+**	B+	B+	329.8	8.71	8.6	3.3	37.4	13.1	**10.0**	15.1	27.6
▲	Bank of Okolona	Okolona	MS	**B-**	C	C-	236.1	2.47	25.9	4.4	11.6	26.5	**7.6**	9.4	0.0
	Bank of Ontario	Ontario	WI	**B-**	C+	B	66.1	30.60	8.1	3.5	27.9	9.0	**9.5**	10.7	0.0
	Bank of Orchard	Orchard	NE	**B-**	B-	B-	31.9	16.07	3.9	4.4	0.1	38.0	**10.0**	11.8	0.0
	Bank of Palmer	Palmer	KS	**C+**	C+	C+	51.9	7.62	1.7	3.2	7.4	46.6	**8.3**	9.9	0.0
	Bank of Pensacola	Pensacola	FL	**C**	C	C	132.6	32.36	8.8	0.8	14.4	39.4	**8.1**	9.7	0.0
	Bank of Perry County	Lobelville	TN	**B**	B	C+	200.6	4.75	5.3	12.0	38.0	3.7	**6.7**	8.7	0.0
	Bank of Pontiac	Pontiac	IL	**A-**	A-	A-	879.8	47.69	11.0	2.8	15.7	13.9	**10.0**	11.8	21.1
	Bank of Prague	Prague	NE	**A-**	A-	A-	34.5	9.96	19.1	10.1	0.9	16.8	**10.0**	12.6	0.0
	Bank of Prairie Du Sac	Prairie Du Sac	WI	**A+**	A+	A+	594.1	11.80	10.3	0.3	7.3	36.5	**10.0**	13.0	22.4
	Bank of Prairie Village	Prairie Village	KS	**A-**	A-	A-	129.0	-2.52	11.2	0.9	27.2	17.2	**9.4**	10.6	0.0
	Bank of Rantoul	Rantoul	IL	**B+**	B	B-	265.6	7.62	13.6	0.4	1.3	54.2	**7.7**	9.5	0.0
	Bank of Richmondville	Cobleskill	NY	**C+**	B-	B-	176.2	13.35	2.3	4.1	25.3	31.2	**8.6**	10.1	23.9
	Bank of Ripley	Ripley	TN	**B-**	B	B	279.3	13.28	0.7	6.6	6.7	56.5	**10.0**	13.0	28.0
	Bank of Saint Elizabeth	Saint Elizabeth	MO	**A**	A-	A-	188.3	6.91	3.1	6.5	37.3	0.0	**9.4**	10.6	17.5
	Bank of Salem	Salem	AR	**B+**	B+	B+	171.8	9.41	9.4	4.8	19.1	9.8	**9.2**	10.5	0.0
	Bank of Salem	Salem	MO	**B-**	B-	B-	125.1	5.86	2.1	3.8	27.7	31.5	**6.8**	8.9	0.0
	Bank of San Francisco	San Francisco	CA	**B**	B+	A-	656.2	-1.81	30.2	0.0	30.3	0.0	**6.8**	8.8	16.6
	Bank of Santa Clarita	Santa Clarita	CA	**B+**	B+	B+	416.1	10.80	10.8	0.2	1.4	3.7	**8.5**	10.0	16.0
▲	Bank of South Texas	Pharr	TX	**A-**	B	B-	136.5	-5.95	5.0	1.2	16.3	4.1	**10.0**	11.6	0.0
	Bank of Southern California	San Diego	CA	**B-**	B-	B	1777.2	14.97	30.4	0.2	4.4	1.2	**8.1**	9.7	17.5
	Bank of Springfield	Springfield	IL	**C-**	C-	C-	1377.0	14.56	17.8	0.4	8.2	5.4	**5.9**	8.1	11.7
	Bank of St. Francisville	Saint Francisville	LA	**B**	B	B	203.9	13.81	12.6	1.7	16.4	6.8	**5.7**	9.9	0.0
	Bank of Steinauer	Steinauer	NE	**C-**	C	C	14.4	15.81	3.9	7.3	33.3	2.8	**6.6**	8.6	0.0
	Bank of Stockton	Stockton	CA	**A**	A-	A	4334.9	14.68	5.5	5.6	4.0	25.9	**10.0**	14.5	17.0

Asset Quality Index	Adjusted Non-Performing Loans as a % of Total Loans	Adjusted Non-Performing Loans as a % of Capital	Net Charge-Offs Avg Loans	Profitability Index	Net Income ($Mil)	Return on Assets (R.O.A.)	Return on Equity (R.O.E.)	Net Interest Spread	Overhead Efficiency Ratio	Liquidity Index	Liquidity Ratio	Hot Money Ratio	Stability Index
9.4	0.00	0.3	-0.01	**4.1**	1.2	0.81	7.47	3.27	67.5	**2.1**	32.0	15.2	**7.1**
8.0	1.19	3.0	-0.09	**8.1**	1.3	1.43	12.71	4.50	56.7	**2.2**	33.1	25.0	**8.2**
7.0	0.02	0.1	0.00	**4.0**	0.4	0.97	8.28	2.87	74.5	**1.0**	10.6	19.7	**6.0**
5.2	1.82	7.3	-0.09	**6.5**	1.9	1.49	15.60	3.05	84.1	**6.3**	53.7	5.6	**4.7**
3.7	1.43	4.6	0.02	**9.9**	0.5	1.88	16.56	5.34	52.3	**2.1**	16.7	18.6	**7.2**
1.6	7.64	32.6	0.03	**2.1**	-0.3	-0.75	-8.54	2.97	133.2	**6.5**	51.1	2.6	**3.9**
5.8	1.58	3.6	-0.07	**2.0**	0.1	0.24	2.20	3.23	93.0	**4.1**	32.9	12.1	**6.6**
7.1	1.76	3.3	0.06	**6.2**	0.3	2.01	13.19	6.48	67.6	**4.8**	45.0	11.6	**6.5**
5.8	1.26	4.2	0.06	**7.6**	3.8	1.56	17.41	3.69	55.4	**4.7**	33.9	9.3	**5.8**
6.8	0.60	3.1	0.00	**5.4**	1.8	1.01	10.43	3.27	61.5	**3.5**	25.8	11.1	**6.6**
8.4	0.18	4.4	-0.01	**4.8**	0.6	1.14	9.16	3.48	61.6	**5.9**	49.7	7.3	**7.6**
7.2	0.62	3.0	-0.01	**6.7**	19.9	1.31	11.67	3.38	57.9	**6.0**	29.2	2.5	**10.0**
8.9	0.36	1.2	-0.01	**9.5**	5.0	2.92	22.32	3.34	37.1	**3.4**	36.1	16.9	**9.1**
8.7	0.19	0.3	-0.02	**4.6**	0.8	0.99	5.87	3.44	63.0	**4.7**	37.4	10.7	**8.3**
8.8	0.00	0.0	0.00	**6.4**	0.2	1.37	12.05	4.34	50.5	**5.4**	36.5	5.7	**6.7**
8.6	0.39	1.5	0.11	**3.0**	0.5	0.32	3.65	1.81	81.5	**6.8**	55.1	2.6	**4.9**
8.8	0.09	0.6	-0.01	**8.9**	1.5	1.73	19.42	3.53	45.8	**4.2**	36.4	12.9	**6.5**
4.9	1.05	7.9	0.04	**2.7**	0.5	0.82	9.10	4.32	79.8	**0.9**	20.1	22.9	**3.0**
8.8	0.64	1.7	-0.12	**6.0**	1.1	1.26	10.03	3.57	62.4	**4.0**	35.6	13.5	**8.3**
8.6	0.00	0.0	0.00	**9.5**	2.6	3.12	33.49	2.80	37.5	**4.9**	46.8	10.5	**7.4**
9.8	0.00	0.0	-0.02	**1.2**	0.1	0.40	4.53	1.84	104.1	**6.1**	76.7	10.2	**3.4**
6.1	0.93	3.9	-0.10	**7.2**	1.3	1.77	19.18	3.87	55.0	**5.5**	44.0	8.3	**6.6**
7.6	0.52	1.8	0.07	**8.2**	1.4	2.08	19.08	3.86	47.0	**4.0**	32.6	12.7	**7.6**
3.7	2.67	18.5	0.19	**6.7**	0.6	1.37	10.42	4.08	67.0	**2.8**	41.7	23.2	**9.5**
6.5	2.71	4.8	0.03	**2.6**	0.3	0.56	6.22	2.47	76.2	**2.7**	37.4	21.7	**5.1**
9.5	0.00	0.0	0.00	**1.7**	0.0	-0.06	-0.50	2.39	102.3	**7.0**	72.4	3.5	**6.0**
6.8	0.70	2.1	0.00	**9.9**	10.5	1.84	12.42	4.00	35.1	**0.9**	17.3	10.5	**10.0**
7.6	0.40	2.3	-0.01	**4.9**	11.9	1.14	11.34	3.27	65.3	**4.0**	18.0	4.3	**8.9**
9.3	0.01	0.4	0.01	**5.1**	0.7	1.19	11.20	3.34	63.1	**2.9**	35.2	19.0	**7.4**
5.5	0.91	5.5	-0.01	**7.2**	1.3	1.62	19.19	5.10	56.5	**1.3**	15.2	27.5	**5.1**
4.7	0.18	11.3	0.62	**1.4**	-0.1	-0.29	-2.67	1.89	113.1	**5.4**	54.5	10.3	**4.7**
8.5	0.25	1.3	0.14	**4.5**	1.8	1.05	7.77	2.40	54.0	**2.3**	33.8	25.0	**8.3**
7.4	0.00	0.0	0.03	**3.8**	0.3	0.84	8.97	4.26	74.5	**0.7**	12.6	35.6	**5.6**
4.8	1.28	7.1	0.35	**6.3**	4.2	1.51	15.10	4.33	58.4	**1.6**	18.7	17.7	**7.3**
9.0	0.08	0.2	0.00	**6.5**	3.1	1.19	13.84	2.83	46.9	**5.8**	47.7	7.6	**6.1**
5.9	0.19	8.6	0.26	**7.0**	2.5	1.49	9.71	3.47	38.5	**2.5**	14.8	16.4	**7.8**
4.3	1.63	10.5	0.01	**5.4**	1.4	1.20	12.02	4.20	68.7	**2.0**	36.3	31.3	**6.6**
2.0	5.00	22.6	-0.05	**7.3**	0.6	1.75	15.88	5.21	62.6	**1.9**	13.1	19.0	**6.8**
9.3	0.00	1.2	-0.06	**3.3**	0.1	0.61	5.11	2.49	73.5	**5.1**	81.8	15.8	**6.4**
8.9	0.00	0.0	-0.26	**3.6**	0.3	1.08	10.14	2.63	78.8	**6.2**	62.9	7.0	**6.0**
9.6	0.00	0.0	0.01	**3.1**	0.3	0.51	5.21	2.04	69.6	**4.7**	64.7	17.3	**4.8**
5.2	0.54	3.9	0.02	**7.8**	1.7	1.79	19.89	4.32	55.9	**1.6**	17.3	19.7	**6.8**
6.4	0.80	3.9	0.05	**6.3**	4.7	1.22	11.45	3.14	54.5	**3.6**	26.9	11.6	**8.0**
7.6	0.00	0.0	-0.01	**9.9**	0.4	2.43	18.41	5.31	62.1	**5.0**	35.5	7.9	**9.1**
8.9	0.14	0.5	0.00	**8.8**	4.7	1.61	11.75	2.91	38.9	**6.5**	54.3	5.1	**10.0**
9.0	0.00	0.0	0.00	**6.3**	0.9	1.35	12.12	3.85	60.7	**3.6**	25.1	11.9	**8.0**
6.1	0.99	3.0	-0.19	**6.6**	2.1	1.60	14.36	3.33	45.4	**4.1**	23.1	8.3	**8.4**
5.8	0.88	6.0	0.08	**3.0**	0.4	0.40	4.02	3.29	82.4	**5.0**	34.5	7.7	**5.0**
7.0	1.54	3.0	0.11	**3.4**	1.1	0.78	5.48	3.31	78.1	**4.3**	50.6	16.1	**7.0**
8.1	0.00	0.0	0.00	**9.6**	2.8	3.08	26.23	5.13	49.2	**4.4**	24.9	7.4	**9.0**
4.8	1.27	7.4	-0.01	**9.3**	2.1	2.44	22.93	4.69	49.5	**1.9**	29.0	25.2	**8.0**
6.4	0.77	4.2	-0.02	**4.0**	0.5	0.82	9.32	3.28	68.3	**3.5**	24.7	12.4	**5.2**
6.5	0.64	1.5	0.00	**6.8**	4.5	1.35	18.47	3.72	46.9	**1.3**	18.5	25.0	**5.5**
5.9	0.51	2.4	0.00	**4.9**	1.8	0.87	8.62	2.82	57.3	**2.1**	29.1	13.3	**6.2**
7.0	0.00	0.0	-0.79	**6.4**	0.9	1.23	8.90	6.34	73.2	**1.8**	25.4	22.8	**7.1**
7.9	0.05	0.1	-0.01	**3.7**	4.5	0.54	4.85	3.60	83.0	**5.2**	25.9	5.1	**8.2**
2.2	2.75	23.0	-0.21	**6.1**	8.1	1.24	15.03	3.74	65.9	**5.2**	22.4	3.3	**6.7**
5.1	1.07	6.0	0.02	**5.7**	1.3	1.41	14.26	4.49	64.1	**3.5**	19.4	11.9	**6.0**
6.2	0.38	3.9	0.00	**2.3**	0.0	0.21	2.36	3.08	92.9	**4.9**	37.9	6.8	**2.3**
8.4	0.67	1.2	-0.04	**8.1**	39.5	1.88	12.27	2.99	45.5	**7.1**	60.2	4.7	**10.0**

Name	City	State	Rating	2020 Rating	2019 Rating	Total Assets ($Mil)	One Year Asset Growth	Asset Mix (As a % of Total Assets) Comm-ercial Loans	Cons-umer Loans	Mort-gage Loans	Secur-ities	Capital-ization Index	Lever-age Ratio	Risk-Based Capital Ratio
Bank of Stronghurst	Stronghurst	IL	**C+**	C+	C+	89.9	12.54	3.9	1.7	5.0	63.7	**10.0**	14.0	0.0
Bank of Sun Prairie	Sun Prairie	WI	**B-**	B-	B	539.9	9.50	11.3	0.7	8.7	7.8	**8.2**	11.5	13.5
Bank of Sunset & Trust Co.	Sunset	LA	**B+**	B+	B+	181.0	5.95	13.2	0.5	21.5	9.3	**6.9**	8.9	0.0
Bank of Tennessee	Kingsport	TN	**B+**	B+	B	1753.1	11.32	11.7	0.4	17.4	9.9	**6.5**	8.5	12.6
Bank of Texas	Midland	TX	**A-**	A-	A-	463.2	10.99	29.7	0.1	2.4	1.1	**7.8**	13.2	13.2
▼ Bank of The Bluegrass and Trust Co.	Lexington	KY	**B+**	A-	A-	311.3	4.69	5.1	0.4	18.5	24.4	**10.0**	11.6	0.0
Bank of the Federated States of Micronesi	Pohnpei	FM	**B+**	A-	A-	213.4	11.30	6.5	6.5	1.4	36.6	**10.0**	12.6	43.2
Bank of the Flint Hills	Wamego	KS	**B-**	B-	B-	382.2	11.53	15.5	1.6	12.7	16.6	**3.6**	9.0	0.0
Bank of the James	Lynchburg	VA	**B-**	C+	B-	908.8	9.84	12.2	2.3	11.3	14.8	**6.2**	8.2	12.6
Bank of the Lowcountry	Walterboro	SC	**B-**	B-	B	291.2	15.75	5.1	1.2	10.1	30.7	**7.8**	9.5	0.0
Bank of the Mountains, Inc.	West Liberty	KY	**C+**	C	C-	81.5	4.79	4.2	16.4	24.1	9.8	**9.1**	10.4	16.8
Bank of the Orient	San Francisco	CA	**B-**	B-	B-	917.2	-4.03	2.6	0.0	16.3	3.1	**10.0**	11.2	0.0
Bank of the Pacific	Aberdeen	WA	**A-**	A-	A-	1290.1	14.28	9.1	4.5	7.1	12.3	**7.3**	9.2	16.6
Bank of the Panhandle	Guymon	OK	**A-**	A-	A-	226.1	17.09	14.5	0.7	6.6	33.6	**10.0**	11.2	18.0
▲ Bank of the Rockies	White Sulphur Spring	MT	**C**	C-	C-	201.5	14.59	13.7	2.2	6.9	10.2	**7.3**	9.2	14.9
▲ Bank of the Sierra	Porterville	CA	**A-**	B+	A-	3272.6	5.23	4.5	0.2	3.3	18.6	**8.6**	10.4	0.0
Bank of the South	Pensacola	FL	**C**	C	C	91.0	8.79	5.1	0.1	3.1	50.0	**10.0**	16.8	0.0
Bank of the Southwest	Roswell	NM	**B**	B	B	202.0	11.67	21.9	3.3	11.5	0.0	**5.2**	7.2	14.6
Bank of the Valley	Bellwood	NE	**C+**	C+	C	408.3	21.28	9.7	1.8	5.2	9.4	**5.5**	8.1	11.4
Bank of the West	San Francisco	CA	**B-**	B-	B	99179.0	-0.82	13.5	14.0	7.4	22.4	**8.8**	10.2	15.7
Bank of the West	Grapevine	TX	**B**	B	B	726.9	21.46	10.7	0.3	5.5	3.6	**5.4**	7.4	14.5
Bank of Travelers Rest	Travelers Rest	SC	**B+**	B+	B+	1181.5	21.49	7.2	2.7	9.7	31.0	**7.2**	9.1	17.8
Bank of Turtle Lake	Turtle Lake	ND	**B**	B	B-	62.9	10.13	6.4	1.0	0.3	18.5	**8.8**	10.2	0.0
Bank of Utah	Ogden	UT	**A**	A	A	1996.9	18.85	8.1	0.3	2.4	10.8	**10.0**	11.0	16.5
Bank of Utica	Utica	NY	**B+**	B	A-	1475.6	15.93	4.6	0.3	0.1	76.5	**10.0**	19.1	0.0
Bank of Versailles	Versailles	MO	**B+**	B	B	306.5	7.87	0.7	0.5	58.8	0.0	**10.0**	12.6	0.0
Bank of Vici	Vici	OK	**D+**	D+	C+	38.5	1.72	18.7	11.5	1.4	21.7	**10.0**	11.3	0.0
Bank of Walker County	Jasper	AL	**C+**	C+	C	85.3	9.12	9.9	2.5	19.2	9.7	**7.8**	9.5	17.3
Bank of Washington	Washington	MO	**C**	C-	D	846.5	2.24	30.2	0.4	5.1	3.9	**8.6**	11.8	13.8
▲ Bank of Western Oklahoma	Elk City	OK	**B**	B-	B-	350.4	6.19	13.4	0.6	14.1	19.1	**5.9**	7.9	12.9
Bank of Weston	Weston	MO	**B-**	B	B	193.9	12.13	9.5	0.5	13.9	25.5	**5.4**	7.4	13.5
Bank of Whittier, N.A.	Whittier	CA	**B**	B-	C+	166.0	95.37	6.1	0.2	6.7	0.0	**10.0**	12.4	0.0
Bank of Wiggins	Wiggins	MS	**B**	B+	B+	190.7	4.94	7.5	4.3	15.0	45.4	**10.0**	15.9	0.0
Bank of Winnfield & Trust Co.	Winnfield	LA	**B-**	B-	B-	162.0	6.85	7.9	3.3	13.6	31.9	**10.0**	12.2	28.8
Bank of Winona	Winona	MS	**B**	B	B	139.5	4.55	3.8	2.4	17.5	47.2	**8.7**	10.1	15.3
▲ Bank of Wisconsin Dells	Wisconsin Dells	WI	**A**	A-	A-	826.1	16.96	8.9	0.2	4.7	17.4	**9.4**	10.6	14.5
Bank of Wolcott	Wolcott	IN	**A-**	B+	A-	204.1	5.82	6.1	1.0	9.7	36.8	**10.0**	11.1	0.0
Bank of Wrightsville	Wrightsville	GA	**B-**	B-	B-	76.3	14.26	9.1	2.0	8.1	27.2	**6.6**	8.6	0.0
Bank of Yates City	Yates City	IL	**C-**	C-	C-	75.0	3.73	10.0	6.1	19.8	28.3	**6.6**	8.6	0.0
Bank of Yazoo City	Yazoo City	MS	**B-**	B	B	299.3	13.70	8.3	1.5	16.8	42.8	**9.3**	10.5	0.0
▼ Bank of York	York	SC	**C+**	B-	B+	283.7	13.88	5.8	2.1	7.7	15.0	**8.0**	9.6	0.0
Bank of Zachary	Zachary	LA	**C+**	C+	B-	323.9	18.78	6.5	1.1	25.0	38.6	**5.9**	7.9	17.2
Bank of Zumbrota	Zumbrota	MN	**B+**	B+	B+	200.6	9.50	13.0	2.4	10.8	16.2	**9.4**	11.4	14.5
Bank OZK	Little Rock	AR	**A-**	A-	A-	26605.9	0.85	2.5	8.4	2.9	17.6	**10.0**	14.5	16.8
▲ Bank Plus	Estherville	IA	**B**	C+	B-	146.9	9.13	5.4	1.4	5.0	10.6	**6.2**	9.1	0.0
Bank Rhode Island	Providence	RI	**B**	B-	B	3202.1	1.74	19.1	0.0	9.3	10.2	**6.3**	8.3	13.1
Bank Star	Pacific	MO	**B**	B	B	170.9	13.17	16.9	1.8	25.4	11.3	**4.2**	8.4	0.0
Bank, N.A.	McAlester	OK	**B+**	A-	A-	478.3	11.17	4.4	2.1	12.3	48.2	**7.6**	9.4	0.0
▲ Bank3	Memphis	TN	**C**	C-	D+	362.1	19.13	37.9	0.4	7.2	8.0	**6.5**	9.2	12.1
Bank7	Oklahoma City	OK	**B+**	B+	A	1132.1	12.86	34.9	0.1	3.4	0.0	**9.4**	11.3	14.5
bankcda	Coeur d'Alene	ID	**B**	B	A-	234.9	37.17	11.2	0.4	2.1	30.3	**9.9**	10.9	0.0
BankChampaign, N.A.	Champaign	IL	**B+**	B+	B+	246.2	-6.89	13.6	0.1	17.6	9.7	**7.8**	9.5	16.5
BankCherokee	Saint Paul	MN	**B**	B	B-	371.4	10.06	20.4	0.3	9.1	34.4	**5.7**	7.7	16.5
Bankers Trust Co.	Des Moines	IA	**B**	B	B	5770.3	6.52	17.6	0.5	5.9	16.1	**6.8**	8.9	12.3
Bankers' Bank	Madison	WI	**B+**	B+	B	1328.0	48.49	0.9	0.5	9.4	10.3	**6.9**	8.9	17.1
▲ Bankers' Bank of Kansas	Wichita	KS	**A-**	B+	B+	183.3	-17.49	12.2	10.8	4.4	1.4	**10.0**	14.9	24.8
▼ Bankers' Bank of the West	Denver	CO	**B**	B+	A-	453.5	-1.48	8.2	0.0	0.6	5.5	**8.2**	9.8	19.7
BankFinancial, N.A.	Olympia Fields	IL	**B-**	B	B+	1655.9	3.99	28.2	0.1	1.6	0.5	**8.6**	10.0	0.0
BankFirst	Norfolk	NE	**B-**	B	B+	864.0	8.58	7.1	0.5	5.2	24.3	**8.9**	10.9	14.1
BankFirst Financial Services	Macon	MS	**B**	B	B	1798.5	17.64	9.7	1.2	14.0	23.8	**6.6**	8.6	14.5

Asset Quality Index	Adjusted Non-Performing Loans as a % of Total Loans	Adjusted Non-Performing Loans as a % of Capital	Net Charge-Offs Avg Loans	Profitability Index	Net Income ($Mil)	Return on Assets (R.O.A.)	Return on Equity (R.O.E.)	Net Interest Spread	Overhead Efficiency Ratio	Liquidity Index	Liquidity Ratio	Hot Money Ratio	Stability Index
9.3	0.21	0.4	0.27	2.4	0.2	0.49	3.21	2.48	87.7	5.3	63.8	12.3	7.1
4.2	0.76	4.9	0.02	5.3	2.8	1.11	9.74	3.53	60.8	3.9	20.9	10.2	8.5
8.6	0.00	0.1	0.13	5.5	1.0	1.18	13.15	3.92	62.2	1.8	21.0	21.6	5.9
8.1	0.36	2.6	0.01	6.3	13.4	1.57	18.17	3.63	60.3	4.9	19.1	3.9	8.4
6.5	0.33	2.1	0.00	7.9	4.0	1.81	13.89	3.01	36.7	0.7	14.7	48.8	9.0
4.5	4.04	17.7	-0.02	6.3	2.0	1.32	11.24	3.37	63.8	5.0	37.6	9.2	8.4
6.9	3.69	4.7	-0.25	4.3	0.8	0.77	5.89	2.86	69.1	7.2	86.5	6.5	7.9
5.7	0.09	7.6	0.06	6.7	3.5	1.86	20.75	3.84	49.5	3.0	17.1	13.3	5.5
6.8	0.39	2.6	-0.02	4.2	4.1	0.92	11.23	3.35	73.4	3.9	27.1	9.2	5.1
5.9	1.74	5.5	-0.10	3.6	0.9	0.63	6.26	2.85	74.7	3.8	47.6	17.9	5.5
3.7	1.60	10.2	-0.05	5.2	0.4	1.01	9.64	5.22	75.8	2.0	24.7	20.0	6.0
4.9	0.94	5.6	0.14	2.9	2.9	0.64	5.68	3.13	75.8	1.8	26.8	25.1	7.2
8.0	0.46	1.9	0.00	6.7	8.3	1.35	12.90	3.20	73.9	6.2	34.5	3.5	8.8
5.7	1.53	6.9	-0.01	6.9	1.8	1.69	14.01	3.87	55.5	2.8	38.7	22.1	8.6
5.8	0.62	3.5	0.00	7.4	2.2	2.22	22.70	4.57	67.7	5.2	35.6	6.6	6.3
6.1	0.84	3.1	-0.05	7.8	23.7	1.47	12.69	3.79	56.9	4.7	29.6	8.1	9.7
9.8	0.00	0.0	0.00	1.8	0.1	0.14	0.77	2.25	92.3	7.3	81.4	3.3	5.9
8.4	0.03	0.3	-0.01	4.6	0.9	0.92	12.70	4.43	79.4	5.8	35.3	2.4	4.5
5.2	0.41	5.4	0.00	4.4	1.9	0.98	11.61	3.29	63.9	1.0	10.6	15.5	5.0
4.7	1.16	4.0	0.07	4.6	527.0	1.10	7.68	2.68	60.7	4.9	29.8	5.2	9.7
7.0	1.80	5.6	0.06	4.3	3.2	0.92	12.05	3.01	69.8	5.7	43.8	6.3	5.3
7.3	0.94	3.7	0.05	5.6	7.2	1.29	14.88	2.74	61.4	5.8	50.3	11.2	8.6
5.8	0.49	2.5	0.02	4.1	0.2	0.64	6.17	3.32	73.7	2.4	34.1	23.0	6.1
7.3	0.03	0.1	0.00	9.2	16.6	1.68	14.74	3.43	54.5	5.0	24.8	3.8	10.0
10.0	2.56	0.9	-0.07	9.7	19.0	2.68	13.87	2.04	29.7	4.7	82.3	21.4	10.0
6.6	1.84	7.2	0.00	5.1	1.5	1.02	7.94	3.01	56.1	4.6	24.0	5.6	7.7
1.1	6.37	27.0	-0.32	3.4	0.2	0.99	8.51	4.04	79.2	2.4	37.4	26.6	4.9
7.0	0.44	2.1	0.08	3.7	0.3	0.64	6.49	3.77	83.3	2.3	40.7	30.2	5.2
2.0	2.57	15.1	-0.07	7.1	7.2	1.68	14.22	3.75	56.9	3.9	10.5	8.6	9.7
5.7	0.00	2.9	0.00	8.9	4.2	2.40	28.57	4.78	49.0	1.3	22.0	29.8	7.0
5.2	1.15	7.9	-0.14	4.4	0.7	0.71	9.82	3.51	69.7	3.9	31.1	12.6	4.9
9.0	0.00	0.0	-0.09	7.2	1.0	1.41	11.16	0.25	44.1	3.3	83.5	66.7	8.0
8.8	0.61	1.5	0.02	3.7	0.8	0.83	5.23	3.21	73.6	3.7	57.2	22.9	7.9
8.0	1.21	3.6	0.36	2.9	0.4	0.54	4.57	3.10	81.8	5.2	53.1	12.3	6.3
7.4	0.84	1.9	0.00	5.0	0.9	1.29	10.79	3.60	61.5	4.9	49.0	13.0	6.6
7.4	0.36	1.1	0.00	9.5	6.6	1.74	16.10	3.62	40.7	3.4	27.1	8.1	8.7
6.6	1.79	5.0	-0.10	7.5	2.1	2.05	17.82	3.36	48.2	5.6	47.9	8.3	8.6
7.6	0.26	1.1	0.00	4.5	0.4	1.09	12.22	3.39	67.2	4.0	36.4	13.8	5.2
3.0	2.10	13.1	0.39	2.8	0.3	0.79	8.99	3.07	72.4	3.9	30.1	12.0	3.0
9.1	0.00	0.0	0.25	3.9	1.1	0.72	7.00	2.95	70.7	3.7	31.1	13.6	5.6
6.3	2.00	5.1	-0.03	3.1	0.6	0.40	3.94	2.24	81.0	6.5	62.8	7.2	5.1
8.0	0.36	1.9	0.02	3.2	1.0	0.60	7.75	3.42	80.0	4.3	32.5	11.0	4.5
5.9	0.90	3.9	-0.04	7.9	2.1	2.19	18.40	3.11	60.3	3.2	29.5	14.4	8.5
6.2	0.31	1.2	0.08	8.9	299.0	2.22	13.64	3.88	39.2	1.8	23.8	25.1	10.0
6.2	0.04	1.7	0.00	6.9	1.3	1.75	16.32	4.64	58.5	3.0	23.5	14.8	7.2
6.9	0.50	2.2	0.01	5.5	21.0	1.33	12.30	3.10	53.0	4.2	17.6	7.6	7.7
8.2	0.00	0.0	0.23	7.4	1.4	1.65	17.38	5.42	54.2	3.2	4.9	11.9	5.5
5.1	1.81	8.1	-0.05	7.7	4.6	1.94	19.87	3.53	51.2	5.7	57.0	10.7	7.1
8.2	0.00	0.0	0.00	3.4	1.3	0.74	8.09	2.91	71.6	1.1	17.7	15.5	5.4
4.5	1.46	9.8	-0.02	9.7	11.2	2.24	20.22	5.29	35.1	1.3	19.0	19.6	10.0
8.0	0.87	1.7	-0.01	4.4	1.0	0.91	8.95	3.00	66.1	7.1	56.8	1.3	6.0
7.6	0.30	1.9	0.00	5.2	1.7	1.32	13.48	3.45	69.2	2.1	18.5	16.9	6.8
8.3	0.23	1.4	-0.04	4.8	1.7	0.91	11.79	3.41	66.2	6.5	45.5	1.7	5.0
6.4	0.97	3.6	0.14	4.7	24.9	0.85	9.39	2.50	62.1	4.1	21.4	10.3	7.7
7.5	0.82	4.0	0.01	5.3	6.7	1.03	11.73	1.73	65.3	5.1	53.4	10.8	8.1
7.7	0.00	0.3	0.17	5.9	1.4	1.26	9.13	3.12	74.0	3.9	32.1	3.9	7.4
8.8	0.12	0.5	0.00	4.2	1.8	0.67	6.81	2.15	80.8	4.2	51.7	9.6	8.5
8.5	0.09	0.5	-0.02	3.5	4.1	0.51	5.04	2.80	80.8	5.9	37.2	6.6	7.9
4.0	2.21	9.0	0.62	8.3	6.6	1.56	12.44	3.58	44.0	3.7	17.1	10.6	9.1
5.5	1.03	5.3	0.06	5.0	9.3	1.04	9.85	3.12	69.2	4.2	22.9	10.5	8.8

Name	City	State	Rating	2020 Rating	2019 Rating	Total Assets ($Mil)	One Year Asset Growth	Asset Mix (As a % of Total Assets) Comm-ercial Loans	Cons-umer Loans	Mort-gage Loans	Secur-ities	Capital-ization Index	Lever-age Ratio	Risk-Based Capital Ratio
▼ BankFlorida	Jupiter	FL	**D-**	D	D-	217.3	79.73	15.0	0.0	10.1	6.3	**10.0**	11.3	15.0
BankGloucester	Gloucester	MA	**C-**	C	C+	337.0	5.11	8.7	0.2	38.1	3.4	**5.9**	7.9	13.0
BankIowa	Cedar Rapids	IA	**C+**	C+	B	775.9	1.00	9.5	1.3	11.5	15.4	**9.0**	10.5	0.0
▲ BankNewport	Middletown	RI	**B+**	B	B+	2213.6	11.93	13.5	3.1	23.5	14.9	**8.5**	10.0	14.1
BankNorth	Arthur	ND	**C+**	C	C	446.0	3.08	7.6	1.1	2.5	6.3	**5.9**	9.2	11.7
BankORION	Orion	IL	**B**	B	B	595.8	9.63	9.2	1.9	13.9	40.9	**8.2**	9.8	0.0
BankPacific, Ltd.	Hagatna	GU	**D**	D+	C+	188.1	11.94	4.1	22.1	25.5	0.0	**7.8**	9.5	19.1
BankPlus	Belzoni	MS	**B+**	B+	B+	5056.1	11.32	11.3	1.5	13.4	12.4	**5.9**	8.2	11.7
BankSouth	Dothan	AL	**B+**	B+	A-	206.2	7.84	6.4	1.2	28.5	32.9	**10.0**	18.7	0.0
▲ BankSouth	Greensboro	GA	**A**	A-	A-	1077.9	19.01	5.0	0.5	30.6	2.0	**8.4**	9.9	16.0
BankStar Financial	Elkton	SD	**B-**	B-	B-	222.9	3.78	11.3	1.7	14.7	14.4	**6.7**	8.7	13.2
BankTennessee	Collierville	TN	**B-**	B-	B	414.9	17.85	11.4	2.1	28.6	4.8	**5.4**	8.1	11.3
BankUnited, N.A.	Miami Lakes	FL	**B**	B	B+	35583.7	2.79	11.5	0.0	19.9	28.5	**8.3**	9.8	15.7
▲ BankVista	Sartell	MN	**B**	C+	C	446.0	-7.25	33.8	1.3	7.0	2.9	**7.1**	9.1	13.6
Bankwell Bank	New Canaan	CT	**C+**	C+	B	2266.9	11.02	12.3	0.0	4.7	4.8	**6.1**	9.2	11.8
▼ BANKWEST	Rockford	MN	**B**	B+	B+	227.5	22.09	11.3	0.7	8.5	31.9	**5.3**	7.3	16.9
Bankwest of Kansas	Goodland	KS	**C+**	B-	B+	139.9	-0.29	2.4	0.9	2.1	7.1	**9.4**	10.6	19.0
BankWest, Inc.	Pierre	SD	**C**	C-	C	1461.2	17.08	7.2	6.9	3.9	28.8	**7.7**	9.5	14.0
Banner Bank	Walla Walla	WA	**B+**	B+	B+	16177.2	14.64	11.2	0.6	4.8	23.2	**6.8**	8.8	13.6
Banner Banks	Birnamwood	WI	**C+**	B-	B-	120.9	8.51	1.6	0.3	3.9	24.6	**9.8**	10.9	0.0
Banner Capital Bank	Harrisburg	NE	**C+**	C	C+	228.2	13.56	13.8	2.7	3.2	11.9	**6.1**	9.4	11.8
Banterra Bank	Eldorado	IL	**B-**	B-	B-	2391.9	12.33	24.8	22.4	4.0	23.9	**5.4**	8.1	11.3
Bar Harbor Bank and Trust Co.	Bar Harbor	ME	**B**	B	B	3637.8	-3.70	7.9	0.3	24.4	17.1	**7.5**	9.3	13.8
Bar Harbor S&L Assn.	Bar Harbor	ME	**C+**	B-	B-	100.7	-2.15	0.0	0.3	55.4	6.1	**10.0**	12.1	0.0
Baraboo State Bank	Baraboo	WI	**B**	B	B	504.8	6.47	9.7	0.8	5.3	8.4	**8.0**	9.7	17.4
Barclays Bank Delaware	Wilmington	DE	**C+**	C+	C	28773.0	-12.61	0.6	69.0	0.0	0.5	**10.0**	15.7	22.7
▲ Barrington Bank & Trust Co., N.A.	Barrington	IL	**B**	B-	B	3317.4	0.73	20.0	17.2	39.2	3.1	**6.9**	11.4	12.5
Barwick Banking Co.	Barwick	GA	**D**	D	D	91.5	436.18	14.1	2.0	4.4	7.6	**10.0**	25.5	28.3
Basile State Bank	Basile	LA	**B-**	B-	B-	71.4	10.20	2.6	7.6	32.0	0.6	**7.8**	9.5	0.0
Bath Savings Institution	Bath	ME	**A**	A	A	1181.3	13.36	6.0	0.8	22.8	32.3	**10.0**	15.0	25.7
Bath State Bank	Bath	IN	**B-**	B-	B-	234.5	26.61	4.2	1.4	13.4	26.7	**6.3**	8.3	0.0
Battle Creek State Bank	Battle Creek	NE	**C+**	C+	B-	40.2	5.65	51.0	0.9	1.0	11.2	**10.0**	11.6	17.6
▼ Bay Bank	Green Bay	WI	**B+**	A-	B+	204.1	61.45	11.6	2.7	7.1	22.3	**7.8**	9.5	20.5
Bay Port State Bank	Bay Port	MI	**C+**	C+	C+	128.9	5.73	10.5	1.9	17.9	1.2	**5.5**	7.5	12.6
Bay State Savings Bank	Worcester	MA	**C**	C	C	486.3	4.08	5.6	0.9	38.8	3.4	**6.9**	8.9	14.1
Baybank	Gladstone	MI	**B-**	C+	C	131.6	8.19	19.7	10.3	16.1	19.5	**6.8**	9.0	0.0
BayCoast Bank	Swansea	MA	**B-**	C+	C+	2244.7	5.58	11.2	3.2	13.5	11.1	**5.1**	9.0	11.1
BayVanguard Bank	Sparrows Point	MD	**B+**	B+	B	800.8	90.24	7.2	2.3	29.0	4.9	**10.0**	11.1	17.8
BBVA USA	Birmingham	AL	**C**	C-	C+	95849.0	-4.96	15.8	7.0	13.4	18.4	**7.0**	9.0	15.7
BCB Community Bank	Bayonne	NJ	**B-**	B-	B-	2893.9	-3.15	4.0	0.0	17.7	2.9	**7.3**	10.0	0.0
BCBank, Inc.	Philippi	WV	**B-**	B-	C+	160.2	9.17	7.6	2.9	17.7	15.3	**6.8**	9.2	0.0
▲ Beach Bank	Fort Walton Beach	FL	**D+**	D-	D-	602.2	5.88	13.0	0.3	11.6	1.6	**8.1**	9.7	14.1
Beacon Business Bank, N.A.	San Francisco	CA	**C**	C	B	154.7	-1.05	10.6	0.0	3.8	14.8	**8.9**	10.3	23.9
Beacon Community Bank	Charleston	SC	**D+**	D	D	337.1	45.74	12.9	0.3	33.5	9.2	**10.0**	11.0	15.6
Beal Bank	Plano	TX	**C+**	C+	C+	1742.9	-18.35	10.6	0.4	23.8	27.6	**10.0**	30.0	46.3
Beal Bank USA	Las Vegas	NV	**C+**	C+	C+	5709.7	-29.49	36.1	0.0	2.2	18.3	**10.0**	41.6	44.7
Beardstown Savings, S.B.	Beardstown	IL	**C+**	C+	C+	68.8	13.24	2.1	9.6	35.7	26.9	**8.6**	10.0	19.0
Beauregard Federal Savings Bank	DeRidder	LA	**B+**	B+	B+	75.5	10.10	5.0	5.3	30.7	14.4	**10.0**	15.5	0.0
▲ Bedford Federal Savings Bank	Bedford	IN	**B+**	B	B	166.3	8.48	5.6	2.3	33.6	5.7	**9.5**	10.7	0.0
▲ Bedford Loan & Deposit Bank	Bedford	KY	**B+**	B	B	114.6	14.11	2.8	5.8	30.4	31.8	**10.0**	12.5	24.4
Belgrade State Bank	Belgrade	MO	**B**	B	B	341.2	7.10	7.0	4.7	28.1	18.6	**6.9**	8.9	16.1
Bell Bank	Fargo	ND	**A-**	A-	B+	10213.7	24.89	15.0	2.0	18.4	0.8	**7.2**	9.2	13.8
Bellevue State Bank	Bellevue	IA	**A**	A-	A-	149.0	12.60	9.3	4.8	16.4	15.3	**10.0**	13.8	0.0
Belmont Bank & Trust Co.	Chicago	IL	**A-**	A-	C+	846.7	22.54	15.7	0.5	5.2	17.5	**8.6**	10.1	17.3
Belmont Savings Bank	Bellaire	OH	**B-**	B-	B	418.7	6.85	4.9	2.5	16.6	54.4	**10.0**	17.6	0.0
Belmont Savings Bank, SSB	Belmont	NC	**C+**	C+	C+	107.6	14.55	0.0	0.0	58.4	3.8	**10.0**	18.7	0.0
Belt Valley Bank	Belt	MT	**B+**	B+	B	75.8	9.05	3.5	2.4	25.4	2.3	**10.0**	13.1	0.0
Benchmark Bank	Plano	TX	**B+**	B+	B+	1067.7	34.74	11.6	1.2	14.5	0.1	**5.3**	7.3	11.8
Benchmark Community Bank	Kenbridge	VA	**A-**	A-	A-	978.4	23.63	6.3	1.5	28.5	6.2	**6.6**	8.6	15.3
Bendena State Bank	Bendena	KS	**B-**	B-	B-	88.0	24.86	7.0	1.9	9.4	31.3	**6.3**	8.3	13.9

Asset Quality Index	Adjusted Non-Performing Loans as a % of Total Loans	Adjusted Non-Performing Loans as a % of Capital	Net Charge-Offs Avg Loans	Profitability Index	Net Income ($Mil)	Return on Assets (R.O.A.)	Return on Equity (R.O.E.)	Net Interest Spread	Overhead Efficiency Ratio	Liquidity Index	Liquidity Ratio	Hot Money Ratio	Stability Index
8.0	0.16	0.9	-0.02	0.3	0.0	0.04	0.36	2.92	88.8	2.4	31.3	12.7	4.8
2.7	2.72	21.6	0.00	3.3	0.8	0.46	5.74	3.24	78.7	3.2	21.7	13.9	4.7
3.3	2.94	13.9	0.11	4.4	4.1	1.07	9.74	2.72	66.7	4.3	25.6	7.6	7.7
5.4	1.50	7.2	0.09	5.3	11.9	1.11	10.63	3.22	64.4	4.4	24.5	10.4	8.6
4.0	0.56	2.7	-0.09	7.5	4.1	1.75	16.35	3.98	59.5	3.7	8.1	10.0	8.9
4.9	2.06	6.8	-0.01	4.3	2.5	0.88	8.07	2.79	64.1	4.9	37.9	9.7	7.9
1.2	3.83	18.2	0.29	2.7	0.2	0.23	2.46	3.54	88.4	6.2	39.3	1.8	4.9
7.2	0.32	3.1	0.00	6.3	31.4	1.28	15.28	3.79	64.0	4.2	17.4	8.5	7.2
9.2	0.08	0.1	-0.04	4.5	0.9	0.92	4.82	2.83	62.8	4.2	39.7	13.8	8.8
7.8	0.48	3.0	-0.02	9.3	16.5	3.17	32.77	3.60	67.9	4.7	24.4	8.1	9.6
4.2	0.93	6.9	-0.06	6.3	1.7	1.58	15.99	4.23	58.3	1.9	8.3	16.9	6.8
4.5	0.71	5.7	-0.15	5.4	2.5	1.22	13.68	3.90	63.2	3.0	13.8	14.1	5.3
5.1	1.52	12.5	0.24	5.4	222.4	1.26	13.06	2.48	49.9	3.1	21.8	5.6	8.3
5.3	0.79	5.3	0.00	8.4	6.4	2.72	33.77	4.86	40.3	3.5	7.8	10.1	5.1
3.1	2.40	16.1	0.48	5.4	14.1	1.25	14.74	3.00	49.7	1.6	19.9	20.6	6.6
7.3	0.90	2.7	-0.01	4.5	1.0	0.90	11.73	2.81	70.3	7.0	56.9	2.5	5.1
1.5	3.02	17.9	0.00	5.6	1.0	1.36	12.93	3.75	63.3	2.7	46.9	7.2	7.5
3.0	2.17	16.5	0.12	5.7	8.8	1.22	12.99	3.51	66.3	4.5	31.6	7.9	7.4
7.8	0.35	1.6	0.06	6.1	105.7	1.35	12.17	3.47	62.5	6.2	35.0	3.6	9.8
7.8	0.56	1.6	0.00	3.3	0.4	0.60	5.29	2.30	76.6	6.7	69.5	7.0	6.8
3.8	1.62	10.9	0.05	6.6	2.4	2.17	22.54	3.61	54.1	0.7	12.8	34.8	6.2
5.7	0.33	2.3	0.13	6.3	18.5	1.61	17.02	3.56	54.0	3.8	20.4	9.8	9.0
6.3	0.69	3.1	0.02	4.9	21.3	1.14	9.15	2.89	62.4	4.0	20.7	9.5	9.2
7.0	1.48	6.3	0.00	2.3	0.1	0.18	1.52	1.83	89.9	1.5	34.1	38.5	6.7
5.6	1.57	5.3	0.00	4.6	2.1	0.86	8.74	2.66	66.6	5.4	40.8	7.8	7.4
3.3	1.34	4.5	3.73	6.2	293.0	1.99	11.04	8.27	62.9	3.8	35.8	5.2	7.5
3.7	0.41	2.5	-0.04	9.4	59.0	3.49	28.04	2.74	64.7	2.2	3.6	6.4	8.5
7.5	0.00	0.0	0.00	0.0	-1.1	-3.49	-12.14	2.86	209.3	1.5	29.2	31.2	5.6
4.0	2.36	11.4	0.00	7.4	0.6	1.57	16.26	4.31	67.9	3.4	41.1	18.3	6.7
9.2	0.16	0.4	0.01	8.3	8.6	1.52	10.48	3.08	61.0	4.7	30.2	9.1	10.0
6.3	0.72	3.3	-0.03	4.4	1.2	1.03	11.97	3.50	71.8	3.0	36.7	18.8	5.7
6.5	0.90	3.5	0.47	3.4	0.1	0.64	5.48	2.43	72.3	2.1	37.0	31.0	6.3
5.9	1.28	4.1	-0.05	4.9	0.8	0.95	8.92	3.44	71.8	6.2	56.8	7.2	7.0
4.9	0.66	6.4	-0.01	4.7	0.6	0.89	12.01	4.17	66.9	2.4	22.2	17.5	4.7
4.2	1.58	12.4	0.01	3.3	2.2	0.91	10.16	3.26	74.4	2.9	17.4	13.3	5.6
4.4	1.83	7.8	0.06	6.0	0.8	1.21	13.36	3.71	61.9	3.4	32.0	15.4	6.0
6.2	0.41	2.5	0.09	4.7	11.9	1.11	13.30	3.40	82.6	2.6	15.9	14.1	7.7
4.8	2.23	9.8	-0.04	6.6	5.6	1.38	10.95	3.55	47.0	3.6	19.1	11.3	7.7
4.1	1.72	9.4	na	0.1	-652.2	-1.36	-12.82	na	60.0	5.8	33.2	2.5	6.8
4.4	1.51	9.3	0.03	5.7	16.0	1.13	11.06	3.62	50.1	1.8	15.4	21.9	7.6
5.4	1.15	5.2	0.02	4.5	0.9	1.11	12.28	4.35	70.9	3.0	15.9	10.1	6.0
8.2	0.13	0.7	-0.04	1.7	1.1	0.39	2.88	2.97	83.5	3.0	22.3	14.6	4.3
7.6	0.18	0.7	-0.56	1.0	-0.1	-0.13	-1.23	3.45	103.6	5.8	50.2	7.9	6.8
8.7	0.00	0.0	0.00	2.7	2.5	1.64	16.79	3.45	67.4	1.3	17.7	28.3	4.2
3.3	13.30	18.6	-0.04	8.9	66.2	7.43	22.81	7.07	29.6	2.8	53.5	10.8	7.9
2.6	15.37	18.4	-0.03	8.2	158.6	5.12	12.52	6.17	39.5	2.1	39.8	15.6	8.6
4.2	1.41	11.3	-0.05	3.4	0.2	0.61	5.96	3.43	74.7	4.5	42.0	12.8	4.8
6.9	0.93	6.7	-0.01	4.9	0.3	0.72	4.65	3.87	79.4	4.9	45.8	11.5	8.7
6.0	0.90	4.3	-0.01	5.5	1.0	1.21	11.34	3.11	60.5	3.1	34.9	17.8	7.1
7.5	0.97	4.0	-0.03	6.5	0.9	1.54	11.89	4.50	55.9	4.7	37.2	10.4	7.4
7.8	0.13	1.1	0.04	6.2	2.4	1.42	16.60	4.37	61.3	2.1	24.1	19.3	5.3
8.1	0.13	0.9	0.21	8.7	242.1	4.95	51.81	3.07	39.8	5.1	20.7	2.3	9.0
7.1	0.98	2.2	0.15	9.0	1.4	1.88	13.67	3.54	41.6	5.5	39.8	6.8	9.6
8.6	0.03	0.2	0.00	7.7	5.7	1.42	14.02	3.26	39.3	2.5	36.9	24.3	7.5
7.5	2.31	4.2	0.00	3.0	1.2	0.56	2.94	2.64	75.3	3.7	53.8	19.8	7.3
10.0	0.76	1.5	0.00	2.6	0.2	0.42	2.17	3.15	81.4	1.7	36.4	39.6	7.3
5.4	1.12	9.2	0.00	8.2	0.6	1.50	11.25	4.16	52.1	3.2	30.7	15.9	8.6
8.5	0.17	1.5	-0.09	5.7	6.1	1.23	16.57	3.13	77.0	5.8	33.1	5.5	7.2
8.0	0.21	1.8	-0.01	6.5	5.7	1.20	13.76	3.61	64.3	4.8	28.8	6.1	6.7
6.1	0.58	4.0	0.12	5.9	0.5	1.17	13.82	2.89	60.4	3.7	25.2	11.7	5.7

Name	City	State	Rating	2020 Rating	2019 Rating	Total Assets ($Mil)	One Year Asset Growth	Asset Mix (As a % of Total Assets): Commercial Loans	Consumer Loans	Mortgage Loans	Securities	Capitalization Index	Leverage Ratio	Risk-Based Capital Ratio
Beneficial State Bank	Oakland	CA	**D+**	D	C-	1456.5	17.51	15.6	11.3	2.6	27.2	**6.0**	9.2	0.0
Benton County State Bank	Blairstown	IA	**B**	B	B	49.9	8.11	2.4	0.1	4.4	19.5	**10.0**	13.3	0.0
Benton State Bank	Benton	WI	**C**	C-	C-	72.3	3.62	8.1	4.9	23.5	2.3	**6.7**	9.4	0.0
Berkshire Bank	Pittsfield	MA	**C-**	C	B-	12266.7	-6.04	11.3	1.6	14.5	19.0	**6.9**	8.9	15.0
Bessemer Trust Co.	New York	NY	**A**	A	A	877.6	-8.79	11.0	35.9	0.0	35.2	**9.3**	10.5	20.6
Bessemer Trust Co. of California, N.A.	San Francisco	CA	**U**	U	U	13.2	9.06	0.0	0.0	0.0	76.4	**10.0**	100.	0.0
Bessemer Trust Co. of Delaware, N.A.	Wilmington	DE	**U**	U	U	23.1	7.99	0.0	0.0	0.0	36.9	**10.0**	82.5	0.0
Bessemer Trust Co., N.A.	New York	NY	**A**	A	A	2632.7	19.33	6.9	13.4	0.0	48.6	**7.1**	9.1	28.2
Better Banks	Peoria	IL	**B-**	B-	B-	380.3	17.94	5.3	27.0	14.4	31.6	**5.4**	7.4	13.0
Beverly Bank & Trust Co., N.A.	Chicago	IL	**B**	B	B	1759.4	0.31	40.0	12.5	3.5	5.7	**6.1**	9.7	11.8
Big Horn Federal Savings Bank	Greybull	WY	**C+**	C+	C+	330.2	14.63	8.8	2.0	8.4	43.2	**7.4**	9.2	22.5
Bison State Bank	Bison	KS	**C-**	C	D	18.2	11.32	17.2	4.3	19.6	2.6	**6.9**	8.9	0.0
Black Hills Community Bank, N.A.	Rapid City	SD	**B**	B-	B	414.9	12.47	10.5	0.3	7.8	15.8	**6.4**	10.8	0.0
Black Mountain Savings Bank, SSB	Black Mountain	NC	**C**	C	C+	42.0	5.45	0.0	0.1	66.4	0.0	**10.0**	12.6	0.0
Black River Country Bank	Black River Falls	WI	**B+**	B+	B+	94.6	0.48	6.6	3.7	28.3	14.7	**8.3**	9.9	16.5
Blackhawk Bank	Beloit	WI	**B**	B	B	1327.4	20.87	20.4	1.9	7.1	33.6	**6.2**	8.3	14.8
Blackhawk Bank & Trust	Milan	IL	**B+**	B+	A-	1736.8	15.83	8.1	0.7	5.7	52.6	**8.5**	10.0	0.0
BLC Community Bank	Little Chute	WI	**A**	A	A-	327.0	2.08	13.4	0.2	11.8	19.9	**10.0**	11.2	16.0
Blissfield State Bank	Blissfield	MI	**C+**	C+	B-	117.4	11.64	6.5	2.4	14.3	46.8	**7.9**	9.6	0.0
Bloomsdale Bank	Bloomsdale	MO	**A-**	A-	B+	308.1	1.84	8.4	1.4	12.6	35.2	**5.8**	7.8	13.6
Blue Foundry Bank	Rutherford	NJ	**C-**	C-	C+	2580.0	31.10	2.5	0.0	20.7	11.5	**8.3**	9.9	20.4
▼ Blue Grass Federal S&L Assn.	Paris	KY	**C+**	B-	B-	38.5	10.64	4.7	1.9	50.3	18.1	**10.0**	22.5	0.0
▲ Blue Grass Savings Bank	Blue Grass	IA	**A-**	B	B	225.7	7.17	10.1	0.6	15.2	43.6	**10.0**	14.1	28.1
Blue Ridge Bank	Walhalla	SC	**C-**	C-	C+	168.9	16.95	1.9	1.8	25.7	18.9	**6.0**	8.0	0.0
Blue Ridge Bank and Trust Co.	Independence	MO	**C-**	C	C	723.9	15.87	11.4	9.6	2.8	18.5	**6.5**	8.6	14.8
▲ Blue Ridge Bank, N.A.	Martinsville	VA	**B+**	B-	C+	2747.5	73.48	14.9	2.3	21.5	9.5	**7.4**	9.2	13.9
Blue Sky Bank	Pawhuska	OK	**B**	B	B	466.4	11.76	24.9	1.0	3.5	12.2	**5.1**	10.2	0.0
BlueHarbor Bank	Mooresville	NC	**A-**	A-	A-	389.9	36.60	9.3	0.5	10.7	10.6	**8.6**	10.1	14.5
Bluestone Bank	Raynham	MA	**B-**	B-	C+	1298.7	82.30	4.9	1.4	28.8	22.3	**8.4**	9.9	17.2
Bluff View Bank	Galesville	WI	**A**	A	A-	127.5	7.73	9.2	2.1	10.9	12.0	**10.0**	17.6	20.6
▲ BMO Harris Bank N.A.	Chicago	IL	**B**	C+	B	159838.7	4.16	20.6	5.1	4.3	23.8	**7.7**	9.5	14.8
BMO Harris Central N.A.	Roselle	IL	**U**	U	U	8.0	0.11	0.0	0.0	0.0	0.0	**10.0**	87.3	446.4
BMW Bank of North America	Salt Lake City	UT	**A-**	A-	A-	11509.3	0.55	0.2	75.1	0.0	21.0	**10.0**	13.5	15.6
BNA Bank	New Albany	MS	**A-**	A-	A-	655.1	7.50	5.7	3.5	21.8	34.4	**10.0**	11.1	19.2
BNC National Bank	Glendale	AZ	**A**	A	B+	1027.9	-6.80	11.6	4.8	11.9	18.1	**9.3**	10.5	19.9
BNY Mellon Trust of Delaware	Wilmington	DE	**B**	B	B	143.1	-7.36	0.0	0.0	9.9	0.0	**10.0**	46.0	130.2
BNY Mellon, N.A.	Pittsburgh	PA	**B**	B	B	28759.0	-4.89	0.5	11.0	26.6	0.7	**5.1**	7.1	11.4
BOC Bank	Amarillo	TX	**A-**	A-	A-	111.2	16.80	51.0	0.1	15.1	7.4	**7.6**	9.4	22.0
Bodcaw Bank	Stamps	AR	**B+**	B+	B-	151.2	16.67	21.4	3.7	26.2	14.8	**10.0**	11.7	17.5
Boelus State Bank	Boelus	NE	**C+**	C+	C+	19.3	12.87	0.8	3.9	0.2	2.9	**10.0**	13.6	0.0
▲ Bogota Savings Bank	Teaneck	NJ	**B-**	C	C+	819.0	10.83	1.3	0.1	42.7	11.0	**10.0**	14.4	0.0
▲ BOKF, N.A.	Tulsa	OK	**B+**	B	B	46909.6	2.82	17.7	0.9	4.5	28.9	**6.4**	8.4	12.8
▲ BOM Bank	Natchitoches	LA	**A-**	B+	B	655.4	7.44	17.0	2.2	22.5	2.5	**7.8**	9.5	0.0
Bonanza Valley State Bank	Brooten	MN	**C+**	C+	C	75.4	9.29	7.8	1.9	25.9	11.0	**6.9**	8.9	14.8
Bonduel State Bank	Bonduel	WI	**B+**	B+	B+	80.6	18.68	6.6	4.0	9.1	35.8	**10.0**	17.6	36.2
Boone Bank & Trust Co.	Boone	IA	**B+**	B+	A-	157.3	6.73	6.5	0.2	3.8	49.6	**7.0**	9.0	0.0
Boonville Federal Savings Bank	Boonville	IN	**C-**	C-	D+	61.7	2.57	10.2	9.6	40.4	11.5	**6.7**	8.7	17.4
Border Bank	Fargo	ND	**B-**	B-	B-	858.8	32.27	13.8	4.4	8.9	11.5	**6.4**	8.5	12.8
Boston Trust Walden Co.	Boston	MA	**A-**	A-	A-	59.6	16.78	0.1	0.0	0.0	2.3	**10.0**	85.9	105.0
Boundary Waters Bank	Ely	MN	**C+**	C+	C+	128.5	4.32	5.2	0.6	9.2	4.8	**8.5**	11.0	13.8
Bradesco BAC Florida Bank	Coral Gables	FL	**B+**	B+	B+	2212.2	-3.44	1.5	0.4	54.6	9.9	**10.0**	11.5	18.2
Brannen Bank	Inverness	FL	**B-**	B-	B-	754.7	21.98	1.5	0.9	25.0	24.8	**3.2**	5.2	17.0
Branson Bank	Branson	MO	**B-**	B-	B	304.7	14.08	8.0	1.9	23.6	3.0	**6.5**	8.5	13.4
Brantley Bank & Trust Co.	Brantley	AL	**A-**	A-	B+	104.8	18.05	10.0	2.0	6.5	40.7	**9.8**	10.9	0.0
Brattleboro S&L Assn.	Brattleboro	VT	**C**	C	C+	290.6	14.88	7.9	0.6	35.0	0.1	**4.7**	6.7	13.6
Brazos National Bank	Richwood	TX	**B+**	B+	B+	32.9	-11.65	0.4	0.8	58.1	0.0	**10.0**	35.7	74.9
Bremer Bank, N.A.	Saint Paul	MN	**B+**	B+	B+	15775.4	4.98	11.9	0.8	8.5	22.6	**6.6**	8.6	13.8
▲ Brentwood Bank	Bethel Park	PA	**B**	B-	B	803.2	6.89	2.7	0.0	30.0	14.0	**10.0**	12.0	0.0
Brickyard Bank	Lincolnwood	IL	**C-**	C-	C-	167.3	5.18	8.7	0.3	8.4	5.3	**6.7**	8.8	19.3
Bridge City State Bank	Bridge City	TX	**B**	B	B	221.4	-14.76	4.4	0.8	10.3	53.0	**9.0**	10.3	23.8

Asset Quality Index	Adjusted Non-Performing Loans as a % of Total Loans	Adjusted Non-Performing Loans as a % of Capital	Net Charge-Offs / Avg Loans	Profitability Index	Net Income ($Mil)	Return on Assets (R.O.A.)	Return on Equity (R.O.E.)	Net Interest Spread	Overhead Efficiency Ratio	Liquidity Index	Liquidity Ratio	Hot Money Ratio	Stability Index
4.7	1.71	8.9	0.01	**3.5**	7.2	1.06	12.04	3.79	70.0	**5.4**	35.7	9.2	**5.5**
7.8	0.00	0.0	0.00	**6.4**	0.3	1.35	9.97	3.88	54.4	**4.7**	39.3	11.4	**7.4**
4.8	1.03	6.1	-0.02	**6.8**	0.7	1.92	20.71	4.73	64.0	**1.9**	22.3	18.0	**5.5**
6.4	0.98	5.0	0.37	**2.7**	36.3	0.58	6.22	2.63	72.4	**3.9**	35.2	13.3	**5.3**
6.8	0.00	0.0	0.00	**9.5**	15.6	3.57	31.90	1.11	72.2	**5.4**	19.4	0.0	**8.3**
10.0	na	0.0	na	**9.5**	0.4	5.98	6.06	0.30	73.2	**4.0**	na	0.0	**7.0**
10.0	na	0.0	na	**10.0**	8.7	70.56	85.08	1.00	56.7	**4.0**	na	0.0	**7.0**
7.7	0.00	0.0	0.00	**9.5**	44.3	3.22	29.31	0.41	86.0	**5.9**	24.4	0.0	**9.1**
3.9	0.65	4.4	0.11	**4.2**	2.0	1.08	12.76	3.18	71.3	**2.5**	31.4	19.6	**5.6**
7.0	0.32	1.6	0.05	**6.1**	11.6	1.32	12.34	2.89	61.3	**2.2**	12.6	9.1	**7.9**
5.4	3.02	8.9	-0.15	**3.1**	0.7	0.45	4.78	2.79	83.2	**5.8**	55.6	9.6	**5.2**
8.9	0.00	0.0	-0.19	**4.4**	0.1	0.77	8.85	3.44	83.1	**5.6**	54.0	6.6	**3.1**
5.7	0.38	2.8	0.00	**7.5**	4.2	2.11	20.76	3.84	53.2	**1.6**	16.0	23.8	**7.3**
10.0	0.00	0.0	0.00	**2.3**	0.1	0.34	2.72	2.78	84.1	**1.5**	33.7	44.8	**6.6**
8.7	0.01	0.1	0.01	**6.0**	0.7	1.55	15.65	3.98	57.1	**2.6**	27.8	17.9	**7.1**
5.5	1.50	6.9	0.01	**6.0**	7.6	1.24	12.74	3.53	64.0	**6.2**	32.9	3.0	**7.4**
8.6	0.75	1.9	-0.04	**4.9**	8.8	1.09	9.46	2.50	51.3	**2.8**	21.6	17.0	**9.0**
7.4	0.00	0.0	-0.01	**8.4**	3.9	2.39	21.14	3.24	42.9	**1.9**	23.8	12.2	**9.1**
5.0	2.26	9.4	0.01	**2.9**	0.3	0.49	4.87	2.76	82.3	**6.3**	61.0	8.0	**5.0**
6.5	0.55	3.3	0.00	**9.6**	3.4	2.22	25.21	3.53	43.2	**2.3**	30.0	21.1	**7.2**
7.1	1.07	6.0	0.00	**0.7**	-1.7	-0.17	-1.67	2.10	116.0	**4.7**	51.0	16.9	**6.2**
8.9	0.03	0.1	0.00	**3.5**	0.1	0.32	1.34	3.64	85.1	**2.1**	37.8	30.6	**5.6**
8.7	0.82	2.6	-0.19	**5.6**	1.5	1.32	9.29	2.31	36.2	**3.5**	54.9	21.4	**7.7**
5.3	2.29	10.6	0.09	**2.2**	0.2	0.29	3.37	2.76	90.1	**6.0**	52.2	7.5	**4.4**
2.4	2.71	15.4	0.29	**4.0**	2.2	0.63	7.20	2.89	72.3	**4.7**	31.8	8.7	**6.0**
5.8	0.60	4.4	0.07	**8.1**	34.5	2.36	29.54	3.76	57.5	**2.5**	21.1	16.7	**8.4**
7.7	0.10	0.2	-0.04	**6.6**	3.6	1.58	13.00	4.60	58.8	**1.6**	12.4	21.9	**8.0**
8.8	0.05	0.3	0.00	**6.1**	2.2	1.27	12.17	3.07	51.5	**4.0**	31.3	11.2	**6.4**
8.9	0.15	1.1	0.01	**4.1**	5.5	0.86	8.50	2.86	71.1	**5.3**	34.6	9.2	**7.9**
7.7	1.08	2.4	0.00	**8.3**	1.0	1.59	8.63	4.11	66.1	**5.2**	29.9	4.2	**10.0**
5.3	1.23	4.7	0.14	**5.2**	956.9	1.20	10.51	2.28	55.4	**6.5**	45.5	4.3	**9.8**
10.0	na	0.0	na	**3.9**	0.0	0.35	0.40	5.65	-300.0	**4.0**	na	0.0	**7.0**
5.6	0.15	0.8	-0.09	**7.9**	112.6	1.87	13.99	2.09	23.1	**1.5**	28.6	2.8	**9.9**
7.1	1.27	4.5	0.03	**7.0**	4.8	1.48	13.26	3.25	47.7	**4.2**	32.1	11.1	**8.7**
8.3	0.40	1.9	0.01	**8.7**	14.3	2.54	22.06	3.13	56.9	**5.9**	34.3	5.6	**10.0**
4.4	18.74	2.3	-1.77	**9.8**	2.9	4.26	6.79	0.77	39.5	**8.8**	117.2	0.0	**8.1**
6.9	0.14	0.7	0.01	**5.9**	171.0	1.11	9.05	1.19	56.2	**2.4**	33.9	22.3	**8.1**
8.5	0.00	0.0	0.00	**7.4**	0.9	1.52	16.68	3.78	58.1	**3.8**	19.2	10.2	**9.5**
6.2	0.72	5.5	0.44	**6.3**	0.9	1.26	10.61	4.70	55.6	**0.7**	11.2	38.7	**6.4**
8.9	0.00	0.0	0.00	**2.2**	0.0	0.10	0.70	1.58	92.3	**4.1**	81.0	19.7	**6.0**
9.5	0.19	0.8	0.00	**4.2**	4.7	1.19	8.39	2.48	54.8	**0.9**	25.2	40.6	**6.9**
5.9	1.17	3.7	0.26	**6.0**	317.2	1.27	12.40	2.55	60.2	**5.5**	29.1	3.9	**9.6**
7.5	0.09	2.1	0.01	**8.3**	6.5	2.04	21.72	4.57	61.3	**3.7**	9.4	10.1	**7.4**
6.9	0.50	3.5	-0.02	**3.8**	0.3	0.67	7.46	3.52	79.7	**4.2**	21.9	7.5	**6.0**
9.0	0.34	0.7	0.00	**4.2**	0.3	0.67	3.63	2.89	71.0	**6.1**	63.2	8.1	**8.1**
9.0	0.00	0.0	-0.02	**5.6**	0.9	1.21	12.18	2.75	53.2	**5.0**	50.0	11.6	**7.4**
6.5	0.03	4.2	0.01	**2.2**	0.1	0.35	4.13	3.14	83.7	**1.4**	27.9	32.6	**3.6**
4.3	1.47	7.7	0.01	**4.1**	3.9	0.91	9.55	3.31	73.1	**3.0**	21.7	10.4	**6.4**
6.5	0.00	0.0	0.00	**10.0**	14.9	60.82	71.12	5.73	55.3	**3.7**	121.9	100.0	**9.7**
5.3	1.14	7.2	0.04	**3.8**	0.4	0.60	5.41	3.48	76.5	**2.1**	20.0	19.0	**5.6**
6.9	1.27	5.3	0.01	**4.3**	6.0	0.54	4.79	2.80	76.0	**1.4**	24.4	37.5	**8.2**
6.3	1.26	6.7	0.00	**5.7**	4.6	1.30	24.90	2.63	60.3	**6.5**	62.2	6.9	**4.8**
6.2	0.50	3.6	0.00	**4.9**	1.4	0.99	11.18	3.80	66.9	**3.5**	23.6	12.2	**5.0**
6.8	0.42	1.9	-0.08	**4.2**	0.4	0.70	6.51	3.74	79.9	**2.9**	45.9	25.9	**7.1**
6.6	0.40	4.6	0.03	**3.0**	0.7	0.47	6.57	2.74	82.2	**4.7**	27.5	6.2	**4.1**
8.5	0.07	0.1	0.00	**9.5**	1.4	6.93	20.21	2.78	78.5	**2.4**	44.2	31.8	**8.0**
7.9	0.38	1.9	-0.06	**6.4**	107.8	1.37	15.33	3.06	56.5	**4.0**	18.7	3.9	**8.6**
8.7	0.24	1.2	0.00	**4.4**	3.8	0.96	7.87	3.15	65.9	**3.1**	13.1	10.6	**7.8**
5.3	2.32	8.1	-0.01	**2.4**	0.2	0.19	2.23	2.11	90.1	**2.8**	48.0	29.4	**5.0**
5.0	4.16	10.7	0.00	**3.8**	0.9	0.79	7.41	2.91	68.5	**6.1**	61.7	9.4	**5.7**

Name	City	State	Rating	2020 Rating	2019 Rating	Total Assets ($Mil)	One Year Asset Growth	Comm-ercial Loans	Cons-umer Loans	Mort-gage Loans	Secur-ities	Capital-ization Index	Lever-age Ratio	Risk-Based Capital Ratio
								Asset Mix (As a % of Total Assets)						
Bridge Community Bank	Mount Vernon	IA	**B+**	A-	B+	135.1	22.62	10.4	2.6	15.6	19.1	**7.5**	9.3	0.0
Bridgewater Bank	Saint Louis Park	MN	**A-**	A-	A-	3158.9	14.90	13.1	0.3	7.4	12.7	**7.0**	10.6	12.5
▲ Brighton Bank	Brighton	TN	**E+**	E-	E-	60.1	38.74	5.5	0.6	35.2	8.3	**5.1**	7.1	19.0
▼ Brighton Bank	Salt Lake City	UT	**B**	B+	A-	283.1	-0.90	7.4	0.3	5.8	17.9	**8.7**	10.2	0.0
Bristol County Savings Bank	Taunton	MA	**B-**	C+	B-	2905.5	11.19	7.4	10.3	24.6	14.5	**10.0**	13.0	15.0
Bristol Morgan Bank	Oakfield	WI	**C**	C	C	159.5	21.59	7.0	3.9	30.8	10.4	**9.8**	10.8	15.2
▲ Broadway National Bank	San Antonio	TX	**B**	B-	B+	5076.8	12.28	8.9	3.3	10.1	44.3	**6.6**	8.6	0.0
Brookline Bank	Brookline	MA	**B**	B-	B	5386.1	-9.72	24.6	0.7	10.0	6.8	**8.3**	10.4	13.6
Brookville Building and Savings Assn.	Brookville	OH	**B-**	B	B	46.9	-4.20	4.8	0.7	45.6	18.0	**10.0**	19.4	0.0
Brown Brothers Harriman Trust Co. of Dela	Wilmington	DE	**U**	U	U	11.9	10.27	0.0	0.0	0.0	53.3	**10.0**	76.0	0.0
Brown Brothers Harriman Trust Co., N.A.	New York	NY	**U**	U	U	14.3	7.21	0.0	0.0	0.0	52.3	**10.0**	68.4	0.0
Bruning Bank	Bruning	NE	**B+**	B+	B	462.4	12.95	9.2	0.5	1.6	33.9	**8.6**	10.7	0.0
Brunswick Bank and Trust Co.	New Brunswick	NJ	**B**	B	B-	362.3	27.72	4.7	0.0	15.5	13.4	**10.0**	12.0	15.9
Brunswick State Bank	Brunswick	NE	**C**	C	C	169.0	16.78	17.0	3.5	1.2	2.7	**5.6**	8.1	11.5
Bryant Bank	Tuscaloosa	AL	**B**	B+	A-	2496.5	15.61	10.4	0.5	5.6	18.2	**6.1**	8.1	16.0
Bryant State Bank	Bryant	SD	**A-**	A-	B+	43.9	10.75	18.3	5.5	0.9	19.3	**10.0**	11.6	18.9
BTC Bank	Bethany	MO	**A-**	B+	B+	708.3	17.46	9.1	1.6	9.1	11.5	**10.0**	12.5	0.0
BTH Bank N.A.	Quitman	TX	**B**	B+	A-	1955.2	-1.23	35.5	0.6	14.5	17.5	**10.0**	12.5	0.0
Buckeye Community Bank	Lorain	OH	**B+**	B+	A-	217.2	5.35	21.9	0.1	5.1	21.0	**10.0**	11.1	18.4
▲ Buckeye State Bank	Powell	OH	**C-**	D+	D-	239.9	-0.18	31.8	4.0	8.2	21.8	**10.0**	11.7	20.6
Buckley State Bank	Buckley	IL	**C+**	B-	B-	51.2	16.76	5.6	0.7	0.2	32.1	**9.1**	10.4	0.0
Buena Vista National Bank	Chester	IL	**A-**	A-	A-	252.5	4.02	3.3	5.3	16.7	33.4	**10.0**	11.1	0.0
▲ Buffalo Federal Bank	Buffalo	WY	**B+**	B-	B	156.9	13.78	11.5	3.5	16.0	15.1	**7.5**	10.1	0.0
Burke & Herbert Bank & Trust Co.	Alexandria	VA	**B-**	B-	B	3554.8	6.57	3.3	0.1	10.5	38.7	**9.5**	10.7	18.9
Burling Bank	Chicago	IL	**B+**	B+	A-	207.7	43.37	12.1	0.2	22.8	17.1	**7.0**	9.0	0.0
Burton State Bank	Burton	TX	**B+**	B+	B+	85.0	7.55	0.8	4.7	9.7	19.4	**10.0**	11.0	0.0
Busey Bank	Champaign	IL	**A-**	A-	A-	10945.6	1.15	13.1	0.3	10.3	28.1	**9.7**	10.8	16.2
Butte State Bank	Butte	NE	**B**	B-	B-	50.9	11.44	6.1	1.9	2.0	32.2	**9.9**	10.9	0.0
Byline Bank	Chicago	IL	**B**	B	B	6531.0	2.24	27.5	0.0	3.1	23.0	**9.1**	10.7	14.2
Byron Bank	Byron	IL	**B**	B-	B-	330.4	9.13	9.8	2.0	11.1	27.3	**8.7**	10.1	0.0
C3bank, N.A.	Encinitas	CA	**B+**	B+	B+	673.1	43.73	15.9	0.0	6.8	0.9	**6.0**	8.0	15.4
▼ Cache Bank & Trust	Greeley	CO	**D-**	D+	C	115.4	7.49	3.6	0.5	3.5	36.8	**10.0**	11.0	37.4
▼ Cache Valley Bank	Logan	UT	**C-**	C+	B	2947.2	9.08	25.9	0.2	3.8	0.7	**2.3**	9.3	0.0
▲ Cadence Bank, N.A.	Atlanta	GA	**B+**	B-	B+	18675.0	-0.95	26.1	0.5	12.2	22.9	**10.0**	11.6	16.2
Caldwell Bank & Trust Co.	Columbia	LA	**C**	C	B-	200.4	-1.13	7.0	2.9	19.9	6.5	**7.3**	9.2	0.0
Calhoun County Bank, Inc.	Grantsville	WV	**B-**	B-	B-	175.7	9.22	2.6	11.6	47.1	12.9	**7.7**	9.4	18.0
California Bank of Commerce	Walnut Creek	CA	**C+**	C+	B-	1873.7	-1.94	33.3	3.4	0.4	3.3	**5.8**	8.4	11.6
California Business Bank	Irvine	CA	**D**	D	D	97.2	-0.97	13.1	4.8	0.2	0.0	**10.0**	11.7	17.7
California First National Bank	Irvine	CA	**A+**	A+	A	144.1	17.40	0.0	0.0	0.0	3.5	**10.0**	36.3	102.4
California International Bank, N.A.	Westminster	CA	**D**	D	D	82.8	35.68	41.4	0.0	0.0	0.4	**10.0**	13.7	50.3
California Pacific Bank	San Francisco	CA	**B+**	B+	A-	79.8	-7.12	5.9	0.0	4.4	0.0	**10.0**	43.1	53.2
▲ CalPrivate Bank	La Jolla	CA	**B+**	B-	C+	1382.3	8.56	26.2	0.2	5.5	6.4	**7.7**	9.5	13.4
Calvin B. Taylor Banking Co.	Berlin	MD	**A**	A	A	836.9	30.21	7.6	0.2	15.8	12.3	**10.0**	12.1	0.0
▲ Cambridge Savings Bank	Cambridge	MA	**B**	B-	B-	5244.1	3.33	12.5	0.1	21.8	11.1	**6.8**	8.8	12.7
▲ Cambridge State Bank	Cambridge	MN	**C**	C-	B-	89.2	3.85	16.4	0.6	13.3	25.7	**9.0**	10.3	0.0
Cambridge Trust Co.	Cambridge	MA	**B+**	B+	B+	4303.0	6.97	8.3	1.1	32.1	16.6	**6.6**	8.6	13.7
Camden National Bank	Camden	ME	**A-**	A-	B+	5131.3	3.99	7.7	0.4	23.8	27.3	**6.7**	8.7	14.1
Camp Grove State Bank	Camp Grove	IL	**D**	D	D+	19.8	10.86	2.3	1.5	2.4	13.2	**10.0**	18.3	41.6
▼ Campbell & Fetter Bank	Kendallville	IN	**C+**	B-	B-	368.3	8.89	4.8	4.9	34.6	33.1	**7.5**	9.4	26.5
Campbell County Bank	Herreid	SD	**B+**	B	B	146.3	3.21	7.2	1.0	0.2	13.6	**10.0**	13.9	0.0
Campus State Bank	Campus	IL	**C-**	C	C	25.5	22.01	0.0	12.9	9.9	6.1	**8.4**	9.9	0.0
Canandaigua National Trust Co. of Florida	Sarasota	FL	**U**	U	U	4.2	2.58	0.0	0.0	0.0	12.2	**10.0**	94.6	429.3
Canton Co-operative Bank	Canton	MA	**B-**	B-	B-	145.5	8.52	1.1	0.0	31.7	20.8	**10.0**	14.2	26.3
▲ Canyon Community Bank, N.A.	Tucson	AZ	**D+**	D-	D	142.1	19.02	28.1	0.0	2.0	6.4	**9.6**	10.7	35.4
▲ Cape Ann Savings Bank	Gloucester	MA	**A**	A-	A-	818.6	12.57	2.9	0.1	40.2	18.3	**10.0**	22.0	39.0
Cape Cod Co-Operative Bank	Hyannis	MA	**C+**	C+	C+	1306.0	20.52	6.1	0.1	40.3	4.8	**6.6**	8.6	0.0
Cape Cod Five Cents Savings Bank	Hyannis	MA	**B**	B-	B-	4625.6	15.98	5.2	1.3	46.7	8.2	**8.6**	10.1	18.3
Capital Bank	Houston	TX	**B**	B-	B-	553.9	5.71	10.0	1.1	10.1	7.7	**6.8**	8.9	12.9
Capital Bank and Trust Co.	Irvine	CA	**U**	U	U	233.8	19.72	0.0	0.0	0.0	58.9	**10.0**	67.7	152.2
Capital Bank of Texas	Carrizo Springs	TX	**B+**	B+	B+	88.4	-4.78	1.9	0.4	2.3	8.6	**10.0**	11.8	0.0

Asset Quality Index	Adjusted Non-Performing Loans as a % of Total Loans	Adjusted Non-Performing Loans as a % of Capital	Net Charge-Offs Avg Loans	Profitability Index	Net Income ($Mil)	Return on Assets (R.O.A.)	Return on Equity (R.O.E.)	Net Interest Spread	Overhead Efficiency Ratio	Liquidity Index	Liquidity Ratio	Hot Money Ratio	Stability Index
8.7	0.00	0.0	0.00	**5.5**	0.7	1.11	12.00	3.15	57.2	**5.1**	46.0	10.8	**5.7**
7.3	0.04	0.2	0.00	**7.7**	22.9	1.53	14.15	3.69	40.5	**0.9**	17.5	19.0	**9.1**
3.7	1.63	14.9	1.20	**6.7**	0.6	2.01	29.10	2.41	83.4	**2.7**	39.9	18.6	**2.7**
4.4	1.38	5.6	0.00	**10.0**	3.3	2.33	21.99	4.68	50.1	**6.3**	38.9	0.8	**9.1**
7.9	0.50	1.6	-0.01	**7.5**	37.6	2.67	21.52	3.08	64.5	**5.2**	30.9	9.3	**9.8**
5.3	1.48	5.3	0.00	**3.2**	0.4	0.57	6.27	3.84	71.4	**0.9**	18.7	22.3	**5.7**
8.7	0.11	0.9	0.06	**4.7**	26.9	1.11	11.82	2.89	68.9	**6.4**	42.2	4.9	**7.9**
4.6	0.75	5.1	0.09	**6.8**	39.7	1.43	13.30	3.58	50.5	**3.0**	7.9	12.8	**7.8**
9.7	0.00	0.1	0.00	**3.0**	0.1	0.40	2.03	3.69	87.0	**5.3**	45.4	9.5	**7.2**
10.0	na	0.0	na	**9.8**	2.5	40.42	68.18	1.10	67.7	**4.0**	222.8	0.0	**6.4**
10.0	na	0.0	na	**10.0**	1.9	26.05	44.21	1.16	77.7	**4.0**	187.0	0.0	**6.8**
8.7	0.00	0.0	0.00	**4.6**	2.4	1.04	9.62	3.10	66.7	**3.8**	28.8	10.7	**7.4**
7.1	0.62	2.8	-0.02	**4.1**	1.4	0.80	6.84	3.49	66.1	**1.0**	18.4	29.7	**7.6**
3.2	1.56	16.9	1.04	**5.0**	1.0	1.34	16.48	3.51	46.0	**1.3**	30.3	32.4	**4.5**
8.9	0.37	2.0	0.02	**4.3**	10.1	0.83	10.23	2.39	68.1	**5.2**	39.3	11.4	**7.2**
8.1	0.21	0.7	1.46	**7.0**	0.4	1.81	16.20	5.54	61.1	**5.4**	38.9	7.0	**6.4**
6.1	1.12	5.8	-0.01	**6.0**	4.6	1.31	10.31	3.27	59.2	**2.8**	24.2	15.9	**8.9**
3.9	3.50	16.5	1.21	**5.5**	10.4	1.03	8.05	2.89	39.7	**2.2**	24.7	23.5	**9.5**
8.5	0.36	1.3	-0.14	**4.1**	0.7	0.66	5.89	3.26	75.5	**2.9**	19.6	11.7	**7.5**
8.0	0.06	0.4	0.10	**2.3**	0.7	0.56	6.29	2.92	76.2	**1.9**	23.6	20.5	**4.5**
8.7	0.00	0.0	0.00	**3.2**	0.1	0.43	4.11	2.67	83.0	**6.1**	54.8	6.3	**4.2**
7.5	1.06	2.9	0.03	**6.0**	1.4	1.13	9.19	3.13	61.9	**5.8**	42.2	5.5	**7.8**
8.4	0.00	0.0	0.00	**5.8**	0.9	1.23	12.88	4.04	64.2	**3.8**	19.4	10.4	**6.6**
7.3	1.80	7.1	-0.02	**4.1**	18.3	1.06	9.58	3.05	63.5	**5.6**	31.5	6.8	**9.3**
9.2	0.00	0.0	0.00	**6.1**	1.5	1.48	16.07	3.69	56.5	**5.9**	36.6	2.6	**6.0**
9.4	0.00	0.7	0.00	**4.1**	0.3	0.69	6.27	1.67	60.6	**4.1**	67.3	18.8	**7.3**
7.6	0.38	1.6	0.04	**7.4**	79.5	1.49	11.07	2.76	55.1	**5.7**	29.8	5.0	**9.6**
6.3	0.67	3.1	-0.22	**6.5**	0.4	1.42	12.56	3.07	67.2	**1.8**	38.2	17.1	**6.5**
4.7	0.84	5.3	0.31	**6.9**	53.4	1.61	12.85	3.83	52.6	**4.2**	22.2	8.4	**8.4**
4.1	2.22	10.8	0.05	**6.9**	2.9	1.85	17.57	3.19	56.6	**2.0**	25.2	20.0	**7.1**
8.6	0.00	0.0	0.00	**5.3**	4.2	1.39	16.92	3.03	46.8	**5.0**	33.1	6.9	**7.5**
9.8	0.00	0.0	0.00	**0.0**	-0.7	-1.14	-9.86	1.35	178.9	**5.3**	79.0	15.7	**4.8**
8.0	0.45	2.5	-0.04	**10.0**	28.1	2.16	28.35	4.19	35.5	**5.4**	35.7	9.4	**9.0**
6.3	1.14	4.5	0.34	**5.7**	218.0	2.33	20.18	3.20	53.4	**5.3**	34.7	7.1	**7.4**
2.9	1.96	17.4	-0.01	**4.6**	1.3	1.26	13.97	4.36	67.2	**0.7**	16.4	48.4	**5.2**
5.3	1.05	5.4	0.02	**3.9**	0.6	0.65	7.08	3.72	74.7	**3.1**	19.9	14.1	**5.7**
7.9	0.09	0.7	0.01	**4.1**	7.5	0.78	9.96	2.95	67.1	**4.5**	26.0	10.3	**6.6**
7.0	0.09	0.5	-0.15	**0.4**	0.1	0.10	0.79	2.93	97.5	**1.6**	31.4	29.9	**6.2**
9.3	0.00	0.0	0.00	**3.7**	-1.9	-5.14	-11.01	1.00	556.3	**4.1**	109.4	14.0	**9.6**
8.5	0.00	0.0	0.00	**0.0**	-0.5	-1.25	-9.16	2.57	139.5	**1.7**	38.4	58.3	**6.0**
5.0	4.31	5.8	0.00	**9.4**	0.6	1.55	3.68	4.14	52.4	**4.0**	55.1	14.5	**9.2**
7.1	0.13	1.1	0.00	**5.9**	9.5	1.39	14.93	4.00	52.8	**4.4**	13.9	5.3	**7.6**
8.9	0.20	0.9	0.01	**6.6**	4.7	1.25	10.03	2.88	50.1	**6.3**	45.8	3.2	**9.0**
6.8	0.63	4.4	0.00	**4.6**	24.7	0.95	10.36	3.04	63.1	**2.9**	14.4	11.0	**7.6**
9.0	0.23	0.5	-0.02	**3.7**	0.4	0.97	9.14	3.29	72.3	**6.5**	52.2	2.7	**4.9**
8.3	0.17	1.2	0.00	**6.1**	27.5	1.33	13.55	3.28	57.8	**4.5**	5.7	4.1	**7.6**
8.3	0.25	1.1	0.03	**7.3**	39.3	1.58	14.23	2.93	53.5	**4.1**	22.3	3.9	**9.8**
5.3	7.18	10.5	0.00	**0.0**	-0.6	-7.25	-46.25	2.26	348.6	**3.3**	71.2	17.1	**3.7**
9.3	0.00	0.1	0.00	**3.0**	0.7	0.39	4.63	2.36	79.8	**6.0**	45.4	5.5	**4.9**
5.0	0.76	4.2	0.33	**9.3**	1.5	2.18	13.55	5.98	49.8	**3.6**	20.6	10.8	**10.0**
5.5	0.40	2.2	0.00	**2.6**	0.0	0.27	2.69	2.41	89.5	**5.5**	49.0	8.7	**4.3**
10.0	na	0.0	na	**7.5**	0.1	3.85	4.11	0.27	90.4	**4.0**	na	0.0	**5.7**
7.4	2.68	7.4	0.00	**2.8**	0.2	0.33	2.28	2.69	84.6	**5.3**	48.1	10.7	**7.7**
8.3	0.00	0.0	0.00	**2.1**	0.6	0.77	8.38	3.37	77.6	**5.0**	20.5	2.5	**4.5**
9.2	0.80	2.3	0.00	**8.2**	7.3	1.87	8.62	2.46	74.8	**3.0**	42.9	21.7	**8.5**
7.1	0.81	4.8	-0.01	**3.6**	3.7	0.60	6.88	2.78	77.5	**5.6**	27.2	4.4	**6.5**
8.3	0.44	3.0	0.00	**5.6**	28.4	1.30	12.80	3.04	60.6	**4.3**	21.8	9.3	**7.8**
7.3	0.02	0.2	-0.01	**6.0**	3.6	1.32	14.83	4.42	62.3	**2.3**	17.7	17.4	**6.6**
10.0	na	0.0	na	**10.0**	33.2	30.19	48.31	1.81	76.0	**9.9**	195.6	0.0	**6.5**
9.5	0.00	0.0	0.00	**2.1**	-0.1	-0.13	-1.00	1.18	107.8	**7.0**	76.0	4.6	**7.3**

Name	City	State	Rating	2020 Rating	2019 Rating	Total Assets ($Mil)	One Year Asset Growth	Asset Mix (As a % of Total Assets): Commercial Loans	Consumer Loans	Mortgage Loans	Securities	Capitalization Index	Leverage Ratio	Risk-Based Capital Ratio
Capital Bank, N.A.	Rockville	MD	**B**	B	B	2120.2	18.48	17.0	5.6	14.3	7.6	**5.6**	7.6	13.5
Capital City Bank	Tallahassee	FL	**B+**	B+	B+	4000.6	14.62	6.0	7.5	9.8	20.1	**6.6**	8.6	16.0
Capital Community Bank	Provo	UT	**A-**	B+	B-	491.9	5.45	15.5	17.9	1.0	2.2	**10.0**	12.1	16.9
▲ Capital One Bank (USA), N.A.	Glen Allen	VA	**B-**	C	B-	107235.1	-3.13	7.8	75.7	0.0	12.3	**10.0**	18.0	21.8
▲ Capital One, N.A.	McLean	VA	**B-**	C	B-	369047.0	1.47	7.2	23.7	0.0	23.8	**5.9**	7.9	13.8
Capitol Bank	Madison	WI	**A-**	A-	A-	455.4	-6.24	12.1	0.3	7.8	18.4	**10.0**	11.7	15.2
Capitol Federal Savings Bank	Topeka	KS	**B**	B-	B	9672.0	0.96	0.8	0.1	63.9	20.8	**10.0**	11.5	0.0
▲ Capitol National Bank	Lansing	MI	**C+**	C	B-	237.0	-1.68	35.2	0.1	1.9	0.2	**4.1**	9.3	0.0
Capon Valley Bank	Wardensville	WV	**B**	B	B	195.7	12.87	4.4	7.0	30.1	16.2	**8.1**	9.8	0.0
▲ CapStar Bank	Nashville	TN	**A-**	B	B+	3198.5	30.86	17.1	1.4	7.8	15.7	**9.6**	10.7	15.6
▲ CapTex Bank	Fort Worth	TX	**D+**	D-	D	263.1	27.73	10.6	5.4	13.4	2.2	**7.2**	9.5	12.7
Carmine State Bank	Carmine	TX	**B+**	B	B	98.9	11.67	3.1	5.4	10.6	45.3	**10.0**	11.9	0.0
Carolina Bank & Trust Co.	Florence	SC	**A-**	A-	A-	677.7	19.92	13.7	1.2	15.3	9.8	**10.0**	12.1	21.7
Carroll Bank and Trust	Huntingdon	TN	**B**	B	B	372.5	12.28	8.5	4.7	25.3	15.1	**7.1**	9.1	0.0
▲ Carroll County Trust Co.	Carrollton	MO	**B-**	C	C	174.9	6.93	4.0	1.5	5.8	52.0	**7.3**	10.7	0.0
Carrollton Bank	Carrollton	IL	**B-**	B-	B-	2913.8	22.29	24.1	0.2	9.9	7.9	**4.2**	6.2	10.8
Carrollton Federal Bank	Carrollton	KY	**C+**	C+	C+	37.5	9.92	0.3	3.4	43.4	10.9	**10.0**	14.5	0.0
Carson Bank	Mulvane	KS	**B-**	B-	C+	165.2	14.32	7.8	1.4	13.3	16.6	**5.5**	7.5	13.1
Carson Community Bank	Stilwell	OK	**B+**	B+	B+	176.5	10.14	18.6	3.7	6.1	34.1	**7.6**	9.4	0.0
Carter Bank & Trust	Martinsville	VA	**C-**	C-	C	4120.5	-0.75	7.1	1.1	11.5	20.5	**8.8**	10.2	14.6
Carthage Federal S&L Assn.	Carthage	NY	**B**	B	B	293.5	8.07	2.3	2.4	51.9	17.4	**10.0**	11.0	27.6
Carver Federal Savings Bank	New York	NY	**D-**	D-	D	683.5	1.87	6.5	0.3	15.3	13.5	**8.6**	10.1	15.2
Carver State Bank	Savannah	GA	**C+**	C	C	70.5	33.75	23.3	1.3	13.8	2.1	**10.0**	12.0	0.0
Casey State Bank	Casey	IL	**B-**	B-	B-	393.4	10.79	16.5	6.8	7.7	15.1	**7.2**	9.4	0.0
Cashmere Valley Bank	Cashmere	WA	**A-**	A-	A	2147.5	16.28	5.7	9.6	3.8	46.9	**8.3**	9.9	0.0
Cass Commercial Bank	Saint Louis	MO	**A**	A	A	1215.8	9.56	26.4	0.0	0.0	0.0	**10.0**	13.6	22.2
Castle Rock Bank	Castle Rock	MN	**B+**	B+	A-	245.5	9.30	8.6	3.4	9.8	57.9	**10.0**	13.6	26.7
Castroville State Bank	Castroville	TX	**B**	B	B	235.0	20.76	5.7	3.0	23.9	29.3	**6.2**	8.2	0.0
Cathay Bank	Los Angeles	CA	**A-**	A-	A-	19330.8	0.50	14.0	0.0	26.4	5.2	**10.0**	11.2	15.2
Catlin Bank	Catlin	IL	**B+**	B	B-	69.8	8.97	10.4	0.9	26.4	23.0	**9.7**	10.8	24.3
Catskill Hudson Bank	Kingston	NY	**C-**	C-	C	555.1	2.39	6.3	0.1	13.3	24.9	**5.0**	7.0	11.9
Cattaraugus County Bank	Little Valley	NY	**C**	C+	B-	323.0	11.00	7.8	0.7	11.8	17.5	**5.7**	7.7	12.3
Cattle Bank & Trust	Seward	NE	**A-**	A-	A-	342.9	8.76	6.0	0.5	18.9	21.2	**10.0**	12.0	0.0
Cayuga Lake National Bank	Union Springs	NY	**B-**	B-	B-	212.1	14.59	14.6	3.9	33.6	29.4	**8.5**	10.0	19.3
CB&S Bank, Inc.	Russellville	AL	**B**	B	B	2252.4	9.21	4.9	1.2	8.2	49.1	**9.3**	10.5	0.0
▲ CBank	Cincinnati	OH	**B+**	B-	B	250.1	-8.74	28.4	1.2	8.4	7.7	**10.0**	11.1	15.6
CBBC Bank	Maryville	TN	**A-**	A-	B	459.2	15.22	4.2	0.4	4.6	33.2	**10.0**	13.7	22.7
CBI Bank & Trust	Muscatine	IA	**B+**	B+	B+	1150.1	68.71	11.8	1.6	10.6	27.8	**8.7**	10.2	16.8
CBW Bank	Weir	KS	**A-**	A-	A	100.6	-16.04	48.9	5.8	0.6	2.9	**10.0**	44.1	97.8
CCB Community Bank	Andalusia	AL	**B+**	B+	A-	576.2	1.36	8.9	1.2	12.6	9.5	**8.2**	10.4	0.0
Cecil Bank	Elkton	MD	**E**	E	E-	194.5	-2.91	28.6	0.1	9.5	20.9	**3.7**	5.7	10.7
Cedar Hill National Bank	Charlotte	NC	**U**	U	U	14.0	3.87	0.0	0.0	0.0	82.3	**10.0**	84.2	128.4
▲ Cedar Rapids Bank and Trust Co.	Cedar Rapids	IA	**A-**	B+	B+	1898.8	-6.19	23.6	0.2	4.1	13.2	**8.6**	12.0	13.9
▲ Cedar Rapids State Bank	Cedar Rapids	NE	**B-**	C+	C-	55.0	6.91	21.4	2.2	18.0	4.0	**7.7**	9.5	13.2
Cedar Security Bank	Fordyce	NE	**B+**	B+	B-	56.8	10.20	13.1	1.9	6.6	15.4	**10.0**	14.0	0.0
Cedar Valley Bank & Trust	La Porte City	IA	**B-**	C+	C+	89.5	12.88	7.8	4.3	34.0	10.1	**5.7**	7.7	12.1
CedarStone Bank	Lebanon	TN	**B**	B	B	250.5	-1.87	7.3	2.1	24.7	21.5	**7.7**	9.5	16.1
Celtic Bank Corp.	Salt Lake City	UT	**C-**	C	B+	3905.1	-7.52	76.6	1.3	0.0	4.1	**0.9**	21.1	0.0
CenBank	Buffalo Lake	MN	**B**	B	B	79.9	9.69	7.8	10.6	2.1	20.3	**5.3**	7.3	11.6
▼ Cendera Bank, N.A.	Bells	TX	**C+**	B+	B+	127.1	1.03	4.9	0.7	33.1	0.0	**10.0**	14.1	20.8
Cenlar FSB	Trenton	NJ	**A-**	A-	A-	1142.8	-2.44	0.0	0.0	31.2	48.5	**7.5**	9.3	25.5
Centennial Bank	Conway	AR	**A-**	A-	A-	17591.9	4.33	9.2	4.7	6.8	17.4	**10.0**	11.2	17.4
Centennial Bank	Trezevant	TN	**B-**	B-	B-	666.3	6.99	8.6	4.0	12.9	5.3	**8.0**	9.7	14.4
Center National Bank	Litchfield	MN	**A-**	A-	A-	240.5	11.54	8.7	4.1	7.7	30.7	**8.1**	9.8	18.8
▲ Centera Bank	Sublette	KS	**B**	B-	B-	323.9	6.62	6.4	0.9	5.3	54.7	**6.0**	8.0	18.0
CenterBank	Milford	OH	**B+**	B+	B	274.7	-0.73	19.5	0.1	19.8	6.2	**8.3**	10.4	0.0
Centier Bank	Merrillville	IN	**A-**	A-	B+	5886.0	9.53	6.3	6.3	8.4	11.6	**8.1**	9.7	13.5
Centinel Bank of Taos	Taos	NM	**A-**	A-	A-	379.2	17.19	7.1	0.7	12.6	56.4	**5.7**	7.7	24.2
Central Bank	Little Rock	AR	**B**	B	B	366.1	22.98	13.9	0.3	16.6	13.1	**6.4**	8.4	12.6
▲ Central Bank	Tampa	FL	**B-**	C+	C+	282.9	4.07	25.1	0.0	20.3	1.3	**6.9**	8.9	14.0

Arrows denote recent upgrades ▲ or downgrades ▼

Asset Quality Index	Adjusted Non-Performing Loans as a % of Total Loans	Adjusted Non-Performing Loans as a % of Capital	Net Charge-Offs Avg Loans	Profitability Index	Net Income ($Mil)	Return on Assets (R.O.A.)	Return on Equity (R.O.E.)	Net Interest Spread	Overhead Efficiency Ratio	Liquidity Index	Liquidity Ratio	Hot Money Ratio	Stability Index
6.2	0.49	4.4	0.08	**9.4**	18.3	1.86	25.27	5.32	67.3	**3.9**	23.9	11.7	**7.3**
7.0	0.67	2.4	-0.08	**5.8**	18.5	1.16	12.80	2.88	75.8	**6.7**	36.7	1.0	**8.0**
6.8	0.08	1.7	1.13	**9.0**	6.0	2.44	20.87	7.98	47.7	**0.8**	20.3	42.2	**6.0**
4.1	0.54	4.0	2.59	**9.0**	4168.1	7.82	42.75	11.08	46.8	**0.7**	20.7	75.4	**8.4**
4.8	1.08	3.4	0.21	**5.6**	2817.1	1.54	13.31	3.44	70.8	**6.9**	47.3	2.0	**7.8**
7.4	0.01	0.0	-0.14	**6.2**	3.1	1.25	11.34	3.12	53.3	**1.9**	22.4	20.2	**8.1**
9.8	0.20	1.3	0.00	**4.0**	38.7	0.80	6.72	1.86	58.4	**1.9**	19.7	21.5	**9.3**
5.4	1.21	4.4	-0.08	**5.0**	1.1	0.98	12.69	3.66	61.9	**5.3**	32.0	4.2	**6.0**
4.5	2.25	9.1	0.09	**4.8**	0.9	1.00	10.13	4.07	71.1	**3.0**	25.1	15.1	**6.1**
7.8	0.29	1.6	0.01	**6.8**	24.1	1.57	13.24	3.22	54.6	**4.5**	26.7	10.6	**8.5**
5.3	0.26	2.6	0.09	**2.1**	1.2	0.92	8.58	4.30	83.6	**1.8**	14.2	13.1	**5.1**
9.2	0.00	0.0	-0.01	**5.5**	0.7	1.51	11.67	3.58	54.3	**3.2**	80.6	42.9	**6.8**
7.9	1.01	3.0	0.02	**6.2**	3.8	1.29	10.59	3.30	54.9	**4.8**	29.3	6.3	**8.0**
5.5	1.03	5.4	0.02	**6.1**	2.3	1.27	13.89	4.59	64.2	**2.0**	16.5	19.1	**5.4**
4.8	4.34	11.8	-0.01	**4.5**	1.3	1.43	13.03	3.28	57.1	**5.0**	47.9	11.9	**5.2**
8.5	0.07	0.5	-0.01	**4.2**	14.2	1.01	16.23	2.71	66.5	**5.0**	30.7	10.3	**6.0**
5.3	4.75	12.6	0.01	**3.1**	0.1	0.48	3.21	3.91	81.1	**2.6**	28.6	18.2	**6.8**
8.7	0.02	0.2	0.00	**6.0**	1.2	1.56	20.07	4.19	66.0	**3.3**	28.3	14.7	**4.6**
4.4	1.65	9.1	0.03	**6.6**	1.2	1.34	13.94	4.26	63.2	**2.8**	28.7	17.1	**6.1**
6.3	0.33	1.9	0.62	**2.5**	16.0	0.78	7.96	2.75	76.6	**3.3**	24.6	15.9	**6.5**
9.6	0.16	0.6	0.02	**4.5**	1.3	0.95	9.08	2.75	57.5	**1.6**	20.4	25.1	**6.3**
2.4	2.67	15.5	0.00	**0.0**	-3.0	-0.86	-9.41	2.86	126.6	**1.5**	26.4	18.7	**5.1**
4.9	2.82	11.7	0.03	**4.6**	0.3	1.02	9.06	4.07	65.6	**2.1**	42.6	13.5	**4.3**
3.7	3.33	14.0	-0.01	**5.1**	2.4	1.20	12.00	3.31	54.9	**2.2**	20.2	18.7	**6.8**
6.5	1.82	3.6	-0.03	**6.2**	14.2	1.39	12.22	2.71	54.6	**6.7**	56.8	6.5	**10.0**
8.2	0.00	0.0	0.00	**8.0**	8.9	1.34	10.84	2.42	43.4	**6.3**	39.0	4.6	**10.0**
8.1	1.19	3.8	-0.15	**4.9**	1.4	1.18	8.67	2.60	45.6	**4.6**	58.9	16.5	**8.1**
6.5	0.45	2.6	0.11	**5.5**	1.4	1.22	14.24	3.35	52.2	**2.7**	19.9	15.9	**5.0**
6.9	0.60	3.0	0.19	**7.8**	155.5	1.62	12.45	3.23	43.6	**1.0**	16.1	29.5	**10.0**
8.3	0.23	1.0	0.03	**7.8**	0.6	1.62	15.13	3.84	60.7	**3.8**	30.9	13.2	**6.3**
4.5	0.95	5.8	-0.03	**2.5**	0.9	0.30	4.24	2.64	84.1	**3.1**	11.5	13.3	**4.3**
4.0	3.33	16.0	-0.11	**3.3**	0.7	0.47	6.13	3.16	85.7	**5.5**	32.9	3.9	**4.7**
8.8	0.30	1.0	-0.19	**6.8**	3.1	1.80	15.09	3.23	51.1	**2.4**	20.2	17.7	**8.3**
6.9	0.46	2.9	0.03	**3.3**	0.7	0.69	6.80	3.27	63.4	**3.2**	23.2	13.9	**5.3**
6.3	1.70	4.8	0.12	**4.5**	12.0	1.08	9.24	3.29	68.3	**5.9**	45.0	8.7	**9.3**
8.1	0.02	0.1	0.02	**6.7**	2.7	1.94	20.23	3.81	51.2	**1.5**	14.0	24.3	**6.5**
9.0	0.55	1.0	0.01	**6.2**	2.6	1.20	8.33	3.52	54.7	**4.1**	49.7	16.7	**8.2**
6.2	0.84	2.4	0.09	**5.8**	7.2	1.25	12.09	3.22	61.5	**5.3**	31.1	8.2	**9.1**
6.0	1.73	2.8	0.00	**8.3**	2.2	5.11	27.78	7.38	46.6	**2.5**	51.3	8.5	**7.9**
6.5	0.46	3.1	0.03	**7.4**	5.0	1.77	17.16	4.29	56.0	**2.5**	23.8	16.5	**8.7**
3.8	2.54	17.3	0.00	**0.3**	-1.8	-1.89	-30.89	1.57	177.0	**2.6**	37.4	22.1	**1.6**
10.0	na	0.0	na	**9.8**	0.2	3.50	4.15	1.72	69.5	**10.0**	427.1	0.0	**7.0**
7.6	0.31	1.6	0.23	**9.8**	22.5	2.40	19.76	3.25	46.1	**4.3**	22.0	9.2	**9.0**
8.1	0.00	0.0	0.00	**6.2**	0.5	1.77	19.20	3.26	59.8	**0.8**	5.1	27.9	**5.6**
6.6	0.93	4.6	-0.08	**4.4**	0.2	0.71	4.97	3.39	74.5	**5.3**	53.9	10.1	**7.2**
5.6	0.06	6.7	0.00	**7.3**	0.8	1.76	22.31	4.71	56.3	**4.0**	2.7	7.1	**5.1**
8.9	0.27	0.8	0.02	**4.4**	1.1	0.85	8.74	3.57	61.2	**3.1**	27.2	15.1	**6.3**
6.1	0.41	3.7	0.06	**9.5**	53.0	2.38	35.55	2.27	33.2	**0.4**	8.0	0.4	**9.2**
6.6	0.49	2.2	0.00	**6.6**	0.8	2.08	28.34	4.80	57.1	**4.3**	21.1	7.4	**5.1**
8.8	0.00	0.0	-0.07	**2.3**	0.0	-0.07	-0.62	4.23	98.8	**0.9**	19.9	31.1	**6.9**
7.8	0.71	5.6	-0.02	**7.6**	8.2	1.38	14.65	1.82	97.4	**7.8**	59.9	0.0	**9.2**
5.9	0.64	2.1	0.09	**9.6**	176.5	2.07	12.59	4.04	37.9	**5.2**	32.9	5.5	**10.0**
4.4	1.15	6.5	0.12	**4.8**	2.6	0.78	7.10	3.97	64.7	**1.9**	27.5	21.7	**6.5**
8.7	0.08	0.4	0.00	**5.6**	1.6	1.31	12.69	3.24	63.0	**3.4**	25.5	13.2	**7.5**
7.6	0.50	2.1	0.01	**5.0**	2.2	1.33	15.06	3.21	59.6	**5.0**	34.4	7.6	**5.9**
8.4	0.01	0.4	0.00	**7.3**	2.0	1.48	15.47	4.05	55.5	**2.2**	20.7	18.3	**6.5**
7.9	0.20	1.4	-0.03	**7.1**	39.5	1.37	14.04	3.10	54.1	**4.6**	20.6	5.9	**9.1**
9.5	0.02	0.1	0.00	**7.9**	3.4	1.89	22.06	3.09	42.8	**6.4**	59.0	7.0	**6.7**
7.6	0.54	2.0	0.00	**5.8**	2.2	1.25	14.40	2.93	44.4	**1.5**	33.4	40.8	**6.2**
6.1	0.20	1.6	0.57	**4.8**	1.6	1.12	14.97	3.13	59.7	**0.9**	15.9	34.2	**4.7**

Name	City	State	Rating	2020 Rating	2019 Rating	Total Assets ($Mil)	One Year Asset Growth	Asset Mix (As a % of Total Assets) Comm-ercial Loans	Cons-umer Loans	Mort-gage Loans	Secur-ities	Capital-ization Index	Lever-age Ratio	Risk-Based Capital Ratio
Central Bank	Storm Lake	IA	**C+**	C+	B	1623.6	14.60	18.2	1.3	13.6	4.9	**1.8**	9.2	0.0
Central Bank	Savannah	TN	**B-**	B-	B	123.1	10.67	4.9	3.7	31.6	26.9	**9.2**	10.5	22.5
Central Bank	Houston	TX	**B+**	B+	B+	883.7	7.90	12.7	0.2	23.3	18.7	**8.0**	9.7	15.0
Central Bank	Provo	UT	**A**	A	A	1702.1	19.34	5.4	0.9	3.2	29.0	**10.0**	13.1	0.0
Central Bank & Trust Co.	Lexington	KY	**B**	B+	A-	3474.6	10.44	14.3	4.4	16.3	10.7	**8.2**	9.8	16.1
Central Bank and Trust	Lander	WY	**B+**	B+	B	203.1	14.74	14.2	1.4	15.1	39.7	**5.7**	7.7	18.1
Central Bank Illinois	Geneseo	IL	**A-**	A-	B+	1082.0	11.87	6.0	0.6	5.4	42.7	**7.7**	9.4	0.0
Central Bank of Audrain County	Mexico	MO	**B**	B	B	231.1	12.55	2.8	2.5	10.2	33.0	**4.9**	6.9	19.4
Central Bank of Boone County	Columbia	MO	**B+**	B+	B+	2680.7	19.18	6.9	3.8	9.0	33.7	**5.9**	7.9	14.9
Central Bank of Branson	Branson	MO	**B+**	B+	B+	560.0	42.34	8.9	3.9	11.4	25.4	**7.0**	9.0	19.7
▲ Central Bank of Kansas City	Kansas City	MO	**A**	A-	A	335.5	28.30	30.2	0.1	0.3	0.0	**10.0**	12.1	18.3
Central Bank of Lake of the Ozarks	Osage Beach	MO	**A-**	B+	B+	1117.7	17.52	4.8	4.4	12.2	34.6	**5.6**	7.6	17.2
Central Bank of Moberly	Moberly	MO	**B+**	B+	B	238.3	11.26	5.7	8.6	6.3	33.7	**5.3**	7.3	17.7
Central Bank of Oklahoma	Tulsa	OK	**B+**	B	B	764.8	-0.50	9.4	0.2	11.9	5.7	**8.5**	11.2	13.7
Central Bank of Sedalia	Sedalia	MO	**B+**	B+	B+	566.0	11.21	6.0	12.9	6.2	27.7	**5.4**	7.4	15.8
Central Bank of St. Louis	Clayton	MO	**B+**	B+	B+	2492.7	7.01	13.8	0.7	8.5	11.4	**6.8**	8.8	12.8
Central Bank of the Midwest	Lee's Summit	MO	**B+**	B+	B+	4017.9	12.30	11.2	5.0	4.3	22.3	**6.4**	8.4	14.6
Central Bank of the Ozarks	Springfield	MO	**B+**	B+	B+	1845.9	12.10	9.4	10.0	11.5	19.9	**7.5**	9.4	14.6
Central Bank of Warrensburg	Warrensburg	MO	**B+**	B+	B	343.4	17.98	5.8	1.5	8.3	25.0	**6.0**	8.0	18.7
Central Federal S&L Assn.	Cicero	IL	**D+**	C-	C-	201.4	4.85	0.1	0.1	50.0	20.4	**8.2**	9.8	0.0
Central National Bank	Junction City	KS	**A-**	A-	B	1215.3	4.77	6.1	1.5	4.3	38.4	**8.9**	10.2	0.0
Central National Bank	Waco	TX	**A-**	A-	A-	1164.9	6.35	11.7	0.8	22.6	9.5	**6.4**	8.4	15.0
Central National Bank of Poteau	Poteau	OK	**A-**	A-	B+	317.4	12.39	8.6	2.8	10.8	35.3	**8.6**	10.1	0.0
Central Pacific Bank	Honolulu	HI	**B+**	A-	A-	7171.8	8.22	12.5	7.6	23.9	19.6	**7.2**	9.1	14.6
Central Savings Bank	Sault Sainte Marie	MI	**B**	B-	B-	374.1	19.08	10.8	4.9	18.8	33.7	**7.1**	9.1	0.0
Central Savings, F.S.B.	Chicago	IL	**C**	C	B	114.0	-4.52	0.0	0.0	27.5	0.0	**10.0**	23.5	33.2
Central State Bank	Calera	AL	**A-**	A-	A-	458.7	19.00	8.9	2.2	15.1	16.9	**8.1**	9.7	0.0
Central State Bank	Elkader	IA	**B**	B	B	391.2	5.43	16.3	1.6	19.0	11.6	**6.6**	8.6	12.7
Central State Bank	State Center	IA	**B-**	C+	C	368.5	4.79	15.8	1.4	2.5	26.4	**5.8**	12.1	0.0
Central State Bank	Clayton	IL	**D+**	D+	C	180.0	10.98	9.4	6.0	19.2	6.8	**10.0**	13.2	0.0
Central Valley Community Bank	Fresno	CA	**B+**	B+	A	2279.7	19.14	8.9	1.7	1.3	41.8	**6.5**	8.5	14.4
CentreBank	Veedersburg	IN	**A-**	A-	A-	104.3	25.35	12.3	3.1	14.9	0.2	**10.0**	11.6	0.0
Centreville Bank	West Warwick	RI	**B-**	B-	C+	1880.2	0.36	3.7	0.1	24.3	15.2	**10.0**	16.4	0.0
Centric Bank	Harrisburg	PA	**B**	B	B+	1110.4	6.83	31.1	0.2	7.3	3.8	**7.5**	9.6	12.9
CenTrust Bank, N.A.	Northbrook	IL	**C+**	C+	C+	161.3	-2.88	34.3	0.0	6.2	10.3	**8.5**	10.0	16.6
Century Bank	Lucedale	MS	**B**	B	B-	439.4	9.58	7.2	8.7	12.5	28.2	**7.2**	9.1	0.0
Century Bank	Santa Fe	NM	**B+**	B+	B+	1239.6	15.45	16.8	3.5	3.0	25.9	**7.2**	9.2	14.5
Century Bank & Trust	Milledgeville	GA	**A-**	A-	B-	338.5	13.63	4.6	0.7	10.1	30.5	**8.1**	9.8	0.0
Century Bank and Trust	Coldwater	MI	**A-**	A-	B	440.9	13.99	7.1	1.4	11.8	13.2	**9.3**	10.6	19.1
Century Bank and Trust Co.	Medford	MA	**C+**	C+	C+	7246.7	22.19	7.4	0.1	6.7	49.6	**3.9**	5.9	12.8
Century Bank of Florida	Tampa	FL	**C+**	C+	C+	110.1	2.50	13.3	2.7	15.4	8.7	**5.4**	7.4	14.0
Century Bank of Georgia	Cartersville	GA	**A-**	A-	A-	308.3	23.65	9.0	1.1	8.9	25.6	**6.0**	8.0	19.9
Century Bank of Kentucky, Inc.	Lawrenceburg	KY	**B**	B	C+	155.5	8.23	3.1	1.1	32.1	17.8	**9.5**	10.7	0.0
Century Bank of the Ozarks	Gainesville	MO	**B**	B+	A-	239.7	19.54	8.4	2.4	15.2	3.1	**5.4**	8.9	0.0
Century Next Bank	Ruston	LA	**B**	B	B	540.2	2.98	15.5	2.3	24.4	0.8	**9.2**	11.0	0.0
Century S&L Assn.	Trinidad	CO	**C-**	C	C+	101.2	4.67	0.0	0.4	16.8	58.7	**10.0**	13.9	0.0
▲ Century Savings Bank	Vineland	NJ	**C**	C-	C+	588.4	14.89	5.6	0.0	14.0	47.4	**10.0**	11.6	0.0
CerescoBank	Ceresco	NE	**B+**	B+	B	65.7	20.44	8.9	4.1	7.6	25.4	**10.0**	13.6	0.0
CFBank N.A.	Worthington	OH	**A-**	A-	B	1501.1	31.24	19.0	0.1	32.8	1.2	**8.1**	9.7	14.1
CFG Community Bank	Baltimore	MD	**B-**	B-	C+	2045.5	18.79	21.5	0.0	1.1	11.3	**9.8**	11.9	0.0
cfsbank	Charleroi	PA	**C**	C	C+	545.2	9.80	0.9	0.8	42.9	31.6	**10.0**	14.0	30.6
Chain Bridge Bank, N.A.	McLean	VA	**C**	C+	C+	990.8	-5.46	7.4	0.4	16.9	55.7	**4.8**	6.8	19.6
Chambers Bank	Danville	AR	**B**	B	B-	1121.5	4.94	9.8	0.6	15.8	3.0	**6.2**	9.5	11.9
Chambers State Bank	Chambers	NE	**B+**	B+	B+	70.0	-0.43	8.6	4.1	1.5	0.5	**10.0**	24.0	0.0
Champion Bank	Parker	CO	**A**	A	A-	86.2	21.67	5.3	0.0	4.6	4.6	**10.0**	17.9	78.9
Champlain National Bank	Willsboro	NY	**B-**	B-	B-	418.0	4.50	10.8	8.6	15.8	23.6	**7.1**	9.1	0.0
Chappell Hill Bank	Chappell Hill	TX	**C**	C	C+	50.4	29.98	2.4	1.4	21.0	9.3	**5.5**	7.5	15.3
▼ Charis Bank	Justin	TX	**D+**	C-	C+	203.5	51.29	30.4	1.7	12.6	0.8	**10.0**	13.8	17.4
Charles River Bank	Medway	MA	**C**	C	C-	313.8	12.21	2.0	2.2	32.1	16.4	**5.2**	7.2	12.9
Charles Schwab Bank, SSB	Westlake	TX	**B**	B+	B+	358095.0	22.47	0.5	2.0	5.0	87.0	**5.1**	7.1	25.6

Asset Quality Index	Adjusted Non-Performing Loans as a % of Total Loans	Adjusted Non-Performing Loans as a % of Capital	Net Charge-Offs Avg Loans	Profitability Index	Net Income ($Mil)	Return on Assets (R.O.A.)	Return on Equity (R.O.E.)	Net Interest Spread	Overhead Efficiency Ratio	Liquidity Index	Liquidity Ratio	Hot Money Ratio	Stability Index
7.9	0.07	1.0	0.08	**8.9**	13.4	1.82	18.32	4.67	56.2	**1.7**	10.1	17.2	**8.7**
7.4	0.36	1.8	-0.16	**4.1**	0.4	0.63	5.82	3.69	80.5	**3.7**	37.5	15.8	**6.7**
6.9	0.18	2.1	0.01	**6.1**	6.3	1.47	14.58	4.96	72.3	**1.8**	15.0	20.1	**7.4**
8.9	0.04	0.1	0.18	**9.0**	12.2	1.48	10.94	3.68	51.9	**5.7**	49.2	11.1	**10.0**
5.1	1.88	7.8	0.07	**4.7**	16.9	0.99	9.75	3.17	72.1	**4.6**	24.1	8.5	**7.5**
8.9	0.00	0.0	0.00	**8.6**	2.0	1.97	25.51	3.60	52.0	**5.3**	30.4	3.5	**5.6**
6.7	0.89	3.7	-0.01	**7.3**	7.8	1.44	13.49	3.47	51.5	**5.7**	34.4	6.6	**10.0**
7.3	0.55	2.4	-0.05	**5.3**	1.2	0.95	13.60	2.21	56.1	**6.1**	40.2	1.8	**6.3**
8.6	0.18	0.7	-0.03	**7.0**	16.6	1.24	15.36	2.28	54.2	**6.0**	34.7	4.7	**7.7**
4.9	1.63	7.4	0.04	**6.0**	2.6	1.06	12.31	2.66	61.6	**5.7**	39.4	4.4	**6.6**
6.3	0.00	0.0	-0.09	**10.0**	7.4	4.65	35.99	3.59	57.2	**2.2**	39.0	8.2	**9.5**
8.0	0.67	2.7	0.05	**8.1**	7.0	1.32	16.02	2.62	57.9	**6.2**	44.6	6.6	**7.5**
8.4	0.03	0.2	-0.09	**5.4**	1.1	0.97	12.90	2.31	61.8	**5.1**	29.7	3.0	**6.4**
4.6	0.28	1.3	-0.02	**8.8**	6.2	1.62	9.06	4.03	45.8	**2.2**	13.9	13.9	**8.7**
6.0	0.61	3.7	0.08	**6.7**	3.1	1.10	13.83	2.61	56.6	**4.6**	30.4	6.8	**7.1**
8.0	0.23	1.4	-0.04	**8.6**	19.3	1.58	16.20	3.09	54.4	**4.6**	16.7	4.4	**8.6**
6.0	0.76	2.4	0.04	**6.0**	22.5	1.15	8.88	3.08	56.9	**6.0**	29.8	2.9	**8.5**
7.8	0.03	0.2	0.01	**6.7**	12.0	1.34	14.75	2.97	58.4	**5.2**	21.4	2.4	**8.0**
7.1	0.32	1.0	0.01	**5.7**	1.8	1.14	9.63	2.95	59.1	**4.2**	23.1	6.7	**8.2**
6.2	2.85	8.4	-0.19	**1.6**	0.1	0.09	0.89	2.52	96.4	**3.2**	44.0	20.5	**5.5**
7.9	1.12	3.6	0.18	**6.6**	9.5	1.58	14.90	3.27	60.1	**5.5**	28.2	5.4	**9.3**
8.9	0.01	0.3	0.00	**7.2**	9.2	1.60	19.09	3.16	48.9	**5.0**	35.6	11.1	**9.1**
6.8	1.14	2.8	0.03	**7.1**	2.6	1.69	16.24	3.67	58.8	**4.4**	35.9	11.6	**7.8**
8.3	0.25	1.6	0.06	**5.4**	39.7	1.16	12.51	3.23	62.0	**3.9**	18.8	10.3	**7.5**
5.9	1.21	4.7	-0.03	**5.5**	2.1	1.16	12.63	3.42	57.1	**5.0**	44.6	11.1	**5.8**
1.9	4.53	14.3	0.02	**2.9**	0.2	0.40	1.68	2.90	79.6	**0.8**	23.0	39.9	**7.5**
8.8	0.09	0.3	0.02	**7.4**	3.7	1.71	17.25	3.92	55.5	**2.8**	24.4	16.2	**7.1**
8.0	0.02	0.1	-0.01	**5.8**	2.8	1.45	14.73	3.74	56.8	**3.3**	15.7	6.3	**7.1**
3.8	2.49	11.5	0.21	**6.2**	3.4	1.89	14.99	2.94	46.1	**1.4**	31.6	41.7	**8.4**
1.2	8.03	36.2	-0.01	**8.7**	2.0	2.25	17.02	3.89	48.0	**2.8**	38.1	20.6	**9.2**
7.1	0.80	2.0	-0.15	**7.0**	15.4	1.43	12.40	3.65	56.4	**6.7**	43.9	3.2	**10.0**
7.7	0.17	0.8	-0.06	**6.3**	0.5	0.99	8.50	3.12	68.3	**5.1**	48.0	11.5	**7.4**
5.7	2.20	6.0	0.00	**8.0**	18.0	1.91	10.94	3.09	69.4	**4.6**	32.7	12.6	**9.2**
4.5	1.08	12.0	0.06	**6.3**	7.7	1.39	14.87	3.92	54.3	**1.2**	9.2	17.9	**8.2**
3.9	1.37	8.3	0.03	**4.9**	0.7	0.89	7.74	4.21	71.8	**0.9**	22.6	38.9	**6.5**
5.1	1.39	5.1	0.13	**4.3**	1.9	0.86	9.65	3.36	74.8	**4.8**	30.0	6.7	**6.0**
6.5	0.10	5.3	0.00	**4.8**	6.7	1.17	11.50	3.97	73.0	**6.2**	41.8	6.2	**8.5**
9.1	0.12	0.6	-0.01	**5.3**	1.5	0.91	9.27	2.88	65.9	**5.5**	39.4	6.7	**6.3**
5.8	0.89	7.5	-0.03	**6.3**	2.6	1.21	11.30	2.62	64.5	**6.5**	44.7	1.8	**7.3**
9.4	0.11	0.5	0.00	**3.5**	22.0	0.61	10.97	1.80	62.2	**4.1**	10.9	5.7	**3.8**
5.2	0.88	5.9	-0.01	**3.2**	0.3	0.53	6.97	3.66	84.0	**4.8**	42.9	11.6	**4.7**
9.1	0.02	0.1	-0.12	**6.0**	1.6	1.10	13.42	3.32	56.7	**6.2**	51.1	5.7	**5.9**
4.7	2.35	10.8	-0.07	**6.9**	1.4	1.74	16.37	3.56	55.3	**3.1**	20.2	14.1	**8.4**
6.6	0.24	1.0	-0.08	**10.0**	3.0	2.75	31.48	4.52	44.8	**4.4**	27.1	8.4	**7.2**
5.7	0.37	2.5	0.81	**4.4**	1.7	0.63	5.42	4.31	68.5	**2.5**	13.6	5.8	**7.5**
8.0	3.26	5.4	-0.18	**1.9**	0.0	0.09	0.64	1.76	115.2	**3.2**	67.5	37.4	**7.0**
7.2	1.82	5.7	-0.07	**2.5**	1.2	0.40	3.67	2.72	77.6	**6.2**	50.2	5.1	**6.4**
8.6	0.08	2.0	-0.06	**4.1**	0.3	0.86	6.30	2.92	62.5	**4.9**	47.0	11.7	**6.7**
8.7	0.25	1.1	-0.01	**7.3**	10.5	1.36	15.66	2.83	61.4	**0.7**	10.8	29.2	**9.1**
3.6	1.22	7.3	-0.12	**9.7**	39.0	4.17	39.11	4.63	40.5	**2.5**	26.1	20.3	**10.0**
9.5	0.67	2.4	-0.05	**2.0**	0.3	0.10	0.71	2.04	94.0	**3.8**	40.3	16.0	**7.9**
9.8	0.00	0.0	0.00	**2.3**	0.5	0.10	1.23	2.30	99.4	**7.6**	70.9	1.2	**4.1**
7.2	0.39	1.5	0.03	**6.8**	9.0	1.62	16.22	4.10	56.0	**1.6**	13.7	23.5	**9.5**
6.8	0.08	0.3	0.06	**8.9**	1.1	2.93	12.32	4.07	36.9	**1.1**	23.9	23.7	**8.1**
9.7	1.09	1.5	0.00	**5.9**	0.2	0.53	2.85	1.55	86.1	**4.9**	86.3	17.3	**9.5**
4.7	0.94	6.2	-0.01	**5.2**	2.1	1.02	11.31	3.72	63.1	**4.3**	13.5	6.3	**5.5**
9.1	0.00	0.0	0.04	**4.1**	0.2	0.77	9.76	3.24	77.9	**3.1**	47.7	22.2	**4.4**
7.7	0.00	0.0	0.00	**0.6**	0.3	0.28	1.73	2.78	81.8	**3.6**	28.2	12.9	**6.1**
5.7	0.34	5.9	0.00	**2.9**	0.7	0.48	6.45	3.14	80.0	**3.0**	34.0	17.9	**3.5**
10.0	0.19	0.2	0.00	**5.0**	1158.0	0.66	9.95	1.28	31.6	**7.8**	85.2	0.0	**6.2**

Name	City	State	Rating	2020 Rating	2019 Rating	Total Assets ($Mil)	One Year Asset Growth	Asset Mix (As a % of Total Assets) Commercial Loans	Consumer Loans	Mortgage Loans	Securities	Capitalization Index	Leverage Ratio	Risk-Based Capital Ratio
Charles Schwab Premier Bank, SSB	Westlake	TX	**U**	U	U	33582.0	29.22	0.0	0.0	0.0	94.7	**5.1**	7.1	38.0
Charles Schwab Trust Bank	Henderson	NV	**U**	U		11939.0	7.06	0.0	0.0	0.0	92.4	**6.9**	8.9	56.8
Charlevoix State Bank	Charlevoix	MI	**B+**	B+	B+	287.1	30.80	6.3	2.1	12.3	38.5	**5.9**	7.9	16.2
Charlotte State Bank & Trust	Port Charlotte	FL	**A-**	A-	A-	580.4	29.40	1.5	0.1	11.5	23.5	**6.5**	8.5	0.0
▲ Charter Bank	Johnston	IA	**A-**	B+	B+	208.2	12.61	9.8	2.4	15.8	28.9	**8.9**	10.3	20.3
Charter Bank	Corpus Christi	TX	**B+**	B+	B	342.5	6.20	17.1	0.1	4.3	43.8	**6.1**	8.1	15.8
Charter Bank	Eau Claire	WI	**A**	A	A	1128.5	9.14	10.1	0.3	12.9	19.2	**10.0**	11.2	16.8
Charter West Bank	West Point	NE	**A-**	A-	B	399.1	20.25	11.7	1.8	18.1	9.8	**7.2**	9.8	0.0
Chelsea Groton Bank	Norwich	CT	**A-**	B+	A-	1532.4	9.65	6.7	0.4	41.1	11.8	**10.0**	14.3	19.9
Chelsea Savings Bank	Belle Plaine	IA	**A-**	A-	A-	198.8	56.74	7.8	0.9	8.3	51.3	**10.0**	12.4	0.0
Chelsea State Bank	Chelsea	MI	**A-**	A-	A	410.8	13.34	16.0	0.3	4.6	19.3	**8.1**	9.7	0.0
Chemung Canal Trust Co.	Elmira	NY	**B-**	B-	B-	2374.7	16.10	13.0	5.4	13.0	29.0	**5.4**	7.4	13.6
Cherokee State Bank	Cherokee	IA	**A-**	B+	B	237.0	2.50	9.9	0.5	6.7	36.2	**10.0**	12.5	0.0
Chesapeake Bank	Kilmarnock	VA	**A-**	B+	B+	1291.9	16.10	11.4	0.6	9.2	42.0	**9.1**	10.4	16.2
Chesapeake Bank & Trust Co.	Chestertown	MD	**B**	B	B+	126.7	14.67	7.3	1.1	27.4	11.9	**6.6**	8.6	0.0
Chesapeake Bank of Maryland	Baltimore	MD	**C+**	C+	B-	249.8	6.31	5.0	0.1	25.7	9.0	**10.0**	18.5	32.1
Chester National Bank	Chester	IL	**C**	C	B-	66.0	-0.35	1.3	1.9	47.6	11.3	**7.6**	9.4	22.3
Chesterfield State Bank	Chesterfield	IL	**C-**	C-	C-	21.3	19.43	17.5	5.6	23.7	0.0	**8.4**	9.9	18.9
Cheyenne State Bank	Cheyenne	WY	**B-**	B-	B-	47.3	5.29	2.3	0.6	15.9	4.7	**10.0**	14.0	24.8
Chickasaw Community Bank	Oklahoma City	OK	**B**	B-	B	334.4	29.54	15.7	1.2	25.7	10.3	**8.2**	9.8	17.4
Chillicothe State Bank	Chillicothe	MO	**B**	B	B	145.1	12.26	4.0	4.6	19.9	43.3	**6.1**	8.2	20.6
Chilton Trust Co., N.A.	Palm Beach	FL	**U**	U		18.7	na	0.0	0.0	0.0	49.5	**10.0**	92.6	163.7
Chino Commercial Bank, N.A.	Chino	CA	**B+**	B+	B+	353.0	16.08	13.2	0.0	5.1	14.2	**8.7**	10.1	0.0
Chippewa Valley Bank	Hayward	WI	**B-**	B-	B-	706.5	21.48	8.3	0.3	11.4	9.2	**5.2**	7.2	13.7
Chisholm Trail State Bank	Park City	KS	**B-**	C+	C-	157.4	21.46	7.1	1.0	13.4	8.1	**8.8**	10.2	15.6
▲ Choice Financial Group	Fargo	ND	**B**	C+	B+	3197.0	16.63	22.6	0.4	4.5	3.5	**5.2**	9.2	0.0
ChoiceOne Bank	Sparta	MI	**B+**	B+	B+	2118.4	37.72	12.7	1.6	7.8	40.4	**5.8**	7.8	13.7
CIBC Bank USA	Chicago	IL	**B**	B-	B	45147.2	16.43	20.1	0.8	4.0	14.4	**8.9**	10.3	14.8
CIBC National Trust Co.	Atlanta	GA	**U**	U	U	309.5	19.38	0.0	0.0	0.0	0.0	**10.0**	57.5	158.8
CIBM Bank	Champaign	IL	**B+**	B	C	745.9	-5.00	8.3	0.0	21.2	14.3	**10.0**	11.6	17.1
Ciera Bank	Graham	TX	**B+**	B+	B-	832.2	6.65	11.1	0.3	6.8	8.3	**7.5**	9.3	13.6
Cincinnati Federal	Cincinnati	OH	**B-**	B-	C+	249.8	6.72	0.2	0.1	41.0	3.7	**10.0**	15.3	19.8
▲ CIT Bank, N.A.	Pasadena	CA	**B**	C+	B+	49309.2	-13.10	22.6	0.0	11.0	10.3	**9.4**	10.6	15.1
▲ Citibank, N.A.	Sioux Falls	SD	**B**	B-	B+	1693227.0	3.64	9.0	9.2	5.1	26.3	**6.9**	8.9	15.6
Citicorp Trust Delaware, N.A.	Greenville	DE	**U**	U	U	26.0	10.08	0.0	0.0	0.0	0.8	**10.0**	95.2	482.7
Citizens & Northern Bank	Wellsboro	PA	**B+**	B+	A-	2322.4	34.34	11.5	0.7	23.0	16.2	**9.0**	10.3	16.4
Citizens 1st Bank	Tyler	TX	**A**	A+	A+	761.6	6.24	0.6	0.6	7.3	56.9	**10.0**	20.2	48.5
Citizens Alliance Bank	Clara City	MN	**B-**	B-	B-	968.4	4.84	13.5	1.1	5.6	22.8	**6.7**	8.8	12.3
Citizens and Farmers Bank	West Point	VA	**A-**	A-	A-	2137.2	9.66	6.1	16.0	19.2	16.7	**8.2**	9.8	14.6
Citizens B&T Co. of Grainger County	Rutledge	TN	**B+**	B+	A-	267.5	15.52	1.7	1.2	9.9	68.3	**10.0**	13.8	0.0
Citizens B&T Co., Hutchinson, Minn.	Hutchinson	MN	**B**	B	B-	335.8	21.25	12.0	0.8	15.4	38.9	**4.6**	6.7	13.4
Citizens Bank	Sac City	IA	**C**	C-	C	58.5	2.90	17.4	2.2	9.1	35.5	**6.4**	8.4	15.8
Citizens Bank	Mooresville	IN	**B**	B	B	634.0	12.47	2.7	30.0	4.5	16.9	**7.7**	9.4	15.9
Citizens Bank	Mount Vernon	KY	**B+**	B	C+	161.9	2.38	7.8	4.5	38.5	6.9	**8.6**	10.1	16.3
Citizens Bank	Butler	MO	**B**	B	B-	190.1	12.24	8.1	1.8	20.6	4.8	**4.7**	6.8	11.4
Citizens Bank	New Haven	MO	**B-**	B-	C+	273.9	8.58	5.4	0.6	13.1	4.7	**8.0**	11.4	13.4
Citizens Bank	Columbia	MS	**B-**	B-	B-	486.6	3.33	8.9	3.3	18.6	9.3	**8.4**	10.0	18.2
Citizens Bank	Corvallis	OR	**B+**	B+	A	1053.4	11.74	6.8	0.3	2.6	43.9	**7.5**	9.4	21.5
Citizens Bank	Carthage	TN	**A**	A	A	733.7	9.60	6.3	3.5	8.1	54.1	**10.0**	16.3	0.0
Citizens Bank	Elizabethton	TN	**A**	A	A	1066.7	1.82	15.1	1.6	7.0	14.4	**10.0**	11.7	16.6
Citizens Bank	Hartsville	TN	**B+**	A-	A-	290.7	5.35	5.5	2.4	18.1	21.3	**8.3**	9.8	14.6
Citizens Bank	Lafayette	TN	**B+**	B+	B+	1069.7	5.86	5.8	3.6	11.2	30.6	**7.2**	9.1	15.8
Citizens Bank	Amarillo	TX	**A-**	A-	A-	214.6	5.79	8.3	0.2	2.7	8.2	**7.2**	9.2	14.5
Citizens Bank	Kilgore	TX	**B**	B	B	450.6	-3.94	21.7	0.6	6.1	5.6	**10.0**	13.6	20.7
Citizens Bank	Mukwonago	WI	**A-**	A-	B+	995.3	11.42	8.7	0.1	5.2	19.2	**10.0**	12.0	0.0
Citizens Bank & Trust	Guntersville	AL	**B-**	B-	B	830.4	19.97	10.0	1.2	10.5	34.8	**7.4**	9.3	17.8
Citizens Bank & Trust	Rock Port	MO	**B-**	B	B	112.3	13.53	12.7	2.1	5.4	44.7	**9.0**	10.3	0.0
Citizens Bank & Trust Co.	Van Buren	AR	**A**	A-	A-	510.0	11.07	4.9	3.5	12.0	28.2	**10.0**	11.4	0.0
Citizens Bank & Trust Co.	Campbellsville	KY	**B**	B	B	293.9	8.32	17.6	2.3	17.7	36.4	**10.0**	13.3	0.0
Citizens Bank & Trust Co.	Covington	LA	**B-**	B-	B	166.5	19.44	4.6	0.3	18.7	16.0	**6.9**	9.0	0.0

Asset Quality Index	Adjusted Non-Performing Loans as a % of Total Loans	Adjusted Non-Performing Loans as a % of Capital	Net Charge-Offs Avg Loans	Profitability Index	Net Income ($Mil)	Return on Assets (R.O.A.)	Return on Equity (R.O.E.)	Net Interest Spread	Overhead Efficiency Ratio	Liquidity Index	Liquidity Ratio	Hot Money Ratio	Stability Index
10.0	na	0.0	na	5.0	107.0	0.65	8.84	1.24	29.7	8.4	85.8	0.0	8.2
10.0	na	0.0	na	5.6	51.0	0.82	8.92	0.99	43.5	7.9	64.4	0.0	7.0
5.8	1.37	5.7	-0.62	9.1	3.1	2.31	28.41	3.60	51.2	7.2	60.0	1.9	6.3
9.6	0.10	0.3	-0.08	7.6	4.3	1.63	18.46	2.54	60.7	7.6	65.7	0.5	7.8
8.9	0.02	0.0	0.00	6.5	1.8	1.77	17.00	2.40	48.3	5.0	52.2	13.0	6.3
7.0	0.27	1.4	0.01	10.0	5.3	3.12	32.43	5.95	55.2	5.8	49.7	8.0	8.0
7.7	0.89	3.8	-0.02	6.9	9.2	1.63	13.85	3.08	49.1	5.1	28.9	7.8	10.0
6.8	0.39	2.7	0.00	8.8	3.6	2.01	20.69	3.11	77.8	1.8	21.4	17.4	7.4
6.2	2.18	8.7	0.10	6.2	9.4	1.28	9.04	2.92	68.9	5.9	34.6	5.4	10.0
7.7	1.23	2.6	1.20	5.8	1.4	1.37	9.65	3.17	51.5	6.2	73.6	10.7	8.6
7.2	0.21	0.5	-0.03	5.9	3.1	1.49	14.55	3.34	55.4	6.3	50.3	4.5	8.4
5.8	0.96	5.4	-0.02	4.9	12.7	1.06	13.32	2.79	62.9	4.8	24.1	7.4	6.8
6.5	0.86	3.8	-0.04	8.1	2.2	1.89	15.05	3.99	46.1	3.7	31.1	10.6	8.1
8.9	0.53	1.8	-0.02	6.4	9.1	1.49	14.20	3.85	65.5	5.2	30.8	8.8	9.4
4.6	1.25	6.8	0.00	5.3	0.8	1.25	14.45	3.05	62.4	4.7	31.1	8.3	6.2
9.2	0.25	0.7	0.00	2.7	0.3	0.27	1.43	2.98	90.6	2.8	43.6	25.5	7.2
9.7	0.12	0.7	0.00	2.4	0.1	0.29	3.10	2.71	86.7	4.6	37.5	11.2	5.0
5.3	0.46	3.0	0.20	5.8	0.2	2.16	21.81	2.94	55.2	3.1	33.8	15.3	3.7
9.0	0.00	0.0	0.00	3.1	0.1	0.22	1.56	5.00	94.0	5.0	43.7	10.8	7.0
5.2	1.32	4.0	-0.02	8.6	2.3	1.47	13.77	4.90	76.1	0.9	23.6	25.8	7.5
5.9	1.01	5.1	0.01	4.3	0.7	0.93	11.39	2.73	70.1	6.5	51.4	4.1	5.6
10.0	na	0.0	na	6.3	2.4	29.20	30.41	0.26	69.9	4.0	na	0.0	5.9
7.7	0.76	2.0	-0.03	5.8	1.8	1.09	12.19	3.35	53.7	6.0	42.8	3.2	6.9
6.9	0.37	2.7	0.03	4.9	3.3	1.02	14.08	2.72	59.4	3.6	32.6	5.7	5.8
8.7	0.01	0.1	0.00	3.8	0.7	0.91	8.75	3.71	71.8	3.5	28.9	12.0	5.9
6.4	0.57	3.5	0.06	9.2	24.0	1.60	14.34	3.79	50.2	2.7	26.9	9.8	10.0
6.8	0.68	1.8	0.01	5.1	11.2	1.09	9.98	3.26	65.0	6.5	50.7	7.0	9.2
5.3	0.75	2.4	0.12	5.6	269.6	1.23	7.66	2.23	42.7	6.0	40.3	4.3	9.4
6.5	na	0.0	na	10.0	21.5	14.91	20.31	0.66	53.3	4.4	156.4	100.0	7.0
8.7	0.31	1.4	-0.11	5.0	3.9	1.05	8.35	3.23	74.2	1.7	16.3	16.4	8.9
5.3	1.30	5.7	0.00	7.1	6.6	1.62	15.83	3.53	54.8	2.7	27.7	17.6	9.8
8.7	0.61	2.0	0.00	5.5	1.6	1.29	8.65	2.65	77.0	1.7	12.3	21.1	7.6
4.8	1.83	10.6	0.30	5.1	487.3	1.91	19.21	2.74	62.6	3.0	22.0	11.1	7.3
6.9	1.04	3.9	0.76	5.6	11519.0	1.37	14.20	2.37	57.1	5.9	46.5	2.6	7.2
10.0	na	0.0	na	10.0	1.2	9.30	9.91	0.63	73.8	4.0	na	0.0	7.0
4.6	1.45	7.8	0.00	6.8	16.4	1.45	11.19	3.78	58.7	3.7	15.5	9.1	9.8
9.4	3.11	2.6	0.00	6.4	6.0	1.66	8.00	2.78	38.8	3.4	55.8	26.3	10.0
4.5	0.94	6.3	-0.07	7.6	6.9	1.45	14.16	3.94	54.3	3.7	20.0	8.2	7.3
7.2	0.38	1.6	-0.02	7.9	16.4	1.58	14.91	4.46	69.4	3.2	19.8	14.2	9.0
7.5	2.73	4.2	0.16	4.5	1.3	1.04	6.53	2.98	64.9	5.4	64.9	13.6	8.0
5.5	1.49	6.9	0.00	7.3	2.8	1.82	25.40	3.51	45.4	4.2	26.3	6.5	5.5
4.8	0.96	9.4	0.42	5.7	0.5	1.72	21.24	2.42	57.3	4.1	44.7	15.4	4.6
5.5	0.62	2.2	-0.02	4.7	2.7	0.87	8.51	2.75	70.1	4.8	29.7	6.8	6.5
5.8	0.69	4.8	-0.11	6.6	1.6	1.99	18.78	4.17	61.5	1.6	13.6	23.1	6.6
6.8	0.40	3.2	-0.02	6.9	1.5	1.53	21.49	3.93	62.2	4.4	30.2	9.7	5.5
8.5	0.33	1.0	-1.01	5.7	1.7	1.26	11.12	3.53	60.0	4.1	30.9	8.0	7.6
4.1	2.81	14.7	0.14	7.4	4.9	2.05	21.47	3.59	53.1	2.8	27.5	16.7	7.1
8.6	0.37	1.3	-0.02	6.0	6.7	1.31	13.81	2.85	64.4	7.6	58.0	0.9	7.1
8.9	0.08	1.6	-0.04	10.0	8.5	2.39	13.38	3.98	25.7	3.4	62.2	30.1	10.0
5.5	0.95	4.1	-0.05	9.2	14.3	3.03	25.57	4.47	51.0	1.4	8.4	18.0	10.0
6.8	0.64	3.5	0.12	5.7	1.5	1.00	10.34	3.60	59.9	2.3	37.1	27.1	6.8
4.4	1.77	9.4	0.06	6.5	6.9	1.33	13.37	3.78	58.9	3.1	33.1	20.4	8.3
7.5	0.00	0.1	0.00	7.1	1.7	1.60	17.53	3.41	51.8	3.9	33.7	13.3	7.0
5.1	1.63	8.5	0.99	3.8	1.2	0.56	4.02	3.89	74.7	4.9	40.9	10.9	7.3
7.1	0.68	2.6	-0.01	6.5	5.9	1.21	10.10	3.19	55.5	4.5	26.0	7.4	7.8
8.2	0.29	1.4	0.13	4.0	3.1	0.79	9.06	3.05	71.6	4.4	32.2	10.4	6.1
8.4	0.33	1.2	-0.04	3.9	0.5	0.89	8.16	2.84	69.8	4.3	31.4	10.6	6.7
7.1	1.17	3.9	0.01	8.0	3.6	1.47	12.43	3.48	49.0	3.6	30.8	14.0	9.1
8.2	0.91	3.4	-0.01	5.8	1.9	1.28	9.16	3.36	55.2	4.9	41.3	10.6	8.7
7.8	0.31	2.0	-0.01	4.1	0.5	0.67	7.72	3.57	77.3	4.7	39.0	10.9	4.9

Name	City	State	Rating	2020 Rating	2019 Rating	Total Assets ($Mil)	One Year Asset Growth	Asset Mix (As a % of Total Assets) Commercial Loans	Consumer Loans	Mortgage Loans	Securities	Capitalization Index	Leverage Ratio	Risk-Based Capital Ratio
Citizens Bank & Trust Co.	Vivian	LA	**B-**	B-	B-	173.1	9.60	3.8	1.8	19.2	28.7	**9.4**	10.6	0.0
▲ Citizens Bank & Trust Co.	Big Timber	MT	**B+**	B-	C+	128.8	4.71	6.8	1.9	5.7	27.8	**7.6**	9.4	0.0
▲ Citizens Bank & Trust Co.	Saint Paul	NE	**C+**	C-	D+	237.3	12.97	8.2	1.3	4.4	18.3	**9.3**	10.6	0.0
Citizens Bank & Trust Co. of Ardmore	Ardmore	OK	**B**	B	B	280.1	9.07	4.9	2.1	23.3	36.0	**6.2**	8.2	0.0
▲ Citizens Bank & Trust Co. of Jackson	Jackson	KY	**C+**	C	C	170.8	5.63	10.9	4.5	25.7	12.6	**5.7**	7.7	14.9
Citizens Bank and Trust	Lake Wales	FL	**B-**	B-	B-	1044.7	16.95	10.0	5.9	8.0	45.9	**4.2**	6.3	12.8
Citizens Bank and Trust Co.	Plaquemine	LA	**B-**	B-	B	403.6	9.91	11.7	0.5	13.6	7.4	**9.4**	10.6	16.2
▲ Citizens Bank and Trust Co.	Kansas City	MO	**C+**	C	B	999.6	0.60	9.3	0.4	8.9	15.4	**7.1**	9.1	15.7
Citizens Bank and Trust Co.	Marks	MS	**E+**	E+	D	124.7	-11.89	6.6	1.8	12.0	27.7	**2.2**	5.5	9.2
Citizens Bank and Trust Co.	Blackstone	VA	**A-**	A-	A-	533.0	16.36	4.9	2.1	18.3	37.5	**10.0**	11.4	0.0
Citizens Bank and Trust, Inc.	Trenton	GA	**B+**	B+	A-	125.8	11.92	3.1	7.2	30.3	28.6	**8.5**	10.0	21.3
▲ Citizens Bank Minnesota	New Ulm	MN	**B+**	B	B	571.2	6.80	6.1	1.2	15.9	29.6	**6.1**	8.2	12.0
Citizens Bank of Ada	Ada	OK	**B-**	B-	B	268.4	21.30	13.4	2.2	12.7	19.3	**6.0**	8.0	0.0
Citizens Bank of Americus	Americus	GA	**B+**	B+	B+	427.3	13.69	9.6	1.3	6.8	25.8	**6.3**	8.4	17.1
Citizens Bank of Cape Vincent	Cape Vincent	NY	**C**	C	C+	82.5	13.83	0.8	2.1	37.6	41.1	**6.4**	8.4	22.9
Citizens Bank of Chatsworth	Chatsworth	IL	**E+**	D-	D	39.8	-6.45	45.7	0.6	4.1	16.5	**6.9**	8.9	19.0
Citizens Bank of Cumberland County, Inc.	Burkesville	KY	**B+**	B+	B	80.3	1.95	4.7	11.7	28.7	10.8	**10.0**	13.0	0.0
Citizens Bank of Edinburg	Edinburg	IL	**C+**	C	C	28.5	8.00	0.4	2.2	11.3	21.6	**6.6**	8.6	0.0
Citizens Bank of Eldon	Eldon	MO	**A-**	B+	A-	198.2	16.05	7.3	6.4	20.7	14.4	**10.0**	11.1	0.0
Citizens Bank of Florida	Oviedo	FL	**B-**	B-	C+	491.7	19.91	8.3	0.5	6.9	23.6	**6.6**	8.6	14.5
Citizens Bank of Kansas	Kingman	KS	**B-**	B-	B-	502.8	12.75	6.1	0.9	15.2	46.5	**6.3**	8.3	14.7
Citizens Bank of Kentucky, Inc	Paintsville	KY	**C+**	C+	B	778.1	5.21	5.1	2.0	13.0	23.1	**8.5**	10.0	19.5
Citizens Bank of Las Cruces	Las Cruces	NM	**A**	A	A-	872.4	23.56	13.0	0.3	4.8	15.9	**7.5**	9.4	15.1
Citizens Bank of Morgantown, Inc.	Morgantown	WV	**B**	B	B-	46.3	9.25	15.8	2.8	46.8	17.9	**10.0**	17.2	0.0
Citizens Bank of Rogersville	Rogersville	MO	**B+**	B	B-	108.8	9.37	19.3	3.6	23.0	9.6	**7.9**	10.5	0.0
Citizens Bank of the Midwest	Rolla	MO	**C-**	C	C	175.2	13.85	7.6	2.3	22.9	23.2	**7.3**	9.2	0.0
▼ Citizens Bank of The South	Sandersville	GA	**B**	B+	B+	319.3	1.81	8.2	3.1	25.4	10.4	**8.7**	10.1	18.5
Citizens Bank of West Virginia, Inc.	Elkins	WV	**B**	B-	B-	343.4	11.08	9.1	24.5	27.2	8.0	**9.6**	10.7	16.3
Citizens Bank, N.A.	Providence	RI	**B-**	B-	B-	185036.2	2.89	20.8	16.1	13.0	14.8	**7.4**	9.3	13.0
Citizens Bank, N.A.	Abilene	TX	**B+**	B+	A-	124.2	5.32	11.7	3.0	13.1	18.5	**7.1**	9.1	0.0
▲ Citizens Building and Loan, SSB	Greer	SC	**B**	B-	B+	150.9	1.63	0.0	0.3	49.2	14.0	**10.0**	20.4	0.0
Citizens Business Bank	Ontario	CA	**A**	A	A-	15534.4	13.00	8.0	0.1	2.4	25.7	**7.2**	9.1	15.5
Citizens Commerce Bank	Versailles	KY	**B-**	B-	C-	307.7	4.75	6.5	0.7	27.8	15.1	**8.9**	10.3	0.0
Citizens Community Bank	Hahira	GA	**B+**	B+	A-	184.0	13.84	6.2	3.0	14.4	33.3	**9.6**	10.8	20.6
Citizens Community Bank	Mascoutah	IL	**B+**	B+	B+	445.0	2.98	5.9	0.8	9.1	39.8	**10.0**	11.0	0.0
Citizens Community Bank	Pilot Grove	MO	**B+**	B	B	123.9	8.36	4.2	1.7	10.0	13.4	**10.0**	11.1	0.0
Citizens Community Bank	Winchester	TN	**A**	A	B+	288.3	13.66	10.9	2.9	16.5	21.4	**10.0**	11.7	20.8
Citizens Community Federal N.A.	Altoona	WI	**B**	B-	B-	1714.4	6.69	9.1	1.8	9.6	17.6	**8.0**	9.7	14.7
Citizens Deposit Bank & Trust, Inc.	Vanceburg	KY	**B**	B	B	654.3	12.67	4.2	1.7	13.1	45.2	**6.2**	8.2	16.2
Citizens Deposit Bank of Arlington, Inc.	Arlington	KY	**A-**	A-	A-	274.9	3.86	15.1	4.6	15.2	25.7	**10.0**	14.4	0.0
Citizens Federal S&L Assn.	Bellefontaine	OH	**C-**	C-	C	168.1	8.06	0.0	0.1	64.9	11.6	**9.8**	10.9	22.4
Citizens Federal S&L Assn. of Covington	Covington	KY	**B-**	B-	B	43.1	2.83	0.0	0.0	51.9	20.5	**10.0**	26.3	62.4
Citizens Federal Savings Bank	Leavenworth	KS	**C**	C	C	191.4	3.96	0.8	0.7	47.6	40.7	**10.0**	20.2	0.0
Citizens First Bank	The Villages	FL	**A+**	A+	A+	3612.7	31.42	10.4	0.2	5.9	67.2	**9.3**	10.6	16.5
Citizens First Bank	Clinton	IA	**C+**	C	B-	264.2	5.33	12.5	1.7	10.2	20.1	**6.3**	8.5	0.0
Citizens First Bank	Viroqua	WI	**B**	B	B-	268.6	5.84	7.6	1.5	6.0	24.9	**7.7**	10.1	0.0
Citizens First National Bank	Storm Lake	IA	**A**	A	A	251.0	6.61	9.2	3.5	4.0	46.9	**7.3**	9.2	0.0
Citizens First State Bank of Walnut	Walnut	IL	**C+**	C+	C+	56.6	7.67	5.9	3.0	17.2	29.9	**6.6**	8.6	20.0
Citizens Guaranty Bank	Irvine	KY	**C-**	C-	D+	242.1	11.75	10.9	9.1	41.3	6.0	**2.9**	6.1	9.9
Citizens Independent Bank	Saint Louis Park	MN	**C+**	B-	B-	357.2	5.89	11.7	5.2	9.9	15.9	**8.4**	9.9	19.8
▲ Citizens National Bank	Greenleaf	KS	**B**	B-	B-	217.4	10.17	3.5	1.7	9.8	59.4	**7.7**	9.5	22.3
Citizens National Bank	Sevierville	TN	**A**	A	A	1442.5	13.38	10.8	0.3	11.1	9.5	**8.8**	10.2	16.3
Citizens National Bank	Cameron	TX	**B+**	B+	B	550.4	21.23	6.1	0.4	7.1	33.4	**8.3**	9.9	15.6
Citizens National Bank	Crockett	TX	**B**	B	B	102.2	12.60	11.0	5.0	5.8	10.8	**10.0**	11.1	0.0
Citizens National Bank at Brownwood	Brownwood	TX	**A**	A	A-	270.7	14.12	7.7	4.8	10.7	51.7	**9.4**	10.6	23.4
Citizens National Bank of Albion	Albion	IL	**B**	B	B	341.0	5.51	8.6	3.7	14.3	23.3	**10.0**	16.0	29.0
Citizens National Bank of Cheboygan	Cheboygan	MI	**B-**	B-	C+	448.8	23.49	6.8	1.4	12.2	46.1	**4.4**	6.4	15.5
▼ Citizens National Bank of Crosbyton	Crosbyton	TX	**B**	B+	B+	57.1	6.48	3.8	2.2	1.3	4.5	**10.0**	16.7	0.0
▲ Citizens National Bank of Texas	Waxahachie	TX	**B+**	B	B-	1776.3	24.25	9.1	0.6	9.0	0.7	**6.2**	8.3	13.6
Citizens National Bank, N.A.	Bossier City	LA	**B+**	B+	B+	1343.6	11.66	9.2	0.3	9.6	20.2	**7.8**	9.5	15.9

Asset Quality Index	Adjusted Non-Performing Loans as a % of Total Loans	Adjusted Non-Performing Loans as a % of Capital	Net Charge-Offs Avg Loans	Profitability Index	Net Income ($Mil)	Return on Assets (R.O.A.)	Return on Equity (R.O.E.)	Net Interest Spread	Overhead Efficiency Ratio	Liquidity Index	Liquidity Ratio	Hot Money Ratio	Stability Index
4.1	4.79	15.7	0.19	3.5	0.6	0.76	6.66	3.08	81.7	4.4	37.9	12.1	7.1
5.5	1.24	4.1	-0.07	6.5	0.9	1.36	12.71	3.82	52.7	5.9	46.6	6.0	7.4
4.3	0.61	7.1	-0.18	5.3	1.4	1.17	10.77	4.30	65.3	4.9	41.9	11.1	5.8
7.4	0.00	0.0	0.10	4.6	1.5	1.10	12.94	3.33	70.7	4.5	37.4	11.5	5.8
4.9	1.01	4.7	0.05	4.1	1.0	1.12	12.76	3.76	74.4	1.9	23.3	20.9	4.0
8.3	0.36	2.0	0.00	5.1	6.5	1.33	18.44	3.36	66.3	6.6	38.3	1.8	5.7
4.2	1.76	13.0	0.00	5.3	2.1	1.07	10.75	3.85	58.3	3.4	23.8	13.0	6.7
4.4	3.15	11.6	0.01	3.9	4.9	0.97	9.39	2.59	81.1	4.7	32.0	8.5	6.9
0.3	11.30	83.8	3.34	0.0	-2.0	-2.81	-46.85	1.84	174.5	2.8	22.6	16.0	1.4
9.3	0.70	1.4	0.00	6.0	3.3	1.27	11.23	2.88	54.9	5.0	48.2	12.1	8.4
7.0	0.44	2.1	0.11	5.9	0.7	1.10	10.81	4.61	68.3	5.2	42.1	9.2	6.2
8.6	0.16	1.0	0.00	7.1	5.7	2.03	22.50	3.24	44.4	4.6	32.1	9.1	6.3
4.3	1.34	8.4	-0.02	3.5	0.9	0.68	8.31	3.33	80.4	5.1	33.4	6.2	4.1
8.9	0.25	1.0	0.03	5.4	2.0	0.96	11.21	2.85	60.2	5.6	39.0	5.5	5.9
6.1	1.39	6.9	-0.03	2.6	0.2	0.47	5.38	2.93	81.9	5.2	27.9	3.5	4.0
2.7	1.61	8.4	-0.75	0.0	-0.1	-0.39	-4.00	3.46	109.3	3.8	9.2	9.5	2.5
4.7	2.72	10.2	0.07	6.8	0.6	1.47	11.21	4.24	66.4	3.3	29.3	14.8	8.8
9.1	0.00	0.0	0.00	3.3	0.1	0.38	4.30	2.82	79.4	5.8	35.6	2.6	4.8
6.1	0.86	5.0	0.13	7.4	1.4	1.52	13.56	4.27	50.4	4.3	32.7	11.1	7.2
6.0	1.02	3.3	-0.01	4.9	2.4	1.00	11.87	3.40	61.5	4.2	37.5	13.1	4.6
7.4	0.32	1.1	0.02	3.7	1.9	0.77	6.48	3.05	77.6	4.9	30.9	6.5	7.3
4.9	1.40	4.8	0.03	3.8	2.8	0.73	5.87	2.67	71.8	4.1	40.6	14.8	8.3
8.7	0.20	0.7	0.00	9.5	8.5	2.11	22.06	3.57	53.1	5.2	32.3	5.1	7.9
8.3	0.70	2.9	0.10	6.9	0.4	1.90	11.80	6.49	55.9	2.9	25.1	15.6	7.3
6.8	0.30	1.9	0.00	7.3	1.1	2.02	18.22	4.14	56.6	3.1	17.1	9.4	8.1
5.6	0.57	6.2	-0.07	2.2	0.4	0.43	4.71	2.96	86.6	1.1	24.4	16.3	4.3
7.6	0.38	2.0	0.16	4.5	1.2	0.80	7.81	3.20	71.1	3.3	27.2	14.1	5.8
4.5	0.61	4.5	0.01	7.6	2.8	1.63	16.78	4.22	55.1	3.8	12.4	9.4	6.4
4.4	1.19	4.7	0.37	5.7	1258.8	1.37	11.33	2.74	61.2	5.3	22.6	2.2	9.2
7.6	0.00	0.0	0.00	7.4	1.0	1.60	12.44	3.91	57.4	2.4	21.4	17.6	9.7
9.9	0.38	1.0	0.00	3.9	0.6	0.76	3.74	3.24	67.4	1.3	31.3	54.7	8.0
7.4	0.21	0.6	0.07	8.9	117.5	1.59	11.77	3.09	39.1	6.2	31.3	2.4	10.0
7.7	0.17	2.3	0.00	7.2	2.9	1.85	18.80	4.71	51.6	1.8	15.7	20.0	6.5
6.5	0.99	3.9	0.07	4.9	1.0	1.16	10.20	3.72	68.1	5.5	52.3	10.8	7.1
5.3	3.00	11.6	-0.01	4.9	2.2	0.97	8.93	2.70	50.4	2.1	20.3	18.1	6.8
8.8	0.52	1.9	-0.01	4.2	0.6	0.89	8.15	3.00	67.8	3.9	34.4	13.7	7.2
8.0	0.55	2.4	0.12	8.5	2.0	1.37	11.61	3.87	49.6	3.6	22.3	11.7	8.0
4.9	1.64	6.6	0.03	6.1	11.6	1.37	11.69	3.45	55.6	5.1	28.5	8.1	8.9
7.5	0.30	1.5	0.03	5.6	3.8	1.26	13.23	3.13	57.5	3.4	24.4	12.8	6.7
6.9	0.21	4.3	0.25	5.7	1.7	1.22	8.28	3.73	55.1	0.8	23.3	40.9	9.5
9.3	0.32	1.3	0.00	2.5	0.4	0.47	4.19	2.32	79.9	0.8	14.0	34.3	5.9
10.0	0.00	0.0	0.00	3.0	0.1	0.32	1.18	2.35	77.2	3.4	53.5	21.5	7.4
10.0	0.05	0.1	0.01	1.9	0.1	0.11	0.55	2.52	96.3	4.1	47.2	16.2	7.2
9.6	0.08	0.2	-0.01	8.1	27.4	1.67	13.94	2.24	46.3	7.1	67.3	5.6	10.0
4.9	0.36	4.8	0.56	4.3	1.4	1.01	12.08	2.98	62.1	3.6	27.2	11.9	5.6
5.1	1.05	5.0	-0.01	7.4	2.6	1.98	16.95	4.24	53.5	3.8	33.9	10.0	8.1
8.6	0.00	0.5	-0.03	8.7	2.4	1.86	18.82	2.48	49.3	5.4	50.5	10.4	7.8
6.6	0.78	3.5	-0.04	4.1	0.3	0.90	10.45	3.73	72.2	6.4	57.5	4.6	4.4
3.8	1.01	11.6	-0.01	3.7	1.0	0.81	12.63	4.47	80.0	1.4	7.5	23.9	3.6
5.0	3.05	8.4	-0.16	3.2	0.7	0.39	3.81	2.79	83.6	6.4	45.2	2.3	6.8
9.4	0.00	0.0	-0.02	5.3	1.5	1.38	13.79	3.18	60.9	5.4	48.1	10.2	5.9
8.7	0.00	0.2	0.01	8.4	13.8	2.02	19.21	3.82	48.5	4.6	25.5	9.6	10.0
8.7	0.19	1.0	0.00	5.2	3.1	1.15	11.54	3.14	52.9	4.1	33.8	12.6	6.9
8.7	0.00	0.0	-0.03	3.8	0.2	0.49	4.38	4.95	83.9	6.1	48.9	5.7	6.3
7.7	0.34	3.4	0.01	7.1	2.0	1.56	14.33	2.79	56.5	5.8	52.9	8.7	8.1
6.2	1.72	5.0	0.03	4.9	1.7	0.98	5.88	2.50	56.8	3.7	37.6	15.5	7.2
6.7	1.14	3.3	-0.02	3.2	1.1	0.53	7.92	2.57	81.7	6.8	61.3	5.2	3.6
9.4	0.00	0.0	-0.08	3.3	0.1	0.37	2.12	1.81	78.0	3.8	82.3	27.8	7.7
6.8	0.27	2.9	-0.02	9.4	14.0	1.67	19.51	3.85	48.2	6.1	31.9	3.4	8.7
6.8	1.11	4.4	0.16	4.9	7.5	1.16	11.69	3.20	63.2	5.3	31.5	8.5	7.9

	Name	City	State	Rating	2020 Rating	2019 Rating	Total Assets ($Mil)	One Year Asset Growth	Comm-ercial Loans	Cons-umer Loans	Mort-gage Loans	Secur-ities	Capital-ization Index	Lever-age Ratio	Risk-Based Capital Ratio
▲	Citizens Progressive Bank	Winnsboro	LA	**C**	C-	C	209.5	8.80	10.6	2.7	18.3	4.9	**4.7**	8.7	0.0
	Citizens Savings Bank	Anamosa	IA	**A-**	A-	A-	162.7	18.39	3.7	0.6	5.9	47.1	**6.6**	8.6	18.8
▼	Citizens Savings Bank	Hawkeye	IA	**B**	B+	A-	30.5	3.07	0.9	0.9	7.0	69.4	**10.0**	14.0	0.0
	Citizens Savings Bank	Marshalltown	IA	**B-**	C+	C+	76.8	13.33	7.1	1.2	14.2	0.2	**5.7**	7.7	15.1
▲	Citizens Savings Bank	Spillville	IA	**A**	A-	A-	127.0	8.74	3.3	0.4	3.0	45.0	**10.0**	17.0	0.0
	Citizens Savings Bank	Bogalusa	LA	**B**	B-	B-	266.7	5.90	2.4	3.9	34.6	10.6	**10.0**	13.9	0.0
	Citizens Savings Bank	Clarks Summit	PA	**B-**	B-	B-	383.4	14.13	0.0	0.1	69.3	16.5	**10.0**	13.9	30.7
▲	Citizens Savings Bank and Trust Co.	Nashville	TN	**D**	E+	E+	127.6	22.62	12.4	1.6	14.0	8.7	**8.8**	10.2	15.4
	Citizens State Bank	Vernon	AL	**B**	B	B	85.4	12.71	7.1	4.3	10.4	56.2	**10.0**	13.0	0.0
▼	Citizens State Bank	Monticello	IA	**B+**	A-	A-	481.4	9.63	5.0	0.8	2.2	52.3	**9.5**	10.6	0.0
	Citizens State Bank	Sheldon	IA	**A-**	A-	A-	161.8	14.83	6.4	4.5	10.6	23.4	**10.0**	11.4	0.0
	Citizens State Bank	Wyoming	IA	**B+**	B+	B	112.5	8.50	8.8	2.5	3.4	30.1	**10.0**	19.5	33.5
▼	Citizens State Bank	Lena	IL	**B-**	B	B	305.0	0.83	9.1	4.6	8.7	27.3	**10.0**	11.6	19.3
	Citizens State Bank	Hugoton	KS	**B**	B	B-	141.3	4.38	6.3	0.6	3.4	29.1	**10.0**	11.7	0.0
	Citizens State Bank	Ontonagon	MI	**C**	C-	C	67.8	7.56	3.1	4.6	17.3	33.1	**10.0**	15.4	0.0
▲	Citizens State Bank	Carleton	NE	**C**	C-	D+	25.9	4.98	8.9	4.3	1.3	0.4	**8.1**	9.8	0.0
	Citizens State Bank	Wisner	NE	**C+**	C	C	444.1	9.33	6.7	1.0	5.8	19.0	**8.9**	10.3	14.2
▼	Citizens State Bank	Anton	TX	**D-**	D	C-	34.2	-1.38	12.5	1.2	3.3	9.4	**6.4**	8.4	15.6
	Citizens State Bank	Buffalo	TX	**B**	B	B+	1330.5	12.45	3.9	1.0	3.1	78.7	**9.2**	10.5	26.3
	Citizens State Bank	Corrigan	TX	**A-**	A-	A-	155.5	9.88	14.6	12.1	14.8	31.1	**9.9**	10.9	0.0
	Citizens State Bank	Miles	TX	**A-**	A-	A-	192.9	16.36	11.3	1.9	21.8	0.1	**7.2**	9.2	0.0
▼	Citizens State Bank	Roma	TX	**C**	C+	B-	90.9	-2.75	3.5	9.6	16.8	39.6	**6.9**	8.9	20.2
	Citizens State Bank	Sealy	TX	**A-**	A-	A-	354.0	9.14	4.9	2.1	24.3	41.7	**9.5**	10.7	0.0
	Citizens State Bank	Somerville	TX	**B+**	B+	B+	828.7	16.28	8.9	2.0	18.8	28.6	**9.2**	10.5	0.0
	Citizens State Bank	Woodville	TX	**C+**	C+	C+	192.0	5.85	3.7	2.1	20.9	16.6	**6.1**	8.1	23.9
	Citizens State Bank	Cadott	WI	**B**	B	B-	151.6	14.38	6.1	2.2	13.2	23.5	**8.8**	10.2	16.5
	Citizens State Bank	Hudson	WI	**B**	B-	B-	300.9	14.81	7.1	0.9	25.5	12.1	**10.0**	11.0	0.0
	Citizens State Bank - La Crosse	La Crosse	WI	**B**	B	B	407.6	7.73	15.0	0.7	16.4	0.5	**5.7**	9.1	11.5
	Citizens State Bank and Trust Co.	Ellsworth	KS	**B**	B	B	234.2	5.04	3.1	2.6	16.7	41.0	**5.8**	7.8	16.1
	Citizens State Bank and Trust Co.	Hiawatha	KS	**B+**	A-	A-	112.7	8.98	4.0	1.6	9.1	42.3	**10.0**	13.5	27.2
	Citizens State Bank Norwood Young Ameri	Norwood Young Ame	MN	**C**	C-	C	112.2	15.78	21.9	1.0	4.1	7.9	**6.6**	8.6	16.6
	Citizens State Bank of Arlington	Arlington	SD	**A-**	B+	B	128.7	9.11	2.7	0.9	2.9	44.5	**10.0**	11.6	0.0
	Citizens State Bank of Hayfield	Hayfield	MN	**D+**	D+	D+	137.8	25.08	9.1	2.2	5.7	24.7	**4.3**	6.3	14.6
▲	Citizens State Bank of Lankin	Lankin	ND	**B**	B-	C+	54.6	8.72	9.0	9.9	5.8	30.2	**8.6**	10.1	14.7
	Citizens State Bank of Loyal	Loyal	WI	**B+**	B+	B+	277.0	17.74	3.1	0.1	4.9	33.2	**9.7**	10.8	18.5
	Citizens State Bank of Luling	Luling	TX	**B**	B	B	73.4	1.64	5.5	0.7	8.8	4.6	**10.0**	14.6	0.0
▲	Citizens State Bank of Milford	Milford	IL	**C**	C-	C-	52.2	10.80	8.1	1.5	0.4	16.2	**5.9**	7.9	15.6
	Citizens State Bank of New Castle	New Castle	IN	**B**	B	B	748.4	11.64	8.3	7.9	14.4	34.2	**6.6**	8.6	16.9
	Citizens State Bank of Roseau	Roseau	MN	**A-**	A-	B+	280.8	13.91	8.3	5.3	5.9	49.1	**10.0**	11.2	0.0
	Citizens State Bank of Tyler, Inc.	Tyler	MN	**C-**	C	C-	29.4	14.75	5.5	3.0	2.4	42.7	**5.6**	7.6	33.8
	Citizens State Bank of Waverly (Inc.)	Waverly	MN	**B**	B	B+	110.8	20.23	3.2	1.0	10.6	32.4	**5.7**	7.7	16.3
▲	Citizens Tri-County Bank	Dunlap	TN	**A-**	B+	C+	1146.4	13.60	5.4	7.0	15.1	24.3	**7.3**	9.2	0.0
	Citizens Trust Bank	Atlanta	GA	**B**	B	B+	637.9	25.96	13.8	0.9	6.6	10.4	**5.9**	7.9	17.7
	Citizens Union Bank of Shelbyville	Shelbyville	KY	**B+**	B+	B	1071.1	7.86	9.6	0.4	13.7	10.1	**7.8**	10.7	0.0
	Citizens' Bank of Charleston	Charleston	MO	**A**	A	A-	164.2	12.84	5.1	5.4	7.1	5.0	**10.0**	16.5	0.0
	Citizens' Bank, Inc.	Robertsdale	AL	**B-**	B-	B	132.0	4.62	8.0	1.4	17.2	29.4	**9.6**	10.8	0.0
	City Bank	Lubbock	TX	**A-**	A-	B+	3712.4	3.63	10.9	8.2	12.3	21.0	**8.8**	10.2	15.6
	City Bank & Trust Co.	Natchitoches	LA	**B**	B	B	318.3	18.91	5.0	1.8	12.3	52.5	**6.7**	8.7	15.2
▲	City Bank & Trust Co.	Lincoln	NE	**C+**	C	B	265.0	21.88	16.6	3.0	10.0	5.4	**6.8**	10.1	0.0
	City First Bank of D.C., N.A.	Washington	DC	**D**	D+	C+	1041.5	183.64	8.4	0.0	5.3	15.3	**8.7**	10.3	0.0
	City National Bank	Los Angeles	CA	**B**	B	B+	84955.4	18.87	12.8	1.0	18.7	21.6	**5.1**	7.1	12.9
	City National Bank	Corsicana	TX	**C+**	C+	B-	62.6	6.13	8.2	3.8	32.1	13.8	**7.3**	9.2	18.3
▲	City National Bank of Florida	Miami	FL	**B**	B-	B	20235.4	15.98	16.8	0.2	9.1	24.1	**7.8**	9.6	16.1
	City National Bank of Taylor	Taylor	TX	**B+**	B+	A-	253.5	16.09	2.9	0.5	26.9	23.6	**8.2**	9.8	26.9
	City National Bank of West Virginia	Charleston	WV	**A-**	A-	B+	5840.7	6.84	5.8	0.8	26.3	22.3	**6.8**	8.8	15.3
	City State Bank	Norwalk	IA	**B**	B	B	611.3	10.91	7.5	0.9	9.9	7.7	**6.1**	8.1	13.2
	Citywide Banks	Denver	CO	**B+**	B+	B+	2611.8	2.55	14.7	0.5	4.5	34.0	**8.2**	9.8	15.1
▲	Civis Bank	Rogersville	TN	**E**	E-	E-	145.6	54.38	3.2	0.6	12.1	29.9	**10.0**	29.9	79.6
	Civista Bank	Sandusky	OH	**A-**	A-	A-	2920.4	4.04	11.1	0.4	10.6	15.7	**7.0**	9.0	14.6
▼	Clackamas County Bank	Sandy	OR	**A-**	A	A	291.9	14.97	1.9	0.2	8.0	30.4	**9.3**	10.5	22.5

Asset Quality Index	Adjusted Non-Performing Loans as a % of Total Loans	Adjusted Non-Performing Loans as a % of Capital	Net Charge-Offs Avg Loans	Profitability Index	Net Income ($Mil)	Return on Assets (R.O.A.)	Return on Equity (R.O.E.)	Net Interest Spread	Overhead Efficiency Ratio	Liquidity Index	Liquidity Ratio	Hot Money Ratio	Stability Index
2.8	1.01	11.2	0.08	**6.5**	1.8	1.85	17.63	5.02	61.6	**0.7**	15.4	45.7	**5.8**
9.1	0.25	0.9	0.01	**5.2**	0.9	1.14	12.04	2.85	57.4	**6.3**	47.6	4.2	**6.9**
10.0	0.70	1.1	0.00	**2.6**	0.0	0.26	1.99	2.07	86.1	**6.5**	88.8	10.0	**6.5**
8.8	0.00	0.0	0.00	**6.9**	0.8	2.15	28.90	4.37	48.7	**5.5**	37.1	5.5	**4.5**
8.0	0.07	0.2	0.00	**7.0**	0.9	1.54	8.61	3.57	44.0	**5.6**	57.9	8.5	**9.1**
3.9	6.87	18.8	0.02	**4.3**	1.1	0.84	5.97	4.18	78.8	**2.3**	30.8	21.1	**7.7**
9.2	0.78	3.2	0.01	**3.0**	1.0	0.51	3.63	2.71	78.6	**3.2**	28.1	15.0	**7.4**
2.7	1.52	20.6	-0.18	**2.2**	0.2	0.24	2.98	4.36	92.8	**1.0**	26.4	46.5	**3.0**
9.3	0.00	1.3	0.11	**4.1**	0.4	0.87	6.54	2.16	59.5	**2.5**	55.0	37.4	**6.2**
4.6	4.80	8.1	0.00	**8.6**	5.6	2.38	18.40	3.66	44.5	**4.7**	52.1	14.0	**9.2**
8.2	0.00	0.2	0.00	**6.3**	1.2	1.53	12.53	3.28	51.3	**6.2**	49.0	4.8	**8.8**
8.4	0.03	0.1	0.00	**4.5**	0.7	1.15	5.61	3.18	64.4	**5.2**	52.0	12.2	**7.4**
3.0	2.43	19.4	-0.11	**6.1**	2.5	1.64	13.40	3.55	56.3	**4.4**	33.4	10.7	**7.6**
6.7	1.59	5.3	-0.05	**3.6**	0.3	0.43	3.64	3.12	79.5	**1.9**	24.3	21.0	**7.0**
8.7	2.25	2.4	-0.20	**1.4**	0.0	-0.07	-0.41	4.48	112.4	**6.8**	65.4	3.7	**5.9**
4.1	1.63	10.7	0.00	**5.2**	0.2	1.24	13.07	3.00	61.9	**1.3**	30.8	36.5	**5.1**
4.1	0.55	3.6	0.17	**5.8**	3.1	1.43	13.15	3.70	62.0	**1.6**	21.3	19.5	**7.7**
8.1	0.00	1.8	1.02	**0.0**	-0.2	-1.02	-12.12	2.09	131.7	**2.5**	48.8	31.3	**2.1**
9.6	1.02	1.2	-0.03	**4.4**	8.7	1.40	11.39	2.79	53.5	**3.4**	60.7	32.7	**8.5**
7.3	0.03	1.6	0.03	**7.7**	1.4	1.78	15.76	3.94	56.5	**1.6**	19.7	23.7	**8.5**
8.7	0.05	0.2	0.00	**9.3**	1.9	2.09	22.79	3.70	45.2	**1.7**	36.4	36.3	**7.3**
6.4	1.25	5.3	0.00	**1.3**	-0.1	-0.14	-1.43	4.09	105.7	**2.4**	48.6	33.8	**4.0**
9.3	0.00	0.0	0.00	**6.4**	2.6	1.48	13.38	3.10	45.0	**3.5**	49.8	20.3	**7.5**
4.9	1.39	9.8	0.10	**8.3**	6.5	1.62	15.30	4.41	50.8	**3.7**	25.6	11.5	**7.7**
5.1	1.64	7.4	0.01	**3.0**	0.1	0.13	1.61	2.78	94.5	**5.5**	45.1	8.4	**4.4**
6.0	0.81	3.3	-0.33	**4.6**	0.7	1.02	9.94	4.07	73.1	**5.6**	35.8	3.9	**6.5**
8.9	0.11	0.4	-0.01	**5.6**	1.8	1.23	14.20	3.67	58.1	**3.7**	24.2	11.2	**5.4**
6.2	0.09	0.6	0.00	**9.8**	6.9	3.42	38.48	4.35	38.1	**1.6**	7.5	13.8	**6.8**
7.7	0.10	0.5	0.03	**4.7**	1.4	1.17	13.24	2.85	62.8	**4.4**	19.7	6.9	**6.3**
9.2	0.00	0.0	0.00	**3.9**	0.4	0.63	4.59	2.42	76.9	**6.4**	42.5	1.7	**9.0**
1.8	3.23	14.9	0.00	**8.0**	1.4	2.54	21.86	3.14	47.4	**5.5**	40.6	6.9	**6.8**
8.8	0.14	0.5	0.00	**6.6**	1.2	1.88	15.80	2.75	50.1	**3.7**	46.6	15.7	**7.9**
2.1	5.03	26.0	0.02	**3.3**	0.7	1.08	16.48	3.40	64.5	**6.6**	53.7	4.2	**2.4**
7.8	0.39	1.0	0.00	**5.4**	0.4	1.28	12.04	4.33	71.7	**4.5**	20.0	6.1	**6.4**
7.7	0.70	2.3	0.00	**5.0**	1.5	1.13	10.22	3.06	59.4	**6.2**	42.7	2.9	**7.4**
7.5	0.38	1.7	-0.01	**3.9**	0.2	0.57	3.85	4.16	83.3	**4.1**	34.1	12.5	**7.6**
4.1	0.00	9.1	0.00	**3.5**	0.2	0.83	10.40	3.62	77.9	**5.8**	40.5	5.1	**3.7**
8.3	0.18	1.1	0.06	**4.8**	3.8	1.03	12.00	3.23	62.6	**6.7**	51.3	2.7	**5.7**
6.6	0.90	5.7	-0.04	**6.3**	2.3	1.67	14.28	2.54	49.4	**2.7**	38.7	23.1	**7.5**
8.4	2.19	2.2	0.00	**2.2**	0.0	-0.02	-0.26	2.23	89.3	**7.4**	72.6	1.0	**2.6**
7.8	0.43	0.9	0.00	**5.8**	0.7	1.45	13.73	3.34	59.1	**6.5**	50.6	3.7	**6.7**
7.1	0.34	2.2	0.01	**7.7**	10.5	1.89	19.26	4.10	54.9	**3.6**	29.1	16.7	**9.8**
5.2	1.63	6.8	0.12	**3.9**	2.1	0.70	8.25	2.69	72.7	**4.3**	45.9	14.9	**5.6**
7.2	0.85	3.6	0.03	**5.4**	6.1	1.16	10.36	3.31	63.6	**5.1**	26.4	6.8	**10.0**
8.3	0.59	1.8	-0.12	**7.4**	1.1	1.37	8.48	3.20	48.5	**4.2**	43.3	14.7	**8.9**
5.2	2.55	7.9	0.00	**4.1**	0.6	0.92	8.39	3.65	72.4	**5.3**	38.5	7.1	**6.9**
7.1	0.52	2.5	0.06	**7.8**	31.5	1.69	14.98	3.58	66.1	**4.6**	25.3	7.7	**9.7**
8.8	0.07	0.4	0.00	**4.3**	1.6	1.05	10.70	3.16	70.3	**6.6**	53.0	3.8	**5.6**
8.3	0.08	0.4	0.00	**3.3**	0.6	0.51	4.99	3.05	79.4	**4.2**	24.0	8.8	**5.4**
5.7	0.52	2.1	0.00	**1.4**	-0.8	-0.32	-5.43	3.78	112.8	**2.1**	33.1	22.6	**5.7**
8.1	0.31	2.5	-0.04	**4.2**	289.5	0.71	8.99	2.29	69.0	**6.4**	32.1	1.1	**6.4**
8.8	0.01	0.0	0.00	**3.3**	0.2	0.57	5.89	3.70	84.2	**2.4**	37.1	25.9	**5.3**
7.0	0.58	3.2	0.01	**5.3**	113.8	1.16	11.05	2.81	50.2	**6.1**	36.2	4.7	**8.3**
6.3	1.33	5.8	-0.77	**5.4**	1.6	1.32	12.75	3.01	75.5	**7.0**	56.2	2.0	**6.5**
6.7	0.92	3.3	0.12	**8.3**	41.4	1.44	13.24	2.85	54.3	**4.2**	24.1	11.2	**10.0**
8.7	0.03	0.6	-0.01	**4.9**	3.6	1.22	14.69	2.73	65.3	**4.1**	31.6	11.6	**6.2**
6.9	0.38	1.4	0.06	**6.0**	16.1	1.24	8.44	3.64	56.1	**5.6**	26.8	3.6	**8.3**
6.3	4.94	3.0	0.10	**2.1**	0.3	0.59	6.27	2.32	22.5	**6.6**	79.8	9.3	**0.4**
7.6	0.29	1.3	-0.03	**5.9**	20.1	1.30	11.62	3.40	64.9	**4.7**	21.2	5.1	**10.0**
9.2	0.00	0.0	-0.01	**5.8**	1.8	1.27	11.72	3.28	65.6	**5.9**	42.8	4.8	**8.5**

Name	City	State	Rating	2020 Rating	2019 Rating	Total Assets ($Mil)	One Year Asset Growth	Asset Mix (As a % of Total Assets) Commercial Loans	Consumer Loans	Mortgage Loans	Securities	Capitalization Index	Leverage Ratio	Risk-Based Capital Ratio
Clare Bank, N.A.	Platteville	WI	**B+**	B+	B+	342.6	15.02	2.2	0.7	16.4	49.7	**9.5**	10.7	0.0
Claremont Savings Bank	Claremont	NH	**C+**	C	B-	490.3	3.85	5.3	0.7	52.8	9.4	**10.0**	13.7	0.0
Clarion County Community Bank	Clarion	PA	**C-**	C	B-	199.9	3.33	7.4	1.9	31.7	17.7	**3.6**	9.1	0.0
▲ Clarkson Bank	Clarkson	NE	**A-**	B+	B+	69.5	9.46	3.4	0.9	0.0	56.7	**10.0**	12.3	0.0
Classic Bank, N.A.	Cameron	TX	**B+**	B	B-	527.7	17.87	5.1	1.4	19.9	13.8	**6.9**	8.9	12.4
Classic City Bank	Athens	GA	**D**	D		109.0	na	4.5	0.2	12.5	0.9	**10.0**	20.1	0.0
▲ Clay City Banking Co.	Clay City	IL	**C+**	C-	C	190.6	14.19	8.8	2.2	23.3	18.4	**6.6**	8.6	14.2
Clay County Bank, Inc.	Clay	WV	**A-**	A-	A-	110.6	7.22	0.7	14.3	33.3	23.3	**10.0**	13.9	0.0
▼ Clay County Savings Bank	Liberty	MO	**C-**	C	C+	149.4	12.05	1.9	0.3	22.2	1.1	**5.9**	7.9	0.0
Clay County State Bank	Louisville	IL	**B**	B	B	96.2	11.62	7.8	6.2	13.8	22.0	**10.0**	12.6	0.0
CLB The Community Bank	Jonesville	LA	**C+**	C+	C+	242.2	9.77	30.1	3.4	6.6	27.7	**7.3**	9.2	0.0
Clear Lake Bank and Trust Co.	Clear Lake	IA	**B+**	B+	B+	543.1	4.07	10.8	3.1	11.3	8.9	**5.5**	7.5	13.2
Clear Mountain Bank, Inc.	Bruceton Mills	WV	**A-**	A-	A-	835.6	13.33	11.5	3.2	24.4	25.4	**10.0**	11.5	0.0
ClearPoint Federal Bank & Trust	Batesville	IN	**U**	U	U	115.7	1.54	0.0	0.0	0.0	95.1	**10.0**	16.8	0.0
Cleo State Bank	Cleo Springs	OK	**B**	B	C+	95.2	3.86	15.4	2.7	0.1	46.6	**10.0**	18.1	0.0
Cleveland State Bank	Cleveland	WI	**B-**	B-	B	172.8	20.25	10.4	2.8	16.7	32.0	**7.8**	10.3	0.0
Climate First Bank	Saint Petersburg	FL	**D**			52.7	na	4.9	0.0	0.0	1.9	**10.0**	91.0	373.1
Clinton Bank	Clinton	KY	**B**	B	B-	66.6	0.09	4.8	1.7	10.2	41.2	**10.0**	18.1	27.9
Clinton Savings Bank	Clinton	MA	**B-**	B-	B	647.4	2.87	6.1	1.3	28.3	22.0	**10.0**	11.2	17.2
▲ CNB Bank	Carlsbad	NM	**A-**	B+	B+	488.6	1.14	17.0	8.3	14.4	27.0	**6.9**	8.9	14.5
CNB Bank	Clearfield	PA	**B**	B	B	5127.9	15.20	13.4	1.5	16.8	13.2	**6.6**	8.6	13.5
CNB Bank & Trust, NA	Carlinville	IL	**C+**	C+	C+	1581.7	7.74	11.3	1.3	6.1	28.9	**6.2**	8.2	0.0
CNB Bank, Inc.	Berkeley Springs	WV	**C+**	C+	B-	514.6	11.96	8.0	0.9	34.7	18.5	**6.2**	8.2	0.0
▲ CNB St. Louis Bank	Maplewood	MO	**B+**	B	C+	650.8	12.66	15.5	0.4	10.8	15.8	**8.0**	9.6	13.9
Coastal Bank & Trust	Jacksonville	NC	**B-**	B	B-	174.5	22.94	8.8	0.8	14.1	13.1	**10.0**	11.9	16.4
Coastal Carolina National Bank	Myrtle Beach	SC	**B-**	B-	B-	706.4	28.52	9.2	2.2	15.2	11.0	**6.4**	8.4	13.2
Coastal Community Bank	Everett	WA	**B+**	B+	A-	2006.1	19.53	28.6	0.3	6.7	1.4	**6.2**	8.2	12.7
Coastal Heritage Bank	Weymouth	MA	**C+**	C+	C	963.6	7.09	5.9	1.4	39.3	10.9	**7.9**	9.6	0.0
Coastal States Bank	Hilton Head Island	SC	**B-**	C+	C-	1259.5	30.80	26.8	8.2	5.4	12.3	**6.3**	8.3	12.0
Coffee County Bank	Manchester	TN	**B+**	B+	B	233.6	5.69	11.2	5.7	26.0	9.2	**9.5**	11.0	14.6
Cogent Bank	Orange City	FL	**D+**	D+	D-	940.3	59.84	34.8	0.2	10.0	12.5	**8.9**	10.8	14.1
Colchester State Bank	Colchester	IL	**B**	B	B	79.9	3.22	4.4	3.3	6.0	60.8	**10.0**	14.2	34.1
Coleman County State Bank	Coleman	TX	**A-**	A-	B+	163.4	12.47	10.5	1.7	12.1	18.4	**6.8**	8.8	14.5
▼ Colfax Banking Co.	Colfax	LA	**B-**	B	B	157.9	22.63	2.5	2.0	15.5	50.6	**6.1**	8.1	0.0
▲ Collins State Bank	Collins	WI	**A-**	B+	B-	126.6	18.54	7.9	2.4	24.8	16.7	**7.2**	9.1	13.9
Collinsville Building and Loan Assn.	Collinsville	IL	**C**	C+	C	136.6	5.09	0.0	0.0	68.3	19.6	**10.0**	24.8	0.0
Colonial Federal Savings Bank	Quincy	MA	**B-**	B-	B	338.8	1.78	0.0	0.5	41.5	32.4	**10.0**	14.4	29.7
▲ Colonial Savings, FA	Fort Worth	TX	**C-**	D+	C	1111.7	-9.86	0.8	0.2	53.3	6.9	**9.8**	10.9	21.4
Colony Bank	Fitzgerald	GA	**B**	B-	B	1751.6	-1.16	7.5	1.1	10.4	26.8	**6.8**	8.8	15.0
▲ Colorado Federal Savings Bank	Greenwood Village	CO	**B**	B-	B	1825.0	-21.92	0.7	0.0	43.4	14.1	**10.0**	12.3	22.0
▲ Columbia Bank	Fair Lawn	NJ	**B**	B-	B	9055.5	1.09	5.2	0.0	23.7	22.7	**8.9**	10.2	16.4
Columbia S&L Assn.	Milwaukee	WI	**E-**	E-	E-	25.5	8.53	0.0	1.3	42.0	0.0	**4.9**	6.9	12.1
Columbia State Bank	Tacoma	WA	**A-**	B+	B+	18005.2	13.16	15.2	0.2	2.8	34.5	**6.6**	8.6	14.0
Columbus Bank and Trust Co.	Columbus	NE	**C+**	C+	B-	178.0	11.07	14.2	0.9	5.5	15.3	**3.5**	8.6	0.0
Columbus State Bank	Columbus	TX	**C+**	B-	B-	121.8	0.88	0.2	0.2	0.4	58.1	**10.0**	11.4	27.9
▲ Comenity Bank	Wilmington	DE	**C**	C-	D+	9127.0	-16.43	0.0	84.2	0.0	1.0	**10.0**	22.1	27.8
Comenity Capital Bank	Draper	UT	**C**	C-	C-	8919.9	5.24	0.1	87.2	0.0	1.0	**10.0**	16.0	18.9
Comerica Bank	Dallas	TX	**B+**	B+	A-	88331.0	4.60	26.9	0.6	2.2	17.9	**7.2**	9.1	13.5
Comerica Bank & Trust, N.A.	Ann Arbor	MI	**U**	U	U	84.3	28.12	0.0	0.0	0.0	0.0	**10.0**	96.6	160.8
Commencement Bank	Tacoma	WA	**B**	B+	A-	561.8	2.43	23.7	0.5	3.9	9.6	**7.1**	9.1	16.3
Commerce Bank	Edina	MN	**B**	B	B-	273.9	23.79	7.6	0.0	7.1	11.4	**10.0**	11.2	17.3
Commerce Bank	Kansas City	MO	**A-**	A-	A	33712.9	10.87	10.8	7.1	9.0	39.4	**6.1**	8.1	13.2
Commerce Bank	Corinth	MS	**B+**	A-	A-	158.9	9.39	12.0	4.3	24.4	24.5	**8.9**	10.3	0.0
Commerce Bank	Laredo	TX	**A**	A	A	613.5	11.54	6.1	0.8	11.5	64.7	**10.0**	16.4	47.9
Commerce Bank of Arizona, Inc.	Tucson	AZ	**C+**	C	D+	335.9	6.57	22.2	0.3	2.7	12.8	**6.4**	8.4	13.2
Commerce Bank Texas	Stockdale	TX	**B-**	B-	B	63.8	12.90	7.9	0.2	10.5	32.5	**10.0**	12.3	0.0
Commerce Community Bank	Oak Grove	LA	**B-**	B-	B	78.0	25.22	10.8	1.0	8.9	10.5	**10.0**	17.0	23.2
Commerce National Bank & Trust	Winter Park	FL	**B+**	B+	A-	148.8	6.43	2.1	1.1	12.6	18.7	**7.6**	9.4	16.3
▲ Commerce State Bank	West Bend	WI	**B**	B-	B-	829.8	8.05	21.3	0.0	13.3	4.2	**7.7**	10.3	13.1
Commerceone Bank	Birmingham	AL	**B-**	C+		399.7	44.99	19.7	0.8	5.9	6.8	**10.0**	13.4	16.3

Asset Quality Index	Adjusted Non-Performing Loans as a % of Total Loans	Adjusted Non-Performing Loans as a % of Capital	Net Charge-Offs Avg Loans	Profitability Index	Net Income ($Mil)	Return on Assets (R.O.A.)	Return on Equity (R.O.E.)	Net Interest Spread	Overhead Efficiency Ratio	Liquidity Index	Liquidity Ratio	Hot Money Ratio	Stability Index
6.9	2.25	5.0	0.01	**4.5**	1.8	1.11	10.02	2.34	57.0	**6.3**	48.6	4.6	**7.2**
7.6	0.84	4.1	0.02	**5.7**	4.2	1.71	12.40	2.78	83.1	**2.2**	21.0	18.6	**7.6**
6.4	0.58	3.6	-0.01	**3.0**	0.7	0.66	7.23	3.42	75.4	**1.5**	16.2	25.6	**5.4**
8.9	0.11	0.4	0.00	**7.7**	0.7	2.09	16.57	2.47	42.2	**3.6**	53.1	19.4	**8.5**
8.5	0.10	0.8	0.00	**6.7**	4.7	1.90	19.78	4.40	54.4	**2.4**	7.6	16.2	**6.2**
9.2	0.00	0.0	0.00	**0.0**	-0.8	-2.15	-8.31	2.90	129.5	**6.7**	46.8	1.1	**2.0**
3.6	1.70	13.2	-0.03	**4.0**	0.8	0.84	9.48	3.08	71.0	**4.5**	24.5	6.9	**4.7**
8.2	0.55	1.8	0.11	**5.7**	0.6	1.03	7.16	3.47	64.5	**4.2**	43.5	14.9	**8.8**
9.2	0.00	0.0	0.00	**2.3**	0.2	0.25	3.04	2.71	90.0	**5.9**	40.9	4.2	**5.4**
4.3	3.65	13.1	0.10	**4.5**	0.5	1.05	8.25	2.89	64.2	**4.7**	32.5	8.4	**7.7**
3.8	1.90	12.4	0.10	**5.7**	1.8	1.49	16.05	4.17	62.0	**4.0**	27.3	10.8	**5.6**
4.7	1.18	7.3	0.01	**7.6**	5.2	1.93	24.15	3.70	51.9	**5.2**	31.7	5.2	**7.3**
7.2	0.90	3.8	-0.02	**7.3**	6.2	1.53	13.19	3.67	58.2	**3.7**	33.3	14.0	**8.0**
10.0	na	0.0	na	**4.8**	0.7	1.35	6.79	2.32	80.7	**8.7**	118.5	0.8	**6.3**
4.5	15.14	15.6	-0.68	**6.8**	1.2	2.61	13.49	5.07	46.7	**4.5**	61.9	16.1	**6.1**
5.7	0.37	1.9	-0.04	**9.1**	1.7	1.98	19.08	4.00	50.2	**5.4**	42.2	5.4	**6.9**
10.0	0.00	0.0	na	**0.0**	-1.7	-6.36	-7.92	na	14680.0	**5.2**	421.3	74.9	**2.0**
8.8	0.95	1.9	0.13	**3.6**	0.2	0.68	3.51	3.34	75.2	**4.1**	35.7	13.0	**7.5**
6.8	1.23	5.1	-0.03	**3.7**	2.3	0.74	6.58	2.94	78.3	**3.2**	27.3	13.1	**7.4**
7.7	0.03	1.2	0.18	**9.5**	6.5	2.62	28.35	4.16	45.1	**4.8**	24.7	4.3	**7.2**
5.6	1.18	7.2	0.06	**5.5**	28.8	1.18	12.61	3.38	57.8	**4.8**	21.4	5.5	**7.3**
3.9	2.33	12.3	0.04	**4.6**	6.6	0.85	8.46	3.08	62.2	**4.1**	30.2	14.3	**7.8**
5.9	0.91	6.0	0.00	**3.6**	1.8	0.74	9.89	3.28	73.9	**3.8**	19.0	10.5	**4.8**
5.9	0.49	3.2	0.00	**6.1**	5.5	1.75	17.79	3.49	51.5	**4.2**	20.0	8.3	**7.4**
8.7	0.10	0.5	0.03	**3.0**	0.4	0.47	3.76	3.44	85.4	**4.4**	31.2	9.8	**7.3**
7.5	0.30	1.3	0.00	**4.5**	3.2	0.98	10.73	3.29	65.0	**3.6**	31.0	14.2	**5.8**
7.1	0.04	0.2	0.00	**6.9**	13.6	1.36	17.58	3.74	58.4	**4.9**	15.3	1.9	**7.6**
6.6	0.51	2.8	0.07	**3.0**	2.4	0.51	5.09	3.13	77.7	**4.3**	28.0	9.4	**6.1**
7.0	0.34	2.4	0.03	**4.9**	6.7	1.13	12.16	3.54	63.4	**4.9**	26.4	8.1	**5.5**
4.6	1.66	7.6	-0.07	**10.0**	3.1	2.67	24.01	4.80	43.2	**1.5**	11.4	23.4	**8.6**
7.6	0.29	1.7	0.00	**3.5**	4.1	0.97	11.24	3.80	60.7	**3.4**	24.2	12.8	**5.2**
7.8	1.50	3.0	0.13	**4.5**	0.4	1.10	7.08	2.73	54.1	**3.6**	37.5	16.0	**7.6**
8.6	0.01	0.1	0.00	**10.0**	2.4	3.06	34.69	4.96	52.6	**4.4**	27.3	8.6	**6.5**
8.8	0.04	0.4	0.00	**3.9**	0.7	0.97	10.89	3.21	74.9	**2.3**	34.2	24.8	**4.9**
8.5	0.25	0.9	0.00	**8.3**	1.9	3.23	34.42	3.56	45.6	**4.9**	32.6	7.1	**6.2**
10.0	0.00	0.0	0.00	**1.9**	0.1	0.07	0.27	1.80	95.6	**2.5**	37.8	24.7	**7.3**
10.0	0.00	0.0	0.00	**3.0**	0.9	0.50	3.51	2.43	75.0	**3.3**	47.9	21.1	**7.9**
2.5	17.47	7.6	0.01	**4.8**	11.7	2.05	9.54	4.78	81.5	**3.6**	19.1	7.1	**7.4**
5.4	1.68	7.2	-0.05	**5.2**	9.3	1.05	10.68	3.61	72.2	**5.3**	31.7	8.4	**8.0**
6.9	0.99	3.7	-0.01	**4.2**	8.0	0.80	6.68	2.14	49.5	**3.9**	29.8	11.7	**9.3**
8.1	0.76	2.4	0.06	**5.0**	47.6	1.07	10.54	2.66	52.1	**3.3**	20.0	13.4	**8.0**
1.7	4.28	35.3	0.00	**0.3**	-0.1	-0.71	-9.48	4.50	120.5	**0.9**	24.4	39.0	**1.8**
7.3	0.32	1.0	0.00	**6.1**	108.3	1.26	9.35	3.31	55.7	**6.8**	39.9	1.2	**9.8**
4.1	1.01	6.8	-0.07	**7.2**	1.7	1.97	20.07	4.25	50.9	**2.2**	14.1	17.8	**6.5**
10.0	0.00	0.0	0.00	**2.0**	0.1	0.11	0.92	1.16	95.6	**7.6**	107.9	7.1	**5.8**
2.3	2.49	9.2	5.36	**10.0**	377.2	7.81	42.39	19.00	54.9	**0.5**	18.6	59.3	**9.5**
2.2	1.80	10.3	4.74	**7.6**	217.8	5.12	39.80	16.65	52.8	**0.8**	18.5	13.7	**8.6**
6.7	0.71	3.7	-0.03	**7.1**	675.0	1.57	16.20	2.27	62.9	**6.5**	36.7	1.6	**8.2**
8.1	na	0.0	na	**10.0**	15.7	41.44	44.78	0.87	54.4	**4.0**	na	0.0	**8.0**
5.2	0.83	5.6	1.13	**4.3**	1.5	0.55	5.87	3.54	56.3	**2.8**	28.7	17.3	**6.4**
8.0	0.44	1.8	0.03	**4.3**	1.4	1.14	9.91	3.08	63.6	**2.3**	43.6	7.5	**7.5**
7.6	0.76	2.2	0.13	**8.1**	277.8	1.69	18.44	2.63	56.0	**6.2**	37.7	4.6	**8.8**
6.2	1.05	5.0	0.06	**5.2**	0.8	1.02	9.61	3.89	69.4	**4.0**	42.6	15.4	**7.8**
9.0	0.48	0.9	0.02	**8.1**	4.9	1.66	9.31	2.09	40.0	**3.5**	77.6	33.6	**9.2**
4.3	0.57	4.2	-0.02	**4.0**	1.6	0.88	10.36	3.73	75.7	**4.1**	25.4	9.2	**5.6**
7.8	0.00	0.0	0.00	**2.9**	0.1	0.32	2.02	3.24	87.3	**4.4**	49.6	14.5	**7.0**
6.5	0.86	1.9	0.04	**3.0**	0.1	0.66	5.42	3.13	76.5	**4.2**	51.5	16.2	**5.0**
8.8	0.00	0.0	0.00	**3.4**	0.4	0.54	5.40	2.87	82.2	**1.9**	37.0	33.5	**7.5**
5.3	0.23	1.5	0.25	**7.1**	5.7	1.47	14.21	3.97	43.1	**1.4**	16.2	17.7	**6.4**
7.4	0.00	0.0	0.00	**3.3**	1.5	0.82	5.80	3.24	54.2	**2.9**	23.0	15.1	**4.8**

Name	City	State	Rating	2020 Rating	2019 Rating	Total Assets ($Mil)	One Year Asset Growth	Asset Mix (As a % of Total Assets) Commercial Loans	Consumer Loans	Mortgage Loans	Securities	Capitalization Index	Leverage Ratio	Risk-Based Capital Ratio
CommerceWest Bank	Irvine	CA	**B**	B	B+	1162.4	27.39	17.5	2.6	0.1	7.7	**6.0**	8.0	16.3
Commercial Bank	Parsons	KS	**B**	B+	B+	417.1	9.94	10.4	7.7	11.5	45.2	**5.6**	7.6	15.3
Commercial Bank	West Liberty	KY	**B**	B-	B-	181.5	11.92	3.9	5.8	29.8	24.7	**9.8**	10.9	20.2
Commercial Bank	Alma	MI	**C+**	C+	B-	587.1	5.92	13.8	1.2	27.2	6.2	**6.8**	8.8	15.9
Commercial Bank	Saint Louis	MO	**C**	C	C	273.8	7.36	18.7	1.2	10.0	27.7	**5.2**	7.2	12.4
Commercial Bank	Harrogate	TN	**B+**	B+	B+	1653.0	5.53	8.8	1.2	18.4	8.8	**7.8**	9.5	14.2
Commercial Bank & Trust Co.	Monticello	AR	**B**	B	B	247.3	0.91	14.6	6.3	11.9	37.1	**7.6**	9.4	0.0
Commercial Bank & Trust Co.	Paris	TN	**A-**	A-	A-	1075.5	16.05	10.9	2.8	12.6	33.8	**7.2**	9.1	17.4
Commercial Bank & Trust of PA	Latrobe	PA	**B+**	B+	B+	449.3	4.21	3.4	0.2	25.8	28.6	**10.0**	12.8	23.9
▲ Commercial Bank of California	Irvine	CA	**B-**	C+	B	1691.8	18.54	15.4	3.9	1.2	9.9	**4.5**	8.7	0.0
▼ Commercial Bank of Mott	Mott	ND	**A-**	A	A-	119.6	11.26	4.2	1.4	1.7	23.1	**9.8**	10.8	0.0
Commercial Bank of Nelson	Nelson	NE	**B+**	B+	B	58.2	7.33	23.9	7.4	0.8	36.3	**10.0**	12.1	18.0
Commercial Bank of Oak Grove	Oak Grove	MO	**B+**	B+	B+	104.0	15.00	10.3	1.1	22.6	19.4	**10.0**	11.9	0.0
Commercial Bank of Texas, N.A.	Nacogdoches	TX	**A-**	A-	B	1211.5	21.23	12.7	3.2	13.3	28.2	**9.5**	10.7	16.4
Commercial Banking Co.	Valdosta	GA	**A-**	A-	A-	298.2	10.86	6.6	1.0	22.8	6.2	**9.0**	10.3	22.4
Commercial Capital Bank	Delhi	LA	**B-**	C+	B-	238.6	4.89	7.9	2.5	15.1	4.1	**8.7**	11.5	0.0
Commercial National Bank of Texarkana	Texarkana	TX	**B+**	B+	B+	281.4	10.76	14.7	1.9	20.6	31.9	**6.0**	8.0	14.7
Commercial Savings Bank	Carroll	IA	**B**	B	B	238.0	9.36	9.6	2.2	29.6	15.6	**5.8**	7.8	14.8
▲ Commercial State Bank	Republican City	NE	**A-**	B+	B+	63.5	1.80	1.6	0.9	0.0	62.7	**10.0**	30.2	37.4
Commercial State Bank	Wausa	NE	**B**	B-	B-	168.4	11.24	18.9	4.9	2.9	6.8	**7.0**	9.5	0.0
Commercial State Bank	Palmer	TX	**C+**	B-	C+	106.1	14.26	9.8	2.7	8.5	31.9	**6.6**	8.6	22.8
▼ Commercial State Bank of Wagner	Wagner	SD	**C**	C+	B-	260.0	27.28	6.5	2.2	6.1	24.1	**8.6**	10.1	0.0
Commercial Trust Co. of Fayette	Fayette	MO	**B+**	B+	B+	169.5	15.59	2.8	5.4	33.2	6.4	**6.6**	8.6	0.0
Commodore Bank	Somerset	OH	**D+**	D+	D+	90.1	15.30	2.2	4.7	26.0	23.4	**5.4**	7.4	16.1
Commonwealth Bank and Trust Co.	Louisville	KY	**B+**	B+	B-	1254.9	-2.29	8.4	2.5	9.7	15.7	**7.4**	9.3	14.9
Commonwealth Business Bank	Los Angeles	CA	**A-**	B+	A-	1612.9	20.07	12.0	0.1	1.3	5.1	**10.0**	11.3	15.6
Commonwealth Community Bank, Inc.	Hartford	KY	**C+**	C+	B-	157.6	2.70	0.7	2.9	15.8	56.5	**10.0**	15.0	33.5
Commonwealth Cooperative Bank	Hyde Park	MA	**B-**	B-	B	199.9	3.52	4.0	0.1	41.5	16.2	**10.0**	14.7	0.0
Commonwealth National Bank	Mobile	AL	**D**	D-	D+	59.8	18.11	4.8	0.3	5.6	30.0	**10.0**	11.0	24.6
▲ Community 1st Bank Las Vegas	Las Vegas	NM	**B**	C+	C+	168.9	7.58	4.0	0.5	8.3	43.6	**8.0**	9.6	26.4
Community Bank	Dunlap	IA	**B-**	C+	B	110.5	12.96	6.1	2.6	12.6	14.4	**10.0**	11.4	20.0
Community Bank	Winslow	IL	**A-**	A-	A-	251.0	-4.58	6.9	1.4	21.6	32.6	**10.0**	14.5	25.6
▲ Community Bank	Topeka	KS	**B+**	B	B+	138.3	4.42	12.0	1.2	25.6	7.3	**5.8**	10.4	0.0
Community Bank	Alva	OK	**B+**	B+	A-	119.9	4.03	8.0	1.8	5.5	56.6	**10.0**	11.1	19.3
Community Bank	Bristow	OK	**B+**	B+	A-	106.8	12.92	6.9	2.7	24.6	10.5	**6.0**	8.1	16.4
▼ Community Bank	Joseph	OR	**C+**	B-	B+	542.9	18.88	3.8	0.3	2.1	57.9	**6.1**	8.2	21.0
Community Bank	Carmichaels	PA	**C**	C+	B-	1459.7	3.71	7.7	7.3	21.7	14.1	**5.2**	7.2	12.9
Community Bank	Avon	SD	**B-**	C+	B-	65.4	20.24	9.0	4.1	5.4	44.3	**10.0**	13.1	0.0
Community Bank	Longview	TX	**A**	A	A	257.0	9.13	7.4	2.6	32.5	0.0	**10.0**	11.2	0.0
Community Bank & Trust - West Georgia	LaGrange	GA	**E+**	E+	E+	96.1	14.92	9.9	0.7	12.0	11.0	**0.0**	2.6	7.7
▲ Community Bank & Trust Co.	Muscatine	IA	**C+**	C-	D+	276.6	5.30	7.0	4.8	10.2	29.0	**6.1**	8.1	15.1
Community Bank & Trust, Waco, Texas	Waco	TX	**B+**	B+	A-	536.8	-1.31	19.9	1.7	20.1	32.0	**10.0**	14.3	26.6
Community Bank & Trust-Alabama	Union Springs	AL	**D-**	D-	D	51.8	4.55	6.5	4.7	9.9	43.4	**5.4**	7.4	19.1
Community Bank and Trust	Neosho	MO	**C+**	B-	B-	404.5	13.64	3.6	1.5	11.4	22.8	**5.3**	7.3	21.4
Community Bank Delaware	Lewes	DE	**B**	B-	B-	279.0	10.84	5.6	0.2	31.2	3.6	**7.3**	9.2	14.6
▲ Community Bank Mankato	Vernon Center	MN	**B-**	C+	C	392.1	5.57	9.7	0.7	12.7	1.2	**6.2**	8.2	12.4
▲ Community Bank of Cameron	Cameron	WI	**B+**	B	B	158.8	12.48	2.4	2.5	24.8	16.1	**6.8**	8.9	14.5
Community Bank of Easton	Easton	IL	**A-**	A-	A-	40.1	5.78	21.3	8.5	2.4	1.3	**10.0**	21.5	0.0
Community Bank of El Dorado Springs	El Dorado Springs	MO	**A-**	A	A	127.8	12.88	1.4	2.1	10.4	20.5	**10.0**	14.0	0.0
▲ Community Bank of Elmhurst	Elmhurst	IL	**B-**	C+	B-	196.7	13.26	10.8	0.1	11.7	42.1	**6.5**	8.5	18.6
Community Bank of Georgia	Baxley	GA	**C+**	C+	C	166.0	14.70	9.8	0.9	5.8	6.2	**7.0**	9.0	0.0
Community Bank of Louisiana	Mansfield	LA	**B**	B	B	648.1	10.81	7.0	1.1	8.3	50.8	**6.8**	8.8	18.7
Community Bank of Marshall	Marshall	MO	**B+**	B+	B	204.0	12.53	5.4	2.2	11.1	50.0	**6.9**	8.9	19.3
Community Bank of Memphis	Memphis	MO	**B-**	B	B-	57.3	13.75	4.0	2.8	13.3	21.7	**9.3**	10.5	0.0
Community Bank of Mississippi	Forest	MS	**B-**	B-	B-	4301.9	15.50	12.6	1.9	18.7	24.4	**5.6**	7.6	16.0
▲ Community Bank of Missouri	Richmond	MO	**A-**	B+	B+	76.9	25.64	6.4	1.4	14.5	2.4	**10.0**	11.6	16.6
Community Bank of Oelwein	Oelwein	IA	**B+**	B+	B	115.5	-1.01	8.4	2.6	11.6	29.2	**10.0**	12.3	20.4
▼ Community Bank of Oklahoma	Verden	OK	**B-**	B	B-	116.5	65.15	8.5	2.2	1.4	52.8	**6.3**	8.4	0.0
Community Bank of Parkersburg	Parkersburg	WV	**B+**	B+	B+	274.9	2.89	6.7	5.7	53.9	8.5	**9.4**	10.6	0.0
Community Bank of Pickens County	Jasper	GA	**B**	B-	C+	486.5	18.82	7.7	1.9	10.7	7.9	**9.9**	11.0	19.3

Asset Quality Index	Adjusted Non-Performing Loans as a % of Total Loans	Adjusted Non-Performing Loans as a % of Capital	Net Charge-Offs Avg Loans	Profitability Index	Net Income ($Mil)	Return on Assets (R.O.A.)	Return on Equity (R.O.E.)	Net Interest Spread	Overhead Efficiency Ratio	Liquidity Index	Liquidity Ratio	Hot Money Ratio	Stability Index
8.6	0.00	0.0	0.05	**6.2**	7.0	1.20	15.72	2.55	42.9	**5.6**	39.0	6.3	**6.7**
6.9	0.48	2.3	0.02	**5.1**	2.7	1.35	15.18	2.99	59.5	**4.1**	37.8	14.0	**6.1**
5.7	0.86	3.9	0.01	**4.4**	1.3	1.45	11.17	3.91	75.3	**2.2**	24.4	19.0	**7.4**
3.3	2.32	12.9	-0.01	**5.2**	3.3	1.17	12.23	3.21	58.4	**2.9**	18.9	4.2	**6.6**
4.9	1.11	8.6	-0.22	**3.4**	0.9	0.70	9.57	3.18	78.7	**4.6**	41.0	12.1	**4.3**
6.2	0.70	4.2	-0.02	**6.6**	10.9	1.32	13.85	3.59	52.0	**1.9**	17.8	15.1	**8.6**
6.7	0.54	1.8	0.20	**4.8**	1.6	1.29	13.73	3.37	62.8	**1.6**	28.0	29.4	**6.1**
7.6	0.73	3.3	0.02	**7.1**	8.7	1.70	17.16	3.44	60.0	**6.4**	48.7	6.8	**9.6**
5.7	3.11	8.6	0.00	**4.9**	2.1	0.97	6.20	3.71	72.4	**6.1**	44.1	3.9	**8.8**
8.2	0.27	1.5	-0.01	**4.7**	7.6	0.93	10.78	2.96	66.2	**6.2**	33.7	2.9	**6.8**
5.2	1.29	3.6	-0.04	**7.8**	1.1	1.83	14.38	2.68	43.4	**1.4**	22.9	27.5	**9.5**
8.0	0.04	0.2	0.00	**6.9**	0.5	1.53	13.05	3.84	58.1	**1.5**	13.8	23.8	**7.9**
7.4	0.25	4.9	0.25	**3.4**	0.3	0.56	4.64	2.48	74.3	**3.4**	34.7	16.3	**6.9**
7.9	0.66	2.7	0.02	**7.2**	7.4	1.52	15.12	3.20	60.8	**5.5**	29.8	6.8	**7.7**
6.8	0.93	3.4	-0.02	**5.6**	2.0	1.25	10.94	3.44	61.1	**5.0**	37.7	9.2	**7.6**
4.2	0.97	12.5	0.37	**7.4**	2.1	1.77	15.81	4.03	57.7	**1.1**	26.1	32.1	**8.0**
8.8	0.04	0.5	0.00	**6.7**	2.0	1.50	17.78	3.77	63.2	**4.0**	25.2	10.2	**6.3**
6.0	0.15	4.1	-0.02	**5.6**	1.7	1.44	18.64	2.85	52.0	**3.7**	32.6	14.0	**5.8**
9.6	0.00	0.0	0.00	**6.1**	0.5	1.50	4.86	3.08	35.2	**4.7**	103.9	22.1	**8.2**
6.9	0.23	1.6	0.44	**7.5**	1.9	2.26	24.21	3.24	46.2	**1.6**	24.9	25.1	**6.3**
3.7	3.08	15.3	-0.08	**4.7**	0.6	1.08	12.30	3.39	72.0	**6.1**	52.3	7.0	**4.8**
2.4	4.72	22.5	0.48	**10.0**	3.1	2.82	26.21	4.86	34.0	**2.1**	26.6	19.8	**7.3**
7.5	0.31	2.5	0.01	**4.4**	0.8	0.97	11.11	2.68	68.7	**4.3**	39.9	13.4	**5.9**
2.4	1.95	24.9	0.06	**1.6**	0.1	0.16	1.98	2.88	95.6	**5.4**	32.7	4.2	**3.0**
7.8	0.57	3.3	0.05	**6.0**	9.7	1.60	16.74	3.10	75.1	**5.3**	26.7	5.8	**9.1**
7.0	0.47	1.7	-0.01	**7.6**	12.0	1.69	14.55	3.80	50.6	**1.2**	20.5	27.8	**8.7**
9.9	0.17	0.8	0.00	**2.3**	0.2	0.25	1.69	1.92	90.0	**4.8**	77.5	18.1	**7.5**
9.3	0.32	1.4	0.00	**3.2**	0.5	0.54	3.62	3.20	86.5	**2.0**	35.4	25.3	**7.8**
7.9	0.49	1.5	-0.01	**0.0**	-0.2	-0.80	-7.41	3.37	122.2	**3.7**	43.8	17.0	**3.2**
9.2	0.93	1.5	-0.04	**4.9**	1.4	1.66	16.53	3.41	65.3	**6.3**	55.3	6.8	**5.3**
6.8	1.74	4.2	-0.02	**3.8**	0.4	0.81	6.73	3.68	77.9	**4.7**	35.4	9.7	**7.3**
6.4	2.50	6.5	0.00	**6.5**	2.2	1.76	11.55	2.97	38.9	**3.6**	32.3	14.6	**8.5**
8.6	0.00	0.0	-0.01	**9.5**	1.4	1.97	19.70	4.12	47.7	**3.2**	16.5	13.2	**8.1**
9.1	0.29	0.8	-0.04	**4.6**	0.7	1.13	9.12	3.14	62.5	**2.4**	49.0	34.9	**7.4**
8.9	0.00	0.3	0.02	**8.7**	0.7	1.42	17.49	4.20	62.1	**5.0**	46.0	11.4	**6.7**
8.0	1.27	4.2	0.01	**3.1**	1.3	0.48	5.34	2.53	86.0	**7.0**	68.9	4.6	**5.8**
4.3	1.51	10.5	0.01	**2.6**	2.4	0.32	3.72	2.90	93.2	**4.3**	19.4	7.7	**6.0**
4.4	4.12	12.4	0.01	**3.0**	0.2	0.54	3.85	3.10	84.0	**3.2**	53.2	23.1	**6.5**
8.7	0.00	0.3	0.00	**9.6**	2.6	2.15	18.92	3.52	43.0	**3.5**	27.0	13.4	**8.7**
3.7	1.07	14.5	0.10	**0.4**	-0.1	-0.22	-8.83	3.24	106.0	**5.8**	47.1	6.1	**0.9**
4.8	1.04	4.6	-0.17	**3.8**	1.4	1.03	10.27	3.19	70.0	**5.4**	46.2	9.1	**4.9**
8.8	0.28	0.5	-0.01	**4.6**	2.6	0.96	6.47	3.03	69.8	**4.2**	50.6	16.6	**8.5**
5.4	1.98	6.7	-0.07	**0.2**	-0.2	-0.60	-7.84	3.36	123.4	**4.9**	52.2	12.6	**1.9**
8.3	0.37	1.4	-0.01	**3.4**	1.2	0.60	7.29	2.51	84.5	**6.7**	47.5	1.4	**4.8**
6.9	0.44	3.0	0.00	**4.7**	1.4	1.05	11.13	3.31	61.1	**0.9**	22.7	38.7	**5.4**
3.9	0.66	5.1	-0.15	**6.2**	2.4	1.23	15.19	3.33	50.1	**3.3**	17.6	12.5	**5.1**
7.3	0.38	2.6	0.00	**7.4**	1.5	1.95	22.31	4.25	53.2	**4.3**	33.4	10.3	**6.3**
7.8	0.00	0.0	0.00	**9.8**	0.5	2.21	10.69	3.73	22.0	**3.9**	38.5	15.2	**9.3**
8.4	1.52	2.9	-0.02	**5.8**	0.9	1.42	9.60	2.72	49.9	**5.4**	64.2	13.6	**9.6**
6.6	1.07	3.7	-0.04	**4.1**	0.9	0.91	10.04	3.53	69.2	**6.2**	48.8	4.8	**4.9**
3.6	2.84	14.9	-0.04	**7.0**	0.8	1.06	11.52	3.77	51.9	**3.0**	41.5	21.1	**6.6**
7.7	0.48	2.0	0.00	**7.0**	5.6	1.77	18.48	3.59	52.0	**2.7**	29.6	18.0	**6.7**
9.2	0.00	0.0	-0.01	**5.1**	1.2	1.14	12.16	2.63	52.5	**5.6**	45.5	7.8	**5.7**
8.4	0.11	0.4	0.00	**3.9**	0.2	0.58	5.00	2.58	64.9	**4.2**	53.8	16.1	**6.8**
7.8	0.35	2.8	0.05	**4.5**	20.3	0.97	12.11	3.28	65.2	**3.5**	25.6	15.3	**7.0**
7.6	0.72	3.7	0.00	**8.7**	0.7	1.87	15.84	3.91	54.3	**5.1**	36.0	7.8	**7.8**
8.6	0.11	1.4	0.15	**5.8**	0.8	1.33	9.64	3.16	46.3	**2.3**	46.7	36.3	**7.2**
4.7	0.50	14.0	0.00	**5.4**	0.4	1.33	13.17	3.45	65.2	**4.4**	23.3	7.3	**6.5**
7.3	0.60	2.5	0.02	**5.7**	2.0	1.48	13.79	3.96	64.8	**3.7**	9.6	10.0	**7.8**
4.4	2.78	9.6	0.08	**9.4**	4.6	1.98	18.37	4.18	42.0	**1.7**	31.3	31.5	**7.0**

								Asset Mix (As a % of Total Assets)						
Name	City	State	Rating	2020 Rating	2019 Rating	Total Assets ($Mil)	One Year Asset Growth	Comm-ercial Loans	Cons-umer Loans	Mort-gage Loans	Secur-ities	Capital-ization Index	Lever-age Ratio	Risk-Based Capital Ratio
Community Bank of Pleasant Hill	Pleasant Hill	MO	B+	B+	B+	118.2	9.43	8.3	1.1	3.6	62.5	6.4	8.4	22.2
Community Bank of Raymore	Raymore	MO	B+	B+	B+	383.9	18.61	10.4	0.4	1.7	52.1	4.6	6.6	13.9
▼ Community Bank of Santa Maria	Santa Maria	CA	B-	B+	A-	371.1	12.19	14.1	0.2	0.8	25.2	4.5	8.3	0.0
Community Bank of the Bay	Oakland	CA	B	B	B	796.1	30.08	21.3	0.1	3.4	2.9	6.3	8.4	14.5
Community Bank of the Chesapeake	Waldorf	MD	B-	B-	B-	2192.9	4.84	7.9	0.1	10.9	15.9	8.9	10.3	14.3
Community Bank of the South	Merritt Island	FL	B+	A-	A-	241.2	22.25	5.6	0.4	2.9	16.6	5.9	7.9	25.9
Community Bank of Trenton	Trenton	IL	B+	B	B	100.2	1.32	12.4	4.2	25.1	16.6	9.8	10.8	15.0
▲ Community Bank of Wichita, Inc.	Wichita	KS	C+	C	C+	102.4	1.86	22.9	3.8	18.6	13.8	6.5	8.5	13.0
Community Bank Owatonna	Owatonna	MN	C+	C+	C+	76.4	9.14	8.6	1.1	16.5	24.6	5.9	7.9	12.6
Community Bank, Lexington, Tennessee	Lexington	TN	B+	B+	B	192.5	10.61	17.8	8.6	26.6	4.4	8.1	9.8	15.1
Community Bank, N.A.	De Witt	NY	B+	B+	B+	14587.7	10.15	5.1	8.6	18.8	27.5	5.6	7.6	16.3
Community Bankers' Bank	Midlothian	VA	C	C	C+	154.2	-4.46	6.2	0.5	4.5	18.2	10.0	11.5	0.0
Community Banking Co. of Fitzgerald	Fitzgerald	GA	B+	B+	A-	220.4	23.93	5.8	8.3	21.0	9.1	7.8	9.5	0.0
▼ Community Banks of Shelby County	Cowden	IL	C-	C+	C+	59.2	10.77	5.1	2.2	9.3	34.5	7.5	9.3	0.0
▲ Community Commerce Bank	Claremont	CA	B+	B	B+	334.1	3.10	7.2	11.7	5.5	1.8	10.0	16.7	24.8
Community Development Bank FSB	Ogema	MN	C	C	C+	208.7	10.93	7.1	1.6	9.3	32.9	6.4	8.4	16.2
Community Federal Savings Bank	New York	NY	C	C-	C	730.4	122.52	53.9	0.7	3.6	2.0	8.8	10.2	38.9
Community Financial Bank	Prentice	WI	C+	C+	C+	52.1	2.51	4.5	1.7	28.0	0.0	8.9	10.3	21.8
▲ Community Financial Services Bank	Benton	KY	C	C-	C+	1452.1	8.74	8.2	12.3	15.5	22.7	7.1	9.1	13.7
▼ Community First Bank	Kansas City	KS	B+	A-	B+	261.8	16.74	11.5	0.5	8.2	1.5	7.7	9.5	13.4
Community First Bank	New Iberia	LA	B	B	B	528.3	12.01	15.7	2.7	17.8	10.5	6.6	8.6	13.6
Community First Bank	Menahga	MN	A-	A	A-	111.5	10.75	9.1	5.9	12.8	32.0	10.0	12.9	0.0
Community First Bank	Butler	MO	B	B	B	258.7	25.04	10.2	2.9	14.1	6.3	6.0	8.0	15.7
Community First Bank	Maywood	NE	D	D-	D-	128.6	5.45	7.5	2.2	2.6	29.3	8.3	9.8	15.4
Community First Bank	Kennewick	WA	B+	B+	B+	583.3	30.57	12.2	2.4	10.0	34.5	5.2	7.2	15.6
Community First Bank	Boscobel	WI	B+	B+	B+	518.1	8.28	9.2	1.2	12.2	28.8	8.4	9.9	15.7
Community First Bank	Rosholt	WI	B+	B+	B	111.1	4.46	6.1	1.2	11.7	30.2	7.0	9.0	0.0
Community First Bank Inc.	Walhalla	SC	C	C	C	638.2	29.13	3.8	20.9	14.9	10.8	5.8	8.8	0.0
Community First Bank of Indiana	Kokomo	IN	C+	C+	B-	513.0	24.38	19.7	0.6	8.7	0.4	2.3	9.2	0.0
▲ Community First Bank of the Heartland	Mount Vernon	IL	B+	B	B	241.8	-3.76	13.0	0.4	7.5	7.5	7.4	9.3	15.0
Community First Bank, N.A.	Forest	OH	D+	C-	C-	58.9	4.97	8.3	2.4	21.7	22.9	6.5	8.5	19.5
Community First Banking Co.	West Plains	MO	A-	A-	A-	249.0	10.09	6.9	3.2	22.8	24.6	8.4	9.9	0.0
Community First National Bank	Manhattan	KS	B+	B	C+	336.6	3.15	14.9	1.7	15.5	1.0	8.5	10.0	13.9
Community National B&T of Texas	Corsicana	TX	A-	A-	A-	967.9	5.80	9.2	0.9	8.1	16.5	6.7	8.7	14.9
Community National Bank	Seneca	KS	B+	B+	A-	570.3	11.48	3.9	0.5	8.5	57.1	6.5	8.5	19.6
Community National Bank	Hondo	TX	B+	B+	B+	261.1	7.86	7.3	1.5	9.3	32.5	7.2	9.2	16.0
Community National Bank	Midland	TX	B+	B+	B+	1476.8	1.15	26.6	0.6	5.9	10.3	8.8	10.2	15.3
Community National Bank	Derby	VT	B	B	B-	925.0	12.46	17.4	0.4	19.2	9.2	6.8	8.8	15.9
Community National Bank & Trust	Chanute	KS	B-	B-	B-	1806.9	22.13	9.5	2.3	14.6	27.6	6.1	8.1	13.4
▲ Community National Bank in Monmouth	Monmouth	IL	B-	C	D+	50.9	5.16	3.8	6.9	14.7	26.7	10.0	12.7	0.0
Community National Bank of Okarche	Okarche	OK	A	A	A	131.2	3.27	7.1	1.7	4.5	57.9	10.0	13.7	0.0
Community Neighbor Bank	Camden	AL	A-	B+	A-	132.6	11.34	16.1	5.2	12.6	11.1	10.0	12.2	0.0
Community Partners Savings Bank	Salem	IL	C+	B-	B-	234.6	6.64	4.6	9.8	23.5	33.2	9.7	10.8	22.5
▲ Community Point Bank	Russellville	MO	B+	B-	B-	155.1	6.90	4.0	3.6	15.7	16.5	7.6	9.4	14.6
Community Resource Bank	Northfield	MN	A-	A-	A-	370.6	9.01	13.0	0.9	14.7	12.3	10.0	11.2	16.4
▲ Community Savings	Caldwell	OH	C	C-	D	60.6	15.01	0.0	15.6	41.6	4.1	10.0	12.8	30.7
Community Savings Bank	Edgewood	IA	C+	C+	D	508.5	5.61	10.7	1.9	7.0	22.2	6.8	8.8	13.8
Community Savings Bank	Chicago	IL	C-	C-	C	447.4	5.81	0.0	0.0	31.9	35.9	10.0	14.8	0.0
Community Savings Bank	Bethel	OH	B	B	B-	88.0	6.47	10.4	0.1	45.7	9.1	10.0	16.7	0.0
Community Spirit Bank	Red Bay	AL	B	B	B	174.5	7.69	12.1	4.3	19.4	21.0	8.0	9.7	0.0
Community State Bank	Bradley	AR	B-	C+	C	30.1	15.82	35.2	5.4	13.7	1.9	7.4	10.1	0.0
Community State Bank	Lamar	CO	A	A	A-	151.2	11.44	11.7	3.2	5.7	10.2	10.0	12.6	17.2
▼ Community State Bank	Starke	FL	D+	C-	C+	195.1	21.34	9.5	2.4	9.4	18.4	4.3	6.3	13.2
Community State Bank	Ankeny	IA	B+	B+	B+	1070.5	18.24	18.2	0.1	6.3	21.4	6.3	9.8	12.0
Community State Bank	Paton	IA	B	B	B	52.2	13.41	5.6	1.7	1.0	57.5	10.0	18.1	39.9
Community State Bank	Spencer	IA	B+	B+	B+	248.9	12.93	12.7	1.3	3.6	47.0	7.3	9.2	0.0
Community State Bank	Galva	IL	B-	B	B-	263.7	2.54	9.6	1.2	7.6	22.3	8.3	9.8	0.0
Community State Bank	Avilla	IN	A-	A-	A-	364.6	2.81	16.2	1.2	21.7	8.8	7.2	9.2	16.0
Community State Bank	Brook	IN	B-	B-	B-	96.7	27.19	7.0	0.9	26.2	8.6	10.0	11.2	0.0
Community State Bank	Royal Center	IN	B-	B-	B-	162.6	18.49	5.9	2.1	10.5	32.8	7.2	9.1	17.7

Asset Quality Index	Adjusted Non-Performing Loans as a % of Total Loans	Adjusted Non-Performing Loans as a % of Capital	Net Charge-Offs Avg Loans	Profitability Index	Net Income ($Mil)	Return on Assets (R.O.A.)	Return on Equity (R.O.E.)	Net Interest Spread	Overhead Efficiency Ratio	Liquidity Index	Liquidity Ratio	Hot Money Ratio	Stability Index
9.3	0.00	0.0	0.00	**5.2**	0.7	1.22	15.52	2.77	65.3	**7.8**	72.8	0.2	**4.9**
9.3	0.00	0.0	-0.01	**8.3**	4.4	2.38	36.80	2.85	43.4	**6.3**	46.1	3.3	**5.6**
6.1	0.60	3.9	-0.01	**5.0**	1.5	0.86	10.06	3.89	66.9	**5.2**	34.7	6.4	**5.1**
8.4	0.03	0.1	0.11	**5.9**	4.4	1.19	13.71	3.38	52.2	**4.3**	34.1	11.5	**6.1**
4.6	0.88	6.1	0.19	**6.4**	14.2	1.36	12.79	3.51	49.0	**3.9**	22.7	10.7	**8.7**
9.5	0.00	0.0	-0.04	**5.2**	1.0	0.86	9.70	2.83	61.5	**7.2**	66.8	3.1	**4.9**
4.8	1.63	9.5	-0.02	**5.8**	0.8	1.56	14.57	3.06	60.6	**2.6**	26.5	17.6	**7.6**
5.5	0.40	3.1	-0.10	**6.3**	0.7	1.30	15.78	4.53	63.1	**1.9**	23.8	20.5	**5.7**
8.9	0.00	0.0	0.00	**4.3**	0.3	0.82	10.26	3.70	68.1	**3.8**	39.1	14.5	**4.1**
8.0	0.12	0.8	0.03	**7.3**	2.3	2.44	25.52	3.99	49.6	**1.3**	9.3	17.1	**6.1**
4.6	0.99	4.1	0.01	**5.6**	82.0	1.15	9.88	2.90	59.8	**5.9**	29.2	3.6	**10.0**
8.7	0.00	0.0	-0.06	**2.5**	0.3	0.29	2.64	2.08	92.7	**2.0**	30.1	14.5	**7.1**
5.1	0.83	4.1	-0.01	**6.5**	1.4	1.34	12.68	3.44	52.4	**3.8**	32.7	13.4	**7.6**
4.4	2.96	12.1	-0.01	**2.1**	0.0	0.14	1.51	1.90	93.8	**5.2**	57.4	11.9	**4.6**
6.4	0.99	2.4	0.00	**5.1**	1.8	1.10	6.67	3.95	62.2	**0.6**	21.7	76.2	**7.2**
5.0	1.09	4.5	0.02	**2.7**	0.5	0.43	4.20	2.41	79.2	**5.2**	45.2	10.2	**5.6**
4.8	0.40	5.5	0.00	**3.1**	1.8	0.62	12.31	1.45	80.1	**3.0**	34.1	17.9	**3.5**
7.4	0.75	2.6	0.00	**2.7**	0.1	0.37	3.57	2.61	83.4	**2.9**	44.6	22.7	**5.9**
3.3	2.07	12.9	0.05	**4.0**	7.5	1.06	11.55	2.83	68.1	**2.0**	25.7	17.9	**5.6**
8.0	0.13	0.5	0.00	**8.2**	1.1	1.75	17.92	5.03	42.8	**0.9**	22.6	39.5	**7.0**
6.4	0.37	3.6	0.00	**5.8**	3.9	1.51	17.55	3.79	64.5	**3.1**	28.1	15.6	**7.1**
8.3	0.03	0.1	0.10	**5.8**	0.7	1.35	9.62	3.59	65.2	**5.5**	50.0	9.2	**8.8**
5.9	0.69	3.9	-0.05	**5.9**	1.6	1.40	17.89	3.41	54.6	**2.8**	33.5	18.3	**6.5**
1.6	5.87	25.5	0.58	**1.3**	0.2	0.33	3.14	4.05	92.3	**2.2**	23.6	16.9	**5.3**
8.6	0.00	0.0	0.00	**5.3**	4.6	1.63	20.36	3.33	66.3	**6.5**	42.7	0.8	**5.2**
6.1	0.57	2.9	-0.02	**5.7**	4.0	1.56	13.69	3.67	63.1	**4.3**	30.5	10.2	**8.0**
8.9	0.17	0.9	0.01	**5.0**	0.7	1.20	12.41	3.84	72.1	**6.6**	47.7	2.1	**7.0**
5.0	0.63	2.9	-0.01	**2.8**	1.4	0.47	5.01	3.35	86.6	**2.6**	20.3	16.7	**5.9**
5.4	0.62	3.4	-0.02	**5.7**	2.4	1.15	10.68	5.22	77.6	**1.8**	16.6	15.9	**6.8**
5.7	0.28	1.9	-0.09	**8.5**	2.8	2.24	22.94	3.60	51.0	**4.1**	18.4	8.5	**7.5**
9.3	0.00	0.0	0.00	**1.8**	0.0	0.00	0.04	2.55	99.9	**6.7**	52.9	1.6	**4.1**
8.4	0.42	1.2	-0.05	**5.9**	1.9	1.54	15.04	3.37	58.5	**3.9**	27.7	11.6	**8.0**
7.1	0.23	2.5	0.00	**7.3**	2.8	1.65	17.05	3.54	69.4	**3.1**	23.5	14.1	**6.4**
8.2	0.26	0.8	0.00	**7.0**	6.7	1.43	14.05	4.07	60.0	**4.7**	31.5	8.0	**8.1**
5.5	2.41	8.5	-0.01	**8.3**	4.9	1.74	19.94	2.78	51.1	**6.3**	51.8	5.2	**7.7**
3.7	2.39	12.3	-0.02	**5.7**	1.7	1.34	12.35	3.92	67.4	**5.5**	42.4	7.7	**6.1**
5.2	1.20	7.1	0.07	**6.5**	7.7	1.05	9.47	3.54	64.6	**5.6**	26.0	3.4	**8.8**
4.7	0.56	6.4	0.01	**6.7**	6.4	1.38	14.10	3.55	55.3	**4.2**	14.1	7.2	**7.3**
5.4	1.35	7.7	0.02	**4.4**	8.9	0.99	11.18	3.49	68.9	**4.6**	25.5	9.7	**7.1**
8.5	0.12	0.5	0.14	**3.8**	0.3	1.10	8.77	3.02	60.6	**6.0**	53.7	6.4	**5.6**
9.1	0.00	0.9	0.00	**7.4**	1.2	1.88	12.79	3.34	43.6	**1.1**	25.7	34.2	**9.9**
6.1	0.81	5.8	0.31	**5.4**	0.6	0.98	7.98	4.12	72.6	**4.2**	37.0	13.1	**8.1**
4.6	1.32	6.9	0.16	**3.9**	0.8	0.69	6.26	3.60	75.5	**4.1**	37.0	13.7	**5.7**
8.2	0.20	1.3	0.00	**6.4**	1.4	1.76	18.79	3.85	47.5	**3.1**	25.5	14.6	**5.9**
7.7	0.44	1.4	0.00	**7.5**	2.5	1.36	11.25	3.87	58.8	**3.3**	18.2	12.0	**8.2**
4.5	1.97	9.3	-0.04	**3.0**	0.2	0.81	6.22	3.95	86.2	**4.3**	32.8	11.3	**6.0**
6.1	0.74	3.5	-0.17	**3.0**	2.2	0.86	8.68	3.19	77.1	**4.1**	24.9	7.4	**5.7**
7.6	2.78	5.6	0.00	**1.3**	-0.1	-0.06	-0.41	2.15	106.2	**3.5**	51.3	20.8	**7.5**
9.0	0.14	0.6	-0.03	**4.0**	0.4	0.80	4.72	3.78	77.0	**2.0**	17.4	19.0	**8.0**
5.7	1.36	5.1	-0.01	**4.7**	1.0	1.14	11.22	4.30	72.5	**2.2**	31.7	23.5	**6.2**
7.6	0.00	0.0	0.05	**8.3**	0.4	2.49	22.24	5.60	52.0	**0.7**	13.2	41.9	**5.7**
8.2	0.07	0.4	0.00	**7.5**	1.3	1.71	13.60	3.64	52.2	**1.1**	26.6	42.5	**9.6**
2.4	3.23	24.5	-0.07	**2.4**	0.0	0.00	0.03	3.75	93.4	**5.5**	33.7	3.6	**2.3**
8.0	0.01	0.0	0.08	**5.2**	5.2	1.00	9.02	3.65	61.5	**4.8**	22.5	6.0	**8.8**
7.0	0.00	4.6	-0.13	**5.6**	0.3	1.25	6.63	2.25	49.1	**5.3**	77.7	14.4	**7.1**
8.5	0.31	0.9	0.02	**7.2**	2.7	2.21	20.94	3.45	41.6	**4.7**	39.5	3.3	**7.0**
3.4	1.85	12.0	2.52	**5.2**	1.5	1.13	11.28	3.88	55.0	**1.8**	21.4	20.7	**7.0**
8.7	0.13	0.5	0.04	**7.1**	2.4	1.32	13.51	3.65	53.8	**5.0**	32.9	6.7	**7.3**
3.8	4.39	20.4	0.72	**7.2**	0.7	1.49	14.05	3.78	48.5	**2.2**	37.0	23.1	**5.6**
6.5	0.43	1.5	0.81	**3.6**	0.5	0.68	6.94	3.30	72.2	**6.3**	50.8	5.1	**5.6**

Name	City	State	Rating	2020 Rating	2019 Rating	Total Assets ($Mil)	One Year Asset Growth	Asset Mix (As a % of Total Assets) Comm-ercial Loans	Cons-umer Loans	Mort-gage Loans	Secur-ities	Capital-ization Index	Lever-age Ratio	Risk-Based Capital Ratio
Community State Bank	Coffeyville	KS	**A-**	A-	A	189.0	1.05	7.1	1.1	3.5	35.3	**8.8**	10.2	0.0
Community State Bank	Shelbina	MO	**B**	B	B-	98.7	14.23	5.3	10.2	26.9	21.2	**7.6**	9.4	0.0
Community State Bank	Colon	NE	**C-**	C-	D+	41.0	9.50	6.1	1.4	3.0	12.4	**6.6**	8.6	0.0
Community State Bank	Hennessey	OK	**C**	C	C-	84.6	6.49	8.9	2.3	5.3	55.5	**5.1**	7.1	23.2
Community State Bank	Union Grove	WI	**B**	B	B-	566.5	15.76	15.8	0.2	9.0	28.5	**5.9**	7.9	15.0
Community State Bank of Canton	Canton	OK	**C**	C	B-	54.9	-4.39	14.3	5.9	4.8	20.4	**8.6**	10.8	0.0
Community State Bank of Missouri	Bowling Green	MO	**B+**	B+	B+	285.1	8.86	11.5	0.6	16.2	19.6	**5.1**	11.4	0.0
Community State Bank of Orbisonia	Orbisonia	PA	**C+**	C+	B	413.6	13.00	3.0	7.7	48.7	17.9	**8.0**	9.6	0.0
Community State Bank of Rock Falls	Rock Falls	IL	**C**	C-	C-	323.8	7.81	8.7	1.3	21.3	28.9	**7.2**	9.1	19.1
Community Trust Bank	Irvington	IL	**B-**	B-	B-	99.9	14.49	8.4	0.9	7.0	37.1	**10.0**	11.8	24.4
Community Trust Bank, Inc.	Pikeville	KY	**B**	B	B	5460.1	9.19	8.3	15.1	14.1	24.4	**10.0**	11.9	0.0
Community Valley Bank	El Centro	CA	**B+**	B+	A-	276.1	12.00	16.9	0.1	4.8	0.3	**7.0**	10.0	0.0
Community West Bank, N.A.	Goleta	CA	**C**	C	C+	1062.9	0.21	9.4	27.0	3.4	2.2	**3.1**	8.9	0.0
Communitybank of Texas, N.A.	Beaumont	TX	**B+**	B+	A-	4067.4	4.24	16.1	0.8	5.0	7.6	**9.9**	10.9	16.7
Compass Savings Bank	Wilmerding	PA	**D-**	D-	D-	53.5	3.89	0.1	1.1	71.8	6.3	**6.2**	8.2	16.4
Computershare Trust Co., N.A.	Canton	MA	**U**	U	U	47.6	47.91	0.0	0.0	0.0	0.0	**10.0**	87.3	402.6
▼ Concorde Bank	Blomkest	MN	**C+**	B-	C+	72.7	22.91	8.9	2.5	19.8	11.5	**6.8**	8.8	14.1
Concordia Bank	Concordia	MO	**A-**	B+	B+	98.4	13.57	7.6	1.4	21.5	9.9	**7.3**	9.2	0.0
Concordia Bank & Trust Co.	Vidalia	LA	**B**	B-	B	614.0	5.77	5.1	1.7	10.3	38.9	**9.1**	10.4	0.0
▲ Congressional Bank	Chevy Chase	MD	**C**	C-	C	2465.0	60.08	31.2	3.9	4.6	1.0	**10.0**	21.9	21.7
▲ Connect Bank	Star City	AR	**A**	A-	B+	111.2	10.76	9.1	1.4	14.5	27.2	**10.0**	14.8	0.0
Connecticut Community Bank, N.A.	Norwalk	CT	**C-**	C-	C	641.9	9.40	34.7	0.0	2.3	0.5	**6.1**	8.2	0.0
Connection Bank	Fort Madison	IA	**B-**	B	B-	373.1	8.70	13.7	1.8	26.6	5.6	**5.3**	7.5	11.2
Connections Bank	Kirksville	MO	**B+**	B+	B	94.6	-0.02	3.7	0.5	30.0	4.7	**10.0**	11.9	0.0
ConnectOne Bank	Englewood Cliffs	NJ	**C+**	C+	C+	7709.8	1.22	12.6	0.0	6.9	6.0	**8.9**	11.3	14.1
Consumers National Bank	Minerva	OH	**B**	B	B	833.4	12.49	11.9	3.5	15.0	25.9	**5.8**	7.8	13.1
Continental Bank	Salt Lake City	UT	**B+**	B	B	290.1	-0.19	75.7	0.0	0.0	3.3	**9.5**	10.7	23.4
▲ Conway Bank	Conway Springs	KS	**C-**	D+	D+	106.0	-1.48	20.6	0.7	11.4	11.7	**5.6**	7.6	16.0
Copiah Bank	Hazlehurst	MS	**B-**	B-	B-	273.9	10.59	4.8	1.9	18.4	25.0	**7.2**	9.3	0.0
Core Bank	Omaha	NE	**B**	B-	C+	718.3	3.03	25.3	0.4	15.1	5.0	**6.5**	9.0	12.1
▲ COREBANK	Waynoka	OK	**C**	C-	C-	78.1	3.26	12.1	2.4	27.4	6.4	**9.3**	10.5	0.0
CoreFirst Bank & Trust	Topeka	KS	**B-**	B-	C+	1179.1	8.07	10.8	3.0	10.6	29.2	**6.2**	8.3	14.6
Corn Growers State Bank	Murdock	NE	**C-**	C-	D+	32.3	19.79	4.2	8.4	6.0	20.5	**5.7**	7.7	0.0
▲ Cornerstone Bank	Atlanta	GA	**D+**	D-	D	223.8	-0.62	17.6	0.1	9.3	15.4	**6.8**	8.8	18.0
Cornerstone Bank	Clarinda	IA	**C**	C-	C-	43.7	5.88	6.5	6.1	27.1	14.1	**10.0**	13.2	27.3
▼ Cornerstone Bank	Overland Park	KS	**C+**	B	B+	315.3	15.09	13.8	0.3	24.7	3.7	**2.9**	8.5	0.0
▲ Cornerstone Bank	Worcester	MA	**C**	C-	C	1394.2	6.60	6.0	0.5	42.6	5.4	**6.2**	8.2	13.3
Cornerstone Bank	Fargo	ND	**B-**	B-	C	1146.7	5.03	14.0	2.0	8.6	16.3	**5.9**	7.9	11.9
Cornerstone Bank	York	NE	**B**	B	B+	1972.0	11.91	13.9	1.2	2.8	18.9	**6.3**	9.1	0.0
Cornerstone Bank	Mount Laurel	NJ	**D+**	D+	D+	287.4	2.96	9.0	0.0	22.6	5.0	**4.7**	6.7	11.7
Cornerstone Bank	Watonga	OK	**C+**	C+	C+	240.9	5.95	6.1	3.4	9.1	38.3	**6.4**	8.4	15.8
▲ CornerStone Bank, N.A.	Lexington	VA	**C+**	C	C+	183.4	-2.01	14.2	1.6	21.6	8.4	**7.9**	9.7	0.0
Cornerstone Community Bank	Red Bluff	CA	**B**	B	B	525.7	14.58	23.8	0.5	2.9	14.3	**6.3**	8.3	13.1
Cornerstone Community Bank	Grafton	WI	**C**	C	C+	228.7	-2.99	12.5	0.1	10.0	0.0	**3.5**	9.7	0.0
▲ Cornerstone National Bank & Trust Co.	Palatine	IL	**B**	B-	B-	959.9	11.33	26.0	0.3	6.7	9.4	**6.3**	8.3	13.6
CornerStone State Bank	Montgomery	MN	**B+**	B+	A-	222.9	13.74	5.1	3.9	19.8	39.7	**8.1**	9.7	0.0
Cornhusker Bank	Lincoln	NE	**B-**	B-	B-	827.5	10.05	8.2	0.6	15.9	25.9	**5.9**	7.9	12.7
▲ CorTrust Bank N.A.	Mitchell	SD	**B**	C+	B-	1524.5	15.24	11.7	2.7	8.4	33.8	**6.5**	8.5	14.5
Corydon State Bank	Corydon	IA	**C+**	C+	B+	113.8	7.74	4.9	1.4	7.9	20.9	**10.0**	19.9	0.0
Cottonwood Valley Bank	Cedar Point	KS	**B-**	B-	C+	40.9	8.92	6.6	1.6	0.3	38.0	**10.0**	12.1	0.0
Coulee Bank	La Crosse	WI	**B**	B-	C+	494.1	11.88	19.9	1.2	6.4	16.9	**6.4**	8.4	12.7
Country Bank for Savings	Ware	MA	**B**	B	B	1758.3	-0.12	2.7	0.5	22.9	17.6	**10.0**	15.2	0.0
Country Club Bank	Kansas City	MO	**B+**	B+	A-	2283.3	20.29	15.6	0.4	6.3	34.3	**5.9**	7.9	14.6
Country Club Trust Co., N.A.	Kansas City	MO	**U**	U	U	15.4	10.42	0.0	0.0	0.0	21.8	**10.0**	102.	0.0
COUNTRY Trust Bank	Bloomington	IL	**U**	U	U	31.9	4.84	0.0	0.0	0.0	66.7	**10.0**	97.3	123.5
Countryside Bank	Unadilla	NE	**B+**	B	B	99.5	12.63	6.1	4.2	14.3	25.1	**10.0**	14.4	0.0
County Bank	Rehoboth Beach	DE	**B+**	B	B-	562.3	24.46	11.1	4.9	8.4	13.8	**8.0**	9.7	16.8
County Bank	Sigourney	IA	**B-**	B-	C	208.5	11.53	13.5	1.9	9.6	15.6	**7.7**	9.5	13.6
County Bank	Brunswick	MO	**B**	B-	B-	125.2	20.66	8.0	3.5	13.4	29.2	**5.6**	7.6	16.4
County National Bank	Hillsdale	MI	**B**	B	B	1046.9	10.37	22.4	3.6	17.4	3.4	**5.7**	7.7	13.5

Asset Quality Index	Adjusted Non-Performing Loans as a % of Total Loans	Adjusted Non-Performing Loans as a % of Capital	Net Charge-Offs Avg Loans	Profitability Index	Net Income ($Mil)	Return on Assets (R.O.A.)	Return on Equity (R.O.E.)	Net Interest Spread	Overhead Efficiency Ratio	Liquidity Index	Liquidity Ratio	Hot Money Ratio	Stability Index
3.7	5.19	22.2	0.03	**5.8**	0.7	0.74	6.97	2.86	49.5	**4.9**	21.2	3.7	**8.1**
5.7	1.14	4.3	0.26	**8.7**	0.9	1.83	19.74	3.88	36.9	**4.0**	26.6	8.9	**6.1**
7.4	0.74	1.7	-0.09	**3.5**	0.2	0.91	10.67	3.25	66.3	**3.1**	52.3	20.8	**3.8**
4.6	3.83	13.4	0.05	**4.6**	0.4	1.01	14.26	3.55	70.3	**6.5**	51.2	2.4	**3.5**
4.9	1.93	9.9	-0.13	**5.7**	4.0	1.41	18.71	3.34	63.3	**5.8**	46.5	6.5	**6.5**
1.2	4.70	28.1	0.87	**4.9**	0.2	0.71	6.59	5.00	67.4	**2.5**	7.0	15.6	**5.3**
6.2	1.38	7.3	-0.04	**5.4**	2.0	1.41	12.02	3.25	59.9	**3.4**	17.6	12.2	**8.3**
4.7	1.54	8.0	0.12	**3.7**	1.4	0.68	6.89	3.63	75.8	**2.3**	20.2	17.9	**5.2**
2.6	3.49	19.2	0.02	**4.2**	1.3	0.81	8.44	2.96	62.2	**3.9**	35.6	13.9	**6.0**
8.2	1.77	3.3	0.00	**3.1**	0.4	0.74	5.78	3.24	83.5	**6.3**	50.7	3.9	**6.3**
4.6	2.21	6.6	-0.02	**7.6**	46.7	1.76	13.64	3.24	50.3	**3.1**	20.0	14.5	**10.0**
6.5	0.23	1.5	0.03	**8.8**	2.1	1.59	15.98	4.84	49.1	**3.0**	20.9	14.6	**6.6**
6.0	0.35	2.3	-0.06	**6.4**	6.6	1.29	14.45	4.18	59.5	**1.7**	12.4	8.8	**8.2**
4.9	1.93	6.5	-0.03	**6.1**	22.5	1.12	8.68	3.50	67.1	**5.6**	30.2	4.1	**9.3**
7.1	0.00	4.7	0.00	**0.0**	-0.1	-0.47	-5.83	1.82	124.9	**0.7**	12.9	36.7	**2.7**
6.7	na	0.0	na	**9.5**	3.1	14.51	16.32	0.19	70.3	**4.0**	460.5	0.0	**6.4**
4.1	0.95	14.2	-0.14	**5.1**	0.4	1.11	12.29	5.07	70.4	**4.0**	39.9	15.0	**5.8**
2.4	5.80	19.5	0.58	**5.8**	0.6	1.21	13.33	3.86	60.9	**4.8**	26.5	5.5	**6.6**
5.4	0.75	5.1	0.01	**5.2**	4.1	1.36	12.01	3.40	63.8	**1.8**	17.1	20.2	**8.0**
3.6	2.03	8.3	0.09	**6.9**	14.0	1.43	10.95	4.77	59.1	**3.3**	22.1	10.5	**9.6**
8.8	0.63	1.7	0.01	**7.8**	1.2	2.28	15.57	5.26	57.1	**3.8**	33.3	13.8	**8.5**
4.0	1.77	10.0	-0.11	**2.5**	1.5	0.47	5.51	3.24	86.3	**4.9**	39.9	10.3	**5.2**
7.5	0.14	1.3	0.01	**3.8**	1.4	0.75	8.57	3.17	78.9	**4.6**	14.0	4.7	**5.8**
8.3	0.16	0.9	0.06	**5.4**	0.6	1.21	9.29	4.45	64.3	**1.6**	15.1	20.4	**7.6**
3.1	1.39	8.2	0.00	**7.9**	68.7	1.83	13.39	3.65	38.9	**1.4**	10.9	13.6	**9.5**
6.6	0.34	2.5	0.01	**5.1**	4.1	1.04	12.25	3.52	63.4	**4.5**	18.7	5.9	**5.9**
5.0	0.57	3.7	-0.01	**8.0**	4.5	3.16	29.09	4.96	50.0	**0.4**	20.9	78.6	**8.8**
3.8	3.33	12.1	0.06	**2.6**	0.2	0.42	4.68	3.92	83.9	**3.8**	29.6	12.8	**4.5**
6.1	0.62	3.6	0.02	**4.4**	1.2	0.88	9.52	3.79	73.3	**3.6**	25.7	12.0	**5.6**
6.4	0.98	1.9	-0.05	**6.9**	6.0	1.68	18.78	4.33	65.0	**4.4**	7.4	1.9	**6.6**
8.6	0.03	0.2	-0.01	**3.0**	0.2	0.62	5.74	3.08	80.1	**0.9**	25.3	55.5	**5.7**
4.2	3.57	17.8	0.03	**5.4**	7.2	1.28	15.27	3.22	72.4	**5.0**	19.4	3.1	**7.7**
5.4	0.18	5.2	-0.03	**3.9**	0.1	0.88	11.74	3.31	77.5	**6.6**	53.4	2.4	**2.0**
2.6	6.16	17.8	-0.01	**2.5**	1.2	1.12	13.09	3.53	76.7	**2.4**	36.8	25.2	**3.3**
5.4	2.01	10.3	0.00	**2.5**	0.1	0.52	3.89	3.80	82.4	**2.8**	42.5	23.6	**6.1**
4.4	0.46	4.3	0.45	**7.3**	2.6	1.75	20.32	4.25	38.7	**0.7**	10.6	35.6	**6.5**
6.8	0.81	6.4	0.08	**2.8**	4.0	0.56	7.01	3.02	76.1	**2.9**	12.6	13.7	**5.5**
3.6	3.44	18.1	0.51	**4.0**	5.0	0.89	10.83	3.49	60.0	**3.2**	17.1	13.7	**7.5**
6.5	0.72	3.0	0.01	**5.1**	11.5	1.16	12.22	3.33	67.0	**2.5**	13.1	14.8	**8.5**
6.8	0.40	2.8	-0.13	**1.4**	0.1	0.07	0.88	2.90	101.7	**4.3**	30.2	10.1	**3.7**
8.8	0.19	0.9	-0.01	**3.6**	1.0	0.90	9.23	3.84	73.5	**5.3**	37.0	6.7	**4.6**
4.8	1.67	8.5	-0.01	**3.8**	1.0	1.13	12.07	3.94	71.2	**1.7**	17.5	21.7	**4.4**
7.4	0.00	0.0	0.00	**7.9**	4.2	1.56	19.79	3.46	36.9	**3.0**	23.1	12.2	**6.2**
7.2	0.08	0.3	0.00	**8.9**	2.1	1.75	18.52	4.38	50.2	**4.0**	8.4	7.5	**7.3**
5.7	0.50	3.6	0.00	**5.7**	5.4	1.14	13.73	3.32	60.6	**5.3**	33.1	4.8	**6.1**
5.4	2.22	6.2	0.00	**4.6**	1.3	1.15	11.27	2.83	67.3	**5.2**	42.5	9.4	**6.1**
7.3	0.26	1.7	0.01	**4.5**	5.8	1.17	14.50	3.31	69.2	**3.1**	30.1	9.6	**5.9**
6.8	1.09	4.6	0.23	**5.0**	8.4	1.13	12.42	3.82	67.3	**5.0**	27.9	8.4	**6.6**
1.2	12.95	27.4	1.20	**4.4**	1.0	1.70	8.36	2.67	40.6	**3.2**	64.4	24.0	**6.7**
9.5	0.00	0.0	-0.05	**3.0**	0.2	0.86	6.77	2.02	68.5	**5.6**	66.4	11.2	**6.8**
5.7	0.74	5.1	-0.16	**6.0**	4.3	1.78	20.01	3.75	66.3	**4.4**	19.2	5.7	**5.8**
5.4	2.88	10.7	0.00	**4.1**	6.0	0.69	4.56	2.98	71.9	**5.2**	37.5	10.3	**9.8**
7.8	0.63	2.7	-0.01	**6.9**	20.5	1.83	21.76	2.86	68.4	**6.1**	41.3	4.3	**8.5**
10.0	na	0.0	na	**10.0**	1.4	19.04	18.74	0.30	80.6	**4.0**	na	0.0	**7.0**
10.0	na	0.0	na	**10.0**	4.2	29.71	30.09	2.88	83.9	**4.0**	na	0.0	**7.0**
8.8	0.00	0.0	-0.04	**5.3**	0.7	1.43	9.85	3.45	58.1	**5.6**	51.2	8.7	**7.6**
6.0	1.35	4.0	-0.49	**5.7**	2.6	0.97	9.98	3.21	65.6	**6.2**	42.8	3.1	**6.1**
3.9	1.34	14.1	-0.01	**8.5**	2.5	2.41	24.80	4.46	49.6	**3.3**	16.0	12.7	**7.0**
8.3	0.00	0.0	0.02	**6.4**	1.0	1.71	20.54	4.35	63.0	**5.1**	39.8	8.8	**5.5**
6.8	0.59	3.6	0.00	**6.4**	6.6	1.27	16.16	3.97	60.3	**5.1**	25.9	6.3	**7.9**

Name	City	State	Rating	2020 Rating	2019 Rating	Total Assets ($Mil)	One Year Asset Growth	Asset Mix (As a % of Total Assets) Commercial Loans	Consumer Loans	Mortgage Loans	Securities	Capitalization Index	Leverage Ratio	Risk-Based Capital Ratio
County Savings Bank	Essington	PA	**C**	C	C	96.6	9.61	0.0	0.1	37.5	15.3	**4.6**	6.6	20.8
▲ Countybank	Greenwood	SC	**B**	B-	B-	675.6	24.25	7.0	0.6	14.2	24.7	**6.2**	8.2	16.1
Covington County Bank	Collins	MS	**C**	C+	C+	82.3	0.47	10.4	4.0	4.8	30.5	**7.2**	9.1	16.7
▲ Cowboy State Bank	Ranchester	WY	**C**	C-	D	55.3	10.11	4.6	4.2	8.5	17.5	**6.8**	8.8	0.0
Craft Bank	Atlanta	GA	**D**	D-		69.1	na	13.0	0.8	1.5	0.0	**10.0**	43.8	80.1
Crawford County Trust and Savings Bank	Denison	IA	**B**	B	C+	247.4	13.26	6.7	3.0	7.2	15.0	**6.0**	8.0	12.4
Credit First N.A.	Brook Park	OH	**U**	U	U	34.9	24.05	0.0	0.0	0.0	0.0	**10.0**	102.	386.1
Credit One Bank, N.A.	Las Vegas	NV	**U**	U	U	803.9	9.58	0.0	57.9	0.0	3.3	**10.0**	40.7	0.0
▲ Crescent Bank & Trust	New Orleans	LA	**C**	C-	C-	931.7	0.08	1.9	78.0	4.1	7.7	**10.0**	18.0	21.0
Crest Savings Bank	Wildwood	NJ	**C**	C	C+	594.3	15.07	3.1	3.8	44.0	3.4	**5.2**	7.2	15.1
Crews Bank & Trust	Arcadia	FL	**A-**	A-	A-	209.9	11.06	3.1	1.4	12.2	27.4	**6.8**	8.8	0.0
Crockett National Bank	San Antonio	TX	**A**	A	A	802.3	11.94	3.1	0.1	35.2	6.0	**10.0**	12.7	22.9
Cross County Bank	Wynne	AR	**B+**	B+	B+	310.7	10.22	9.8	1.1	10.1	2.2	**8.7**	11.8	0.0
Cross County Savings Bank	Middle Village	NY	**C+**	C+	B	559.0	13.75	0.0	0.1	48.5	3.2	**8.1**	9.7	17.3
Cross Keys Bank	Saint Joseph	LA	**B+**	B+	B+	460.3	1.48	11.3	0.8	10.1	33.0	**9.8**	10.9	16.4
Cross River Bank	Fort Lee	NJ	**B+**	B+	A-	14323.1	44.49	81.8	9.6	0.3	0.5	**8.5**	10.0	22.0
CrossFirst Bank	Leawood	KS	**C+**	C+	B-	5309.4	-2.78	31.9	0.5	7.6	13.4	**7.7**	10.3	13.1
▲ Crossroads Bank	Effingham	IL	**A**	A-	A-	212.8	4.91	17.2	0.7	5.8	26.6	**10.0**	13.4	0.0
Crossroads Bank	Wabash	IN	**B**	B	B	488.7	5.41	7.0	2.9	23.8	23.8	**7.2**	9.1	15.3
Crossroads Bank	Yoakum	TX	**A-**	A-	A	294.1	16.21	10.3	5.2	18.7	43.8	**7.8**	9.5	0.0
Crowell State Bank	Crowell	TX	**B**	B	B-	47.9	15.21	13.1	5.1	7.5	23.2	**8.7**	10.1	0.0
Crown Bank	Edina	MN	**C+**	C	C-	301.1	23.77	38.6	0.6	1.2	14.8	**6.1**	8.2	12.0
▲ Crown Bank	Elizabeth	NJ	**B**	B-	C+	563.4	6.95	5.7	0.1	2.4	5.3	**10.0**	20.8	0.0
Crystal Lake Bank & Trust Co., N.A.	Crystal Lake	IL	**B**	B	B	1318.8	0.84	32.7	14.8	4.6	10.0	**6.3**	9.4	12.0
CS Bank	Eureka Springs	AR	**B+**	B	B-	445.0	12.91	5.5	4.0	20.1	7.7	**7.4**	9.2	0.0
CTBC Bank Corp. (USA)	Los Angeles	CA	**A-**	B+	A-	4022.3	4.20	8.5	0.0	30.2	6.9	**10.0**	14.4	0.0
Culbertson Bank	Culbertson	NE	**C-**	C-	C	14.5	3.06	5.3	0.2	0.1	24.5	**10.0**	13.9	0.0
Cullman Savings Bank	Cullman	AL	**A-**	A-	A-	374.3	13.71	5.2	0.9	32.3	5.3	**10.0**	15.5	0.0
Cumberland Federal Bank, FSB	Cumberland	WI	**A-**	A-	B+	198.5	7.55	3.6	1.0	16.8	50.6	**10.0**	11.0	16.0
Cumberland Security Bank, Inc.	Somerset	KY	**A**	A	A	268.2	3.42	8.7	4.6	28.5	11.0	**10.0**	13.3	19.6
Cumberland Valley National B&T Co.	London	KY	**B-**	C+	C+	683.5	11.33	9.4	1.6	10.8	16.5	**6.8**	8.8	15.2
▲ Currie State Bank	Currie	MN	**C-**	D+	C-	89.8	1.37	8.8	1.6	5.8	0.1	**6.5**	10.3	0.0
CUSB Bank	Cresco	IA	**A-**	A-	B+	547.5	1.20	8.4	4.5	6.4	18.5	**10.0**	14.1	0.0
Custer Federal State Bank	Broken Bow	NE	**B-**	B-	B-	126.5	10.07	4.7	1.2	12.2	34.4	**10.0**	11.1	0.0
Customers Bank	Phoenixville	PA	**B-**	B-	B-	19634.8	9.74	38.4	8.2	2.0	7.8	**7.1**	9.1	13.8
Cypress Bank, SSB	Pittsburg	TX	**B-**	B-	B-	217.1	3.90	5.5	6.6	27.8	24.0	**8.7**	10.1	18.0
▲ D.L. Evans Bank	Burley	ID	**A-**	B+	A-	2695.7	27.97	7.8	1.2	3.6	29.6	**6.8**	8.9	0.0
▲ Dacotah Bank	Aberdeen	SD	**B**	B-	B-	3282.0	12.00	12.4	2.8	3.0	13.3	**8.9**	10.3	15.3
Dairy State Bank	Rice Lake	WI	**B-**	B	B	693.8	16.00	8.0	0.6	5.3	59.6	**9.5**	10.6	26.4
Dakota Community Bank & Trust, N.A.	Hebron	ND	**B+**	B+	B+	1015.0	9.78	8.8	1.7	3.7	35.0	**6.0**	8.0	14.4
Dakota Heritage Bank	Hunter	ND	**B**	B	C+	281.0	20.43	8.1	3.8	4.5	13.3	**7.0**	9.4	0.0
▲ Dakota Prairie Bank	Fort Pierre	SD	**A-**	B+	A-	121.0	17.61	8.3	2.2	2.9	14.5	**9.4**	10.6	19.3
Dakota Western Bank	Bowman	ND	**B**	B	B+	309.2	0.25	10.9	2.4	1.0	24.5	**10.0**	11.3	16.9
Dalhart Federal S&L Assn., SSB	Dalhart	TX	**C**	C	C	118.3	-1.21	0.7	2.0	47.5	35.0	**10.0**	11.8	27.2
Dallas Capital Bank, N.A.	Dallas	TX	**C+**	C+	C-	953.4	-1.21	13.1	0.0	8.3	9.7	**7.0**	9.8	0.0
Danville State Savings Bank	Danville	IA	**B+**	B+	B+	178.6	14.05	4.7	3.7	20.4	34.1	**10.0**	11.2	0.0
Davidson Trust Co.	Great Falls	MT	**U**	U	U	9.7	-10.66	0.0	0.0	0.0	54.6	**10.0**	75.7	128.2
Davis Trust Co.	Elkins	WV	**B-**	B-	B	175.9	-2.01	8.1	3.2	22.7	9.3	**6.4**	10.5	0.0
De Witt Bank & Trust Co.	De Witt	IA	**C+**	C+	B	221.9	8.52	12.5	1.8	8.7	28.0	**5.1**	8.7	11.1
Dean Co-operative Bank	Franklin	MA	**B-**	B-	C+	426.1	15.45	6.5	0.7	43.8	16.9	**5.9**	7.9	15.0
Dearborn Federal Savings Bank	Dearborn	MI	**C**	C+	B	283.7	4.61	0.3	0.0	61.5	6.4	**10.0**	27.6	55.8
Decatur County Bank	Decaturville	TN	**B-**	C+	C-	195.6	15.93	17.9	2.8	15.8	12.2	**7.6**	9.4	13.5
Decorah Bank and Trust Co.	Decorah	IA	**A-**	A-	A-	588.3	6.74	13.7	2.4	9.3	21.9	**8.6**	10.1	14.8
▲ Dedham Institution for Savings	Dedham	MA	**A-**	B	B	1825.5	8.89	3.4	0.0	34.5	18.4	**10.0**	12.5	17.0
Dedicated Community Bank	Darlington	SC	**C**	C+	C	80.6	-5.67	17.1	1.9	14.2	12.1	**7.0**	9.0	13.2
Deerwood Bank	Waite Park	MN	**B**	B	B	1000.8	12.93	20.5	0.9	11.5	9.3	**6.0**	8.0	13.4
Defiance State Bank	Defiance	IA	**C+**	C+	C-	38.7	2.19	7.2	5.3	9.6	9.2	**7.2**	9.1	0.0
Del Norte Bank, A S&L Assn.	Del Norte	CO	**B**	B	B-	114.5	1.78	10.5	1.0	21.1	8.6	**7.7**	9.5	0.0
Delta Bank	Vidalia	LA	**B**	B	B-	428.0	20.21	8.5	1.9	16.5	17.4	**5.7**	7.7	12.5
▼ Delta National Bank and Trust Co.	New York	NY	**D**	D+	C	305.1	-12.14	28.8	9.6	0.0	24.3	**10.0**	16.3	0.0

Asset Quality Index	Adjusted Non-Performing Loans as a % of Total Loans	Adjusted Non-Performing Loans as a % of Capital	Net Charge-Offs Avg Loans	Profitability Index	Net Income ($Mil)	Return on Assets (R.O.A.)	Return on Equity (R.O.E.)	Net Interest Spread	Overhead Efficiency Ratio	Liquidity Index	Liquidity Ratio	Hot Money Ratio	Stability Index
9.9	0.24	1.3	-0.37	**2.3**	0.1	0.20	3.02	2.62	96.3	**6.2**	52.1	4.7	**3.2**
7.1	0.42	2.2	-0.13	**5.8**	4.8	1.57	21.88	2.86	77.4	**6.5**	41.8	0.9	**5.6**
6.1	1.04	4.9	-0.01	**2.9**	0.2	0.37	4.22	2.76	81.1	**3.2**	50.7	21.6	**4.4**
4.9	2.83	8.6	0.00	**4.9**	0.4	1.28	15.50	5.11	74.0	**4.3**	40.9	13.9	**3.8**
9.6	0.00	0.0	0.00	**0.0**	-0.9	-4.11	-9.48	3.12	148.9	**6.8**	87.2	7.5	**1.5**
5.8	0.19	1.8	0.00	**6.0**	1.5	1.23	15.02	3.01	57.0	**3.5**	18.9	11.7	**6.4**
10.0	na	0.0	na	**9.5**	3.4	21.78	22.12	0.01	80.5	**4.0**	na	100.0	**6.5**
5.5	0.00	2.0	7.65	**10.0**	159.2	41.53	96.18	16.69	63.9	**2.4**	58.7	99.8	**8.7**
2.0	1.69	9.3	2.65	**7.1**	18.6	4.12	24.35	13.66	41.8	**0.6**	14.0	59.0	**7.4**
8.8	0.16	0.7	0.00	**2.5**	0.8	0.28	3.91	2.54	86.0	**4.3**	25.5	8.4	**4.3**
6.3	1.50	5.9	-0.01	**3.7**	0.8	0.79	8.56	2.72	76.0	**6.5**	52.2	4.2	**7.3**
8.7	0.07	1.2	-0.01	**9.5**	15.7	6.31	47.11	2.90	63.9	**2.8**	21.0	15.6	**9.8**
5.6	0.52	4.5	0.00	**7.9**	2.4	1.54	12.99	4.49	55.0	**1.2**	8.8	23.8	**7.8**
5.9	1.06	7.7	0.00	**2.8**	1.1	0.39	3.95	3.48	84.6	**2.1**	23.9	19.5	**5.8**
6.0	1.20	4.2	0.01	**6.3**	4.0	1.75	15.11	3.88	64.7	**2.5**	31.3	18.2	**6.9**
6.9	0.08	1.8	0.23	**9.0**	144.3	2.26	64.40	3.88	34.0	**0.5**	2.9	18.7	**6.8**
4.3	2.27	11.3	0.48	**4.0**	28.8	1.01	9.76	3.06	50.1	**2.8**	19.9	13.2	**6.9**
8.5	0.10	0.5	0.00	**7.8**	1.7	1.59	11.53	3.49	38.4	**4.5**	36.2	11.1	**8.4**
5.3	1.41	5.5	-0.02	**5.5**	2.9	1.19	12.08	3.34	67.1	**4.3**	31.9	10.7	**7.2**
6.0	0.70	5.5	0.00	**8.3**	3.0	2.07	20.54	3.65	45.8	**2.9**	43.8	24.0	**7.6**
8.1	0.08	1.6	0.01	**8.0**	0.5	2.03	20.53	4.45	54.7	**2.0**	26.9	21.2	**6.3**
8.0	0.13	0.9	0.20	**4.2**	1.8	1.35	15.88	4.04	65.1	**1.1**	26.2	26.4	**5.2**
4.1	2.84	7.8	-0.11	**10.0**	7.6	2.73	13.01	5.29	35.9	**0.9**	22.1	35.5	**10.0**
7.2	0.14	0.7	0.04	**6.1**	7.5	1.12	12.27	2.39	56.1	**1.7**	13.1	10.5	**7.5**
8.5	0.13	1.2	0.00	**7.4**	4.1	1.85	20.46	4.33	56.0	**2.6**	17.9	16.4	**6.6**
8.7	0.37	1.9	0.00	**6.0**	23.9	1.20	8.39	3.13	53.6	**1.7**	18.9	22.8	**9.7**
8.9	0.00	0.2	0.00	**1.1**	0.0	0.10	0.68	2.96	96.6	**4.5**	54.8	13.2	**6.1**
8.2	1.69	4.4	0.00	**5.7**	1.7	1.01	6.51	3.63	66.5	**2.2**	32.3	20.2	**8.4**
9.3	0.40	0.8	0.00	**7.3**	1.5	1.54	13.48	3.23	44.2	**2.5**	44.8	6.2	**7.1**
8.4	0.04	0.9	-0.16	**9.8**	4.1	3.11	23.22	4.41	43.5	**4.4**	19.7	6.4	**10.0**
5.0	1.31	8.0	0.03	**4.1**	2.9	0.88	9.87	2.98	70.4	**2.4**	32.2	21.7	**5.8**
2.3	2.52	12.5	0.69	**7.3**	0.6	1.25	12.59	4.94	58.9	**1.0**	12.4	12.4	**7.3**
5.8	1.84	5.7	0.02	**8.0**	5.4	1.99	13.26	3.83	46.8	**3.2**	26.6	7.6	**9.5**
7.1	0.02	0.6	0.34	**4.0**	0.7	1.08	9.56	2.96	72.0	**2.3**	31.3	22.1	**5.6**
5.9	0.34	3.6	0.24	**4.8**	97.9	1.04	15.10	3.00	53.5	**1.8**	10.8	3.6	**6.5**
6.5	0.35	2.4	-0.01	**3.4**	0.6	0.56	5.44	3.48	82.3	**2.6**	36.8	21.7	**6.3**
8.5	0.72	2.9	-0.03	**7.4**	18.4	1.46	16.96	3.65	56.3	**5.8**	37.7	7.1	**8.0**
4.9	1.63	8.2	0.01	**5.4**	17.9	1.11	10.43	3.29	64.4	**4.3**	19.2	7.3	**9.3**
8.5	0.24	0.5	-1.25	**4.6**	3.1	0.96	8.27	2.39	66.4	**6.1**	58.1	8.5	**7.6**
8.6	0.22	1.5	-0.10	**8.1**	10.0	2.04	24.21	3.52	52.4	**5.6**	39.9	7.4	**8.4**
6.2	0.67	2.5	0.06	**5.6**	1.6	1.15	12.16	3.40	64.3	**3.1**	29.6	16.0	**7.7**
8.3	0.02	0.2	0.00	**7.6**	1.2	1.96	18.67	4.95	56.0	**3.0**	23.7	15.0	**7.4**
3.7	1.84	9.9	-0.16	**8.1**	2.8	1.82	15.82	3.91	49.1	**3.5**	16.2	11.2	**8.7**
7.0	1.31	8.0	0.00	**2.2**	0.2	0.33	2.81	3.56	91.8	**2.1**	42.1	35.6	**6.3**
7.9	0.00	0.0	-0.06	**3.6**	4.5	0.90	8.45	2.80	61.2	**1.9**	17.5	12.3	**7.2**
6.2	0.92	6.4	0.02	**3.9**	0.7	0.77	6.31	2.26	70.7	**4.8**	58.7	15.4	**6.6**
10.0	na	0.0	na	**10.0**	0.5	11.14	15.06	1.33	84.3	**10.0**	324.6	0.0	**6.2**
5.3	1.24	9.2	0.30	**4.2**	0.6	0.73	9.76	4.14	76.5	**4.5**	16.3	5.3	**4.7**
3.6	2.88	13.8	0.00	**4.9**	1.4	1.29	13.99	3.04	66.0	**4.7**	32.5	8.9	**6.2**
6.2	1.32	6.3	-0.07	**3.2**	1.1	0.54	6.69	3.20	80.0	**4.7**	28.4	7.0	**4.4**
8.7	2.51	3.7	0.00	**2.0**	0.0	0.00	0.01	2.21	101.7	**4.5**	42.7	13.1	**7.5**
7.1	0.28	2.0	0.05	**6.1**	1.7	1.77	20.24	5.19	58.7	**3.0**	16.8	13.6	**4.3**
8.0	0.03	0.3	0.08	**7.8**	5.0	1.72	15.11	3.70	57.8	**4.3**	22.1	7.5	**9.8**
9.0	0.20	1.0	0.00	**6.0**	12.3	1.39	12.23	3.29	67.3	**3.2**	26.2	10.8	**9.4**
4.0	2.15	12.1	0.04	**2.9**	0.1	0.35	3.78	3.67	83.0	**3.8**	20.0	10.7	**4.6**
4.6	1.60	9.7	0.05	**5.6**	4.8	0.97	10.67	3.19	65.0	**5.7**	26.3	2.8	**8.4**
8.5	0.00	0.0	0.00	**4.1**	0.2	1.23	13.47	3.06	69.7	**4.5**	49.3	14.3	**4.4**
5.3	0.87	9.1	0.00	**6.9**	0.9	1.53	16.33	4.27	60.0	**1.6**	12.1	16.9	**5.9**
6.6	0.51	2.7	0.05	**7.8**	4.1	1.95	24.89	3.97	55.8	**1.3**	14.7	26.8	**6.0**
8.6	0.00	0.0	0.00	**0.0**	-1.5	-0.91	-5.84	1.30	130.6	**2.5**	46.0	13.3	**6.2**

							One	Asset Mix (As a % of Total Assets)						Risk-
Name	City	State	Rating	2020 Rating	2019 Rating	Total Assets ($Mil)	Year Asset Growth	Commercial Loans	Consumer Loans	Mortgage Loans	Securities	Capitalization Index	Leverage Ratio	Based Capital Ratio
DeMotte State Bank	Demotte	IN	**B+**	B+	B+	530.7	10.65	9.8	0.6	9.3	38.8	**10.0**	11.4	21.6
Denali State Bank	Fairbanks	AK	**B**	B	B-	454.2	20.54	22.4	7.6	5.5	28.1	**8.2**	9.8	16.6
▲ Denmark State Bank	Denmark	WI	**B**	B-	B	655.0	6.10	15.7	1.5	6.8	5.6	**6.8**	8.8	13.6
▲ Denver Savings Bank	Denver	IA	**B**	C+	C	214.6	15.22	12.9	1.0	9.7	25.7	**8.9**	10.8	0.0
Department Stores National Bank	Sioux Falls	SD	**B**	B	B+	709.7	119.79	0.0	5.7	0.0	0.0	**10.0**	62.6	247.1
Desjardins Bank, N.A.	Hallandale Beach	FL	**C+**	B-	B-	269.2	21.22	1.5	3.0	54.4	8.3	**10.0**	12.3	0.0
Deutsche Bank National Trust Co.	Los Angeles	CA	**U**	U	U	366.5	19.48	0.0	0.0	0.0	28.0	**10.0**	67.5	0.0
Deutsche Bank Trust Co. Americas	New York	NY	**B+**	B+	A	42726.0	-5.49	6.6	0.7	5.0	1.8	**10.0**	24.7	64.2
▼ Deutsche Bank Trust Co. Delaware	Wilmington	DE	**A-**	A+	A+	118.1	-61.11	0.0	0.0	0.0	0.0	**10.0**	93.1	0.0
Deutsche Bank Trust Co., N.A.	New York	NY	**U**	U	U	169.4	9.44	0.0	0.0	0.0	62.6	**10.0**	86.9	0.0
Devon Bank	Chicago	IL	**C+**	C+	C	434.6	21.76	10.2	1.4	10.9	36.7	**4.8**	6.8	11.3
▲ Dewey Bank	Dewey	IL	**C**	C-	C-	28.7	8.59	12.0	2.2	12.3	19.6	**5.1**	7.1	13.0
DeWitt Savings Bank	Clinton	IL	**B-**	B-	B-	139.8	6.55	0.3	15.7	25.7	38.6	**10.0**	11.7	25.3
Diamond Bank	Glenwood	AR	**B**	B	B	731.2	6.73	6.7	2.0	16.1	21.9	**8.4**	9.9	16.5
▲ Dickinson County Bank	Enterprise	KS	**D+**	D-	E+	17.3	-0.83	10.5	4.9	31.9	0.0	**9.2**	10.5	21.3
Dieterich Bank	Effingham	IL	**B-**	B-	B-	1266.5	50.00	5.1	1.1	7.1	29.9	**5.3**	7.3	12.0
Dilley State Bank	Dilley	TX	**B-**	B-	B+	128.1	-10.88	0.9	0.7	0.1	63.7	**8.0**	9.7	0.0
▲ Dime Bank	Norwich	CT	**B**	B-	B-	1069.4	11.38	7.0	0.1	22.7	31.5	**10.0**	11.3	19.8
Dime Community Bank	Bridgehampton	NY	**B-**	B	B+	12688.4	106.30	10.6	0.2	5.0	9.9	**7.4**	9.2	13.7
▲ Discover Bank	Greenwood	DE	**C-**	D+	D+	108936.3	-2.94	0.2	78.4	1.8	8.1	**10.0**	12.2	17.8
Dixon Bank	Dixon	KY	**C**	C+	B	83.6	3.99	1.7	1.6	7.7	45.0	**10.0**	25.1	0.0
DMB Community Bank	De Forest	WI	**A-**	A-	A-	606.7	12.53	0.4	0.3	19.0	11.7	**10.0**	11.8	18.1
▲ DNB National Bank	Clear Lake	SD	**B+**	B-	C+	105.8	21.60	12.5	1.9	5.3	54.0	**6.9**	8.9	27.8
Dogwood State Bank	Raleigh	NC	**C-**	D+	D+	807.9	37.17	26.8	0.2	6.3	9.0	**10.0**	14.6	22.1
▼ Dollar Bank, A Federal Savings Bank	Pittsburgh	PA	**B-**	B	B	10215.8	3.76	7.4	2.6	43.0	19.6	**7.9**	9.6	17.7
Dominion Bank	Dallas	TX	**D+**	D+	C	384.1	44.71	55.0	0.4	2.8	0.8	**10.0**	15.4	17.4
Douglas National Bank	Douglas	GA	**A**	A	A	242.3	5.51	11.3	1.9	16.3	9.2	**8.7**	10.1	17.3
▲ DR Bank	Darien	CT	**D**	D-	D-	431.8	5.14	12.7	16.3	30.3	9.1	**8.8**	10.2	14.7
▲ Drake Bank	Saint Paul	MN	**B-**	C+	C+	182.4	8.80	32.1	1.0	10.8	7.3	**6.8**	8.9	0.0
Drummond Community Bank	Chiefland	FL	**A-**	A-	A-	917.7	17.84	7.7	5.3	10.8	40.8	**8.7**	10.1	0.0
DSRM National Bank	Albuquerque	NM	**U**	U	U	4.1	5.06	0.0	0.0	0.0	73.9	**10.0**	83.0	0.0
Du Quoin State Bank	Du Quoin	IL	**B**	B+	B+	130.9	10.89	4.7	1.5	11.7	71.0	**6.4**	8.4	23.7
Dubuque Bank and Trust Co.	Dubuque	IA	**B+**	B+	B+	1990.0	7.63	15.4	0.8	3.5	33.6	**6.6**	8.7	14.1
Dundee Bank	Omaha	NE	**B-**	B-	B-	436.5	17.93	15.6	0.1	21.4	8.1	**5.2**	8.8	0.0
Durand State Bank	Durand	IL	**B-**	B-	B	128.6	11.19	4.6	1.6	9.2	27.5	**8.2**	9.8	19.7
Durden Banking Co., Inc.	Twin City	GA	**A**	A	A	231.0	15.56	10.3	4.6	22.8	16.5	**10.0**	14.2	30.1
Dysart State Bank	Dysart	IA	**D**	D	D-	17.7	26.66	6.8	1.1	21.3	5.8	**5.7**	7.7	17.9
E*TRADE Bank	Arlington	VA	**B**	B	B	77868.2	53.12	0.0	1.5	0.1	65.5	**6.2**	8.2	53.1
E*TRADE Savings Bank	Arlington	VA	**B**	B	B	9833.0	105.29	0.0	11.7	0.0	69.6	**10.0**	16.2	113.4
▲ Eagle Bank	Everett	MA	**B-**	C+	B-	524.0	6.57	11.3	0.1	26.4	19.4	**10.0**	12.2	0.0
Eagle Bank	Glenwood	MN	**A-**	A	A	204.3	11.34	10.9	3.7	10.9	27.8	**10.0**	11.3	21.8
▲ Eagle Bank	Polson	MT	**A-**	B+	B+	94.7	12.33	10.0	2.2	10.8	27.8	**9.2**	10.4	0.0
Eagle Bank and Trust Co.	Little Rock	AR	**A**	A-	B	476.4	11.49	1.8	0.5	19.9	42.7	**10.0**	14.0	0.0
▼ Eagle.Bank	Cincinnati	OH	**B+**	A-	B-	167.2	8.26	5.0	0.0	42.6	0.0	**10.0**	15.3	17.8
EagleBank	Bethesda	MD	**A-**	A-	A	10934.4	11.78	11.8	0.0	2.6	15.2	**10.0**	11.7	17.1
Eaglemark Savings Bank	Reno	NV	**A-**	A-	A-	362.2	314.85	0.0	78.8	0.0	0.0	**10.0**	19.4	15.1
Earlham Savings Bank	West Des Moines	IA	**C**	C	C	373.8	10.39	10.0	1.4	9.4	46.7	**5.6**	7.6	18.2
East Boston Savings Bank	East Boston	MA	**B+**	B	B	6286.4	-2.04	2.4	0.2	7.9	0.2	**8.0**	11.3	0.0
East Cambridge Savings Bank	Cambridge	MA	**C+**	C+	C+	1248.2	6.42	3.7	0.8	39.0	9.5	**9.6**	10.8	17.0
East West Bank	Pasadena	CA	**A-**	A-	A-	59838.9	21.11	16.7	0.0	15.5	14.0	**6.7**	8.7	13.4
East Wisconsin Savings Bank	Kaukauna	WI	**D+**	D+	D+	293.6	14.63	2.1	14.2	40.0	33.9	**6.0**	8.1	17.1
▼ Eastbank, N.A.	New York	NY	**C-**	C+	B-	169.5	-2.56	0.7	0.0	10.1	24.2	**10.0**	20.0	31.0
Eastern Bank	Boston	MA	**B+**	B	B+	17035.4	21.75	13.0	1.3	10.3	28.5	**10.0**	13.9	22.1
Eastern Connecticut Savings Bank	Norwich	CT	**D**	D	D+	236.7	11.25	7.2	1.7	48.8	0.1	**4.8**	6.8	11.2
Eastern International Bank	Los Angeles	CA	**C+**	C+	B	137.3	-2.98	0.0	0.0	0.1	12.1	**10.0**	14.9	0.0
Eastern Michigan Bank	Croswell	MI	**B**	B	B	502.2	14.07	15.3	2.8	6.6	28.9	**8.3**	9.9	18.8
Eastern National Bank	Miami	FL	**D-**	D	D+	320.1	-6.28	12.7	0.2	18.2	0.9	**5.0**	7.0	12.1
Eastern Savings Bank FSB	Hunt Valley	MD	**B**	B	B	340.0	4.04	4.3	0.0	39.2	0.0	**10.0**	25.2	41.9
▲ Easthampton Savings Bank	Easthampton	MA	**B**	B-	B-	1650.1	2.49	10.6	0.3	23.5	9.9	**7.2**	9.1	0.0
▲ Eaton Community Bank	Charlotte	MI	**B-**	C+	B-	442.4	11.07	3.3	1.8	22.5	41.0	**10.0**	13.3	0.0

Asset Quality Index	Adjusted Non-Performing Loans as a % of Total Loans	Adjusted Non-Performing Loans as a % of Capital	Net Charge-Offs Avg Loans	Profitability Index	Net Income ($Mil)	Return on Assets (R.O.A.)	Return on Equity (R.O.E.)	Net Interest Spread	Overhead Efficiency Ratio	Liquidity Index	Liquidity Ratio	Hot Money Ratio	Stability Index
7.1	1.28	4.5	-0.20	**4.7**	2.4	0.93	8.33	3.27	66.3	**6.2**	55.1	7.2	**7.1**
5.5	1.49	4.6	0.08	**6.1**	2.7	1.34	12.79	4.45	60.5	**5.5**	33.4	3.9	**5.3**
7.5	0.56	2.4	-0.01	**4.9**	3.2	0.97	11.00	3.13	66.5	**4.2**	23.0	8.1	**6.6**
8.4	0.10	0.5	0.00	**6.5**	1.5	1.53	13.39	4.24	52.2	**1.7**	34.8	33.1	**6.3**
9.4	0.84	0.1	0.44	**4.1**	2.2	0.61	0.96	1.27	45.2	**5.0**	247.7	99.9	**7.6**
8.8	0.87	3.2	0.00	**2.4**	0.2	0.12	0.97	3.05	95.1	**5.4**	40.6	7.4	**7.1**
10.0	na	0.0	na	**6.5**	1.1	0.58	0.86	0.65	99.0	**4.0**	225.3	0.0	**6.3**
9.5	0.71	0.9	0.02	**3.2**	25.0	0.13	0.54	0.73	93.5	**8.1**	83.0	0.4	**9.1**
10.0	0.00	0.0	0.00	**9.4**	1.1	1.80	2.01	0.11	79.3	**4.0**	na	100.0	**5.7**
10.0	na	0.0	na	**9.5**	4.1	5.08	5.79	0.88	77.7	**4.0**	na	0.0	**6.3**
5.4	1.00	4.3	-0.07	**3.9**	1.6	0.79	11.17	2.68	82.4	**3.0**	36.4	18.7	**3.8**
6.2	0.00	0.2	0.00	**3.4**	0.1	0.79	7.78	3.98	78.8	**4.4**	21.3	6.6	**4.2**
6.9	0.80	2.9	0.13	**3.4**	0.4	0.54	4.42	2.91	78.8	**5.4**	48.9	10.0	**6.8**
5.2	1.55	6.3	0.09	**5.1**	4.7	1.30	12.44	3.63	60.3	**1.6**	14.8	23.4	**7.9**
5.0	2.46	7.9	0.00	**3.4**	0.1	1.42	13.93	2.90	62.7	**2.2**	40.1	24.3	**3.8**
6.0	0.85	3.6	0.19	**4.2**	5.1	0.82	8.99	2.69	60.3	**5.7**	32.9	6.3	**6.9**
9.1	0.02	0.1	-0.04	**2.8**	0.2	0.34	3.33	1.55	68.1	**6.7**	75.6	8.0	**5.9**
7.0	1.49	5.2	-0.04	**4.0**	4.7	0.90	8.49	2.54	74.1	**4.4**	34.3	14.0	**8.2**
5.2	0.49	3.8	0.11	**4.2**	35.0	0.60	6.32	3.18	68.3	**3.6**	17.0	8.1	**8.3**
2.7	2.09	8.1	2.28	**8.9**	2760.5	4.96	49.48	8.54	36.6	**2.0**	25.6	9.9	**10.0**
9.3	1.91	1.6	-0.14	**2.1**	0.0	0.05	0.18	1.68	96.8	**4.2**	88.4	23.5	**7.2**
7.5	0.00	0.0	0.00	**6.5**	3.9	1.37	11.38	3.16	47.9	**0.7**	15.5	22.9	**8.1**
9.3	0.00	0.0	0.00	**6.9**	1.5	2.99	31.91	6.90	57.4	**4.9**	52.6	13.8	**5.6**
8.0	0.13	0.7	0.04	**2.2**	2.6	0.71	4.76	3.44	73.4	**3.0**	24.0	9.4	**7.4**
6.1	1.50	8.8	0.08	**3.0**	20.2	0.40	3.72	2.52	79.4	**4.5**	23.8	6.4	**7.0**
7.9	0.01	0.1	0.02	**0.8**	0.4	0.23	1.82	3.02	78.2	**3.4**	16.3	12.2	**5.8**
6.6	1.41	3.4	-0.01	**9.8**	3.1	2.61	26.12	4.36	48.0	**4.0**	35.9	13.4	**8.3**
7.5	0.00	0.0	0.04	**1.3**	0.8	0.36	3.84	3.17	83.4	**0.8**	14.9	35.4	**7.1**
8.4	0.00	0.0	0.28	**4.9**	1.0	1.18	15.03	4.54	69.9	**2.6**	30.5	18.9	**4.7**
8.1	0.43	1.5	0.04	**6.0**	5.4	1.25	11.10	3.51	66.8	**5.3**	38.7	7.2	**8.2**
10.0	na	0.0	na	**5.8**	0.0	0.93	1.13	0.85	89.6	**4.0**	na	100.0	**4.8**
9.0	0.37	0.4	-0.02	**4.2**	0.6	0.96	7.06	3.37	68.8	**4.1**	73.4	23.7	**7.9**
5.4	2.04	9.0	0.16	**7.3**	12.7	1.33	14.12	2.90	56.8	**6.8**	42.0	2.2	**7.9**
4.7	0.31	8.0	0.01	**9.3**	7.2	3.47	38.50	4.61	45.0	**1.0**	12.2	26.4	**6.6**
5.8	2.72	6.3	-0.03	**3.5**	0.4	0.63	6.15	2.96	72.8	**5.0**	39.9	10.1	**5.8**
8.4	0.31	1.4	-0.08	**9.5**	3.4	3.04	20.67	5.80	49.1	**3.8**	29.7	12.6	**9.3**
5.6	1.32	8.0	0.00	**3.4**	0.1	1.09	14.31	2.10	71.2	**6.4**	48.0	0.0	**1.3**
7.9	0.33	0.6	0.00	**3.5**	175.4	0.45	5.49	1.14	63.0	**3.5**	82.9	0.0	**6.4**
7.7	0.00	0.0	0.00	**1.6**	-2.4	-0.05	-0.26	1.52	105.2	**3.7**	104.5	0.0	**7.6**
8.9	0.24	1.4	0.00	**4.3**	2.4	0.96	8.48	3.22	75.8	**2.1**	29.4	17.4	**7.7**
8.6	0.01	0.1	0.02	**5.4**	1.2	1.17	9.77	2.75	63.9	**5.8**	34.7	2.6	**9.0**
8.6	0.03	0.1	-0.04	**9.4**	0.8	1.60	15.05	4.54	50.6	**2.0**	25.7	9.4	**7.3**
9.6	0.62	0.9	0.08	**8.1**	4.4	1.89	12.89	3.40	80.1	**5.4**	47.3	9.6	**8.0**
8.6	0.73	2.7	0.43	**4.4**	0.6	0.75	4.91	3.05	80.9	**3.3**	26.3	14.2	**8.5**
5.8	0.68	3.3	0.28	**9.1**	97.8	1.71	14.20	3.13	35.8	**2.4**	31.6	3.7	**10.0**
5.6	0.00	0.0	0.00	**10.0**	4.6	4.46	31.39	9.01	56.9	**0.4**	20.8	0.2	**9.5**
7.9	0.00	0.7	-0.04	**2.7**	0.6	0.32	4.17	2.62	85.9	**6.6**	55.7	4.3	**3.7**
7.2	0.24	1.3	0.00	**5.9**	41.8	1.28	11.08	3.10	51.7	**2.9**	20.2	12.8	**9.1**
9.0	0.04	0.3	0.01	**3.4**	4.1	0.67	6.51	3.06	72.1	**2.0**	19.4	20.4	**7.7**
6.5	0.82	4.5	0.13	**7.1**	433.1	1.53	16.86	2.72	43.2	**3.5**	29.3	12.7	**9.0**
7.5	0.23	1.1	0.02	**1.9**	0.7	0.51	6.35	2.36	88.2	**2.8**	38.8	21.1	**3.7**
7.9	0.00	0.0	0.00	**1.2**	-0.1	-0.15	-0.71	2.93	105.1	**2.4**	49.0	40.7	**6.9**
7.8	0.76	1.9	0.07	**5.3**	85.7	1.04	6.46	2.67	65.2	**7.1**	44.0	0.8	**9.1**
2.1	2.57	24.2	0.00	**2.8**	0.6	0.48	6.78	3.60	84.6	**2.2**	6.1	17.0	**3.2**
7.5	0.00	0.0	0.00	**2.2**	0.1	0.16	1.12	3.01	93.7	**1.3**	31.4	52.4	**7.4**
8.5	0.78	1.1	-0.01	**4.9**	2.6	1.02	11.82	2.64	61.1	**6.9**	54.0	1.8	**5.2**
3.7	3.10	13.8	-0.29	**0.0**	-0.7	-0.44	-6.23	3.01	132.6	**1.6**	35.0	43.1	**2.4**
4.2	4.33	13.8	-0.01	**5.1**	2.0	1.18	4.75	5.10	81.2	**3.4**	36.4	16.8	**8.7**
7.7	0.44	3.0	0.00	**4.8**	8.2	1.02	11.18	2.98	57.9	**2.2**	23.7	22.4	**7.1**
8.7	1.21	2.6	-0.01	**3.5**	1.6	0.73	5.18	2.69	72.4	**6.0**	58.8	9.2	**7.5**

	Name	City	State	Rating	2020 Rating	2019 Rating	Total Assets ($Mil)	One Year Asset Growth	Comm-ercial Loans	Cons-umer Loans	Mort-gage Loans	Secur-ities	Capital-ization Index	Lever-age Ratio	Risk-Based Capital Ratio
	Eclipse Bank, Inc.	Louisville	KY	**B-**	B-	C+	258.9	24.21	3.4	0.4	24.8	14.8	**7.8**	10.0	13.2
	Edison National Bank	Fort Myers	FL	**B-**	B-	B-	528.4	41.32	4.7	0.8	14.7	8.9	**5.2**	7.2	26.3
	Edmonton State Bank	Edmonton	KY	**A**	A	A-	699.8	12.46	6.9	7.1	14.0	7.8	**10.0**	12.6	0.0
	Edward Jones Trust Co.	Saint Louis	MO	**U**	U	U	112.1	8.35	0.0	0.0	0.0	0.1	**10.0**	93.8	369.2
	EH National Bank	Beverly Hills	CA	**C-**	C-	C	332.5	22.16	6.3	0.1	3.0	3.9	**8.8**	10.2	15.7
	El Dorado Savings Bank, F.S.B.	Placerville	CA	**C+**	C+	B	2699.1	13.68	0.0	0.0	20.0	51.9	**7.8**	9.6	38.6
	Elberton Federal S&L Assn.	Elberton	GA	**C-**	C-	C-	29.3	11.60	0.0	0.5	72.2	10.1	**10.0**	17.4	0.0
	Elderton State Bank	Elderton	PA	**B**	B	B+	333.8	6.34	14.1	0.8	12.4	7.3	**10.0**	11.2	0.0
	Elgin State Bank	Elgin	IA	**D**	D-	D-	32.2	31.56	3.9	2.3	13.5	17.2	**4.4**	6.4	15.0
	Elizabethton Federal Savings Bank	Elizabethton	TN	**A-**	A-	A	318.5	4.53	0.0	0.6	33.0	39.6	**10.0**	39.7	0.0
	Elkhorn Valley Bank & Trust	Norfolk	NE	**B+**	B+	B	1005.0	18.50	11.9	2.1	5.9	19.2	**10.0**	11.5	18.5
	Elkton Bank & Trust Co.	Elkton	KY	**B+**	B+	A-	165.6	7.56	4.6	3.4	13.5	50.0	**10.0**	12.0	25.8
	Elmira Savings Bank	Elmira	NY	**C+**	C+	C+	648.9	-4.02	4.8	4.6	46.7	1.8	**6.2**	8.2	15.0
▼	Elysian Bank	Elysian	MN	**B**	A-	B+	62.2	16.35	7.0	6.9	19.9	10.1	**8.9**	10.3	18.3
	Embassy Bank for the Lehigh Valley	Bethlehem	PA	**B**	B	B	1515.7	10.73	5.8	0.0	45.4	14.5	**5.7**	7.7	13.2
	Embassy National Bank	Lawrenceville	GA	**A**	A	A	119.5	8.76	7.5	0.0	1.9	0.0	**10.0**	15.7	24.4
	Emerald Bank	Burden	KS	**C-**	C-	D+	21.6	12.74	6.8	6.4	27.2	12.4	**8.2**	9.8	21.1
	Emigrant Bank	New York	NY	**B-**	B-	B-	5748.0	-15.53	34.7	0.7	12.0	5.6	**10.0**	20.6	21.3
	Emigrant Mercantile Bank	New York	NY	**U**	U	U	3.4	-0.90	0.0	0.0	0.0	0.0	**10.0**	85.2	424.3
▲	Empire State Bank	Newburgh	NY	**C+**	C-	C	516.5	0.91	14.2	0.0	34.0	0.9	**7.9**	9.6	16.9
	Emprise Bank	Wichita	KS	**B**	B	B+	2345.8	13.82	9.3	1.9	14.1	27.2	**5.4**	7.4	13.4
	Encore Bank	Little Rock	AR	**D**	D+	D+	1129.8	93.17	11.9	0.3	15.2	14.8	**6.6**	11.7	0.0
▲	Endeavor Bank	San Diego	CA	**C-**	D	D	463.9	26.41	46.8	0.5	3.6	0.0	**7.5**	9.5	12.9
	EnerBank USA	Salt Lake City	UT	**B+**	B+	B+	3074.8	8.27	0.0	95.6	0.0	1.1	**7.8**	12.6	0.0
	Englewood Bank & Trust	Englewood	FL	**A-**	A-	A-	505.7	34.70	2.2	0.7	11.5	19.4	**5.5**	7.5	19.9
	Ennis State Bank	Ennis	TX	**A-**	B+	B+	316.1	7.88	14.2	0.6	7.6	24.7	**7.0**	9.0	0.0
	Enterprise Bank	Omaha	NE	**B-**	B-	B-	429.0	4.30	12.3	0.6	3.1	1.9	**6.3**	8.7	12.0
	Enterprise Bank	Allison Park	PA	**D-**	D-	D-	383.7	-6.33	13.0	0.0	3.1	0.0	**5.6**	8.6	11.4
	Enterprise Bank & Trust	Clayton	MO	**A-**	A-	B+	10311.6	23.74	28.1	1.3	2.5	14.9	**7.5**	9.3	13.4
	Enterprise Bank and Trust Co.	Lowell	MA	**B**	B	B	4428.0	9.68	12.4	0.2	9.1	14.3	**6.8**	8.8	14.5
▲	Enterprise Bank of South Carolina	Ehrhardt	SC	**C+**	C-	C-	439.9	13.66	8.2	3.1	14.3	31.6	**5.8**	7.8	16.7
	Envision Bank	Stoughton	MA	**C+**	C	C	744.1	2.58	2.1	1.2	48.5	6.8	**10.0**	12.6	16.8
	Ephrata National Bank	Ephrata	PA	**B**	B-	B	1577.4	21.45	6.2	0.3	19.2	37.0	**7.3**	9.2	15.6
	Equitable Bank	Grand Island	NE	**B-**	C+	C+	422.5	7.14	16.0	1.0	15.5	5.2	**6.7**	8.7	12.5
	Equitable S&L Assn.	Sterling	CO	**B**	B	B	169.5	3.34	0.0	0.7	79.5	4.9	**10.0**	16.0	30.3
▲	Equity Bank	Andover	KS	**B-**	C	C+	4267.4	1.56	16.6	1.3	14.6	24.4	**8.3**	9.9	15.6
	Ergo Bank	Markesan	WI	**B-**	B-	B-	128.5	21.26	17.4	0.6	7.7	16.5	**6.7**	9.6	0.0
	ESB Bank	Caledonia	MN	**A-**	B+	C+	144.6	13.53	10.8	3.4	10.2	6.7	**6.0**	8.8	0.0
	ESB Financial	Emporia	KS	**C**	C	C+	338.9	13.57	8.2	1.0	14.6	16.7	**6.0**	8.0	14.1
▲	Esquire Bank, N.A.	Jericho	NY	**A+**	A	A	1051.8	25.11	35.2	3.4	4.2	12.0	**10.0**	12.3	17.9
	ESSA Bank & Trust	Stroudsburg	PA	**C+**	C+	C+	1815.5	-9.50	5.1	1.1	35.3	9.2	**7.6**	9.4	14.3
▲	Essex Bank	Richmond	VA	**A-**	B+	B+	1754.1	8.62	12.4	0.5	7.1	19.5	**8.9**	10.3	14.1
	Essex Savings Bank	Essex	CT	**C**	C	B-	534.6	13.28	5.8	0.2	34.6	1.8	**6.6**	8.6	0.0
	ETHIC	Boston	MA	**D-**	D-	D	248.2	-9.91	0.9	10.6	40.2	0.0	**7.5**	9.3	14.9
▲	Eureka Homestead	Metairie	LA	**C+**	C	C	107.0	2.02	0.0	0.2	65.3	5.2	**10.0**	18.7	39.3
	Eureka Savings Bank	La Salle	IL	**C+**	C+	C+	417.2	16.28	2.8	0.6	32.7	43.6	**10.0**	19.0	0.0
	EvaBank	Cullman	AL	**B**	B	B-	423.9	0.85	1.8	3.8	26.0	20.7	**10.0**	25.1	0.0
▲	Evans Bank, N.A.	Angola	NY	**B**	B-	B-	2144.6	4.66	15.7	0.0	19.2	10.9	**7.0**	9.0	14.3
	Evercore Trust Co., N.A.	New York	NY	**U**	U	U	13.1	-1.51	0.0	0.0	0.0	77.2	**10.0**	97.2	950.4
	Everence Trust Co.	Goshen	IN	**U**	U	U	11.4	12.43	0.0	0.0	0.0	51.9	**10.0**	116.	297.1
	Everett Co-operative Bank	Everett	MA	**B+**	B+	B+	629.6	15.80	1.4	0.1	40.3	10.5	**10.0**	12.1	18.2
	Evergreen Bank Group	Oak Brook	IL	**A-**	B+	B+	1215.2	-3.54	2.6	54.3	2.4	8.0	**10.0**	12.2	15.3
	Evergreen Federal Bank	Grants Pass	OR	**B**	B	B	610.9	13.92	1.2	0.2	21.2	9.1	**9.9**	10.9	0.0
	Evergreen National Bank	Evergreen	CO	**C+**	C+	C+	142.7	8.93	8.2	0.5	11.1	21.7	**6.5**	8.5	0.0
	EverTrust Bank	Pasadena	CA	**A-**	B+	B+	1029.7	12.06	8.8	0.0	6.5	8.9	**10.0**	16.9	0.0
	Evolve Bank & Trust	Memphis	TN	**B-**	B-	B-	711.7	17.90	16.0	0.7	28.0	2.1	**8.6**	10.1	14.4
	Exchange Bank	Milledgeville	GA	**A-**	A-	A-	332.7	13.92	3.4	0.7	14.1	36.6	**10.0**	11.9	0.0
▲	Exchange Bank	Kearney	NE	**A-**	B+	B+	1183.2	7.60	7.2	0.6	10.0	26.3	**7.0**	9.8	0.0
	Exchange Bank & Trust	Atchison	KS	**A-**	A-	A-	537.9	13.13	9.1	12.6	12.1	25.4	**8.2**	9.8	0.0
▼	Exchange Bank (Santa Rosa, CA)	Santa Rosa	CA	**A-**	A	A	3434.0	13.12	9.5	1.3	9.4	32.1	**7.4**	9.3	19.7

Asset Quality Index	Adjusted Non-Performing Loans as a % of Total Loans	Adjusted Non-Performing Loans as a % of Capital	Net Charge-Offs Avg Loans	Profitability Index	Net Income ($Mil)	Return on Assets (R.O.A.)	Return on Equity (R.O.E.)	Net Interest Spread	Overhead Efficiency Ratio	Liquidity Index	Liquidity Ratio	Hot Money Ratio	Stability Index
5.3	1.28	6.0	-0.01	4.4	1.2	0.95	9.74	3.17	73.1	0.9	21.0	31.1	5.4
9.8	0.00	0.0	0.00	3.4	1.4	0.61	8.25	2.17	73.6	7.3	66.3	2.2	3.7
7.3	0.48	3.0	0.00	9.0	7.8	2.28	18.02	3.40	47.9	4.0	29.7	11.4	10.0
10.0	na	0.0	na	9.5	3.7	6.77	7.26	1.13	78.2	4.0	na	0.0	6.7
1.7	3.03	14.0	-0.30	2.5	0.6	0.36	2.90	3.56	86.3	3.5	29.8	14.4	7.0
10.0	0.74	1.1	0.01	2.8	4.0	0.30	3.04	1.46	80.8	6.9	83.9	9.8	7.0
8.8	1.00	4.2	0.00	1.1	0.0	-0.13	-0.74	2.97	101.6	1.7	27.3	27.1	6.3
3.8	4.50	18.6	-0.10	6.0	2.1	1.26	11.24	3.45	49.4	2.7	13.9	15.2	7.5
9.0	0.00	0.0	0.00	2.8	0.1	0.70	11.51	3.52	82.4	6.1	44.4	4.0	1.0
10.0	0.00	0.1	0.00	5.5	1.5	0.97	2.44	2.26	47.9	4.7	89.7	20.5	8.4
8.4	0.27	1.4	-0.01	5.1	5.4	1.12	9.52	2.75	56.0	5.6	36.4	7.8	8.5
9.3	0.21	0.6	0.09	5.0	0.9	1.05	8.24	2.95	63.9	4.8	56.3	15.2	7.4
4.3	1.29	8.2	0.05	4.2	2.6	0.80	8.48	3.52	71.0	2.5	20.3	16.9	6.7
3.4	2.94	15.0	-0.02	8.1	0.5	1.68	16.23	3.75	60.8	6.4	39.1	0.2	7.8
9.3	0.29	1.7	0.00	4.9	8.3	1.14	14.65	3.03	51.0	3.9	15.1	9.6	6.9
7.3	0.00	0.0	0.00	7.8	0.9	1.56	9.89	3.92	70.3	1.9	33.3	30.2	9.3
5.2	1.48	8.9	0.36	3.9	0.1	0.88	9.00	3.87	71.8	4.7	48.0	11.0	3.7
3.1	4.98	16.7	-0.03	6.4	34.7	1.21	5.83	3.64	79.6	2.1	14.1	5.7	10.0
10.0	na	0.0	na	0.1	0.0	-0.53	-0.62	1.12	163.2	4.0	na	0.0	6.4
6.0	0.54	3.9	0.11	4.3	2.5	0.98	10.75	3.63	62.1	3.1	10.6	13.1	5.1
8.4	0.30	1.6	0.03	5.1	13.0	1.16	13.44	2.90	66.4	6.0	39.9	4.5	7.5
8.7	0.03	0.1	0.01	0.8	1.1	0.23	2.29	2.73	90.7	2.0	23.9	5.1	6.5
8.2	0.00	0.0	0.00	3.1	2.0	0.85	14.47	3.16	61.0	5.3	22.6	1.0	4.6
5.5	0.02	1.2	1.01	10.0	55.4	3.55	35.10	7.16	34.6	0.2	5.9	9.8	9.5
9.4	0.36	0.9	-0.01	6.1	2.7	1.17	14.92	2.39	63.2	7.5	64.4	0.6	7.5
7.5	0.57	1.6	-0.01	7.6	2.8	1.82	18.82	4.05	59.9	5.2	34.8	6.7	7.6
7.3	0.00	0.0	0.00	4.4	2.0	0.93	10.75	2.65	57.0	0.8	20.6	36.2	5.4
0.3	3.77	32.4	0.11	4.2	1.6	0.84	10.38	3.59	70.0	0.7	13.2	3.3	4.5
6.3	0.60	3.1	0.18	7.2	73.3	1.46	12.24	3.58	53.1	4.6	22.6	3.5	9.4
5.3	1.40	8.1	0.13	5.7	23.7	1.13	11.99	3.60	60.8	4.7	18.8	3.5	8.0
4.1	1.96	9.1	-0.08	4.0	1.8	0.88	10.74	3.25	76.5	5.2	37.2	7.7	4.9
5.6	1.30	7.4	0.01	7.2	5.7	1.54	12.63	2.98	76.3	1.5	12.7	14.5	8.0
8.9	0.57	1.9	0.00	4.6	8.4	1.11	11.65	2.84	65.5	6.5	39.1	2.9	8.0
5.3	0.67	4.6	0.00	4.3	2.0	0.94	10.36	3.28	73.0	3.3	13.3	12.3	5.7
9.9	0.00	0.0	0.00	3.5	0.5	0.57	3.61	3.04	80.5	2.0	21.4	19.6	8.0
4.6	2.01	10.9	0.05	4.9	33.9	1.63	14.90	3.58	57.8	3.2	11.2	11.4	6.9
4.5	3.27	11.3	0.00	4.0	0.4	0.63	6.34	4.36	69.5	3.9	25.1	6.6	5.5
8.3	0.00	0.0	0.00	8.6	1.7	2.43	24.84	3.43	44.7	3.5	24.1	12.7	7.5
2.6	5.05	23.6	-0.01	3.5	1.1	0.68	8.36	2.90	75.6	5.0	35.0	8.0	4.4
8.1	0.32	1.7	0.01	10.0	9.6	2.02	16.61	4.45	50.7	6.6	34.7	1.1	9.8
4.8	1.93	11.5	-0.01	3.8	8.5	0.89	8.85	2.93	65.0	1.7	11.8	6.4	7.8
8.4	0.30	2.2	-0.01	6.7	12.5	1.48	14.13	3.63	56.5	2.3	25.1	21.0	8.8
2.8	1.96	11.6	0.06	3.2	1.3	0.51	4.93	2.83	88.3	5.5	36.9	5.5	5.8
5.3	1.26	6.6	-0.36	0.0	-2.5	-1.95	-20.42	3.78	162.5	0.7	16.3	56.1	3.4
10.0	0.00	0.0	-0.02	2.8	0.3	0.54	2.87	1.82	80.8	0.7	26.4	76.1	7.3
8.2	1.33	3.3	0.00	2.7	0.7	0.37	1.78	2.31	80.1	6.3	64.7	8.6	6.7
4.7	4.55	9.5	0.12	10.0	5.6	2.76	9.82	6.10	38.3	1.6	34.1	28.3	9.1
4.8	1.68	10.4	0.00	5.7	12.1	1.15	13.08	3.52	61.9	4.3	10.4	5.5	6.9
10.0	na	0.0	na	10.0	0.3	4.53	4.70	-0.28	90.7	4.0	na	0.0	6.8
10.0	na	0.0	na	10.0	1.4	31.10	27.95	2.46	89.0	4.0	na	100.0	6.5
8.8	0.45	2.8	0.00	4.5	2.7	0.89	7.28	3.06	59.6	1.2	20.3	30.6	7.9
5.7	0.18	1.2	0.23	8.6	11.8	1.95	16.65	4.96	46.1	0.9	16.9	31.5	9.0
8.1	0.30	1.5	-0.02	4.2	2.4	0.79	7.24	3.01	73.6	5.5	36.2	4.9	7.6
6.0	0.40	3.6	0.00	3.4	0.4	0.61	7.21	3.30	82.9	7.1	51.8	0.1	4.9
5.9	0.92	2.9	0.00	6.9	6.3	1.23	6.23	3.19	46.2	2.1	36.1	58.6	9.6
4.2	1.89	10.0	-0.05	8.9	6.8	2.09	23.10	3.91	84.9	3.2	22.4	10.2	6.4
8.6	0.91	2.5	0.00	5.7	1.7	1.04	8.77	3.55	65.9	5.5	44.8	8.5	7.9
8.5	0.13	0.6	0.06	7.5	12.4	2.13	19.71	3.33	41.6	1.8	25.3	30.2	10.0
7.9	0.01	0.1	0.01	6.6	3.5	1.30	12.97	3.32	53.7	4.9	30.3	6.1	7.2
8.7	0.70	2.6	-0.01	5.9	16.7	1.02	10.94	3.01	56.6	6.6	44.8	4.2	8.5

Name	City	State	Rating	2020 Rating	2019 Rating	Total Assets ($Mil)	One Year Asset Growth	Asset Mix (As a % of Total Assets) Comm-ercial Loans	Cons-umer Loans	Mort-gage Loans	Secur-ities	Capital-ization Index	Lever-age Ratio	Risk-Based Capital Ratio
Exchange Bank and Trust Co.	Natchitoches	LA	**B+**	A-	A-	183.9	8.31	2.5	1.6	18.1	61.5	**6.7**	8.7	22.8
Exchange Bank and Trust Co.	Perry	OK	**B**	B	B-	359.1	12.40	6.3	3.9	17.5	33.7	**8.0**	9.7	16.6
Exchange Bank of Missouri	Fayette	MO	**A-**	A-	B+	285.4	17.89	8.0	1.2	7.9	11.6	**8.6**	10.1	15.8
▲ Exchange Bank of Northeast Missouri	Kahoka	MO	**B**	B-	C+	210.0	14.71	6.5	1.0	9.1	28.1	**7.2**	9.1	14.6
Exchange State Bank	Adair	IA	**B+**	B+	B	43.0	8.49	4.9	1.8	4.4	21.8	**10.0**	11.4	25.7
Exchange State Bank	Ames	IA	**B**	B	B	136.1	13.48	7.7	0.9	13.7	14.5	**7.6**	9.4	0.0
Exchange State Bank	Lanark	IL	**B+**	B+	B	107.2	9.03	10.6	1.2	7.2	54.2	**10.0**	11.6	0.0
Exchange State Bank	Saint Paul	KS	**B-**	B-	B-	84.3	5.90	9.9	2.4	12.7	21.2	**8.2**	9.8	0.0
Exchange State Bank	Carsonville	MI	**B+**	A-	A-	207.9	11.69	6.1	2.0	8.6	41.7	**9.5**	10.7	0.0
Extraco Banks, N.A.	Temple	TX	**B-**	C+	B	1966.6	11.80	3.2	5.5	15.9	21.1	**6.3**	8.3	17.1
F & C Bank	Holden	MO	**B**	B-	C+	283.3	10.30	7.2	1.9	20.3	9.2	**8.6**	10.2	0.0
F & M Bank and Trust Co.	Manchester	GA	**E-**	E-	E-	82.1	1.08	18.9	2.0	10.0	7.2	**2.4**	5.0	9.4
▲ F & M Community Bank, N.A.	Preston	MN	**B+**	B	B	177.5	10.03	7.4	1.2	15.1	25.5	**8.1**	10.0	0.0
F&M Bank	Washington	GA	**B+**	B+	B+	346.0	14.39	3.0	2.1	15.5	35.4	**10.0**	14.2	0.0
F&M Bank	Falls City	NE	**B+**	B+	B+	123.3	4.95	3.6	1.9	8.1	31.9	**8.6**	10.0	0.0
F&M Bank	West Point	NE	**B+**	B+	B+	333.0	-1.06	6.0	1.1	9.3	7.0	**8.0**	10.1	0.0
F&M Bank	Edmond	OK	**A-**	A-	A-	608.5	11.89	10.8	1.6	9.1	31.6	**8.2**	9.8	0.0
▲ F&M Bank	Clarksville	TN	**B**	B-	C+	1311.3	1.85	6.0	1.1	21.3	10.3	**5.5**	9.0	11.4
F&M Bank and Trust Co.	Hannibal	MO	**B**	B	B-	162.3	17.67	7.6	2.2	22.8	28.3	**6.7**	8.7	0.0
▲ Fairfax State Savings Bank	Fairfax	IA	**B-**	C+	B	224.8	21.16	9.6	1.8	10.3	47.5	**8.4**	9.9	0.0
Fairfield County Bank	Ridgefield	CT	**B**	B	B	1896.7	7.86	15.3	0.0	17.0	18.1	**10.0**	12.5	0.0
Fairfield Federal S&L Assn. of Lancaster	Lancaster	OH	**C**	C	C+	281.5	1.90	0.0	0.3	74.9	3.3	**10.0**	11.1	0.0
Fairview S&L Assn.	Fairview	OK	**B+**	B+	B+	50.5	5.82	5.7	2.3	22.4	0.6	**10.0**	19.9	0.0
Fairview State Banking Co.	Fairview	IL	**C+**	C+	C+	34.2	9.54	6.8	5.2	22.6	17.7	**10.0**	12.2	0.0
Falcon International Bank	Laredo	TX	**A**	A	A	1670.5	13.01	8.0	1.1	6.1	19.7	**10.0**	11.1	19.3
▼ Falcon National Bank	Foley	MN	**C+**	B-	B	746.3	18.98	38.4	0.4	6.1	13.4	**2.5**	8.2	0.0
Fall River Five Cents Savings Bank	Fall River	MA	**B-**	C+	C	1334.9	12.47	11.6	1.3	28.5	18.5	**6.2**	8.2	12.6
Family Bank	Pelham	GA	**B+**	B+	B+	135.9	12.16	5.6	6.5	44.2	3.7	**10.0**	11.3	21.0
Fannin Bank	Bonham	TX	**B-**	B-	B	136.7	10.45	10.1	1.8	14.3	39.8	**6.0**	8.0	15.0
Farm Bureau Bank FSB	Reno	NV	**C**	C	C-	768.8	-1.60	8.8	57.9	0.4	3.3	**10.0**	11.8	15.6
FarmBank	Green City	MO	**D+**	C-	C	70.9	15.23	15.5	3.9	12.7	23.3	**5.8**	7.8	12.0
Farmers & Merchants Bank	Piedmont	AL	**B**	B+	B+	291.5	12.43	5.1	1.6	10.7	34.1	**10.0**	11.6	19.9
Farmers & Merchants Bank	Waterloo	AL	**B**	B+	B+	107.3	16.12	1.2	1.0	0.1	87.3	**10.0**	20.4	0.0
Farmers & Merchants Bank	Lodi	CA	**A-**	A-	A-	4924.9	15.71	10.7	0.2	6.7	16.2	**7.0**	9.0	13.2
Farmers & Merchants Bank	Eatonton	GA	**B-**	B-	B-	228.1	12.68	5.1	1.5	6.4	50.2	**10.0**	12.4	24.1
Farmers & Merchants Bank	Lakeland	GA	**E-**	E-	E-	624.1	2.08	13.2	4.3	14.1	12.0	**3.7**	5.7	10.4
Farmers & Merchants Bank	Tolna	ND	**B**	B	C+	123.5	13.32	5.1	2.5	2.6	45.8	**7.2**	9.1	16.0
Farmers & Merchants Bank	Miamisburg	OH	**B+**	B+	B+	255.6	15.63	14.0	0.7	9.9	16.4	**6.7**	8.7	13.7
Farmers & Merchants Bank	New Castle	VA	**B+**	A-	A-	76.7	16.38	2.0	3.7	24.4	31.9	**10.0**	17.3	0.0
Farmers & Merchants Bank	Timberville	VA	**B**	B-	C+	1104.7	12.62	5.1	9.6	15.0	17.1	**7.9**	9.6	16.0
Farmers & Merchants Bank & Trust	Burlington	IA	**C**	C	C-	250.2	10.80	6.4	1.3	23.7	35.1	**6.1**	8.1	17.4
Farmers & Merchants Bank & Trust	Marinette	WI	**B-**	B-	B-	175.7	9.86	10.1	1.1	18.7	38.7	**8.4**	10.0	16.9
Farmers & Merchants Bank of Colby	Colby	KS	**A**	A	A-	296.8	13.22	10.2	0.3	1.7	25.1	**9.7**	13.3	0.0
Farmers & Merchants Bank of Hutsonville	Hutsonville	IL	**B**	B	B	49.3	7.91	4.8	8.6	24.3	5.4	**10.0**	17.3	0.0
Farmers & Merchants Bank of Long Beach	Long Beach	CA	**B+**	B+	A-	10684.2	13.08	3.2	0.8	5.5	38.6	**10.0**	11.9	19.0
▲ Farmers & Merchants Savings Bank	Lone Tree	IA	**A-**	B	B	93.3	-2.48	10.5	1.0	18.4	14.6	**10.0**	13.0	17.6
Farmers & Merchants Savings Bank	Manchester	IA	**A-**	B+	B-	665.0	-0.92	31.1	0.3	4.4	11.7	**10.0**	11.0	15.5
Farmers & Merchants State Bank	Winterset	IA	**A-**	A-	B+	222.0	8.22	4.3	3.1	7.3	22.8	**7.8**	9.5	15.2
▲ Farmers & Merchants State Bank	New York Mills	MN	**B+**	B	B	82.0	18.10	5.7	2.9	3.9	50.9	**10.0**	12.8	26.5
Farmers & Merchants State Bank	Springfield	MN	**C+**	C+	C+	142.0	6.41	6.6	1.1	4.2	24.3	**5.6**	7.6	16.4
Farmers & Merchants State Bank	Waterloo	WI	**B+**	B+	B-	203.2	0.26	2.3	0.8	16.3	8.5	**7.6**	11.1	0.0
▲ Farmers & Merchants Union Bank	Columbus	WI	**A-**	B+	C+	430.6	2.53	9.5	0.5	5.4	10.6	**10.0**	12.4	18.0
Farmers & Stockmens Bank	Clayton	NM	**A**	A	B	397.8	-3.22	18.8	0.8	3.8	0.7	**8.2**	9.8	16.7
Farmers & Traders Bank of Campton	Campton	KY	**B-**	B-	B-	63.5	18.99	3.3	3.2	19.8	52.6	**6.8**	8.8	12.4
Farmers & Traders Savings Bank	Bancroft	IA	**B-**	B-	B-	65.2	10.39	2.2	1.3	3.7	44.5	**7.8**	9.6	21.2
Farmers and Drovers Bank	Council Grove	KS	**B+**	B+	A-	210.1	2.83	3.1	8.5	13.9	36.1	**10.0**	24.9	0.0
Farmers and Mechanics FSB	Bloomfield	IN	**D**	D	C-	95.3	20.29	7.5	0.1	30.8	43.9	**10.0**	12.0	24.0
Farmers and Merchants Bank	LaFayette	AL	**A-**	A-	A-	235.6	22.90	7.8	4.4	7.7	52.5	**10.0**	11.4	19.9
Farmers and Merchants Bank	Sylvania	GA	**B+**	B	B	142.4	10.96	3.1	1.8	7.6	38.1	**10.0**	13.5	0.0
Farmers and Merchants Bank	Laotto	IN	**A-**	A-	A-	209.1	15.29	11.6	2.1	21.8	31.0	**7.7**	9.5	16.5

Asset Quality Index	Adjusted Non-Performing Loans as a % of Total Loans	Adjusted Non-Performing Loans as a % of Capital	Net Charge-Offs Avg Loans	Profitability Index	Net Income ($Mil)	Return on Assets (R.O.A.)	Return on Equity (R.O.E.)	Net Interest Spread	Overhead Efficiency Ratio	Liquidity Index	Liquidity Ratio	Hot Money Ratio	Stability Index
5.4	2.58	9.4	-0.01	6.2	1.2	1.35	14.28	3.04	55.9	4.7	14.8	3.7	7.6
6.4	0.60	3.1	-0.04	5.5	2.7	1.50	14.22	4.05	62.7	1.4	23.7	26.3	6.7
7.1	0.60	3.4	0.01	8.9	2.4	1.72	16.37	4.25	47.1	3.4	27.2	13.9	7.7
6.0	0.73	3.2	-0.18	4.7	1.3	1.26	12.89	3.60	65.3	4.3	39.8	13.5	7.0
6.2	3.87	5.5	0.00	7.4	0.4	1.85	13.55	4.06	52.4	5.2	56.6	12.0	8.1
8.6	0.00	0.0	0.00	6.0	1.0	1.53	17.14	3.69	53.8	3.6	30.8	13.8	5.5
8.4	0.00	0.0	-0.71	5.3	1.1	2.07	16.77	2.38	60.2	4.8	51.8	11.1	7.6
5.7	1.11	5.8	-0.07	4.5	0.4	0.86	8.87	3.52	67.7	3.2	44.8	19.9	5.9
6.4	1.36	4.7	0.00	4.8	1.0	0.93	8.56	2.96	64.7	6.1	54.5	7.3	6.9
8.7	0.03	0.2	0.01	4.1	9.1	0.97	11.08	2.79	73.1	6.4	40.4	3.6	7.2
5.0	1.57	7.5	-0.01	9.8	3.6	2.59	25.21	5.31	51.4	4.1	12.8	7.6	8.2
2.5	2.89	23.7	-0.09	3.5	0.3	0.78	16.23	4.79	84.0	2.1	27.0	20.6	0.7
7.0	0.04	1.1	0.03	6.7	1.5	1.78	17.60	4.50	63.2	4.4	16.7	6.2	6.4
8.6	0.40	1.4	0.07	5.1	1.8	1.07	7.17	3.82	62.7	3.6	34.5	15.4	7.7
8.8	0.00	0.8	0.00	5.4	0.9	1.41	13.78	3.34	53.5	6.0	42.1	4.3	6.9
7.6	0.00	2.7	-0.07	6.9	2.7	1.63	16.45	3.50	60.9	5.3	32.1	4.6	7.7
8.7	0.15	1.0	0.01	7.7	5.4	1.80	17.64	3.45	61.2	3.3	24.7	13.7	8.3
8.1	0.18	1.2	-0.01	5.6	10.8	1.66	15.17	3.21	74.7	2.8	11.8	13.1	9.0
5.6	0.79	3.8	0.04	4.7	0.8	0.97	10.70	3.04	65.6	3.9	21.8	10.0	4.9
9.1	0.07	0.3	-0.14	4.0	1.1	0.98	9.71	2.75	65.3	4.3	55.4	17.4	5.7
6.7	1.33	4.7	-0.04	4.4	9.0	0.99	7.80	3.44	70.0	5.7	29.9	5.0	9.0
6.9	1.24	8.1	-0.04	2.2	0.2	0.15	1.38	2.83	93.6	2.2	17.2	18.2	6.2
8.7	0.00	0.0	0.00	7.2	0.4	1.49	7.59	3.92	52.4	3.4	32.1	15.4	8.1
1.6	8.22	32.6	0.07	5.8	0.2	1.35	11.40	4.54	56.4	2.0	26.9	22.5	5.8
6.6	2.16	6.1	0.00	6.1	8.6	1.04	9.43	3.01	60.7	3.1	34.6	21.4	10.0
7.6	0.19	1.5	0.08	4.7	3.2	0.90	10.70	4.31	63.7	1.7	11.0	14.8	5.9
8.3	0.35	2.6	0.00	4.2	6.1	0.95	12.44	2.71	67.2	2.4	23.2	18.5	6.2
5.6	1.17	7.4	0.03	5.9	0.7	1.19	10.54	4.66	66.7	1.8	24.3	22.2	6.7
6.9	0.27	1.5	0.31	4.7	0.8	1.18	14.31	3.93	70.4	3.5	39.8	13.2	4.5
4.0	0.70	3.9	0.60	5.6	5.3	1.39	12.02	4.28	75.9	0.9	17.6	30.6	6.2
5.5	1.30	7.6	0.00	2.8	0.1	0.29	3.68	4.12	85.8	0.8	15.9	39.3	3.5
6.3	3.69	12.0	0.00	3.7	0.8	0.59	4.87	3.32	77.4	4.9	44.7	11.9	7.0
10.0	0.00	1.2	-0.81	4.1	0.5	0.98	4.78	2.00	44.7	4.1	84.0	27.0	6.1
8.6	0.28	0.9	-0.01	8.1	33.8	1.43	15.52	3.58	57.9	5.2	27.2	6.7	9.0
6.0	4.40	8.4	-0.07	4.2	0.9	0.83	6.77	3.02	70.7	5.4	46.0	9.5	6.8
1.6	3.04	28.4	0.47	3.5	2.1	0.69	12.09	3.67	71.0	1.2	23.0	31.0	2.4
5.1	2.45	5.4	0.05	4.0	0.5	0.82	8.06	2.74	69.1	4.9	51.9	13.3	6.1
4.8	1.51	8.5	0.00	6.5	1.7	1.34	15.04	3.84	56.4	4.5	21.1	6.2	6.2
9.8	0.00	0.0	0.00	4.6	0.3	0.76	4.32	2.98	68.6	5.6	50.8	8.5	7.9
5.8	0.99	5.6	-0.07	5.2	6.9	1.35	14.12	3.29	72.2	5.8	37.3	5.8	7.7
5.6	1.37	7.9	0.15	3.3	0.8	0.69	8.84	2.91	77.9	6.1	39.9	2.7	3.4
4.2	3.95	15.0	0.07	4.1	0.7	0.84	8.21	3.43	71.3	5.1	46.5	11.0	5.8
8.4	0.05	0.0	-0.08	9.3	3.2	2.15	15.87	4.13	34.2	0.7	15.0	40.2	8.9
8.5	0.00	0.0	0.00	4.9	0.3	1.23	7.20	2.54	51.5	2.6	39.1	25.8	8.0
9.1	0.87	2.4	0.00	5.1	55.7	1.07	9.55	2.92	53.0	5.5	33.1	7.9	9.9
8.1	0.00	0.0	0.00	6.1	0.7	1.40	9.66	4.34	56.0	3.9	18.6	8.3	7.7
7.8	0.33	1.6	-0.05	7.2	5.0	1.45	13.01	3.25	56.7	4.2	38.6	13.4	9.7
8.5	0.44	1.1	-0.01	6.6	1.6	1.44	14.82	2.87	50.8	5.3	41.4	8.4	6.7
9.0	0.00	0.0	-0.03	5.0	0.6	1.44	10.96	3.47	60.4	4.9	51.3	12.5	7.2
5.9	0.93	3.1	0.00	6.1	1.2	1.68	21.63	3.77	55.3	4.9	31.6	5.8	4.7
7.6	0.10	0.3	0.00	7.0	1.2	1.22	11.17	3.12	57.1	4.2	16.4	7.7	7.9
5.8	3.35	7.3	-1.58	7.9	3.9	1.83	14.99	3.34	39.1	2.0	30.4	25.9	7.7
8.1	0.07	0.2	0.00	9.3	6.0	2.73	29.28	4.39	62.0	5.4	31.3	3.7	8.4
6.5	1.22	3.0	-0.01	4.1	0.3	1.13	10.45	3.55	74.1	3.0	47.5	24.4	5.7
8.8	0.08	0.3	0.00	3.5	0.2	0.72	7.23	2.64	70.5	4.0	52.3	17.2	6.0
8.4	0.18	0.4	0.00	4.9	1.1	1.05	4.13	3.17	58.0	2.2	31.4	23.1	8.1
9.9	0.06	0.1	0.00	0.2	0.0	0.00	0.02	2.53	112.2	4.7	53.0	13.9	6.0
8.0	1.58	3.9	0.03	5.5	1.3	1.13	9.28	3.09	59.2	3.4	50.5	21.1	7.2
7.6	2.85	4.3	0.03	5.1	0.8	1.14	8.12	2.51	59.0	4.7	56.7	15.5	6.9
8.9	0.17	0.9	0.00	5.5	1.4	1.39	14.78	3.17	59.4	6.7	46.8	1.1	6.6

Name	City	State	Rating	2020 Rating	2019 Rating	Total Assets ($Mil)	One Year Asset Growth	Asset Mix (As a % of Total Assets) Commercial Loans	Consumer Loans	Mortgage Loans	Securities	Capitalization Index	Leverage Ratio	Risk-Based Capital Ratio
Farmers and Merchants Bank	Mound City	KS	**D**	D	D+	46.7	7.79	10.9	5.3	31.0	13.4	**4.9**	6.9	15.1
Farmers and Merchants Bank	Upperco	MD	**C+**	C+	B-	707.9	40.23	7.2	0.1	10.5	17.0	**7.0**	9.0	12.6
Farmers and Merchants Bank	Baldwyn	MS	**A-**	A-	A-	446.7	15.98	10.6	5.6	12.8	28.2	**10.0**	12.8	0.0
Farmers and Merchants Bank	Salisbury	NC	**A-**	A-	A-	848.2	16.90	5.2	0.3	8.6	0.0	**8.1**	9.7	19.5
Farmers and Merchants Bank	Axtell	NE	**D**	D+	D+	10.5	14.18	6.1	3.3	1.0	57.3	**5.5**	7.5	27.0
Farmers and Merchants Bank	Milford	NE	**C+**	C+	B	905.3	1.25	2.0	2.3	2.8	57.3	**7.5**	9.3	19.6
Farmers and Merchants Bank	Milligan	NE	**B**	B-	B	134.1	6.56	7.3	0.9	3.8	0.0	**10.0**	11.1	15.8
Farmers and Merchants Bank	Arnett	OK	**B**	B	B	60.5	7.07	3.3	6.9	0.8	41.2	**10.0**	13.5	0.0
Farmers and Merchants Bank	Duke	OK	**C**	C+	C+	21.3	9.36	5.6	0.9	0.0	18.5	**8.3**	9.9	0.0
▼ Farmers and Merchants Bank	Maysville	OK	**C+**	B-	B-	21.0	2.46	45.1	9.2	0.1	13.8	**5.3**	7.3	12.3
Farmers and Merchants Bank	Holly Hill	SC	**B-**	B	B+	371.8	9.97	2.1	1.7	6.7	34.9	**10.0**	11.6	43.2
Farmers and Merchants Bank	De Leon	TX	**C**	C+	C+	128.2	20.62	5.3	3.9	20.2	19.6	**5.4**	7.4	14.9
Farmers and Merchants Bank of Ashland	Ashland	NE	**B**	B	B	110.2	12.47	3.6	1.2	19.1	8.5	**7.0**	9.0	0.0
Farmers and Merchants Bank of Kendall	Kendall	WI	**B-**	B-	C+	81.0	5.60	5.1	1.4	7.9	0.0	**10.0**	15.6	0.0
Farmers and Merchants Bank of St. Clair	Saint Clair	MO	**B+**	B+	A-	282.1	20.16	8.0	1.5	20.0	23.9	**10.0**	11.1	17.0
Farmers and Merchants State Bank	Bushnell	IL	**B**	B	B-	87.0	11.90	7.7	3.3	9.3	28.8	**5.7**	7.7	20.5
▼ Farmers and Merchants State Bank	Alpha	MN	**D+**	C-	C-	42.5	6.77	5.8	2.5	9.1	3.7	**9.8**	10.8	19.9
Farmers and Merchants State Bank	Appleton	MN	**B**	B-	B-	55.8	8.84	10.1	1.7	1.5	7.8	**9.5**	11.4	0.0
Farmers and Merchants State Bank	Blooming Prairie	MN	**C+**	C+	C+	111.8	12.89	7.8	1.5	10.0	12.7	**5.6**	7.6	16.2
Farmers and Merchants State Bank	Pierz	MN	**B+**	B+	B-	288.0	12.76	9.2	1.8	9.0	24.7	**6.4**	8.5	0.0
▲ Farmers and Merchants State Bank	Langdon	ND	**A**	A-	B	122.1	4.10	5.3	2.0	1.5	35.6	**10.0**	14.7	0.0
Farmers and Merchants State Bank	Bloomfield	NE	**A-**	A-	B	174.2	22.69	6.5	2.1	0.0	17.9	**10.0**	12.3	18.4
Farmers and Merchants State Bank	Plankinton	SD	**C**	C	C	135.2	14.63	12.1	3.3	5.8	12.1	**8.9**	10.3	14.1
Farmers and Merchants Trust Co.	Chambersburg	PA	**B**	B	B+	1676.6	17.86	7.4	0.4	9.0	30.6	**6.5**	8.5	16.3
▲ Farmers and Miners Bank	Pennington Gap	VA	**A-**	B+	A-	161.9	11.80	11.4	5.9	16.8	17.4	**10.0**	13.1	0.0
Farmers Bank	Greenwood	AR	**B+**	B+	B+	260.9	9.44	6.2	4.7	24.2	34.0	**10.0**	15.5	0.0
Farmers Bank	Ault	CO	**A**	A	A	283.7	8.20	7.5	0.3	4.6	18.2	**10.0**	12.6	0.0
Farmers Bank	Buhl	ID	**A**	A	A	622.2	21.86	10.0	1.3	3.8	43.6	**10.0**	12.7	24.6
Farmers Bank	Nicholasville	KY	**B**	B	B	206.4	16.84	3.6	1.1	28.0	26.9	**8.2**	9.8	21.0
Farmers Bank	Parsons	TN	**C+**	C+	C+	44.8	4.16	3.3	9.8	14.8	8.7	**10.0**	11.3	34.9
▲ Farmers Bank & Trust	Atwood	KS	**B**	B-	B-	125.4	6.76	2.9	0.8	2.4	38.7	**6.7**	8.7	17.6
Farmers Bank & Trust	Great Bend	KS	**A**	A	A	1064.6	7.05	3.5	0.2	9.2	41.0	**10.0**	17.2	27.6
Farmers Bank & Trust Co.	Magnolia	AR	**B**	B	B	1934.6	8.20	13.2	1.2	14.1	17.8	**7.6**	9.4	13.3
Farmers Bank & Trust Co.	Marion	KY	**B+**	B+	B+	470.8	14.13	8.2	2.3	29.8	14.0	**7.5**	9.4	13.6
Farmers Bank and Trust Co.	Blytheville	AR	**B**	B	B	306.6	-9.92	11.8	2.7	17.2	5.0	**7.5**	9.4	14.2
▼ Farmers Bank and Trust Co.	Princeton	KY	**A-**	A	A	183.9	20.40	5.2	1.1	12.7	26.5	**9.4**	10.6	0.0
Farmers Bank of Lohman	Jefferson City	MO	**B**	B-	B-	79.3	7.36	3.3	3.4	15.2	54.9	**10.0**	14.5	0.0
Farmers Bank of Northern Missouri	Unionville	MO	**A-**	A-	B+	473.8	15.85	4.7	1.2	6.9	46.8	**10.0**	11.4	0.0
▲ Farmers Bank, Windsor VA	Windsor	VA	**A-**	B+	B+	589.5	12.73	8.9	0.7	5.3	44.6	**9.0**	10.4	17.5
Farmers Building and Savings Bank	Rochester	PA	**B**	B	B	123.8	15.01	0.1	0.0	35.3	22.7	**10.0**	17.9	49.8
Farmers National Bank	Prophetstown	IL	**A**	A	A	845.5	9.57	3.2	0.6	3.2	50.2	**10.0**	13.0	0.0
▲ Farmers National Bank	Phillipsburg	KS	**A-**	B+	A-	164.9	9.29	12.0	2.5	6.6	16.6	**10.0**	15.5	26.1
Farmers National Bank of Griggsville	Griggsville	IL	**C**	C	C	119.5	14.65	6.3	6.6	12.1	9.4	**8.3**	9.9	15.1
Farmers Savings Bank	Colesburg	IA	**B+**	B+	B	233.2	2.92	7.7	2.1	4.9	33.2	**10.0**	11.7	0.0
Farmers Savings Bank	Fostoria	IA	**B-**	B	B	165.4	18.54	6.5	1.8	14.6	25.1	**10.0**	12.7	0.0
Farmers Savings Bank	Frederika	IA	**B**	B	B	54.8	12.43	3.5	2.4	6.9	8.8	**10.0**	16.4	0.0
Farmers Savings Bank	Marshalltown	IA	**A-**	A-	A-	139.1	17.22	7.5	1.6	10.0	23.3	**10.0**	13.1	0.0
▲ Farmers Savings Bank	Wever	IA	**B+**	B-	C	142.1	14.74	10.3	0.9	17.5	29.7	**10.0**	13.3	0.0
Farmers Savings Bank	Spencer	OH	**A-**	A-	A-	319.3	6.01	1.1	0.5	18.2	69.1	**10.0**	24.0	65.5
Farmers Savings Bank	Mineral Point	WI	**B+**	B+	B	412.3	15.22	7.1	4.4	11.8	45.2	**7.1**	9.1	17.5
Farmers Savings Bank & Trust	Traer	IA	**A-**	A-	A-	206.2	16.35	4.3	1.1	6.7	45.9	**6.6**	8.7	0.0
Farmers Security Bank	Washburn	ND	**B**	B	B-	70.6	15.11	5.7	2.8	1.6	28.0	**8.0**	9.7	0.0
Farmers State Bank	Dublin	GA	**A-**	A-	A-	150.0	9.16	10.1	6.4	16.7	13.3	**10.0**	11.2	16.8
Farmers State Bank	Lincolnton	GA	**A**	A	A	167.7	12.30	4.1	5.0	17.5	22.9	**10.0**	14.0	26.6
Farmers State Bank	Algona	IA	**B+**	B+	A-	131.9	15.59	14.2	1.1	13.8	19.7	**9.7**	10.8	0.0
Farmers State Bank	Lake View	IA	**B**	B	B	39.8	7.23	6.4	3.8	10.7	24.2	**10.0**	11.1	0.0
Farmers State Bank	Marcus	IA	**B+**	B+	B+	72.4	5.33	5.0	2.1	5.7	51.6	**10.0**	12.6	0.0
Farmers State Bank	Marion	IA	**A-**	A-	A	1084.6	13.94	8.9	1.0	6.8	12.6	**10.0**	11.6	0.0
Farmers State Bank	Mason City	IA	**A-**	A-	A-	221.3	9.09	5.1	1.6	15.5	41.3	**10.0**	11.8	23.4
Farmers State Bank	Waterloo	IA	**A-**	A-	B	1335.0	6.70	8.9	4.9	21.2	11.6	**8.7**	10.1	14.6

Asset Quality Index	Adjusted Non-Performing Loans as a % of Total Loans	Adjusted Non-Performing Loans as a % of Capital	Net Charge-Offs Avg Loans	Profitability Index	Net Income ($Mil)	Return on Assets (R.O.A.)	Return on Equity (R.O.E.)	Net Interest Spread	Overhead Efficiency Ratio	Liquidity Index	Liquidity Ratio	Hot Money Ratio	Stability Index
2.1	7.95	33.0	0.00	**6.0**	0.4	1.55	21.99	3.28	61.1	**2.5**	25.7	17.8	**4.4**
3.5	1.28	7.6	0.00	**4.8**	3.7	1.05	10.60	3.56	60.4	**2.1**	20.3	16.7	**5.5**
6.5	1.74	5.3	0.08	**8.6**	4.2	1.92	14.20	3.90	56.7	**2.6**	30.2	18.8	**8.3**
6.7	0.83	3.3	-0.16	**5.9**	4.0	1.00	9.98	2.98	68.4	**6.4**	49.6	4.0	**7.1**
9.6	0.00	0.0	0.00	**1.2**	0.0	0.04	0.44	4.12	98.6	**6.3**	70.6	3.2	**1.0**
8.5	0.04	0.2	0.11	**3.8**	5.0	1.11	11.63	1.97	63.9	**3.0**	65.5	5.5	**6.1**
4.5	1.02	6.3	0.00	**7.7**	1.3	1.96	16.60	4.09	46.5	**0.9**	22.0	18.9	**8.3**
8.6	0.35	0.8	0.13	**4.5**	0.3	1.08	7.77	2.88	61.7	**5.7**	48.5	7.2	**7.4**
9.5	0.00	0.0	0.00	**2.9**	0.0	0.39	4.00	2.39	83.7	**5.8**	71.1	9.6	**4.5**
7.8	0.00	0.0	0.00	**7.5**	0.2	1.48	19.58	4.23	66.6	**4.8**	42.6	8.9	**4.3**
7.5	4.15	5.3	-0.01	**2.9**	0.4	0.19	1.69	1.65	88.9	**6.6**	67.8	7.2	**6.1**
7.0	0.45	2.8	0.02	**2.5**	0.2	0.25	3.10	2.94	89.1	**6.2**	42.9	3.2	**4.0**
9.0	0.00	0.0	0.00	**4.6**	0.5	0.96	10.54	3.87	71.0	**4.9**	31.1	6.5	**5.4**
3.0	5.89	17.2	0.00	**10.0**	0.9	2.29	14.64	4.51	49.1	**3.2**	26.0	14.6	**9.3**
8.8	0.30	1.4	-0.03	**5.0**	1.5	1.14	10.05	3.60	67.2	**4.3**	25.4	8.2	**6.7**
8.9	0.00	0.2	0.06	**5.0**	0.5	1.05	13.72	3.07	64.5	**6.3**	45.3	2.8	**4.0**
1.7	6.10	42.3	1.07	**2.7**	0.1	0.30	2.74	3.57	74.7	**2.7**	42.8	20.0	**2.8**
3.6	1.48	7.5	0.14	**6.8**	0.5	1.57	13.43	3.23	49.0	**5.0**	32.0	6.5	**8.7**
6.3	0.55	3.3	0.00	**8.9**	1.2	2.16	29.38	4.35	51.0	**6.1**	42.9	3.4	**5.0**
4.5	3.28	11.7	0.00	**9.0**	3.5	2.44	27.38	3.70	45.6	**4.8**	31.9	7.7	**7.0**
7.5	0.71	3.5	-0.03	**8.8**	1.2	1.98	13.38	3.54	43.0	**4.5**	36.7	11.3	**10.0**
8.1	0.21	2.9	0.01	**7.2**	1.0	1.22	9.88	3.53	56.6	**3.6**	29.6	13.5	**7.6**
2.9	0.86	6.1	-0.06	**10.0**	1.8	2.71	26.32	4.82	41.4	**1.0**	23.3	15.1	**7.9**
5.6	1.72	7.9	-0.03	**6.0**	11.1	1.37	15.51	3.18	65.1	**6.3**	31.7	1.9	**7.7**
7.5	1.17	3.5	0.11	**5.8**	0.9	1.18	9.05	4.33	69.0	**4.7**	45.9	13.2	**7.4**
8.6	0.46	1.4	0.06	**4.5**	1.4	1.11	6.94	3.88	71.2	**4.2**	25.0	8.6	**8.1**
8.7	0.24	1.2	0.00	**8.5**	2.5	1.85	15.27	3.81	53.2	**2.2**	21.8	18.6	**9.8**
8.9	0.87	1.8	-0.01	**5.9**	3.1	1.04	7.98	2.71	59.0	**5.9**	62.0	10.6	**8.9**
9.1	0.17	0.9	-0.10	**4.4**	0.9	0.94	9.51	2.77	61.4	**2.3**	29.7	20.1	**6.1**
8.4	0.00	0.7	0.00	**2.7**	0.1	0.33	2.89	2.61	96.0	**4.2**	58.7	16.9	**6.4**
5.1	2.61	7.7	-0.04	**6.4**	1.1	1.76	18.41	3.84	54.7	**5.0**	30.0	5.3	**6.1**
9.2	0.82	1.0	0.00	**7.6**	8.6	1.65	8.73	3.13	63.4	**2.8**	52.9	40.2	**10.0**
5.4	1.07	6.7	0.07	**6.7**	12.7	1.37	13.03	3.92	52.3	**1.7**	17.1	23.5	**9.6**
6.6	0.31	2.3	0.04	**7.8**	5.3	2.30	22.79	4.87	51.9	**1.6**	12.5	11.1	**6.6**
5.3	0.81	5.0	0.07	**7.0**	2.7	1.69	17.97	3.37	52.7	**0.9**	22.4	36.7	**7.7**
8.9	0.02	0.7	-0.02	**6.2**	1.3	1.49	13.60	3.47	60.4	**4.8**	31.0	7.4	**9.1**
9.7	0.00	0.0	0.02	**4.6**	0.4	1.09	7.19	2.96	52.8	**6.6**	79.7	7.3	**7.7**
8.7	0.29	0.7	0.09	**8.1**	4.9	2.08	16.96	4.10	40.8	**5.3**	42.5	8.7	**7.9**
8.3	0.28	0.5	0.17	**7.1**	5.8	2.08	17.09	3.14	56.8	**4.5**	44.9	13.8	**8.2**
8.0	3.62	7.3	0.00	**3.4**	0.4	0.61	3.36	2.54	61.6	**7.8**	71.0	0.0	**7.7**
8.5	0.20	1.7	0.06	**7.3**	6.6	1.58	11.33	2.91	39.9	**2.3**	44.0	33.8	**9.9**
6.7	1.11	3.4	0.00	**6.6**	1.2	1.53	9.13	2.72	52.0	**4.7**	45.1	13.0	**8.4**
4.8	0.64	5.3	-0.01	**7.5**	1.1	1.80	18.19	5.00	58.2	**1.8**	27.5	24.7	**7.8**
3.7	2.03	20.4	-0.01	**3.6**	0.8	0.73	5.83	3.01	66.0	**1.4**	32.1	35.2	**8.1**
6.5	1.68	7.3	0.04	**3.6**	0.3	0.44	3.27	2.68	68.3	**5.0**	42.4	10.7	**7.7**
9.0	0.17	0.4	-0.06	**3.8**	0.2	0.55	3.29	1.80	61.4	**6.3**	70.9	8.0	**7.0**
8.8	0.16	0.7	0.00	**5.3**	0.8	1.13	8.68	3.15	60.7	**5.3**	41.7	7.8	**8.0**
5.8	2.43	6.7	-0.02	**5.2**	0.9	1.32	9.67	3.84	63.2	**5.3**	49.5	11.1	**7.9**
7.7	4.86	4.6	-0.16	**6.4**	2.5	1.63	6.12	3.15	47.1	**4.5**	89.5	24.2	**9.7**
8.6	0.17	0.4	-0.02	**6.9**	3.2	1.61	16.48	3.04	51.5	**6.4**	47.1	2.8	**6.7**
9.1	0.00	0.0	-0.01	**5.8**	1.5	1.39	15.72	3.00	57.6	**6.0**	52.1	7.1	**5.9**
5.3	2.15	5.8	0.20	**5.0**	0.4	1.09	11.16	3.57	61.2	**4.7**	30.6	7.7	**5.4**
6.1	1.86	6.3	0.00	**5.4**	1.0	1.33	10.97	4.02	67.2	**4.2**	33.6	11.9	**8.5**
8.8	0.19	1.3	-0.03	**7.6**	1.5	1.87	12.89	4.49	61.8	**4.9**	38.8	10.1	**8.7**
5.7	0.88	7.1	0.02	**6.9**	1.2	1.79	16.25	3.60	52.5	**5.5**	41.1	7.1	**7.4**
9.4	0.00	0.0	-0.08	**4.0**	0.1	0.60	5.46	3.51	70.2	**7.2**	75.8	3.3	**5.9**
6.3	3.47	10.2	-0.04	**5.0**	0.5	1.27	9.85	2.52	56.8	**6.4**	63.7	6.1	**7.9**
8.6	0.14	0.8	0.00	**5.4**	6.2	1.16	9.75	2.72	60.2	**5.5**	36.0	8.9	**10.0**
8.2	0.51	1.7	0.05	**7.1**	1.9	1.71	13.92	4.18	49.1	**3.3**	49.7	21.8	**7.5**
8.1	0.09	0.9	0.01	**8.6**	16.2	2.41	24.40	4.22	38.8	**1.6**	9.5	9.6	**8.0**

Name	City	State	Rating	2020 Rating	2019 Rating	Total Assets ($Mil)	One Year Asset Growth	Asset Mix (As a % of Total Assets)				Capital-ization Index	Lever-age Ratio	Risk-Based Capital Ratio
								Comm-ercial Loans	Cons-umer Loans	Mort-gage Loans	Secur-ities			
Farmers State Bank	Yale	IA	**B**	B	B	58.8	6.08	6.8	1.5	12.8	49.6	**9.2**	10.4	0.0
Farmers State Bank	Elmwood	IL	**C-**	C	C-	62.5	8.80	4.2	1.4	21.1	47.3	**6.6**	8.6	19.1
Farmers State Bank	Pittsfield	IL	**A**	A-	A-	310.0	8.94	5.1	0.9	3.3	13.3	**10.0**	12.7	18.5
Farmers State Bank	Lagrange	IN	**A-**	B+	B+	1067.1	13.96	3.7	1.6	27.6	20.6	**6.6**	8.6	17.1
Farmers State Bank	Dwight	KS	**C-**	C-	C-	17.3	9.85	3.6	0.8	5.9	6.8	**10.0**	11.2	0.0
▼ Farmers State Bank	Fairview	KS	**D+**	C	D+	24.1	21.28	2.3	4.2	7.5	17.4	**7.0**	9.0	0.0
Farmers State Bank	Phillipsburg	KS	**D+**	D+	C	39.3	8.58	10.3	6.5	7.7	27.4	**10.0**	11.2	0.0
Farmers State Bank	Wathena	KS	**B-**	B-	B	71.9	8.32	9.0	3.9	16.8	56.4	**10.0**	14.5	37.2
Farmers State Bank	Cameron	MO	**B-**	B-	B-	307.4	12.77	2.4	2.5	38.7	15.5	**6.2**	8.2	13.7
▲ Farmers State Bank	Victor	MT	**B+**	B-	B	614.6	21.49	6.2	1.9	9.9	32.0	**7.2**	9.2	15.5
▼ Farmers State Bank	Dodge	NE	**C+**	B-	C+	342.9	13.57	11.2	1.1	1.6	8.4	**5.8**	7.8	11.8
▲ Farmers State Bank	West Salem	OH	**C+**	C	C+	173.3	17.30	21.5	1.7	20.7	18.2	**5.1**	7.1	13.0
Farmers State Bank	Hosmer	SD	**C+**	C+	B-	22.1	-0.11	44.2	3.3	0.0	13.5	**10.0**	14.2	15.4
Farmers State Bank	Parkston	SD	**B**	B	B	257.9	12.13	5.1	2.4	0.0	46.5	**6.8**	8.8	0.0
▲ Farmers State Bank	Mountain City	TN	**B**	B-	B	183.8	18.89	5.7	3.0	20.9	40.4	**10.0**	13.3	24.2
▲ Farmers State Bank	Center	TX	**C+**	C	B-	422.3	15.63	13.5	1.7	7.0	23.4	**10.0**	12.1	22.7
Farmers State Bank	Groesbeck	TX	**B+**	B+	B+	165.8	7.78	10.6	4.3	13.6	29.0	**6.1**	8.1	0.0
Farmers State Bank	Winthrop	WA	**C**	C	B-	57.4	25.70	4.3	0.7	0.4	64.3	**5.8**	7.8	83.3
▲ Farmers State Bank	Pine Bluffs	WY	**C-**	D+	C-	29.8	9.25	13.5	1.6	8.8	1.1	**5.7**	7.7	21.1
Farmers State Bank & Trust Co.	Mount Sterling	IL	**B**	B	B-	112.7	9.10	10.9	4.5	15.5	18.6	**6.4**	8.4	14.5
Farmers State Bank & Trust Co.	Church Point	LA	**B-**	B-	B-	146.3	6.23	14.5	1.8	8.1	25.0	**7.0**	9.0	0.0
Farmers State Bank of Alto Pass, Ill.	Harrisburg	IL	**C+**	C	C-	321.1	2.56	31.9	0.8	13.2	4.9	**6.1**	8.1	12.7
Farmers State Bank of Calhan	Calhan	CO	**B+**	B+	B	359.8	13.33	5.0	2.3	12.1	49.9	**7.3**	9.2	17.8
Farmers State Bank of Canton	Canton	SD	**C+**	B-	B-	61.2	23.94	2.1	3.2	20.8	32.8	**8.5**	10.0	18.3
Farmers State Bank of Emden	Emden	IL	**B-**	B-	B-	38.1	7.20	3.7	1.5	0.4	55.2	**10.0**	25.0	63.0
Farmers State Bank of Hamel	Hamel	MN	**B+**	B+	B	183.5	17.22	4.1	1.1	8.3	49.3	**6.8**	8.8	0.0
Farmers State Bank of Hoffman	Hoffman	IL	**B-**	B-	B	190.7	16.77	5.0	0.9	8.2	53.3	**10.0**	13.1	0.0
Farmers State Bank of Hoffman	Hoffman	MN	**B**	B	B	32.5	2.34	4.8	3.3	8.4	42.8	**10.0**	11.7	0.0
Farmers State Bank of Medora	Medora	IL	**C-**	C-	C	23.9	11.75	7.2	4.6	1.7	57.3	**10.0**	12.9	37.1
Farmers State Bank of Munith	Munith	MI	**B-**	B	B-	104.9	20.61	2.2	3.7	20.5	23.7	**6.5**	8.5	23.6
▲ Farmers State Bank of Newcastle	Newcastle	TX	**B**	B-	B-	62.2	13.87	15.8	1.8	6.3	34.0	**7.3**	9.2	0.0
▲ Farmers State Bank of Trimont	Trimont	MN	**B+**	B	B	70.2	8.20	7.6	1.8	5.3	47.8	**10.0**	15.1	28.3
Farmers State Bank of Underwood	Underwood	MN	**B-**	B-	B-	93.9	15.54	16.4	3.0	13.6	17.5	**5.4**	7.4	11.8
Farmers State Bank of Western Illinois	Alpha	IL	**B+**	B+	A-	163.4	11.01	5.9	1.8	4.8	34.2	**10.0**	11.5	0.0
Farmers State Bank, Allen, Oklahoma	Allen	OK	**B-**	B-	B	50.2	12.24	19.8	8.9	15.0	8.0	**10.0**	11.6	19.3
Farmers State Bank, Inc	Booneville	KY	**B-**	B-	B-	63.3	14.44	5.1	3.3	12.4	58.3	**9.7**	10.8	15.9
Farmers State Bank-Hillsboro	Hillsboro	WI	**B+**	B+	A	206.7	10.54	2.6	1.3	7.8	38.5	**10.0**	18.3	0.0
▲ Farmers Trust & Savings Bank	Buffalo Center	IA	**A**	A-	A-	290.4	8.00	13.3	1.2	4.9	0.4	**10.0**	11.9	0.0
Farmers Trust & Savings Bank	Earling	IA	**B+**	B+	B+	125.0	13.92	10.8	1.3	6.1	11.4	**6.1**	8.1	17.2
Farmers Trust and Savings Bank	Spencer	IA	**C**	C+	C+	475.8	-2.51	11.9	0.6	5.6	16.5	**6.2**	9.3	11.9
Farmers Trust and Savings Bank	Williamsburg	IA	**A**	A	A	183.7	8.02	8.1	2.5	9.6	27.5	**10.0**	20.1	0.0
▲ Farmers-Merchants Bank & Trust Co.	Breaux Bridge	LA	**C+**	C	D+	406.5	10.33	6.8	3.9	11.3	9.6	**10.0**	11.3	20.1
Farmers-Merchants Bank of Illinois	Joy	IL	**B-**	B-	B	286.4	8.45	1.0	0.7	3.7	3.7	**5.3**	9.6	0.0
Farmington State Bank	Farmington	WA	**D+**	C-	C	16.6	60.38	15.4	3.1	3.0	0.4	**10.0**	33.2	0.0
Fayette County National Bank of Fayettevill	Fayetteville	WV	**A-**	B+	B+	128.5	22.38	2.2	2.2	36.0	41.8	**9.8**	10.9	0.0
Fayette Savings Bank, SSB	La Grange	TX	**B-**	B-	B	295.2	15.91	6.3	2.0	39.2	11.7	**6.6**	8.6	14.3
▲ Fayetteville Bank	Fayetteville	TX	**B+**	B	B	674.1	15.44	4.8	0.8	3.7	79.1	**9.6**	10.7	25.3
FBT Bank & Mortgage	Fordyce	AR	**B+**	B+	B+	206.7	1.82	9.8	5.3	15.4	33.8	**9.6**	10.8	0.0
FCB Banks	Collinsville	IL	**B**	B	B	2073.8	7.12	3.7	3.5	29.2	12.9	**6.1**	8.1	15.6
FCN Bank, N.A.	Brookville	IN	**B+**	B+	B+	721.1	8.35	5.7	1.1	14.8	43.2	**7.5**	9.3	18.3
FDS Bank	Mason	OH	**A+**	A+	A+	111.8	-22.97	0.9	0.3	0.0	15.9	**10.0**	48.4	81.3
Federated Bank	Onarga	IL	**C+**	C+	C	113.8	12.55	17.2	2.0	11.1	26.1	**6.0**	8.0	18.8
Federation Bank	Washington	IA	**C+**	C+	C+	158.3	13.39	6.6	3.2	9.6	31.9	**6.0**	8.0	0.0
Feliciana Bank & Trust Co.	Clinton	LA	**B+**	B+	B+	149.1	11.05	9.0	1.7	26.2	20.2	**8.9**	10.3	0.0
Fidelity Bank	West Memphis	AR	**A-**	A-	A-	523.6	12.62	5.1	0.7	4.1	53.6	**8.9**	10.3	0.0
Fidelity Bank	West Des Moines	IA	**B+**	B+	B-	108.6	20.75	2.7	0.4	46.8	1.7	**7.6**	9.4	14.8
Fidelity Bank	New Orleans	LA	**B+**	B	B	1045.8	4.43	15.5	0.6	26.2	6.2	**10.0**	15.7	27.6
▲ Fidelity Bank	Edina	MN	**A**	A-	A-	674.6	-12.27	22.9	0.3	0.0	5.7	**10.0**	12.2	0.0
Fidelity Bank & Trust	Dubuque	IA	**B**	B	B	1631.3	12.65	10.8	1.1	7.1	21.5	**6.4**	8.4	14.2
Fidelity Bank of Texas	Waco	TX	**B-**	B+	B+	105.6	0.12	4.0	0.6	14.8	0.5	**10.0**	14.6	0.0

Asset Quality Index	Adjusted Non-Performing Loans as a % of Total Loans	Adjusted Non-Performing Loans as a % of Capital	Net Charge-Offs Avg Loans	Profitability Index	Net Income ($Mil)	Return on Assets (R.O.A.)	Return on Equity (R.O.E.)	Net Interest Spread	Overhead Efficiency Ratio	Liquidity Index	Liquidity Ratio	Hot Money Ratio	Stability Index
9.0	0.00	0.0	0.00	**5.6**	0.4	1.39	12.82	3.44	55.7	**4.4**	60.8	16.5	**6.3**
3.7	6.01	26.1	-0.03	**3.8**	0.3	0.96	11.53	3.32	71.1	**4.2**	45.4	15.0	**4.3**
7.7	0.30	4.4	0.00	**6.6**	2.5	1.64	12.68	3.67	57.5	**5.1**	31.0	5.6	**8.3**
9.0	0.22	1.0	0.00	**7.1**	7.3	1.44	15.71	3.41	56.8	**6.0**	41.2	6.4	**8.4**
8.2	0.00	0.0	0.00	**1.7**	0.0	0.32	2.78	3.27	88.8	**5.5**	63.8	10.0	**5.0**
7.6	0.36	2.1	0.00	**2.6**	0.1	0.42	4.41	3.47	87.0	**4.6**	52.9	12.6	**3.4**
1.1	8.62	37.6	-0.02	**5.6**	0.3	1.66	14.27	4.64	63.7	**2.8**	38.1	20.8	**4.8**
9.1	0.05	0.1	-0.18	**3.4**	0.3	0.74	4.94	3.47	80.7	**6.1**	57.1	6.3	**7.2**
7.9	0.19	1.5	-0.06	**4.5**	1.4	0.91	10.16	3.71	70.0	**4.5**	29.7	8.5	**5.2**
7.8	0.42	1.4	-0.06	**6.3**	5.3	1.81	20.62	3.83	64.5	**5.3**	36.9	6.5	**6.6**
5.6	0.54	6.7	-0.01	**3.1**	0.4	0.24	2.76	3.77	87.3	**1.8**	26.0	22.3	**4.9**
6.9	0.52	3.0	0.02	**3.6**	0.5	0.58	8.34	3.53	81.7	**5.2**	19.5	1.6	**3.8**
8.0	0.00	0.0	0.52	**6.0**	0.2	1.36	9.81	4.87	68.0	**0.7**	17.7	41.1	**5.0**
8.7	0.02	0.1	0.00	**6.3**	1.8	1.41	15.80	3.74	51.1	**5.5**	50.2	9.9	**5.5**
6.6	2.92	6.2	0.03	**4.5**	0.8	0.91	6.86	4.05	70.4	**3.3**	28.2	14.5	**7.2**
3.7	6.07	21.9	0.13	**3.6**	1.4	0.75	5.97	3.56	78.2	**5.6**	51.0	9.7	**5.0**
7.4	0.55	2.0	0.00	**7.5**	1.8	2.15	23.92	5.31	59.4	**4.5**	27.1	7.8	**6.3**
10.0	1.13	0.7	-0.04	**2.6**	0.1	0.22	2.72	1.31	81.3	**8.1**	93.8	0.0	**3.4**
8.6	0.00	0.0	0.00	**2.5**	0.1	0.54	6.73	3.92	83.9	**5.9**	46.6	5.5	**3.7**
8.1	0.00	0.6	0.03	**6.7**	0.7	1.29	14.60	3.02	54.5	**2.4**	32.6	21.0	**6.1**
4.5	1.31	9.3	-0.01	**5.3**	0.9	1.19	12.25	3.71	68.3	**3.9**	29.8	12.3	**6.5**
4.1	1.77	11.1	-0.06	**6.5**	3.2	1.91	26.31	3.19	64.9	**4.0**	21.3	9.3	**4.6**
8.5	0.29	1.3	0.26	**6.1**	2.7	1.58	16.02	3.64	59.5	**4.7**	34.1	9.7	**6.1**
8.9	0.07	0.4	0.04	**3.7**	0.2	0.77	7.85	3.58	70.0	**5.8**	40.1	4.5	**4.4**
9.8	1.30	0.6	0.00	**3.4**	0.1	0.55	2.25	1.92	69.8	**3.7**	67.5	23.5	**7.0**
9.6	0.00	0.0	0.00	**4.2**	0.9	1.02	11.11	2.41	59.9	**6.5**	66.6	7.5	**5.3**
9.5	0.80	1.7	-0.02	**3.5**	0.6	0.64	4.71	2.72	69.8	**6.4**	61.2	7.6	**7.6**
8.9	0.00	0.0	0.00	**4.1**	0.2	1.01	8.10	3.43	71.1	**4.5**	63.0	16.2	**7.3**
6.5	0.32	7.6	-0.07	**0.3**	-0.1	-0.46	-2.93	2.32	119.6	**5.9**	86.8	11.6	**4.6**
5.5	1.73	6.4	0.02	**3.4**	0.2	0.44	5.08	2.77	86.2	**7.0**	59.7	3.3	**5.2**
6.7	0.21	1.4	0.07	**8.0**	0.5	1.82	18.91	4.53	48.0	**6.5**	41.3	0.0	**5.7**
8.8	0.11	0.6	-0.13	**5.2**	0.4	1.00	6.58	3.32	63.1	**4.3**	53.1	12.9	**7.5**
8.3	0.00	0.0	-0.05	**4.2**	0.2	0.52	6.62	3.88	85.1	**1.9**	24.5	21.6	**5.0**
9.1	0.15	0.8	0.10	**4.1**	0.7	0.91	7.64	3.34	70.5	**6.4**	51.6	4.6	**6.8**
3.7	4.02	23.3	0.30	**7.4**	0.5	2.10	17.97	5.40	59.5	**2.3**	26.2	18.9	**7.0**
5.9	2.98	5.8	0.02	**4.6**	0.4	1.19	9.91	3.50	77.3	**3.9**	47.9	17.1	**6.3**
9.4	0.10	0.3	-0.06	**8.9**	1.9	1.87	10.38	3.20	32.4	**6.2**	62.0	9.2	**7.0**
7.1	0.03	0.0	0.00	**7.6**	2.6	1.81	14.86	3.78	51.9	**4.5**	26.9	7.6	**9.0**
8.7	0.04	0.3	-0.11	**7.1**	1.0	1.59	19.44	3.55	54.5	**5.7**	46.3	7.6	**6.6**
2.2	3.11	19.1	-0.01	**5.3**	3.2	1.31	14.14	3.45	53.3	**3.3**	9.5	7.0	**6.7**
8.8	0.80	1.4	0.00	**9.0**	1.9	2.10	9.91	3.91	41.5	**5.9**	58.5	9.9	**9.9**
3.6	4.23	18.8	0.18	**4.4**	2.0	1.03	8.62	3.65	71.1	**5.0**	41.6	10.6	**7.4**
5.6	0.35	2.4	0.01	**6.9**	2.1	1.46	11.72	3.08	41.9	**0.9**	2.1	18.3	**7.4**
6.8	0.00	0.0	0.00	**0.7**	0.0	-0.59	-1.48	2.50	126.8	**7.3**	73.6	0.0	**5.5**
5.8	1.66	6.9	0.05	**5.3**	0.6	1.03	9.39	3.59	68.4	**4.5**	25.5	7.0	**5.9**
6.4	0.50	4.1	0.00	**5.4**	1.9	1.38	16.08	3.85	52.9	**1.1**	15.6	30.2	**5.5**
10.0	0.13	0.2	0.01	**5.0**	4.8	1.49	12.82	2.66	42.4	**3.1**	64.7	38.2	**8.2**
4.5	6.69	13.0	0.00	**6.2**	1.9	1.82	17.16	4.08	64.1	**3.6**	46.1	18.4	**6.2**
6.6	0.82	5.5	0.00	**5.1**	10.6	1.06	12.81	2.47	55.9	**4.6**	27.6	11.0	**7.3**
6.3	1.47	4.8	-0.03	**5.5**	4.4	1.27	12.09	2.91	56.5	**5.3**	51.1	11.4	**7.4**
10.0	0.00	0.0	1.87	**9.5**	278.7	485.66	1324.29	0.16	14.1	**8.7**	113.8	0.0	**8.3**
7.9	0.00	0.0	0.00	**2.9**	0.3	0.55	4.82	3.18	83.1	**5.4**	36.8	5.9	**6.6**
4.2	1.50	10.7	0.08	**4.4**	0.8	1.05	11.55	3.78	72.2	**5.3**	42.3	8.2	**5.5**
6.4	0.58	3.1	0.20	**5.7**	1.0	1.44	13.67	4.02	64.7	**1.0**	25.2	35.7	**6.9**
9.2	0.00	0.0	-0.01	**5.5**	3.3	1.31	11.89	2.84	56.1	**2.0**	25.2	20.2	**8.3**
7.2	0.12	1.7	0.00	**5.5**	0.5	0.81	7.69	2.27	91.7	**1.4**	22.4	22.6	**8.5**
8.4	0.68	1.9	0.13	**5.2**	4.1	0.81	4.85	4.42	87.9	**3.8**	22.2	8.0	**9.4**
6.8	0.00	0.0	-0.02	**8.8**	8.1	2.16	14.99	4.39	51.2	**4.3**	10.8	0.5	**9.9**
6.2	0.64	2.8	0.00	**5.3**	8.3	1.05	9.28	2.50	58.2	**5.7**	38.2	7.9	**9.8**
9.6	0.39	0.9	0.00	**1.9**	0.0	-0.08	-0.52	2.03	102.6	**6.8**	73.5	6.8	**7.3**

Name	City	State	Rating	2020 Rating	2019 Rating	Total Assets ($Mil)	One Year Asset Growth	Asset Mix (As a % of Total Assets) Comm-ercial Loans	Cons-umer Loans	Mort-gage Loans	Secur-ities	Capital-ization Index	Lever-age Ratio	Risk-Based Capital Ratio
Fidelity Bank, N.A.	Wichita	KS	**B-**	C+	B-	2734.2	0.01	10.6	4.3	13.2	10.8	**6.4**	9.3	12.1
▲ Fidelity Co-operative Bank	Leominster	MA	**B-**	C+	C+	1200.4	3.47	13.5	0.2	24.8	15.5	**8.6**	10.1	15.2
Fidelity Federal S&L Assn. of Delaware	Delaware	OH	**C-**	C-	C-	130.6	14.97	0.0	1.0	29.1	45.3	**10.0**	17.6	41.1
Fidelity Personal Trust Co., F.S.B.	Boston	MA	**U**	U	U	124.4	23.94	0.0	0.0	0.0	0.0	**10.0**	103.	0.0
Fidelity State Bank and Trust Co.	Topeka	KS	**C+**	C+	C+	157.7	4.21	9.9	14.5	6.3	17.3	**6.3**	8.3	0.0
Field & Main Bank	Henderson	KY	**B-**	B-	C+	606.0	13.04	14.5	0.6	17.1	7.6	**6.2**	8.2	13.1
▼ Fieldpoint Private Bank & Trust	Greenwich	CT	**C**	C+	B	1150.7	20.64	5.7	9.2	30.6	9.7	**8.5**	10.0	14.3
Fifth District Savings Bank	New Orleans	LA	**B-**	B-	B-	452.4	0.70	0.3	0.2	66.4	18.8	**10.0**	17.4	38.1
Fifth Third Bank, N.A.	Cincinnati	OH	**B**	B	B	203979.3	1.34	21.2	9.8	10.7	18.4	**6.5**	8.5	13.3
▲ Finance Factors, Ltd.	Honolulu	HI	**B+**	B	B	559.2	-5.43	0.0	1.0	31.4	11.7	**10.0**	13.5	19.5
Financial Federal Bank	Memphis	TN	**A-**	A-	A-	751.2	6.61	17.2	3.3	21.7	0.0	**7.8**	11.9	0.0
Financial Security Bank	Kerkhoven	MN	**B-**	B-	C+	125.1	0.82	17.3	0.5	8.4	2.6	**6.0**	8.0	12.5
FineMark National Bank & Trust	Fort Myers	FL	**B-**	B-	B-	2979.6	18.33	6.2	5.0	36.3	24.3	**7.8**	9.5	17.7
Finwise Bank	Murray	UT	**A-**	B+	A-	281.8	5.42	10.6	26.2	7.0	0.6	**10.0**	19.2	0.0
First & Farmers National Bank, Inc.	Somerset	KY	**B-**	B-	B-	617.5	8.82	3.4	2.5	26.5	34.7	**8.6**	10.1	15.8
▲ First & Peoples Bank and Trust Co.	Russell	KY	**B**	B-	B	237.5	9.66	9.0	21.9	7.5	46.1	**10.0**	17.5	0.0
▲ First American Bank	Elk Grove Village	IL	**C**	C-	C+	5731.7	-4.37	10.3	2.8	4.7	51.2	**5.1**	7.1	16.3
First American Bank	Artesia	NM	**A**	A	A	1519.0	4.14	10.8	0.2	6.7	42.0	**7.7**	9.5	18.6
First American Bank	Stonewall	OK	**B-**	B-	B	32.1	-0.96	18.1	8.1	20.1	7.8	**10.0**	11.9	0.0
First American Bank and Trust	Vacherie	LA	**A-**	A	A	1149.4	9.90	5.1	1.1	22.4	31.5	**10.0**	12.9	23.0
First American Bank and Trust Co.	Athens	GA	**B+**	B+	A-	853.4	28.39	5.1	0.3	12.3	13.7	**6.8**	8.8	19.1
▲ First American National Bank	Iuka	MS	**B**	B-	B-	365.1	16.88	7.9	5.6	23.0	35.6	**8.0**	9.6	0.0
First American State Bank	Greenwood Village	CO	**B-**	B-	B-	263.4	-2.21	3.1	0.0	32.3	17.3	**7.9**	9.6	15.3
First American Trust, F.S.B.	Santa Ana	CA	**U**	U	U	6792.9	53.82	0.0	0.0	0.0	76.2	**4.0**	6.0	26.4
First Arkansas Bank and Trust	Jacksonville	AR	**B-**	C+	B-	946.3	12.49	18.1	7.9	7.9	20.6	**7.6**	9.5	0.0
First Bank	Ketchikan	AK	**B**	B-	B-	759.0	15.27	8.9	1.1	3.6	46.6	**6.6**	8.6	22.4
First Bank	Wadley	AL	**B+**	B+	B+	116.9	17.16	6.5	1.6	3.9	56.7	**6.7**	8.7	13.9
First Bank	Clewiston	FL	**B**	B	B	573.3	17.74	7.8	1.5	11.9	18.1	**5.8**	7.8	13.9
First Bank	Dalton	GA	**B-**	C+	B-	506.9	8.47	9.2	1.3	13.1	15.5	**7.7**	9.8	0.0
First Bank	Waverly	IA	**B+**	B+	B+	628.6	7.90	11.4	1.1	8.2	19.1	**9.3**	10.5	19.2
First Bank	Sterling	KS	**A-**	A-	B+	146.3	-10.30	8.5	0.8	11.0	39.5	**10.0**	11.8	0.0
First Bank	Creve Coeur	MO	**A-**	A-	B+	6728.2	-3.07	13.0	0.3	8.3	36.9	**7.3**	9.2	16.7
First Bank	McComb	MS	**C**	C+	B	626.4	2.04	6.5	1.1	16.6	9.8	**7.5**	9.3	16.7
First Bank	Southern Pines	NC	**A-**	A-	B+	8201.6	19.16	6.1	0.7	11.4	29.4	**7.5**	9.4	15.0
▲ First Bank	Hamilton	NJ	**B+**	B	B	2443.1	6.19	15.6	0.2	4.7	4.9	**8.0**	9.8	13.3
▲ First Bank	Erick	OK	**A**	A-	A-	94.9	12.92	28.8	3.5	8.7	5.8	**10.0**	11.5	16.8
First Bank	Burkburnett	TX	**B+**	B	B-	576.1	4.28	17.2	0.8	33.2	1.0	**8.7**	11.0	14.0
First Bank	Strasburg	VA	**B+**	B+	A-	1023.6	8.77	10.0	0.5	19.9	22.8	**6.8**	8.8	16.3
First Bank & Trust	Brookings	SD	**B+**	B+	B+	3833.7	68.98	16.1	2.0	6.5	24.6	**6.2**	9.4	0.0
First Bank & Trust	Lubbock	TX	**B+**	B+	B+	2883.0	129.41	11.7	0.7	10.5	34.8	**7.9**	9.6	15.0
First Bank & Trust Co.	Duncan	OK	**B+**	B+	B+	767.0	22.07	6.6	2.4	20.8	9.8	**10.0**	12.6	19.8
First Bank & Trust Co.	Perry	OK	**B**	B	A-	228.9	2.00	6.1	5.3	12.7	40.4	**8.0**	9.6	0.0
▲ First Bank and Trust	New Orleans	LA	**B**	C+	B-	1277.4	9.72	11.4	2.6	21.9	4.0	**6.9**	8.9	13.5
▲ First Bank and Trust Co.	Minden	NE	**B**	C+	C+	84.3	10.44	7.9	2.5	15.6	39.3	**7.9**	9.6	19.1
First Bank and Trust Co.	Clinton	OK	**C+**	C+	B	69.3	18.51	4.5	6.4	12.8	36.2	**10.0**	11.1	0.0
▲ First Bank and Trust Co. of Illinois	Palatine	IL	**C-**	D+	C-	217.7	14.45	16.5	0.0	1.2	0.0	**6.1**	8.1	12.9
First Bank and Trust of Childress	Childress	TX	**C+**	C+	C+	154.4	13.53	12.4	2.7	7.0	47.6	**5.6**	7.6	18.5
First Bank and Trust of Fullerton	Fullerton	NE	**B+**	B+	B+	98.3	0.09	9.3	0.7	0.2	14.2	**10.0**	14.5	0.0
First Bank and Trust of Memphis	Memphis	TX	**B-**	B	B+	63.4	6.56	6.7	0.4	14.0	0.0	**10.0**	12.0	21.3
First Bank Blue Earth	Blue Earth	MN	**A-**	A-	A-	297.5	10.84	8.2	1.3	4.5	42.5	**6.9**	8.9	0.0
First Bank Elk River	Elk River	MN	**C+**	C	C+	376.3	12.97	18.1	0.7	6.0	20.5	**6.3**	8.3	15.0
First Bank Hampton	Hampton	IA	**A-**	A-	A-	206.8	9.57	16.4	3.7	10.9	14.3	**9.8**	10.8	0.0
First Bank Kansas	Salina	KS	**B+**	B+	B+	574.2	16.11	5.9	2.6	13.2	42.8	**5.9**	7.9	17.2
▼ First Bank of Alabama	Talladega	AL	**B+**	A-	A-	832.4	28.71	11.1	1.1	10.7	27.8	**9.6**	10.8	17.1
First Bank of Bancroft	Bancroft	NE	**B-**	B-	B-	28.1	14.84	6.3	1.7	3.1	55.0	**10.0**	14.3	0.0
First Bank of Beloit	Beloit	KS	**B+**	B	B-	96.5	13.24	9.6	1.5	14.7	33.4	**10.0**	12.0	23.6
First Bank of Berne	Berne	IN	**A-**	A-	B+	975.5	13.62	3.4	0.6	14.5	28.9	**6.5**	8.5	13.2
First Bank of Boaz	Boaz	AL	**A+**	A+	A+	274.2	-2.00	5.4	1.6	4.6	72.6	**10.0**	17.2	32.1
First Bank of Central Ohio	Worthington	OH	**D-**			35.8	na	9.0	0.0	1.3	0.0	**9.8**	103.	0.0
First Bank of Coastal Georgia	Pembroke	GA	**B-**	B-	B-	150.5	12.78	1.6	0.4	7.2	69.4	**10.0**	12.6	33.5

Asset Quality Index	Adjusted Non-Performing Loans as a % of Total Loans	Adjusted Non-Performing Loans as a % of Capital	Net Charge-Offs Avg Loans	Profitability Index	Net Income ($Mil)	Return on Assets (R.O.A.)	Return on Equity (R.O.E.)	Net Interest Spread	Overhead Efficiency Ratio	Liquidity Index	Liquidity Ratio	Hot Money Ratio	Stability Index
4.0	1.77	7.9	0.00	**4.8**	9.3	0.68	7.62	3.59	73.3	**1.8**	6.4	11.2	**8.3**
6.1	1.58	6.2	0.00	**4.2**	6.8	1.20	13.29	3.54	67.1	**2.6**	15.6	12.5	**6.2**
9.8	0.15	0.4	-0.01	**1.8**	0.2	0.26	1.40	2.70	94.8	**6.5**	66.1	7.9	**7.1**
10.0	na	0.0	na	**9.5**	23.2	41.06	42.11	1.70	38.9	**4.0**	na	100.0	**6.5**
7.4	0.21	1.2	-0.02	**3.1**	0.4	0.57	6.45	2.58	79.0	**6.0**	48.8	6.2	**5.2**
4.5	1.07	6.4	-0.10	**5.3**	3.5	1.21	12.68	3.40	66.4	**1.9**	22.6	21.1	**6.5**
4.4	1.73	12.6	0.09	**2.5**	1.3	0.23	2.23	2.63	88.9	**2.2**	12.1	18.0	**6.9**
10.0	0.11	0.2	0.03	**2.9**	0.9	0.38	2.14	2.60	81.9	**2.3**	28.9	20.0	**7.8**
5.1	1.16	4.1	0.20	**7.1**	1448.9	1.44	12.01	2.72	60.0	**6.6**	36.7	0.5	**10.0**
9.1	0.27	2.2	0.06	**5.6**	3.3	1.20	9.10	3.77	66.8	**1.5**	20.0	26.2	**8.2**
7.1	0.09	0.4	0.05	**7.8**	7.6	2.00	17.18	3.17	43.4	**0.4**	3.7	60.8	**9.7**
5.4	0.62	5.3	0.00	**5.7**	0.9	1.46	18.11	3.93	65.9	**4.6**	19.8	5.4	**5.7**
8.9	0.13	1.0	0.00	**4.3**	12.9	0.90	9.73	2.35	62.9	**5.4**	22.4	2.3	**7.4**
7.0	0.38	1.4	0.89	**10.0**	12.3	7.99	52.90	12.70	41.0	**1.3**	17.4	20.1	**8.0**
7.8	0.23	1.1	-0.06	**4.4**	3.0	0.97	8.03	3.76	69.7	**3.8**	37.4	15.1	**8.7**
6.5	0.79	3.4	0.28	**4.8**	1.2	1.03	5.89	4.14	63.2	**5.3**	38.1	7.2	**7.5**
6.7	1.46	4.2	-0.12	**2.7**	39.0	1.38	16.24	2.33	84.2	**6.3**	37.7	3.1	**6.3**
8.8	0.31	1.2	0.03	**8.3**	14.0	1.89	18.29	3.49	53.0	**5.9**	32.4	4.8	**10.0**
4.4	0.51	7.7	-0.01	**6.5**	0.3	1.52	12.80	4.49	65.9	**2.3**	24.8	18.6	**6.9**
7.4	0.88	3.6	-0.12	**5.5**	6.3	1.11	8.38	3.47	64.3	**5.4**	35.9	9.0	**10.0**
7.6	0.63	2.4	0.01	**5.3**	4.0	1.02	11.37	2.60	63.6	**5.7**	37.3	4.1	**6.5**
5.0	1.71	8.7	0.09	**5.4**	2.5	1.43	14.12	4.52	70.3	**4.9**	36.7	9.4	**5.3**
9.1	0.00	0.0	0.00	**4.1**	1.1	0.86	9.24	3.65	69.2	**0.9**	24.1	44.0	**5.4**
10.0	na	0.0	na	**5.6**	22.0	0.82	11.56	1.29	39.4	**8.7**	105.3	0.0	**6.1**
3.3	1.37	5.5	0.49	**8.4**	11.3	2.46	16.58	3.84	64.4	**4.7**	28.1	6.7	**8.8**
8.8	0.31	1.0	-0.15	**5.0**	4.7	1.34	13.43	2.54	68.6	**6.0**	55.1	8.7	**6.5**
9.0	0.08	0.3	-0.01	**7.6**	1.6	2.84	26.79	5.14	51.3	**6.5**	72.7	8.8	**7.0**
7.3	0.00	0.0	0.00	**4.8**	2.7	0.98	12.40	3.49	64.3	**5.2**	35.4	6.4	**5.6**
4.6	1.28	7.8	0.00	**9.1**	4.5	1.83	19.32	4.57	52.7	**4.1**	36.1	13.3	**6.6**
6.4	0.66	3.1	0.05	**5.2**	3.4	1.07	9.48	3.04	54.9	**4.4**	35.7	11.6	**7.7**
9.0	0.01	0.1	-0.22	**5.3**	0.9	1.19	9.49	3.62	59.7	**4.6**	31.4	8.5	**8.1**
6.8	1.03	4.9	0.31	**6.0**	28.8	0.86	8.81	2.75	67.0	**6.0**	41.2	6.1	**8.9**
3.4	2.03	18.9	0.01	**2.5**	0.7	0.23	2.44	2.61	87.2	**5.2**	37.3	7.7	**6.2**
6.3	0.85	3.1	0.08	**7.5**	58.6	1.52	12.53	3.26	52.1	**5.3**	28.6	7.0	**10.0**
5.6	0.49	3.5	0.01	**6.6**	18.6	1.55	15.07	3.56	47.2	**1.8**	12.0	12.1	**8.4**
8.2	0.00	0.0	-0.12	**10.0**	1.1	2.77	24.11	5.67	50.3	**5.1**	33.4	5.7	**8.5**
4.9	0.77	5.4	-0.01	**9.7**	8.8	3.11	27.28	4.07	63.9	**3.5**	8.1	11.0	**9.6**
7.6	0.34	2.2	0.32	**6.1**	6.3	1.26	14.27	3.28	65.4	**5.9**	31.6	4.4	**8.6**
6.7	0.96	4.0	0.04	**8.0**	27.4	1.47	13.90	3.88	56.8	**3.5**	19.6	9.6	**9.8**
4.7	0.97	3.1	0.08	**6.0**	17.8	1.19	7.58	3.67	68.6	**4.4**	36.2	14.7	**8.4**
4.2	2.62	12.1	0.20	**8.4**	5.9	1.67	11.99	4.60	61.5	**4.0**	24.8	9.9	**9.9**
5.0	1.89	6.2	0.08	**7.2**	1.9	1.65	15.48	4.04	59.1	**4.6**	37.6	11.1	**8.9**
5.7	0.25	2.1	-0.01	**8.1**	12.1	1.99	21.89	4.08	62.9	**1.6**	14.9	24.6	**9.5**
8.3	0.00	0.0	0.02	**4.7**	0.5	1.25	12.65	3.45	63.9	**4.0**	33.5	12.9	**5.8**
9.1	0.00	0.1	0.71	**3.1**	0.2	0.52	4.49	2.73	82.2	**4.7**	49.5	13.2	**5.4**
7.4	0.00	0.0	0.00	**2.9**	1.3	1.22	15.20	4.43	69.0	**1.6**	33.7	33.8	**3.9**
8.2	0.10	0.3	0.00	**3.3**	0.5	0.62	7.65	2.05	70.2	**0.8**	21.3	45.8	**4.5**
7.4	0.00	0.3	-0.01	**5.9**	0.6	1.29	8.85	3.72	55.1	**2.0**	26.4	15.2	**8.1**
8.9	0.00	0.0	0.00	**2.8**	0.1	0.31	2.62	2.35	87.8	**2.4**	42.9	31.2	**7.4**
8.2	0.25	1.4	-0.16	**6.4**	2.4	1.66	17.28	3.06	52.8	**3.5**	22.9	12.1	**7.4**
8.0	0.23	1.6	0.02	**3.3**	1.4	0.75	8.93	2.55	74.6	**3.7**	25.0	9.6	**4.7**
5.4	1.83	5.6	0.08	**6.2**	1.5	1.43	12.75	3.26	56.3	**4.5**	31.8	9.6	**8.7**
7.8	0.00	1.1	-0.05	**7.9**	5.5	1.98	22.71	3.27	59.0	**4.4**	42.2	13.5	**7.4**
4.6	2.74	12.7	0.06	**8.1**	6.5	1.70	15.28	3.84	49.9	**1.7**	27.7	27.5	**8.9**
6.5	8.00	8.1	-0.08	**4.2**	0.1	0.80	5.53	3.02	67.7	**6.6**	63.5	4.4	**6.9**
9.0	0.00	0.4	0.00	**5.6**	0.6	1.24	10.71	4.13	60.1	**4.5**	26.3	7.0	**6.7**
6.6	0.52	3.4	-0.01	**9.0**	9.5	2.00	22.31	3.19	46.1	**5.9**	33.9	1.6	**8.0**
9.7	0.11	0.2	-0.01	**7.8**	2.8	1.99	11.09	3.41	36.3	**4.1**	75.0	23.7	**9.6**
9.3	0.00	0.0	0.00	**0.0**	-0.5	-9.20	-3.89	1.09	859.0	**10.0**	246.8	0.0	**1.3**
9.9	0.15	0.1	0.00	**3.0**	0.5	0.68	4.98	2.66	79.9	**5.5**	40.3	6.5	**7.1**

	Name	City	State	Rating	2020 Rating	2019 Rating	Total Assets ($Mil)	One Year Asset Growth	Asset Mix (As a % of Total Assets) Comm-ercial Loans	Cons-umer Loans	Mort-gage Loans	Secur-ities	Capital-ization Index	Lever-age Ratio	Risk-Based Capital Ratio
	First Bank of Highland Park	Highland Park	IL	**C**	C	C+	1959.3	0.38	29.9	0.1	2.5	16.1	**5.3**	10.2	0.0
	First Bank of Manhattan	Manhattan	IL	**C+**	C+	B-	233.4	15.19	6.9	1.1	17.3	22.9	**6.0**	8.0	20.8
	First Bank of Ohio	Tiffin	OH	**A-**	A-	B+	249.0	15.90	0.0	78.6	0.0	15.3	**10.0**	31.4	0.0
	First Bank of Okarche	Okarche	OK	**A-**	A-	A	128.3	10.85	6.0	1.5	1.4	33.7	**9.6**	10.7	0.0
	First Bank of Owasso	Owasso	OK	**A**	A	A-	578.5	7.44	8.8	0.3	7.1	3.7	**9.2**	10.4	16.7
▲	First Bank of Pike	Molena	GA	**C**	C-	C-	69.5	18.64	5.6	9.8	20.6	17.6	**6.1**	8.1	16.0
▲	First Bank of the Lake	Osage Beach	MO	**B**	C+	C	962.6	58.07	84.5	0.1	0.5	1.8	**8.9**	10.3	27.8
	First Bank of Thomas	Thomas	OK	**B+**	B+	B+	50.3	4.72	3.9	0.4	9.1	17.3	**10.0**	14.8	31.6
▲	First Bank of Utica	Utica	NE	**B**	C+	C+	78.6	9.98	8.1	3.7	8.1	2.5	**10.0**	11.0	17.0
	First Bank Richmond	Richmond	IN	**B-**	B-	B-	1186.0	3.96	9.3	1.3	10.9	28.7	**10.0**	13.7	19.1
	First Bank, Upper Michigan	Gladstone	MI	**C**	C	D+	575.0	10.00	14.8	8.7	12.5	17.3	**8.3**	9.9	15.0
	First Bankers Trust Co., N.A.	Quincy	IL	**B-**	B-	B-	1181.9	8.30	5.9	3.3	5.7	52.2	**6.1**	8.1	16.9
	First Bethany Bank & Trust	Bethany	OK	**B+**	B+	B	265.7	6.06	6.5	0.4	10.9	46.0	**7.4**	9.2	0.0
	First Business Bank	Madison	WI	**B-**	C+	B-	2860.8	16.49	24.5	0.3	0.8	6.7	**5.0**	9.2	11.0
▼	First Cahawba Bank	Selma	AL	**B-**	B	B	181.8	25.83	14.1	2.6	12.2	27.9	**5.9**	7.9	15.4
	First Capital Bank	Laurinburg	NC	**D+**	D+	C-	331.6	60.93	4.8	1.3	19.4	10.9	**7.6**	9.4	14.3
	First Capital Bank	Germantown	TN	**B-**	B-	B-	377.7	6.25	13.6	0.3	10.9	1.4	**5.7**	10.2	0.0
	First Capital Bank	Quanah	TX	**C-**	C-	C	74.0	-6.36	15.4	6.6	16.2	0.0	**6.7**	8.9	12.2
▲	First Carolina Bank	Rocky Mount	NC	**A-**	B	B	1249.9	37.82	10.3	0.1	6.3	12.3	**10.0**	14.1	15.5
	First Central Bank	Cambridge	NE	**D+**	C-	C-	119.0	0.64	13.8	4.6	2.3	9.9	**6.2**	10.4	0.0
	First Central Bank McCook	McCook	NE	**D**	D	C-	121.9	0.92	19.6	2.8	3.7	9.9	**7.6**	11.9	0.0
▲	First Central Savings Bank	Glen Cove	NY	**C+**	C-	D+	678.1	4.53	7.5	0.0	30.5	4.8	**7.3**	9.2	13.4
	First Central State Bank	De Witt	IA	**A-**	A-	A-	707.0	16.31	11.1	1.6	11.5	29.2	**9.5**	10.6	0.0
	First Century Bank	Tazewell	TN	**B+**	B+	B+	515.4	9.33	5.9	1.1	24.5	0.7	**6.7**	8.7	13.8
	First Century Bank, N.A.	Commerce	GA	**A**	A	B	324.2	-1.25	4.7	0.1	1.8	24.5	**10.0**	18.9	0.0
	First Chatham Bank	Savannah	GA	**B-**	C+	C-	528.7	21.76	10.2	0.3	5.6	6.3	**5.9**	7.9	14.5
	First Choice Bank	Pontotoc	MS	**B+**	A-	A-	387.8	12.34	9.5	4.7	20.2	32.4	**10.0**	11.3	0.0
	First Citizens Bank	Luverne	AL	**A-**	A-	A-	323.7	9.74	7.9	3.6	10.8	35.5	**10.0**	11.9	0.0
	First Citizens Bank	Mason City	IA	**A-**	A-	A-	1559.8	7.34	13.1	1.1	6.8	20.5	**10.0**	11.3	16.9
	First Citizens Bank of Butte	Butte	MT	**B-**	B	B-	88.6	13.26	11.8	4.6	14.1	16.7	**6.9**	8.9	0.0
	First Citizens Community Bank	Mansfield	PA	**B**	B	B	1999.9	11.20	4.9	0.5	16.1	18.5	**6.4**	8.7	0.0
	First Citizens National Bank	Dyersburg	TN	**B+**	B+	B+	2117.7	8.61	4.8	1.2	9.0	38.9	**7.9**	9.6	0.0
	First Citizens State Bank	Whitewater	WI	**A-**	A-	A-	388.8	12.67	5.7	0.6	18.2	23.7	**10.0**	17.6	0.0
	First Citrus Bank	Tampa	FL	**C+**	C+	B-	631.3	14.89	18.4	0.0	5.8	0.1	**2.9**	8.1	0.0
	First City Bank	Columbus	OH	**B**	B-	C+	71.9	-7.06	10.1	0.0	14.8	1.1	**10.0**	12.2	0.0
	First Colony Bank of Florida	Maitland	FL	**B+**	B+	B	263.3	-0.30	10.5	0.2	0.8	17.6	**7.4**	9.2	13.7
	First Colorado National Bank	Paonia	CO	**C**	C+	B	90.0	19.28	0.7	0.2	0.6	0.0	**7.1**	9.1	120.5
	First Columbia Bank & Trust Co.	Bloomsburg	PA	**A-**	A-	A-	913.4	11.42	4.5	0.6	24.3	30.7	**9.3**	10.5	0.0
	First Command Bank	Fort Worth	TX	**B+**	B+	A-	1008.8	14.13	11.3	19.9	0.0	54.3	**5.6**	7.6	14.7
	First Commerce Bank	Marysville	KS	**B+**	B+	B+	130.2	17.88	9.6	4.4	23.1	12.6	**6.6**	8.6	0.0
▲	First Commerce Bank	Lakewood	NJ	**A-**	B	C+	1095.1	2.00	8.9	0.0	19.4	4.9	**10.0**	14.8	20.0
	First Commerce Bank	Lewisburg	TN	**B**	B	B	507.0	3.46	5.0	2.8	16.0	10.6	**6.8**	8.8	13.1
	First Commercial Bank	Jackson	MS	**C+**	C+	B	634.4	29.54	18.4	1.1	18.5	2.6	**8.2**	11.2	0.0
	First Commercial Bank (U.S.A)	Alhambra	CA	**A-**	A-	A-	792.5	8.05	7.1	0.0	14.0	4.3	**10.0**	19.4	25.2
	First Commercial Bank, N.A.	Seguin	TX	**B**	B	B	484.0	17.07	5.9	1.1	13.2	17.6	**5.7**	7.7	14.5
	First Commonwealth Bank	Indiana	PA	**B+**	B+	B+	9377.3	0.40	13.1	9.8	13.6	17.6	**7.1**	9.1	14.5
	First Community Bank	Batesville	AR	**B-**	B-	B-	1895.0	12.39	13.3	4.2	18.3	13.3	**5.2**	8.8	11.1
	First Community Bank	Newell	IA	**B**	B	B	112.5	10.51	3.9	2.2	5.7	26.6	**6.3**	8.3	14.4
	First Community Bank	Harbor Springs	MI	**B+**	B+	B+	422.5	16.70	12.9	0.6	7.1	7.7	**6.3**	8.3	13.8
	First Community Bank	Lester Prairie	MN	**B-**	B-	B-	78.7	13.72	5.8	1.1	10.0	28.3	**7.1**	9.0	0.0
	First Community Bank	Glasgow	MT	**A-**	A-	B	373.6	9.39	7.3	1.4	6.7	34.4	**9.4**	10.6	15.9
	First Community Bank	Beemer	NE	**B-**	B-	B-	174.1	4.56	12.5	1.5	5.8	17.1	**9.2**	10.4	17.9
	First Community Bank	Lexington	SC	**B**	B	B+	1515.0	14.30	7.0	0.5	9.5	31.0	**6.5**	8.5	14.7
	First Community Bank	Corpus Christi	TX	**B+**	B+	A-	576.5	8.22	19.3	1.5	13.6	15.1	**9.3**	10.5	17.8
	First Community Bank	San Benito	TX	**B+**	B	B	667.7	17.13	12.2	0.6	6.5	24.3	**6.1**	8.1	15.3
	First Community Bank	Bluefield	VA	**B**	B	B	3124.3	5.97	4.6	3.9	27.8	2.6	**7.2**	9.1	14.9
	First Community Bank	Milton	WI	**A-**	A-	A-	130.7	2.80	6.4	1.0	17.3	26.7	**8.1**	9.8	13.9
▼	First Community Bank and Trust	Beecher	IL	**B**	B+	A-	195.0	16.73	14.3	1.3	5.0	14.6	**9.9**	10.9	0.0
	First Community Bank of Central Alabama	Wetumpka	AL	**B+**	B+	B+	513.8	10.77	6.0	3.3	11.1	34.5	**6.1**	8.1	11.8
	First Community Bank of Cullman	Cullman	AL	**C+**	C+	C+	124.8	-1.55	4.7	2.3	31.2	0.9	**7.5**	9.3	0.0

Asset Quality Index	Adjusted Non-Performing Loans as a % of Total Loans	Adjusted Non-Performing Loans as a % of Capital	Net Charge-Offs Avg Loans	Profitability Index	Net Income ($Mil)	Return on Assets (R.O.A.)	Return on Equity (R.O.E.)	Net Interest Spread	Overhead Efficiency Ratio	Liquidity Index	Liquidity Ratio	Hot Money Ratio	Stability Index
6.7	0.93	3.2	0.00	**3.0**	4.1	0.45	4.41	2.41	72.8	**1.8**	25.3	21.1	**7.6**
6.9	0.65	2.0	0.03	**3.1**	0.6	0.56	6.86	3.01	80.4	**5.7**	37.4	4.4	**5.1**
5.6	0.06	0.2	0.34	**9.4**	2.3	1.94	6.09	6.01	34.5	**0.5**	23.5	64.3	**7.5**
9.3	0.00	0.0	0.27	**6.1**	0.9	1.38	12.89	2.64	49.3	**5.9**	75.4	12.6	**7.8**
7.5	0.00	0.4	-0.02	**9.6**	7.5	2.62	25.41	3.89	38.0	**4.1**	28.4	6.4	**9.6**
5.8	0.43	4.1	0.21	**3.9**	0.2	0.64	8.18	4.78	80.8	**4.8**	39.1	10.8	**3.0**
6.6	0.11	1.0	0.19	**7.3**	9.4	1.99	77.08	3.47	46.6	**0.5**	6.1	46.3	**6.0**
8.5	0.81	2.3	0.02	**4.4**	0.2	0.92	5.97	3.46	70.5	**5.0**	53.9	12.6	**8.8**
6.6	0.65	3.8	-0.01	**4.9**	0.4	0.99	9.03	3.70	65.4	**1.8**	29.0	27.4	**6.9**
7.4	0.72	4.5	0.02	**3.8**	6.5	1.14	8.20	3.39	58.6	**1.9**	19.1	16.7	**9.1**
3.0	2.75	10.1	0.12	**7.8**	4.7	1.70	13.77	3.52	60.4	**3.7**	31.3	13.7	**8.9**
5.2	2.43	10.0	-0.02	**3.7**	3.8	0.65	7.10	2.16	68.9	**3.4**	20.6	9.7	**7.4**
9.1	0.23	1.0	0.00	**5.0**	2.1	1.57	15.92	2.68	65.0	**4.7**	37.4	9.7	**7.0**
5.0	0.53	3.8	-0.02	**6.9**	20.3	1.57	16.82	3.61	58.8	**4.3**	20.9	1.8	**7.2**
8.8	0.03	0.2	2.16	**2.1**	-0.2	-0.18	-2.16	3.95	74.0	**5.5**	37.9	5.8	**5.1**
7.4	0.44	2.4	0.00	**1.5**	0.4	0.27	2.69	3.09	78.3	**1.5**	32.1	36.6	**5.5**
6.0	0.44	1.8	0.02	**5.0**	1.9	1.02	9.86	3.15	53.3	**0.8**	19.0	51.4	**6.1**
3.9	1.25	12.3	0.19	**4.2**	0.2	0.65	7.27	4.80	76.6	**1.6**	15.5	23.0	**4.3**
7.4	0.00	0.0	0.00	**5.9**	7.6	1.33	10.50	3.37	42.0	**1.2**	23.3	29.5	**9.3**
0.0	6.47	39.3	-0.08	**5.9**	0.8	1.27	12.29	4.23	60.5	**0.8**	17.9	27.0	**5.4**
0.0	10.68	60.6	0.29	**6.2**	0.8	1.23	10.52	4.02	55.1	**0.7**	16.5	36.7	**5.7**
3.8	2.19	9.4	0.09	**3.9**	3.0	0.87	9.30	3.69	66.4	**0.7**	12.3	33.3	**5.0**
6.9	0.42	2.2	0.04	**5.5**	3.8	1.13	10.03	2.91	57.1	**4.9**	35.7	8.8	**7.9**
8.7	0.20	1.1	0.00	**7.6**	3.6	1.45	16.72	3.88	52.6	**4.1**	25.8	8.9	**6.1**
9.9	1.35	0.7	8.01	**8.1**	3.4	1.43	9.66	4.51	42.3	**8.4**	97.6	0.5	**6.9**
5.0	1.25	6.5	0.75	**6.1**	4.0	1.64	18.65	3.31	62.2	**5.2**	38.3	8.0	**4.2**
8.6	0.19	1.4	0.05	**5.3**	2.0	1.06	9.24	3.66	62.7	**2.0**	26.8	22.1	**7.2**
6.5	1.51	5.7	-0.17	**7.6**	2.5	1.58	12.76	3.84	53.4	**3.2**	32.2	16.6	**8.1**
5.7	1.41	6.7	0.24	**7.1**	13.0	1.67	14.13	2.88	49.9	**4.4**	22.1	8.7	**10.0**
6.3	0.91	4.3	0.43	**3.4**	0.3	0.68	7.31	3.00	78.6	**5.7**	46.0	6.6	**5.3**
5.7	1.14	5.2	0.00	**7.4**	15.4	1.57	15.49	3.58	50.5	**3.3**	13.2	11.5	**9.5**
8.5	0.25	1.2	0.04	**5.2**	12.7	1.24	10.86	3.36	62.9	**3.7**	31.5	16.8	**9.3**
9.5	0.00	0.0	0.00	**5.9**	2.3	1.20	6.88	3.02	57.9	**4.9**	48.3	12.8	**8.2**
7.4	0.17	0.0	0.00	**6.5**	3.9	1.32	16.29	3.94	53.9	**4.7**	27.8	6.3	**5.2**
7.5	0.00	0.0	0.00	**4.5**	0.4	1.18	9.62	4.46	72.4	**3.3**	24.4	13.3	**6.5**
6.3	0.77	2.5	0.00	**7.9**	2.4	1.79	19.29	3.55	46.5	**4.8**	37.2	9.9	**8.0**
9.7	0.00	0.0	0.00	**0.0**	-0.7	-1.55	-9.84	0.92	210.0	**7.9**	104.2	3.3	**7.0**
6.8	0.76	2.8	0.02	**5.2**	4.5	1.02	9.02	2.62	60.9	**4.2**	24.6	8.8	**8.3**
7.6	0.17	0.5	0.15	**8.5**	9.8	2.01	28.13	2.49	60.9	**7.7**	62.6	1.1	**7.0**
5.7	0.63	3.8	0.00	**7.4**	1.1	1.70	18.11	3.60	51.4	**2.7**	35.1	20.3	**7.1**
5.3	1.39	5.9	-0.09	**7.3**	8.7	1.60	10.89	3.90	47.2	**1.8**	17.7	21.6	**9.9**
8.6	0.06	0.4	0.00	**6.3**	3.1	1.25	13.98	3.53	54.1	**1.2**	17.6	30.1	**7.2**
8.3	0.13	0.9	-0.03	**3.5**	1.6	0.51	4.44	3.31	80.6	**1.7**	15.8	11.7	**7.4**
7.3	0.00	0.0	0.00	**5.5**	3.6	0.98	5.06	2.90	51.2	**0.6**	12.3	42.1	**9.3**
5.4	0.89	5.5	0.00	**5.3**	3.0	1.26	15.11	3.50	67.4	**6.0**	38.7	3.1	**5.5**
4.9	0.78	4.0	0.21	**6.8**	72.4	1.57	13.04	3.30	52.8	**4.9**	8.9	2.1	**9.4**
6.3	0.48	3.7	0.04	**6.0**	11.7	1.27	14.55	3.73	60.4	**1.2**	11.8	29.2	**7.5**
7.9	0.00	0.0	-0.01	**4.5**	0.6	0.99	8.68	3.17	67.5	**5.3**	43.1	8.8	**7.2**
7.5	0.03	0.4	-0.01	**6.5**	3.1	1.51	18.06	3.95	63.6	**5.3**	28.8	3.4	**6.6**
9.1	0.00	0.0	0.00	**4.5**	0.4	1.09	11.31	3.69	69.0	**5.1**	46.8	10.6	**5.4**
6.8	0.71	2.2	0.00	**7.8**	3.1	1.71	15.38	4.43	60.3	**4.9**	31.1	6.5	**7.5**
8.0	0.04	0.1	-0.02	**4.5**	0.8	0.94	8.63	3.75	73.6	**2.0**	32.4	23.8	**7.1**
6.2	0.59	5.5	0.02	**4.9**	7.3	1.00	10.02	3.25	66.3	**5.5**	29.0	6.2	**8.3**
6.8	0.51	2.8	0.04	**5.7**	3.6	1.33	12.16	4.78	69.4	**4.2**	30.5	10.7	**8.1**
8.8	0.00	0.3	-0.03	**8.1**	5.6	1.81	20.87	4.28	52.1	**5.1**	39.0	8.9	**6.1**
4.2	1.67	6.8	0.11	**9.1**	28.3	1.82	13.80	3.78	56.1	**5.2**	24.4	5.2	**10.0**
7.2	0.94	2.5	-0.03	**8.8**	1.6	2.42	24.59	3.58	47.1	**5.3**	43.6	9.0	**7.8**
4.2	3.82	13.4	-0.14	**7.0**	1.3	1.34	11.95	4.28	65.1	**6.6**	51.0	3.2	**6.8**
7.7	0.37	1.5	0.00	**8.4**	4.2	1.71	21.08	3.45	54.7	**4.5**	36.3	11.3	**7.5**
5.3	1.67	6.2	0.02	**3.7**	0.4	0.70	7.58	3.04	74.6	**0.9**	23.3	33.0	**5.9**

Name	City	State	Rating	2020 Rating	2019 Rating	Total Assets ($Mil)	One Year Asset Growth	Asset Mix (As a % of Total Assets) Commercial Loans	Consumer Loans	Mortgage Loans	Securities	Capitalization Index	Leverage Ratio	Risk-Based Capital Ratio
▼ First Community Bank of East Tennessee	Rogersville	TN	**B-**	B+	B	198.0	2.79	5.6	1.3	19.5	8.1	**9.8**	10.9	0.0
First Community Bank of Hillsboro	Hillsboro	IL	**B**	B	B	144.5	10.05	7.6	2.1	12.4	42.5	**6.7**	8.7	0.0
First Community Bank of Moultrie County	Sullivan	IL	**B**	B	B	104.9	12.76	4.9	4.0	19.8	26.3	**6.9**	8.9	0.0
First Community Bank of Tennessee	Shelbyville	TN	**A-**	A-	B+	793.3	8.81	3.8	0.4	44.0	10.0	**10.0**	12.1	16.7
First Community Bank of the Heartland, Inc	Clinton	KY	**B-**	B-	B-	343.5	19.02	5.8	3.7	14.2	14.1	**5.9**	8.4	11.7
First Community Bank of the Ozarks	Branson	MO	**B-**	B-	B+	136.0	16.57	6.5	1.8	22.6	18.9	**8.8**	10.2	0.0
First Community Bank Xenia-Flora	Xenia	IL	**B**	B	B	53.1	12.46	4.3	5.8	21.4	32.8	**7.8**	9.6	0.0
▲ First Community National Bank	Cuba	MO	**C-**	D+	C-	157.3	8.81	4.4	1.7	15.9	33.5	**6.2**	8.3	14.5
First Community Trust, N.A.	Dubuque	IA	**U**	U	U	13.6	10.17	0.0	0.0	0.0	36.1	**10.0**	81.6	0.0
▲ First County Bank	Stamford	CT	**C+**	C	C+	2013.6	5.32	7.1	0.8	36.1	16.2	**7.0**	9.0	17.7
▲ First Credit Bank	Los Angeles	CA	**B+**	B	B-	441.3	5.56	2.6	0.0	15.1	2.0	**10.0**	45.3	54.5
First Dakota National Bank	Yankton	SD	**B+**	B+	B	2427.7	23.42	10.2	1.2	5.1	20.0	**6.9**	9.0	12.4
First Eagle Bank	Chicago	IL	**A**	A	A	619.0	8.78	5.6	0.0	18.4	29.3	**10.0**	17.1	0.0
First Electronic Bank	Salt Lake City	UT	**A-**	A-	A-	74.2	107.23	8.9	33.0	0.0	0.0	**10.0**	34.0	58.8
First Enterprise Bank	Oklahoma City	OK	**B+**	B+	B-	199.5	3.91	12.0	0.4	11.9	0.0	**9.0**	10.3	0.0
First Exchange Bank	White Hall	WV	**C**	C-	C-	330.3	4.47	9.2	2.9	35.7	10.6	**7.1**	9.0	0.0
First FarmBank	Greeley	CO	**B**	B-	C+	313.0	9.25	7.8	0.3	9.9	10.1	**7.3**	9.2	14.2
First Farmers & Merchants Bank	Cannon Falls	MN	**B+**	B+	B+	441.0	18.57	9.6	1.5	7.1	31.1	**10.0**	11.2	19.1
First Farmers & Merchants National Bank	Fairmont	MN	**B-**	B	B	135.7	8.36	15.2	2.8	15.1	7.8	**9.3**	10.5	17.1
First Farmers & Merchants National Bank	Luverne	MN	**B-**	B	B	216.2	8.53	12.2	1.2	2.0	15.9	**10.0**	14.0	18.8
First Farmers & Merchants State Bank	Brownsdale	MN	**B**	B	B	91.9	8.99	8.7	0.5	3.0	23.9	**10.0**	15.0	21.6
First Farmers & Merchants State Bank	Grand Meadow	MN	**B**	B	B	78.1	7.04	9.2	0.5	4.6	13.7	**7.2**	9.1	14.0
First Farmers and Commercial Bank	Pikeville	TN	**B-**	B-	B-	189.7	22.09	9.6	2.6	14.9	11.9	**6.7**	8.7	14.1
First Farmers and Merchants Bank	Columbia	TN	**B**	B+	B+	1876.8	16.83	6.6	0.6	14.8	41.8	**6.0**	8.0	14.8
First Farmers Bank & Trust Co.	Converse	IN	**B-**	C+	B-	2298.1	11.35	16.4	0.8	3.5	17.3	**8.5**	10.0	14.1
First Federal Bank	Lake City	FL	**A-**	A-	A-	3175.3	8.76	3.8	1.3	20.0	26.7	**8.4**	9.9	19.3
First Federal Bank	Dunn	NC	**C-**	C	C+	210.5	6.54	5.7	0.3	27.7	27.4	**9.2**	10.4	20.0
First Federal Bank	Dickson	TN	**A-**	A-	A-	867.5	9.75	2.8	2.0	18.8	39.3	**8.1**	9.7	0.0
First Federal Bank & Trust	Sheridan	WY	**A-**	A-	B	406.3	9.35	11.2	1.0	21.4	21.8	**10.0**	16.6	20.1
First Federal Bank Littlefield, Texas, SSB	Littlefield	TX	**B-**	B-	B	53.1	7.17	11.6	9.8	14.5	0.0	**10.0**	18.9	0.0
First Federal Bank Of Kansas City	Kansas City	MO	**C**	C-	D+	786.8	-0.80	0.0	5.6	54.3	13.6	**10.0**	15.3	0.0
▼ First Federal Bank of Louisiana	Lake Charles	LA	**C**	C+	C+	1277.1	27.89	4.2	1.1	19.3	14.0	**7.4**	9.2	23.2
▼ First Federal Bank of Ohio	Galion	OH	**C-**	C+	C+	268.5	8.41	0.1	0.7	29.4	34.2	**10.0**	13.7	34.2
First Federal Bank of Wisconsin	Waukesha	WI	**B**	B	B-	352.5	20.15	5.0	0.1	14.0	14.1	**10.0**	21.7	34.7
▲ First Federal Bank, A FSB	Tuscaloosa	AL	**B**	B-	C	161.1	4.80	0.2	0.2	76.7	0.5	**10.0**	12.8	22.5
First Federal Community Bank of Bucyrus	Bucyrus	OH	**B-**	C+	C+	222.0	7.40	9.7	3.6	39.2	12.3	**6.2**	8.3	13.3
First Federal Community Bank, N.A.	Dover	OH	**B**	B	B	589.4	13.47	9.8	1.3	25.5	7.4	**6.3**	8.3	13.5
First Federal Community Bank, SSB	Paris	TX	**B-**	B	B	533.2	9.58	10.7	2.2	33.1	3.3	**9.5**	10.7	16.3
▲ First Federal S&L Assn.	Hazard	KY	**C+**	C-	C+	90.8	10.64	0.0	1.1	72.0	0.2	**10.0**	20.9	0.0
▼ First Federal S&L Assn.	Morehead	KY	**C**	C+	C+	35.2	4.00	4.5	1.1	50.2	0.0	**10.0**	28.3	53.4
First Federal S&L Assn.	Aberdeen	MS	**C+**	C+	C+	46.7	5.55	0.0	1.9	65.7	11.0	**10.0**	16.4	35.2
▲ First Federal S&L Assn.	Ravenswood	WV	**C**	C-	D+	26.1	6.72	0.0	0.4	66.6	0.0	**6.7**	8.7	18.5
First Federal S&L Assn. of Bath	Bath	ME	**B**	B	B	174.4	17.35	1.5	1.0	54.0	4.4	**10.0**	14.3	29.9
First Federal S&L Assn. of Centerburg	Centerburg	OH	**C**	C+	C+	25.5	6.44	0.0	0.5	54.5	11.2	**10.0**	19.3	0.0
First Federal S&L Assn. of Central Illinois,	Shelbyville	IL	**B+**	B+	B+	162.9	8.52	8.6	4.3	21.9	27.1	**9.4**	10.6	15.8
First Federal S&L Assn. of Delta	Delta	OH	**C-**	C-	C+	212.6	15.98	1.2	0.3	36.8	25.2	**8.7**	10.1	29.3
First Federal S&L Assn. of Greene County	Waynesburg	PA	**C+**	C+	B-	1017.9	3.54	0.0	0.3	60.3	16.2	**10.0**	13.6	32.3
First Federal S&L Assn. of Greensburg	Greensburg	IN	**C+**	C+	C+	175.8	4.48	0.6	1.6	35.0	29.3	**8.8**	10.2	21.9
▼ First Federal S&L Assn. of Lakewood	Lakewood	OH	**C+**	B-	C-	2175.2	1.39	5.2	4.2	49.1	6.0	**9.0**	10.3	0.0
First Federal S&L Assn. of Lorain	Lorain	OH	**D+**	C-	C	484.4	5.78	0.0	0.1	49.3	35.5	**10.0**	13.7	32.7
First Federal S&L Assn. of McMinnville	McMinnville	OR	**B-**	B-	B	597.6	17.71	0.7	0.1	34.3	35.5	**10.0**	11.9	25.4
First Federal S&L Assn. of Newark	Newark	OH	**B-**	B-	C	242.2	5.96	0.0	0.2	35.4	19.7	**10.0**	15.5	0.0
First Federal S&L Assn. of Pascagoula-Mo	Pascagoula	MS	**C**	C	C	325.0	-2.95	0.1	0.3	75.6	10.4	**7.6**	9.4	20.7
First Federal S&L Assn. of Port Angeles	Port Angeles	WA	**B-**	B-	B-	1784.3	21.25	3.8	10.2	18.3	20.8	**9.8**	10.9	15.6
First Federal S&L Assn. of San Rafael	San Rafael	CA	**B-**	B-	B-	225.9	4.40	0.0	0.0	0.8	0.0	**10.0**	18.9	23.8
First Federal S&L Assn. of Valdosta	Valdosta	GA	**C**	C+	B-	221.2	7.23	0.0	2.3	56.2	1.5	**10.0**	13.3	0.0
First Federal S&L Assn. of Van Wert, OH	Van Wert	OH	**B-**	B-	C+	133.2	9.41	0.0	0.2	47.6	32.5	**10.0**	18.3	0.0
First Federal S&L Bank	Olathe	KS	**B+**	B	B	95.0	-2.08	0.4	0.0	74.9	0.0	**10.0**	13.9	0.0
▲ First Federal Savings Bank	Ottawa	IL	**C+**	C-	C	378.0	-2.60	1.7	0.8	40.5	7.4	**10.0**	11.5	25.7
First Federal Savings Bank	Evansville	IN	**C+**	C	C	480.7	1.71	18.9	0.8	22.3	10.5	**6.4**	8.4	13.9

Arrows denote recent upgrades ▲ or downgrades ▼

Asset Quality Index	Adjusted Non-Performing Loans as a % of Total Loans	Adjusted Non-Performing Loans as a % of Capital	Net Charge-Offs / Avg Loans	Profitability Index	Net Income ($Mil)	Return on Assets (R.O.A.)	Return on Equity (R.O.E.)	Net Interest Spread	Overhead Efficiency Ratio	Liquidity Index	Liquidity Ratio	Hot Money Ratio	Stability Index
8.5	0.12	0.6	0.00	**3.4**	0.5	0.53	4.74	3.20	80.9	**4.9**	31.6	7.2	**7.5**
7.5	0.44	2.2	0.00	**5.5**	1.0	1.43	17.07	2.92	53.5	**4.6**	21.7	5.3	**5.0**
7.0	0.54	2.6	-0.01	**4.4**	0.6	1.05	12.08	3.10	69.9	**5.4**	43.9	8.5	**5.6**
7.1	0.09	2.5	0.01	**8.9**	14.7	3.73	29.44	2.74	73.2	**0.7**	13.9	27.9	**9.6**
5.8	0.26	2.9	0.03	**6.1**	2.9	1.83	17.99	4.27	60.1	**1.5**	14.3	19.0	**5.7**
7.5	0.74	2.3	-0.01	**4.6**	0.8	1.14	11.02	3.68	68.3	**4.4**	25.4	7.5	**5.9**
8.8	0.27	1.1	-0.14	**4.6**	0.3	1.02	10.37	2.82	65.4	**4.7**	50.7	13.5	**6.4**
6.0	1.55	6.0	-0.05	**2.8**	0.6	0.73	9.69	3.49	90.7	**5.7**	48.3	8.3	**2.8**
10.0	na	0.0	na	**10.0**	0.5	7.66	8.78	0.34	78.8	**4.0**	367.0	0.0	**6.5**
5.4	2.16	12.9	0.00	**3.4**	6.8	0.69	8.35	2.83	74.4	**3.1**	31.2	15.9	**6.7**
5.6	3.27	4.0	0.00	**10.0**	10.2	4.61	10.23	5.87	17.6	**1.9**	42.4	36.8	**9.0**
6.9	0.36	2.8	-0.03	**8.4**	22.3	1.93	21.21	4.02	52.0	**5.0**	20.3	3.6	**7.9**
8.9	0.86	2.2	-0.05	**9.7**	7.0	2.38	12.93	3.85	39.5	**2.4**	30.1	18.0	**10.0**
7.1	0.00	0.0	0.00	**10.0**	3.6	13.30	37.84	17.85	56.9	**6.4**	75.0	5.4	**9.0**
4.9	2.14	13.2	0.22	**6.1**	1.3	1.26	12.21	3.79	72.6	**1.4**	32.2	28.9	**9.1**
2.7	3.30	19.2	0.58	**4.3**	1.2	0.76	8.34	3.52	67.8	**2.6**	20.7	16.7	**6.6**
7.6	0.00	2.6	0.00	**5.0**	1.6	1.00	10.87	4.07	65.3	**1.7**	16.2	21.6	**5.2**
5.9	1.45	6.5	0.50	**7.6**	4.0	1.85	15.88	3.40	52.2	**5.7**	40.8	5.5	**7.9**
3.0	3.21	18.0	1.17	**4.4**	0.8	1.05	10.42	3.08	62.9	**2.7**	29.2	17.8	**6.8**
1.1	4.66	30.9	1.72	**5.1**	1.1	0.99	7.18	3.25	61.4	**3.6**	17.0	11.0	**8.0**
5.1	1.59	13.4	0.77	**4.9**	0.6	1.20	7.90	3.38	64.5	**5.8**	34.5	1.9	**7.1**
1.8	5.27	32.3	1.06	**3.3**	0.4	0.91	10.35	3.99	63.4	**3.8**	25.1	10.9	**5.1**
5.0	1.02	6.0	0.32	**4.9**	0.9	1.01	11.43	3.79	57.3	**1.1**	20.0	29.1	**4.6**
9.0	0.17	0.8	0.00	**4.6**	8.5	0.92	10.85	2.54	66.7	**5.4**	29.0	4.6	**7.5**
4.0	2.82	14.1	0.46	**7.3**	16.6	1.46	13.60	3.54	51.2	**3.9**	20.7	5.4	**9.1**
7.4	0.67	1.8	0.02	**8.5**	29.0	1.79	15.86	3.18	65.1	**4.6**	39.9	8.3	**10.0**
5.4	1.62	8.2	0.00	**1.9**	0.1	0.07	0.69	3.41	97.4	**3.9**	36.9	14.7	**6.3**
7.1	0.98	2.8	-0.03	**6.1**	5.9	1.40	12.29	3.26	52.5	**4.8**	41.8	11.4	**8.8**
5.6	2.02	8.0	-0.05	**7.6**	2.7	1.66	9.83	3.58	67.0	**3.7**	30.3	13.2	**8.1**
7.8	0.00	0.0	0.00	**3.5**	0.1	0.47	2.49	4.45	83.0	**1.0**	23.1	34.3	**6.3**
8.8	0.33	1.4	0.05	**2.3**	1.5	0.37	2.71	2.38	83.6	**2.3**	27.1	19.3	**8.0**
8.9	0.78	2.4	0.00	**2.6**	1.7	0.27	2.82	2.04	86.7	**6.1**	45.0	7.6	**7.0**
9.6	1.14	1.9	0.00	**1.3**	-0.2	-0.11	-0.84	2.08	103.7	**6.8**	61.8	4.8	**7.3**
8.9	0.43	0.8	0.40	**4.1**	1.3	0.74	3.28	3.64	74.2	**5.4**	48.9	10.4	**7.1**
8.4	0.67	2.9	0.08	**8.7**	5.6	6.93	53.00	2.93	64.8	**0.5**	6.1	49.7	**8.8**
5.0	1.49	7.6	-0.05	**4.0**	0.9	0.77	9.40	3.47	84.1	**3.0**	17.1	14.3	**5.1**
7.9	0.23	1.5	-0.01	**6.9**	3.9	1.36	16.18	3.21	52.3	**4.2**	18.7	7.9	**6.9**
5.2	0.91	7.9	0.01	**3.8**	1.8	0.68	6.33	3.13	72.2	**1.6**	21.0	24.7	**7.4**
5.2	2.86	12.6	0.00	**4.3**	0.4	0.86	4.14	3.07	60.2	**1.4**	5.2	23.7	**6.2**
6.1	4.71	8.9	0.00	**2.0**	0.0	0.13	0.44	2.91	94.7	**2.1**	32.8	26.2	**6.6**
9.5	0.00	0.7	0.11	**2.7**	0.1	0.49	3.03	2.41	68.4	**1.2**	29.9	41.4	**7.0**
7.7	0.31	2.6	0.00	**3.6**	0.1	0.72	8.43	3.09	69.3	**1.4**	23.2	27.8	**5.2**
5.5	4.99	15.2	0.01	**3.8**	0.4	0.51	3.68	4.09	79.5	**4.6**	38.7	11.6	**7.3**
9.9	0.00	0.0	0.00	**2.0**	0.0	0.04	0.20	2.89	95.6	**3.4**	43.6	18.7	**7.1**
5.9	0.87	3.3	0.22	**5.3**	1.0	1.19	10.56	3.40	60.3	**2.9**	30.9	17.3	**6.7**
9.8	0.29	1.1	0.00	**2.0**	0.2	0.17	1.62	2.28	92.4	**7.0**	59.9	3.3	**5.1**
9.8	0.38	1.4	0.00	**2.3**	1.0	0.20	1.42	2.01	88.7	**3.2**	38.6	22.8	**9.0**
4.8	3.99	14.0	0.00	**3.1**	0.4	0.50	4.64	2.74	78.8	**6.9**	53.1	1.8	**6.2**
8.6	0.23	1.4	-0.02	**3.3**	6.8	0.63	6.14	2.35	77.1	**3.2**	16.4	11.0	**7.8**
6.1	4.03	12.4	-0.36	**0.9**	-0.4	-0.15	-1.13	2.22	116.3	**4.3**	43.4	14.4	**7.3**
9.8	0.34	0.7	0.00	**3.1**	1.1	0.37	2.98	2.51	82.2	**5.7**	50.9	8.8	**8.3**
6.9	2.44	5.8	0.00	**3.2**	0.8	0.63	4.08	2.88	79.2	**2.9**	37.1	19.5	**7.7**
7.1	0.82	4.4	0.03	**2.2**	0.4	0.26	2.80	2.73	87.5	**0.7**	18.1	50.4	**4.8**
8.0	0.29	1.3	0.01	**3.7**	7.3	0.86	8.05	3.49	74.3	**2.9**	20.7	10.6	**8.2**
7.2	0.00	0.0	0.00	**2.7**	0.4	0.31	1.65	3.43	87.4	**1.5**	12.8	23.8	**7.6**
5.7	2.67	11.4	-0.01	**1.9**	0.3	0.26	1.94	3.37	88.9	**3.1**	26.3	14.7	**7.2**
10.0	0.08	0.2	0.00	**3.2**	0.3	0.52	2.71	2.89	79.8	**4.8**	42.7	11.8	**7.8**
5.1	3.25	17.3	-0.02	**10.0**	1.7	3.47	24.97	4.72	21.2	**0.6**	21.8	39.5	**9.6**
5.8	2.90	10.2	-0.09	**2.9**	1.3	0.67	5.84	1.87	80.4	**4.6**	46.4	13.7	**6.5**
6.4	0.45	2.3	0.00	**3.8**	2.2	0.95	9.85	3.26	70.0	**3.2**	20.4	10.5	**5.3**

Name	City	State	Rating	2020 Rating	2019 Rating	Total Assets ($Mil)	One Year Asset Growth	Asset Mix (As a % of Total Assets) Commercial Loans	Consumer Loans	Mortgage Loans	Securities	Capitalization Index	Leverage Ratio	Risk-Based Capital Ratio
▲ First Federal Savings Bank	Huntington	IN	B+	B-	B-	409.9	1.19	21.1	1.8	9.4	22.9	10.0	11.5	17.1
First Federal Savings Bank	Rochester	IN	B-	B-	B-	513.6	5.12	1.5	0.1	41.2	0.0	8.0	9.7	20.2
First Federal Savings Bank of Angola	Angola	IN	B-	B	B	141.7	4.61	0.1	2.4	55.6	0.0	10.0	19.6	0.0
▲ First Federal Savings Bank of Kentucky	Frankfort	KY	C	C-	C	249.8	3.32	0.9	0.3	63.9	0.1	10.0	12.3	0.0
First Federal Savings Bank of Mascoutah	Mascoutah	IL	C+	C+	C	143.5	14.86	9.9	1.2	42.3	22.8	9.6	10.7	18.7
First Federal Savings of Middletown	Middletown	NY	C+	C+	C+	168.9	9.13	0.2	0.0	0.3	20.7	10.0	33.2	0.0
First Fidelity Bank	Fort Payne	AL	C+	C+	C+	131.8	18.70	6.7	1.6	21.4	37.5	6.6	8.6	17.6
▲ First Fidelity Bank	Oklahoma City	OK	B	B-	B	2510.9	20.57	9.0	10.2	5.7	22.5	4.8	7.8	0.0
First Fidelity Bank	Burke	SD	B+	B+	B+	476.4	14.21	4.3	1.8	1.5	33.4	7.1	9.0	15.2
First Financial Bank	Bessemer	AL	C+	C+	C+	228.9	15.38	9.8	1.1	11.1	31.8	6.4	8.5	16.9
First Financial Bank	El Dorado	AR	B+	B+	B+	1551.5	2.93	7.4	1.5	4.4	6.8	9.1	10.4	0.0
First Financial Bank	Cincinnati	OH	B+	B+	B+	15955.9	0.98	15.1	0.7	7.7	25.5	8.3	9.9	14.0
First Financial Bank in Winnebago	Winnebago	MN	B+	B+	B	52.2	3.78	13.5	2.4	8.1	29.7	10.0	14.3	22.1
First Financial Bank, N.A.	Terre Haute	IN	A-	A-	A-	4621.2	8.89	13.4	8.0	7.9	26.4	8.8	10.2	17.9
First Financial Bank, N.A.	Abilene	TX	A	A	A	12292.0	19.28	7.8	4.0	10.4	45.1	8.6	10.1	19.3
First Financial Northwest Bank	Renton	WA	B	B	B+	1430.8	0.88	3.1	2.3	25.5	13.3	8.7	10.2	15.7
First Financial Trust & Asset Mgmt Co.	Abilene	TX	U	U	U	37.7	9.78	0.0	0.0	0.0	78.0	10.0	102.	341.4
First Financial Trust N.A.	Wellesley	MA	U	U	U	11.8	11.49	0.0	0.0	0.0	4.4	10.0	95.8	0.0
First Florida Integrity Bank	Naples	FL	B	B-	B	2323.2	23.67	8.6	0.1	5.2	16.9	5.8	7.8	14.9
First Foundation Bank	Irvine	CA	B	B	B-	7917.2	11.12	9.5	0.2	10.2	9.3	6.3	8.3	12.2
▲ First Freedom Bank	Lebanon	TN	C+	C	B-	596.6	-3.92	20.3	5.1	9.0	0.0	3.9	10.0	0.0
First FSB of Champaign-Urbana	Champaign	IL	B-	C+	B-	211.5	6.79	5.3	0.9	19.3	0.0	6.2	8.2	0.0
First FSB of Lincolnton	Lincolnton	NC	B+	B+	A-	441.7	7.50	0.7	0.4	45.0	18.3	10.0	15.8	36.4
First FSB of Twin Falls	Twin Falls	ID	A-	A-	A-	1103.0	30.37	6.3	2.7	25.4	15.1	7.0	9.0	15.3
▲ First FSB of Washington	Washington	IN	C	C-	C-	78.5	-1.69	6.7	1.6	45.5	5.6	10.0	12.0	0.0
First General Bank	Rowland Heights	CA	A	A	A-	1178.3	12.52	5.4	0.0	3.7	0.7	10.0	14.9	0.0
First Guaranty Bank	Hammond	LA	B-	B-	B	2746.6	12.76	13.1	1.2	10.1	16.2	6.0	9.1	11.8
First Harrison Bank	Corydon	IN	B+	B+	B+	1074.0	17.33	6.2	5.1	9.7	33.1	6.8	8.8	0.0
First Hawaiian Bank	Honolulu	HI	B+	B+	B+	24246.1	5.45	9.2	4.8	15.3	28.7	5.6	7.6	13.9
▲ First Heritage Bank	Shenandoah	IA	B	B-	B-	54.9	15.51	11.5	2.2	15.1	29.3	7.5	9.3	0.0
First Heritage Bank	Centralia	KS	B+	B+	B	225.5	6.34	16.3	0.6	6.7	34.7	7.7	9.5	0.0
▲ First Home Bank	Saint Petersburg	FL	B+	B-	B+	1196.7	-18.59	54.9	0.3	15.1	1.9	10.0	12.1	22.6
First Hope Bank, A National Banking Assn.	Hope	NJ	C+	C+	C	670.9	11.56	8.3	0.1	12.4	19.0	5.9	7.9	13.9
First Horizon Bank	Memphis	TN	B	B	B-	87574.1	80.69	18.5	0.8	10.8	9.6	6.2	8.2	12.9
▲ First IC Bank	Doraville	GA	A-	B+	B+	881.5	19.11	10.6	0.0	8.3	5.5	9.3	10.5	17.9
First Independence Bank	Detroit	MI	C+	C+	B-	348.9	23.37	10.2	0.0	9.9	1.9	8.1	9.8	0.0
First Independent Bank	Russell	MN	B+	B	C	376.6	17.81	9.8	1.8	9.9	30.9	7.8	9.5	16.8
First Independent Bank	Aurora	MO	B-	B-	B	120.4	16.44	7.8	4.0	20.9	39.1	8.7	10.2	0.0
First International Bank and Trust	Watford City	ND	B	B	B	4362.0	10.20	15.4	2.0	8.8	16.4	5.7	7.7	11.7
▲ First Internet Bank of Indiana	Fishers	IN	B	B-	B-	4197.0	-2.89	13.3	6.7	4.0	17.4	7.9	9.6	14.5
First Interstate Bank	Billings	MT	B+	B+	B+	18879.3	15.04	8.5	5.1	8.1	30.0	5.5	7.5	12.5
First Iowa State Bank	Albia	IA	B+	B+	B+	184.6	14.78	6.1	1.0	10.2	39.5	8.6	10.1	0.0
First Iowa State Bank	Keosauqua	IA	B	B	B+	153.9	8.78	11.8	2.4	13.5	30.8	8.4	9.9	0.0
First Jackson Bank	Stevenson	AL	A-	A-	A-	364.5	12.86	5.8	2.9	14.1	14.6	9.4	10.6	0.0
First Kansas Bank	Hoisington	KS	B+	B+	B+	267.0	30.11	2.5	1.5	16.3	59.2	5.1	7.1	19.1
First Kentucky Bank, Inc.	Mayfield	KY	B	B	B	524.8	7.25	5.0	4.3	20.5	31.9	6.5	8.5	14.0
▲ First Keystone Community Bank	Berwick	PA	B+	B	B	1307.7	22.53	5.7	0.4	17.7	30.9	9.5	10.6	16.8
▲ First Liberty Bank	Oklahoma City	OK	B+	B-	B-	539.5	1.51	27.6	0.2	15.3	5.4	9.0	10.4	14.2
First Merchants Bank	Muncie	IN	A-	A-	A-	14904.1	8.02	17.9	0.9	7.8	28.1	7.2	9.1	13.3
First Metro Bank	Muscle Shoals	AL	A	A	A	873.2	9.37	9.0	1.9	14.6	26.1	8.5	10.0	21.5
First Mid Bank & Trust, N.A.	Mattoon	IL	B+	B+	B+	5753.8	29.91	15.0	1.5	6.1	21.3	8.2	9.8	15.3
First Midwest Bank	Chicago	IL	B	B	B	21484.7	1.53	20.9	2.8	16.2	14.7	5.8	8.0	11.6
First Midwest Bank of Dexter	Dexter	MO	B	B-	B-	428.3	1.69	32.0	1.8	11.4	6.7	8.4	10.0	13.6
First Midwest Bank of Poplar Bluff	Poplar Bluff	MO	B+	B	B-	491.4	0.23	21.3	3.4	23.5	3.7	8.3	9.9	13.6
First Midwest Bank of the Ozarks	Piedmont	MO	B-	B-	B-	143.1	2.46	13.0	4.5	10.6	24.7	8.6	10.1	14.9
First Minnetonka City Bank	Minnetonka	MN	B+	A-	A-	271.6	3.24	8.8	1.2	14.0	41.9	7.8	9.6	21.4
First Missouri Bank	Brookfield	MO	C+	C	B-	365.3	2.64	13.0	0.9	11.3	4.0	8.5	10.0	14.8
First Missouri Bank of SEMO	Kennett	MO	B	B	B+	205.3	6.30	10.6	2.3	22.4	1.6	7.0	9.0	13.2
First Missouri State Bank	Poplar Bluff	MO	B	B	B+	212.3	9.38	7.3	3.9	31.2	0.3	7.2	9.1	14.4
First Missouri State Bank of Cape County	Cape Girardeau	MO	B+	B	B-	186.9	2.51	11.6	1.7	18.0	6.3	6.7	8.8	12.3

Asset Quality Index	Adjusted Non-Performing Loans as a % of Total Loans	Adjusted Non-Performing Loans as a % of Capital	Net Charge-Offs Avg Loans	Profitability Index	Net Income ($Mil)	Return on Assets (R.O.A.)	Return on Equity (R.O.E.)	Net Interest Spread	Overhead Efficiency Ratio	Liquidity Index	Liquidity Ratio	Hot Money Ratio	Stability Index
5.9	0.79	3.9	-0.01	**8.5**	3.9	1.95	16.91	3.77	47.0	**3.4**	25.8	8.9	**8.0**
3.7	5.16	16.4	0.00	**6.5**	3.6	1.33	13.88	3.17	73.5	**2.4**	32.6	21.0	**7.7**
9.7	0.22	1.0	0.01	**3.2**	0.4	0.52	2.64	2.47	74.2	**5.4**	47.5	9.8	**8.0**
5.1	1.99	13.7	0.00	**2.2**	0.6	0.52	4.05	3.16	77.0	**1.2**	9.6	28.0	**6.0**
9.4	0.00	0.0	0.01	**3.1**	0.4	0.61	5.48	2.70	67.9	**1.7**	20.8	22.7	**6.5**
8.7	0.00	0.0	0.00	**2.9**	0.3	0.37	1.10	2.68	73.3	**5.0**	58.4	14.5	**7.5**
7.2	0.69	3.2	-0.03	**3.6**	0.5	0.81	8.76	2.84	68.8	**4.3**	53.2	16.6	**5.3**
7.3	0.46	2.1	0.00	**6.1**	17.8	1.50	17.59	3.49	53.6	**6.1**	31.9	2.0	**7.9**
5.6	1.02	6.7	0.16	**9.0**	5.7	2.45	25.49	5.33	44.4	**5.4**	36.7	6.1	**7.1**
9.1	0.29	1.0	0.04	**3.9**	1.3	1.16	13.71	3.29	73.3	**5.8**	41.2	4.9	**4.7**
5.5	4.69	7.2	0.18	**7.5**	12.5	1.62	13.77	3.01	67.1	**2.6**	34.2	27.7	**10.0**
5.0	0.99	3.3	0.30	**6.5**	108.9	1.36	9.30	3.46	57.4	**4.4**	20.2	3.9	**10.0**
8.2	0.67	1.3	-0.01	**4.5**	0.3	0.99	6.70	3.39	71.5	**5.0**	37.4	9.0	**7.9**
6.8	0.62	2.7	0.03	**5.9**	26.1	1.15	9.37	3.12	64.2	**5.4**	26.3	4.6	**10.0**
7.2	0.56	1.8	0.00	**9.7**	109.0	1.91	14.12	3.50	45.4	**6.0**	29.6	2.9	**10.0**
8.5	0.12	0.4	-0.02	**4.5**	7.0	0.99	9.79	3.33	65.3	**1.7**	19.2	24.4	**8.5**
10.0	na	0.0	na	**10.0**	8.3	50.48	47.99	2.22	41.2	**4.0**	na	0.0	**7.0**
6.5	na	0.0	na	**10.0**	0.5	8.13	8.44	1.06	64.2	**4.0**	na	0.0	**5.7**
8.9	0.00	0.0	0.00	**5.1**	11.4	1.03	12.86	2.71	51.6	**6.3**	38.4	4.1	**6.8**
6.3	0.32	2.4	0.00	**6.4**	48.0	1.29	13.44	3.29	46.1	**4.3**	21.1	7.0	**7.7**
6.2	0.34	2.4	0.15	**6.9**	4.3	1.42	15.22	4.17	47.9	**1.2**	16.1	24.7	**6.9**
7.1	0.15	0.4	0.31	**3.4**	0.4	0.39	4.83	2.18	86.4	**7.0**	59.2	3.4	**5.1**
8.9	0.96	3.1	-0.02	**4.2**	1.6	0.73	4.58	2.83	67.1	**3.0**	43.1	22.8	**7.9**
8.7	0.13	0.5	0.01	**6.0**	6.0	1.13	12.35	3.80	69.1	**6.1**	35.0	4.7	**7.8**
5.9	2.25	11.9	0.00	**2.1**	0.2	0.38	3.14	3.44	84.0	**2.1**	34.4	25.7	**6.2**
7.1	0.18	1.1	0.00	**10.0**	12.5	2.22	15.27	3.82	25.2	**0.6**	9.1	38.0	**10.0**
4.7	0.83	8.9	0.05	**4.4**	12.6	0.96	10.84	3.13	64.9	**1.8**	15.1	18.5	**7.7**
8.3	0.61	2.2	0.03	**5.0**	5.1	0.99	9.93	2.89	65.6	**7.1**	50.4	2.7	**8.4**
7.5	0.25	0.9	0.09	**6.5**	147.4	1.26	10.94	2.48	54.1	**5.8**	32.5	5.8	**10.0**
8.6	0.03	0.1	0.00	**7.0**	0.5	1.85	20.22	4.43	54.1	**4.6**	39.7	12.0	**6.0**
8.6	0.05	0.3	0.00	**6.2**	1.8	1.53	17.19	3.56	55.8	**3.2**	38.1	7.9	**7.1**
7.1	0.95	3.0	0.34	**7.8**	21.2	2.67	48.59	3.37	68.7	**4.4**	11.9	6.1	**7.5**
7.0	0.44	2.8	-0.01	**3.1**	1.8	0.53	6.55	2.65	80.1	**5.3**	33.0	5.1	**4.5**
5.6	0.91	4.7	-0.01	**6.4**	587.2	1.37	13.81	2.58	62.8	**4.8**	22.7	3.4	**9.4**
6.1	0.00	0.0	-0.30	**8.4**	6.7	1.61	15.15	3.57	52.8	**3.1**	33.6	17.5	**9.3**
7.4	0.36	2.9	-0.01	**4.5**	0.7	0.92	11.13	3.55	90.2	**2.6**	34.8	20.0	**3.6**
5.4	0.92	7.2	0.00	**7.2**	3.6	1.98	19.49	3.76	50.6	**4.3**	42.6	14.4	**7.8**
6.0	1.59	5.9	0.00	**4.1**	0.5	0.80	7.79	2.97	66.2	**4.8**	54.5	14.4	**5.6**
5.4	1.25	7.0	0.16	**6.9**	37.0	1.72	20.09	4.02	62.3	**4.3**	12.7	6.7	**7.7**
7.5	0.35	2.3	0.18	**5.1**	25.0	1.20	13.09	2.32	47.8	**0.8**	14.8	28.9	**7.1**
6.8	0.33	1.7	0.08	**6.1**	102.7	1.13	10.55	2.76	59.8	**6.3**	36.3	3.4	**9.5**
4.8	0.00	10.1	0.02	**8.7**	2.5	2.68	24.71	3.58	40.0	**4.9**	38.2	9.7	**7.9**
5.0	1.45	8.0	-0.02	**7.2**	1.4	1.82	17.90	4.97	60.2	**5.3**	35.6	5.7	**7.0**
6.5	0.98	2.6	0.02	**6.0**	2.1	1.17	10.86	2.98	48.2	**1.7**	36.3	33.5	**6.9**
9.6	0.00	0.0	0.01	**5.4**	1.7	1.35	15.00	3.06	51.4	**5.0**	29.7	5.7	**6.6**
7.5	0.64	2.2	-0.02	**4.7**	3.3	1.26	13.67	3.23	64.2	**3.3**	30.8	12.6	**7.1**
5.4	2.14	7.3	0.02	**5.4**	7.9	1.33	10.22	3.37	57.3	**4.2**	14.4	5.9	**9.0**
8.4	0.00	0.0	0.06	**5.8**	3.3	1.23	13.21	3.96	60.7	**1.2**	18.7	29.3	**6.3**
6.1	0.63	2.7	0.11	**6.8**	109.4	1.51	11.69	3.27	51.1	**5.8**	29.7	2.5	**10.0**
9.0	0.08	0.2	0.01	**6.4**	4.7	1.12	11.41	2.75	52.3	**3.7**	34.5	14.9	**7.7**
5.9	0.79	3.8	0.06	**4.0**	14.7	0.56	5.24	3.43	69.6	**3.6**	17.6	8.5	**9.1**
4.6	0.83	4.6	0.40	**5.7**	116.1	1.10	9.51	3.04	57.0	**4.5**	14.7	5.5	**9.1**
4.5	0.90	6.7	0.00	**7.4**	4.0	1.81	18.08	4.10	54.1	**2.3**	13.6	17.2	**7.7**
5.6	0.32	3.2	0.05	**7.8**	5.1	2.07	20.76	4.22	52.9	**1.5**	12.2	19.6	**7.7**
2.6	2.64	16.3	0.03	**5.9**	1.0	1.48	14.32	4.07	65.4	**2.1**	26.9	20.4	**7.3**
9.4	0.00	0.0	-0.02	**5.1**	1.6	1.22	12.15	2.90	60.3	**6.4**	54.8	5.5	**6.7**
6.3	0.10	0.6	0.00	**7.3**	3.5	1.98	19.80	3.96	52.6	**3.2**	17.8	13.3	**7.6**
5.7	1.68	7.7	0.02	**5.2**	1.3	1.29	14.34	3.40	63.5	**3.5**	15.1	11.3	**6.4**
5.7	0.63	4.7	-0.01	**7.6**	2.1	2.02	21.98	3.57	49.3	**1.6**	17.1	22.3	**7.3**
8.5	0.02	0.1	0.00	**5.2**	1.2	1.36	14.54	3.24	66.3	**1.6**	18.6	18.6	**6.6**

Name	City	State	Rating	2020 Rating	2019 Rating	Total Assets ($Mil)	One Year Asset Growth	Asset Mix (As a % of Total Assets) Commercial Loans	Consumer Loans	Mortgage Loans	Securities	Capitalization Index	Leverage Ratio	Risk-Based Capital Ratio
First Montana Bank, Inc.	Missoula	MT	**B-**	B-	C+	456.5	25.56	11.6	2.7	8.4	25.6	**6.2**	8.2	13.4
▼ First Mutual Bank, FSB	Belpre	OH	**C+**	B-	C-	102.2	11.01	4.1	0.5	40.4	32.0	**7.7**	9.5	0.0
First National B&T Co. of Ardmore	Ardmore	OK	**B**	B	B	611.6	4.33	13.9	3.1	8.7	34.6	**7.3**	9.2	0.0
First National B&T Co. of Bottineau	Bottineau	ND	**B-**	B-	B-	161.1	6.61	4.0	2.2	5.0	35.5	**10.0**	11.4	0.0
First National B&T Co. of McAlester	McAlester	OK	**B**	B-	B	553.6	7.02	5.8	1.7	8.0	28.6	**8.5**	10.0	17.0
▲ First National B&T Co. of Weatherford	Weatherford	OK	**B+**	B	B+	308.9	2.14	16.9	1.4	5.5	2.3	**10.0**	11.1	15.8
First National B&T Co. of Weatherford	Weatherford	TX	**B-**	B-	B-	875.2	155.22	15.6	1.2	10.3	10.7	**6.7**	8.7	14.5
First National B&T, Elk City, Oklahoma	Elk City	OK	**A-**	A-	A-	313.8	0.09	9.6	0.6	10.1	44.4	**10.0**	11.7	0.0
▼ First National Bank	Hamilton	AL	**B+**	A-	A	364.2	13.97	5.4	5.5	9.1	26.1	**10.0**	14.3	0.0
First National Bank	Paragould	AR	**B+**	B+	A-	1860.1	2.88	7.4	2.2	24.1	7.6	**9.5**	11.1	14.6
▲ First National Bank	Mattoon	IL	**C+**	C	C-	101.5	1.57	10.8	2.7	7.6	20.6	**6.2**	8.3	14.7
First National Bank	Cloverdale	IN	**C**	C	C+	425.8	18.48	5.8	0.9	12.8	24.3	**5.8**	7.8	18.9
First National Bank	Damariscotta	ME	**B**	B	B	2416.3	8.23	10.5	1.0	21.7	28.5	**6.5**	8.5	14.5
▲ First National Bank	Bagley	MN	**B-**	C+	C+	108.0	14.01	8.0	8.3	19.6	23.5	**5.8**	7.8	15.1
First National Bank	Alamogordo	NM	**A-**	A	A-	465.2	14.41	5.0	3.6	3.9	54.0	**8.6**	10.0	0.0
First National Bank	Heavener	OK	**B+**	B+	B+	95.2	2.76	6.4	2.7	17.5	10.7	**6.4**	8.4	14.7
First National Bank	Fort Pierre	SD	**A**	A-	A-	1593.8	10.65	9.5	10.7	5.6	19.0	**10.0**	18.2	26.4
▲ First National Bank	Oldham	SD	**A-**	B+	A-	412.7	10.79	5.4	12.9	7.0	26.6	**10.0**	11.6	19.0
First National Bank	Oneida	TN	**B+**	B+	A-	294.2	17.40	5.8	2.2	19.9	20.6	**7.7**	9.5	18.4
First National Bank	Rotan	TX	**C+**	B-	C+	87.7	11.55	7.4	3.0	0.2	60.2	**8.9**	10.3	24.5
▼ First National Bank	Spearman	TX	**B-**	B+	A-	244.0	1.63	14.9	2.3	6.7	24.9	**10.0**	13.8	19.6
First National Bank	Wichita Falls	TX	**B**	B	B	939.7	11.49	7.9	0.8	24.1	6.6	**7.5**	9.3	14.2
First National Bank	Altavista	VA	**B-**	B-	B-	931.5	65.57	10.2	12.3	10.9	9.7	**5.7**	7.7	13.0
First National Bank & Trust of Newtown	Newtown	PA	**B**	B	B+	1270.6	14.27	2.6	0.2	10.9	47.6	**6.4**	8.4	0.0
First National Bank Alaska	Anchorage	AK	**A**	A	A	5338.1	16.19	11.6	0.3	1.5	41.8	**9.7**	10.8	21.5
First National Bank Ames, Iowa	Ames	IA	**B+**	B+	A-	1075.3	9.53	4.0	0.5	11.8	35.4	**6.5**	8.5	0.0
First National Bank and Trust	Atmore	AL	**B**	B-	B-	205.1	11.43	13.0	2.9	13.3	27.9	**9.9**	10.9	0.0
First National Bank and Trust	Phillipsburg	KS	**A-**	A-	B	258.6	3.79	11.5	4.0	8.5	35.4	**10.0**	14.9	0.0
First National Bank and Trust Co.	Clinton	IL	**C+**	C	C+	218.0	12.13	4.1	0.2	4.1	70.5	**8.6**	10.0	20.1
▼ First National Bank and Trust Co.	Shawnee	OK	**C-**	C+	C+	241.8	-25.28	13.2	0.8	6.5	19.6	**9.3**	10.5	25.2
First National Bank at Darlington	Darlington	WI	**B+**	B+	B+	177.4	11.87	5.3	2.5	4.6	9.9	**10.0**	13.7	21.2
First National Bank in Cimarron	Cimarron	KS	**B**	B	B	127.6	7.71	11.3	2.2	6.0	55.7	**5.5**	7.5	15.8
▼ First National Bank in DeRidder	DeRidder	LA	**B-**	B	B	412.4	20.24	8.5	1.9	16.9	21.6	**5.4**	7.4	18.4
▲ First National Bank in Fairfield	Fairfield	IA	**C**	C-	C+	155.0	4.41	6.1	0.8	10.5	20.6	**7.5**	9.3	16.3
First National Bank in Frankfort	Frankfort	KS	**B**	B	B	57.4	13.44	4.3	2.7	5.9	51.1	**8.1**	9.7	0.0
First National Bank in Fredonia	Fredonia	KS	**B+**	A-	A-	103.5	2.03	9.0	5.8	9.0	62.5	**10.0**	15.7	0.0
First National Bank in Howell	Howell	MI	**A-**	A-	B	643.2	26.39	11.3	5.3	13.5	14.6	**8.2**	9.8	15.6
First National Bank in New Bremen	New Bremen	OH	**B+**	B+	B+	401.6	15.70	5.7	0.6	7.3	27.3	**6.8**	8.8	26.4
First National Bank in Okeene	Okeene	OK	**C**	C	C	82.5	-3.32	7.3	0.2	0.0	40.3	**10.0**	16.6	25.9
First National Bank in Olney	Olney	IL	**B+**	B+	B+	418.7	10.84	4.7	2.2	12.3	37.1	**8.9**	10.3	0.0
▲ First National Bank in Ord	Ord	NE	**B-**	C+	B	151.7	-2.64	4.8	1.6	10.5	38.4	**6.5**	8.5	19.0
▲ First National Bank in Philip	Philip	SD	**A**	A-	A-	333.6	15.88	3.7	0.5	0.0	16.6	**10.0**	12.3	18.4
First National Bank in Pinckneyville	Pinckneyville	IL	**B+**	A-	A-	144.1	17.46	2.1	3.0	18.7	48.1	**9.0**	10.3	26.3
First National Bank in Port Lavaca	Port Lavaca	TX	**B+**	B+	B	374.3	5.47	4.4	1.6	28.9	38.6	**8.3**	9.8	0.0
First National Bank in Taylorville	Taylorville	IL	**B+**	A-	A-	237.7	11.95	7.3	2.3	6.6	50.0	**10.0**	15.9	0.0
First National Bank in Tigerton	Tigerton	WI	**C+**	C	C+	28.0	13.30	1.9	2.6	22.8	14.3	**10.0**	12.1	0.0
First National Bank in Trinidad	Trinidad	CO	**C+**	C+	B-	270.5	16.00	1.0	0.5	22.2	44.9	**8.5**	10.0	0.0
First National Bank Minnesota	Saint Peter	MN	**A-**	B+	C+	388.7	8.93	10.1	1.3	8.9	22.1	**7.2**	9.2	13.8
First National Bank North	Walker	MN	**A-**	A-	A	730.7	12.21	5.0	6.9	17.9	14.6	**7.0**	9.0	0.0
▼ First National Bank Northwest Florida	Panama City	FL	**B-**	B	B+	217.3	15.92	6.7	0.0	7.0	3.5	**7.7**	9.4	31.4
▼ First National Bank of Absecon	Absecon	NJ	**C**	C+	C+	173.7	8.22	9.2	0.2	26.6	28.5	**7.9**	9.6	0.0
▼ First National Bank of Albany/Breckenridge	Albany	TX	**B-**	B+	A-	617.2	7.39	23.5	1.9	8.5	17.8	**8.8**	10.2	0.0
First National Bank of Alvin	Alvin	TX	**B**	B+	B+	177.3	10.30	1.2	0.9	0.3	79.3	**8.4**	10.0	0.0
▲ First National Bank of America	East Lansing	MI	**B+**	B	B-	3061.7	12.59	0.2	0.1	86.5	1.8	**9.7**	10.8	21.0
First National Bank of Benton	Benton	LA	**B**	B	A-	72.1	7.95	2.8	1.1	35.0	11.3	**10.0**	17.0	0.0
First National Bank of Bosque County	Valley Mills	TX	**B**	B	B+	162.2	12.47	14.0	4.7	23.0	9.0	**7.3**	9.2	16.3
First National Bank of Brookfield	Brookfield	IL	**B+**	B+	A-	295.6	19.25	1.0	4.5	12.8	3.5	**7.4**	9.3	13.7
First National Bank of Burleson	Burleson	TX	**A-**	A-	A-	242.3	11.61	8.9	1.8	3.6	32.5	**7.8**	9.5	0.0
First National Bank of Central Texas	Waco	TX	**B+**	B+	B+	1162.5	9.42	13.5	0.8	11.5	4.9	**6.4**	8.4	12.1
First National Bank of Clarksdale	Clarksdale	MS	**B+**	A-	B+	386.0	3.08	5.7	2.5	6.9	35.4	**10.0**	11.9	0.0

Asset Quality Index	Adjusted Non-Performing Loans as a % of Total Loans	Adjusted Non-Performing Loans as a % of Capital	Net Charge-Offs Avg Loans	Profitability Index	Net Income ($Mil)	Return on Assets (R.O.A.)	Return on Equity (R.O.E.)	Net Interest Spread	Overhead Efficiency Ratio	Liquidity Index	Liquidity Ratio	Hot Money Ratio	Stability Index
3.8	1.61	14.1	0.07	4.3	1.6	0.76	8.88	3.39	71.2	5.3	29.0	3.1	5.2
4.1	1.42	4.9	0.14	0.3	-0.2	-0.34	-2.63	2.66	120.8	4.8	47.1	12.6	6.0
4.7	1.36	5.9	0.05	4.7	3.3	1.10	12.62	3.78	70.2	4.0	15.4	8.8	6.9
5.9	3.20	8.6	-0.01	3.1	0.3	0.36	3.09	1.92	77.6	4.8	35.5	9.4	6.9
4.5	3.25	11.4	0.11	5.0	2.8	1.05	9.39	3.19	62.8	4.3	30.1	10.4	8.1
5.2	0.89	4.7	0.40	5.8	2.0	1.32	11.16	4.07	61.5	2.2	28.9	21.0	7.7
5.5	1.22	9.1	-0.05	5.5	4.3	0.99	13.38	4.15	72.2	3.0	27.9	16.1	6.2
7.3	0.53	2.9	0.02	8.4	3.5	2.26	17.02	3.86	48.5	2.7	38.9	23.2	9.3
8.9	0.55	1.0	0.15	4.9	1.7	0.99	6.50	2.71	66.7	6.3	61.4	8.5	8.1
8.2	0.30	1.8	0.00	5.5	10.7	1.14	9.99	3.23	57.9	1.4	6.2	23.7	9.0
4.8	1.43	8.6	0.00	3.6	0.5	0.89	10.21	3.30	73.2	3.8	42.0	16.7	5.0
7.7	0.70	3.1	-0.04	2.7	0.6	0.28	3.49	2.31	88.3	6.9	63.3	4.3	4.5
7.6	0.54	3.5	0.04	6.7	18.2	1.55	18.26	3.11	45.1	1.2	20.9	18.8	8.2
7.7	0.23	1.4	-0.01	7.0	1.1	2.05	25.41	4.65	54.4	4.4	29.7	9.3	5.3
6.7	1.33	3.4	0.03	5.3	2.9	1.30	12.52	3.62	61.5	6.1	46.8	5.1	7.2
6.2	0.61	4.8	-0.02	7.6	0.7	1.48	17.71	5.44	62.5	3.6	25.2	12.2	6.2
6.8	0.45	1.0	1.90	10.0	24.2	3.12	16.12	7.67	39.0	5.2	31.5	9.1	9.5
6.7	0.94	2.3	2.74	8.1	4.3	2.16	19.80	7.20	52.5	4.3	27.4	8.9	6.6
8.5	0.25	1.2	-0.16	5.1	1.7	1.21	12.16	3.02	63.1	2.7	36.8	21.0	7.2
5.1	2.16	7.2	-0.02	4.6	0.6	1.25	12.96	3.57	69.1	4.3	32.1	10.9	5.1
1.9	5.42	23.5	0.09	5.8	2.1	1.73	12.08	3.94	61.9	1.3	17.1	28.2	8.8
6.8	0.18	1.5	-0.01	5.3	5.9	1.30	13.16	3.86	70.3	1.7	17.1	21.8	7.6
6.4	0.43	2.4	0.00	3.6	2.6	0.59	7.96	2.89	79.2	5.7	38.5	4.9	4.5
9.1	1.05	3.0	0.00	4.4	4.8	0.79	9.77	2.47	66.5	7.4	55.3	1.8	6.3
7.9	1.15	3.0	0.07	6.4	27.7	1.13	9.60	3.03	53.7	6.2	30.3	2.2	10.0
5.4	1.46	8.2	0.00	5.4	6.2	1.17	12.44	2.85	54.4	5.9	36.8	6.0	8.1
4.8	1.71	8.4	0.00	6.4	3.0	3.08	29.58	3.29	50.5	4.3	35.3	11.7	6.8
6.0	1.37	5.8	-0.05	7.6	2.7	2.05	13.53	4.33	56.6	3.1	28.0	15.6	8.7
9.9	0.48	0.7	0.01	2.9	0.9	0.88	9.58	2.63	77.4	2.3	45.7	17.8	5.8
5.0	1.92	6.6	0.01	1.8	0.3	0.17	1.39	2.47	94.9	5.5	40.1	6.6	6.9
8.5	0.15	0.3	-0.01	3.3	0.3	0.37	2.66	2.57	81.8	3.9	43.8	16.3	7.8
8.9	0.00	0.0	0.00	6.5	1.1	1.76	21.91	3.37	57.7	3.8	36.6	15.0	5.4
7.0	0.78	3.3	0.01	3.8	1.4	0.69	9.59	2.71	73.2	5.6	42.0	6.8	4.5
3.0	2.67	13.9	0.18	1.4	0.1	0.14	1.56	2.82	92.5	3.9	14.9	8.0	4.0
5.1	2.18	8.7	-0.34	7.2	0.6	1.97	19.36	3.50	52.7	5.6	57.8	9.8	5.7
7.7	1.75	3.2	-0.06	4.8	0.6	1.04	6.44	2.74	63.9	3.9	55.9	19.3	8.2
6.7	0.40	2.6	0.00	5.3	3.0	0.97	9.75	3.33	69.0	5.3	32.9	5.0	7.6
9.5	0.20	0.7	0.00	5.0	2.2	1.14	12.33	2.29	53.2	6.5	59.9	6.8	6.3
5.3	3.15	8.2	-0.04	4.6	0.5	1.14	6.39	3.35	51.7	2.3	40.4	25.9	7.3
4.9	1.84	6.2	0.14	5.7	2.5	1.18	10.23	3.11	53.9	5.1	35.8	7.6	7.3
9.1	0.00	0.0	-0.02	4.9	1.0	1.30	15.59	3.15	57.3	4.2	28.5	6.7	5.2
7.1	0.03	0.1	0.00	8.7	4.1	2.53	19.98	4.10	36.4	3.7	35.4	5.9	9.0
6.3	1.66	4.5	0.00	4.9	0.7	1.07	8.87	2.89	61.0	5.7	32.6	2.3	8.2
9.5	0.00	0.3	-0.01	5.3	1.9	1.02	9.92	2.98	54.0	4.8	29.5	6.6	6.9
9.2	0.09	0.2	-0.08	4.3	1.1	0.98	5.76	2.45	59.0	5.7	68.3	12.8	8.4
9.6	0.32	1.6	0.00	2.2	0.0	0.24	1.90	2.20	90.5	5.7	52.2	8.1	6.4
6.5	2.15	5.2	0.06	1.8	0.5	0.39	3.45	2.97	104.5	5.7	43.5	6.5	6.4
8.1	0.19	0.6	0.01	7.3	3.5	1.88	16.79	4.28	57.6	5.0	22.5	3.0	7.5
6.8	0.73	2.2	0.04	7.1	5.6	1.60	16.54	3.40	54.1	3.6	40.4	17.2	8.2
9.6	0.00	0.0	0.00	3.4	0.5	0.51	5.05	2.35	76.2	6.0	71.2	11.2	5.8
8.4	0.47	2.2	0.00	2.4	0.2	0.25	2.48	3.05	90.7	6.7	49.2	1.7	5.9
2.7	3.11	16.5	2.51	8.0	6.2	1.91	16.67	4.03	38.3	1.0	21.6	15.7	9.2
10.0	0.10	0.1	0.01	3.9	0.8	0.86	7.57	1.89	54.9	4.8	73.4	17.7	6.1
5.5	1.99	14.5	0.00	10.0	58.1	3.88	37.78	6.25	25.0	0.4	6.5	35.2	9.7
6.5	0.90	3.0	0.00	5.1	0.3	0.73	4.30	2.95	70.3	5.5	33.2	3.5	7.1
4.7	1.07	9.1	0.55	6.1	1.2	1.51	16.39	3.77	54.7	5.0	36.4	8.2	6.0
7.3	0.00	0.0	-0.13	6.0	1.8	1.27	13.47	3.36	56.3	2.2	27.0	19.5	6.5
9.7	0.00	0.0	0.00	5.1	1.5	1.25	12.85	2.83	55.2	7.2	66.7	3.4	6.3
7.5	0.05	0.5	0.00	7.6	11.9	2.06	23.68	3.94	47.5	3.8	24.6	13.2	8.8
7.8	1.10	4.4	0.02	4.0	1.8	0.91	7.70	3.05	67.5	4.0	33.1	12.7	7.6

Name	City	State	Rating	2020 Rating	2019 Rating	Total Assets ($Mil)	One Year Asset Growth	Asset Mix (As a % of Total Assets) Commercial Loans	Consumer Loans	Mortgage Loans	Securities	Capitalization Index	Leverage Ratio	Risk-Based Capital Ratio
First National Bank of Coffee County	Douglas	GA	B+	B+	B+	370.4	31.27	6.6	0.6	9.7	7.7	6.2	8.2	17.9
First National Bank of Decatur County	Bainbridge	GA	B-	B-	B-	224.6	13.46	10.5	2.0	18.4	7.9	6.2	8.2	15.2
First National Bank of Dublin	Dublin	TX	B+	B+	B+	119.9	14.49	10.6	8.7	3.7	0.6	7.2	9.2	15.8
First National Bank of Eagle Lake	Eagle Lake	TX	B-	B-	B	122.9	-1.76	10.8	0.2	3.9	13.2	9.4	10.9	0.0
First National Bank of Eastern Arkansas	Forrest City	AR	B-	B	B+	541.7	12.75	7.4	1.7	6.8	37.4	7.0	9.0	0.0
First National Bank of Elmer	Elmer	NJ	B-	B-	C	371.4	13.63	9.2	0.1	27.1	4.2	5.9	7.9	13.6
First National Bank of Fort Stockton	Fort Stockton	TX	B+	B+	B	142.9	0.93	13.3	1.2	4.8	42.3	9.1	10.4	0.0
First National Bank of Giddings	Giddings	TX	B	B	B	273.3	13.66	3.9	1.5	18.3	36.2	9.3	10.6	0.0
First National Bank of Gillette	Gillette	WY	B	B	B	637.4	0.75	11.6	1.1	1.4	68.4	10.0	11.7	39.6
First National Bank of Griffin	Griffin	GA	C	C	C	366.3	10.35	3.4	1.2	4.6	29.0	4.6	6.6	16.4
First National Bank of Hartford	Hartford	AL	B	B	B	140.8	8.72	4.4	4.1	20.4	34.4	10.0	13.3	0.0
▼ First National Bank of Harveyville	Harveyville	KS	D	D+	C-	17.0	7.86	11.5	5.7	20.5	1.5	6.7	8.7	0.0
First National Bank of Hugo	Hugo	CO	B+	B+	A-	148.3	11.25	2.9	1.7	5.1	30.4	8.5	10.0	0.0
First National Bank of Huntsville	Huntsville	TX	B+	B+	B+	556.8	5.35	6.3	4.7	14.1	29.4	9.6	10.8	0.0
First National Bank of Izard County	Calico Rock	AR	A-	A-	A	199.0	9.96	2.3	5.1	14.7	26.5	10.0	31.1	0.0
First National Bank of Jasper	Jasper	TX	B	B	B	323.1	23.46	4.8	3.6	6.9	59.3	10.0	11.6	0.0
First National Bank of Johnson	Johnson	NE	C+	C+	C+	88.6	17.84	1.1	2.2	3.6	55.1	10.0	17.0	0.0
First National Bank of Kansas	Burlington	KS	C	C	C+	99.3	6.41	6.1	1.7	7.7	63.8	6.1	8.1	21.2
First National Bank of Kentucky	Carrollton	KY	B	B	B+	155.9	13.72	5.3	2.3	32.8	12.4	7.1	9.1	15.1
First National Bank of Lacon	Lacon	IL	C+	C+	C+	81.8	12.32	5.7	5.4	11.2	14.0	5.9	7.9	0.0
First National Bank of Lake Jackson	Lake Jackson	TX	C+	B-	B	280.5	4.68	1.3	0.3	0.0	73.3	7.3	9.2	43.7
First National Bank of Las Animas	Las Animas	CO	A	A	A	517.8	15.20	6.7	0.8	8.5	24.4	9.2	10.4	0.0
First National Bank of Louisiana	Crowley	LA	A	A	A	582.8	10.41	21.0	0.9	9.0	5.1	7.9	9.6	19.6
First National Bank of Manchester	Manchester	KY	C+	B-	B	173.3	5.66	3.9	3.2	13.2	18.7	8.7	10.2	0.0
First National Bank of Michigan	Kalamazoo	MI	B-	B-	B-	803.7	6.08	20.3	0.1	2.3	21.1	6.3	8.4	12.2
First National Bank of Middle Tennessee	McMinnville	TN	A-	A-	A-	606.4	7.24	5.4	0.3	25.5	10.6	10.0	12.2	19.5
First National Bank of Muscatine	Muscatine	IA	C	C	B-	369.6	7.32	11.1	1.4	20.8	20.7	8.7	10.1	20.8
▼ First National Bank of Nokomis	Nokomis	IL	B-	B	B	182.3	9.25	4.1	2.0	10.1	34.6	8.0	9.7	18.0
▲ First National Bank of North Arkansas	Berryville	AR	B	B-	B	261.4	20.38	7.7	8.6	23.4	0.4	7.8	9.5	0.0
First National Bank of Oklahoma	Oklahoma City	OK	B	B	B-	674.5	4.04	11.5	1.3	15.7	5.1	6.9	8.9	13.7
First National Bank of Omaha	Omaha	NE	B	B	B-	25479.6	6.66	8.3	24.7	4.4	17.8	9.3	10.5	15.2
▲ First National Bank of Orwell	Orwell	VT	C	C-	C-	86.5	3.15	3.6	2.1	45.8	0.0	6.8	8.8	19.0
First National Bank of Pana	Pana	IL	B+	B+	A-	240.7	14.20	11.8	1.4	16.3	14.3	8.9	10.2	0.0
First National Bank of Pasco	Dade City	FL	B-	B-	C+	272.4	29.52	15.5	1.7	6.5	22.2	9.1	10.4	0.0
First National Bank of Pennsylvania	Pittsburgh	PA	B	B-	B-	38437.7	2.03	16.5	3.6	15.0	16.5	6.4	8.4	12.9
First National Bank of Pulaski	Pulaski	TN	A-	A-	A-	1103.7	13.57	4.2	2.2	11.5	33.4	8.3	9.9	0.0
First National Bank of Scotia	Scotia	NY	C+	C+	C+	649.7	16.21	10.7	21.9	16.8	15.2	5.2	7.2	12.7
First National Bank of South Carolina	Holly Hill	SC	B	B	B	259.0	13.69	6.0	1.1	8.5	31.0	9.1	10.4	28.6
First National Bank of South Miami	South Miami	FL	C+	C+	B-	958.4	14.54	8.3	0.3	8.5	9.0	7.0	9.0	17.4
▼ First National Bank of South Padre Island	South Padre Island	TX	C+	B-	B	83.8	29.05	2.6	0.2	21.8	3.2	6.9	8.9	0.0
First National Bank of Spearville	Spearville	KS	B+	B+	B	48.4	15.01	8.4	3.9	0.0	7.1	10.0	12.2	0.0
First National Bank of Steeleville	Steeleville	IL	B	B+	B+	244.2	4.54	4.8	3.5	17.4	52.9	10.0	12.8	27.9
First National Bank of Syracuse	Syracuse	KS	B-	B	B	429.6	3.82	16.9	1.3	4.6	20.8	8.3	9.9	14.9
First National Bank of Tennessee	Livingston	TN	B	B+	A-	1136.3	15.88	6.4	2.1	9.8	15.1	8.0	9.6	0.0
First National Bank of Waterloo	Waterloo	IL	B-	B-	C+	801.3	16.15	5.4	0.4	14.0	33.1	6.1	8.1	14.4
First National Bank of Wauchula	Wauchula	FL	C	C	C+	84.0	0.61	5.9	2.0	29.8	10.2	9.1	10.4	0.0
First National Bank Texas	Killeen	TX	B+	B+	B+	3737.7	38.91	1.4	9.8	9.2	47.9	6.1	8.1	24.7
First National Bank USA	Boutte	LA	A-	B+	A-	155.7	-2.96	9.4	0.8	19.2	1.4	10.0	11.3	0.0
First National Bank, Cortez	Cortez	CO	B-	B	B	126.2	12.77	3.6	2.7	8.8	18.8	8.3	9.9	17.5
▲ First National Bankers Bank	Baton Rouge	LA	B	B-	B-	1029.4	6.53	2.3	0.0	0.7	1.8	10.0	14.0	0.0
First National Community Bank	Chatsworth	GA	A-	A-	B	353.9	16.06	7.1	0.8	11.4	2.8	10.0	11.2	0.0
First National Community Bank	New Richmond	WI	C+	C	C-	299.5	18.88	7.5	2.2	12.8	28.3	5.9	7.9	14.2
First National Trust Co.	Hermitage	PA	U	U	U	43.5	25.03	0.0	0.0	0.0	0.0	10.0	73.8	141.7
First Nations Bank	Chicago	IL	B+	B+	A-	482.9	23.94	3.7	0.3	4.8	0.5	10.0	11.2	18.0
First NaturalState Bank	McGehee	AR	C+	B-	B-	79.8	19.58	15.8	5.4	16.3	16.5	7.7	9.5	15.6
First Nebraska Bank	Valley	NE	B	B+	B+	364.6	15.23	9.0	0.8	7.8	19.6	6.9	8.9	0.0
First Neighbor Bank, N.A.	Toledo	IL	C	C	B-	545.0	6.13	16.4	3.9	10.4	5.2	6.6	9.8	0.0
First Neighborhood Bank, Inc.	Spencer	WV	C+	C+	C+	151.0	-11.02	8.9	2.0	26.0	29.4	9.6	10.8	0.0
First New Mexico Bank	Deming	NM	A	A	A	246.5	8.56	19.4	1.6	7.0	31.8	10.0	12.5	0.0
First New Mexico Bank of Silver City	Silver City	NM	A	A	A	136.7	7.50	1.8	0.4	6.2	31.3	9.7	10.8	0.0

Arrows denote recent upgrades ▲ or downgrades ▼

Asset Quality Index	Adjusted Non-Performing Loans as a % of Total Loans	Adjusted Non-Performing Loans as a % of Capital	Net Charge-Offs Avg Loans	Profitability Index	Net Income ($Mil)	Return on Assets (R.O.A.)	Return on Equity (R.O.E.)	Net Interest Spread	Overhead Efficiency Ratio	Liquidity Index	Liquidity Ratio	Hot Money Ratio	Stability Index
7.8	0.69	2.2	0.00	**6.1**	2.6	1.53	18.67	3.52	64.2	**6.2**	49.2	4.8	**5.1**
5.4	0.84	6.2	0.10	**4.0**	0.7	0.62	7.35	3.50	78.4	**2.0**	30.1	25.1	**4.5**
8.0	0.07	0.5	-0.05	**7.5**	1.2	2.10	22.58	3.51	58.7	**5.2**	38.0	7.8	**6.2**
6.5	0.62	3.1	0.02	**4.2**	0.6	0.86	8.01	4.04	78.8	**4.8**	21.8	4.5	**6.6**
7.6	0.37	2.1	0.18	**4.2**	2.0	0.77	8.30	2.63	71.7	**4.0**	39.6	14.8	**6.6**
4.8	2.47	12.0	0.01	**3.7**	1.0	0.55	6.77	3.59	75.5	**4.4**	26.1	8.0	**4.7**
7.8	0.00	0.0	-0.02	**4.5**	0.7	1.06	8.77	3.77	77.1	**3.3**	36.3	17.4	**7.7**
6.5	0.91	3.5	0.00	**4.3**	1.3	0.94	8.32	2.91	62.9	**4.3**	40.2	13.5	**6.5**
7.5	3.11	4.4	-0.03	**4.7**	3.3	1.06	8.64	2.29	58.1	**5.9**	74.8	12.5	**7.0**
8.8	0.35	1.5	-0.01	**3.1**	1.2	0.70	9.51	2.66	84.0	**6.9**	63.1	4.2	**3.5**
6.3	2.48	7.6	0.57	**4.0**	0.6	0.93	6.61	4.29	79.3	**3.3**	41.1	18.8	**7.0**
5.1	0.60	11.4	0.00	**2.6**	0.0	0.27	3.15	3.31	89.7	**2.4**	41.3	22.7	**2.3**
8.2	0.00	0.4	0.02	**5.6**	1.0	1.37	12.49	3.48	62.9	**5.6**	34.3	3.2	**7.8**
8.5	0.02	0.1	0.00	**3.6**	1.3	0.48	4.03	2.37	78.9	**5.2**	43.8	10.0	**8.3**
8.3	2.53	3.1	-0.01	**6.3**	1.4	1.43	4.53	3.73	54.7	**4.6**	63.4	17.2	**8.1**
9.5	0.15	0.3	0.02	**3.4**	0.8	0.55	4.47	2.47	74.8	**3.7**	41.0	16.6	**6.7**
7.1	2.63	3.9	-0.05	**3.4**	0.3	0.65	3.68	2.52	72.5	**7.0**	78.7	5.0	**6.7**
7.4	1.12	2.9	0.00	**3.3**	0.3	0.65	6.97	2.25	77.6	**5.0**	41.6	10.1	**4.5**
8.4	0.24	1.2	0.02	**3.9**	0.5	0.68	7.21	3.70	76.8	**2.2**	15.5	18.2	**5.7**
8.2	0.04	0.4	0.00	**3.2**	0.2	0.56	7.06	3.39	81.7	**4.5**	30.1	9.1	**4.5**
10.0	0.00	0.0	0.00	**3.1**	0.6	0.44	4.34	1.43	69.9	**4.3**	38.1	12.7	**5.6**
8.8	0.10	0.2	0.00	**9.0**	5.4	2.17	18.88	4.08	52.6	**4.6**	31.7	9.1	**9.8**
8.6	0.02	0.1	0.00	**5.7**	3.7	1.31	13.49	2.98	59.0	**5.5**	38.2	5.6	**7.9**
5.6	1.43	5.6	0.00	**3.7**	0.7	0.75	7.01	2.92	74.3	**2.0**	36.0	30.7	**7.6**
7.4	0.00	0.0	0.00	**4.3**	3.4	0.84	10.47	3.12	60.8	**1.4**	17.0	18.7	**5.8**
8.8	0.21	1.2	-0.04	**6.9**	4.0	1.35	10.81	3.26	65.5	**1.4**	14.8	23.2	**9.0**
3.8	3.76	15.4	0.09	**4.1**	1.3	0.71	6.92	2.60	64.4	**5.5**	42.6	7.7	**6.5**
7.4	0.34	1.7	-0.03	**4.0**	0.8	0.87	8.30	2.81	70.8	**5.7**	49.0	8.1	**7.0**
4.8	0.90	5.7	0.09	**6.8**	2.1	1.68	17.74	4.79	68.7	**4.8**	35.4	9.2	**6.1**
4.9	0.88	7.2	-0.03	**7.5**	6.3	1.94	21.32	3.97	48.8	**2.9**	20.6	15.0	**7.3**
5.1	0.97	3.8	1.22	**8.8**	302.1	2.41	22.52	4.94	55.0	**4.9**	19.8	2.1	**9.0**
3.0	2.73	18.7	-0.12	**4.9**	0.5	1.10	12.72	3.37	67.0	**2.0**	31.1	26.8	**5.5**
4.8	2.82	11.1	-0.01	**5.9**	1.8	1.50	14.56	3.30	53.8	**3.5**	25.6	12.2	**7.7**
7.0	0.33	1.8	-0.03	**4.3**	1.1	0.89	8.31	4.27	75.1	**5.1**	32.9	6.2	**5.2**
5.0	0.70	2.7	0.08	**5.2**	200.7	1.07	8.04	2.73	57.6	**4.5**	11.4	4.9	**9.9**
8.8	0.25	1.2	-0.04	**5.5**	5.8	1.08	10.80	3.25	60.7	**4.1**	33.5	15.5	**8.7**
5.8	0.15	2.5	0.05	**4.0**	2.4	0.77	11.56	3.30	71.7	**5.3**	27.0	2.2	**4.3**
7.8	0.63	2.1	0.01	**2.8**	0.4	0.31	2.94	2.41	86.2	**6.8**	61.3	4.8	**5.7**
4.5	1.71	12.0	0.00	**3.4**	2.3	0.51	5.58	2.90	78.9	**4.5**	34.8	10.6	**5.9**
6.4	1.67	6.4	-0.01	**2.8**	0.1	0.30	3.26	2.79	87.9	**6.9**	68.2	3.8	**5.3**
7.9	0.00	0.0	-0.05	**8.5**	0.6	2.22	15.87	2.48	33.5	**4.2**	51.9	14.1	**7.0**
7.4	1.57	3.8	0.64	**3.5**	1.0	0.78	5.90	2.38	75.7	**4.8**	43.4	11.7	**7.0**
4.0	0.43	10.6	-0.12	**7.1**	3.4	1.55	14.91	4.20	54.1	**1.0**	26.1	38.6	**6.4**
7.3	1.29	5.1	-0.01	**4.3**	3.9	0.71	7.26	2.43	74.8	**6.3**	59.0	9.7	**8.1**
5.6	1.17	5.4	0.04	**3.6**	2.5	0.64	7.21	2.53	71.3	**3.7**	25.0	11.4	**5.7**
5.0	1.56	9.3	-0.07	**2.9**	0.2	0.46	4.69	4.41	98.7	**2.0**	24.7	20.0	**5.6**
8.5	0.16	0.6	0.32	**6.2**	25.4	1.45	16.82	2.75	86.2	**7.6**	61.3	0.9	**7.0**
8.3	0.34	2.2	-0.04	**4.9**	0.8	0.90	7.85	4.06	71.6	**3.3**	23.0	13.5	**8.5**
4.8	2.19	11.0	0.06	**3.6**	0.3	0.51	4.95	3.35	77.0	**4.7**	32.6	8.7	**6.1**
6.4	1.95	5.9	-0.23	**4.1**	4.0	0.75	5.20	2.31	81.7	**7.5**	51.8	0.0	**8.3**
6.8	1.95	5.7	-0.01	**5.6**	1.9	1.08	9.09	3.82	65.0	**4.9**	32.8	7.4	**7.8**
3.4	2.84	14.8	0.06	**5.7**	2.2	1.52	18.52	3.39	61.7	**5.5**	32.4	3.2	**5.2**
6.6	na	0.0	na	**10.0**	8.1	40.04	55.96	0.46	65.6	**4.0**	184.4	0.0	**6.3**
7.6	0.00	0.0	0.50	**4.4**	1.4	0.65	5.63	2.78	61.0	**1.9**	39.0	43.7	**7.8**
4.1	2.26	9.9	0.01	**4.1**	0.3	0.86	9.08	3.37	65.4	**3.7**	25.2	11.4	**5.5**
4.5	1.55	10.3	0.05	**5.5**	2.2	1.26	13.31	3.58	69.9	**5.5**	32.6	3.6	**6.7**
1.4	5.13	27.6	0.02	**5.6**	3.1	1.13	11.23	3.20	62.5	**2.0**	25.2	20.5	**7.4**
8.3	0.04	0.3	0.01	**2.9**	0.5	0.60	5.65	3.13	79.9	**5.0**	38.5	9.6	**5.8**
7.7	1.11	3.9	0.03	**6.7**	1.6	1.29	10.30	3.40	55.1	**6.7**	48.4	1.7	**8.9**
9.9	0.05	0.2	-0.01	**7.1**	0.9	1.26	11.75	3.25	61.7	**7.4**	66.7	1.5	**8.6**

	Name	City	State	Rating	2020 Rating	2019 Rating	Total Assets ($Mil)	One Year Asset Growth	Asset Mix (As a % of Total Assets) Comm-ercial Loans	Cons-umer Loans	Mort-gage Loans	Secur-ities	Capital-ization Index	Lever-age Ratio	Risk-Based Capital Ratio
	First New Mexico Bank, Las Cruces	Las Cruces	NM	**A**	A	A	158.6	19.73	5.2	1.0	10.5	16.1	**10.0**	11.6	0.0
	First Northeast Bank of Nebraska	Lyons	NE	**B**	B	A-	357.5	13.26	5.3	1.0	1.4	39.7	**10.0**	12.4	0.0
	First Northern Bank and Trust Co.	Palmerton	PA	**B**	B	B	894.6	11.46	6.0	0.3	22.3	12.9	**10.0**	12.3	0.0
	First Northern Bank of Dixon	Dixon	CA	**B+**	B+	A-	1834.6	13.80	11.6	0.0	4.1	30.6	**6.2**	8.2	17.5
	First Northern Bank of Wyoming	Buffalo	WY	**B-**	B-	B-	527.5	11.70	12.0	3.0	8.9	24.7	**5.7**	7.7	13.9
▲	First Oklahoma Bank	Jenks	OK	**C-**	D+	C	933.2	5.83	22.0	0.3	13.1	0.8	**2.8**	9.0	0.0
	First Option Bank	Osawatomie	KS	**B**	B	B	554.5	17.98	4.5	2.5	19.9	48.1	**6.1**	8.1	19.1
	First Palmetto Bank	Camden	SC	**B+**	B+	B+	861.7	8.03	9.9	0.7	19.3	4.9	**8.1**	9.7	16.9
	First Peoples Bank	Pine Mountain	GA	**B**	B+	A-	221.1	9.14	10.1	1.2	16.9	18.4	**6.7**	8.7	16.3
	First Peoples Bank of Tennessee	Jefferson City	TN	**C+**	C+	B-	196.0	12.38	7.8	1.4	11.0	24.7	**6.4**	8.4	13.1
	First Piedmont Federal S&L Assn.	Gaffney	SC	**A**	A	A	524.5	11.62	1.4	0.7	30.0	1.2	**10.0**	23.1	0.0
	First Pioneer National Bank	Wray	CO	**A-**	A-	A-	237.6	12.59	3.7	3.2	2.2	31.6	**10.0**	11.3	0.0
	First Port City Bank	Bainbridge	GA	**B**	B	B+	325.2	13.35	9.4	1.4	24.7	10.1	**6.1**	8.1	13.1
	First Premier Bank	Sioux Falls	SD	**A**	A-	A	3014.1	14.10	4.9	33.0	2.3	18.7	**10.0**	11.0	19.6
▼	First Progressive Bank	Brewton	AL	**D+**		C	32.2	5.64	8.3	1.7	12.7	52.3	**9.8**	26.4	0.0
	First Pryority Bank	Pryor	OK	**B**	B	B	287.2	12.67	31.1	4.4	9.3	4.0	**6.0**	9.7	0.0
	First Reliance Bank	Florence	SC	**B+**	B	C+	829.9	9.08	7.4	9.0	16.9	6.9	**9.2**	10.4	14.4
	First Republic Bank	San Francisco	CA	**B**	B	B	161646.7	25.99	7.9	3.6	43.1	15.0	**6.0**	8.1	12.6
	First Resource Bank	Lino Lakes	MN	**B**	B-	B-	307.8	15.35	18.9	0.1	19.4	1.2	**6.9**	8.9	14.7
	First Resource Bank	Exton	PA	**C+**	C+	C+	457.6	18.74	10.8	0.1	19.4	3.9	**5.4**	7.4	12.9
	First Robinson Savings Bank, N.A.	Robinson	IL	**C+**	C+	B-	420.2	-5.74	7.2	3.6	14.2	39.4	**6.0**	8.0	16.3
	First S&L Assn.	Mebane	NC	**C+**	C+	C+	59.9	3.46	0.0	0.0	51.4	19.3	**10.0**	21.8	54.5
	First Savanna Savings Bank	Savanna	IL	**E+**	E+	D-	10.8	-10.22	0.0	10.6	54.0	4.5	**3.2**	5.2	10.9
	First Savings Bank	Danville	IL	**C+**	B-	C	40.7	-5.33	0.0	0.1	31.9	55.2	**10.0**	22.8	75.2
	First Savings Bank	Jeffersonville	IN	**B+**	B+	B+	1753.8	5.75	9.9	0.6	21.2	11.9	**7.6**	10.6	13.0
	First Savings Bank	Beresford	SD	**A**	A-	A-	1177.3	21.59	7.2	12.3	5.6	20.8	**10.0**	13.9	21.8
	First Savings Bank of Hegewisch	Chicago	IL	**C+**	C+	B	774.5	9.06	0.0	0.1	49.2	27.6	**10.0**	14.4	41.9
▲	First Seacoast Bank	Dover	NH	**C**	C-	C	478.4	1.49	7.8	0.7	47.4	14.0	**9.2**	10.5	18.2
	First Secure Bank and Trust Co.	Palos Hills	IL	**C**	C+	B-	394.0	12.96	28.4	0.7	10.5	6.7	**6.1**	8.1	13.8
▼	First Secure Community Bank	Sugar Grove	IL	**C-**	C	C+	495.4	19.58	23.2	2.7	2.4	17.3	**5.3**	7.5	11.3
	First Security Bank	Searcy	AR	**A+**	A+	A+	7895.0	17.20	6.6	0.5	4.3	38.0	**10.0**	14.9	22.8
▼	First Security Bank	Mapleton	IA	**B+**	A-	A-	82.4	8.70	4.2	3.2	3.4	30.4	**9.9**	10.9	18.4
	First Security Bank	Mackinaw	IL	**C-**	C-	D+	95.1	2.59	6.6	0.5	16.3	2.4	**7.5**	9.3	14.7
	First Security Bank	Byron	MN	**B-**	B-	C+	87.5	12.62	8.2	2.8	15.8	21.0	**6.3**	8.3	12.1
	First Security Bank	Union Star	MO	**C-**	C-	C	44.3	21.48	10.0	9.5	32.7	25.7	**5.3**	7.3	14.0
	First Security Bank	Batesville	MS	**B+**	B+	A-	760.7	7.30	6.7	2.9	15.5	34.9	**6.7**	8.7	15.2
	First Security Bank - Canby	Canby	MN	**B+**	A-	B+	79.6	10.98	19.0	1.8	0.8	18.8	**10.0**	11.6	21.4
	First Security Bank - Hendricks	Hendricks	MN	**B+**	B+	B+	45.3	15.13	14.2	1.7	3.4	36.0	**8.8**	10.2	23.0
	First Security Bank - Sleepy Eye	Sleepy Eye	MN	**B+**	A-	B+	250.1	12.12	7.9	1.1	3.7	49.0	**10.0**	11.1	25.5
	First Security Bank - West	Beulah	ND	**A-**	A-	A-	73.4	8.26	13.1	1.4	0.6	16.4	**8.7**	10.1	23.8
▲	First Security Bank and Trust Co.	Charles City	IA	**B-**	C+	C	592.3	8.67	6.1	1.1	11.5	29.8	**6.7**	8.7	14.8
	First Security Bank and Trust Co.	Oklahoma City	OK	**C-**	C-	C-	63.4	-1.93	25.4	2.0	37.4	1.9	**10.0**	12.9	15.4
	First Security Bank of Deer Lodge	Deer Lodge	MT	**B+**	B+	B+	66.7	28.09	17.8	4.5	27.3	0.0	**7.3**	9.2	17.1
	First Security Bank of Nevada	Las Vegas	NV	**A**	A	A	323.1	13.21	6.9	0.0	0.6	1.0	**10.0**	15.7	0.0
	First Security Bank of Roundup	Roundup	MT	**C+**	B-	B	83.2	11.81	8.6	3.2	3.7	39.7	**8.8**	10.2	22.5
	First Security State Bank	Evansdale	IA	**B**	B	C+	100.0	-0.11	28.5	25.3	5.9	8.9	**10.0**	12.3	0.0
	First Security State Bank	Cranfills Gap	TX	**B**	B	B	154.2	13.38	3.4	2.6	15.8	38.0	**4.2**	6.2	17.6
	First Security Trust and Savings Bank	Elmwood Park	IL	**C+**	B-	B-	341.4	15.37	11.4	6.3	3.7	22.2	**6.4**	8.4	15.3
	First Sentinel Bank	Richlands	VA	**B-**	B-	B-	319.4	-0.21	10.6	34.8	18.9	0.5	**7.2**	9.1	13.3
▲	First Service Bank	Greenbrier	AR	**B+**	B-	C+	449.7	11.87	10.6	0.8	16.6	10.6	**9.0**	11.4	0.0
	First Shore Federal S&L Assn.	Salisbury	MD	**B-**	B-	B	341.5	5.27	2.0	9.6	44.1	4.5	**10.0**	15.1	27.2
	First Sound Bank	Seattle	WA	**D+**	D+	C-	165.2	12.65	30.7	1.1	5.2	4.8	**5.3**	10.2	0.0
	First Southeast Bank	Harmony	MN	**C+**	C	D+	118.9	8.95	9.9	2.7	6.7	5.0	**5.7**	7.7	12.4
	First Southern Bank	Florence	AL	**B**	B	B	371.3	15.14	16.8	1.2	14.3	4.2	**5.7**	8.5	0.0
	First Southern Bank	Patterson	GA	**D-**	D-	E	256.7	36.74	9.1	1.4	7.2	15.7	**5.6**	7.6	16.0
	First Southern Bank	Marion	IL	**B+**	B+	A-	765.0	3.09	7.1	6.0	11.2	28.7	**10.0**	12.0	0.0
	First Southern Bank	Columbia	MS	**B+**	B+	B+	240.4	6.93	6.9	5.1	13.0	21.0	**8.6**	10.1	0.0
	First Southern National Bank	Lancaster	KY	**B**	B	B	1119.7	13.92	7.8	2.0	19.4	19.6	**6.3**	8.3	15.9
	First Southern State Bank	Stevenson	AL	**B+**	B+	B+	713.0	17.30	9.0	3.8	14.9	36.4	**6.8**	8.8	0.0
	First Southwest Bank	Alamosa	CO	**B**	B	B-	427.4	12.19	18.6	1.3	3.8	27.6	**5.7**	7.7	16.3

Asset Quality Index	Adjusted Non-Performing Loans as a % of Total Loans	Adjusted Non-Performing Loans as a % of Capital	Net Charge-Offs Avg Loans	Profitability Index	Net Income ($Mil)	Return on Assets (R.O.A.)	Return on Equity (R.O.E.)	Net Interest Spread	Overhead Efficiency Ratio	Liquidity Index	Liquidity Ratio	Hot Money Ratio	Stability Index
9.4	0.00	0.0	-0.01	7.2	0.9	1.24	10.37	3.89	61.2	6.4	59.2	7.2	9.1
8.7	0.37	1.3	0.77	4.5	1.7	0.98	7.45	2.89	61.4	3.5	29.5	10.5	7.7
8.2	0.64	3.0	-0.08	3.9	3.2	0.74	5.83	3.13	68.9	4.6	27.3	6.9	7.9
5.5	1.96	10.3	0.07	4.7	6.6	0.74	8.97	2.73	65.0	7.2	51.6	2.1	7.2
5.1	0.93	6.5	0.15	7.4	4.9	1.93	24.31	3.55	62.7	2.0	27.8	14.4	6.4
7.3	0.35	1.4	0.06	4.9	4.8	1.03	11.84	3.65	69.0	0.7	14.8	47.1	5.1
8.7	0.08	0.4	-0.05	6.0	4.4	1.62	18.90	3.02	61.0	4.7	28.5	6.6	6.3
6.7	0.49	2.9	-0.04	6.1	5.5	1.31	13.44	3.39	61.9	2.3	25.0	18.4	7.2
6.3	0.73	3.6	0.00	5.6	1.2	1.07	12.47	4.01	65.0	4.6	26.1	6.8	5.5
7.1	0.14	0.9	-0.43	3.8	1.0	1.09	13.40	3.77	78.7	4.9	28.8	6.0	2.2
9.5	0.49	0.9	0.00	6.5	2.6	1.03	4.22	3.30	66.9	6.4	53.8	5.6	9.7
6.0	3.31	12.2	0.06	5.9	1.4	1.21	10.25	3.46	52.5	2.8	28.6	17.2	7.9
8.7	0.11	0.5	0.00	4.5	1.5	0.92	11.91	4.08	67.9	3.2	13.1	12.6	5.1
6.8	0.13	0.4	-0.02	6.2	21.1	1.43	12.68	2.70	62.4	5.0	29.3	1.8	9.9
9.6	2.22	1.1	0.00	1.2	0.0	-0.15	-0.57	2.30	107.8	6.7	98.1	9.9	6.7
7.0	0.63	1.8	0.08	9.0	2.8	2.04	21.43	4.35	39.5	0.7	12.0	35.9	6.2
6.2	0.49	2.2	-0.02	5.9	3.7	0.97	8.86	3.51	77.5	3.0	26.8	13.6	7.5
9.0	0.12	1.0	0.00	4.2	707.9	0.90	11.12	2.69	62.5	4.6	18.0	4.8	7.4
8.0	0.06	0.4	0.01	5.6	1.7	1.13	12.30	3.69	58.4	2.8	17.2	10.4	6.9
6.3	0.37	2.1	0.05	4.4	2.0	0.90	12.12	3.67	63.0	2.6	13.4	14.7	3.9
5.3	1.31	6.7	0.01	4.0	1.4	0.69	8.25	2.70	71.3	5.2	33.3	5.8	4.3
9.5	2.33	3.6	0.00	2.4	0.1	0.45	2.05	3.29	83.5	2.3	54.8	53.8	7.5
1.9	1.60	27.8	-0.05	0.0	-0.1	-2.19	-35.66	4.07	166.3	1.5	22.4	24.9	1.6
9.9	0.43	0.6	0.00	2.1	0.1	0.31	1.31	1.87	88.6	4.2	87.4	23.6	6.4
5.6	1.27	4.7	0.01	9.1	15.0	1.73	16.31	3.80	80.2	2.5	14.8	11.1	9.8
6.9	0.54	1.8	2.16	10.0	17.8	3.09	23.07	7.17	44.9	5.2	27.5	7.1	9.3
10.0	0.18	0.6	0.00	2.3	0.8	0.21	1.46	1.79	85.4	3.6	53.8	21.8	7.9
9.1	0.00	0.0	-0.02	2.9	1.7	0.75	7.08	3.32	78.9	4.0	21.2	5.6	5.8
5.4	0.49	3.1	0.00	5.3	2.2	1.12	18.53	2.54	46.6	1.1	23.1	33.7	5.0
1.7	3.50	24.1	0.00	3.4	1.3	0.55	6.86	2.84	63.3	2.2	35.1	25.8	4.6
9.2	0.16	0.4	0.09	8.1	63.2	1.72	10.22	3.27	41.1	5.5	29.5	6.0	10.0
7.3	0.00	0.0	0.00	5.7	0.6	1.47	10.02	3.29	56.5	4.5	49.2	14.1	7.7
8.2	0.00	0.0	0.00	5.8	1.1	2.28	24.86	3.92	53.1	3.1	25.3	14.6	4.0
8.7	0.05	0.4	-0.01	5.9	0.6	1.53	17.94	3.82	61.8	3.6	27.4	13.0	5.4
5.0	1.08	4.9	0.16	5.4	0.2	1.12	15.02	4.50	61.0	3.8	16.5	10.3	3.6
4.6	1.92	9.7	-0.01	5.7	4.0	1.06	11.23	3.58	65.1	4.7	26.3	6.2	7.2
5.2	1.76	6.3	0.00	7.8	0.8	2.06	15.15	3.98	48.0	6.5	45.4	1.2	8.1
9.0	0.00	0.0	0.00	7.1	0.4	1.69	16.11	3.12	48.4	6.5	61.9	4.6	6.7
8.8	0.03	0.3	0.00	4.7	1.5	1.21	10.27	2.99	61.3	6.7	53.4	3.1	7.6
3.1	5.47	20.6	0.10	3.0	-0.6	-1.57	-13.22	3.69	63.0	7.0	62.8	1.7	7.4
4.6	2.33	6.4	-0.11	4.3	3.0	1.05	10.02	3.32	70.3	5.6	36.7	3.7	6.3
5.4	2.17	7.8	-0.25	6.3	2.9	8.99	97.03	13.85	33.1	1.5	8.7	22.4	5.5
8.4	0.00	0.0	0.00	10.0	1.1	3.49	39.36	5.98	36.5	5.0	22.2	2.9	6.5
7.0	0.00	0.0	0.00	8.6	2.5	1.61	8.86	3.56	43.7	6.8	50.7	1.5	9.6
3.0	4.93	17.7	0.18	5.9	0.5	1.26	11.75	3.35	60.4	5.9	49.0	6.0	7.6
4.6	0.00	5.7	0.00	5.7	0.7	1.31	10.73	3.62	64.3	2.8	28.4	16.5	6.7
9.4	0.00	0.0	-0.03	4.0	0.6	0.85	11.69	2.91	74.4	6.6	65.5	7.1	4.0
4.9	1.49	7.0	-0.06	2.7	0.7	0.38	4.65	2.10	83.5	6.6	53.9	3.9	5.0
3.9	0.64	5.0	0.14	5.9	1.9	1.18	13.19	4.81	59.7	1.5	10.4	23.6	5.1
5.4	0.95	5.3	-0.01	6.7	3.4	1.50	13.53	4.34	60.3	1.7	14.4	10.2	6.8
6.1	1.21	5.4	-0.02	3.6	1.0	0.58	3.82	3.03	73.9	2.1	27.0	21.1	7.8
3.0	1.29	12.5	0.02	2.3	0.5	0.60	7.38	2.74	77.9	4.7	20.0	4.4	4.0
5.9	0.54	2.2	0.56	5.0	0.7	1.24	15.89	4.89	67.1	2.1	28.7	17.1	5.4
8.3	0.20	0.9	0.01	6.6	2.4	1.34	15.69	3.98	52.5	4.1	23.9	9.4	5.4
6.5	0.90	3.2	0.00	2.6	2.4	2.04	25.57	3.50	90.1	5.7	42.5	6.5	2.8
4.6	0.93	8.3	0.16	7.2	5.3	1.37	10.20	3.58	50.9	4.1	25.2	9.6	9.1
7.1	0.86	4.2	-0.04	5.3	1.6	1.33	12.87	3.56	71.2	4.6	30.7	8.5	7.0
5.0	1.44	8.0	0.00	5.1	5.2	0.96	9.66	3.45	66.5	5.8	34.1	5.8	8.5
8.5	0.22	0.9	0.01	5.9	4.4	1.27	12.91	3.68	54.6	3.4	35.7	16.7	6.9
6.0	0.99	3.4	0.00	4.5	1.6	0.76	8.93	4.42	73.7	4.2	31.2	11.3	5.0

Name	City	State	Rating	2020 Rating	2019 Rating	Total Assets ($Mil)	One Year Asset Growth	Asset Mix (As a % of Total Assets): Commercial Loans	Consumer Loans	Mortgage Loans	Securities	Capitalization Index	Leverage Ratio	Risk-Based Capital Ratio
▲ First State Bank	Lonoke	AR	**B-**	C	C	283.8	9.62	4.0	0.4	13.7	27.0	**8.3**	9.8	0.0
First State Bank	Russellville	AR	**B+**	B+	A-	450.1	26.48	9.6	0.5	14.8	23.1	**7.4**	9.2	16.2
First State Bank	Wrens	GA	**B+**	B	B	274.4	51.92	13.1	1.4	20.1	14.9	**5.9**	7.9	13.0
First State Bank	Belmond	IA	**B+**	B+	B	132.6	20.38	8.8	2.2	7.6	48.1	**8.1**	9.7	0.0
First State Bank	Britt	IA	**A**	A	A	128.2	8.49	5.6	1.3	11.4	28.2	**10.0**	12.3	0.0
First State Bank	Ida Grove	IA	**A-**	A-	B	182.6	2.59	9.2	3.6	8.9	19.2	**9.2**	11.9	0.0
First State Bank	Lynnville	IA	**A**	A	A-	273.5	28.48	6.6	1.3	10.8	25.8	**9.1**	10.4	16.5
First State Bank	Nashua	IA	**A-**	B+	B+	56.7	-1.93	8.9	3.3	25.8	4.9	**9.8**	10.9	0.0
First State Bank	Stuart	IA	**C+**	C+	B-	130.0	14.88	5.4	1.7	6.2	50.6	**6.9**	8.9	23.3
First State Bank	Webster City	IA	**A-**	A-	A-	536.7	1.70	7.2	0.6	9.3	9.9	**10.0**	13.2	0.0
First State Bank	Mendota	IL	**B+**	B+	B-	1368.4	8.82	9.9	0.8	20.2	9.3	**8.3**	9.9	15.5
First State Bank	Monticello	IL	**B-**	B-	B-	314.9	11.45	3.5	0.9	6.2	36.2	**5.4**	7.4	17.2
First State Bank	Irvington	KY	**B+**	B+	B+	244.1	12.32	3.7	3.7	26.9	28.3	**10.0**	11.0	20.3
First State Bank	Saint Clair Shores	MI	**B-**	B	B	987.0	6.50	11.1	0.3	8.3	14.4	**6.7**	8.7	0.0
First State Bank	Holly Springs	MS	**C**	C	C	137.0	9.21	7.2	1.2	12.2	33.2	**10.0**	11.1	0.0
First State Bank	Waynesboro	MS	**B+**	B+	B+	894.8	3.13	5.8	1.5	15.2	30.6	**10.0**	11.3	0.0
First State Bank	Buxton	ND	**B**	B	B	294.1	5.31	13.1	0.9	7.8	9.1	**5.3**	10.2	0.0
First State Bank	Farnam	NE	**A**	A-	A-	152.7	3.76	9.8	2.7	4.7	22.4	**9.6**	13.3	0.0
▲ First State Bank	Gothenburg	NE	**B**	C+	C	807.5	21.62	10.8	0.6	2.0	25.9	**7.0**	10.3	0.0
First State Bank	Hordville	NE	**B-**	B-	B-	45.2	10.00	10.9	0.7	5.9	6.1	**10.0**	11.6	0.0
First State Bank	Loomis	NE	**B+**	B+	B-	166.7	8.87	9.5	3.0	4.9	15.4	**10.0**	11.6	15.3
First State Bank	Randolph	NE	**B+**	B+	B+	71.9	12.35	2.7	1.3	1.9	11.5	**10.0**	12.5	0.0
First State Bank	Scottsbluff	NE	**A-**	A-	A-	361.1	8.09	8.7	1.2	6.6	10.8	**7.1**	9.2	0.0
First State Bank	Socorro	NM	**B-**	B-	B	171.3	6.59	0.8	0.4	3.0	78.2	**8.9**	10.3	46.4
First State Bank	Winchester	OH	**B-**	B	B	802.0	35.77	1.2	4.9	15.1	36.4	**6.9**	8.9	17.8
First State Bank	Anadarko	OK	**B+**	B+	B	116.6	18.19	1.6	2.0	2.3	65.7	**10.0**	12.5	0.0
First State Bank	Elmore City	OK	**B-**	B-	C+	17.4	-8.07	15.3	1.2	29.9	5.4	**10.0**	14.3	33.4
First State Bank	Noble	OK	**C-**	C-	C+	58.2	8.81	1.4	3.0	15.1	40.0	**8.4**	9.9	0.0
▼ First State Bank	Tahlequah	OK	**C-**	C	C-	70.2	-12.66	16.8	1.5	10.0	22.1	**10.0**	12.1	0.0
First State Bank	Valliant	OK	**C+**	C	C-	89.7	14.72	9.0	4.8	20.6	6.0	**6.2**	8.2	12.2
First State Bank	Watonga	OK	**A-**	A-	B+	82.1	4.55	7.3	2.5	1.6	38.7	**10.0**	11.0	0.0
First State Bank	Abilene	TX	**C**	C-	C	46.0	-10.80	11.5	1.0	0.9	1.1	**5.1**	7.1	28.4
First State Bank	Athens	TX	**B+**	B+	A-	620.9	18.12	6.0	2.2	23.7	29.8	**8.2**	9.8	0.0
First State Bank	Clute	TX	**B+**	B	B-	270.6	-0.74	16.8	6.5	14.9	13.2	**7.0**	9.0	0.0
First State Bank	Gainesville	TX	**B+**	B+	B+	1466.1	14.06	8.4	1.4	7.6	37.0	**6.4**	8.4	14.9
First State Bank	Graham	TX	**B+**	B+	B+	215.3	22.36	18.0	1.6	10.2	14.1	**6.2**	8.2	16.4
First State Bank	Junction	TX	**C+**	C+	C+	65.1	8.35	4.9	1.3	9.9	32.6	**5.9**	7.9	15.9
First State Bank	Paint Rock	TX	**A-**	A-	A-	136.6	11.58	7.3	2.9	2.5	31.8	**10.0**	11.2	0.0
First State Bank	Shallowater	TX	**A-**	B+	B-	115.3	10.96	10.8	2.3	2.7	10.5	**10.0**	15.9	26.2
First State Bank	Spearman	TX	**B-**	B-	B	135.6	-10.89	12.1	0.8	4.5	6.2	**8.4**	9.9	0.0
First State Bank	Stratford	TX	**A-**	A-	A-	293.4	12.46	8.0	0.7	6.0	45.1	**9.5**	10.7	0.0
▼ First State Bank	New London	WI	**B-**	B	B-	515.8	5.89	7.6	2.8	12.7	32.9	**7.9**	9.7	0.0
▲ First State Bank & Trust	Williston	ND	**A**	A-	A-	484.5	-2.43	7.2	1.1	2.3	59.8	**10.0**	13.8	29.3
▲ First State Bank & Trust Co.	Fremont	NE	**A-**	B+	B+	288.1	6.99	17.5	1.8	17.8	9.4	**7.5**	9.4	0.0
First State Bank and Trust	Tonganoxie	KS	**B**	B	B-	406.7	14.23	8.8	1.4	12.1	18.9	**5.8**	7.8	14.4
First State Bank and Trust	Bayport	MN	**B+**	B+	B	353.1	24.29	7.2	3.7	25.0	25.2	**6.1**	8.2	17.9
First State Bank and Trust Co.	Carthage	TX	**B+**	B+	A-	572.9	12.10	1.5	4.1	15.4	64.5	**10.0**	14.2	0.0
First State Bank and Trust Co., Inc.	Caruthersville	MO	**A-**	A-	A-	449.3	5.69	7.6	2.8	10.9	28.4	**10.0**	11.8	0.0
▲ First State Bank in Temple	Temple	OK	**B-**	C+	C+	26.6	4.73	3.8	3.7	1.7	52.2	**10.0**	19.6	0.0
First State Bank Minnesota	Le Roy	MN	**B-**	B-	B	89.1	17.65	5.9	1.3	4.3	5.8	**7.7**	9.4	0.0
First State Bank Nebraska	Lincoln	NE	**B**	B	B	827.9	22.80	11.3	0.8	10.3	17.0	**6.4**	8.4	13.8
First State Bank of Bedias	Bedias	TX	**A**	A	A	187.0	5.73	10.4	4.1	10.2	16.5	**10.0**	15.6	0.0
First State Bank of Beecher City	Beecher City	IL	**B+**	B+	B+	91.1	14.95	6.8	10.4	15.6	7.2	**10.0**	12.7	20.5
First State Bank of Ben Wheeler, Texas	Ben Wheeler	TX	**A-**	A-	A-	184.6	11.40	5.7	2.7	13.0	53.8	**10.0**	12.5	0.0
First State Bank of Bigfork	Bigfork	MN	**D-**	D-	D+	94.2	4.19	11.5	10.1	30.3	0.3	**9.9**	10.9	0.0
▲ First State Bank of Blakely	Blakely	GA	**A-**	B+	A-	541.6	-1.39	8.9	2.1	11.7	14.9	**10.0**	15.3	0.0
First State Bank of Bloomington	Bloomington	IL	**B-**	B-	C+	157.7	13.40	14.5	1.4	14.5	26.9	**5.7**	7.7	18.4
▼ First State Bank of Brownsboro	Brownsboro	TX	**B-**	B	B-	127.7	11.72	5.3	6.2	15.5	53.0	**6.9**	8.9	0.0
First State Bank of Burnet	Burnet	TX	**B+**	B+	A-	316.0	10.91	7.2	1.2	6.5	60.1	**10.0**	11.2	0.0
▲ First State Bank of Campbell Hill	Campbell Hill	IL	**A-**	B+	B+	139.1	8.59	5.3	4.5	22.8	25.7	**10.0**	11.1	20.0

Arrows denote recent upgrades ▲ or downgrades ▼

Asset Quality Index	Adjusted Non-Performing Loans as a % of Total Loans	Adjusted Non-Performing Loans as a % of Capital	Net Charge-Offs Avg Loans	Profitability Index	Net Income ($Mil)	Return on Assets (R.O.A.)	Return on Equity (R.O.E.)	Net Interest Spread	Overhead Efficiency Ratio	Liquidity Index	Liquidity Ratio	Hot Money Ratio	Stability Index
6.2	0.00	6.3	0.00	**4.2**	1.3	0.95	8.85	3.48	61.6	**1.9**	20.2	20.5	**5.8**
8.9	0.15	0.6	-0.01	**5.7**	2.3	1.10	12.10	3.16	58.1	**4.1**	40.5	13.6	**5.7**
8.0	0.18	1.4	0.04	**8.7**	1.9	1.54	19.59	4.62	53.6	**2.2**	33.7	25.2	**5.3**
9.3	0.14	0.7	-0.12	**3.9**	0.5	0.73	7.30	1.99	61.8	**5.0**	58.6	14.4	**5.8**
9.1	0.00	0.0	-0.01	**6.6**	0.8	1.25	9.60	2.70	40.0	**5.7**	51.5	9.1	**8.7**
5.8	0.00	3.4	0.00	**8.1**	2.3	2.53	21.03	4.40	35.5	**1.8**	27.6	25.4	**8.2**
8.4	0.20	1.0	-0.07	**8.0**	2.2	1.68	15.11	3.53	50.0	**4.3**	30.2	8.3	**8.9**
8.6	0.00	0.0	-0.01	**9.9**	0.8	2.63	23.31	4.61	34.6	**2.5**	34.0	21.6	**7.7**
9.1	0.00	0.0	0.12	**3.5**	0.4	0.65	7.26	2.73	70.5	**6.4**	57.4	6.4	**5.1**
8.4	0.00	0.0	0.00	**6.0**	3.3	1.16	8.90	3.05	63.2	**3.7**	27.2	10.9	**9.2**
6.9	0.32	2.9	0.11	**6.2**	7.7	1.14	10.92	3.35	71.1	**2.6**	20.2	17.1	**9.3**
5.4	2.19	6.7	-0.02	**4.2**	1.2	0.79	9.34	2.35	76.2	**6.1**	50.3	6.5	**5.6**
6.5	0.73	3.8	0.01	**6.5**	1.5	1.23	10.91	3.86	61.4	**5.1**	35.8	7.2	**7.7**
7.2	0.78	2.6	-0.10	**3.3**	2.3	0.48	5.19	3.25	76.5	**6.2**	53.0	6.1	**7.6**
6.7	1.99	6.2	-0.05	**2.4**	0.3	0.38	3.59	2.90	84.4	**3.2**	24.1	14.0	**6.6**
6.0	1.78	6.1	-0.03	**4.2**	3.6	0.81	6.60	3.28	63.4	**2.6**	27.8	17.9	**7.9**
7.4	0.18	1.3	0.00	**6.3**	2.4	1.64	15.53	3.59	57.2	**2.2**	3.6	13.0	**8.1**
5.2	0.55	5.1	0.02	**9.3**	2.3	3.09	21.45	4.91	45.2	**1.6**	16.4	23.2	**9.8**
4.9	1.41	5.7	0.00	**9.5**	9.6	2.50	22.92	4.18	37.9	**0.8**	19.0	21.8	**9.1**
8.4	0.17	0.9	0.00	**3.5**	0.1	0.65	5.64	3.22	73.3	**5.1**	37.7	8.0	**6.2**
4.6	0.82	4.0	0.00	**7.5**	1.1	1.29	9.68	3.48	54.2	**1.6**	10.2	20.6	**9.2**
7.4	0.00	0.0	-0.14	**6.7**	0.6	1.68	13.51	2.56	53.7	**3.2**	21.3	9.9	**8.0**
8.8	0.16	0.8	-0.11	**7.6**	2.8	1.58	16.86	3.20	58.3	**4.1**	46.6	16.2	**7.9**
10.0	1.53	0.5	-0.07	**4.0**	0.7	0.82	8.05	3.02	69.7	**7.0**	63.1	3.6	**6.1**
6.1	0.98	4.2	0.02	**3.7**	3.3	0.88	9.11	2.82	81.9	**5.0**	40.1	10.1	**6.2**
9.7	0.72	1.4	0.48	**3.7**	0.8	1.32	11.30	2.78	56.8	**5.3**	46.8	10.4	**6.0**
5.5	3.38	10.8	0.00	**10.0**	0.2	2.19	16.24	8.03	88.8	**6.3**	52.3	2.1	**7.5**
7.1	1.12	4.6	-0.01	**2.3**	0.1	0.40	3.98	3.32	90.4	**6.5**	47.8	1.6	**4.6**
1.6	6.36	26.9	0.08	**2.7**	0.2	0.52	4.24	3.23	85.0	**2.9**	34.4	18.4	**6.4**
7.4	0.23	1.6	-0.03	**3.2**	0.2	0.51	6.06	4.08	84.5	**3.2**	22.5	13.7	**4.3**
7.9	0.97	2.7	-0.06	**7.5**	0.8	1.88	15.74	4.37	55.1	**5.2**	57.1	11.9	**7.7**
8.7	0.00	0.0	0.00	**3.0**	0.1	0.36	4.16	2.31	81.2	**6.6**	68.7	5.6	**3.1**
5.3	1.54	8.0	-0.02	**5.8**	3.6	1.19	11.87	3.46	61.9	**4.8**	30.1	7.0	**6.9**
6.3	0.38	2.5	0.04	**7.9**	2.4	1.88	20.50	4.58	58.0	**4.8**	32.1	7.6	**6.6**
7.1	0.63	3.9	0.00	**4.6**	7.6	1.07	11.55	3.78	73.4	**6.2**	39.3	5.4	**8.3**
8.9	0.03	0.2	-0.08	**8.6**	2.9	3.00	32.99	5.92	49.9	**4.0**	44.9	16.3	**6.3**
9.1	0.05	0.3	0.02	**4.0**	0.3	0.84	9.66	3.13	73.6	**4.9**	32.5	7.1	**5.0**
6.0	2.62	8.3	0.07	**6.7**	1.1	1.55	14.04	3.29	54.0	**4.6**	56.1	16.0	**7.3**
7.0	1.13	3.5	0.40	**7.2**	0.9	1.57	8.59	3.74	65.1	**3.9**	29.5	12.1	**9.3**
8.4	0.00	0.0	0.00	**4.4**	0.7	0.88	8.89	3.19	75.5	**1.7**	24.7	24.9	**4.5**
8.8	0.00	0.0	0.00	**6.4**	2.3	1.57	14.19	3.05	55.0	**3.8**	42.3	16.7	**8.0**
3.4	3.24	13.6	-0.11	**4.8**	2.5	0.99	8.94	3.66	68.1	**5.2**	34.0	6.3	**7.7**
9.1	0.04	0.1	-0.08	**6.7**	4.1	1.72	11.19	3.41	51.6	**6.0**	59.1	9.5	**7.5**
8.5	0.06	0.5	-0.07	**8.4**	3.1	2.10	23.13	4.22	55.3	**4.3**	23.3	8.0	**7.4**
8.7	0.00	0.0	-0.03	**4.7**	2.1	1.04	12.86	3.46	72.2	**4.9**	28.5	5.8	**5.2**
8.8	0.06	0.2	-0.05	**4.6**	1.8	1.07	12.00	2.88	75.7	**5.4**	39.9	7.2	**5.6**
8.3	1.57	3.0	-0.02	**4.7**	2.8	1.02	6.53	2.83	59.4	**2.3**	46.3	35.2	**8.5**
8.3	0.31	2.6	0.14	**6.6**	3.5	1.53	12.98	3.84	62.9	**3.9**	27.1	11.4	**8.7**
8.6	0.06	0.1	0.00	**3.5**	0.1	0.73	3.52	3.27	72.4	**3.3**	53.2	22.0	**6.9**
3.8	2.27	8.8	-0.01	**5.3**	0.6	1.26	13.25	3.31	61.3	**6.3**	39.0	1.0	**6.0**
7.6	0.11	0.2	0.01	**5.5**	5.4	1.37	13.89	3.29	55.6	**3.9**	24.1	8.7	**6.9**
7.5	0.87	3.1	0.10	**7.0**	1.5	1.58	9.83	3.44	55.4	**2.9**	49.9	28.3	**9.7**
3.4	4.64	16.6	1.06	**9.1**	0.9	1.87	14.56	3.94	44.1	**4.2**	31.1	11.0	**8.9**
9.5	0.00	0.0	-0.05	**5.1**	1.1	1.21	9.51	2.72	62.4	**3.0**	48.6	25.8	**8.4**
0.1	5.72	37.8	-0.17	**7.3**	0.9	1.92	17.96	4.89	55.1	**3.3**	25.2	13.5	**6.1**
5.9	1.50	6.0	0.13	**6.0**	3.1	1.13	7.36	3.67	59.8	**1.3**	17.9	23.3	**8.5**
4.7	1.69	10.3	0.35	**4.2**	0.7	0.92	11.12	3.22	67.5	**5.8**	43.6	5.9	**5.5**
6.3	1.06	3.7	0.17	**3.9**	0.5	0.81	8.33	3.35	76.4	**4.4**	40.6	13.2	**5.8**
9.4	1.11	1.6	-0.01	**4.3**	1.6	1.03	8.40	2.80	64.0	**6.3**	66.8	8.9	**7.3**
6.1	1.23	6.5	0.01	**6.2**	0.9	1.32	12.16	3.14	54.0	**5.2**	36.5	6.9	**7.0**

Name	City	State	Rating	2020 Rating	2019 Rating	Total Assets ($Mil)	One Year Asset Growth	Asset Mix (As a % of Total Assets) Commercial Loans	Consumer Loans	Mortgage Loans	Securities	Capitalization Index	Leverage Ratio	Risk-Based Capital Ratio
First State Bank of Cando	Cando	ND	**C+**	C+	C+	75.3	4.42	4.8	4.2	2.9	47.4	**6.6**	8.6	18.4
First State Bank of Decatur	Decatur	MI	**B-**	B-	B	60.6	11.69	6.1	3.1	32.5	26.8	**10.0**	19.0	0.0
First State Bank of Dekalb County, Inc.	Fort Payne	AL	**B-**	B-	B-	291.5	30.56	6.4	4.6	14.7	19.7	**6.7**	8.7	15.0
▲ First State Bank of DeQueen	De Queen	AR	**B**	B-	B+	318.7	5.03	8.7	3.7	12.7	18.4	**7.3**	9.2	0.0
▲ First State Bank of Forrest	Forrest	IL	**C+**	C-	C-	239.6	1.71	16.6	5.0	32.9	10.3	**6.6**	8.6	13.1
First State Bank of Forsyth	Forsyth	MT	**B+**	B+	B	147.2	11.72	6.1	3.1	8.2	52.6	**9.7**	10.8	0.0
First State Bank of Golva	Golva	ND	**B+**	B+	A-	99.1	13.58	4.9	1.8	4.2	52.1	**6.6**	8.6	15.5
First State Bank of Harvey	Harvey	ND	**B-**	B-	B	94.6	10.28	3.5	3.1	3.9	53.8	**8.1**	9.7	0.0
First State Bank of Le Center	Le Center	MN	**A-**	B+	B+	103.9	11.29	11.4	5.3	14.8	20.7	**7.9**	9.6	17.6
First State Bank of Livingston	Livingston	TX	**B**	B	B	420.8	7.81	1.5	2.1	3.7	49.9	**10.0**	13.1	0.0
First State Bank of Middlebury	Middlebury	IN	**A-**	A-	B+	709.1	5.11	13.4	1.6	18.3	25.4	**10.0**	11.3	17.9
First State Bank of Newcastle	Newcastle	WY	**B-**	B	B	177.8	7.10	5.5	2.2	6.0	54.1	**10.0**	11.8	39.1
First State Bank of Odem	Odem	TX	**A-**	A	A	167.9	7.63	17.6	1.4	4.5	13.9	**10.0**	11.6	23.7
First State Bank of Olmsted	Olmsted	IL	**B**	B	B-	65.4	4.10	12.1	3.6	22.4	32.2	**10.0**	11.9	21.8
First State Bank of Porter	Porter	IN	**B+**	B+	B+	162.7	5.43	1.9	0.1	16.9	42.5	**10.0**	15.2	0.0
▼ First State Bank of Purdy	Monett	MO	**C+**	B-	B-	192.5	9.46	15.2	0.9	10.2	14.6	**5.4**	7.4	13.2
First State Bank of Randolph County	Cuthbert	GA	**C-**	C-	D+	95.2	12.81	8.3	2.8	3.6	52.9	**6.3**	8.3	16.2
First State Bank of Roscoe	Roscoe	SD	**B+**	B+	A-	131.8	11.99	4.6	0.4	0.1	13.8	**9.5**	10.7	18.1
First State Bank of San Diego	San Diego	TX	**C+**	C+	C+	74.7	-0.19	21.3	2.2	2.7	32.8	**6.4**	8.4	24.1
First State Bank of Sauk Centre	Sauk Centre	MN	**A-**	A-	A-	138.1	11.57	8.4	3.0	12.0	26.8	**10.0**	11.3	20.4
First State Bank of St. Charles, Missouri	Saint Charles	MO	**A**	A-	A-	463.0	0.97	11.7	0.1	31.6	9.7	**10.0**	15.0	21.4
First State Bank of St. Peter	Saint Peter	IL	**B+**	B+	B+	34.7	16.66	0.5	2.7	3.0	29.5	**10.0**	14.4	39.7
First State Bank of Swanville	Swanville	MN	**C**	C	C+	26.4	5.15	18.1	3.6	11.5	5.7	**10.0**	15.1	26.6
First State Bank of Texas	Orange	TX	**C+**	B-	B-	239.9	20.64	20.4	5.5	8.4	9.9	**7.1**	9.1	0.0
First State Bank of the Florida Keys	Key West	FL	**B**	B	B	1268.3	21.79	9.4	0.4	13.0	26.9	**6.0**	8.0	18.5
First State Bank of the South, Inc.	Sulligent	AL	**B+**	B+	B+	121.0	7.40	5.8	6.0	11.3	36.8	**10.0**	15.0	0.0
First State Bank of The Southeast, Inc	Middlesboro	KY	**C+**	C+	C+	358.2	0.10	11.3	2.3	27.1	8.4	**7.2**	9.1	14.1
First State Bank of Uvalde	Uvalde	TX	**B+**	B+	B+	1971.6	7.01	3.0	0.5	5.2	55.6	**8.0**	9.6	26.9
First State Bank of Van Orin	Van Orin	IL	**C-**	C	C	44.6	8.54	2.5	1.1	1.3	42.6	**7.2**	9.1	25.7
First State Bank of Warren	Warren	AR	**C**	C	B-	133.1	9.84	17.8	1.4	3.7	42.6	**8.0**	9.7	0.0
First State Bank of Wyoming	Wyoming	MN	**B+**	B+	A-	227.5	14.69	5.4	1.4	11.6	58.1	**10.0**	15.1	0.0
▼ First State Bank Shannon-Polo	Shannon	IL	**C+**	B-	C+	219.2	17.80	8.1	2.1	7.1	43.9	**5.6**	7.6	0.0
First State Bank Southwest	Worthington	MN	**A**	A	A	357.9	23.60	8.5	2.1	7.2	49.3	**8.1**	9.8	20.9
First State Community Bank	Farmington	MO	**A-**	A-	B+	3577.0	23.18	7.5	1.8	19.6	16.1	**5.9**	8.4	11.7
First Summit Bank	Ryan	OK	**C+**	C	C	28.9	5.43	11.0	2.0	4.9	0.0	**10.0**	12.9	0.0
First Texas Bank	Georgetown	TX	**B+**	B+	B+	896.1	18.25	4.2	0.5	2.5	59.1	**5.9**	7.9	0.0
▲ First Texas Bank	Killeen	TX	**B+**	B	B	408.0	20.34	3.0	0.4	9.5	49.7	**6.8**	8.8	0.0
First Texas Bank	Lampasas	TX	**A-**	A-	A-	183.0	15.32	3.0	1.1	13.9	46.4	**7.4**	9.3	0.0
First Texoma National Bank	Durant	OK	**B**	B+	A-	220.1	8.03	6.1	4.5	20.9	29.7	**9.2**	10.5	17.5
First Tri-County Bank	Swanton	NE	**C+**	C+	C	70.8	19.07	6.1	3.9	14.8	6.3	**6.3**	8.4	0.0
First Trust & Savings Bank	Coralville	IA	**D+**	D+	C-	64.4	8.82	3.5	1.0	2.1	77.0	**8.9**	10.3	23.1
First Trust and Savings Bank	Wheatland	IA	**B-**	B-	B-	236.8	10.54	14.5	3.2	7.1	4.5	**5.4**	9.4	0.0
First Trust Bank of Illinois	Kankakee	IL	**B-**	C+	B	385.8	13.86	10.9	0.6	5.5	45.2	**6.4**	8.4	13.6
First United Bank	Park River	ND	**B+**	B	C+	299.7	4.85	6.7	1.6	3.2	31.9	**6.9**	8.9	0.0
First United Bank	Dimmitt	TX	**A-**	A-	A-	1637.9	5.56	17.5	0.4	6.0	26.7	**8.6**	10.1	15.6
First United Bank & Trust	Oakland	MD	**B**	B	B	1743.5	7.29	12.5	3.3	17.5	17.4	**7.3**	9.2	14.9
First United Bank and Trust Co.	Durant	OK	**B**	B	B	11646.3	17.88	9.7	1.2	24.3	10.7	**5.1**	8.7	11.1
First United Bank and Trust Co., Inc.	Madisonville	KY	**A-**	A-	A-	448.2	20.32	10.8	1.9	21.2	20.1	**8.1**	9.7	0.0
First United National Bank	Fryburg	PA	**B-**	B-	B	345.8	18.51	4.4	4.9	31.5	42.1	**5.6**	7.6	0.0
First US Bank	Birmingham	AL	**C+**	C+	B-	946.8	11.99	5.6	24.8	6.1	13.1	**6.6**	8.6	12.2
▲ First Utah Bank	Salt Lake City	UT	**B+**	B	B-	631.0	5.04	19.4	0.5	0.5	6.7	**7.1**	9.1	15.4
First Vision Bank of Tennessee	Tullahoma	TN	**B+**	B+	B+	357.9	13.99	5.7	2.0	15.2	6.8	**8.2**	9.8	16.3
First Volunteer Bank	Chattanooga	TN	**A**	A-	A-	1307.3	13.78	7.3	1.5	9.8	0.8	**9.4**	10.6	18.6
▲ First Western Bank	Booneville	AR	**B+**	B	B-	511.7	5.38	3.9	0.8	37.5	9.2	**7.0**	9.0	14.4
First Western Bank and Trust	Minot	ND	**C**	C	B-	1892.5	51.38	14.1	2.6	8.7	12.9	**2.7**	8.9	0.0
First Western Federal Savings Bank	Rapid City	SD	**A-**	A-	A-	61.7	-2.88	0.4	0.0	88.2	0.0	**10.0**	16.0	0.0
First Western Trust Bank	Denver	CO	**B**	B-	C+	2003.0	11.23	17.7	4.3	22.7	1.3	**6.0**	8.0	12.0
First Westroads Bank, Inc.	Omaha	NE	**A-**	A-	A	355.8	-3.36	13.9	0.1	5.7	6.3	**9.5**	10.7	19.1
First Whitney Bank and Trust	Atlantic	IA	**B+**	B+	B+	262.5	8.19	14.6	1.2	4.9	34.7	**5.7**	9.7	11.5
First-Citizens Bank & Trust Co.	Raleigh	NC	**B+**	B+	B+	55098.9	15.20	10.4	3.4	10.7	19.5	**6.3**	8.3	13.8

Asset Quality Index	Adjusted Non-Performing Loans as a % of Total Loans	Adjusted Non-Performing Loans as a % of Capital	Net Charge-Offs Avg Loans	Profitability Index	Net Income ($Mil)	Return on Assets (R.O.A.)	Return on Equity (R.O.E.)	Net Interest Spread	Overhead Efficiency Ratio	Liquidity Index	Liquidity Ratio	Hot Money Ratio	Stability Index
8.8	0.00	0.0	0.00	**3.5**	0.3	0.69	7.03	2.81	74.4	**4.3**	52.3	15.6	**5.4**
9.5	0.00	1.0	0.04	**3.3**	0.2	0.59	2.93	3.09	79.5	**5.3**	69.1	13.3	**7.1**
4.5	1.30	9.5	0.06	**6.2**	1.6	1.23	12.58	4.17	57.6	**4.8**	43.9	12.2	**5.3**
5.4	0.82	5.5	0.01	**6.8**	3.1	1.95	21.66	3.57	53.3	**0.8**	18.4	15.2	**6.3**
4.9	0.48	6.1	-0.01	**3.5**	1.1	0.92	10.91	2.76	62.4	**2.4**	15.9	16.7	**4.7**
5.2	3.85	7.2	-0.02	**5.6**	0.8	1.12	9.97	3.19	49.3	**4.6**	44.3	13.1	**6.7**
8.9	0.00	0.0	0.00	**8.5**	1.1	2.19	23.45	4.16	43.2	**5.7**	40.1	5.6	**7.2**
8.9	0.00	1.1	-0.07	**4.1**	0.5	1.05	9.46	3.07	69.7	**6.3**	68.1	7.5	**6.4**
7.3	0.72	2.1	0.05	**7.1**	0.7	1.46	14.39	3.69	63.3	**4.8**	30.1	6.6	**7.0**
9.0	0.64	1.7	-0.01	**3.7**	1.5	0.71	4.98	2.78	77.5	**5.5**	44.8	8.4	**7.8**
6.8	1.08	4.8	-0.03	**6.9**	5.0	1.44	12.18	3.70	61.6	**4.1**	35.8	12.4	**8.7**
9.6	0.77	0.9	-0.06	**3.1**	0.5	0.60	4.69	2.21	74.2	**3.8**	55.7	20.2	**7.6**
8.7	0.00	0.0	0.00	**5.6**	0.8	0.94	8.22	3.50	67.5	**5.7**	36.4	3.8	**7.6**
7.7	0.07	1.3	0.00	**4.8**	0.4	1.22	10.47	3.48	62.6	**3.3**	27.0	14.2	**6.8**
9.1	1.20	2.6	0.00	**4.1**	0.7	0.87	5.46	3.40	72.0	**3.6**	52.8	20.4	**8.3**
2.9	5.70	31.4	0.55	**4.1**	1.0	0.96	13.20	3.36	69.0	**3.7**	26.5	8.3	**5.4**
2.8	5.48	20.0	0.06	**2.1**	0.1	0.27	3.33	2.55	88.8	**5.1**	48.8	11.2	**3.4**
5.7	2.38	11.0	-0.03	**7.1**	1.4	2.05	18.99	3.63	43.9	**4.0**	39.7	15.0	**7.8**
7.2	0.83	3.3	0.00	**4.2**	0.4	1.03	11.53	2.43	67.7	**4.5**	37.6	11.5	**5.1**
8.3	0.00	0.0	0.00	**5.8**	0.7	1.02	8.48	3.00	53.8	**4.0**	34.7	13.5	**7.8**
7.8	1.04	3.7	0.00	**9.4**	7.8	3.40	23.11	3.41	73.6	**4.5**	34.0	10.5	**9.7**
9.4	0.00	2.6	-0.09	**5.2**	0.2	0.96	6.45	2.12	56.7	**6.8**	87.2	7.6	**7.8**
7.0	2.16	4.3	0.02	**2.0**	0.0	0.02	0.10	3.74	96.9	**5.3**	39.8	7.9	**5.9**
6.6	0.47	2.1	0.00	**3.2**	0.8	0.73	6.64	3.22	78.0	**2.2**	33.5	24.8	**6.8**
8.0	0.80	2.8	-0.29	**5.1**	8.0	1.35	16.22	3.00	63.6	**6.6**	39.3	2.2	**7.6**
8.7	0.13	0.9	0.05	**4.8**	0.6	1.04	6.74	4.81	70.5	**3.5**	50.6	21.2	**7.9**
3.7	1.96	14.6	0.55	**3.9**	2.1	1.14	12.21	3.77	70.1	**2.6**	21.5	15.1	**5.3**
9.7	0.32	0.8	0.02	**4.5**	7.9	0.81	7.88	1.75	44.8	**3.0**	56.1	49.6	**7.7**
8.7	0.68	1.3	0.00	**1.9**	0.0	0.09	0.87	2.18	87.9	**5.5**	75.6	13.2	**3.8**
8.8	0.22	0.8	0.19	**2.8**	0.3	0.53	5.17	2.71	77.4	**4.0**	31.6	12.0	**5.2**
8.2	1.87	3.8	-0.01	**3.4**	0.4	0.37	2.34	2.43	84.1	**7.0**	71.7	5.6	**7.8**
3.4	1.75	14.6	-0.32	**2.9**	0.6	0.55	6.12	2.25	81.8	**4.7**	35.4	10.1	**4.8**
8.8	0.06	0.1	0.00	**8.4**	3.7	2.20	20.83	2.59	50.8	**5.1**	34.6	6.9	**7.6**
5.9	0.80	3.7	0.00	**7.3**	26.8	1.52	14.50	3.31	57.4	**4.2**	13.0	7.3	**10.0**
7.3	0.26	2.0	-0.03	**3.0**	0.1	0.67	5.02	4.45	87.8	**1.8**	24.8	22.6	**6.3**
8.6	0.77	1.7	0.01	**6.7**	6.1	1.43	18.11	2.64	42.2	**7.0**	66.1	4.3	**6.2**
9.9	0.24	0.6	-0.02	**5.0**	2.2	1.14	12.75	2.86	57.1	**7.2**	63.4	2.3	**6.5**
9.6	0.17	0.7	-0.01	**6.2**	1.0	1.11	11.52	3.02	59.6	**6.9**	60.1	4.2	**7.1**
4.3	1.73	9.3	0.11	**5.6**	1.3	1.19	10.99	4.20	68.0	**4.9**	36.4	9.3	**7.2**
5.4	0.00	5.6	0.01	**3.5**	0.3	0.79	8.82	3.49	72.6	**5.2**	35.7	6.9	**4.3**
6.0	3.39	10.4	0.02	**3.7**	0.4	1.45	13.35	3.79	59.3	**2.5**	57.5	34.1	**5.2**
6.0	0.31	2.4	-0.01	**4.8**	1.2	1.01	10.43	3.39	65.6	**1.8**	21.5	21.8	**6.5**
4.9	1.87	8.0	0.00	**4.8**	1.9	1.02	10.30	2.57	52.9	**4.6**	39.8	12.0	**5.5**
5.1	0.67	3.4	-0.01	**5.9**	1.9	1.27	13.03	3.32	61.2	**4.8**	27.9	5.9	**8.2**
8.3	0.11	0.7	-0.01	**8.6**	16.3	2.03	18.74	3.83	52.2	**1.8**	12.4	20.5	**10.0**
7.2	0.94	5.6	0.01	**5.7**	11.0	1.26	14.94	3.14	57.8	**3.4**	21.1	8.1	**7.7**
7.1	0.43	2.5	0.02	**6.7**	76.4	1.40	15.13	3.69	64.2	**2.4**	10.6	8.7	**8.2**
7.6	0.37	2.1	0.00	**6.0**	3.3	1.54	15.01	3.95	62.9	**4.4**	16.2	6.3	**7.0**
6.7	0.68	4.1	0.00	**3.3**	0.8	0.46	5.87	2.63	82.9	**5.7**	46.3	7.7	**3.9**
5.3	0.29	1.7	0.20	**3.5**	2.4	0.52	5.52	4.45	79.9	**2.9**	17.3	11.0	**5.0**
5.9	1.22	4.5	0.01	**7.6**	5.1	1.62	17.63	4.45	52.6	**2.9**	30.0	17.1	**7.3**
6.0	1.37	4.5	0.11	**7.4**	2.4	1.45	14.98	3.58	62.6	**3.1**	33.2	17.0	**6.4**
8.3	0.43	2.0	0.03	**7.8**	9.1	1.45	13.40	3.57	54.8	**5.7**	37.2	8.0	**9.5**
7.0	0.48	2.5	0.06	**7.6**	3.8	1.48	16.51	4.22	55.9	**2.9**	13.4	14.3	**6.6**
3.7	3.42	12.2	0.08	**6.0**	11.3	1.19	11.35	4.12	62.8	**2.4**	23.2	16.5	**9.1**
9.9	0.17	0.5	0.00	**10.0**	0.9	3.01	19.05	5.87	47.5	**0.9**	7.3	30.9	**9.0**
7.7	0.19	1.7	0.00	**6.0**	13.1	1.27	15.88	3.02	70.3	**3.4**	17.1	7.7	**7.3**
8.6	0.00	0.0	-0.03	**5.9**	1.8	1.05	9.56	3.07	60.2	**6.1**	39.8	2.5	**8.5**
8.6	0.00	0.4	-0.07	**8.4**	2.4	1.86	17.84	2.92	36.7	**3.8**	35.7	14.6	**8.1**
6.2	0.96	5.0	0.03	**5.1**	288.3	1.09	12.27	2.78	68.5	**5.8**	27.3	2.6	**8.2**

Name	City	State	Rating	2020 Rating	2019 Rating	Total Assets ($Mil)	One Year Asset Growth	Asset Mix (As a % of Total Assets) Commercial Loans	Consumer Loans	Mortgage Loans	Securities	Capitalization Index	Leverage Ratio	Risk-Based Capital Ratio
First-Lockhart National Bank	Lockhart	TX	**B**	B	B	346.1	9.11	1.5	0.5	14.4	12.6	**6.7**	8.7	15.9
Firstar Bank	Sallisaw	OK	**C+**	C+	B-	784.0	0.79	18.8	1.9	15.9	7.4	**4.8**	7.9	10.9
▼ FirstBank	Lakewood	CO	**B+**	A-	A-	26751.6	18.89	2.8	0.3	25.5	40.1	**5.0**	7.0	15.3
FirstBank	Antlers	OK	**B**	B	B	565.9	7.78	7.1	9.4	24.3	6.1	**6.5**	8.5	0.0
FirstBank	Nashville	TN	**B+**	B+	B+	11880.7	63.86	11.3	2.3	15.4	11.8	**8.1**	9.7	14.3
FirstBank of Nebraska	Wahoo	NE	**A-**	A-	B+	345.6	9.86	5.1	1.0	6.6	48.4	**8.2**	9.8	0.0
FirstBank Puerto Rico	San Juan	PR	**B-**	C+	C-	21361.1	51.68	7.4	10.3	15.2	30.9	**10.0**	11.1	19.9
FirstBank Southwest	Amarillo	TX	**B**	B+	B+	1267.9	12.73	16.2	2.2	7.6	37.6	**5.9**	7.9	13.1
FirstCapital Bank of Texas, N.A.	Midland	TX	**B-**	B-	B-	1963.5	3.36	21.7	0.6	12.8	4.3	**5.9**	10.3	0.0
FirsTier Bank	Kimball	NE	**A-**	A-	A-	601.3	21.89	37.2	1.3	6.6	3.1	**6.3**	10.7	12.0
FirstOak Bank	Independence	KS	**A-**	A-	A-	215.9	-2.32	10.7	1.2	16.4	8.4	**6.5**	8.5	0.0
Firstrust Savings Bank	Conshohocken	PA	**B+**	B+	B+	5129.7	11.73	21.5	2.9	8.3	7.4	**6.9**	8.9	13.3
FirstState Bank	Lineville	AL	**B+**	B+	A-	316.3	10.78	3.7	3.8	7.4	35.9	**8.9**	10.2	0.0
Five Points Bank	Grand Island	NE	**A-**	A-	A-	1818.7	21.59	16.5	0.8	5.2	37.6	**6.9**	8.9	0.0
Five Points Bank of Hastings	Hastings	NE	**A-**	A-	A-	464.2	30.16	8.2	0.7	3.3	37.3	**8.8**	10.2	0.0
▲ Five Star Bank	Rancho Cordova	CA	**A-**	B+	B+	2327.4	10.39	10.8	0.3	1.1	7.2	**9.5**	10.6	16.1
▲ Five Star Bank	Warsaw	NY	**B+**	B-	B	5257.8	13.19	12.3	17.4	11.8	21.5	**6.9**	8.9	12.7
Flagler Bank	West Palm Beach	FL	**A-**	A-	B+	477.5	16.91	20.5	0.0	6.1	12.9	**6.9**	8.9	13.5
Flagship Bank	Clearwater	FL	**C**	C	B	394.7	53.77	15.1	0.4	3.1	0.8	**6.5**	9.4	0.0
Flagship Bank Minnesota	Wayzata	MN	**B**	B	B	327.6	7.79	10.7	0.1	22.2	2.4	**6.5**	8.5	15.7
Flagstar Bank, FSB	Troy	MI	**B+**	B+	B+	27043.0	-1.43	3.4	4.2	37.3	7.8	**6.9**	8.9	12.9
Flanagan State Bank	Flanagan	IL	**B-**	B-	B-	249.4	19.08	5.1	1.7	13.5	44.6	**9.1**	10.4	0.0
Flatirons Bank	Boulder	CO	**B**	B	B	286.6	16.83	16.8	0.0	31.7	27.6	**6.1**	8.1	14.9
Flatwater Bank	Gothenburg	NE	**C**	C-	C	220.6	-0.65	13.4	2.1	4.5	28.3	**9.2**	10.5	0.0
Fleetwood Bank	Fleetwood	PA	**C+**	C+	C+	339.2	13.05	3.3	0.1	32.2	33.3	**6.0**	8.0	0.0
Flint Community Bank	Albany	GA	**C+**	C	C	290.7	-2.29	11.6	1.2	27.1	0.9	**6.0**	8.2	11.8
Flint Hills Bank	Eskridge	KS	**B+**	A-	A-	155.7	6.98	4.6	2.7	11.5	51.6	**10.0**	11.6	0.0
Flora Bank & Trust	Flora	IL	**B-**	B-	B-	101.9	14.07	6.9	8.5	12.5	36.0	**6.9**	8.9	19.7
Florence Bank	Florence	MA	**B-**	B	B	1835.9	13.42	2.8	0.0	33.5	27.6	**8.3**	9.9	0.0
▲ Florida Business Bank	Melbourne	FL	**A**	A-	A-	188.4	-4.06	16.1	0.2	1.5	15.4	**10.0**	11.2	17.3
Florida Capital Bank, N.A.	Jacksonville	FL	**B-**	C+	C	491.5	-6.41	9.1	0.0	18.6	4.0	**10.0**	12.4	25.0
▲ Flushing Bank	Uniondale	NY	**B**	B-	B	8160.3	13.87	11.3	0.0	10.5	10.7	**7.5**	9.5	12.9
FM BANK	Granite Falls	MN	**A-**	A-	A-	487.2	218.24	4.8	0.3	2.1	39.7	**6.0**	8.1	15.5
▼ FMB Bank	Wright City	MO	**D+**	C-	D+	46.5	8.83	5.6	2.8	11.9	35.0	**5.2**	7.2	16.8
FMS Bank	Fort Morgan	CO	**C+**	C+	C+	243.6	4.89	18.1	10.6	7.9	13.6	**6.1**	9.4	11.8
FNB Bank	Fontanelle	IA	**A-**	A-	B+	222.7	3.02	5.1	1.0	7.2	15.7	**10.0**	12.9	0.0
▲ FNB Bank	Goodland	KS	**A-**	B+	B+	233.0	10.87	5.9	0.9	1.3	23.7	**10.0**	11.8	18.5
FNB Bank, Inc.	Mayfield	KY	**B-**	C+	B-	585.8	7.42	12.3	7.7	17.2	20.3	**6.1**	8.1	12.4
FNB Bank, Inc.	Romney	WV	**B-**	B-	B	247.2	5.19	6.9	4.8	26.9	21.1	**7.4**	9.2	14.8
FNB Community Bank	Midwest City	OK	**C**	C	C+	570.3	8.37	5.4	3.1	4.7	39.3	**6.0**	8.0	16.9
▲ FNB Coweta	Coweta	OK	**B-**	C+	C+	100.3	18.11	10.1	1.5	9.0	45.7	**7.4**	9.3	0.0
FNB Oxford Bank	Oxford	MS	**B**	B	B+	466.7	9.10	6.6	0.6	13.3	39.8	**8.0**	9.7	0.0
FNB Picayune Bank	Picayune	MS	**A-**	B+	B	256.7	11.31	7.6	5.0	20.3	34.7	**10.0**	12.7	26.4
FNB South	Alma	GA	**A**	A	A	485.9	5.91	8.4	4.9	14.0	7.7	**10.0**	15.4	25.5
FNB Washington	Washington	KS	**B+**	B+	B+	80.5	-1.45	2.2	1.8	10.3	45.2	**10.0**	25.0	0.0
FNBC Bank	Ash Flat	AR	**B**	B-	C	610.4	7.90	8.2	4.2	12.8	28.1	**8.6**	10.1	15.6
▼ FNBC Bank and Trust	La Grange	IL	**B-**	B	B	644.7	7.04	4.5	0.2	15.6	36.8	**6.7**	8.7	19.4
▼ FNBT Bank	Fort Walton Beach	FL	**B+**	A-	A-	619.2	17.01	3.4	0.6	8.1	0.7	**6.7**	8.7	18.1
FNCB Bank	Dunmore	PA	**B+**	B	B	1520.1	7.56	16.1	5.5	12.6	28.5	**8.4**	9.9	15.8
FNNB Bank	Newton	IA	**C+**	C	D+	104.1	16.54	15.8	0.6	5.4	19.5	**5.2**	7.2	15.0
Focus Bank	Charleston	MO	**B+**	B+	B+	804.3	2.06	8.8	1.9	24.9	5.9	**9.2**	11.1	0.0
Forcht Bank, N.A.	Lexington	KY	**C+**	C+	B-	1501.9	8.46	4.0	1.3	23.9	29.6	**6.4**	8.4	0.0
Ford County State Bank	Spearville	KS	**C+**	B-	C+	49.7	12.25	7.6	0.8	1.7	38.4	**10.0**	11.1	24.8
Foresight Bank	Plainview	MN	**B-**	C+	B-	301.9	8.34	8.2	1.5	28.5	19.4	**7.5**	9.3	13.8
Forest Park National Bank and Trust Co.	Forest Park	IL	**B-**	B-	B-	317.4	12.52	10.5	0.1	12.5	11.0	**5.2**	7.2	12.5
Fort Davis State Bank	Fort Davis	TX	**C**	C	C+	111.0	9.34	6.9	3.0	4.3	40.0	**6.2**	8.2	16.9
Forte Bank	Hartford	WI	**B+**	B	B	305.8	11.65	8.6	0.3	16.5	8.6	**7.8**	9.9	0.0
Fortifi Bank	Berlin	WI	**B**	B-	C+	559.2	2.69	13.5	1.1	10.4	11.5	**8.3**	9.9	13.7
Fortis Private Bank	Denver	CO	**C+**	C+	C-	1144.7	15.40	6.4	5.7	21.4	18.5	**6.8**	8.8	13.6
Fortress Bank	Peoria	IL	**C+**	C+	C	552.5	5.96	17.1	1.3	15.4	13.3	**5.5**	8.6	11.4

Asset Quality Index	Adjusted Non-Performing Loans as a % of Total Loans	Adjusted Non-Performing Loans as a % of Capital	Net Charge-Offs Avg Loans	Profitability Index	Net Income ($Mil)	Return on Assets (R.O.A.)	Return on Equity (R.O.E.)	Net Interest Spread	Overhead Efficiency Ratio	Liquidity Index	Liquidity Ratio	Hot Money Ratio	Stability Index
8.8	0.00	1.5	0.00	**4.0**	1.3	0.76	8.36	3.05	73.5	**4.7**	34.1	9.7	**6.1**
4.2	0.75	5.1	0.12	**8.3**	6.9	1.75	17.66	4.36	56.0	**2.8**	12.3	13.9	**8.1**
9.6	0.13	2.0	0.02	**6.5**	159.7	1.26	17.54	2.77	47.7	**6.9**	45.1	2.6	**7.6**
6.1	0.25	1.6	0.04	**8.8**	7.5	2.74	27.80	5.94	56.9	**2.1**	29.1	22.6	**7.4**
5.5	0.94	4.8	0.03	**7.4**	97.6	1.67	14.41	3.18	65.2	**4.2**	20.2	8.2	**9.0**
6.3	0.33	3.5	0.00	**9.5**	4.6	2.67	24.89	4.12	35.3	**3.3**	24.1	11.4	**8.7**
3.6	5.01	16.6	0.26	**6.9**	131.4	1.34	11.18	3.88	62.7	**4.5**	30.0	10.6	**7.9**
8.1	0.35	2.4	0.00	**4.7**	7.2	1.14	14.45	3.18	67.8	**2.2**	24.2	22.6	**7.1**
4.5	1.23	5.6	0.04	**7.7**	15.0	1.56	12.01	4.64	54.4	**1.5**	13.6	24.8	**9.9**
7.9	0.11	0.8	-0.04	**8.2**	5.6	1.93	17.69	4.16	47.4	**1.1**	15.9	31.1	**10.0**
8.4	0.02	0.2	-0.01	**7.7**	1.8	1.61	16.81	4.44	60.4	**3.7**	23.3	11.1	**7.9**
6.1	0.93	5.0	-0.04	**6.3**	38.9	1.60	17.83	3.10	54.3	**6.0**	32.4	3.8	**8.5**
8.1	0.67	1.7	0.00	**4.6**	1.7	1.08	10.13	3.45	67.6	**2.7**	40.4	24.7	**7.2**
8.7	0.00	0.2	-0.02	**6.9**	15.7	1.83	18.97	2.99	44.5	**4.5**	26.0	10.7	**8.8**
8.9	0.01	0.0	-0.01	**5.4**	2.6	1.12	11.21	2.62	48.7	**5.4**	33.2	4.4	**7.6**
7.4	0.03	0.2	0.03	**9.6**	23.5	2.20	26.30	3.73	38.3	**6.2**	32.3	2.5	**9.3**
7.1	0.18	1.1	0.03	**6.8**	42.5	1.65	17.50	3.23	48.9	**1.8**	5.5	14.6	**7.9**
8.5	0.04	0.3	-0.70	**8.8**	5.7	2.51	27.81	3.83	36.3	**2.3**	32.1	21.3	**7.1**
7.7	0.00	0.0	0.00	**1.2**	0.4	0.21	1.90	3.19	85.2	**5.4**	34.7	5.1	**6.3**
8.3	0.31	1.3	0.00	**6.3**	1.8	1.10	12.87	3.59	57.7	**4.3**	25.7	8.7	**5.4**
6.2	2.19	4.2	-0.10	**8.5**	300.7	2.07	22.83	2.88	68.9	**3.3**	9.2	6.1	**9.7**
5.7	1.35	4.5	0.06	**8.8**	3.0	2.39	21.85	2.75	81.3	**5.7**	52.1	9.2	**7.3**
8.2	0.43	1.5	0.00	**7.4**	2.9	2.08	22.86	4.36	52.2	**2.6**	21.4	12.6	**6.8**
1.4	1.77	28.3	0.05	**6.9**	2.0	1.76	14.02	4.46	55.1	**2.7**	23.6	12.7	**8.3**
8.9	0.28	1.8	0.01	**3.2**	0.8	0.51	6.38	3.03	80.1	**5.8**	41.6	5.4	**4.4**
3.7	1.59	15.1	0.00	**6.3**	2.1	1.48	17.91	3.70	58.7	**3.5**	12.1	10.8	**6.5**
9.0	0.03	0.1	0.00	**5.9**	1.2	1.56	13.54	2.86	52.7	**3.5**	40.0	17.3	**8.2**
4.6	0.59	10.4	-0.01	**3.6**	0.4	0.70	7.90	2.74	68.3	**3.0**	32.5	17.6	**5.1**
9.7	0.33	1.8	0.05	**3.7**	5.0	0.56	5.90	2.73	67.0	**5.7**	44.7	10.0	**7.4**
7.3	0.00	0.0	-0.15	**8.0**	1.7	1.77	16.30	4.27	47.8	**5.1**	30.3	4.8	**8.2**
7.9	1.85	0.7	0.33	**6.4**	2.9	1.16	9.71	2.63	81.4	**3.5**	39.4	10.5	**7.8**
6.3	0.49	3.1	0.11	**4.9**	45.9	1.12	12.18	3.32	53.0	**2.1**	9.8	10.2	**7.2**
7.0	0.62	4.5	-0.17	**8.9**	3.9	2.40	32.74	5.09	54.2	**4.9**	29.4	6.3	**7.1**
4.8	4.69	9.2	-0.04	**2.3**	0.1	0.21	2.71	2.95	94.6	**5.8**	45.4	6.2	**3.8**
3.6	2.92	6.7	0.15	**6.0**	1.8	1.45	15.07	5.00	73.6	**2.6**	17.8	15.7	**6.1**
6.7	0.04	0.2	-0.10	**5.5**	1.6	1.38	9.40	3.48	65.0	**3.6**	21.1	11.6	**9.1**
8.5	0.14	0.5	0.01	**5.4**	1.6	1.35	11.54	4.11	69.3	**4.2**	21.5	7.9	**7.7**
4.5	1.41	5.2	-0.01	**4.7**	3.2	1.09	11.48	3.49	65.5	**3.6**	14.0	6.5	**6.6**
5.3	1.69	6.8	-0.02	**4.5**	1.2	0.96	10.40	3.40	66.3	**1.9**	27.2	23.1	**4.6**
8.6	0.30	1.1	-0.03	**2.9**	1.5	0.55	6.25	2.81	78.8	**5.4**	33.9	4.7	**5.2**
6.0	1.00	4.3	0.47	**6.3**	0.9	1.93	20.97	4.59	51.6	**5.4**	48.7	10.3	**4.7**
9.1	0.26	0.6	0.00	**5.3**	2.5	1.11	10.31	3.14	54.9	**3.4**	31.3	10.2	**7.0**
5.7	1.94	8.0	-0.01	**9.6**	2.7	2.19	16.44	4.22	51.8	**4.2**	46.7	15.6	**9.4**
8.5	1.05	0.2	-1.15	**10.0**	7.0	2.98	19.78	4.65	39.0	**3.5**	26.3	12.9	**9.0**
9.1	2.34	2.1	0.00	**5.4**	0.5	1.26	4.90	2.83	55.9	**4.5**	29.8	8.6	**8.3**
4.8	1.28	7.1	-0.02	**5.9**	5.1	1.70	17.06	4.15	64.5	**3.0**	24.0	14.7	**7.4**
5.9	1.07	5.2	0.00	**3.7**	2.2	0.69	7.34	2.91	79.7	**6.5**	47.1	2.1	**7.0**
9.5	0.18	0.5	0.08	**4.7**	2.5	0.86	9.51	2.01	74.5	**7.0**	69.5	4.9	**7.3**
6.2	1.15	4.5	0.00	**6.2**	10.9	1.47	14.11	3.61	52.0	**4.2**	10.6	5.7	**8.8**
8.8	0.00	0.0	-0.03	**4.3**	0.6	1.15	15.34	4.54	67.8	**6.0**	42.6	4.3	**3.7**
6.2	0.28	3.2	-0.01	**6.0**	6.3	1.57	14.26	3.55	64.6	**1.8**	16.1	18.9	**8.1**
8.1	0.40	1.3	0.02	**3.2**	4.7	0.63	5.66	3.27	79.7	**5.6**	33.2	6.8	**9.3**
7.9	0.20	0.5	2.87	**1.5**	0.0	-0.10	-0.88	2.15	106.3	**5.4**	59.1	11.0	**5.8**
3.7	3.75	15.9	0.00	**6.2**	2.3	1.57	15.43	3.55	58.5	**1.2**	24.8	29.5	**8.0**
5.4	0.58	4.9	0.00	**4.7**	1.7	1.11	14.79	4.02	71.4	**4.6**	20.6	5.2	**4.8**
5.7	0.73	5.9	0.06	**2.4**	0.2	0.34	3.89	3.37	90.0	**6.0**	54.6	8.3	**4.7**
8.2	0.28	2.0	-0.01	**5.8**	1.8	1.21	12.31	3.61	60.1	**4.5**	24.9	6.4	**5.9**
4.9	1.13	6.8	0.00	**7.5**	5.0	1.89	19.49	4.09	51.6	**5.0**	28.8	5.2	**6.6**
8.6	0.07	0.6	0.00	**3.7**	4.3	0.86	9.48	2.87	60.6	**6.8**	38.2	1.0	**6.3**
3.2	1.84	11.3	0.17	**4.6**	2.7	0.99	10.20	3.03	65.9	**1.8**	18.0	19.4	**7.0**

Name	City	State	Rating	2020 Rating	2019 Rating	Total Assets ($Mil)	One Year Asset Growth	Commercial Loans	Consumer Loans	Mortgage Loans	Securities	Capitalization Index	Leverage Ratio	Risk-Based Capital Ratio
FortuneBank	Arnold	MO	**C**	C-	C-	253.1	-1.87	25.9	0.1	6.9	6.2	**5.3**	8.3	11.2
▲ Forward Bank	Marshfield	WI	**B**	C+	C+	806.7	12.83	12.3	3.2	13.4	17.8	**7.6**	9.4	14.0
Foundation One Bank	Waterloo	NE	**C+**	C+	C+	163.0	4.59	39.1	2.3	13.5	5.2	**6.4**	9.5	0.0
Founders Bank	Washington	DC	**D-**	D-		120.7	154.65	1.8	0.0	11.8	16.7	**9.8**	22.2	0.0
▲ Four Corners Community Bank	Farmington	NM	**C+**	C-	C-	473.6	7.88	16.7	4.0	4.1	20.6	**9.2**	10.5	0.0
Fourth Capital Bank	Nashville	TN	**D-**	D-	D	367.5	12.42	19.2	5.3	7.9	10.7	**3.1**	9.8	0.0
Fowler State Bank	Fowler	CO	**A-**	B+	B	110.0	17.07	5.2	0.7	3.0	43.6	**10.0**	13.0	0.0
▼ Fowler State Bank	Fowler	IN	**B+**	A-	A-	207.8	17.24	11.7	4.4	6.9	43.0	**10.0**	12.1	0.0
Fowler State Bank	Fowler	KS	**D-**	D	D+	73.5	-16.31	4.3	1.1	1.9	59.7	**7.5**	9.4	28.3
Fox Valley Savings Bank	Fond du Lac	WI	**B**	B	B	395.9	6.94	1.8	0.7	30.1	39.1	**10.0**	14.4	0.0
Foxboro Federal Savings	Foxboro	MA	**B-**	B-	B-	200.2	10.97	0.0	0.8	51.2	31.1	**10.0**	15.0	35.8
Frandsen Bank & Trust	Lonsdale	MN	**B+**	B+	B	2614.8	37.53	10.2	1.4	14.3	27.9	**5.1**	7.1	11.8
Franklin Bank	Pilesgrove	NJ	**C**	C	C+	311.2	8.91	4.2	1.0	34.6	16.7	**6.5**	8.5	18.2
▲ Franklin Bank & Trust Co.	Franklin	KY	**A-**	B+	A-	687.5	12.01	22.5	0.7	13.1	0.3	**8.6**	11.6	0.0
Franklin Savings Bank	Farmington	ME	**B+**	B+	B+	527.8	11.86	9.9	2.5	30.8	4.4	**10.0**	22.5	32.8
Franklin Savings Bank	Franklin	NH	**B-**	B-	C+	665.9	10.38	4.3	0.2	25.0	26.5	**7.7**	9.5	16.5
Franklin State Bank	Franklin	MN	**B-**	B-	B-	36.4	5.26	7.0	5.1	11.8	17.1	**10.0**	15.1	0.0
Franklin State Bank & Trust Co.	Winnsboro	LA	**B+**	B+	B+	201.9	9.94	5.7	4.4	12.8	16.2	**6.7**	8.7	19.7
Frazer Bank	Altus	OK	**D+**	D+	C-	333.9	11.28	8.7	0.6	5.6	24.9	**6.5**	8.5	12.5
Fredonia Valley Bank	Fredonia	KY	**B+**	B+	B+	94.7	3.60	4.8	2.1	39.9	24.5	**10.0**	14.7	0.0
Freedom Bank	Huntingburg	IN	**A-**	A-	A-	537.6	8.30	5.3	4.7	33.2	7.3	**8.9**	10.3	14.6
Freedom Bank	Overland Park	KS	**C+**	B-	C+	218.8	15.13	11.6	0.0	3.8	13.0	**7.7**	10.2	13.1
Freedom Bank	Columbia Falls	MT	**B**	B	C+	125.5	30.64	22.9	1.5	11.2	0.0	**5.6**	8.6	0.0
▲ Freedom Bank	Maywood	NJ	**B**	B-	B-	611.1	20.16	4.6	0.0	18.7	1.4	**8.4**	9.9	13.9
▼ Freedom Bank	Freer	TX	**C**	C+	C	81.6	31.31	11.9	1.4	11.2	6.4	**4.0**	8.4	0.0
Freedom Bank of Southern Missouri	Cassville	MO	**B+**	B+	B	551.5	13.17	8.1	2.4	16.4	9.2	**6.9**	8.9	0.0
▲ Freedom Bank, Inc.	Belington	WV	**B-**	C	C-	200.5	8.54	8.4	5.7	32.2	18.1	**7.3**	9.2	0.0
Freedom Financial Bank	West Des Moines	IA	**B-**	B-	B	226.7	-3.57	9.4	0.2	10.5	4.9	**6.1**	8.7	11.8
FreedomBank	Elkader	IA	**C**	C+	C+	471.8	8.51	6.3	2.1	11.9	22.8	**6.8**	8.8	13.9
Freehold Bank	Freehold	NJ	**C**	C	C+	305.6	2.60	2.5	0.0	22.2	37.5	**10.0**	13.0	0.0
▼ Freeland State Bank	Freeland	MI	**D+**	C-	C-	57.5	10.03	0.0	0.3	7.0	53.8	**10.0**	15.5	0.0
Freeport State Bank	Freeport	MN	**B**	B	B	137.4	6.25	8.0	2.4	7.3	24.7	**7.9**	9.6	16.5
Fremont Bank	Fremont	CA	**B**	B	B+	5462.1	9.49	11.0	0.0	22.1	11.0	**5.2**	7.2	12.1
Fresno First Bank	Fresno	CA	**A**	A-	B+	988.0	30.58	28.4	0.0	1.6	25.5	**10.0**	11.3	19.4
Friend Bank	Slocomb	AL	**B+**	B+	B	173.7	15.52	11.9	2.5	17.3	10.0	**6.6**	8.6	0.0
Friendly Hills Bancorp	Whittier	CA	**C+**	C+	B	223.3	-4.98	10.0	0.0	9.2	7.9	**7.4**	9.2	21.3
Frontier Bank	Lamar	CO	**A-**	A-	A-	370.7	5.79	2.5	0.5	8.9	45.9	**8.6**	10.1	18.8
▲ Frontier Bank	Omaha	NE	**B**	B-	C+	1094.1	13.49	12.6	1.1	16.7	9.7	**5.7**	9.1	11.5
▲ Frontier Bank	Sioux Falls	SD	**B**	B-	B-	261.5	5.32	5.1	1.1	9.7	38.3	**6.8**	8.8	13.2
Frontier Bank of Texas	Elgin	TX	**A-**	B+	B+	545.2	22.83	5.6	1.1	17.3	8.1	**9.3**	10.6	14.8
Frontier Community Bank	Waynesboro	VA	**C+**	C+	C+	142.5	-1.50	14.1	1.5	32.5	4.4	**9.5**	10.7	15.8
Frontier State Bank	Oklahoma City	OK	**B**	B	C	510.7	-16.66	10.8	0.6	10.3	6.6	**10.0**	14.5	19.5
Frost Bank	San Antonio	TX	**B+**	B+	A-	46734.2	18.49	14.4	1.0	2.2	27.2	**5.1**	7.1	14.3
Frost State Bank	Frost	MN	**B-**	C+	C-	49.7	-3.06	12.4	2.6	1.1	5.3	**10.0**	14.3	20.7
FSNB, N.A.	Lawton	OK	**A**	A	A	503.7	12.58	3.7	1.1	6.3	55.5	**10.0**	12.5	0.0
▲ Fulton Bank, N.A.	Lancaster	PA	**B+**	B	B	25922.8	5.84	11.9	1.8	15.9	15.1	**8.7**	10.2	14.3
▲ Fulton Savings Bank	Fulton	NY	**A**	B+	A	453.5	11.37	0.3	0.7	30.6	30.8	**10.0**	26.7	55.3
Fusion Bank	Larned	KS	**A-**	A-	A-	194.5	7.86	9.1	0.3	1.2	35.1	**10.0**	12.0	0.0
FVCbank	Fairfax	VA	**B+**	B+	B+	1971.1	10.84	11.9	0.6	6.7	10.1	**7.7**	11.5	0.0
G.W. Jones Exchange Bank	Marcellus	MI	**B-**	B-	C+	104.5	50.07	2.2	0.9	8.0	28.7	**5.9**	7.9	30.6
Garden Plain State Bank	Wichita	KS	**A**	A	A	141.1	21.32	7.0	1.1	8.6	26.0	**10.0**	12.5	22.2
Garfield County Bank	Jordan	MT	**D+**	D+	D	100.9	-0.72	2.9	1.7	2.5	8.7	**10.0**	12.4	19.5
Garrison State Bank and Trust	Garrison	ND	**B**	B	B	172.0	10.63	3.7	3.5	1.8	26.7	**9.3**	10.5	0.0
▼ Gate City Bank	Fargo	ND	**B-**	B	B	2985.1	15.56	3.0	25.2	37.3	6.4	**8.7**	10.1	0.0
Gates Banking and Trust Co.	Gates	TN	**B**	B	B	54.4	5.21	6.0	0.4	2.3	62.6	**8.8**	10.2	20.5
Gateway Bank	Rison	AR	**B**	B-	B-	91.7	8.80	14.4	3.5	31.7	1.6	**9.2**	11.2	0.0
Gateway Bank	Mendota Heights	MN	**B+**	B+	A-	268.3	10.64	27.3	2.2	9.9	2.6	**5.7**	7.7	14.9
▲ Gateway Bank, F.S.B.	Oakland	CA	**D**	D-	D	201.8	17.80	20.0	0.0	45.2	10.2	**6.0**	8.0	17.3
Gateway Commercial Bank	Mesa	AZ	**B+**	B+	A-	202.0	23.18	12.7	0.3	2.7	30.1	**7.4**	9.3	0.0
Gateway First Bank	Jenks	OK	**B-**	B-		1990.6	26.28	5.3	0.1	59.3	2.6	**10.0**	16.2	26.0

Asset Quality Index	Adjusted Non-Performing Loans as a % of Total Loans	Adjusted Non-Performing Loans as a % of Capital	Net Charge-Offs / Avg Loans	Profitability Index	Net Income ($Mil)	Return on Assets (R.O.A.)	Return on Equity (R.O.E.)	Net Interest Spread	Overhead Efficiency Ratio	Liquidity Index	Liquidity Ratio	Hot Money Ratio	Stability Index
3.7	0.03	5.9	-0.07	**5.7**	1.7	1.27	16.13	3.88	69.0	**0.9**	10.8	25.3	**4.6**
5.4	0.47	2.4	0.03	**5.7**	5.0	1.31	13.07	3.76	62.3	**4.6**	27.8	7.1	**7.1**
4.3	2.03	16.6	0.37	**3.1**	0.4	0.53	5.62	3.04	66.3	**1.1**	17.3	31.1	**5.6**
9.6	0.00	0.0	0.00	**0.0**	-1.5	-2.93	-11.58	1.86	237.2	**5.7**	57.7	11.1	**0.8**
3.8	2.09	6.9	0.11	**5.3**	3.0	1.33	12.44	3.32	56.8	**4.2**	41.4	14.4	**8.5**
6.9	0.45	1.8	0.36	**0.3**	-0.4	-0.23	-2.56	4.13	103.3	**2.7**	19.1	11.9	**1.3**
8.4	0.12	0.6	-0.18	**5.1**	0.6	1.10	8.35	2.57	50.3	**2.9**	51.1	29.6	**8.1**
8.0	0.49	1.7	0.06	**5.0**	1.2	1.10	8.55	3.37	65.9	**6.8**	54.8	3.2	**8.5**
7.3	0.25	0.6	1.58	**0.0**	-0.1	-0.37	-3.85	1.79	117.9	**5.1**	69.5	14.2	**3.6**
8.9	0.68	2.1	-0.02	**4.2**	2.1	1.07	7.01	2.84	68.2	**4.5**	38.9	11.8	**7.6**
10.0	0.00	0.0	0.00	**3.3**	0.5	0.54	3.51	2.43	76.6	**5.3**	50.0	11.1	**7.6**
7.2	0.27	1.4	0.00	**7.7**	22.5	1.78	15.64	3.53	58.0	**5.2**	20.8	2.7	**10.0**
7.8	0.57	2.5	0.22	**2.2**	0.2	0.11	1.27	2.55	89.9	**5.4**	37.9	6.1	**4.5**
8.3	0.12	0.7	0.19	**6.2**	4.1	1.26	10.95	3.37	54.8	**3.3**	19.5	13.0	**7.7**
8.2	0.76	2.3	-0.02	**4.6**	2.4	0.93	4.27	4.25	75.6	**4.3**	21.4	7.4	**8.4**
6.8	0.65	3.1	0.00	**3.9**	2.8	0.87	9.44	3.23	69.7	**3.6**	31.1	11.7	**5.7**
6.5	2.14	4.0	0.01	**4.4**	0.2	0.89	6.00	3.02	60.7	**4.7**	44.9	12.2	**7.4**
7.5	0.48	3.2	0.06	**6.9**	1.8	1.73	20.37	4.02	59.3	**1.6**	27.3	28.5	**5.1**
4.0	1.98	13.6	0.01	**2.0**	0.7	0.46	5.26	3.07	82.7	**1.8**	22.8	15.2	**2.8**
5.7	3.14	10.0	0.03	**5.3**	0.5	1.09	7.26	3.89	67.4	**5.6**	37.3	4.9	**8.0**
5.8	0.60	4.0	0.01	**8.8**	5.7	2.14	20.71	2.73	40.5	**3.5**	25.3	12.6	**9.5**
8.6	0.00	0.0	0.00	**3.1**	0.5	0.47	4.42	3.01	80.9	**5.4**	27.5	1.8	**5.4**
7.0	0.15	1.2	-0.02	**8.6**	0.8	1.38	15.70	4.91	62.7	**2.2**	26.8	19.8	**7.0**
4.7	0.60	4.7	0.00	**5.6**	3.3	1.17	12.29	3.75	54.3	**1.2**	17.2	29.8	**6.4**
6.2	0.00	1.9	0.00	**3.6**	0.3	0.69	5.85	4.77	78.5	**2.0**	32.7	27.4	**6.2**
7.0	0.58	1.8	0.04	**5.6**	3.7	1.37	13.21	3.40	58.5	**2.7**	31.1	18.3	**7.5**
4.5	2.47	11.3	0.08	**4.6**	0.8	0.77	7.95	3.58	69.9	**4.9**	33.3	8.0	**5.2**
7.5	0.00	0.0	-0.03	**3.8**	0.9	0.77	8.86	2.41	63.9	**0.9**	20.3	17.3	**5.1**
1.2	3.70	19.2	0.24	**4.3**	2.2	0.90	8.19	3.27	62.6	**4.5**	30.0	7.6	**7.4**
9.5	0.06	0.1	0.00	**2.0**	0.3	0.20	1.56	2.04	87.1	**2.3**	34.0	23.9	**6.8**
9.4	9.32	2.6	-0.44	**0.6**	-0.1	-0.32	-2.06	1.54	126.7	**7.8**	108.0	4.6	**6.8**
8.6	0.19	0.6	0.06	**4.1**	0.4	0.60	6.47	4.11	77.8	**5.2**	35.6	6.6	**5.7**
5.5	1.35	9.4	-0.01	**7.2**	53.0	2.03	27.80	3.18	62.7	**5.9**	27.1	2.0	**7.6**
8.3	0.15	0.2	0.02	**10.0**	10.6	2.23	19.61	4.34	36.1	**3.3**	25.9	9.4	**7.5**
8.3	0.22	0.9	0.05	**7.3**	1.4	1.67	19.14	3.80	58.8	**4.8**	35.5	9.6	**6.3**
8.9	0.00	0.0	-0.54	**3.2**	0.4	0.38	3.95	2.72	81.7	**6.7**	53.9	3.0	**5.2**
9.3	0.03	0.1	0.00	**7.6**	3.8	2.04	18.50	3.23	50.4	**3.9**	30.9	12.5	**9.0**
6.2	0.54	3.8	0.12	**6.6**	9.4	1.79	17.11	3.44	49.4	**1.9**	16.2	14.2	**9.6**
7.0	0.90	2.5	0.03	**5.4**	1.9	1.51	15.42	3.33	60.6	**3.4**	32.2	13.5	**6.4**
8.5	0.04	0.3	0.01	**6.4**	3.6	1.42	13.01	4.01	55.9	**1.1**	27.1	35.0	**6.8**
8.6	0.07	0.2	0.00	**3.6**	0.5	0.67	6.41	3.09	73.2	**1.4**	13.8	25.9	**6.5**
4.8	1.42	11.4	0.21	**5.5**	4.4	1.63	11.35	3.27	46.5	**0.9**	26.2	58.3	**7.1**
8.4	0.35	1.9	0.04	**5.1**	238.6	1.09	11.55	2.61	61.5	**7.3**	54.0	2.1	**8.1**
3.5	2.42	9.5	0.67	**7.4**	0.5	1.83	13.42	3.09	37.0	**1.1**	28.7	45.3	**6.2**
10.0	0.08	0.2	0.31	**9.8**	8.4	3.37	22.62	2.73	75.1	**7.6**	72.8	1.3	**8.9**
5.5	1.04	5.3	0.14	**5.3**	166.0	1.29	10.92	2.82	65.2	**4.7**	17.9	3.7	**9.7**
10.0	0.67	0.9	0.03	**7.4**	4.7	2.17	7.97	3.68	48.4	**7.2**	69.5	3.5	**8.0**
8.9	0.41	1.7	0.04	**5.6**	1.0	1.06	8.72	2.82	70.4	**5.1**	36.3	6.2	**8.9**
7.0	0.28	1.7	0.08	**6.1**	12.4	1.30	10.84	3.27	49.4	**3.6**	23.3	11.5	**9.5**
8.5	0.68	2.2	0.00	**3.7**	0.5	0.98	12.93	3.06	70.9	**7.9**	80.5	1.0	**4.7**
9.3	0.00	0.0	-0.58	**6.3**	0.8	1.21	9.37	2.47	52.3	**5.8**	65.3	11.5	**7.8**
1.4	8.09	33.0	0.64	**3.7**	0.3	0.60	5.18	2.44	70.4	**2.2**	45.2	43.4	**6.3**
7.1	0.42	2.9	0.10	**4.7**	0.8	0.92	8.31	3.44	65.6	**4.7**	40.4	11.6	**6.3**
5.9	0.66	3.5	0.12	**4.0**	10.2	0.70	6.84	2.75	79.2	**5.5**	26.1	4.0	**8.1**
9.7	0.40	0.5	0.00	**3.5**	0.2	0.86	7.34	2.68	72.4	**1.8**	38.9	48.9	**7.2**
3.5	3.02	16.0	0.00	**6.2**	0.7	1.63	14.70	4.79	61.6	**0.7**	13.9	40.1	**6.4**
8.4	0.09	0.3	0.00	**5.8**	2.0	1.50	19.32	3.24	51.3	**3.0**	37.0	16.4	**5.7**
5.3	1.57	8.9	0.00	**1.4**	0.4	0.44	5.66	3.25	87.2	**1.4**	23.4	28.6	**3.2**
9.0	0.00	0.0	-0.02	**5.5**	1.1	1.08	11.75	3.49	48.8	**5.7**	50.1	8.8	**6.0**
3.9	1.72	6.0	0.06	**7.4**	55.4	5.91	35.72	2.00	58.7	**0.8**	13.4	30.1	**6.8**

Name	City	State	Rating	2020 Rating	2019 Rating	Total Assets ($Mil)	One Year Asset Growth	Asset Mix (As a % of Total Assets) Comm-ercial Loans	Cons-umer Loans	Mort-gage Loans	Secur-ities	Capital-ization Index	Lever-age Ratio	Risk-Based Capital Ratio
▲ GBC International Bank	Los Angeles	CA	**B**	B-	B-	697.5	-0.59	21.9	0.0	0.3	0.6	**8.5**	10.4	0.0
Geddes Federal S&L Assn.	Syracuse	NY	**C+**	C+	B-	595.8	2.32	0.0	0.1	74.4	10.9	**10.0**	15.8	0.0
▲ Generations Bank	Rogers	AR	**B+**	B	B	663.0	10.07	12.2	1.4	20.0	17.6	**8.9**	10.2	14.3
Generations Bank	Exeter	NE	**C**	C	C-	44.7	9.37	13.4	1.7	7.7	23.1	**8.4**	10.1	0.0
Generations Bank	Seneca Falls	NY	**C-**	D+	D+	380.5	2.18	3.5	30.9	32.0	9.9	**9.4**	10.6	14.9
Generations Commercial Bank	Seneca Falls	NY	**U**	U		15.5	-68.72	0.0	0.0	0.0	71.3	**10.0**	59.6	316.1
▲ Genesee Regional Bank	Rochester	NY	**A**	A-	A-	824.5	15.32	24.9	0.3	12.6	19.1	**10.0**	11.0	0.0
▼ Genesis Bank	Benoit	MS	**C-**	C	C-	23.1	8.28	2.6	21.9	0.1	12.1	**10.0**	17.0	39.1
Genoa Community Bank	Genoa	NE	**B**	B	B	67.1	7.93	4.1	0.9	1.5	21.9	**10.0**	11.1	16.8
▼ GENUBANK	Las Vegas	NV	**C+**	B+	B+	152.6	6.92	10.2	0.0	1.8	0.0	**10.0**	18.5	0.0
Georgia Banking Co.	Sandy Springs	GA	**C**	C	C+	738.5	4.82	4.1	3.1	46.8	3.4	**10.0**	15.6	27.2
Georgia Community Bank	Dawson	GA	**B**	B	B	391.3	12.85	6.5	2.7	22.5	17.0	**9.3**	10.5	0.0
Georgia Primary Bank	Atlanta	GA	**B**	B	C+	273.4	-1.72	18.3	0.2	4.3	15.6	**7.5**	9.4	13.3
German American Bank	Jasper	IN	**A-**	A-	A-	5339.1	10.25	10.0	0.9	9.0	29.7	**6.8**	8.8	13.4
German-American State Bank	German Valley	IL	**B-**	B-	B	301.2	10.70	14.3	5.9	8.0	22.1	**5.2**	9.2	0.0
Germantown Trust & Savings Bank	Breese	IL	**A**	A	A	454.6	5.95	3.1	0.8	12.6	47.3	**10.0**	11.7	0.0
▼ Gibsland Bank & Trust Co.	Gibsland	LA	**C**	C+	C	462.7	-2.84	14.0	1.9	11.2	20.3	**9.7**	10.8	16.4
Gilmer National Bank	Gilmer	TX	**B+**	B	B	247.6	-0.73	7.1	9.9	20.4	18.3	**10.0**	13.3	21.8
Glacier Bank	Kalispell	MT	**A-**	A-	A-	20475.5	21.18	8.1	0.9	5.6	35.1	**7.0**	9.0	13.7
Glasford State Bank	Glasford	IL	**B-**	B-	B-	54.0	-1.66	1.4	8.0	20.1	43.2	**5.1**	7.1	21.3
Glen Burnie Mutual Savings Bank	Glen Burnie	MD	**C-**	C-	C-	106.7	4.08	0.0	0.0	73.7	0.2	**5.5**	7.5	16.6
▲ Glen Rock Savings Bank	Glen Rock	NJ	**C**	C-	D+	294.4	9.10	0.0	0.0	43.4	13.3	**10.0**	11.7	18.2
Glenmede Trust Co., N.A.	Philadelphia	PA	**U**	U	U	144.5	17.20	0.0	0.0	0.0	6.7	**10.0**	49.4	57.8
Glennville Bank	Glennville	GA	**A-**	A-	A-	337.4	17.50	3.8	2.7	18.2	25.3	**8.8**	10.2	20.0
Glens Falls National Bank and Trust Co.	Glens Falls	NY	**B+**	B+	B+	3049.9	7.94	5.1	24.1	20.1	16.9	**6.9**	8.9	15.3
▲ Glenview State Bank	Glenview	IL	**B+**	B-	B	1435.5	3.29	6.0	10.6	8.5	27.3	**5.4**	7.4	0.0
Glenwood State Bank	Glenwood	IA	**C+**	C+	B-	281.0	15.39	3.9	1.7	7.2	45.7	**7.0**	9.0	0.0
Glenwood State Bank (Inc.)	Glenwood	MN	**B-**	B-	C+	425.4	17.82	17.4	1.6	13.9	1.1	**5.5**	8.1	11.4
▲ Global Bank	New York	NY	**B**	B-	C+	215.5	0.59	1.4	0.0	24.9	1.4	**9.8**	12.9	0.0
Global Innovations Bank	Kiester	MN	**C-**	C	D+	32.7	25.29	15.0	3.7	15.4	2.4	**5.9**	7.9	19.6
GN Bank	Chicago	IL	**D-**	D-	D-	91.1	-15.79	1.7	6.4	20.1	7.1	**8.9**	10.3	17.2
▲ GNB Bank	Grundy Center	IA	**A-**	B+	B+	594.0	3.97	16.8	0.8	6.7	11.3	**10.0**	11.1	16.2
GNBank, N.A.	Girard	KS	**B-**	B-	B-	928.8	11.58	11.6	1.5	6.2	24.3	**8.1**	9.7	0.0
Gogebic Range Bank	Ironwood	MI	**B**	B	B-	154.2	11.13	18.0	4.1	7.0	35.6	**6.9**	8.9	0.0
Gold Coast Bank	Chicago	IL	**B+**	B+	A-	447.0	11.37	7.9	0.4	32.1	0.0	**10.0**	11.7	0.0
▲ Golden Bank, N.A.	Houston	TX	**A**	A-	A-	1294.4	14.96	7.8	0.1	7.5	7.9	**10.0**	12.5	17.4
▲ Golden Belt Bank, FSA	Hays	KS	**A**	A-	B+	276.4	3.96	8.3	2.6	28.9	15.5	**10.0**	11.5	0.0
▲ Golden Pacific Bank, N.A.	Sacramento	CA	**C**	D+	C	166.1	-1.92	13.2	0.4	2.6	6.7	**7.6**	9.4	0.0
▲ Golden State Bank	Glendale	CA	**C**	C-	C+	494.7	13.86	9.9	0.1	8.0	0.0	**5.4**	7.8	11.3
Golden Valley Bank	Chico	CA	**B+**	B+	B+	442.8	6.26	13.7	0.2	6.4	30.7	**6.0**	8.0	15.8
Goldman Sachs Bank USA	New York	NY	**B-**	C+	B	351163.0	24.27	4.6	4.3	3.7	6.8	**7.7**	10.7	13.1
▲ Goldwater Bank, N.A.	Phoenix	AZ	**B**	B-	C	345.1	21.45	6.5	0.1	68.7	0.3	**9.2**	10.5	0.0
Goodfield State Bank	Goodfield	IL	**A**	A	A-	174.0	13.86	15.8	2.2	16.3	14.6	**10.0**	11.6	17.3
Goppert Financial Bank	Lathrop	MO	**B**	B	B	220.2	15.65	7.8	0.4	6.5	27.2	**7.2**	9.2	0.0
Goppert State Service Bank	Garnett	KS	**B**	B	B	244.1	15.50	19.6	4.3	13.0	15.1	**6.9**	9.1	0.0
Gorham Savings Bank	Gorham	ME	**C+**	C+	C+	1469.0	5.91	11.2	0.2	15.8	17.7	**6.0**	9.4	0.0
Gorham State Bank	Gorham	KS	**B-**	B-	C+	36.3	15.88	11.3	3.1	8.9	2.6	**10.0**	11.0	19.9
Gouverneur S&L Assn.	Gouverneur	NY	**C+**	C	B-	132.8	-5.53	1.1	1.8	54.1	18.0	**10.0**	20.4	35.1
Graham S&L, SSB	Graham	TX	**C+**	C+	B	153.2	6.23	1.9	0.7	40.5	12.2	**9.4**	10.6	19.0
Grand Bank	Tulsa	OK	**B-**	B-	B-	471.0	2.59	16.0	0.1	13.8	9.2	**9.5**	11.4	14.5
Grand Bank for Savings, F.S.B.	Hattiesburg	MS	**B+**	B+	B+	109.0	28.74	0.0	0.2	63.7	0.0	**10.0**	11.5	0.0
Grand Marais State Bank	Grand Marais	MN	**B**	B	B	127.1	17.07	12.2	1.6	22.0	36.2	**4.8**	6.8	16.8
Grand Rapids State Bank	Grand Rapids	MN	**B-**	B-	B-	274.0	-1.75	13.0	2.7	6.2	20.1	**6.9**	8.9	0.0
Grand Ridge National Bank	Grand Ridge	IL	**B+**	A-	A	302.1	16.43	16.0	0.0	6.0	0.1	**8.2**	11.2	0.0
Grand River Bank	Grandville	MI	**B-**	B-	C+	464.9	17.01	12.8	0.0	11.6	3.5	**7.3**	9.2	13.0
Grand Rivers Community Bank	Grand Chain	IL	**E-**	E-	E-	19.9	-30.23	10.1	0.8	16.8	4.9	**0.0**	3.3	5.8
Grand Savings Bank	Grove	OK	**B+**	B+	B+	723.8	20.53	9.3	5.9	18.7	6.2	**6.5**	8.5	0.0
Grand Timber Bank	McGregor	MN	**B**	B	B-	54.7	6.23	7.1	6.8	28.8	12.0	**10.0**	11.1	19.6
Grand Valley Bank	Heber City	UT	**B+**	B+	B+	549.7	13.71	2.4	0.3	5.9	55.6	**6.7**	8.7	0.0
GrandSouth Bank	Greenville	SC	**B+**	B+	B	1163.2	17.25	18.6	2.9	10.1	11.3	**7.9**	9.9	13.3

Asset Quality Index	Adjusted Non-Performing Loans as a % of Total Loans	Adjusted Non-Performing Loans as a % of Capital	Net Charge-Offs Avg Loans	Profitability Index	Net Income ($Mil)	Return on Assets (R.O.A.)	Return on Equity (R.O.E.)	Net Interest Spread	Overhead Efficiency Ratio	Liquidity Index	Liquidity Ratio	Hot Money Ratio	Stability Index
7.1	0.22	0.2	0.02	**5.3**	3.9	1.08	10.69	3.09	56.9	**0.8**	19.9	42.1	**7.7**
9.9	0.34	1.6	0.00	**2.7**	1.0	0.34	2.13	1.98	77.5	**1.0**	23.8	37.3	**8.5**
6.7	0.50	2.5	0.02	**6.3**	4.3	1.31	12.71	3.87	59.3	**1.8**	21.3	21.4	**6.4**
3.2	2.66	13.5	0.00	**5.7**	0.3	1.50	14.18	2.69	57.7	**3.2**	28.5	10.1	**5.9**
2.0	2.36	12.1	0.08	**2.5**	0.8	0.40	3.92	3.61	83.2	**1.9**	13.9	19.4	**4.8**
10.0	na	0.0	na	**2.4**	0.1	0.60	1.05	1.85	49.2	**6.4**	201.0	21.4	**3.1**
8.0	0.31	1.7	0.00	**9.2**	8.9	2.23	20.89	3.72	49.4	**2.7**	7.6	12.0	**8.2**
7.3	0.85	2.0	0.02	**1.3**	-0.1	-0.62	-3.61	3.21	100.5	**3.6**	77.7	24.8	**5.1**
8.4	0.00	0.0	0.00	**5.4**	0.4	1.29	11.57	4.16	60.9	**2.3**	23.0	18.3	**6.5**
7.2	0.00	0.0	0.00	**0.8**	-0.1	-0.17	-0.91	3.10	103.4	**4.7**	64.5	17.1	**6.3**
7.3	0.63	3.1	0.28	**1.6**	-4.3	-1.35	-9.36	2.92	117.3	**1.0**	25.3	36.0	**6.0**
4.5	3.32	11.2	0.15	**4.9**	1.8	0.93	8.55	3.23	71.5	**1.8**	30.0	27.5	**6.6**
7.4	0.05	0.4	0.00	**4.8**	1.4	1.00	11.24	3.45	65.8	**1.4**	15.6	26.6	**6.2**
6.9	0.57	2.6	0.02	**7.9**	44.6	1.72	14.88	3.41	55.3	**6.2**	37.0	4.1	**9.8**
1.8	2.89	20.2	0.00	**4.1**	1.0	0.68	7.19	3.43	64.1	**2.6**	11.9	15.8	**6.4**
9.3	0.00	0.0	-0.03	**7.4**	3.9	1.77	13.55	2.62	35.3	**4.6**	50.5	14.7	**9.2**
2.5	4.32	30.4	0.94	**3.1**	1.0	0.45	4.15	4.23	57.0	**2.0**	27.1	21.0	**4.2**
6.0	0.58	4.5	0.05	**5.0**	1.2	0.96	7.16	3.63	62.8	**1.9**	31.4	28.4	**7.6**
7.4	0.61	2.3	0.03	**8.8**	163.5	1.69	13.88	3.62	49.1	**6.0**	31.1	3.4	**10.0**
7.8	0.04	1.4	0.20	**2.9**	0.1	0.44	5.64	2.52	80.1	**6.1**	55.3	6.0	**4.9**
5.4	1.29	14.2	0.00	**1.8**	0.1	0.12	1.65	0.88	85.5	**5.6**	25.8	0.0	**4.0**
7.6	0.52	4.0	0.00	**2.6**	0.7	0.47	4.23	2.75	73.2	**1.3**	8.5	25.4	**6.3**
10.0	na	0.0	na	**10.0**	17.4	25.14	52.88	0.69	79.7	**4.0**	67.8	0.0	**6.7**
6.5	0.71	3.2	0.01	**6.3**	2.0	1.26	12.05	3.57	59.1	**2.6**	37.4	23.9	**7.3**
7.0	0.17	1.4	0.05	**6.4**	20.2	1.37	14.73	3.03	56.7	**5.2**	18.9	1.9	**8.2**
7.3	1.03	3.4	-0.01	**1.7**	-4.3	-3.50	-32.03	1.62	177.0	**6.8**	65.7	7.5	**8.1**
8.1	0.24	3.8	0.00	**3.3**	0.8	0.56	6.00	2.23	73.9	**6.9**	67.3	5.0	**4.9**
3.5	0.87	13.4	0.04	**6.2**	2.9	1.40	17.03	3.51	60.1	**3.2**	17.4	12.7	**6.6**
7.0	0.20	1.4	0.00	**5.5**	1.3	1.22	9.65	4.33	70.6	**0.4**	3.3	54.6	**7.3**
8.7	0.00	0.0	0.02	**4.3**	0.1	0.52	6.18	2.73	82.4	**5.4**	49.4	9.4	**2.3**
2.0	6.14	30.3	0.28	**0.1**	0.1	0.20	1.91	2.79	109.8	**4.0**	28.9	10.4	**3.0**
6.3	1.01	3.6	0.04	**5.7**	4.3	1.41	11.37	3.97	63.1	**2.2**	22.4	13.7	**8.5**
3.6	2.78	11.2	0.14	**6.7**	6.4	1.42	12.93	4.00	53.4	**4.3**	27.4	8.8	**7.8**
4.4	2.84	12.8	-0.01	**5.1**	0.8	1.03	11.16	3.54	64.0	**6.0**	53.6	7.9	**5.6**
7.1	0.50	2.9	0.00	**5.3**	2.1	0.97	8.30	3.30	71.6	**0.8**	21.3	36.8	**7.3**
7.4	0.08	0.8	-0.07	**8.8**	12.0	1.93	15.17	3.89	41.0	**1.2**	21.8	34.9	**10.0**
7.7	0.64	2.2	-0.08	**7.8**	2.4	1.77	13.65	3.14	60.5	**4.3**	23.2	7.8	**9.3**
3.0	1.98	9.6	-0.04	**3.0**	0.4	0.54	4.95	3.66	81.9	**5.0**	35.2	7.5	**6.0**
6.0	0.22	1.7	0.00	**3.4**	1.5	0.62	7.39	3.58	67.2	**1.7**	28.0	27.6	**4.9**
8.8	0.00	0.0	0.00	**6.4**	2.8	1.29	15.77	3.61	45.7	**5.7**	43.5	6.4	**5.1**
6.4	1.74	5.5	0.30	**4.4**	1515.0	1.03	9.85	1.28	49.4	**3.7**	69.5	9.6	**7.5**
8.0	0.77	4.8	0.49	**9.8**	3.1	1.86	18.41	3.58	89.5	**0.5**	6.2	55.3	**7.1**
6.0	1.02	5.4	0.03	**9.3**	1.8	2.22	18.53	3.21	48.6	**3.8**	34.4	14.2	**9.0**
8.9	0.01	0.1	0.05	**3.9**	0.8	0.74	8.11	3.14	70.0	**5.3**	32.1	4.5	**5.2**
8.1	0.04	0.8	0.06	**5.2**	1.2	1.03	11.21	3.72	63.7	**3.1**	17.3	13.8	**5.6**
5.6	1.06	7.6	0.47	**3.4**	4.8	0.67	7.33	3.40	72.6	**3.1**	4.7	3.4	**7.7**
4.8	2.38	12.1	0.20	**4.4**	0.2	0.88	8.11	3.19	67.2	**5.9**	42.2	4.6	**5.8**
9.6	0.39	1.2	0.02	**2.8**	0.7	1.07	5.04	3.90	77.0	**4.8**	26.9	5.5	**6.3**
8.6	0.29	1.8	0.00	**3.7**	0.6	0.84	7.74	3.36	76.7	**1.8**	30.7	28.9	**6.7**
4.4	0.61	4.4	0.09	**9.3**	4.4	2.08	17.79	4.77	47.0	**0.8**	15.8	31.3	**7.8**
7.5	1.16	6.1	-0.01	**5.7**	0.8	1.51	12.76	6.20	75.7	**1.4**	31.2	33.8	**6.9**
5.6	0.85	6.4	0.02	**7.1**	1.1	1.86	27.90	3.48	49.1	**4.9**	19.4	3.4	**5.2**
8.6	0.00	0.0	0.00	**4.1**	1.3	0.92	9.94	3.32	76.3	**5.1**	26.8	3.8	**6.0**
5.4	0.35	2.3	0.00	**9.2**	2.1	1.48	13.24	5.61	53.2	**1.4**	19.8	26.6	**8.3**
7.4	0.00	0.0	0.00	**4.2**	2.2	0.95	10.56	2.84	66.6	**2.2**	18.0	12.6	**5.4**
0.3	5.80	179.2	0.00	**0.0**	-0.3	-2.52	-78.36	4.03	157.1	**3.1**	19.6	13.9	**0.0**
6.9	0.21	1.3	-0.06	**7.5**	4.7	1.37	16.54	4.43	55.8	**2.9**	23.0	14.7	**6.9**
4.2	3.60	15.4	-0.04	**8.0**	0.4	1.69	14.06	4.36	66.0	**5.6**	34.5	3.6	**8.8**
9.4	0.04	0.1	-0.02	**4.9**	2.5	0.96	9.54	3.18	62.6	**6.2**	58.9	8.4	**7.2**
8.2	0.20	0.8	-0.05	**6.9**	8.3	1.46	14.79	4.67	56.8	**3.0**	21.0	14.0	**7.8**

Name	City	State	Rating	2020 Rating	2019 Rating	Total Assets ($Mil)	One Year Asset Growth	Asset Mix (As a % of Total Assets) Commercial Loans	Consumer Loans	Mortgage Loans	Securities	Capitalization Index	Leverage Ratio	Risk-Based Capital Ratio
▼ Grandview Bank	Grandview	TX	B+	A-	A-	383.3	31.23	17.0	4.5	8.9	13.9	6.5	8.5	17.4
Granite Community Bank	Cold Spring	MN	B-	B-	C+	142.0	-5.32	17.2	1.8	10.1	10.8	6.8	8.8	13.8
Granite Mountain Bank, Inc.	Philipsburg	MT	B-	B-	B	133.4	35.14	8.4	1.8	10.3	8.9	5.1	7.1	22.7
Grant County Bank	Ulysses	KS	A-	B+	B-	269.5	2.43	9.5	1.9	22.5	32.7	10.0	12.5	0.0
Grant County Bank	Medford	OK	C-	C-	C	63.2	3.44	3.6	4.6	0.9	41.4	10.0	14.5	0.0
Grant County State Bank	Swayzee	IN	B	B	B	233.9	10.99	12.4	5.8	30.8	0.0	10.0	12.1	19.7
Grant County State Bank	Carson	ND	B+	B+	A-	41.4	11.51	3.8	0.1	0.0	0.0	10.0	11.1	0.0
Grasshopper Bank, N.A.	New York	NY	D	D		257.2	94.84	21.1	0.0	0.0	32.9	10.0	24.8	41.5
Great American Bank	Lawrence	KS	B+	B+	B	256.1	9.82	7.5	0.3	22.7	0.0	6.5	10.3	0.0
Great Midwest Bank, State Savings Bank	Brookfield	WI	A-	A-	B+	845.9	-6.12	0.0	0.1	55.0	6.4	10.0	17.5	0.0
Great Nations Bank	Norman	OK	C+	C+	B-	77.9	-0.11	18.1	0.3	6.8	5.9	10.0	12.4	17.0
Great North Bank	Florence	WI	D+	D+	D+	143.1	-5.38	20.6	1.7	13.6	27.7	8.3	9.8	14.9
Great Oaks Bank	Eastman	GA	B-	B-	B-	263.9	30.61	13.9	1.2	12.1	13.0	4.8	6.8	13.9
Great Plains Bank	Eureka	SD	D+	D+	D+	143.6	15.02	26.9	0.6	3.0	12.1	8.4	12.8	0.0
Great Plains National Bank	Hollis	OK	B+	B	B	1016.2	6.62	25.5	3.1	15.1	5.9	7.7	9.5	13.6
Great Plains State Bank	Petersburg	NE	B-	B-	C	349.2	12.02	20.2	0.3	0.2	5.2	8.5	10.9	0.0
Great Rivers Bank	Barry	IL	B	B	C+	181.3	24.98	10.2	1.7	4.3	17.3	7.1	9.1	14.8
Great Southern Bank	Springfield	MO	A-	A-	A-	5580.8	0.20	4.4	1.8	12.5	8.1	10.0	11.7	15.7
Great Southern Bank	Meridian	MS	B	B	B	351.7	6.01	4.9	8.3	10.8	55.5	6.2	8.2	0.0
▲ Great Western Bank	Sioux Falls	SD	B-	C+	C+	13056.2	0.97	11.0	0.4	4.1	18.3	8.7	10.1	15.6
▲ Greater Community Bank	Rome	GA	A-	B+	B+	305.2	7.77	22.7	6.6	7.0	3.5	9.0	10.3	16.7
Greater State Bank	McAllen	TX	C+	C+	C	115.0	12.75	18.1	1.1	15.2	7.2	6.0	8.0	14.4
Green Belt Bank & Trust	Iowa Falls	IA	B-	B-	C	614.0	10.18	6.7	1.3	4.7	13.5	6.6	8.6	12.3
▼ Green Dot Bank	Provo	UT	A-	A	A+	3481.0	39.19	0.1	0.8	0.0	31.3	5.9	7.9	0.0
Greene County Commercial Bank	Catskill	NY	U	U	U	875.4	29.63	0.0	0.0	0.0	101.9	5.9	7.9	40.2
Greeneville Federal Bank, F.S.B.	Greeneville	TN	C+	C+	B-	159.2	-1.23	9.2	1.1	30.9	0.8	10.0	13.8	21.5
Greenfield Banking Co.	Greenfield	IN	B+	B+	A-	797.4	17.88	5.7	0.5	3.3	10.2	7.2	9.2	18.1
▲ Greenfield Banking Co.	Greenfield	TN	C	D+	D	81.6	13.37	16.8	8.0	14.9	22.1	6.2	8.2	12.1
Greenfield Co-operative Bank	Greenfield	MA	C+	C+	B	799.2	7.63	5.1	0.4	33.4	17.3	9.3	10.5	0.0
Greenfield Savings Bank	Greenfield	MA	B	B	B	1081.7	10.50	7.3	0.0	43.9	11.5	10.0	11.1	22.8
Greenleaf Bank	Greenleaf	WI	B-	B	B	125.7	10.21	5.0	0.7	18.9	40.7	7.0	9.0	0.0
▲ Greenville Federal	Greenville	OH	C	C-	C	221.9	2.14	8.8	0.5	43.3	9.3	7.5	9.4	14.4
Greenville National Bank	Greenville	OH	B+	B+	B+	569.5	9.69	5.8	8.2	15.6	13.7	8.3	9.9	0.0
Greenville Savings Bank	Greenville	PA	B-	B-	B	282.6	8.12	1.4	0.5	54.6	16.1	10.0	13.1	0.0
Grinnell State Bank	Grinnell	IA	B+	B+	B	425.4	17.03	7.1	0.3	3.2	24.6	9.5	10.7	15.8
▲ Grove Bank	Grove City	MN	B	B-	B-	40.5	16.04	21.0	1.6	25.5	0.7	10.0	11.4	0.0
Grove Bank & Trust	Miami	FL	C	C+	B-	1002.8	19.82	6.7	0.5	2.2	18.6	10.0	12.3	24.7
Grundy Bank	Morris	IL	B+	B+	B	345.5	15.91	6.8	0.4	15.2	9.1	6.9	8.9	19.6
GSL Savings Bank	Guttenberg	NJ	D+	D+	D+	118.4	1.00	1.4	0.0	53.1	6.3	7.7	9.5	16.4
Guadalupe Bank	Kerrville	TX	A-	A-	B+	235.2	18.49	5.5	0.9	22.8	0.1	6.6	8.6	14.3
Guaranty Bank	Springfield	MO	B-	B-	C	1195.9	6.23	10.1	0.4	9.7	16.4	6.3	9.6	0.0
Guaranty Bank & Trust Co. of Delhi	Delhi	LA	B+	B+	B+	341.6	6.44	2.6	1.4	26.5	4.1	6.2	8.2	16.1
Guaranty Bank & Trust, N.A.	Mount Pleasant	TX	A-	B+	B+	2932.9	9.95	11.2	1.8	13.2	15.2	7.3	9.2	15.0
Guaranty Bank and Trust Co.	New Roads	LA	A-	A-	A-	269.3	10.20	4.2	1.4	24.8	15.5	10.0	11.1	22.2
Guaranty Bank and Trust Co.	Belzoni	MS	B	B	B	1359.5	12.18	16.7	0.7	8.3	18.0	4.1	8.4	0.0
Guaranty State Bank and Trust Co.	Beloit	KS	C+	C	C+	340.9	9.31	8.6	1.1	6.9	22.1	10.0	11.3	0.0
Guardian Bank	Valdosta	GA	B+	B+	B+	499.4	9.26	8.5	1.2	14.1	30.3	9.6	10.7	0.0
Guardian Savings Bank	Granite City	IL	D	D	D	36.6	-5.43	0.0	10.1	25.5	31.4	10.0	18.5	0.0
Guardian Savings Bank	West Chester	OH	A	A	B+	1109.3	4.22	0.0	0.0	50.7	0.0	10.0	12.2	31.8
Gulf Atlantic Bank	Key West	FL	D	D		57.0	285.34	10.9	0.6	18.6	21.2	10.0	18.7	34.7
Gulf Capital Bank	Houston	TX	D	D		318.8	135.40	39.9	0.2	0.0	2.4	10.0	31.6	59.9
Gulf Coast Bank	Abbeville	LA	A-	B+	A-	519.1	11.46	13.7	5.4	11.3	7.2	10.0	11.5	0.0
Gulf Coast Bank and Trust Co.	New Orleans	LA	B-	C+	B-	2575.1	15.08	31.8	1.4	12.1	18.0	6.2	8.2	12.2
Gulfside Bank	Sarasota	FL	D	D		216.3	58.27	7.3	0.1	8.0	27.0	8.4	10.1	0.0
▲ Gunnison S&L Assn.	Gunnison	CO	B	C+	B-	107.4	6.18	0.0	0.7	35.7	9.3	10.0	12.6	0.0
Guthrie County State Bank	Panora	IA	B+	B	B-	166.6	6.22	7.0	2.6	14.8	38.2	8.4	9.9	17.0
Habib American Bank	New York	NY	B+	B+	B+	1886.6	1.59	2.7	0.4	9.6	16.7	7.4	9.3	17.3
Haddon Savings Bank	Haddon Heights	NJ	C-	C-	C	412.1	9.13	11.1	0.0	27.3	46.2	6.7	8.7	19.1
Hamlin Bank and Trust Co.	Smethport	PA	A-	B+	A-	457.3	13.39	1.3	3.9	44.0	21.7	10.0	19.8	0.0
Hancock Bank & Trust Co.	Hawesville	KY	C+	B-	B-	333.8	5.63	6.4	0.9	20.7	15.2	8.1	10.2	0.0

Asset Quality Index	Adjusted Non-Performing Loans as a % of Total Loans	Adjusted Non-Performing Loans as a % of Capital	Net Charge-Offs Avg Loans	Profitability Index	Net Income ($Mil)	Return on Assets (R.O.A.)	Return on Equity (R.O.E.)	Net Interest Spread	Overhead Efficiency Ratio	Liquidity Index	Liquidity Ratio	Hot Money Ratio	Stability Index
6.0	0.51	3.1	0.09	**7.9**	2.5	1.51	16.68	3.87	50.0	**5.2**	45.6	10.5	**5.6**
5.0	1.05	6.2	0.01	**7.0**	1.1	1.46	17.74	4.33	59.2	**2.5**	18.0	16.9	**5.5**
6.8	0.70	5.0	-0.03	**4.5**	0.5	0.77	10.56	2.88	66.1	**7.4**	62.7	1.1	**3.8**
5.9	1.84	8.7	0.16	**5.6**	1.9	1.45	11.18	3.43	64.0	**1.7**	23.2	23.4	**9.1**
5.7	9.15	8.9	0.04	**1.6**	0.0	0.07	0.47	2.20	96.8	**2.9**	60.3	32.0	**5.9**
4.1	2.28	12.7	0.04	**9.8**	2.9	2.55	21.27	3.69	27.3	**1.0**	24.8	36.8	**8.6**
7.5	0.00	0.0	0.23	**5.9**	0.3	1.28	11.65	3.50	60.4	**4.7**	42.3	12.0	**6.7**
9.4	0.00	0.0	0.00	**0.0**	-9.1	-7.70	-27.96	2.14	475.2	**4.0**	79.8	0.0	**1.5**
6.5	0.00	0.0	0.01	**9.5**	3.0	2.41	18.17	4.81	50.3	**1.4**	11.0	25.3	**10.0**
6.9	1.21	5.1	0.00	**6.3**	5.8	1.37	7.95	2.61	53.0	**0.9**	23.4	29.8	**8.9**
6.2	0.98	5.3	0.00	**2.5**	0.2	0.51	4.10	3.08	83.2	**1.3**	29.1	34.0	**7.3**
3.5	2.48	13.0	0.37	**1.4**	0.2	0.29	2.89	3.19	84.0	**1.6**	35.8	33.3	**5.0**
8.8	0.02	0.1	0.01	**4.1**	1.1	0.85	11.48	3.68	77.9	**5.4**	44.0	9.0	**4.2**
1.7	3.68	25.2	0.00	**9.4**	3.1	4.36	34.28	6.98	26.8	**0.7**	9.8	22.8	**8.8**
6.0	0.81	5.7	0.07	**8.5**	9.7	1.93	19.76	5.36	70.1	**1.7**	8.6	20.9	**9.0**
4.9	1.03	6.7	0.04	**5.5**	2.3	1.31	12.29	4.05	52.0	**0.7**	17.2	33.1	**6.3**
6.0	0.55	3.2	0.02	**4.6**	1.1	1.27	13.00	3.04	62.9	**5.2**	36.8	7.5	**5.6**
7.3	0.24	1.2	0.00	**8.0**	43.6	1.58	12.70	3.54	52.8	**2.6**	19.2	16.7	**10.0**
8.1	0.20	1.2	0.04	**4.1**	1.2	0.72	8.30	3.55	80.0	**6.3**	62.1	8.7	**4.5**
4.1	2.96	15.2	0.29	**5.8**	114.1	1.76	19.44	3.32	48.5	**5.4**	25.0	3.2	**7.2**
8.0	0.17	1.0	0.04	**6.9**	2.7	1.83	19.21	3.77	64.3	**4.2**	30.6	10.1	**6.6**
5.9	0.83	6.9	0.09	**3.4**	0.3	0.60	7.50	4.42	77.3	**1.6**	26.1	27.6	**4.0**
5.7	0.71	3.6	0.03	**6.7**	5.4	1.81	20.31	3.52	43.0	**3.3**	24.9	12.4	**4.9**
10.0	2.48	0.3	21.59	**9.8**	35.1	2.05	25.81	0.67	12.6	**8.6**	99.0	0.1	**7.5**
10.0	na	0.0	na	**5.5**	3.9	0.94	11.88	1.67	17.5	**5.0**	0.2	0.0	**7.0**
7.0	0.27	1.3	-0.02	**3.0**	0.6	0.81	5.87	4.47	77.7	**3.2**	17.7	13.2	**5.6**
7.8	0.48	2.2	-0.01	**5.1**	3.4	0.91	10.26	2.71	62.7	**7.2**	56.6	1.2	**5.9**
3.9	1.25	8.9	-0.23	**4.7**	0.4	0.88	10.89	3.60	66.2	**1.1**	26.3	37.3	**3.9**
6.5	1.12	4.7	-0.02	**3.0**	1.6	0.41	3.82	2.38	78.7	**4.2**	42.1	14.4	**7.0**
8.7	0.49	3.0	0.01	**4.1**	4.1	0.79	7.05	3.18	70.9	**2.9**	28.1	17.7	**8.8**
9.4	0.00	0.0	0.00	**3.7**	0.4	0.67	7.14	2.81	73.1	**6.6**	57.2	5.0	**5.9**
8.6	0.10	0.8	0.00	**2.9**	0.6	0.53	5.81	2.93	81.1	**1.5**	19.5	26.2	**5.3**
4.5	1.75	8.7	-0.05	**5.5**	3.1	1.09	10.82	2.99	59.1	**4.8**	33.4	8.3	**7.6**
8.8	0.73	3.7	0.02	**3.1**	0.7	0.49	3.71	2.60	74.7	**3.0**	27.8	15.9	**7.4**
5.7	0.57	2.3	0.02	**5.8**	2.2	1.07	9.90	3.54	56.0	**3.8**	26.0	11.1	**6.2**
7.1	0.01	0.1	0.00	**5.4**	0.2	1.16	7.35	3.71	60.0	**5.1**	30.8	5.2	**6.9**
9.2	0.14	0.3	0.00	**2.0**	0.8	0.18	1.38	2.09	95.3	**7.1**	51.8	3.0	**7.8**
5.6	1.43	4.0	0.03	**8.3**	2.8	1.70	17.51	2.88	56.5	**5.9**	39.1	3.4	**7.8**
8.0	0.67	4.8	0.00	**1.0**	-0.1	-0.09	-0.85	2.34	103.7	**1.3**	14.3	27.4	**5.2**
8.3	0.30	2.2	0.02	**7.9**	1.7	1.48	17.13	4.15	57.9	**5.4**	30.8	3.2	**5.9**
4.8	1.26	8.0	-0.05	**4.8**	5.9	0.98	10.08	3.05	64.2	**4.8**	27.4	9.9	**7.8**
6.4	0.24	2.9	0.18	**8.6**	3.2	1.96	23.81	4.08	60.3	**2.7**	38.3	22.7	**6.5**
7.4	0.69	2.5	0.11	**7.2**	22.7	1.60	14.56	3.68	56.1	**4.3**	22.7	9.5	**9.1**
7.3	0.27	3.0	0.00	**7.1**	1.7	1.29	11.22	4.14	60.7	**3.8**	27.1	11.5	**7.7**
6.6	0.76	3.7	-0.03	**7.7**	12.4	1.87	20.50	4.09	58.5	**3.1**	18.8	14.4	**9.3**
6.6	0.42	2.2	0.07	**7.0**	3.0	1.76	14.45	3.14	59.7	**3.8**	32.0	9.6	**7.1**
5.4	1.98	5.8	0.08	**5.6**	3.4	1.39	13.11	3.20	58.3	**3.2**	30.2	15.6	**7.6**
9.3	1.00	1.6	0.00	**0.4**	0.0	-0.11	-0.62	2.43	104.5	**3.8**	68.0	21.4	**5.7**
7.5	0.90	3.3	-0.06	**9.0**	16.8	2.97	23.97	2.08	41.1	**3.4**	44.7	24.4	**10.0**
9.5	0.00	0.0	0.00	**0.0**	-0.9	-3.95	-18.40	2.83	211.4	**3.1**	60.8	15.1	**1.0**
8.4	0.00	0.0	0.00	**0.0**	-1.6	-1.23	-3.69	2.65	130.8	**5.7**	59.2	8.8	**1.5**
5.8	1.12	5.9	0.08	**8.1**	4.7	1.84	15.59	4.39	57.0	**5.4**	35.4	5.2	**8.1**
4.4	1.05	9.5	1.35	**8.2**	21.8	1.81	21.73	6.58	68.7	**5.1**	27.0	6.4	**7.2**
9.1	0.00	0.0	0.00	**0.9**	0.2	0.17	1.58	2.36	86.1	**6.8**	56.9	3.5	**1.7**
10.0	0.39	1.3	-0.02	**4.4**	0.6	1.07	8.51	1.95	60.7	**4.0**	62.9	20.4	**6.7**
8.4	0.35	1.3	0.09	**5.7**	1.2	1.47	13.38	3.71	61.9	**4.9**	24.8	4.3	**6.7**
7.5	0.34	1.9	0.00	**6.1**	11.2	1.14	12.09	2.29	55.0	**2.5**	40.8	36.5	**8.2**
7.5	0.56	2.1	0.18	**2.5**	0.8	0.38	4.38	1.68	70.6	**2.0**	40.4	13.1	**4.1**
8.1	0.43	3.1	0.02	**6.8**	7.5	3.37	16.49	3.48	54.8	**5.6**	46.0	8.0	**7.1**
5.4	0.89	7.6	-0.04	**3.1**	0.9	0.57	5.36	2.97	85.2	**2.6**	15.6	15.8	**6.8**

	Name	City	State	Rating	2020 Rating	2019 Rating	Total Assets ($Mil)	One Year Asset Growth	Asset Mix (As a % of Total Assets) Commercial Loans	Consumer Loans	Mortgage Loans	Securities	Capitalization Index	Leverage Ratio	Risk-Based Capital Ratio
	Hancock County Savings Bank, F.S.B.	Chester	WV	**B**	B	B	442.9	11.19	0.1	2.6	72.6	12.7	**10.0**	17.2	32.2
▲	Hancock Whitney Bank	Gulfport	MS	**C+**	C-	B-	35074.8	5.65	21.3	2.0	7.9	24.9	**6.0**	8.0	12.5
	Hanmi Bank	Los Angeles	CA	**B-**	B-	B+	6577.1	5.82	15.2	0.1	5.6	13.1	**9.8**	10.9	15.3
	Hanover Community Bank	Garden City Park	NY	**B+**	B+	B+	1541.0	83.89	17.6	0.0	27.9	1.1	**10.0**	11.2	15.0
	Happy State Bank	Happy	TX	**A-**	B+	A-	6257.9	37.68	11.6	0.6	8.0	23.3	**9.6**	10.7	16.6
▲	HarborOne Bank	Brockton	MA	**A-**	B	C+	4620.7	3.32	8.1	4.0	23.0	7.7	**10.0**	12.0	16.9
▲	Hardin County Bank	Savannah	TN	**C+**	C	C+	570.0	-0.10	26.8	2.4	13.2	14.4	**4.8**	9.3	0.0
	Hardin County Savings Bank	Eldora	IA	**B**	B	B	269.0	7.30	7.7	1.6	13.2	38.7	**6.0**	8.1	14.1
	Harford Bank	Aberdeen	MD	**B-**	B-	B-	519.4	14.27	11.9	1.5	16.0	13.4	**7.4**	9.3	15.6
	Harleysville Bank	Harleysville	PA	**B**	B	B	905.9	6.21	2.4	0.1	31.7	11.0	**6.9**	8.9	15.5
	Harrison County Bank	Lost Creek	WV	**B**	B	B	151.9	15.01	4.4	4.2	27.4	39.8	**7.4**	9.3	0.0
	Hart County Bank and Trust Co.	Munfordville	KY	**B**	B	B	30.9	4.17	26.9	1.0	0.0	16.3	**10.0**	22.4	29.3
▼	Hartsburg State Bank	Hartsburg	IL	**C-**	C+	C+	19.2	9.66	5.9	0.9	3.0	41.4	**8.9**	10.2	0.0
	Harvest Bank	Kimball	MN	**B**	B-	B-	193.5	12.09	9.4	2.5	13.8	25.6	**6.0**	8.0	13.8
	Harwood State Bank	Harwood	ND	**C**	C	C	46.0	6.25	9.9	3.2	1.6	4.5	**7.5**	9.3	0.0
▼	Haskell National Bank	Haskell	TX	**C**	C+	B	85.1	4.77	4.8	3.5	8.0	58.5	**9.5**	10.7	27.1
	Hatboro Federal Savings	Hatboro	PA	**B**	B	B	582.8	7.92	0.0	0.0	53.1	9.3	**10.0**	21.7	52.3
	Hatch Bank	San Marcos	CA	**C+**	B-	C+	386.8	378.70	3.2	13.3	2.3	8.1	**6.5**	8.5	0.0
▲	Haven Savings Bank	Hoboken	NJ	**D+**	D	C-	997.2	-1.45	1.9	0.0	42.0	13.7	**9.2**	10.5	0.0
	Haverhill Bank	Haverhill	MA	**B-**	B-	C+	527.0	13.85	5.9	0.7	39.2	15.1	**8.2**	9.8	16.8
	Hawaii National Bank	Honolulu	HI	**C+**	C+	C+	883.7	18.47	22.2	0.4	12.7	10.8	**5.9**	7.9	17.4
▼	Hawthorn Bank	Jefferson City	MO	**B-**	B+	A-	1700.8	1.51	11.5	1.4	14.3	16.1	**9.5**	10.6	14.6
	Headwaters State Bank	Land O'Lakes	WI	**A-**	B+	B+	80.4	15.13	3.4	1.9	30.2	16.1	**10.0**	13.1	0.0
	Hearthside Bank Corp.	Middlesboro	KY	**B**	B	B	450.7	5.26	5.1	1.9	34.2	17.9	**9.8**	10.8	18.5
	Heartland Bank	Somers	IA	**A**	A	A-	192.0	3.94	17.4	1.4	7.4	18.1	**10.0**	11.8	15.9
	Heartland Bank	Geneva	NE	**B+**	B	C+	745.0	10.46	4.8	0.8	1.5	33.9	**7.6**	9.5	0.0
	Heartland Bank	Whitehall	OH	**B+**	B+	A-	1507.0	-0.19	12.7	0.5	19.2	10.6	**8.0**	9.6	14.8
	Heartland Bank and Trust Co.	Bloomington	IL	**A**	A-	A-	3951.2	25.43	8.1	0.3	6.5	29.1	**8.3**	9.9	17.2
▼	Heartland National Bank	Sebring	FL	**B**	B+	A-	640.1	26.72	2.9	0.8	5.6	28.1	**5.4**	7.4	25.3
	Heartland State Bank	Edgeley	ND	**C+**	C+	B-	69.4	10.98	2.1	1.9	1.2	22.8	**8.3**	9.9	0.0
▲	Heartland State Bank	Redfield	SD	**A-**	B+	B-	114.0	18.07	8.2	1.2	0.0	26.0	**8.2**	9.8	14.2
	Heartland Tri-State Bank	Elkhart	KS	**C+**	B-	B-	132.6	0.93	5.7	1.9	2.0	34.5	**7.3**	9.2	16.7
	Hebron Savings Bank	Hebron	MD	**C+**	C	C-	778.8	11.48	8.9	0.3	17.3	2.4	**6.5**	8.6	13.7
	Helm Bank USA	Miami	FL	**B-**	B	B	1023.0	20.71	0.4	0.8	43.8	24.2	**9.4**	10.6	29.7
	Henderson Federal Savings Bank	Henderson	TX	**B**	B	B	116.8	6.73	3.0	3.5	45.1	11.2	**10.0**	21.3	0.0
	Henderson State Bank	Henderson	NE	**C+**	C+	C-	266.0	-6.36	12.0	0.5	0.3	15.7	**8.7**	12.7	0.0
▼	Hendricks County Bank and Trust Co.	Brownsburg	IN	**C-**	C+	C+	212.8	13.39	6.3	1.1	12.4	38.0	**8.1**	9.8	0.0
▲	Heritage Bank	Marion	IA	**C**	D+	C-	42.6	7.13	7.2	1.0	19.4	28.7	**7.6**	9.4	0.0
	Heritage Bank	Topeka	KS	**C**	C	C	84.0	11.43	15.5	0.9	13.2	5.8	**6.0**	8.0	14.1
	Heritage Bank	Wood River	NE	**A**	A	A	582.9	6.25	4.7	0.6	2.2	52.0	**10.0**	14.7	0.0
	Heritage Bank	Olympia	WA	**B-**	B-	B+	7099.7	8.18	12.2	2.4	3.0	14.8	**6.9**	8.9	14.8
▲	Heritage Bank & Trust	Columbia	TN	**B**	B-	B-	210.0	6.86	4.4	1.4	27.8	14.1	**6.8**	8.8	12.6
	Heritage Bank Minnesota	West Concord	MN	**C**	C	C+	74.0	13.43	11.1	8.3	29.2	16.3	**6.2**	8.2	13.4
	Heritage Bank of Commerce	San Jose	CA	**A-**	A-	A-	5071.0	9.94	14.0	0.4	4.1	11.3	**7.0**	9.0	15.0
	Heritage Bank of Saint Tammany	Covington	LA	**B-**	B-	B-	152.5	9.54	3.6	0.3	41.3	11.5	**10.0**	13.8	0.0
	Heritage Bank of Schaumburg	Schaumburg	IL	**B-**	B-	B-	162.1	12.85	3.5	0.0	9.4	19.7	**6.1**	8.1	23.6
	Heritage Bank of the Ozarks	Lebanon	MO	**B-**	B-	B-	233.0	31.70	7.8	2.2	16.6	12.9	**5.0**	8.7	0.0
	Heritage Bank, Inc.	Burlington	KY	**B-**	B-	C+	1390.8	19.30	10.4	0.4	6.5	24.0	**5.8**	7.8	13.1
	Heritage Bank, N.A.	Spicer	MN	**B-**	B-	C	448.4	-6.81	18.1	6.6	15.3	11.9	**8.2**	9.8	16.8
	Heritage Community Bank	Chamois	MO	**C+**	C+	B-	179.7	11.88	11.6	2.1	25.9	3.1	**4.6**	8.7	0.0
	Heritage Community Bank	Greeneville	TN	**B-**	B-	B-	131.4	-2.61	7.7	5.5	34.2	3.0	**8.0**	9.6	15.5
▲	Heritage Southeast Bank	Jonesboro	GA	**B-**	C+	C+	1652.0	9.67	14.7	0.8	6.9	10.5	**7.0**	9.0	13.6
▲	Herring Bank	Amarillo	TX	**B**	B-	C+	524.1	3.79	6.6	11.5	6.8	7.7	**8.4**	9.9	13.9
▲	Hertford Savings Bank, SSB	Hertford	NC	**C**	C-	C	15.5	5.77	0.0	2.3	52.7	0.1	**10.0**	14.2	28.3
▲	Hiawatha Bank & Trust Co.	Hiawatha	IA	**A-**	B+	B	102.6	15.88	8.9	2.2	26.1	12.4	**8.9**	10.2	0.0
	Hiawatha National Bank	Hager City	WI	**C+**	C	C	533.3	42.53	20.7	0.4	7.6	21.2	**8.3**	9.9	15.4
	Hibernia Bank	New Orleans	LA	**B-**	B-	B-	214.3	3.25	1.4	0.0	46.3	0.7	**10.0**	13.4	0.0
	Hickory Point Bank and Trust	Decatur	IL	**B-**	B-	B	757.7	5.19	10.7	0.2	4.9	20.4	**7.4**	9.3	15.4
	High Country Bank	Salida	CO	**A-**	A-	A-	404.6	21.94	8.4	0.6	22.7	9.1	**7.7**	9.7	0.0
	High Plains Bank	Flagler	CO	**B+**	B+	A-	280.3	11.31	12.6	0.9	9.9	2.0	**4.7**	8.7	0.0

Asset Quality Index	Adjusted Non-Performing Loans as a % of Total Loans	Adjusted Non-Performing Loans as a % of Capital	Net Charge-Offs Avg Loans	Profitability Index	Net Income ($Mil)	Return on Assets (R.O.A.)	Return on Equity (R.O.E.)	Net Interest Spread	Overhead Efficiency Ratio	Liquidity Index	Liquidity Ratio	Hot Money Ratio	Stability Index
9.3	0.66	2.1	0.01	**4.3**	1.7	0.80	4.57	3.03	67.9	**4.0**	19.6	9.2	**7.7**
6.6	0.41	2.3	0.27	**4.2**	206.5	1.20	11.74	3.05	63.8	**5.7**	26.6	3.0	**7.4**
4.5	0.83	5.2	0.16	**5.8**	44.4	1.40	12.84	3.22	49.6	**2.5**	25.9	17.8	**9.1**
6.3	0.76	6.9	0.08	**4.0**	1.7	0.34	3.03	3.87	82.3	**1.2**	13.3	29.7	**6.6**
6.2	0.68	2.7	0.12	**7.6**	53.6	1.81	13.93	4.00	59.7	**3.5**	28.1	6.2	**9.6**
5.4	1.20	4.9	0.00	**6.5**	34.8	1.53	11.59	3.09	64.7	**3.8**	19.3	8.2	**9.3**
4.1	1.45	10.2	0.00	**6.3**	3.7	1.30	14.19	3.89	56.0	**1.4**	7.7	22.3	**6.6**
8.6	0.16	1.0	-0.01	**5.2**	1.7	1.29	14.34	2.69	53.7	**2.2**	36.3	18.4	**5.9**
4.3	1.51	10.9	0.00	**5.1**	2.7	1.06	11.56	3.46	61.7	**2.4**	22.3	15.9	**6.2**
5.7	1.27	8.2	0.00	**4.8**	3.9	0.86	9.61	2.45	58.3	**5.1**	34.2	6.8	**6.3**
8.8	0.03	0.5	-0.01	**4.6**	0.6	0.87	8.32	3.79	66.0	**5.8**	46.7	6.9	**6.0**
8.5	0.00	0.0	0.00	**4.5**	0.2	1.01	4.65	3.41	70.2	**4.8**	43.0	11.4	**7.4**
7.2	0.00	3.5	0.06	**1.8**	0.0	-0.01	-0.10	2.42	100.5	**4.6**	53.6	12.7	**5.5**
5.8	0.72	4.1	0.00	**6.7**	1.6	1.68	20.03	3.59	56.3	**5.2**	30.5	4.2	**6.3**
8.6	0.12	0.3	-0.01	**2.4**	0.1	0.30	3.22	2.36	91.4	**4.7**	55.4	14.1	**4.7**
9.3	0.04	0.2	0.07	**2.4**	0.1	0.28	2.49	2.73	89.9	**6.4**	63.9	6.0	**6.1**
7.6	3.15	5.9	-0.01	**3.8**	2.0	0.71	3.22	2.02	67.5	**2.6**	44.6	29.8	**8.7**
8.4	0.06	0.1	0.36	**2.0**	0.6	0.45	4.52	1.06	65.1	**8.1**	86.5	0.2	**5.7**
6.2	0.66	4.2	0.00	**1.4**	0.8	0.16	1.50	2.35	91.0	**0.9**	22.7	34.8	**6.3**
9.4	0.04	0.2	0.00	**4.5**	2.8	1.06	10.97	2.46	81.1	**2.5**	35.3	23.2	**6.5**
8.8	0.00	0.0	0.00	**2.8**	1.7	0.40	4.81	3.09	86.1	**5.4**	39.2	7.0	**4.9**
3.8	2.78	17.0	-0.03	**6.6**	11.7	1.36	12.99	3.51	60.2	**3.5**	9.6	9.1	**9.2**
8.9	0.12	0.4	0.00	**5.9**	0.6	1.42	10.46	3.74	63.9	**5.9**	57.2	8.1	**7.6**
6.1	0.95	4.6	0.01	**4.2**	1.8	0.82	7.48	3.68	73.5	**3.0**	26.1	15.1	**7.0**
7.8	0.05	0.3	0.00	**9.5**	2.1	2.19	17.14	4.77	51.3	**1.8**	11.7	15.7	**9.7**
5.6	1.12	3.2	0.01	**8.7**	6.6	1.80	14.75	4.16	50.7	**4.5**	29.7	9.1	**8.6**
8.2	0.31	2.0	0.22	**5.6**	9.5	1.24	12.09	3.47	59.0	**3.5**	13.8	11.8	**8.9**
8.2	0.33	1.7	-0.02	**8.7**	30.9	1.62	15.34	3.31	54.3	**6.5**	37.9	2.6	**9.6**
9.2	0.00	0.0	0.10	**3.9**	1.5	0.48	6.41	1.74	68.4	**7.0**	77.8	6.1	**5.2**
7.0	0.00	0.0	0.00	**3.9**	0.3	0.83	7.41	3.69	76.2	**3.4**	29.7	12.2	**6.6**
7.3	0.00	0.5	0.01	**8.8**	1.1	2.06	20.10	4.78	54.8	**2.6**	32.5	10.0	**7.5**
4.6	0.21	7.9	0.01	**5.2**	0.8	1.21	12.27	3.27	56.8	**3.3**	29.2	15.0	**6.5**
4.4	2.66	12.1	0.04	**4.3**	3.2	0.84	9.67	2.99	63.4	**3.0**	31.7	17.0	**5.6**
6.0	3.02	11.6	-0.03	**4.0**	4.1	0.85	7.85	2.93	75.8	**4.0**	60.1	24.3	**7.9**
7.2	1.56	4.3	0.27	**3.7**	0.3	0.55	2.56	2.93	69.2	**1.5**	32.7	39.6	**7.6**
3.2	1.63	9.2	-0.08	**6.3**	2.1	1.53	12.05	3.31	52.4	**0.6**	14.7	42.0	**7.5**
7.4	0.34	1.0	-0.17	**2.1**	0.4	0.38	3.84	3.32	92.0	**5.5**	49.3	9.7	**5.2**
9.3	0.00	0.0	0.00	**3.3**	0.2	0.96	10.29	4.02	75.8	**5.9**	54.9	7.2	**3.4**
5.4	0.99	5.4	-0.04	**3.0**	0.2	0.46	5.65	3.58	74.9	**2.3**	29.3	19.9	**4.4**
9.6	0.00	0.9	-0.20	**8.1**	4.5	1.56	10.65	2.25	29.6	**6.7**	50.0	2.3	**9.8**
4.0	2.15	6.8	-0.01	**6.9**	60.5	1.75	14.40	3.47	57.6	**6.1**	33.6	4.0	**9.6**
7.6	0.24	1.8	0.01	**4.8**	0.9	0.86	9.71	3.93	70.6	**3.2**	23.1	13.2	**6.0**
7.3	0.16	0.9	0.03	**3.5**	0.3	0.78	9.63	3.76	81.1	**4.3**	18.7	7.3	**4.1**
7.6	0.19	0.9	-0.12	**5.2**	22.3	0.91	7.46	3.14	62.2	**6.6**	41.5	3.3	**9.3**
7.3	0.92	4.2	0.00	**3.9**	0.6	0.80	5.85	3.57	75.9	**1.8**	26.6	24.7	**7.8**
6.8	0.06	0.1	0.00	**3.9**	0.6	0.74	5.54	2.64	71.2	**6.3**	54.7	6.1	**7.6**
7.7	0.29	1.5	-0.01	**6.6**	1.7	1.55	17.95	4.48	61.4	**2.9**	13.8	11.8	**5.2**
7.1	1.14	4.1	0.06	**5.0**	6.9	1.07	13.40	3.32	59.9	**5.0**	31.4	9.7	**6.9**
4.2	1.00	7.3	0.16	**9.3**	5.2	2.25	22.22	5.09	63.5	**3.8**	16.1	8.4	**6.9**
5.7	0.77	4.9	0.05	**6.0**	1.4	1.60	18.28	4.10	59.4	**3.1**	11.6	13.4	**6.1**
8.5	0.14	0.9	-0.01	**4.0**	0.6	0.84	8.67	3.78	78.0	**1.7**	15.0	22.0	**6.5**
6.5	0.45	1.5	-0.19	**4.4**	8.6	1.06	9.31	3.58	68.5	**4.3**	25.0	10.9	**7.7**
5.8	0.40	2.5	0.06	**6.1**	5.0	1.87	21.12	5.05	68.0	**4.1**	21.9	8.9	**7.1**
6.9	1.25	6.1	0.00	**3.0**	0.1	0.82	5.88	4.36	76.1	**1.7**	32.6	25.8	**5.6**
8.7	0.00	0.0	-0.01	**7.1**	0.7	1.47	14.03	3.57	55.8	**5.4**	31.0	3.1	**7.3**
3.6	3.62	9.5	-0.01	**4.6**	2.8	1.03	10.15	2.99	59.8	**2.3**	34.8	10.6	**7.2**
8.2	0.27	1.3	0.00	**1.9**	0.2	0.19	1.20	3.23	90.4	**0.8**	14.1	36.4	**7.0**
5.2	1.50	7.2	-0.01	**3.9**	2.5	0.65	6.89	2.36	74.4	**4.8**	26.7	5.4	**6.7**
7.4	0.60	4.2	0.00	**8.6**	2.9	1.50	15.69	4.48	67.5	**4.6**	23.0	5.9	**6.8**
8.3	0.08	0.6	0.02	**8.1**	3.5	2.57	30.10	6.36	56.5	**3.5**	20.0	12.2	**6.6**

	Name	City	State	Rating	2020 Rating	2019 Rating	Total Assets ($Mil)	One Year Asset Growth	Asset Mix (As a % of Total Assets) Commercial Loans	Consumer Loans	Mortgage Loans	Securities	Capitalization Index	Leverage Ratio	Risk-Based Capital Ratio
	High Plains Bank	Keyes	OK	**B**	B	B	148.8	0.31	10.3	2.9	6.2	6.9	**9.4**	11.9	0.0
▲	Highland Bank	Saint Michael	MN	**B+**	B	B	667.0	9.82	17.7	0.3	4.3	30.5	**7.4**	9.3	15.0
▼	Highland Federal S&L Assn.	Crossville	TN	**C+**	B	C+	73.5	11.39	0.0	0.2	23.2	4.3	**10.0**	20.3	59.0
	Highland State Bank	Highland	WI	**B+**	B+	B	37.5	7.48	2.2	5.8	23.0	20.1	**9.8**	10.9	0.0
	Highlands Community Bank	Covington	VA	**B+**	B+	B+	181.7	9.64	8.9	14.1	18.3	34.5	**10.0**	11.7	0.0
	Highpoint Community Bank	Hastings	MI	**C+**	C+	C+	432.1	20.58	6.9	2.2	20.5	14.9	**6.2**	8.2	19.0
	Hill Bank & Trust Co.	Weimar	TX	**B-**	B-	B	158.4	5.46	0.6	0.6	2.9	69.4	**10.0**	15.9	31.3
	Hills Bank and Trust Co.	Hills	IA	**A**	A-	A	3924.4	9.76	6.9	0.8	24.3	11.9	**10.0**	11.8	0.0
▼	Hillsboro Bank	Plant City	FL	**B+**	A	A	237.6	28.79	2.2	0.9	10.5	13.1	**8.8**	10.2	22.7
	Hillsboro State Bank	Hillsboro	KS	**D**	D+	C-	23.0	5.29	6.9	0.7	9.0	28.8	**6.0**	8.0	21.1
	Hilltop National Bank	Casper	WY	**B+**	B+	A-	977.0	11.55	8.0	1.8	11.7	51.7	**9.1**	10.4	0.0
	Hingham Institution for Savings	Hingham	MA	**A-**	A-	A-	2973.8	9.18	0.2	0.0	33.3	0.1	**8.8**	11.4	14.0
	Hinsdale Bank & Trust Co., N.A.	Hinsdale	IL	**B**	B	B	3959.8	5.44	26.1	9.1	4.8	15.7	**6.3**	8.5	12.0
	HNB First Bank	Headland	AL	**B+**	B+	A-	209.5	16.82	13.7	2.5	13.0	8.6	**7.2**	9.1	14.9
	HNB National Bank	Hannibal	MO	**A**	A	A	658.8	15.90	5.1	1.2	12.0	15.7	**10.0**	11.5	0.0
	Hodge Bank & Trust Co.	Hodge	LA	**B+**	B+	B	83.8	9.69	11.2	8.2	22.3	17.3	**10.0**	16.5	0.0
	Holcomb Bank	Rochelle	IL	**B-**	B	C+	251.2	13.43	13.1	1.2	13.8	26.3	**8.6**	10.1	15.9
▲	Holladay Bank and Trust	Salt Lake City	UT	**A-**	B+	A-	70.1	3.86	3.8	1.7	9.9	3.5	**10.0**	15.3	0.0
	Holmes County Bank	Lexington	MS	**C+**	B-	B	138.5	7.51	8.6	1.9	6.4	42.0	**10.0**	12.5	27.5
	Home Bank and Trust Co.	Eureka	KS	**B**	B	B-	150.8	22.40	12.9	3.1	30.6	3.8	**4.9**	6.9	11.6
	Home Bank of California	San Diego	CA	**A**	A	A	205.6	3.62	1.5	0.0	23.6	0.2	**10.0**	12.7	0.0
	Home Bank SB	Martinsville	IN	**B**	B	B-	399.3	10.88	3.5	0.8	21.4	38.0	**10.0**	11.8	0.0
▲	Home Bank, N.A.	Lafayette	LA	**B+**	B	B	2759.1	4.84	13.5	1.3	13.2	10.4	**8.3**	9.9	16.1
	Home Banking Co.	Selmer	TN	**C-**	C-	C+	126.9	22.45	5.7	5.5	13.7	43.5	**6.4**	8.4	0.0
▲	Home Exchange Bank	Jamesport	MO	**A**	A-	A-	148.6	-13.47	2.5	0.5	3.3	46.2	**10.0**	15.2	0.0
	Home Federal Bank	Shreveport	LA	**B+**	B+	B+	565.9	9.06	12.4	0.2	19.9	14.8	**7.9**	9.6	17.9
▼	Home Federal Bank of Hollywood	Hallandale Beach	FL	**D-**	D	D	46.8	-19.00	2.2	0.0	37.7	4.5	**10.0**	11.0	21.5
	Home Federal Bank of Tennessee	Knoxville	TN	**B-**	B-	B	2660.7	9.51	2.5	0.2	16.3	50.2	**10.0**	16.5	0.0
	Home Federal S&L Assn.	Bamberg	SC	**C+**	C+	C+	41.6	2.46	0.0	3.1	59.2	1.2	**10.0**	13.6	0.0
▼	Home Federal S&L Assn. of Grand Island	Grand Island	NE	**C**	B-	B-	373.4	14.39	10.3	3.9	21.4	21.1	**9.0**	10.3	15.6
	Home Federal S&L Assn. of Niles Ohio	Niles	OH	**C**	C	C+	112.8	6.87	1.9	0.1	35.8	10.7	**10.0**	11.1	0.0
	Home Federal Savings Bank	Rochester	MN	**A-**	B+	A-	981.0	13.80	6.8	1.7	16.9	21.6	**8.5**	10.0	15.4
▲	Home Loan Investment Bank, F.S.B.	Warwick	RI	**C-**	D	D+	362.3	3.68	1.7	26.4	33.0	0.3	**10.0**	12.0	17.7
	Home Loan State Bank	Grand Junction	CO	**C+**	C+	C+	193.4	10.68	15.6	1.6	2.3	31.3	**4.6**	6.7	16.5
	Home National Bank	Racine	OH	**C**	C	C-	78.3	3.95	11.6	9.5	30.1	30.3	**10.0**	11.7	0.0
	Home S&L Assn. of Carroll County, F.A.	Norborne	MO	**C+**	C+	C+	91.2	4.86	2.3	5.3	43.7	11.0	**10.0**	20.1	38.2
	Home Savings Bank	Chanute	KS	**B-**	B-	B-	79.8	2.61	4.9	5.2	35.5	23.1	**10.0**	18.7	34.4
	Home Savings Bank	Salt Lake City	UT	**B+**	A-	A-	119.4	-8.19	0.0	0.0	28.7	0.3	**10.0**	14.5	0.0
	Home Savings Bank	Madison	WI	**C+**	C+	D+	182.9	-0.06	1.4	0.2	39.9	0.5	**7.5**	9.3	15.8
	Home Savings Bank of Wapakoneta	Wapakoneta	OH	**C**	C	B-	40.2	7.34	0.0	0.1	56.3	13.0	**10.0**	12.0	0.0
	Home Savings Bank, FSB	Ludlow	KY	**D**	D	D	27.3	2.45	0.0	0.0	46.8	0.9	**10.0**	13.0	0.0
	Home State Bank	Jefferson	IA	**B-**	B-	B-	293.4	2.64	16.9	1.4	3.6	13.4	**4.6**	8.9	0.0
	Home State Bank	Royal	IA	**A-**	B+	B+	49.3	13.65	3.2	0.4	1.9	39.3	**10.0**	27.9	0.0
	Home State Bank	Litchfield	MN	**B+**	B+	B+	199.9	12.64	11.7	1.8	7.5	40.7	**8.0**	9.6	15.1
	Home State Bank/N.A.	Crystal Lake	IL	**B**	B	B	755.3	10.60	8.5	0.3	13.9	20.9	**9.2**	10.5	20.8
	HOMEBANK	Palmyra	MO	**B**	B	B-	456.1	1.92	17.1	1.8	11.4	10.7	**5.8**	9.5	0.0
▲	HomeBank of Arkansas	Portland	AR	**D**	D-	D+	75.2	11.02	11.8	2.8	22.8	0.0	**8.4**	9.9	0.0
	HomeBank Texas	Seagoville	TX	**A-**	A-	A-	271.0	6.96	14.9	0.6	24.4	4.3	**8.5**	10.0	17.0
	Homeland Community Bank	McMinnville	TN	**C+**	C+	C+	220.7	25.18	5.8	2.1	17.4	26.9	**5.2**	7.2	14.1
	Homeland Federal Savings Bank	Columbia	LA	**B-**	B-	B-	391.7	1.30	12.2	8.5	29.8	1.1	**5.4**	9.5	0.0
▲	HomePride Bank	Mansfield	MO	**D+**	D-	D-	105.1	-4.20	2.3	2.2	46.4	6.6	**6.9**	8.9	18.2
	Homestead Bank	Cozad	NE	**A**	A-	B+	329.8	14.17	5.9	0.9	0.7	33.2	**10.0**	15.3	0.0
	Homestead Savings Bank	Albion	MI	**D**	D	D-	79.0	7.60	6.7	1.3	36.9	10.3	**4.4**	6.4	14.9
	HomeStreet Bank	Seattle	WA	**B**	B	C+	7122.7	-2.48	7.7	0.1	14.8	14.1	**8.4**	10.0	14.4
▲	Hometown Bank	Oxford	MA	**B**	B-	B-	1288.1	10.27	8.0	0.3	16.1	11.0	**7.3**	9.2	0.0
	HomeTown Bank	Redwood Falls	MN	**A-**	A-	A-	513.0	22.05	10.1	1.6	12.6	42.7	**6.0**	8.0	15.6
	Hometown Bank	Kent	OH	**C-**	C-	C-	254.0	6.37	15.1	0.9	21.5	19.0	**5.8**	7.8	12.6
	Hometown Bank	Fond du Lac	WI	**A**	A	A-	630.0	9.39	20.5	0.2	7.9	4.5	**10.0**	11.3	19.0
	Hometown Bank of Corbin Inc.	Corbin	KY	**B-**	B-	B-	247.3	17.28	9.6	2.6	21.5	27.4	**6.0**	8.0	14.8
	Hometown Bank of Pennsylvania	Bedford	PA	**C**	C	B-	279.4	12.39	11.7	0.7	23.2	11.6	**5.0**	7.0	11.5

Asset Quality Index	Adjusted Non-Performing Loans as a % of Total Loans	Adjusted Non-Performing Loans as a % of Capital	Net Charge-Offs Avg Loans	Profitability Index	Net Income ($Mil)	Return on Assets (R.O.A.)	Return on Equity (R.O.E.)	Net Interest Spread	Overhead Efficiency Ratio	Liquidity Index	Liquidity Ratio	Hot Money Ratio	Stability Index
4.7	1.09	5.8	0.37	**7.4**	1.5	2.10	16.65	4.83	46.1	**0.9**	22.3	33.2	**7.2**
8.5	0.03	0.7	-0.01	**6.7**	6.7	2.12	21.11	4.13	54.1	**4.3**	27.8	6.0	**7.6**
10.0	0.31	0.4	0.00	**2.4**	0.0	0.09	0.41	2.08	93.6	**6.0**	79.4	11.0	**7.6**
9.1	0.00	0.0	0.00	**4.0**	0.1	0.71	6.55	2.53	85.4	**5.7**	56.4	8.7	**6.8**
5.0	1.53	8.6	0.43	**5.0**	0.9	0.97	7.77	3.80	65.7	**2.9**	41.6	22.0	**7.5**
7.4	0.30	1.5	0.00	**3.5**	1.4	0.67	7.88	2.93	77.2	**6.1**	43.1	3.8	**4.4**
10.0	0.00	0.0	0.00	**3.6**	0.5	0.57	3.57	1.57	57.8	**5.5**	98.0	17.3	**7.2**
8.3	0.62	2.5	-0.09	**7.2**	29.0	1.48	12.45	2.77	52.8	**5.1**	33.9	8.7	**10.0**
9.6	0.13	0.3	0.00	**4.3**	0.6	0.63	5.52	2.62	69.7	**6.5**	73.4	9.1	**6.9**
5.4	12.95	14.7	0.00	**2.5**	0.0	0.38	4.53	2.56	82.2	**7.0**	72.9	1.7	**2.3**
8.9	0.51	0.9	0.00	**5.1**	6.7	1.34	12.55	2.44	60.7	**6.4**	57.8	6.7	**8.2**
7.7	0.04	0.2	0.00	**9.7**	36.8	2.58	23.77	3.47	20.7	**0.7**	10.9	27.9	**9.5**
5.5	0.49	2.6	0.12	**6.0**	22.5	1.13	10.09	2.55	57.3	**3.0**	24.0	9.9	**8.1**
8.5	0.05	0.3	0.03	**7.0**	1.7	1.75	19.10	3.03	57.1	**2.3**	32.5	22.2	**6.0**
8.5	0.57	1.6	-0.05	**9.8**	8.7	2.64	21.56	3.70	44.2	**4.3**	34.7	11.6	**9.7**
4.2	4.58	15.8	0.51	**6.7**	0.5	1.23	7.38	3.44	53.2	**2.5**	37.3	24.0	**8.6**
5.5	1.07	4.4	0.09	**4.4**	1.5	1.21	11.77	3.41	62.8	**3.3**	30.9	12.8	**5.1**
8.0	0.63	1.0	-0.02	**7.7**	0.5	1.46	9.74	4.59	54.7	**4.0**	52.4	17.3	**8.3**
5.4	5.42	11.4	0.00	**3.5**	0.5	0.72	5.85	2.92	82.1	**4.0**	33.2	12.5	**6.5**
7.8	0.11	0.9	-0.01	**6.0**	1.0	1.34	19.69	3.27	65.7	**2.2**	28.5	20.1	**5.2**
7.5	0.00	0.0	0.00	**10.0**	2.9	2.83	22.75	5.17	43.1	**0.7**	11.5	36.7	**10.0**
7.9	2.03	5.8	-0.02	**3.9**	1.6	0.87	7.06	2.90	77.6	**6.0**	54.0	7.7	**7.3**
5.4	1.00	4.6	0.12	**7.5**	23.4	1.75	14.63	3.96	57.4	**4.3**	21.7	7.7	**9.9**
8.2	0.28	1.3	0.07	**1.8**	0.3	0.53	5.63	2.96	99.5	**3.6**	45.2	18.1	**4.0**
9.3	0.00	0.0	0.00	**7.5**	4.6	6.09	46.45	3.34	18.7	**2.3**	45.6	14.1	**9.3**
7.0	0.27	1.5	0.09	**4.8**	2.9	1.03	10.70	3.23	61.4	**3.7**	36.6	13.2	**6.5**
2.3	6.57	29.1	0.00	**0.0**	-1.0	-4.02	-34.42	3.03	262.1	**1.7**	38.9	60.9	**6.2**
9.3	0.82	2.1	0.00	**2.9**	5.4	0.42	2.57	2.05	77.9	**5.4**	57.4	13.9	**9.2**
6.5	1.28	6.6	0.01	**2.9**	0.1	0.47	3.52	3.51	87.8	**0.7**	19.5	55.5	**6.1**
4.5	1.65	10.6	0.00	**2.6**	0.5	0.27	2.69	3.10	81.9	**4.6**	18.2	5.0	**6.6**
7.8	0.67	3.7	0.00	**2.1**	0.1	0.21	1.86	1.82	86.7	**1.5**	33.8	48.6	**6.6**
7.5	0.27	1.6	-0.21	**8.2**	8.3	1.73	17.51	3.23	55.0	**5.2**	31.6	4.7	**7.8**
2.2	4.25	17.0	0.58	**8.1**	7.8	4.21	39.26	3.96	50.4	**0.8**	20.7	38.7	**7.3**
5.5	2.24	6.5	0.00	**4.1**	0.7	0.72	10.01	2.91	69.1	**5.5**	37.3	5.4	**4.0**
2.3	4.82	22.2	0.04	**4.9**	0.5	1.16	9.39	4.72	70.8	**2.9**	13.4	14.1	**7.2**
8.0	1.06	3.1	0.02	**2.5**	0.2	0.48	2.36	3.16	82.7	**2.4**	35.9	24.8	**7.3**
8.9	0.08	0.2	-0.01	**3.5**	0.3	0.69	3.40	3.41	74.4	**2.0**	30.3	16.4	**7.6**
7.4	0.00	0.0	0.58	**5.1**	0.5	0.78	5.43	3.65	62.8	**0.7**	16.8	53.7	**8.2**
8.3	0.08	0.3	0.17	**3.2**	0.5	0.57	5.74	2.88	72.2	**1.6**	16.1	16.2	**5.6**
9.8	0.00	0.0	0.00	**2.0**	0.1	0.41	3.30	3.33	84.4	**4.2**	28.2	10.0	**6.0**
6.0	2.18	10.0	0.00	**0.0**	0.0	-0.25	-1.79	2.54	108.8	**2.5**	39.6	25.5	**5.9**
4.4	1.42	9.6	0.01	**6.8**	2.5	1.68	18.76	4.43	60.8	**2.0**	17.1	8.5	**6.9**
8.7	0.00	0.0	0.01	**6.4**	0.3	1.37	4.79	3.01	50.4	**6.9**	67.9	3.3	**9.4**
8.9	0.00	0.0	-0.17	**4.5**	1.4	1.44	14.31	3.35	72.9	**5.9**	40.0	3.9	**6.3**
6.2	0.52	3.3	0.15	**4.1**	3.6	0.99	8.98	3.38	76.1	**5.8**	41.6	5.1	**7.3**
6.6	0.22	2.1	0.02	**5.5**	3.2	1.44	15.10	4.14	67.6	**3.8**	15.9	9.9	**6.7**
4.1	1.15	6.9	-0.30	**1.6**	0.1	0.30	3.05	3.97	89.9	**1.3**	30.8	40.9	**4.6**
8.6	0.15	0.8	0.00	**8.9**	2.9	2.17	21.43	4.19	47.8	**3.1**	27.7	15.2	**8.1**
4.7	1.69	10.9	-0.01	**3.8**	0.6	0.58	8.05	2.66	75.7	**3.4**	47.3	19.8	**3.9**
3.8	1.64	12.7	-0.01	**5.8**	2.7	1.35	14.45	4.64	66.0	**0.6**	7.4	41.8	**6.4**
5.7	0.79	6.5	-0.10	**2.2**	0.4	0.78	8.86	3.70	79.7	**2.0**	24.1	20.2	**3.3**
8.4	0.00	0.5	0.00	**7.6**	2.3	1.43	9.11	3.74	57.8	**5.4**	38.8	6.7	**9.2**
3.7	2.54	15.0	0.10	**2.1**	0.1	0.19	2.86	3.00	94.2	**5.9**	38.5	3.0	**3.0**
4.9	1.20	5.1	0.00	**7.0**	59.7	1.66	15.49	3.54	60.5	**3.5**	14.3	8.6	**9.5**
6.3	1.18	5.1	0.07	**4.1**	4.9	0.78	7.60	2.77	68.4	**4.7**	36.7	13.3	**6.9**
7.9	0.32	1.5	-0.04	**6.6**	2.0	0.81	8.82	2.82	71.6	**6.6**	48.7	2.4	**7.0**
2.7	2.14	17.1	-0.04	**3.3**	0.8	0.64	8.12	3.09	80.1	**1.8**	27.2	25.3	**4.4**
8.1	0.31	1.0	-0.02	**7.3**	4.1	1.33	10.89	2.98	51.8	**5.8**	36.5	3.4	**9.1**
7.8	0.23	1.5	0.01	**5.0**	1.2	0.99	12.01	3.73	70.6	**4.3**	29.5	10.0	**4.7**
5.2	1.69	8.6	0.00	**3.2**	0.8	0.55	7.77	2.86	75.2	**2.5**	30.6	19.1	**4.1**

Name	City	State	Rating	2020 Rating	2019 Rating	Total Assets ($Mil)	One Year Asset Growth	Asset Mix (As a % of Total Assets) Commercial Loans	Consumer Loans	Mortgage Loans	Securities	Capitalization Index	Leverage Ratio	Risk-Based Capital Ratio
Hometown Bank, N.A.	Galveston	TX	**A-**	A-	A-	845.6	15.34	7.2	1.2	9.5	33.8	**9.8**	10.9	18.7
Hometown Community Bank	Cyrus	MN	**C+**	C+	C+	75.8	12.51	8.2	1.3	13.0	10.0	**6.9**	8.9	0.0
Hometown National Bank	LaSalle	IL	**B**	B	B+	318.6	7.03	16.1	0.3	4.6	21.8	**6.4**	8.4	15.5
HomeTrust Bank	Asheville	NC	**C+**	C+	B-	3524.5	-5.32	16.5	3.5	12.4	9.8	**5.6**	9.8	11.4
▼ Homewood Federal Savings Bank	Baltimore	MD	**C**	C+	B-	61.3	-1.21	4.0	1.7	41.6	0.6	**10.0**	26.9	51.3
Honor Bank	Honor	MI	**B-**	B-	B-	340.1	22.12	14.8	1.0	15.1	6.1	**6.4**	8.4	13.4
Hoosier Heartland State Bank	Crawfordsville	IN	**B-**	B-	B-	271.0	20.09	7.0	4.3	8.6	29.7	**5.4**	7.4	11.6
Horatio State Bank	Horatio	AR	**B**	B	B	240.1	-0.54	5.9	17.2	26.5	11.6	**10.0**	12.5	0.0
▲ Horicon Bank	Horicon	WI	**C+**	C	C-	1168.2	12.13	11.7	0.5	11.3	3.6	**6.9**	8.9	12.6
Horizon Bank	Michigan City	IN	**B+**	B+	B+	6090.3	6.31	8.3	6.5	9.9	30.4	**6.8**	8.8	14.1
Horizon Bank	Waverly	NE	**A-**	A-	A-	352.4	-7.81	6.4	0.4	10.7	6.1	**10.0**	15.9	18.2
Horizon Bank, SSB	Austin	TX	**B+**	B+	B+	1970.8	28.17	15.5	0.1	7.4	11.4	**6.3**	8.3	15.4
Horizon Community Bank	Lake Havasu City	AZ	**B**	B-	B-	532.5	15.17	15.2	0.2	5.5	24.6	**5.8**	7.8	15.6
Horizon Financial Bank	Munich	ND	**B+**	B+	B+	167.0	10.40	6.6	1.3	3.1	14.5	**10.0**	11.1	0.0
▲ Houghton State Bank	Red Oak	IA	**A-**	B+	B	209.2	9.88	6.4	0.5	5.6	14.8	**9.4**	10.6	15.7
▲ Howard Bank	Baltimore	MD	**C+**	C-	C+	2598.9	5.50	19.1	3.3	15.8	14.4	**9.5**	10.8	14.6
Howard State Bank	Howard	KS	**B+**	B+	B+	63.9	13.10	2.7	5.6	4.4	35.1	**9.1**	10.4	15.9
Hoyne Savings Bank	Chicago	IL	**C-**	C-	C-	533.3	17.82	0.2	0.0	25.4	36.9	**10.0**	17.2	0.0
HSBC Bank USA, N.A.	Tysons	VA	**C-**	C-	C	194764.2	-7.71	10.8	0.6	9.5	21.4	**9.7**	10.8	22.3
HSBC Trust Co. (Delaware), N.A.	Wilmington	DE	**U**	U	U	55.3	0.51	0.0	0.0	0.0	0.0	**9.8**	98.8	0.0
Huntingdon Savings Bank	Huntingdon	PA	**C+**	C	C	16.1	-2.39	0.0	0.0	74.1	0.0	**10.0**	22.9	50.8
▲ Huntingdon Valley Bank	Doylestown	PA	**C+**	C	C-	546.5	29.22	18.1	0.9	39.7	5.7	**6.1**	8.1	14.1
Huntington Federal Savings Bank	Huntington	WV	**C**	C	C+	560.6	1.84	0.0	0.3	37.4	48.6	**10.0**	16.5	0.0
Huron Community Bank	East Tawas	MI	**B**	B	B	287.2	11.41	10.6	0.9	7.6	29.8	**8.5**	10.0	0.0
Huron State Bank	Rogers City	MI	**B-**	B	B-	72.6	13.00	1.6	6.1	30.7	25.8	**10.0**	13.7	0.0
Huron Valley State Bank	Milford	MI	**B**	B	B	223.2	17.35	19.0	0.4	2.3	4.6	**6.6**	8.6	15.4
Hustisford State Bank	Hustisford	WI	**B+**	B+	B+	73.4	18.66	3.6	1.3	33.1	26.8	**10.0**	15.4	0.0
Hyden Citizens Bank, Inc	Hyden	KY	**B-**	B-	B-	146.7	9.01	8.4	2.7	18.6	42.3	**6.7**	8.7	12.7
▲ Hyperion Bank	Philadelphia	PA	**C+**	C-	D+	279.5	25.67	13.2	0.6	31.5	1.5	**10.0**	11.6	16.7
i3 Bank	Bennington	NE	**B**	B	B-	188.0	9.03	20.6	1.2	6.9	10.9	**8.6**	10.1	15.2
Idaho First Bank	McCall	ID	**C+**	C+	C+	683.7	-25.42	39.1	0.7	6.9	1.5	**7.5**	9.4	13.7
▲ Idaho Trust Bank	Boise	ID	**B-**	C+	C	207.4	16.45	11.8	2.6	2.5	2.2	**6.5**	8.5	14.3
▲ Illini State Bank	Tonica	IL	**A-**	B+	B	155.0	12.11	6.3	0.6	11.3	32.5	**10.0**	11.9	0.0
Illinois Bank & Trust	Rockford	IL	**B+**	B+	B+	1671.6	13.71	17.2	0.9	5.3	39.1	**5.6**	7.6	13.3
Impact Bank	Wellington	KS	**B-**	B-	B-	159.2	9.21	12.9	1.9	2.8	29.1	**7.4**	9.2	15.2
INB, N.A.	Springfield	IL	**B-**	B-	B-	1529.4	13.25	9.1	0.1	7.1	8.5	**6.0**	8.0	14.0
▲ InBank	Raton	NM	**C-**	D+	C+	705.7	22.71	16.3	0.2	5.8	27.3	**6.8**	8.8	12.8
Incommons Bank, N.A.	Mexia	TX	**B**	B	B-	205.5	8.40	14.2	4.2	21.3	24.4	**6.8**	8.8	15.6
IncredibleBank	Wausau	WI	**B**	B-	B-	1734.5	4.72	29.8	4.6	5.6	15.8	**5.6**	7.6	11.4
Independence Bank	Havre	MT	**A**	A	A-	1137.3	26.05	5.1	1.8	4.4	15.6	**10.0**	11.5	16.2
Independence Bank	Independence	OH	**B**	B	B	195.8	5.19	22.8	0.4	5.0	15.1	**10.0**	12.3	0.0
Independence Bank	East Greenwich	RI	**B**	B	B	64.1	-4.65	65.1	0.3	1.0	0.0	**10.0**	28.5	0.0
Independence Bank of Kentucky	Owensboro	KY	**B+**	B+	B+	3044.7	6.71	4.7	0.2	14.4	41.8	**5.6**	7.6	13.4
Independence State Bank	Independence	WI	**C**	C	D	89.1	17.31	8.9	1.1	8.8	17.0	**5.6**	7.6	12.5
▲ Independent Bank	Grand Rapids	MI	**B+**	B	B-	4459.5	10.33	9.7	11.7	20.3	29.8	**6.7**	8.7	13.7
Independent Bank	Memphis	TN	**B+**	B	B-	1203.2	3.11	8.8	39.2	1.9	0.3	**8.0**	11.4	13.4
Independent Bank	McKinney	TX	**A-**	A-	B+	18442.2	8.60	10.5	0.4	7.0	8.5	**9.4**	10.8	14.5
Independent Farmers Bank	Maysville	MO	**B+**	B+	B	147.8	12.96	6.5	2.8	9.7	52.4	**6.7**	8.7	17.6
Industrial & Commerc. Bank of China (USA	New York	NY	**B-**	B-	B	2999.7	3.93	27.5	0.0	13.2	0.4	**10.0**	13.6	16.4
Industrial Bank	Washington	DC	**C-**	D+	C-	592.2	-1.27	5.9	0.1	15.8	29.7	**8.3**	9.9	18.9
Industry State Bank	Industry	TX	**A-**	A-	B+	965.9	3.42	3.7	1.1	4.6	74.2	**10.0**	11.0	25.0
▲ Infinity Bank (Santa Ana, CA)	Santa Ana	CA	**C-**	D	D	204.3	13.49	40.3	2.2	3.0	6.2	**10.0**	13.0	16.4
InFirst Bank	Indiana	PA	**C+**	C+	B-	464.1	2.36	7.5	1.3	54.1	5.2	**8.0**	9.6	15.1
Inland Bank and Trust	Oak Brook	IL	**A-**	B+	B	1287.4	6.63	9.3	0.1	11.8	17.9	**10.0**	12.9	16.0
InsBank	Nashville	TN	**C+**	B-	B	658.0	11.21	24.6	1.3	6.1	2.5	**7.9**	10.4	13.3
INSOUTH Bank	Brownsville	TN	**B-**	B-	B	418.9	12.22	16.1	2.2	17.1	11.8	**4.9**	9.3	0.0
Institution for Savings	Newburyport	MA	**B**	B	A-	4230.2	8.81	0.7	0.2	55.1	4.9	**10.0**	11.9	15.7
▲ Integrity Bank & Trust	Monument	CO	**B+**	B	B	304.1	18.31	6.3	0.7	16.9	15.2	**6.3**	8.3	15.6
Integrity Bank for Business	Virginia Beach	VA	**U**			25.6	na	0.0	0.0	0.0	0.0	**9.8**	140.	0.0
Integrity Bank Plus	Wabasso	MN	**D+**	D+	C+	85.7	16.62	11.9	1.0	5.8	27.4	**8.0**	9.7	16.4

Arrows denote recent upgrades ▲ or downgrades ▼

Asset Quality Index	Adjusted Non-Performing Loans as a % of Total Loans	Adjusted Non-Performing Loans as a % of Capital	Net Charge-Offs Avg Loans	Profitability Index	Net Income ($Mil)	Return on Assets (R.O.A.)	Return on Equity (R.O.E.)	Net Interest Spread	Overhead Efficiency Ratio	Liquidity Index	Liquidity Ratio	Hot Money Ratio	Stability Index
8.8	0.09	0.4	0.00	**6.5**	4.9	1.23	10.78	3.58	56.9	**4.1**	44.6	15.7	**8.0**
5.0	0.92	6.3	-0.01	**4.8**	0.5	1.28	13.67	3.00	60.7	**2.8**	28.2	17.1	**5.2**
4.8	1.42	7.5	-0.01	**4.5**	1.4	0.87	9.60	2.93	65.3	**5.3**	38.6	7.5	**6.4**
6.2	0.84	4.4	-0.04	**2.2**	0.8	0.04	0.40	3.02	106.6	**4.1**	10.8	8.0	**8.2**
7.4	2.22	3.9	0.00	**1.9**	0.0	-0.03	-0.10	2.47	99.4	**2.2**	48.3	49.5	**6.8**
7.9	0.17	1.2	-0.03	**7.6**	2.8	1.75	20.84	3.77	54.0	**5.0**	23.8	3.2	**4.7**
5.2	1.54	5.7	0.03	**3.8**	1.2	0.92	11.14	3.70	78.2	**5.5**	35.1	4.2	**4.5**
4.6	0.95	7.8	0.46	**8.5**	1.9	1.55	12.81	4.32	42.3	**0.7**	16.4	42.8	**8.1**
4.2	3.16	15.8	-0.03	**6.3**	8.0	1.39	15.20	3.32	61.3	**5.5**	27.3	4.3	**9.0**
5.8	0.63	2.9	0.01	**6.6**	44.9	1.50	13.12	3.32	56.2	**5.3**	27.7	6.3	**9.6**
6.8	0.47	2.3	0.30	**9.8**	3.7	2.05	14.75	4.06	34.5	**0.6**	7.4	26.1	**9.4**
8.6	0.15	0.9	0.03	**8.1**	15.3	1.71	23.71	3.58	52.0	**5.8**	43.4	4.9	**8.5**
7.1	0.67	2.2	0.00	**5.1**	2.9	1.10	14.08	3.38	64.4	**5.3**	43.2	9.4	**5.4**
8.4	0.02	1.4	0.00	**4.3**	0.7	0.85	7.60	3.21	68.8	**4.6**	33.4	8.2	**6.8**
6.3	0.12	0.7	0.00	**7.7**	1.6	1.52	12.04	4.11	49.9	**4.3**	16.1	6.5	**8.2**
5.3	0.84	6.1	0.20	**3.9**	14.7	1.14	9.08	3.46	53.8	**1.4**	9.2	15.5	**7.2**
8.9	0.04	0.1	-0.03	**6.5**	0.5	1.64	15.47	4.33	57.4	**5.7**	35.8	3.7	**5.6**
8.7	1.27	3.1	0.04	**1.9**	0.5	0.18	1.07	2.05	94.4	**4.0**	67.1	23.3	**7.8**
6.3	3.55	7.9	0.39	**2.5**	585.0	0.59	5.41	1.18	83.3	**5.3**	71.1	5.5	**7.9**
10.0	na	0.0	na	**8.6**	0.5	1.71	1.73	0.27	46.7	**4.0**	na	0.0	**4.3**
7.6	1.64	5.5	0.00	**3.3**	0.0	0.45	1.97	3.03	74.4	**1.4**	24.9	27.6	**7.9**
5.7	0.69	6.1	0.09	**4.3**	2.7	0.86	13.90	2.25	71.9	**4.4**	21.5	6.8	**4.2**
10.0	0.56	1.6	0.03	**2.2**	0.9	0.32	1.98	2.15	79.7	**3.8**	63.9	24.8	**8.3**
5.0	2.09	8.1	-0.06	**5.0**	1.5	1.12	10.65	3.56	65.1	**6.1**	43.1	3.6	**6.9**
6.1	2.64	7.3	-0.28	**3.7**	0.3	0.73	5.24	2.97	72.9	**5.1**	53.0	11.6	**6.8**
8.4	0.12	0.5	0.00	**4.7**	1.0	0.95	10.89	3.36	61.7	**4.0**	28.2	10.9	**5.4**
5.5	6.15	14.0	-0.01	**4.7**	0.3	0.85	5.52	3.31	65.5	**3.9**	46.9	14.6	**7.7**
6.8	0.32	2.8	0.02	**4.1**	0.7	0.97	10.13	3.54	75.2	**2.2**	27.2	20.0	**5.9**
5.1	1.90	11.4	0.17	**3.6**	1.2	0.92	10.02	3.96	67.9	**0.9**	20.6	24.1	**5.2**
8.3	0.00	0.0	0.03	**4.7**	0.8	0.90	8.28	3.53	73.9	**5.0**	29.1	4.9	**6.2**
8.0	0.00	0.0	0.01	**4.0**	3.3	0.81	17.64	2.91	56.6	**4.0**	19.4	8.3	**4.0**
8.6	0.00	0.0	0.00	**4.2**	1.0	0.99	8.93	3.12	76.3	**6.5**	44.7	1.6	**7.1**
7.9	0.35	0.7	0.00	**5.4**	1.1	1.46	10.10	3.17	50.7	**4.7**	33.1	4.7	**8.3**
8.1	0.23	1.0	0.02	**6.3**	12.6	1.57	16.81	3.27	53.7	**6.5**	37.9	2.6	**7.1**
6.9	0.58	2.7	-0.01	**3.9**	0.7	0.91	9.38	3.07	70.2	**4.0**	35.7	13.4	**6.1**
6.6	0.80	5.3	-0.01	**4.3**	8.5	1.10	13.88	2.60	70.6	**4.2**	33.2	2.6	**7.4**
5.2	1.09	3.7	-0.01	**2.6**	1.7	0.49	4.71	3.87	81.1	**3.7**	26.8	11.9	**6.3**
6.6	0.45	2.3	0.14	**6.7**	1.6	1.58	16.67	4.82	65.5	**4.1**	16.5	8.2	**5.8**
5.2	0.90	5.2	0.04	**7.3**	16.0	1.87	21.82	3.95	59.8	**4.6**	23.1	7.3	**8.6**
6.5	1.62	4.6	0.00	**9.7**	9.0	1.78	15.19	3.88	39.5	**1.6**	23.4	11.2	**10.0**
7.2	1.37	3.9	-0.01	**3.6**	0.7	0.66	5.18	2.72	68.3	**1.1**	26.8	38.2	**7.4**
6.2	2.02	3.1	3.10	**5.7**	0.2	0.69	2.37	4.00	83.9	**2.4**	55.7	47.6	**7.5**
9.9	0.14	0.8	0.02	**6.0**	24.8	1.63	21.10	3.44	54.6	**4.4**	16.2	3.0	**7.8**
4.6	0.88	10.7	0.00	**4.2**	0.4	0.86	10.43	3.66	71.3	**4.4**	34.3	11.3	**4.1**
5.4	1.60	5.4	-0.05	**7.3**	35.1	1.62	16.93	3.13	61.0	**6.0**	34.4	4.9	**9.0**
5.6	0.49	3.3	0.10	**6.6**	8.0	1.32	10.84	4.40	65.5	**2.7**	11.9	11.9	**9.3**
6.4	0.41	1.6	0.07	**7.5**	130.4	1.45	9.10	3.32	48.3	**3.7**	22.3	6.5	**10.0**
7.2	0.64	2.3	0.04	**5.3**	0.7	0.98	10.01	3.59	66.9	**4.1**	36.9	13.7	**5.8**
3.5	1.83	11.2	0.00	**2.9**	8.0	0.54	4.01	2.64	72.6	**0.4**	9.9	42.9	**7.7**
2.4	3.15	19.7	-0.03	**5.3**	2.8	0.96	10.88	3.81	74.3	**4.6**	35.6	10.5	**6.3**
9.5	0.35	0.5	0.11	**6.7**	8.5	1.82	14.31	2.87	50.2	**3.1**	62.9	35.9	**8.7**
6.8	0.67	3.7	0.00	**2.1**	0.6	0.55	4.24	3.93	76.9	**5.4**	20.9	0.0	**3.8**
4.6	1.63	13.5	0.11	**3.7**	1.4	0.60	6.15	3.86	73.9	**2.1**	11.8	18.3	**6.1**
4.9	2.10	8.3	0.06	**5.9**	8.4	1.31	10.20	2.95	69.0	**2.9**	21.5	16.1	**9.7**
4.2	0.55	4.0	0.44	**4.8**	3.2	0.98	9.58	3.04	51.1	**0.8**	15.1	37.3	**6.7**
5.4	0.33	5.0	-0.28	**8.1**	3.9	1.95	21.12	4.59	58.4	**3.3**	7.4	12.0	**5.5**
9.6	0.10	0.4	0.00	**7.3**	50.1	2.45	20.87	2.09	56.3	**2.2**	27.3	27.2	**9.8**
8.9	0.12	0.8	0.00	**7.0**	2.1	1.42	17.06	4.21	60.8	**5.5**	31.7	3.2	**5.4**
10.0	na	0.0	na	**0.0**	-0.9	-36.04	-8.27	0.41	9988.9	**4.0**	na	0.0	**1.3**
1.7	6.70	31.0	0.00	**7.1**	0.7	1.74	16.91	5.37	63.1	**4.5**	29.3	8.7	**7.3**

Name	City	State	Rating	2020 Rating	2019 Rating	Total Assets ($Mil)	One Year Asset Growth	Asset Mix (As a % of Total Assets) Commercial Loans	Consumer Loans	Mortgage Loans	Securities	Capitalization Index	Leverage Ratio	Risk-Based Capital Ratio
Interamerican Bank, A FSB	Miami	FL	**C+**	C+	C	259.8	19.76	0.2	0.2	20.4	0.0	**10.0**	11.5	21.2
Interaudi Bank	New York	NY	**B**	B+	B+	2294.9	10.26	7.7	0.2	17.7	15.3	**6.0**	8.1	23.3
InterBank	Oklahoma City	OK	**C**	C-	C-	3656.4	-0.77	21.0	0.5	4.7	0.0	**7.3**	11.6	0.0
Intercity State Bank	Schofield	WI	**A**	A	A	242.1	18.99	9.7	0.9	18.1	10.6	**10.0**	19.0	27.5
▼ Intercredit Bank, N.A.	Miami	FL	**D**	D+	D+	421.4	11.47	12.6	1.2	24.0	14.9	**8.4**	10.2	0.0
▼ International Bank of Chicago	Chicago	IL	**C**	C+	B-	866.9	16.88	12.1	0.0	20.6	18.4	**8.6**	10.1	18.5
International Bank of Commerce	Oklahoma City	OK	**A-**	A-	A-	1903.7	13.85	13.2	0.1	0.8	42.6	**10.0**	11.8	19.1
International Bank of Commerce	Brownsville	TX	**A**	A	A	1497.6	19.64	13.7	0.3	2.5	47.5	**10.0**	13.8	26.0
International Bank of Commerce	Laredo	TX	**A**	A	A	10810.4	10.51	11.3	0.4	6.5	24.3	**10.0**	11.9	19.1
International Bank of Commerce	Zapata	TX	**A**	A	A	468.8	8.11	4.8	1.1	13.8	60.6	**10.0**	15.8	42.3
▲ International City Bank	Long Beach	CA	**B-**	C+	B+	504.5	16.48	4.9	0.0	2.4	50.5	**6.9**	9.0	22.0
International Finance Bank	Miami	FL	**C+**	C	C+	926.9	15.10	26.5	2.2	16.6	5.8	**6.1**	8.1	12.6
Interstate Bank	Perryton	TX	**C+**	C+	B	210.8	8.04	21.4	0.7	7.1	36.9	**7.8**	9.6	0.0
Interstate Federal S&L Assn.	McGregor	IA	**D+**	C-	C-	8.2	-4.23	0.0	0.4	65.1	0.0	**10.0**	20.9	50.3
Intracoastal Bank	Palm Coast	FL	**B+**	B+	B	527.3	17.75	5.6	0.1	1.0	25.7	**6.4**	8.4	13.4
INTRUST Bank, N.A.	Wichita	KS	**B-**	B-	B	7272.7	-0.98	19.8	3.5	2.2	33.1	**5.3**	7.3	12.2
▲ Investar Bank, N.A.	Baton Rouge	LA	**B**	B-	B	2671.1	13.34	13.7	0.8	12.4	10.5	**7.7**	9.5	13.1
Investment Savings Bank	Altoona	PA	**C**	C	C+	109.1	2.88	0.4	0.7	32.7	43.9	**10.0**	20.1	0.0
Investors Bank	Short Hills	NJ	**B**	B-	B	26765.4	-1.49	5.1	1.7	15.1	14.1	**7.5**	9.4	12.9
Investors Community Bank	Chillicothe	MO	**A-**	A-	B+	83.0	11.24	1.5	3.4	14.6	58.0	**10.0**	14.2	38.3
Investors Community Bank	Manitowoc	WI	**B-**	B-	B-	1513.7	0.22	6.5	0.0	0.8	23.1	**10.0**	13.9	16.6
Inwood National Bank	Dallas	TX	**A-**	A-	A-	3883.7	12.99	3.9	0.1	7.8	42.5	**6.9**	8.9	0.0
▲ Ion Bank	Naugatuck	CT	**B-**	C	B-	1772.1	9.02	14.2	9.0	15.7	6.3	**7.1**	9.0	14.9
Iowa Falls State Bank	Iowa Falls	IA	**B-**	B-	B-	154.2	9.75	11.4	1.7	12.3	44.3	**10.0**	11.1	0.0
▲ Iowa Prairie Bank	Brunsville	IA	**D**	D-	D	69.2	-3.83	8.7	2.0	0.5	55.1	**5.0**	7.0	17.8
Iowa Savings Bank	Carroll	IA	**B**	B	B	251.4	13.04	13.8	0.6	5.0	20.0	**5.4**	8.2	0.0
Iowa State Bank	Algona	IA	**B+**	B+	A-	401.0	18.53	6.7	1.1	7.8	24.0	**9.3**	10.6	19.7
Iowa State Bank	Clarksville	IA	**D-**	D-	D-	424.0	7.27	10.3	0.6	2.5	19.4	**6.5**	8.5	14.9
Iowa State Bank	Des Moines	IA	**A**	A	A	464.6	7.57	6.2	0.2	10.5	29.7	**10.0**	12.6	0.0
Iowa State Bank	Hull	IA	**A**	A-	A-	751.2	8.62	5.3	0.8	2.8	24.2	**10.0**	12.9	0.0
Iowa State Bank	Sac City	IA	**A**	A	A-	172.4	14.47	8.1	4.8	19.9	11.4	**8.8**	10.2	0.0
Iowa State Bank and Trust Co.	Fairfield	IA	**B**	B	B	173.8	11.58	9.6	2.1	18.7	4.6	**7.2**	9.1	13.9
Iowa State Savings Bank	Creston	IA	**B-**	B-	C	251.5	7.03	2.6	1.1	9.0	29.2	**7.1**	9.1	0.0
Iowa Trust & Savings Bank	Emmetsburg	IA	**A-**	A-	B+	371.9	4.52	3.3	0.4	6.5	22.7	**10.0**	12.4	16.0
Iowa Trust and Savings Bank	Centerville	IA	**A**	A	A	232.1	17.29	6.0	1.4	4.2	45.7	**7.7**	9.4	0.0
Ipava State Bank	Ipava	IL	**B+**	B+	B+	205.0	13.54	9.6	2.5	15.8	17.5	**5.4**	7.4	17.1
Ipswich State Bank	Ipswich	SD	**B+**	B+	B	66.7	9.81	4.5	0.7	0.0	33.2	**10.0**	14.1	28.4
Ireland Bank	Malad City	ID	**B+**	B+	B+	336.0	17.23	13.9	0.9	4.4	36.0	**7.5**	9.4	20.3
Iron Workers Savings Bank	Aston	PA	**C-**	C-	C	203.8	7.29	0.3	0.0	41.5	18.5	**7.0**	9.0	0.0
Iroquois Farmers State Bank	Iroquois	IL	**B-**	B-	B-	147.7	21.44	3.6	2.3	8.5	25.8	**5.6**	7.6	13.4
Iroquois Federal S&L Assn.	Watseka	IL	**B-**	B-	B-	797.3	8.41	10.0	1.0	14.8	23.8	**9.2**	10.5	0.0
Isabella Bank	Mount Pleasant	MI	**B-**	B-	B-	1982.7	6.42	9.5	3.8	16.3	22.6	**6.3**	8.3	14.3
Israel Discount Bank of New York	New York	NY	**C+**	B-	B+	11431.0	10.60	26.2	0.2	0.5	24.5	**8.6**	10.0	14.9
Itasca Bank & Trust Co.	Itasca	IL	**B**	B	B+	732.3	6.80	26.1	0.1	8.9	29.2	**5.7**	8.6	0.0
ITS Bank	Johnston	IA	**U**	U	U	9.0	6.01	0.0	0.0	0.0	28.9	**10.0**	94.2	0.0
▲ Ixonia Bank	Ixonia	WI	**B+**	B-	B-	546.7	13.89	18.6	0.1	16.1	13.9	**9.2**	10.5	16.9
Jackson County Bank	Seymour	IN	**B-**	B-	B-	730.6	6.90	6.0	0.8	19.9	15.1	**6.7**	8.7	12.8
Jackson County Bank	McKee	KY	**A**	A	A	166.0	8.29	2.5	8.6	16.6	30.3	**10.0**	23.7	0.0
Jackson County Bank	Black River Falls	WI	**D+**	D	D-	200.1	-2.90	0.2	0.6	9.2	33.9	**7.5**	9.3	23.1
▼ Jackson Federal S&L Assn.	Jackson	MN	**C-**	C	C	41.1	7.70	4.9	1.8	24.5	51.4	**10.0**	22.4	41.5
Jackson Parish Bank	Jonesboro	LA	**B-**	B-	B-	72.8	3.19	4.2	4.6	11.8	65.3	**10.0**	15.1	0.0
Jackson Savings Bank, SSB	Sylva	NC	**C-**	C-	B-	35.4	2.02	0.0	0.4	46.0	0.0	**10.0**	19.3	47.7
James Polk Stone Community Bank	Portales	NM	**B+**	A-	A-	301.7	11.66	7.8	3.3	17.0	38.3	**6.9**	9.0	0.0
Janesville State Bank	Janesville	MN	**A-**	A-	B+	87.0	8.95	4.8	2.3	18.7	21.4	**10.0**	11.7	0.0
Jarrettsville Federal S&L Assn.	Jarrettsville	MD	**C**	C	C+	133.2	8.57	4.0	0.0	41.7	10.4	**10.0**	14.1	0.0
JD Bank	Jennings	LA	**B**	B	B+	1360.4	33.02	9.4	2.3	11.8	36.0	**5.8**	7.8	15.6
▼ Jeff Bank	Jeffersonville	NY	**C+**	B-	B+	668.5	15.60	4.7	0.3	16.5	25.9	**8.1**	9.7	0.0
Jefferson Bank	San Antonio	TX	**B+**	B+	B+	2535.3	17.39	6.7	1.0	16.1	26.9	**6.6**	8.6	15.5
Jefferson Bank and Trust Co.	Saint Louis	MO	**B**	B	B	697.2	2.14	14.5	1.4	4.5	16.9	**9.1**	10.6	14.3
Jefferson Bank of Missouri	Jefferson City	MO	**B+**	B+	B+	825.1	7.91	13.3	18.8	18.5	12.0	**6.9**	8.9	14.7

Asset Quality Index	Adjusted Non-Performing Loans as a % of Total Loans	Adjusted Non-Performing Loans as a % of Capital	Net Charge-Offs Avg Loans	Profitability Index	Net Income ($Mil)	Return on Assets (R.O.A.)	Return on Equity (R.O.E.)	Net Interest Spread	Overhead Efficiency Ratio	Liquidity Index	Liquidity Ratio	Hot Money Ratio	Stability Index
3.9	5.31	19.5	-0.32	**3.0**	0.5	0.38	3.26	3.14	93.0	**5.1**	41.0	9.4	**7.4**
7.6	0.88	4.7	0.00	**4.2**	6.1	0.55	6.71	1.64	66.1	**3.3**	61.4	34.7	**6.1**
4.6	0.95	6.8	0.00	**8.3**	40.6	2.23	16.48	3.87	45.2	**4.5**	19.6	6.9	**10.0**
7.1	0.82	2.9	0.05	**9.2**	2.0	1.66	8.80	3.35	41.8	**4.4**	33.9	11.1	**9.0**
3.9	1.89	13.1	-0.06	**0.8**	-0.1	-0.03	-0.24	3.07	102.4	**0.9**	21.4	27.3	**6.1**
2.0	3.98	23.3	-0.08	**6.1**	7.7	1.85	17.45	3.45	51.2	**1.5**	26.6	21.5	**7.1**
8.3	0.02	0.1	0.19	**3.5**	4.6	0.52	3.64	2.52	76.1	**5.1**	23.8	4.9	**7.0**
7.9	0.06	0.2	0.07	**9.5**	13.2	1.86	13.16	3.06	41.1	**4.5**	54.5	17.9	**9.3**
8.2	0.09	0.9	0.07	**7.3**	73.6	1.33	9.42	2.69	50.9	**4.8**	37.6	12.9	**9.5**
9.2	0.29	0.8	0.41	**4.4**	1.8	0.79	4.62	2.33	71.3	**4.4**	65.2	18.6	**8.3**
10.0	0.01	0.0	0.00	**5.2**	6.4	2.63	19.37	2.92	45.3	**2.2**	43.1	19.7	**6.6**
3.5	1.60	13.6	0.03	**4.2**	3.6	0.82	10.03	2.92	62.9	**2.7**	24.3	16.3	**4.9**
3.2	4.58	17.3	-0.02	**3.6**	0.5	0.47	4.85	3.15	79.2	**4.0**	47.4	17.0	**4.6**
10.0	0.63	1.0	0.00	**0.8**	0.0	-0.27	-1.27	2.89	107.2	**2.8**	37.6	17.8	**7.4**
7.3	0.88	2.9	0.00	**6.7**	3.9	1.56	18.18	3.41	53.6	**5.3**	48.0	10.4	**7.3**
4.8	3.28	12.3	0.39	**4.5**	30.8	0.85	12.54	2.71	60.5	**4.2**	26.2	6.1	**6.0**
5.4	1.02	6.6	0.05	**4.6**	12.4	0.99	8.75	3.65	70.1	**1.9**	18.1	15.7	**8.3**
10.0	0.00	0.0	0.00	**1.9**	0.1	0.20	0.99	2.35	89.6	**5.3**	61.8	13.8	**7.1**
6.3	0.41	3.0	-0.02	**5.4**	151.9	1.17	12.26	3.00	51.9	**3.6**	11.0	6.5	**9.0**
9.4	0.38	0.8	-0.01	**5.7**	0.6	1.45	10.23	3.56	59.4	**6.6**	74.0	5.6	**7.8**
3.8	3.71	12.6	-0.14	**7.5**	13.1	1.75	12.80	3.49	54.7	**2.4**	29.7	15.1	**9.8**
8.8	0.03	0.2	0.00	**7.7**	32.9	1.78	18.11	2.86	41.0	**5.7**	44.3	9.8	**9.4**
4.2	2.08	13.3	0.01	**4.2**	7.7	0.88	11.19	2.85	72.9	**5.8**	30.0	4.0	**6.6**
6.6	1.31	5.8	-0.02	**6.5**	1.4	1.76	15.10	4.19	54.6	**5.8**	54.8	9.7	**6.0**
6.6	0.67	2.7	-0.01	**1.3**	0.1	0.39	5.78	2.83	86.6	**5.2**	42.6	9.1	**1.3**
7.8	0.19	1.3	0.00	**6.8**	2.1	1.68	20.27	3.09	51.7	**5.6**	38.2	4.5	**6.1**
4.8	2.19	7.1	0.99	**6.1**	2.4	1.24	10.52	4.06	53.0	**3.8**	26.6	11.6	**7.5**
0.3	10.01	52.3	0.01	**3.7**	2.0	0.96	11.22	1.90	50.3	**2.4**	44.6	23.6	**4.0**
9.2	0.31	1.0	-0.05	**6.1**	3.4	1.49	9.86	2.95	61.3	**6.3**	52.5	5.5	**9.7**
7.1	0.71	5.7	0.00	**8.4**	6.3	1.72	12.85	3.72	47.6	**5.1**	34.7	6.7	**9.5**
8.1	0.04	0.2	-0.02	**9.0**	1.9	2.18	19.67	3.70	39.2	**3.9**	28.2	11.5	**9.2**
6.0	1.03	5.1	0.00	**6.5**	1.3	1.52	16.71	4.30	52.3	**3.7**	24.5	11.6	**5.4**
7.7	0.28	1.3	0.00	**3.6**	1.1	0.89	8.24	3.14	63.4	**5.0**	32.5	6.6	**6.5**
8.2	0.00	0.3	-0.01	**7.1**	3.1	1.67	11.57	4.00	53.3	**1.7**	21.6	21.1	**9.0**
9.3	0.00	0.0	0.00	**7.4**	2.2	1.95	17.95	3.48	45.4	**5.2**	44.8	10.4	**7.6**
8.9	0.00	0.0	-0.03	**7.1**	2.0	1.99	26.78	2.93	55.6	**4.6**	36.5	10.8	**5.3**
9.0	0.00	0.0	0.00	**4.8**	0.4	1.11	7.58	2.06	59.3	**3.4**	54.9	21.8	**8.3**
7.0	0.94	2.5	-0.15	**4.9**	1.4	0.92	9.60	3.51	71.7	**6.4**	48.6	3.7	**5.6**
8.9	0.10	0.8	0.00	**1.7**	0.1	0.09	1.05	2.81	95.9	**3.0**	29.4	16.3	**4.8**
5.7	0.83	5.3	0.06	**4.6**	0.9	1.20	15.89	3.15	57.7	**5.1**	35.1	6.9	**3.6**
8.6	0.22	0.8	0.17	**3.8**	2.6	0.71	6.37	2.87	69.1	**1.9**	22.1	19.1	**6.4**
5.2	2.49	9.2	-0.02	**4.8**	10.9	1.12	12.94	2.87	62.3	**4.8**	31.6	11.4	**6.8**
7.2	0.68	3.6	0.19	**3.6**	35.1	0.63	6.13	2.37	68.9	**2.8**	31.4	11.2	**7.5**
7.1	0.59	2.1	-0.11	**6.2**	4.3	1.19	13.55	3.47	56.6	**2.3**	30.8	20.8	**6.7**
10.0	na	0.0	na	**10.0**	0.3	6.12	6.53	5.45	9.7	**4.0**	na	100.0	**5.8**
8.7	0.01	0.0	-0.13	**7.8**	3.9	1.45	13.43	4.53	87.0	**3.2**	40.1	15.8	**8.8**
5.0	1.30	6.1	-0.06	**5.1**	4.5	1.23	13.39	3.18	68.8	**4.5**	26.3	7.4	**6.9**
8.7	0.82	0.9	0.01	**7.6**	1.3	1.56	6.48	3.63	51.3	**5.2**	56.1	12.9	**8.4**
5.0	9.51	17.5	-0.03	**4.1**	0.6	0.58	6.06	1.86	76.8	**3.8**	56.8	10.0	**6.8**
9.7	0.00	0.0	0.03	**1.4**	0.1	0.23	1.01	2.31	102.2	**3.7**	38.9	16.3	**6.9**
8.8	1.10	2.0	0.46	**3.3**	0.2	0.60	3.85	2.20	82.5	**5.7**	51.6	8.2	**6.1**
7.6	0.69	5.4	0.00	**1.7**	0.0	-0.04	-0.20	2.00	102.1	**2.4**	55.1	45.4	**7.5**
5.2	2.51	9.4	0.74	**6.5**	2.2	1.47	15.41	4.28	68.3	**6.0**	36.0	1.5	**6.5**
8.7	0.00	0.0	0.00	**6.8**	0.7	1.57	13.40	3.44	53.3	**4.2**	19.8	8.2	**9.3**
6.8	2.26	8.3	-0.06	**2.2**	0.1	0.18	1.27	2.13	95.3	**3.2**	47.6	22.2	**7.5**
6.2	0.91	4.6	0.16	**4.1**	5.1	0.77	9.26	2.99	72.4	**6.6**	53.2	6.5	**7.3**
2.7	4.91	20.8	0.00	**4.4**	2.7	0.83	8.56	3.06	70.0	**6.3**	48.8	4.2	**6.3**
7.4	0.74	4.0	0.02	**4.5**	12.3	1.02	13.10	2.91	71.2	**5.7**	46.5	10.8	**7.8**
6.4	0.18	1.1	3.24	**2.8**	0.5	0.14	1.29	2.78	52.6	**2.3**	17.1	17.6	**8.0**
6.1	0.27	1.8	0.03	**10.0**	8.8	2.24	24.79	3.88	40.7	**4.0**	22.9	8.1	**7.8**

Name	City	State	Rating	2020 Rating	2019 Rating	Total Assets ($Mil)	One Year Asset Growth	Asset Mix (As a % of Total Assets): Commercial Loans	Consumer Loans	Mortgage Loans	Securities	Capitalization Index	Leverage Ratio	Risk-Based Capital Ratio
Jefferson Security Bank	Shepherdstown	WV	**B-**	B-	B-	414.3	18.27	5.5	0.8	31.1	34.4	**6.3**	8.3	16.6
Jersey Shore State Bank	Williamsport	PA	**B-**	B-	B-	1307.4	-1.50	4.0	10.2	17.5	10.5	**4.3**	8.1	10.7
Jersey State Bank	Jerseyville	IL	**B**	B	B+	183.8	5.24	7.0	0.5	5.2	42.5	**10.0**	12.2	0.0
Jewett City Savings Bank	Jewett City	CT	**B-**	B-	B	387.6	13.43	11.8	0.7	34.1	7.6	**10.0**	13.4	21.0
Jim Thorpe Neighborhood Bank	Jim Thorpe	PA	**C+**	C+	C+	225.8	12.54	3.1	0.7	20.3	30.0	**7.5**	9.3	20.8
John Deere Financial, F.S.B.	Madison	WI	**A-**	A-	A-	3621.2	-5.07	4.1	16.3	0.0	0.0	**10.0**	20.8	0.0
John Marshall Bank	Reston	VA	**B+**	B+	B+	2064.0	14.56	6.6	0.1	13.3	14.5	**9.6**	10.7	15.0
Johnson Bank	Racine	WI	**A**	A	A-	5734.7	-7.64	16.8	1.4	14.2	10.9	**10.0**	12.6	19.4
▼ Johnson City Bank	Johnson City	TX	**B**	B+	A-	152.4	18.93	9.5	5.6	21.3	10.8	**8.3**	9.8	0.0
▲ Johnson County Bank	Mountain City	TN	**A-**	B	B	146.8	9.80	2.9	3.6	28.4	34.6	**10.0**	14.6	0.0
Johnson State Bank	Johnson	KS	**B**	B-	B	92.4	2.56	7.0	1.3	4.0	50.0	**10.0**	15.0	0.0
Jonah Bank of Wyoming	Casper	WY	**A-**	B+	B	479.7	8.20	16.7	0.3	7.4	9.7	**8.3**	9.9	0.0
Jones Bank	Seward	NE	**A-**	A-	B+	380.4	8.31	8.7	1.1	5.8	46.5	**8.6**	10.1	0.0
Jonesboro State Bank	Jonesboro	LA	**B+**	B+	A-	495.2	33.51	2.1	6.5	2.4	82.1	**8.7**	10.1	24.2
Jonesburg State Bank	Jonesburg	MO	**B**	B	B	127.7	14.22	7.8	1.5	18.8	2.0	**5.3**	7.3	16.2
▲ Jonestown Bank & Trust Co.	Jonestown	PA	**C**			800.0	12.73	3.5	27.8	16.3	3.4	**5.9**	8.2	0.0
JPMorgan Chase Bank, Dearborn	Dearborn	MI	**U**	U	U	61.7	0.12	0.0	0.0	0.0	0.0	**10.0**	99.3	510.6
JPMorgan Chase Bank, N.A.	Columbus	OH	**B**	B	B+	3190100.0	13.04	5.9	6.4	7.1	18.0	**5.9**	7.9	17.7
▼ Junction National Bank	Junction	TX	**B-**	B	B	87.5	9.99	4.5	1.6	6.9	63.5	**6.3**	8.3	29.3
▼ Kahoka State Bank	Kahoka	MO	**C+**	B-	B-	64.1	12.21	4.6	4.0	22.3	25.1	**6.8**	8.8	0.0
Kalamazoo County State Bank	Schoolcraft	MI	**C**	C	C+	122.5	9.45	6.2	10.1	12.8	49.0	**8.7**	10.2	22.1
Kansas State Bank	Ottawa	KS	**B+**	B+	B+	181.0	12.24	6.9	1.4	13.1	48.0	**6.2**	8.2	0.0
▲ Kansas State Bank	Overbrook	KS	**A-**	B	B+	83.4	16.37	9.4	3.0	6.2	51.2	**10.0**	11.8	21.3
KansasLand Bank	Quinter	KS	**D+**	D+	C-	54.2	1.46	5.5	1.6	7.6	29.2	**7.2**	9.2	23.6
Kanza Bank	Kingman	KS	**C+**	C+	B-	280.7	5.95	5.5	0.6	19.0	21.9	**6.4**	8.4	0.0
Katahdin Trust Co.	Patten	ME	**B**	B	B-	947.4	-3.46	17.0	0.6	18.4	11.7	**8.3**	9.8	15.0
Kaw Valley Bank	Topeka	KS	**C+**	C+	B-	329.6	-3.31	15.7	2.0	18.5	4.4	**8.6**	10.7	0.0
Kaw Valley State Bank	Eudora	KS	**C+**	C+	B-	72.9	24.15	4.0	3.3	13.9	50.3	**6.0**	8.0	21.1
Kearney Trust Co.	Kearney	MO	**B+**	B+	A-	268.6	13.42	6.0	2.4	11.5	30.9	**6.6**	8.6	17.2
▲ Kearny Bank	Fairfield	NJ	**B**	B-	B-	7264.7	7.86	2.3	0.0	20.3	23.4	**8.9**	10.2	17.2
Kearny County Bank	Lakin	KS	**A**	A	A-	253.2	5.30	18.1	2.1	11.0	33.2	**10.0**	15.3	0.0
KEB Hana Bank USA, N.A.	New York	NY	**D**	D	D	284.3	25.66	17.4	0.0	2.0	7.1	**10.0**	12.8	24.9
▼ Kendall Bank	Overland Park	KS	**D+**	D+	C-	92.9	104.06	28.6	1.3	4.7	0.0	**10.0**	11.2	17.3
▲ Kennebec Savings Bank	Augusta	ME	**A**	A-	A-	1363.8	11.67	3.8	0.2	57.2	7.6	**10.0**	14.2	0.0
Kennebunk Savings Bank	Kennebunk	ME	**B-**	B-	B	1723.0	17.51	6.9	0.1	18.9	16.5	**8.3**	10.0	0.0
Kennett Trust Bank	Kennett	MO	**B-**	B-	B	119.6	14.51	10.6	3.2	30.4	27.5	**10.0**	11.0	0.0
Kensington Bank	Kensington	MN	**C+**	C	C-	335.8	10.91	10.2	1.7	6.3	20.1	**5.8**	7.9	11.6
▼ Kentland Bank	Kentland	IN	**A-**	A	A	346.1	4.71	10.1	1.0	6.7	27.7	**10.0**	12.9	21.0
Kentland Federal S&L Assn.	Kentland	IN	**D**	D	D	3.4	-12.18	2.2	0.0	81.6	1.2	**10.0**	14.8	0.0
Kentucky Farmers Bank Corp.	Ashland	KY	**A**	A	A	263.7	15.50	5.3	3.3	23.1	33.8	**10.0**	16.7	28.2
Kerndt Brothers Savings Bank	Lansing	IA	**C+**	C+	B-	332.5	6.48	9.9	1.1	6.7	28.6	**7.8**	9.5	15.5
Key Community Bank	Inver Grove Heights	MN	**C+**	C+	C+	70.0	12.68	16.1	2.7	6.6	0.0	**7.0**	9.0	0.0
Key National Trust Co. of Delaware	Wilmington	DE	**U**	U	U	5.5	12.71	0.0	0.0	0.0	0.0	**10.0**	95.7	447.3
▲ KeyBank N.A.	Cleveland	OH	**B+**	B	B	178935.7	5.38	22.8	5.8	9.4	23.0	**6.5**	8.6	12.9
KeySavings Bank	Wisconsin Rapids	WI	**C-**	C-	C-	91.4	2.54	0.5	0.9	38.8	33.9	**10.0**	12.5	28.8
▲ Keystone Bank, SSB	Austin	TX	**C**	D+	C	432.8	26.34	22.2	1.5	14.9	8.8	**10.0**	12.8	20.6
Keystone Savings Bank	Keystone	IA	**B-**	B	B-	176.7	11.35	6.0	1.2	12.7	38.3	**7.4**	9.3	17.5
Kindred State Bank	Kindred	ND	**C-**	C-	C	42.1	33.78	6.1	6.3	2.8	1.8	**4.6**	6.6	16.3
Kingston National Bank	Kingston	OH	**B-**	B-	B	454.6	12.39	11.9	2.3	20.9	20.4	**5.7**	7.7	12.5
Kingstree Federal S&L Assn.	Kingstree	SC	**C+**	C+	C+	39.8	5.14	0.6	0.2	36.9	23.1	**10.0**	14.7	0.0
▲ Kinmundy Bank	Kinmundy	IL	**A-**	B+	B	60.2	16.12	5.3	14.0	22.7	20.4	**9.3**	10.5	20.7
Kirkpatrick Bank	Edmond	OK	**A-**	A-	B+	1056.0	15.39	8.2	0.7	5.8	29.6	**8.1**	9.8	16.1
Kirkwood Bank and Trust Co.	Bismarck	ND	**B**	B	B	320.5	14.58	12.2	3.1	7.9	11.3	**6.6**	8.8	0.0
Kish Bank	Belleville	PA	**B-**	B-	C+	1150.9	10.13	11.9	0.7	21.0	15.2	**5.3**	7.7	11.2
Kitsap Bank	Port Orchard	WA	**B+**	A-	A-	1638.1	17.32	9.7	0.2	3.6	34.8	**7.0**	9.0	17.0
Kleberg Bank, N.A.	Kingsville	TX	**B-**	B-	B-	678.8	9.54	14.4	10.0	10.9	29.5	**6.1**	8.1	15.5
KodaBank	Drayton	ND	**A-**	B+	B	373.2	20.08	9.4	4.1	5.5	11.7	**10.0**	11.3	0.0
▼ Kress National Bank	Kress	TX	**B-**	B	B	44.0	22.25	12.0	2.7	0.5	31.2	**9.3**	10.5	23.7
KS Bank, Inc.	Smithfield	NC	**B**	B	B-	533.4	13.81	4.8	0.3	17.0	15.0	**6.3**	8.4	13.8
KS StateBank	Manhattan	KS	**A-**	A-	A-	2389.8	4.13	10.4	0.3	16.7	15.5	**9.0**	10.4	0.0

Arrows denote recent upgrades ▲ or downgrades ▼

Asset Quality Index	Adjusted Non-Performing Loans as a % of Total Loans	Adjusted Non-Performing Loans as a % of Capital	Net Charge-Offs Avg Loans	Profitability Index	Net Income ($Mil)	Return on Assets (R.O.A.)	Return on Equity (R.O.E.)	Net Interest Spread	Overhead Efficiency Ratio	Liquidity Index	Liquidity Ratio	Hot Money Ratio	Stability Index
5.1	1.81	10.6	0.03	4.2	1.8	0.90	11.76	3.05	65.5	4.6	22.2	5.6	4.3
5.4	1.21	6.7	0.04	4.4	5.9	0.91	11.28	2.87	63.5	3.7	12.2	8.6	6.7
9.3	0.49	1.2	0.00	4.2	0.7	0.82	6.21	2.72	69.5	6.5	58.0	5.9	7.9
6.2	1.48	6.5	0.02	3.8	1.3	0.69	4.95	3.44	81.4	4.2	17.3	7.5	7.1
7.4	0.60	2.8	0.04	2.8	0.6	0.51	5.06	2.67	81.0	4.8	30.0	7.2	5.8
5.8	0.16	0.8	-0.10	10.0	76.0	5.06	22.74	6.00	35.5	0.0	0.0	99.4	9.8
7.5	0.03	0.1	0.01	5.7	12.1	1.22	11.40	3.43	47.8	1.1	21.1	23.8	9.1
7.7	0.42	2.0	-0.02	7.2	40.6	1.38	10.72	3.00	61.1	5.1	21.0	3.1	10.0
6.3	1.11	3.5	0.35	4.2	0.7	0.89	8.90	2.92	66.6	3.3	46.0	20.7	5.8
7.1	2.70	5.8	0.02	6.6	1.8	2.49	16.81	3.01	50.2	2.9	46.4	26.1	8.1
7.8	1.50	3.0	3.11	4.0	0.3	0.71	4.62	2.75	76.4	4.5	39.6	12.2	8.5
7.3	0.30	1.2	0.08	9.7	5.7	2.39	25.06	3.93	50.5	5.5	33.4	3.7	7.7
8.5	0.10	0.5	-0.05	6.0	2.9	1.52	13.65	3.41	55.6	4.6	32.1	9.5	7.9
8.4	1.62	1.7	0.15	5.5	5.0	2.17	19.16	3.03	36.4	2.9	75.2	71.3	8.5
8.3	0.01	0.0	0.00	4.9	0.7	1.11	14.87	3.16	66.5	5.1	41.4	9.9	5.5
3.6	0.89	6.9	0.06	4.2	3.2	0.82	9.99	3.51	71.0	3.4	10.7	11.6	5.4
10.0	na	0.0	na	4.7	0.2	0.54	0.54	0.75	0.0	4.0	na	100.0	8.5
6.5	1.31	4.0	0.35	6.1	20415.0	1.28	14.67	1.73	61.6	7.0	63.8	2.9	7.3
9.8	0.45	1.0	-0.10	4.0	0.3	0.75	8.20	2.12	70.4	5.1	72.6	14.7	5.7
8.2	0.06	2.5	-0.01	3.0	0.1	0.43	4.79	2.79	79.4	2.5	43.2	28.9	4.1
8.3	0.08	1.4	0.01	2.8	0.4	0.59	5.63	3.12	82.0	7.0	66.1	4.7	5.3
9.4	0.00	0.0	0.01	5.0	1.0	1.09	12.88	3.03	62.2	4.5	17.9	5.7	5.4
8.1	0.64	2.1	0.02	6.2	0.5	1.35	10.71	3.82	56.8	3.9	52.3	17.4	7.5
1.5	12.47	37.7	-0.16	0.9	0.0	0.15	1.49	3.52	97.5	2.6	46.2	28.6	4.3
8.8	0.08	0.3	-0.17	3.5	1.1	0.76	8.22	3.15	75.9	3.4	25.0	13.1	5.8
6.1	0.48	2.6	-0.02	5.2	5.3	1.12	10.97	3.60	64.4	1.6	8.1	9.3	7.3
3.7	2.28	13.3	-0.05	6.1	2.0	1.20	11.03	3.75	63.8	2.2	17.4	17.7	6.8
5.6	0.91	6.0	0.00	4.0	0.3	0.85	9.38	2.86	70.4	5.9	45.3	5.1	4.5
9.0	0.00	0.0	-0.01	5.2	1.7	1.32	14.83	2.99	55.2	5.7	49.1	8.2	5.8
4.7	1.77	8.4	0.06	4.7	35.5	0.97	7.32	2.90	57.6	1.9	18.7	13.1	8.8
6.2	1.26	4.6	0.02	8.5	2.3	1.86	11.70	3.93	55.2	4.1	30.0	9.9	10.0
8.6	0.16	0.8	-0.09	0.0	-0.4	-0.31	-2.42	3.01	110.7	5.0	41.8	10.5	6.0
7.9	0.11	0.6	0.33	0.4	-0.2	-0.55	-4.16	9.13	103.7	1.5	28.2	31.0	4.7
8.9	0.40	2.6	0.00	8.4	11.9	1.79	12.99	3.43	70.7	3.9	16.9	4.4	10.0
7.5	0.97	6.1	0.00	4.2	6.7	0.83	8.63	3.40	69.1	5.9	25.4	1.1	7.3
8.8	0.25	1.4	0.12	3.5	0.3	0.56	4.83	3.56	80.1	2.5	40.2	22.5	6.1
4.1	1.11	7.1	0.00	3.6	1.2	0.71	7.57	3.46	73.7	4.9	34.2	8.3	5.2
8.9	0.21	1.3	0.03	5.1	1.7	0.97	7.16	3.20	67.1	4.3	48.2	15.6	8.8
6.6	1.71	9.1	0.00	0.0	0.0	-1.34	-9.25	3.91	135.8	1.4	17.2	26.0	6.1
8.9	0.27	1.2	-0.06	9.4	3.2	2.64	14.68	4.39	47.6	5.4	47.6	9.5	9.4
3.2	0.55	14.8	-0.01	3.7	1.4	0.83	7.50	3.46	76.0	4.7	41.2	12.0	7.0
4.2	3.06	13.2	0.00	3.3	0.2	0.61	6.82	3.46	82.7	6.3	43.6	2.4	4.4
10.0	na	0.0	na	10.0	0.2	8.86	9.25	7.81	49.5	4.0	na	0.0	7.0
5.6	0.87	4.8	0.27	6.5	1341.7	1.54	15.30	2.57	57.5	6.3	31.3	1.4	8.4
9.8	0.53	2.1	-0.03	0.9	0.0	0.02	0.14	2.16	103.6	5.4	52.5	9.8	6.6
7.9	0.02	0.1	0.00	2.9	1.4	0.72	6.49	3.43	69.1	2.2	30.7	22.8	6.7
5.9	0.96	6.0	0.07	3.9	0.8	0.98	9.19	3.24	73.6	5.1	49.9	11.9	5.7
5.2	0.00	6.5	0.01	3.3	0.1	0.60	8.88	2.92	78.7	6.4	61.3	5.6	2.1
8.6	0.00	0.0	-0.01	4.3	2.1	0.94	11.75	3.30	65.6	2.1	18.0	19.0	4.7
5.2	3.20	12.3	0.00	3.3	0.1	0.67	4.31	2.77	74.5	2.1	40.5	33.1	7.2
6.4	0.00	1.0	0.07	10.0	0.6	2.08	16.65	4.16	39.1	5.3	40.2	8.3	8.3
8.6	0.31	1.4	-0.01	5.6	6.5	1.31	13.32	2.98	59.8	4.0	19.3	9.8	8.9
8.6	0.27	0.8	0.00	4.9	1.9	1.21	13.19	2.89	67.4	4.7	31.1	8.1	6.0
8.6	0.16	0.9	0.00	4.2	5.7	1.01	13.01	3.35	69.9	2.7	12.8	15.5	6.9
8.6	0.12	0.5	0.13	5.3	8.8	1.13	10.37	3.52	65.3	7.4	53.1	1.2	9.4
4.7	0.82	3.8	0.07	4.8	3.9	1.14	10.42	3.50	70.2	4.3	25.8	8.3	7.8
6.0	0.93	5.1	0.08	6.5	2.3	1.28	10.66	3.09	59.1	3.7	31.2	13.3	8.4
8.3	0.43	1.5	0.00	3.2	0.1	0.50	4.62	2.85	87.0	3.2	55.2	24.4	5.0
6.8	0.75	3.2	0.00	6.0	3.2	1.23	14.26	3.69	58.9	3.2	29.0	13.3	6.0
8.1	0.37	2.6	0.00	8.7	26.9	2.29	21.64	3.30	47.7	1.6	25.9	29.0	9.9

Name	City	State	Rating	2020 Rating	2019 Rating	Total Assets ($Mil)	One Year Asset Growth	Asset Mix (As a % of Total Assets): Commercial Loans	Consumer Loans	Mortgage Loans	Securities	Capitalization Index	Leverage Ratio	Risk-Based Capital Ratio
La Monte Community Bank	La Monte	MO	**B+**	B+	B+	44.6	30.22	2.4	1.6	11.5	39.4	**5.7**	7.7	17.0
Labette Bank	Altamont	KS	**B**	B+	B+	498.5	11.83	2.4	1.8	18.6	32.0	**8.2**	9.8	0.0
▲ Ladysmith Federal S&L Assn.	Ladysmith	WI	**C+**	C	B-	79.2	19.18	13.4	5.0	39.5	21.8	**6.8**	8.8	18.1
Lafayette State Bank	Mayo	FL	**D**	D	E+	174.3	29.48	11.2	2.2	11.4	14.8	**4.8**	6.8	12.3
Lake Area Bank	Lindstrom	MN	**B+**	B	B	438.4	4.06	8.4	0.1	22.7	26.1	**7.8**	11.2	13.1
Lake Central Bank	Annandale	MN	**A**	A	A	203.5	12.99	8.0	0.5	12.3	41.1	**10.0**	11.4	19.6
Lake City Bank	Warsaw	IN	**A**	A	A-	6221.6	14.48	24.1	1.6	2.9	18.1	**9.0**	10.3	14.7
▲ Lake City Federal Bank	Lake City	MN	**B**	B-	B	80.9	6.97	3.9	2.1	40.5	11.2	**10.0**	12.0	0.0
Lake Community Bank	Long Lake	MN	**B+**	B+	B+	146.8	5.38	6.2	0.3	6.7	13.5	**9.8**	10.8	15.5
Lake Country Community Bank	Morristown	MN	**D+**	D+	C	32.9	9.28	8.0	0.9	13.2	46.4	**6.4**	8.4	24.4
Lake Elmo Bank	Lake Elmo	MN	**B+**	B+	A-	511.3	15.02	9.1	1.7	21.4	11.0	**6.4**	8.4	18.6
Lake Forest Bank & Trust Co., N.A.	Lake Forest	IL	**B+**	B	B+	6044.1	13.24	46.5	7.6	1.8	10.9	**6.1**	9.1	11.8
Lake Region Bank	New London	MN	**B**	B	B-	151.5	16.28	12.3	2.7	6.1	46.7	**6.8**	8.8	20.4
Lake Shore Savings Bank	Dunkirk	NY	**B-**	B-	B	710.7	4.76	4.7	0.2	23.6	11.0	**10.0**	11.4	0.0
▲ Lake-Osceola State Bank	Baldwin	MI	**B-**	C+	C+	396.7	18.76	5.9	13.3	12.1	16.8	**10.0**	11.2	20.5
Lakeland Bank	Oak Ridge	NJ	**B+**	B+	B+	7851.9	4.91	7.1	0.1	8.1	13.8	**6.8**	9.2	12.4
Lakeside Bank	Chicago	IL	**B+**	A-	A-	2177.5	1.78	8.1	0.0	5.7	6.0	**8.5**	10.0	14.5
Lakeside Bank	Lake Charles	LA	**C+**	C+	B-	360.9	42.60	8.0	1.1	10.6	14.6	**5.4**	7.4	17.8
Lakeside Bank	Rockwall	TX	**C**	C	C+	201.2	52.52	15.2	1.3	2.5	0.0	**10.0**	15.9	0.0
Lakeside Bank of Salina	Salina	OK	**B**	B	B	50.2	11.23	12.4	25.2	21.3	9.8	**9.8**	10.9	0.0
▲ Lakeside State Bank	Oologah	OK	**C**	D+	C	83.5	16.23	4.3	5.0	10.8	37.3	**6.0**	8.0	0.0
Lakeview Bank	Lakeville	MN	**B**	B	B	146.7	8.80	27.9	0.2	19.9	10.5	**5.9**	7.9	16.4
Lamar Bank and Trust Co.	Lamar	MO	**B+**	B+	A-	218.7	18.55	8.6	2.3	14.7	10.1	**9.7**	10.8	0.0
Lamar National Bank	Paris	TX	**B-**	B-	C+	279.9	6.68	16.7	1.0	23.9	21.8	**10.0**	11.6	17.3
Lamont Bank of St. John	Saint John	WA	**B+**	B+	B+	62.3	15.84	6.0	11.0	0.3	36.7	**10.0**	13.1	0.0
Landmark Bank	Clinton	LA	**B-**	C+	C+	158.4	3.96	14.1	2.0	22.9	24.9	**9.0**	10.3	0.0
Landmark Community Bank	Collierville	TN	**B**	B	B	986.7	3.57	8.0	0.7	41.5	12.1	**9.0**	10.4	15.7
Landmark National Bank	Manhattan	KS	**B+**	B+	B	1246.8	11.74	15.3	0.1	13.6	27.1	**9.0**	10.3	18.4
Laona State Bank	Laona	WI	**C+**	C+	B-	260.1	10.90	6.1	3.2	23.5	40.5	**8.1**	9.7	21.2
LaSalle State Bank	La Salle	IL	**C+**	C+	C+	173.9	17.06	8.5	1.0	9.1	38.6	**6.4**	8.5	20.7
Latimer State Bank	Wilburton	OK	**C+**	B-	B	72.1	0.92	7.4	1.9	4.2	27.6	**10.0**	19.8	62.4
Lawrenceburg Federal Bank	Lawrenceburg	TN	**B-**	B-	B	74.0	0.52	0.0	3.1	73.8	0.0	**10.0**	21.1	0.0
LCA Bank Corp.	Park City	UT	**B+**	A-	A	211.3	-8.03	26.2	0.0	0.0	0.2	**9.3**	18.2	0.0
LCNB National Bank	Lebanon	OH	**B+**	B+	B	1852.7	6.96	5.2	1.9	17.2	18.1	**7.7**	9.7	13.1
Lea County State Bank	Hobbs	NM	**B+**	A-	A-	479.0	7.18	19.3	2.6	0.8	61.3	**8.2**	9.8	23.4
Lead Bank	Kansas City	MO	**C**	C-	C	723.6	58.68	7.6	46.9	3.1	2.9	**5.9**	7.9	22.8
Leader Bank, N.A.	Arlington	MA	**A**	A	A	2651.5	32.98	5.2	0.0	40.9	7.1	**10.0**	13.9	20.5
Ledyard National Bank	Norwich	VT	**B**	B	B+	715.0	14.56	8.5	2.4	19.5	38.3	**6.3**	8.3	16.5
▲ Lee Bank	Lee	MA	**B-**	C+	C+	502.4	16.26	7.1	2.2	30.0	14.3	**6.6**	8.6	0.0
Lee Bank and Trust Co.	Pennington Gap	VA	**B+**	B+	B+	170.7	3.82	30.5	2.6	18.6	12.6	**10.0**	15.4	24.4
Lee County Bank	Fort Madison	IA	**A**	A-	A-	228.7	9.13	8.8	4.2	44.7	0.9	**10.0**	11.6	0.0
Legacy Bank	Wiley	CO	**B+**	B+	B+	471.3	12.55	16.5	0.6	4.3	20.1	**10.0**	12.9	15.6
Legacy Bank	Altoona	IA	**C+**	C+	C	161.3	16.74	20.1	1.4	17.4	6.5	**5.1**	7.1	14.8
Legacy Bank	Wichita	KS	**B**	B-	C+	588.6	9.59	11.4	0.4	12.0	17.7	**7.9**	9.6	0.0
▼ Legacy Bank	Hinton	OK	**C**	B-	B-	1134.1	42.34	51.9	0.5	7.0	3.7	**5.3**	7.3	14.4
Legacy Bank	Grundy	VA	**B-**	B-	C	339.7	6.54	5.4	3.6	7.7	35.9	**10.0**	21.2	38.3
Legacy Bank & Trust Co.	Rogersville	MO	**A-**	B+	B	666.4	48.29	18.3	0.7	17.7	0.0	**8.0**	9.6	13.6
Legacy National Bank	Springdale	AR	**C+**	C+	B-	876.0	37.55	8.4	1.2	15.1	4.7	**5.7**	8.5	11.5
▲ Legacy State Bank	Loganville	GA	**B+**	B-	C-	140.6	6.18	7.7	0.2	7.2	14.9	**9.1**	10.4	14.5
Legacy Trust Co., N.A.	Houston	TX	**U**	U	U	30.4	4.23	0.0	0.0	0.0	25.9	**10.0**	85.6	114.3
Legence Bank	Eldorado	IL	**B**	B	B	618.0	9.99	17.7	4.9	2.7	24.6	**6.8**	8.8	15.2
Legend Bank, N. A.	Bowie	TX	**B+**	B+	B+	942.3	11.84	10.4	0.7	12.3	22.1	**7.5**	9.3	14.3
Legends Bank	Linn	MO	**A**	A	A-	471.9	7.62	5.0	6.8	15.5	20.6	**10.0**	13.8	0.0
Legends Bank	Clarksville	TN	**B+**	B+	B+	660.6	17.10	11.1	1.4	8.0	17.7	**6.9**	8.9	13.2
Leighton State Bank	Pella	IA	**B+**	B+	A-	213.3	6.07	12.0	1.0	17.1	18.4	**9.2**	10.5	16.0
Lena State Bank	Lena	IL	**B+**	B+	B+	94.3	-0.27	6.1	0.6	2.7	43.4	**10.0**	11.7	0.0
LendingClub Bank, N.A.	Lehi	UT	**C**	C	C+	3357.9	51.01	19.6	36.8	4.5	5.4	**10.0**	13.5	19.9
Level One Bank	Farmington Hills	MI	**B-**	B-	B	2507.0	-1.26	24.0	0.0	12.1	15.0	**6.1**	8.1	13.7
Lewis & Clark Bank	Oregon City	OR	**B+**	B+	B+	437.9	44.26	15.1	0.0	4.1	0.4	**8.5**	10.0	21.2
Lewisburg Banking Co.	Lewisburg	KY	**B+**	B+	B+	164.5	10.83	9.7	4.2	26.6	19.2	**7.9**	9.6	0.0

Asset Quality Index	Adjusted Non-Performing Loans as a % of Total Loans	Adjusted Non-Performing Loans as a % of Capital	Net Charge-Offs Avg Loans	Profitability Index	Net Income ($Mil)	Return on Assets (R.O.A.)	Return on Equity (R.O.E.)	Net Interest Spread	Overhead Efficiency Ratio	Liquidity Index	Liquidity Ratio	Hot Money Ratio	Stability Index
3.7	0.00	20.4	0.00	**1.9**	0.0	0.05	0.69	2.13	96.2	**4.4**	33.9	11.0	**5.2**
7.6	0.43	1.7	0.01	**4.2**	1.9	0.78	7.87	3.03	72.3	**3.7**	27.5	12.2	**6.1**
5.4	1.33	6.1	0.00	**4.3**	0.3	0.92	10.17	3.34	64.5	**2.3**	35.0	26.1	**4.0**
2.3	4.08	24.6	0.02	**3.6**	0.5	0.53	7.94	3.65	77.4	**5.8**	38.3	3.9	**1.2**
4.9	1.66	6.3	0.00	**8.8**	5.6	2.60	22.26	3.97	76.1	**3.8**	27.2	11.2	**8.5**
9.5	0.00	0.0	0.00	**9.0**	1.9	1.89	14.92	3.56	54.2	**6.4**	47.4	2.9	**8.8**
8.1	0.36	1.8	-0.07	**8.5**	49.9	1.67	15.46	3.11	44.8	**3.7**	24.7	13.7	**10.0**
9.1	0.36	1.7	0.03	**4.5**	0.3	0.79	6.44	3.39	71.5	**4.5**	37.0	11.2	**6.9**
7.7	0.05	0.3	0.00	**4.6**	0.5	0.71	6.35	2.85	66.0	**5.0**	37.6	8.7	**7.2**
6.4	3.30	6.1	-0.38	**1.4**	0.0	-0.01	-0.07	2.48	100.2	**6.0**	63.3	8.3	**3.6**
7.2	0.66	2.0	-0.05	**6.1**	3.5	1.43	16.30	3.02	59.6	**5.6**	36.5	4.6	**6.5**
7.7	0.30	1.5	-0.09	**9.8**	57.3	1.96	20.79	2.70	47.2	**3.4**	22.2	3.9	**8.1**
5.9	1.16	3.9	-0.05	**5.5**	1.1	1.54	16.34	3.37	69.5	**7.4**	68.4	1.8	**5.7**
7.8	0.53	3.2	0.01	**3.8**	2.8	0.80	6.72	3.23	67.1	**3.1**	17.0	13.8	**8.4**
6.2	1.08	3.4	-0.03	**4.5**	1.7	0.94	10.59	3.16	64.7	**5.3**	47.4	9.0	**5.9**
5.4	0.44	2.6	0.09	**6.3**	49.4	1.28	11.65	3.28	52.0	**3.7**	11.7	8.2	**9.5**
5.1	0.90	6.0	0.00	**6.5**	18.7	1.63	17.41	3.23	51.0	**2.1**	21.6	12.3	**10.0**
7.6	0.31	4.2	0.01	**2.9**	0.7	0.42	5.49	2.18	76.8	**3.1**	44.5	21.9	**5.2**
8.4	0.00	0.0	0.00	**2.3**	0.8	0.89	5.26	2.66	63.2	**6.9**	55.0	2.5	**5.5**
2.3	3.40	14.0	0.03	**9.4**	0.5	1.80	16.96	5.45	50.2	**1.6**	18.8	23.7	**6.8**
2.3	4.01	5.0	0.00	**0.8**	-0.2	-0.44	-3.39	2.22	110.3	**5.7**	46.1	6.9	**4.2**
6.5	0.37	3.0	-0.01	**8.4**	1.2	1.59	19.93	4.79	52.3	**4.2**	25.9	8.0	**5.4**
3.8	2.57	13.3	0.02	**7.6**	2.1	1.89	17.70	3.66	54.1	**5.3**	37.9	7.3	**8.2**
5.1	2.15	10.4	-0.01	**3.5**	0.6	0.43	4.47	3.62	81.3	**4.6**	26.1	6.6	**6.5**
7.8	1.05	2.0	-0.33	**8.0**	0.6	1.87	14.28	4.58	35.1	**6.6**	42.7	0.0	**6.3**
4.8	1.59	8.5	0.08	**6.5**	2.6	3.24	32.96	6.72	49.6	**3.7**	28.9	12.7	**5.8**
5.7	0.90	6.0	0.04	**5.1**	5.6	1.12	11.06	3.33	57.1	**1.0**	16.1	25.3	**7.5**
5.0	2.13	8.6	0.03	**7.7**	10.4	1.68	14.10	3.56	59.1	**4.5**	14.9	5.6	**9.7**
3.8	3.53	14.5	0.16	**3.9**	1.0	0.82	8.19	2.83	60.3	**5.0**	50.2	12.6	**5.8**
4.5	4.25	16.4	-0.07	**3.7**	0.7	0.81	8.98	3.04	72.0	**4.5**	32.9	10.2	**5.2**
8.3	3.72	3.2	-0.34	**2.2**	0.0	0.11	0.53	1.24	92.6	**3.6**	93.0	34.2	**6.6**
6.1	0.67	9.0	0.02	**3.1**	0.2	0.39	1.85	3.17	83.1	**1.1**	18.6	31.6	**7.5**
6.0	1.28	7.3	0.28	**8.8**	2.4	2.22	18.06	6.53	57.2	**0.3**	13.4	0.0	**7.5**
6.8	0.48	2.0	0.00	**5.7**	10.7	1.18	9.09	3.54	64.5	**4.4**	13.1	6.2	**9.9**
6.2	3.02	7.4	0.00	**5.3**	4.4	1.87	17.79	3.03	66.3	**6.2**	48.5	5.2	**6.9**
2.0	0.34	6.2	0.02	**6.4**	4.2	1.31	17.34	9.81	88.9	**0.8**	19.2	2.3	**5.4**
8.7	0.04	0.2	0.00	**9.5**	37.5	3.12	23.52	2.88	34.6	**3.4**	17.8	6.1	**10.0**
7.6	0.49	1.9	-0.02	**5.0**	4.0	1.17	12.58	2.98	73.8	**2.7**	9.2	3.6	**6.8**
5.4	0.80	6.0	0.03	**4.2**	2.0	0.85	10.70	3.07	75.5	**5.1**	28.5	4.3	**4.3**
6.5	0.73	4.8	0.14	**3.9**	0.5	0.59	4.22	3.68	75.5	**1.9**	22.0	21.1	**7.7**
8.6	0.15	1.0	0.00	**8.2**	2.5	2.14	19.12	3.90	44.3	**5.1**	17.3	1.6	**8.0**
4.0	1.86	13.0	0.27	**7.9**	3.9	1.74	11.93	3.77	51.0	**2.3**	22.6	16.8	**9.6**
4.4	1.65	12.3	-0.02	**4.2**	0.8	1.03	14.77	3.43	74.7	**5.9**	38.8	3.6	**4.3**
7.1	0.55	2.2	0.14	**4.2**	1.8	0.62	6.25	3.11	71.1	**3.7**	30.9	12.7	**6.4**
2.4	1.33	20.4	0.12	**4.1**	4.6	0.84	20.86	2.90	62.0	**4.7**	15.0	4.2	**5.0**
7.9	1.50	3.1	-0.13	**3.8**	1.4	0.84	3.93	2.77	63.0	**4.0**	56.5	18.9	**6.8**
8.2	0.03	0.2	0.00	**8.3**	4.5	1.47	14.92	3.66	51.1	**0.8**	14.3	30.3	**7.8**
4.6	0.96	7.8	-0.01	**5.9**	4.2	1.12	13.41	3.90	60.2	**3.0**	11.9	13.2	**6.4**
7.6	0.00	0.0	0.00	**6.4**	1.3	1.81	18.35	3.56	50.0	**2.3**	24.7	18.4	**5.6**
10.0	na	0.0	na	**10.0**	2.0	12.82	14.48	0.65	72.8	**4.0**	na	0.0	**7.0**
2.7	2.37	12.9	0.12	**6.7**	5.1	1.66	15.21	4.55	63.4	**4.9**	30.6	6.8	**8.1**
5.2	1.44	4.8	-0.08	**6.6**	7.7	1.68	15.57	4.34	61.5	**3.6**	23.2	11.9	**8.3**
6.8	0.22	4.0	0.05	**7.9**	3.2	1.36	9.73	3.43	52.6	**3.9**	22.8	10.2	**9.2**
8.3	0.16	0.9	0.02	**6.9**	4.6	1.46	15.99	3.77	60.3	**3.1**	21.6	6.0	**6.6**
4.0	0.90	11.3	-0.03	**6.2**	1.9	1.68	14.76	3.49	59.8	**4.2**	27.7	9.7	**7.6**
8.9	0.00	0.1	0.00	**5.1**	0.5	1.02	8.59	2.52	54.7	**2.7**	43.6	26.1	**7.5**
5.2	0.69	2.8	-0.01	**2.2**	12.4	0.76	6.66	3.91	78.4	**3.9**	18.0	2.4	**6.0**
5.3	0.80	5.1	0.00	**5.9**	17.4	1.38	14.55	3.39	56.7	**1.9**	22.2	22.8	**8.5**
5.8	1.70	8.2	-0.01	**5.3**	2.5	1.21	11.52	3.45	54.3	**5.8**	46.1	6.8	**5.5**
5.5	0.93	3.8	0.02	**7.5**	1.6	2.05	21.13	4.44	54.9	**3.7**	25.7	11.9	**6.8**

Name	City	State	Rating	2020 Rating	2019 Rating	Total Assets ($Mil)	One Year Asset Growth	Asset Mix (As a % of Total Assets) Commercial Loans	Consumer Loans	Mortgage Loans	Securities	Capitalization Index	Leverage Ratio	Risk-Based Capital Ratio
▲ Lexicon Bank	Las Vegas	NV	**D+**	D-		290.3	16.83	44.7	0.0	1.6	8.1	**9.8**	11.4	0.0
▲ Liberty Bank	Geraldine	AL	**B+**	B	B	180.2	12.65	6.1	5.1	16.3	19.7	**9.6**	10.8	17.1
Liberty Bank	South San Francisco	CA	**C**	C+	B	293.1	-4.47	4.2	0.1	1.5	15.4	**9.0**	12.5	0.0
Liberty Bank	Middletown	CT	**B**	B	A-	7286.0	9.44	12.5	0.1	12.8	14.3	**10.0**	11.7	16.6
Liberty Bank	Liberty	IL	**A-**	B+	B+	121.7	9.92	8.1	5.2	15.0	16.2	**10.0**	11.4	19.9
Liberty Bank	Ironton	OH	**C+**	C+	B-	60.5	9.73	1.8	3.8	34.2	20.6	**10.0**	15.1	0.0
Liberty Bank	Poulsbo	WA	**C**	C	C-	168.5	-6.32	17.8	3.2	14.2	12.2	**7.2**	9.1	18.1
Liberty Bank and Trust Co.	New Orleans	LA	**B-**	B-	B-	889.3	20.59	8.2	3.0	18.6	21.6	**8.0**	9.7	15.5
Liberty Bank for Savings	Chicago	IL	**C+**	C+	C+	904.5	3.63	0.0	0.0	48.6	39.5	**10.0**	22.6	55.3
Liberty Bank Minnesota	Saint Cloud	MN	**A**	A	A	295.4	15.32	0.1	1.9	31.8	29.7	**9.7**	10.8	24.5
Liberty Bank, Inc.	Salt Lake City	UT	**D**	D-	E+	12.5	27.55	1.1	43.7	9.6	4.8	**10.0**	14.5	22.9
Liberty Capital Bank	Addison	TX	**A-**	A-	A-	330.3	-0.38	14.0	0.0	19.6	0.9	**7.0**	9.0	15.6
Liberty First Bank	Monroe	GA	**B-**	B	B+	191.9	16.89	2.8	0.3	9.5	46.2	**6.8**	8.8	0.0
Liberty National Bank	Sioux City	IA	**A-**	B+	B+	492.3	-3.36	10.3	0.5	11.1	11.5	**7.0**	9.0	14.0
Liberty National Bank	Ada	OH	**A-**	A-	B+	441.0	8.62	8.8	0.1	10.9	11.0	**10.0**	12.0	16.7
Liberty National Bank	Lawton	OK	**A-**	A-	A-	865.3	18.05	11.0	0.9	8.2	11.7	**6.9**	8.9	15.6
Liberty Savings Bank, F.S.B.	Wilmington	OH	**B**	B	B-	923.6	12.84	0.1	1.4	48.3	37.2	**8.4**	9.9	22.2
Liberty State Bank	Powers Lake	ND	**A**	A	A-	108.5	10.46	3.4	1.9	7.2	53.5	**10.0**	11.9	0.0
Liberty Trust & Savings Bank	Durant	IA	**A**	A	A	174.3	13.76	9.1	1.7	7.2	41.6	**10.0**	18.8	0.0
Libertyville Bank & Trust Co., N.A.	Libertyville	IL	**B**	B	B	2160.1	3.13	30.1	12.8	4.5	12.8	**5.7**	8.6	11.5
▲ Libertyville Savings Bank	Fairfield	IA	**B+**	B	B-	418.7	10.73	9.5	1.0	9.3	31.4	**8.3**	9.9	16.7
Lifestore Bank	West Jefferson	NC	**B+**	B+	B	385.2	12.50	5.2	0.5	20.0	21.1	**8.6**	10.1	18.6
▲ LimeBank	Bolivar	MO	**C+**	C	C	76.5	1.36	1.5	2.5	27.3	7.6	**8.3**	9.8	0.0
▲ Limestone Bank, Inc	Louisville	KY	**B+**	B	C	1331.5	2.58	15.5	2.4	10.3	17.2	**8.9**	10.6	14.1
Lincoln 1st Bank	Lincoln Park	NJ	**D**	D-	D	284.6	-3.33	3.3	0.1	39.0	25.0	**4.9**	6.9	14.5
▲ Lincoln FSB of Nebraska	Lincoln	NE	**B+**	B-	C+	321.6	-5.87	0.0	0.0	40.4	31.3	**10.0**	15.7	30.4
Lincoln Savings Bank	Reinbeck	IA	**B**	B	B	1430.5	-3.52	10.1	0.6	9.4	13.9	**8.9**	10.3	14.6
Lincoln State Bank	Hankinson	ND	**B**	B	B	102.6	19.59	8.6	4.1	2.4	49.5	**6.9**	8.9	0.0
LincolnWay Community Bank	New Lenox	IL	**C**	C-	C	274.5	0.96	11.5	0.0	11.3	1.3	**9.7**	10.8	15.0
Lindell Bank & Trust Co.	Saint Louis	MO	**A**	A-	A	880.6	51.93	8.9	0.5	14.6	37.4	**10.0**	11.9	0.0
Lineage Bank	Franklin	TN	**D+**	C-	C-	55.8	123.15	0.6	1.3	11.0	16.3	**10.0**	18.2	35.1
▲ LINKBANK	Camp Hill	PA	**C-**	D	E	463.8	36.72	28.0	0.7	9.1	0.7	**8.3**	11.2	13.6
Lisle Savings Bank	Lisle	IL	**B**	B	A-	610.5	9.93	0.2	0.0	39.8	43.7	**10.0**	21.9	0.0
Little Horn State Bank	Hardin	MT	**C+**	C+	B-	137.7	21.04	16.1	1.6	7.8	1.2	**6.9**	9.0	13.3
▼ Live Oak Banking Co.	Wilmington	NC	**B-**	B+	A-	8145.7	-0.51	40.4	0.0	0.9	10.0	**5.6**	7.6	12.6
Llano National Bank	Llano	TX	**A-**	A-	A-	259.3	23.26	2.4	2.4	11.1	52.4	**10.0**	11.1	0.0
▼ LNB Community Bank	Lynnville	IN	**B**	B+	C+	150.8	14.55	3.6	2.7	32.1	11.1	**7.8**	9.5	0.0
Logan Bank & Trust Co.	Logan	WV	**B-**	B-	B-	319.6	7.37	10.9	3.2	19.3	40.1	**6.5**	8.5	0.0
Logan County Bank	Scranton	AR	**B+**	B+	B+	96.2	10.59	3.4	8.7	19.7	53.4	**10.0**	19.3	42.4
Logan State Bank	Logan	IA	**C**	C-	C-	78.0	11.30	7.5	3.1	7.1	0.4	**5.4**	7.4	13.7
Logansport Savings Bank	Logansport	IN	**A**	A	A-	243.3	9.64	15.2	0.6	12.5	27.4	**9.1**	10.4	0.0
Lone Star Bank	Houston	TX	**B**	B	B-	141.0	-11.87	9.5	0.1	21.1	0.0	**10.0**	12.6	19.3
Lone Star Capital Bank, N.A.	San Antonio	TX	**C+**	C+	B-	444.1	55.68	11.4	0.6	10.7	23.3	**9.0**	10.3	16.6
Lone Star National Bank	McAllen	TX	**B+**	B+	B+	2875.7	11.87	8.6	0.7	6.4	32.2	**9.6**	10.7	0.0
▲ Lone Star State Bank of West Texas	Lubbock	TX	**B+**	B-	C+	1063.4	3.76	26.1	0.6	4.2	7.3	**9.5**	11.4	14.6
Longview Bank	Ogden	IL	**B-**	C+	C	247.6	14.32	10.2	1.3	9.2	4.9	**6.5**	8.5	14.6
Longview Bank & Trust	Chrisman	IL	**B-**	B-	C	217.8	11.01	6.9	1.1	6.0	4.4	**6.0**	8.0	12.8
Louisiana National Bank	Ruston	LA	**B-**	B-	B-	294.8	9.00	5.9	0.8	15.2	1.1	**3.9**	8.7	0.0
Lovelady State Bank	Lovelady	TX	**B-**	B-	B-	53.5	12.89	8.9	9.2	13.0	19.3	**8.2**	9.8	0.0
Lowry State Bank	Lowry	MN	**B**	B	C+	63.0	7.91	14.7	5.6	25.2	0.0	**5.9**	7.9	12.5
Loyal Trust Bank	Johns Creek	GA	**D+**	D		108.7	99.27	36.5	0.0	0.0	1.8	**10.0**	21.4	27.8
▼ Luana Savings Bank	Luana	IA	**B+**	A-	B+	1903.1	11.19	0.9	1.0	19.5	18.0	**7.3**	9.2	13.7
Lumbee Guaranty Bank	Pembroke	NC	**B-**	B-	B	454.6	19.61	3.9	1.6	8.4	45.6	**8.5**	10.0	0.0
Lusitania Savings Bank	Newark	NJ	**B+**	B+	B+	382.9	9.73	0.0	0.3	37.7	34.3	**10.0**	14.2	35.8
Lusk State Bank	Lusk	WY	**A-**	A-	A-	62.8	4.52	2.4	3.2	0.3	21.3	**10.0**	12.1	0.0
▲ Luther Burbank Savings	Santa Rosa	CA	**B**	B-	B	7255.0	1.24	0.0	0.0	26.8	9.1	**9.5**	10.7	20.1
Luzerne Bank	Luzerne	PA	**B-**	B-	C+	586.9	15.41	8.2	5.2	12.3	5.9	**5.4**	7.4	12.6
Lyons Federal Bank	Lyons	KS	**B+**	B+	B	145.3	10.80	4.4	3.5	17.3	2.9	**10.0**	12.9	0.0
M C Bank & Trust Co.	Morgan City	LA	**B**	B	B-	367.4	10.28	13.1	1.2	9.4	20.6	**10.0**	20.6	0.0
M.Y. Safra Bank, FSB	New York	NY	**D**	D	D+	349.5	-9.43	0.0	4.7	25.2	21.9	**10.0**	12.5	24.8

Asset Quality Index	Adjusted Non-Performing Loans as a % of Total Loans	Adjusted Non-Performing Loans as a % of Capital	Net Charge-Offs Avg Loans	Profitability Index	Net Income ($Mil)	Return on Assets (R.O.A.)	Return on Equity (R.O.E.)	Net Interest Spread	Overhead Efficiency Ratio	Liquidity Index	Liquidity Ratio	Hot Money Ratio	Stability Index
8.4	0.00	0.0	0.00	**2.4**	1.2	0.83	13.37	2.86	66.9	**5.0**	38.4	9.6	**3.4**
7.1	0.51	2.3	0.04	**7.0**	1.5	1.78	15.89	6.34	57.2	**3.9**	44.7	16.6	**6.1**
5.4	1.25	3.3	0.00	**2.8**	0.4	0.28	2.21	3.20	88.6	**4.5**	31.8	10.0	**7.2**
8.0	0.86	2.8	0.04	**4.9**	38.3	1.08	8.85	2.45	73.4	**6.4**	43.7	5.2	**8.7**
6.2	0.00	4.1	0.56	**7.1**	0.9	1.41	12.39	3.00	44.0	**4.9**	39.5	10.4	**7.3**
7.7	1.20	3.9	0.01	**2.1**	0.0	0.14	0.86	3.17	91.9	**5.3**	43.4	9.0	**6.7**
8.4	0.00	0.0	0.00	**2.6**	0.3	0.32	3.90	3.63	86.7	**5.0**	24.4	3.4	**4.4**
5.3	2.23	7.1	0.01	**3.5**	3.2	0.75	7.52	3.23	78.3	**3.4**	31.8	11.7	**5.2**
10.0	0.61	1.6	0.02	**2.6**	1.4	0.32	1.38	2.21	83.2	**5.3**	57.0	12.5	**8.3**
8.8	0.00	0.0	-0.01	**8.3**	3.4	2.37	22.17	1.90	59.9	**7.2**	59.2	1.8	**7.8**
6.8	0.00	0.0	0.00	**0.0**	-0.5	-8.09	-49.72	3.47	201.0	**1.0**	36.1	70.6	**4.2**
8.7	0.00	0.0	0.00	**5.8**	2.3	1.33	14.69	3.15	55.0	**5.0**	27.3	4.6	**7.1**
9.5	0.10	0.2	-0.01	**3.6**	0.9	0.96	11.60	2.74	78.6	**5.4**	59.0	12.7	**6.1**
7.9	0.01	0.1	0.02	**7.6**	4.0	1.55	13.75	3.78	52.4	**2.8**	18.5	15.4	**8.7**
7.4	0.30	0.9	0.02	**6.8**	3.2	1.48	12.01	4.08	56.6	**2.7**	15.1	12.2	**7.4**
7.9	0.17	1.1	0.00	**6.1**	5.8	1.49	15.31	3.81	60.8	**3.8**	33.0	13.5	**7.5**
4.9	2.71	10.4	-0.03	**7.8**	9.7	2.06	21.34	2.87	50.6	**1.9**	41.5	40.9	**8.3**
9.1	0.00	0.0	0.00	**6.7**	0.9	1.75	13.62	3.41	46.2	**3.4**	44.7	19.3	**9.0**
8.9	0.00	0.0	0.00	**7.5**	1.2	1.41	7.32	3.62	51.1	**6.4**	62.9	6.3	**8.7**
7.1	0.32	1.9	-0.01	**6.1**	12.6	1.22	14.00	2.32	50.4	**2.2**	16.6	8.3	**6.8**
6.6	0.79	2.7	-0.10	**5.6**	2.8	1.37	11.94	3.83	59.7	**5.5**	48.2	9.6	**7.2**
5.7	1.25	5.6	-0.07	**5.2**	2.2	1.16	10.85	3.14	67.0	**4.6**	47.3	13.7	**7.0**
5.0	0.67	3.9	0.00	**5.5**	1.1	3.10	28.36	5.89	55.7	**2.3**	20.0	17.8	**6.3**
8.2	0.20	1.0	0.03	**5.9**	8.4	1.26	10.82	3.62	57.3	**2.8**	18.6	15.9	**9.4**
4.3	2.00	13.9	0.00	**0.2**	0.0	0.02	0.32	1.67	108.0	**0.7**	12.6	20.7	**2.1**
9.1	0.63	2.2	0.00	**6.2**	2.3	1.45	8.89	2.67	70.6	**2.5**	38.0	25.3	**8.0**
4.7	1.62	8.4	-0.08	**6.1**	9.9	1.37	11.99	4.13	69.4	**2.5**	22.7	9.7	**8.2**
8.1	0.28	1.3	0.01	**4.6**	0.5	1.03	10.57	3.22	69.5	**4.1**	19.5	8.9	**6.0**
2.7	1.97	12.3	0.00	**8.2**	2.1	1.59	14.04	4.74	56.3	**1.9**	24.8	21.4	**7.9**
8.5	0.33	1.0	-0.14	**7.0**	5.8	1.60	13.60	4.13	64.3	**5.3**	33.0	4.7	**10.0**
8.3	0.00	1.2	0.10	**0.6**	-1.8	-8.35	-43.79	2.98	535.6	**3.8**	67.5	22.2	**3.9**
7.1	0.12	0.9	0.00	**2.2**	3.7	1.77	15.30	3.59	81.5	**1.2**	8.4	21.6	**5.1**
7.7	3.70	5.6	-0.04	**4.6**	2.7	0.90	4.04	2.34	60.1	**4.3**	61.4	18.4	**8.6**
3.5	1.06	7.6	-0.01	**8.0**	1.5	2.25	24.62	6.36	48.0	**4.0**	23.7	9.8	**6.2**
4.6	2.48	9.9	0.04	**6.1**	74.0	1.82	27.27	3.70	54.0	**0.9**	16.3	21.4	**7.7**
8.1	1.01	3.2	-0.19	**5.8**	1.4	1.16	9.89	3.73	66.1	**5.8**	64.4	11.7	**7.8**
6.4	0.44	2.3	-0.01	**4.3**	0.8	1.11	11.72	2.86	74.4	**6.6**	48.6	2.1	**5.9**
8.4	0.53	2.3	0.01	**4.2**	1.6	1.01	11.10	2.60	66.0	**4.8**	44.5	12.3	**5.5**
8.8	0.09	1.1	0.00	**4.3**	0.5	1.00	5.10	2.81	56.8	**3.8**	48.0	17.5	**7.1**
6.4	0.00	2.4	0.01	**6.9**	0.7	1.95	27.30	4.34	54.0	**2.3**	22.6	12.0	**4.1**
7.1	0.82	2.2	0.00	**6.6**	1.7	1.38	11.88	3.49	58.4	**5.5**	41.8	7.0	**9.1**
7.2	0.38	2.1	-0.06	**4.7**	0.7	0.99	7.64	3.97	68.8	**0.9**	19.3	37.0	**7.6**
4.2	1.33	5.1	0.00	**3.9**	1.6	0.86	7.88	3.73	71.7	**2.6**	38.5	17.9	**6.9**
4.9	3.72	14.1	-0.36	**5.5**	16.7	1.24	10.61	3.25	62.7	**3.1**	22.1	15.4	**9.2**
7.3	0.12	0.7	0.02	**6.7**	8.7	1.66	13.83	3.38	51.5	**1.7**	18.7	24.6	**10.0**
5.0	0.71	7.0	0.02	**5.8**	1.3	1.10	13.25	3.35	56.4	**3.1**	29.8	16.0	**5.7**
6.7	0.37	2.0	-0.02	**6.5**	1.3	1.16	13.51	3.13	56.4	**3.9**	31.7	12.8	**5.8**
4.2	1.06	6.8	0.01	**5.6**	1.6	1.07	12.03	5.20	77.2	**3.2**	15.2	12.8	**7.4**
5.0	1.71	7.4	0.09	**4.0**	0.2	0.55	5.42	4.54	84.7	**4.6**	41.9	12.2	**5.1**
5.8	0.49	3.7	0.02	**6.5**	0.4	1.29	16.31	3.57	65.9	**4.3**	21.7	7.7	**5.7**
8.2	0.00	0.0	0.00	**1.1**	0.1	0.28	1.25	4.54	86.4	**2.6**	34.8	20.5	**2.6**
8.6	0.04	0.3	0.00	**4.7**	5.9	0.61	6.53	2.26	76.4	**0.7**	21.9	59.5	**9.2**
4.8	3.62	12.3	-0.02	**4.2**	2.1	0.95	9.71	3.41	70.2	**4.8**	39.6	10.8	**5.4**
10.0	0.47	1.6	0.00	**4.0**	1.3	0.71	4.98	2.43	58.8	**4.8**	60.5	16.2	**8.0**
5.9	2.39	5.6	0.00	**8.6**	0.6	1.97	15.92	4.15	51.7	**5.1**	45.8	4.5	**9.1**
7.6	0.03	0.2	0.00	**5.4**	42.3	1.20	11.20	2.39	34.7	**0.7**	11.4	40.0	**8.5**
4.4	0.96	4.5	0.01	**4.0**	2.0	0.73	7.29	2.72	67.0	**3.6**	30.6	14.1	**6.2**
8.4	0.23	0.7	0.11	**4.4**	0.7	0.97	7.56	2.81	70.0	**3.4**	31.0	15.1	**7.5**
6.8	3.27	3.9	0.40	**3.6**	0.9	0.50	2.32	3.48	78.6	**4.1**	40.8	14.6	**7.5**
8.8	0.02	0.1	0.38	**0.0**	-0.9	-0.56	-4.34	2.18	114.9	**1.2**	29.2	33.0	**5.1**

Name	City	State	Rating	2020 Rating	2019 Rating	Total Assets ($Mil)	One Year Asset Growth	Comm-ercial Loans	Cons-umer Loans	Mort-gage Loans	Secur-ities	Capital-ization Index	Lever-age Ratio	Risk-Based Capital Ratio
								Asset Mix (As a % of Total Assets)						
M1 Bank	Macks Creek	MO	**C+**	C+	B-	577.6	52.75	47.7	0.0	1.6	0.0	**2.0**	9.1	0.0
MA Bank	Macon	MO	**B-**	B-	B	335.9	9.56	6.6	2.2	5.8	34.1	**7.7**	9.5	0.0
Mabrey Bank	Bixby	OK	**B**	B	B-	1524.3	6.89	19.0	1.7	17.5	23.1	**5.7**	7.7	12.2
▼ Macatawa Bank	Holland	MI	**A-**	A	A	2940.2	19.99	17.8	0.2	4.5	12.4	**6.5**	8.5	17.7
Machias Savings Bank	Machias	ME	**A-**	B+	B+	1982.5	14.75	13.8	0.8	21.9	13.2	**10.0**	11.7	16.0
Macon Bank and Trust Co.	Lafayette	TN	**C+**	B-	B	569.5	20.86	2.6	3.1	9.1	46.6	**8.8**	10.2	0.0
Madison County Bank	Madison	NE	**A**	A	A-	491.1	13.75	1.5	1.5	18.8	17.6	**10.0**	16.5	20.2
Madison County Community Bank	Madison	FL	**B-**	B-	B-	163.8	12.55	5.6	1.5	6.5	40.7	**6.1**	8.1	16.6
Madison Valley Bank	Ennis	MT	**B+**	B+	B	253.2	25.43	8.8	2.7	15.3	30.3	**6.1**	8.2	14.2
Magnolia Bank, Inc	Magnolia	KY	**A**	A	A-	474.1	29.05	4.0	0.6	22.1	29.9	**10.0**	11.6	0.0
Magnolia State Bank	Eastman	GA	**B**	B	C	198.1	11.21	9.4	3.4	17.0	6.2	**9.3**	10.5	0.0
Magnolia State Bank	Bay Springs	MS	**B-**	B-	B-	413.2	7.91	10.5	3.2	19.5	9.9	**6.2**	8.2	13.0
Magyar Bank	New Brunswick	NJ	**C+**	C	C	842.3	11.07	10.3	0.4	24.2	7.4	**6.3**	8.3	13.6
Mahopac Bank	Brewster	NY	**B**	B	B	1583.2	3.88	13.1	2.1	18.8	22.8	**6.2**	8.2	13.4
Main Bank	Albuquerque	NM	**B+**	B+	B+	236.1	7.02	19.1	0.1	3.8	1.3	**5.9**	7.9	14.1
Main Street Bank	Marlborough	MA	**C+**	C+	C+	1296.6	9.28	6.3	1.0	28.5	16.6	**8.3**	10.3	0.0
Main Street Bank Corp.	Wheeling	WV	**B-**	B-	C+	554.4	7.50	12.3	3.2	33.8	16.6	**7.3**	9.2	0.0
Maine Community Bank	Biddeford	ME	**B**	B	B	1004.8	1.39	8.2	0.4	37.0	6.8	**10.0**	12.8	0.0
▲ MainStreet Bank	Fairfax	VA	**A-**	B+	B+	1708.0	11.74	12.9	2.0	7.1	10.8	**10.0**	11.8	16.3
▲ Mainstreet Community Bank of Florida	Deland	FL	**B-**	C+	C+	740.2	26.68	12.1	0.8	7.1	21.6	**5.5**	8.6	0.0
Malaga Bank, FSB	Palos Verdes Estates	CA	**A-**	A-	A-	1392.6	5.87	0.9	0.0	7.6	0.0	**10.0**	12.7	21.9
▲ Malvern Bank	Malvern	IA	**B-**	C+	C	170.7	5.59	25.1	17.1	12.6	0.3	**6.6**	8.6	12.7
▼ Malvern Bank NA	Paoli	PA	**B-**	B	B	1183.9	-1.54	9.2	0.2	19.2	5.6	**10.0**	13.5	17.8
▲ Manasquan Bank	Manasquan	NJ	**B-**	C+	B	2524.5	25.61	11.1	0.1	26.8	3.5	**6.0**	9.1	0.0
Manhattan Bank	Manhattan	MT	**B+**	B+	B+	248.5	16.46	4.4	1.7	19.0	31.6	**6.2**	8.2	14.6
Manson State Bank	Manson	IA	**C+**	C+	B-	40.5	13.17	10.3	1.4	5.4	53.4	**8.7**	10.1	0.0
Manufacturers and Traders Trust Co.	Buffalo	NY	**C+**	C+	C+	150227.9	7.96	13.6	9.1	11.1	3.8	**6.3**	8.3	13.2
Manufacturers Bank	Los Angeles	CA	**C+**	B-	B	3776.2	-17.35	25.6	0.0	0.3	16.5	**9.7**	10.8	14.8
Manufacturers Bank & Trust Co.	Forest City	IA	**A**	A-	A-	442.7	12.08	12.5	1.7	9.6	22.5	**10.0**	12.6	0.0
▲ Maple Bank	Champlin	MN	**D+**	D-	D+	106.9	7.60	43.2	0.5	7.1	4.9	**2.9**	9.6	0.0
Maple City Savings Bank, FSB	Hornell	NY	**C**	C	C-	99.4	4.03	7.0	1.1	49.6	14.3	**7.4**	9.3	16.0
MapleMark Bank	Dallas	TX	**D**	D-	D	945.4	34.00	22.8	0.9	13.8	13.6	**8.7**	10.1	15.7
Maquoketa State Bank	Maquoketa	IA	**A-**	A-	A-	403.0	5.89	6.8	2.7	4.3	43.8	**10.0**	15.1	0.0
Marathon Bank	Wausau	WI	**C+**	C+	B-	213.9	25.34	8.8	0.2	22.6	5.5	**7.8**	12.5	0.0
Marblehead Bank	Marblehead	MA	**C-**	C-	C	288.2	20.11	3.4	0.2	39.2	3.3	**5.6**	7.6	15.8
Marine Bank	Springfield	IL	**B-**	B-	C	722.0	5.23	5.4	0.3	4.5	12.4	**7.0**	9.7	0.0
Marine Bank & Trust Co.	Vero Beach	FL	**B-**	B-	B-	488.3	29.74	10.3	0.2	24.4	10.1	**4.9**	6.9	13.8
▼ Mariner's Bank	Edgewater	NJ	**C-**	C	C	422.1	1.64	9.4	0.9	13.8	1.0	**7.9**	9.6	14.5
▼ Marion Bank and Trust Co.	Marion	AL	**D+**	C	B-	312.6	1.19	12.0	2.4	8.7	38.3	**8.4**	9.9	0.0
Marion Center Bank	Indiana	PA	**C**	C	C	381.9	12.83	12.6	2.1	24.5	25.3	**4.9**	6.9	11.5
Marion County State Bank	Pella	IA	**B**	B	B	611.3	10.36	12.2	1.5	15.0	34.4	**6.3**	8.3	14.5
▲ Marion State Bank	Marion	LA	**B**	B-	B	210.4	8.99	11.4	2.8	17.1	20.9	**9.4**	10.6	17.1
Marion State Bank	Marion	TX	**B+**	B+	A-	128.9	8.29	8.3	4.8	0.0	33.5	**10.0**	12.9	0.0
▲ Marlin Business Bank	Salt Lake City	UT	**B+**	B	A-	918.1	-14.73	55.0	0.0	0.0	1.0	**10.0**	18.9	21.2
Marquette Bank	Orland Park	IL	**C+**	C+	C+	1948.1	10.34	1.2	0.0	11.8	22.7	**5.7**	7.7	13.8
Marquette Farmers State Bank Kansas	Marquette	KS	**C**	C	C-	31.6	5.09	8.7	3.0	9.9	33.8	**10.0**	15.8	0.0
Marquette Savings Bank	Erie	PA	**B-**	B-	B	1086.7	5.94	7.2	0.1	38.2	35.1	**10.0**	16.0	0.0
Mars Bank	Mars	PA	**C**	C	C	472.5	6.77	4.0	0.1	33.7	28.6	**6.1**	8.2	16.0
Marseilles Bank	Marseilles	IL	**B-**	B-	B-	74.0	10.83	0.5	6.4	23.2	55.2	**7.5**	9.3	0.0
Marshall County State Bank	Newfolden	MN	**C-**	C	B	35.7	10.82	0.6	4.7	9.4	18.4	**10.0**	15.8	90.7
Martha's Vineyard Bank	Edgartown	MA	**B+**	B+	B+	1142.8	17.90	6.0	0.5	46.7	7.1	**10.0**	11.0	0.0
Martinsville First Savings Bank	Martinsville	VA	**C**	C	C+	38.1	-4.13	0.0	0.3	40.6	4.2	**10.0**	14.2	0.0
Mascoma Bank	Lebanon	NH	**C+**	C+	C+	2521.7	17.04	7.4	0.3	36.1	9.4	**6.7**	8.7	14.4
Mason Bank	Mason	TX	**A-**	A	A	141.3	15.81	6.6	4.3	8.0	61.0	**10.0**	16.7	0.0
Mason City National Bank	Mason City	IL	**A-**	B+	B+	82.1	17.39	1.8	1.2	8.6	50.0	**10.0**	15.2	0.0
Maspeth Federal S&L Assn.	Maspeth	NY	**B+**	B+	A-	2129.5	5.49	0.0	0.0	46.0	2.0	**10.0**	31.7	46.2
Massena S&L	Massena	NY	**B**	B	B	186.1	4.92	1.3	7.6	64.5	0.0	**10.0**	12.6	22.0
Mauch Chunk Trust Co.	Jim Thorpe	PA	**C+**	C+	C+	578.2	13.88	6.3	0.5	17.3	55.8	**5.0**	7.0	12.2
▼ Maxwell State Bank	Maxwell	IA	**C**	B-	B+	30.9	-0.27	4.8	1.5	3.6	39.8	**6.8**	8.8	0.0
Maynard Savings Bank	Maynard	IA	**B+**	B+	A-	67.4	7.83	3.4	2.7	19.3	42.1	**10.0**	14.1	0.0

Asset Quality Index	Adjusted Non-Performing Loans as a % of Total Loans	Adjusted Non-Performing Loans as a % of Capital	Net Charge-Offs Avg Loans	Profitability Index	Net Income ($Mil)	Return on Assets (R.O.A.)	Return on Equity (R.O.E.)	Net Interest Spread	Overhead Efficiency Ratio	Liquidity Index	Liquidity Ratio	Hot Money Ratio	Stability Index
8.1	0.00	0.0	0.00	8.7	5.0	1.98	22.52	3.88	29.0	0.9	25.5	33.5	6.1
5.3	1.29	4.2	0.31	4.2	2.0	1.18	11.77	2.79	70.0	3.2	26.7	14.9	5.9
7.6	0.10	0.8	-0.01	5.5	8.4	1.11	14.44	3.94	64.1	2.7	15.1	12.3	7.3
9.0	0.45	1.2	-0.02	6.6	16.2	1.18	12.89	2.28	54.3	7.4	58.6	1.8	8.6
5.9	1.76	6.6	0.03	7.0	14.6	1.52	13.08	3.89	63.3	3.8	19.7	5.2	9.5
8.6	0.12	1.9	0.00	3.4	1.7	0.65	6.02	2.81	72.8	3.4	53.2	24.5	6.3
8.5	0.20	0.8	0.00	8.4	4.3	1.84	10.79	3.23	52.1	5.1	23.3	2.2	9.0
6.6	0.94	3.8	0.01	3.9	0.6	0.80	9.41	3.04	68.5	4.3	48.1	15.5	4.8
7.1	0.32	2.1	0.00	7.2	3.2	2.69	34.17	4.27	52.6	5.6	41.0	6.3	5.3
8.5	0.09	0.4	0.00	9.5	7.2	2.86	24.59	2.41	85.7	2.1	44.1	10.9	8.9
4.1	1.99	13.8	0.15	3.8	0.8	0.80	7.41	3.88	79.3	5.2	44.4	9.8	6.1
5.3	0.61	6.5	0.02	3.7	1.6	0.79	9.22	2.98	73.6	2.6	25.0	16.8	5.2
3.6	1.99	15.9	0.01	4.4	3.3	0.86	10.88	3.68	63.1	3.9	24.3	10.2	4.4
6.4	0.61	3.7	0.01	5.3	8.8	1.12	11.92	3.18	60.1	4.6	15.8	5.1	7.5
7.4	0.00	0.0	0.00	9.3	2.7	2.35	29.81	4.20	38.1	3.7	30.6	13.3	6.9
5.9	1.18	6.2	0.00	3.9	4.8	0.77	7.14	3.20	66.7	4.7	24.0	8.2	8.1
3.3	2.50	17.6	0.03	4.9	2.5	0.94	10.09	3.35	59.3	1.6	21.7	22.8	6.9
7.9	0.80	3.1	0.00	4.8	4.1	0.83	6.67	3.54	67.0	3.0	15.3	7.7	8.9
7.3	0.00	0.0	0.00	6.9	13.2	1.56	14.22	3.42	51.8	1.3	23.9	33.1	8.9
7.3	0.45	2.3	0.01	5.0	3.6	1.02	12.77	3.17	61.5	4.8	35.7	7.3	5.9
7.3	0.00	0.0	0.00	8.1	9.8	1.46	11.56	2.95	30.3	1.2	10.8	19.5	10.0
6.3	0.11	0.7	0.32	4.4	0.9	1.09	12.70	3.44	63.8	1.5	19.9	23.6	4.9
2.7	4.92	20.3	0.29	3.8	4.6	0.75	5.68	2.75	65.9	4.3	16.5	6.7	8.1
6.9	0.60	4.4	0.04	5.0	14.3	1.21	13.90	2.87	61.2	3.5	25.2	15.2	6.5
8.9	0.01	0.2	0.00	5.3	1.4	1.22	13.57	3.58	62.6	5.9	39.8	4.2	5.8
3.3	4.88	17.3	0.00	3.2	0.1	0.56	5.57	2.11	77.7	6.3	64.6	6.6	6.3
2.8	2.54	13.1	0.25	6.6	903.9	1.21	11.21	2.84	57.6	5.7	27.9	0.9	8.8
8.6	0.50	1.7	-0.04	2.8	4.5	0.24	2.29	1.73	81.3	5.1	45.0	5.4	8.4
8.5	0.15	0.7	-0.04	8.4	3.9	1.79	13.76	3.71	56.9	4.7	33.4	8.9	9.2
6.3	0.00	0.0	0.08	4.4	0.7	1.34	15.66	4.17	54.5	1.4	16.0	10.9	3.9
6.0	0.92	6.1	-0.22	6.9	1.2	2.36	24.87	3.63	56.1	4.3	18.3	4.2	5.4
8.4	0.06	0.4	0.00	0.9	0.9	0.23	2.11	2.63	89.4	2.7	35.1	20.1	5.2
7.8	0.75	2.0	0.00	5.6	2.3	1.18	7.57	2.86	57.8	6.3	54.8	5.9	8.8
8.0	0.44	1.5	-0.10	3.1	0.6	0.60	5.37	3.05	76.8	1.8	31.2	19.0	6.3
7.8	0.47	2.8	0.00	2.2	0.3	0.21	3.05	2.79	94.5	5.4	33.2	4.3	3.0
3.8	1.17	6.1	0.00	4.3	3.5	0.98	9.73	2.78	72.3	4.0	26.1	8.1	8.1
8.9	0.02	0.1	-0.03	5.3	2.7	1.17	16.76	3.65	58.7	5.1	30.4	5.4	3.8
2.1	2.81	19.0	0.25	4.2	2.4	1.12	11.46	3.24	66.4	2.6	18.2	16.2	5.7
4.8	4.81	19.5	3.93	1.1	-0.4	-0.29	-2.72	2.86	88.2	2.7	44.2	24.7	4.3
4.0	1.87	14.5	0.11	3.4	1.4	0.77	11.07	3.19	74.7	3.2	28.1	15.1	3.3
4.6	0.64	4.0	0.01	7.7	5.3	1.74	16.60	2.98	48.8	5.5	34.4	4.0	8.7
6.3	0.53	2.2	0.00	5.0	1.2	1.10	10.43	4.38	69.0	3.1	28.0	15.3	6.4
8.1	0.96	3.1	0.02	4.2	0.6	0.98	7.29	3.01	66.7	2.1	32.6	25.9	7.7
7.3	1.09	3.9	1.14	6.6	16.7	3.76	23.23	7.27	70.7	0.3	16.1	31.6	7.2
3.5	1.38	8.7	0.09	3.6	6.0	0.63	6.65	3.05	75.3	4.7	24.1	8.0	7.0
3.6	4.10	11.5	0.52	3.5	0.1	0.75	4.64	3.87	69.6	3.8	61.8	19.5	5.5
9.5	0.48	1.5	0.00	3.9	4.6	0.87	5.22	3.00	65.9	5.0	41.6	12.8	9.4
8.8	0.02	0.1	0.00	2.9	1.2	0.50	6.08	2.66	82.1	5.1	26.8	3.8	4.7
7.3	0.03	1.9	0.21	3.3	0.2	0.62	6.68	2.58	72.5	3.1	55.2	25.4	3.6
9.5	0.01	0.0	0.00	2.0	0.0	0.02	0.11	1.42	98.9	6.7	73.7	6.0	6.3
9.0	0.13	0.8	0.04	5.4	6.1	1.13	10.41	3.45	58.5	4.6	14.2	3.4	9.0
2.8	8.26	21.0	0.00	0.0	-0.2	-1.87	-11.19	1.90	193.8	3.2	61.8	28.2	6.5
8.8	0.29	1.6	0.00	3.8	10.8	0.89	10.03	3.32	71.4	4.6	20.8	6.8	6.8
9.0	0.55	1.3	-0.01	5.5	0.8	1.27	7.16	3.37	62.5	5.9	73.5	12.1	8.9
8.4	0.34	0.7	0.01	5.0	0.5	1.24	7.65	2.70	55.1	5.8	63.6	9.8	7.8
5.9	3.11	7.7	0.00	5.0	10.2	0.97	3.06	3.12	59.4	2.5	18.4	17.2	9.7
5.0	2.66	12.4	0.08	3.2	0.5	0.52	4.08	2.78	74.9	0.9	18.2	34.3	6.9
8.9	0.61	1.7	0.03	3.6	2.5	0.92	10.89	2.95	69.3	4.9	31.2	6.5	4.8
7.6	0.00	0.0	0.00	1.0	-0.1	-0.72	-4.87	2.86	141.5	5.7	78.7	12.2	7.0
7.5	0.24	0.8	-0.09	3.6	0.3	0.83	6.08	2.61	56.0	5.4	58.8	10.9	6.1

Name	City	State	Rating	2020 Rating	2019 Rating	Total Assets ($Mil)	One Year Asset Growth	Asset Mix (As a % of Total Assets) Comm-ercial Loans	Cons-umer Loans	Mort-gage Loans	Secur-ities	Capital-ization Index	Lever-age Ratio	Risk-Based Capital Ratio
Mayville Savings Bank	Mayville	WI	**B-**	B-	B-	74.0	5.96	6.8	0.8	34.4	5.9	**9.6**	10.7	23.1
Mayville State Bank	Mayville	MI	**C+**	C+	B-	107.5	16.23	4.9	3.7	24.0	33.8	**7.7**	9.5	0.0
▲ mBank	Manistique	MI	**B+**	B	B	1516.6	0.01	13.7	1.2	12.4	6.7	**7.6**	9.4	15.7
MCBank	Goldthwaite	TX	**B+**	B+	C	403.6	9.73	5.0	4.3	8.1	54.5	**9.4**	10.6	21.2
McClain Bank	Purcell	OK	**A-**	A-	A-	260.3	1.86	10.6	1.3	19.5	4.4	**9.2**	10.4	0.0
McClave State Bank	McClave	CO	**B**	B	B	46.3	4.62	10.0	1.5	5.1	9.0	**10.0**	14.1	0.0
McCurtain County National Bank	Broken Bow	OK	**A-**	A-	A-	337.7	13.31	3.5	5.7	23.5	4.7	**10.0**	11.6	0.0
McGehee Bank	McGehee	AR	**A-**	A-	A-	150.0	9.81	12.8	1.0	1.8	18.8	**10.0**	12.1	0.0
McHenry Savings Bank	McHenry	IL	**D+**	D+	E+	267.9	4.04	4.6	27.8	14.9	18.6	**6.7**	8.8	13.8
McIntosh County Bank	Ashley	ND	**B**	B-	C	110.1	12.31	5.7	1.9	0.1	33.7	**8.6**	10.1	16.8
▲ McKenzie Banking Co.	McKenzie	TN	**A-**	B	B-	179.1	16.34	11.2	5.1	16.0	18.6	**10.0**	11.5	0.0
MCNB Bank and Trust Co.	Welch	WV	**D+**	C-	C+	339.1	4.99	2.8	1.0	21.5	15.3	**10.0**	11.2	0.0
MCS Bank	Lewistown	PA	**C+**	C+	C+	175.2	9.17	8.9	6.2	34.7	14.6	**10.0**	11.7	0.0
Meade County Bank, Inc.	Brandenburg	KY	**B+**	B+	B+	269.9	6.87	3.7	3.4	34.7	23.6	**6.5**	8.5	14.9
Meadows Bank	Las Vegas	NV	**A-**	A-	B+	1305.0	14.79	14.9	0.0	1.3	1.0	**7.7**	10.5	0.0
▲ Mechanics & Farmers Bank	Durham	NC	**C+**	C-	C-	358.4	23.03	18.7	0.3	5.7	18.7	**10.0**	11.9	22.3
▲ Mechanics Bank	Walnut Creek	CA	**B**	B-	B-	18797.5	-0.38	5.6	18.2	9.6	29.0	**6.9**	8.9	15.5
Mechanics Bank	Water Valley	MS	**B**	B	B	276.7	9.23	11.0	1.7	23.4	13.6	**8.4**	10.0	0.0
Mechanics Bank	Mansfield	OH	**B-**	B-	B-	747.4	19.12	2.7	0.9	60.0	14.1	**5.6**	7.6	17.5
Mechanics Cooperative Bank	Taunton	MA	**A-**	A-	B+	675.6	0.75	8.8	1.2	27.7	10.9	**10.0**	11.4	17.8
▲ Medallion Bank	Salt Lake City	UT	**C**	D+	C+	1413.9	7.10	0.9	89.1	0.0	3.4	**10.0**	18.1	19.2
▲ Mediapolis Savings Bank	Mediapolis	IA	**B+**	B	C+	191.4	2.38	6.8	1.3	17.0	13.0	**9.7**	10.8	0.0
Mega Bank	San Gabriel	CA	**C**	C+	B	436.6	6.99	7.5	1.1	13.1	0.0	**9.8**	11.0	0.0
MEMBERS Trust Co.	Tampa	FL	**U**	U	U	41.1	0.77	0.0	0.0	0.0	67.5	**10.0**	92.3	0.0
Menard Bank	Menard	TX	**B-**	B-	B-	66.0	35.40	1.2	0.6	4.1	68.4	**4.4**	6.4	17.6
Meramec Valley Bank	Ellisville	MO	**B-**	C+	C	148.0	-4.49	15.2	0.8	16.9	3.2	**6.3**	8.3	13.3
Mercantile Bank of Michigan	Grand Rapids	MI	**A-**	A-	A-	4737.4	10.27	21.7	0.3	8.7	10.7	**7.6**	9.4	13.0
Mercer County State Bank	Sandy Lake	PA	**B-**	B-	C+	539.0	14.38	10.4	0.5	18.4	34.6	**6.6**	8.6	0.0
Mercer Savings Bank	Celina	OH	**C**	C	C+	152.6	3.06	1.5	0.6	47.4	6.6	**7.2**	9.1	16.0
Merchants & Farmers Bank	Eutaw	AL	**C**	C+	C+	90.8	3.08	8.8	7.6	11.8	31.1	**6.4**	8.4	15.9
▼ Merchants & Farmers Bank	Holly Springs	MS	**C**	C+	B	128.4	12.56	7.3	3.1	8.9	41.5	**7.0**	9.0	0.0
▼ Merchants & Farmers Bank & Trust Co.	Leesville	LA	**B-**	B	B	485.9	12.98	4.8	0.7	19.5	43.7	**9.5**	10.7	0.0
▼ Merchants & Marine Bank	Pascagoula	MS	**C+**	B-	B-	731.8	13.92	6.4	2.2	9.6	14.0	**9.3**	10.5	20.4
Merchants & Planters Bank	Newport	AR	**C+**	C+	C+	351.6	16.71	7.6	3.2	6.3	20.5	**7.0**	9.0	0.0
Merchants and Farmers Bank	Dumas	AR	**B**	B-	B-	181.8	3.41	16.0	2.2	10.6	10.2	**8.2**	9.8	13.6
Merchants and Manufacturers Bank	Joliet	IL	**C**	C	C+	361.2	14.04	20.8	43.4	5.3	1.8	**4.6**	8.5	10.8
Merchants and Planters Bank	Raymond	MS	**B+**	B+	B	113.8	11.94	7.2	0.9	11.9	20.3	**7.8**	9.5	0.0
Merchants Bank	Rugby	ND	**B**	B	B	209.2	15.27	11.4	1.2	2.1	30.3	**6.3**	8.4	12.0
Merchants Bank of Alabama	Cullman	AL	**B+**	B+	B+	388.8	13.42	6.9	2.7	16.5	25.4	**7.2**	9.2	18.0
Merchants Bank of Commerce	Sacramento	CA	**B+**	B+	B+	1916.5	11.99	7.5	0.9	4.1	30.3	**8.2**	9.8	15.7
Merchants Bank of Indiana	Carmel	IN	**B-**	B-	B+	9623.1	4.37	4.7	0.1	0.9	3.2	**4.4**	10.8	0.0
Merchants Bank, N.A.	Winona	MN	**B+**	B	B	2707.3	12.10	16.6	1.4	9.1	5.9	**7.3**	9.2	14.4
Merchants Commercial Bank	Saint Thomas	VI	**B**	B	C	358.7	23.00	8.1	0.3	14.7	56.2	**6.0**	8.0	0.0
Merchants National Bank	Hillsboro	OH	**B**	B	B-	1175.5	11.55	6.0	2.1	28.3	9.7	**5.8**	7.8	12.3
▲ Merchants State Bank	Freeman	SD	**A-**	B	B-	215.1	11.92	5.4	1.1	1.2	27.8	**10.0**	12.4	0.0
Meredith Village Savings Bank	Meredith	NH	**B**	B	B	1220.6	9.01	5.9	9.8	45.4	6.2	**9.3**	10.5	16.7
▲ Meridian Bank	Malvern	PA	**B**	B-		1709.0	8.23	27.0	0.0	19.9	8.7	**9.8**	11.3	0.0
Merit Bank	Huntsville	AL	**D+**	C-	C	180.8	46.74	22.0	1.1	2.7	8.3	**7.1**	9.8	0.0
▲ Merrick Bank Corp.	South Jordan	UT	**C+**	C	C	4349.5	4.80	0.0	82.2	0.0	2.2	**10.0**	25.5	34.9
Merrimack County Savings Bank	Concord	NH	**B-**	B-	B-	1120.4	6.43	13.1	10.1	28.1	9.0	**7.3**	9.2	14.4
▼ MetaBank, N.A.	Sioux Falls	SD	**B**	B+	B+	7055.0	-19.71	33.5	4.0	0.1	28.1	**5.8**	7.8	16.2
Metairie Bank & Trust Co.	Metairie	LA	**B**	B-	B-	543.5	16.58	8.5	0.8	21.2	13.4	**6.3**	8.3	0.0
Methuen Co-operative Bank	Methuen	MA	**C**	C	C	116.2	13.84	6.8	0.9	48.7	15.6	**7.1**	9.1	0.0
Metro Bank	Pell City	AL	**A**	A	A-	953.0	13.40	4.4	1.4	7.9	28.9	**10.0**	13.4	0.0
Metro City Bank	Doraville	GA	**A**	A	A	2520.4	46.03	5.3	0.0	56.7	0.7	**9.4**	10.6	17.9
Metro Phoenix Bank	Phoenix	AZ	**C**			395.4	22.11	30.3	0.0	3.5	0.4	**8.4**	10.1	0.0
Metropolitan Bank	Oakland	CA	**A-**	A-	B	210.0	19.10	1.9	0.3	22.9	2.1	**10.0**	11.2	0.0
▲ Metropolitan Capital Bank & Trust	Chicago	IL	**C-**	D+	D+	244.5	10.06	40.4	0.3	1.4	26.1	**7.7**	9.4	14.4
▼ Metropolitan Commercial Bank	New York	NY	**B+**	A-	A-	5785.5	45.77	10.3	0.7	2.2	9.4	**5.3**	7.3	12.2
Metz Banking Co.	Nevada	MO	**B+**	B+	B+	96.5	13.18	6.2	0.9	10.6	24.5	**9.1**	10.4	0.0

Asset Quality Index	Adjusted Non-Performing Loans as a % of Total Loans	Adjusted Non-Performing Loans as a % of Capital	Net Charge-Offs Avg Loans	Profitability Index	Net Income ($Mil)	Return on Assets (R.O.A.)	Return on Equity (R.O.E.)	Net Interest Spread	Overhead Efficiency Ratio	Liquidity Index	Liquidity Ratio	Hot Money Ratio	Stability Index
4.5	2.79	11.6	-0.02	**3.4**	0.2	0.57	5.18	2.85	71.7	**5.7**	44.9	6.5	**6.0**
8.3	0.85	1.8	0.06	**3.2**	0.3	0.55	5.62	2.89	79.9	**6.9**	60.1	3.8	**5.5**
5.9	1.11	4.6	0.05	**5.6**	8.1	1.07	9.93	4.52	70.0	**5.6**	32.2	5.7	**8.5**
5.2	2.61	7.1	0.00	**6.0**	3.1	1.58	12.88	3.95	59.1	**6.2**	59.3	8.5	**7.5**
7.7	0.46	2.5	0.00	**6.7**	1.8	1.28	12.64	3.74	62.7	**5.0**	31.2	6.0	**6.4**
7.1	0.30	0.8	-0.11	**7.7**	0.4	1.54	11.08	4.59	57.4	**0.6**	13.6	44.4	**6.3**
6.9	1.44	5.2	-0.15	**5.7**	1.3	0.79	6.75	2.91	55.1	**5.5**	57.1	11.8	**7.5**
6.7	1.11	2.8	0.00	**7.5**	1.4	1.89	15.41	3.43	56.8	**1.6**	11.7	21.4	**9.2**
3.9	0.51	3.8	0.03	**3.8**	2.0	1.46	16.85	3.67	76.0	**1.3**	19.3	18.9	**3.3**
5.6	1.84	4.4	0.00	**5.4**	0.7	1.30	12.78	3.34	59.9	**5.2**	41.3	8.8	**7.4**
5.6	1.80	7.4	0.42	**10.0**	2.4	2.79	25.09	5.96	49.7	**5.8**	55.0	9.7	**8.8**
3.0	4.30	17.9	0.14	**4.9**	1.8	1.08	9.65	3.84	65.5	**3.5**	20.8	12.1	**6.2**
5.9	0.97	5.9	0.24	**2.5**	0.3	0.38	3.14	3.06	74.8	**1.8**	19.7	17.4	**6.5**
8.9	0.00	0.6	0.00	**6.0**	1.7	1.25	14.72	3.51	55.6	**3.4**	26.7	13.6	**5.5**
5.1	1.52	7.0	0.02	**9.7**	11.3	1.82	16.59	3.98	46.7	**5.0**	29.6	8.6	**10.0**
6.0	1.88	5.8	0.02	**3.5**	1.2	0.71	6.68	3.23	80.5	**2.2**	29.0	20.4	**3.0**
6.3	0.41	1.9	0.13	**4.9**	100.2	1.07	8.08	3.57	55.7	**5.9**	30.6	3.9	**8.5**
4.8	1.17	7.1	0.00	**5.3**	1.5	1.15	11.22	3.78	65.5	**2.0**	29.6	23.9	**6.0**
7.3	0.60	3.6	0.00	**3.8**	2.7	0.75	9.80	2.70	69.1	**3.7**	27.0	12.0	**4.9**
8.7	0.13	0.5	0.00	**6.2**	4.1	1.23	11.58	3.76	58.1	**1.6**	13.9	19.5	**7.1**
2.4	1.56	6.7	2.52	**7.9**	31.3	4.81	27.27	10.00	27.5	**0.2**	9.5	0.4	**7.1**
5.8	0.52	5.2	0.26	**5.8**	1.4	1.45	13.82	3.08	51.2	**3.8**	33.7	13.9	**6.6**
2.4	1.26	9.3	-0.01	**4.3**	2.5	1.17	10.88	3.14	53.5	**0.6**	19.7	63.3	**6.3**
9.3	na	0.0	na	**7.4**	0.6	3.10	3.35	1.25	95.5	**4.0**	na	0.0	**7.0**
10.0	0.00	0.0	0.00	**3.3**	0.3	0.65	10.07	1.93	67.4	**4.9**	70.1	15.7	**5.0**
8.5	0.18	0.7	0.00	**4.8**	1.0	1.42	17.54	3.46	65.3	**3.8**	21.4	10.3	**5.4**
7.5	0.71	2.5	-0.04	**7.1**	34.9	1.50	15.05	2.79	54.6	**4.3**	21.3	7.8	**9.0**
4.3	4.07	13.9	0.00	**5.3**	3.0	1.16	12.39	3.59	62.2	**4.0**	28.5	11.3	**6.0**
8.3	0.08	0.6	0.06	**2.6**	0.2	0.29	3.18	2.89	82.7	**3.8**	25.2	11.0	**5.2**
4.3	2.47	12.8	0.00	**2.5**	0.1	0.20	2.30	2.99	95.0	**2.7**	29.6	17.9	**4.8**
6.3	1.26	4.9	0.04	**1.1**	-0.3	-0.43	-4.57	3.25	117.7	**3.2**	42.5	19.8	**4.4**
5.3	1.55	5.5	0.06	**3.6**	1.8	0.78	6.60	3.25	77.0	**4.9**	38.0	9.0	**6.5**
4.5	2.64	9.7	0.14	**3.1**	1.5	0.43	3.80	3.53	87.0	**5.9**	52.4	7.9	**7.2**
4.8	1.54	7.7	0.09	**3.6**	1.1	0.65	7.10	2.91	76.5	**2.3**	29.0	19.5	**5.1**
5.1	1.45	7.7	0.34	**4.7**	0.8	0.88	8.95	3.87	69.4	**1.8**	23.2	21.7	**6.4**
2.4	1.21	12.8	0.00	**5.1**	1.7	0.97	12.57	4.12	66.2	**1.6**	8.3	14.0	**4.4**
8.9	0.00	0.0	-0.08	**4.1**	0.4	0.66	6.58	3.10	79.4	**5.5**	41.3	7.1	**6.0**
5.5	0.00	8.3	0.00	**7.4**	1.5	1.43	16.51	3.65	46.3	**2.5**	23.7	17.1	**5.8**
6.3	1.30	4.1	0.10	**5.3**	2.0	1.04	11.14	3.29	62.6	**5.1**	46.9	11.5	**5.6**
7.2	0.71	2.7	-0.05	**5.8**	10.8	1.18	11.01	3.36	54.5	**6.0**	38.5	6.3	**9.2**
7.6	0.07	0.4	0.00	**9.5**	113.2	2.38	24.85	2.89	26.5	**3.2**	4.8	5.8	**9.6**
5.7	1.09	5.1	0.05	**7.2**	19.1	1.45	14.65	3.40	57.9	**5.8**	32.8	6.0	**9.6**
6.6	1.32	3.9	-0.26	**7.9**	2.5	1.43	15.47	3.38	46.4	**7.1**	55.8	1.5	**5.1**
6.0	0.63	5.0	0.00	**5.6**	6.5	1.13	12.49	3.45	59.8	**4.1**	20.7	8.2	**8.4**
7.5	0.38	1.6	0.10	**7.3**	1.6	1.53	12.15	3.71	52.6	**3.8**	32.4	12.6	**8.5**
6.8	0.66	4.0	0.01	**4.6**	5.1	0.87	8.39	3.65	68.5	**4.0**	4.2	7.5	**7.3**
6.3	0.71	4.5	0.01	**9.1**	19.5	2.28	21.23	3.79	67.8	**2.1**	7.3	2.4	**9.4**
7.0	0.32	3.4	0.03	**0.0**	-0.3	-0.30	-2.82	3.05	95.2	**4.9**	29.8	6.3	**4.4**
2.8	3.05	7.1	6.17	**10.0**	231.6	9.87	40.17	15.14	30.0	**1.6**	28.1	11.8	**9.5**
7.8	0.27	1.7	0.00	**3.8**	4.1	0.77	8.03	3.49	70.1	**4.4**	8.6	5.8	**6.7**
4.3	1.43	4.7	0.83	**8.5**	102.5	2.22	22.53	3.48	55.7	**5.4**	28.7	0.3	**8.9**
8.6	0.23	1.3	0.07	**5.4**	3.0	1.12	13.51	3.85	65.4	**5.4**	37.6	6.2	**5.6**
7.1	0.74	4.5	0.00	**3.1**	0.3	0.51	5.52	2.76	76.9	**3.8**	34.4	14.1	**4.8**
8.9	0.45	1.9	0.00	**7.0**	6.0	1.31	9.81	3.48	55.5	**4.5**	46.9	14.5	**8.9**
7.4	0.45	3.0	0.01	**10.0**	27.5	2.56	22.88	4.54	35.9	**0.8**	14.6	19.0	**9.3**
8.3	0.01	0.1	-0.04	**8.6**	3.3	1.79	16.59	4.16	43.1	**4.1**	29.4	11.1	**4.3**
7.1	0.87	2.9	0.00	**5.9**	0.9	0.89	7.80	3.91	67.9	**1.1**	19.4	31.7	**7.2**
4.1	2.72	12.8	-0.01	**2.7**	0.2	0.20	2.26	4.80	93.8	**2.0**	42.3	25.2	**4.2**
7.4	0.18	1.4	0.05	**5.8**	26.6	1.05	13.50	2.87	50.1	**5.4**	42.2	1.5	**8.1**
9.0	0.00	0.0	-0.01	**5.8**	0.7	1.55	14.60	3.45	56.2	**3.9**	44.6	16.3	**6.2**

Name	City	State	Rating	2020 Rating	2019 Rating	Total Assets ($Mil)	One Year Asset Growth	Asset Mix (As a % of Total Assets) Commercial Loans	Consumer Loans	Mortgage Loans	Securities	Capitalization Index	Leverage Ratio	Risk-Based Capital Ratio
Mi Bank	Bloomfield Hills	MI	**D**	D		147.0	56.21	29.3	0.0	1.3	1.6	**10.0**	12.0	19.6
▼ Miami Savings Bank	Miamitown	OH	**C-**	C	A-	144.3	4.09	4.1	0.2	31.1	1.1	**0.0**	15.8	0.0
Mid America Bank	Jefferson City	MO	**B+**	B+	A-	535.4	-13.68	13.0	1.8	16.3	15.8	**9.5**	10.7	0.0
▲ Mid Penn Bank	Millersburg	PA	**B**	B-	B-	3461.0	18.48	21.2	0.2	10.8	4.8	**6.6**	8.6	13.4
▲ Mid-America Bank	Baldwin City	KS	**A-**	B+	B-	310.8	16.21	4.4	1.0	37.6	1.3	**8.0**	9.7	14.4
Mid-Central National Bank	Wadena	MN	**C+**	C	B-	140.9	13.90	2.8	11.8	33.7	0.7	**10.0**	12.1	27.3
Mid-Missouri Bank	Springfield	MO	**B**	B-	B	863.7	11.71	6.5	0.8	14.4	13.4	**6.1**	8.1	14.1
Mid-Southern Savings Bank, F.S.B.	Salem	IN	**B-**	B-		249.1	14.56	2.8	0.6	24.6	44.9	**9.8**	16.3	0.0
MidAmerica National Bank	Canton	IL	**B**	B	B-	529.0	9.56	5.3	6.3	8.5	26.8	**8.8**	10.2	0.0
MidCountry Bank	Minneapolis	MN	**B**	B-	B-	880.6	5.85	19.0	3.6	7.4	12.8	**9.1**	12.2	14.2
▲ Middlesex Federal Savings, F.A.	Somerville	MA	**C**	C-	C	701.1	52.89	8.8	0.0	21.6	14.5	**5.0**	7.0	15.6
Middlesex Savings Bank	Natick	MA	**B-**	B-	B	5925.6	4.95	6.9	0.1	19.8	34.3	**10.0**	11.9	17.9
Middletown State Bank	Middletown	IL	**B-**	B-	B-	39.7	-0.71	1.3	1.6	34.2	12.1	**7.0**	9.0	0.0
Middletown Valley Bank	Middletown	MD	**C+**	C+	B-	722.5	8.14	22.8	0.1	17.3	12.0	**6.0**	9.1	0.0
▲ MidFirst Bank	Oklahoma City	OK	**B+**	B	B	31048.2	27.60	7.8	0.5	51.6	10.7	**6.7**	8.7	18.9
Midland Community Bank	Kincaid	IL	**B+**	B+	B+	76.8	2.88	12.8	3.0	30.0	30.0	**8.4**	10.6	13.7
Midland Federal S&L Assn.	Bridgeview	IL	**D**	D	D+	127.8	8.23	0.0	0.4	22.1	37.1	**5.9**	7.9	39.5
Midland States Bank	Effingham	IL	**B-**	B-	B-	6616.6	-0.19	16.6	12.8	5.9	11.3	**6.3**	9.2	12.0
▼ MidSouth Bank	Dothan	AL	**C**	B-	B+	557.7	17.74	11.2	0.5	7.2	15.1	**8.3**	9.9	0.0
Midstates Bank, N.A.	Council Bluffs	IA	**C+**	C+	B-	632.7	1.51	5.7	0.5	8.3	40.4	**6.6**	8.7	15.3
Midwest Bank	Monmouth	IL	**C+**	C	C+	634.3	16.33	8.0	2.5	6.6	35.4	**6.6**	8.7	16.6
Midwest Bank	Detroit Lakes	MN	**B+**	B+	B+	645.1	11.08	14.9	1.7	11.7	2.6	**6.5**	8.5	13.7
Midwest Bank	Pierce	NE	**B+**	B+	B+	915.4	5.00	9.6	1.5	2.4	24.8	**8.0**	9.7	14.3
▲ Midwest BankCentre	Saint Louis	MO	**B-**	C+	C+	2325.0	-0.48	22.7	2.4	13.9	12.1	**7.6**	10.2	13.0
Midwest Community Bank	Freeport	IL	**A-**	B+	B-	367.1	-10.67	4.3	0.1	43.1	0.4	**10.0**	11.0	20.0
Midwest Heritage Bank, FSB	West Des Moines	IA	**A**	A	A	368.2	12.98	7.5	11.0	20.2	10.3	**10.0**	11.6	19.0
Midwest Independent BankersBank	Jefferson City	MO	**A-**	A-	B+	249.7	-6.68	1.7	0.0	0.4	10.0	**10.0**	16.0	20.6
▲ Midwest Regional Bank	Festus	MO	**B-**	C+	C	898.0	8.21	23.6	0.2	5.4	7.4	**7.0**	9.1	12.5
▲ MidWestOne Bank	Iowa City	IA	**B**	C+	B	5742.5	9.92	12.0	1.2	6.2	36.1	**7.2**	9.2	13.0
Mifflinburg Bank and Trust Co.	Mifflinburg	PA	**B**	B	B	538.2	8.31	10.6	1.6	16.7	19.9	**7.4**	9.3	0.0
Milford Building and Loan Assn., SB	Milford	IL	**D+**	D+	D+	32.2	2.48	0.0	0.0	54.2	0.0	**7.0**	9.0	20.3
Milford Federal Bank	Milford	MA	**C+**	C+	C+	453.1	4.53	0.4	1.3	70.1	2.3	**10.0**	11.5	19.9
Millbury National Bank	Millbury	MA	**C**	C	C	103.2	1.91	3.7	1.1	26.0	19.4	**8.9**	10.3	16.7
Milledgeville State Bank	Milledgeville	IL	**A-**	A-	A-	163.9	7.82	13.4	0.6	5.1	24.2	**9.7**	10.8	16.4
Millennial Bank	Leeds	AL	**C-**	C-	D	112.9	-0.87	16.7	0.5	9.3	15.9	**5.0**	9.4	0.0
▼ Millennium Bank	Des Plaines	IL	**A-**	A	A-	259.8	31.56	13.4	0.0	4.3	0.0	**9.4**	10.6	18.3
Millennium Bank	Ooltewah	TN	**C+**	C+	B-	509.8	7.56	14.5	0.2	8.2	6.8	**6.2**	9.1	0.0
Millville Savings Bank	Millville	NJ	**C+**	C+	C+	151.4	6.45	0.1	0.0	21.8	48.7	**10.0**	13.0	27.9
Milton Savings Bank	Milton	PA	**B-**	B	B	72.2	3.50	0.0	1.3	48.8	13.5	**10.0**	22.3	64.2
▼ Minden Exchange Bank & Trust Co.	Minden	NE	**A-**	A	A	174.9	12.26	5.2	1.8	0.7	31.3	**10.0**	18.0	0.0
Mineola Community Bank, SSB	Mineola	TX	**C**	C	C+	350.0	22.44	2.0	1.1	43.2	15.0	**7.5**	9.3	0.0
Miners and Merchants Bank	Thomas	WV	**C+**	C	B-	63.2	5.86	0.6	1.1	22.9	48.8	**10.0**	14.4	0.0
Miners Exchange Bank	Coeburn	VA	**C**	C+	B-	92.9	6.93	2.1	5.4	32.1	13.3	**10.0**	12.4	0.0
Minnesota Bank & Trust	Edina	MN	**B**	B	B	961.1	1.04	22.9	1.4	4.3	33.6	**7.2**	9.1	14.5
Minnesota First Credit and Savings, Inc.	Rochester	MN	**C+**	C+	C+	25.3	-1.41	1.6	36.2	47.0	0.0	**10.0**	16.6	24.8
Minnesota Lakes Bank	Delano	MN	**B-**	B-	B-	144.6	-7.53	24.3	0.9	4.4	10.3	**5.6**	7.6	15.5
Minnesota National Bank	Sauk Centre	MN	**B+**	B+	B+	254.3	11.73	8.7	2.8	12.1	30.4	**7.2**	9.1	15.2
▲ MinnStar Bank N.A.	Lake Crystal	MN	**B+**	B	B-	164.6	14.91	13.0	0.5	15.0	1.4	**6.7**	8.7	13.8
Minnwest Bank	Redwood Falls	MN	**A-**	B+	B+	2323.1	4.31	6.6	0.7	2.1	15.4	**9.3**	10.5	16.1
Minster Bank	Minster	OH	**B+**	B+	B+	674.0	13.01	8.0	0.5	6.8	29.8	**5.9**	7.9	18.1
Mission Bank	Kingman	AZ	**C+**	C+	B-	178.7	15.25	4.0	0.2	3.0	49.9	**4.5**	6.5	16.2
Mission Bank	Bakersfield	CA	**B+**	B+	B+	1421.0	28.58	11.2	0.0	1.8	13.8	**6.0**	8.9	0.0
▼ Mission National Bank	San Francisco	CA	**C+**	B-	B+	221.2	-14.79	1.3	0.0	11.9	0.0	**10.0**	16.6	0.0
Mission Valley Bank	Sun Valley	CA	**B+**	B+	A-	423.0	-16.47	17.1	0.0	1.4	10.4	**9.8**	10.9	16.4
Mississippi River Bank	Belle Chasse	LA	**B+**	B+	A-	125.5	5.94	21.9	0.7	10.0	3.5	**10.0**	13.1	37.4
Mizuho Bank (USA)	New York	NY	**B-**	B-	B	7855.2	-0.42	31.2	0.0	0.0	0.0	**10.0**	18.7	21.0
MNB Bank	McCook	NE	**B**	B-	C+	408.3	5.07	5.5	0.4	4.9	34.8	**10.0**	13.9	0.0
▲ Modern Bank, N.A.	New York	NY	**C+**	C-	C	807.0	-7.28	49.5	0.0	4.0	13.0	**8.9**	11.1	14.1
Monona Bank	Monona	WI	**B**	B	B-	1128.6	8.76	11.5	0.5	14.2	7.3	**6.0**	9.5	11.7
Monroe Federal S&L Assn.	Tipp City	OH	**C-**	C-	C	137.7	15.66	7.6	0.6	29.1	27.2	**6.9**	8.9	0.0

Asset Quality Index	Adjusted Non-Performing Loans as a % of Total Loans	Adjusted Non-Performing Loans as a % of Capital	Net Charge-Offs Avg Loans	Profitability Index	Net Income ($Mil)	Return on Assets (R.O.A.)	Return on Equity (R.O.E.)	Net Interest Spread	Overhead Efficiency Ratio	Liquidity Index	Liquidity Ratio	Hot Money Ratio	Stability Index
8.3	0.00	0.0	0.00	**0.5**	-0.1	-0.10	-0.81	3.12	90.7	**2.9**	28.8	16.8	**2.0**
8.0	0.62	2.2	-0.02	**3.6**	0.4	0.55	3.50	1.99	72.8	**3.0**	43.3	23.0	**8.4**
4.6	1.41	7.5	0.41	**7.4**	5.3	1.78	17.11	3.70	52.4	**4.5**	15.6	5.7	**8.9**
6.4	0.34	2.3	0.06	**5.5**	21.7	1.31	14.35	3.43	54.4	**3.9**	21.7	8.9	**7.8**
8.8	0.00	0.4	0.00	**9.2**	3.8	2.52	26.58	3.36	42.1	**1.0**	24.8	31.1	**6.9**
5.4	0.72	4.6	0.06	**3.1**	0.3	0.44	3.01	3.34	81.3	**4.7**	41.1	11.6	**6.0**
7.7	0.30	1.6	-0.01	**5.7**	5.0	1.21	14.91	3.44	63.0	**3.0**	25.3	7.0	**5.8**
7.3	1.56	3.0	-0.04	**3.4**	0.9	0.78	4.49	3.20	75.2	**6.3**	63.1	8.3	**7.6**
4.5	1.57	5.1	-0.02	**6.6**	3.4	1.39	11.41	4.05	59.8	**4.2**	14.1	7.1	**7.5**
5.3	0.94	4.0	0.06	**5.6**	5.2	1.19	9.56	3.97	59.6	**3.8**	16.9	9.5	**8.4**
8.9	0.15	1.4	0.00	**2.8**	1.2	0.43	6.25	2.54	99.8	**4.6**	40.6	11.3	**4.6**
6.5	1.46	6.4	-0.03	**3.1**	11.3	0.39	3.32	2.21	77.6	**5.3**	46.3	12.7	**8.8**
8.1	0.00	0.0	0.00	**7.7**	0.4	1.92	22.07	3.11	37.1	**1.6**	20.1	24.0	**5.7**
6.9	0.46	3.0	1.56	**3.9**	2.3	0.66	7.37	3.72	55.7	**3.9**	19.2	9.4	**5.5**
6.0	0.41	3.1	0.05	**8.2**	437.2	2.82	36.37	3.51	36.1	**1.8**	13.7	4.4	**9.2**
7.8	0.23	3.1	-0.01	**8.6**	0.6	1.51	14.39	2.83	47.7	**2.3**	30.4	21.6	**7.5**
6.2	3.27	10.3	0.00	**0.2**	-0.4	-0.58	-7.13	1.61	134.6	**6.8**	78.9	7.8	**3.2**
4.0	1.25	6.8	0.23	**5.5**	41.6	1.24	10.71	3.53	63.8	**4.1**	12.6	7.4	**8.0**
8.8	0.02	0.1	-0.02	**2.5**	0.8	0.31	3.06	2.85	88.6	**4.9**	40.1	10.5	**6.6**
2.1	4.57	16.5	1.20	**4.7**	4.4	1.40	13.70	3.84	60.2	**5.7**	44.3	7.1	**6.4**
4.0	2.22	7.8	-0.05	**4.0**	2.6	0.85	7.45	3.08	63.6	**3.4**	25.4	9.7	**6.7**
5.1	1.00	7.4	-0.07	**7.7**	5.6	1.76	20.24	3.03	49.1	**4.4**	31.2	10.1	**7.4**
7.1	0.15	0.9	0.00	**8.5**	8.3	1.84	18.52	4.13	49.1	**1.9**	17.2	19.0	**8.6**
7.5	0.37	2.3	0.03	**4.3**	11.0	0.96	9.56	3.17	66.0	**3.8**	9.3	9.5	**8.4**
8.5	0.16	0.8	0.00	**10.0**	12.8	7.58	75.50	2.57	70.1	**1.2**	13.4	18.7	**8.1**
7.7	0.02	0.2	0.05	**9.5**	4.0	2.03	17.66	2.97	65.0	**5.4**	31.3	3.7	**8.9**
8.5	0.00	0.0	-0.28	**6.6**	2.0	1.51	9.87	2.27	65.2	**4.5**	37.2	5.4	**8.9**
5.2	0.40	2.3	0.29	**4.8**	5.1	1.11	13.31	3.12	56.5	**1.7**	17.9	22.6	**4.8**
5.6	1.28	5.8	0.04	**5.7**	42.4	1.50	14.10	3.08	54.4	**4.8**	31.9	11.3	**7.3**
5.6	1.02	4.8	0.00	**5.1**	3.0	1.15	11.93	3.15	59.1	**4.1**	21.7	8.7	**7.0**
4.2	0.74	17.0	0.28	**2.8**	0.1	0.43	4.83	2.47	70.7	**1.9**	39.0	41.4	**4.9**
8.7	0.62	3.5	0.01	**2.5**	0.6	0.27	2.37	2.74	88.7	**3.3**	14.1	12.2	**6.7**
6.2	0.91	3.5	0.00	**3.2**	0.2	0.39	4.02	3.93	88.8	**1.3**	21.0	28.9	**5.3**
6.6	0.59	2.8	0.00	**6.2**	1.2	1.53	13.21	3.55	43.0	**1.5**	36.0	48.5	**8.3**
8.7	0.00	0.0	0.00	**2.4**	0.2	0.36	3.89	4.24	87.5	**3.0**	21.4	14.7	**5.0**
5.4	1.43	9.1	-0.02	**9.8**	3.2	2.65	24.75	3.24	51.0	**1.5**	32.8	30.8	**8.2**
3.0	4.08	17.3	-0.17	**4.4**	2.5	1.03	10.40	3.52	72.7	**2.9**	30.2	15.3	**5.7**
7.2	4.88	9.9	0.26	**2.4**	0.2	0.27	1.98	2.32	90.0	**7.2**	66.2	3.3	**7.1**
9.9	0.48	1.3	0.00	**2.0**	0.0	-0.03	-0.15	2.56	107.1	**6.1**	59.5	7.2	**7.5**
8.6	0.00	0.5	-0.02	**5.5**	0.8	0.92	5.05	2.87	62.9	**4.7**	20.1	4.6	**9.0**
7.0	0.64	4.4	0.01	**2.4**	0.4	0.27	2.74	2.76	88.9	**3.4**	35.1	16.1	**5.3**
9.3	0.59	2.9	0.05	**3.1**	0.2	0.65	4.49	2.17	75.9	**7.2**	72.8	2.5	**6.8**
6.5	2.23	6.8	0.17	**2.2**	0.1	0.16	1.26	4.41	95.9	**4.8**	41.6	11.1	**5.8**
4.5	1.03	3.2	-0.02	**7.6**	8.0	1.65	12.90	3.36	48.5	**5.5**	30.9	2.7	**7.6**
6.8	0.08	1.6	0.03	**2.9**	0.1	0.35	2.13	5.27	92.8	**2.6**	15.2	10.9	**6.7**
8.1	0.04	0.1	0.00	**4.8**	0.8	1.13	12.47	4.81	75.3	**5.6**	30.9	2.1	**5.1**
7.9	0.26	1.2	0.00	**6.1**	1.9	1.58	14.54	3.88	61.8	**5.2**	37.5	7.8	**6.9**
8.5	0.07	0.5	-0.02	**6.8**	1.5	1.91	21.76	4.06	57.0	**3.8**	19.7	10.4	**5.7**
5.8	1.44	6.6	0.01	**6.1**	14.2	1.21	11.30	3.66	55.8	**4.5**	30.2	7.0	**9.6**
8.8	0.33	1.6	0.00	**5.9**	3.7	1.12	13.79	2.68	56.1	**6.0**	43.8	4.7	**6.1**
8.0	0.62	2.4	-0.02	**2.0**	0.2	0.28	4.06	2.73	98.5	**7.4**	70.2	2.7	**4.0**
8.6	0.05	0.3	0.00	**7.1**	8.3	1.22	14.89	3.32	50.1	**6.5**	34.7	1.4	**8.4**
7.9	0.00	0.0	0.00	**1.0**	-0.7	-0.59	-3.53	3.38	117.2	**2.1**	43.0	31.1	**6.7**
7.4	0.20	0.7	-0.15	**6.3**	2.8	1.24	12.10	4.10	66.2	**5.0**	32.0	6.3	**6.2**
4.2	4.48	16.8	-0.08	**5.9**	0.8	1.20	8.99	3.11	62.9	**6.5**	50.7	3.6	**8.4**
8.2	0.00	0.0	0.00	**3.4**	17.2	0.44	2.33	0.81	88.3	**1.4**	24.7	16.4	**8.6**
5.4	3.28	9.4	0.00	**5.0**	2.3	1.12	7.78	3.15	60.8	**3.6**	31.2	14.1	**7.5**
4.9	1.00	5.7	0.00	**3.6**	3.5	0.81	8.16	2.71	66.8	**0.3**	4.3	68.3	**6.6**
6.3	0.35	2.5	0.00	**5.6**	6.1	1.12	10.34	3.65	61.7	**4.0**	13.5	8.3	**8.8**
5.2	1.65	9.7	-0.02	**1.7**	0.1	0.10	1.12	2.65	94.9	**4.5**	38.4	11.1	**4.9**

Name	City	State	Rating	2020 Rating	2019 Rating	Total Assets ($Mil)	One Year Asset Growth	Asset Mix (As a % of Total Assets) Commercial Loans	Consumer Loans	Mortgage Loans	Securities	Capitalization Index	Leverage Ratio	Risk-Based Capital Ratio
Monroe Savings Bank	Williamstown	NJ	**B-**	B-	B-	103.7	6.79	1.7	9.4	49.9	8.5	**10.0**	13.5	27.0
Monson Savings Bank	Monson	MA	**B**	B-	B-	554.6	10.43	8.4	0.4	26.5	9.7	**6.5**	8.7	0.0
Montecito Bank & Trust	Santa Barbara	CA	**B-**	B	B+	2185.6	16.12	12.9	0.8	10.1	28.7	**6.3**	8.5	0.0
Monterey County Bank	Monterey	CA	**D+**	D+	C-	239.9	20.52	16.0	0.1	3.9	28.9	**6.7**	8.7	15.2
Montezuma State Bank	Montezuma	IA	**B-**	B-	B-	50.1	15.47	10.7	8.1	6.2	17.7	**10.0**	11.3	0.0
Montgomery Bank	Sikeston	MO	**B-**	B-	C+	1156.6	7.30	14.7	0.4	18.6	2.9	**5.2**	7.2	11.9
Monticello Banking Co.	Monticello	KY	**B**	B	B	989.9	13.80	5.7	2.1	17.4	26.7	**6.4**	8.8	0.0
▲ Montrose Savings Bank	Montrose	MO	**A-**	B+	B	53.1	18.51	5.9	3.2	12.0	28.1	**10.0**	13.5	0.0
Moody National Bank	Galveston	TX	**B+**	B+	A-	1545.5	16.44	9.2	0.5	4.0	28.4	**10.0**	13.0	0.0
Morgan Stanley Bank, N.A.	Salt Lake City	UT	**A-**	A-	A	173043.0	3.57	3.8	5.1	0.3	36.8	**9.0**	10.4	20.5
Morgan Stanley Private Bank, N.A.	New York	NY	**A-**	A-	A	135856.0	32.51	4.1	15.5	28.6	16.2	**5.4**	7.4	25.2
Morganton Savings Bank, S.S.B.	Morganton	NC	**B-**	B-	B+	123.1	9.17	0.2	0.1	26.8	10.8	**10.0**	21.8	0.0
Morgantown Bank & Trust Co., Inc.	Morgantown	KY	**B-**	B-	B-	254.6	15.36	6.9	3.2	33.8	16.5	**5.8**	7.8	0.0
Morris Bank	Dublin	GA	**B+**	B	C+	1329.3	18.19	9.5	1.6	12.1	20.9	**9.7**	10.9	14.8
Morton Community Bank	Morton	IL	**B+**	B+	B	4948.9	13.18	10.7	1.7	6.4	35.1	**6.8**	8.8	14.4
▲ Mound City Bank	Platteville	WI	**B**	B-	C+	435.5	5.66	2.5	0.6	16.3	17.2	**10.0**	11.6	17.9
Mount Vernon Bank	Mount Vernon	GA	**B**	B	B	163.6	12.62	8.9	2.0	12.7	29.3	**8.7**	10.2	0.0
▲ Mount Vernon Bank and Trust Co.	Mount Vernon	IA	**A**	A-	A-	161.0	13.00	7.5	4.7	27.9	35.8	**10.0**	12.6	0.0
Mountain Commerce Bank	Knoxville	TN	**A-**	B+	B+	1238.1	5.93	12.4	0.9	20.8	8.1	**8.2**	10.6	13.5
Mountain Pacific Bank	Everett	WA	**C-**	C-		579.9	14.96	14.7	0.6	6.7	2.0	**6.3**	8.9	12.0
Mountain Valley Bank	Walden	CO	**B**	B	B	328.4	21.74	12.5	1.6	16.8	27.4	**6.9**	8.9	0.0
Mountain Valley Bank	Dunlap	TN	**C+**	C+	C+	130.7	13.85	9.5	5.4	34.2	17.5	**5.9**	7.9	15.6
Mountain Valley Bank, N.A.	Elkins	WV	**B+**	B+	A-	177.3	7.18	9.6	1.8	23.8	28.3	**10.0**	12.3	0.0
Mountain View Bank of Commerce	Westminster	CO	**C+**	C+	C	157.4	-3.95	12.3	0.0	6.6	1.7	**7.5**	9.7	13.0
▲ MountainOne Bank	North Adams	MA	**B+**	B-	B	890.7	-3.42	13.8	0.7	21.7	9.2	**10.0**	13.4	18.7
▲ Movement Bank	Danville	VA	**C**	D+	D	86.9	21.00	3.0	0.9	15.7	12.4	**10.0**	21.4	34.2
MRV Banks	Sainte Genevieve	MO	**B+**	B+	B	540.6	23.74	29.4	0.4	6.0	2.1	**3.5**	9.7	0.0
Mt. McKinley Bank	Fairbanks	AK	**B+**	B+	A-	609.5	16.08	9.7	0.3	4.6	43.4	**10.0**	17.1	0.0
▼ Mt. Victory State Bank	Mount Victory	OH	**D**	C-	C	23.8	23.81	3.6	6.4	12.1	20.2	**6.6**	8.6	0.0
Muenster State Bank	Muenster	TX	**A**	A	A	195.5	5.64	5.6	2.2	7.6	63.1	**10.0**	14.5	0.0
▲ MUFG Union Bank, N.A.	San Francisco	CA	**C**	C-	C+	133207.2	-2.25	14.6	2.2	18.6	21.5	**10.0**	11.2	16.9
Municipal Trust and Savings Bank	Bourbonnais	IL	**A**	A	A	347.9	7.10	2.8	0.5	22.0	5.7	**10.0**	14.4	29.7
Murphy Bank	Fresno	CA	**A-**	A-	B+	351.7	13.63	30.8	20.6	12.4	0.0	**7.9**	11.4	0.0
Murphy-Wall State Bank and Trust Co.	Pinckneyville	IL	**C-**	C	B-	158.6	5.71	9.6	3.3	14.9	32.0	**8.1**	9.8	0.0
▼ Mutual Federal Bank	Chicago	IL	**B-**	B	C	99.9	18.04	0.0	0.0	43.6	0.1	**10.0**	16.1	25.6
Mutual S&L Assn.	Metairie	LA	**B-**	B-	B-	45.3	0.73	0.0	0.3	67.2	0.0	**10.0**	30.2	67.1
Mutual Savings Assn.	Leavenworth	KS	**A**	A	A-	275.2	12.27	3.5	1.3	25.4	35.4	**10.0**	26.8	43.7
Mutual Savings Bank	Franklin	IN	**B-**	B-	B-	229.9	14.20	3.9	1.3	13.2	33.5	**6.4**	8.7	12.1
Mutual Savings Bank	Hartsville	SC	**D+**	D	C-	57.4	4.59	3.8	2.6	22.1	21.3	**10.0**	23.4	47.4
MutualOne Bank	Framingham	MA	**A**	A	A-	1040.3	6.37	20.2	0.6	15.3	6.4	**10.0**	18.8	0.0
MVB Bank, Inc.	Fairmont	WV	**A-**	A-	B+	2741.8	24.01	23.5	0.1	7.5	16.4	**8.1**	11.0	0.0
Nano Banc	Irvine	CA	**C-**	C	C+	1298.2	13.10	26.2	0.0	3.4	2.1	**8.2**	10.2	13.5
Nantahala Bank & Trust Co.	Franklin	NC	**D**	D	E+	214.7	20.61	4.2	0.8	22.9	15.1	**4.5**	6.5	11.9
Nashville Savings Bank	Nashville	IL	**B**	B	B	79.3	13.41	9.4	2.4	18.5	11.0	**10.0**	11.4	0.0
▲ Natbank, N.A.	Hollywood	FL	**B**	B-	B	210.7	12.08	0.5	0.9	62.5	2.1	**10.0**	16.6	33.2
National Advisors Trust Co.	Kansas City	MO	**U**	U	U	15.0	4.73	0.0	0.0	0.0	4.7	**10.0**	96.0	293.9
National Bank & Trust	La Grange	TX	**B**	B	B-	230.8	6.17	2.1	2.8	20.4	52.2	**10.0**	11.1	0.0
National Bank of Commerce	Superior	WI	**A-**	A-	B	1175.0	11.94	15.5	1.4	16.2	17.2	**9.0**	11.3	14.2
National Bank of Middlebury	Middlebury	VT	**B-**	B-	B	520.9	17.93	6.0	2.2	27.6	27.9	**5.9**	7.9	16.9
▲ National Bank of New York City	Flushing	NY	**C+**	C	B	203.6	-8.72	1.2	0.0	18.5	1.6	**10.0**	18.6	23.3
▲ National Bank of St. Anne	Saint Anne	IL	**B**	B-	B-	107.8	18.33	9.9	3.1	10.4	6.1	**7.1**	9.1	13.3
National Cooperative Bank, N.A.	Hillsboro	OH	**B**	B	B-	3042.9	6.66	21.3	2.6	17.8	9.5	**10.0**	11.3	15.4
National Exchange Bank and Trust	Fond du Lac	WI	**A-**	A-	A	2552.4	10.74	9.3	0.8	4.7	31.8	**10.0**	16.2	0.0
National Grand Bank of Marblehead	Marblehead	MA	**B+**	B+	A-	428.0	12.30	3.1	0.3	59.3	21.3	**8.2**	9.8	0.0
Nationwide Trust Co., FSB	Columbus	OH	**U**	U	U	195.7	0.32	0.0	0.0	0.0	60.3	**10.0**	18.2	53.2
Native American Bank, N.A.	Denver	CO	**C**	C	C-	166.3	-18.28	61.7	0.3	0.4	4.8	**10.0**	11.1	0.0
NBC Oklahoma	Oklahoma City	OK	**B-**	B-	B-	792.2	6.86	20.1	0.5	9.4	15.1	**6.0**	8.0	12.8
NBH Bank	Greenwood Village	CO	**A-**	B+	B	7129.2	11.70	19.6	0.3	9.8	18.1	**7.0**	9.0	14.0
NBKC Bank	Overland Park	KS	**A**	A	B+	1110.6	3.76	3.4	1.3	28.8	7.3	**10.0**	15.8	26.0
NBT Bank, N.A.	Norwich	NY	**B+**	B	B+	11477.6	6.63	12.5	13.3	14.4	18.9	**8.3**	9.9	15.3

Asset Quality Index	Adjusted Non-Performing Loans as a % of Total Loans	Adjusted Non-Performing Loans as a % of Capital	Net Charge-Offs Avg Loans	Profitability Index	Net Income ($Mil)	Return on Assets (R.O.A.)	Return on Equity (R.O.E.)	Net Interest Spread	Overhead Efficiency Ratio	Liquidity Index	Liquidity Ratio	Hot Money Ratio	Stability Index
8.5	0.14	0.8	0.00	**3.2**	0.2	0.39	2.82	2.57	77.9	**2.5**	32.6	20.7	**7.2**
8.6	0.18	1.0	0.00	**5.3**	2.8	1.05	11.94	3.62	63.3	**3.9**	23.8	10.6	**6.1**
7.1	0.63	3.4	-0.05	**4.1**	8.5	0.81	9.08	3.32	71.9	**6.4**	36.6	2.8	**7.2**
3.1	3.75	18.6	0.02	**1.7**	0.3	0.22	2.71	3.55	102.0	**5.0**	44.2	11.1	**4.3**
4.1	3.72	13.5	-0.03	**4.5**	0.2	0.78	6.51	2.61	61.8	**6.1**	46.3	4.4	**6.9**
8.3	0.67	2.9	0.00	**4.2**	5.7	0.98	12.93	2.76	70.1	**5.3**	27.3	6.0	**7.3**
5.0	1.95	8.1	0.01	**4.7**	5.1	1.05	11.45	3.35	61.3	**2.2**	25.3	19.0	**6.5**
7.1	0.60	6.8	-0.01	**8.1**	0.6	2.11	15.71	4.36	45.2	**5.1**	40.6	9.2	**8.4**
4.5	4.33	15.4	0.03	**5.7**	7.9	1.07	8.08	3.04	61.6	**3.4**	35.0	19.3	**10.0**
8.3	0.76	2.8	0.29	**7.6**	1333.0	1.53	15.23	1.70	18.3	**5.4**	61.5	0.0	**8.7**
7.1	0.29	2.8	0.00	**6.2**	708.0	1.11	16.33	1.74	24.6	**4.4**	30.4	0.0	**6.9**
9.4	0.60	1.5	0.00	**3.9**	0.4	0.60	2.84	2.74	90.7	**3.0**	40.5	21.0	**7.1**
8.9	0.06	0.2	-0.03	**3.5**	0.9	0.70	8.92	3.06	74.6	**2.9**	19.8	15.2	**4.2**
5.8	1.71	5.5	0.02	**8.7**	11.7	1.80	15.24	4.42	49.8	**5.1**	31.4	9.5	**10.0**
5.3	1.55	8.9	0.06	**6.2**	37.9	1.58	16.56	2.81	45.3	**3.7**	29.4	8.6	**8.9**
5.0	3.39	10.7	0.02	**7.7**	3.6	1.67	14.66	3.32	48.5	**3.3**	24.3	13.6	**7.3**
6.6	0.75	4.0	-0.02	**5.1**	1.0	1.21	11.67	3.55	67.5	**4.0**	48.3	17.0	**7.1**
8.9	0.00	0.0	0.00	**6.8**	1.2	1.51	11.96	3.47	51.0	**6.1**	43.7	4.1	**7.8**
8.5	0.24	1.7	0.03	**8.3**	13.4	2.33	22.22	3.79	36.9	**1.9**	17.2	17.2	**8.0**
0.5	2.78	22.1	0.00	**5.8**	3.0	1.10	12.01	3.66	54.1	**2.2**	18.7	18.2	**6.2**
8.0	0.59	1.6	-0.01	**5.7**	1.9	1.21	13.67	3.38	58.2	**2.6**	33.2	18.8	**6.3**
5.5	1.03	5.6	0.08	**3.4**	0.3	0.48	5.89	3.86	81.6	**2.8**	20.1	15.2	**3.8**
9.0	0.04	0.2	0.00	**3.9**	0.5	0.62	5.33	3.18	77.6	**5.5**	34.1	4.3	**7.3**
2.5	1.65	12.9	0.00	**4.1**	0.7	0.86	9.32	3.15	72.5	**1.5**	10.8	23.3	**5.4**
6.5	1.08	4.1	0.19	**5.5**	5.8	1.31	9.66	3.48	66.0	**1.8**	20.5	15.6	**8.0**
5.9	3.26	6.1	-0.09	**3.1**	0.4	0.98	5.28	3.01	90.6	**6.1**	45.5	3.7	**5.1**
8.3	0.00	0.0	-0.02	**9.5**	4.9	1.91	20.64	4.15	38.2	**2.6**	12.6	10.6	**5.9**
9.4	0.74	1.6	0.00	**4.3**	2.3	0.80	4.60	2.99	70.0	**6.0**	57.2	8.8	**8.6**
8.7	0.00	0.2	-0.09	**2.3**	0.0	0.26	2.92	2.42	89.0	**5.0**	57.4	11.2	**3.0**
8.2	1.81	3.7	0.03	**6.9**	1.7	1.85	11.99	2.96	42.0	**5.8**	61.1	11.4	**9.2**
6.2	1.17	5.0	0.14	**2.6**	615.6	0.91	7.73	2.13	85.3	**5.5**	38.4	4.6	**8.7**
8.2	0.16	0.7	0.00	**9.1**	3.4	2.00	14.21	3.05	42.4	**4.3**	44.4	12.3	**10.0**
5.4	0.23	2.0	0.10	**9.6**	4.4	2.66	23.45	5.03	41.6	**0.4**	13.0	73.0	**8.5**
1.8	4.12	21.0	0.59	**3.8**	0.6	0.71	6.83	3.79	70.4	**4.0**	19.5	5.7	**6.6**
6.5	2.48	8.9	-0.01	**3.0**	0.1	0.11	0.67	3.01	98.9	**2.5**	41.4	28.7	**7.8**
9.9	0.35	0.8	0.00	**2.9**	0.1	0.37	1.21	3.08	84.6	**1.3**	30.8	50.5	**7.8**
9.4	0.43	0.4	-0.01	**6.8**	1.5	1.17	4.14	3.45	63.8	**3.6**	50.6	14.2	**8.6**
8.8	0.07	0.5	0.00	**4.0**	0.9	0.85	9.39	3.17	74.7	**4.2**	38.6	11.3	**5.6**
8.9	0.52	0.9	0.16	**0.8**	0.0	-0.12	-0.49	2.93	103.5	**2.8**	67.2	50.5	**6.3**
7.9	0.66	1.8	0.02	**9.2**	8.6	1.69	8.93	3.73	48.4	**1.8**	24.7	29.7	**10.0**
5.8	1.31	7.2	0.00	**9.0**	22.0	1.75	16.06	3.18	63.2	**4.3**	22.9	6.3	**9.8**
5.9	1.45	7.3	0.00	**2.6**	1.5	0.25	2.38	3.97	76.6	**5.6**	22.9	0.0	**8.4**
3.6	1.96	17.2	-0.05	**2.6**	0.7	0.63	10.01	3.62	78.9	**5.1**	37.7	8.1	**2.0**
8.8	0.00	0.0	0.00	**3.7**	0.2	0.54	4.72	2.11	67.0	**2.9**	40.4	21.1	**6.9**
9.8	0.19	0.9	0.00	**4.0**	0.7	0.72	4.34	3.78	79.4	**4.0**	39.1	10.5	**7.4**
9.2	na	0.0	na	**10.0**	1.4	20.38	22.69	0.36	83.4	**4.0**	na	100.0	**6.3**
9.5	0.70	1.3	0.04	**3.7**	1.0	0.90	6.98	2.55	67.2	**4.4**	50.4	15.5	**7.1**
5.6	0.85	6.7	0.03	**8.6**	13.3	2.43	19.43	4.26	52.1	**4.0**	14.7	7.3	**10.0**
8.6	0.22	1.4	-0.01	**4.3**	2.4	0.93	11.59	2.80	68.4	**5.7**	33.7	2.4	**5.3**
4.3	1.92	8.6	0.00	**3.4**	0.8	0.85	4.64	2.81	81.8	**0.6**	16.3	52.1	**7.1**
5.7	0.22	4.3	0.00	**6.5**	0.7	1.32	13.45	3.80	60.1	**1.5**	21.4	27.0	**7.3**
7.8	0.44	2.3	0.00	**7.2**	31.9	2.09	18.48	3.14	57.7	**4.7**	24.1	6.4	**9.7**
8.4	1.40	2.3	-1.49	**6.3**	15.5	1.22	7.23	2.80	53.8	**7.2**	51.8	2.6	**8.8**
8.8	0.64	2.1	0.00	**4.7**	1.9	0.91	8.98	2.77	59.4	**5.2**	33.2	5.7	**6.2**
10.0	na	0.0	na	**10.0**	27.9	26.81	89.33	-0.61	76.2	**8.5**	99.2	0.0	**8.7**
4.2	2.44	9.9	-0.01	**6.0**	2.5	2.62	29.03	3.81	53.6	**0.4**	4.8	44.3	**5.9**
4.8	1.09	6.9	0.00	**4.4**	4.0	1.00	12.10	4.10	72.4	**3.6**	27.0	12.6	**5.9**
7.1	0.58	2.5	0.04	**7.4**	53.6	1.58	14.64	2.89	62.0	**5.2**	27.3	6.7	**8.8**
8.2	1.46	2.9	-0.03	**9.5**	34.4	6.22	39.39	1.55	68.7	**5.4**	50.1	10.9	**10.0**
5.7	0.72	3.2	0.09	**6.4**	77.9	1.39	11.79	3.13	56.8	**4.9**	16.2	2.4	**9.1**

Name	City	State	Rating	2020 Rating	2019 Rating	Total Assets ($Mil)	One Year Asset Growth	Asset Mix (As a % of Total Assets) Commercial Loans	Consumer Loans	Mortgage Loans	Securities	Capitalization Index	Leverage Ratio	Risk-Based Capital Ratio
Nebraska Bank of Commerce	Lincoln	NE	**C+**	C+	C	157.1	-3.99	16.0	0.2	12.8	6.5	**8.7**	10.1	14.8
Nebraska State Bank	Bristow	NE	**C**	C	C	21.2	9.43	9.3	1.7	2.2	0.0	**10.0**	12.6	0.0
Nebraska State Bank	Lynch	NE	**C+**	C	C	20.3	14.64	2.0	1.4	0.3	0.0	**10.0**	11.3	0.0
Nebraska State Bank	Oshkosh	NE	**A-**	A-	A-	65.6	9.70	4.8	0.1	0.0	2.4	**10.0**	14.4	0.0
Nebraska State Bank and Trust Co.	Broken Bow	NE	**B**	B	B	297.3	5.91	7.9	2.4	7.2	9.1	**5.9**	9.4	0.0
NebraskaLand Bank	North Platte	NE	**B**	B-	B	827.6	-3.42	13.3	0.5	9.1	28.6	**9.2**	10.4	0.0
Needham Bank	Needham	MA	**B-**	B-	B-	2843.0	9.50	5.8	0.6	28.3	6.8	**9.7**	11.2	0.0
Neighborhood National Bank	El Cajon	CA	**D**	D-	D	133.2	-6.59	32.3	0.0	3.4	0.1	**9.0**	10.3	25.4
▼ Neighborhood National Bank	Mora	MN	**B**	B+	A-	287.4	17.28	13.1	3.0	15.8	37.4	**7.5**	9.4	15.5
Neighbors Bank	Clarence	MO	**B-**	C+	C-	77.4	10.61	1.8	0.4	19.5	11.9	**10.0**	13.7	16.7
Nekoosa Port Edwards State Bank	Nekoosa	WI	**A-**	A-	A-	247.5	11.86	5.4	2.2	30.1	17.8	**10.0**	13.0	25.5
Nelnet Bank	Draper	UT	**D-**	D		407.6	na	0.0	47.1	0.0	46.6	**9.8**	26.4	0.0
Nelsonville Home & Savings	Nelsonville	OH	**B-**	B-	B-	35.9	12.08	0.0	2.5	48.9	6.1	**10.0**	11.4	30.5
Neuberger Berman Trust Co. N.A.	New York	NY	**U**	U	U	26.6	19.61	0.0	0.0	0.0	0.0	**10.0**	56.2	111.0
Neuberger Berman Trust Co. of Delaware	Wilmington	DE	**U**	U	U	8.1	17.63	0.0	0.0	0.0	0.0	**10.0**	85.9	174.9
Nevada Bank and Trust Co.	Caliente	NV	**B-**	B-	C+	212.1	16.71	7.1	2.7	1.6	40.7	**5.6**	7.6	17.8
New Albin Savings Bank	New Albin	IA	**A-**	A-	A	292.0	3.68	2.0	1.0	12.6	69.3	**10.0**	16.3	50.4
▲ New Carlisle Federal Savings Bank	New Carlisle	OH	**B-**	C+	C+	179.7	7.91	20.8	1.1	26.1	3.0	**6.4**	10.1	0.0
New Century Bank	Belleville	KS	**B+**	B	B	59.9	0.05	2.2	3.8	29.6	0.0	**10.0**	11.5	19.7
New Covenant Trust Co., N.A.	Jeffersonville	IN	**U**	U	U	7.2	12.77	0.0	0.0	0.0	1.8	**10.0**	91.9	263.7
New Era Bank	Fredericktown	MO	**A-**	A-	A-	428.2	-1.71	3.8	1.1	20.4	23.1	**8.6**	10.0	0.0
New Foundation Savings Bank	Cincinnati	OH	**C+**	C	C+	28.0	13.78	5.3	0.3	72.6	0.7	**7.0**	9.0	0.0
▲ New Frontier Bank	Saint Charles	MO	**B**	B-	B-	125.6	5.51	8.0	0.1	8.7	19.8	**6.5**	9.1	12.1
▲ New Haven Bank	New Haven	CT	**C+**	C	C+	166.3	3.89	13.9	6.8	26.6	3.9	**8.1**	9.7	16.1
▲ New Horizon Bank, N.A.	Powhatan	VA	**C**	C-	C+	126.1	31.68	12.4	0.6	10.5	17.3	**10.0**	12.0	20.5
New Market Bank	Elko New Market	MN	**C+**	C+	C+	189.7	18.72	12.7	0.6	8.9	21.5	**4.7**	6.7	15.1
New Mexico Bank & Trust	Albuquerque	NM	**B+**	B+	A-	2497.2	31.49	11.3	0.4	3.3	39.8	**6.2**	8.2	13.4
New Millennium Bank	Fort Lee	NJ	**B-**	C+	C+	527.1	13.14	20.8	0.0	10.7	0.4	**7.1**	9.1	15.2
New OMNI Bank, N.A.	Alhambra	CA	**A-**	A-	A-	577.3	15.93	2.7	0.1	31.0	0.2	**10.0**	13.2	21.9
▲ New Peoples Bank, Inc.	Honaker	VA	**B-**	C	C	796.5	5.72	10.7	2.4	25.5	12.1	**7.3**	9.2	16.1
▼ New Republic Bank	Charlotte	NC	**D**	C-	C-	71.0	0.10	2.7	0.1	29.3	1.5	**10.0**	15.0	35.2
New Tripoli Bank	New Tripoli	PA	**A-**	B+	B	545.0	6.44	6.5	0.3	41.1	18.8	**10.0**	11.0	0.0
New Valley Bank & Trust	Springfield	MA	**C**	D		264.4	36.41	31.8	0.0	11.7	11.3	**7.9**	9.6	17.3
New York Community Bank	Hicksville	NY	**B**	B	B	57445.0	6.01	3.2	0.0	0.3	10.6	**7.2**	9.2	12.7
NewBank	Flushing	NY	**A-**	B+	A-	553.3	14.78	19.3	0.0	0.3	0.0	**10.0**	11.1	0.0
Newburyport Five Cents Savings Bank	Newburyport	MA	**C+**	C+	C+	1244.8	6.79	9.7	2.9	25.1	9.8	**10.0**	11.3	15.5
Newfield National Bank	Newfield	NJ	**C+**	C+	C+	877.8	13.39	4.7	0.1	14.3	34.2	**5.9**	7.9	16.1
NewFirst National Bank	El Campo	TX	**B+**	B+	B	876.7	1.58	10.8	0.4	6.1	4.4	**8.9**	10.3	0.0
Newport Federal Bank	Newport	TN	**C+**	C+	B	250.7	10.84	0.2	1.0	30.7	49.5	**7.1**	9.1	0.0
Newtown Savings Bank	Newtown	CT	**C+**	C+	C+	1616.4	-1.23	7.9	1.1	27.8	15.3	**5.8**	7.8	16.1
NexBank	Dallas	TX	**B+**	B+	B+	9274.8	4.90	1.6	0.2	33.5	19.3	**6.9**	8.9	14.3
NexTier Bank, NA	Butler	PA	**B-**	B	B+	1782.0	10.46	10.4	7.8	20.7	7.8	**4.4**	8.9	0.0
Nicolet National Bank	Green Bay	WI	**B+**	B+	B+	4573.6	0.96	18.3	0.8	10.9	12.3	**5.6**	8.0	11.4
Ninnescah Valley Bank	Cunningham	KS	**B**	B	B	41.0	18.72	5.5	1.8	4.2	55.2	**10.0**	11.5	0.0
Noah Bank	Elkins Park	PA	**D+**	D+	C-	362.5	-2.91	11.8	0.0	0.8	0.6	**5.3**	7.3	14.8
▲ NobleBank & Trust	Anniston	AL	**B-**	C+	B-	371.0	18.32	17.3	1.4	11.4	22.4	**6.9**	9.1	0.0
Nokomis Savings Bank	Nokomis	IL	**D+**	C-	C	33.2	-4.54	7.7	2.3	16.6	44.6	**10.0**	14.2	0.0
Normangee State Bank	Normangee	TX	**B**	B	B-	137.1	3.78	2.0	7.2	21.9	41.5	**10.0**	14.9	32.3
North Adams State Bank	Ursa	IL	**B-**	B-	B-	47.3	8.31	11.1	3.7	15.1	19.2	**10.0**	12.9	0.0
North Alabama Bank	Hazel Green	AL	**B+**	B+	B-	142.4	11.71	6.6	1.6	10.5	6.6	**7.0**	9.3	0.0
North American Banking Co.	Roseville	MN	**A-**	A-	A-	871.6	10.52	15.7	0.3	4.9	32.7	**5.3**	7.3	13.3
North American Savings Bank, FSB	Kansas City	MO	**A**	A	A-	2297.1	-11.23	0.3	0.0	66.8	6.3	**10.0**	16.6	24.1
North Arundel Savings Bank	Pasadena	MD	**C**	C	C	47.5	6.78	0.0	0.8	54.3	5.5	**10.0**	12.3	24.9
North Brookfield Savings Bank	North Brookfield	MA	**C+**	C+	B-	354.4	2.88	2.9	2.0	43.2	18.7	**10.0**	11.6	0.0
North Cambridge Co-operative Bank	Cambridge	MA	**C+**	C+	C+	88.7	-3.11	0.0	0.1	55.5	5.7	**10.0**	24.7	60.3
North Central Bank	Hennepin	IL	**B+**	A-	B	149.6	9.82	5.6	3.4	17.2	31.3	**9.6**	12.0	0.0
North County Savings Bank	Red Bud	IL	**C**	C	C+	66.1	12.04	0.1	1.6	33.8	26.4	**5.9**	7.9	0.0
▼ North Dallas Bank & Trust Co.	Dallas	TX	**B-**	B	B	1591.9	9.13	4.5	0.4	12.5	37.1	**9.4**	10.6	0.0
North Easton Savings Bank	South Easton	MA	**C+**	C	C	1323.7	6.33	7.2	1.8	35.5	19.0	**6.3**	8.3	14.4
North Georgia National Bank	Calhoun	GA	**B-**	B-	B-	184.7	27.06	7.2	0.7	11.8	32.7	**7.0**	9.0	0.0

Asset Quality Index	Adjusted Non-Performing Loans as a % of Total Loans	Adjusted Non-Performing Loans as a % of Capital	Net Charge-Offs Avg Loans	Profitability Index	Net Income ($Mil)	Return on Assets (R.O.A.)	Return on Equity (R.O.E.)	Net Interest Spread	Overhead Efficiency Ratio	Liquidity Index	Liquidity Ratio	Hot Money Ratio	Stability Index
7.5	0.01	0.1	0.00	**3.8**	0.6	0.79	8.06	2.96	70.5	**1.6**	21.7	25.4	**5.7**
8.4	0.00	0.0	-0.06	**2.9**	0.1	0.81	6.49	3.31	70.3	**2.0**	50.9	24.2	**5.7**
9.0	0.54	1.1	-0.03	**4.9**	0.2	1.53	12.99	2.50	60.1	**6.3**	77.1	6.0	**5.1**
6.1	0.55	3.2	0.00	**10.0**	1.4	4.25	29.86	3.99	34.6	**1.7**	11.2	20.8	**9.5**
7.3	0.41	2.8	0.10	**7.3**	2.6	1.77	19.12	3.88	52.1	**2.2**	28.0	14.3	**7.1**
8.7	0.00	0.0	0.00	**4.0**	4.1	0.99	9.20	3.08	68.2	**2.6**	8.1	10.9	**7.8**
7.0	0.59	3.2	0.33	**3.5**	7.7	0.56	4.98	2.76	69.8	**1.9**	25.3	30.0	**9.0**
2.1	3.21	21.8	-0.08	**0.7**	0.2	0.34	3.70	2.53	84.8	**3.4**	38.6	17.6	**4.5**
7.7	0.48	2.4	0.36	**4.4**	1.3	0.95	9.93	3.30	71.5	**4.4**	28.9	9.4	**6.0**
9.9	0.00	0.0	0.00	**7.1**	0.8	2.05	15.76	0.84	92.0	**7.1**	71.7	3.1	**8.8**
8.5	0.91	2.0	-0.01	**6.0**	1.9	1.55	11.49	2.93	46.9	**2.3**	43.2	33.0	**8.2**
6.8	0.00	0.0	0.01	**0.0**	-1.2	-0.72	-2.28	1.76	137.0	**3.2**	69.9	12.0	**1.3**
9.3	0.00	0.0	0.07	**3.2**	0.1	0.45	3.92	2.94	77.3	**4.1**	43.6	14.9	**5.9**
10.0	na	0.0	na	**10.0**	0.6	4.81	8.57	6.47	97.1	**4.0**	107.0	0.0	**6.7**
10.0	na	0.0	na	**10.0**	0.1	3.23	3.71	6.98	97.7	**4.0**	228.1	0.0	**5.5**
9.2	0.05	0.2	-0.02	**3.4**	0.6	0.55	6.54	2.70	78.7	**7.6**	66.7	0.7	**4.8**
9.8	0.20	0.4	-0.03	**6.2**	2.1	1.50	8.62	2.52	26.6	**4.8**	72.2	17.5	**8.8**
4.4	0.77	10.4	-0.03	**7.1**	1.5	1.73	20.11	4.26	58.5	**2.6**	16.9	16.0	**5.4**
8.5	0.30	1.9	0.10	**8.2**	1.0	3.36	30.07	5.94	55.3	**0.8**	17.0	36.1	**8.0**
10.0	na	0.0	na	**10.0**	0.4	10.51	11.72	0.80	81.6	**4.0**	na	0.0	**5.5**
8.9	0.03	0.1	0.00	**6.4**	3.1	1.48	13.98	2.51	52.1	**5.3**	38.7	7.6	**8.6**
8.2	0.36	2.2	0.00	**7.9**	0.1	2.85	30.16	2.66	82.0	**1.6**	7.3	20.5	**4.9**
5.5	0.27	1.2	-0.04	**6.4**	1.2	1.88	19.80	3.54	56.2	**4.0**	23.1	9.6	**7.0**
8.2	0.04	0.3	0.00	**3.5**	0.5	0.59	5.27	3.43	75.3	**0.7**	15.4	37.0	**7.4**
7.7	0.62	2.8	0.05	**2.4**	0.1	0.23	1.85	3.55	91.5	**2.2**	34.5	26.6	**6.0**
5.5	1.07	5.6	0.00	**6.1**	1.3	1.41	20.88	3.39	66.6	**6.6**	45.1	1.3	**3.9**
7.7	0.68	3.6	0.09	**7.4**	16.4	1.44	15.24	3.34	54.2	**6.1**	33.8	4.1	**7.5**
6.0	0.42	2.0	-0.11	**5.8**	2.9	1.21	13.18	3.39	55.4	**1.2**	27.9	38.5	**5.6**
7.8	0.00	0.0	0.00	**7.2**	3.9	1.36	10.24	3.93	50.4	**0.7**	20.3	67.3	**8.4**
5.2	0.92	5.7	0.29	**4.3**	3.5	0.88	9.38	3.59	73.0	**3.1**	22.0	14.0	**5.9**
7.2	0.96	2.3	0.00	**0.0**	-0.3	-0.69	-4.44	4.40	131.2	**2.4**	50.9	34.9	**5.8**
7.1	0.95	4.8	-0.01	**5.9**	3.7	1.36	11.96	3.62	52.1	**3.3**	18.6	12.8	**8.2**
8.4	0.00	0.0	0.00	**2.6**	1.2	0.95	11.34	3.37	58.4	**3.4**	24.1	13.1	**3.4**
6.2	0.11	0.5	-0.03	**5.1**	314.8	1.10	8.59	2.55	37.9	**1.1**	13.6	16.1	**10.0**
8.6	0.09	0.5	-0.08	**6.6**	5.3	2.18	19.72	3.01	45.7	**2.6**	45.4	30.6	**5.2**
8.4	0.09	0.7	0.13	**2.9**	3.3	0.53	4.73	3.42	76.3	**2.4**	16.5	8.6	**8.9**
7.2	0.47	2.2	0.07	**3.2**	2.5	0.59	7.18	2.70	74.1	**6.0**	41.3	4.0	**5.2**
5.4	0.72	4.8	0.01	**10.0**	14.4	3.24	31.59	4.39	44.2	**5.7**	34.3	2.6	**9.2**
8.0	0.72	2.5	0.00	**3.5**	0.8	0.61	6.21	2.39	65.3	**2.5**	40.1	27.9	**5.1**
6.3	1.65	6.9	0.05	**3.3**	4.9	0.60	8.11	2.52	76.9	**5.9**	39.1	6.3	**6.4**
6.4	0.69	7.9	0.01	**5.2**	57.9	1.23	17.27	2.00	34.8	**5.1**	17.2	2.1	**6.3**
6.7	0.41	3.1	0.01	**5.3**	8.8	1.03	11.03	2.95	60.2	**4.2**	8.9	5.5	**7.9**
7.2	0.38	1.4	0.01	**7.9**	31.9	1.42	12.37	3.42	55.7	**5.3**	30.8	3.8	**10.0**
9.3	0.00	0.0	0.07	**5.8**	0.4	1.80	14.47	3.99	61.8	**6.3**	66.5	7.0	**6.5**
0.3	4.23	28.7	0.41	**0.5**	0.4	0.22	2.90	3.14	96.7	**1.0**	26.2	47.8	**2.9**
6.3	0.61	2.9	-0.02	**5.3**	2.5	1.40	15.93	3.94	62.5	**4.7**	35.1	10.0	**4.6**
6.7	1.85	5.2	0.00	**1.2**	0.0	-0.13	-0.90	2.07	105.0	**3.6**	58.8	20.2	**6.3**
5.3	4.17	9.1	0.08	**4.0**	0.6	0.90	5.92	3.61	71.1	**4.4**	51.0	15.5	**6.9**
7.0	0.57	3.7	0.17	**4.4**	0.2	0.83	6.09	3.69	65.2	**5.3**	46.8	9.5	**6.8**
6.3	0.64	2.0	-0.14	**5.4**	0.6	0.86	8.20	4.60	74.1	**2.2**	29.9	21.2	**7.4**
8.7	0.00	0.0	0.01	**8.0**	8.5	1.87	27.34	2.47	48.5	**4.5**	41.6	12.9	**6.5**
7.0	1.55	5.4	0.52	**9.8**	37.2	3.08	18.90	4.25	63.8	**1.4**	16.4	28.2	**10.0**
8.1	0.65	3.5	-0.01	**1.4**	0.0	0.14	1.11	3.26	99.7	**2.0**	36.8	31.9	**5.2**
9.3	0.37	1.5	-0.01	**3.0**	0.9	0.52	4.53	3.22	83.3	**4.7**	31.8	8.2	**6.5**
10.0	0.00	0.0	0.00	**3.0**	0.1	0.19	0.77	2.62	98.9	**3.5**	51.6	19.2	**7.7**
5.6	1.53	3.6	0.01	**4.8**	0.8	1.19	8.14	3.34	67.3	**5.2**	44.3	10.1	**8.9**
10.0	0.00	0.0	0.00	**2.6**	0.1	0.37	4.63	2.18	82.2	**3.5**	62.2	23.2	**3.4**
9.6	0.00	0.3	0.00	**3.3**	3.7	0.48	4.30	2.24	73.6	**6.3**	59.3	9.3	**8.7**
6.9	0.60	3.1	0.00	**3.3**	4.4	0.69	7.06	3.07	76.8	**5.0**	27.1	7.8	**6.6**
8.2	0.72	1.9	-0.02	**4.6**	0.9	1.00	11.02	3.52	65.5	**5.2**	35.5	6.9	**4.8**

Name	City	State	Rating	2020 Rating	2019 Rating	Total Assets ($Mil)	One Year Asset Growth	Asset Mix (As a % of Total Assets) Commercial Loans	Consumer Loans	Mortgage Loans	Securities	Capitalization Index	Leverage Ratio	Risk-Based Capital Ratio
North Shore Bank of Commerce	Duluth	MN	A-	A-	B	404.0	12.20	4.8	0.4	44.6	11.0	8.5	10.0	0.0
▲ North Shore Bank, a Co-operative Bank	Peabody	MA	B	B-	B-	1587.4	6.48	12.0	0.2	19.8	9.0	8.9	10.3	16.9
North Shore Bank, F.S.B.	Brookfield	WI	B-	B-	B	2539.5	6.92	1.9	19.2	7.7	17.7	9.3	10.5	0.0
North Shore Trust and Savings	Waukegan	IL	D+	D+	C	239.4	-2.70	0.1	0.1	36.1	41.1	10.0	18.5	0.0
North Side Federal S&L Assn. of Chicago	Chicago	IL	D-	D-	D+	49.7	4.95	4.7	0.0	37.4	19.6	6.1	8.1	20.7
North Star Bank	Roseville	MN	B+	B+	B+	347.8	8.21	18.5	1.0	3.6	23.6	7.3	9.6	0.0
North State Bank	Raleigh	NC	B	B	B	1284.0	5.53	12.0	0.3	15.5	3.2	5.5	7.5	12.5
North Valley Bank	Thornton	CO	A	A	A	218.7	13.94	3.7	0.0	34.7	1.4	10.0	11.3	0.0
North Valley Bank	Zanesville	OH	C+	C+	B-	313.2	3.85	13.6	3.2	16.4	13.1	5.2	8.9	0.0
Northbrook Bank & Trust Co., N.A.	Northbrook	IL	B	B	B	4035.9	26.42	27.4	9.9	3.1	10.5	5.6	8.2	11.4
▲ Northeast Bank	Portland	ME	B	C+	C+	2174.4	72.90	0.4	0.1	2.5	2.8	10.0	13.6	24.3
Northeast Bank	Minneapolis	MN	A-	A-	A-	760.8	16.41	20.1	0.1	6.0	19.1	6.4	8.4	14.4
▲ NorthEast Community Bank	White Plains	NY	A-	B+	B	1070.3	13.48	7.4	0.0	0.5	1.0	8.3	14.8	13.6
Northeast Georgia Bank	Lavonia	GA	A-	A-	A-	580.0	8.93	6.0	2.5	6.4	20.4	8.3	9.8	0.0
Northeast Missouri State Bank	Kirksville	MO	A-	A-	A-	135.5	14.00	2.4	2.8	8.7	49.3	10.0	11.2	24.0
Northeast Security Bank	Sumner	IA	B+	B+	A-	441.4	39.32	7.6	0.8	9.6	33.9	8.8	10.2	18.2
Northern Bank & Trust Co.	Woburn	MA	A	A	B+	2556.6	-4.96	39.6	0.0	9.0	2.6	10.0	13.5	16.4
Northern California National Bank	Chico	CA	B	B+	B+	310.7	2.31	5.5	3.2	4.3	31.8	7.3	9.2	0.0
Northern Interstate Bank, N.A.	Norway	MI	C+	C+	B	192.2	12.30	5.4	2.8	17.1	44.8	8.2	9.8	0.0
Northern State Bank	Ashland	WI	B+	B+	B+	322.3	15.09	5.2	0.6	18.0	23.5	5.9	7.9	17.8
Northern State Bank of Thief River Falls	Thief River Falls	MN	B-	B-	B+	451.7	22.41	4.7	3.7	7.7	18.9	6.2	8.3	27.3
Northern State Bank of Virginia	Virginia	MN	B	B-	B-	87.4	3.14	15.5	1.7	20.7	25.8	7.4	9.2	0.0
▲ Northfield Bank	Woodbridge	NJ	B+	B-	B	5426.1	7.44	4.0	0.0	4.6	20.4	9.1	11.4	0.0
Northfield Savings Bank	Berlin	VT	C+	C	B-	1330.7	13.24	9.0	0.1	38.2	21.3	8.9	10.3	0.0
Northmark Bank	North Andover	MA	B+	B+	A-	457.8	6.81	8.2	0.3	33.4	7.6	10.0	11.6	0.0
Northpointe Bank	Grand Rapids	MI	A-	B+	B	3666.8	22.38	0.0	0.0	50.0	0.1	10.0	11.2	0.0
Northrim Bank	Anchorage	AK	B+	B+	B	2438.1	21.74	25.9	0.2	5.7	14.6	5.9	7.9	12.6
Northside Community Bank	Gurnee	IL	A-	A-	B	292.8	0.04	4.4	0.7	6.2	2.4	10.0	20.0	26.9
▲ NorthStar Bank	Estherville	IA	A-	B+	A-	218.2	14.75	2.5	1.2	9.8	7.5	9.0	10.3	21.2
Northstar Bank	Bad Axe	MI	C+	C+	C+	859.4	16.54	12.0	1.3	9.9	6.7	4.4	8.2	0.0
Northview Bank	Sandstone	MN	A-	A-	B	410.7	13.54	5.3	2.9	17.2	25.1	8.6	10.1	0.0
Northway Bank	Berlin	NH	C+	C	B	1204.6	13.45	5.2	1.2	19.2	23.8	7.1	9.1	15.3
Northwest Bank	Spencer	IA	B+	B+	B+	2131.3	8.17	15.0	1.4	11.7	12.7	6.3	8.3	12.0
Northwest Bank	Boise	ID	B+	A-	A-	993.5	-5.42	39.1	0.0	0.5	10.0	8.8	10.7	0.0
Northwest Bank	Warren	PA	C+	B-	B	14401.2	2.85	6.5	12.1	27.6	15.5	8.3	9.9	14.8
Northwest Bank & Trust Co.	Davenport	IA	B	B-	B-	221.2	-3.60	16.8	0.3	5.9	5.8	6.9	8.9	16.7
Northwest Bank of Rockford	Rockford	IL	B-	B-	B	368.0	6.96	20.1	3.4	9.0	20.2	6.2	8.2	0.0
Northwest Community Bank	Winsted	CT	C+	C+	B-	984.6	128.08	7.3	1.8	35.8	17.6	7.4	9.2	0.0
Northwestern Bank	Orange City	IA	A-	A-	A-	249.8	6.08	6.3	1.0	11.6	9.8	10.0	12.9	0.0
Northwestern Bank, N.A.	Dilworth	MN	B-	C+	C+	162.4	-1.38	14.2	3.1	10.4	11.8	6.0	9.6	0.0
Northwestern Mutual Wealth Mgmt Co.	Milwaukee	WI	U	U	U	327.2	1.62	0.0	0.0	0.0	88.8	10.0	57.1	0.0
Northwoods Bank of Minnesota	Park Rapids	MN	B+	B+	B-	144.6	13.84	4.6	1.3	20.3	36.5	8.1	9.7	0.0
▲ Norway Savings Bank	Norway	ME	A	B+	A	1654.4	16.67	7.8	3.9	22.6	16.7	10.0	13.5	0.0
Norwood Co-operative Bank	Norwood	MA	A-	A-	B	683.7	8.78	4.2	0.0	28.9	7.4	10.0	13.7	0.0
NSB Bank	Mason City	IA	A-	A-	A-	242.8	-0.03	22.3	0.9	5.0	14.0	6.0	8.1	11.7
NVE Bank	Englewood	NJ	B-	B	B	724.7	0.58	1.3	0.0	27.1	20.6	10.0	15.9	29.7
NXT Bank	Central City	IA	B	B	B-	237.7	-8.27	11.2	0.4	10.4	8.2	10.0	13.5	19.1
O'Bannon Banking Co.	Buffalo	MO	B-	B-	B-	261.8	8.80	7.0	1.4	20.5	14.7	6.4	8.4	13.1
▲ Oak Bank	Fitchburg	WI	A-	B+	B	423.9	4.60	14.5	0.7	13.0	14.7	8.0	9.6	16.5
Oak Valley Community Bank	Oakdale	CA	B+	B+	B+	1764.4	20.45	10.8	0.0	1.2	13.4	5.5	7.5	13.7
Oak View National Bank	Warrenton	VA	B-	C+	B-	313.7	11.96	10.7	1.0	29.8	1.1	6.8	8.8	0.0
Oakdale State Bank	Oakdale	IL	C+	C+	C+	28.4	21.24	5.6	4.6	19.1	6.6	8.0	9.7	19.4
OakStar Bank	Springfield	MO	B-	B-	B-	1687.0	41.31	11.7	1.1	14.6	1.5	5.6	8.9	0.0
Oakwood Bank	Dallas	TX	C	C-	D	667.6	24.96	20.6	0.4	6.6	2.7	7.7	9.4	13.3
Oakwood Bank	Pigeon Falls	WI	C+	C	C	108.9	9.91	9.7	0.4	10.1	1.3	4.3	8.4	10.6
Oakworth Capital Bank	Birmingham	AL	B	B	A-	925.0	13.25	32.5	1.4	1.9	9.4	5.1	9.4	0.0
▲ Ocean Bank	Miami	FL	B	B-	B+	4806.7	5.13	8.1	0.5	4.7	8.3	9.7	11.2	14.7
▲ OceanFirst Bank, N.A.	Toms River	NJ	B	B-	B	11410.5	0.64	3.9	0.5	21.8	12.4	7.1	9.1	13.0
▼ Oconee Federal S&L Assn.	Seneca	SC	B	B+	B+	545.7	5.46	1.1	1.1	49.5	25.1	10.0	15.0	30.6
Oconee State Bank	Watkinsville	GA	C+	C	C+	529.1	12.79	8.9	0.6	6.9	23.9	6.4	8.4	14.9

Arrows denote recent upgrades ▲ or downgrades ▼

Asset Quality Index	Adjusted Non-Performing Loans as a % of Total Loans	Adjusted Non-Performing Loans as a % of Capital	Net Charge-Offs Avg Loans	Profitability Index	Net Income ($Mil)	Return on Assets (R.O.A.)	Return on Equity (R.O.E.)	Net Interest Spread	Overhead Efficiency Ratio	Liquidity Index	Liquidity Ratio	Hot Money Ratio	Stability Index
6.9	0.99	6.1	0.00	9.1	4.4	2.31	21.93	5.24	65.3	4.8	16.0	3.2	6.9
7.5	0.49	3.0	0.00	4.7	7.7	0.99	9.50	3.45	61.3	4.7	27.0	10.2	8.3
7.1	0.39	1.8	-0.22	3.5	7.1	0.57	5.14	2.83	82.7	5.5	28.9	6.1	8.7
9.4	2.08	3.0	0.19	1.0	0.0	0.00	0.00	1.89	108.1	5.2	64.2	14.7	7.3
2.8	5.69	33.6	0.00	0.4	0.0	-0.12	-1.65	3.23	104.7	4.8	43.9	11.9	3.6
6.4	1.02	2.9	-0.11	5.6	2.4	1.38	13.65	3.45	60.9	4.9	37.9	9.6	7.3
7.5	0.39	3.5	-0.08	6.5	11.0	1.74	23.42	3.38	64.7	5.6	26.8	4.0	7.8
7.8	0.00	0.0	0.00	10.0	2.9	2.72	24.24	5.01	43.4	3.2	8.8	12.4	8.9
5.6	0.68	5.2	-0.01	5.0	1.8	1.20	14.18	3.99	65.9	4.6	22.3	4.0	5.2
6.7	0.47	2.6	0.14	5.8	18.4	1.01	11.89	2.32	46.5	3.9	31.8	7.0	7.1
4.2	3.59	11.7	0.07	10.0	55.5	6.86	52.38	3.93	20.2	5.7	52.3	11.7	10.0
7.2	0.30	3.1	-0.01	6.5	5.3	1.50	17.04	3.65	57.0	6.1	38.7	2.2	7.6
6.9	0.44	2.3	0.00	7.2	6.9	1.41	9.41	4.55	58.7	1.4	20.0	28.7	9.4
7.6	0.44	2.0	0.02	3.5	0.1	0.03	0.28	2.96	98.2	5.7	42.0	6.3	7.4
8.5	0.00	0.0	0.00	5.5	0.9	1.43	10.55	2.94	54.4	4.8	56.0	14.9	8.9
8.3	0.06	0.3	-0.01	5.9	2.6	1.32	11.38	3.35	54.2	5.2	40.1	8.6	7.4
6.2	0.47	5.2	0.04	10.0	30.6	2.43	19.06	4.90	30.5	2.9	8.4	9.9	10.0
5.3	2.16	8.0	0.30	4.4	1.1	0.69	7.79	2.52	64.4	4.1	23.2	6.2	5.7
2.8	5.73	19.9	-0.53	3.9	0.7	0.77	7.78	3.20	72.3	6.4	55.9	6.2	5.7
8.6	0.55	1.6	0.07	5.2	1.8	1.14	14.03	2.78	63.0	5.9	45.5	5.6	5.4
7.7	0.11	3.2	-0.02	3.4	1.1	0.54	6.20	1.75	72.4	7.1	65.7	3.6	5.0
8.1	0.28	1.5	0.00	5.5	0.6	1.34	12.96	4.22	63.6	4.1	31.7	11.7	6.5
6.9	0.40	2.2	0.12	5.8	38.6	1.39	11.44	2.99	45.7	4.2	15.7	5.7	9.1
8.9	0.35	2.1	-0.02	4.1	5.7	0.89	8.44	3.24	72.4	3.4	19.1	12.9	8.4
9.1	0.00	0.0	0.00	4.4	1.5	0.69	5.95	3.04	69.8	2.1	31.8	25.4	7.6
6.4	0.50	4.2	-0.02	9.3	53.7	3.05	28.20	2.42	69.3	0.4	5.8	19.7	9.2
5.7	0.95	6.1	0.00	9.1	21.5	1.88	21.37	3.76	62.1	5.6	29.1	5.6	9.1
7.6	0.00	0.0	-0.01	5.7	1.3	0.89	4.34	3.23	67.8	3.4	27.9	12.0	8.3
7.2	0.00	0.0	0.01	6.8	1.9	1.77	14.63	2.96	58.3	5.3	43.7	9.1	8.2
4.5	2.30	9.3	-0.02	5.3	4.3	1.03	12.05	3.24	65.1	4.7	31.0	6.0	6.4
5.9	0.72	3.3	0.00	7.3	3.3	1.63	14.85	4.41	63.7	4.8	36.2	9.4	8.8
8.0	0.37	2.0	-0.01	3.8	4.0	0.70	7.14	2.76	84.9	4.6	7.6	4.2	7.4
6.1	0.62	4.5	-0.01	6.2	13.5	1.29	15.09	3.08	60.5	3.8	19.8	10.9	8.3
4.0	2.19	10.3	0.05	7.7	7.5	1.47	13.87	3.73	51.2	3.4	30.1	6.1	8.4
3.1	2.19	12.4	0.22	5.6	93.1	1.31	11.74	3.26	61.6	5.3	23.7	4.0	8.6
5.6	1.33	7.3	-0.01	8.0	2.7	2.23	26.96	3.76	62.9	4.9	35.2	8.8	6.4
6.5	0.40	2.5	0.24	4.2	1.7	0.92	11.15	3.06	69.1	3.7	32.5	13.8	5.7
6.9	0.57	3.2	-0.05	3.6	2.7	0.57	6.94	3.03	81.9	4.2	28.4	9.8	6.0
4.5	2.07	5.5	-0.08	9.2	2.2	1.71	12.93	3.20	42.6	3.9	23.6	9.1	8.9
5.6	0.42	2.8	0.00	5.3	1.1	1.36	13.19	5.50	75.5	4.2	18.9	6.8	6.4
10.0	na	0.0	na	10.0	62.7	31.22	58.34	0.99	87.4	5.0	297.5	100.0	6.7
6.4	0.63	2.7	-0.09	5.0	0.8	1.16	10.69	3.80	66.5	5.1	35.0	7.4	7.0
7.6	0.63	3.0	0.01	8.7	14.8	1.85	13.70	3.60	69.9	6.1	34.0	4.3	10.0
8.2	0.55	2.7	0.00	5.7	3.8	1.14	8.67	3.11	55.0	3.0	25.5	15.0	9.2
8.2	0.00	0.8	-0.02	9.4	2.7	2.25	26.65	4.18	44.3	4.3	13.8	6.3	7.6
7.2	1.49	5.5	0.00	3.1	1.2	0.34	2.13	2.34	81.7	5.0	35.2	7.6	8.6
7.2	0.02	0.0	0.00	4.5	1.3	1.06	7.65	3.48	65.9	2.8	10.5	14.4	7.2
7.0	0.36	2.3	-0.08	4.8	1.2	0.91	10.93	3.65	65.6	2.9	23.0	15.3	5.2
8.6	0.00	0.0	0.00	6.5	2.4	1.15	11.91	2.82	53.8	4.6	30.0	6.7	7.2
8.6	0.04	0.2	-0.01	5.5	8.6	1.06	13.03	3.23	57.7	6.6	36.4	1.7	7.0
8.7	0.01	0.1	0.00	3.8	1.0	0.65	7.28	3.39	79.0	2.5	19.0	17.0	5.0
7.4	0.03	0.3	0.45	4.4	0.1	0.59	5.93	3.02	68.5	4.9	49.1	12.2	5.5
6.8	0.94	3.1	-0.01	5.8	11.1	1.39	14.74	3.41	62.9	2.8	21.7	11.0	7.5
8.0	0.02	0.1	0.01	2.7	1.6	0.50	4.72	2.93	72.9	2.5	33.2	20.5	6.6
3.5	1.93	5.1	0.01	5.0	0.6	1.10	8.61	4.04	64.5	1.5	20.3	25.6	7.7
8.2	0.00	0.0	0.02	5.7	5.4	1.17	12.45	3.37	63.8	4.2	24.1	8.8	6.8
6.3	0.55	2.5	-0.14	5.3	25.5	1.10	9.70	3.60	65.5	2.2	19.0	18.7	9.1
5.7	0.62	2.8	0.00	5.0	60.4	1.05	7.95	2.97	58.3	4.6	15.2	5.1	8.6
8.4	0.82	3.3	0.00	3.7	1.9	0.70	4.47	2.94	70.4	2.7	32.0	18.7	9.0
4.3	1.89	11.8	-0.01	4.1	1.9	0.75	8.69	3.29	76.3	5.4	39.6	7.4	5.4

Name	City	State	Rating	2020 Rating	2019 Rating	Total Assets ($Mil)	One Year Asset Growth	Asset Mix (As a % of Total Assets) Commercial Loans	Consumer Loans	Mortgage Loans	Securities	Capitalization Index	Leverage Ratio	Risk-Based Capital Ratio
Odin State Bank	Odin	MN	**C-**	D+	D	51.8	2.52	10.4	6.9	15.6	26.0	**7.9**	9.7	0.0
Ohio State Bank	Bexley	OH	**D**	D-		241.0	72.45	6.0	0.0	26.8	8.9	**9.8**	17.0	0.0
Ohnward Bank & Trust	Cascade	IA	**A-**	A-	A-	374.4	11.00	12.8	1.7	8.6	17.7	**10.0**	11.6	0.0
Oklahoma Bank and Trust Co.	Clinton	OK	**A**	A-	A-	181.3	4.40	4.0	0.7	6.7	59.9	**10.0**	14.0	35.5
Oklahoma Capital Bank	Tulsa	OK	**B**	B	B	158.0	-10.67	20.6	1.0	8.9	13.3	**10.0**	14.1	0.0
▲ Oklahoma Heritage Bank	Stratford	OK	**C+**	C	C+	94.0	0.71	13.9	4.0	26.6	13.2	**8.7**	10.1	15.8
▼ Oklahoma State Bank	Buffalo	OK	**B-**	B+	B+	60.9	-1.37	8.2	9.6	5.4	17.1	**8.0**	9.7	16.9
▲ Oklahoma State Bank	Guthrie	OK	**C**	D+	D+	201.2	22.13	17.1	0.9	21.7	1.6	**8.7**	10.1	15.4
Oklahoma State Bank	Vinita	OK	**B+**	B+	A-	216.6	21.93	6.2	1.9	14.6	15.5	**7.4**	9.3	16.6
Old Dominion National Bank	North Garden	VA	**C**	C-	D	827.5	23.38	27.6	0.0	10.6	2.2	**10.0**	11.6	15.6
Old Mission Bank	Sault Sainte Marie	MI	**B+**	A-	B	142.4	6.74	5.7	2.1	9.4	50.4	**9.5**	10.7	24.8
Old Missouri Bank	Springfield	MO	**C+**	C+	C+	686.3	17.33	15.0	1.7	13.1	2.8	**5.3**	9.3	11.2
Old National Bank	Evansville	IN	**B-**	B-	B-	23577.3	7.17	12.7	4.2	10.3	28.7	**6.6**	8.7	12.8
▲ Old Plank Trail Community Bank, N.A.	Mokena	IL	**B**	C+	B	2151.4	12.43	28.8	13.8	3.1	19.1	**5.6**	8.2	11.5
Old Point Trust & Financial Services, N.A.	Newport News	VA	**U**	U	U	7.2	2.93	0.0	0.0	0.0	32.8	**10.0**	88.6	327.9
Old Second National Bank	Aurora	IL	**A-**	A-	A-	3256.2	10.98	14.5	0.1	4.9	17.8	**9.5**	10.6	16.3
Olpe State Bank	Olpe	KS	**B**	B	B	48.0	8.67	4.9	1.9	13.3	26.1	**10.0**	13.7	28.1
Olympia Federal S&L Assn.	Olympia	WA	**C+**	C+	B-	813.1	7.83	0.3	0.5	57.8	9.2	**10.0**	13.4	0.0
OmniBank	Bay Springs	MS	**C**	C-	D+	55.0	2.03	17.0	7.0	17.0	4.4	**6.5**	8.6	18.3
ONB Bank	Rochester	MN	**A-**	A-	B	141.1	6.73	15.9	1.3	17.0	8.9	**8.5**	10.4	13.7
▲ One American Bank	Sioux Falls	SD	**B-**	C+	C	365.8	116.69	4.6	5.5	70.8	0.4	**10.0**	14.2	23.3
One Bank of Tennessee	Cookeville	TN	**B**	B	B	1375.9	11.64	6.4	1.8	18.6	30.3	**5.1**	7.1	15.0
One Community Bank	Oregon	WI	**B+**	B+	A	1530.8	15.81	9.6	0.1	11.3	8.1	**4.4**	10.3	0.0
▲ One Florida Bank	Orlando	FL	**C-**	D+	C	1090.8	61.74	24.1	0.1	4.9	5.7	**9.0**	10.8	14.2
▲ One World Bank	Dallas	TX	**B**	C+	B	142.6	13.12	26.4	0.0	1.4	1.3	**9.5**	12.1	0.0
OneSouth Bank	Blakely	GA	**C+**	C+	C+	165.5	4.55	6.8	0.6	14.4	0.2	**8.6**	10.1	17.2
OneUnited Bank	Boston	MA	**D-**	D-	D	616.4	-10.00	0.1	0.5	2.8	21.6	**5.3**	7.3	15.1
▲ Oostburg State Bank	Oostburg	WI	**A**	A-	B+	326.0	17.13	13.7	0.5	15.4	23.4	**10.0**	11.4	15.9
Open Bank	Los Angeles	CA	**A-**	A-	A-	1601.4	24.36	13.9	0.1	7.5	7.0	**8.2**	9.8	13.6
Opportunity Bank of Montana	Helena	MT	**A-**	A-	B	1353.1	10.51	7.1	1.4	12.3	16.9	**10.0**	11.4	16.2
▲ OptimumBank	Fort Lauderdale	FL	**C**	D+	C-	294.0	62.74	11.5	3.7	11.4	8.1	**10.0**	11.3	0.0
Optum Bank, Inc.	Draper	UT	**A+**	A+	A+	14446.0	22.43	2.8	0.7	0.0	74.4	**10.0**	11.6	20.5
Optus Bank	Columbia	SC	**C+**	C+	C	315.2	103.69	22.8	1.8	3.6	3.4	**9.6**	10.7	0.0
Orange Bank & Trust Co.	Middletown	NY	**B-**	B-	B-	2043.5	29.89	16.9	0.8	5.8	18.5	**5.6**	7.6	13.4
Oregon Coast Bank	Newport	OR	**B+**	B+	A-	387.9	32.27	8.3	1.3	9.9	37.6	**6.9**	8.9	0.0
Oregon Pacific Banking Co.	Florence	OR	**B**	B	B+	665.8	29.64	16.9	0.2	5.2	9.8	**5.5**	7.5	16.5
▲ Oriental Bank	San Juan	PR	**D+**	D	C-	10367.0	4.78	11.3	18.9	20.5	6.0	**7.0**	9.0	14.6
▲ Origin Bank	Choudrant	LA	**B**	C+	B	7233.0	9.39	20.5	0.2	9.3	14.0	**7.2**	9.2	13.9
Orrstown Bank	Shippensburg	PA	**B**	B	B-	2912.3	5.09	17.8	0.7	11.3	15.5	**6.5**	8.5	14.7
Osgood State Bank	Osgood	OH	**B+**	B+	B+	358.7	10.38	33.8	1.2	7.3	24.4	**7.3**	9.2	13.1
Ottawa Savings Bank	Ottawa	IL	**B**	B	B	330.2	5.90	7.9	6.2	45.8	5.3	**10.0**	13.7	21.1
Our Community Bank	Spencer	IN	**C**	C	C+	74.2	0.68	0.0	0.5	49.6	11.7	**9.1**	10.4	0.0
Owen County State Bank	Spencer	IN	**B-**	B-	B	300.2	8.73	5.9	2.2	23.8	32.6	**8.3**	9.9	0.0
Owingsville Banking Co.	Owingsville	KY	**C**	C	C-	80.1	9.06	1.9	3.8	29.0	22.1	**7.5**	9.3	0.0
Oxford Bank	Oxford	MI	**B**	B	B	723.7	-3.65	30.3	0.4	3.7	12.5	**6.3**	8.3	15.0
Oxford Bank & Trust	Oak Brook	IL	**B**	B	C+	753.1	8.89	3.0	12.6	4.8	7.8	**6.8**	8.9	0.0
Oxford University Bank	Oxford	MS	**B**	B	B	198.0	4.63	11.4	4.2	25.3	17.8	**8.6**	10.0	0.0
Ozark Bank	Ozark	MO	**B**	B	B	304.0	10.31	6.9	0.8	20.8	12.3	**7.0**	9.0	0.0
Ozarks Federal S&L Assn.	Farmington	MO	**B-**	B-	B-	251.9	-6.22	0.0	0.1	53.5	8.7	**10.0**	15.0	25.0
Ozona Bank	Ozona	TX	**B-**	B-	B	330.9	8.40	6.5	0.6	7.3	39.2	**8.3**	9.9	29.9
Pacific Alliance Bank	Rosemead	CA	**B**	B+	B+	348.4	6.50	8.6	0.0	18.4	8.1	**9.1**	11.9	0.0
Pacific City Bank	Los Angeles	CA	**A**	A	A	2059.9	1.94	17.0	1.0	10.3	6.6	**10.0**	11.5	16.1
Pacific Coast Bankers' Bank	Walnut Creek	CA	**A-**	A	A-	1309.7	-7.02	2.8	0.0	0.1	8.8	**7.5**	9.3	24.8
Pacific Crest Savings Bank	Lynnwood	WA	**B+**	B+	B+	252.6	4.19	0.0	0.0	14.9	11.2	**10.0**	11.4	18.3
▲ Pacific Enterprise Bank	Irvine	CA	**B+**	B-	B	646.6	5.45	43.4	0.0	3.8	0.0	**10.0**	12.3	21.6
▲ Pacific Mercantile Bank	Costa Mesa	CA	**C**	C-	B-	1534.2	-8.97	29.9	5.2	1.7	1.6	**10.0**	11.3	18.0
▲ Pacific National Bank	Miami	FL	**C**	C-	B-	844.6	12.69	8.2	0.1	11.0	25.2	**8.0**	9.7	15.3
Pacific Premier Bank	Irvine	CA	**A-**	B+	A-	20533.7	0.09	7.4	0.0	1.9	22.0	**10.0**	11.3	15.4
Pacific Valley Bank	Salinas	CA	**B-**	B-	B	477.2	12.48	21.6	0.1	3.9	0.0	**5.1**	8.9	0.0
Pacific West Bank	West Linn	OR	**C-**	C-	C	284.0	50.46	27.2	0.1	4.1	13.2	**10.0**	12.0	0.0

Asset Quality Index	Adjusted Non-Performing Loans as a % of Total Loans	Adjusted Non-Performing Loans as a % of Capital	Net Charge-Offs Avg Loans	Profitability Index	Net Income ($Mil)	Return on Assets (R.O.A.)	Return on Equity (R.O.E.)	Net Interest Spread	Overhead Efficiency Ratio	Liquidity Index	Liquidity Ratio	Hot Money Ratio	Stability Index
2.5	2.37	17.0	0.02	**4.1**	0.3	1.11	11.24	3.34	68.6	**3.1**	31.7	14.2	**5.0**
7.9	0.00	0.0	0.00	**0.9**	0.0	0.00	0.02	2.36	75.7	**5.1**	12.3	1.0	**1.7**
8.4	0.01	0.6	0.00	**5.7**	2.1	1.16	9.72	3.31	62.7	**4.0**	36.4	12.8	**8.1**
9.5	0.00	0.4	-0.01	**6.4**	1.5	1.70	11.49	3.23	50.1	**2.8**	40.0	22.3	**9.1**
6.1	0.42	7.5	0.03	**3.4**	0.4	0.48	2.88	2.96	83.4	**1.3**	29.6	34.0	**6.8**
5.7	0.39	4.9	-0.04	**5.5**	0.8	1.77	17.93	5.64	66.2	**1.2**	10.9	27.2	**4.6**
2.8	2.07	12.6	-0.02	**9.5**	0.7	2.15	22.54	4.74	57.3	**3.7**	24.3	11.4	**7.2**
4.6	1.34	6.6	-0.21	**4.0**	1.0	1.04	9.46	4.01	70.4	**2.8**	22.5	15.9	**5.4**
7.0	0.70	2.2	-0.01	**4.6**	1.0	0.94	9.31	3.36	73.0	**2.6**	41.0	24.7	**6.7**
7.0	0.16	1.1	0.04	**2.8**	2.7	0.68	6.23	3.22	65.8	**4.1**	20.0	8.9	**6.6**
7.3	0.85	2.1	0.07	**4.0**	0.6	0.84	7.18	3.33	76.3	**6.2**	67.8	9.9	**7.6**
4.7	0.63	5.5	0.07	**6.5**	4.6	1.39	14.81	4.00	51.6	**0.5**	3.6	38.8	**6.6**
4.6	1.06	4.1	0.00	**5.9**	153.3	1.32	10.10	2.97	59.2	**5.4**	23.5	2.8	**10.0**
7.0	0.29	2.1	0.04	**3.9**	8.5	0.83	9.46	2.38	70.0	**3.8**	22.5	6.5	**6.6**
10.0	na	0.0	na	**10.0**	0.5	13.28	15.08	0.35	77.6	**4.0**	na	0.0	**5.0**
6.0	1.20	5.7	-0.05	**8.1**	23.7	1.50	13.07	3.13	61.8	**5.6**	29.5	5.9	**9.9**
9.0	0.00	0.0	0.00	**5.2**	0.3	1.37	9.89	2.34	64.7	**4.9**	46.6	11.6	**7.6**
8.2	0.66	3.7	0.00	**3.0**	1.6	0.41	3.08	3.12	83.4	**2.9**	20.4	15.1	**8.5**
4.9	0.80	6.5	-0.11	**3.1**	0.1	0.53	5.51	4.81	87.9	**4.7**	34.7	9.8	**4.1**
5.4	1.76	11.0	0.02	**5.7**	1.0	1.48	13.90	4.10	61.6	**2.6**	18.6	15.1	**7.3**
8.6	0.05	0.3	0.29	**3.4**	-6.2	-2.86	-21.15	2.78	147.4	**0.4**	2.0	39.1	**8.0**
7.6	0.02	0.2	0.84	**5.5**	8.7	1.30	18.16	3.36	63.6	**4.9**	39.7	13.0	**5.6**
6.9	0.10	0.6	-0.08	**8.1**	10.1	1.38	12.45	3.45	51.2	**3.9**	12.9	6.4	**9.2**
8.4	0.16	1.0	0.00	**2.1**	3.6	0.77	6.83	3.25	67.1	**5.5**	31.8	7.3	**6.6**
6.5	0.10	0.6	0.22	**5.2**	0.8	1.22	10.01	3.97	71.8	**1.0**	16.3	32.7	**7.7**
5.0	1.17	6.8	-0.12	**3.8**	0.7	0.87	8.52	3.93	76.4	**2.2**	25.1	18.8	**5.3**
5.9	0.52	2.2	0.00	**0.0**	-1.9	-0.60	-8.54	2.03	93.6	**0.9**	25.9	34.2	**3.0**
8.5	0.09	0.5	0.00	**7.3**	2.4	1.58	13.51	3.67	51.9	**5.0**	34.8	7.0	**7.8**
7.1	0.06	0.2	0.00	**8.4**	11.7	1.59	16.14	3.87	50.6	**1.3**	16.8	23.7	**8.5**
5.9	0.78	4.2	0.00	**8.1**	8.8	1.36	10.15	4.11	74.6	**4.7**	22.5	6.8	**10.0**
6.9	0.00	0.0	0.06	**2.6**	1.2	0.93	10.20	3.28	62.8	**5.6**	37.0	4.5	**5.1**
8.8	0.00	0.0	0.00	**9.5**	136.0	1.92	13.74	2.03	30.6	**8.5**	91.1	0.0	**10.0**
5.7	1.86	4.9	0.01	**3.7**	0.8	0.74	7.95	2.23	58.1	**3.1**	66.5	42.5	**3.0**
6.3	1.26	5.8	0.00	**5.0**	10.3	1.10	14.48	3.24	57.4	**5.5**	24.6	3.5	**5.9**
6.5	0.63	3.2	0.00	**6.0**	2.6	1.40	15.01	3.58	58.2	**5.6**	47.7	8.3	**6.3**
5.8	0.71	3.7	-0.12	**6.1**	4.0	1.29	16.56	3.42	60.4	**6.2**	40.9	2.1	**6.2**
1.7	4.03	19.1	0.34	**6.1**	69.7	1.38	13.78	4.37	61.2	**5.0**	32.9	10.7	**8.2**
6.7	0.63	4.2	0.20	**5.8**	54.2	1.47	16.00	3.17	53.6	**4.1**	19.1	7.9	**7.1**
6.8	0.55	3.5	0.04	**5.9**	20.7	1.44	15.25	3.36	57.2	**4.5**	18.0	6.6	**8.0**
6.7	0.77	2.3	0.00	**6.1**	2.5	1.45	15.00	4.24	62.4	**3.6**	22.5	11.9	**6.6**
7.5	0.54	3.1	-0.02	**4.4**	1.4	0.85	5.95	3.77	70.2	**1.4**	11.4	25.3	**7.6**
6.5	1.13	5.8	0.00	**2.7**	0.2	0.62	5.87	3.67	82.0	**4.5**	35.0	10.9	**5.1**
7.8	0.54	2.5	0.01	**3.8**	0.9	0.65	6.41	3.46	79.2	**5.4**	46.5	9.6	**6.4**
5.5	0.71	8.4	0.02	**3.6**	0.3	0.75	12.44	4.24	76.4	**1.8**	20.7	21.1	**2.7**
4.7	1.09	5.6	-0.01	**7.5**	6.4	1.73	22.04	3.67	47.5	**4.9**	22.9	3.7	**5.8**
5.0	0.74	4.3	0.01	**4.7**	5.0	1.33	14.05	3.30	67.4	**4.8**	43.0	10.4	**7.4**
7.6	0.26	2.0	-0.01	**4.9**	1.0	1.03	10.07	3.90	64.1	**1.8**	26.0	23.3	**6.3**
8.9	0.09	0.3	-0.02	**4.6**	1.8	1.17	13.06	3.33	63.7	**4.0**	18.6	9.3	**5.6**
7.5	1.37	5.2	-0.03	**2.7**	0.5	0.41	2.99	2.55	85.4	**3.0**	27.7	15.9	**7.4**
7.8	1.68	2.5	0.01	**3.4**	0.6	0.40	4.00	2.71	88.8	**6.8**	68.2	5.8	**5.4**
7.6	0.00	0.0	0.00	**4.6**	1.8	1.01	8.67	3.01	56.8	**0.7**	18.9	60.5	**7.8**
7.1	0.12	0.7	-0.06	**8.2**	18.7	1.87	15.98	3.74	45.5	**1.1**	10.9	25.7	**9.4**
10.0	0.00	0.0	0.00	**5.9**	2.9	0.42	4.33	1.01	81.4	**6.9**	54.0	4.7	**8.9**
5.3	1.23	5.9	0.00	**5.1**	1.6	1.25	10.87	3.06	58.0	**1.9**	33.0	23.2	**7.8**
8.0	0.11	0.5	0.03	**5.2**	3.4	1.04	11.66	4.06	63.7	**0.7**	12.1	40.4	**6.4**
2.9	2.63	13.6	0.03	**4.8**	8.4	1.08	9.64	3.26	60.2	**4.3**	28.6	12.5	**7.2**
8.5	0.60	1.8	0.00	**3.1**	2.6	0.65	6.97	2.80	67.3	**2.8**	41.1	24.2	**5.7**
6.1	0.25	1.0	0.04	**7.4**	175.0	1.74	11.59	3.64	48.8	**5.5**	28.8	5.9	**9.4**
6.4	0.23	1.8	0.00	**5.2**	2.2	0.97	11.13	3.63	62.8	**4.4**	24.7	7.3	**5.5**
8.5	0.25	0.7	0.00	**1.7**	0.7	0.52	4.09	3.28	74.7	**5.2**	33.5	6.0	**6.5**

Name	City	State	Rating	2020 Rating	2019 Rating	Total Assets ($Mil)	One Year Asset Growth	Asset Mix (As a % of Total Assets): Commercial Loans	Consumer Loans	Mortgage Loans	Securities	Capitalization Index	Leverage Ratio	Risk-Based Capital Ratio
▲ Pacific Western Bank	Beverly Hills	CA	B+	B-	B+	34820.5	27.37	9.5	1.0	1.7	20.7	6.5	8.5	14.2
Palmetto State Bank	Hampton	SC	A	A-	A	676.1	9.61	6.9	3.1	8.1	60.9	10.0	12.3	25.6
Palo Savings Bank	Palo	IA	B-	B-	B	49.8	20.17	4.2	2.9	19.9	44.0	8.5	10.0	0.0
Pan American Bank & Trust	Melrose Park	IL	C-	C	C	404.8	7.06	8.1	0.2	16.0	11.0	6.8	8.8	13.2
Paper City Savings Assn.	Wisconsin Rapids	WI	B+	B+	B+	216.6	9.28	0.7	1.9	33.9	0.5	10.0	12.2	20.6
Paradise Bank	Boca Raton	FL	A	A	A	393.1	10.69	11.2	0.3	8.5	7.9	8.4	9.9	14.7
Paragon Bank	Memphis	TN	B-	B-	B	479.1	-3.73	23.9	3.5	16.1	11.5	8.7	10.1	16.7
Paramount Bank	Saint Louis	MO	C+	C	C-	225.2	31.52	1.1	1.3	47.0	0.7	5.9	7.9	0.0
Park Bank	Holmen	WI	B-	B-	B-	68.8	9.72	6.7	3.1	14.2	47.6	10.0	14.2	27.5
Park Ridge Community Bank	Park Ridge	IL	A	A	A	451.3	20.03	6.3	0.0	13.2	12.8	10.0	13.6	0.0
Park State Bank	Duluth	MN	B+	B+	B	1073.8	73.60	15.8	1.2	15.8	16.7	6.0	8.0	13.8
Park State Bank & Trust	Woodland Park	CO	B	B	B-	133.8	13.10	4.2	0.6	12.1	8.5	8.1	9.7	16.7
Parke Bank	Sewell	NJ	A	A	A	2101.1	8.56	4.5	0.4	32.3	0.8	10.0	12.4	0.0
Parkside Financial Bank and Trust	Clayton	MO	B+	B+	B+	742.9	12.62	37.5	0.1	2.5	11.0	6.6	9.2	12.2
Parkway Bank and Trust Co.	Harwood Heights	IL	B-	B-	B-	2874.8	4.38	13.7	0.0	1.0	8.3	9.7	10.8	15.0
▲ Partners Bank	Helena	AR	C+	C	C+	345.0	12.05	14.5	0.4	11.8	9.7	7.1	9.0	13.1
Partners Bank	Spencer	WI	B+	B+	B+	247.7	8.12	12.4	1.6	14.3	31.2	10.0	13.1	0.0
▲ Partners Bank of California	Mission Viejo	CA	B	B-	B	406.0	-10.48	26.1	0.1	7.3	0.5	7.3	9.2	15.7
▲ Partners Bank of New England	Sanford	ME	A-	B	B+	767.1	17.40	7.5	0.5	39.2	10.6	10.0	11.0	16.0
Passumpsic Savings Bank	Saint Johnsbury	VT	B-	B-	C	854.2	7.83	5.0	4.6	41.0	8.4	9.7	10.8	19.6
Pathfinder Bank	Oswego	NY	U	U	U	1253.9	7.84	14.8	6.3	18.9	25.8	6.8	8.8	14.8
▲ Pathway Bank	Cairo	NE	C-	D+	C-	207.7	5.78	5.9	0.8	4.4	18.3	8.5	10.7	0.0
Patriot Bank	Millington	TN	B+	B	B	456.7	5.43	8.2	2.0	11.5	40.2	6.9	8.9	13.4
Patriot Bank, N.A.	Stamford	CT	D+	D+	D+	962.8	-1.73	10.6	3.1	18.2	11.3	7.9	10.1	13.3
▲ Patriot Community Bank	Woburn	MA	A-	B+	B+	211.8	8.12	3.9	0.0	17.3	0.0	10.0	14.7	22.8
Patriots Bank	Garnett	KS	B	B	B	164.1	13.60	7.1	2.8	15.0	15.3	5.7	9.2	0.0
Patterson State Bank	Patterson	LA	C+	C+	B-	280.4	-2.38	9.1	1.4	36.9	25.0	6.7	8.7	18.6
Pavillion Bank	Richardson	TX	B	B	B	80.3	0.05	7.1	0.7	27.8	2.9	10.0	12.4	20.1
PBK Bank, Inc	Stanford	KY	A-	A-	B+	151.3	17.47	2.1	4.8	19.4	20.4	10.0	11.3	0.0
▲ PCSB Bank	Clarinda	IA	B	B-	C+	317.3	15.51	6.9	2.6	6.2	35.7	7.6	9.4	0.0
PCSB Bank	Yorktown Heights	NY	B-	B-	B-	1874.2	4.61	5.5	0.0	12.0	21.8	10.0	12.5	18.5
Peach State Bank & Trust	Gainesville	GA	B	B+	B+	491.1	24.65	7.1	1.3	11.9	22.7	7.7	9.5	16.4
▲ Peapack-Gladstone Bank	Bedminster	NJ	B	B-	B+	5792.3	-7.72	17.1	0.5	8.9	14.2	8.7	10.1	14.6
Pearland State Bank	Pearland	TX	B+	B+	A-	209.0	0.56	5.2	1.3	4.6	72.5	8.9	10.3	0.0
Pee Dee Federal Savings Bank	Marion	SC	D+	D+	C	36.4	1.90	9.9	2.9	3.3	46.0	10.0	17.1	50.0
Pegasus Bank	Dallas	TX	B+	B+	A-	966.8	24.55	27.7	2.2	7.6	3.9	5.2	7.2	12.6
Pendleton Community Bank, Inc.	Franklin	WV	B-	C+	B	619.9	26.23	9.8	3.5	18.3	14.0	5.9	7.9	14.0
▲ Penn Community Bank	Doylestown	PA	B	B-	B-	2694.0	6.86	5.0	0.1	23.2	26.9	10.0	11.7	19.6
PennCrest BANK	Altoona	PA	C+	C+	B-	211.5	6.59	0.3	5.9	52.3	25.8	10.0	14.6	0.0
Pennian Bank	Mifflintown	PA	B-	B-	B-	664.2	15.83	9.0	0.2	19.4	31.2	6.5	8.5	15.9
▲ Pentucket Bank	Haverhill	MA	B-	C+	B-	929.2	6.45	10.0	0.1	35.6	12.6	10.0	11.4	0.0
People's B&T Co. of Pickett County	Byrdstown	TN	B	B	B-	148.5	12.03	16.3	8.7	20.1	16.2	10.0	11.8	0.0
People's Bank of Commerce	Medford	OR	B+	B+	B	806.1	63.12	16.6	0.3	3.8	12.9	5.9	8.8	0.0
People's Bank of Seneca	Seneca	MO	C	C	B-	338.4	26.87	17.2	1.8	21.4	6.9	2.5	8.2	0.0
People's United Bank, N.A.	Bridgeport	CT	B	B	B	63075.2	2.94	16.2	0.1	12.9	16.8	6.8	8.8	13.5
PeopleFirst Bank	Joliet	IL	B	B-	B	206.2	29.15	10.9	0.1	4.5	1.9	8.2	11.1	0.0
Peoples B&T Co. of Pointe Coupee Parish	New Roads	LA	A-	A-	B	371.6	13.43	8.1	1.5	34.3	1.0	10.0	13.8	0.0
Peoples Bank	Sheridan	AR	A	A	A	191.7	5.46	11.7	3.7	6.1	36.4	10.0	14.4	0.0
▲ Peoples Bank	Eatonton	GA	D	D-	E+	191.3	16.35	3.9	2.3	14.3	6.7	9.8	10.9	0.0
Peoples Bank	Lyons	GA	B	B-	B-	144.6	10.69	7.1	1.2	11.0	3.5	6.2	8.2	18.0
▲ Peoples Bank	Clive	IA	C	C-	C-	401.0	10.63	7.0	0.6	7.7	28.7	5.5	8.3	0.0
▲ Peoples Bank	Rock Valley	IA	B-	C	C	747.4	12.77	15.4	1.4	3.3	9.4	9.8	10.9	15.0
Peoples Bank	Munster	IN	B-	B-	B-	1603.0	8.98	9.2	2.3	17.3	29.5	6.2	8.2	14.1
Peoples Bank	Coldwater	KS	B+	B+	B+	54.5	-1.89	3.4	1.2	8.2	40.2	10.0	12.5	0.0
▲ Peoples Bank	Lebanon	KY	C+	C	B-	114.0	33.41	30.3	1.3	8.3	22.5	3.5	9.4	0.0
Peoples Bank	Chatham	LA	B-	C+	D+	84.0	-2.77	8.8	8.3	26.0	2.5	10.0	12.0	18.6
Peoples Bank	Cuba	MO	B+	B+	B+	251.2	6.80	5.2	2.2	29.7	22.0	8.0	9.7	0.0
▼ Peoples Bank	Mendenhall	MS	D	D+	C-	422.8	5.09	19.4	2.8	11.2	8.2	7.8	9.6	16.2
Peoples Bank	Newton	NC	B+	B+	A	1598.7	12.20	5.9	0.4	12.5	23.0	8.1	9.7	16.2
Peoples Bank	Marietta	OH	B	B	B	5060.4	1.64	17.6	12.2	12.0	20.3	5.3	7.3	11.9

Asset Quality Index	Adjusted Non-Performing Loans as a % of Total Loans	Adjusted Non-Performing Loans as a % of Capital	Net Charge-Offs Avg Loans	Profitability Index	Net Income ($Mil)	Return on Assets (R.O.A.)	Return on Equity (R.O.E.)	Net Interest Spread	Overhead Efficiency Ratio	Liquidity Index	Liquidity Ratio	Hot Money Ratio	Stability Index
7.2	0.50	1.2	-0.03	**6.8**	320.3	1.96	16.22	3.54	48.0	**6.0**	40.9	3.5	**8.2**
9.4	0.26	0.4	-1.26	**7.4**	5.7	1.74	14.18	3.40	44.9	**5.9**	53.5	8.7	**9.1**
9.3	0.06	1.0	0.00	**4.4**	0.3	1.07	10.24	2.58	61.1	**4.7**	63.3	15.6	**5.1**
7.7	0.75	2.9	0.03	**2.8**	1.0	0.53	5.84	3.47	81.8	**1.7**	27.2	22.3	**4.8**
7.0	1.13	4.5	0.14	**4.3**	0.8	0.73	5.97	1.96	64.9	**3.2**	44.5	20.2	**7.6**
6.4	0.53	3.3	0.00	**9.1**	6.5	3.40	34.91	4.14	46.5	**5.5**	32.8	3.3	**7.6**
8.2	0.64	0.6	-0.24	**4.4**	2.1	0.86	8.34	3.83	66.0	**3.8**	13.4	5.3	**6.4**
9.6	0.05	0.3	0.00	**3.3**	-3.0	-2.64	-31.07	1.70	115.8	**1.9**	40.7	41.3	**7.2**
5.5	8.69	10.2	0.12	**2.8**	0.1	0.39	2.72	3.24	91.0	**4.7**	8.7	3.0	**6.0**
8.8	0.19	0.9	0.00	**9.4**	4.8	2.25	18.01	4.16	39.0	**4.8**	32.0	7.5	**9.3**
7.4	0.44	3.5	-0.02	**7.8**	7.4	1.72	22.60	5.02	56.6	**4.9**	27.0	7.5	**7.0**
5.0	1.50	8.4	0.00	**6.8**	1.2	1.84	18.64	4.73	66.2	**6.3**	45.7	3.6	**5.8**
7.7	0.74	2.8	0.02	**9.9**	21.5	2.06	17.34	3.50	28.0	**2.3**	29.8	27.9	**10.0**
8.3	0.03	0.2	-0.30	**5.4**	3.6	1.01	10.86	2.89	67.9	**3.4**	19.7	3.1	**6.7**
3.5	2.97	11.6	-0.01	**6.1**	17.3	1.21	11.07	3.11	42.9	**1.4**	18.9	19.0	**9.5**
8.4	0.01	0.1	0.02	**5.4**	2.5	1.48	16.96	3.52	61.9	**0.6**	11.3	33.8	**6.0**
6.1	2.26	5.8	0.00	**4.8**	1.2	0.98	6.82	3.17	64.6	**4.0**	34.4	12.1	**7.1**
7.1	0.08	0.6	0.09	**4.7**	1.7	0.84	9.34	3.58	66.1	**4.7**	20.0	2.2	**5.2**
8.9	0.18	1.1	0.00	**6.2**	6.0	1.62	15.11	3.65	68.4	**2.0**	18.8	13.2	**6.6**
4.7	1.22	5.9	0.01	**6.4**	5.6	1.33	10.88	2.74	73.6	**4.7**	22.4	5.3	**8.2**
4.4	2.55	14.3	0.03	**4.3**	6.2	0.99	11.37	3.32	57.6	**1.5**	22.0	17.2	**6.7**
4.4	0.67	6.3	-0.15	**6.4**	1.6	1.54	14.27	3.03	56.9	**2.3**	30.5	21.0	**7.5**
8.5	0.35	1.7	-0.01	**8.1**	4.0	1.76	18.13	3.37	61.8	**1.3**	8.1	24.9	**6.4**
1.0	4.46	26.6	0.06	**2.2**	2.6	0.58	5.62	3.16	75.2	**1.8**	25.4	21.1	**5.7**
6.0	2.62	7.8	0.00	**7.0**	1.4	1.39	9.65	2.53	50.7	**1.8**	36.2	33.7	**8.2**
6.9	0.13	0.5	0.00	**4.6**	0.8	0.97	10.35	4.28	73.9	**2.3**	10.3	17.1	**6.3**
6.2	0.78	4.2	0.52	**3.0**	0.8	0.54	6.07	3.38	75.3	**2.7**	20.3	16.1	**4.7**
8.8	0.53	1.2	0.07	**5.1**	0.4	0.86	6.89	4.06	73.8	**2.4**	28.1	19.1	**6.9**
7.0	1.02	4.4	0.00	**7.3**	0.9	1.24	10.74	3.84	65.8	**5.9**	43.2	5.3	**8.5**
6.8	0.86	2.8	0.10	**4.8**	2.1	1.34	13.68	3.09	58.5	**6.3**	54.3	6.4	**5.5**
7.3	0.68	3.2	-0.02	**3.8**	7.1	0.77	6.14	2.75	68.5	**3.1**	23.7	14.3	**8.8**
8.8	0.00	0.3	0.05	**4.5**	1.6	0.71	7.64	3.52	68.4	**5.7**	40.8	5.5	**5.3**
6.7	0.26	1.7	0.22	**5.2**	31.6	1.07	10.49	2.43	57.9	**3.8**	4.9	6.7	**7.8**
9.7	0.00	0.0	0.00	**4.5**	1.0	0.93	7.83	1.98	55.7	**4.1**	71.4	23.3	**7.2**
8.0	7.42	7.4	0.00	**0.2**	-0.2	-0.92	-5.26	1.96	141.2	**6.3**	92.5	11.5	**5.4**
8.5	0.00	0.0	0.00	**3.2**	2.8	0.59	8.13	2.35	67.3	**6.0**	40.5	3.6	**5.8**
6.3	0.24	1.3	0.35	**5.2**	2.6	0.95	10.26	3.54	66.7	**4.2**	32.5	11.3	**6.6**
9.1	0.33	1.0	-0.02	**4.0**	12.3	0.94	7.85	2.63	64.3	**4.7**	36.9	11.0	**9.0**
9.1	0.34	1.7	0.00	**2.8**	0.4	0.42	2.76	2.93	83.8	**4.8**	36.2	9.8	**7.1**
5.3	1.83	8.1	0.00	**3.7**	2.7	0.84	8.99	3.06	69.2	**4.1**	21.8	8.8	**6.1**
7.8	0.55	3.0	-0.01	**4.4**	4.8	1.03	9.28	2.97	78.6	**3.7**	16.9	10.6	**7.3**
5.0	1.84	7.8	0.41	**8.3**	1.4	1.99	17.01	4.94	52.5	**1.0**	25.4	36.3	**7.2**
8.3	0.15	1.0	0.00	**7.5**	5.9	1.62	17.18	4.24	67.3	**5.5**	33.8	2.9	**6.6**
5.3	0.95	6.1	0.01	**7.8**	2.2	1.42	17.19	3.67	44.5	**3.2**	18.4	9.6	**5.0**
5.0	1.01	4.6	0.11	**4.8**	331.2	1.04	8.64	2.76	62.2	**4.2**	14.9	4.5	**9.1**
4.7	0.64	4.0	1.19	**6.9**	1.4	1.50	13.64	3.78	58.4	**1.7**	26.1	23.3	**7.0**
5.9	0.81	7.9	0.15	**9.3**	3.3	1.79	13.26	4.31	45.0	**1.1**	20.4	31.7	**9.0**
8.7	0.05	0.1	-0.01	**9.4**	1.5	1.65	10.96	3.68	42.7	**4.6**	29.2	7.8	**9.5**
7.6	0.03	0.2	-0.14	**1.5**	0.1	0.15	1.34	3.47	90.3	**5.3**	34.8	5.4	**2.8**
6.0	0.05	9.6	0.00	**6.2**	0.8	1.17	14.37	3.67	60.5	**3.6**	39.2	16.8	**5.3**
3.1	1.95	8.1	-0.15	**4.9**	2.4	1.21	9.82	3.81	67.9	**3.1**	34.0	13.4	**4.1**
4.7	0.68	4.6	0.01	**8.0**	6.5	1.74	14.59	3.42	51.6	**2.5**	20.5	12.9	**9.6**
5.1	1.30	7.5	-0.01	**4.4**	8.1	1.03	10.80	3.42	68.6	**5.0**	34.2	11.0	**8.2**
8.5	0.13	0.2	0.00	**3.9**	0.2	0.80	5.77	3.34	75.1	**2.2**	34.4	16.5	**6.8**
8.5	0.00	0.0	0.00	**7.2**	1.4	2.60	29.91	5.72	40.5	**3.1**	25.6	14.7	**5.3**
4.6	1.78	10.8	-0.08	**4.8**	0.4	0.98	8.28	4.13	68.3	**0.6**	16.9	56.3	**5.6**
6.2	0.82	3.5	0.10	**6.9**	1.9	1.56	15.32	3.59	62.9	**4.1**	23.6	8.9	**8.0**
0.7	5.24	29.1	0.04	**10.0**	8.6	4.17	43.46	5.44	49.8	**2.0**	26.1	20.5	**7.7**
8.8	0.38	2.0	-0.01	**5.7**	9.1	1.20	11.93	3.26	69.2	**6.3**	39.9	4.3	**8.5**
4.1	1.02	5.3	0.11	**5.4**	27.6	1.10	9.84	3.30	68.9	**4.0**	12.7	4.8	**9.6**

Name	City	State	Rating	2020 Rating	2019 Rating	Total Assets ($Mil)	One Year Asset Growth	Asset Mix (As a % of Total Assets) Commercial Loans	Consumer Loans	Mortgage Loans	Securities	Capitalization Index	Leverage Ratio	Risk-Based Capital Ratio
▲ Peoples Bank	Clifton	TN	B-	C+	C-	246.7	11.54	26.9	7.4	11.8	4.5	8.4	9.9	14.2
Peoples Bank	Lubbock	TX	B+	B+	A-	889.9	32.76	9.5	1.8	6.6	20.7	7.3	9.2	0.0
Peoples Bank	Paris	TX	B	B	B-	172.9	16.82	3.4	1.0	25.6	16.0	7.2	9.1	0.0
Peoples Bank	Bellingham	WA	B+	B+	A-	2635.0	15.77	9.3	5.7	7.8	5.1	6.7	9.2	0.0
Peoples Bank & Trust	Buford	GA	B-	B	B	438.4	16.05	4.3	0.5	6.3	53.4	7.9	9.6	0.0
Peoples Bank & Trust	Pana	IL	B-	C+	C-	559.2	21.40	29.9	0.2	3.4	27.0	6.1	8.1	16.9
▲ Peoples Bank & Trust Co.	Troy	MO	B	B-	B-	684.1	24.64	4.1	1.3	5.8	47.0	7.2	9.1	14.1
▲ Peoples Bank & Trust Co.	Ryan	OK	B	B-	B-	79.7	-5.60	41.3	0.2	1.9	0.0	10.0	13.6	19.6
▲ Peoples Bank & Trust Co.	Manchester	TN	A-	B+	A-	141.5	25.84	9.2	3.7	21.4	6.9	9.8	10.9	0.0
Peoples Bank & Trust Co. of Hazard	Hazard	KY	E-	E-	E	251.4	-1.04	14.0	2.0	17.9	27.9	3.6	5.6	10.6
Peoples Bank and Trust Co.	McPherson	KS	B+	B+	B+	980.1	36.64	17.2	2.3	2.9	36.7	8.1	9.7	13.5
Peoples Bank Mt Washington	Mount Washington	KY	A-	A-	A-	109.7	14.24	5.4	0.4	5.7	23.9	9.2	10.5	16.7
▲ Peoples Bank of Alabama	Cullman	AL	B+	B-	B-	1136.0	13.34	15.3	1.3	6.4	12.2	5.9	8.2	0.0
▲ Peoples Bank of Altenburg	Altenburg	MO	B	B-	B-	74.9	7.48	5.3	1.3	27.4	21.9	8.3	9.8	17.9
Peoples Bank of Deer Lodge	Deer Lodge	MT	C	C	C-	45.7	27.79	12.8	4.9	13.1	18.7	6.9	8.9	0.0
▼ Peoples Bank of East Tennessee	Madisonville	TN	B+	A-	A-	325.7	25.05	13.1	2.5	22.5	16.4	7.8	9.5	0.0
Peoples Bank of Graceville	Graceville	FL	B+	B+	A-	125.5	14.55	4.8	1.5	10.2	53.6	8.2	9.8	33.3
▲ Peoples Bank of Greensboro	Greensboro	AL	B-	C+	B-	114.5	15.07	6.5	5.2	11.1	50.6	6.3	8.3	17.5
Peoples Bank of Kankakee County	Bourbonnais	IL	B-	B-	C+	311.8	11.99	6.2	2.7	8.1	46.8	5.1	7.1	14.3
Peoples Bank of Kentucky, Inc.	Flemingsburg	KY	B+	B	B	365.5	5.25	6.9	6.5	18.3	8.6	9.6	10.8	15.6
Peoples Bank of Macon	Macon	IL	C+	C+	C+	24.2	8.66	8.1	6.4	3.4	35.8	10.0	11.9	0.0
▼ Peoples Bank of Middle Tennessee	Shelbyville	TN	B+	A-	A-	163.0	2.92	3.4	4.3	17.4	31.0	10.0	12.8	0.0
▲ Peoples Bank of Moniteau County	Jamestown	MO	C	D+	C-	68.6	7.82	3.4	3.7	16.5	37.4	6.9	8.9	16.0
▲ Peoples Bank of the South	La Follette	TN	A-	B	C	187.0	8.99	4.0	1.7	24.8	13.7	10.0	11.7	20.5
Peoples Bank of Wyaconda	Kahoka	MO	B+	B+	B+	119.6	16.15	3.8	3.6	14.7	24.2	8.4	10.0	0.0
Peoples Bank, A Codorus Valley Co.	York	PA	B	B+	B+	2232.8	7.98	11.8	0.4	9.7	9.3	8.5	10.0	16.1
Peoples Community Bank	Greenville	MO	A	A	A-	607.3	13.13	6.1	6.3	31.5	23.1	10.0	16.1	0.0
Peoples Community Bank Sb of Monticello,	Monticello	IN	C	C	C+	33.2	8.74	1.2	2.8	56.6	1.5	10.0	38.4	0.0
Peoples Exchange Bank	Monroeville	AL	B+	B	B	92.3	12.49	16.6	5.0	10.4	27.9	10.0	12.1	0.0
Peoples Exchange Bank	Winchester	KY	B	B	B	488.4	11.07	4.2	1.1	30.2	3.8	7.0	9.0	0.0
Peoples Federal S&L Assn.	Sidney	OH	B-	B-	B-	127.1	4.87	3.2	2.0	46.2	10.3	10.0	12.3	21.0
Peoples First Savings Bank	Mason	OH	C+	C+	C	69.5	-2.18	0.0	0.2	43.1	0.3	10.0	12.2	19.9
Peoples Independent Bank	Boaz	AL	B+	B+	B	403.2	17.54	8.8	1.0	6.0	42.2	6.3	8.3	13.8
Peoples National Bank of Kewanee	Kewanee	IL	B-	B	B+	547.6	36.96	3.6	0.8	3.5	57.1	6.8	8.8	15.8
Peoples National Bank, N.A.	Mount Vernon	IL	B-	B-	C+	1469.5	1.28	19.8	0.3	4.0	4.0	6.2	8.5	11.9
Peoples Savings Bank	Crawfordsville	IA	B+	B	B	39.3	10.08	8.6	0.7	8.0	50.5	6.9	8.9	0.0
▲ Peoples Savings Bank	Indianola	IA	B+	B	B	439.5	23.12	15.0	0.5	5.3	46.4	8.0	9.6	17.0
Peoples Savings Bank	Montezuma	IA	B-	B-	B-	49.0	10.54	6.9	4.9	12.8	22.0	9.0	10.4	0.0
▲ Peoples Savings Bank	Wellsburg	IA	B-	C	C	126.1	29.95	15.6	2.2	7.6	27.9	6.5	10.1	0.0
Peoples Savings Bank of Rhineland	Rhineland	MO	B-	B-	B-	432.5	31.21	11.5	1.7	19.0	17.1	6.4	8.4	12.6
Peoples Security Bank and Trust Co.	Scranton	PA	B+	B+	B+	2999.6	11.14	14.8	2.6	11.3	11.5	8.3	9.9	14.9
▲ Peoples State Bank	Cherryvale	KS	B-	C+	C-	17.2	-2.08	18.0	4.9	18.4	6.2	10.0	26.3	0.0
Peoples State Bank	Manhattan	KS	D+	D	C+	251.2	-7.05	14.5	1.0	11.5	2.4	6.9	9.8	0.0
▲ Peoples State Bank	Fairmount	ND	D+	D-	D+	34.8	7.09	16.0	2.0	5.8	26.0	4.5	6.6	11.0
Peoples State Bank	Westhope	ND	A-	B+	B+	72.3	9.31	7.4	1.8	0.1	41.5	10.0	13.2	0.0
▼ Peoples State Bank	New Lexington	OH	C+	B-	B-	183.1	13.21	5.0	6.3	32.4	23.1	5.4	7.4	14.8
▼ Peoples State Bank	Blair	OK	C+	B-	B-	19.8	10.87	28.8	5.3	2.4	9.7	5.7	7.7	14.8
Peoples State Bank	Rocksprings	TX	A-	A-	A-	100.8	17.87	1.6	1.4	8.9	46.1	10.0	11.7	24.7
Peoples State Bank	Shepherd	TX	B-	B-	B-	154.2	12.84	3.2	3.4	6.1	43.7	6.4	8.4	22.1
Peoples State Bank	Prairie Du Chien	WI	C	C-	C	911.6	4.21	4.8	0.5	9.0	39.7	8.7	10.1	18.5
Peoples State Bank	Wausau	WI	B+	B+	B+	1253.7	14.79	9.9	0.4	17.5	20.7	6.7	8.7	14.4
Peoples State Bank of Colfax	Colfax	IL	B+	B+	B+	43.6	10.10	9.1	5.6	14.1	14.6	8.8	10.2	24.4
Peoples State Bank of Hallettsville	Hallettsville	TX	B	B-	B-	332.5	9.37	2.4	1.5	11.9	39.5	9.7	10.8	0.0
Peoples State Bank of Munising	Munising	MI	A-	B+	A-	185.4	15.42	9.6	3.8	9.2	33.9	9.8	10.8	0.0
Peoples State Bank of Plainview	Plainview	MN	B	B	B-	347.2	11.62	7.0	2.6	14.2	35.0	6.0	8.1	15.2
Peoples State Bank of Velva	Velva	ND	D+	D+	C-	135.8	8.43	12.3	2.7	7.2	12.4	7.2	9.1	13.9
Peoples State Bank of Wells	Wells	MN	C+	C+	B-	61.7	6.40	2.3	1.2	7.8	9.6	7.1	9.1	17.1
Peoples Trust and Savings Bank	Riverside	IA	B+	B	B	34.9	28.26	3.8	0.6	9.3	38.0	10.0	11.2	0.0
Peoples Trust and Savings Bank	Boonville	IN	B	B-	B	233.1	13.69	2.9	0.5	35.2	27.1	10.0	14.2	0.0
Peoples Trust Co. of St. Albans	Saint Albans	VT	B-	B-	B	369.5	12.21	4.9	1.9	16.1	16.0	8.4	10.0	22.0

Asset Quality Index	Adjusted Non-Performing Loans as a % of Total Loans	Adjusted Non-Performing Loans as a % of Capital	Net Charge-Offs Avg Loans	Profitability Index	Net Income ($Mil)	Return on Assets (R.O.A.)	Return on Equity (R.O.E.)	Net Interest Spread	Overhead Efficiency Ratio	Liquidity Index	Liquidity Ratio	Hot Money Ratio	Stability Index
5.7	0.40	2.7	0.16	**5.5**	1.3	1.08	10.97	5.26	66.1	**1.1**	22.8	32.4	**5.5**
8.5	0.11	0.1	0.00	**7.2**	5.3	3.64	43.29	9.59	59.6	**4.5**	37.2	11.8	**7.0**
8.5	0.22	1.4	0.04	**5.4**	1.0	1.18	12.55	3.25	70.8	**5.0**	36.4	8.0	**6.0**
7.8	0.34	2.0	0.01	**5.1**	11.9	0.97	10.08	2.85	70.8	**5.8**	32.0	5.1	**7.8**
9.4	0.19	0.6	0.00	**3.9**	1.6	0.78	7.51	2.89	69.9	**3.5**	56.0	23.8	**6.2**
5.8	0.54	3.9	-0.07	**7.0**	3.6	1.36	15.73	3.60	48.5	**2.6**	18.9	14.2	**6.2**
6.5	0.98	3.5	-0.09	**4.9**	4.2	1.28	14.12	2.92	66.0	**5.5**	35.6	4.9	**7.5**
4.3	1.20	13.0	0.00	**8.6**	2.2	4.93	58.09	2.75	36.3	**0.7**	17.5	49.9	**6.7**
6.9	0.02	3.1	0.02	**7.9**	1.4	2.04	18.69	5.58	49.2	**4.2**	39.3	13.7	**6.7**
0.3	8.39	65.9	0.05	**0.6**	0.0	0.03	0.67	3.00	101.0	**2.2**	30.5	22.4	**1.2**
5.1	0.42	4.4	0.00	**5.6**	6.0	1.23	11.94	3.70	59.5	**4.4**	22.1	7.3	**7.9**
5.3	2.18	5.4	-0.02	**7.0**	1.0	1.78	15.79	3.68	63.1	**6.0**	41.6	4.1	**8.4**
6.6	1.24	4.2	0.05	**7.2**	9.6	1.71	20.40	3.72	63.2	**6.0**	33.2	4.1	**8.5**
7.7	0.51	2.5	0.00	**6.4**	0.6	1.57	15.28	4.25	62.3	**5.8**	40.6	4.6	**6.3**
4.9	0.74	6.6	0.13	**7.3**	0.4	2.15	23.29	4.35	54.5	**5.6**	33.7	3.0	**3.9**
5.3	1.18	6.9	0.28	**5.7**	1.7	1.11	11.08	4.04	66.4	**4.4**	28.2	9.0	**5.7**
7.2	1.73	3.8	0.00	**5.4**	0.8	1.43	13.36	2.97	54.3	**4.9**	71.2	16.7	**6.3**
5.0	1.63	8.2	0.10	**5.0**	0.7	1.26	15.77	3.37	63.4	**4.4**	52.8	16.3	**5.1**
8.0	0.46	1.8	0.00	**4.2**	1.6	1.08	14.51	2.51	69.2	**5.3**	43.2	9.2	**4.9**
4.3	1.19	7.3	0.03	**6.7**	2.5	1.36	12.17	4.21	51.4	**1.5**	11.9	23.9	**7.4**
9.2	0.00	1.1	0.00	**2.2**	0.0	0.13	1.11	1.88	91.7	**5.4**	48.8	6.8	**6.1**
8.3	0.54	2.6	0.04	**4.9**	0.6	0.77	6.00	3.06	66.8	**2.6**	37.1	22.9	**7.9**
3.8	2.68	14.1	-0.03	**5.4**	0.5	1.57	17.39	3.76	52.3	**5.3**	46.2	9.2	**3.8**
5.7	1.31	7.2	-0.03	**9.6**	2.1	2.24	19.30	5.05	50.6	**2.4**	30.8	20.0	**9.8**
8.7	0.00	0.0	-0.01	**5.3**	0.7	1.11	11.24	3.44	54.0	**1.8**	27.6	21.5	**6.4**
4.2	2.65	15.3	0.11	**4.1**	8.1	0.73	7.32	2.97	69.6	**3.8**	22.2	12.0	**7.2**
8.1	0.59	1.9	-0.03	**10.0**	10.7	3.60	20.68	5.53	35.4	**2.6**	25.6	17.0	**10.0**
9.3	0.50	1.0	0.00	**1.9**	0.0	0.10	0.25	3.16	96.9	**3.8**	37.3	15.3	**6.4**
5.0	2.48	11.2	0.16	**5.6**	0.5	1.03	8.28	4.65	66.7	**4.0**	39.3	11.0	**7.4**
7.9	0.30	1.7	-0.02	**4.9**	2.5	1.05	11.58	3.47	67.5	**2.8**	23.3	16.0	**5.8**
8.2	0.77	3.8	0.00	**3.4**	0.4	0.58	4.78	3.47	79.9	**4.6**	21.7	5.3	**7.6**
9.0	0.00	0.0	0.00	**3.0**	0.2	0.57	4.58	3.16	84.0	**2.4**	17.5	17.0	**6.7**
6.7	1.09	2.2	-0.02	**6.3**	3.4	1.80	17.66	3.77	60.4	**6.1**	53.8	7.4	**6.9**
5.2	3.38	6.9	0.10	**3.6**	1.5	0.59	5.53	2.71	72.4	**5.9**	63.4	11.1	**6.1**
4.2	1.59	13.0	-0.04	**5.1**	10.1	1.37	16.29	3.39	68.1	**3.7**	13.1	10.3	**7.7**
8.7	0.11	0.3	0.00	**4.8**	0.3	1.27	12.68	2.33	61.4	**6.7**	67.6	4.6	**6.1**
8.4	0.68	1.5	0.00	**5.4**	3.6	1.69	16.24	3.37	55.2	**4.7**	40.7	8.8	**6.1**
8.2	0.67	2.3	0.04	**3.9**	0.2	0.76	7.11	4.54	73.4	**6.5**	70.0	6.7	**4.8**
3.7	1.79	10.0	0.17	**4.5**	0.5	0.92	9.01	3.67	74.3	**1.5**	29.7	32.3	**5.3**
7.9	0.32	2.0	-0.18	**4.4**	1.5	0.73	8.67	3.75	69.3	**4.5**	14.6	5.3	**4.7**
7.4	0.32	1.7	0.02	**5.6**	18.8	1.28	10.86	3.10	55.6	**4.2**	15.9	7.4	**9.5**
5.2	1.42	5.2	-0.08	**9.5**	0.2	2.72	10.36	5.63	52.0	**2.6**	28.2	16.6	**8.0**
2.2	2.79	18.4	-0.36	**2.4**	0.7	0.55	5.25	4.31	76.8	**1.6**	19.2	24.8	**3.4**
7.3	0.00	0.0	0.00	**3.6**	0.1	0.57	8.71	3.69	79.9	**5.0**	13.6	2.0	**2.7**
8.8	0.00	0.0	0.00	**7.0**	0.7	1.95	15.08	3.66	48.9	**5.6**	62.9	10.7	**8.3**
4.4	1.48	9.9	0.00	**3.0**	0.4	0.45	5.47	3.15	86.1	**3.7**	28.2	12.4	**4.6**
8.0	0.00	0.2	0.00	**3.4**	0.0	0.23	2.84	4.02	93.9	**5.6**	48.6	5.4	**3.9**
9.5	0.00	0.0	0.00	**5.4**	0.6	1.26	10.19	2.63	50.0	**5.8**	53.2	9.0	**8.2**
9.2	0.00	0.0	0.00	**3.9**	0.7	0.95	11.26	3.02	71.5	**3.8**	37.8	15.1	**5.1**
2.5	5.46	18.4	0.00	**4.2**	5.3	1.19	10.43	3.03	66.7	**4.8**	39.4	10.7	**8.0**
6.1	1.31	7.5	0.00	**6.5**	7.8	1.30	13.92	3.73	56.9	**4.1**	18.0	8.9	**8.6**
8.7	0.00	0.0	0.00	**6.4**	0.2	1.07	10.46	3.61	55.0	**6.1**	58.2	6.8	**5.9**
9.4	0.17	0.5	0.00	**4.0**	1.4	0.89	7.54	2.86	62.8	**2.8**	58.0	37.0	**6.8**
5.9	1.08	3.3	-0.04	**6.2**	1.0	1.19	10.03	3.55	61.0	**5.1**	46.5	11.4	**8.2**
6.8	0.50	2.4	0.00	**7.0**	3.2	1.89	21.63	3.46	54.5	**4.9**	36.4	8.6	**6.4**
1.4	6.28	29.9	-0.03	**6.6**	1.1	1.71	18.81	4.53	60.4	**2.5**	26.8	18.1	**5.9**
5.7	0.15	1.6	0.00	**4.6**	0.3	0.80	7.53	2.65	72.0	**4.1**	35.7	13.1	**7.4**
7.7	0.00	2.8	2.01	**5.2**	0.2	1.41	11.93	4.03	58.1	**6.0**	58.9	7.5	**5.4**
9.4	0.12	0.4	-0.03	**4.3**	1.2	1.04	6.65	3.59	72.7	**3.9**	36.2	14.2	**7.7**
6.0	1.52	4.0	-0.12	**3.5**	1.3	0.71	6.83	2.74	77.4	**6.0**	51.7	7.3	**5.9**

Name	City	State	Rating	2020 Rating	2019 Rating	Total Assets ($Mil)	One Year Asset Growth	Asset Mix (As a % of Total Assets) Commercial Loans	Consumer Loans	Mortgage Loans	Securities	Capitalization Index	Leverage Ratio	Risk-Based Capital Ratio
PeoplesBank	Holyoke	MA	**C**	C+	B-	3576.3	11.90	9.3	2.6	20.8	11.7	**7.0**	9.0	13.2
PeoplesSouth Bank	Colquitt	GA	**B**	B	B	991.1	7.45	7.2	2.3	12.0	30.5	**7.2**	9.1	16.0
PeoplesTrust Bank	Hamilton	AL	**B-**	B-	B-	131.2	13.26	18.4	5.6	12.3	15.9	**7.7**	10.7	0.0
Perennial Bank	Darwin	MN	**B**	B	B	144.7	20.24	4.8	4.0	11.9	36.8	**5.6**	7.6	23.8
Perpetual Federal Savings Bank	Urbana	OH	**A**	A	A	394.8	0.22	5.1	0.6	48.3	3.3	**10.0**	20.1	34.7
Persons Banking Co.	Forsyth	GA	**D+**	D+	D+	405.4	10.50	4.8	0.9	10.0	39.1	**3.9**	5.9	13.5
Peru Federal Savings Bank	Peru	IL	**B-**	B-	B-	181.7	7.19	2.1	1.4	30.9	39.2	**10.0**	12.3	29.9
Peshtigo National Bank	Peshtigo	WI	**C+**	B-	B-	261.6	9.42	7.7	1.5	16.3	31.9	**7.2**	9.1	0.0
Petefish, Skiles & Co.	Virginia	IL	**A-**	A-	A-	255.6	14.35	5.7	5.6	10.0	22.7	**9.4**	10.6	0.0
Petit Jean State Bank	Morrilton	AR	**A-**	A-	A-	217.4	7.86	14.4	1.8	11.2	33.0	**10.0**	14.2	0.0
Phelps County Bank	Rolla	MO	**B**	B	B	484.0	14.24	5.8	1.3	24.4	18.7	**5.2**	7.2	16.2
Phenix-Girard Bank	Phenix City	AL	**A**	A	B+	268.3	21.88	1.1	0.3	7.4	47.2	**10.0**	14.2	0.0
▼ Philo Exchange Bank	Philo	IL	**B-**	B+	B+	132.1	21.94	2.4	1.0	5.0	33.5	**7.1**	9.1	17.9
Phoenixville Federal Bank and Trust	Phoenixville	PA	**B-**	B-	B-	571.2	9.93	2.8	0.0	33.6	15.8	**9.8**	10.9	0.0
Pickens S&L Assn., Federal Assn.	Pickens	SC	**C+**	C+	B-	117.3	8.24	1.3	0.6	37.5	36.2	**8.4**	9.9	23.7
Piedmont Federal Savings Bank	Winston-Salem	NC	**C-**	C-	C+	949.4	6.33	1.6	0.0	54.3	28.6	**10.0**	25.0	0.0
Piermont Bank	New York	NY	**D**	D		287.3	145.73	6.3	0.0	3.3	19.7	**10.0**	11.1	25.6
Piggott State Bank	Piggott	AR	**B-**	B-	B	114.2	8.22	9.7	3.8	14.7	36.5	**6.1**	8.1	17.3
▲ Pike National Bank	McComb	MS	**A-**	B+	B+	314.4	12.04	9.8	3.1	13.3	29.8	**10.0**	12.5	23.1
Pikes Peak National Bank	Colorado Springs	CO	**C+**	C+	B-	117.6	5.85	7.8	0.3	3.7	0.0	**10.0**	12.0	30.4
Pilgrim Bank	Pittsburg	TX	**B**	B	B	599.2	2.54	5.6	0.7	12.0	25.3	**10.0**	11.4	16.2
Pilot Bank	Tampa	FL	**C**	C+	C	646.4	10.33	35.4	14.3	2.3	12.1	**4.0**	9.3	0.0
Pilot Grove Savings Bank	Pilot Grove	IA	**B+**	A-	A-	761.8	12.87	7.7	3.1	26.1	18.7	**7.8**	9.5	15.2
▼ Pine Country Bank	Little Falls	MN	**B**	B+	B+	244.6	17.81	10.1	0.5	4.4	22.7	**7.0**	9.0	0.0
Pine Island Bank	Pine Island	MN	**B+**	B+	B+	114.9	-2.09	7.3	1.2	30.8	8.3	**8.5**	10.0	14.6
Pine River State Bank	Pine River	MN	**B-**	B-	B-	163.1	18.13	7.6	1.4	14.3	23.6	**5.3**	7.3	17.0
Pineland Bank	Alma	GA	**B-**	B-	B	380.2	12.61	7.8	1.6	10.7	6.3	**7.5**	9.4	0.0
Pinnacle Bank	Jasper	AL	**A-**	A-	A-	321.3	18.29	14.5	1.7	6.4	51.0	**8.7**	10.1	18.4
Pinnacle Bank	Gilroy	CA	**B+**	B+	A-	695.9	11.35	13.9	0.0	3.9	2.1	**7.1**	9.0	14.9
Pinnacle Bank	Elberton	GA	**B+**	B+	B+	1658.7	11.27	7.9	1.5	9.5	12.5	**6.2**	8.2	12.4
Pinnacle Bank	Marshalltown	IA	**A**	A	A	261.1	14.61	15.3	1.7	4.6	19.0	**10.0**	15.8	20.1
Pinnacle Bank	Lincoln	NE	**A-**	A-	A-	6966.8	14.32	6.7	0.9	7.6	20.5	**7.8**	9.6	14.2
▲ Pinnacle Bank	Nashville	TN	**A-**	B+	B+	35216.9	6.09	20.5	1.3	6.8	15.2	**7.7**	9.6	13.1
Pinnacle Bank	Fort Worth	TX	**A-**	A-	A-	1941.9	14.44	7.0	0.8	9.3	32.9	**7.0**	9.0	16.1
Pinnacle Bank - Wyoming	Cody	WY	**A-**	A-	A-	1260.4	14.69	7.3	1.3	10.0	35.1	**7.8**	9.5	15.3
Pinnacle Bank, Inc	Vanceburg	KY	**B-**	B-	B-	51.5	1.81	5.8	3.5	29.8	11.7	**10.0**	14.8	0.0
Pioneer Bank	Sergeant Bluff	IA	**B**	B	B	241.5	13.72	10.1	0.6	16.3	7.3	**6.4**	8.4	0.0
Pioneer Bank	Mapleton	MN	**C+**	C+	C	716.5	5.47	16.5	1.0	8.3	16.7	**7.2**	9.1	16.3
Pioneer Bank	Roswell	NM	**B-**	B-	B-	954.1	14.08	9.5	1.0	10.9	32.3	**7.3**	9.2	17.5
▼ Pioneer Bank	Albany	NY	**C**	B-	B	1795.1	17.73	9.6	0.2	19.8	15.4	**8.9**	10.3	18.5
Pioneer Bank	Stanley	VA	**B**	B	B	281.9	15.67	8.5	8.2	21.0	17.8	**9.3**	10.5	18.0
Pioneer Bank & Trust	Spearfish	SD	**A**	A	A	928.9	23.23	7.8	1.4	3.8	46.1	**8.0**	9.7	18.9
▲ Pioneer Bank, SSB	Austin	TX	**C+**	C	C+	1631.3	-10.36	10.5	2.4	10.3	10.8	**7.0**	9.0	14.0
Pioneer Commercial Bank	Albany	NY	**U**	U	U	420.6	38.51	0.0	0.0	0.0	11.4	**5.5**	7.5	37.7
Pioneer Community Bank, Inc.	Iaeger	WV	**B**	B	B	144.9	11.24	24.9	2.4	38.3	15.1	**10.0**	12.0	0.0
Pioneer Federal S&L Assn.	Dillon	MT	**C+**	B-	B-	107.2	10.52	3.2	1.1	54.5	16.1	**10.0**	16.1	0.0
Pioneer State Bank	Earlville	IL	**C+**	C+	C	132.7	17.97	6.2	0.8	11.4	16.3	**9.3**	10.5	0.0
Pioneer Trust Bank, N.A.	Salem	OR	**A+**	A+	A	705.5	11.34	18.7	0.2	4.5	15.1	**9.9**	10.9	19.9
Piqua State Bank	Piqua	KS	**C+**	C+	B	38.7	31.25	4.3	1.5	7.3	37.5	**7.6**	9.4	28.0
Piscataqua Savings Bank	Portsmouth	NH	**C+**	C+	B-	335.1	9.03	0.0	0.9	48.4	32.3	**10.0**	14.5	0.0
Pittsfield Co-operative Bank	Pittsfield	MA	**B**	B	B	380.2	7.79	6.0	0.4	37.1	20.0	**10.0**	12.4	20.4
▲ Plains Commerce Bank	Hoven	SD	**B**	C+	C	1063.7	14.14	6.9	0.5	22.7	5.5	**10.0**	12.6	0.0
Plains State Bank	Plains	KS	**C-**	C	C	246.2	-0.98	17.2	0.8	17.2	15.8	**7.6**	9.7	13.0
Plains State Bank	Humble	TX	**B**	B-	C	722.7	10.11	16.0	0.3	4.2	10.1	**10.0**	12.2	0.0
PlainsCapital Bank	Dallas	TX	**A-**	A-	A-	14199.6	2.88	8.4	0.2	26.4	14.9	**8.8**	10.2	16.0
Planters and Citizens Bank	Camilla	GA	**C+**	C+	B-	125.5	6.84	5.3	2.0	4.9	42.0	**8.1**	9.7	0.0
Planters Bank & Trust Co.	Indianola	MS	**B**	B	B	1309.6	5.64	8.1	1.7	9.8	44.3	**6.8**	8.8	16.5
Planters Bank, Inc.	Hopkinsville	KY	**A**	A-	B+	1288.3	0.82	10.2	0.9	13.1	17.0	**10.0**	12.0	15.2
Planters First Bank	Cordele	GA	**B-**	B-	B-	368.8	-10.33	13.5	1.3	7.1	16.1	**7.6**	9.4	14.0
Plaquemine Bank and Trust Co.	Plaquemine	LA	**B-**	B-	B-	184.6	2.49	9.4	2.6	7.6	26.0	**9.3**	10.6	23.6

Asset Quality Index	Adjusted Non-Performing Loans as a % of Total Loans	Adjusted Non-Performing Loans as a % of Capital	Net Charge-Offs Avg Loans	Profitability Index	Net Income ($Mil)	Return on Assets (R.O.A.)	Return on Equity (R.O.E.)	Net Interest Spread	Overhead Efficiency Ratio	Liquidity Index	Liquidity Ratio	Hot Money Ratio	Stability Index
6.7	0.66	4.4	0.06	**3.6**	11.7	0.68	7.32	2.67	75.4	**5.7**	26.0	2.7	**7.2**
5.4	1.32	6.3	0.02	**6.6**	5.8	1.20	13.95	3.80	59.1	**4.3**	34.8	11.7	**6.5**
4.6	1.10	6.5	0.00	**5.6**	0.7	1.12	9.88	3.59	62.1	**2.1**	27.8	21.2	**6.9**
8.2	0.40	2.2	0.01	**4.3**	0.8	1.12	13.41	2.34	58.3	**7.4**	65.8	1.4	**4.6**
8.9	0.37	1.2	0.09	**6.3**	2.3	1.18	5.82	2.58	44.0	**0.8**	18.5	41.8	**9.2**
7.3	1.32	2.6	0.03	**2.4**	0.8	0.41	6.85	2.76	87.3	**5.5**	43.8	7.9	**1.8**
9.5	0.89	2.0	0.00	**3.0**	0.4	0.43	3.36	2.25	73.4	**4.4**	50.0	15.2	**6.9**
9.0	0.09	0.5	-0.02	**3.3**	0.8	0.61	6.17	3.12	77.8	**5.4**	39.0	7.0	**6.3**
6.4	0.34	1.6	-0.02	**7.9**	2.4	1.97	16.15	3.89	56.9	**4.2**	21.9	8.2	**8.8**
7.8	1.40	3.4	0.11	**7.3**	1.5	1.40	9.93	3.50	44.9	**3.0**	41.6	21.7	**8.5**
7.7	0.43	2.7	0.01	**7.1**	4.2	1.82	24.92	3.30	58.6	**5.8**	35.7	2.7	**5.3**
9.7	0.51	1.2	0.03	**5.7**	2.6	2.09	14.66	2.92	66.9	**6.4**	49.8	3.8	**8.4**
6.2	1.04	3.2	0.01	**3.9**	0.5	0.73	6.96	2.25	72.5	**5.5**	43.4	8.2	**6.4**
6.2	0.75	4.4	0.01	**3.6**	1.7	0.63	5.68	2.85	74.1	**3.9**	27.2	11.3	**7.5**
8.5	0.37	1.2	-0.19	**3.5**	0.4	0.70	6.53	3.42	75.5	**4.3**	50.9	16.4	**6.8**
10.0	0.19	0.4	0.00	**1.9**	1.1	0.24	0.97	2.50	87.8	**2.5**	43.2	29.9	**8.1**
9.0	0.00	0.0	0.00	**0.0**	-1.3	-1.09	-8.33	2.21	122.2	**6.4**	62.5	4.5	**1.5**
9.0	0.05	0.2	0.02	**4.6**	0.7	1.23	14.27	3.15	65.5	**4.1**	35.8	13.1	**5.6**
5.8	3.00	8.0	0.06	**7.0**	2.5	1.62	13.00	3.47	57.4	**3.4**	27.6	13.9	**7.5**
8.1	0.88	2.9	0.24	**2.1**	-0.1	-0.16	-1.28	4.29	104.1	**7.1**	61.2	2.7	**6.9**
6.7	1.54	4.0	0.01	**4.4**	3.2	1.06	8.40	3.38	69.2	**2.8**	21.4	15.7	**8.2**
6.3	0.37	2.1	-0.02	**7.3**	6.1	1.86	22.48	3.56	42.6	**3.0**	16.6	6.3	**5.8**
5.8	0.85	6.3	0.22	**7.4**	6.7	1.77	17.28	3.30	46.1	**4.3**	27.8	9.4	**8.8**
4.5	1.73	8.2	-0.01	**8.3**	1.9	1.72	18.88	4.43	51.2	**5.7**	38.4	4.8	**5.5**
5.7	0.78	3.3	-0.08	**9.6**	1.5	2.60	24.03	4.26	39.6	**1.3**	3.0	17.7	**8.1**
6.7	1.05	3.5	0.00	**3.5**	0.5	0.64	8.57	3.04	80.3	**6.4**	55.1	5.9	**4.1**
4.9	1.21	6.7	0.12	**5.4**	2.3	1.30	13.70	4.21	66.3	**4.2**	26.1	9.2	**5.0**
9.1	0.09	0.5	0.07	**6.3**	2.0	1.30	11.78	3.60	57.6	**4.1**	39.4	14.2	**7.8**
7.2	0.02	0.1	-0.03	**6.5**	3.6	1.07	11.94	3.72	65.5	**5.0**	33.0	6.7	**6.1**
8.0	0.21	1.0	0.05	**6.2**	9.5	1.20	12.02	3.95	63.1	**5.4**	33.0	8.7	**8.5**
5.8	1.66	5.9	0.04	**10.0**	2.6	2.20	12.67	4.06	36.5	**4.7**	32.7	1.6	**9.3**
8.4	0.18	1.6	0.00	**7.2**	51.9	1.55	15.78	3.30	51.0	**4.9**	25.5	7.4	**8.8**
6.9	0.24	1.0	0.18	**6.9**	253.9	1.47	10.04	3.04	48.8	**4.4**	26.5	5.4	**10.0**
7.8	0.00	0.0	0.02	**5.9**	11.1	1.21	9.85	3.64	56.6	**5.7**	39.3	8.7	**9.0**
8.3	0.39	2.6	0.03	**8.9**	10.6	1.74	18.13	3.66	48.3	**4.8**	34.4	11.9	**8.8**
5.4	1.29	5.0	-0.02	**5.3**	0.3	1.17	6.90	4.99	66.3	**1.1**	18.7	27.9	**6.7**
8.8	0.01	0.0	0.00	**5.0**	1.6	1.33	15.80	3.09	57.9	**3.2**	31.1	16.1	**5.8**
2.8	3.46	14.9	0.44	**5.4**	5.1	1.39	13.35	3.88	63.6	**3.5**	22.6	12.2	**6.3**
4.8	2.16	6.7	0.02	**5.2**	6.5	1.42	14.98	3.29	63.1	**5.0**	32.5	6.4	**5.9**
5.6	1.70	10.5	0.33	**2.4**	2.2	0.26	2.55	2.50	84.5	**5.4**	23.2	2.7	**6.6**
5.4	1.03	4.6	0.01	**4.6**	1.3	0.98	9.09	3.87	75.6	**5.3**	36.4	6.1	**6.6**
9.1	0.20	0.8	0.00	**7.6**	6.8	1.52	15.99	2.84	45.4	**5.8**	45.3	6.2	**7.0**
7.0	0.45	2.6	0.00	**3.8**	6.4	0.72	7.79	2.80	72.1	**2.2**	28.2	29.0	**6.8**
10.0	na	0.0	na	**3.8**	1.0	0.53	7.17	0.87	18.1	**8.4**	97.7	0.0	**5.1**
7.5	0.70	4.9	0.02	**4.7**	0.8	1.17	9.54	3.53	69.0	**4.0**	23.8	9.7	**6.8**
9.9	0.00	0.0	0.00	**1.6**	0.1	0.19	1.14	3.04	90.4	**3.6**	39.3	16.7	**7.6**
5.1	2.05	7.3	-0.03	**2.8**	0.4	0.65	5.97	3.47	79.6	**4.0**	26.2	10.3	**6.1**
8.7	0.00	0.0	-0.02	**9.5**	7.3	2.10	18.92	3.19	33.9	**6.5**	45.4	2.0	**9.3**
6.5	0.00	15.0	0.00	**3.1**	0.1	0.42	4.15	3.06	88.5	**7.2**	76.1	3.2	**4.4**
9.8	0.54	2.0	0.00	**2.7**	0.7	0.43	3.05	1.88	82.7	**3.4**	45.5	19.3	**7.7**
6.5	1.23	4.0	-0.01	**3.3**	1.0	0.51	3.57	2.83	78.7	**3.1**	34.2	16.1	**7.7**
4.3	1.61	6.6	0.67	**8.8**	11.6	2.11	16.41	3.75	79.7	**1.7**	23.3	26.5	**10.0**
2.4	2.65	15.8	-0.04	**4.3**	1.3	1.05	10.05	3.53	69.2	**2.3**	21.0	15.6	**6.8**
4.8	2.91	9.9	-0.03	**6.9**	4.9	1.36	11.60	3.74	56.5	**1.3**	27.9	25.9	**8.3**
5.6	0.70	3.7	0.00	**9.5**	219.6	3.21	26.85	3.01	66.2	**4.4**	24.7	8.2	**10.0**
6.0	1.18	4.7	-0.01	**3.4**	0.4	0.57	5.78	3.34	75.4	**6.6**	53.1	3.6	**5.8**
6.0	1.69	7.5	0.20	**4.4**	5.4	0.81	8.74	2.73	65.4	**3.7**	39.1	18.7	**8.1**
8.1	0.24	1.0	0.00	**8.9**	12.5	1.93	16.13	4.00	40.2	**2.9**	10.0	11.8	**10.0**
5.4	1.13	5.5	-0.19	**4.6**	2.1	1.12	12.28	3.71	74.7	**4.3**	14.8	6.7	**5.7**
5.4	2.39	7.6	0.14	**3.2**	0.4	0.42	3.93	3.00	80.4	**3.1**	41.3	19.7	**6.3**

	Name	City	State	Rating	2020 Rating	2019 Rating	Total Assets ($Mil)	One Year Asset Growth	Asset Mix (As a % of Total Assets) Commercial Loans	Consumer Loans	Mortgage Loans	Securities	Capitalization Index	Leverage Ratio	Risk-Based Capital Ratio
	Platinum Bank	Oakdale	MN	**B+**	B+	B	425.6	22.87	36.2	0.8	6.0	4.9	**5.7**	7.7	14.9
▲	Platte Valley Bank	North Bend	NE	**A-**	B+	A-	100.5	7.30	7.0	2.4	2.9	18.0	**10.0**	12.9	0.0
	Platte Valley Bank	Scottsbluff	NE	**B**	B-	B-	913.1	8.50	14.1	6.5	16.3	16.2	**5.9**	8.7	0.0
	Platte Valley Bank	Torrington	WY	**B+**	B	B	536.1	8.74	26.4	5.0	12.2	14.7	**7.4**	10.3	0.0
	Plumas Bank	Quincy	CA	**A-**	A-	B	1266.7	22.30	10.6	7.7	0.8	19.6	**7.1**	9.0	16.2
	Plus International Bank	Miami	FL	**D+**	D	C-	80.4	28.87	13.0	0.0	33.6	0.8	**10.0**	17.5	29.4
	PNB Community Bank	Niceville	FL	**B-**	B-	B-	133.0	12.79	3.2	0.8	27.1	15.7	**7.9**	9.6	0.0
	PNC Bank, N.A.	Wilmington	DE	**B-**	B-	B-	453973.6	-0.29	20.6	5.7	7.7	24.0	**6.0**	8.0	13.4
	Pocahontas State Bank	Pocahontas	IA	**B+**	B+	B+	104.9	5.60	4.3	0.4	3.1	43.4	**10.0**	24.6	0.0
	Pointbank	Pilot Point	TX	**B+**	B+	B+	753.8	12.29	12.5	1.9	6.7	42.7	**7.6**	9.4	17.6
	Points West Community Bank	Windsor	CO	**A-**	A-	A-	826.4	9.45	6.1	1.0	5.0	37.3	**6.9**	8.9	0.0
▼	POINTWEST Bank	West	TX	**C+**	B	B	127.7	11.83	2.4	5.4	17.5	21.8	**6.9**	8.9	25.3
▲	Ponce Bank	Bronx	NY	**B-**	C+	C+	1525.4	25.37	16.0	2.2	27.3	3.3	**8.9**	10.2	16.1
	Pony Express Bank	Liberty	MO	**B+**	B+	B	283.0	42.46	17.0	1.1	13.4	16.7	**5.3**	7.3	12.0
▼	Poppy Bank	Santa Rosa	CA	**A-**	A	A	3734.8	28.96	12.0	0.0	4.6	13.5	**8.0**	9.7	17.7
▲	Popular Bank	New York	NY	**C+**	C-	C+	10197.2	-3.75	4.5	1.3	11.9	10.8	**10.0**	13.1	17.9
	Port Richmond Savings	Philadelphia	PA	**A-**	A-	A-	97.1	-2.36	13.5	0.0	50.2	0.0	**10.0**	17.6	0.0
	Portage Bank	Ceylon	MN	**C-**	D+	D+	30.6	67.87	3.9	2.4	35.2	9.0	**10.0**	13.8	18.1
▼	Portage Community Bank	Ravenna	OH	**C+**	B	B	475.5	15.14	6.4	1.2	23.9	20.2	**8.2**	9.8	18.6
	Powell State Bank	Powell	TX	**C-**	C-	C-	35.8	18.74	9.7	10.9	6.0	31.5	**6.6**	8.6	0.0
	Powell Valley National Bank	Jonesville	VA	**B-**	B-	B	413.0	12.26	6.9	2.3	19.4	10.7	**9.0**	10.3	18.9
	Prairie Bank of Kansas	Stafford	KS	**C+**	C+	C	133.8	9.10	7.7	1.1	4.9	33.9	**6.1**	8.1	0.0
	Prairie Community Bank	Marengo	IL	**D+**	C-	C	165.8	13.10	14.7	1.2	12.8	10.5	**5.9**	7.9	14.2
	Prairie State Bank & Trust	Springfield	IL	**A-**	A-	A-	826.8	10.59	8.6	0.6	14.1	21.4	**8.8**	10.2	0.0
▲	Prairie Sun Bank	Milan	MN	**C+**	C-	C-	76.7	24.54	7.0	3.1	3.9	25.9	**6.1**	8.1	13.8
	Preferred Bank	Los Angeles	CA	**A-**	A-	B+	5577.1	11.40	24.3	0.0	9.9	5.3	**8.6**	10.1	15.6
	Preferred Bank	Casey	IL	**C-**	C-	C-	69.4	8.17	20.0	4.1	15.4	14.5	**6.2**	8.2	14.5
	Preferred Bank	Rothville	MO	**B-**	B-	B-	140.5	13.57	3.0	1.8	9.6	57.6	**5.0**	7.0	20.7
	Premier Bank	Dubuque	IA	**B**	B	B	385.0	0.42	13.7	0.8	15.8	24.4	**6.1**	8.1	13.2
▲	Premier Bank	Rock Valley	IA	**B-**	C	C+	553.9	-7.28	10.6	1.7	4.6	9.0	**10.0**	11.3	15.4
	Premier Bank	Maplewood	MN	**B+**	B+	B-	995.6	3.65	8.7	0.3	4.9	8.8	**6.9**	9.0	13.1
	Premier Bank	Omaha	NE	**B+**	B+	B+	378.9	10.76	12.4	0.1	6.8	5.2	**6.8**	10.4	0.0
	Premier Bank	Youngstown	OH	**B**	B	B	7535.3	8.13	13.3	1.6	17.2	17.0	**7.1**	9.8	12.6
	Premier Bank Minnesota	Farmington	MN	**A-**	B+	B	344.7	11.27	10.9	0.3	5.9	11.4	**7.4**	9.3	14.3
▲	Premier Bank of Arkansas	Jonesboro	AR	**A-**	B+	A-	196.5	7.24	10.6	1.2	18.5	1.7	**10.0**	13.6	18.0
	Premier Bank of the South	Cullman	AL	**B**	B	B	290.5	25.16	13.0	4.9	21.9	16.0	**6.7**	8.7	17.8
	Premier Bank Rochester	Rochester	MN	**B**	B	B-	269.7	3.51	10.7	0.1	9.2	8.6	**7.0**	9.0	12.7
	Premier Bank, Inc.	Huntington	WV	**B**	B	B	1418.7	6.86	9.1	0.8	17.3	19.5	**8.6**	10.3	0.0
	Premier Community Bank	Marion	WI	**B-**	B-	B-	419.4	17.31	5.2	1.8	7.4	19.6	**6.0**	8.0	13.2
	Premier Valley Bank	Fresno	CA	**B+**	B+	A-	1126.8	9.20	17.1	1.1	1.9	27.9	**6.5**	8.7	12.2
	PremierBank	Fort Atkinson	WI	**B**	B	B	525.0	11.87	7.6	0.8	12.6	40.3	**8.0**	9.7	17.3
	Prescott State Bank	Prescott	KS	**B-**	B-	B-	15.1	11.62	8.6	2.9	14.6	18.9	**10.0**	15.2	0.0
	Presence Bank	Coatesville	PA	**D+**	D+	C	348.6	35.96	7.0	0.0	28.0	8.0	**4.0**	7.5	0.0
	Presidential Bank, FSB	Bethesda	MD	**A-**	A-	B	885.0	28.53	7.0	3.1	16.3	3.9	**9.4**	10.6	19.8
	Prevail Bank	Medford	WI	**C+**	C+	C+	895.9	7.20	5.5	0.1	38.0	23.1	**10.0**	13.4	24.1
	Primary Bank	Bedford	NH	**B-**	C+	C+	635.2	24.89	27.4	0.0	4.3	0.2	**7.4**	9.3	14.0
▼	Prime Alliance Bank	Woods Cross	UT	**C-**	C+	B-	500.0	-6.75	45.3	0.0	0.1	12.9	**9.0**	12.0	14.1
▲	Prime Meridian Bank	Tallahassee	FL	**B+**	B	B+	756.5	25.64	15.4	0.8	16.9	8.4	**7.0**	9.0	15.1
▲	Prime Security Bank	Karlstad	MN	**B+**	B	B-	98.9	-3.93	18.9	0.4	14.4	5.0	**7.3**	9.2	13.9
	Primebank	Le Mars	IA	**A-**	B+	B	554.0	7.92	11.0	1.3	14.4	10.6	**10.0**	11.5	15.4
	PrimeSouth Bank	Waycross	GA	**B+**	B+	B	953.1	13.02	10.6	2.5	20.7	9.0	**6.9**	8.9	13.7
	Primis Bank	Glen Allen	VA	**A-**	B+	A-	3396.8	10.51	10.7	0.8	15.2	6.8	**10.0**	11.0	18.4
	Princeville State Bank	Princeville	IL	**C+**	C	C	114.6	7.18	11.7	2.0	4.9	33.7	**5.9**	7.9	14.7
	Principal Bank	Des Moines	IA	**B+**	B+	B+	4780.3	12.38	0.0	0.0	25.3	70.7	**5.4**	7.4	13.3
	PrinsBank	Prinsburg	MN	**A**	A	A-	166.1	-7.74	6.1	3.4	1.9	2.2	**10.0**	14.6	23.0
	Priority Bank	Fayetteville	AR	**B**	B-	B-	95.1	4.54	1.7	1.1	66.3	2.1	**8.1**	9.7	0.0
	PriorityOne Bank	Magee	MS	**B+**	B+	B	844.0	8.41	9.0	3.2	15.6	17.4	**7.5**	9.6	0.0
	Produce State Bank	Hollandale	MN	**B**	B	B+	120.7	14.70	11.6	3.8	4.2	6.9	**4.9**	6.9	15.9
▲	Professional Bank	Coral Gables	FL	**B-**	C	C+	2560.5	26.05	13.8	0.6	14.6	4.8	**5.4**	7.4	12.8
	Profile Bank	Rochester	NH	**C-**	C	C	284.9	16.36	2.3	1.0	22.3	24.8	**9.2**	10.5	20.6

Arrows denote recent upgrades ▲ or downgrades ▼

Asset Quality Index	Adjusted Non-Performing Loans as a % of Total Loans	Adjusted Non-Performing Loans as a % of Capital	Net Charge-Offs Avg Loans	Profitability Index	Net Income ($Mil)	Return on Assets (R.O.A.)	Return on Equity (R.O.E.)	Net Interest Spread	Overhead Efficiency Ratio	Liquidity Index	Liquidity Ratio	Hot Money Ratio	Stability Index
6.5	0.76	5.5	-0.09	**7.2**	4.3	1.92	26.14	3.59	47.6	**5.4**	27.7	1.9	**5.5**
8.8	0.04	0.1	-0.03	**5.3**	0.5	1.08	8.25	3.27	59.8	**7.1**	62.1	3.2	**7.0**
4.6	0.77	5.7	0.07	**7.2**	6.9	1.56	17.35	3.77	54.3	**2.2**	24.6	18.3	**7.0**
5.3	0.75	3.9	0.30	**10.0**	6.8	2.53	25.04	5.28	46.1	**1.4**	20.4	24.7	**7.7**
6.6	1.05	5.8	0.11	**8.9**	9.2	1.54	16.51	3.68	46.0	**6.3**	30.7	1.8	**8.7**
4.2	4.44	14.9	0.00	**0.7**	-0.1	-0.22	-1.43	4.39	102.4	**3.0**	42.4	20.7	**6.0**
7.5	0.80	2.6	-0.12	**3.2**	0.2	0.37	3.74	3.62	86.9	**5.1**	36.2	7.7	**5.2**
5.0	1.39	5.7	0.17	**5.7**	3231.6	1.41	14.20	2.23	64.7	**6.7**	40.0	1.0	**8.1**
8.9	0.00	0.0	0.00	**8.6**	1.1	2.08	7.86	3.46	28.1	**5.9**	90.2	14.2	**7.0**
8.8	0.12	0.5	-0.02	**4.7**	4.5	1.25	12.40	3.47	68.5	**5.4**	35.9	5.5	**7.2**
6.7	0.62	2.7	0.00	**7.3**	6.7	1.63	16.67	3.69	55.6	**4.2**	30.1	10.5	**8.6**
9.3	0.10	0.2	-0.14	**3.1**	0.3	0.53	5.81	2.30	87.0	**6.7**	69.4	6.8	**5.1**
5.3	1.16	7.4	0.04	**4.5**	9.6	1.35	13.11	3.93	60.0	**1.1**	8.5	21.9	**7.4**
8.0	0.00	0.0	-0.06	**8.5**	2.6	2.03	22.71	4.03	52.9	**1.8**	22.9	3.5	**7.5**
6.0	1.64	6.8	0.04	**7.8**	30.3	1.75	21.97	2.80	36.9	**1.8**	21.5	21.5	**9.2**
5.6	0.58	2.1	0.04	**4.6**	66.5	1.30	7.24	3.32	63.0	**1.9**	15.1	13.5	**6.7**
8.9	0.30	1.2	0.00	**8.1**	1.1	2.34	13.90	4.29	44.1	**3.7**	15.2	10.7	**8.3**
7.0	0.51	1.6	-0.01	**6.5**	0.3	2.04	15.62	6.06	61.4	**0.6**	15.6	34.2	**5.0**
5.5	1.55	7.4	0.02	**3.3**	1.1	0.48	4.71	2.59	81.4	**4.1**	36.8	13.4	**6.0**
3.5	4.23	13.7	1.60	**1.0**	-0.1	-0.37	-4.05	3.13	91.2	**4.9**	33.2	7.9	**3.3**
6.1	0.82	4.3	0.01	**3.5**	1.3	0.63	5.94	2.99	77.1	**3.4**	36.3	16.8	**7.7**
6.4	1.35	3.5	0.00	**3.5**	0.5	0.77	9.07	3.03	69.8	**3.1**	31.4	16.5	**4.7**
2.2	3.88	23.1	0.00	**0.3**	-0.3	-0.38	-4.64	2.95	73.5	**3.5**	31.1	14.5	**4.6**
7.9	0.34	2.0	-0.07	**5.6**	5.6	1.38	13.45	2.98	63.2	**4.5**	25.2	6.8	**7.8**
6.0	0.33	2.8	0.02	**8.1**	1.0	2.74	31.70	5.22	42.1	**3.1**	20.0	9.5	**5.6**
6.2	1.06	5.6	0.06	**8.9**	42.7	1.60	15.78	3.41	33.4	**0.9**	18.9	27.9	**9.5**
7.0	0.39	2.4	-0.04	**2.0**	0.1	0.26	3.07	2.79	93.5	**2.3**	32.4	23.0	**3.8**
8.7	0.00	2.5	0.03	**4.1**	0.7	0.96	13.18	2.62	64.4	**6.8**	58.6	4.4	**4.5**
8.2	0.03	0.1	0.00	**5.6**	3.3	1.65	19.60	3.08	52.4	**4.5**	22.8	4.4	**6.2**
4.6	1.29	4.7	-0.01	**9.0**	6.0	2.13	17.15	3.56	39.3	**1.2**	16.8	25.8	**9.0**
4.6	1.08	7.0	-0.04	**8.7**	7.3	1.52	15.82	3.51	44.5	**4.5**	25.8	7.0	**7.3**
8.6	0.00	0.0	0.00	**5.2**	1.6	0.87	8.10	3.06	66.4	**4.7**	35.7	8.2	**7.3**
4.8	0.85	3.8	-0.02	**7.6**	69.9	1.89	14.09	3.39	48.8	**4.2**	12.2	7.6	**9.6**
7.2	0.15	0.8	0.02	**7.9**	3.1	1.95	20.22	3.98	52.9	**4.8**	28.2	6.2	**7.3**
6.8	0.40	2.3	0.00	**5.4**	1.0	1.01	7.29	4.20	63.3	**2.9**	14.3	14.5	**8.0**
6.9	0.79	2.8	0.21	**5.6**	1.7	1.30	16.11	3.70	68.3	**4.4**	27.9	8.6	**4.7**
6.6	0.25	1.9	-0.01	**7.0**	2.6	1.93	21.20	3.90	51.5	**3.1**	17.1	13.5	**6.8**
5.2	1.18	6.4	0.27	**7.6**	9.1	1.34	10.19	3.78	52.1	**4.6**	22.4	7.3	**8.9**
4.4	3.11	11.7	0.01	**3.9**	1.4	0.68	8.24	3.05	71.3	**6.0**	43.1	4.3	**5.2**
7.0	0.44	0.9	0.21	**5.8**	6.6	1.24	8.93	3.68	54.3	**5.5**	26.2	4.3	**7.6**
4.3	4.26	9.3	-0.01	**5.3**	2.8	1.11	9.56	3.02	66.3	**5.4**	32.5	4.3	**8.1**
8.8	0.00	0.0	0.00	**3.9**	0.1	0.71	4.65	3.91	77.7	**2.7**	51.7	25.0	**6.1**
5.1	1.07	8.6	0.00	**1.7**	0.3	0.23	3.01	2.58	86.1	**3.1**	29.9	15.5	**3.2**
5.7	1.24	4.6	0.07	**8.2**	9.6	2.28	21.64	3.09	67.7	**4.6**	37.0	11.0	**7.5**
7.1	1.26	2.6	0.00	**3.3**	2.8	0.65	3.89	2.76	66.2	**3.6**	34.3	15.2	**8.2**
4.4	0.49	3.7	0.08	**5.4**	3.6	1.19	12.92	3.46	43.7	**1.9**	23.1	20.4	**6.3**
1.8	4.90	26.7	-0.03	**7.7**	5.8	2.30	20.39	4.57	27.0	**0.7**	17.0	42.1	**7.1**
8.2	0.00	0.0	0.00	**5.7**	4.7	1.34	15.11	3.23	52.0	**5.2**	33.8	5.7	**6.0**
7.3	0.00	0.0	0.00	**7.7**	1.5	2.92	32.66	5.54	44.0	**3.7**	4.6	7.7	**6.1**
5.9	0.89	4.6	-0.03	**7.7**	5.8	2.16	18.49	3.44	45.9	**2.3**	20.0	15.0	**8.1**
5.2	0.81	4.5	-0.05	**6.5**	5.5	1.20	12.58	3.68	60.1	**3.6**	16.2	11.1	**7.1**
6.6	0.76	2.9	-0.04	**6.3**	22.3	1.36	9.79	3.30	60.4	**4.5**	24.4	9.3	**9.2**
3.9	3.29	12.9	0.12	**4.7**	0.8	1.28	14.89	2.63	57.9	**3.7**	46.0	14.7	**5.3**
9.0	0.42	1.2	-0.24	**6.9**	34.3	1.50	17.66	1.92	23.1	**7.6**	79.9	4.2	**6.2**
6.8	0.00	3.5	-1.06	**9.7**	2.1	2.44	17.13	3.92	54.9	**3.2**	41.0	19.1	**8.5**
5.6	0.92	6.4	0.06	**10.0**	1.9	3.88	39.11	4.54	59.6	**0.8**	16.8	32.7	**7.9**
5.8	0.44	4.6	0.05	**6.7**	7.1	1.73	17.37	4.41	65.2	**3.3**	15.3	12.7	**7.9**
6.5	0.38	1.9	-0.03	**5.6**	0.8	1.35	16.07	3.33	60.8	**6.7**	53.6	3.4	**5.5**
7.2	0.18	1.3	0.90	**4.3**	12.1	1.04	12.36	3.18	56.1	**5.0**	32.7	10.5	**5.9**
6.8	1.31	3.9	0.00	**2.2**	0.3	0.25	2.39	2.71	89.4	**4.7**	47.9	13.4	**4.9**

Name	City	State	Rating	2020 Rating	2019 Rating	Total Assets ($Mil)	One Year Asset Growth	Asset Mix (As a % of Total Assets) Comm-ercial Loans	Cons-umer Loans	Mort-gage Loans	Secur-ities	Capital-ization Index	Lever-age Ratio	Risk-Based Capital Ratio
Profinium, Inc.	Truman	MN	**B**	B	B	533.9	14.22	8.0	0.3	7.8	19.6	**6.1**	8.1	14.3
Progress Bank and Trust	Huntsville	AL	**B**	B	B	1632.6	11.68	18.7	1.3	12.4	4.5	**6.7**	9.2	12.3
▲ Progressive Bank	Monroe	LA	**B-**	C+	B	739.1	0.52	11.3	0.9	15.8	12.3	**7.5**	9.3	13.1
Progressive National Bank	Mansfield	LA	**C**	C	C+	102.8	19.74	6.7	2.7	24.4	14.1	**6.3**	8.3	17.1
Progressive Ozark Bank	Salem	MO	**B+**	B+	A-	163.4	19.34	6.2	5.0	34.7	3.4	**7.2**	9.1	15.1
ProGrowth Bank	Nicollet	MN	**B**	B	B	231.6	51.34	8.6	0.6	7.5	61.0	**10.0**	11.2	25.4
PromiseOne Bank	Duluth	GA	**A-**	A-	A-	561.6	4.25	13.3	0.0	13.2	14.8	**10.0**	11.6	19.6
Prospect Bank	Paris	IL	**B-**	B-	B-	689.1	13.20	9.5	0.5	7.2	36.2	**6.3**	8.3	13.6
Prosperity Bank	El Campo	TX	**A-**	A-	A-	36098.0	9.47	8.1	0.3	14.0	33.3	**7.7**	9.4	15.6
Providence Bank	Rocky Mount	NC	**A-**	A-	A-	626.7	10.99	11.0	1.0	8.1	8.8	**9.0**	11.3	14.2
Providence Bank & Trust	South Holland	IL	**A-**	A-	B+	1323.8	11.18	14.0	0.0	3.4	24.4	**8.5**	10.0	0.0
Providence Bank of Texas, SSB	Southlake	TX	**B**	B	B	199.1	12.32	5.6	0.4	10.4	0.0	**10.0**	11.0	16.6
Provident Bank	Iselin	NJ	**B-**	B-	B-	13211.3	25.67	7.8	0.2	11.9	15.2	**5.9**	9.1	11.7
▲ Provident Savings Bank, F.S.B.	Riverside	CA	**B-**	C+	C+	1183.6	0.57	0.1	0.0	22.9	19.2	**8.8**	10.2	19.8
Provident State Bank, Inc.	Preston	MD	**B**	B	B-	570.4	8.95	7.0	0.3	13.1	24.0	**7.4**	9.2	14.0
Prudential Bank	Philadelphia	PA	**C+**	C+	B-	1124.4	-5.34	4.7	0.1	17.9	31.9	**9.8**	10.8	17.8
Prudential Bank and Trust, FSB	Hartford	CT	**U**	U	U	28.4	15.84	0.0	0.0	0.0	71.3	**10.0**	87.7	210.0
▲ PS Bank	Wyalusing	PA	**A-**	B+	B	462.4	4.79	12.5	0.5	18.3	21.1	**8.6**	10.1	0.0
Pulaski Savings Bank	Chicago	IL	**D**	D	D	47.8	-0.75	0.0	0.5	71.7	1.1	**5.7**	7.7	18.6
Putnam 1st Mercantile Bank	Cookeville	TN	**A-**	A-	A-	148.3	5.26	14.1	1.8	19.4	19.2	**9.4**	10.6	0.0
Putnam County Bank	Hurricane	WV	**B-**	B-	B-	666.8	7.26	3.4	0.5	26.7	30.4	**10.0**	14.5	34.2
▼ Putnam County National Bank	Carmel	NY	**C+**	B	B	195.6	18.00	0.8	0.3	22.5	7.2	**10.0**	19.3	0.0
▲ Putnam County State Bank	Unionville	MO	**A-**	B+	B	262.5	11.27	9.0	1.4	6.7	1.9	**10.0**	12.8	0.0
PyraMax Bank, F.S.B.	Greenfield	WI	**C**	C	D+	602.9	21.71	6.8	0.0	16.9	14.9	**8.1**	9.7	16.1
QNB Bank	Quakertown	PA	**B-**	B-	B-	1560.2	13.11	12.0	0.3	12.5	35.2	**5.7**	7.7	13.0
▲ Quad City Bank and Trust Co.	Bettendorf	IA	**A-**	B+	B+	2065.9	3.23	25.0	0.4	8.5	12.2	**7.8**	9.8	13.2
▲ Quail Creek Bank, N.A.	Oklahoma City	OK	**B**	C+	C-	834.0	11.26	2.7	0.8	19.3	16.4	**6.4**	8.4	16.0
Quaint Oak Bank	Southampton	PA	**B-**	B	B	526.5	29.44	42.3	0.0	15.3	0.9	**5.2**	7.2	12.6
Quantum National Bank	Suwanee	GA	**A-**	A-	A	614.9	1.12	13.6	0.0	8.9	1.1	**6.9**	10.0	0.0
Quarry City S&L Assn.	Warrensburg	MO	**B-**	B-	C+	72.4	16.03	0.7	1.0	31.0	0.0	**10.0**	13.5	22.3
Queensborough National Bank & Trust Co.	Louisville	GA	**C**	C	C-	1815.3	20.57	10.0	0.8	8.7	33.8	**6.2**	8.2	14.7
Queenstown Bank of Maryland	Queenstown	MD	**A-**	A-	A-	621.9	13.17	4.3	1.0	25.7	18.2	**10.0**	11.5	19.6
Quoin Financial Bank	Miller	SD	**A**	A-	A-	205.3	10.24	11.9	1.2	6.7	13.2	**10.0**	11.4	20.6
Quontic Bank	New York	NY	**D+**	C-	B	1280.2	26.79	48.8	0.0	32.3	0.4	**1.6**	10.8	0.0
R Bank	Round Rock	TX	**B-**	B-	B-	792.8	19.10	20.5	0.5	11.2	11.7	**6.3**	8.3	12.3
Rabun County Bank	Clayton	GA	**B+**	B+	B+	244.9	18.79	2.3	3.9	25.5	3.8	**9.6**	10.7	0.0
Raccoon Valley Bank	Perry	IA	**B-**	B-	C+	355.5	7.15	11.5	0.3	7.6	16.5	**6.5**	8.5	12.4
Ramsey National Bank	Devils Lake	ND	**A-**	A	A	317.5	17.15	10.2	1.2	5.4	28.5	**7.1**	9.1	0.0
Randall State Bank	Randall	MN	**B**	B	B-	56.5	12.41	7.2	2.8	16.3	0.4	**8.9**	10.3	0.0
Range Bank	Marquette	MI	**B-**	B-	B-	489.3	13.80	12.7	0.8	16.9	35.1	**6.2**	8.2	15.0
Raritan State Bank	Raritan	IL	**B-**	C+	C+	231.0	17.38	8.0	6.4	22.0	26.5	**8.5**	10.0	0.0
Raymond Federal Bank	Raymond	WA	**C-**	C-	C-	65.7	5.14	0.0	0.9	71.1	16.4	**8.3**	9.9	22.5
Raymond James Bank	Saint Petersburg	FL	**B+**	B+	A-	34576.2	18.96	25.1	13.0	14.9	23.7	**5.5**	7.5	14.7
Raymond James Trust, N.A.	Saint Petersburg	FL	**U**	U	U	46.6	18.07	0.0	0.0	0.0	2.4	**10.0**	81.3	236.7
Rayne Building & Loan Assn.	Rayne	LA	**B-**	B-	B-	61.1	2.09	5.7	0.8	16.4	49.3	**10.0**	26.5	0.0
Rayne State Bank & Trust Co.	Rayne	LA	**A**	A	A	471.4	-1.53	19.0	0.4	14.2	20.4	**10.0**	11.9	22.3
▼ RBC Bank (Georgia), N.A.	Raleigh	NC	**B**	B+	A-	5706.7	20.09	0.0	2.1	26.4	67.0	**7.3**	9.2	29.0
RCB Bank	Claremore	OK	**B**	B	B	3797.5	7.53	4.5	4.7	8.4	18.1	**5.9**	7.9	14.0
Reading Co-Operative Bank	Reading	MA	**B-**	B-	B-	656.6	2.61	8.3	0.0	39.3	12.8	**7.4**	9.2	15.5
Red River Bank	Alexandria	LA	**A-**	A-	A-	2877.7	21.85	11.6	0.8	16.0	17.8	**7.6**	9.4	17.8
Red River State Bank	Halstad	MN	**B**	B	B	143.7	44.68	35.7	8.8	5.0	2.6	**6.0**	8.1	15.4
Red Rock Bank	Sanborn	MN	**A-**	A-	A-	46.7	20.15	4.3	2.7	11.4	15.6	**5.8**	7.8	20.0
Redstone Bank	Centennial	CO	**B+**	B+	A-	219.5	11.96	9.5	0.1	8.7	33.5	**9.7**	10.8	17.9
Redwood Capital Bank	Eureka	CA	**B+**	B+	B+	578.6	25.68	10.3	0.2	4.4	10.2	**6.4**	8.4	15.6
Regal Bank	Livingston	NJ	**C**	C	C	574.8	5.36	3.4	0.0	1.9	2.8	**7.6**	9.4	0.0
▲ Regent Bank	Tulsa	OK	**B-**	C+	C+	903.0	0.68	22.5	0.5	13.1	4.0	**6.2**	8.5	11.9
▲ Regional Missouri Bank	Marceline	MO	**B**	C+	C	497.9	24.00	9.3	2.5	12.5	24.3	**7.6**	9.5	0.0
Regions Bank	Birmingham	AL	**B**	B	B	154735.0	7.87	17.9	3.3	12.9	19.6	**7.2**	9.1	14.2
▲ Reliabank Dakota	Estelline	SD	**B**	B-	B-	667.7	28.58	12.7	0.7	6.8	30.5	**6.6**	8.6	12.8
▲ Reliance Bank	Faribault	MN	**B**	B-	B-	198.4	9.03	30.9	1.1	10.4	12.0	**6.5**	9.7	0.0

Asset Quality Index	Adjusted Non-Performing Loans as a % of Total Loans	Adjusted Non-Performing Loans as a % of Capital	Net Charge-Offs Avg Loans	Profitability Index	Net Income ($Mil)	Return on Assets (R.O.A.)	Return on Equity (R.O.E.)	Net Interest Spread	Overhead Efficiency Ratio	Liquidity Index	Liquidity Ratio	Hot Money Ratio	Stability Index
4.5	2.91	11.8	0.00	**4.5**	2.4	0.90	10.30	3.04	63.3	**4.1**	25.0	6.3	**6.1**
8.1	0.33	1.3	0.00	**5.6**	9.4	1.18	11.48	3.33	64.2	**2.4**	18.8	14.9	**9.2**
8.1	0.21	1.5	-0.04	**4.2**	3.0	0.81	9.34	3.51	73.7	**4.4**	22.8	7.2	**6.0**
8.8	0.09	1.1	0.00	**4.2**	0.5	0.92	11.68	3.24	76.0	**3.2**	29.9	15.4	**4.8**
7.2	0.44	2.3	0.03	**6.9**	1.3	1.64	18.23	4.69	68.5	**5.3**	25.7	1.8	**7.1**
9.3	0.27	0.5	-0.01	**4.9**	1.1	1.07	9.86	3.29	60.4	**1.9**	42.1	32.8	**4.7**
6.8	2.79	3.8	0.08	**9.3**	7.7	2.84	24.90	3.61	38.6	**1.0**	23.8	31.0	**9.3**
5.5	0.90	3.8	-0.01	**4.9**	4.5	1.32	16.04	2.77	58.6	**1.0**	18.9	16.8	**6.0**
6.8	0.17	0.5	0.14	**7.8**	270.1	1.53	8.72	3.23	40.1	**4.5**	21.3	7.4	**10.0**
7.1	0.02	0.2	0.00	**8.3**	5.0	1.63	13.59	3.66	39.7	**1.1**	15.6	27.3	**8.2**
8.0	0.59	2.3	-0.03	**9.2**	12.0	1.88	17.32	4.73	48.7	**5.6**	37.8	7.2	**9.5**
4.9	2.54	8.2	0.00	**4.1**	0.8	0.76	6.91	3.65	70.9	**2.3**	33.1	24.1	**7.0**
3.8	1.06	5.3	-0.11	**6.4**	94.0	1.43	11.82	3.05	55.4	**3.7**	10.0	4.4	**9.4**
4.4	1.87	9.9	0.00	**4.1**	5.2	0.88	8.87	2.65	66.3	**4.1**	6.7	7.3	**7.9**
6.5	0.61	3.3	0.00	**5.0**	2.8	1.01	10.90	3.51	63.0	**3.5**	23.6	12.4	**6.1**
6.1	1.44	6.5	-0.01	**3.5**	4.2	0.72	6.50	2.17	69.0	**2.5**	41.7	15.4	**8.2**
9.9	na	0.0	na	**10.0**	4.0	30.70	36.03	1.00	16.1	**4.0**	na	100.0	**6.7**
8.3	0.19	1.5	-0.01	**6.8**	3.4	1.56	15.42	3.25	54.1	**4.0**	30.0	11.9	**6.3**
5.5	2.20	12.7	0.00	**1.6**	0.0	0.11	1.40	3.29	96.4	**4.1**	19.5	8.3	**2.9**
6.5	0.00	3.2	0.08	**5.8**	1.0	1.31	12.31	3.45	57.1	**2.3**	37.2	27.3	**7.5**
7.0	3.30	6.7	0.71	**3.4**	1.7	0.51	3.61	2.07	69.8	**2.3**	44.7	34.0	**7.5**
5.7	4.97	9.9	-0.14	**2.5**	0.2	0.18	0.94	2.30	92.3	**6.1**	46.4	5.0	**7.2**
6.1	0.29	2.9	-0.03	**9.7**	2.3	1.79	14.01	3.68	29.8	**1.1**	28.1	42.9	**8.4**
7.3	0.44	2.2	-0.02	**2.8**	1.1	0.41	3.99	2.57	82.9	**5.5**	43.6	7.9	**5.0**
5.8	1.35	7.8	0.02	**4.3**	7.3	0.97	12.28	2.87	61.3	**5.0**	24.1	5.8	**7.0**
8.2	0.26	1.7	0.18	**6.4**	15.8	1.48	15.65	3.12	47.3	**5.3**	21.0	2.2	**8.2**
4.6	1.90	10.9	-0.01	**6.5**	6.2	1.51	16.26	3.25	52.2	**5.1**	43.1	10.3	**7.8**
7.6	0.03	0.2	0.01	**5.0**	2.7	0.98	14.56	3.31	70.5	**1.1**	6.7	27.7	**5.0**
7.2	0.00	0.0	0.00	**10.0**	9.3	3.00	29.78	4.76	45.4	**3.7**	11.4	7.3	**9.2**
6.0	1.71	7.6	0.00	**2.6**	0.1	0.26	1.93	2.54	91.9	**2.9**	38.9	20.2	**6.9**
4.9	1.61	11.9	0.00	**5.9**	10.5	1.20	14.58	3.30	65.0	**4.9**	26.1	8.2	**7.3**
6.7	1.58	5.8	0.00	**6.2**	3.3	1.08	9.47	3.21	57.0	**3.3**	33.3	16.2	**8.3**
8.7	0.31	1.0	-0.12	**8.6**	2.0	1.91	16.87	4.27	48.1	**2.5**	28.5	17.0	**7.5**
4.6	0.62	13.0	-0.01	**6.8**	18.7	2.64	58.59	2.05	47.7	**0.8**	13.6	36.0	**5.1**
8.1	0.15	1.2	0.00	**4.1**	3.1	0.81	8.84	3.89	71.8	**2.2**	21.9	18.8	**5.7**
8.9	0.12	0.4	-0.09	**4.7**	1.0	0.85	7.73	2.95	69.1	**6.0**	45.1	5.1	**7.4**
8.4	0.32	1.1	0.01	**6.5**	3.0	1.72	19.68	3.70	57.4	**3.1**	25.5	14.9	**6.3**
7.8	0.00	0.0	0.08	**6.1**	2.0	1.25	9.97	2.87	58.6	**4.7**	27.4	6.7	**8.8**
4.5	1.92	8.6	0.00	**8.3**	0.4	1.50	14.61	4.83	55.2	**4.5**	37.1	11.5	**8.0**
4.9	1.58	7.1	0.05	**4.6**	2.5	1.01	11.41	3.13	65.9	**5.5**	36.7	5.1	**5.4**
4.2	2.10	11.1	0.11	**5.3**	1.3	1.13	10.97	2.63	52.7	**2.6**	39.2	24.9	**5.6**
9.0	0.31	1.8	0.00	**1.8**	0.0	0.10	0.96	3.43	96.6	**2.7**	24.1	16.5	**5.1**
7.7	0.19	1.6	0.05	**6.1**	202.4	1.22	16.66	1.94	37.4	**6.1**	31.6	0.7	**6.8**
10.0	na	0.0	na	**10.0**	5.8	24.60	31.36	0.10	78.5	**4.0**	496.4	0.0	**6.3**
9.2	0.31	0.4	0.00	**3.8**	0.2	0.74	2.73	3.29	57.9	**3.0**	76.4	58.8	**7.5**
8.6	0.00	0.0	0.00	**6.7**	4.1	1.74	14.53	4.08	58.8	**4.8**	27.6	6.0	**9.1**
9.7	0.55	2.0	0.20	**4.8**	17.6	0.67	6.97	1.38	63.3	**8.0**	75.6	0.6	**6.7**
5.4	1.34	7.1	0.01	**4.7**	21.3	1.13	11.20	2.99	65.6	**4.6**	25.0	8.6	**9.2**
8.4	0.07	1.6	0.00	**3.8**	2.5	0.75	8.24	3.37	70.5	**2.6**	22.0	9.0	**6.0**
8.9	0.25	1.1	0.01	**5.8**	16.6	1.18	12.51	2.65	55.8	**5.7**	41.0	9.0	**8.3**
4.7	0.46	3.8	-0.03	**8.3**	2.1	3.42	39.73	5.41	34.2	**0.5**	5.9	35.6	**5.7**
8.0	0.00	0.0	0.00	**3.4**	0.1	0.44	4.14	2.54	75.6	**4.7**	60.5	14.7	**6.4**
8.2	0.00	0.0	0.00	**4.7**	1.0	0.89	6.63	3.90	68.8	**2.6**	46.1	22.5	**8.1**
7.6	0.29	1.6	0.00	**6.6**	3.4	1.23	15.06	3.15	53.1	**5.3**	36.8	6.4	**6.0**
6.6	0.28	1.7	0.00	**2.8**	1.3	0.46	4.76	3.00	75.8	**2.3**	36.2	26.4	**6.5**
5.2	0.48	3.6	0.47	**5.2**	4.9	1.08	12.33	4.05	59.2	**1.5**	14.9	23.3	**5.9**
5.9	0.85	3.6	0.00	**7.1**	4.0	1.64	16.05	3.49	52.5	**4.1**	30.5	8.3	**7.6**
5.1	1.42	5.3	0.30	**7.5**	1484.0	1.99	16.27	2.94	55.2	**6.5**	34.1	1.5	**10.0**
6.9	0.73	4.4	0.02	**5.6**	4.2	1.37	15.92	3.33	62.9	**3.8**	12.8	9.5	**6.8**
7.2	0.23	1.6	-0.11	**5.8**	1.5	1.51	15.85	3.88	57.0	**3.6**	23.1	11.8	**6.3**

Name	City	State	Rating	2020 Rating	2019 Rating	Total Assets ($Mil)	One Year Asset Growth	Asset Mix (As a % of Total Assets) Commercial Loans	Consumer Loans	Mortgage Loans	Securities	Capital-ization Index	Lever-age Ratio	Risk-Based Capital Ratio
Reliance Savings Bank	Altoona	PA	**B-**	B-	C+	664.0	9.78	6.9	1.0	19.3	26.5	**8.6**	10.1	16.6
Reliance State Bank	Story City	IA	**B**	B	B+	275.2	14.94	5.1	0.8	9.4	35.0	**7.0**	9.0	0.0
Reliant Bank	Brentwood	TN	**A-**	B+	B	3090.1	3.61	13.8	7.3	17.9	8.6	**8.0**	11.1	13.3
Relyance Bank, N.A.	White Hall	AR	**B+**	B+	B	1102.2	15.30	10.5	0.7	8.2	11.4	**8.5**	11.3	13.7
Renasant Bank	Tupelo	MS	**B+**	B+	A-	16005.7	7.56	9.7	1.0	15.9	13.5	**8.1**	9.7	13.8
Republic Bank & Trust Co.	Louisville	KY	**A**	A	A-	6175.7	-4.28	8.0	4.6	19.0	9.2	**10.0**	12.2	17.2
▲ Republic Bank of Arizona	Phoenix	AZ	**B-**	C+	B+	231.0	40.42	11.6	3.0	6.8	19.1	**9.3**	10.5	0.0
Republic Bank of Chicago	Oak Brook	IL	**B+**	B+	B+	2598.9	13.06	18.5	0.1	4.6	14.3	**8.9**	10.3	15.5
Republic First Bank	Philadelphia	PA	**C-**	D+	D+	5367.4	21.29	10.1	0.0	11.1	34.0	**5.0**	7.0	12.8
Resource Bank	Covington	LA	**A-**	A-	B	968.6	8.25	2.6	0.7	15.1	16.3	**9.3**	10.5	0.0
Resource Bank, N.A.	DeKalb	IL	**C+**	C	C	695.4	13.14	6.6	0.6	12.4	36.8	**5.8**	7.8	14.8
RG Bank, a S&L Assn.	Monte Vista	CO	**C**	C	C+	136.1	12.73	1.6	1.8	43.3	15.9	**7.9**	9.6	0.0
▲ Rhinebeck Bank	Poughkeepsie	NY	**B**	C+	C	1210.0	7.26	14.4	29.3	4.9	16.7	**8.0**	9.7	14.1
Richland County Bank	Richland Center	WI	**A**	A	B	117.7	5.40	4.1	2.4	8.7	49.2	**10.0**	16.8	0.0
Richland State Bank	Bruce	SD	**A-**	A-	B+	50.5	38.24	8.9	14.0	2.1	47.2	**7.7**	9.5	19.7
▼ Richton Bank & Trust Co.	Richton	MS	**C+**	B-	B	57.7	-10.75	15.4	2.7	7.7	35.3	**10.0**	13.4	0.0
Ridgewood Savings Bank	Ridgewood	NY	**B-**	B-	B	6619.9	7.73	0.6	0.1	27.9	24.3	**10.0**	12.4	0.0
▲ Rio Bank	McAllen	TX	**B-**	C	B-	745.2	14.08	12.2	0.8	6.1	31.3	**6.8**	8.9	14.5
River Bank	La Crosse	WI	**B**	B	B	912.6	20.75	4.2	0.2	10.1	7.6	**6.8**	10.2	12.3
River Bank & Trust	Prattville	AL	**B+**	B+	A-	2226.0	30.54	11.1	1.9	13.1	35.1	**6.3**	8.3	14.1
▲ River City Bank	Sacramento	CA	**B-**	C+	B+	3359.5	5.20	7.4	0.0	5.4	21.1	**4.3**	8.5	0.0
River City Bank	Rome	GA	**B**	B+	A-	208.1	18.57	9.7	0.9	10.3	16.1	**8.7**	10.1	15.0
River City Bank, Inc.	Louisville	KY	**B+**	B+	B+	384.9	7.86	1.8	0.3	19.4	22.9	**10.0**	12.6	22.3
River Falls State Bank	River Falls	WI	**A**	A	B+	125.6	14.12	2.0	2.6	30.0	27.1	**10.0**	11.5	0.0
▲ River Valley Community Bank	Yuba City	CA	**B**	B-	B	503.1	-2.25	9.2	0.0	2.2	34.1	**6.4**	8.4	14.2
RiverBank	Pocahontas	AR	**C+**	C+	B-	93.0	-6.23	5.1	0.7	10.0	5.6	**10.0**	13.2	23.1
▲ RiverBank	Spokane	WA	**C+**	C	C+	192.7	8.71	13.1	0.1	8.1	15.2	**5.1**	9.2	0.0
RiverHills Bank	Vicksburg	MS	**A-**	A-	B+	388.1	4.78	9.9	1.1	6.9	46.8	**8.9**	10.2	0.0
▼ RiverHills Bank	Milford	OH	**C+**	B-	B-	238.9	4.54	7.1	0.3	4.8	28.8	**7.6**	9.4	14.0
▲ Riverland Bank	Jordan	MN	**B-**	C	C+	190.3	8.54	17.2	0.5	19.1	1.2	**7.2**	11.1	0.0
Rivers Edge Bank	Marion	SD	**B-**	B-	C	260.5	18.81	8.3	1.9	5.6	20.1	**5.8**	7.8	14.0
Riverside Bank	Sparkman	AR	**B-**	B	B	61.5	-4.00	17.4	6.3	40.9	2.3	**6.9**	8.9	13.1
Riverside Bank of Dublin	Dublin	OH	**B-**			41.2	na	4.8	0.0	4.4	13.0	**10.0**	64.2	0.0
▲ Riverstone Bank	Eagle	NE	**B-**	C	C	113.5	107.46	13.3	1.5	12.6	3.5	**6.8**	9.4	12.4
▲ Riverview Bank	Marysville	PA	**C**	C-	C	1214.1	-9.85	12.6	0.5	12.3	12.2	**8.5**	10.0	0.0
Riverview Community Bank	Vancouver	WA	**A-**	A-	A	1616.3	17.42	9.1	0.1	4.2	19.0	**7.6**	9.4	17.5
Riverwind Bank	Augusta	AR	**C**	C	B	122.6	-4.62	9.2	2.1	17.7	30.3	**7.7**	9.5	0.0
RiverWood Bank	Baxter	MN	**B-**	B-	C+	524.5	7.25	12.7	5.0	11.3	23.5	**6.0**	8.0	13.3
RNB State Bank	Rawlins	WY	**C+**	C+	C+	243.2	12.05	8.1	1.4	4.9	37.4	**6.5**	8.5	0.0
Roanoke Rapids Savings Bank, SSB	Roanoke Rapids	NC	**C**	C	C+	88.0	19.84	0.3	1.5	31.1	21.4	**10.0**	20.6	0.0
Robert Lee State Bank	Robert Lee	TX	**C+**	C+	B-	45.6	-6.39	3.5	5.2	16.9	45.8	**10.0**	13.4	0.0
Robertson Banking Co.	Demopolis	AL	**A-**	A-	A-	387.9	-0.66	9.6	0.9	15.8	13.3	**7.7**	9.5	14.1
Rochelle State Bank	Rochelle	GA	**C-**	C	C+	46.5	46.26	1.7	4.2	0.1	33.4	**10.0**	26.1	31.0
▲ Rock Canyon Bank	Provo	UT	**A-**	B+	B+	752.3	17.75	10.9	0.1	3.2	0.0	**7.5**	9.3	0.0
Rockefeller Trust Co., N.A.	New York	NY	**U**	U	U	17.7	3.03	0.0	0.0	0.0	0.6	**10.0**	86.8	362.4
▲ Rockhold Bank	Bainbridge	OH	**D-**	E+	D-	47.3	3.61	15.4	0.6	39.4	0.0	**5.1**	7.1	13.9
Rockland Savings Bank, FSB	Rockland	ME	**D+**	C-	C+	86.8	-1.12	12.0	1.2	57.9	1.2	**8.3**	9.9	0.0
▲ Rockland Trust Co.	Rockland	MA	**A-**	B+	B+	14194.4	9.06	12.1	0.2	14.7	11.8	**7.9**	9.6	15.4
▲ RockPoint Bank, N.A.	Chattanooga	TN	**D**			72.0	na	14.3	0.2	0.4	15.4	**10.0**	49.9	116.8
Rocky Mountain Bank	Billings	MT	**B**	B	B	646.8	9.49	14.0	1.1	4.3	40.2	**6.4**	8.5	13.7
Rocky Mountain Bank	Jackson	WY	**B+**	B+	B+	420.5	9.35	16.1	3.7	13.4	3.1	**8.4**	9.9	16.7
Rocky Mountain Bank and Trust	Florence	CO	**B**	B-	C+	95.2	12.54	24.8	0.5	7.4	25.5	**7.6**	9.4	0.0
Rolette State Bank	Rolette	ND	**D**	D-	D-	44.8	6.24	9.0	1.5	2.0	8.5	**6.0**	8.0	15.4
▲ Rolling Hills Bank & Trust	Atlantic	IA	**B-**	C	D+	381.7	11.88	6.8	0.7	2.7	2.6	**6.4**	9.3	0.0
Rollstone Bank & Trust	Fitchburg	MA	**B-**	C+	C+	845.0	10.03	5.5	0.1	15.7	24.5	**9.0**	10.4	14.9
▲ Rondout Savings Bank	Kingston	NY	**C+**	C	C	466.0	8.12	6.5	0.3	40.7	11.2	**8.4**	9.9	17.9
Root River State Bank	Chatfield	MN	**C+**	C+	C+	81.4	8.71	4.5	0.4	6.7	50.6	**9.1**	10.4	21.8
▲ Rosedale Federal S&L Assn.	Baltimore	MD	**B-**	C+	B	1053.8	5.09	2.2	0.0	38.2	18.7	**10.0**	24.0	0.0
Round Top State Bank	Round Top	TX	**A-**	A-	A-	777.3	15.62	3.2	1.7	18.9	28.9	**9.6**	10.8	0.0
Roundbank	Waseca	MN	**B+**	B+	B	384.2	4.57	10.6	1.3	17.1	31.8	**9.5**	10.7	15.8

Asset Quality Index	Adjusted Non-Performing Loans as a % of Total Loans	Adjusted Non-Performing Loans as a % of Capital	Net Charge-Offs Avg Loans	Profitability Index	Net Income ($Mil)	Return on Assets (R.O.A.)	Return on Equity (R.O.E.)	Net Interest Spread	Overhead Efficiency Ratio	Liquidity Index	Liquidity Ratio	Hot Money Ratio	Stability Index
5.3	2.58	7.4	0.09	**4.5**	3.3	1.02	9.81	2.70	63.7	**4.1**	23.0	8.4	**7.2**
4.4	1.11	5.1	0.20	**5.7**	1.6	1.20	10.94	3.26	49.2	**5.2**	36.4	6.8	**7.9**
7.4	0.25	1.5	-0.02	**7.6**	27.0	1.85	14.20	4.35	56.5	**1.4**	10.4	17.5	**10.0**
6.8	0.62	3.5	-0.21	**5.5**	5.3	1.04	8.56	3.97	67.0	**3.9**	13.1	9.8	**9.5**
5.4	0.75	2.7	0.07	**6.1**	105.5	1.36	9.01	3.33	63.5	**4.8**	23.1	6.6	**9.0**
7.1	0.71	3.3	0.51	**6.4**	49.8	1.15	9.40	3.48	65.5	**3.7**	19.1	4.2	**9.8**
8.7	0.21	0.5	-0.05	**4.3**	1.1	1.00	11.06	3.11	58.5	**4.1**	53.1	17.2	**6.2**
5.2	1.92	9.4	0.16	**8.6**	20.9	1.75	16.99	3.80	44.0	**5.2**	40.2	9.7	**8.9**
7.5	0.48	3.9	-0.01	**2.7**	14.3	0.60	9.69	2.86	73.2	**5.8**	27.6	3.0	**3.7**
7.4	0.33	1.2	0.00	**5.3**	4.7	0.99	9.32	3.52	67.3	**4.3**	27.9	9.4	**7.2**
4.3	2.34	11.0	0.27	**4.7**	5.4	1.59	18.96	3.25	72.8	**5.1**	33.4	6.2	**6.0**
5.7	1.03	6.4	0.00	**2.9**	0.3	0.43	4.52	3.65	85.1	**2.3**	30.4	20.9	**5.1**
4.8	0.76	5.3	0.07	**4.7**	6.3	1.08	11.39	3.43	71.1	**4.4**	23.7	9.8	**6.6**
9.2	0.02	0.0	0.00	**6.4**	0.9	1.63	9.82	3.51	58.1	**6.9**	68.5	5.6	**8.9**
8.1	0.00	0.0	0.00	**9.8**	0.7	2.97	28.58	4.05	47.2	**5.4**	66.8	12.7	**8.6**
9.2	0.00	0.0	0.00	**1.7**	0.0	0.09	0.64	3.91	97.0	**5.9**	59.9	8.2	**5.5**
5.9	0.88	4.8	0.00	**3.6**	20.6	0.63	5.01	1.97	76.6	**3.5**	41.2	20.6	**9.0**
4.4	1.59	7.8	0.09	**4.8**	3.3	0.95	9.25	4.31	72.9	**5.4**	37.0	6.3	**6.0**
5.1	0.68	2.6	0.00	**7.7**	7.8	1.83	16.52	3.39	36.1	**1.1**	4.6	23.6	**9.0**
7.7	0.38	1.7	0.04	**6.5**	13.6	1.34	13.70	3.58	50.7	**5.1**	34.9	10.5	**8.1**
7.5	0.00	0.0	-0.02	**6.6**	23.0	1.35	16.38	2.61	28.8	**4.9**	10.9	2.8	**8.4**
5.8	1.93	7.1	0.23	**5.0**	0.9	0.90	8.60	4.12	73.0	**4.6**	28.4	7.7	**6.3**
9.1	0.46	1.6	0.00	**4.4**	1.8	0.94	7.59	3.35	66.3	**4.1**	43.4	15.1	**8.0**
9.1	0.09	0.4	-0.01	**6.1**	1.0	1.59	13.46	3.05	57.6	**5.8**	38.7	3.8	**8.6**
8.9	0.09	0.5	0.08	**5.1**	2.7	1.07	11.61	3.35	55.6	**5.7**	38.6	4.9	**5.7**
3.4	2.87	13.7	0.06	**8.6**	0.8	1.75	13.53	4.26	44.0	**0.8**	18.0	41.0	**7.8**
8.5	0.00	0.0	-0.85	**3.8**	0.7	0.79	9.31	3.64	79.9	**5.3**	34.0	5.6	**5.3**
7.1	0.51	2.2	0.16	**7.3**	3.6	1.89	17.05	3.51	47.3	**3.6**	41.2	17.5	**7.6**
2.8	2.12	10.8	1.48	**5.9**	1.6	1.30	15.48	4.14	65.9	**1.7**	21.3	4.5	**6.4**
6.4	0.03	0.2	0.00	**4.4**	0.9	1.01	9.32	3.86	71.5	**0.9**	20.0	40.2	**6.5**
4.0	1.08	10.5	0.02	**5.9**	1.9	1.47	16.03	3.61	56.9	**4.2**	14.8	6.9	**6.3**
5.4	1.22	6.6	0.00	**9.6**	0.8	2.43	26.99	3.83	53.1	**0.9**	16.4	33.6	**7.1**
8.9	0.00	0.0	0.00	**0.0**	-0.9	-11.23	-7.98	2.26	536.7	**4.0**	105.2	32.5	**6.8**
6.3	0.09	0.4	0.00	**7.6**	1.3	2.21	24.76	4.30	46.2	**1.5**	10.0	22.9	**6.4**
7.6	0.25	1.8	0.11	**3.5**	8.6	1.29	14.27	3.44	65.0	**3.8**	9.9	7.2	**5.8**
8.1	0.25	0.7	0.00	**6.4**	9.5	1.24	11.18	3.24	64.4	**6.3**	43.5	5.8	**9.6**
7.7	0.42	2.5	0.08	**3.2**	0.4	0.59	6.64	2.96	77.2	**2.9**	31.5	17.5	**4.4**
6.7	0.33	2.3	0.01	**5.4**	2.8	1.08	13.15	3.36	63.1	**4.0**	27.5	10.5	**6.2**
8.9	0.03	0.2	0.00	**3.7**	1.0	0.84	9.95	3.47	78.1	**5.2**	32.1	5.3	**4.8**
8.8	0.48	0.9	0.00	**2.6**	0.2	0.40	1.81	3.26	85.4	**4.3**	41.3	13.9	**6.8**
6.0	3.61	7.9	-0.50	**1.5**	0.0	-0.06	-0.40	2.92	101.9	**3.0**	34.9	18.1	**6.0**
8.5	0.22	1.2	-0.05	**6.0**	2.8	1.43	15.32	3.41	58.7	**1.9**	21.3	17.0	**6.9**
8.6	0.00	0.0	na	**0.0**	-0.1	-0.30	-1.30	na	237.5	**4.3**	83.9	20.8	**4.9**
8.4	0.15	0.8	0.00	**9.6**	7.3	2.05	22.31	4.38	55.0	**4.2**	40.9	11.3	**7.4**
10.0	na	0.0	na	**9.8**	0.7	8.24	9.67	0.07	82.0	**4.0**	na	0.0	**6.4**
4.7	1.19	10.5	0.60	**2.3**	0.1	0.51	7.49	4.98	87.0	**2.7**	19.7	15.6	**1.7**
5.0	1.91	9.9	-0.03	**1.1**	0.0	-0.09	-0.87	3.39	102.3	**1.2**	12.5	28.1	**5.1**
5.9	0.75	3.0	0.08	**6.4**	81.1	1.19	9.05	3.14	59.5	**5.9**	28.9	3.6	**9.9**
9.5	0.00	0.0	0.00	**0.0**	-2.0	-14.49	-13.36	0.50	2714.9	**8.6**	118.2	0.0	**2.0**
5.3	2.61	4.9	-0.04	**4.9**	3.6	1.15	12.20	3.35	67.2	**5.3**	35.6	5.7	**7.1**
8.3	0.02	0.2	0.21	**5.0**	2.5	1.21	11.97	3.06	56.3	**4.7**	33.2	6.5	**5.3**
8.8	0.13	0.6	-0.01	**6.0**	0.6	1.35	13.72	4.74	70.0	**5.7**	38.7	4.6	**5.1**
3.1	4.66	16.4	0.34	**2.1**	0.1	0.32	3.99	3.78	85.6	**4.0**	31.3	12.2	**2.4**
4.7	0.55	3.1	0.00	**5.6**	2.2	1.16	10.74	3.31	53.5	**4.8**	32.1	7.7	**7.4**
7.3	0.70	2.5	-0.03	**4.4**	4.2	1.01	10.07	2.65	74.3	**1.7**	33.7	13.3	**6.5**
5.0	1.94	11.1	-0.02	**3.7**	1.6	0.71	7.51	2.96	76.0	**2.6**	18.7	16.5	**5.6**
9.6	0.00	0.0	-0.01	**2.7**	0.2	0.40	3.80	3.03	83.6	**5.6**	54.5	9.1	**5.9**
6.1	3.71	7.7	-0.03	**3.4**	2.5	0.49	2.02	2.50	76.8	**3.4**	40.2	21.2	**8.9**
8.9	0.01	0.1	0.00	**6.1**	4.9	1.35	12.37	3.09	49.4	**2.4**	37.6	27.1	**7.8**
5.4	1.16	5.3	-0.04	**9.3**	5.1	2.62	23.30	3.99	57.2	**4.1**	32.3	10.3	**8.4**

Name	City	State	Rating	2020 Rating	2019 Rating	Total Assets ($Mil)	One Year Asset Growth	Asset Mix (As a % of Total Assets) Commercial Loans	Consumer Loans	Mortgage Loans	Securities	Capitalization Index	Leverage Ratio	Risk-Based Capital Ratio
Rowley Savings Bank	Rowley	IA	C-	C-	C-	18.1	10.90	5.9	4.8	4.4	0.0	5.6	7.6	42.1
Roxboro Savings Bank, SSB	Roxboro	NC	A-	A-	B+	285.5	16.44	0.8	0.2	20.6	47.4	10.0	19.0	47.0
Royal Bank	Elroy	WI	A-	A-	B+	665.0	25.81	8.2	3.1	16.2	25.1	8.0	9.7	16.8
Royal Banks of Missouri	Saint Louis	MO	B+	B+	B-	906.2	19.11	10.3	0.4	2.8	5.6	9.5	10.9	14.6
Royal Business Bank	Los Angeles	CA	A	A	A	3885.3	23.94	4.2	0.2	28.8	8.9	10.0	12.3	19.8
Royal Savings Bank	Chicago	IL	B	B	B+	532.6	23.46	1.7	0.2	35.4	6.0	7.4	9.3	14.0
RSI Bank	Rahway	NJ	C+	C+	B-	608.8	1.76	3.7	0.0	34.2	26.7	10.0	15.0	0.0
RSNB Bank	Rock Springs	WY	A	A	A	419.4	7.05	5.8	0.7	4.4	61.4	10.0	11.1	0.0
▲ Rushford State Bank (Inc.)	Rushford	MN	C-	D+	C-	72.1	14.72	4.7	2.7	13.5	16.7	5.2	7.2	13.9
▼ Rushville State Bank	Rushville	IL	B+	A-	A-	119.9	5.18	5.7	1.4	3.6	50.3	10.0	12.7	0.0
S & T Bank	Indiana	PA	C+	C+	B	9487.4	0.33	16.7	0.9	10.3	8.9	7.5	9.3	13.7
Sabal Palm Bank	Sarasota	FL	B	B	B-	412.2	21.96	14.3	0.1	14.6	1.8	6.2	8.2	0.0
Sabine State Bank and Trust Co.	Many	LA	B+	B+	B+	1245.3	13.04	8.4	1.2	7.4	6.7	7.3	9.2	15.2
Saco & Biddeford Savings Institution	Saco	ME	B-	B-	B	1149.6	5.63	3.1	0.5	49.7	13.2	10.0	11.7	0.0
Safra National Bank of New York	New York	NY	B	B	B+	9724.6	4.32	11.0	0.0	0.1	42.8	7.1	9.1	22.2
Sage Capital Bank	Gonzales	TX	B+	B+	B+	555.9	12.45	7.8	0.3	7.4	8.7	7.7	9.5	15.7
▲ Saint Clair State Bank (Inc.)	Saint Clair	MN	A-	B+	B+	105.6	6.77	11.6	4.7	9.4	3.9	8.8	10.2	16.0
▼ Saint John's Bank and Trust Co.	Saint Louis	MO	C+	B-	C+	344.7	5.71	4.8	0.5	8.7	16.6	6.7	8.7	0.0
Saint Landry Homestead FSB	Opelousas	LA	C	C+	B	238.6	0.10	3.0	2.0	38.5	24.0	10.0	21.3	43.1
Saint Louis Bank	Saint Louis	MO	C+	C+	C	673.2	6.38	23.2	0.3	5.5	7.2	5.7	7.7	12.5
Saint Martin National Bank	Saint Martin	MN	B+	B+	B	31.8	35.51	5.4	2.1	15.8	40.9	10.0	11.5	0.0
Sainte Marie State Bank	Sainte Marie	IL	D	D	D	16.1	-1.55	2.6	0.8	0.8	3.9	10.0	19.4	27.9
Salem Co-operative Bank	Salem	NH	C	C	C	478.0	3.10	3.1	0.7	51.4	12.4	10.0	14.6	29.2
Salem Five Cents Savings Bank	Salem	MA	A-	A-	A-	5785.3	4.72	10.9	2.2	21.8	22.4	10.0	11.4	16.5
Salisbury Bank and Trust Co.	Lakeville	CT	B+	B	B	1436.7	11.62	12.9	0.7	24.7	10.5	7.5	9.3	14.7
Sallie Mae Bank	Salt Lake City	UT	D+	D+	D+	28835.8	-5.20	0.0	73.8	0.0	7.2	8.8	10.5	14.0
San Luis Valley Federal Bank	Alamosa	CO	B	B	B	355.8	12.19	5.8	1.5	38.3	15.7	10.0	15.9	23.4
Sanborn Savings Bank	Sanborn	IA	B	B-	C+	70.6	3.49	4.6	3.5	15.5	21.9	8.4	9.9	0.0
Sandhills Bank	North Myrtle Beach	SC	C+	C	C	230.6	7.07	7.6	1.4	29.8	11.4	6.2	8.2	0.0
Sandhills State Bank	Bassett	NE	B-	C+	C+	332.4	4.97	16.5	0.8	2.0	17.6	6.8	8.8	13.5
Sandy Spring Bank	Olney	MD	B-	B-	B-	12912.4	-2.74	13.5	0.2	12.2	11.1	8.9	10.3	14.8
Sanger Bank	Sanger	TX	B+	B+	A	179.1	16.20	6.6	2.1	12.9	13.3	10.0	14.5	31.2
▼ Sanibel Captiva Community Bank	Sanibel	FL	B-	B	B-	778.3	37.41	7.6	1.0	26.9	0.9	3.7	5.7	12.2
Santa Cruz County Bank	Santa Cruz	CA	A	A	A	1631.1	17.79	24.0	0.0	3.0	5.1	8.0	9.7	15.3
Santander Bank, N.A.	Boston	MA	C	C	C+	95192.6	8.48	14.5	12.4	6.5	18.2	10.0	12.0	17.4
Saratoga National Bank and Trust Co.	Saratoga Springs	NY	B+	B+	B+	845.2	10.62	6.0	18.7	19.4	15.7	7.2	9.2	14.8
Sauk Valley Bank & Trust Co.	Sterling	IL	B-	B-	B-	581.4	-1.69	15.1	0.3	6.4	31.0	6.5	8.6	13.9
Savanna-Thomson State Bank	Savanna	IL	C+	C+	B	119.8	19.03	6.2	0.3	4.7	44.3	7.6	9.4	18.9
Savannah Bank, N.A.	Savannah	NY	C	C	B-	164.2	5.49	8.2	0.7	19.2	41.5	6.1	8.2	17.5
Savers Co-operative Bank	Southbridge	MA	B-	B-	B-	663.9	3.74	5.7	2.8	28.6	9.8	9.4	10.6	0.0
▲ SaviBank	Burlington	WA	C+	C	C+	468.5	18.13	17.9	7.4	6.2	3.1	5.9	7.9	11.7
▲ Savings Bank	Primghar	IA	A	A-	A-	237.4	5.12	11.2	4.1	5.3	17.9	10.0	12.6	0.0
Savings Bank of Mendocino County	Ukiah	CA	A	A	A	1386.0	12.47	4.9	0.4	3.6	43.9	10.0	14.8	0.0
Savings Bank of Walpole	Walpole	NH	B-	B-	B-	606.4	14.94	7.6	10.0	36.5	19.9	4.6	6.7	12.2
Sawyer Savings Bank	Saugerties	NY	C-	D+	D+	268.3	4.33	4.1	0.1	39.7	21.1	8.9	10.3	17.2
▲ Schaumburg Bank & Trust Co., N.A.	Schaumburg	IL	B	B-	B	1567.1	10.04	27.4	13.6	3.8	17.7	5.8	8.7	11.6
Schertz Bank & Trust	Schertz	TX	B+	B+	A-	595.7	17.60	7.4	0.2	3.8	1.3	5.3	10.3	0.0
Schuyler Savings Bank	Kearny	NJ	C	C	C	124.5	3.03	0.0	0.0	62.1	6.7	10.0	15.8	0.0
Scott State Bank	Bethany	IL	B	B	B	197.3	7.57	8.8	2.0	10.2	45.3	10.0	12.9	0.0
Scottsburg Building and Loan Assn.	Scottsburg	IN	C	C+	C+	85.8	-0.71	1.2	0.1	40.6	40.5	10.0	16.3	36.0
Scribner Bank	Scribner	NE	A-	A-	A-	87.1	19.85	10.9	0.7	1.7	7.5	10.0	12.6	28.1
Seacoast National Bank	Stuart	FL	A-	A-	B+	9317.5	15.26	12.7	1.9	10.2	19.5	9.6	10.7	17.6
Seamens Bank	Provincetown	MA	C	C	C+	535.2	21.11	6.3	0.1	26.4	12.4	6.8	8.9	0.0
▲ Seattle Bank	Seattle	WA	B	B-	B	691.8	-7.46	12.1	6.6	8.1	0.2	10.0	11.1	21.6
Sebree Deposit Bank	Sebree	KY	D-	D-	D+	22.3	-2.87	5.1	5.8	30.8	8.0	8.7	10.1	0.0
▲ Second Federal S&L Assn. of Philadelphia	Philadelphia	PA	C	D+	D	27.2	44.51	0.0	0.0	48.9	19.2	10.0	22.7	38.4
Securian Trust Co., N.A.	Saint Paul	MN	U	U	U	15.7	1.26	0.0	0.0	0.0	69.3	10.0	87.2	98.4
Security Bank	Stephens	AR	B+	B+	B+	64.1	-9.52	3.5	6.1	52.3	7.1	9.3	10.5	0.0
Security Bank	Laurel	NE	A-	A-	A-	281.1	11.37	11.6	1.9	2.1	39.4	9.8	10.8	17.0
Security Bank	Tulsa	OK	B	B-	B-	782.8	6.07	24.7	0.6	6.1	2.6	8.1	9.7	15.6

Arrows denote recent upgrades ▲ or downgrades ▼

Asset Quality Index	Adjusted Non-Performing Loans as a % of Total Loans	Adjusted Non-Performing Loans as a % of Capital	Net Charge-Offs Avg Loans	Profitability Index	Net Income ($Mil)	Return on Assets (R.O.A.)	Return on Equity (R.O.E.)	Net Interest Spread	Overhead Efficiency Ratio	Liquidity Index	Liquidity Ratio	Hot Money Ratio	Stability Index
9.5	0.41	0.8	0.00	1.2	-0.1	-0.49	-6.32	1.17	134.8	7.5	89.3	1.5	2.8
9.1	2.05	2.8	0.00	5.2	1.7	1.20	6.29	2.58	59.7	4.2	68.5	20.1	8.4
7.5	0.36	2.0	0.00	7.1	4.4	1.33	13.17	3.78	58.8	4.8	32.7	8.0	7.7
4.2	0.73	3.7	0.03	4.6	4.0	0.89	6.74	2.87	59.6	2.7	24.8	16.5	8.0
7.6	0.66	2.3	0.01	9.1	29.3	1.61	11.11	3.73	40.6	1.5	25.1	34.0	10.0
5.1	0.47	3.5	-0.13	5.7	3.2	1.22	12.35	3.51	57.5	0.6	9.1	33.2	6.2
6.1	3.10	11.0	-0.01	2.8	1.2	0.39	2.71	2.63	77.7	4.5	40.3	12.7	8.3
9.6	0.14	0.3	-0.05	6.4	4.5	2.15	17.55	3.05	55.5	5.8	50.8	8.1	8.8
3.9	3.24	14.9	-0.36	3.8	0.3	0.81	10.99	3.84	76.2	3.6	37.7	16.4	3.5
6.6	2.41	6.4	0.08	4.7	0.6	1.02	7.54	2.19	61.3	5.6	52.7	10.2	8.9
3.2	1.80	9.0	0.37	5.4	62.4	1.35	10.54	3.32	52.4	4.2	17.5	8.0	8.0
8.7	0.00	0.0	0.00	7.8	3.5	1.79	23.14	3.66	53.0	5.5	36.4	4.8	5.0
8.6	0.35	1.5	0.01	4.9	5.9	0.97	10.26	3.06	75.8	6.4	37.9	3.2	8.4
8.0	0.66	4.1	0.00	3.5	4.1	0.72	6.54	2.58	82.2	1.4	16.3	17.2	8.6
9.5	0.00	0.0	0.00	5.2	63.2	1.30	11.60	1.14	48.3	1.7	28.5	8.3	8.9
8.5	0.00	0.0	0.00	5.9	3.5	1.30	12.65	3.96	59.6	3.2	31.2	16.1	7.1
8.2	0.08	0.5	0.06	6.5	0.8	1.57	15.51	3.11	45.1	2.6	34.0	20.6	8.9
7.7	0.01	0.0	0.00	3.2	0.7	0.40	4.57	3.26	82.0	5.4	29.0	2.3	5.0
6.9	3.04	5.5	0.12	2.4	0.4	0.35	1.63	3.03	94.4	2.6	41.8	26.7	6.7
5.5	0.53	4.0	-0.05	3.8	2.7	0.79	10.34	3.43	68.1	0.7	20.3	40.0	5.1
9.5	0.00	0.0	0.00	7.3	0.3	1.88	15.99	4.04	49.6	7.1	71.4	3.1	8.2
7.7	0.00	0.0	0.00	0.0	-0.3	-2.90	-14.57	2.75	260.4	2.8	47.2	20.8	4.8
9.4	0.58	2.1	0.00	2.5	1.0	0.42	2.80	2.68	82.0	2.3	28.9	20.1	7.6
7.3	0.62	3.5	0.01	6.2	35.9	1.26	11.14	2.44	58.2	4.1	24.5	11.7	9.7
6.5	0.72	4.0	0.02	6.1	9.5	1.37	13.33	3.13	57.2	4.5	20.5	7.0	8.7
1.7	5.19	17.6	0.84	10.0	795.5	5.25	66.18	4.67	21.1	1.1	22.4	6.8	9.2
8.6	0.78	2.7	-0.11	4.2	1.3	0.77	4.99	3.66	72.9	4.7	34.5	9.3	7.7
6.4	0.70	2.9	0.00	7.0	0.7	1.88	18.04	4.01	51.2	4.6	31.2	8.5	6.2
8.1	0.17	1.2	0.06	3.8	0.9	0.81	9.30	3.44	68.7	3.9	32.1	12.6	4.8
4.3	0.41	2.6	0.09	7.0	4.3	2.58	24.12	4.94	50.4	2.6	12.6	10.2	6.4
3.9	0.92	5.1	0.05	7.9	136.6	2.14	16.81	3.61	48.4	2.5	13.7	10.9	9.3
9.1	0.13	0.4	-0.07	4.4	0.7	0.75	5.61	3.23	71.8	3.4	48.2	20.5	8.3
8.4	0.32	1.6	0.00	8.9	5.2	1.47	25.23	3.74	52.6	6.0	38.8	2.9	5.0
6.7	0.01	0.1	0.00	8.3	11.1	1.45	12.77	4.09	44.4	4.3	16.4	7.3	9.7
5.1	1.72	5.8	0.24	2.4	337.1	0.76	5.65	2.46	79.6	6.0	33.8	1.4	8.0
5.7	0.60	4.3	0.01	7.6	6.5	1.57	17.47	3.19	42.3	3.7	12.9	10.3	7.2
4.3	1.26	9.9	0.67	4.2	2.5	0.86	10.01	3.34	60.4	3.0	17.1	7.6	5.7
4.8	1.26	4.2	0.00	3.0	0.3	0.45	3.59	2.61	78.3	6.3	46.4	3.7	6.5
8.2	0.26	1.4	0.00	2.9	0.4	0.54	6.46	2.83	79.7	2.4	18.3	17.1	4.6
5.9	0.87	4.5	0.00	3.5	1.9	0.59	5.52	2.88	73.9	3.9	27.6	11.2	7.2
4.2	1.06	7.5	0.03	4.6	2.4	1.08	13.02	4.02	69.5	2.3	25.1	16.0	5.2
8.1	0.00	0.7	0.00	7.8	2.3	1.90	15.03	2.73	41.2	3.1	16.2	13.6	9.2
9.0	0.48	0.9	0.00	5.8	6.9	1.02	6.78	3.30	54.0	7.0	51.4	3.8	10.0
5.6	0.71	6.9	0.26	3.1	1.4	0.49	7.26	3.04	78.4	4.8	24.5	4.8	4.9
6.3	0.89	3.9	-0.05	2.4	0.8	0.58	5.45	3.25	80.9	1.2	28.4	29.3	5.7
7.1	0.12	0.6	-0.05	4.5	7.6	1.00	10.53	2.30	59.7	1.9	18.0	12.1	6.8
7.4	0.30	0.6	0.01	8.0	4.6	1.62	15.29	3.68	42.3	1.1	18.9	32.3	7.4
7.6	1.77	5.6	0.02	2.3	0.2	0.34	2.10	2.88	84.0	1.6	25.3	25.8	7.3
9.1	0.27	1.3	0.12	3.7	0.7	0.70	5.24	2.70	75.0	6.1	52.9	7.1	7.9
10.0	0.20	0.5	0.00	2.5	0.2	0.34	2.07	2.16	80.3	1.9	42.2	43.1	7.6
8.7	0.33	1.2	0.00	6.9	0.5	1.22	9.67	2.95	69.9	6.6	54.8	2.9	8.8
6.7	0.67	2.8	0.04	7.2	66.0	1.51	11.51	3.36	55.2	5.8	35.4	4.1	9.5
3.0	4.80	21.0	0.00	2.6	0.7	0.26	2.83	2.23	85.2	4.9	51.7	13.3	5.5
6.6	4.89	6.6	-0.05	4.3	2.4	0.68	6.05	3.60	68.7	0.6	11.6	35.6	8.9
8.8	0.00	0.4	-0.02	0.0	-0.1	-0.77	-6.86	2.98	126.1	2.1	35.7	23.1	4.2
9.9	0.00	0.0	0.00	2.8	0.1	0.87	3.59	3.73	59.3	2.2	51.6	58.1	6.0
10.0	na	0.0	na	8.0	0.2	3.09	3.33	2.64	90.5	4.0	na	0.0	6.3
8.7	0.12	1.2	0.00	6.3	0.6	1.65	15.11	3.98	61.4	0.7	16.7	42.2	6.3
7.4	0.33	0.7	-0.02	8.3	3.2	2.28	19.55	4.91	57.3	5.3	33.7	5.0	8.1
5.2	0.81	5.1	0.00	8.1	7.2	1.89	19.29	3.50	36.9	1.7	32.8	26.3	9.4

Name	City	State	Rating	2020 Rating	2019 Rating	Total Assets ($Mil)	One Year Asset Growth	Asset Mix (As a % of Total Assets) Comm-ercial Loans	Cons-umer Loans	Mort-gage Loans	Secur-ities	Capital-ization Index	Lever-age Ratio	Risk-Based Capital Ratio
Security Bank	Dyersburg	TN	**B-**	B-	B-	231.7	-3.05	8.6	1.2	3.9	58.8	**7.5**	9.3	17.2
Security Bank	New Auburn	WI	**B-**	B-	B	146.9	11.33	14.8	1.4	10.0	5.8	**8.6**	11.8	0.0
Security Bank & Trust Co.	Glencoe	MN	**B+**	B+	B+	729.3	9.68	6.3	0.6	4.8	17.7	**6.4**	8.4	18.7
Security Bank and Trust Co.	Maysville	KY	**B+**	B+	B+	64.3	9.89	1.2	1.4	15.6	31.8	**10.0**	16.9	0.0
Security Bank and Trust Co.	Miami	OK	**B-**	B-	B-	93.1	-7.43	9.5	4.4	24.3	14.2	**7.6**	9.4	0.0
Security Bank and Trust Co.	Paris	TN	**B+**	B+	B+	793.1	29.54	27.9	1.3	11.5	13.9	**6.7**	9.3	12.2
Security Bank Minnesota	Albert Lea	MN	**B+**	B+	B+	152.3	4.98	52.4	2.2	2.8	6.1	**7.3**	9.2	13.8
Security Bank of Crawford	Crawford	TX	**C+**	C+	C+	101.3	21.91	12.0	1.9	35.3	7.9	**5.7**	8.7	0.0
Security Bank of Kansas City	Kansas City	KS	**A-**	A-	A-	3632.4	7.76	6.0	0.3	1.2	37.9	**10.0**	12.6	0.0
Security Bank of Pulaski County	Waynesville	MO	**C+**	C+	C+	128.4	4.67	11.8	4.6	14.7	23.5	**6.0**	8.1	13.8
Security Bank of Southwest Missouri	Cassville	MO	**B+**	B+	B+	107.9	24.43	6.5	4.9	24.3	16.3	**8.2**	9.8	0.0
▲ Security Bank of the Ozarks	Eminence	MO	**B-**	C+	C+	130.8	21.68	10.9	6.2	13.0	13.9	**5.4**	7.4	12.2
Security Bank USA	Bemidji	MN	**B+**	B+	B+	196.4	7.84	16.0	4.9	14.8	7.5	**7.2**	9.2	0.0
▼ Security Bank, s.b.	Springfield	IL	**D+**	C	C	241.6	31.30	8.0	2.3	14.1	27.6	**4.6**	6.6	17.1
▲ Security Federal Bank	Aiken	SC	**B**	B-	B-	1199.7	8.90	7.1	1.8	7.0	51.6	**8.3**	9.8	20.2
Security Federal Savings Bank	Jasper	AL	**C**	C	C+	39.0	4.26	0.0	5.3	27.0	9.5	**10.0**	11.8	27.8
Security Federal Savings Bank	Logansport	IN	**B-**	B-	B-	340.7	8.22	6.6	0.7	27.8	11.4	**9.6**	10.7	16.9
Security Financial Bank	Durand	WI	**B**	B-	B-	636.4	6.95	16.0	0.1	7.3	17.7	**6.5**	8.5	12.5
Security First Bank	Lincoln	NE	**B-**	B-	C+	1383.5	16.35	6.9	11.8	7.9	15.3	**5.8**	7.8	11.7
Security First Bank of North Dakota	Center	ND	**A**	A	A-	221.7	12.42	7.6	2.2	4.5	5.0	**9.7**	12.2	0.0
Security First National Bank of Hugo	Hugo	OK	**B+**	B+	A-	137.8	7.41	4.1	1.8	20.6	7.3	**6.9**	8.9	0.0
Security FSB of McMinnville	McMinnville	TN	**B+**	B+	A-	284.2	16.81	12.7	4.7	21.4	14.6	**7.9**	9.6	15.1
Security National Bank	Witt	IL	**B-**	B-	B	99.5	9.94	11.5	1.4	14.3	27.9	**7.1**	9.0	16.1
Security National Bank of Omaha	Omaha	NE	**B+**	B+	A	1242.6	18.54	21.1	3.9	4.1	18.3	**6.9**	10.1	0.0
Security National Bank of South Dakota	Dakota Dunes	SD	**A**	A	A	247.4	6.72	3.7	2.4	13.8	25.4	**9.6**	10.7	0.0
Security National Trust Co.	Wheeling	WV	**U**	U	U	7.1	11.48	0.0	0.0	0.0	78.1	**10.0**	119.	0.0
Security Savings Bank	Gowrie	IA	**B+**	B+	A-	152.5	8.09	9.1	2.3	10.1	16.8	**9.6**	10.7	16.8
Security Savings Bank	Monmouth	IL	**C+**	B-	B-	244.8	16.31	3.1	5.5	6.9	42.3	**8.2**	9.8	0.0
Security Savings Bank	Canton	SD	**C+**	C+	C+	506.6	12.40	3.6	0.7	5.4	11.0	**6.4**	8.4	15.6
Security State Bank	Algona	IA	**A-**	B+	A-	124.8	15.98	15.0	0.9	1.7	6.9	**10.0**	15.4	24.8
Security State Bank	Radcliffe	IA	**C**	C-	C-	120.6	12.10	7.3	1.4	9.1	31.9	**5.6**	7.6	19.4
Security State Bank	Sutherland	IA	**B+**	B+	B+	275.2	4.36	13.4	2.8	5.3	0.2	**5.9**	10.4	0.0
▼ Security State Bank	Waverly	IA	**B**	B+	A-	91.2	4.20	3.7	2.1	8.8	56.0	**10.0**	11.6	0.0
Security State Bank	Scott City	KS	**A**	A	A-	343.4	0.32	13.0	2.9	2.2	16.3	**10.0**	16.2	0.0
▲ Security State Bank	Wellington	KS	**B**	C+	C+	55.6	5.77	5.9	0.7	5.1	50.4	**10.0**	14.1	0.0
Security State Bank	Cheyenne	OK	**B+**	B+	A-	247.6	43.01	10.5	3.2	8.0	37.3	**8.8**	10.2	0.0
Security State Bank	Alexandria	SD	**B**	B-	B	94.0	10.56	9.8	2.9	1.8	35.9	**8.6**	10.1	0.0
Security State Bank	Tyndall	SD	**B**	B-	B	253.1	9.94	8.2	0.5	1.8	22.9	**6.9**	9.9	0.0
Security State Bank	Farwell	TX	**A**	A	A-	189.5	23.85	18.2	0.8	14.5	16.0	**10.0**	12.6	0.0
Security State Bank	Pearsall	TX	**A-**	A-	A-	766.1	8.33	4.1	0.6	2.4	36.1	**10.0**	12.2	0.0
Security State Bank	Centralia	WA	**A-**	A	A	648.0	16.57	5.5	0.9	3.1	2.4	**9.5**	10.7	30.6
Security State Bank	Iron River	WI	**B-**	B-	B-	130.5	5.98	20.9	0.9	13.8	10.6	**10.0**	17.2	0.0
Security State Bank	Basin	WY	**B-**	B-	B	427.5	9.54	6.7	2.5	7.5	42.1	**8.2**	9.8	19.3
Security State Bank & Trust	Fredericksburg	TX	**A**	A	A	1549.3	19.01	7.9	1.4	8.0	23.2	**9.0**	10.4	0.0
Security State Bank of Aitkin	Aitkin	MN	**B+**	A-	A-	122.5	7.41	13.7	1.6	7.1	31.7	**10.0**	11.2	0.0
Security State Bank of Hibbing	Hibbing	MN	**B**	B	B	164.3	3.32	18.1	1.4	10.4	24.1	**6.7**	8.7	20.9
Security State Bank of Kenyon	Kenyon	MN	**D-**	D-	D-	73.0	24.64	3.7	1.0	12.0	1.3	**7.9**	9.6	14.8
Security State Bank of Marine	Marine On Saint Croi	MN	**A-**	A-	A-	181.0	13.95	5.6	1.5	29.3	4.8	**7.5**	9.3	18.6
Security State Bank of Oklahoma	Wewoka	OK	**B**	B	C	381.1	32.77	13.3	7.1	9.8	12.7	**10.0**	12.1	18.7
Security State Bank of Oklee	Oklee	MN	**B+**	B+	B+	38.8	9.33	2.8	4.9	12.9	19.5	**10.0**	14.9	46.9
Security State Bank of Wanamingo, Inc.	Wanamingo	MN	**B+**	B+	B+	75.4	10.78	12.0	0.8	2.8	13.8	**10.0**	11.9	0.0
▲ Security State Bank of Warroad	Warroad	MN	**C+**	C	D	126.9	12.03	16.1	9.4	1.6	44.1	**10.0**	14.4	0.0
▼ Security Trust & Savings Bank	Storm Lake	IA	**C+**	B-	B-	278.3	18.86	4.3	0.7	5.8	28.7	**6.5**	8.5	28.7
SEI Private Trust Co.	Oaks	PA	**U**	U	U	219.2	11.01	0.0	0.0	0.0	53.5	**10.0**	98.7	330.8
▲ Seiling State Bank	Seiling	OK	**B+**	B	B	141.2	10.89	12.5	2.1	8.2	29.8	**10.0**	12.1	19.8
Select Bank	Forest	VA	**C+**	C+	B-	368.9	14.48	29.1	1.2	26.2	0.3	**5.6**	7.6	15.9
Select Bank & Trust Co.	Dunn	NC	**B-**	B-	B	1867.9	15.44	4.8	0.2	9.7	11.7	**7.0**	9.6	12.5
Senath State Bank	Senath	MO	**A**	A	A	93.4	9.28	2.4	7.3	27.5	9.2	**10.0**	13.2	0.0
SENB Bank	Moline	IL	**B-**	B-	B-	363.6	5.62	13.0	0.7	13.1	19.7	**6.5**	8.6	12.7
▲ Seneca Savings	Baldwinsville	NY	**B-**	C	C	222.5	-6.44	12.0	0.3	40.5	17.4	**9.4**	10.6	0.0

Asset Quality Index	Adjusted Non-Performing Loans as a % of Total Loans	Adjusted Non-Performing Loans as a % of Capital	Net Charge-Offs Avg Loans	Profitability Index	Net Income ($Mil)	Return on Assets (R.O.A.)	Return on Equity (R.O.E.)	Net Interest Spread	Overhead Efficiency Ratio	Liquidity Index	Liquidity Ratio	Hot Money Ratio	Stability Index
7.1	2.09	3.8	-0.01	4.2	1.3	1.13	9.91	3.06	76.5	4.4	41.3	13.2	7.2
2.2	2.93	18.7	-0.12	7.8	1.0	1.34	11.38	3.64	54.6	2.6	19.7	9.8	7.1
7.2	0.44	2.0	0.00	6.5	6.1	1.70	19.14	2.87	49.9	5.2	38.2	7.6	7.8
9.6	0.19	0.5	-0.02	4.8	0.3	1.02	5.94	2.72	63.6	5.6	56.1	9.7	8.4
6.0	0.43	3.1	-0.01	5.3	0.7	1.42	14.37	4.42	69.5	1.8	15.2	16.9	6.5
8.3	0.11	0.5	0.00	8.1	8.4	2.19	22.01	3.50	43.2	3.7	12.3	7.2	7.9
7.9	0.00	0.9	-0.24	6.5	1.3	1.66	17.60	3.94	53.9	2.9	20.6	14.8	6.9
6.9	0.49	4.0	-0.01	4.1	0.4	0.77	9.11	4.47	74.4	1.0	25.1	31.3	4.7
7.3	1.56	2.5	-0.02	5.1	16.3	0.91	6.22	2.58	58.7	6.4	46.5	6.0	9.9
5.6	0.93	4.8	0.00	3.9	0.5	0.78	9.23	3.90	74.3	2.2	15.1	15.8	5.1
5.4	0.08	4.3	0.03	9.5	1.4	2.68	26.77	4.40	48.2	4.3	33.3	11.4	7.1
4.0	1.26	8.6	0.00	7.3	1.4	2.25	27.57	5.35	55.1	3.5	26.7	13.2	5.0
6.6	0.42	2.4	0.00	8.4	2.0	2.06	22.55	3.89	59.1	4.8	28.8	6.1	7.4
2.4	2.68	25.8	0.03	2.4	0.3	0.22	3.05	2.21	87.4	6.9	56.2	2.8	3.5
8.7	0.59	2.2	-0.07	5.0	6.8	1.16	10.92	3.13	68.5	4.8	29.2	8.8	8.7
9.6	0.00	0.1	0.18	0.8	-0.1	-0.27	-2.29	2.06	117.9	3.5	69.8	27.1	4.8
5.3	1.84	6.2	-0.02	3.7	1.1	0.67	6.09	3.67	80.5	4.6	21.3	5.7	6.7
5.1	1.05	4.0	0.00	5.5	3.7	1.17	12.04	3.40	59.6	4.6	24.0	5.7	7.4
6.2	0.62	2.9	0.06	4.2	6.4	0.94	10.88	3.24	68.7	4.4	25.4	10.5	7.2
7.5	0.46	1.3	-0.08	6.8	1.6	1.45	11.38	4.04	68.8	4.5	23.1	6.7	8.8
7.5	0.13	0.4	0.06	10.0	1.6	2.40	28.20	6.16	48.8	2.8	24.8	16.2	7.1
8.5	0.13	0.8	0.00	5.1	1.3	0.97	9.93	3.21	62.0	2.5	28.0	18.7	6.0
5.2	1.94	6.0	0.22	3.3	0.2	0.49	5.46	3.00	76.6	4.8	45.5	11.7	5.8
8.2	0.30	1.6	0.00	5.8	6.8	1.20	11.14	3.35	65.1	6.3	31.2	2.1	9.4
9.1	0.00	0.0	0.00	7.4	1.7	1.40	12.74	2.08	52.2	4.8	42.4	11.4	8.4
10.0	na	0.0	na	10.0	1.3	49.18	43.67	1.80	63.6	4.0	na	0.0	5.5
8.4	0.11	0.4	0.34	4.9	0.9	1.18	10.65	3.13	61.8	4.2	32.1	11.4	7.1
7.8	0.23	1.2	0.01	2.9	0.5	0.41	4.17	2.74	78.7	3.5	42.1	18.2	5.5
5.1	0.12	4.6	-0.40	3.0	1.0	0.42	4.41	2.45	83.4	4.4	39.4	12.4	5.0
6.3	0.52	2.6	0.00	7.2	0.9	1.35	8.91	2.73	47.5	3.9	39.9	15.2	8.6
5.2	1.62	6.7	0.00	3.2	0.5	0.76	9.18	2.55	68.5	6.6	66.6	6.9	3.5
4.3	0.95	8.2	0.17	9.8	3.2	2.36	22.99	3.61	36.1	1.7	11.7	15.9	8.0
9.4	0.00	0.0	-0.01	4.5	0.5	1.10	10.38	2.59	55.8	6.9	63.3	2.7	6.4
7.1	0.00	0.0	0.00	7.5	2.3	1.49	9.34	3.59	48.7	0.7	15.4	39.2	8.6
8.9	0.45	1.1	-0.78	6.0	0.6	2.02	13.96	4.76	58.1	6.2	59.4	6.2	6.2
4.5	1.01	4.7	0.07	8.8	3.1	2.49	20.84	3.61	46.2	1.4	15.0	25.3	8.8
8.1	0.10	0.5	0.00	5.1	0.7	1.46	14.51	2.62	59.8	2.5	38.2	25.2	5.5
5.0	1.06	3.5	0.13	8.5	2.6	2.13	21.81	4.80	53.1	1.7	17.5	18.7	7.4
8.6	0.00	0.7	0.00	7.4	1.6	1.77	14.36	3.84	52.8	0.9	21.8	35.7	8.2
7.1	2.53	4.7	-0.01	5.6	4.4	1.19	9.11	2.95	50.9	1.6	29.6	30.9	8.0
9.1	0.09	0.2	-0.19	5.2	2.6	0.84	7.59	2.10	66.6	7.2	71.9	4.1	9.0
4.4	3.87	13.2	-0.07	6.9	1.0	1.52	8.87	3.58	61.0	3.1	40.6	16.9	6.7
4.6	3.02	11.5	0.11	4.3	2.1	1.00	9.63	2.57	64.4	2.9	40.0	19.9	5.6
7.6	0.67	2.8	-0.02	6.4	10.8	1.45	13.58	3.72	62.4	5.2	32.8	9.7	9.8
4.2	4.96	18.0	0.40	4.7	0.5	0.78	7.07	3.27	71.3	6.5	48.7	3.0	8.3
5.2	2.26	11.1	0.00	4.2	0.6	0.65	7.81	3.75	71.6	5.6	51.0	10.0	4.9
0.3	13.35	81.1	-0.11	2.0	0.0	0.05	0.54	3.80	98.1	4.6	41.3	12.0	4.0
7.2	0.44	3.1	-0.01	7.5	1.6	1.75	18.56	3.22	55.2	5.4	40.8	7.8	7.7
4.8	2.72	12.1	0.07	10.0	3.0	2.07	16.51	4.12	45.7	2.9	41.5	19.9	7.6
8.9	0.00	0.0	0.00	4.4	0.2	0.86	5.72	2.01	69.2	6.3	63.7	6.4	8.0
8.4	0.00	0.0	-0.03	8.0	0.9	2.50	20.42	5.12	49.7	3.7	21.5	11.2	7.6
7.5	1.53	2.6	-0.21	2.6	0.5	0.80	5.54	3.27	73.1	5.7	50.4	9.1	5.7
9.2	0.02	0.1	-0.17	2.8	0.6	0.44	4.35	1.79	74.8	6.4	66.5	8.6	5.6
10.0	na	0.0	na	10.0	49.0	47.96	50.14	1.86	53.6	4.0	na	100.0	6.7
6.7	0.01	0.1	-0.04	6.9	1.3	1.89	18.85	4.85	54.5	1.4	22.2	27.6	6.5
5.1	0.63	5.3	0.04	3.5	1.1	0.60	8.09	3.05	70.7	0.7	13.2	39.5	4.2
4.5	1.00	5.1	0.03	6.3	13.1	1.45	12.52	3.86	56.0	3.1	21.2	15.2	8.7
8.2	0.00	3.7	-0.04	6.7	0.7	1.39	10.36	2.95	59.0	6.5	51.8	2.5	9.7
6.7	0.10	0.8	-0.01	4.2	2.0	1.08	11.43	3.33	73.3	4.5	20.2	6.3	5.8
8.4	0.21	1.5	-0.04	4.2	1.0	0.86	9.09	3.62	70.0	1.8	16.2	18.5	4.4

Name	City	State	Rating	2020 Rating	2019 Rating	Total Assets ($Mil)	One Year Asset Growth	Comm-ercial Loans	Cons-umer Loans	Mort-gage Loans	Secur-ities	Capital-ization Index	Lever-age Ratio	Risk-Based Capital Ratio
								Asset Mix (As a % of Total Assets)						
▲ Sentry Bank	Saint Joseph	MN	**B+**	B	B-	274.2	0.64	9.6	2.2	14.2	26.4	**6.5**	8.5	14.0
ServisFirst Bank	Birmingham	AL	**A-**	A-	A-	13206.1	19.94	22.6	0.5	4.1	7.7	**6.6**	8.6	12.3
Settlers Bank	Marietta	OH	**B+**	B+	A-	142.2	1.19	4.2	3.0	33.7	3.1	**10.0**	12.1	0.0
▲ Settlers bank	Windsor	WI	**B**	B-	C+	339.3	-11.24	28.8	1.7	8.5	1.9	**8.7**	11.2	13.9
Severn Savings Bank, FSB	Annapolis	MD	**A-**	B+	A-	1142.5	25.03	6.0	0.1	17.9	13.6	**10.0**	11.9	0.0
▲ Sevier County Bank	Sevierville	TN	**D**	E+	E-	475.2	28.06	8.5	0.6	11.4	15.2	**5.9**	7.9	13.3
▲ Sewickley Savings Bank	Sewickley	PA	**B-**	C+	B-	318.7	0.75	1.5	0.1	4.3	63.5	**10.0**	29.3	65.7
Shamrock Bank, N.A.	Coalgate	OK	**B+**	A-	A-	416.7	8.64	6.0	3.1	12.4	40.7	**8.7**	10.1	0.0
Sharon Bank	Springfield	PA	**D**	D+	D+	193.6	1.63	2.4	0.1	28.0	14.5	**6.0**	8.8	0.0
Shelby County State Bank	Harlan	IA	**A-**	A-	B-	331.7	16.95	4.8	1.6	5.7	19.7	**8.4**	10.0	16.5
Shelby County State Bank	Shelbyville	IL	**B+**	B+	B+	282.8	7.22	7.3	2.3	14.9	25.5	**7.6**	9.4	0.0
Shelby Savings Bank, SSB	Center	TX	**A-**	A-	A-	349.8	3.87	14.9	4.2	11.6	12.0	**10.0**	12.2	16.2
Shell Lake State Bank	Shell Lake	WI	**B+**	A-	A-	274.7	17.64	3.3	3.4	23.8	40.6	**10.0**	14.3	0.0
Sherburne State Bank	Becker	MN	**B+**	B	B	208.4	27.82	12.8	1.1	9.0	17.2	**5.8**	7.8	11.6
Sherwood Community Bank	Creighton	MO	**B-**	B-	C+	63.1	13.54	8.1	1.4	19.7	28.8	**6.4**	8.5	16.5
▼ Shinhan Bank America	New York	NY	**D+**	C-	C	1863.8	8.12	16.0	0.2	15.8	4.1	**10.0**	11.0	16.8
Shore United Bank	Easton	MD	**B+**	B+	B+	2119.3	23.29	7.9	3.0	15.7	14.7	**7.5**	9.3	14.2
Sibley State Bank	Sibley	IA	**B+**	B	B	99.7	16.30	1.5	0.8	2.5	17.2	**10.0**	11.2	18.0
Sicily Island State Bank	Sicily Island	LA	**C+**	C	B-	70.6	5.84	7.8	3.9	28.9	4.0	**10.0**	13.4	20.3
Sidney Federal S&L Assn.	Sidney	NE	**E+**	E+	E+	19.2	-1.64	12.1	1.4	40.4	6.4	**3.4**	5.4	10.9
Sidney State Bank	Sidney	MI	**C+**	C	C	105.7	12.99	3.9	3.7	37.3	17.4	**5.7**	7.7	15.5
Signature Bank	Rosemont	IL	**A-**	A-	A-	1353.5	14.68	38.1	0.1	1.7	12.1	**7.5**	9.3	14.4
Signature Bank	New York	NY	**B+**	B+	B+	97209.7	61.08	24.4	0.2	0.5	16.2	**5.9**	7.9	12.8
▲ Signature Bank of Arkansas	Fayetteville	AR	**B**	B-	B	810.4	7.49	11.9	1.2	16.4	10.8	**8.0**	10.7	13.3
▲ Signature Bank of Georgia	Sandy Springs	GA	**C+**	C-	C-	194.3	7.46	5.1	0.1	0.9	10.2	**8.9**	10.2	17.2
Signature Bank, N.A.	Toledo	OH	**A-**	A-	A-	1272.9	0.24	23.6	0.5	5.9	8.5	**7.8**	9.5	15.7
▲ Silex Banking Co.	Silex	MO	**B**	B-	B+	91.4	20.36	4.1	0.4	7.5	28.3	**10.0**	14.2	0.0
Silicon Valley Bank	Santa Clara	CA	**B+**	B+	A-	161200.3	90.79	9.2	0.2	2.6	52.0	**5.0**	7.0	14.3
Silver Lake Bank	Topeka	KS	**B+**	B+	B+	393.3	11.18	13.7	0.7	16.2	11.9	**7.9**	9.6	0.0
Silvergate Bank	La Jolla	CA	**B+**	A-	A-	12297.2	425.51	1.7	0.0	7.2	50.2	**5.9**	7.9	47.7
▲ Simmesport State Bank	Simmesport	LA	**B-**	C+	B-	147.0	20.38	5.9	14.6	34.0	3.1	**10.0**	12.1	18.6
Simmons Bank	Pine Bluff	AR	**B+**	B+	B+	23379.8	6.97	9.0	1.2	6.6	32.0	**7.7**	9.4	15.5
Simply Bank	Dayton	TN	**B-**	B-	C+	688.8	65.09	7.0	1.0	13.9	14.1	**6.7**	9.2	0.0
Siouxland Bank	South Sioux City	NE	**C+**	C+	C+	82.4	13.68	5.9	2.2	13.1	0.0	**5.6**	7.6	19.8
▼ SJN Bank of Kansas	Saint John	KS	**C**	C+	B	224.5	7.01	11.9	0.9	3.4	42.1	**6.1**	8.1	14.6
Skowhegan Savings Bank	Skowhegan	ME	**B**	B	B+	754.2	12.72	3.7	5.8	31.4	20.6	**10.0**	13.3	23.3
Skyline National Bank	Independence	VA	**B-**	B-	B-	946.7	19.23	9.5	0.7	19.9	10.9	**6.9**	8.9	12.7
Sloan State Bank	Sloan	IA	**B+**	B+	B+	68.1	11.81	3.8	7.3	10.9	55.7	**8.9**	10.2	0.0
Slovenian S&L Assn. of Canonsburg, PA	Strabane	PA	**A-**	A-	A-	523.4	11.72	0.0	0.4	29.6	61.9	**10.0**	14.4	0.0
Slovenian S&L Assn. of Franklin-Conemau	Conemaugh	PA	**D+**	C-	C+	168.2	8.12	0.0	1.8	45.1	42.8	**9.1**	10.4	0.0
Smackover State Bank	Smackover	AR	**B**	B	B	197.0	3.45	2.4	3.3	22.3	42.9	**10.0**	12.6	0.0
Small Business Bank	Lenexa	KS	**B**	B	C+	77.3	5.70	43.2	3.7	10.0	0.0	**10.0**	13.7	0.0
SmartBank	Pigeon Forge	TN	**B+**	B	B	3645.8	11.63	13.1	0.3	9.8	6.9	**6.6**	8.8	12.2
SNB Bank, N.A.	Shattuck	OK	**C+**	C	C+	136.1	0.28	19.4	4.7	1.8	12.1	**6.8**	8.8	0.0
Solera National Bank	Lakewood	CO	**B+**	B+	A-	532.0	34.61	33.4	2.5	6.9	15.8	**5.9**	9.6	0.0
Solomon State Bank	Solomon	KS	**A-**	A-	A-	197.9	-1.50	3.0	1.8	44.3	9.7	**10.0**	15.3	0.0
Solon State Bank	Solon	IA	**A**	A-	A-	126.7	18.74	15.4	1.3	8.8	35.3	**10.0**	19.4	0.0
Solutions Bank	Forreston	IL	**B+**	B+	B+	316.0	30.39	4.8	0.3	6.1	45.3	**9.3**	10.5	0.0
Solutions North Bank	Stockton	KS	**A-**	A-	B+	304.4	13.84	6.7	2.8	5.6	27.0	**10.0**	11.4	17.2
Solvay Bank	Solvay	NY	**B-**	B-	B	1126.2	3.09	11.5	5.6	23.6	33.1	**6.9**	8.9	0.0
Somerset Savings Bank, SLA	Bound Brook	NJ	**C+**	C+	B-	639.4	4.80	0.0	0.0	47.1	37.6	**10.0**	19.4	0.0
Somerset Trust Co.	Somerset	PA	**B-**	B-	B-	1778.4	13.60	22.2	3.2	11.7	24.8	**5.5**	7.5	12.0
Somerville Bank	Somerville	OH	**B-**	B-	B-	255.3	12.55	10.5	0.9	10.2	29.1	**6.9**	8.9	0.0
Sooner State Bank	Tuttle	OK	**B+**	B+	A	328.9	11.13	2.5	1.2	14.6	22.7	**6.6**	8.6	0.0
Sound Banking Co.	Lakewood	WA	**B**	B+	B+	77.9	29.61	4.1	0.4	13.7	0.0	**4.5**	6.5	13.9
▲ Sound Community Bank	Seattle	WA	**B+**	B	B-	923.4	5.90	5.7	8.8	21.4	0.8	**8.9**	10.3	0.0
South Atlantic Bank	Myrtle Beach	SC	**B**	B-	B-	1142.4	24.11	8.6	0.7	17.2	19.3	**6.0**	8.0	12.3
South Central Bank, Inc.	Glasgow	KY	**B+**	B+	B+	1569.3	14.48	8.6	1.2	11.2	22.7	**8.4**	9.9	16.2
▲ South Central State Bank	Campbell	NE	**A-**	B+	A-	156.5	12.13	2.7	0.7	0.3	24.2	**10.0**	11.9	16.1
South Coast Bank & Trust	Brunswick	GA	**B**	B	B	183.0	3.68	5.5	0.7	20.2	14.6	**6.9**	8.9	13.2

Arrows denote recent upgrades ▲ or downgrades ▼

Asset Quality Index	Adjusted Non-Performing Loans as a % of Total Loans	Adjusted Non-Performing Loans as a % of Capital	Net Charge-Offs Avg Loans	Profitability Index	Net Income ($Mil)	Return on Assets (R.O.A.)	Return on Equity (R.O.E.)	Net Interest Spread	Overhead Efficiency Ratio	Liquidity Index	Liquidity Ratio	Hot Money Ratio	Stability Index
7.6	0.26	1.3	0.20	**7.4**	2.0	1.37	13.09	3.00	43.9	**4.5**	38.2	11.3	**7.3**
8.4	0.14	1.4	0.01	**8.5**	102.8	1.65	18.82	3.04	27.9	**5.6**	30.9	6.1	**8.4**
7.0	1.34	5.7	0.06	**4.2**	0.4	0.52	4.28	2.51	73.1	**4.5**	44.7	13.8	**7.8**
6.0	0.30	2.3	0.00	**5.3**	2.0	1.15	11.14	4.20	52.8	**2.4**	12.7	14.8	**6.2**
7.5	1.09	3.1	-0.08	**5.4**	5.9	1.13	9.54	2.91	70.2	**5.8**	45.8	9.9	**9.4**
5.4	0.75	5.1	0.00	**1.7**	2.7	1.19	13.73	3.01	87.6	**2.3**	20.9	17.9	**3.3**
10.0	0.05	0.0	0.00	**4.1**	1.8	1.14	3.93	1.82	44.0	**4.3**	108.2	32.4	**7.5**
7.0	0.21	1.0	2.27	**5.3**	2.5	1.23	11.61	4.33	58.4	**3.9**	47.4	15.0	**5.7**
5.1	1.65	10.0	0.27	**0.7**	-0.1	-0.05	-0.53	2.70	94.4	**2.5**	30.5	19.1	**3.9**
7.3	0.51	1.6	0.06	**6.1**	1.9	1.16	10.38	3.49	53.6	**5.5**	35.4	4.7	**7.3**
4.7	1.30	8.4	-0.03	**3.9**	1.1	0.77	7.79	2.90	77.3	**4.6**	25.7	6.6	**6.9**
7.2	0.42	2.9	0.23	**5.7**	2.4	1.41	11.51	4.19	68.3	**2.4**	21.5	17.5	**7.9**
9.2	0.25	0.7	0.09	**5.9**	2.0	1.55	10.19	3.31	56.5	**5.9**	52.1	8.3	**8.7**
7.1	0.63	2.4	-0.01	**9.7**	2.2	2.24	29.09	3.89	44.6	**5.1**	40.9	9.9	**6.5**
6.3	0.18	7.5	-0.02	**5.3**	0.5	1.53	18.06	4.18	65.2	**6.2**	41.9	2.5	**4.6**
5.5	0.84	5.7	-0.02	**1.6**	1.0	0.10	0.88	3.05	94.8	**1.3**	18.1	27.5	**8.2**
7.1	0.53	2.9	-0.02	**5.0**	9.2	0.91	8.94	2.99	60.1	**5.0**	25.5	7.1	**8.1**
7.5	1.17	0.9	-0.16	**7.2**	0.8	1.59	14.40	3.21	45.4	**2.7**	37.5	21.5	**6.4**
2.7	4.54	21.1	-0.01	**6.5**	0.6	1.84	13.64	4.70	65.2	**0.8**	19.9	34.7	**7.3**
6.2	0.26	7.8	0.00	**0.0**	-0.2	-2.17	-35.82	2.81	180.6	**2.2**	37.1	21.8	**0.8**
6.1	0.42	3.1	-0.06	**3.6**	0.3	0.65	8.50	3.40	75.5	**4.6**	31.5	9.0	**4.4**
6.5	0.40	2.9	0.05	**9.1**	10.6	1.61	17.96	3.57	42.4	**5.7**	29.7	4.8	**8.7**
7.4	0.78	3.9	0.13	**5.0**	405.0	0.94	12.48	2.05	37.1	**6.7**	41.6	2.2	**6.9**
7.4	0.00	0.0	0.00	**5.2**	4.0	1.01	9.37	3.77	70.3	**1.6**	16.4	16.9	**7.7**
7.9	0.47	0.6	0.27	**3.7**	1.0	1.04	9.88	2.66	73.4	**5.2**	44.4	10.1	**5.6**
8.4	0.01	0.0	-0.03	**6.0**	7.7	1.21	12.94	2.92	48.8	**5.6**	35.7	7.8	**8.7**
9.4	0.00	0.0	0.00	**5.0**	0.6	1.32	9.13	3.38	58.2	**6.1**	54.3	6.0	**7.4**
9.4	0.16	0.8	0.42	**5.8**	587.0	0.87	13.41	2.15	54.1	**8.0**	68.2	0.0	**5.5**
6.7	0.69	2.2	0.15	**7.4**	3.0	1.58	16.42	3.57	48.3	**2.3**	25.3	18.7	**6.1**
10.0	0.56	0.8	0.00	**4.3**	35.2	0.78	10.75	1.24	53.3	**8.6**	93.5	0.0	**5.7**
4.1	1.71	10.9	0.04	**7.9**	1.3	2.11	17.80	5.19	47.8	**0.9**	24.4	43.8	**7.0**
5.8	0.74	2.4	0.01	**6.2**	156.4	1.36	10.08	2.96	57.2	**4.2**	29.4	11.4	**10.0**
3.2	4.22	17.5	0.04	**3.9**	2.0	0.59	7.02	4.62	82.2	**3.3**	21.5	12.9	**6.6**
9.2	0.00	0.0	-0.01	**3.4**	0.3	0.66	8.91	2.10	65.4	**5.3**	62.4	12.5	**3.7**
1.8	3.48	23.6	0.77	**5.9**	1.5	1.35	15.83	4.23	52.1	**3.9**	19.3	9.7	**5.6**
7.8	0.79	3.2	0.01	**4.5**	3.5	0.95	7.03	3.34	73.1	**5.2**	35.0	6.4	**8.4**
5.6	0.71	3.8	-0.02	**4.8**	4.2	0.93	9.85	3.64	69.4	**3.2**	19.5	13.3	**5.8**
5.0	1.58	10.0	0.00	**6.5**	0.5	1.45	14.00	2.96	49.0	**6.5**	58.8	3.9	**7.7**
6.4	5.03	12.7	0.00	**6.6**	3.1	1.20	8.37	2.67	28.5	**3.2**	73.0	53.0	**8.9**
6.7	0.00	5.7	-0.02	**1.4**	0.1	0.06	0.56	2.14	96.7	**3.4**	50.7	22.3	**5.1**
9.4	0.19	0.6	0.17	**4.0**	0.8	0.80	6.08	2.73	66.1	**2.6**	44.9	29.1	**7.5**
5.7	1.64	7.7	0.17	**4.6**	0.4	1.13	8.05	2.96	74.6	**5.4**	21.3	0.0	**7.2**
7.8	0.15	1.0	0.01	**5.4**	20.7	1.20	10.63	3.41	60.8	**4.2**	24.5	9.6	**8.8**
4.0	0.71	5.2	-0.03	**5.9**	1.4	2.00	22.42	2.90	55.8	**0.8**	16.1	28.2	**4.7**
3.8	1.61	11.5	0.00	**8.5**	5.1	1.99	20.58	3.76	33.2	**4.3**	16.2	5.4	**9.3**
9.2	0.00	0.0	0.00	**5.9**	1.4	1.40	8.99	3.12	44.2	**1.9**	27.8	23.4	**8.3**
5.0	1.00	13.2	-0.01	**10.0**	1.4	2.27	10.58	4.53	45.0	**6.6**	61.7	6.6	**9.2**
7.8	0.74	1.3	-0.06	**5.9**	4.0	2.48	21.26	3.17	57.2	**2.9**	47.3	21.6	**7.4**
8.6	0.00	0.0	0.03	**7.2**	2.4	1.60	13.35	3.89	48.4	**3.1**	18.8	13.8	**7.8**
7.4	0.77	3.7	0.01	**4.3**	4.7	0.86	9.54	2.59	61.6	**3.8**	24.7	13.2	**7.7**
10.0	0.03	0.3	0.00	**2.4**	0.9	0.28	1.45	1.85	82.9	**4.7**	39.1	11.2	**8.0**
5.4	1.24	8.0	0.05	**4.2**	7.5	0.87	11.37	3.94	73.4	**4.1**	22.4	7.4	**6.4**
5.8	1.06	5.0	0.00	**4.2**	1.3	1.05	11.54	3.06	67.0	**3.7**	37.7	15.8	**5.7**
8.8	0.10	0.5	0.05	**4.7**	1.5	0.92	9.93	3.29	71.6	**5.1**	41.7	10.1	**6.1**
9.2	0.00	0.0	0.00	**6.1**	0.6	1.42	21.67	3.19	55.9	**4.4**	48.1	14.2	**5.8**
5.8	0.65	2.8	0.03	**5.4**	5.2	1.15	11.17	3.33	63.5	**3.9**	29.5	12.0	**7.5**
8.7	0.04	0.2	0.00	**5.1**	6.2	1.22	14.01	3.73	66.3	**5.5**	34.5	6.8	**7.1**
5.8	1.15	6.9	-0.01	**7.1**	11.6	1.52	15.74	3.17	55.0	**4.5**	25.1	10.1	**8.5**
5.9	1.27	4.8	1.02	**5.7**	1.1	1.39	11.14	2.61	55.2	**4.0**	15.0	8.8	**7.8**
4.1	1.95	8.0	0.00	**5.2**	1.2	1.29	15.07	3.60	64.8	**1.7**	18.7	20.5	**6.6**

Name	City	State	Rating	2020 Rating	2019 Rating	Total Assets ($Mil)	One Year Asset Growth	Asset Mix (As a % of Total Assets) Commercial Loans	Consumer Loans	Mortgage Loans	Securities	Capitalization Index	Leverage Ratio	Risk-Based Capital Ratio
South Georgia Bank	Glennville	GA	A	A	A	201.5	13.40	4.4	3.0	12.5	26.9	9.9	10.9	20.0
South Georgia Banking Co.	Tifton	GA	B+	B+	A-	563.5	13.48	5.8	1.4	8.9	18.2	9.2	10.4	17.7
▲ South Lafourche Bank & Trust Co.	Larose	LA	C	C-	C-	145.5	-4.02	18.0	4.0	34.4	8.1	10.0	11.2	0.0
South Louisiana Bank	Houma	LA	A-	A-	A-	629.2	6.71	23.6	1.3	6.4	10.4	10.0	12.0	0.0
South Ottumwa Savings Bank	Ottumwa	IA	B+	B+	A-	571.0	2.18	6.4	1.3	15.4	42.6	8.5	10.0	17.6
▲ South Shore Bank	South Weymouth	MA	B-	C+	C+	1995.6	8.96	14.0	0.3	19.1	17.9	6.6	8.6	14.8
▲ South State Bank, N.A.	Winter Haven	FL	B+	B	B+	40262.7	6.74	8.5	2.2	10.7	13.8	6.7	8.7	13.7
South Story Bank & Trust	Slater	IA	B-	B	B	318.6	7.60	10.6	0.5	18.1	4.6	8.3	9.8	14.7
SouthEast Bank	Farragut	TN	B	B	B	2197.3	17.90	5.0	54.5	4.8	0.0	6.7	8.7	13.0
Southeast First National Bank	Summerville	GA	C+	C+	C	75.8	48.65	3.3	1.7	11.1	34.7	8.4	9.9	0.0
Southeastern Bank	Darien	GA	A	A	A	586.9	15.43	6.5	1.5	14.5	26.9	8.3	9.9	0.0
Southern Bancorp Bank	Arkadelphia	AR	B	B	B-	1963.6	20.27	10.7	1.8	15.9	21.1	6.7	8.7	14.0
▼ Southern Bank	Waynesboro	GA	C-	C	B-	123.9	46.74	3.8	7.2	23.4	19.0	10.0	11.7	0.0
Southern Bank	Poplar Bluff	MO	A-	A-	B+	2687.5	6.28	10.5	1.4	17.6	7.7	8.8	10.4	14.0
Southern Bank and Trust Co.	Mount Olive	NC	B+	B+	A-	4139.6	19.62	8.5	0.7	11.8	32.5	6.6	8.6	13.5
Southern Bank of Tennessee	Mount Juliet	TN	B	B	B+	363.1	12.32	7.0	1.3	19.3	10.2	10.0	11.2	15.7
Southern First Bank	Greenville	SC	A-	B+	B+	2650.6	6.77	8.5	1.1	30.9	3.4	9.3	10.7	14.4
Southern Heritage Bank	Jonesville	LA	B+	B+	A-	363.2	8.56	9.7	3.6	27.3	29.8	8.5	10.0	0.0
Southern Hills Community Bank	Leesburg	OH	C	C	C	177.7	6.10	3.7	3.1	33.3	20.0	10.0	13.9	23.3
Southern Illinois Bank	Johnston City	IL	B+	B+	B+	157.6	20.74	6.3	1.1	10.3	29.4	9.6	10.7	17.4
▲ Southern Independent Bank	Opp	AL	A-	B+	B+	303.8	5.55	12.6	1.9	12.7	37.6	9.5	10.7	0.0
▲ Southern Michigan Bank & Trust	Coldwater	MI	B+	B	B	1118.2	22.72	12.3	0.3	8.7	23.2	7.5	9.3	14.0
Southern States Bank	Anniston	AL	B	B-	B-	1513.4	16.77	13.7	0.6	5.4	8.3	6.3	9.5	12.0
SouthernTrust Bank	Marion	IL	B-	B-	C	235.9	275.61	23.7	1.9	17.4	8.2	6.6	10.7	0.0
SouthPoint Bank	Birmingham	AL	C+	C+	B-	633.7	18.43	24.5	0.4	12.0	13.2	3.0	9.7	0.0
▲ Southside Bank	Tyler	TX	A	A-	A-	7176.5	-2.03	6.2	1.2	9.5	40.0	10.0	11.9	19.1
▲ SouthStar Bank, S.S.B.	Moulton	TX	A-	B+	A-	1062.7	2.64	4.3	0.3	19.3	10.3	9.1	10.4	14.7
SouthTrust Bank, N.A.	George West	TX	C+	C+	B-	512.1	9.82	9.8	0.8	12.9	15.4	6.8	8.8	17.6
Southwest Bank	Odessa	TX	B	B	B+	580.0	-1.42	33.4	0.4	5.8	11.3	6.7	8.7	0.0
Southwest Bank of Weatherford	Weatherford	OK	B+	B+	B+	81.3	5.07	5.3	4.5	12.4	16.2	10.0	12.0	22.6
Southwest Capital Bank	Albuquerque	NM	C-	C-	C	414.9	5.59	7.5	0.1	2.9	31.4	8.2	9.8	0.0
Southwest Missouri Bank	Carthage	MO	B	B	B	1024.2	15.29	6.4	5.9	15.9	45.5	5.8	7.8	16.4
▼ Southwest National Bank	Wichita	KS	C-	C+	B-	526.7	-2.59	10.1	35.6	6.0	8.2	3.4	8.8	0.0
▲ Southwestern National Bank	Houston	TX	B	B-	B+	799.2	11.11	9.9	0.0	2.9	1.6	10.0	12.3	16.8
Southwind Bank	Natoma	KS	B+	B+	B	155.2	10.98	7.5	3.2	10.6	50.2	8.8	10.2	0.0
Spectra Bank	Fort Worth	TX	D+	D+	C	100.0	18.00	11.6	0.5	1.5	7.2	3.4	5.4	13.2
▼ Spencer County Bank	Santa Claus	IN	C+	B-	B	129.9	10.35	5.4	5.5	24.6	27.0	10.0	11.1	0.0
Spencer Savings Bank, S&L Assn.	Elmwood Park	NJ	C+	C+	B-	3453.3	7.37	1.3	0.1	17.4	10.5	9.2	10.5	16.7
▲ Spirit of Texas Bank, SSB	Conroe	TX	A-	B+	B+	3082.4	4.13	16.4	0.3	11.5	14.1	8.9	10.5	14.1
SpiritBank	Tulsa	OK	B-	B-	C	712.6	3.56	21.0	1.8	12.7	4.7	7.9	10.1	13.3
Spiro State Bank	Spiro	OK	D+	D+	C+	61.3	4.62	3.6	2.9	6.5	47.9	8.9	10.3	0.0
Spratt Savings Bank	Chester	SC	C+	C+	C+	147.2	3.31	4.0	0.4	11.3	40.1	10.0	20.1	0.0
Spring Bank	Bronx	NY	B-	B	B+	354.7	3.87	37.5	0.4	7.8	7.9	6.0	10.8	0.0
▲ Spring Bank	Brookfield	WI	B+	B	B-	370.6	5.82	17.8	0.0	10.6	6.0	8.2	11.4	0.0
Spring Hill State Bank	Longview	TX	B+	B+	B+	223.8	7.51	7.1	5.8	42.1	2.4	10.0	12.4	25.9
Spring Valley Bank	Wyoming	OH	A	A	A-	92.8	3.84	0.3	0.1	37.9	0.0	10.0	35.8	44.7
Spring Valley City Bank	Spring Valley	IL	B+	B+	B+	230.0	10.40	13.6	2.1	14.4	33.7	10.0	13.0	24.5
▲ Springfield First Community Bank	Springfield	MO	A-	B+	B+	850.1	13.92	16.4	0.5	8.5	9.4	7.1	10.5	12.6
Springfield State Bank	Springfield	KY	B+	B+	A-	378.5	8.38	3.9	2.0	22.9	43.7	10.0	14.6	0.0
Springfield State Bank	Springfield	NE	B-	B	B+	76.3	15.01	8.3	2.1	5.2	33.4	7.0	9.0	0.0
▲ Springs Valley Bank & Trust Co.	Jasper	IN	B+	B-	B-	497.5	0.67	6.8	2.4	18.8	13.0	10.0	11.1	15.2
Spur Security Bank	Spur	TX	D+	C-	C+	55.1	14.63	2.0	2.4	0.5	65.9	8.7	10.1	33.4
Square Financial Services, Inc.	Salt Lake City	UT	B+			125.4	na	30.8	0.0	0.0	0.0	10.0	60.8	115.7
SSB Bank	Pittsburgh	PA	D+	D+	C	245.2	1.16	24.2	1.4	27.7	1.8	6.2	8.3	12.7
SSB Community Bank	Strasburg	OH	C+	C+	C+	143.0	22.43	11.1	1.1	30.8	0.0	5.0	7.6	11.0
St. Ansgar State Bank	Saint Ansgar	IA	A-	B+	A-	145.0	9.75	9.2	1.3	8.5	23.6	8.7	10.1	0.0
St. Charles Bank & Trust Co., N.A.	Saint Charles	IL	B	B-	B	1855.6	5.68	28.5	18.6	3.8	8.2	5.8	9.1	11.6
St. Clair County State Bank	Osceola	MO	A	A	A	173.5	12.83	8.5	3.5	13.7	11.8	10.0	13.0	0.0
St. Landry Bank and Trust Co.	Opelousas	LA	C-	C	C+	348.9	1.87	3.6	0.4	2.4	67.0	5.5	7.5	29.8
▲ Stafford Savings Bank	Stafford Springs	CT	A+	A-	A-	375.8	19.37	0.0	0.3	16.0	5.8	10.0	44.7	31.0

Asset Quality Index	Adjusted Non-Performing Loans as a % of Total Loans	Adjusted Non-Performing Loans as a % of Capital	Net Charge-Offs Avg Loans	Profitability Index	Net Income ($Mil)	Return on Assets (R.O.A.)	Return on Equity (R.O.E.)	Net Interest Spread	Overhead Efficiency Ratio	Liquidity Index	Liquidity Ratio	Hot Money Ratio	Stability Index
8.8	0.00	0.1	0.49	**8.7**	1.9	1.89	16.55	4.08	53.6	**2.4**	34.8	24.4	**8.8**
8.0	0.15	0.6	0.00	**4.7**	2.7	0.97	7.95	3.28	67.9	**5.1**	40.9	9.9	**8.3**
4.9	1.92	10.7	-0.13	**3.1**	0.9	1.24	11.33	3.41	72.2	**1.9**	23.1	21.3	**4.2**
7.3	0.83	3.4	-0.16	**6.0**	3.5	1.12	9.24	3.15	64.4	**3.7**	38.4	16.0	**8.9**
7.8	0.28	1.2	0.01	**5.4**	3.7	1.33	10.39	3.17	57.1	**4.5**	44.1	13.0	**9.0**
7.5	0.49	2.8	0.00	**4.4**	9.4	0.95	10.48	3.01	62.7	**5.8**	32.9	5.5	**7.4**
7.1	0.35	1.4	0.02	**6.1**	266.4	1.37	10.90	2.99	68.6	**5.3**	28.0	5.0	**9.3**
6.9	0.16	1.0	0.06	**3.4**	1.0	0.63	5.06	3.74	72.9	**2.0**	21.2	12.1	**6.6**
4.2	0.44	4.4	0.01	**4.9**	9.9	0.93	10.96	3.34	62.6	**0.7**	9.8	22.3	**6.9**
9.6	0.14	0.4	0.02	**3.3**	0.3	0.79	7.51	2.58	66.8	**6.3**	62.8	6.7	**4.8**
8.9	0.28	1.0	-1.10	**7.1**	4.1	1.48	14.34	3.27	59.5	**6.1**	40.2	3.0	**8.1**
5.2	1.99	7.4	0.03	**4.9**	9.0	1.01	9.42	3.20	64.3	**3.8**	16.7	9.2	**8.5**
6.5	0.41	2.2	0.14	**1.7**	0.2	0.30	3.00	4.19	84.0	**1.4**	26.0	29.7	**4.5**
7.6	0.41	2.3	0.02	**8.7**	25.6	1.91	18.70	3.76	50.3	**2.5**	7.0	14.6	**9.5**
8.0	0.35	2.5	-0.01	**7.2**	31.5	1.61	18.86	3.06	59.4	**5.9**	29.6	3.9	**8.1**
8.6	0.22	1.2	0.00	**4.2**	1.7	0.97	8.17	3.37	72.0	**2.2**	30.0	22.5	**7.0**
7.8	0.50	2.9	0.00	**7.4**	21.4	1.69	16.16	3.63	52.9	**4.4**	10.4	5.9	**8.5**
5.9	0.75	4.6	0.05	**6.3**	2.6	1.43	13.91	4.00	66.2	**3.3**	26.9	14.4	**7.4**
6.2	2.71	7.5	-0.03	**2.1**	0.2	0.24	1.70	3.66	92.9	**3.9**	40.6	15.9	**6.5**
6.1	0.92	3.3	0.09	**5.2**	0.8	1.00	9.20	3.78	61.0	**5.2**	33.9	6.1	**6.6**
9.0	0.21	0.8	0.04	**7.1**	2.7	1.79	17.11	2.90	39.6	**3.3**	52.9	25.0	**6.7**
8.0	0.24	1.2	-0.01	**5.5**	6.4	1.20	12.43	3.26	60.4	**5.3**	32.7	8.8	**8.9**
6.7	0.28	1.5	0.00	**6.2**	10.0	1.40	12.79	3.91	54.3	**2.6**	20.9	15.0	**9.1**
4.3	0.86	7.0	0.00	**7.7**	1.7	1.56	16.16	4.52	51.3	**1.7**	18.0	23.0	**5.0**
6.1	0.02	5.8	0.05	**7.7**	4.6	1.54	18.59	4.39	62.7	**0.8**	16.3	34.8	**7.1**
8.0	0.18	0.5	0.01	**7.2**	61.0	1.77	11.71	3.29	50.2	**4.6**	24.7	8.4	**10.0**
7.2	0.52	3.3	-0.01	**6.5**	7.6	1.43	13.89	4.37	61.1	**1.4**	14.6	26.5	**9.2**
8.1	0.37	1.6	-0.01	**3.3**	1.3	0.51	5.35	4.18	85.2	**4.4**	40.4	13.4	**6.0**
6.3	0.12	3.3	-0.15	**7.5**	5.2	1.85	21.46	4.20	64.9	**4.4**	26.8	8.2	**7.0**
5.2	2.28	9.7	0.34	**5.6**	0.5	1.15	9.26	4.24	64.2	**4.7**	48.4	12.8	**7.9**
2.5	6.47	24.2	-0.01	**2.5**	1.8	0.90	9.70	3.09	73.3	**5.7**	47.8	6.3	**3.9**
7.0	0.98	4.4	0.10	**4.3**	4.5	0.91	11.33	3.16	71.0	**5.7**	39.9	8.4	**6.6**
0.6	1.39	27.2	0.48	**5.3**	3.1	1.16	12.81	4.14	65.3	**1.7**	14.6	18.5	**7.0**
7.3	0.00	0.0	-0.12	**6.9**	8.3	2.13	18.34	4.65	45.9	**0.9**	16.0	30.4	**7.3**
7.3	0.63	2.5	-0.07	**6.2**	1.0	1.32	11.85	3.86	53.3	**5.0**	41.8	10.7	**6.8**
5.3	0.00	10.4	-3.03	**3.0**	0.7	1.59	29.06	2.66	100.4	**3.2**	62.0	32.4	**1.6**
5.2	1.88	8.8	1.58	**2.6**	0.2	0.26	2.28	2.50	84.3	**3.5**	44.0	18.7	**6.5**
4.9	1.35	8.0	0.11	**3.0**	10.4	0.61	5.78	2.55	72.0	**3.1**	20.2	14.8	**8.3**
7.2	0.34	1.9	0.16	**7.2**	24.3	1.55	12.86	4.18	49.7	**2.0**	13.1	19.2	**9.5**
3.3	1.53	8.5	-0.29	**5.1**	4.0	1.10	10.46	4.15	69.4	**0.6**	10.7	33.2	**6.7**
9.2	0.05	1.3	-0.02	**1.8**	0.1	0.29	2.44	3.04	93.8	**6.6**	70.1	6.1	**6.3**
10.0	0.92	1.2	0.00	**2.5**	0.2	0.33	1.59	2.07	83.4	**4.9**	84.7	18.6	**7.6**
3.8	1.66	14.0	0.00	**5.5**	1.5	0.88	10.47	3.28	63.7	**0.9**	20.0	23.0	**5.3**
5.3	0.57	3.6	0.00	**7.3**	2.5	1.39	12.14	3.51	43.7	**1.3**	21.5	30.0	**7.6**
6.1	0.43	5.3	0.02	**5.5**	1.1	1.02	8.18	3.54	62.9	**2.2**	29.0	20.3	**7.6**
8.1	1.67	3.2	0.06	**10.0**	1.8	3.88	10.64	5.31	33.0	**2.0**	41.4	36.6	**9.8**
8.2	0.56	2.3	0.23	**4.6**	1.1	1.04	7.49	2.99	56.5	**4.2**	37.0	13.2	**7.9**
5.8	0.05	0.1	0.00	**7.9**	6.0	1.47	9.06	3.49	48.0	**3.0**	11.9	13.5	**9.0**
9.2	0.22	0.8	0.05	**5.5**	2.3	1.26	8.81	3.34	51.8	**2.7**	39.9	24.2	**8.1**
4.7	2.12	8.0	2.13	**3.8**	0.2	0.59	6.16	2.30	67.7	**6.7**	48.9	0.8	**5.3**
6.1	1.54	6.2	-0.33	**6.6**	4.1	1.67	14.62	4.09	59.9	**2.9**	20.3	12.7	**7.0**
9.8	0.00	0.0	0.00	**1.1**	0.1	0.17	1.61	1.55	116.4	**3.3**	75.7	33.3	**4.5**
9.2	0.00	0.0	0.00	**10.0**	4.4	16.08	14.18	8.31	71.5	**7.4**	117.7	9.1	**7.0**
1.9	3.05	25.6	0.23	**2.3**	0.4	0.35	4.42	2.42	82.2	**0.7**	15.0	32.7	**4.3**
4.6	1.10	8.7	0.00	**5.7**	0.9	1.34	17.72	3.78	66.6	**2.1**	14.4	18.5	**5.4**
8.8	0.00	0.1	-0.01	**5.8**	1.1	1.46	14.37	3.41	51.2	**5.7**	41.3	5.5	**6.5**
5.1	0.57	3.3	0.05	**5.5**	13.1	1.43	13.06	2.64	59.1	**1.7**	16.4	11.3	**7.6**
8.5	0.01	1.4	0.03	**7.8**	1.2	1.47	11.31	3.58	49.5	**3.4**	26.5	13.5	**8.5**
6.1	9.50	10.8	-0.88	**0.2**	-0.6	-0.34	-4.39	0.98	127.7	**6.2**	51.7	6.2	**3.3**
10.0	0.44	0.2	0.00	**10.0**	13.6	7.89	18.54	1.79	73.1	**7.8**	135.4	8.0	**9.6**

Name	City	State	Rating	2020 Rating	2019 Rating	Total Assets ($Mil)	One Year Asset Growth	Comm-ercial Loans	Cons-umer Loans	Mort-gage Loans	Secur-ities	Capital-ization Index	Lever-age Ratio	Risk-Based Capital Ratio
								Asset Mix (As a % of Total Assets)						
▼ Standard Bank	Monroeville	PA	**B-**	B	B	1084.3	2.19	4.6	0.0	33.1	17.5	**10.0**	11.5	17.9
Standing Stone Bank	Lancaster	OH	**B-**	C+	C+	111.4	4.37	13.6	13.2	18.4	23.2	**6.6**	8.7	16.7
Stanton State Bank	Stanton	NE	**C+**	C+	C+	56.9	10.39	11.2	3.9	14.8	20.0	**7.1**	9.0	18.5
Star Bank	Maple Lake	MN	**C-**	C-	C	357.0	10.05	10.1	2.0	7.2	10.3	**6.5**	8.5	13.0
STAR Financial Bank	Fort Wayne	IN	**B+**	B+	B+	2854.2	14.92	18.6	0.9	9.3	26.9	**6.7**	8.7	14.3
Starion Bank	Bismarck	ND	**B+**	B+	B+	1599.8	2.99	11.6	1.6	5.4	35.6	**8.9**	10.3	16.9
State Bank	Spencer	IA	**C+**	C+	C+	84.5	14.08	8.4	2.7	14.3	14.5	**6.1**	8.1	15.9
State Bank	Freeport	IL	**B**	B	B+	319.5	6.39	13.4	0.2	2.1	30.4	**8.3**	9.9	0.0
▼ State Bank	Waterloo	IL	**C+**	B-	C	296.1	33.34	4.7	1.0	9.1	27.7	**5.9**	7.9	11.9
▲ State Bank	Wonder Lake	IL	**C**	C-	C	284.1	11.29	13.0	0.7	15.5	15.6	**6.4**	8.4	18.1
State Bank	Brownsburg	IN	**B+**	B+	B+	623.3	4.25	10.5	0.7	6.9	16.2	**7.5**	9.4	13.2
▲ State Bank	Green River	WY	**D**	D-	D-	35.9	22.53	6.2	1.2	7.4	0.0	**10.0**	21.1	0.0
▲ State Bank & Trust	Winfield	AL	**B**	B-	B-	296.1	6.98	4.0	6.5	14.8	59.5	**8.4**	9.9	0.0
State Bank & Trust Co.	Nevada	IA	**B+**	B+	A-	216.3	17.78	8.5	0.4	9.0	32.8	**6.3**	8.3	0.0
State Bank & Trust Co.	Golden Meadow	LA	**B-**	B-	C+	129.5	2.72	22.6	4.4	14.5	14.9	**10.0**	11.0	18.9
State Bank & Trust of Kenmare	Kenmare	ND	**B-**	B-	B-	148.4	7.68	10.7	1.9	6.8	41.6	**7.7**	9.5	18.0
State Bank Financial	La Crosse	WI	**B-**	B-	B	440.2	-0.11	9.2	0.5	4.0	26.9	**6.8**	8.8	16.2
State Bank Northwest	Spokane Valley	WA	**A-**	A-	B-	216.2	15.01	17.1	0.2	8.3	2.1	**7.5**	9.3	16.2
State Bank of Arcadia	Arcadia	WI	**B-**	B-	B	212.5	7.64	4.1	1.0	16.3	31.1	**8.1**	9.8	27.3
State Bank of Bellingham	Bellingham	MN	**B-**	B-	C	54.6	9.89	9.7	0.3	0.0	26.5	**10.0**	11.6	16.7
State Bank of Bement	Bement	IL	**C**	C+	B-	140.1	27.63	16.1	7.8	6.6	15.4	**8.8**	10.2	18.0
▲ State Bank of Bern	Bern	KS	**A**	A-	A-	110.7	12.24	2.7	1.6	0.7	47.0	**10.0**	15.4	0.0
▼ State Bank of Bottineau	Bottineau	ND	**C+**	B-	B-	85.4	9.58	7.7	2.4	17.5	1.3	**2.9**	9.0	0.0
State Bank of Brooks	Corning	IA	**C-**	C-	C	22.1	16.02	1.1	4.0	9.3	52.6	**8.4**	9.9	41.7
▼ State Bank of Burrton	Burrton	KS	**C-**	C	C	12.5	10.03	5.7	3.1	13.9	27.1	**8.2**	9.8	0.0
▼ State Bank of Bussey	Bussey	IA	**C-**	C	C	49.8	8.66	5.0	1.2	26.2	1.5	**5.7**	7.7	17.1
State Bank of Canton	Canton	KS	**B**	B	B	34.1	7.49	10.7	1.5	0.8	27.2	**10.0**	19.7	45.8
State Bank of Cerro Gordo	Cerro Gordo	IL	**C**	C+	B-	36.1	1.14	14.6	4.1	8.2	47.1	**8.0**	9.7	23.4
State Bank of Chandler	Chandler	MN	**B**	B	B-	56.8	15.11	10.5	3.2	2.4	16.1	**10.0**	11.1	17.7
State Bank of Cherry	Cherry	IL	**B+**	B+	A-	114.4	12.29	10.2	4.6	13.6	12.8	**8.4**	11.4	0.0
State Bank of Chilton	Chilton	WI	**B-**	B-	B	377.2	7.72	11.8	0.9	9.8	4.8	**8.9**	10.3	15.2
State Bank of Cochran	Cochran	GA	**B+**	B+	B+	252.1	10.20	5.2	6.3	16.0	12.5	**10.0**	13.5	28.2
State Bank of Cold Spring	Cold Spring	MN	**C+**	C+	C+	79.7	6.89	3.8	4.3	17.4	34.0	**6.4**	8.5	0.0
State Bank of Cross Plains	Cross Plains	WI	**B+**	B	C+	1611.6	6.83	11.7	0.8	10.7	14.5	**7.3**	9.5	12.7
State Bank of Danvers	Benson	MN	**A-**	A-	B+	62.6	14.80	2.4	1.1	0.1	41.9	**8.9**	10.3	26.6
State Bank of Davis	Davis	IL	**B+**	B+	B+	169.6	-4.52	14.2	0.9	1.6	45.7	**10.0**	11.1	0.0
State Bank of De Kalb	De Kalb	TX	**B**	B+	B+	397.6	21.00	15.2	1.2	10.9	0.0	**7.1**	9.1	0.0
State Bank of Downs	Downs	KS	**B+**	B	C+	120.7	15.84	15.3	1.6	24.6	3.8	**10.0**	11.6	0.0
State Bank of Eagle Butte	Eagle Butte	SD	**C**	C-	C-	91.8	25.11	4.6	13.2	2.0	44.9	**5.6**	7.6	16.5
State Bank of Easton	Easton	MN	**C-**	C-	C-	21.4	-1.26	17.1	6.1	3.2	9.1	**10.0**	13.1	0.0
State Bank of Fairmont	Fairmont	MN	**C-**	C-	C+	127.2	7.97	24.1	5.9	2.9	17.8	**9.1**	10.4	15.2
State Bank of Graymont	Graymont	IL	**B**	B	B	264.0	16.41	4.3	1.3	5.7	34.9	**9.2**	10.4	0.0
State Bank of Herscher	Herscher	IL	**B**	B+	B+	161.7	6.65	12.7	0.1	4.2	44.5	**10.0**	11.9	0.0
State Bank of India (California)	Los Angeles	CA	**B+**	B+	B+	883.9	-2.62	17.8	0.0	0.0	12.7	**10.0**	17.2	22.2
State Bank of Industry	Industry	IL	**B+**	B	B	56.9	-1.44	7.7	3.7	12.4	21.7	**10.0**	14.7	25.8
State Bank of Jeffers	Jeffers	MN	**B-**	B	B	37.9	30.79	7.5	4.2	0.8	17.3	**7.3**	10.6	12.7
State Bank of Lake Park	Lake Park	MN	**C**	C+	C+	45.1	7.87	5.9	6.1	21.3	29.7	**7.0**	9.0	0.0
State Bank of Lakota	Lakota	ND	**B-**	B-	B-	69.1	23.75	4.7	2.9	8.9	14.5	**6.3**	8.4	15.2
State Bank of Lismore	Lismore	MN	**C+**	C+	C	64.0	1.16	9.0	2.6	0.0	0.0	**7.8**	9.5	14.4
State Bank of Medora	Medora	IN	**B-**	B-	B	101.2	9.14	3.6	4.1	15.6	58.4	**10.0**	14.0	0.0
State Bank of Missouri	Concordia	MO	**B**	B	B	128.6	16.38	4.9	1.4	18.6	34.1	**6.1**	8.1	19.1
State Bank of Nauvoo	Nauvoo	IL	**D-**	D-	D	34.5	11.44	7.1	7.5	28.6	1.6	**6.3**	8.3	16.6
▲ State Bank of New Richland	New Richland	MN	**B-**	C+	C	109.6	-6.68	4.2	1.3	14.7	9.3	**7.2**	10.0	12.7
State Bank of Newburg	Newburg	WI	**A-**	A-	A-	218.7	7.34	2.5	0.6	28.7	9.0	**10.0**	18.2	0.0
State Bank of Odell	Odell	NE	**D**	D	C	33.9	12.91	1.8	6.7	2.1	5.3	**5.9**	7.9	19.2
State Bank of Reeseville	Reeseville	WI	**B-**	B-	B-	119.4	9.94	7.6	1.7	8.8	49.9	**8.5**	10.0	20.0
State Bank of Saunemin	Saunemin	IL	**B**	B	B-	40.6	8.90	10.6	1.7	2.6	37.6	**10.0**	11.5	0.0
State Bank of Schaller	Schaller	IA	**B+**	B+	B	40.3	9.83	5.0	1.9	1.7	62.4	**9.0**	10.4	23.0
▲ State Bank of Scotia	Scotia	NE	**B+**	B	B-	56.6	12.43	4.8	1.8	5.9	15.0	**10.0**	20.2	28.1
State Bank of Southern Utah	Cedar City	UT	**A**	A	A	1954.0	26.77	7.0	1.9	3.4	27.1	**9.0**	10.3	0.0

Asset Quality Index	Adjusted Non-Performing Loans as a % of Total Loans	Adjusted Non-Performing Loans as a % of Capital	Net Charge-Offs Avg Loans	Profitability Index	Net Income ($Mil)	Return on Assets (R.O.A.)	Return on Equity (R.O.E.)	Net Interest Spread	Overhead Efficiency Ratio	Liquidity Index	Liquidity Ratio	Hot Money Ratio	Stability Index
7.1	0.53	2.4	0.00	**2.6**	0.4	0.39	2.85	2.25	79.1	**4.5**	28.9	11.8	**7.1**
7.8	0.02	0.3	0.07	**3.8**	0.5	0.78	9.05	3.43	75.5	**2.7**	32.5	5.0	**5.0**
5.8	1.81	4.3	0.00	**4.4**	0.3	1.19	13.32	3.54	65.9	**6.1**	41.5	3.0	**4.5**
2.2	3.77	25.7	-0.18	**6.1**	2.6	1.46	17.12	4.19	65.0	**4.3**	25.8	8.4	**6.0**
7.6	0.69	2.4	0.58	**4.9**	13.8	1.01	10.94	3.09	65.9	**6.7**	40.1	2.0	**7.7**
7.1	0.88	4.3	0.06	**5.2**	10.2	1.26	11.57	3.11	60.3	**4.2**	25.9	12.0	**10.0**
8.7	0.03	0.2	0.02	**5.8**	0.6	1.57	19.32	4.19	63.5	**4.0**	43.6	15.8	**3.7**
7.1	0.45	2.0	0.09	**6.5**	1.9	1.21	11.97	3.00	46.8	**3.3**	28.6	14.8	**6.3**
6.7	1.00	3.5	-0.13	**2.8**	0.6	0.44	5.11	2.62	82.4	**2.9**	46.1	25.7	**4.3**
3.8	2.32	12.1	-0.19	**2.2**	0.2	0.17	1.73	3.57	82.0	**5.5**	38.6	6.3	**5.3**
6.1	0.67	3.2	-0.02	**5.0**	3.2	1.04	10.78	3.46	65.5	**4.8**	24.7	4.0	**6.7**
9.4	0.00	0.0	0.00	**0.0**	-0.3	-1.76	-15.39	2.00	185.8	**4.9**	65.9	15.0	**4.7**
5.5	2.03	5.7	0.00	**4.6**	2.0	1.36	12.36	3.02	59.6	**2.4**	48.9	42.6	**6.5**
6.8	0.32	1.8	-0.46	**8.3**	1.8	1.74	20.40	2.69	44.7	**5.9**	39.3	2.6	**6.9**
4.0	1.47	8.7	1.48	**4.2**	0.6	0.85	7.39	4.58	59.0	**3.4**	22.3	13.0	**5.5**
3.7	5.87	14.6	-0.10	**3.5**	0.6	0.79	7.54	2.39	70.6	**4.0**	48.0	16.9	**5.8**
7.6	1.08	1.8	0.00	**4.0**	1.7	0.76	8.16	2.35	72.6	**5.7**	37.9	4.2	**6.0**
8.3	0.47	0.0	0.00	**6.5**	1.5	1.45	14.75	4.38	69.8	**4.6**	33.5	9.7	**6.8**
7.4	0.67	1.8	0.01	**3.7**	0.9	0.81	7.54	2.30	65.1	**6.4**	57.1	6.3	**7.2**
5.6	2.14	8.9	0.00	**2.7**	0.0	0.06	0.55	2.40	97.3	**2.2**	48.4	29.3	**8.3**
5.2	0.36	2.9	0.26	**2.9**	0.3	0.47	4.60	2.99	81.9	**5.7**	46.6	7.3	**5.1**
8.8	0.92	1.2	-0.12	**7.5**	0.9	1.64	10.56	3.66	41.0	**4.6**	63.5	17.2	**8.0**
7.2	0.00	0.0	-0.05	**5.9**	0.6	1.43	15.57	4.62	66.3	**2.7**	8.0	14.4	**6.8**
6.3	1.82	7.2	0.00	**1.9**	0.0	0.07	0.72	1.88	93.4	**7.1**	88.3	4.3	**3.9**
9.4	0.00	0.0	-0.27	**1.5**	0.0	0.02	0.16	3.28	99.5	**4.1**	31.1	9.8	**3.4**
6.9	1.02	4.5	0.08	**3.4**	0.3	1.00	13.04	4.49	75.4	**5.3**	46.9	9.9	**2.4**
9.1	0.00	0.0	0.02	**3.1**	0.0	0.22	1.11	2.77	89.5	**7.6**	82.7	1.5	**6.9**
8.5	0.00	0.0	0.00	**2.2**	0.0	0.18	1.61	2.00	91.0	**6.3**	58.6	5.8	**5.2**
7.1	0.10	0.6	0.01	**5.7**	0.3	1.08	9.73	3.67	59.7	**4.3**	30.2	10.5	**6.9**
6.1	0.44	2.8	0.00	**6.2**	0.8	1.48	12.13	3.79	53.9	**2.0**	20.5	19.5	**8.4**
3.3	1.84	10.0	0.03	**7.0**	3.1	1.67	16.28	3.69	51.7	**4.0**	21.5	9.3	**7.4**
4.1	4.45	14.5	-0.16	**8.6**	2.4	1.93	14.26	3.19	55.2	**5.1**	40.7	9.4	**9.7**
4.7	3.56	14.1	-0.01	**4.8**	0.5	1.25	14.83	3.06	62.1	**6.2**	58.7	6.0	**4.9**
5.8	1.15	7.2	0.02	**5.4**	9.9	1.21	11.70	3.45	57.4	**5.1**	22.0	4.0	**9.1**
9.3	0.00	0.0	0.01	**7.0**	0.5	1.44	12.89	2.96	49.5	**6.3**	61.6	5.8	**7.7**
5.8	2.82	7.8	-0.02	**5.7**	1.0	1.14	9.85	2.65	50.9	**3.4**	45.5	19.2	**7.7**
4.6	1.37	8.9	-0.02	**6.7**	2.8	1.51	16.00	3.13	60.0	**4.7**	39.7	11.3	**7.3**
5.2	3.89	11.0	0.00	**7.2**	1.1	1.75	15.39	3.76	54.3	**4.9**	29.4	6.0	**7.5**
5.2	1.18	4.8	2.39	**2.8**	0.2	0.54	6.43	3.42	73.4	**1.8**	23.9	22.1	**2.6**
5.0	1.69	8.2	-0.03	**4.4**	0.1	1.16	8.89	3.16	71.7	**2.2**	31.6	19.3	**4.3**
1.9	3.25	18.1	-0.03	**5.0**	0.9	1.37	13.12	3.44	55.5	**3.0**	27.5	15.6	**6.4**
4.2	2.69	11.5	-0.02	**4.3**	1.2	0.94	8.79	2.51	55.1	**5.3**	41.1	8.2	**6.5**
5.4	3.20	9.8	0.00	**4.4**	0.6	0.66	5.56	2.95	73.6	**5.2**	37.0	7.3	**7.7**
2.6	3.74	15.6	0.00	**4.8**	4.8	1.08	6.35	3.00	60.3	**0.9**	20.7	34.5	**8.8**
8.5	0.00	0.8	0.08	**6.5**	0.5	1.78	12.05	3.26	50.5	**1.9**	35.2	31.4	**7.5**
8.7	0.00	0.0	0.04	**5.1**	0.3	1.37	13.15	2.23	58.1	**6.5**	70.7	6.5	**4.7**
4.9	1.39	7.0	0.00	**4.5**	0.2	0.91	10.04	3.94	74.7	**5.0**	50.6	11.9	**4.3**
6.4	0.70	4.5	0.02	**4.9**	0.4	1.22	14.61	2.73	59.4	**3.9**	41.3	15.6	**4.5**
7.0	0.00	0.0	0.00	**3.5**	0.3	0.80	8.43	3.21	77.3	**1.6**	22.8	25.9	**6.1**
9.7	1.15	2.5	-0.02	**3.8**	0.4	0.87	6.23	2.57	63.0	**3.9**	67.1	24.2	**7.8**
6.8	0.69	3.7	0.00	**5.0**	0.7	1.11	13.56	2.85	65.1	**5.6**	38.7	5.3	**5.6**
1.9	3.29	27.3	-0.22	**1.5**	0.0	0.04	0.39	3.44	92.1	**5.2**	37.5	7.3	**2.3**
4.0	0.70	5.4	0.19	**10.0**	1.6	2.84	27.93	4.53	38.4	**1.5**	9.8	12.9	**7.6**
6.6	2.98	6.5	-0.01	**7.9**	1.6	1.50	8.28	3.11	45.2	**1.8**	31.6	24.4	**9.2**
5.9	0.53	3.6	0.30	**2.5**	0.1	0.58	7.43	2.09	83.5	**7.1**	73.9	3.1	**1.9**
9.1	0.18	0.6	0.15	**3.4**	0.5	0.76	7.35	3.18	71.9	**2.8**	48.1	12.0	**6.4**
8.8	0.00	0.0	0.00	**4.7**	0.3	1.32	11.28	2.36	59.8	**5.4**	53.6	10.4	**7.1**
5.3	1.38	12.4	-0.02	**6.0**	0.3	1.21	11.26	3.10	57.3	**5.6**	48.9	8.1	**7.6**
7.3	0.25	0.9	-0.03	**8.0**	0.6	2.04	10.08	4.38	33.9	**1.9**	34.3	30.3	**7.0**
7.4	0.90	3.4	0.00	**8.6**	14.7	1.61	14.94	3.51	46.0	**6.1**	47.7	8.5	**10.0**

Name	City	State	Rating	2020 Rating	2019 Rating	Total Assets ($Mil)	One Year Asset Growth	Asset Mix (As a % of Total Assets) Commercial Loans	Consumer Loans	Mortgage Loans	Securities	Capitalization Index	Leverage Ratio	Risk-Based Capital Ratio
State Bank of Southwest Missouri	Springfield	MO	C+	B-	B-	185.0	13.56	12.8	3.8	29.5	10.1	3.7	5.7	11.2
State Bank of St. Jacob	Saint Jacob	IL	B+	B+	B+	78.2	13.13	5.5	11.5	11.6	35.9	10.0	14.4	0.0
▲ State Bank of Table Rock	Table Rock	NE	B-	C	C-	121.4	15.23	10.0	2.5	10.5	2.2	5.9	8.2	0.0
▲ State Bank of Taunton	Taunton	MN	B	C+	B-	55.4	9.04	4.9	0.5	3.9	13.8	10.0	11.0	15.3
State Bank of Texas	Dallas	TX	B+	A-	B+	1118.5	22.18	2.6	0.3	3.7	4.0	10.0	15.8	0.0
State Bank of the Lakes, N.A.	Antioch	IL	B	B-	B	1627.8	6.66	23.5	21.7	3.5	8.5	5.6	8.3	11.4
▲ State Bank of Toulon	Toulon	IL	B	B-	B-	293.6	12.88	14.8	1.0	4.8	32.3	7.6	9.5	13.0
State Bank of Wapello	Wapello	IA	B	B	B	42.9	5.05	2.9	3.8	8.4	18.1	10.0	13.0	30.9
▲ State Bank of Wheaton	Wheaton	MN	A	A-	A-	96.3	8.66	4.1	0.5	0.6	0.5	10.0	22.8	34.8
State Bank of Whittington	Benton	IL	B	B	B	163.2	13.77	5.5	12.6	13.5	33.9	7.8	9.5	16.8
State Central Bank	Bonaparte	IA	D+	D+	D+	48.9	11.62	14.4	1.8	10.0	22.5	6.5	8.5	0.0
State Nebraska Bank & Trust	Wayne	NE	A-	A-	A-	196.4	16.48	14.5	1.9	9.9	28.7	10.0	11.9	21.3
State Savings Bank	Creston	IA	B	B-	B-	148.3	11.48	12.2	5.4	19.8	0.0	6.5	9.4	0.0
▲ State Savings Bank	Rake	IA	C-	D	D-	76.6	-1.76	13.0	0.7	0.2	4.3	10.0	12.0	0.0
State Savings Bank	West Des Moines	IA	B+	B+	B+	197.6	16.61	13.0	0.5	11.4	0.3	8.1	9.7	15.8
State Savings Bank	Frankfort	MI	D+	D+	D+	334.6	23.24	9.4	0.4	15.6	9.2	6.2	8.3	0.0
State Street B&T Co. of California, N.A.	Boston	MA	U	U	U	6.3	-62.08	0.0	0.0	0.0	0.0	10.0	84.1	306.7
State Street Bank and Trust Co.	Quincy	IL	B	B	B	283.2	8.45	4.7	22.8	21.0	23.9	6.0	8.4	11.8
State Street Bank and Trust Co.	Boston	MA	B	B+	B+	322958.0	16.67	1.4	0.0	0.0	35.0	4.0	6.0	15.8
State Street Bank and Trust Co., N.A.	New York	NY	U	U	U	33.4	-14.19	0.0	0.0	0.0	0.0	10.0	101.	270.1
Stearns Bank N.A.	Saint Cloud	MN	A-	A-	A-	2166.0	-5.90	42.9	0.1	0.7	0.9	10.0	20.6	32.5
Stearns Bank of Holdingford, N.A.	Holdingford	MN	A-	A-	A-	102.3	8.23	64.9	0.4	0.6	3.1	10.0	18.2	26.3
Stearns Bank of Upsala, N.A.	Upsala	MN	A-	A-	A-	82.9	12.56	64.7	0.2	0.5	4.0	10.0	16.6	24.5
Sterling Bank	Poplar Bluff	MO	A-	A-	A-	1391.6	7.33	29.1	0.6	3.3	3.2	9.5	10.6	15.2
Sterling Bank	Barron	WI	B+	B+	B	308.0	10.18	7.1	0.3	8.8	25.9	6.5	8.5	16.4
Sterling Bank and Trust, FSB	Southfield	MI	B+	B+	A	3403.0	-8.96	0.0	0.0	58.1	5.6	9.3	10.5	24.5
Sterling Federal Bank, FSB	Sterling	IL	D+	D+	D+	483.1	0.84	4.9	0.2	22.8	39.8	6.1	8.1	16.0
Sterling National Bank	Pearl River	NY	B	B	B	29057.0	-5.54	17.8	0.0	5.0	15.4	10.0	12.1	15.2
Sterling State Bank	Austin	MN	C+	C+	C+	463.6	3.30	16.5	1.0	7.7	37.5	5.4	7.4	17.5
Stifel Bank	Clayton	MO	B	B	B	4584.6	62.07	25.4	16.4	0.4	49.1	5.1	7.1	20.9
Stifel Bank and Trust	Saint Louis	MO	B+	B+	B+	15498.0	9.13	28.0	6.9	29.9	25.8	5.1	7.1	11.8
Stifel Trust Co. Delaware, N.A.	Wilmington	DE	U	U	U	334.9	13.52	0.0	0.0	0.0	74.2	7.9	9.6	44.3
Stifel Trust Co. N.A.	Saint Louis	MO	U	U	U	870.0	7.41	0.0	0.0	0.0	88.4	6.1	8.1	34.1
Stillman BancCorp, N.A.	Stillman Valley	IL	B+	B+	B	593.2	13.90	5.3	0.9	4.8	60.8	6.3	8.3	23.4
Stock Exchange Bank	Caldwell	KS	C+	C+	C+	67.9	11.07	5.0	3.0	38.3	15.6	6.7	8.7	0.0
Stock Growers Bank	Forman	ND	A-	A-	A-	293.4	45.47	3.6	1.7	1.1	51.1	8.2	9.8	0.0
▼ Stock Yards Bank & Trust Co.	Louisville	KY	A-	A	A	6074.4	40.27	19.6	1.3	10.8	16.6	6.9	10.0	12.5
Stockgrowers State Bank	Ashland	KS	B+	B+	B+	152.3	7.86	9.0	0.7	1.1	39.6	10.0	12.9	0.0
Stockman Bank of Montana	Miles City	MT	A-	A-	A-	5178.4	14.51	5.7	0.6	5.4	36.1	7.3	9.2	15.2
Stockmans Bank	Altus	OK	B-	B-	C+	389.9	21.11	3.1	0.4	6.5	1.1	4.8	8.7	0.0
Stockmens Bank	Colorado Springs	CO	B+	B+	B	423.0	2.23	11.4	0.6	15.2	3.5	6.6	9.7	0.0
Stockmens Bank	Cascade	MT	C+	B-	B-	42.3	9.77	5.2	1.9	4.4	7.8	9.6	10.7	36.1
Stockmens National Bank in Cotulla	Cotulla	TX	B-	B	B+	98.5	-5.86	2.3	3.6	2.0	50.2	10.0	11.4	0.0
Stone Bank	Mountain View	AR	B	B-	C+	565.2	0.92	12.2	0.6	7.4	12.2	9.3	10.5	14.9
StonehamBank	Stoneham	MA	C	C	C+	687.6	2.40	11.7	0.1	30.2	16.4	8.3	9.9	16.7
Stoughton Co-operative Bank	Stoughton	MA	C	C	C-	126.3	3.47	0.7	2.0	62.1	14.1	6.8	8.8	0.0
Strasburg State Bank	Strasburg	ND	C	C	C+	89.4	16.61	4.1	0.3	0.0	17.2	4.2	7.2	10.6
Streator Home Savings Bank	Streator	IL	C+	C+	B-	172.4	4.12	0.0	1.0	21.0	68.0	10.0	25.0	0.0
Stride Bank, N.A.	Enid	OK	C-	C-	C+	1893.3	56.51	12.3	27.0	3.9	3.7	4.4	6.4	16.8
▲ Studio Bank	Nashville	TN	C	D+		470.2	40.53	14.7	0.7	13.3	14.7	10.0	11.5	15.1
Sturdy Savings Bank	Cape May Court Hou	NJ	C	C	C+	1135.7	18.01	5.2	0.0	20.7	37.9	6.0	8.0	15.4
Sturgis Bank & Trust Co.	Sturgis	MI	B-	B-	B-	706.6	14.45	8.0	1.0	29.7	13.1	6.6	8.6	0.0
Success Bank	Bloomfield	IA	B+	B+	B-	231.4	5.42	7.8	1.4	15.2	8.1	8.0	11.1	0.0
Sugar River Bank	Newport	NH	B-	B-	B-	362.7	8.22	5.2	1.5	41.6	23.1	10.0	13.6	0.0
▲ Sullivan Bank	Sullivan	MO	B+	B-	B-	664.2	13.56	8.3	2.4	31.8	5.9	8.1	9.7	13.5
Sumitomo Mitsui Trust Bank (U.S.A.) Ltd.	Hoboken	NJ	C+	B-	B+	3735.7	-5.57	0.0	0.0	0.0	0.0	6.9	9.0	24.3
Summit Bank	Oakland	CA	A-	A-	A-	338.5	12.61	11.7	0.1	1.4	0.1	10.0	11.0	18.8
Summit Bank	Eugene	OR	C	C+	B-	811.3	12.66	26.9	0.1	1.1	3.5	2.8	8.3	0.0
Summit Community Bank, Inc.	Moorefield	WV	B+	B+	B+	3271.3	14.40	9.2	1.0	14.4	13.7	7.5	9.8	12.9
Summit National Bank	Hulett	WY	B-	B-	C	88.3	3.49	5.2	2.0	2.3	29.9	8.8	10.2	19.9

Asset Quality Index	Adjusted Non-Performing Loans as a % of Total Loans	Adjusted Non-Performing Loans as a % of Capital	Net Charge-Offs Avg Loans	Profitability Index	Net Income ($Mil)	Return on Assets (R.O.A.)	Return on Equity (R.O.E.)	Net Interest Spread	Overhead Efficiency Ratio	Liquidity Index	Liquidity Ratio	Hot Money Ratio	Stability Index
7.7	0.00	0.0	0.00	**5.9**	1.4	1.61	27.43	2.76	59.6	**4.7**	27.2	6.5	**3.2**
5.3	0.55	7.3	-0.04	**5.8**	0.6	1.52	10.15	2.97	41.0	**6.0**	61.7	8.4	**7.8**
6.6	0.34	2.4	0.00	**5.3**	0.9	1.57	19.37	4.50	62.7	**4.0**	28.7	11.1	**4.7**
8.4	0.00	0.0	-0.06	**6.4**	0.7	2.58	25.58	3.63	58.0	**3.7**	20.6	11.1	**5.9**
5.0	1.23	6.1	-0.02	**10.0**	19.5	3.74	22.98	5.48	25.2	**0.9**	18.5	40.9	**10.0**
6.0	0.32	1.6	0.10	**4.9**	8.0	1.00	8.69	2.43	58.9	**2.7**	16.8	8.4	**8.2**
5.8	0.68	3.2	-0.01	**5.6**	2.2	1.57	14.23	3.07	53.9	**3.4**	27.6	13.8	**5.9**
9.3	0.00	0.0	-0.03	**3.9**	0.2	0.78	5.74	2.70	68.2	**7.5**	70.0	0.0	**6.7**
7.7	0.00	0.0	0.00	**10.0**	1.5	3.17	13.92	4.00	38.4	**3.9**	46.2	16.7	**9.4**
6.7	0.13	1.4	0.16	**4.8**	0.9	1.11	11.08	3.69	72.1	**6.0**	42.1	4.1	**6.1**
0.3	32.17	49.3	-0.98	**1.7**	0.1	0.36	3.27	2.51	90.8	**7.0**	55.4	0.2	**6.2**
5.3	0.72	10.2	0.00	**6.5**	1.2	1.30	10.75	3.78	54.7	**4.4**	24.0	7.1	**7.7**
6.4	0.04	0.3	-0.29	**8.2**	2.2	2.95	31.98	3.15	38.9	**2.2**	22.5	18.6	**7.7**
1.9	4.03	18.3	1.16	**5.0**	0.5	1.18	10.24	3.00	45.3	**1.4**	33.3	46.0	**5.5**
6.7	0.41	2.7	0.00	**5.7**	1.3	1.41	14.63	3.23	59.8	**4.9**	31.6	6.9	**7.6**
5.5	0.77	4.7	0.00	**3.4**	1.4	0.89	10.61	3.24	73.8	**5.5**	30.6	2.7	**4.6**
10.0	na	0.0	na	**8.9**	0.2	3.26	4.00	0.06	82.5	**4.0**	na	0.0	**5.7**
6.8	0.11	0.8	-0.03	**7.6**	2.7	1.88	21.81	3.63	58.9	**4.7**	28.2	7.0	**6.5**
8.8	0.00	0.0	0.01	**4.3**	1290.0	0.87	9.79	0.80	72.3	**6.7**	55.7	0.1	**8.0**
10.0	na	0.0	na	**9.8**	3.3	17.98	19.42	0.05	59.7	**4.0**	na	0.0	**5.7**
5.3	5.51	7.6	1.36	**10.0**	31.8	2.70	13.13	4.98	47.3	**2.9**	40.2	11.0	**9.2**
7.9	0.88	2.1	0.92	**7.9**	1.3	2.53	14.54	3.70	19.4	**1.7**	36.1	38.3	**7.9**
7.5	1.16	2.6	1.45	**7.2**	1.0	2.41	15.02	3.91	16.9	**1.5**	34.0	39.0	**7.4**
8.1	0.10	0.6	0.01	**8.4**	12.4	1.82	16.12	4.20	42.9	**1.8**	19.2	15.7	**9.8**
9.0	0.22	0.9	0.00	**7.9**	3.0	2.01	24.02	3.68	51.5	**4.6**	47.5	14.1	**6.7**
3.7	3.90	20.5	-0.07	**3.7**	9.4	0.51	5.08	2.68	75.0	**2.2**	29.6	29.9	**7.8**
4.4	3.86	11.5	0.07	**1.0**	0.5	0.22	2.58	2.54	103.2	**3.6**	42.0	17.5	**5.1**
4.8	0.95	3.5	0.26	**6.7**	217.5	1.48	8.82	3.49	44.2	**4.6**	12.5	2.8	**9.3**
8.8	0.05	0.4	-0.06	**3.4**	1.8	0.79	10.02	3.27	77.7	**4.9**	25.3	4.4	**4.7**
7.7	0.00	0.0	0.00	**7.5**	34.9	1.64	24.80	2.32	20.6	**6.3**	29.9	0.6	**6.5**
8.2	0.09	0.8	0.10	**8.3**	112.6	1.50	21.15	2.48	27.8	**5.8**	23.3	0.1	**7.4**
10.0	na	0.0	na	**6.1**	1.6	0.99	10.03	1.13	52.7	**8.6**	109.1	0.0	**7.0**
10.0	na	0.0	na	**6.1**	5.4	1.25	14.47	1.38	48.3	**8.6**	108.3	0.0	**7.0**
9.0	0.18	1.3	-0.05	**6.0**	4.3	1.50	15.30	2.65	58.8	**5.3**	57.4	13.1	**7.0**
8.9	0.00	0.3	-0.16	**6.4**	0.5	1.59	18.54	3.48	55.8	**1.5**	27.3	29.7	**4.5**
8.8	0.00	0.0	0.00	**7.0**	2.6	1.75	15.86	3.56	45.6	**5.2**	41.2	9.2	**7.9**
7.6	0.30	2.0	0.15	**7.0**	29.4	1.19	12.27	3.36	62.9	**4.6**	16.0	4.5	**9.8**
8.7	0.00	0.0	-0.05	**4.0**	0.6	0.82	6.27	2.93	73.1	**1.9**	24.7	21.1	**7.4**
7.6	0.62	3.1	-0.03	**7.5**	42.9	1.71	17.96	2.90	54.0	**5.5**	32.5	6.3	**9.6**
4.4	0.96	9.1	0.00	**6.4**	2.9	1.58	18.06	4.65	64.6	**0.9**	15.5	28.4	**5.0**
7.1	0.51	3.4	0.00	**5.7**	2.5	1.19	11.80	3.86	55.8	**3.9**	15.8	9.3	**6.1**
8.2	0.68	1.8	0.00	**2.9**	0.1	0.48	4.32	2.65	81.5	**5.4**	77.0	13.7	**6.3**
9.6	0.00	0.0	0.01	**3.0**	0.1	0.27	2.54	1.38	83.4	**6.4**	56.6	4.5	**5.5**
4.7	1.83	6.0	0.29	**6.1**	4.2	1.54	14.06	3.40	49.2	**0.8**	18.2	39.2	**6.4**
4.1	2.24	13.7	0.00	**3.2**	1.9	0.57	5.77	2.92	86.7	**3.5**	13.0	11.1	**6.9**
7.7	0.36	2.7	0.00	**2.6**	0.3	0.44	4.88	2.47	81.6	**1.7**	27.2	27.1	**4.7**
9.2	0.00	0.8	0.00	**3.2**	0.2	0.38	5.14	2.12	77.7	**5.0**	56.4	12.5	**3.9**
9.9	1.95	1.5	0.03	**2.2**	0.2	0.26	1.02	1.01	83.1	**5.0**	98.1	19.6	**7.5**
2.9	0.98	17.6	0.16	**4.9**	8.7	1.00	17.52	2.30	63.9	**2.2**	34.4	1.9	**5.1**
8.7	0.00	0.0	0.00	**2.8**	2.0	0.93	8.09	3.19	76.3	**4.6**	30.0	2.4	**4.3**
5.7	1.58	9.6	0.00	**2.8**	2.5	0.46	5.47	3.01	79.4	**6.9**	41.5	1.0	**6.2**
5.9	0.78	3.1	0.09	**4.9**	3.3	0.94	10.71	2.99	65.1	**2.3**	13.9	10.0	**6.6**
7.6	0.51	2.1	-0.28	**7.6**	2.2	1.96	17.93	4.35	53.7	**2.8**	11.9	11.9	**7.6**
7.6	1.27	4.8	0.13	**3.0**	0.9	0.50	3.57	3.35	83.3	**4.6**	35.5	10.5	**7.4**
6.5	0.63	1.8	-0.38	**6.4**	4.1	1.29	13.12	3.69	54.6	**2.7**	9.1	14.7	**7.1**
10.0	0.00	0.0	0.00	**3.0**	5.0	0.25	2.78	0.12	88.3	**8.8**	108.9	0.0	**6.9**
7.5	0.35	0.9	0.00	**5.5**	1.3	0.76	6.76	3.80	62.9	**4.8**	37.7	10.0	**7.4**
6.5	0.07	0.5	0.15	**6.4**	4.9	1.23	15.04	3.99	52.8	**5.3**	23.3	1.4	**5.9**
5.5	0.94	5.8	0.03	**6.7**	22.5	1.40	13.13	3.65	51.0	**3.6**	15.2	10.5	**9.0**
5.8	0.89	5.6	-0.01	**3.7**	0.3	0.74	6.96	3.27	74.9	**5.4**	35.3	5.3	**6.3**

Name	City	State	Rating	2020 Rating	2019 Rating	Total Assets ($Mil)	One Year Asset Growth	Asset Mix (As a % of Total Assets) Comm-ercial Loans	Cons-umer Loans	Mort-gage Loans	Secur-ities	Capital-ization Index	Lever-age Ratio	Risk-Based Capital Ratio
Summit State Bank	Santa Rosa	CA	**B**	B	B	901.6	5.99	10.9	0.0	6.6	7.4	**6.3**	8.3	12.3
Sumner Bank & Trust	Gallatin	TN	**B+**	B	B	202.7	7.85	5.1	0.6	19.4	8.4	**8.5**	10.0	15.4
▲ Suncrest Bank	Visalia	CA	**A-**	B+	B+	1372.0	6.64	11.0	0.0	3.7	27.6	**7.7**	9.5	14.8
Sundance State Bank	Sundance	WY	**B**	B	B-	237.0	12.30	13.5	2.6	7.1	34.6	**8.6**	10.1	14.2
Sundown State Bank	Sundown	TX	**B+**	B+	B+	202.7	10.19	17.6	0.1	0.4	8.2	**7.8**	9.5	13.4
Sunflower Bank, N.A.	Denver	CO	**B**	B	C	5549.5	15.30	26.6	0.3	9.2	9.6	**7.1**	9.2	12.6
SunMark Community Bank	Hawkinsville	GA	**A-**	A-	B+	379.0	15.79	12.5	1.4	16.7	5.9	**7.9**	9.6	0.0
▼ Sunnyside Federal S&L Assn. of Irvington	Irvington	NY	**D-**	D+	D+	95.5	-3.42	7.2	3.7	18.7	50.7	**9.5**	10.7	24.1
▼ Sunrise Bank	Orlando	FL	**B-**	B+	A-	361.0	35.65	7.0	0.5	7.8	10.2	**6.5**	8.6	0.0
Sunrise Bank Dakota	Onida	SD	**C+**	C	D+	65.0	15.27	3.8	1.3	3.0	41.5	**9.0**	10.3	24.6
▼ Sunrise Banks, N.A.	Saint Paul	MN	**B**	B+	B	1669.9	14.86	16.8	6.9	8.0	12.1	**6.1**	8.1	14.6
▲ SunSouth Bank	Dothan	AL	**D+**	D	E	124.1	-1.87	25.2	0.9	10.8	50.8	**5.8**	7.8	18.0
Sunstate Bank	Miami	FL	**C+**	C+	B	524.4	1.86	5.7	0.2	20.8	11.5	**7.2**	9.1	15.8
Sunwest Bank	Irvine	CA	**B**	B	B+	2051.4	3.25	30.3	2.1	2.9	3.9	**5.5**	10.5	0.0
Superior National Bank	Hancock	MI	**B+**	B+	A-	1021.8	63.75	9.2	4.8	19.7	25.2	**7.6**	9.4	0.0
Superior Savings Bank	Superior	WI	**B**	B	B	77.5	6.54	2.0	0.8	50.9	0.7	**10.0**	17.6	0.0
Surety Bank	Deland	FL	**B+**	B	B-	182.6	19.88	5.2	0.1	4.0	12.3	**7.2**	9.1	23.3
Surrey Bank & Trust	Mount Airy	NC	**A**	A	A-	461.8	14.45	17.9	0.5	4.6	6.1	**10.0**	11.1	23.9
Susquehanna Community Bank	West Milton	PA	**B+**	B+	B+	513.9	10.98	7.4	2.3	6.8	35.3	**5.5**	9.3	0.0
Susser Bank	Bedford	TX	**B**	B-	B	1320.0	13.83	19.6	0.3	14.2	2.5	**8.0**	9.6	15.5
Sutton Bank	Attica	OH	**A-**	A-	B	1193.7	44.19	7.9	0.4	2.3	11.2	**6.2**	8.2	26.7
▲ Swedish-American State Bank	Courtland	KS	**B+**	B-	C+	49.2	5.20	10.6	2.1	7.2	24.0	**10.0**	11.3	20.4
Sweet Water State Bank	Sweet Water	AL	**C+**	C+	B-	113.9	2.71	14.2	2.9	7.0	16.4	**8.6**	10.1	0.0
▼ Sycamore Bank	Senatobia	MS	**B-**	B	B	309.7	17.42	4.2	2.2	15.8	24.8	**5.9**	7.9	0.0
Synchrony Bank	Draper	UT	**C+**	C+	C	81927.0	-3.91	1.6	85.2	0.0	6.9	**10.0**	16.0	20.6
Synergy Bank	Houma	LA	**B+**	B+	B	744.6	11.84	14.7	2.0	9.4	39.0	**8.6**	10.1	0.0
Synovus Bank	Columbus	GA	**B**	B	B+	54872.5	1.54	17.4	4.7	10.6	17.2	**6.9**	8.9	12.7
Synovus Trust Co., N.A.	Columbus	GA	**U**	U	U	115.5	10.38	0.0	0.0	0.0	17.6	**10.0**	96.2	125.0
▲ Systematic Savings Bank	Springfield	MO	**C-**	D+	D	53.0	32.53	4.3	0.6	44.1	3.0	**10.0**	18.8	0.0
T Bank, N.A.	Dallas	TX	**A-**	A-	B+	552.0	5.29	42.4	0.7	1.0	3.8	**10.0**	12.2	20.3
Table Grove State Bank	Table Grove	IL	**B**	B	B	52.4	8.98	3.2	7.3	1.0	18.4	**9.5**	10.7	0.0
Table Rock Community Bank	Kimberling City	MO	**B**	B	B-	128.6	29.57	3.2	3.7	20.3	13.2	**5.9**	7.9	15.2
Talbot State Bank	Woodland	GA	**D+**	D+	C-	62.7	10.07	0.0	0.3	46.6	14.9	**9.4**	10.6	28.2
Tampa State Bank	Tampa	KS	**C+**	C+	C+	69.2	11.80	11.9	2.4	14.2	41.6	**6.8**	8.9	0.0
Tandem Bank	Tucker	GA	**D**	D		113.6	45.23	21.1	0.1	8.4	2.7	**10.0**	16.2	29.3
Tarboro Savings Bank, SSB	Tarboro	NC	**D+**	D+	C+	58.7	-2.73	0.0	0.1	51.7	0.0	**8.3**	11.6	13.6
Taylor County Bank	Campbellsville	KY	**A**	A	A-	216.5	7.56	11.6	3.5	17.0	19.7	**10.0**	13.6	0.0
▲ Taylorsville Savings Bank, SSB	Taylorsville	NC	**C+**	C	B-	128.6	11.99	1.2	0.7	38.9	12.1	**8.8**	10.2	20.4
TBK Bank, SSB	Dallas	TX	**C+**	C+	B	5997.4	7.13	45.9	0.2	1.7	3.2	**6.0**	10.4	11.8
▲ TC Federal Bank	Thomasville	GA	**B-**	C+	C+	406.2	19.54	7.1	0.3	25.2	6.5	**10.0**	11.3	18.4
TCM Bank, N.A.	Tampa	FL	**B**	B-	B-	258.2	-4.52	26.1	63.1	0.0	1.2	**10.0**	20.9	23.1
TD Bank USA, N.A.	Wilmington	DE	**B**	B-	B-	28622.1	20.61	0.6	27.6	0.0	29.2	**9.6**	10.7	32.7
TD Bank, N.A.	Wilmington	DE	**C+**	C	B-	415513.5	8.22	8.4	7.2	7.2	40.7	**6.2**	8.2	19.0
Tecumseh Federal Bank	Tecumseh	NE	**C+**	B-	B	51.0	3.54	1.4	1.0	33.3	24.9	**10.0**	22.2	0.0
Tejas Bank	Monahans	TX	**A**	A	A-	184.0	-9.17	20.4	2.1	1.7	26.5	**10.0**	11.3	18.4
Templeton Savings Bank	Templeton	IA	**A-**	A-	A-	157.7	15.01	10.3	1.8	11.4	23.3	**10.0**	12.6	0.0
Tempo Bank	Trenton	IL	**C-**	D+	C-	92.9	-8.61	0.0	0.7	62.8	0.0	**10.0**	11.2	25.1
Tennessee State Bank	Pigeon Forge	TN	**A-**	A-	A-	945.4	25.55	4.0	2.0	16.6	19.3	**6.7**	8.7	15.8
Tensas State Bank	Newellton	LA	**B+**	B+	B+	167.0	7.30	8.1	1.3	13.1	30.9	**10.0**	12.8	0.0
Terrabank, N.A.	Miami	FL	**C**	C	C+	602.3	17.96	3.5	0.2	14.0	45.7	**5.1**	7.1	15.5
Terre Haute Savings Bank	Terre Haute	IN	**C**	C	C	466.8	13.69	6.0	1.1	18.0	30.3	**5.6**	7.6	14.2
Territorial Savings Bank	Honolulu	HI	**B+**	B+	B+	2131.8	2.08	0.4	0.0	59.9	28.9	**10.0**	11.6	28.2
Teutopolis State Bank	Teutopolis	IL	**A**	A	A	319.3	16.77	5.5	2.1	7.9	32.6	**10.0**	12.0	24.0
▲ Texan Bank, N.A.	Houston	TX	**C+**	C	C	434.2	5.62	16.0	0.5	4.3	1.7	**6.3**	10.8	0.0
▼ Texana Bank, N.A.	Linden	TX	**C**	B-	C-	235.6	0.64	14.1	1.4	28.6	4.5	**6.3**	8.3	12.1
Texas Advantage Community Bank, N.A.	Alvin	TX	**B**	B	B-	170.4	12.19	25.1	0.9	4.0	5.6	**6.4**	8.4	16.3
Texas Bank	Brownwood	TX	**A**	A	A	688.8	21.68	6.4	0.9	10.1	8.7	**10.0**	11.4	19.3
Texas Bank	Henderson	TX	**B-**	B-	B-	654.5	13.25	8.8	4.4	18.2	23.9	**6.8**	9.5	0.0
Texas Bank and Trust Co.	Longview	TX	**A-**	A-	A-	3502.9	14.03	12.5	1.1	19.0	8.3	**8.8**	10.2	15.3
Texas Bank Financial	Weatherford	TX	**A-**	A-	B+	620.5	22.95	1.0	0.1	67.3	2.9	**10.0**	11.2	19.8

Asset Quality Index	Adjusted Non-Performing Loans as a % of Total Loans	Adjusted Non-Performing Loans as a % of Capital	Net Charge-Offs Avg Loans	Profitability Index	Net Income ($Mil)	Return on Assets (R.O.A.)	Return on Equity (R.O.E.)	Net Interest Spread	Overhead Efficiency Ratio	Liquidity Index	Liquidity Ratio	Hot Money Ratio	Stability Index
6.4	0.34	1.6	0.00	**8.1**	7.2	1.64	18.89	4.20	48.0	**1.6**	14.5	15.0	**6.9**
9.0	0.05	0.3	0.00	**5.8**	1.2	1.21	12.08	3.41	59.6	**4.2**	26.7	9.2	**6.0**
6.7	0.57	2.7	0.00	**6.8**	8.5	1.29	10.15	3.83	51.5	**5.5**	36.1	4.7	**9.6**
4.7	2.21	10.8	0.04	**5.5**	1.5	1.32	12.38	3.41	49.5	**2.7**	31.3	18.4	**6.1**
7.7	0.25	1.7	0.00	**4.8**	0.8	0.80	8.42	3.27	72.1	**2.8**	25.2	16.3	**5.9**
5.3	0.95	6.2	0.16	**4.6**	28.6	1.09	10.58	3.24	76.9	**4.2**	18.2	4.0	**7.9**
6.9	0.55	3.4	-0.08	**6.5**	2.9	1.55	16.34	4.01	60.5	**4.6**	24.8	6.2	**6.7**
5.6	2.33	7.4	0.30	**0.0**	-0.8	-1.61	-15.95	2.38	164.3	**3.3**	54.1	22.8	**4.4**
8.1	0.33	1.8	0.00	**3.7**	1.2	0.74	8.21	3.18	71.6	**5.0**	40.8	10.0	**5.8**
3.2	13.27	22.0	-0.08	**3.0**	0.2	0.56	5.38	2.29	79.2	**4.5**	56.4	13.7	**4.8**
7.4	0.24	2.1	0.05	**5.0**	9.9	1.23	17.49	3.68	79.7	**2.3**	28.8	3.2	**6.8**
8.8	0.02	0.1	-0.14	**1.9**	0.3	0.41	5.36	2.68	89.6	**2.6**	40.0	25.5	**1.6**
6.0	0.99	3.8	-0.02	**4.0**	1.6	0.59	5.50	2.14	76.4	**2.9**	51.8	30.6	**6.8**
6.2	0.27	1.8	-0.03	**8.9**	16.7	1.62	15.70	3.91	49.9	**4.2**	17.7	1.6	**10.0**
6.9	0.83	3.1	-0.04	**7.0**	7.8	1.57	15.87	3.66	66.3	**4.4**	38.5	14.8	**8.5**
7.3	1.94	4.7	0.05	**3.7**	0.2	0.55	3.12	2.58	73.9	**5.4**	37.9	6.2	**7.8**
6.0	1.52	4.6	0.02	**8.7**	2.1	2.37	24.90	3.35	56.2	**5.1**	59.8	14.6	**7.6**
7.6	1.42	5.6	0.01	**7.2**	3.2	1.39	12.21	3.08	51.4	**5.6**	44.7	7.8	**8.8**
8.3	0.30	1.6	0.01	**4.6**	2.7	1.08	10.55	3.32	66.2	**4.5**	20.9	5.9	**7.1**
7.7	0.29	1.0	0.00	**4.3**	5.1	0.78	6.70	3.55	75.8	**3.3**	28.7	17.2	**9.4**
9.6	0.86	1.5	0.00	**9.5**	13.4	2.30	27.77	1.89	49.2	**4.5**	70.9	0.6	**8.0**
8.4	0.00	0.0	-0.05	**9.0**	0.5	2.18	18.64	4.76	54.0	**2.7**	32.7	19.3	**5.7**
4.6	1.37	10.2	-0.05	**3.8**	0.4	0.72	6.96	4.93	84.9	**2.3**	34.8	25.5	**6.1**
6.7	0.78	4.3	-0.02	**3.8**	0.9	0.59	7.19	3.22	78.8	**4.6**	29.1	7.4	**4.9**
3.2	1.32	5.8	3.63	**10.0**	2103.0	4.98	37.94	9.81	38.9	**1.2**	22.0	22.2	**10.0**
5.2	2.17	6.9	0.08	**6.7**	5.0	1.39	13.86	3.40	55.3	**4.2**	44.3	14.9	**7.3**
6.5	0.72	3.7	0.24	**6.2**	382.1	1.40	14.59	3.00	53.0	**3.6**	18.5	5.7	**8.3**
6.6	na	0.0	na	**10.0**	7.3	12.87	13.39	0.45	69.4	**4.0**	na	0.0	**7.0**
9.2	0.35	1.4	0.21	**1.4**	0.0	0.16	0.85	3.28	87.7	**1.0**	27.0	37.8	**5.8**
7.3	0.86	1.8	0.09	**9.7**	6.1	2.31	19.53	4.42	59.7	**0.8**	20.0	42.6	**8.9**
8.0	0.09	0.7	0.00	**4.5**	0.3	0.95	8.24	3.22	77.5	**5.6**	38.5	5.4	**7.2**
8.1	0.30	1.4	0.00	**6.0**	0.7	1.13	14.31	3.63	63.3	**5.8**	38.2	4.0	**4.9**
4.8	3.57	13.3	0.00	**0.2**	0.1	0.19	1.62	3.12	126.2	**2.1**	46.5	36.4	**5.4**
7.5	0.53	3.2	-0.20	**4.5**	0.4	1.28	14.37	2.67	66.2	**2.8**	34.1	18.9	**4.9**
8.6	0.00	0.0	0.00	**0.4**	-0.3	-0.50	-2.89	3.50	106.4	**3.8**	37.3	4.2	**1.9**
8.9	0.03	0.1	0.00	**1.2**	0.1	0.20	1.75	2.91	92.6	**1.2**	29.1	41.6	**2.5**
7.7	0.78	2.9	0.00	**7.9**	1.9	1.82	12.84	3.96	57.6	**4.5**	34.1	10.3	**9.5**
5.1	4.33	17.2	0.31	**3.6**	0.5	0.77	8.63	3.00	81.1	**2.8**	38.7	21.9	**5.2**
3.4	0.47	6.5	1.72	**8.9**	66.9	2.22	16.08	6.33	63.3	**1.4**	10.6	13.1	**9.8**
6.8	1.28	5.9	-0.01	**3.3**	1.3	0.74	6.59	3.46	76.3	**4.6**	32.4	9.0	**6.6**
5.0	0.22	1.9	2.65	**6.5**	2.3	1.79	8.39	7.31	79.6	**0.2**	11.3	99.6	**5.8**
5.7	1.32	3.4	3.05	**6.8**	192.3	1.32	12.81	5.74	85.7	**8.0**	78.7	0.0	**7.4**
6.5	0.79	2.5	0.22	**3.8**	1437.0	0.70	6.24	1.66	64.7	**7.6**	60.4	0.7	**7.8**
9.6	0.37	0.8	0.37	**5.2**	0.5	1.80	8.37	2.87	66.6	**4.5**	60.9	16.0	**7.0**
7.2	0.22	4.0	0.15	**7.4**	1.4	1.57	12.39	3.37	54.0	**5.7**	37.6	4.4	**8.3**
8.3	0.04	0.5	0.00	**6.9**	1.1	1.40	10.16	3.63	48.7	**5.1**	47.1	11.4	**8.0**
8.2	0.52	2.4	0.50	**4.5**	1.5	3.26	30.14	2.19	129.1	**2.6**	34.2	20.4	**4.6**
7.6	0.31	1.8	-0.03	**5.4**	5.9	1.34	14.64	3.27	66.1	**5.4**	35.4	5.4	**6.2**
4.6	2.84	13.9	0.13	**5.1**	1.0	1.23	9.29	3.78	66.8	**2.5**	37.9	25.0	**7.8**
8.5	0.11	0.7	0.01	**3.0**	1.1	0.38	5.10	2.68	83.2	**5.0**	50.8	12.1	**4.5**
5.9	0.75	6.0	0.17	**2.7**	1.0	0.45	5.52	2.53	82.5	**5.2**	52.7	12.4	**4.1**
10.0	0.36	1.8	0.00	**4.5**	9.6	0.91	8.17	2.58	63.9	**4.6**	29.7	11.7	**9.0**
9.0	0.00	0.3	0.03	**8.3**	2.6	1.67	13.45	2.67	36.9	**6.3**	53.9	5.7	**8.0**
4.2	0.84	4.5	-0.01	**4.4**	2.2	1.09	9.90	4.30	70.1	**1.4**	21.6	28.1	**5.8**
8.4	0.07	0.8	-0.01	**2.5**	-0.6	-0.51	-5.94	4.39	106.4	**1.5**	9.9	18.0	**4.4**
8.5	0.00	0.0	0.00	**4.4**	0.7	0.82	9.88	3.73	68.6	**4.1**	40.6	13.4	**5.1**
8.8	0.05	0.2	-0.01	**8.7**	5.5	1.71	14.54	3.63	59.2	**5.3**	42.9	9.3	**9.8**
5.8	0.51	3.8	0.11	**6.3**	6.0	1.85	19.81	4.30	60.3	**1.8**	21.9	20.7	**6.3**
7.5	0.54	3.0	0.00	**6.6**	22.5	1.31	12.09	3.05	55.5	**4.7**	26.6	9.6	**9.8**
7.8	0.34	2.5	0.00	**10.0**	9.4	3.16	29.56	5.37	52.3	**0.8**	16.6	42.2	**8.8**

Name	City	State	Rating	2020 Rating	2019 Rating	Total Assets ($Mil)	One Year Asset Growth	Asset Mix (As a % of Total Assets) Commercial Loans	Consumer Loans	Mortgage Loans	Securities	Capitalization Index	Leverage Ratio	Risk-Based Capital Ratio
Texas Brand Bank	Dallas	TX	B+	B+	B+	327.9	14.88	24.3	0.1	5.2	0.8	8.4	9.9	14.5
▲ Texas Capital Bank, N.A.	Dallas	TX	B-	C+	B-	35217.1	-3.66	20.9	0.3	1.2	10.7	5.9	7.9	12.9
Texas Champion Bank	Corpus Christi	TX	C	C	C-	370.5	-9.88	28.5	1.0	4.5	2.1	7.3	12.1	0.0
Texas Citizens Bank, N.A.	Pasadena	TX	D+	D	C-	537.6	-7.19	20.1	1.4	3.7	1.4	9.3	10.6	16.0
Texas Community Bank	Laredo	TX	B+	A-	A	1783.8	16.04	11.3	1.0	9.4	8.3	8.7	10.2	21.0
Texas Exchange Bank, SSB	Crowley	TX	A	A	A	2636.7	90.08	26.5	0.0	0.0	26.7	10.0	12.4	21.2
Texas Financial Bank	Eden	TX	A-	A-	A-	118.3	2.57	2.7	0.9	0.5	34.7	8.0	9.7	0.0
Texas First Bank	Texas City	TX	A-	A-	A-	1924.0	15.67	12.0	0.4	7.1	39.8	6.5	8.5	0.0
Texas Gulf Bank, N.A.	Houston	TX	B+	B+	B-	666.5	-2.06	11.3	0.6	18.3	28.1	9.9	11.0	0.0
Texas Heritage Bank	Boerne	TX	B	B	B	199.0	9.74	8.7	0.9	14.3	3.2	5.8	7.8	13.9
▲ Texas Heritage National Bank	Daingerfield	TX	B-	C+	B	287.6	41.03	20.7	2.9	19.2	3.8	7.9	10.4	13.3
Texas National Bank	Mercedes	TX	B	B	B	725.4	72.48	35.6	0.6	6.9	12.5	7.0	9.0	18.1
Texas National Bank	Sweetwater	TX	C+	C+	C+	175.7	11.03	7.3	1.3	5.0	59.6	6.6	8.6	22.9
Texas National Bank of Jacksonville	Jacksonville	TX	B	B	B	684.5	14.01	11.4	3.4	23.8	3.4	7.9	9.6	14.6
Texas Partners Bank	San Antonio	TX	B	B-	B	1744.6	67.86	23.2	0.5	8.6	12.3	6.4	8.5	12.8
Texas Regional Bank	Harlingen	TX	B-	B-	B-	1708.0	29.74	10.3	0.7	6.4	33.4	6.8	8.8	15.6
Texas Republic Bank, N.A.	Frisco	TX	A-	A-	A-	399.7	10.76	12.1	0.2	19.7	0.0	9.7	10.8	17.2
Texas Security Bank	Dallas	TX	B+	B+	A-	1014.9	4.66	23.7	0.1	7.6	13.8	7.1	9.1	15.2
Texas State Bank	San Angelo	TX	A-	A-	A	371.5	10.70	8.2	0.7	12.7	33.1	9.0	10.3	19.8
▼ Texico State Bank	Texico	IL	E-	E+	D-	10.1	8.88	12.1	1.1	17.5	0.0	3.6	5.6	19.5
TexStar National Bank	Universal City	TX	B	B	B+	433.9	20.19	8.2	0.4	4.0	8.6	6.7	8.7	17.1
▲ Thayer County Bank	Hebron	NE	B-	C+	C	81.4	7.90	12.6	2.0	9.5	28.8	9.2	10.4	0.0
▲ The Adirondack Trust Co.	Saratoga Springs	NY	B	B-	B	1623.6	15.78	9.6	0.8	11.0	21.1	6.5	8.5	17.6
The Alden State Bank	Sterling	KS	D+	D+	C	21.3	-1.36	8.9	6.6	14.6	25.1	10.0	11.7	22.1
The American Bank	Wagoner	OK	C-	C-	C+	37.0	14.40	0.7	3.1	1.8	38.9	10.0	17.5	0.0
The American National Bank of Mount Plea	Mount Pleasant	TX	A-	A-	A-	137.8	12.18	6.9	6.9	11.0	48.6	8.8	10.2	0.0
The American National Bank of Texas	Terrell	TX	B+	B+	B+	4929.6	24.75	7.5	0.5	7.7	44.2	6.3	8.3	15.4
The Andover Bank	Andover	OH	B-	B-	B-	566.5	16.04	2.2	0.6	27.0	47.5	5.5	7.5	19.5
The Antwerp Exchange Bank Co.	Antwerp	OH	C+	C+	B-	141.5	8.64	6.4	5.2	21.0	26.1	6.9	9.0	13.9
The Apple Creek Banking Co.	Apple Creek	OH	B-	B-	B-	188.0	16.27	19.3	0.3	20.4	11.1	5.7	7.7	12.2
The Atlanta National Bank	Atlanta	IL	B-	B-	B-	69.7	5.14	4.9	2.7	9.4	61.3	10.0	11.8	28.5
The Baldwin State Bank	Baldwin City	KS	B-	B-	C+	97.5	5.74	5.5	2.7	28.6	22.2	7.9	9.6	0.0
The Baltic State Bank	Baltic	OH	C-	C	C+	90.3	6.27	12.7	2.9	34.0	9.1	5.0	7.1	11.0
The Bancorp Bank	Wilmington	DE	B	B	B	6562.7	5.44	7.9	24.8	0.5	16.9	6.7	8.7	16.1
The Bank	Oberlin	KS	C-	D+	D+	397.7	3.52	4.0	0.4	1.3	22.2	10.0	12.7	26.7
The Bank	Jennings	LA	B+	B+	A-	359.7	26.38	13.9	10.4	22.8	13.3	8.0	9.7	0.0
The Bank and Trust, SSB	Del Rio	TX	B+	B+	B+	546.3	13.53	5.3	2.1	27.9	24.7	5.7	7.7	17.6
The Bank of Advance	Advance	MO	A	A	A-	410.1	18.39	8.4	5.8	27.3	14.0	10.0	11.6	0.0
The Bank of Baker	Baker	MT	C+	C	B-	178.1	3.79	9.6	0.7	2.7	15.0	8.4	9.9	0.0
The Bank of Beaver City	Beaver	OK	C+	B-	B	147.9	7.77	12.4	2.3	11.1	46.1	9.0	10.3	0.0
The Bank of Bennington	Bennington	VT	C+	C+	B	529.7	11.87	5.4	0.1	48.8	18.0	8.3	9.9	0.0
The Bank of Brodhead	Brodhead	WI	A-	A-	B+	243.5	5.77	7.8	1.7	13.0	23.2	10.0	12.2	0.0
The Bank of Canton	Canton	MA	B+	B	B	987.0	38.58	3.5	0.1	15.8	5.9	9.8	10.9	19.3
The Bank of Carbondale	Carbondale	IL	B	B	B+	272.2	4.80	8.1	1.9	13.1	34.6	10.0	12.7	0.0
The Bank of Castile	Castile	NY	B	B	B	1903.1	7.90	11.2	0.5	13.4	23.8	6.0	8.0	12.8
The Bank of Charlotte County	Phenix	VA	B+	A-	A-	172.5	13.19	3.9	2.4	28.0	19.3	10.0	12.9	19.1
▼ The Bank of Clarendon	Manning	SC	B+	A-	A	357.4	16.04	7.5	2.4	9.1	24.8	10.0	11.6	0.0
The Bank of Clovis	Clovis	NM	A-	A-	A-	275.1	8.90	10.3	2.7	12.8	38.7	9.7	10.8	0.0
The Bank of Commerce	Ammon	ID	A	A	A	1696.2	10.70	13.9	0.5	1.5	20.2	10.0	13.3	18.7
▼ The Bank of Commerce	White Castle	LA	C	B-	B-	67.0	6.42	7.9	2.2	9.4	18.7	10.0	11.2	20.0
The Bank of Commerce and Trust Co.	Wellington	KS	B-	B-	B-	98.1	8.56	5.6	5.5	14.8	45.9	6.2	8.2	17.7
The Bank of Deerfield	Deerfield	WI	A	A	A-	174.7	2.00	7.0	1.0	26.8	4.9	10.0	12.2	16.7
The Bank of Denton	Denton	KS	C	C	C	22.5	22.52	0.8	7.0	25.2	30.6	10.0	15.5	0.0
The Bank of Denver	Denver	CO	B-	B-	C+	276.2	7.62	0.5	2.1	7.2	24.3	6.9	8.9	15.0
The Bank of Edison	Edison	GA	D+	C-	C	65.7	16.89	21.1	4.7	11.1	28.1	6.1	8.2	17.9
The Bank of Elk River	Elk River	MN	B+	B+	B+	609.8	11.59	19.0	1.7	6.8	32.4	5.7	7.7	16.2
The Bank of Fayette County	Piperton	TN	B	B-	B-	720.5	-1.46	6.3	7.0	29.6	8.5	7.4	9.8	0.0
The Bank of Glen Burnie	Glen Burnie	MD	C	C	C	432.7	3.46	5.0	15.2	16.5	36.4	6.6	8.6	14.3
The Bank of Grain Valley	Kansas City	MO	A	A	A-	108.0	2.93	15.3	0.9	19.8	12.2	10.0	19.9	0.0
The Bank of Greene County	Catskill	NY	B+	B+	B+	2196.7	31.26	6.5	0.2	17.6	41.4	6.0	8.0	16.9

Asset Quality Index	Adjusted Non-Performing Loans as a % of Total Loans	Adjusted Non-Performing Loans as a % of Capital	Net Charge-Offs Avg Loans	Profitability Index	Net Income ($Mil)	Return on Assets (R.O.A.)	Return on Equity (R.O.E.)	Net Interest Spread	Overhead Efficiency Ratio	Liquidity Index	Liquidity Ratio	Hot Money Ratio	Stability Index
7.2	0.00	0.0	0.00	**6.4**	2.3	1.45	14.66	4.02	55.0	**1.2**	16.8	29.8	**7.3**
7.1	0.36	2.9	0.08	**4.2**	153.0	0.78	10.37	2.09	61.4	**5.2**	33.6	1.8	**6.3**
3.1	1.80	11.3	-0.01	**4.0**	1.7	0.90	8.33	4.07	75.5	**4.3**	13.2	6.6	**5.7**
0.6	5.48	22.4	0.13	**3.9**	2.4	0.87	8.58	3.66	83.0	**3.8**	23.9	10.7	**5.4**
8.8	0.03	0.3	-0.01	**4.7**	6.0	0.71	6.68	2.65	64.2	**3.8**	42.2	19.1	**9.2**
9.3	0.00	0.0	0.00	**8.7**	30.1	2.93	24.61	2.30	17.5	**2.4**	46.6	11.2	**9.2**
9.4	0.11	0.2	0.01	**4.4**	0.4	0.67	7.14	2.57	74.4	**5.3**	46.9	10.3	**6.4**
6.9	1.00	3.9	0.00	**6.8**	14.9	1.63	17.11	3.65	56.1	**5.9**	39.0	7.1	**9.2**
5.4	0.96	4.6	0.00	**6.1**	5.1	1.51	12.83	3.78	62.8	**4.2**	22.2	8.5	**8.5**
7.5	0.31	2.4	-0.21	**6.9**	1.7	1.79	23.04	4.04	64.6	**4.4**	34.0	10.9	**5.6**
6.8	0.12	1.5	0.00	**5.4**	2.3	1.61	17.06	4.11	58.7	**1.6**	7.6	21.2	**5.8**
7.0	0.21	2.1	0.01	**8.1**	5.5	2.17	28.73	5.99	53.3	**1.9**	21.6	20.4	**4.9**
9.4	0.00	0.0	-0.03	**2.8**	0.3	0.41	3.90	2.57	83.3	**6.0**	50.0	6.7	**5.3**
6.0	0.40	3.3	0.04	**5.2**	3.5	1.06	11.03	3.86	61.9	**0.8**	14.8	37.2	**6.6**
8.1	0.01	0.1	0.09	**6.3**	13.3	1.60	17.30	3.41	51.1	**5.7**	30.8	5.4	**5.8**
7.8	0.28	0.8	0.01	**4.6**	10.6	1.33	14.80	3.53	73.0	**3.8**	49.9	22.8	**7.8**
8.6	0.00	0.0	0.00	**7.8**	2.6	1.40	12.54	4.10	59.1	**2.7**	29.2	17.9	**7.8**
8.5	0.11	0.6	0.00	**7.4**	7.8	1.72	19.82	3.42	49.5	**2.2**	36.0	24.2	**7.0**
9.2	0.00	0.0	0.00	**5.7**	2.4	1.32	12.23	3.03	63.1	**6.2**	43.9	3.6	**7.8**
3.7	0.69	20.7	0.97	**0.7**	-0.2	-2.90	-46.26	2.37	204.5	**7.0**	64.2	0.0	**0.3**
8.7	0.00	0.0	0.00	**4.0**	1.8	0.88	9.73	3.01	62.3	**2.0**	40.3	24.5	**5.7**
4.8	3.72	8.9	-0.21	**4.4**	0.4	1.03	9.82	3.10	61.0	**3.3**	17.4	12.7	**6.3**
8.5	0.24	1.3	-0.02	**5.0**	7.8	1.00	10.91	2.74	68.5	**5.8**	38.0	7.2	**7.6**
8.7	0.00	0.0	0.00	**1.3**	0.0	-0.07	-0.65	2.71	102.6	**3.2**	41.4	16.9	**5.2**
10.0	0.00	0.0	0.05	**1.1**	-0.1	-0.28	-1.56	2.00	113.0	**7.2**	96.9	6.5	**6.2**
8.6	0.00	0.0	-0.12	**6.3**	1.1	1.61	14.29	3.57	58.7	**2.9**	45.4	24.9	**7.7**
8.5	0.35	1.1	0.03	**4.7**	21.7	0.97	10.50	3.17	67.3	**5.5**	28.0	5.4	**7.5**
8.1	0.54	2.2	0.02	**4.4**	2.9	1.06	12.25	2.84	63.6	**5.5**	41.9	7.1	**5.7**
4.7	0.94	8.6	0.05	**3.2**	0.4	0.61	6.74	3.33	78.5	**4.6**	29.3	8.2	**5.5**
8.7	0.02	0.1	0.00	**4.8**	0.9	0.98	13.28	4.22	68.3	**4.9**	19.3	3.3	**4.5**
8.8	0.17	0.5	-0.02	**3.3**	0.2	0.57	4.65	2.65	75.2	**5.6**	57.3	9.9	**6.6**
6.9	0.52	3.5	0.40	**3.7**	0.4	0.91	8.98	2.78	67.3	**5.0**	43.2	10.5	**5.5**
8.9	0.02	0.1	0.03	**3.1**	0.3	0.59	8.89	3.59	81.7	**2.9**	21.9	11.5	**3.5**
6.0	0.53	2.1	0.02	**8.4**	63.0	1.82	20.80	3.35	50.9	**2.5**	28.6	0.0	**7.3**
2.0	8.40	20.9	0.00	**7.9**	3.8	1.86	14.53	3.45	46.1	**5.0**	33.5	7.1	**9.7**
5.0	0.46	4.4	0.22	**8.6**	3.2	1.81	19.05	5.71	54.5	**3.1**	24.8	13.9	**5.8**
8.9	0.05	0.2	0.01	**5.4**	3.6	1.38	15.92	3.21	68.2	**4.3**	32.8	10.9	**6.1**
7.3	0.59	3.2	0.01	**9.4**	4.3	2.12	18.60	4.10	48.3	**2.9**	19.0	15.0	**8.8**
3.6	3.47	15.9	-0.16	**6.6**	1.4	1.56	17.07	2.63	52.2	**5.9**	40.6	4.4	**6.2**
8.8	0.08	0.2	0.00	**4.3**	0.8	1.08	10.15	3.82	66.8	**2.8**	43.8	26.2	**5.9**
8.6	0.52	2.0	-0.01	**3.8**	2.2	0.85	8.51	2.69	67.3	**3.9**	27.5	11.3	**6.5**
6.4	1.55	4.6	-0.07	**5.3**	1.4	1.12	8.34	3.44	58.7	**4.2**	46.4	15.7	**8.0**
7.0	0.53	3.1	-0.06	**4.5**	3.7	0.96	9.38	2.77	72.1	**6.4**	47.4	3.0	**5.7**
3.8	5.78	19.0	0.00	**6.6**	1.9	1.40	11.38	2.31	59.0	**5.7**	38.2	4.4	**7.0**
5.0	1.42	11.5	0.00	**6.5**	11.9	1.30	16.84	3.02	52.9	**4.9**	23.8	5.9	**7.1**
7.9	1.05	3.4	0.02	**4.8**	0.7	0.87	6.40	3.60	72.6	**3.9**	23.0	10.2	**8.4**
8.9	0.45	1.0	-0.01	**5.0**	1.7	1.00	8.28	2.94	63.6	**5.6**	39.6	5.8	**7.7**
7.3	0.47	3.2	-0.10	**6.4**	1.9	1.39	12.48	4.01	57.9	**4.0**	34.8	13.5	**7.5**
8.6	0.13	0.5	-0.04	**9.1**	13.7	1.68	12.60	3.45	39.3	**5.6**	45.4	10.9	**10.0**
6.2	0.92	9.3	-0.01	**2.0**	0.0	0.10	0.87	2.69	96.4	**3.1**	33.7	17.2	**5.6**
4.1	3.29	9.4	0.01	**4.1**	0.5	1.10	12.37	3.61	74.0	**4.0**	35.8	11.5	**5.3**
6.5	1.31	5.8	0.00	**9.5**	2.1	2.37	19.84	3.29	48.1	**0.6**	16.3	35.4	**9.2**
6.9	1.62	4.9	0.04	**3.1**	0.1	0.46	2.92	2.44	79.0	**5.2**	44.9	7.0	**6.1**
8.8	0.07	0.4	0.02	**3.7**	0.8	0.58	6.35	3.23	81.4	**4.7**	28.4	6.9	**5.3**
7.8	0.36	1.5	0.11	**4.9**	0.5	1.62	21.23	5.44	68.5	**2.5**	16.2	16.5	**2.4**
8.7	0.13	0.9	-0.01	**5.3**	3.7	1.24	14.88	3.27	66.7	**5.6**	45.2	7.5	**6.4**
5.3	0.54	4.4	0.05	**6.8**	4.9	1.36	14.18	4.19	57.1	**1.1**	7.6	24.1	**6.6**
3.6	1.75	10.8	-0.25	**3.1**	1.2	0.56	6.84	2.95	85.3	**5.7**	46.2	7.6	**4.4**
9.0	0.00	0.0	0.00	**8.0**	1.1	1.98	9.89	4.06	49.1	**5.4**	38.9	6.6	**9.5**
9.6	0.66	2.6	0.01	**5.5**	12.7	1.22	16.01	2.95	51.7	**5.1**	8.1	0.6	**7.1**

Name	City	State	Rating	2020 Rating	2019 Rating	Total Assets ($Mil)	One Year Asset Growth	Asset Mix (As a % of Total Assets) Commercial Loans	Consumer Loans	Mortgage Loans	Securities	Capitalization Index	Leverage Ratio	Risk-Based Capital Ratio
The Bank of Hemet	Riverside	CA	**A**	A	A-	991.9	16.00	1.0	0.0	0.1	13.2	**7.1**	9.0	14.4
The Bank of Herrin	Herrin	IL	**B-**	C+	B-	302.0	10.22	10.4	1.0	8.6	36.1	**6.7**	8.7	15.2
The Bank of Holly Springs	Holly Springs	MS	**B**	B	B	369.5	31.44	10.9	5.8	22.0	12.9	**8.2**	9.8	0.0
The Bank of Holyrood	Holyrood	KS	**B**	B	B	69.4	6.22	19.2	3.4	17.8	16.5	**10.0**	14.5	25.4
The Bank of Houston	Houston	MO	**D+**	D	D-	55.8	25.00	31.5	0.5	10.6	8.5	**10.0**	11.6	0.0
The Bank of Jackson	Jackson	TN	**B**	B	B-	226.4	1.43	6.0	1.1	4.4	65.0	**7.6**	9.4	18.4
The Bank of Kaukauna	Kaukauna	WI	**B-**	B-	C	121.2	5.26	31.0	0.5	6.7	2.8	**7.0**	9.0	14.9
The Bank of Kremlin	Kremlin	OK	**C+**	C+	B-	341.3	1.60	13.3	1.4	5.9	11.2	**8.9**	10.3	15.6
The Bank of Lafayette	Lafayette	GA	**C+**	B-	B	346.6	16.92	1.7	5.0	15.8	62.7	**9.3**	10.5	0.0
The Bank of Landisburg	Landisburg	PA	**B+**	B+	B+	349.4	9.48	2.3	1.8	40.1	24.8	**10.0**	16.3	0.0
The Bank of Magnolia Co.	Magnolia	OH	**B+**	A-	B	95.9	5.02	8.7	3.5	24.8	28.5	**9.8**	10.8	25.9
The Bank of Marion	Marion	VA	**B+**	B+	A-	525.2	16.83	4.7	2.1	31.7	37.6	**8.0**	9.7	19.8
The Bank of Milan	Milan	TN	**B-**	B-	B-	90.4	8.24	10.2	1.2	18.7	30.2	**6.3**	8.3	0.0
The Bank of Missouri	Perryville	MO	**A-**	A-	B+	2648.3	29.52	9.9	2.3	17.7	22.3	**8.6**	10.0	14.2
The Bank of New Glarus	New Glarus	WI	**B-**	B-	B-	411.2	15.93	17.0	1.4	8.7	23.7	**9.3**	10.5	16.1
The Bank of New York Mellon	New York	NY	**B**	B	B	384538.0	7.42	0.4	0.0	0.1	40.5	**4.1**	6.1	16.8
The Bank of New York Mellon Trust Co., N.	Los Angeles	CA	**U**	U	U	1419.1	-2.39	0.0	0.0	0.0	5.4	**10.0**	65.4	396.5
The Bank of Old Monroe	Old Monroe	MO	**A**	A	A	554.1	17.53	8.2	0.4	7.4	35.4	**10.0**	12.4	0.0
The Bank of Orrick	Orrick	MO	**D**	D+	C-	45.3	22.96	1.5	1.8	10.7	62.1	**5.3**	7.3	17.1
The Bank of Princeton	Princeton	NJ	**B+**	B+	B+	1636.2	2.70	11.7	0.0	6.3	4.5	**10.0**	12.2	15.3
▲ The Bank of Protection	Protection	KS	**A-**	B+	B	79.2	4.34	4.6	2.5	5.7	21.6	**10.0**	14.7	22.2
The Bank of Romney	Romney	WV	**B+**	B+	B	353.8	8.18	1.7	4.8	39.9	23.2	**10.0**	11.6	0.0
The Bank of San Jacinto County, Coldsprin	Coldspring	TX	**B-**	B-	B	48.6	9.26	2.5	2.4	18.2	13.5	**10.0**	12.5	0.0
The Bank of Soperton	Soperton	GA	**B+**	B+	B	119.9	15.08	16.4	6.6	25.0	3.4	**8.7**	10.1	14.6
The Bank of South Carolina	Charleston	SC	**A-**	A-	A	581.6	7.16	7.7	0.7	15.2	28.0	**8.0**	9.7	0.0
The Bank of Southside Virginia	Carson	VA	**B+**	B+	A	659.0	6.08	2.4	13.4	3.4	32.7	**10.0**	16.4	0.0
The Bank of Star Valley	Afton	WY	**A-**	A-	B+	332.6	18.15	6.2	5.6	7.1	32.6	**7.1**	9.1	17.2
The Bank of Tampa	Tampa	FL	**B**	B+	B+	2768.2	10.07	15.1	2.0	4.0	24.6	**5.1**	7.1	14.7
The Bank of Tescott	Tescott	KS	**B+**	B+	A-	433.8	3.67	4.5	1.8	22.0	28.7	**10.0**	13.4	20.9
▲ The Bank of the West	Thomas	OK	**A**	A-	A	158.0	3.42	12.2	0.3	6.4	0.0	**9.9**	12.6	0.0
The Bank of Tioga	Tioga	ND	**C+**	C+	C+	344.7	-3.29	3.0	1.1	3.8	69.8	**8.1**	9.7	19.8
▼ The Bank of Vernon	Vernon	AL	**B+**	A-	A-	220.5	14.03	19.4	1.6	12.0	14.7	**10.0**	12.4	0.0
The Bank of Wyandotte	Wyandotte	OK	**C-**	D+	C-	20.1	49.31	11.7	8.2	7.9	17.5	**10.0**	30.6	61.1
▲ The Bankers Bank	Oklahoma City	OK	**B-**	C	B-	195.5	-4.89	6.7	0.5	4.4	0.3	**10.0**	14.8	0.0
▲ The Bankers' Bank of Kentucky, Inc.	Frankfort	KY	**B-**	C	C+	110.6	-84.12	2.3	0.0	2.1	0.9	**10.0**	14.4	33.8
The Baxter State Bank	Baxter Springs	KS	**C**	C	C+	27.1	6.04	1.8	6.8	28.0	15.5	**10.0**	19.2	0.0
The Bennington State Bank	Salina	KS	**B+**	B	B-	931.3	11.16	9.5	0.8	15.7	30.6	**9.2**	10.5	16.9
The Berkshire Bank	New York	NY	**C+**	C+	B	665.8	-9.77	1.1	0.2	6.2	9.6	**10.0**	18.5	37.1
The Big Bend Banks, N.A.	Marfa	TX	**B+**	B+	A-	171.5	-6.01	1.5	2.2	1.9	73.7	**10.0**	13.5	44.7
The Bippus State Bank	Huntington	IN	**A-**	A-	B	245.8	14.18	15.3	2.0	13.4	12.3	**9.3**	10.6	15.7
The Blue Grass Valley Bank	Blue Grass	VA	**C+**	C+	C+	54.6	16.63	5.6	4.5	24.6	15.1	**8.4**	9.9	0.0
The Bradford National Bank of Greenville	Greenville	IL	**A-**	A-	A-	463.4	16.97	4.3	1.5	9.2	59.5	**10.0**	11.8	18.4
▲ The Brady National Bank	Brady	TX	**B**	B-	B-	151.2	3.68	8.6	2.8	10.9	40.8	**6.8**	8.8	18.0
The Breda Savings Bank	Breda	IA	**A-**	A-	A-	74.6	12.62	6.7	1.0	12.0	41.7	**8.8**	10.2	0.0
The Brenham National Bank	Brenham	TX	**B+**	B+	A-	440.2	5.28	4.7	1.1	6.6	52.9	**8.5**	10.0	18.3
▲ The Bryn Mawr Trust Co.	Bryn Mawr	PA	**B+**	B	B+	4954.9	-5.94	9.2	0.9	12.2	15.0	**8.1**	10.0	13.4
The Buckholts State Bank	Buckholts	TX	**A-**	A-	A-	95.6	14.45	22.8	1.6	11.4	38.5	**10.0**	14.9	30.0
The Callaway Bank	Fulton	MO	**B-**	B-	B-	467.2	8.86	9.8	0.9	17.5	16.6	**5.9**	8.7	0.0
The Canandaigua National B&T Co.	Canandaigua	NY	**B**	B	B+	3955.1	12.51	12.7	21.3	17.0	16.2	**6.6**	8.6	12.8
▼ The Casey County Bank, Inc.	Liberty	KY	**B**	B+	B+	295.6	12.43	5.7	4.5	18.3	35.0	**6.8**	8.8	15.4
The Cecilian Bank	Cecilia	KY	**B+**	B+	B+	1385.7	17.62	6.5	3.8	16.0	32.7	**6.6**	8.6	0.0
The Central Trust Bank	Jefferson City	MO	**B+**	B+	B+	3713.5	6.54	5.8	5.3	8.7	45.3	**4.7**	6.7	16.5
The Chasewood Bank	Houston	TX	**D**	D	C-	111.2	16.12	4.4	0.2	6.2	11.7	**6.3**	8.4	0.0
The Chicago Trust Co., N. A.	Lake Forest	IL	**U**	U	U	116.2	2.33	0.0	0.0	0.0	15.4	**10.0**	99.3	455.1
▲ The Cincinnatus S&L Co.	Cincinnati	OH	**B+**	B-	B-	113.4	9.21	1.5	3.7	33.5	4.3	**10.0**	20.7	0.0
The Citizens Bank	Enterprise	AL	**B**	B	B	193.2	15.45	9.3	1.1	17.8	16.9	**7.0**	9.0	0.0
The Citizens Bank	Greensboro	AL	**B+**	B+	A-	117.4	4.81	6.7	4.0	5.0	50.6	**10.0**	11.7	27.8
The Citizens Bank	Batesville	AR	**B-**	B-	B-	1193.4	5.51	6.5	1.6	14.0	9.1	**6.7**	8.9	12.3
▲ The Citizens Bank	Hickman	KY	**B+**	B	B	168.1	10.83	6.3	2.3	12.4	23.8	**10.0**	11.4	0.0
The Citizens Bank	Morehead	KY	**C**	C	B-	212.3	18.31	6.9	3.0	24.7	16.3	**4.2**	6.2	15.0

Asset Quality Index	Adjusted Non-Performing Loans as a % of Total Loans	Adjusted Non-Performing Loans as a % of Capital	Net Charge-Offs Avg Loans	Profitability Index	Net Income ($Mil)	Return on Assets (R.O.A.)	Return on Equity (R.O.E.)	Net Interest Spread	Overhead Efficiency Ratio	Liquidity Index	Liquidity Ratio	Hot Money Ratio	Stability Index
7.6	0.00	0.0	0.00	**9.3**	9.8	2.04	22.01	3.26	40.0	**5.4**	26.3	1.5	**8.2**
5.5	1.25	5.6	0.17	**4.3**	1.5	1.01	11.89	3.45	68.5	**5.2**	30.8	4.5	**4.8**
4.3	1.37	7.2	0.01	**5.0**	1.9	1.04	9.47	4.01	70.8	**1.9**	20.5	20.3	**8.6**
5.8	1.52	6.1	0.65	**6.4**	0.5	1.55	10.79	3.78	47.7	**1.8**	37.5	30.2	**7.0**
8.0	0.00	0.0	0.00	**4.7**	0.7	2.70	24.89	5.21	51.9	**1.8**	21.4	9.7	**3.2**
9.1	0.67	1.1	-0.02	**4.2**	1.2	1.09	9.55	2.97	62.5	**4.4**	64.9	18.8	**6.6**
3.7	2.43	9.1	0.00	**6.7**	0.9	1.67	19.16	3.92	64.6	**4.6**	19.6	4.6	**6.8**
3.6	1.97	8.4	0.00	**7.6**	4.3	2.52	21.34	4.74	44.0	**1.7**	17.6	20.5	**8.3**
6.3	1.79	4.8	0.00	**3.3**	0.9	0.56	5.56	2.47	73.2	**4.3**	34.7	11.6	**4.8**
5.7	4.09	10.6	-0.01	**5.1**	1.9	1.07	6.52	3.00	57.8	**2.7**	21.8	16.0	**8.4**
8.8	0.33	1.3	0.05	**4.0**	0.4	0.79	7.10	3.39	76.2	**5.7**	36.2	3.4	**6.8**
5.9	1.05	5.1	0.09	**5.3**	2.7	1.08	9.88	3.88	64.9	**5.5**	34.7	4.6	**7.0**
9.3	0.00	0.0	0.00	**4.5**	0.5	1.04	12.12	3.80	66.9	**5.3**	49.5	10.0	**5.1**
6.1	1.58	4.8	0.06	**6.7**	17.9	1.40	12.12	3.35	63.5	**4.3**	20.0	8.1	**9.3**
4.3	2.48	11.0	0.00	**7.8**	3.0	1.56	14.44	3.28	53.1	**5.0**	36.7	8.6	**7.1**
9.4	0.34	0.3	-0.04	**3.8**	1194.0	0.64	8.19	0.66	75.5	**6.9**	57.4	0.1	**6.6**
6.5	na	0.0	na	**9.5**	79.4	11.28	13.87	0.56	49.7	**9.5**	162.4	0.0	**6.3**
8.9	0.68	1.6	0.00	**9.4**	7.1	2.64	20.62	3.47	43.5	**5.5**	41.6	5.1	**10.0**
5.5	2.10	6.6	-0.61	**0.6**	-0.1	-0.38	-4.58	2.16	117.7	**5.5**	61.7	7.9	**3.5**
6.3	0.76	3.0	0.30	**5.7**	10.4	1.27	9.80	4.02	52.3	**2.3**	10.7	10.3	**9.9**
7.6	0.01	0.2	-0.01	**7.1**	0.6	1.46	9.86	4.31	55.3	**2.0**	25.1	19.2	**8.1**
5.5	2.03	9.7	-0.01	**5.9**	2.2	1.27	12.04	3.84	59.6	**1.8**	23.2	14.1	**6.7**
9.9	0.00	0.0	0.00	**3.0**	0.1	0.46	3.60	2.33	86.8	**6.1**	78.6	10.7	**6.4**
7.4	0.33	1.6	0.00	**7.1**	1.0	1.69	17.52	5.09	62.2	**1.4**	15.6	25.6	**7.7**
5.9	1.43	4.9	0.00	**7.7**	3.6	1.34	13.59	3.80	59.5	**6.1**	39.5	2.5	**7.7**
8.4	0.39	0.6	-0.07	**4.7**	2.6	0.79	4.80	2.84	69.8	**7.2**	73.2	4.0	**9.1**
8.6	0.43	1.0	-0.03	**6.7**	2.8	1.76	18.61	2.82	54.7	**4.7**	46.3	13.1	**7.2**
8.6	0.39	1.6	-0.03	**4.9**	12.8	0.94	13.37	2.54	62.5	**7.3**	47.7	0.7	**6.1**
4.6	2.96	12.8	-0.01	**7.8**	4.6	2.14	15.27	4.08	45.5	**2.2**	24.4	18.9	**9.0**
8.3	0.13	0.7	0.02	**9.7**	1.8	2.26	17.71	4.82	52.8	**1.3**	23.6	30.5	**9.5**
9.7	0.00	0.0	-0.01	**4.3**	2.9	1.65	15.56	2.71	62.3	**3.1**	65.1	10.3	**6.5**
8.6	0.55	1.3	0.17	**4.9**	0.8	0.69	5.48	3.01	64.6	**2.9**	34.6	18.8	**7.7**
6.4	1.18	1.4	0.35	**2.0**	0.0	-0.41	-1.46	3.84	106.3	**5.2**	74.1	11.0	**4.0**
7.5	0.00	0.0	0.03	**4.7**	1.4	1.40	9.72	3.56	71.4	**0.8**	12.8	21.6	**6.2**
9.1	0.00	0.0	0.00	**3.5**	0.3	0.60	4.14	1.88	77.1	**4.1**	65.5	9.0	**7.0**
2.4	8.80	19.6	0.02	**2.4**	0.0	0.19	0.91	3.82	95.1	**6.8**	52.2	0.5	**6.0**
5.1	2.84	9.5	-0.06	**7.5**	7.7	1.70	15.80	2.97	43.8	**3.5**	21.4	12.2	**8.2**
6.5	3.73	9.3	0.00	**2.2**	0.5	0.16	0.88	2.41	95.9	**5.2**	62.6	14.3	**7.3**
9.9	0.00	0.0	-3.12	**4.5**	0.9	1.03	6.27	3.06	67.0	**7.3**	90.1	6.4	**7.6**
5.7	0.54	4.6	-0.01	**9.7**	3.6	3.01	27.69	3.97	47.1	**4.6**	18.4	5.0	**7.9**
4.5	1.89	7.8	0.07	**3.8**	0.2	0.81	8.05	3.49	71.0	**5.1**	51.0	11.5	**5.0**
7.0	1.71	4.1	0.04	**6.5**	3.8	1.74	11.98	3.69	47.7	**4.6**	32.7	9.2	**8.3**
6.5	0.92	3.5	-0.13	**5.7**	1.2	1.52	15.59	3.51	60.4	**5.1**	40.2	9.8	**6.1**
8.9	0.00	0.0	0.00	**8.4**	0.8	2.17	21.46	4.25	40.4	**5.8**	50.5	7.0	**7.5**
8.3	0.25	0.5	0.72	**5.0**	2.6	1.20	10.60	3.25	62.4	**5.1**	55.0	13.2	**7.5**
7.3	0.44	1.9	0.17	**6.5**	40.7	1.65	12.60	3.28	63.0	**4.5**	15.0	3.7	**8.1**
6.7	1.94	5.9	0.00	**6.9**	0.8	1.69	11.33	3.19	49.0	**4.7**	52.8	13.5	**9.3**
5.9	0.77	4.4	0.06	**4.8**	2.7	1.15	13.18	3.46	64.9	**4.3**	14.5	6.7	**5.5**
4.3	0.87	7.2	0.07	**6.7**	27.3	1.43	16.28	3.38	57.8	**3.5**	8.7	11.2	**7.7**
5.7	1.02	4.7	0.04	**5.0**	1.3	0.89	10.07	2.69	61.8	**4.1**	24.0	9.3	**6.0**
8.0	0.36	2.1	0.02	**5.4**	7.5	1.11	11.97	3.03	59.8	**3.1**	23.5	16.5	**8.1**
8.7	0.23	1.0	-0.05	**5.9**	22.6	1.25	17.07	2.03	69.1	**5.4**	24.5	3.2	**7.3**
6.7	0.47	1.5	0.00	**1.1**	0.0	0.02	0.21	2.77	98.8	**2.2**	45.8	43.3	**3.4**
9.1	na	0.0	na	**10.0**	1.5	2.55	2.57	1.34	76.0	**4.0**	na	0.0	**7.0**
6.8	1.86	4.0	-0.30	**5.1**	0.7	1.24	5.92	4.22	67.6	**2.1**	23.5	16.0	**7.8**
5.8	1.21	5.2	-0.02	**4.2**	0.7	0.74	8.14	3.30	75.1	**3.9**	29.2	12.0	**4.9**
8.9	0.19	1.2	0.04	**4.5**	0.6	0.99	8.07	2.52	55.9	**3.9**	53.4	19.0	**7.1**
7.7	0.39	2.0	-0.04	**4.3**	4.6	0.81	8.26	3.60	67.4	**4.2**	19.9	8.7	**8.5**
8.6	0.27	1.7	-0.01	**5.5**	1.2	1.43	12.37	3.81	59.6	**2.1**	14.6	18.1	**6.6**
5.5	0.77	5.0	0.04	**4.9**	1.4	1.36	18.64	3.95	67.1	**5.2**	31.9	5.2	**3.4**

Name	City	State	Rating	2020 Rating	2019 Rating	Total Assets ($Mil)	One Year Asset Growth	Asset Mix (As a % of Total Assets) Commercial Loans	Consumer Loans	Mortgage Loans	Securities	Capitalization Index	Leverage Ratio	Risk-Based Capital Ratio
The Citizens Bank	Farmington	NM	A-	A-	A-	846.6	8.13	9.7	0.3	10.8	55.9	6.4	8.4	20.2
The Citizens Bank	Olanta	SC	B	B	B	758.0	15.48	7.9	3.8	16.5	12.9	6.5	8.5	16.9
The Citizens Bank Co.	Beverly	OH	B+	B+	A-	297.4	13.23	10.4	1.4	25.5	28.4	10.0	11.1	0.0
The Citizens Bank of Clovis	Clovis	NM	A-	A-	A-	425.8	8.99	2.5	0.3	3.4	33.7	10.0	11.1	0.0
▲ The Citizens Bank of Cochran	Cochran	GA	B	B-	B-	120.9	3.39	7.4	3.8	29.5	17.7	7.9	9.6	15.7
The Citizens Bank of Edina	Edina	MO	A	A	B+	83.8	9.77	7.2	2.6	5.7	5.1	10.0	11.5	0.0
The Citizens Bank of Edmond	Edmond	OK	B-	B-	B-	352.1	11.05	14.1	0.5	17.6	3.0	5.6	9.0	0.0
The Citizens Bank of Fayette	Fayette	AL	A-	A-	B+	221.2	6.07	3.5	2.6	2.1	72.6	10.0	19.2	0.0
The Citizens Bank of Georgia	Cumming	GA	A-	A-	B	459.5	16.16	6.1	1.1	8.2	27.0	7.6	9.4	17.1
The Citizens Bank of Philadelphia	Philadelphia	MS	C+	C+	B-	1338.0	-4.57	6.9	1.0	6.6	40.5	6.2	8.2	15.3
The Citizens Bank of Swainsboro	Swainsboro	GA	B+	B+	B+	279.1	11.11	14.3	4.4	22.7	6.9	8.1	9.8	17.7
The Citizens Bank of Weston, Inc.	Weston	WV	B+	B+	B+	223.0	6.25	30.1	3.3	18.3	21.8	10.0	11.0	17.8
The Citizens Bank of Winfield	Winfield	AL	A	A	A	299.3	5.92	2.8	5.4	4.2	72.6	10.0	20.3	0.0
The Citizens National Bank of Bluffton	Bluffton	OH	A-	B+	B-	947.3	-1.66	13.5	0.2	9.1	19.0	7.3	10.5	0.0
The Citizens National Bank of Hammond	Hammond	NY	C-	C-	C-	26.8	11.54	5.4	13.3	41.6	19.5	6.6	8.6	0.0
The Citizens National Bank of Hillsboro	Hillsboro	TX	B+	B+	B+	224.5	14.50	7.5	2.4	6.5	61.4	10.0	11.9	32.5
The Citizens National Bank of Lebanon	Lebanon	KY	B-	B-	B	156.9	15.69	3.0	2.4	9.4	59.3	8.0	9.7	28.4
The Citizens National Bank of McConnelsvi	McConnelsville	OH	C+	B-	B	110.2	12.53	3.4	4.9	40.3	23.7	9.3	10.5	0.0
The Citizens National Bank of Meridian	Meridian	MS	A-	A-	A-	1718.0	6.98	10.7	1.2	14.3	22.5	9.0	10.3	15.5
The Citizens National Bank of Park Rapids	Park Rapids	MN	A-	A-	A-	334.3	9.15	9.3	6.5	21.3	18.3	8.7	10.1	0.0
The Citizens National Bank of Quitman	Quitman	GA	A-	A-	B+	123.2	11.35	7.1	10.4	11.1	13.4	10.0	12.2	23.8
The Citizens National Bank of Somerset	Somerset	KY	B+	B+	B+	606.3	20.64	3.5	3.0	19.3	34.0	6.4	8.4	0.0
The Citizens National Bank of Woodsfield	Woodsfield	OH	C+	C+	C+	152.3	5.20	3.8	0.9	24.8	51.0	4.7	6.7	21.2
The Citizens State Bank	Gridley	KS	B+	B+	B+	255.9	12.57	8.0	2.1	9.9	21.4	6.6	8.6	0.0
The Citizens State Bank	Marysville	KS	B+	A-	A-	382.7	2.68	5.6	0.9	7.4	18.4	6.5	9.3	0.0
The Citizens State Bank	Moundridge	KS	B+	B+	B+	494.7	3.92	5.3	0.7	3.8	47.7	8.7	10.2	0.0
The Citizens State Bank and Trust Co.	Council Grove	KS	C	C	D+	71.5	28.41	16.9	1.5	7.8	7.4	5.7	7.7	12.0
The Citizens State Bank at Mohall	Mohall	ND	B-	B-	B-	63.9	0.20	10.5	2.9	12.0	23.4	10.0	11.7	18.1
▲ The Citizens State Bank of Cheney, Kansa	Cheney	KS	B+	B	B	80.1	9.43	8.3	8.2	7.6	29.5	7.5	9.3	16.1
The Citizens State Bank of Finley	Finley	ND	B+	B+	A-	141.4	3.83	6.3	1.3	0.4	32.7	10.0	14.9	23.2
The Citizens State Bank of Ganado	Ganado	TX	D-	D-	D	61.5	5.23	1.3	1.6	5.8	53.0	6.0	8.0	31.4
▲ The Citizens State Bank of Ouray	Ouray	CO	B	C+	C	175.5	20.67	14.7	0.5	24.4	18.1	7.2	9.1	14.8
The Citizens-Farmers Bank of Cole Camp	Cole Camp	MO	B+	B+	B+	161.2	12.73	5.7	6.2	25.4	29.6	10.0	14.5	0.0
The City National B&T Co. of Lawton, Okla	Lawton	OK	A	A	A	448.9	11.52	3.9	2.0	15.0	19.7	10.0	11.3	20.5
The City National Bank of Colorado City	Colorado City	TX	B-	B-	B-	189.7	16.72	3.0	5.4	37.8	1.6	7.6	9.4	15.8
The City National Bank of Metropolis	Metropolis	IL	B-	B-	B	476.0	10.95	9.4	2.3	17.6	42.5	10.0	11.7	27.6
The City National Bank of San Saba	San Saba	TX	C+	C+	C+	83.8	13.41	1.5	2.3	0.2	75.0	10.0	11.2	0.0
The City National Bank of Sulphur Springs	Sulphur Springs	TX	A-	A-	A-	1080.1	26.90	6.7	4.6	22.5	29.7	6.4	8.4	14.5
The City State Bank	Fort Scott	KS	C+	C+	C+	53.1	14.64	5.5	3.5	20.5	18.9	5.9	7.9	0.0
The Claxton Bank	Claxton	GA	B	B-	C	146.8	9.82	6.3	1.1	8.0	21.2	8.0	9.7	15.3
The Cleveland State Bank	Cleveland	MS	B+	B+	A-	300.9	14.66	9.1	4.4	12.9	43.4	8.0	9.7	0.0
The Clinton National Bank	Clinton	IA	C+	C+	B-	445.4	8.94	8.8	1.3	7.2	48.8	10.0	11.6	0.0
The Colorado B&T Co. of La Junta	La Junta	CO	A-	A-	B+	183.0	4.50	12.2	2.4	12.3	23.0	9.1	10.4	0.0
The Commercial & Savings Bank of Millers	Millersburg	OH	B+	B+	B+	1128.7	16.96	10.7	1.5	13.3	19.4	6.0	8.0	17.9
▼ The Commercial Bank	Crawford	GA	B+	A-	A	359.3	21.19	13.5	1.3	15.5	17.8	6.1	8.1	14.5
▲ The Commercial Bank	De Kalb	MS	B	B-	B	215.2	15.28	11.3	11.4	9.4	40.4	7.3	9.2	0.0
The Commercial Bank	Honea Path	SC	B+	B+	A-	246.7	14.35	1.6	2.5	10.6	53.1	10.0	12.1	40.8
The Commercial Bank	Mason	TX	B-	B-	B-	78.5	24.43	4.4	1.9	22.9	37.9	6.0	8.0	17.5
The Commercial Bank of Grayson	Grayson	KY	B	B	B	221.2	13.15	6.6	6.5	13.2	44.9	10.0	12.2	23.0
The Commercial Bank of Ozark	Ozark	AL	C	C	C	122.1	13.46	4.8	3.9	12.3	39.6	5.2	7.2	17.9
The Commercial National Bank of Brady	Brady	TX	A	A	A	179.2	12.76	9.4	2.4	16.1	29.8	10.0	11.4	23.9
The Community Bank	Liberal	KS	B-	B-	B-	154.9	1.97	10.9	11.9	0.0	31.3	7.8	9.6	16.1
The Community Bank	Zanesville	OH	B-	B-	B-	565.3	10.49	7.6	4.3	24.7	15.4	6.4	8.4	0.0
The Community Bank	Bridgeport	TX	B-	B-	B-	141.4	17.49	11.7	1.7	17.1	18.6	6.7	8.7	0.0
The Community State Bank	Poteau	OK	B-	B-	B-	338.6	11.65	8.0	2.7	15.5	26.6	6.3	8.3	14.8
The Conneaut Savings Bank	Conneaut	OH	C-	C-	C	85.2	6.25	2.9	0.4	47.1	25.3	10.0	13.1	0.0
The Converse County Bank	Douglas	WY	B+	B+	B+	802.4	7.03	8.0	3.2	3.7	63.7	6.1	8.1	30.5
The Conway National Bank	Conway	SC	B+	B+	B+	1694.0	19.36	6.0	2.7	9.5	58.2	6.3	8.3	19.0
▲ The Cooperative Bank	Roslindale	MA	C+	C	C+	482.6	2.97	4.3	0.6	37.8	10.4	7.6	9.4	14.8
The Corder Bank	Corder	MO	D+	D+	C	23.8	8.72	8.0	3.6	13.6	33.5	7.5	9.4	18.1

Asset Quality Index	Adjusted Non-Performing Loans as a % of Total Loans	Adjusted Non-Performing Loans as a % of Capital	Net Charge-Offs Avg Loans	Profitability Index	Net Income ($Mil)	Return on Assets (R.O.A.)	Return on Equity (R.O.E.)	Net Interest Spread	Overhead Efficiency Ratio	Liquidity Index	Liquidity Ratio	Hot Money Ratio	Stability Index
7.1	1.93	4.1	0.00	**6.2**	6.1	1.49	16.69	2.96	54.7	**5.0**	52.3	12.9	**7.2**
7.7	0.26	1.3	0.03	**4.5**	3.4	0.92	9.94	3.14	70.9	**5.8**	40.6	5.1	**6.2**
9.0	0.00	0.0	0.04	**5.3**	1.5	1.06	8.75	3.66	59.7	**4.3**	22.8	7.7	**8.1**
8.9	0.16	0.6	-0.01	**5.2**	2.3	1.12	9.63	2.67	57.4	**3.0**	45.3	21.1	**8.3**
8.7	0.07	0.4	0.00	**5.0**	0.6	1.01	10.53	3.95	67.6	**1.4**	15.3	26.8	**6.1**
7.2	0.27	1.4	0.00	**9.8**	0.9	2.12	18.21	4.45	35.9	**4.0**	31.4	12.1	**8.6**
6.5	0.14	1.3	0.35	**4.5**	1.8	1.02	12.76	4.49	73.5	**4.1**	14.6	8.1	**5.0**
9.5	4.05	1.7	-3.35	**5.1**	1.1	1.06	5.13	2.53	61.0	**4.6**	92.5	23.6	**8.9**
8.9	0.22	0.6	-0.23	**6.6**	2.6	1.20	12.33	3.32	53.1	**5.4**	49.7	10.7	**6.3**
6.8	0.69	3.3	0.22	**3.1**	4.0	0.54	7.14	2.40	80.2	**3.2**	19.2	14.1	**6.7**
7.0	0.40	2.1	0.04	**5.9**	1.5	1.09	11.02	3.97	66.5	**3.2**	27.5	14.8	**6.7**
4.8	2.31	10.6	0.00	**7.3**	1.5	1.32	12.03	3.57	53.1	**4.7**	28.4	7.1	**7.4**
9.3	2.12	1.1	0.22	**8.9**	3.1	2.22	9.88	3.84	40.9	**2.5**	50.1	40.7	**8.6**
5.5	1.22	6.2	0.00	**9.4**	12.6	2.65	24.35	3.85	49.3	**4.2**	14.4	5.4	**9.3**
5.8	0.49	3.3	0.07	**3.3**	0.1	0.47	5.28	3.45	80.6	**5.3**	21.5	0.9	**3.6**
9.5	0.10	0.3	0.00	**4.3**	0.9	0.87	6.88	2.14	68.9	**5.8**	61.5	5.9	**7.4**
8.5	0.69	1.8	0.00	**3.5**	0.6	0.79	8.28	2.74	71.5	**5.9**	49.8	7.1	**5.5**
4.8	1.80	12.4	0.01	**2.9**	0.2	0.32	2.98	3.01	87.6	**4.1**	16.5	8.4	**6.5**
7.9	0.44	2.4	0.07	**7.0**	14.5	1.74	16.61	3.30	58.5	**4.8**	26.1	8.8	**10.0**
7.0	0.27	2.0	-0.02	**7.9**	3.4	2.12	20.65	3.57	50.3	**2.4**	6.7	16.3	**7.7**
7.1	1.49	3.4	-0.06	**5.1**	0.6	0.99	7.94	3.43	64.9	**2.7**	35.3	19.9	**7.4**
6.9	0.65	3.0	-0.09	**5.8**	4.3	1.49	17.14	3.06	59.7	**4.0**	35.1	13.2	**6.3**
9.7	0.00	0.2	0.00	**3.3**	0.3	0.43	5.99	2.18	76.9	**7.4**	62.5	1.0	**3.5**
7.2	0.35	1.9	0.00	**4.6**	1.0	0.77	8.68	3.07	69.7	**5.2**	34.2	5.8	**5.4**
7.7	0.04	1.4	0.00	**8.5**	3.6	1.81	18.50	3.26	42.2	**1.7**	14.9	21.9	**8.5**
7.4	0.48	1.8	0.00	**5.0**	2.3	0.93	7.81	3.06	75.0	**5.7**	41.8	5.8	**8.4**
8.2	0.00	0.0	0.21	**5.4**	0.4	1.07	14.24	3.82	72.4	**0.9**	23.1	39.6	**4.8**
7.1	0.76	3.9	0.05	**3.9**	0.3	0.75	6.45	3.81	78.1	**3.0**	13.9	13.7	**5.8**
8.3	0.09	0.5	0.18	**7.8**	0.7	1.89	19.36	4.84	52.6	**5.2**	41.8	9.4	**6.7**
8.3	1.36	2.4	0.00	**3.3**	0.1	0.14	0.95	0.88	83.5	**4.2**	27.9	9.5	**7.2**
10.0	0.00	0.0	0.02	**0.3**	-0.2	-0.53	-5.84	1.68	138.1	**6.1**	90.5	12.3	**3.0**
8.7	0.27	1.0	0.01	**7.0**	1.8	2.14	25.17	5.24	47.2	**4.5**	20.7	5.9	**4.7**
4.9	3.06	9.9	-0.17	**7.5**	1.4	1.79	12.24	3.93	43.7	**3.9**	32.3	12.8	**8.2**
8.7	0.48	2.2	-0.06	**6.3**	3.0	1.36	11.40	3.60	86.5	**6.2**	41.4	2.7	**8.3**
5.5	0.65	4.6	0.41	**5.5**	1.1	1.18	12.57	4.11	62.2	**1.8**	25.6	23.9	**6.1**
6.7	1.48	5.4	-0.08	**3.4**	1.4	0.62	5.05	2.52	67.0	**2.1**	43.3	28.1	**6.5**
10.0	0.00	0.0	0.12	**2.5**	0.1	0.28	2.39	2.73	87.7	**7.1**	72.8	3.0	**6.7**
8.0	0.44	2.4	0.00	**8.0**	9.4	1.84	18.12	3.91	61.3	**5.2**	39.0	11.1	**9.3**
8.9	0.00	0.0	0.00	**4.7**	0.3	1.04	12.75	3.80	67.9	**3.8**	42.3	16.5	**4.7**
5.2	1.47	5.7	0.00	**4.6**	0.8	1.15	11.45	4.17	73.1	**4.2**	31.9	11.1	**6.0**
7.5	0.51	2.8	0.00	**5.9**	1.9	1.27	14.96	4.06	60.7	**5.7**	46.0	7.6	**5.0**
7.5	1.36	4.1	0.06	**2.5**	0.7	0.32	2.48	2.34	88.1	**5.8**	51.3	8.4	**7.4**
7.1	0.30	2.7	-0.13	**9.8**	1.7	1.89	18.22	4.46	56.0	**5.0**	28.2	4.8	**7.8**
7.1	0.96	4.0	-0.02	**5.6**	5.8	1.05	12.48	2.61	61.1	**6.1**	41.0	6.1	**7.9**
6.1	0.96	6.9	0.00	**9.2**	3.8	2.25	27.42	4.16	47.5	**3.8**	25.8	11.5	**7.0**
6.3	0.63	2.4	0.08	**5.0**	1.1	1.08	11.18	3.86	65.4	**3.2**	39.2	16.0	**5.8**
7.7	2.70	4.7	0.11	**4.1**	0.9	0.78	6.61	2.37	68.6	**6.3**	77.7	10.4	**7.5**
9.4	0.00	0.1	-0.01	**6.8**	0.6	1.65	18.32	4.36	53.9	**4.3**	33.9	11.6	**5.6**
8.3	0.50	2.3	0.08	**3.7**	0.7	0.63	4.93	3.24	78.1	**6.4**	50.4	4.0	**7.5**
4.8	1.15	7.9	0.01	**2.8**	0.3	0.57	7.55	3.07	80.5	**4.5**	34.3	10.6	**3.8**
9.0	0.00	0.6	0.01	**6.9**	1.4	1.60	13.13	3.66	61.8	**5.1**	36.9	8.1	**8.5**
4.0	2.74	8.4	0.00	**4.4**	0.7	0.88	8.69	3.21	67.3	**2.6**	34.8	21.4	**6.9**
4.9	1.56	7.1	-0.04	**4.5**	2.5	0.88	9.62	3.13	73.3	**4.1**	26.0	10.1	**5.6**
8.3	0.21	1.4	-0.01	**4.6**	0.6	0.89	9.81	4.56	72.3	**4.2**	31.8	11.1	**5.2**
4.5	1.73	11.1	0.12	**4.8**	2.0	1.18	14.04	4.03	74.1	**1.9**	29.6	25.4	**5.5**
9.2	0.73	3.3	0.00	**1.3**	0.1	0.22	1.64	2.78	91.2	**5.5**	39.0	6.1	**6.2**
9.4	0.00	0.0	0.03	**5.4**	4.8	1.19	13.07	1.74	47.2	**3.0**	51.2	28.1	**7.0**
9.1	0.26	1.1	-0.07	**5.1**	8.2	1.02	12.15	2.46	56.0	**6.0**	52.5	10.4	**7.1**
6.0	0.72	4.1	0.00	**3.2**	1.3	0.56	5.64	3.32	81.4	**3.0**	19.8	14.3	**6.2**
3.4	3.00	16.9	0.09	**3.4**	0.1	0.53	5.64	3.03	78.6	**5.3**	54.9	8.9	**3.0**

Name	City	State	Rating	2020 Rating	2019 Rating	Total Assets ($Mil)	One Year Asset Growth	Asset Mix (As a % of Total Assets) Comm-ercial Loans	Cons-umer Loans	Mort-gage Loans	Secur-ities	Capital-ization Index	Lever-age Ratio	Risk-Based Capital Ratio
The Corn City State Bank	Deshler	OH	**B+**	B+	B+	82.0	9.50	1.1	1.9	27.2	51.6	**10.0**	13.0	0.0
The Cornerstone Bank	South West City	MO	**B**	B	B-	178.1	15.41	10.6	7.6	24.7	11.3	**10.0**	12.3	21.2
The Cortland Savings and Banking Co.	Cortland	OH	**B**	B	B	789.5	1.64	10.0	0.4	9.3	21.7	**7.8**	9.5	15.8
The Cottonport Bank	Cottonport	LA	**B+**	B+	B+	479.0	15.92	7.9	2.4	12.7	10.4	**10.0**	11.2	0.0
The Covington S&L Assn.	Covington	OH	**B-**	B-	B-	84.5	16.65	0.0	0.3	43.2	14.4	**10.0**	14.0	0.0
The Cowboy Bank of Texas	Maypearl	TX	**A-**	A-	A-	107.1	13.34	0.5	3.3	21.6	8.9	**9.8**	10.9	15.0
The Croghan Colonial Bank	Fremont	OH	**A-**	A-	B+	1090.0	9.16	10.4	9.2	7.2	27.8	**9.0**	10.3	14.5
The Dart Bank	Mason	MI	**B**	B-	C+	676.7	12.15	14.6	0.7	26.5	6.3	**7.4**	9.2	0.0
The Delaware National Bank of Delhi	Delhi	NY	**B-**	B-	B-	369.3	12.69	7.4	1.1	23.2	27.4	**7.5**	9.3	0.0
The Denison State Bank	Holton	KS	**A**	A	A-	435.2	9.22	10.5	1.7	10.2	36.6	**10.0**	13.4	0.0
The Depository Trust Co.	New York	NY	**U**	U	U	7369.2	89.47	0.0	0.0	0.0	0.0	**10.0**	15.7	51.7
The Dime Bank	Honesdale	PA	**B-**	B-	B-	985.7	16.32	17.3	1.1	10.1	20.1	**7.9**	9.6	14.4
▲ The Dolores State Bank	Dolores	CO	**A**	A-	A-	347.6	18.42	3.6	3.8	26.7	28.4	**10.0**	12.7	22.4
▲ The Donley County State Bank	Clarendon	TX	**C**	C-	C+	47.0	15.61	4.0	1.1	0.1	51.2	**10.0**	16.2	51.7
The Eastern Colorado Bank	Cheyenne Wells	CO	**A-**	A-	A-	541.2	7.42	5.5	0.3	8.2	27.2	**9.9**	10.9	16.1
▲ The Elk State Bank	Clyde	KS	**B-**	C+	C+	109.2	8.42	4.9	1.2	9.8	43.3	**7.4**	9.3	19.0
The Equitable Bank, S.S.B.	Wauwatosa	WI	**C**	C-	D	315.9	3.46	0.8	0.1	31.6	9.8	**10.0**	11.3	0.0
The Equitable S&L Co.	Cadiz	OH	**D**	D	D+	12.3	-9.62	0.0	0.2	54.0	1.3	**10.0**	19.6	0.0
▲ The Evangeline Bank and Trust Co.	Ville Platte	LA	**A-**	B+	B+	795.0	19.90	9.4	3.3	23.7	13.4	**10.0**	14.9	0.0
▼ The Exchange Bank	Skiatook	OK	**B+**	A-	A-	146.6	15.19	20.3	0.9	7.6	35.8	**8.0**	9.7	0.0
The Exchange Bank of Alabama	Altoona	AL	**B+**	B+	B+	361.9	11.57	3.7	2.2	12.8	22.8	**10.0**	12.6	25.0
The Exchange State Bank	Springville	IA	**B+**	B	B	55.8	16.69	4.5	1.2	16.1	27.7	**6.1**	8.1	14.5
▼ The Fahey Banking Co.	Marion	OH	**B-**	B	B+	292.5	-2.69	6.7	0.4	4.2	15.0	**10.0**	17.6	0.0
The Fairfield National Bank	Fairfield	IL	**B**	B	B+	652.4	9.88	18.6	1.7	9.5	40.8	**10.0**	11.7	0.0
The Fairmount State Bank	Fairmount	IN	**C+**	C+	C+	54.4	13.54	1.8	9.9	21.7	23.2	**9.8**	10.9	18.9
The Falls City National Bank	Falls City	TX	**A**	A	B	488.2	7.60	3.1	2.5	7.6	41.9	**10.0**	11.9	0.0
The Farmers & Merchants Bank	Stuttgart	AR	**B**	B+	B+	1652.2	3.30	8.4	1.1	14.5	22.1	**7.8**	9.6	0.0
The Farmers & Merchants Bank	Berlin	WI	**B-**	B-	C+	438.7	27.08	10.0	1.8	19.6	15.3	**7.2**	9.1	13.7
The Farmers & Merchants State Bank	Archbold	OH	**B+**	B+	A-	2142.7	21.72	10.1	2.6	7.2	18.6	**6.2**	8.2	11.9
The Farmers and Merchants Bank	Boswell	IN	**C+**	B-	B	173.9	22.91	7.3	0.6	11.2	24.4	**7.6**	9.4	0.0
The Farmers and Merchants Bank	Caldwell	OH	**B**	B	B-	120.1	6.29	6.0	5.1	39.3	26.8	**10.0**	14.2	0.0
The Farmers and Merchants National Bank	Fairview	OK	**A**	A	A	128.2	5.05	3.9	2.1	7.3	59.0	**10.0**	11.0	0.0
The Farmers and Merchants National Bank	Nashville	IL	**B+**	A-	A-	242.5	14.55	4.0	0.8	9.5	25.8	**8.7**	10.2	0.0
▼ The Farmers and Merchants State Bank	Scotland	SD	**C**	C+	C+	36.0	6.30	7.4	7.0	1.5	43.7	**7.2**	9.1	22.3
The Farmers Bank	Greensboro	GA	**B-**	B-	B-	126.5	11.93	7.1	0.7	14.8	50.4	**10.0**	12.1	24.5
The Farmers Bank	Carnegie	OK	**D-**	D-	D-	77.0	-9.76	9.0	2.3	24.5	10.1	**9.5**	10.7	16.0
The Farmers Bank	Portland	TN	**A-**	A-	A-	814.4	11.85	5.4	1.1	15.2	24.6	**10.0**	11.9	17.7
The Farmers Bank and Savings Co.	Pomeroy	OH	**B**	B	B	390.3	5.98	7.9	3.7	30.8	23.1	**7.7**	9.5	0.0
The Farmers Bank of Appomattox	Appomattox	VA	**B+**	B+	B+	296.5	14.89	4.7	14.3	19.7	31.7	**10.0**	12.7	20.1
The Farmers Bank of Milton	Milton	KY	**B**	B	B	307.7	11.98	3.5	1.8	24.9	43.2	**10.0**	12.0	20.8
The Farmers Bank of Mt. Pulaski	Mount Pulaski	IL	**C**	C	C	57.2	4.33	2.5	2.4	17.4	58.6	**10.0**	12.3	38.8
The Farmers Bank of Willards	Willards	MD	**B**	B	B	489.2	11.11	6.9	1.9	27.0	5.9	**8.3**	9.8	19.0
The Farmers Bank, Frankfort, Indiana, Inc.	Frankfort	IN	**A-**	A-	B-	755.5	12.53	10.4	1.9	5.0	26.2	**9.2**	10.5	14.3
The Farmers National Bank of Canfield	Canfield	OH	**B+**	B+	B+	3243.6	12.99	9.5	5.9	11.5	30.5	**7.0**	9.0	14.4
The Farmers National Bank of Danville	Danville	KY	**B**	B	B+	805.0	7.90	7.5	1.2	20.2	22.3	**6.0**	8.1	14.8
The Farmers National Bank of Emlenton	Emlenton	PA	**B-**	C+	B-	1101.6	10.39	5.8	4.2	35.3	16.7	**5.4**	7.4	12.7
▲ The Farmers National Bank of Lebanon	Lebanon	KY	**B+**	B	B	119.1	8.82	6.9	2.3	6.3	48.0	**10.0**	11.2	19.5
▲ The Farmers State Bank	Holton	KS	**A-**	B+	B+	70.3	10.08	2.0	1.2	20.1	33.2	**10.0**	12.6	0.0
The Farmers State Bank	McPherson	KS	**A-**	A-	A-	146.5	7.75	9.1	3.1	15.9	43.5	**7.4**	9.2	16.4
▲ The Farmers State Bank	Westmoreland	KS	**B-**	C+	B+	225.9	6.28	13.0	2.0	9.0	25.4	**7.0**	12.8	0.0
The Farmers State Bank	New Madison	OH	**B**	B	B	218.4	7.30	4.2	3.5	21.6	22.9	**10.0**	11.4	19.3
The Farmers State Bank	Quinton	OK	**B-**	B-	B-	146.5	14.37	10.2	8.3	13.8	35.8	**5.6**	7.6	13.0
The Farmers State Bank and Trust Co.	Jacksonville	IL	**B**	B	B-	239.4	0.77	4.0	6.2	8.6	44.6	**10.0**	11.1	0.0
The Farmers State Bank of Aliceville, Kans	Westphalia	KS	**A-**	A-	A-	171.7	6.01	4.9	6.1	15.5	11.3	**10.0**	14.9	0.0
▲ The Farmers State Bank of Blue Mound	Blue Mound	KS	**B+**	B-	B-	55.0	16.98	11.1	2.8	0.7	11.0	**10.0**	16.2	0.0
The Farmers State Bank of Brush	Brush	CO	**A**	A	A-	118.7	5.36	4.0	1.4	2.8	31.0	**10.0**	18.9	32.3
▲ The Farmers State Bank of Bucklin, Kansa	Bucklin	KS	**B-**	C+	C+	56.3	7.72	6.2	0.7	1.1	19.2	**6.5**	8.6	21.4
The Farmers State Bank of Oakley, Kansa	Oakley	KS	**A**	A	A-	177.9	5.77	13.0	0.4	0.6	23.9	**10.0**	14.8	0.0
The Farmers State Bank of Turton	Turton	SD	**B+**	B	B	41.8	39.29	1.8	1.5	0.0	26.7	**9.1**	10.4	24.3
The Farmers State Bank of Waupaca	Waupaca	WI	**A**	A	A-	248.7	10.87	6.4	3.0	23.7	31.4	**10.0**	11.6	0.0

Arrows denote recent upgrades ▲ or downgrades ▼

Asset Quality Index	Adjusted Non-Performing Loans as a % of Total Loans	Adjusted Non-Performing Loans as a % of Capital	Net Charge-Offs Avg Loans	Profitability Index	Net Income ($Mil)	Return on Assets (R.O.A.)	Return on Equity (R.O.E.)	Net Interest Spread	Overhead Efficiency Ratio	Liquidity Index	Liquidity Ratio	Hot Money Ratio	Stability Index
9.7	0.13	0.2	-0.09	**3.5**	0.5	1.14	8.60	2.07	78.0	**3.1**	39.7	19.5	**8.4**
4.4	1.89	10.7	-0.05	**7.2**	2.2	2.61	21.15	5.55	55.6	**1.8**	30.3	25.3	**6.7**
5.6	1.40	4.9	0.02	**5.7**	5.3	1.34	13.67	3.49	60.4	**4.9**	25.3	4.2	**6.8**
7.8	0.44	1.8	0.05	**4.6**	2.0	0.88	7.76	3.30	70.2	**4.6**	36.9	10.7	**7.1**
10.0	0.02	0.0	0.00	**2.6**	0.1	0.24	1.68	2.23	87.5	**6.3**	49.1	3.6	**7.5**
6.7	0.08	2.9	0.00	**10.0**	1.5	2.77	25.68	3.95	46.9	**1.3**	24.4	25.4	**8.3**
7.2	0.47	1.4	0.02	**6.6**	7.3	1.37	10.97	3.78	58.9	**4.8**	14.0	3.8	**10.0**
5.3	0.73	3.3	0.08	**8.7**	6.8	2.06	22.58	4.73	65.7	**4.5**	14.0	5.3	**6.5**
7.0	0.54	3.3	-0.03	**3.7**	1.1	0.61	6.47	2.43	68.2	**2.9**	23.7	15.4	**5.2**
8.7	0.32	1.5	0.00	**8.2**	4.3	1.98	14.58	2.92	49.3	**3.6**	18.9	11.2	**9.7**
10.0	na	0.0	na	**9.4**	37.2	1.73	9.62	0.29	79.1	**4.0**	109.8	0.0	**7.0**
2.6	3.00	16.8	0.08	**5.3**	5.4	1.16	11.66	3.57	62.3	**4.0**	20.2	9.2	**6.8**
7.9	0.54	2.3	-0.01	**7.6**	2.3	1.43	10.68	4.04	51.2	**5.5**	39.1	6.2	**8.5**
9.8	0.00	0.0	0.02	**2.9**	0.1	0.55	3.36	2.12	79.9	**2.8**	59.5	32.1	**6.0**
8.3	0.08	0.2	-0.05	**6.8**	4.7	1.74	13.88	4.09	57.6	**1.8**	19.1	20.6	**9.5**
5.5	2.54	6.1	-0.07	**4.8**	0.6	1.06	10.90	3.79	61.5	**3.5**	31.6	13.1	**6.1**
8.3	0.40	2.5	0.08	**5.9**	2.7	1.79	18.87	3.25	72.2	**4.0**	28.8	11.4	**2.6**
9.9	0.72	2.2	0.00	**0.0**	-0.1	-2.25	-11.28	2.72	186.8	**4.1**	42.1	12.7	**6.1**
6.6	0.96	4.7	0.00	**5.3**	4.1	1.08	7.12	3.89	65.6	**1.7**	16.2	22.1	**8.2**
6.2	0.72	3.2	1.39	**5.8**	0.8	1.10	11.03	4.08	66.5	**3.1**	39.3	19.0	**6.2**
8.9	0.00	0.0	-0.01	**3.7**	1.0	0.58	4.41	2.68	76.0	**4.4**	37.1	11.9	**7.7**
6.0	0.97	4.7	-0.01	**5.3**	0.4	1.34	16.18	3.26	61.5	**6.0**	54.1	6.4	**5.9**
3.0	4.03	13.8	-0.13	**5.3**	1.6	1.12	6.24	3.44	65.2	**1.3**	18.2	23.3	**8.1**
4.6	2.70	10.7	0.09	**4.7**	3.9	1.22	9.54	2.36	53.1	**1.5**	24.7	26.2	**8.3**
4.4	1.70	7.7	0.53	**2.1**	0.0	0.11	1.02	3.14	82.2	**5.3**	35.8	5.9	**5.3**
7.1	3.16	6.6	0.20	**7.6**	3.4	1.41	11.97	2.54	33.3	**6.1**	58.7	8.6	**8.1**
6.6	0.38	1.8	0.07	**4.2**	6.6	0.79	6.38	3.27	66.6	**3.9**	20.5	10.6	**9.5**
4.4	1.57	10.7	0.10	**6.5**	3.2	1.51	16.39	3.81	47.4	**0.8**	13.7	22.4	**4.7**
5.9	0.49	2.9	0.13	**4.8**	9.3	0.93	8.74	3.32	63.4	**4.8**	24.8	8.2	**9.1**
7.7	1.26	3.4	-0.01	**3.0**	0.3	0.41	4.30	2.74	83.8	**4.4**	33.1	10.5	**5.4**
4.6	3.13	13.3	-0.09	**5.8**	0.7	1.14	7.75	4.54	61.1	**5.0**	30.9	6.2	**7.9**
9.4	0.00	0.4	-0.01	**7.6**	1.3	2.06	17.27	3.98	49.3	**3.5**	35.3	16.0	**8.9**
6.0	1.60	4.3	0.00	**5.8**	1.7	1.42	13.03	3.35	61.2	**4.9**	24.8	4.0	**7.7**
5.2	0.50	9.4	-0.12	**3.7**	0.2	0.84	8.57	2.64	65.7	**4.9**	43.4	11.3	**4.6**
9.3	0.00	0.0	0.00	**3.3**	0.4	0.65	5.23	2.68	70.7	**4.1**	15.5	7.8	**6.8**
1.5	5.55	31.8	-0.01	**0.5**	0.1	0.19	1.80	3.30	94.2	**0.8**	22.6	49.6	**2.3**
8.3	1.04	3.0	-0.07	**7.5**	5.6	1.45	12.10	4.12	61.0	**2.2**	28.3	20.3	**8.2**
5.8	1.07	5.4	0.02	**4.3**	1.8	0.95	9.93	3.43	72.3	**3.0**	26.1	15.3	**6.0**
6.3	0.99	4.3	0.17	**5.0**	1.6	1.10	8.72	3.78	65.8	**3.5**	30.1	14.2	**7.3**
6.5	2.09	8.0	-0.01	**4.1**	1.3	0.85	6.83	3.12	65.1	**3.5**	36.5	16.6	**7.6**
9.7	0.00	0.0	-0.62	**2.3**	0.1	0.34	2.80	2.47	85.5	**4.0**	50.6	16.6	**6.6**
7.5	0.46	2.1	0.11	**4.3**	1.7	0.72	7.18	3.46	73.4	**3.9**	38.9	14.8	**5.0**
7.3	0.40	1.9	0.04	**6.5**	5.0	1.36	12.47	3.60	61.2	**5.0**	32.9	6.9	**7.9**
6.1	0.76	3.8	0.03	**8.1**	28.1	1.77	16.65	3.52	47.8	**4.5**	22.2	8.3	**9.3**
5.3	1.19	6.5	0.06	**4.6**	3.9	0.98	10.98	3.19	71.5	**5.5**	33.5	3.5	**6.4**
6.7	0.35	3.5	0.06	**4.0**	4.4	0.84	10.01	3.05	65.7	**3.7**	16.8	11.0	**6.8**
6.5	1.60	6.1	0.01	**5.3**	0.7	1.17	10.65	4.01	65.1	**5.1**	47.7	11.2	**5.9**
9.1	0.35	1.4	-0.28	**7.6**	0.5	1.58	12.72	4.14	54.0	**4.0**	30.1	11.8	**6.8**
9.0	0.00	0.0	0.01	**6.2**	1.1	1.55	14.94	3.90	58.9	**5.1**	51.6	12.6	**7.2**
4.3	3.11	11.5	-0.12	**5.5**	1.5	1.34	10.25	3.59	54.2	**3.3**	30.5	15.2	**7.3**
8.0	0.70	4.0	-0.02	**4.5**	1.0	0.93	8.73	3.05	66.5	**1.9**	20.3	20.6	**7.2**
5.1	1.60	5.5	0.09	**5.7**	1.1	1.56	20.44	5.11	68.5	**5.8**	43.9	5.8	**4.8**
6.2	1.76	6.1	1.02	**4.0**	0.9	0.73	6.57	2.42	71.7	**6.8**	54.1	2.7	**5.9**
8.2	0.00	0.1	0.00	**5.5**	0.9	1.06	7.10	2.96	50.2	**1.8**	26.6	25.1	**8.7**
7.9	0.30	1.2	0.02	**6.8**	0.5	2.08	12.51	3.56	60.6	**4.2**	40.0	14.1	**7.1**
8.6	0.00	2.5	0.00	**7.6**	0.8	1.33	7.01	3.90	63.3	**2.8**	30.8	18.0	**8.6**
9.0	0.00	0.0	0.00	**4.4**	0.3	1.10	11.01	3.15	63.8	**5.6**	56.6	9.4	**6.1**
7.3	0.00	0.0	0.00	**8.3**	1.5	1.70	11.18	4.22	45.9	**1.1**	9.2	29.4	**9.3**
8.8	0.00	0.0	0.00	**8.5**	0.5	2.70	24.25	4.77	47.8	**3.6**	61.2	21.2	**7.0**
8.9	0.16	0.7	-0.17	**7.4**	1.9	1.58	12.65	4.15	56.5	**5.3**	41.2	8.2	**7.5**

Name	City	State	Rating	2020 Rating	2019 Rating	Total Assets ($Mil)	One Year Asset Growth	Asset Mix (As a % of Total Assets) Commercial Loans	Consumer Loans	Mortgage Loans	Securities	Capitalization Index	Leverage Ratio	Risk-Based Capital Ratio
The Federal Savings Bank	Chicago	IL	A	A	A	814.8	-29.54	0.2	1.9	80.0	0.7	10.0	15.8	29.1
The Fidelity Bank	Fuquay-Varina	NC	A-	A-	A-	3243.5	22.89	8.2	0.4	3.3	27.8	5.7	7.7	14.9
The Fidelity Deposit and Discount Bank	Dunmore	PA	B+	B+	A-	1944.1	9.04	9.9	5.5	17.6	28.6	6.0	8.0	15.6
The Fidelity State Bank and Trust Co.	Dodge City	KS	A	A-	A-	213.8	10.65	1.7	0.2	0.7	21.5	10.0	17.1	90.9
The First B&T Co. of Murphysboro	Murphysboro	IL	C-	C-	D	92.0	10.04	8.0	6.0	18.4	26.6	6.1	8.4	0.0
The First Bank and Trust Co.	Lebanon	VA	A	A	A	2616.8	12.80	11.5	2.5	12.9	0.6	8.5	10.0	16.7
The First Bank of Baldwin	Baldwin	WI	B	B	B-	244.8	13.39	6.4	1.0	10.1	43.3	6.9	8.9	16.6
The First Bank of Celeste	Celeste	TX	C+	C+	C+	66.7	14.34	9.3	5.7	3.8	31.6	5.0	7.0	20.1
The First Bank of Greenwich	Cos Cob	CT	C+	C+	B-	540.0	7.14	12.8	0.2	34.4	2.9	6.0	8.0	12.5
The First Central National Bank of Saint Pa	Saint Paris	OH	C+	B-	B	108.4	10.79	5.5	1.6	9.9	7.7	10.0	15.7	24.1
▼ The First Citizens National Bank of Upper	Upper Sandusky	OH	C+	B-	B-	355.7	15.05	3.4	0.6	11.7	21.3	10.0	12.0	0.0
▲ The First Farmers National Bank of Waurik	Waurika	OK	B+	B	B	53.0	7.89	1.4	2.4	0.4	62.4	10.0	18.2	0.0
The First Liberty National Bank	Liberty	TX	B+	B+	A-	406.2	2.79	9.5	3.0	18.3	30.0	9.2	10.5	19.1
The First National B&T Co. of Broken Arro	Broken Arrow	OK	B+	B+	B	243.9	9.15	9.0	0.4	15.8	6.5	8.0	9.7	20.2
The First National B&T Co. of Iron Mountai	Iron Mountain	MI	B-	B-	C+	403.4	6.48	12.7	2.1	9.2	39.0	6.7	8.7	0.0
The First National B&T Co. of Miami	Miami	OK	B-	B	B	242.1	46.32	3.0	1.7	7.5	32.0	4.9	6.9	19.4
The First National B&T Co. of Okmulgee	Okmulgee	OK	B-	B-	B	287.3	1.76	8.1	2.3	16.3	33.8	10.0	11.2	16.5
The First National Bank and Trust Co.	Chickasha	OK	A-	A-	B+	852.5	10.99	10.6	0.9	7.7	34.7	10.0	11.3	0.0
The First National Bank and Trust Co.	Beloit	WI	B-	B-	B-	1443.9	12.26	9.3	0.7	13.7	31.4	6.4	8.4	0.0
The First National Bank at Paris	Paris	AR	B+	B+	B+	230.7	12.47	6.3	7.7	15.7	14.9	9.4	10.6	18.2
The First National Bank at Saint James	Saint James	MN	D+	D+	D+	33.5	12.07	6.0	4.3	17.9	12.6	6.1	8.1	16.0
The First National Bank in Amboy	Amboy	IL	B-	B	B	264.6	16.53	5.9	1.9	6.8	50.2	7.3	9.2	0.0
The First National Bank in Carlyle	Carlyle	IL	B	B	B	250.2	13.69	6.4	1.0	5.2	37.0	8.3	9.9	0.0
The First National Bank in Cooper	Cooper	TX	B	B	B	52.9	19.03	2.9	3.9	20.7	18.3	10.0	12.8	0.0
The First National Bank in Creston	Creston	IA	B+	B+	B+	407.0	9.86	8.6	1.8	11.9	30.3	6.2	8.2	13.5
▲ The First National Bank in Falfurrias	Falfurrias	TX	B-	C+	C+	91.8	1.00	32.4	3.3	2.3	18.4	7.1	9.1	0.0
The First National Bank in Marlow	Marlow	OK	C+	C+	C+	63.5	2.03	6.5	7.9	14.6	27.7	7.1	9.1	0.0
The First National Bank in Sioux Falls	Sioux Falls	SD	B+	B+	A-	1573.0	10.12	11.9	0.7	19.7	22.1	10.0	11.3	17.6
The First National Bank in Tremont	Tremont	IL	C+	B-	B	142.5	9.52	7.2	2.0	21.6	23.7	9.7	10.8	0.0
The First National Bank of Allendale	Allendale	IL	B	B	B	317.8	10.99	10.0	5.2	14.7	28.4	7.5	9.4	0.0
The First National Bank of Anderson	Anderson	TX	B	B	B	205.9	3.12	8.2	3.1	11.0	10.6	9.0	10.3	0.0
The First National Bank of Anson	Anson	TX	C+	B-	B-	69.5	-3.01	8.6	10.9	20.0	13.8	5.9	7.9	18.3
The First National Bank of Arenzville	Arenzville	IL	B-	B-	B-	113.4	18.77	7.1	4.4	10.8	18.3	6.6	8.6	0.0
The First National Bank of Aspermont	Aspermont	TX	B+	B+	B+	70.0	4.01	4.7	2.5	8.4	66.6	10.0	14.7	0.0
The First National Bank of Assumption	Assumption	IL	C	C	C	24.5	5.49	2.4	3.8	9.4	29.6	7.8	9.5	0.0
▲ The First National Bank of Ava	Ava	IL	B+	B	B	81.1	10.70	5.5	2.2	13.8	54.8	10.0	11.1	22.8
▲ The First National Bank of Ballinger	Ballinger	TX	B	B-	B-	243.3	12.80	11.7	0.8	8.0	20.6	6.7	8.7	15.7
The First National Bank of Bangor	Bangor	WI	A	A	A	263.7	8.17	4.1	1.2	18.6	14.1	10.0	29.8	0.0
The First National Bank of Bastrop	Bastrop	TX	A-	A-	A-	844.0	21.13	2.5	1.3	12.3	40.1	7.0	9.0	18.5
The First National Bank of Beardstown	Beardstown	IL	A-	A-	A-	158.2	12.73	4.7	4.7	9.1	18.2	9.5	10.7	0.0
▲ The First National Bank of Bellevue	Bellevue	OH	B-	C+	C+	304.1	12.38	14.9	0.9	6.0	23.0	5.8	9.1	0.0
The First National Bank of Bellville	Bellville	TX	B+	B+	B+	849.2	8.26	2.3	1.3	8.3	71.5	9.7	10.8	25.6
The First National Bank of Bemidji	Bemidji	MN	A-	A-	A	963.4	18.98	7.9	5.1	5.8	53.9	10.0	11.2	0.0
▼ The First National Bank of Blanchester	Blanchester	OH	B	B+	B+	75.8	14.56	1.3	3.4	45.0	19.8	8.4	9.9	22.8
The First National Bank of Brooksville	Brooksville	KY	C+	B-	B-	73.1	6.02	0.9	1.9	28.2	46.3	8.9	10.2	0.0
The First National Bank of Brownstown	Brownstown	IL	C+	C+	C+	47.1	4.66	7.1	5.7	12.1	41.6	8.4	9.9	24.2
The First National Bank of Buhl	Mountain Iron	MN	D	D	D	30.3	2.08	12.7	9.4	34.4	0.0	5.2	7.2	17.3
The First National Bank of Carmi	Carmi	IL	B-	B-	B	614.8	33.43	12.5	0.4	3.2	12.7	5.7	7.7	13.7
▲ The First National Bank of Chisholm	Chisholm	MN	C	C-	C-	84.1	8.45	1.9	16.4	16.1	44.6	5.6	8.5	0.0
The First National Bank of Cokato	Cokato	MN	B	B	B	95.8	25.50	14.7	2.0	15.8	29.4	5.3	7.3	17.3
The First National Bank of Coleraine	Coleraine	MN	B-	B-	C+	107.0	15.19	3.0	2.6	12.2	48.9	5.5	7.5	20.4
The First National Bank of Dennison, Ohio	Dennison	OH	B-	B-	B	286.9	10.39	5.9	16.3	11.2	40.0	7.0	9.0	0.0
The First National Bank of Dighton	Dighton	KS	B-	B-	B-	68.2	6.79	9.9	2.3	2.8	31.8	10.0	17.3	30.1
The First National Bank of Dozier	Dozier	AL	B-	B-	B-	40.5	8.56	7.3	2.6	8.7	53.8	10.0	13.5	0.0
▼ The First National Bank of Dryden	Dryden	NY	B	B+	B+	220.6	5.80	5.6	4.6	13.3	38.4	7.5	9.3	0.0
The First National Bank of East Texas	Gilmer	TX	B+	B	B-	461.7	2.28	13.3	5.1	16.8	24.0	9.8	10.9	0.0
The First National Bank of Eldorado	Eldorado	TX	A-	A-	A-	72.5	13.97	18.9	2.6	15.3	20.5	10.0	16.4	0.0
The First National Bank of Ely	Ely	NV	B	B	B+	139.9	8.40	5.5	0.2	0.5	82.7	8.2	9.8	0.0
The First National Bank of Evant	Evant	TX	A-	A-	B+	137.0	22.94	7.7	5.2	25.7	8.8	6.3	8.3	0.0
The First National Bank of Fairfax	Fairfax	MN	B+	B+	B+	36.4	8.37	15.2	0.6	0.3	35.0	10.0	33.5	0.0

Asset Quality Index	Adjusted Non-Performing Loans as a % of Total Loans	Adjusted Non-Performing Loans as a % of Capital	Net Charge-Offs Avg Loans	Profitability Index	Net Income ($Mil)	Return on Assets (R.O.A.)	Return on Equity (R.O.E.)	Net Interest Spread	Overhead Efficiency Ratio	Liquidity Index	Liquidity Ratio	Hot Money Ratio	Stability Index
7.3	0.57	2.7	-0.16	**9.5**	33.7	5.96	43.55	1.39	82.8	**0.4**	5.4	57.0	**9.3**
6.7	1.19	4.5	-0.09	**6.6**	20.6	1.34	15.62	3.07	54.4	**6.9**	44.3	2.1	**8.0**
7.9	0.40	2.1	0.01	**6.3**	12.9	1.41	15.71	3.33	55.4	**5.1**	20.3	3.0	**7.7**
10.0	0.59	0.4	-0.01	**5.9**	1.0	0.94	5.33	1.91	64.0	**7.5**	93.4	5.8	**8.2**
3.2	1.54	16.1	0.00	**3.2**	0.4	0.79	9.30	3.48	77.0	**3.6**	24.8	11.9	**3.6**
8.2	0.06	0.8	0.01	**8.3**	20.3	1.64	16.24	3.62	50.7	**4.3**	17.6	7.8	**9.3**
6.9	0.76	2.5	0.00	**5.3**	1.8	1.54	15.44	3.49	61.8	**5.9**	34.2	1.5	**7.0**
8.8	0.00	0.0	0.04	**3.7**	0.2	0.75	10.56	2.78	77.0	**5.6**	54.8	9.5	**3.7**
5.9	0.63	4.6	0.00	**4.3**	2.4	0.93	11.43	3.29	60.6	**1.3**	13.9	20.0	**5.3**
9.1	0.00	0.0	0.00	**2.4**	0.1	0.18	1.12	2.08	92.0	**5.7**	56.3	10.7	**7.3**
9.1	0.45	1.5	-0.08	**2.2**	0.3	0.16	1.28	2.99	95.2	**6.1**	41.9	3.1	**6.9**
9.0	0.09	1.4	-0.01	**5.4**	0.4	1.45	7.51	3.31	55.7	**3.3**	50.1	20.0	**8.0**
7.5	0.33	2.0	0.06	**5.5**	2.5	1.27	11.66	3.80	72.6	**5.0**	27.7	4.8	**7.2**
5.2	3.96	10.0	-0.04	**4.5**	0.9	0.76	7.90	3.36	70.4	**6.3**	48.4	4.4	**6.3**
5.0	3.10	8.6	0.01	**5.0**	2.4	1.24	13.88	3.43	63.5	**6.5**	55.8	5.6	**5.2**
7.7	0.22	1.3	0.03	**4.6**	0.8	0.82	11.53	3.27	64.6	**5.5**	30.4	2.5	**4.1**
3.7	4.40	16.8	-0.02	**5.7**	2.0	1.40	11.06	3.68	63.3	**3.2**	30.6	15.7	**8.1**
5.3	1.91	7.8	-0.05	**9.0**	7.0	1.73	13.74	4.00	49.4	**4.5**	30.0	7.6	**8.9**
6.5	1.24	3.4	0.00	**3.9**	5.4	0.76	7.77	2.86	72.9	**6.2**	38.8	4.7	**7.7**
4.5	0.82	4.1	0.01	**9.2**	2.9	2.51	20.31	4.96	53.4	**1.8**	22.2	21.4	**8.7**
5.9	0.43	2.3	0.00	**2.6**	0.0	0.25	3.00	3.52	91.4	**5.2**	44.7	10.0	**3.8**
9.2	0.18	0.6	-0.07	**4.3**	1.6	1.20	11.76	3.22	64.0	**6.3**	53.9	6.2	**6.6**
8.7	0.08	0.9	0.00	**4.4**	1.1	0.91	9.35	2.76	61.0	**5.2**	30.6	4.9	**5.7**
7.5	0.00	4.5	0.02	**3.7**	0.1	0.55	4.16	2.24	76.1	**5.6**	60.6	10.6	**6.8**
6.1	0.48	2.8	0.05	**5.9**	2.3	1.15	12.59	3.48	65.1	**4.3**	26.5	8.5	**6.9**
7.3	0.49	1.7	-0.04	**5.2**	0.7	1.56	17.79	3.27	52.9	**5.0**	35.4	7.8	**4.2**
8.4	0.00	0.0	0.02	**2.9**	0.1	0.39	4.18	3.95	91.2	**3.2**	31.0	16.0	**4.9**
5.2	1.82	9.5	-0.04	**5.5**	7.7	1.00	8.25	3.38	67.2	**4.8**	9.7	3.3	**9.7**
7.1	0.42	2.4	0.01	**2.9**	0.3	0.39	3.39	2.95	84.2	**4.2**	35.6	12.7	**6.7**
5.5	0.82	4.1	0.01	**5.1**	1.5	1.00	10.15	3.19	60.1	**3.2**	26.6	14.3	**5.4**
8.6	0.15	0.7	-0.03	**4.1**	0.7	0.69	6.77	3.61	72.3	**2.2**	33.3	25.0	**6.5**
4.4	1.63	9.6	-0.24	**5.7**	0.4	0.98	12.58	3.90	74.3	**6.3**	41.1	1.9	**5.7**
7.8	0.08	0.5	0.00	**4.3**	0.6	1.05	11.96	3.04	68.2	**5.3**	40.0	7.8	**5.8**
9.5	0.00	0.0	-0.02	**5.0**	0.5	1.34	8.41	2.51	59.8	**3.4**	55.0	21.0	**8.3**
7.6	0.86	3.2	-0.04	**3.3**	0.1	0.70	7.39	2.64	72.9	**6.7**	69.9	3.4	**4.4**
5.4	5.22	11.8	-0.12	**5.2**	0.4	1.06	8.86	3.66	61.1	**5.8**	59.6	9.1	**7.3**
5.3	1.09	5.4	0.00	**6.4**	1.8	1.57	16.89	4.20	58.7	**3.7**	39.7	16.6	**6.5**
8.7	1.44	1.8	0.00	**9.8**	3.2	2.40	8.24	4.07	22.0	**5.4**	29.7	2.7	**9.7**
5.6	1.25	6.0	0.02	**6.6**	6.0	1.52	15.48	3.37	58.3	**4.6**	44.1	13.1	**7.9**
8.5	0.00	0.5	0.01	**5.7**	1.1	1.44	13.34	3.51	63.1	**4.9**	30.8	6.5	**7.1**
5.4	0.74	3.8	0.27	**5.5**	1.7	1.10	11.86	3.73	64.0	**2.3**	30.3	6.8	**6.3**
8.7	0.02	0.0	0.00	**5.4**	6.3	1.53	11.05	2.94	49.6	**2.8**	56.5	37.6	**8.7**
6.4	1.41	4.4	-0.01	**8.1**	8.8	2.12	15.59	3.47	43.6	**3.4**	36.2	16.9	**10.0**
6.3	1.05	5.9	0.06	**3.7**	0.2	0.60	5.87	3.15	77.0	**5.6**	37.6	4.7	**5.3**
7.1	1.01	3.9	-0.02	**3.8**	0.3	0.89	8.10	3.36	75.7	**4.8**	27.5	5.7	**6.2**
5.9	0.77	4.1	-0.04	**3.3**	0.1	0.51	4.85	2.45	77.2	**5.4**	54.8	10.6	**5.3**
5.4	0.39	2.8	0.00	**2.0**	0.0	0.10	1.16	3.80	97.6	**3.8**	33.7	13.8	**4.1**
3.5	2.09	12.7	0.06	**3.6**	1.7	0.57	6.13	2.93	77.9	**5.5**	38.8	5.8	**5.8**
7.6	0.03	1.5	0.21	**3.2**	0.3	0.68	7.11	3.59	73.8	**5.8**	39.7	4.4	**4.3**
8.8	0.02	0.1	0.00	**7.0**	0.8	1.73	23.62	3.79	53.6	**5.7**	48.2	7.1	**5.1**
9.5	0.00	0.0	-0.01	**3.3**	0.3	0.54	7.00	2.35	72.3	**5.7**	53.5	9.9	**3.9**
7.9	0.10	0.6	-0.05	**3.5**	0.7	0.48	5.53	3.22	83.0	**6.4**	54.6	5.5	**4.8**
8.7	0.17	0.8	0.05	**3.6**	0.4	1.03	6.08	2.46	58.7	**6.2**	43.5	2.7	**6.0**
9.5	0.00	0.2	0.00	**3.0**	0.1	0.63	4.42	2.62	78.0	**4.2**	73.8	19.7	**7.0**
5.2	2.86	9.2	0.08	**4.2**	1.0	0.96	10.00	2.63	61.8	**6.7**	48.9	1.9	**5.9**
4.8	0.78	5.2	-0.10	**7.0**	3.8	1.75	13.90	4.30	61.7	**1.9**	24.0	21.9	**8.0**
7.3	1.02	3.0	0.00	**10.0**	1.0	2.76	17.10	5.82	52.3	**5.5**	29.3	1.9	**9.2**
9.7	2.69	0.9	0.00	**4.6**	0.8	1.14	9.78	2.27	48.0	**7.8**	72.9	0.0	**6.4**
8.8	0.00	0.0	-0.02	**6.7**	1.0	1.54	17.50	3.95	64.7	**5.6**	47.2	8.4	**6.0**
8.7	0.29	0.0	0.29	**4.7**	0.2	0.90	2.67	2.90	73.3	**7.2**	74.4	3.1	**7.8**

Name	City	State	Rating	2020 Rating	2019 Rating	Total Assets ($Mil)	One Year Asset Growth	Asset Mix (As a % of Total Assets): Commercial Loans	Consumer Loans	Mortgage Loans	Securities	Capitalization Index	Leverage Ratio	Risk-Based Capital Ratio
▲ The First National Bank of Fleming	Fleming	CO	C-	D+	C	26.8	11.05	7.7	1.6	3.7	11.6	10.0	11.1	0.0
The First National Bank of Fletcher	Fletcher	OK	A-	A-	B+	24.0	16.53	7.2	4.5	2.7	42.8	7.2	9.2	0.0
The First National Bank of Floydada	Floydada	TX	B+	B+	A-	117.2	5.89	10.0	1.7	0.1	22.3	8.6	10.0	17.6
The First National Bank of Fort Smith	Fort Smith	AR	A-	A-	A-	1792.5	1.71	11.3	0.5	9.2	4.3	6.3	8.9	0.0
▲ The First National Bank of Frederick	Frederick	SD	C+	C	C+	28.3	31.53	5.2	0.9	0.4	29.1	10.0	11.7	0.0
▲ The First National Bank of Germantown	Germantown	OH	B-	C	C	76.3	10.80	7.5	3.5	35.1	28.1	6.5	8.5	0.0
The First National Bank of Gilbert	Gilbert	MN	D+	D+	D+	65.6	18.67	6.0	5.4	53.0	6.7	4.3	6.3	13.1
▼ The First National Bank of Gordon	Gordon	NE	B+	A-	B+	299.5	29.93	7.6	1.8	0.0	54.3	9.9	10.9	25.1
The First National Bank of Granbury	Granbury	TX	B+	A-	A-	833.8	21.05	3.4	2.4	16.2	43.2	8.8	10.2	0.0
The First National Bank of Grayson	Grayson	KY	B+	A-	A-	320.2	12.31	5.2	9.2	19.9	24.9	4.6	10.6	0.0
The First National Bank of Groton	Groton	NY	A-	A-	A-	207.6	4.79	9.5	6.7	21.6	46.3	10.0	13.2	0.0
▼ The First National Bank of Hebbronville	Hebbronville	TX	B+	A-	A-	97.8	6.78	1.7	8.6	8.8	57.5	10.0	16.7	47.0
The First National Bank of Henning	Ottertail	MN	A-	A-	A-	279.8	16.60	6.7	5.3	13.6	41.2	9.0	10.3	18.6
▲ The First National Bank of Hereford	Hereford	TX	B+	B	B	201.9	5.52	16.9	1.2	7.8	10.2	7.8	9.6	13.1
The First National Bank of Hooker	Hooker	OK	B+	B+	B	88.8	10.49	6.4	2.4	12.6	31.2	10.0	13.2	22.3
▲ The First National Bank of Hope	Hope	KS	D+	D	D-	90.4	-6.80	3.6	1.1	2.1	35.6	10.0	11.1	17.9
The First National Bank of Hughes Springs	Hughes Springs	TX	B	B	B	334.0	11.48	15.1	3.9	14.4	7.9	9.2	10.5	20.7
The First National Bank of Hutchinson	Hutchinson	KS	B+	B+	A-	885.0	-0.15	11.7	1.1	9.1	24.0	9.5	11.0	14.6
The First National Bank of Jeanerette	Jeanerette	LA	B	B	B	377.7	21.31	8.8	1.8	20.3	7.7	7.0	9.0	15.2
The First National Bank of Kemp	Kemp	TX	B-	B-	B-	122.8	12.15	13.7	0.8	14.3	32.4	7.2	9.1	0.0
▼ The First National Bank of Lawrence Count	Walnut Ridge	AR	B	B+	B+	272.7	5.28	7.9	1.6	11.4	39.6	7.7	9.5	0.0
The First National Bank of Le Center	Lonsdale	MN	B+	B+	A-	134.6	2.96	10.4	4.0	8.9	14.5	9.3	10.5	0.0
The First National Bank of Lindsay	Lindsay	OK	B+	B+	B+	84.3	4.00	28.7	3.3	14.5	11.8	10.0	11.3	17.1
▲ The First National Bank of Lipan	Lipan	TX	C-	D+	C-	28.0	3.17	2.3	11.3	7.6	16.9	5.6	7.6	25.4
The First National Bank of Litchfield	Litchfield	IL	A-	A-	B+	123.9	15.35	12.4	2.6	10.5	21.8	10.0	11.3	16.4
The First National Bank of Livingston	Livingston	TX	B+	A-	B+	495.5	15.64	3.4	2.8	13.0	53.6	10.0	11.9	40.4
The First National Bank of Long Island	Glen Head	NY	B	B	B	4110.2	-3.22	4.4	0.0	30.3	19.6	8.3	9.8	0.0
The First National Bank of Louisburg	Louisburg	KS	B+	B+	A-	166.4	13.71	6.2	0.5	21.1	46.1	8.1	9.7	0.0
The First National Bank of Manning	Manning	IA	B+	B+	B+	76.9	13.47	5.5	1.4	6.8	20.8	10.0	16.2	35.6
The First National Bank of McConnelsville	McConnelsville	OH	C	C	C+	193.2	12.98	4.7	3.6	32.2	25.3	4.0	6.0	15.2
▼ The First National Bank of McGregor	McGregor	TX	C+	B+	B+	716.7	7.77	10.9	2.3	21.4	8.9	7.7	9.5	14.2
The First National Bank of McIntosh	McIntosh	MN	B-	B-	B	33.0	19.07	1.5	4.5	8.7	20.2	10.0	20.6	78.8
The First National Bank of Mertzon	Mertzon	TX	B-	B-	B-	486.2	-4.93	3.7	0.8	1.4	44.3	6.3	8.3	47.3
The First National Bank of Milaca	Milaca	MN	B+	B+	A-	269.8	14.16	13.4	3.8	14.2	35.7	8.8	10.2	21.4
The First National Bank of Monterey	Monterey	IN	B	B	B	386.7	11.43	3.2	0.9	10.2	32.1	10.0	12.0	0.0
The First National Bank of Moody	Moody	TX	B	B	B-	52.7	7.41	4.3	3.0	16.4	33.3	10.0	20.1	0.0
The First National Bank of Moose Lake	Moose Lake	MN	A-	A-	A-	124.4	-5.08	6.8	3.6	22.2	15.6	10.0	13.4	0.0
The First National Bank of Mount Dora	Mount Dora	FL	A-	A-	A-	370.3	24.74	3.4	1.5	8.2	56.1	9.2	10.4	19.9
The First National Bank of Nevada	Nevada	MO	B	B	B	114.8	10.83	4.3	1.3	9.6	38.0	10.0	12.9	23.7
The First National Bank of Okawville	Okawville	IL	C+	B-	B	76.0	11.16	1.6	1.0	5.6	60.3	8.6	10.1	21.2
The First National Bank of Osakis	Osakis	MN	B-	B-	B-	87.4	14.27	5.4	2.1	18.3	19.5	5.6	7.6	12.6
The First National Bank of Ottawa	Ottawa	IL	C+	C+	B	958.5	21.93	35.8	0.2	8.0	6.4	2.8	8.6	0.0
The First National Bank of Pandora	Pandora	OH	B-	B-	C+	229.9	11.55	10.2	2.7	17.3	24.7	6.3	8.3	13.0
The First National Bank of Peterstown	Peterstown	WV	C+	B-	B	84.0	11.89	3.5	3.3	29.1	28.8	9.2	10.4	22.4
The First National Bank of Primghar	Primghar	IA	B	B-	B-	39.8	19.73	5.1	1.1	0.3	24.3	10.0	15.8	29.3
▼ The First National Bank of Proctor	Proctor	MN	D+	C-	C-	31.0	16.64	1.1	3.4	31.0	16.4	6.3	8.4	0.0
The First National Bank of Quitaque	Quitaque	TX	B-	B	B	89.9	20.71	5.8	4.2	0.0	12.3	9.4	10.6	0.0
The First National Bank of Raymond	Raymond	IL	B-	B-	C+	181.4	9.48	4.8	1.6	6.6	50.0	7.8	9.6	0.0
The First National Bank of River Falls	River Falls	WI	B+	B+	A-	339.3	5.59	6.0	1.0	9.3	42.8	8.2	9.8	20.4
The First National Bank of Russell Springs	Russell Springs	KY	B	B	B	279.4	7.95	5.4	1.5	10.4	24.9	10.0	11.3	0.0
The First National Bank of Saint Ignace	Saint Ignace	MI	D+	C-	C-	333.3	14.10	2.8	1.6	6.0	58.2	4.4	6.4	14.7
▼ The First National Bank of Sandoval	Sandoval	IL	B-	B	B	73.4	14.70	10.0	7.8	32.6	18.6	9.1	10.4	18.6
▲ The First National Bank of Scott City	Scott City	KS	A-	B	B	149.0	10.83	9.6	5.0	5.6	27.6	10.0	11.2	0.0
The First National Bank of Sedan	Sedan	KS	D-	D-	C-	60.2	-4.54	7.4	2.0	8.5	19.2	9.3	10.5	0.0
The First National Bank of Shiner	Shiner	TX	B+	B+	B+	1002.0	11.56	2.2	0.5	4.2	76.0	9.3	10.5	27.8
The First National Bank of Sonora	Sonora	TX	B-	B-	B	548.8	7.48	7.1	2.9	18.1	3.0	6.8	8.8	15.5
The First National Bank of Sparta	Sparta	IL	A-	A-	A-	109.5	18.18	9.7	7.5	16.7	41.4	9.5	10.6	25.7
The First National Bank of Stanton	Stanton	TX	B+	B+	B+	270.7	10.32	2.9	1.0	1.8	61.0	7.8	9.6	28.9
The First National Bank of Sterling City	Sterling City	TX	C	C	C	213.3	5.78	2.2	1.7	4.5	72.6	6.5	8.5	37.3
The First National Bank of Stigler	Stigler	OK	B+	B+	B	146.7	12.73	7.2	1.6	3.2	50.3	5.5	7.5	21.2

Asset Quality Index	Adjusted Non-Performing Loans as a % of Total Loans	Adjusted Non-Performing Loans as a % of Capital	Net Charge-Offs Avg Loans	Profitability Index	Net Income ($Mil)	Return on Assets (R.O.A.)	Return on Equity (R.O.E.)	Net Interest Spread	Overhead Efficiency Ratio	Liquidity Index	Liquidity Ratio	Hot Money Ratio	Stability Index
7.0	0.33	1.8	0.00	**4.9**	0.2	1.83	16.88	5.07	60.8	**0.9**	21.3	40.1	**3.9**
9.2	0.30	0.3	0.00	**3.2**	0.1	0.69	6.32	3.59	85.7	**6.5**	66.4	3.6	**5.8**
8.8	0.00	0.0	-0.01	**5.8**	0.9	1.42	14.40	2.31	50.0	**3.6**	45.0	18.3	**7.3**
8.2	0.29	1.6	-0.12	**8.5**	14.1	1.59	15.86	3.32	49.0	**5.9**	30.7	4.3	**9.6**
9.4	0.00	0.0	0.00	**2.9**	0.1	0.45	3.67	1.73	80.3	**6.6**	68.2	5.7	**5.3**
6.9	0.47	2.5	0.01	**5.1**	0.4	1.03	12.03	3.69	64.5	**5.1**	31.0	5.6	**4.5**
5.1	0.81	8.5	0.00	**4.3**	0.3	0.95	15.56	3.79	66.6	**4.0**	17.7	8.8	**3.0**
5.0	2.42	7.7	1.32	**7.9**	2.7	2.04	17.44	4.17	44.5	**2.7**	9.3	14.4	**7.1**
6.0	1.74	5.2	0.16	**5.3**	5.0	1.25	11.86	3.21	61.8	**5.5**	56.1	11.4	**7.1**
5.7	0.96	4.4	-0.01	**6.6**	1.8	1.11	10.36	3.18	63.8	**5.1**	37.7	8.6	**7.2**
5.5	3.36	10.9	0.43	**5.3**	1.0	0.93	6.71	3.70	65.2	**4.4**	26.2	8.1	**7.8**
8.4	0.80	1.2	-0.08	**4.8**	0.6	1.14	6.69	2.95	67.4	**2.5**	50.5	32.1	**8.2**
7.9	0.11	2.2	0.02	**6.3**	2.0	1.50	13.65	3.19	59.1	**4.1**	37.2	13.6	**7.9**
7.5	0.09	2.5	-0.07	**6.2**	1.5	1.46	15.21	3.65	63.3	**3.1**	28.0	15.4	**5.5**
5.9	1.54	7.1	0.00	**5.0**	0.5	1.05	7.82	3.73	67.4	**3.5**	36.3	16.4	**7.9**
1.4	10.25	39.1	1.39	**1.4**	-0.1	-0.12	-1.10	2.25	90.6	**4.4**	42.2	13.1	**5.4**
4.0	3.30	12.1	-0.16	**7.7**	2.7	1.65	15.48	3.83	64.1	**5.1**	36.3	7.4	**8.4**
8.5	0.00	0.0	0.00	**5.7**	6.7	1.47	13.10	3.49	64.3	**4.4**	20.4	6.5	**8.1**
4.4	1.81	10.8	0.02	**5.3**	2.1	1.13	12.34	3.63	64.6	**4.1**	35.7	13.0	**6.1**
8.3	0.22	1.1	0.00	**4.5**	0.6	0.98	9.37	3.67	72.7	**5.4**	41.0	7.6	**5.9**
7.4	0.78	3.6	0.13	**3.8**	1.0	0.73	7.59	2.90	74.8	**3.1**	43.2	21.2	**6.7**
2.0	4.38	22.2	-0.06	**4.9**	0.8	1.15	11.23	2.86	61.4	**4.4**	29.1	9.2	**7.6**
4.0	2.71	15.0	0.00	**7.6**	0.8	1.94	17.70	4.12	45.7	**1.1**	15.4	30.7	**7.8**
8.5	0.00	0.0	0.00	**2.1**	0.0	0.14	1.85	2.59	91.8	**7.0**	76.5	4.2	**3.2**
8.2	0.02	1.5	0.02	**6.0**	1.0	1.60	13.66	3.10	59.1	**3.1**	23.6	14.3	**7.7**
9.2	0.12	0.3	0.08	**4.7**	2.5	1.05	7.83	2.40	71.7	**7.1**	69.0	4.0	**8.2**
9.0	0.03	0.1	0.03	**5.2**	23.6	1.14	11.58	2.70	53.2	**4.7**	15.7	4.4	**8.7**
9.7	0.18	0.7	-0.01	**4.7**	0.9	1.06	9.80	2.82	63.8	**5.1**	48.4	11.5	**8.2**
9.0	0.00	0.0	-0.01	**4.1**	0.3	0.74	4.65	2.22	62.2	**5.2**	64.6	12.9	**7.7**
6.7	0.27	1.6	0.01	**3.1**	0.5	0.54	5.85	2.87	77.2	**4.8**	17.2	3.9	**4.8**
2.7	2.54	17.9	0.31	**4.7**	3.3	0.90	9.83	4.18	67.7	**0.8**	22.6	23.5	**6.0**
9.2	0.00	0.0	0.00	**2.8**	0.1	0.33	1.52	1.87	86.3	**6.4**	79.1	9.1	**6.3**
10.0	0.04	0.1	-0.09	**3.8**	1.4	0.58	7.01	1.50	53.1	**7.0**	78.5	6.2	**4.3**
5.3	1.43	6.0	0.15	**6.1**	2.0	1.50	14.58	3.59	63.4	**6.3**	46.5	3.8	**6.5**
7.7	0.60	5.4	0.00	**3.9**	1.4	0.75	6.02	2.80	69.2	**4.8**	46.2	12.8	**7.1**
6.3	3.21	6.4	-0.25	**4.3**	0.2	0.89	4.26	3.76	77.4	**5.7**	47.5	6.9	**8.2**
6.3	0.86	6.1	0.00	**8.4**	1.3	2.11	16.12	4.23	55.0	**1.9**	22.0	11.1	**9.1**
5.9	3.94	5.6	0.18	**5.9**	2.2	1.29	10.00	2.96	68.8	**6.9**	62.5	4.5	**8.1**
6.7	2.24	6.4	0.00	**3.4**	0.4	0.72	5.39	3.07	70.8	**6.5**	66.7	7.9	**7.6**
10.0	0.00	0.0	0.01	**3.3**	0.3	0.66	6.64	2.63	74.1	**6.8**	68.4	4.6	**5.3**
6.9	0.06	0.7	0.00	**3.9**	0.4	0.97	9.05	3.48	65.6	**4.3**	31.2	10.7	**6.0**
5.9	0.55	3.2	0.15	**5.5**	6.1	1.28	14.94	3.84	56.7	**3.6**	7.1	10.2	**6.0**
5.8	1.12	4.4	0.01	**4.8**	1.2	1.05	12.62	3.68	69.2	**3.3**	19.9	13.0	**5.2**
6.2	0.97	4.3	0.06	**3.2**	0.2	0.58	5.56	2.71	76.5	**4.5**	48.9	13.9	**5.1**
8.9	0.00	0.0	0.00	**4.2**	0.2	0.93	5.93	2.46	69.6	**4.0**	59.7	18.2	**7.0**
7.1	0.58	3.0	0.00	**1.5**	0.0	0.06	0.72	2.73	96.9	**6.6**	60.7	4.0	**3.3**
6.5	0.54	2.1	0.02	**3.8**	0.2	0.48	4.49	2.39	77.6	**4.7**	60.7	15.1	**6.4**
6.3	0.97	4.0	0.00	**3.8**	1.0	1.10	10.75	3.10	64.5	**5.2**	56.3	13.2	**6.0**
9.1	0.06	0.2	-0.01	**5.8**	2.7	1.58	14.86	3.23	59.1	**6.4**	45.7	2.6	**7.4**
8.5	0.79	2.1	0.01	**5.8**	2.0	1.45	12.21	3.24	55.5	**2.1**	17.7	18.7	**7.9**
5.1	4.17	11.4	0.00	**2.6**	0.8	0.47	6.44	2.41	85.2	**5.7**	71.6	13.1	**3.0**
3.4	1.21	14.2	0.82	**5.4**	0.5	1.25	11.50	4.19	57.1	**3.0**	20.8	14.4	**7.2**
6.2	0.80	6.8	-0.06	**5.8**	1.0	1.29	11.47	3.73	59.1	**5.8**	42.9	5.8	**5.8**
7.6	0.39	4.0	0.01	**0.1**	-0.1	-0.38	-3.45	2.67	114.8	**5.2**	44.6	9.9	**4.1**
9.9	0.74	0.9	0.96	**5.3**	7.5	1.60	13.09	2.76	40.2	**3.4**	61.1	33.0	**8.7**
3.9	2.44	13.5	0.02	**3.7**	1.7	0.64	7.29	3.60	76.5	**2.7**	33.1	19.1	**6.0**
6.0	0.71	3.7	0.21	**6.6**	0.8	1.47	13.12	3.89	61.2	**5.8**	38.1	4.0	**7.5**
9.8	0.01	0.0	-0.04	**4.5**	1.0	0.74	6.66	2.65	66.1	**7.1**	67.8	3.8	**6.1**
9.3	1.53	2.8	0.04	**3.9**	0.9	0.87	11.48	1.73	60.9	**6.2**	65.1	9.4	**3.1**
8.3	0.46	1.8	0.00	**8.1**	1.5	2.08	24.44	3.52	46.4	**6.5**	60.4	6.9	**5.8**

Name	City	State	Rating	2020 Rating	2019 Rating	Total Assets ($Mil)	One Year Asset Growth	Comm-ercial Loans	Cons-umer Loans	Mort-gage Loans	Secur-ities	Capital-ization Index	Lever-age Ratio	Risk-Based Capital Ratio
								Asset Mix (As a % of Total Assets)						
▲ The First National Bank of Sycamore	Sycamore	OH	B-	C+	C	190.1	14.36	4.9	1.2	21.2	44.6	7.3	9.2	18.9
The First National Bank of Tom Bean	Tom Bean	TX	C+	C	D+	130.5	1.99	13.9	9.2	21.5	7.3	8.3	9.9	17.1
The First National Bank of Trinity	Trinity	TX	B-	B	B	77.8	20.33	3.4	12.2	10.8	48.3	6.9	8.9	0.0
The First National Bank of Wakefield	Wakefield	MI	C+	C+	C+	59.5	10.67	1.6	9.7	16.7	27.2	6.4	8.4	0.0
The First National Bank of Waseca	Waseca	MN	B+	B+	B	178.3	19.09	6.2	2.0	24.5	8.3	6.2	8.2	0.0
The First National Bank of Waverly	Waverly	OH	C+	C+	C	196.1	19.81	2.4	1.7	13.5	39.7	5.7	7.7	18.5
The First National Bank of Waynesboro	Waynesboro	GA	A	A	A	183.2	13.76	5.1	8.1	23.8	16.5	10.0	15.0	32.7
▼ The First National Bank of Williamson	Williamson	WV	C	C+	B	109.8	13.99	7.5	4.9	28.5	24.6	6.0	8.0	16.2
▼ The First National Bank of Winnsboro	Winnsboro	TX	B+	A-	B+	150.5	5.36	5.4	2.0	14.6	20.3	10.0	19.7	0.0
▲ The First Security Bank	Overbrook	KS	B-	C+	C+	75.3	-3.97	10.5	2.1	26.0	3.7	6.2	8.2	12.0
The First Security Bank	Beaver	OK	C-	D+	D+	119.9	-2.12	6.9	0.9	5.7	24.3	7.4	9.3	13.6
The First State Bank	Ness City	KS	A-	B+	B+	75.1	4.07	6.0	1.9	0.0	62.7	10.0	16.6	32.8
The First State Bank	Norton	KS	B-	B-	B-	482.1	-1.85	9.4	2.4	1.9	49.5	9.8	10.9	0.0
The First State Bank	Boise City	OK	C+	C+	C+	102.5	8.89	15.7	4.7	1.7	14.7	3.7	9.9	0.0
The First State Bank	Pond Creek	OK	B	B	B	53.3	5.88	13.8	2.7	21.7	9.2	10.0	11.6	0.0
▲ The First State Bank	Abernathy	TX	B-	C+	C+	49.7	22.77	37.0	6.9	0.3	6.1	9.4	10.6	22.6
The First State Bank	Columbus	TX	C+	C+	B-	171.6	7.82	2.4	3.2	5.3	54.3	10.0	12.5	30.5
The First State Bank	Louise	TX	B+	B+	A-	654.5	11.31	11.5	0.5	8.6	21.8	4.8	8.6	0.0
The First State Bank	Rice	TX	C+	B-	B-	190.5	12.35	13.2	2.7	9.2	19.3	7.0	9.0	0.0
The First State Bank of Dongola	Dongola	IL	B-	B-	C+	31.0	7.06	6.6	8.8	19.8	10.4	8.4	9.9	21.3
▲ The First State Bank of Fountain	Fountain	MN	C	D+	D	41.2	17.97	5.0	1.3	5.7	51.6	6.4	8.4	18.2
▲ The First State Bank of Healy	Healy	KS	B+	B	B-	84.6	8.74	9.2	0.8	0.9	42.5	10.0	20.9	0.0
The First State Bank of Malta	Malta	MT	D	D	D	163.8	9.64	3.2	1.4	0.0	41.6	10.0	14.5	0.0
▲ The First State Bank of Ransom	Ransom	KS	B+	B	B	49.3	5.19	4.4	0.9	0.6	58.3	10.0	19.8	45.6
The First State Bank of Red Wing	Red Wing	MN	C-	D+	D+	94.4	12.19	3.9	9.3	9.2	45.0	5.6	7.6	20.6
The First State Bank of Rosemount	Rosemount	MN	C-	D+	D-	92.9	13.52	13.1	7.6	16.5	19.8	6.6	8.7	14.8
The First State Bank of Shelby	Shelby	MT	B+	B+	A	152.4	14.94	3.4	0.6	0.0	78.5	10.0	20.1	63.3
The First Trust and Savings Bank of Watse	Watseka	IL	A-	A-	A	296.0	10.13	6.4	1.0	5.5	28.7	10.0	14.5	0.0
The First, A National Banking Assn.	Hattiesburg	MS	B	B	B+	5500.8	8.38	8.5	0.7	12.0	23.3	9.3	10.5	17.6
The Fisher National Bank	Fisher	IL	A	A	A-	174.2	20.14	6.1	1.7	28.8	33.0	10.0	11.5	19.0
The FNB Community Bank	Vandalia	IL	A	A-	A-	447.4	13.67	4.6	0.7	9.9	43.5	10.0	11.4	22.3
The Fort Jennings State Bank	Fort Jennings	OH	B	B	B	220.0	7.97	14.0	2.8	21.7	8.2	9.0	10.3	16.4
The Fountain Trust Co.	Covington	IN	B+	B+	A-	578.3	27.87	5.0	1.2	14.5	42.6	7.7	9.5	18.6
The Four County Bank	Allentown	GA	A-	A-	B+	82.9	8.44	9.5	9.3	19.1	16.6	10.0	12.9	0.0
▼ The Frederick Community Bank	Cissna Park	IL	B+	A-	B+	163.6	10.21	9.8	2.1	4.3	21.3	7.5	9.4	0.0
The Freedom Bank of Virginia	Fairfax	VA	B	B	B-	837.1	19.97	22.0	1.5	9.0	15.5	8.6	10.6	13.9
The Friendship State Bank	Friendship	IN	B+	A-	A-	516.5	18.78	2.2	2.0	29.7	32.0	6.3	8.3	17.1
The Galion Building and Loan Bank	Galion	OH	D	D	C	72.8	9.71	10.0	1.3	48.3	12.0	8.6	10.1	0.0
The Garrett State Bank	Garrett	IN	B+	B+	B	304.9	0.85	7.3	1.9	53.1	8.0	8.4	10.0	20.4
▲ The Gary State Bank	Gary	MN	B	B-	B-	17.3	18.76	9.6	5.6	0.7	0.0	10.0	12.6	22.4
The Genoa Banking Co.	Genoa	OH	B-	B-	C+	501.5	10.69	8.9	4.2	21.7	17.3	5.7	7.7	13.9
The Geo. D. Warthen Bank	Sandersville	GA	B-	B-	B-	222.1	7.06	10.2	6.9	18.6	15.1	6.2	8.3	0.0
▼ The Gerber State Bank	Argenta	IL	C+	B-	B-	91.6	12.22	9.3	0.9	8.2	52.5	9.7	10.8	26.2
The Gifford State Bank	Gifford	IL	C	C+	C-	182.7	13.47	6.7	2.5	22.9	1.4	6.5	8.5	0.0
The Goldman Sachs Trust Co., N.A.	New York	NY	U	U	U	115.3	17.98	0.0	0.0	0.0	21.8	10.0	84.6	282.9
The Goose River Bank	Mayville	ND	B+	B+	B	137.9	4.15	19.6	2.4	0.6	20.4	5.8	9.1	0.0
The Granger National Bank	Granger	TX	C+	C+	B	40.8	17.56	4.3	2.0	2.9	67.6	10.0	14.2	0.0
The Grant County Bank	Petersburg	WV	B	B	B	318.0	13.49	9.4	2.1	21.8	18.3	10.0	11.8	0.0
The Granville National Bank	Granville	IL	B-	B-	B-	110.8	10.51	3.0	4.0	21.2	39.3	7.5	9.4	0.0
The Gratz Bank	Gratz	PA	B	B	B	420.8	6.45	6.0	0.3	23.6	27.6	6.3	8.3	14.5
The Greenwood's State Bank	Lake Mills	WI	C+	C+	C-	509.8	38.82	25.7	0.4	7.9	8.1	5.5	8.2	11.4
The Guilford Savings Bank	Guilford	CT	B	B-	B	1007.4	7.49	3.9	0.3	32.9	19.7	10.0	11.1	0.0
The Gunnison Bank and Trust Co.	Gunnison	CO	A-	A-	A-	177.4	23.65	7.5	0.1	13.9	5.5	7.1	9.0	18.1
The Halstead Bank	Halstead	KS	B	B	B	154.2	4.93	9.9	6.2	12.8	20.6	5.9	8.3	0.0
The Hamilton Bank	Hamilton	MO	B	B	B	101.5	12.65	3.4	2.1	14.1	47.9	6.5	8.5	14.1
The Hamler State Bank	Hamler	OH	B+	A-	A-	97.5	10.36	6.9	0.8	14.3	21.3	10.0	14.7	0.0
▲ The Harbor Bank of Maryland	Baltimore	MD	D+	D	D-	333.5	1.70	15.2	0.7	16.3	10.6	6.0	8.0	16.1
The Harrison Building and Loan Assn.	Harrison	OH	B-	B-	B	270.3	10.45	4.8	0.1	24.8	47.6	10.0	13.9	0.0
The Harvard State Bank	Harvard	IL	C+	C+	B-	317.1	7.83	3.1	0.8	11.9	45.3	6.3	8.3	16.6
The Havana National Bank	Havana	IL	C+	C	D+	324.4	10.67	4.8	0.9	5.5	17.8	7.0	9.0	0.0

Asset Quality Index	Adjusted Non-Performing Loans as a % of Total Loans	Adjusted Non-Performing Loans as a % of Capital	Net Charge-Offs Avg Loans	Profitability Index	Net Income ($Mil)	Return on Assets (R.O.A.)	Return on Equity (R.O.E.)	Net Interest Spread	Overhead Efficiency Ratio	Liquidity Index	Liquidity Ratio	Hot Money Ratio	Stability Index
8.5	0.12	0.3	0.05	**4.1**	0.9	0.92	8.85	3.31	67.8	**3.5**	38.3	17.1	**6.4**
4.8	0.93	5.5	0.52	**2.8**	0.3	0.43	4.33	4.06	88.0	**1.8**	25.0	22.6	**4.9**
7.7	0.06	0.3	0.21	**3.9**	0.3	0.65	6.96	3.65	82.2	**5.3**	44.5	9.1	**5.3**
7.2	1.52	3.2	0.09	**3.0**	0.2	0.54	6.51	3.15	81.1	**5.5**	62.6	11.5	**3.5**
7.4	0.52	2.2	0.00	**6.8**	1.3	1.57	17.43	3.69	64.6	**5.2**	30.5	4.6	**6.6**
5.4	1.81	8.6	-1.15	**3.9**	0.9	0.94	12.11	2.86	77.1	**4.9**	30.5	6.4	**3.8**
8.6	0.24	0.9	-0.05	**8.3**	1.5	1.57	10.44	3.77	52.7	**4.8**	42.7	11.5	**8.6**
4.5	0.20	6.1	2.57	**1.2**	-0.3	-0.62	-7.16	3.04	73.7	**1.4**	28.9	32.6	**4.8**
5.6	5.61	9.7	-0.15	**4.9**	0.5	0.67	3.28	4.16	80.6	**4.6**	37.3	11.1	**7.7**
8.4	0.00	0.0	-0.01	**6.8**	0.7	1.81	20.36	4.39	59.6	**3.1**	17.7	14.0	**6.0**
6.0	0.26	4.5	0.27	**5.7**	0.7	1.25	13.74	2.98	61.2	**0.9**	20.9	37.3	**6.6**
9.3	2.22	1.8	-0.01	**7.0**	0.7	1.76	10.20	2.90	51.3	**5.1**	47.4	10.9	**8.2**
4.2	2.54	9.8	0.04	**7.1**	4.3	1.80	14.43	3.87	53.7	**2.2**	29.2	16.7	**7.8**
5.2	0.32	2.8	-0.04	**8.4**	1.9	3.89	45.88	4.30	32.9	**0.6**	8.9	23.7	**6.5**
8.5	0.00	0.1	-0.08	**5.2**	0.3	1.27	10.92	4.47	72.7	**3.9**	31.3	12.6	**5.9**
6.3	0.23	0.9	-0.01	**7.5**	1.4	6.27	55.44	15.70	54.4	**3.0**	9.2	13.3	**6.1**
9.5	0.00	0.4	0.00	**3.3**	0.7	0.75	5.48	2.20	72.9	**3.3**	67.6	32.8	**7.1**
8.4	0.15	0.9	0.05	**9.7**	6.5	2.04	23.45	4.82	56.4	**4.8**	26.0	5.2	**7.3**
8.1	0.32	1.3	-0.08	**2.9**	0.5	0.44	4.29	2.84	83.4	**4.6**	33.7	9.8	**6.9**
4.7	2.72	8.9	-0.01	**5.8**	0.2	1.60	15.82	3.81	65.4	**5.9**	53.8	7.0	**5.4**
9.5	0.00	0.0	0.00	**3.1**	0.2	0.90	10.24	3.44	65.5	**5.8**	63.4	9.9	**3.8**
5.8	2.47	8.3	-0.14	**7.0**	0.7	1.77	8.12	3.79	50.4	**2.0**	32.6	27.5	**7.5**
0.3	21.33	50.1	0.05	**2.8**	0.7	0.91	6.18	3.33	57.3	**5.1**	54.9	13.3	**6.5**
8.7	1.03	1.7	0.05	**5.4**	0.3	1.17	5.71	3.11	53.9	**6.0**	69.9	9.7	**6.8**
8.5	0.00	0.0	0.00	**2.3**	0.2	0.32	4.09	2.42	82.0	**5.3**	55.7	11.0	**3.4**
4.9	0.91	6.4	-0.02	**5.1**	0.5	1.16	15.75	4.47	63.9	**5.1**	28.2	4.4	**2.2**
10.0	1.06	0.6	-0.06	**5.1**	0.7	0.97	4.77	2.65	51.2	**7.0**	105.8	10.6	**7.8**
9.1	0.76	1.1	-0.09	**5.6**	1.6	1.10	7.49	2.53	48.3	**6.0**	48.3	6.4	**8.0**
5.3	1.10	4.7	0.24	**6.6**	36.4	1.36	9.95	3.40	53.0	**5.0**	25.8	6.9	**9.8**
8.5	0.85	2.3	0.00	**6.5**	1.2	1.39	11.41	3.39	62.2	**3.9**	33.7	13.5	**8.7**
8.2	0.65	2.6	0.00	**6.8**	3.1	1.38	11.04	3.51	53.8	**5.4**	42.6	8.3	**7.9**
5.6	0.77	4.7	0.15	**5.0**	0.9	0.83	7.91	3.72	65.9	**3.7**	26.0	11.8	**7.4**
5.4	1.10	4.8	-0.04	**6.3**	3.9	1.43	13.54	3.24	62.5	**6.0**	51.7	7.2	**7.9**
8.0	0.25	1.7	0.28	**7.4**	0.7	1.71	12.83	3.95	58.1	**1.8**	35.5	34.0	**9.4**
9.0	0.00	0.0	0.00	**4.4**	0.8	0.94	9.59	2.24	67.5	**5.6**	48.7	9.0	**6.5**
7.1	0.14	1.0	-0.02	**5.0**	5.1	1.24	13.42	3.42	65.3	**1.2**	23.7	24.5	**6.4**
7.4	0.38	2.3	-0.01	**6.1**	3.0	1.21	13.71	3.36	67.4	**5.1**	45.2	11.0	**5.7**
6.6	0.62	4.4	0.00	**1.3**	0.0	0.06	0.57	2.92	97.1	**4.4**	34.4	11.2	**4.8**
5.6	1.62	8.4	0.03	**6.8**	2.6	1.75	17.44	3.40	50.6	**3.7**	27.5	9.6	**7.9**
8.1	0.00	0.0	0.00	**8.7**	0.2	2.25	18.09	6.75	59.2	**5.6**	42.0	3.5	**6.3**
8.6	0.04	0.3	0.00	**4.3**	2.3	0.94	12.08	3.70	73.0	**2.6**	20.5	12.9	**5.2**
4.6	1.49	8.5	0.06	**3.7**	0.7	0.65	7.65	4.06	79.7	**5.7**	38.4	4.9	**4.5**
5.2	4.47	9.2	0.20	**3.0**	0.2	0.50	4.28	2.28	78.0	**5.5**	41.2	7.3	**6.2**
6.1	0.36	6.4	0.00	**2.9**	0.5	0.49	5.82	2.94	80.9	**4.7**	35.8	9.9	**4.0**
10.0	na	0.0	na	**9.5**	25.2	52.91	66.94	0.11	46.4	**4.0**	364.4	0.0	**6.3**
6.9	0.00	3.6	0.00	**5.1**	0.8	1.16	12.42	3.45	67.5	**3.4**	10.5	11.7	**7.3**
8.2	2.05	2.7	0.53	**3.0**	0.1	0.53	3.49	2.27	70.7	**5.2**	81.9	15.5	**5.8**
5.1	1.78	9.6	-0.07	**4.7**	1.4	0.93	8.15	3.77	70.8	**3.3**	24.8	13.2	**7.4**
8.2	0.40	1.6	0.03	**3.8**	0.4	0.76	6.91	2.48	62.5	**6.3**	56.5	6.9	**6.1**
8.5	0.18	1.3	0.00	**4.8**	2.3	1.07	11.64	2.82	59.2	**4.5**	27.7	7.9	**6.2**
4.2	1.20	5.6	0.00	**6.1**	3.1	1.40	14.37	4.62	61.8	**3.7**	25.5	11.7	**6.1**
7.2	0.80	4.0	-0.01	**4.3**	4.7	0.95	8.49	2.96	70.3	**3.3**	30.7	18.7	**8.4**
9.0	0.00	0.0	-0.15	**9.7**	1.8	2.09	23.44	4.39	50.5	**5.9**	44.4	4.8	**6.1**
7.7	0.35	2.0	0.02	**5.3**	0.9	1.21	14.20	3.58	68.3	**2.9**	19.9	8.7	**5.7**
5.7	0.26	10.3	0.00	**6.0**	0.7	1.48	16.45	3.58	60.6	**5.1**	46.3	11.2	**6.3**
8.7	0.00	0.6	0.00	**5.4**	0.7	1.37	9.10	3.32	54.2	**2.5**	24.2	17.3	**8.4**
3.4	3.10	19.1	-0.01	**1.3**	0.5	0.32	4.98	2.75	90.7	**2.1**	27.7	20.8	**2.6**
7.5	2.09	5.2	0.00	**3.2**	0.7	0.49	3.21	3.00	77.1	**5.4**	63.0	13.4	**7.4**
5.3	1.37	4.9	0.15	**3.9**	1.6	1.06	10.74	2.93	67.6	**4.2**	35.0	12.5	**5.5**
4.5	1.49	10.9	-0.01	**3.3**	0.6	0.39	4.08	2.02	76.7	**4.0**	37.0	13.8	**5.2**

Name	City	State	Rating	2020 Rating	2019 Rating	Total Assets ($Mil)	One Year Asset Growth	Asset Mix (As a % of Total Assets) Comm-ercial Loans	Cons-umer Loans	Mort-gage Loans	Secur-ities	Capital-ization Index	Lever-age Ratio	Risk-Based Capital Ratio
The Haverford Trust Co.	Radnor	PA	**A**	A	A	186.7	9.83	1.8	37.2	0.0	0.1	**10.0**	17.5	20.0
The Haviland State Bank	Haviland	KS	**B**	B	B	43.2	4.01	6.5	0.7	0.5	20.8	**10.0**	13.6	0.0
The Henry County Bank	Napoleon	OH	**C+**	C+	C	333.3	7.29	3.4	3.8	13.0	45.4	**7.4**	9.3	0.0
The Hershey State Bank	Hershey	NE	**B+**	B+	B+	86.8	7.11	14.9	3.4	12.6	5.9	**10.0**	13.3	19.7
The Hicksville Bank	Hicksville	OH	**B**	B	B	152.3	16.51	5.0	0.9	13.5	26.2	**10.0**	11.0	0.0
▲ The Hill-Dodge Banking Co.	Warsaw	IL	**C+**	C	B-	50.2	22.65	14.3	3.2	5.6	8.9	**10.0**	12.9	0.0
The Hocking Valley Bank	Athens	OH	**B**	B	B	335.7	9.91	5.5	0.9	24.3	36.3	**7.6**	9.4	0.0
The Home Loan Savings Bank	Coshocton	OH	**A-**	A-	B	253.4	3.32	10.3	2.3	34.8	3.7	**9.6**	10.8	16.3
The Home National Bank of Thorntown	Thorntown	IN	**B-**	B-	B-	146.0	12.38	12.0	1.7	14.1	48.0	**6.9**	8.9	19.1
The Home S&L Co. of Kenton	Kenton	OH	**B-**	B-	B	147.9	3.57	22.7	0.4	16.8	14.9	**10.0**	24.9	0.0
The Home Trust & Savings Bank	Osage	IA	**B+**	B+	B+	260.2	3.82	5.0	1.7	16.2	35.1	**9.0**	10.3	17.9
The HomeTown Bank of Alabama	Oneonta	AL	**A-**	A-	A-	510.2	12.24	5.3	7.5	30.1	26.5	**10.0**	12.7	23.8
▼ The Hondo National Bank	Hondo	TX	**C+**	B-	B+	348.9	9.46	10.3	1.7	10.0	37.6	**7.4**	9.3	16.7
The Honesdale National Bank	Honesdale	PA	**A-**	A-	A-	877.4	13.18	11.1	2.6	18.1	16.9	**10.0**	13.1	0.0
The Hopeton State Bank	Hopeton	OK	**D+**	C-	D+	27.9	4.80	25.7	4.0	0.0	25.5	**9.1**	10.6	14.3
The Huntington National Bank	Columbus	OH	**B-**	B-	B-	174866.0	47.84	18.7	11.7	12.6	19.8	**7.6**	10.8	13.0
▲ The Idabel National Bank	Idabel	OK	**A-**	B+	B+	171.7	19.04	3.7	6.0	14.3	29.1	**10.0**	11.0	0.0
The International Bank of Amherst	Amherst	WI	**A-**	A-	A-	90.9	10.47	7.7	0.6	7.7	28.9	**10.0**	13.0	0.0
▼ The Iuka State Bank	Salem	IL	**C-**	C	C	113.1	-1.66	9.3	12.8	9.3	12.2	**6.6**	8.8	0.0
The Jacksboro National Bank	Jacksboro	TX	**B+**	B+	B+	281.7	12.20	5.8	2.3	9.0	57.8	**8.9**	10.3	22.6
The Jefferson Bank	Greenville	MS	**A-**	A-	A-	144.9	-4.46	11.4	0.2	3.0	27.9	**10.0**	15.9	17.6
The Juniata Valley Bank	Mifflintown	PA	**B-**	B-	B-	834.8	8.77	7.3	0.6	15.7	41.0	**5.9**	7.9	13.1
The Karnes County National Bank	Karnes City	TX	**B**	B	B	426.6	2.33	2.3	0.7	3.1	61.0	**10.0**	11.1	32.2
The Kaw Valley State B&T Co., of Wameg	Wamego	KS	**A-**	A-	A-	227.2	7.92	9.7	1.7	12.6	38.8	**9.9**	10.9	0.0
The Killbuck Savings Bank Co.	Killbuck	OH	**B+**	B+	A-	720.9	15.71	6.4	0.7	17.0	38.1	**6.9**	8.9	15.7
The Lamesa National Bank	Lamesa	TX	**C+**	C+	B-	399.4	4.25	3.1	0.1	0.0	59.6	**6.9**	8.9	20.9
The Lauderdale County Bank	Halls	TN	**C+**	B-	B-	61.7	10.02	16.6	6.3	9.9	34.0	**7.8**	9.5	0.0
▲ The Leaders Bank	Oak Brook	IL	**C+**	C	C+	359.9	-2.40	14.6	0.7	7.3	4.3	**10.0**	12.0	19.8
The Lemont National Bank	Lemont	IL	**D+**	D+	D+	59.0	5.25	0.0	0.0	7.6	36.3	**3.7**	5.7	29.7
The Liberty National Bank in Paris	Paris	TX	**A**	A-	A-	384.6	18.66	6.1	5.3	24.9	34.0	**10.0**	13.9	0.0
The Liberty Savings Assn., FSA	Fort Scott	KS	**C-**	C-	C	31.7	-0.23	0.4	3.4	20.2	49.7	**10.0**	20.7	0.0
The Lincoln National Bank of Hodgenville	Hodgenville	KY	**A-**	A-	A-	378.3	9.44	4.2	4.3	39.3	12.1	**10.0**	12.2	23.7
The Litchfield National Bank	Litchfield	IL	**C+**	C+	C+	123.3	4.97	3.9	4.9	18.2	26.6	**5.7**	7.7	15.0
The Lowell Five Cent Savings Bank	Tewksbury	MA	**B+**	B+	A-	1525.2	11.69	6.1	0.1	20.4	9.7	**10.0**	11.2	16.4
▲ The Lyndon State Bank	Lyndon	KS	**B-**	C	C	88.6	9.40	7.2	2.9	33.5	11.9	**7.9**	9.6	14.8
The Lyon County State Bank	Emporia	KS	**B**	B	B	176.3	12.78	6.9	2.1	22.1	51.1	**6.0**	8.0	21.1
The Lyons National Bank	Lyons	NY	**B**	B	B	1579.9	16.09	10.0	2.0	28.2	23.9	**5.8**	7.8	13.0
The Lytle State Bank of Lytle, Texas	Lytle	TX	**B**	B	B+	108.5	10.41	5.7	14.4	2.7	60.2	**10.0**	14.0	0.0
The Malvern National Bank	Malvern	AR	**C**	C	C	625.2	1.02	5.7	0.6	7.5	32.7	**7.2**	9.2	16.2
The Marblehead Bank	Marblehead	OH	**C-**	C	C	62.5	19.59	2.5	5.7	13.3	63.1	**6.8**	8.8	0.0
The Maries County Bank	Vienna	MO	**B+**	A-	A-	564.6	11.76	3.2	6.7	11.2	44.6	**10.0**	13.9	0.0
▲ The Marion National Bank	Marion	KS	**B**	B-	C+	26.0	1.80	3.7	0.8	6.9	46.7	**10.0**	13.2	0.0
The MassMutual Trust Co., FSB	Enfield	CT	**U**	U	U	90.6	0.26	0.0	0.0	0.0	77.2	**10.0**	32.2	41.8
The Mer Rouge State Bank	Mer Rouge	LA	**C-**	C	C+	52.2	19.70	13.5	0.8	3.6	19.2	**8.7**	10.1	0.0
The Mercantile Bank of Louisiana, Missouri	Louisiana	MO	**B+**	A-	A-	123.2	5.88	3.4	0.7	10.0	12.3	**10.0**	19.1	0.0
The Merchants & Citizens Bank	McRae	GA	**C+**	C+	B-	125.2	12.65	4.0	2.6	12.1	54.0	**10.0**	13.1	31.2
The Merchants & Planters Bank	Clarendon	AR	**C-**	C-	C-	43.1	2.63	17.8	1.8	0.9	60.9	**10.0**	12.1	0.0
The Merchants and Farmers Bank of Salis	Salisbury	MO	**C+**	C+	C+	112.9	9.82	3.2	1.6	11.1	26.5	**6.3**	8.3	15.8
The Metamora State Bank	Metamora	OH	**C**	C	C	96.7	12.35	7.3	0.9	22.4	20.8	**6.1**	8.1	12.9
▲ The Middlefield Banking Co.	Middlefield	OH	**B+**	B	B	1358.4	1.18	14.5	0.7	16.9	11.1	**7.5**	9.6	12.9
▲ The Milford Bank	Milford	CT	**C**	C-	C+	528.4	7.16	10.0	2.3	34.5	8.7	**8.2**	9.8	17.2
The Millyard Bank	Nashua	NH	**D**	D		100.5	75.71	19.9	0.0	13.0	2.0	**10.0**	21.0	27.2
The Miners National Bank of Eveleth	Eveleth	MN	**B-**	B-	C+	83.0	17.40	3.0	3.9	38.8	14.4	**6.0**	8.0	18.4
The Miners State Bank	Iron River	MI	**B-**	B	B	161.5	4.20	8.2	0.3	10.8	17.0	**7.2**	9.2	0.0
▲ The MINT National Bank	Kingwood	TX	**B+**	B-	B-	339.2	9.65	20.9	0.2	7.2	0.0	**7.6**	11.7	0.0
The Missouri Bank	Warrenton	MO	**A-**	A-	A-	396.4	8.32	3.8	0.7	17.2	25.7	**10.0**	11.1	0.0
The Morris Plan Co. of Terre Haute	Terre Haute	IN	**A-**	A-	A-	121.3	8.93	0.1	97.9	1.3	0.7	**10.0**	25.0	26.7
The Muncy Bank and Trust Co.	Muncy	PA	**B+**	B	B	562.2	9.62	5.8	2.1	37.5	17.3	**7.7**	9.5	0.0
The Murray Bank	Murray	KY	**B**	B	B	397.7	17.70	10.1	2.3	20.8	23.9	**6.6**	8.7	15.5
The Napoleon State Bank	Napoleon	IN	**A-**	A-	A-	390.3	24.59	8.3	5.1	14.5	5.6	**7.3**	9.2	0.0

Asset Quality Index	Adjusted Non-Performing Loans as a % of Total Loans	Adjusted Non-Performing Loans as a % of Capital	Net Charge-Offs Avg Loans	Profitability Index	Net Income ($Mil)	Return on Assets (R.O.A.)	Return on Equity (R.O.E.)	Net Interest Spread	Overhead Efficiency Ratio	Liquidity Index	Liquidity Ratio	Hot Money Ratio	Stability Index
6.8	0.00	0.0	0.00	10.0	7.7	8.76	50.57	0.97	72.7	2.9	69.6	84.5	10.0
7.5	1.00	3.2	0.00	5.7	0.3	1.20	8.56	4.02	58.0	4.8	35.0	9.1	7.8
5.4	2.47	6.2	-0.05	3.1	0.9	0.54	5.59	2.67	77.7	2.0	25.4	19.1	5.3
4.1	3.40	12.1	0.03	7.3	0.7	1.65	11.26	3.83	53.2	0.7	16.5	36.7	8.1
5.8	1.09	4.9	0.00	3.9	0.7	0.89	7.42	3.47	71.4	4.7	30.6	8.0	7.2
6.0	2.09	6.4	-0.01	4.6	0.4	1.57	12.15	3.65	51.0	6.0	62.0	8.4	4.2
8.9	0.37	1.9	-0.01	4.1	1.2	0.73	7.63	2.36	66.7	4.9	31.4	6.7	6.2
6.7	0.30	1.9	0.00	7.8	1.9	1.49	13.28	3.79	53.5	3.2	19.3	13.4	8.0
8.2	0.01	0.0	-0.02	4.4	0.6	0.87	9.25	3.50	68.1	4.4	37.7	12.2	5.4
5.3	3.17	8.4	0.00	3.9	0.6	0.79	3.16	2.85	72.3	1.3	30.3	26.9	7.5
7.8	0.16	0.8	0.01	5.7	1.9	1.44	13.40	2.49	37.5	4.2	40.0	14.0	7.3
8.6	0.51	2.2	0.04	7.2	3.7	1.58	12.15	3.37	61.7	2.1	25.8	20.0	9.3
2.0	6.26	29.7	-0.50	4.0	1.7	1.04	12.04	3.40	71.2	4.5	42.5	13.4	5.4
7.7	0.27	1.1	0.06	6.8	6.3	1.50	11.14	3.64	57.2	4.3	28.1	9.3	8.9
8.2	0.00	0.0	-0.01	2.2	0.1	0.44	3.87	4.20	88.3	1.4	31.7	36.7	6.0
4.4	1.37	6.0	0.30	5.0	633.9	0.98	9.23	3.08	64.4	5.1	18.7	1.6	9.1
6.4	0.76	4.3	0.04	8.5	1.7	2.12	18.91	4.01	44.7	1.4	24.4	28.4	7.7
9.4	0.00	0.0	0.04	6.5	0.7	1.62	12.57	3.47	53.0	6.4	59.5	4.8	8.5
2.0	2.23	15.8	0.54	4.3	0.3	0.58	6.58	3.73	70.1	2.4	21.0	17.6	5.1
7.0	1.00	3.2	0.12	4.9	1.8	1.31	10.22	3.46	69.4	5.3	45.1	9.7	6.9
7.4	0.35	1.3	-0.16	6.6	1.1	1.46	9.64	4.07	55.1	0.8	23.0	45.6	7.7
6.3	1.25	3.9	-0.04	3.9	3.4	0.84	9.35	2.73	74.6	4.8	35.8	7.0	6.1
6.1	6.62	11.4	-0.06	3.3	1.0	0.44	3.80	2.01	82.5	7.0	75.2	6.0	5.5
5.2	1.69	6.9	-0.02	7.4	2.1	1.91	16.58	3.01	48.7	5.9	46.4	6.1	8.5
9.4	0.16	0.8	-0.02	4.5	2.8	0.79	8.60	2.60	69.0	5.4	43.0	8.0	6.6
7.1	2.36	5.2	-5.18	3.6	1.7	0.80	9.01	0.99	79.2	3.9	63.0	22.6	4.2
6.8	0.92	2.3	-0.09	2.9	0.1	0.44	4.48	3.33	83.9	3.1	50.8	23.7	4.5
6.9	1.09	3.4	0.14	3.0	0.9	0.50	3.96	2.86	80.1	1.6	33.9	38.4	6.6
10.0	0.00	0.0	0.00	1.3	0.0	-0.10	-1.61	1.73	106.1	7.8	88.5	1.1	2.0
8.8	0.02	0.4	0.09	6.3	2.5	1.39	9.81	3.46	50.7	4.7	32.4	8.6	8.1
10.0	0.00	0.0	0.00	1.2	0.0	-0.09	-0.43	2.00	104.4	4.4	90.2	21.6	6.5
8.8	0.26	1.3	0.02	5.5	2.0	1.08	8.60	3.42	62.1	4.1	30.7	11.4	8.2
4.2	0.95	12.5	-0.01	3.8	0.4	0.64	8.63	3.26	75.6	4.8	40.1	11.0	4.5
4.2	3.25	19.5	-0.03	4.1	4.8	0.65	5.97	3.08	71.4	5.1	27.5	7.5	8.3
7.6	0.00	1.2	0.01	4.5	0.4	0.99	9.88	4.70	79.4	4.0	17.4	9.0	5.4
9.5	0.02	0.1	0.00	4.7	1.1	1.23	12.73	3.21	69.8	6.8	54.3	3.0	6.7
8.2	0.45	2.8	0.00	4.2	6.1	0.80	10.58	3.02	72.5	4.1	19.4	9.1	6.9
8.1	0.66	1.7	0.16	3.4	0.3	0.61	4.25	2.98	78.7	5.4	51.4	10.8	6.7
8.2	0.35	1.6	0.01	3.1	2.1	0.69	7.06	2.82	77.0	3.4	32.5	15.5	6.3
9.1	0.00	0.0	0.00	2.1	0.1	0.50	5.16	2.63	98.0	6.2	54.8	5.1	4.7
8.3	0.84	2.3	0.24	5.1	2.9	1.04	7.16	3.76	66.0	4.1	34.3	12.5	8.4
8.1	0.00	0.0	0.00	4.0	0.1	0.78	4.56	3.19	68.6	5.9	63.8	9.2	7.3
10.0	na	0.0	na	9.5	1.6	3.86	12.28	0.52	89.7	3.9	131.6	100.0	7.0
8.9	0.28	1.1	-0.02	1.8	0.0	0.14	1.34	2.89	95.0	4.2	57.1	17.1	3.4
6.4	3.37	4.8	-0.02	5.6	0.9	1.40	7.20	3.50	59.5	5.4	41.2	8.1	9.2
8.5	0.09	0.4	-0.03	2.8	0.4	0.63	3.96	2.81	83.1	3.5	53.1	22.6	6.7
9.1	0.49	1.1	0.00	1.3	0.0	0.12	0.94	2.76	95.9	5.5	50.0	8.8	4.6
9.0	0.07	0.5	-0.05	3.5	0.4	0.79	9.41	3.45	77.5	5.4	39.5	7.3	5.2
5.7	1.24	5.2	0.00	3.0	0.2	0.52	6.13	3.59	83.1	3.6	28.9	12.8	4.1
5.8	0.96	5.5	0.03	6.3	9.7	1.41	12.92	3.81	53.7	3.5	14.4	10.9	8.8
6.6	0.53	3.0	0.00	2.6	1.1	0.42	4.30	3.34	86.7	4.7	21.9	4.8	6.1
7.3	0.00	0.0	0.00	0.1	-0.1	-0.31	-1.57	3.75	97.9	1.7	21.5	15.8	1.6
9.3	0.10	0.7	0.00	3.9	0.3	0.69	8.38	4.86	77.0	5.0	29.8	5.7	4.0
8.9	0.02	0.3	0.05	3.3	0.5	0.57	5.98	3.02	80.2	4.0	40.3	15.1	5.5
7.0	0.12	0.8	0.00	9.0	3.5	1.94	18.60	5.12	43.5	0.6	12.4	47.9	7.6
9.2	0.78	1.8	0.01	6.4	3.2	1.65	14.66	3.38	52.0	4.9	30.4	6.5	8.0
5.3	0.49	1.7	0.31	10.0	3.3	5.50	22.30	11.34	27.8	0.1	1.5	67.2	8.6
6.6	0.43	2.4	0.03	6.7	4.3	1.55	15.72	3.59	59.0	1.9	10.9	18.9	7.4
8.0	0.27	1.7	0.01	5.3	2.7	1.40	16.07	3.28	55.1	3.9	28.8	11.7	5.6
6.7	0.44	2.4	0.00	6.6	2.5	1.31	14.17	3.40	54.9	3.9	39.6	15.2	6.1

	Name	City	State	Rating	2020 Rating	2019 Rating	Total Assets ($Mil)	One Year Asset Growth	Comm-ercial Loans	Cons-umer Loans	Mort-gage Loans	Secur-ities	Capital-ization Index	Lever-age Ratio	Risk-Based Capital Ratio
	The National Bank of Adams County	West Union	OH	**B-**	B	B	101.5	5.61	2.1	2.4	19.7	23.4	**7.4**	9.3	0.0
	The National Bank of Andrews	Andrews	TX	**C-**	C-	C+	250.9	1.69	26.7	2.8	7.3	13.2	**8.3**	9.9	13.9
	The National Bank of Blacksburg	Blacksburg	VA	**A-**	A-	A	1658.3	15.90	4.2	1.9	11.0	37.3	**10.0**	11.2	19.5
▲	The National Bank of Coxsackie	Coxsackie	NY	**B-**	C	C	464.0	27.36	8.3	1.9	31.7	32.7	**6.3**	8.3	18.3
	The National Bank of Indianapolis	Indianapolis	IN	**B**	B	B	3009.9	18.32	11.3	0.9	8.6	19.7	**5.1**	7.1	14.3
▲	The National Bank of Malvern	Malvern	PA	**A-**	B+	B+	191.7	11.15	8.1	0.4	17.1	13.5	**10.0**	13.2	0.0
	The National Bank of Texas at Fort Worth	Fort Worth	TX	**C+**	C	B-	381.5	10.97	14.8	3.3	32.6	4.2	**8.3**	9.8	15.3
	The National Capital Bank of Washington	Washington	DC	**D+**			653.3	10.70	12.7	0.1	22.4	18.8	**8.2**	9.8	17.4
▲	The National Iron Bank	Salisbury	CT	**C+**	C	C	226.0	27.10	6.3	0.9	56.7	6.0	**5.9**	7.9	17.3
	The Neffs National Bank	Neffs	PA	**B+**	B+	A-	448.6	13.98	3.0	2.7	22.5	48.8	**10.0**	16.6	0.0
	The New Washington State Bank	New Washington	IN	**B+**	B+	B+	439.3	12.27	11.8	7.9	13.7	14.0	**6.2**	8.9	0.0
	The Nodaway Valley Bank	Maryville	MO	**A**	A	A	1275.8	18.00	7.1	0.7	4.3	26.7	**7.6**	9.4	15.6
	The North Country Savings Bank	Canton	NY	**B-**	B-	B-	320.2	7.63	1.4	1.5	65.8	0.6	**10.0**	13.6	26.2
	The North Salem State Bank	North Salem	IN	**B**	B	B	512.0	12.01	9.6	2.9	13.6	5.0	**5.8**	7.8	13.1
	The North Side Bank and Trust Co.	Cincinnati	OH	**B+**	B+	A-	992.9	11.81	17.9	0.7	11.4	22.8	**7.0**	10.0	12.5
▼	The Northern State Bank of Gonvick	Gonvick	MN	**C+**	B-	B	40.8	1.55	1.8	4.7	6.3	39.5	**10.0**	16.0	86.3
	The Northern Trust Co.	Chicago	IL	**B+**	B+	B+	171870.0	13.88	2.5	0.2	3.4	33.5	**4.7**	6.7	13.6
	The Northumberland National Bank	Northumberland	PA	**C+**	C+	C+	653.3	13.65	9.3	0.8	27.8	35.6	**7.6**	9.4	17.9
	The Northwestern Bank	Chippewa Falls	WI	**A**	A-	A	577.0	17.11	22.5	0.6	5.7	23.3	**8.4**	9.9	14.7
	The Ohio Valley Bank Co.	Gallipolis	OH	**B-**	B-	B	1220.3	12.07	7.3	9.1	22.8	15.1	**9.0**	10.3	0.0
	The Old Exchange National Bank of Okaw	Okawville	IL	**B**	B+	B+	87.2	7.25	1.4	0.5	5.5	52.6	**8.4**	10.0	24.2
	The Old Fort Banking Co.	Old Fort	OH	**B**	B	B	762.5	13.72	15.4	0.3	13.4	29.4	**5.5**	7.5	14.8
	The Old Point National Bank of Phoebus	Hampton	VA	**C+**	C+	C+	1267.5	4.36	9.3	9.2	10.3	16.3	**6.5**	8.5	12.5
	The Ottoville Bank Co.	Ottoville	OH	**B+**	A-	A-	89.7	6.24	5.1	0.3	9.1	32.7	**10.0**	19.7	0.0
▲	The Paducah Bank and Trust Co.	Paducah	KY	**A**	A-	A-	811.6	3.47	16.0	0.9	17.3	18.9	**10.0**	12.6	18.2
▲	The Park Bank	Madison	WI	**B+**	B-	B-	1257.4	6.77	17.8	0.5	11.7	7.9	**7.7**	10.3	13.1
	The Park National Bank	Newark	OH	**C+**	C+	C+	9914.5	2.43	9.9	17.0	14.4	14.2	**6.4**	8.4	12.5
	The Pataskala Banking Co.	Pataskala	OH	**D-**	D-	D	39.7	6.79	4.4	5.9	25.9	26.6	**4.4**	6.4	14.3
	The Pauls Valley National Bank	Pauls Valley	OK	**C+**	C+	B-	308.1	12.50	13.3	7.5	3.2	32.3	**7.4**	9.3	0.0
	The Payne County Bank	Perkins	OK	**A**	A	A	210.6	8.57	8.4	5.3	21.1	31.7	**10.0**	16.9	0.0
	The Pecos County State Bank	Fort Stockton	TX	**B**	B	B	318.4	3.03	8.8	3.5	7.7	55.8	**6.5**	8.5	20.8
	The Pennsville National Bank	Pennsville	NJ	**C**	C	C	247.4	11.38	4.2	0.7	14.9	58.7	**5.7**	7.7	16.4
	The Peoples Bank	Magnolia	AR	**C+**	C+	C+	219.2	1.76	5.1	23.5	38.6	5.7	**9.4**	10.6	18.9
	The Peoples Bank	Willacoochee	GA	**B-**	B-	B	98.4	15.47	2.1	3.3	9.0	23.8	**10.0**	11.2	0.0
	The Peoples Bank	Brownstown	IN	**C**	C	B-	262.8	11.59	2.0	4.3	18.2	59.0	**6.7**	8.7	0.0
	The Peoples Bank	Pratt	KS	**C**	C-	C+	512.5	7.22	6.0	0.7	7.2	47.5	**7.2**	9.1	18.1
	The Peoples Bank	Marion	KY	**C-**	D+	D+	96.4	15.06	16.5	3.2	8.3	6.3	**3.2**	9.0	0.0
	The Peoples Bank	Taylorsville	KY	**A-**	A-	B+	133.0	14.88	1.8	2.5	17.5	29.5	**10.0**	11.2	22.0
▼	The Peoples Bank	Chestertown	MD	**B-**	B	B-	317.6	15.37	3.0	0.2	22.1	8.7	**6.9**	8.9	0.0
	The Peoples Bank	Ripley	MS	**B**	B	B	529.4	15.83	5.5	4.3	12.9	58.3	**7.4**	9.3	22.9
	The Peoples Bank	Gambier	OH	**C**	C	C	64.7	5.52	1.8	6.7	30.3	35.8	**7.5**	9.3	0.0
	The Peoples Bank	Iva	SC	**B-**	B-	B	408.6	21.33	3.7	1.7	13.0	40.5	**7.8**	9.5	15.9
	The Peoples Bank	Sardis	TN	**B+**	B+	A-	113.8	11.23	3.2	3.3	21.1	9.9	**6.2**	8.2	0.0
	The Peoples Bank Co.	Coldwater	OH	**A**	A	A	656.7	12.24	3.5	1.5	10.7	50.1	**9.3**	10.6	21.1
	The Peoples Bank of Georgia	Talbotton	GA	**B-**	B-	B-	124.4	22.69	10.1	7.3	32.2	17.5	**7.8**	9.5	0.0
	The Peoples Bank of Red Level	Red Level	AL	**C**	C	C	17.3	11.52	0.1	15.8	10.5	6.0	**10.0**	11.0	0.0
▲	The Peoples Bank, Biloxi, Mississippi	Biloxi	MS	**C-**	D+	C	765.2	17.03	4.9	0.5	7.2	48.3	**10.0**	11.4	21.7
	The Peoples Community Bank	Mazomanie	WI	**A-**	A-	A-	345.9	6.30	5.1	0.9	6.9	34.1	**10.0**	11.5	0.0
	The Peoples National Bank of Checotah	Checotah	OK	**A-**	B+	A-	166.3	10.58	1.3	9.2	8.4	48.3	**10.0**	15.3	40.8
▼	The Peoples S&L Co.	Bucyrus	OH	**C-**	C+	C+	156.1	7.02	0.8	1.1	31.4	44.4	**10.0**	18.7	0.0
	The Peoples S&L Co.	West Liberty	OH	**B-**	B-	B-	67.8	14.67	1.0	1.9	63.8	3.7	**10.0**	11.8	0.0
	The Peoples Savings Bank	New Matamoras	OH	**B**	B	B	66.6	1.62	3.1	3.5	28.0	52.1	**10.0**	12.1	0.0
	The Peoples Savings Bank	Urbana	OH	**C-**	C	C	140.7	8.38	1.2	1.3	47.6	9.9	**7.8**	9.5	0.0
	The Peoples State Bank	Ellettsville	IN	**B+**	B+	B	405.0	13.39	4.6	0.9	7.4	41.8	**7.5**	9.4	0.0
	The Peoples State Bank of Newton, Illinois	Newton	IL	**B+**	B	B-	561.4	16.96	11.5	2.0	9.3	36.1	**8.4**	9.9	0.0
	The Perryton National Bank	Perryton	TX	**A-**	B+	A-	163.0	-10.98	11.6	5.0	5.3	54.3	**10.0**	16.1	0.0
	The Philadelphia Trust Co.	Philadelphia	PA	**B+**	B+	B+	22.7	0.64	1.6	26.2	1.8	0.0	**10.0**	70.8	0.0
	The Piedmont Bank	Peachtree Corners	GA	**A-**	A-	B	1654.3	26.18	12.8	0.4	5.9	9.6	**7.4**	9.3	13.4
	The Pineries Bank	Stevens Point	WI	**B+**	B+	B+	129.8	9.31	4.6	1.6	28.7	15.1	**7.2**	9.1	20.9
	The Pioneer Savings Bank	Cleveland	OH	**C-**	C-	C	42.7	2.82	0.0	0.3	40.5	28.5	**10.0**	15.8	37.4

Asset Mix columns (Comm-ercial Loans, Cons-umer Loans, Mort-gage Loans, Secur-ities): As a % of Total Assets

Asset Quality Index	Adjusted Non-Performing Loans as a % of Total Loans	Adjusted Non-Performing Loans as a % of Capital	Net Charge-Offs Avg Loans	Profitability Index	Net Income ($Mil)	Return on Assets (R.O.A.)	Return on Equity (R.O.E.)	Net Interest Spread	Overhead Efficiency Ratio	Liquidity Index	Liquidity Ratio	Hot Money Ratio	Stability Index
5.3	1.32	10.1	0.35	**4.1**	0.4	0.69	7.38	2.46	71.1	**5.9**	49.4	7.0	**6.1**
2.0	3.28	19.3	0.01	**9.7**	2.8	2.28	22.74	4.67	56.8	**5.0**	32.4	6.8	**8.0**
8.4	0.85	2.8	0.12	**5.7**	9.4	1.20	10.57	2.80	53.1	**6.2**	33.2	2.9	**10.0**
7.7	0.38	1.9	0.00	**4.7**	2.3	1.03	12.38	3.51	61.1	**5.0**	16.5	2.5	**4.2**
8.3	0.64	2.9	-0.01	**5.1**	15.6	1.07	15.19	2.40	60.7	**6.9**	45.6	2.4	**6.4**
6.8	0.95	4.8	0.00	**5.7**	1.1	1.22	9.07	3.45	56.1	**4.1**	25.3	9.7	**7.5**
8.6	0.03	0.5	-0.06	**4.0**	1.7	0.95	9.58	3.80	63.1	**1.8**	17.3	20.5	**5.1**
6.8	0.60	3.0	0.02	**3.8**	2.3	0.73	8.37	3.37	72.1	**4.7**	25.1	5.3	**3.0**
9.6	0.00	0.0	0.02	**3.8**	1.0	0.88	11.38	3.03	68.6	**4.3**	25.0	8.0	**3.7**
9.7	0.44	1.0	0.00	**4.5**	2.1	0.98	5.80	2.86	59.0	**4.9**	59.2	15.2	**8.1**
6.9	0.34	2.0	0.00	**6.3**	3.0	1.44	15.55	3.71	64.5	**5.4**	30.5	3.3	**6.7**
8.3	0.06	0.3	-0.05	**6.6**	8.7	1.39	13.25	3.14	62.4	**5.9**	37.2	6.7	**10.0**
8.9	0.55	3.1	0.07	**3.1**	0.8	0.52	4.23	3.14	81.5	**4.8**	20.4	4.1	**6.9**
7.4	0.46	2.2	0.00	**6.0**	3.0	1.18	15.60	3.51	56.4	**3.6**	30.1	13.7	**6.1**
8.9	0.10	1.0	0.01	**6.3**	6.2	1.26	13.01	2.73	47.5	**3.3**	21.9	13.0	**7.2**
8.2	1.85	3.6	0.49	**2.4**	0.0	0.17	1.04	1.42	88.6	**7.2**	84.0	4.7	**6.4**
9.6	0.36	1.2	-0.02	**5.2**	756.6	0.99	14.09	1.00	69.8	**7.4**	54.5	1.5	**5.8**
8.0	0.37	2.1	0.03	**3.3**	2.0	0.63	6.54	2.67	79.1	**4.6**	29.7	8.2	**5.9**
7.7	0.42	1.4	0.38	**9.2**	6.0	2.16	20.37	3.71	40.1	**5.5**	32.3	3.4	**9.3**
5.3	1.36	6.4	0.08	**4.5**	5.6	0.93	8.38	3.52	72.6	**3.4**	16.2	10.8	**8.5**
9.3	0.11	1.0	-0.16	**4.5**	0.5	1.07	9.91	2.59	56.7	**5.1**	71.9	15.0	**7.1**
8.8	0.01	0.2	0.00	**6.8**	6.7	1.78	23.25	3.08	51.8	**5.1**	31.0	5.3	**6.2**
8.0	0.26	1.8	0.05	**3.6**	4.7	0.76	8.47	3.30	76.8	**4.8**	25.8	8.9	**6.7**
9.2	0.00	0.0	0.00	**4.8**	0.4	0.96	4.79	2.77	61.9	**3.7**	40.2	16.5	**8.7**
8.2	0.30	1.1	0.11	**7.0**	7.0	1.75	14.00	3.67	59.5	**3.2**	17.9	7.9	**9.5**
5.7	0.58	3.8	0.00	**5.5**	6.7	1.09	10.80	3.44	55.9	**4.9**	12.1	2.7	**9.1**
3.2	1.62	9.9	-0.01	**8.1**	86.0	1.78	17.83	3.72	57.3	**4.8**	16.6	4.4	**8.9**
4.9	2.10	11.3	-0.01	**1.2**	0.0	-0.20	-2.99	3.37	103.8	**6.5**	47.1	1.7	**2.3**
6.2	0.38	3.0	0.24	**3.7**	1.1	0.70	7.60	3.26	70.0	**3.0**	43.0	22.8	**4.6**
8.0	0.59	3.1	0.09	**8.8**	2.5	2.47	14.29	4.62	45.1	**4.7**	42.7	12.4	**9.5**
7.7	0.26	2.4	0.24	**6.2**	2.9	1.76	18.82	3.49	56.9	**3.8**	20.6	10.7	**6.1**
6.6	1.85	4.8	0.09	**2.7**	0.5	0.39	4.41	2.44	78.4	**7.3**	66.6	2.4	**3.9**
3.4	1.61	9.8	0.40	**8.1**	2.7	2.52	22.80	5.49	50.7	**0.8**	21.6	26.8	**6.9**
8.0	1.91	4.3	0.00	**3.4**	0.3	0.65	5.70	2.77	77.6	**2.9**	45.8	23.7	**6.1**
7.7	0.61	2.0	0.04	**3.1**	0.6	0.49	4.90	2.44	79.0	**6.7**	67.3	6.3	**4.7**
3.1	3.19	10.9	-0.03	**7.1**	4.2	1.66	14.59	3.56	55.8	**2.3**	33.4	23.4	**8.9**
5.3	0.78	4.6	-0.01	**5.4**	0.5	1.05	11.70	4.28	60.1	**1.5**	15.4	24.4	**4.4**
5.6	2.91	8.6	-0.16	**7.1**	1.1	1.75	15.01	3.88	58.6	**5.0**	36.3	8.1	**8.2**
5.3	1.62	6.3	-0.27	**3.4**	0.6	0.42	4.27	2.60	86.4	**5.9**	46.4	6.0	**6.0**
9.4	0.03	0.1	-0.11	**4.6**	2.9	1.13	11.24	2.84	59.2	**3.8**	59.6	23.0	**5.8**
9.0	0.03	0.2	0.07	**2.8**	0.1	0.42	4.28	3.13	87.1	**4.7**	40.1	11.4	**5.1**
7.5	0.81	1.8	0.19	**3.9**	1.7	0.89	8.32	2.83	73.6	**5.8**	53.8	9.5	**5.7**
6.3	0.65	5.2	0.07	**3.8**	0.3	0.56	6.62	3.23	77.0	**3.0**	43.7	18.1	**5.6**
9.2	0.00	0.0	0.00	**7.4**	4.6	1.43	12.82	2.67	43.9	**6.1**	50.8	6.1	**8.7**
4.6	0.67	8.9	0.12	**6.0**	0.8	1.30	13.66	5.40	63.7	**1.0**	9.7	17.1	**5.1**
3.4	10.69	21.2	0.08	**3.6**	0.0	0.22	1.99	5.79	90.3	**7.1**	76.9	2.2	**4.5**
8.5	1.19	3.0	-3.32	**3.6**	5.6	1.46	12.17	2.74	94.1	**4.0**	23.7	9.5	**5.3**
6.1	2.29	6.1	0.00	**6.9**	2.4	1.35	11.50	3.10	53.8	**5.5**	40.8	7.1	**8.0**
8.7	0.31	0.8	0.00	**6.2**	1.3	1.62	10.11	2.61	57.6	**6.0**	69.2	11.3	**8.2**
8.6	0.37	3.5	0.00	**1.5**	0.0	0.04	0.21	2.60	98.4	**5.9**	72.5	12.0	**6.8**
9.3	0.00	0.0	0.02	**3.2**	0.2	0.54	4.58	3.18	79.3	**2.7**	11.3	15.2	**6.9**
8.7	0.71	2.0	-0.02	**3.3**	0.2	0.47	3.66	3.11	84.7	**6.6**	53.3	2.3	**6.2**
4.7	1.76	13.3	0.27	**2.5**	0.1	0.21	2.64	3.06	88.0	**2.4**	29.8	19.6	**4.3**
8.8	0.01	0.0	0.00	**5.9**	3.2	1.66	16.48	3.02	62.4	**4.9**	33.8	7.9	**7.0**
5.6	1.03	4.4	0.02	**6.0**	3.5	1.28	12.07	3.34	48.1	**3.9**	26.4	10.6	**7.3**
7.9	1.47	2.9	0.05	**6.2**	1.3	1.57	9.39	3.14	49.7	**4.2**	59.4	18.9	**8.3**
7.5	0.00	0.0	0.00	**10.0**	1.0	9.72	13.97	1.92	71.4	**4.2**	145.0	65.6	**6.3**
7.1	0.32	1.8	0.00	**7.0**	9.6	1.19	11.95	3.69	55.2	**2.3**	23.2	20.2	**7.0**
9.3	0.00	0.0	-0.02	**4.6**	0.7	1.13	11.93	2.56	58.4	**4.0**	49.0	17.4	**6.1**
6.4	2.99	8.6	-0.09	**1.5**	0.1	0.28	1.72	2.66	89.1	**2.3**	51.2	46.7	**7.3**

Name	City	State	Rating	2020 Rating	2019 Rating	Total Assets ($Mil)	One Year Asset Growth	Asset Mix (As a % of Total Assets) Comm-ercial Loans	Cons-umer Loans	Mort-gage Loans	Secur-ities	Capital-ization Index	Lever-age Ratio	Risk-Based Capital Ratio
The Pitney Bowes Bank Inc.	Salt Lake City	UT	**A-**	A-	A-	779.2	0.08	25.0	0.0	0.0	40.1	**8.5**	10.0	0.0
The Pleasants County Bank	Saint Marys	WV	**C+**	C+	C	70.5	6.89	5.9	9.1	25.7	16.2	**9.0**	10.3	0.0
The Poca Valley Bank, Inc.	Walton	WV	**C+**	C+	B-	458.9	7.94	15.2	5.5	30.2	12.5	**5.7**	7.7	13.3
The Port Austin State Bank	Port Austin	MI	**B+**	B+	B+	67.5	17.74	4.0	3.1	27.7	23.7	**10.0**	15.1	0.0
The Port Washington State Bank	Port Washington	WI	**B**	B	B	857.9	20.32	7.7	2.1	12.3	30.8	**5.8**	7.8	13.8
The Portage County Bank	Almond	WI	**B-**	B-	B-	182.7	1.17	10.0	0.4	14.6	21.7	**8.9**	10.2	17.6
The Potter State Bank of Potter	Potter	NE	**B-**	B	B	44.1	8.28	14.4	2.3	1.5	32.1	**10.0**	14.6	0.0
The Private Trust Co., N.A.	Cleveland	OH	**U**	U	U	23.6	1.07	0.0	0.0	0.0	50.8	**10.0**	93.8	807.5
The Provident Bank	Amesbury	MA	**B+**	B+	B+	1583.0	11.94	40.4	0.2	2.2	2.1	**10.0**	12.4	15.1
The Pueblo Bank and Trust Co.	Pueblo	CO	**B+**	B+	B+	614.2	20.79	8.9	0.1	4.4	19.5	**7.1**	9.1	14.7
The Readlyn Savings Bank	Readlyn	IA	**A-**	A-	A-	82.5	-0.19	6.0	1.2	21.5	17.5	**10.0**	15.6	24.7
▲ The Republic Banking Co.	Republic	OH	**A-**	B	B-	56.8	6.90	5.1	8.0	31.6	6.7	**10.0**	15.4	0.0
The Richwood Banking Co., Inc.	Richwood	OH	**B-**	B-	B-	1049.4	26.38	8.2	0.4	14.4	30.1	**5.6**	7.6	13.6
The Riddell National Bank	Brazil	IN	**C+**	C+	C+	267.6	1.19	11.8	4.7	30.1	14.9	**7.1**	9.1	13.5
The Riley State Bank of Riley Kansas	Riley	KS	**C+**	B-	B	116.3	16.58	10.2	2.8	5.6	33.3	**7.7**	9.5	0.0
The Roscoe State Bank	Roscoe	TX	**B+**	B+	A-	210.6	11.57	3.3	1.0	10.6	42.2	**7.2**	9.1	0.0
The Sacramento Deposit Bank	Sacramento	KY	**A-**	A-	A-	131.1	10.07	5.5	4.6	16.7	27.4	**8.9**	10.3	17.1
The Salyersville National Bank	Salyersville	KY	**B**	B	B	127.9	7.78	4.3	2.0	15.4	32.1	**10.0**	13.5	27.3
The Samson Banking Co.	Samson	AL	**A-**	A-	A-	109.3	18.62	12.4	4.9	14.5	39.1	**10.0**	11.4	0.0
The Santa Anna National Bank	Santa Anna	TX	**B+**	B+	B+	56.2	7.68	17.9	8.2	0.7	37.7	**10.0**	11.2	0.0
▲ The Savings Bank	Wakefield	MA	**B-**	C+	B-	691.6	6.38	2.2	0.1	44.2	10.9	**10.0**	11.5	0.0
The Savings Bank	Circleville	OH	**C+**	C+	B-	415.2	9.09	8.1	2.3	31.4	36.5	**8.0**	9.7	20.4
The Savings Bank of Danbury	Danbury	CT	**B**	B+	A-	1356.1	9.50	9.7	0.1	39.8	3.5	**10.0**	11.6	0.0
The Security National Bank of Enid	Enid	OK	**B+**	B+	B+	409.9	13.18	4.7	0.7	20.5	34.7	**5.9**	7.9	16.3
The Security National Bank of Sioux City, I	Sioux City	IA	**A-**	A-	A-	1420.5	17.49	5.4	1.3	11.2	25.4	**7.6**	9.4	0.0
The Security State Bank	McRae	GA	**A-**	A-	A-	54.9	14.60	26.7	2.0	8.2	18.7	**10.0**	13.5	28.6
▼ The Security State Bank	Emery	SD	**B-**	B+	B+	62.0	16.48	11.7	2.3	0.0	3.5	**10.0**	12.1	37.8
The Security State Bank	Winters	TX	**B-**	B-	B-	71.2	11.42	11.2	6.9	6.6	20.0	**7.3**	9.2	0.0
The Seymour Bank	Seymour	MO	**B+**	B	B	197.9	16.99	3.3	4.0	17.1	37.3	**9.3**	10.5	0.0
The Shelby State Bank	Shelby	MI	**C+**	C+	B-	345.5	7.87	6.6	1.1	10.6	36.7	**5.3**	7.3	13.2
The Sherwood State Bank	Sherwood	OH	**B-**	B-	C+	85.2	10.73	6.5	4.0	33.0	17.0	**9.5**	10.6	0.0
▲ The Southern Bank Co.	Gadsden	AL	**C+**	C	C	112.9	9.04	16.8	0.5	6.8	39.5	**8.8**	10.2	0.0
The St. Henry Bank	Saint Henry	OH	**A**	A	A	364.1	4.97	5.5	0.5	10.8	29.0	**10.0**	13.2	0.0
▲ The State Bank	La Junta	CO	**A-**	B+	B	127.5	8.58	2.7	1.7	7.2	24.9	**10.0**	14.3	25.9
The State Bank	Spirit Lake	IA	**C**	C	C+	79.5	8.69	4.9	1.2	13.4	47.2	**10.0**	11.5	0.0
▼ The State Bank	Fenton	MI	**B+**	A-	B+	1309.2	5.79	7.5	0.3	19.4	9.5	**8.4**	9.9	14.0
The State Bank	Richmond	MO	**B**	B	B	42.1	15.87	5.3	3.3	14.6	53.7	**5.8**	7.8	25.4
The State Bank and Trust Co.	Defiance	OH	**A-**	A-	B+	1306.5	9.19	10.7	1.0	16.8	16.2	**8.0**	9.7	14.4
The State Bank of Faribault	Faribault	MN	**B**	B	B	292.5	17.47	8.6	2.6	11.3	35.6	**6.3**	8.3	14.6
▲ The State Bank of Geneva	Geneva	IL	**C+**	C	C-	110.8	18.66	8.3	0.5	15.1	23.1	**7.3**	9.2	18.1
The State Bank of Pearl City	Pearl City	IL	**B-**	B-	B-	70.0	12.40	1.7	31.2	8.0	17.0	**9.7**	10.8	0.0
The State Bank of Spring Hill	Spring Hill	KS	**C-**	C	C+	61.0	12.99	2.4	0.4	4.1	56.8	**5.7**	7.7	24.3
The State Bank of Toledo	Toledo	IA	**D+**	D+	D	134.5	16.08	7.6	4.5	24.2	6.8	**5.5**	8.1	0.0
The State Bank of Wynnewood	Wynnewood	OK	**A-**	B+	B+	103.1	6.83	7.2	1.7	8.2	55.1	**10.0**	15.4	0.0
The State Exchange Bank	Mankato	KS	**B-**	B-	B-	42.3	13.43	3.8	2.9	3.8	58.5	**10.0**	11.4	23.6
The State Exchange Bank	Lamont	OK	**D+**	D	D+	80.0	12.08	22.5	0.8	5.4	4.0	**7.1**	11.8	0.0
The State National Bank of Big Spring	Big Spring	TX	**B+**	B+	A-	463.6	7.01	4.3	0.4	1.2	59.5	**8.9**	10.3	0.0
The State National Bank of Groom	Groom	TX	**C+**	B-	C	40.8	9.54	11.5	1.9	4.0	13.3	**9.1**	10.4	16.9
▼ The State Savings Bank of Manistique	Manistique	MI	**B-**	B	B	156.1	15.26	6.0	4.2	11.6	48.2	**8.9**	10.3	0.0
The Stephenson National Bank and Trust	Marinette	WI	**B**	B	B	661.9	8.34	13.6	4.1	13.1	29.2	**6.7**	8.9	0.0
The Stock Exchange Bank	Woodward	OK	**A-**	A-	A	297.4	12.21	7.2	3.1	5.2	28.9	**10.0**	14.6	0.0
The Stockgrowers State Bank	Maple Hill	KS	**A-**	B+	B+	98.1	13.23	12.2	1.3	15.8	26.7	**10.0**	11.4	18.8
The Tipton Latham Bank, N.A.	Tipton	MO	**B+**	B+	B	161.2	7.77	11.9	2.6	18.4	24.6	**9.5**	10.7	0.0
▲ The Torrington Savings Bank	Torrington	CT	**C+**	C	B	946.9	9.62	2.3	0.1	46.0	14.0	**10.0**	18.8	44.2
The Tri-County Bank	Stuart	NE	**B**	B	B-	193.6	19.89	14.8	1.7	15.9	24.4	**3.9**	8.3	0.0
The Trust Bank	Lenox	GA	**C+**	C+	C	45.3	15.05	2.7	5.7	13.4	3.9	**8.5**	10.0	21.8
The Trust Co. of Toledo, N.A.	Holland	OH	**U**	U	U	6.1	16.09	0.0	0.0	0.0	26.5	**10.0**	100.	286.5
The Turbotville National Bank	Turbotville	PA	**A-**	A-	B+	174.9	10.63	6.5	1.3	21.6	20.8	**10.0**	16.4	0.0
The Twin Valley Bank	West Alexandria	OH	**B-**	C+	C+	112.5	21.19	11.5	1.6	14.7	34.5	**6.2**	8.2	0.0
The Union Bank Co.	Columbus Grove	OH	**A-**	B+	B	1049.4	3.25	10.2	0.7	12.6	21.7	**7.8**	9.5	16.4

Asset Quality Index	Adjusted Non-Performing Loans as a % of Total Loans	Adjusted Non-Performing Loans as a % of Capital	Net Charge-Offs Avg Loans	Profitability Index	Net Income ($Mil)	Return on Assets (R.O.A.)	Return on Equity (R.O.E.)	Net Interest Spread	Overhead Efficiency Ratio	Liquidity Index	Liquidity Ratio	Hot Money Ratio	Stability Index
7.4	1.02	2.8	1.11	**10.0**	24.7	6.57	72.44	7.44	5.8	**7.9**	74.2	0.0	**6.8**
2.2	3.89	20.4	0.02	**3.6**	0.3	0.72	6.92	2.93	76.5	**4.8**	34.8	9.1	**5.6**
4.9	1.07	6.3	0.07	**3.9**	1.6	0.72	8.70	3.66	78.6	**4.5**	26.6	7.7	**4.9**
9.0	0.02	0.0	0.08	**5.4**	0.4	1.27	8.34	2.96	55.9	**5.3**	46.0	9.1	**8.1**
8.2	0.30	1.2	0.06	**4.1**	2.9	0.68	8.77	2.49	68.5	**4.3**	29.0	9.9	**4.8**
8.7	0.13	0.7	0.00	**3.9**	0.9	0.92	8.89	3.46	70.8	**5.6**	38.7	5.7	**6.3**
6.8	0.00	6.2	-0.03	**3.7**	0.1	0.60	4.08	3.40	78.5	**3.5**	57.9	22.0	**7.3**
8.1	na	0.0	na	**10.0**	2.7	23.47	26.00	1.60	48.0	**4.0**	na	0.0	**6.4**
5.2	2.05	7.6	0.23	**5.2**	7.5	0.97	7.92	4.06	59.3	**4.0**	11.0	3.5	**9.3**
8.6	0.25	0.9	-0.06	**6.2**	4.7	1.63	16.61	3.62	65.1	**5.7**	32.9	2.1	**6.8**
8.8	0.13	0.8	0.05	**7.6**	0.7	1.77	11.29	3.57	40.6	**3.5**	41.4	17.8	**9.6**
7.5	0.00	0.1	0.01	**8.8**	0.5	1.72	11.20	4.18	49.7	**2.7**	22.3	16.2	**8.6**
4.7	1.85	11.0	0.03	**4.3**	5.1	0.99	12.01	3.27	64.3	**4.6**	25.7	10.0	**6.8**
4.3	1.42	9.5	0.23	**4.8**	1.4	1.07	12.60	3.47	64.7	**2.4**	26.7	18.6	**5.0**
7.0	0.00	0.0	0.04	**5.3**	0.9	1.54	16.55	3.43	54.7	**3.7**	27.0	12.4	**5.3**
9.1	0.20	1.6	0.13	**5.0**	1.3	1.24	11.92	3.24	65.4	**4.7**	50.7	14.2	**6.8**
6.0	0.49	4.7	0.26	**7.6**	1.2	1.87	18.10	4.14	51.5	**3.2**	46.3	21.5	**7.5**
8.9	0.00	0.6	0.00	**4.0**	0.6	0.95	6.92	3.13	65.7	**1.4**	19.9	27.6	**7.4**
8.9	0.12	0.5	-0.03	**5.3**	0.6	1.21	9.99	3.11	63.2	**5.7**	54.3	10.1	**7.7**
8.0	0.00	0.0	0.05	**7.6**	0.4	1.62	13.49	4.30	56.3	**3.1**	38.4	19.0	**7.5**
9.1	0.26	1.4	0.00	**3.4**	1.8	0.52	4.34	2.86	85.7	**3.0**	30.9	16.7	**7.4**
6.1	1.25	4.9	-0.01	**3.4**	1.4	0.67	6.66	2.90	77.1	**4.2**	26.5	9.1	**6.1**
3.7	3.17	19.5	0.09	**5.4**	7.7	1.18	10.38	3.10	57.1	**1.9**	19.0	18.2	**9.5**
7.6	0.41	2.1	0.00	**6.7**	3.3	1.67	19.09	3.31	45.7	**4.7**	21.9	4.6	**6.0**
7.2	1.82	4.8	0.00	**6.2**	7.5	1.11	11.47	2.13	59.4	**6.2**	41.2	5.2	**8.2**
8.7	0.05	0.2	-0.07	**7.1**	0.5	1.87	12.89	5.14	62.1	**4.4**	31.6	10.2	**7.4**
9.2	0.00	0.0	0.00	**3.2**	0.1	0.35	2.86	1.87	75.9	**6.2**	81.1	10.5	**7.0**
7.1	0.42	3.1	0.09	**4.7**	0.3	1.00	10.52	3.58	74.5	**5.7**	39.6	5.2	**3.8**
8.4	0.34	0.8	-0.02	**5.3**	1.2	1.33	12.06	4.04	66.9	**4.1**	32.0	9.9	**6.2**
5.1	2.41	7.9	0.00	**4.1**	1.4	0.85	11.09	3.36	74.6	**5.9**	37.9	2.9	**4.4**
4.5	1.88	10.7	0.12	**5.6**	0.5	1.28	11.92	4.64	63.9	**4.6**	28.0	7.3	**5.7**
4.7	2.25	9.7	0.01	**3.9**	0.3	0.57	5.34	4.58	83.5	**2.6**	40.9	26.5	**4.9**
9.2	0.00	0.0	0.01	**8.9**	3.7	2.04	14.69	3.11	39.6	**5.9**	49.1	7.0	**9.9**
7.5	0.62	1.9	-0.71	**5.9**	0.8	1.20	8.43	3.94	72.7	**5.4**	39.0	7.0	**8.3**
6.9	5.16	7.9	0.03	**2.1**	0.1	0.36	3.08	2.25	82.5	**3.6**	60.2	20.6	**5.0**
5.0	0.86	5.9	0.06	**7.3**	9.8	1.53	15.22	3.67	59.0	**3.9**	21.5	9.6	**8.8**
7.4	0.66	2.7	0.00	**4.6**	0.2	1.16	15.17	3.11	68.9	**7.0**	59.4	0.9	**4.9**
6.7	0.51	2.5	0.00	**7.5**	10.9	1.69	15.14	3.15	59.3	**4.6**	24.9	9.3	**10.0**
8.7	0.07	0.2	0.03	**4.8**	1.7	1.20	13.93	3.68	69.3	**5.3**	39.3	7.4	**6.0**
9.0	0.18	1.0	0.01	**5.9**	1.5	2.82	32.67	3.25	52.6	**3.4**	39.2	17.7	**5.1**
6.9	0.10	0.5	0.20	**3.6**	0.3	0.80	7.29	3.79	77.2	**4.1**	42.5	14.9	**5.6**
9.9	0.00	0.1	0.00	**2.4**	0.0	0.15	1.91	2.19	91.0	**6.3**	47.2	3.2	**3.8**
1.7	3.89	30.3	0.00	**6.4**	1.1	1.54	19.38	3.71	60.4	**4.8**	28.1	5.6	**6.7**
8.8	2.58	2.9	0.07	**6.7**	1.3	2.55	15.04	4.17	47.4	**3.3**	52.6	24.7	**8.9**
8.9	0.24	0.7	-0.08	**4.2**	0.3	1.16	9.65	2.77	62.6	**5.2**	42.8	9.2	**5.4**
1.2	6.16	28.7	-0.65	**8.6**	1.2	3.03	26.27	5.25	41.1	**0.6**	15.0	40.7	**7.2**
9.9	0.00	0.0	0.03	**4.6**	2.0	0.89	7.75	1.96	53.8	**7.6**	86.4	3.7	**6.8**
5.2	1.52	5.6	-0.13	**2.8**	0.1	0.39	3.78	3.57	86.7	**4.2**	25.2	8.9	**5.7**
7.3	0.99	2.3	0.00	**3.7**	0.5	0.68	6.25	3.36	73.5	**6.4**	62.0	7.4	**5.6**
4.7	1.46	8.1	0.00	**6.5**	5.2	1.62	16.93	3.49	58.1	**4.2**	23.9	8.2	**7.9**
8.8	0.25	0.7	0.32	**5.9**	1.6	1.09	7.19	3.18	55.6	**5.1**	39.9	9.6	**7.8**
8.7	0.00	0.0	0.00	**6.3**	0.7	1.50	11.73	3.65	60.2	**3.5**	25.1	12.6	**7.4**
6.4	1.18	4.2	-0.01	**6.1**	1.6	2.03	19.55	3.17	46.5	**2.2**	36.0	28.4	**7.4**
9.8	0.65	1.9	0.00	**4.0**	4.7	1.02	5.35	2.26	87.6	**4.2**	46.7	15.7	**7.8**
8.3	0.27	1.1	0.01	**7.7**	1.6	1.75	21.71	5.06	54.1	**4.0**	24.5	9.6	**5.1**
4.1	2.04	9.2	-0.02	**4.4**	0.2	0.78	7.75	4.58	85.8	**4.8**	46.4	11.9	**6.3**
10.0	na	0.0	na	**10.0**	2.2	84.34	94.00	0.57	58.7	**4.0**	na	0.0	**5.5**
6.2	1.46	5.2	-0.01	**8.4**	2.0	2.29	13.93	2.97	34.3	**3.6**	40.6	16.9	**8.8**
8.5	0.14	1.1	0.01	**5.9**	1.0	1.91	23.19	5.24	63.2	**5.0**	30.8	6.2	**4.3**
7.9	0.35	1.0	0.00	**6.9**	7.3	1.44	11.18	3.81	66.2	**5.5**	34.0	7.8	**10.0**

Name	City	State	Rating	2020 Rating	2019 Rating	Total Assets ($Mil)	One Year Asset Growth	Asset Mix (As a % of Total Assets) Commercial Loans	Consumer Loans	Mortgage Loans	Securities	Capitalization Index	Leverage Ratio	Risk-Based Capital Ratio
The Union Bank of Mena	Mena	AR	**A-**	A-	B+	335.2	8.70	6.8	10.4	26.9	25.1	**7.7**	9.5	19.3
The Union Banking Co.	West Mansfield	OH	**B-**	B	B+	63.2	4.79	0.2	0.1	4.2	87.5	**8.0**	9.6	38.8
The Union State Bank of Everest	Everest	KS	**B**	B	B-	374.2	10.89	8.1	2.3	15.8	26.6	**7.2**	9.1	14.3
The University National Bank of Lawrence	Lawrence	KS	**B**	B	B	91.9	6.50	7.3	0.4	32.3	6.8	**6.7**	8.7	19.7
The Upstate National Bank	Rochester	NY	**B-**	B-	C	231.6	26.61	4.8	0.0	37.6	9.3	**6.0**	8.0	12.6
The Valley State Bank	Syracuse	KS	**B**	B	B-	184.3	2.16	15.1	6.6	13.7	11.2	**7.1**	9.2	12.6
The Versailles S&L Co.	Versailles	OH	**B-**	B-	B	62.2	4.69	1.2	1.5	44.4	9.1	**10.0**	18.6	0.0
The Victory Bank	Limerick	PA	**B-**	B-	B-	452.1	9.17	16.7	1.9	8.1	4.1	**5.5**	7.5	12.8
The Village Bank	Saint Libory	IL	**B**	B	B	113.8	18.50	8.5	5.6	16.7	19.4	**6.6**	8.6	0.0
The Village Bank	Auburndale	MA	**B**	B	B	1624.2	14.05	3.0	0.3	38.1	16.3	**8.0**	9.7	17.2
The Waggoner National Bank of Vernon	Vernon	TX	**A**	A	A	350.2	8.23	5.3	3.7	5.2	43.6	**10.0**	13.0	0.0
The Walton State Bank	Walton	KS	**E+**	E+	D-	11.7	15.01	19.5	4.5	8.8	13.1	**4.2**	6.3	21.5
▼ The Wanda State Bank	Wanda	MN	**B+**	A-	B+	177.7	17.86	2.6	1.7	2.0	33.6	**10.0**	14.1	0.0
The Warrington Bank	Pensacola	FL	**C**	C	C	116.4	22.01	1.7	0.1	0.7	55.2	**10.0**	14.6	0.0
The Washington Trust Co. of Westerly	Westerly	RI	**B+**	B+	B+	5851.5	-0.42	6.1	0.2	27.7	18.0	**7.0**	9.0	13.5
The Waterford Commercial and Savings B	Waterford	OH	**B+**	B	B	58.8	13.41	3.4	10.6	26.0	27.2	**10.0**	12.1	0.0
The Watkins Savings Bank	Watkins	IA	**B+**	B+	B+	84.6	13.65	0.9	1.1	6.2	66.1	**10.0**	14.9	0.0
The Westchester Bank	White Plains	NY	**A-**	A-	A-	1328.1	14.59	20.3	0.2	2.6	11.1	**8.8**	10.2	15.3
▲ The Wilmington Savings Bank	Wilmington	OH	**B**	B-	B	182.3	4.54	0.7	1.6	50.8	6.7	**10.0**	18.1	0.0
▼ The Yoakum National Bank	Yoakum	TX	**B+**	A-	A-	225.9	-5.23	5.4	3.5	17.7	51.4	**10.0**	13.8	0.0
Think Mutual Bank	Rochester	MN	**B+**	B+	B+	2137.7	14.36	1.7	8.7	41.6	34.2	**10.0**	14.3	0.0
Third Coast Bank, SSB	Humble	TX	**B-**	B-	C	2011.0	10.03	30.4	0.2	5.8	1.3	**6.8**	9.2	12.3
Third Federal S&L Assn. of Cleveland	Cleveland	OH	**C+**	C+	B-	14220.3	-4.03	0.0	0.0	75.3	3.0	**9.7**	10.8	20.7
▲ Thomaston Savings Bank	Thomaston	CT	**B-**	C+	C+	1512.4	15.97	11.5	2.2	17.3	29.5	**7.9**	9.6	0.0
Thomasville National Bank	Thomasville	GA	**A-**	A-	A-	1397.0	25.47	16.7	1.7	21.8	9.6	**6.3**	8.3	12.5
Three Rivers Bank of Montana	Kalispell	MT	**B-**	B-	B+	240.7	19.13	18.6	1.8	11.0	8.1	**6.2**	8.6	0.0
Thrivent Trust Co.	Appleton	WI	**U**	U	U	20.9	-70.94	0.0	0.0	0.0	59.9	**10.0**	51.2	224.3
Thumb Bank & Trust	Pigeon	MI	**B-**	B-	C+	369.1	14.14	12.3	1.0	7.8	25.1	**5.5**	7.5	14.2
▲ TIAA, FSB	Jacksonville	FL	**C**	C-	C+	38435.4	-10.34	2.1	0.0	34.4	9.2	**7.0**	9.0	14.0
TIB, N.A.	Farmers Branch	TX	**B-**	B-	B	3794.2	-0.05	2.7	1.7	0.4	9.1	**6.4**	8.4	21.9
Timberland Bank	Hoquiam	WA	**A**	A	A	1737.6	14.39	9.7	0.2	7.5	6.9	**9.8**	10.9	22.2
▲ Timberline Bank	Grand Junction	CO	**B**	B-	B-	599.5	24.19	17.8	1.0	12.5	26.7	**5.8**	7.8	12.5
Tioga State Bank, N.A.	Spencer	NY	**A-**	A-	A-	547.6	4.16	13.9	1.0	24.1	25.9	**10.0**	12.2	22.4
Tioga-Franklin Savings Bank	Philadelphia	PA	**D+**	C-	C	74.4	-16.89	38.8	0.1	35.1	1.1	**6.5**	8.5	17.1
▼ Titan Bank, N.A.	Mineral Wells	TX	**B+**	A-	A-	512.8	73.46	23.5	0.0	8.8	13.9	**5.0**	7.0	22.9
TNB Bank	Tuscola	IL	**D+**	C-	C+	99.5	3.64	4.0	1.1	8.3	8.5	**10.0**	11.0	19.3
▲ TNBANK	Oak Ridge	TN	**C+**	C	C	287.8	3.50	7.4	1.1	15.3	13.1	**5.6**	8.8	11.5
▲ Today's Bank	Huntsville	AR	**B-**	C+	C+	285.3	-0.71	8.5	1.2	19.7	18.4	**7.0**	9.0	13.4
Tolleson Private Bank	Dallas	TX	**B+**	B+	A-	870.7	49.30	9.7	3.4	35.8	4.7	**6.1**	8.1	13.4
Tomahawk Community Bank S.S.B.	Tomahawk	WI	**B**	B	B	184.0	11.38	6.3	3.7	31.9	7.9	**10.0**	12.0	21.6
Tompkins State Bank	Avon	IL	**B**	B	B-	259.1	3.10	10.0	1.3	6.1	31.7	**6.2**	8.3	13.8
Tompkins Trust Co.	Ithaca	NY	**B+**	B+	B+	2490.8	6.35	5.2	0.9	22.9	30.8	**6.2**	8.2	14.4
Touchmark National Bank	Alpharetta	GA	**B**	B	B	414.1	-9.68	24.2	0.0	0.6	3.8	**10.0**	12.6	29.2
▲ Touchstone Bank	Prince George	VA	**B-**	C+	B-	563.7	11.10	9.5	0.6	20.8	15.3	**7.6**	9.4	0.0
▲ Tower Community Bank	Jasper	TN	**B-**	C+	C+	250.5	8.91	8.3	2.4	16.1	7.8	**5.3**	9.0	0.0
Town & Country Bank	Salem	MO	**A-**	A-	A-	693.3	14.89	3.3	2.5	26.1	22.3	**8.0**	9.7	18.8
Town & Country Bank	Ravenna	NE	**A**	A-	A-	188.1	8.62	6.8	1.4	2.2	29.8	**10.0**	12.5	0.0
Town & Country Bank	Las Vegas	NV	**B+**	B+	B+	262.2	19.98	11.4	0.0	2.3	0.0	**8.9**	10.3	0.0
Town & Country Bank and Trust Co.	Bardstown	KY	**A-**	A-	A	402.1	14.51	6.1	1.0	15.9	21.5	**9.4**	10.6	0.0
▲ Town and Country Bank	Springfield	IL	**B+**	B	B-	878.3	-2.27	11.3	0.3	13.5	15.1	**8.3**	9.9	14.7
Town and Country Bank Midwest	Quincy	IL	**A**	A	A-	222.8	14.51	19.3	1.0	11.0	7.5	**9.6**	10.7	0.0
Town Bank, N.A.	Hartland	WI	**B**	B	B	3096.9	1.25	24.3	18.9	4.5	16.1	**5.6**	8.3	11.4
Town Center Bank	New Lenox	IL	**C+**	C+	C+	152.1	-5.43	36.6	0.9	0.8	8.8	**7.9**	9.6	16.4
Town-Country National Bank	Camden	AL	**A-**	A-	A-	130.0	9.78	12.7	12.0	12.5	30.2	**10.0**	17.3	0.0
TowneBank	Portsmouth	VA	**A-**	B+	A-	15803.8	1.44	9.8	2.2	10.9	9.3	**7.7**	9.4	15.8
▲ Toyota Financial Savings Bank	Henderson	NV	**C+**	C	C	2682.6	51.99	7.4	0.1	43.1	16.8	**10.0**	34.0	86.7
TPNB Bank	Paris	MO	**B+**	B+	B+	94.0	7.18	4.0	1.3	7.2	48.4	**10.0**	14.4	25.2
Tradition Capital Bank	Wayzata	MN	**B-**	B-	C+	1429.7	27.60	11.3	0.5	11.8	11.1	**5.3**	8.1	11.3
Traditional Bank, Inc.	Mount Sterling	KY	**A-**	A-	A-	2150.3	14.31	8.1	0.2	17.3	29.8	**6.9**	8.9	15.8
Traditions Bank	Cullman	AL	**B+**	B+	B+	513.1	16.86	15.3	6.5	30.7	4.7	**6.9**	8.9	13.4

Asset Quality Index	Adjusted Non-Performing Loans as a % of Total Loans	Adjusted Non-Performing Loans as a % of Capital	Net Charge-Offs Avg Loans	Profitability Index	Net Income ($Mil)	Return on Assets (R.O.A.)	Return on Equity (R.O.E.)	Net Interest Spread	Overhead Efficiency Ratio	Liquidity Index	Liquidity Ratio	Hot Money Ratio	Stability Index
7.3	0.45	1.7	0.04	**8.5**	3.3	2.01	20.04	4.14	53.8	**4.0**	27.5	10.7	**7.0**
9.7	0.03	1.0	0.00	**3.5**	0.3	0.81	6.65	2.13	63.0	**2.8**	40.7	22.8	**7.0**
5.9	0.46	2.8	0.15	**6.8**	3.4	1.79	17.29	3.98	59.8	**4.2**	13.8	7.4	**7.3**
9.2	0.09	0.6	0.09	**4.5**	0.5	1.07	11.73	3.47	71.6	**4.4**	32.7	10.4	**5.9**
7.8	0.00	0.0	0.01	**4.9**	1.3	1.17	13.01	3.28	47.7	**0.6**	12.1	46.8	**5.5**
4.5	1.09	7.4	-0.03	**5.8**	1.3	1.33	14.50	3.47	65.1	**1.0**	17.3	32.5	**6.9**
9.7	0.00	0.0	0.00	**2.9**	0.1	0.30	1.62	2.49	83.6	**4.4**	48.2	14.2	**7.3**
8.5	0.05	0.4	0.01	**5.1**	2.1	0.99	13.27	3.57	62.7	**4.8**	31.7	8.0	**4.0**
8.7	0.02	0.8	0.01	**4.9**	0.7	1.19	13.95	2.58	56.8	**6.0**	40.5	3.4	**4.9**
8.4	0.32	2.0	0.00	**4.0**	6.0	0.77	7.94	2.86	66.2	**2.7**	29.7	24.1	**7.5**
8.4	0.53	1.7	0.00	**9.4**	4.8	2.76	21.04	3.29	43.3	**3.9**	27.4	11.4	**9.6**
2.3	4.00	27.2	0.00	**2.7**	0.0	0.38	6.04	2.19	83.2	**5.7**	49.0	5.3	**0.3**
8.0	0.54	2.9	0.05	**4.5**	0.9	0.99	6.74	2.19	58.9	**5.1**	57.2	13.6	**8.3**
9.9	0.00	0.0	0.00	**1.9**	0.1	0.10	0.67	1.83	93.3	**7.9**	90.6	2.5	**5.8**
7.7	0.43	2.4	0.01	**6.4**	38.4	1.33	13.86	2.50	58.9	**1.7**	17.0	8.3	**9.0**
8.5	0.00	0.0	0.00	**6.2**	0.4	1.46	11.72	4.16	62.0	**4.9**	35.3	8.9	**6.8**
9.5	0.00	0.0	0.00	**4.2**	0.4	0.93	6.12	2.39	57.2	**5.0**	79.9	16.4	**7.6**
8.4	0.23	1.2	0.00	**6.7**	8.5	1.31	12.87	3.04	42.4	**5.6**	32.5	6.6	**9.5**
5.3	4.22	11.0	-0.29	**4.1**	0.8	0.85	4.70	2.50	68.3	**3.0**	24.1	14.8	**7.6**
9.1	0.52	1.5	-0.01	**4.3**	1.1	0.98	6.36	3.16	74.7	**4.0**	57.8	19.5	**8.7**
8.7	0.11	0.4	0.02	**4.6**	9.3	0.90	6.12	2.58	66.9	**6.9**	45.6	2.6	**9.5**
5.7	0.71	4.7	0.01	**4.6**	9.4	0.95	12.21	4.64	70.9	**1.3**	20.5	18.2	**6.6**
7.7	1.12	6.3	-0.04	**3.2**	38.7	0.53	5.45	1.63	66.8	**0.7**	7.8	29.4	**7.9**
6.3	1.34	5.9	-0.02	**4.2**	7.1	0.98	11.48	3.11	65.4	**4.5**	37.7	14.3	**6.7**
8.4	0.13	1.1	0.00	**9.2**	11.3	1.75	20.74	3.18	47.0	**4.4**	17.2	6.7	**9.2**
5.4	0.64	4.1	-0.08	**6.6**	1.5	1.24	14.18	4.97	64.7	**3.6**	26.1	9.9	**5.9**
6.7	na	0.0	na	**5.6**	1.5	5.26	13.01	-0.04	91.9	**5.0**	250.0	100.0	**5.3**
7.9	0.07	0.5	-0.01	**5.1**	2.5	1.39	17.55	3.87	65.0	**4.1**	40.5	14.6	**5.0**
4.1	1.73	12.8	0.13	**2.7**	135.0	0.70	7.65	2.12	70.4	**1.7**	12.4	16.6	**6.6**
9.0	0.05	0.1	0.10	**4.3**	18.4	0.91	12.11	1.24	68.0	**6.3**	69.4	5.2	**7.3**
8.3	0.43	1.5	-0.01	**8.9**	14.4	1.70	14.70	3.22	48.8	**6.1**	36.1	5.0	**10.0**
8.6	0.12	0.4	0.01	**7.1**	6.6	2.22	30.58	4.82	47.1	**5.4**	27.6	1.8	**5.3**
5.4	2.12	10.1	-0.02	**6.6**	3.9	1.44	11.35	4.08	60.9	**4.5**	15.9	4.5	**8.4**
1.3	1.07	35.1	0.00	**4.0**	0.4	0.92	14.53	4.09	70.7	**0.6**	12.7	53.1	**4.9**
9.0	0.01	0.1	0.00	**9.5**	9.4	3.89	55.83	2.31	26.4	**6.8**	51.2	0.6	**7.2**
3.1	1.84	23.2	-0.01	**1.4**	0.0	0.05	0.45	2.35	97.6	**3.8**	43.1	16.8	**6.2**
4.1	2.14	15.6	-0.05	**6.0**	2.0	1.44	16.39	3.69	61.3	**4.0**	22.3	9.7	**5.8**
8.6	0.12	0.8	0.05	**4.3**	1.3	0.90	9.93	3.89	76.4	**1.1**	20.9	32.7	**5.1**
7.3	0.00	0.0	0.00	**8.8**	8.2	2.12	28.10	2.57	46.4	**4.0**	26.4	10.3	**6.8**
8.1	0.52	2.2	0.01	**4.1**	0.7	0.74	6.13	3.32	75.1	**5.6**	36.0	4.3	**7.3**
8.2	0.09	0.6	-0.01	**4.7**	1.5	1.18	11.50	3.54	64.4	**4.2**	23.3	8.7	**6.7**
6.9	0.85	6.9	-0.09	**7.5**	18.5	1.51	22.99	2.81	67.7	**4.3**	10.1	5.9	**6.4**
4.6	1.29	7.0	-0.02	**7.3**	3.4	1.59	12.94	3.18	42.9	**0.7**	17.9	43.4	**7.0**
6.2	0.65	3.5	-0.04	**4.0**	2.3	0.82	8.43	3.65	76.5	**4.2**	29.1	10.5	**6.0**
7.4	0.32	2.6	0.14	**6.0**	1.5	1.24	13.64	4.72	67.3	**3.2**	14.2	12.8	**5.0**
6.9	0.40	2.2	0.02	**6.8**	5.6	1.68	15.88	3.56	59.4	**4.0**	25.7	10.3	**8.9**
7.5	0.00	0.0	0.00	**8.8**	2.0	2.15	16.90	4.66	45.1	**2.9**	30.3	17.0	**8.2**
4.3	2.83	9.9	0.00	**5.7**	1.5	1.22	12.13	2.90	57.1	**5.7**	48.9	8.1	**7.8**
5.8	2.14	5.7	0.00	**5.4**	2.2	1.09	10.09	3.41	64.4	**6.1**	41.6	3.0	**7.8**
6.0	0.43	2.9	-0.03	**6.5**	6.1	1.37	13.07	3.51	60.4	**4.4**	20.4	6.6	**7.0**
7.6	0.38	1.9	0.01	**8.8**	2.0	1.90	16.84	3.30	52.2	**5.4**	43.0	8.2	**8.4**
6.6	0.21	1.2	0.02	**4.9**	15.8	1.02	10.03	2.18	59.6	**3.8**	22.3	5.1	**7.3**
3.0	2.17	14.6	0.00	**4.2**	0.7	0.83	8.43	4.07	69.1	**3.2**	21.2	13.6	**6.2**
6.8	1.01	3.0	1.14	**7.2**	0.8	1.24	7.04	4.15	71.1	**2.4**	45.1	33.4	**8.8**
7.6	0.22	0.9	0.01	**7.3**	124.8	1.76	14.47	2.99	66.0	**4.8**	29.9	7.2	**9.8**
9.3	0.20	0.3	-0.03	**3.1**	6.7	0.58	1.86	1.64	52.0	**2.9**	55.1	19.4	**8.3**
8.1	0.24	0.3	0.00	**5.1**	0.6	1.25	8.35	3.41	58.0	**4.5**	36.9	11.6	**8.2**
8.5	0.07	0.4	-0.01	**4.9**	7.6	1.10	14.35	3.23	54.4	**3.7**	25.6	10.7	**7.2**
6.1	1.71	9.2	-0.01	**7.2**	20.5	1.94	20.88	3.23	40.7	**3.4**	36.0	13.4	**9.3**
5.7	0.71	5.1	0.24	**6.9**	3.3	1.29	14.66	5.18	60.5	**2.1**	14.4	14.0	**6.0**

Name	City	State	Rating	2020 Rating	2019 Rating	Total Assets ($Mil)	One Year Asset Growth	Asset Mix (As a % of Total Assets) Commercial Loans	Consumer Loans	Mortgage Loans	Securities	Capitalization Index	Leverage Ratio	Risk-Based Capital Ratio
▲ Traditions Bank	York	PA	**B**			705.7	13.38	12.4	0.0	20.7	14.6	**8.4**	9.9	15.9
Traditions First Bank	Erin	TN	**B-**	C+	B-	200.8	12.26	3.4	1.2	14.0	28.3	**5.7**	7.7	13.7
TrailWest Bank	Lolo	MT	**B+**	B+	B+	880.3	13.33	8.3	1.6	25.5	3.3	**6.7**	8.7	14.7
▼ Transact Bank, N.A.	Denver	CO	**D-**	D	D	21.8	-10.87	0.0	0.0	0.0	4.2	**9.6**	10.7	83.0
TransPecos Banks, SSB	Pecos	TX	**C**	C+	C+	501.2	27.99	48.0	1.2	15.4	5.1	**6.4**	8.4	13.1
Transportation Alliance Bank, Inc.	Ogden	UT	**C**	C	C	1330.9	47.66	69.1	3.4	0.0	4.3	**1.5**	11.0	0.0
Tri City National Bank	Oak Creek	WI	**B**	B+	A-	1950.6	15.92	4.0	0.2	7.1	34.3	**7.9**	9.6	0.0
Tri Counties Bank	Chico	CA	**A-**	A-	A	8162.2	10.92	5.5	0.9	8.3	25.7	**8.1**	9.7	15.1
Tri-County Bank	Brown City	MI	**A**	A	A-	459.9	20.83	8.6	0.8	5.3	24.1	**9.5**	10.7	0.0
Tri-County Bank & Trust Co.	Roachdale	IN	**C+**	B-	B	230.1	5.95	11.9	2.8	14.3	38.6	**10.0**	11.6	0.0
Tri-County Trust Co.	Glasgow	MO	**B-**	B-	B-	63.1	1.70	9.4	6.5	22.0	29.6	**10.0**	11.6	0.0
Tri-State Bank of Memphis	Memphis	TN	**D**	D+	C-	113.2	9.61	4.7	5.4	6.7	35.5	**5.6**	7.6	14.1
Tri-Valley Bank	Randolph	IA	**C+**	C+	B-	79.6	18.76	4.6	1.4	7.6	34.9	**7.2**	9.1	0.0
Triad Bank	Frontenac	MO	**B**	B	C+	610.0	16.71	23.3	0.2	12.9	4.4	**6.1**	9.1	11.8
Triad Bank, N.A.	Tulsa	OK	**B+**	B+	B	221.1	5.65	9.5	1.6	28.2	0.0	**8.0**	9.6	0.0
Triad Business Bank	Greensboro	NC	**D**	D		266.5	67.28	26.1	0.2	3.1	23.8	**10.0**	18.0	24.7
TriCentury Bank	De Soto	KS	**A-**	A-	A-	120.4	-2.33	10.4	0.8	24.4	0.0	**9.3**	12.1	0.0
Trinity Bank, N.A.	Fort Worth	TX	**A**	A	A-	389.9	10.79	38.1	0.1	2.9	25.7	**9.2**	10.5	18.5
TriStar Bank	Dickson	TN	**B-**	C+	C+	396.8	12.44	9.9	4.5	18.3	18.1	**6.0**	8.1	13.2
TriState Capital Bank	Pittsburgh	PA	**B-**	B-	B-	11461.3	26.54	29.9	27.3	0.2	11.5	**5.3**	7.3	13.3
Triumph Bank	Memphis	TN	**B-**	B-	C+	886.6	-0.17	16.1	0.5	18.8	15.8	**7.4**	9.9	12.8
Triumph State Bank	Trimont	MN	**C+**	C+	C+	89.3	19.69	9.1	2.9	1.1	7.4	**6.7**	8.7	0.0
Troy Bank & Trust Co.	Troy	AL	**B+**	B+	B+	1262.7	29.61	9.5	2.1	11.6	29.5	**9.3**	10.5	0.0
TruBank	Indianola	IA	**B**	B	B-	395.0	17.51	7.4	0.7	7.8	18.5	**7.3**	9.2	0.0
Truist Bank	Charlotte	NC	**B+**	B+	B+	510294.0	3.30	13.1	10.8	9.2	27.4	**6.5**	8.5	13.0
TruPoint Bank	Grundy	VA	**B-**	B-	B-	531.2	9.43	17.5	3.7	10.7	31.7	**7.4**	9.3	0.0
▼ Trustar Bank	Great Falls	VA	**D-**	D		416.0	74.64	18.0	0.3	14.9	0.0	**8.8**	11.4	14.0
TrustBank	Olney	IL	**B+**	B+	B+	326.3	26.12	8.0	2.5	19.2	7.6	**6.5**	9.9	0.0
TrustCo Bank	Glenville	NY	**B+**	B+	A-	6121.8	7.84	0.8	0.1	63.7	8.1	**7.1**	9.1	20.0
Trustmark National Bank	Jackson	MS	**B+**	B+	B+	17096.0	8.96	8.7	0.9	10.5	17.6	**7.0**	9.0	13.0
Trusttexas Bank, S.S.B.	Cuero	TX	**C**	C+	B-	371.1	3.96	3.4	0.8	29.0	39.6	**10.0**	11.8	0.0
Truxton Trust Co.	Nashville	TN	**A-**	A-	A	805.3	21.08	7.8	3.8	15.1	29.2	**7.7**	9.5	14.7
▲ TS Bank	Treynor	IA	**C**	D+	D	424.0	2.24	7.3	0.6	4.2	41.2	**6.4**	8.4	12.4
TSB Bank	Lomira	WI	**B+**	B+	A-	163.8	5.78	9.8	0.8	14.1	8.3	**9.5**	11.0	0.0
Tucumcari Federal S&L Assn.	Tucumcari	NM	**C**	C-	C+	38.9	12.77	0.0	0.7	49.3	16.6	**10.0**	13.9	0.0
Turtle Mountain State Bank	Belcourt	ND	**D+**	C-	C	218.0	125.29	8.1	1.0	0.6	73.8	**4.9**	6.9	24.9
Tustin Community Bank	Tustin	CA	**B**	B	B	85.7	-0.63	12.5	33.5	4.3	0.0	**10.0**	12.8	0.0
Twin City Bank	Longview	WA	**B**	B-	B-	80.8	8.89	18.2	0.1	11.6	12.3	**6.4**	8.4	0.0
Twin River Bank	Lewiston	ID	**B+**	B+	B+	134.5	10.98	13.2	2.8	9.0	2.3	**6.3**	8.4	17.4
Two Rivers Bank	Blair	NE	**A-**	A-	B+	148.6	-2.65	5.5	1.6	11.3	25.9	**10.0**	12.7	20.8
Two Rivers Bank & Trust	Burlington	IA	**B**	B-	B-	1005.3	6.75	15.5	0.9	13.1	17.6	**7.1**	9.0	14.9
U.S. Bank N.A.	Minneapolis	MN	**B**	B	B	547852.7	2.16	13.8	11.4	14.6	29.0	**6.5**	8.5	13.7
U.S. Bank Trust Co., N.A.	Portland	OR	**U**	U	U	21.0	6.56	0.0	0.0	0.0	0.0	**10.0**	101.	498.4
U.S. Bank Trust N.A.	Wilmington	DE	**U**	U	U	680.5	1.43	0.0	0.0	0.0	0.0	**10.0**	98.2	492.4
U.S. Bank Trust N.A. SD	Sioux Falls	SD	**U**	U	U	118.2	8.17	0.0	0.0	0.0	0.0	**10.0**	100.	448.4
▲ U.S. Century Bank	Doral	FL	**B**	B-	B-	1667.0	16.40	10.4	2.4	12.4	23.7	**5.9**	7.9	12.7
▼ UBank	Jellico	TN	**B-**	B	B	80.4	7.72	7.7	5.9	13.5	7.6	**10.0**	16.5	0.0
UBank	Huntington	TX	**B**	B	B+	350.7	14.93	12.1	1.5	12.6	5.5	**7.4**	9.8	0.0
UBS Bank USA	Salt Lake City	UT	**B+**	A-	A	94957.1	25.59	8.8	38.0	21.9	7.7	**5.8**	7.8	31.6
Uinta Bank	Mountain View	WY	**B-**	B-	B-	273.8	8.76	9.1	0.5	2.0	64.6	**6.1**	8.1	21.7
Ulster Savings Bank	Kingston	NY	**B-**	B-	C+	1289.4	18.05	3.5	1.6	30.8	11.9	**7.0**	9.0	15.8
Ultima Bank Minnesota	Winger	MN	**B+**	B	C+	211.5	2.31	15.7	1.6	5.9	0.0	**7.6**	10.8	0.0
UMB Bank & Trust, N.A.	Saint Louis	MO	**U**	U	U	3.0	0.10	0.0	0.0	0.0	0.0	**10.0**	100.	103.1
UMB Bank, N.A.	Kansas City	MO	**B-**	B-	B-	36376.3	22.59	21.6	0.8	5.0	31.4	**5.7**	7.7	12.2
▲ Umpqua Bank	Roseburg	OR	**B**	B-	B+	30290.3	2.22	15.3	0.7	13.8	11.5	**8.4**	9.9	14.4
UNB Bank	Mount Carmel	PA	**C-**	C-	C-	168.8	9.89	1.8	0.8	37.6	35.8	**6.8**	8.9	0.0
▲ UniBank	Lynnwood	WA	**A**	A-	A-	417.1	9.65	15.2	0.0	1.2	13.4	**10.0**	15.5	22.0
▼ UniBank for Savings	Whitinsville	MA	**C-**	C+	B-	2577.5	15.48	5.0	15.1	15.6	30.2	**5.4**	7.4	13.8
UNICO Bank	Mineral Point	MO	**D+**	D+	C	396.0	8.59	7.8	5.1	27.5	10.3	**3.6**	7.2	10.3
Unified Bank	Martins Ferry	OH	**A-**	A-	B+	733.2	4.37	13.5	1.0	15.0	19.7	**9.3**	10.5	15.6

Asset Quality Index	Adjusted Non-Performing Loans as a % of Total Loans	Adjusted Non-Performing Loans as a % of Capital	Net Charge-Offs Avg Loans	Profitability Index	Net Income ($Mil)	Return on Assets (R.O.A.)	Return on Equity (R.O.E.)	Net Interest Spread	Overhead Efficiency Ratio	Liquidity Index	Liquidity Ratio	Hot Money Ratio	Stability Index
5.8	0.82	4.9	0.00	**6.0**	4.4	1.32	13.03	3.24	67.9	**4.3**	21.5	7.5	**7.2**
9.1	0.00	0.1	-0.01	**4.4**	1.0	0.99	11.91	3.30	66.8	**2.6**	34.9	21.3	**5.0**
8.5	0.21	1.5	-0.31	**6.4**	6.9	1.61	18.41	3.61	57.0	**5.2**	30.4	3.6	**7.2**
9.9	0.00	0.0	0.00	**0.0**	-0.8	-6.75	-48.77	0.91	242.4	**7.1**	81.3	2.8	**5.3**
3.0	1.56	11.3	0.29	**4.3**	2.7	1.13	19.05	4.04	73.7	**1.3**	12.1	12.1	**3.4**
5.9	0.38	3.3	0.89	**6.6**	12.2	2.08	22.11	7.71	59.8	**0.6**	12.1	26.4	**7.6**
7.1	1.37	4.4	-0.06	**4.4**	6.8	0.72	7.23	2.85	76.6	**6.8**	40.1	1.3	**8.4**
6.6	0.78	3.2	-0.02	**8.0**	63.2	1.59	12.79	3.67	51.3	**6.1**	31.7	3.0	**10.0**
7.6	0.25	1.1	-0.07	**9.2**	3.9	1.74	16.40	3.90	48.7	**6.0**	43.1	4.3	**7.8**
8.0	0.26	0.7	0.23	**3.0**	0.5	0.45	3.82	2.93	80.3	**5.4**	50.6	10.4	**6.4**
4.8	3.24	10.4	0.01	**5.5**	0.5	1.44	11.75	3.77	60.2	**1.3**	30.0	31.6	**7.4**
2.6	4.98	15.2	-0.07	**2.4**	0.4	0.72	7.59	2.93	78.8	**4.9**	40.1	10.6	**4.2**
4.6	2.98	11.0	0.01	**1.9**	0.1	0.18	1.81	2.99	91.0	**4.7**	58.4	12.0	**4.4**
7.2	0.00	0.0	0.00	**5.4**	3.4	1.14	13.71	3.29	52.2	**2.1**	10.9	5.6	**5.9**
6.3	0.41	2.6	-0.04	**5.7**	1.3	1.26	12.62	4.31	65.7	**4.9**	30.4	6.6	**7.0**
8.5	0.00	0.0	0.00	**0.0**	-0.7	-0.55	-3.20	2.71	112.7	**6.3**	46.9	3.8	**1.5**
7.5	0.00	0.0	0.00	**7.1**	0.9	1.45	12.57	3.72	47.5	**1.3**	9.6	25.3	**7.1**
8.4	0.12	0.6	0.00	**6.7**	2.8	1.44	13.24	3.86	42.5	**4.4**	40.1	10.3	**7.8**
7.2	0.25	1.8	0.10	**4.0**	1.5	0.76	9.19	3.38	75.5	**2.8**	30.0	17.5	**4.9**
6.8	0.12	1.4	0.06	**3.8**	36.7	0.70	9.55	1.65	51.5	**2.2**	17.0	8.1	**4.3**
5.9	1.11	4.0	0.00	**3.9**	3.1	0.70	7.01	2.89	73.4	**1.5**	16.6	25.7	**6.6**
4.9	1.65	6.2	0.10	**3.8**	0.2	0.40	4.40	3.95	77.9	**5.9**	52.6	6.5	**4.8**
5.8	1.50	5.8	-1.19	**5.6**	7.7	1.28	12.34	3.12	70.8	**4.1**	36.5	16.2	**9.1**
8.6	0.00	0.0	0.00	**4.1**	1.7	0.89	8.85	3.01	67.5	**2.2**	27.4	19.8	**6.0**
5.6	0.69	2.5	0.19	**5.4**	2708.0	1.08	8.41	2.82	71.1	**6.1**	33.5	1.7	**10.0**
8.4	0.13	0.8	-0.02	**4.2**	2.2	0.86	9.10	3.12	70.1	**3.8**	6.6	8.6	**6.1**
7.3	0.00	0.0	0.00	**0.2**	-0.7	-0.36	-2.94	3.08	93.9	**3.0**	16.5	14.3	**1.1**
5.7	0.51	3.5	-0.01	**7.5**	2.8	1.84	17.27	4.11	68.0	**4.8**	20.4	4.3	**7.9**
8.3	0.74	4.3	-0.01	**5.2**	30.3	1.01	10.92	2.74	54.8	**4.2**	25.2	11.6	**8.7**
6.7	0.51	2.5	-0.02	**5.2**	102.9	1.22	11.46	2.97	69.9	**4.9**	20.4	4.0	**9.6**
9.1	0.52	2.2	0.06	**1.7**	0.7	0.39	3.15	3.15	90.3	**4.7**	49.4	13.7	**6.4**
6.9	0.51	2.7	0.00	**8.7**	6.5	1.75	18.12	2.90	53.5	**5.3**	39.3	3.0	**7.4**
7.2	0.65	1.5	-0.16	**3.7**	3.1	1.55	16.58	3.48	64.8	**2.7**	43.9	10.8	**4.0**
8.4	0.10	0.6	0.39	**3.8**	0.4	0.52	4.88	3.73	61.4	**3.5**	29.3	11.2	**5.3**
6.6	0.82	7.1	0.00	**3.0**	0.1	0.73	5.19	3.19	72.3	**0.8**	19.4	51.7	**6.3**
8.5	0.18	0.9	0.01	**4.1**	0.4	0.88	23.76	2.44	63.3	**7.8**	89.1	2.6	**2.1**
6.8	0.05	0.3	0.50	**5.8**	0.6	1.39	11.00	5.49	67.3	**1.2**	25.4	32.8	**6.9**
8.6	0.00	0.0	0.16	**4.8**	0.3	0.86	9.92	3.68	74.3	**4.6**	39.4	11.5	**5.3**
8.8	0.00	0.0	0.00	**7.6**	1.1	1.68	19.70	4.03	58.2	**6.1**	50.1	6.0	**6.1**
8.9	0.00	0.7	0.00	**5.3**	0.9	1.32	9.37	3.69	67.1	**5.1**	35.3	7.3	**8.2**
4.9	1.48	7.7	0.34	**4.9**	5.5	1.08	11.22	3.28	63.5	**5.9**	31.1	4.2	**8.7**
5.4	1.19	4.5	0.27	**7.1**	4309.2	1.60	16.82	2.57	59.5	**5.4**	35.4	1.8	**9.1**
10.0	na	0.0	na	**10.0**	0.8	7.34	7.29	6.67	16.8	**4.0**	na	0.0	**7.0**
9.3	na	0.0	na	**9.4**	5.8	1.72	1.75	0.23	47.4	**4.0**	na	0.0	**7.0**
10.0	na	0.0	na	**10.0**	5.5	9.47	9.59	0.12	14.2	**4.0**	na	0.0	**7.0**
8.3	0.38	1.2	0.01	**5.0**	8.8	1.09	10.42	3.26	60.8	**4.2**	28.9	13.4	**8.4**
7.9	0.00	0.0	0.50	**3.0**	0.1	0.14	0.86	3.65	88.7	**2.4**	36.7	26.2	**7.8**
4.8	0.53	3.6	-0.05	**5.7**	2.0	1.20	12.90	4.69	67.4	**3.2**	17.0	13.3	**6.6**
6.8	0.05	0.5	0.00	**6.7**	476.5	1.03	12.99	1.75	19.2	**4.0**	27.0	0.0	**7.8**
8.4	0.00	0.9	0.00	**4.9**	1.5	1.16	13.19	2.47	45.0	**2.4**	49.6	28.0	**4.9**
3.9	3.38	18.4	-0.03	**3.3**	3.0	0.49	5.28	2.77	82.8	**4.3**	36.5	13.2	**7.2**
3.9	0.78	11.0	0.00	**10.0**	3.8	3.65	35.58	6.37	44.2	**1.5**	8.5	20.3	**8.5**
10.0	na	0.0	na	**2.3**	0.0	0.13	0.13	6.67	99.9	**4.0**	na	0.0	**7.0**
8.3	0.35	1.9	0.41	**4.6**	167.3	1.01	11.67	2.68	60.4	**6.1**	28.1	1.3	**7.2**
8.4	0.14	0.8	0.28	**5.3**	226.9	1.53	15.47	3.25	56.9	**4.6**	20.4	5.5	**7.6**
9.5	0.04	1.0	0.00	**2.0**	0.2	0.18	2.01	2.05	92.7	**4.7**	42.1	11.8	**4.8**
7.2	0.21	0.9	0.00	**9.8**	3.9	2.00	13.00	4.29	53.4	**1.1**	23.5	12.6	**9.3**
5.2	0.79	4.6	1.59	**2.1**	1.8	0.15	1.92	2.30	77.8	**5.2**	22.6	4.1	**5.6**
2.0	2.03	19.2	0.11	**3.9**	1.9	0.95	12.39	3.65	74.1	**1.7**	10.2	20.1	**4.6**
7.5	0.64	3.2	0.05	**7.3**	5.7	1.61	13.05	3.70	56.8	**4.9**	25.4	4.4	**8.0**

Name	City	State	Rating	2020 Rating	2019 Rating	Total Assets ($Mil)	One Year Asset Growth	Asset Mix (As a % of Total Assets): Commercial Loans	Consumer Loans	Mortgage Loans	Securities	Capitalization Index	Leverage Ratio	Risk-Based Capital Ratio
▼ Union Bank	Lake Odessa	MI	**D+**	C-	C	308.9	28.18	12.3	0.7	6.5	8.2	**4.6**	6.7	11.7
▲ Union Bank	Greenville	NC	**B**	C+	B	1079.6	7.84	7.7	0.3	12.2	27.8	**6.9**	8.9	15.1
▲ Union Bank	Halliday	ND	**B-**	C+	C+	268.1	55.87	4.8	3.3	6.2	14.3	**6.6**	8.6	0.0
Union Bank	Jamestown	TN	**D+**	D+	C+	230.4	9.39	6.5	2.8	15.9	41.8	**9.2**	10.4	22.4
Union Bank	Morrisville	VT	**B**	B	B	1065.3	16.22	9.2	0.2	23.2	14.9	**5.0**	7.0	13.4
Union Bank & Trust Co.	Monticello	AR	**B+**	B+	B-	273.4	10.66	18.3	4.6	16.4	16.8	**7.4**	9.3	14.3
Union Bank & Trust Co.	Livingston	TN	**B+**	B+	B+	102.0	9.07	8.2	4.4	25.4	17.4	**10.0**	11.3	0.0
Union Bank and Trust Co.	Minneapolis	MN	**B-**	B-	B-	201.1	16.06	13.5	0.1	0.4	20.7	**6.2**	8.2	18.2
Union Bank and Trust Co.	Lincoln	NE	**B+**	A-	A-	5969.9	9.79	14.2	9.3	2.7	17.1	**7.5**	9.3	13.7
Union Bank, Inc.	Middlebourne	WV	**B+**	B+	B+	331.2	14.31	5.1	2.0	13.2	47.2	**6.5**	8.5	0.0
▲ Union County Savings Bank	Elizabeth	NJ	**C+**	C	C+	1900.3	5.94	0.0	0.0	4.2	75.9	**10.0**	13.6	49.7
Union Federal S&L Assn.	Kewanee	IL	**C+**	C+	B-	163.5	2.37	1.7	0.2	48.0	3.3	**10.0**	13.7	0.0
Union National Bank	Elgin	IL	**B+**	B+	B+	451.2	-2.37	30.7	0.0	1.8	1.1	**9.8**	10.8	19.7
Union S&L Assn.	Connersville	IN	**B-**	B-	B-	198.7	12.52	2.9	11.0	33.8	9.5	**7.7**	9.4	0.0
▼ Union Savings Bank	Danbury	CT	**B-**	B+	B+	2962.9	14.14	4.6	0.2	19.7	23.8	**9.2**	10.5	0.0
UNION Savings BANK	Freeport	IL	**C-**	C-	C	188.4	8.71	5.0	1.5	35.5	26.7	**6.7**	8.7	16.6
Union Savings Bank	Cincinnati	OH	**A**	A	A-	3354.4	2.08	0.2	0.2	57.2	0.0	**9.1**	10.4	0.0
Union State Bank	Pell City	AL	**D+**	D+	D+	266.5	17.51	3.4	0.6	4.9	23.0	**4.0**	6.0	12.5
▲ Union State Bank	Greenfield	IA	**B**	C+	C-	91.8	11.18	4.5	1.4	16.2	15.2	**8.7**	10.1	0.0
Union State Bank	Winterset	IA	**B-**	B-	C+	118.6	8.68	7.1	1.7	21.9	35.4	**5.6**	7.6	14.3
Union State Bank	Arkansas City	KS	**B**	B	B	567.5	5.62	5.9	3.8	15.5	26.1	**6.9**	8.9	13.9
Union State Bank	Clay Center	KS	**B**	B	B-	162.1	4.82	7.0	1.0	12.1	46.2	**10.0**	11.0	0.0
Union State Bank	Olsburg	KS	**C-**	C-	C+	37.2	9.61	8.2	3.0	2.4	27.2	**9.9**	11.0	34.1
Union State Bank	Uniontown	KS	**C+**	C	C	62.4	14.28	9.8	4.0	20.6	13.5	**6.0**	8.0	14.6
▲ Union State Bank	West Salem	WI	**B-**	C+	B-	113.9	17.70	7.5	3.0	20.7	30.0	**8.1**	9.7	0.0
Union State Bank of Hazen	Hazen	ND	**C**	C	C	207.3	13.92	3.6	4.5	12.9	32.9	**6.4**	8.5	15.9
Unison Bank	Jamestown	ND	**B+**	B+	B	505.5	30.87	3.3	6.9	15.0	24.9	**6.4**	8.4	14.2
▲ United Bank	Atmore	AL	**A-**	B+	B	1013.4	16.30	18.5	2.1	7.8	17.6	**7.6**	9.4	16.5
United Bank	Springdale	AR	**B+**	B+	B+	239.7	8.17	10.3	0.5	29.4	1.9	**8.6**	10.1	13.9
United Bank	Zebulon	GA	**A**	A	A	2086.5	18.46	4.8	1.9	7.3	19.1	**6.6**	8.6	22.7
United Bank	Vienna	VA	**B+**	B	B	27158.3	3.62	9.4	4.3	13.9	12.0	**9.5**	10.7	14.9
United Bank & Trust	Marysville	KS	**B+**	B+	A-	737.7	1.52	8.4	1.4	7.1	19.7	**9.8**	10.9	0.0
United Bank & Trust N.A.	Marshalltown	IA	**B**	B	B+	120.3	0.35	6.5	0.7	6.9	33.7	**6.8**	8.8	0.0
United Bank and Trust Co.	Hampton	IA	**A**	A	A	211.1	16.14	4.0	2.8	10.5	39.1	**10.0**	12.9	0.0
▲ United Bank of El Paso del Norte	El Paso	TX	**B**	B-	C	319.6	5.88	19.3	0.3	2.3	9.2	**9.9**	11.0	17.3
United Bank of Iowa	Ida Grove	IA	**A-**	A-	A-	1938.8	5.11	4.6	3.0	6.9	24.9	**8.6**	10.2	0.0
United Bank of Michigan	Grand Rapids	MI	**B**	B-	C+	826.4	5.71	4.9	0.8	12.7	3.4	**7.4**	9.9	0.0
United Bank of Philadelphia	Philadelphia	PA	**E**	E-	E-	64.2	27.71	24.6	0.9	5.5	2.1	**7.6**	9.4	23.0
United Bank of Union	Union	MO	**B-**	C+	C	448.8	5.99	14.1	0.7	12.9	20.9	**8.4**	10.0	13.9
▲ United Bankers Bank	Bloomington	MN	**B**	B-	B-	1100.3	5.85	6.0	0.3	0.9	23.0	**8.9**	10.3	15.4
▲ United Business Bank	Walnut Creek	CA	**B+**	B	A-	2315.4	5.81	13.4	0.2	5.1	5.3	**9.3**	10.5	16.3
United Citizens Bank & Trust Co.	Campbellsburg	KY	**B+**	B+	B+	145.1	13.57	6.8	1.2	22.5	12.8	**10.0**	11.0	19.3
United Citizens Bank of Southern Kentucky	Columbia	KY	**A**	A-	A-	190.7	7.36	9.0	5.9	31.4	7.7	**10.0**	12.7	17.7
United Community Bank	Milford	IA	**B-**	B-	B	248.7	12.02	8.2	1.3	8.1	15.8	**6.2**	8.2	14.1
United Community Bank	Chatham	IL	**B**	B	B-	3385.8	14.22	10.7	0.9	10.2	28.6	**6.6**	8.6	15.7
United Community Bank	Raceland	LA	**B+**	B	C+	619.0	3.16	22.6	0.4	8.0	8.4	**10.0**	13.8	0.0
United Community Bank	Perham	MN	**B**	B	B+	326.3	10.42	14.5	2.9	6.5	32.6	**7.9**	9.6	0.0
United Community Bank	Greenville	SC	**A-**	A-	A-	18867.0	25.98	16.6	0.7	9.5	26.1	**7.2**	9.2	14.0
United Community Bank of North Dakota	Leeds	ND	**B**	B	B	358.8	-0.24	20.6	1.3	3.3	12.1	**7.4**	9.3	12.9
United Community Bank of W Kentucky	Morganfield	KY	**A**	A	A	361.1	17.65	11.3	4.3	14.0	39.4	**10.0**	11.2	0.0
United Cumberland Bank	Whitley City	KY	**A-**	B+	B-	366.8	11.52	8.6	8.6	23.0	25.6	**10.0**	11.6	0.0
▲ United Farmers State Bank	Adams	MN	**A-**	B	B	180.4	14.26	6.1	0.8	2.8	3.4	**7.3**	11.4	12.8
United Fidelity Bank, FSB	Evansville	IN	**B+**	B	B+	1780.3	51.22	3.3	0.1	7.2	46.5	**7.0**	9.0	17.1
United Midwest Savings Bank, N.A.	De Graff	OH	**C**	C+	C-	467.5	41.06	30.7	10.2	7.0	0.1	**6.9**	8.9	15.9
United Minnesota Bank	New London	MN	**D+**	D+	C	43.7	17.55	12.3	7.3	26.3	8.0	**4.2**	6.2	12.4
United Mississippi Bank	Natchez	MS	**C+**	C+	C+	419.0	9.01	15.8	2.9	10.4	23.9	**5.7**	9.5	0.0
United National Bank	Cairo	GA	**B**	B-	B	271.7	16.78	14.5	3.1	12.4	4.0	**10.0**	12.8	21.0
▼ United Orient Bank	New York	NY	**D+**	C	B	91.5	8.16	0.8	0.0	24.0	2.2	**10.0**	14.2	0.0
United Pacific Bank	City of Industry	CA	**B-**	B-	B	177.1	4.89	2.8	0.0	1.6	0.1	**10.0**	14.4	23.4
United Prairie Bank	Mountain Lake	MN	**B-**	B-	C+	754.6	3.34	13.9	0.6	4.3	10.7	**5.2**	8.5	11.2

Asset Quality Index	Adjusted Non-Performing Loans as a % of Total Loans	Adjusted Non-Performing Loans as a % of Capital	Net Charge-Offs Avg Loans	Profitability Index	Net Income ($Mil)	Return on Assets (R.O.A.)	Return on Equity (R.O.E.)	Net Interest Spread	Overhead Efficiency Ratio	Liquidity Index	Liquidity Ratio	Hot Money Ratio	Stability Index
1.6	4.50	25.2	0.15	**3.3**	0.8	0.50	7.05	3.07	81.7	**5.3**	35.3	5.7	**4.6**
7.5	0.40	2.5	0.00	**5.4**	6.6	1.26	12.73	3.52	57.1	**4.1**	33.6	9.6	**7.7**
5.3	0.49	3.0	-0.02	**5.2**	1.8	1.32	13.42	4.92	61.5	**4.0**	30.8	11.7	**5.2**
2.9	7.36	19.9	-0.01	**1.3**	0.2	0.17	1.62	2.93	95.5	**2.7**	48.3	31.2	**5.2**
6.2	1.04	7.7	0.00	**5.5**	6.1	1.10	15.25	3.32	67.3	**5.0**	23.8	6.2	**7.7**
6.7	0.62	2.7	0.01	**6.5**	2.0	1.51	15.86	3.47	58.8	**1.6**	22.2	21.8	**6.9**
3.2	4.79	22.0	-0.05	**9.9**	1.1	2.15	19.17	4.86	48.9	**4.1**	37.2	13.7	**8.4**
9.2	0.00	0.0	-0.13	**3.6**	0.4	0.50	5.92	2.90	82.8	**7.4**	64.9	1.4	**4.1**
5.4	0.78	4.4	0.38	**6.6**	39.4	1.31	13.98	2.64	58.0	**2.4**	24.2	12.9	**9.2**
6.6	0.76	2.2	0.00	**5.2**	1.8	1.10	9.40	2.88	60.5	**5.7**	37.2	3.9	**7.6**
9.8	0.90	0.0	0.00	**2.8**	4.0	0.43	3.19	0.85	54.9	**4.0**	108.4	62.5	**8.7**
7.8	1.33	6.4	0.05	**2.7**	0.4	0.46	3.18	2.98	77.7	**3.3**	23.0	13.5	**6.8**
4.9	0.38	2.7	-0.01	**6.5**	3.3	1.43	16.71	3.25	35.2	**0.9**	11.7	33.2	**6.6**
4.7	0.89	5.8	-0.01	**3.7**	0.6	0.56	5.86	2.86	80.1	**2.4**	25.7	18.0	**5.4**
5.1	2.34	11.6	-0.04	**3.8**	8.8	0.61	5.75	2.47	71.3	**4.4**	11.4	6.0	**8.5**
9.3	0.02	0.3	-0.02	**1.9**	0.1	0.11	1.30	2.60	95.1	**5.2**	39.4	8.6	**4.6**
7.3	0.66	3.8	-0.01	**9.2**	74.7	4.36	41.74	2.34	31.9	**1.5**	23.8	32.7	**10.0**
5.5	2.39	9.5	0.00	**1.0**	-0.4	-0.29	-4.59	2.21	112.6	**6.4**	50.0	4.2	**2.3**
7.2	0.16	0.6	-0.02	**7.6**	0.9	1.95	13.38	5.85	53.3	**2.0**	33.2	24.0	**7.0**
9.2	0.02	0.1	0.00	**4.1**	0.6	1.06	13.95	3.23	69.6	**3.7**	25.1	11.4	**4.7**
6.5	0.29	1.9	0.00	**4.0**	2.8	0.98	8.20	3.21	70.2	**3.7**	29.1	13.0	**7.9**
9.0	0.00	0.4	-0.05	**3.8**	0.6	0.74	6.27	2.96	69.2	**1.8**	14.7	12.8	**6.5**
5.3	13.29	8.8	-0.06	**2.1**	0.1	0.65	5.64	2.34	66.7	**6.4**	65.8	6.4	**5.3**
5.7	0.00	11.6	0.06	**6.3**	0.5	1.69	21.49	4.73	65.3	**4.3**	31.1	10.6	**4.0**
4.0	3.04	12.8	-0.01	**4.8**	0.7	1.17	12.35	3.47	55.2	**5.2**	43.3	9.2	**5.7**
2.2	4.56	21.1	0.02	**2.2**	0.1	0.06	0.62	3.05	78.3	**4.0**	39.4	14.7	**4.8**
7.3	0.30	0.8	0.00	**6.9**	3.0	1.30	14.20	3.89	55.7	**3.0**	25.9	13.4	**6.8**
7.5	0.62	3.2	-0.06	**8.4**	11.3	2.41	26.72	3.47	43.6	**6.1**	40.4	6.1	**7.6**
6.6	0.55	2.8	-0.07	**5.1**	1.4	1.26	12.18	3.55	73.7	**1.1**	20.3	23.2	**7.1**
8.0	0.90	3.3	-0.04	**7.8**	16.8	1.66	18.86	2.50	57.7	**7.0**	56.6	4.1	**9.0**
5.7	0.50	2.0	0.11	**7.0**	200.0	1.50	8.94	3.21	54.0	**4.7**	22.2	7.1	**10.0**
6.5	0.00	0.0	0.04	**5.5**	4.1	1.10	9.46	3.12	53.5	**4.5**	24.4	6.8	**7.7**
4.2	2.68	13.3	-0.01	**4.3**	0.5	0.89	9.45	2.61	64.0	**5.9**	48.3	7.1	**7.2**
8.8	0.30	1.6	0.00	**6.5**	1.6	1.57	11.71	3.16	45.8	**6.0**	60.3	9.9	**9.1**
8.4	0.14	0.4	0.00	**6.9**	2.0	1.34	11.99	5.22	55.2	**4.4**	31.4	9.5	**7.0**
6.1	0.64	2.7	0.00	**7.1**	16.9	1.75	16.12	3.36	50.3	**2.8**	31.0	23.2	**10.0**
6.1	0.64	2.3	0.00	**5.3**	4.8	1.20	12.09	3.34	69.5	**5.1**	28.9	4.4	**7.0**
1.2	8.08	41.8	-0.03	**3.5**	0.0	0.05	0.57	4.20	100.5	**5.2**	31.6	4.6	**1.1**
3.5	2.39	15.1	0.03	**6.3**	3.6	1.61	15.82	3.46	59.4	**2.7**	12.0	15.4	**8.0**
7.6	1.33	3.3	0.00	**4.9**	6.8	1.10	11.88	2.05	62.7	**6.4**	43.8	0.1	**8.1**
6.0	0.59	2.7	0.00	**5.4**	11.3	1.00	8.04	3.53	64.5	**5.0**	29.4	9.4	**8.6**
4.8	2.23	12.9	0.00	**8.0**	1.2	1.76	15.79	5.18	54.9	**4.8**	24.6	4.6	**7.2**
8.1	0.47	2.2	-0.01	**9.6**	2.5	2.69	21.01	5.66	41.2	**1.7**	17.6	21.6	**8.7**
3.9	2.54	9.3	1.05	**5.9**	1.8	1.39	14.58	3.58	56.0	**4.3**	20.9	7.2	**6.7**
6.0	1.27	6.0	0.01	**5.3**	19.3	1.17	12.32	2.50	59.4	**5.4**	30.2	6.7	**7.7**
5.2	1.70	7.8	0.08	**8.3**	6.7	2.16	15.85	3.92	54.8	**4.0**	27.1	10.5	**8.1**
7.1	0.78	2.1	0.01	**5.2**	2.1	1.33	13.10	3.54	64.2	**4.8**	47.8	13.0	**6.3**
6.7	0.74	2.9	-0.01	**7.8**	147.7	1.61	14.69	3.24	52.7	**5.6**	31.2	5.1	**9.5**
4.7	0.69	8.3	0.00	**8.3**	3.3	1.76	18.64	4.82	42.0	**3.9**	10.0	8.6	**7.3**
8.6	0.18	0.8	0.05	**7.2**	2.5	1.43	12.52	3.63	52.5	**3.3**	32.8	11.4	**8.6**
5.9	2.24	6.1	-0.11	**6.4**	2.4	1.38	11.68	3.49	65.9	**3.2**	31.3	15.9	**8.2**
7.3	0.03	0.2	-0.02	**8.9**	2.2	2.45	22.04	3.05	40.3	**4.5**	31.8	8.5	**8.8**
8.5	1.72	2.8	0.06	**5.9**	9.7	1.25	11.13	2.23	66.9	**4.1**	29.6	9.6	**9.5**
2.4	2.59	13.6	0.88	**6.8**	2.3	1.06	11.38	3.72	76.7	**0.9**	25.1	48.0	**5.5**
5.9	1.52	7.6	0.00	**4.9**	0.3	1.30	21.21	2.95	65.9	**5.3**	33.6	5.3	**2.5**
4.5	1.30	8.4	0.09	**4.4**	2.3	1.12	11.20	3.51	76.2	**3.6**	22.3	11.8	**6.1**
4.2	2.83	13.5	-0.02	**7.2**	1.6	1.20	9.03	3.95	54.1	**1.8**	21.6	19.0	**8.3**
4.2	1.84	9.5	0.00	**0.7**	-0.4	-0.81	-5.47	4.37	117.6	**1.6**	19.8	23.7	**6.7**
7.4	0.01	0.0	-0.02	**3.8**	0.6	0.70	4.91	3.06	70.0	**1.3**	31.2	46.6	**7.4**
5.7	0.58	2.1	0.05	**7.2**	6.9	1.81	18.59	4.21	59.7	**4.1**	14.8	7.1	**7.6**

Name	City	State	Rating	2020 Rating	2019 Rating	Total Assets ($Mil)	One Year Asset Growth	Asset Mix (As a % of Total Assets) Commercial Loans	Consumer Loans	Mortgage Loans	Securities	Capitalization Index	Leverage Ratio	Risk-Based Capital Ratio
United Republic Bank	Elkhorn	NE	D+	D+	D+	150.9	7.78	10.2	0.2	13.2	10.3	6.6	10.9	0.0
▲ United Roosevelt Savings Bank	Carteret	NJ	C	C-	C-	211.7	19.57	17.9	0.1	35.1	11.2	8.1	9.8	16.0
United Savings Bank	Philadelphia	PA	B-	B-	B-	432.7	6.72	1.5	0.0	23.6	12.1	10.0	15.0	0.0
United Security Bank	Fresno	CA	B+	B+	B+	1229.8	19.21	5.8	4.5	14.8	13.6	7.0	10.1	0.0
United Security Bank	Auxvasse	MO	B+	B+	B+	84.4	32.00	4.1	5.1	23.6	29.2	9.8	10.9	0.0
United Southern Bank	Umatilla	FL	B	B	B	775.1	23.67	4.6	0.9	9.7	41.2	5.9	7.9	0.0
United Southern Bank	Hopkinsville	KY	B+	B+	B+	274.4	13.82	5.8	2.2	19.1	17.9	9.8	10.9	0.0
▼ United Southwest Bank	Cottonwood	MN	D+	C-	C	58.8	20.19	1.6	1.5	0.2	17.1	4.7	6.7	17.4
United State Bank	Lewistown	MO	B-	B-	B	245.9	26.70	6.3	1.1	10.6	7.3	6.1	8.1	13.8
United Texas Bank	Dallas	TX	B	B	B-	1109.6	15.73	7.9	0.1	2.3	38.1	7.6	9.4	0.0
▲ United Trust Bank	Palos Heights	IL	E+	E-	E+	77.9	127.89	0.9	0.6	55.7	0.1	9.3	10.5	15.9
United Valley Bank	Cavalier	ND	B-	B-	B-	547.4	33.36	12.1	1.9	5.5	23.5	6.0	8.0	13.2
Unity Bank	Clinton	NJ	B+	B+	A-	1966.0	3.80	11.3	0.1	22.7	1.8	6.3	10.0	0.0
Unity Bank	Augusta	WI	C	C-	D+	604.5	3.73	8.9	1.9	9.9	5.5	6.0	8.0	13.0
▲ Unity National Bank of Houston	Houston	TX	C-	D	D-	227.6	74.42	41.5	0.2	5.9	16.5	10.0	11.3	0.0
Universal Bank	West Covina	CA	C+	C+	C+	392.3	-3.92	0.4	0.0	3.7	1.4	10.0	15.5	0.0
University Bank	Ann Arbor	MI	A	A	B+	700.8	29.76	2.3	0.0	26.4	0.9	10.0	11.1	0.0
Univest Bank and Trust Co.	Souderton	PA	B	B-	B	6337.0	3.80	17.1	0.4	14.5	6.3	6.0	9.4	11.7
Upper Peninsula State Bank	Escanaba	MI	A-	A-	A-	279.9	13.79	6.7	4.7	9.8	9.9	10.0	13.9	0.0
▲ US Metro Bank	Garden Grove	CA	A-	B	A-	872.0	31.09	14.4	0.0	0.4	5.8	9.7	10.8	16.6
USAA Federal Savings Bank	San Antonio	TX	C	C+	C+	115631.2	14.67	0.0	29.1	3.5	57.2	6.4	8.4	19.2
USAA Savings Bank	Las Vegas	NV	U	U	U	1862.1	10.98	0.0	0.0	0.0	10.1	10.0	25.7	83.0
▲ Utah Independent Bank	Salina	UT	A+	A	A-	127.1	10.38	13.6	3.8	9.0	13.1	10.0	13.0	0.0
Uwharrie Bank	Albemarle	NC	B-	C+	C+	842.3	13.33	12.1	1.2	10.6	27.2	6.1	8.1	14.1
Valley Bank of Commerce	Roswell	NM	A-	A	A	203.5	0.11	16.2	0.3	7.2	0.1	8.0	9.7	21.5
Valley Bank of Kalispell	Kalispell	MT	B+	B	B	167.9	17.22	14.2	3.6	13.7	20.0	7.6	9.4	0.0
▼ Valley Bank of Nevada	North Las Vegas	NV	C-	C	D+	235.5	16.77	9.4	0.4	0.8	4.2	4.3	6.3	14.2
Valley Bank of Ronan	Ronan	MT	C	C-	D+	155.6	28.38	12.8	4.1	9.8	4.4	6.5	8.5	0.0
▼ Valley Central Bank	Liberty Township	OH	C+	B-	C-	157.5	0.76	1.6	0.4	38.4	5.3	10.0	23.6	0.0
▼ Valley Exchange Bank	Lennox	SD	C-	C+	B	72.5	16.33	3.1	0.9	0.7	7.2	9.7	10.8	38.0
Valley National Bank	Wayne	NJ	B-	B-	C+	41294.2	-0.99	13.1	5.6	10.6	8.8	8.2	10.1	13.5
Valley Premier Bank	Hawley	MN	B	B	B	130.3	9.06	14.0	3.4	12.0	37.1	7.6	9.4	0.0
Valley Republic Bank	Bakersfield	CA	B+	B+	B+	1364.9	11.99	23.0	0.1	2.8	17.0	6.5	10.1	0.0
Valley State Bank	Russellville	AL	B	B	B	144.0	10.38	7.6	3.2	18.5	43.6	10.0	16.6	0.0
Valley State Bank	Belle Plaine	KS	B+	B+	B	179.7	13.86	7.8	7.8	13.5	29.8	10.0	11.2	0.0
Valliance Bank	Oklahoma City	OK	C+	C	C	555.8	2.67	19.9	0.2	12.1	5.1	5.7	9.0	0.0
Valor Bank	Edmond	OK	B+	B+	B	165.6	39.69	3.2	0.2	38.3	0.0	6.0	8.0	15.7
ValueBank Texas	Corpus Christi	TX	A-	A-	A	303.1	6.74	2.8	0.3	11.0	13.8	8.4	10.0	0.0
Van Wert Federal Savings Bank	Van Wert	OH	C	C	C+	127.6	5.71	0.3	0.6	47.5	22.4	10.0	19.5	0.0
Vanguard National Trust Co., N.A.	Malvern	PA	U	U	U	108.6	11.44	0.0	0.0	0.0	0.0	10.0	66.9	279.9
▼ Vantage Bank	Kent	MN	C	C+	C-	48.4	18.11	14.8	6.7	19.5	0.0	5.7	7.7	11.8
Vantage Bank Texas	San Antonio	TX	B	B	B	2789.3	11.21	15.9	0.3	5.2	5.2	7.3	9.9	12.8
Varo Bank, N.A.	Draper	UT	D-	D		247.9	na	0.0	1.8	0.0	12.3	9.8	17.9	0.0
Vast Bank, N.A.	Tulsa	OK	B-	B-	B-	784.6	-2.44	22.6	2.4	11.5	5.1	8.2	10.1	13.5
VCC Bank	Richmond	VA	C	C-	D	233.4	-4.98	17.3	0.0	8.2	11.3	9.2	11.7	0.0
VeraBank, N.A.	Henderson	TX	B+	B+	B	3286.6	15.69	8.3	2.4	12.3	19.1	6.4	8.4	16.3
▲ Vergas State Bank	Vergas	MN	C+	C	B-	54.3	3.64	4.5	2.3	8.6	23.1	10.0	14.4	0.0
Veritex Community Bank	Dallas	TX	B-	B	B	9343.4	8.84	19.8	0.1	5.2	12.1	5.8	10.7	11.6
Vermilion Bank & Trust Co.	Kaplan	LA	B-	B-	B-	153.3	21.42	7.2	3.5	17.0	28.8	6.3	8.3	18.0
Vermilion Valley Bank	Piper City	IL	A	A	A-	159.9	10.68	3.8	0.9	7.4	30.3	10.0	15.3	28.6
Vermillion State Bank	Vermillion	MN	A+	A+	A+	764.5	12.28	12.6	1.1	10.2	41.3	10.0	12.2	0.0
▼ Vermont State Bank	Vermont	IL	D-	D	D	29.7	0.71	4.7	14.4	31.0	11.4	9.6	10.7	17.5
Verus Bank of Commerce	Fort Collins	CO	A	A	A-	264.2	-6.97	5.7	0.0	7.8	0.0	10.0	13.9	0.0
Vidalia Federal Savings Bank	Vidalia	GA	C	C	C+	214.6	5.25	0.0	1.4	25.9	44.8	10.0	14.5	0.0
Viking Bank, N.A.	Alexandria	MN	B+	B	B	236.6	7.12	11.5	1.9	16.0	4.9	7.4	9.5	0.0
Villa Grove State Bank	Villa Grove	IL	B+	B+	B+	80.8	9.08	7.5	2.2	35.5	11.5	10.0	11.0	0.0
Village Bank	Saint Francis	MN	B-	B-	C+	428.8	14.38	16.5	0.5	5.6	24.1	5.4	7.4	14.1
Village Bank	Midlothian	VA	B	B-	C	717.7	-0.89	20.7	4.4	11.9	6.8	8.1	9.7	14.6
Village Bank & Trust, N.A.	Arlington Heights	IL	B	B	B	2238.5	3.90	43.8	15.1	3.0	7.9	5.6	8.4	11.5
Vinings Bank	Smyrna	GA	B-	B-	C+	677.5	0.87	16.8	0.1	0.4	46.2	5.7	7.7	13.4

Arrows denote recent upgrades ▲ or downgrades ▼

Asset Quality Index	Adjusted Non-Performing Loans as a % of Total Loans	Adjusted Non-Performing Loans as a % of Capital	Net Charge-Offs Avg Loans	Profitability Index	Net Income ($Mil)	Return on Assets (R.O.A.)	Return on Equity (R.O.E.)	Net Interest Spread	Overhead Efficiency Ratio	Liquidity Index	Liquidity Ratio	Hot Money Ratio	Stability Index
6.5	0.00	0.0	0.02	**4.5**	0.8	1.02	7.38	3.80	58.1	**0.7**	18.4	33.9	**3.2**
7.6	0.39	2.6	0.00	**3.2**	0.6	0.67	8.04	3.11	69.5	**1.8**	19.7	21.1	**4.6**
10.0	0.01	0.0	0.00	**3.2**	0.8	0.37	2.35	1.83	76.5	**4.3**	52.0	16.4	**7.8**
5.0	1.39	8.5	0.15	**5.5**	4.8	0.81	7.57	3.18	57.8	**4.9**	20.5	4.5	**9.4**
7.7	0.00	0.0	0.11	**4.1**	0.4	0.94	8.15	3.15	69.4	**4.2**	39.2	13.7	**7.8**
5.8	1.33	5.6	0.00	**4.4**	2.7	0.73	8.77	3.27	63.0	**6.8**	53.1	2.1	**5.7**
4.9	2.08	9.6	-0.04	**5.6**	1.5	1.10	9.95	3.15	63.8	**4.6**	38.3	11.2	**6.5**
7.9	1.15	5.0	0.00	**1.6**	0.0	-0.04	-0.63	1.47	102.1	**7.2**	74.1	2.9	**2.5**
5.3	0.88	5.6	0.01	**5.1**	1.4	1.14	13.14	3.47	59.3	**4.6**	33.3	9.5	**6.0**
9.1	0.00	2.0	0.00	**5.0**	6.5	1.20	11.71	2.48	35.5	**3.7**	64.1	17.2	**9.2**
7.0	0.41	3.6	0.00	**2.2**	0.3	1.20	10.24	2.86	96.2	**0.7**	21.1	58.6	**3.3**
3.8	2.80	9.1	0.00	**3.9**	2.5	0.90	9.56	3.22	72.2	**3.9**	19.9	9.9	**7.5**
5.3	0.65	5.0	0.10	**8.7**	16.1	1.72	17.49	4.14	48.9	**2.2**	14.2	8.3	**8.8**
2.7	2.46	19.0	-0.02	**4.2**	2.8	0.92	11.26	3.60	75.8	**1.8**	21.7	17.8	**5.4**
3.6	2.52	11.7	0.83	**2.5**	0.6	0.65	6.89	4.12	82.5	**1.0**	27.8	56.8	**4.3**
6.5	1.07	3.4	-0.10	**2.7**	0.7	0.35	2.32	3.10	85.4	**1.9**	23.8	21.6	**7.5**
7.5	5.72	3.0	-0.01	**9.1**	15.2	6.71	60.37	2.52	69.9	**7.2**	54.7	0.3	**7.3**
5.4	0.70	4.7	0.02	**7.3**	58.0	1.81	15.84	3.26	56.2	**4.4**	6.0	4.6	**9.5**
8.4	0.40	1.9	0.01	**5.9**	1.5	1.09	8.16	3.47	63.1	**3.5**	35.9	7.4	**8.5**
6.2	0.32	1.9	-0.01	**7.3**	7.1	1.71	15.73	3.25	44.2	**2.0**	30.1	25.1	**8.4**
5.4	5.64	3.8	0.80	**1.1**	-105.7	-0.19	-2.26	3.23	108.7	**6.4**	71.2	2.2	**5.5**
10.0	na	0.0	0.00	**10.0**	104.7	12.07	52.68	0.46	73.1	**4.0**	99.0	34.9	**4.3**
8.6	0.23	1.0	0.01	**9.7**	1.7	2.73	21.44	3.99	46.6	**6.4**	50.5	4.2	**9.5**
5.2	1.54	6.6	0.02	**5.9**	6.4	1.55	19.06	3.41	70.1	**5.4**	35.2	5.5	**5.5**
3.6	7.49	32.5	0.00	**6.1**	1.2	1.20	12.50	2.86	46.3	**6.2**	55.0	7.3	**8.1**
6.1	0.67	3.9	0.00	**9.0**	1.2	1.45	15.38	4.69	59.5	**4.9**	40.1	10.6	**6.9**
5.0	3.05	9.7	0.00	**1.8**	0.0	-0.02	-0.33	2.61	96.7	**6.9**	55.7	2.4	**4.3**
3.1	3.86	15.1	-0.37	**5.0**	0.7	1.02	11.75	4.39	70.1	**6.5**	47.2	2.6	**5.1**
9.1	0.59	1.1	0.00	**2.0**	0.1	0.12	0.52	3.53	96.3	**1.9**	28.7	16.0	**7.8**
7.3	0.00	2.9	0.00	**1.9**	0.0	-0.07	-0.66	1.74	115.9	**7.2**	79.6	3.4	**5.1**
3.8	0.94	4.7	0.09	**5.8**	242.1	1.18	9.44	3.20	49.3	**3.0**	9.5	7.9	**10.0**
8.8	0.00	0.5	0.00	**4.6**	0.7	1.13	11.28	3.63	68.2	**5.8**	43.7	6.1	**6.6**
8.4	0.44	2.1	0.00	**6.8**	9.1	1.39	13.63	3.29	39.8	**6.0**	28.1	2.4	**8.3**
9.0	0.29	1.9	-0.01	**3.9**	0.5	0.75	4.46	3.08	67.2	**2.8**	41.8	24.9	**7.8**
6.2	1.27	5.7	-0.05	**5.4**	0.9	1.08	9.42	3.59	60.6	**2.7**	33.6	18.7	**7.0**
6.9	0.28	2.1	0.00	**3.7**	2.4	0.84	9.59	3.71	63.5	**1.9**	24.8	14.5	**5.4**
9.3	0.00	0.0	0.00	**8.7**	1.6	2.06	26.88	3.07	66.6	**1.5**	32.3	32.5	**6.1**
8.5	0.00	0.0	0.00	**6.0**	1.3	0.91	8.68	3.59	75.3	**6.0**	47.6	6.2	**7.0**
9.9	0.17	0.8	0.00	**2.3**	0.1	0.22	1.13	2.28	88.9	**3.8**	42.4	16.6	**7.6**
10.0	na	0.0	na	**6.5**	0.6	1.11	1.74	0.03	98.7	**4.0**	225.3	0.0	**6.7**
5.9	0.37	3.2	0.00	**6.4**	0.3	1.47	17.38	2.73	65.9	**3.0**	22.4	15.0	**4.3**
4.8	1.57	7.4	-0.01	**5.0**	15.4	1.15	10.82	3.77	69.3	**2.7**	24.5	19.0	**9.2**
8.3	0.03	0.0	na	**0.0**	-103.9	-58.79	-246.29	-0.29	355.3	**8.6**	108.5	0.0	**1.3**
7.8	0.21	1.4	-0.02	**3.4**	1.9	0.48	5.23	3.40	77.7	**0.8**	17.9	37.1	**6.1**
3.2	1.73	10.3	0.00	**4.2**	1.1	0.96	8.23	3.27	64.9	**0.8**	18.9	43.2	**5.8**
7.1	0.86	3.5	0.06	**5.2**	20.3	1.30	12.16	3.02	62.4	**6.2**	37.1	4.1	**8.7**
9.3	0.00	0.2	0.00	**2.6**	0.1	0.35	2.41	2.59	80.7	**5.0**	74.3	15.6	**6.9**
4.0	1.16	5.0	0.16	**6.5**	67.0	1.47	9.75	3.31	48.2	**2.0**	17.7	18.5	**9.8**
4.8	3.07	12.6	0.16	**4.6**	0.8	1.07	12.64	3.00	65.2	**2.8**	38.7	22.0	**5.8**
8.6	0.05	0.2	-0.12	**7.8**	1.5	1.88	12.10	3.50	38.5	**4.4**	39.0	12.6	**9.6**
8.5	0.74	2.5	-0.05	**8.6**	6.9	1.85	14.95	2.42	29.4	**6.3**	60.2	8.2	**10.0**
0.3	9.26	47.2	4.56	**0.0**	-0.2	-1.27	-10.63	3.43	101.1	**0.9**	26.4	54.2	**3.2**
7.6	0.00	0.0	-0.05	**9.4**	2.3	1.61	12.17	3.62	45.5	**2.6**	30.4	5.8	**9.6**
9.0	1.28	2.7	0.00	**0.7**	-0.4	-0.33	-2.20	1.48	127.5	**3.9**	79.3	29.3	**6.5**
6.4	0.12	1.0	0.01	**6.7**	2.1	1.75	12.55	3.46	52.8	**3.2**	25.5	14.0	**9.4**
9.1	0.07	0.3	0.00	**4.9**	0.4	1.07	9.74	3.05	64.9	**4.8**	35.9	9.6	**7.8**
5.5	1.52	5.7	-0.01	**5.5**	3.2	1.56	21.29	3.42	66.0	**5.8**	40.4	4.9	**5.1**
4.7	1.42	6.6	0.01	**8.1**	7.5	2.12	22.77	3.94	54.8	**4.3**	18.6	7.1	**6.9**
5.8	0.65	2.8	0.06	**6.4**	15.7	1.39	14.37	2.67	49.1	**2.6**	13.2	6.7	**7.3**
6.3	0.57	3.5	0.06	**5.8**	8.3	2.28	37.38	3.33	48.0	**6.0**	41.2	3.6	**5.1**

Name	City	State	Rating	2020 Rating	2019 Rating	Total Assets ($Mil)	One Year Asset Growth	Asset Mix (As a % of Total Assets) Comm-ercial Loans	Cons-umer Loans	Mort-gage Loans	Secur-ities	Capital-ization Index	Lever-age Ratio	Risk-Based Capital Ratio
Vintage Bank Kansas	Leon	KS	**B**	B	B	181.8	9.29	5.6	2.2	12.2	35.7	**7.8**	9.6	0.0
Vinton County National Bank	McArthur	OH	**B**	B	B	1253.4	12.62	4.1	15.2	24.9	22.0	**8.0**	9.7	16.7
Virginia National Bank	Charlottesville	VA	**A-**	A-	A-	1847.5	131.08	8.5	3.9	17.8	14.5	**5.9**	7.9	13.8
Virginia Partners Bank	Fredericksburg	VA	**C+**	C+	C+	593.4	2.44	14.3	0.3	13.7	10.2	**6.6**	9.0	12.2
Vision Bank, N.A.	Ada	OK	**B-**	B-	B-	873.2	5.96	8.2	4.8	19.1	27.2	**5.6**	7.6	14.1
VisionBank	Topeka	KS	**C+**	C	C+	213.5	-4.33	28.9	1.7	14.4	3.7	**4.5**	8.8	0.0
VisionBank	Saint Louis Park	MN	**A-**	A-	A-	203.2	20.65	32.2	0.7	14.6	0.0	**6.4**	8.4	13.4
VISIONBank	Fargo	ND	**D+**	D+	D	263.7	16.53	21.4	3.8	12.6	0.0	**6.3**	8.4	13.5
VisionBank of Iowa	Ames	IA	**B-**	B-	B	604.3	4.91	4.6	0.1	8.8	4.4	**7.7**	9.9	13.1
VIST Bank	Wyomissing	PA	**B+**	B+	B+	2038.5	6.86	7.9	0.2	17.0	28.6	**6.4**	8.4	13.7
▲ Vista Bank	Dallas	TX	**B**	C+	B-	1320.7	17.78	23.8	0.4	6.9	2.7	**7.5**	9.3	16.0
Volunteer Federal Savings Bank	Madisonville	TN	**B**	B	B	271.9	17.04	1.0	3.3	37.9	17.6	**10.0**	11.9	24.1
Volunteer State Bank	Portland	TN	**B**	B	B	935.7	11.28	8.3	0.7	11.5	4.5	**4.5**	8.0	10.8
Wabash Savings Bank	Mount Carmel	IL	**D-**	D-	D-	10.1	10.85	2.5	7.1	25.0	11.6	**8.2**	9.8	23.8
Wadena State Bank	Wadena	MN	**B+**	B+	B+	211.9	12.00	12.1	3.0	11.6	28.2	**7.3**	9.2	0.0
Wahoo State Bank	Wahoo	NE	**C**	C-	C	116.0	7.76	11.1	3.3	32.9	20.0	**5.0**	7.0	12.0
Wake Forest Federal S&L Assn.	Wake Forest	NC	**A-**	A-	A	111.9	5.53	0.0	0.4	31.3	3.6	**10.0**	22.9	0.0
Wakefield Co-operative Bank	Wakefield	MA	**C+**	C+	C	272.1	-0.37	1.4	0.0	47.0	18.1	**6.0**	8.0	16.0
Walden Savings Bank	Montgomery	NY	**B-**	B-	B	801.4	15.21	6.5	0.4	24.3	30.1	**6.5**	8.6	17.0
Waldo State Bank	Waldo	WI	**B**	B	B	108.7	14.04	14.9	1.6	29.4	12.9	**10.0**	11.1	0.0
Walker State Bank	Walker	IA	**B+**	B	B	47.1	5.47	3.0	2.0	7.8	32.9	**9.1**	10.4	0.0
Wallis Bank	Wallis	TX	**A-**	A-	A-	1226.7	11.68	26.7	0.2	1.2	0.8	**7.2**	9.1	13.4
Wallkill Valley Federal S&L Assn.	Wallkill	NY	**C+**	C	C	391.5	10.25	4.1	0.9	40.7	16.2	**8.0**	9.7	15.6
Walpole Co-operative Bank	Walpole	MA	**B**	B	B	574.4	4.49	3.8	0.0	20.3	10.3	**10.0**	17.7	0.0
▲ Walters Bank and Trust Co.	Walters	OK	**B+**	B	B	63.6	10.01	3.8	4.5	16.7	20.2	**10.0**	20.0	55.8
Warren Bank and Trust Co.	Warren	AR	**B-**	B-	B-	140.7	6.40	4.8	4.8	17.9	57.8	**10.0**	16.2	40.5
Warren-Boynton State Bank	New Berlin	IL	**A-**	A-	A-	204.0	11.99	11.3	1.9	16.0	25.9	**10.0**	12.5	21.4
Warsaw Federal S&L Assn.	Cincinnati	OH	**C**	C-	D	54.9	-5.44	0.0	0.0	42.6	28.0	**7.9**	9.6	0.0
Washington Business Bank	Olympia	WA	**A-**	A-	B+	103.3	-1.54	34.5	0.0	10.9	0.0	**10.0**	11.8	21.2
Washington County Bank	Blair	NE	**B+**	B+	B+	521.9	11.46	6.5	1.3	6.1	19.8	**7.6**	9.4	13.9
Washington Federal Bank, N.A.	Seattle	WA	**B+**	B+	A-	19651.7	8.09	10.8	0.5	25.6	13.9	**6.9**	9.0	13.1
Washington Financial Bank	Washington	PA	**B**	B	B	1450.6	16.07	4.5	0.3	25.8	20.8	**10.0**	12.0	19.6
Washington Savings Bank	Effingham	IL	**B**	B	B-	479.0	13.36	5.6	1.0	24.3	32.4	**10.0**	14.7	26.9
Washington Savings Bank	Lowell	MA	**C+**	C+	C	268.5	3.72	0.3	0.1	50.5	9.8	**7.8**	9.6	17.5
Washington State Bank	Washington	IA	**A-**	A-	A-	444.5	12.45	5.8	0.5	21.1	41.4	**9.9**	10.9	20.0
Washington State Bank	Washington	IL	**C+**	C+	B-	67.5	9.91	2.9	4.5	29.0	51.0	**8.3**	9.8	0.0
Washington State Bank	Washington	LA	**C**	C	B-	283.2	24.11	9.9	2.4	15.1	12.2	**5.7**	7.7	12.8
Washington Trust Bank	Spokane	WA	**B+**	B+	A-	10270.2	16.52	17.0	1.3	8.1	30.0	**5.6**	7.6	13.7
▼ Washita State Bank	Burns Flat	OK	**C+**	B-	C+	59.6	-36.83	10.8	6.6	9.1	28.1	**10.0**	17.1	0.0
Washita Valley Bank	Fort Cobb	OK	**B**	B	B	49.9	8.14	5.6	7.2	0.6	20.9	**10.0**	15.8	0.0
▲ Waterford Bank, NA	Toledo	OH	**B**	B-	B+	1514.4	20.20	22.6	1.3	2.4	9.1	**5.6**	7.6	12.4
Waterman Bank	Waterman	IL	**B-**	C+	C-	77.7	23.75	20.9	0.4	16.1	8.0	**10.0**	24.7	38.4
▲ Watermark Bank	Oklahoma City	OK	**C+**	D		211.8	54.69	36.9	0.7	12.0	5.0	**10.0**	17.7	0.0
WaterStone Bank	Wauwatosa	WI	**A**	A	A	2197.0	-0.90	2.1	0.0	33.0	7.9	**10.0**	17.5	25.3
Watertown Savings Bank	Watertown	MA	**C-**	C-	C+	1451.2	6.80	1.5	0.1	29.1	46.1	**8.0**	9.7	26.2
Watertown Savings Bank	Watertown	NY	**A-**	A-	B	950.0	18.61	9.0	1.1	11.7	18.8	**10.0**	11.8	0.0
Wauchula State Bank	Wauchula	FL	**A-**	A-	B+	920.4	12.61	2.9	0.4	13.0	20.9	**9.0**	10.3	0.0
Waukesha State Bank	Waukesha	WI	**A**	A	A	1337.8	12.24	14.3	0.5	15.0	18.1	**8.7**	10.2	0.0
Waukon State Bank	Waukon	IA	**A**	A	A	351.6	5.12	11.8	2.0	14.9	12.7	**7.5**	10.2	0.0
Waumandee State Bank	Waumandee	WI	**B-**	B-	B	322.5	61.83	13.6	1.9	13.6	14.9	**6.9**	8.9	13.5
Waycross Bank & Trust	Waycross	GA	**B+**	B+	B+	223.7	6.07	7.0	0.5	6.7	36.7	**9.1**	10.4	21.2
Wayland State Bank	Mount Pleasant	IA	**A-**	A-	A-	133.5	10.37	7.0	1.6	10.5	29.3	**10.0**	15.1	29.8
Wayne Bank	Honesdale	PA	**B**	B	B+	2026.5	50.48	10.4	7.7	13.7	16.5	**6.4**	8.4	13.2
Wayne Bank and Trust Co.	Cambridge City	IN	**A-**	B+	B-	210.2	7.70	9.7	3.8	15.7	19.7	**9.1**	10.4	15.4
▲ Wayne County Bank	Waynesboro	TN	**B**	B-	C+	371.4	10.06	13.0	6.0	15.1	9.6	**10.0**	13.7	0.0
Wayne Savings Community Bank	Wooster	OH	**B**	B	B	629.6	17.56	7.4	0.4	22.2	20.3	**6.0**	8.0	12.9
Waypoint Bank	Cozad	NE	**B+**	B+	A-	352.9	14.36	6.4	1.1	1.4	26.8	**9.5**	10.7	15.2
WCF Financial Bank	Webster City	IA	**C**	C-	C	136.9	1.61	1.3	3.2	34.9	20.7	**10.0**	15.1	26.5
WebBank	Salt Lake City	UT	**A-**	A-	B+	2650.6	-1.79	80.4	9.1	0.0	0.8	**10.0**	28.4	36.5
▲ Webster Bank, N.A.	Waterbury	CT	**B+**	B	B	33737.4	3.10	21.6	0.3	16.2	26.9	**6.8**	8.8	13.8

Asset Quality Index	Adjusted Non-Performing Loans as a % of Total Loans	Adjusted Non-Performing Loans as a % of Capital	Net Charge-Offs Avg Loans	Profitability Index	Net Income ($Mil)	Return on Assets (R.O.A.)	Return on Equity (R.O.E.)	Net Interest Spread	Overhead Efficiency Ratio	Liquidity Index	Liquidity Ratio	Hot Money Ratio	Stability Index
5.6	1.36	4.3	0.00	4.5	0.8	0.87	8.40	3.59	71.2	4.6	34.9	7.1	7.2
6.8	0.39	2.5	0.05	4.4	6.1	0.99	9.52	3.33	67.0	3.8	24.4	13.3	8.9
8.1	0.09	2.0	0.03	3.8	3.3	0.48	6.57	3.01	81.5	5.6	33.8	7.1	7.0
7.5	0.13	2.3	0.04	3.2	1.8	0.73	7.53	3.49	68.6	1.2	25.5	26.5	6.0
4.8	1.21	7.6	0.10	4.9	5.4	1.23	14.88	3.63	67.2	2.4	19.4	17.5	6.4
7.0	0.30	2.5	0.01	5.6	1.3	1.24	14.09	3.77	60.5	3.2	8.5	12.2	5.2
8.1	0.03	0.2	0.01	8.6	2.7	2.84	43.45	4.01	29.2	0.7	15.5	47.0	6.7
1.9	2.19	21.5	0.45	3.6	0.8	0.63	7.30	3.18	75.2	4.5	31.5	9.7	4.6
5.4	0.34	2.5	0.00	4.4	2.7	0.92	9.21	2.91	72.0	3.8	20.0	5.3	7.2
6.0	1.25	6.9	-0.06	4.3	9.9	0.99	9.66	2.95	64.4	4.4	15.5	6.2	7.5
7.3	0.85	5.1	0.02	6.1	10.3	1.53	17.08	3.69	51.7	4.1	29.9	14.0	7.7
9.5	0.07	1.8	0.06	3.9	0.9	0.70	5.87	3.07	72.6	5.2	37.9	7.6	7.1
6.8	0.26	0.6	-0.01	4.6	4.9	1.07	7.44	4.00	69.9	4.0	29.2	10.9	8.4
6.7	0.45	2.0	0.94	0.0	-0.1	-0.97	-9.57	2.50	140.0	3.2	64.1	24.0	3.1
6.9	0.00	0.2	0.00	7.5	2.0	1.92	19.09	4.38	55.5	5.8	47.4	7.4	7.3
7.4	0.20	0.8	0.00	3.3	0.4	0.74	10.64	3.14	76.4	4.8	20.8	4.3	3.9
9.4	0.00	0.0	0.00	5.9	0.6	1.10	4.81	3.11	53.2	2.9	46.1	25.4	8.6
6.5	0.52	3.7	0.00	2.8	0.6	0.40	4.99	2.67	84.8	2.1	29.4	20.5	4.8
5.5	2.51	8.5	-0.06	3.7	2.8	0.74	8.59	2.85	75.6	6.1	41.0	3.1	5.5
6.5	1.69	7.5	0.00	4.4	0.5	0.95	8.60	3.36	64.8	2.5	32.4	17.7	7.0
9.1	0.00	0.0	0.00	6.1	0.4	1.49	14.28	3.18	51.4	5.7	59.2	9.3	6.9
7.0	0.05	0.3	0.08	10.0	23.9	3.82	47.65	4.56	37.2	1.7	14.0	21.5	8.7
4.7	2.55	8.8	-0.07	3.5	0.9	0.49	4.45	3.52	82.7	3.1	28.6	13.6	6.5
6.1	0.98	4.1	-0.01	4.1	2.3	0.82	4.60	3.17	62.4	1.0	21.3	34.4	8.7
8.2	0.27	0.9	0.12	5.2	0.5	1.48	7.21	3.03	61.6	5.8	51.0	6.9	7.1
7.1	3.84	4.9	0.05	2.9	0.4	0.59	3.40	2.69	79.5	3.9	57.6	20.2	7.6
6.8	1.69	4.2	0.01	6.4	1.3	1.28	9.66	3.68	56.2	3.7	31.1	13.5	8.2
6.4	1.01	4.1	-0.24	0.0	-0.4	-1.39	-13.24	2.06	147.2	3.0	51.0	25.7	5.8
8.2	0.00	0.0	-0.01	6.9	0.8	1.47	13.08	4.12	55.2	3.5	18.0	11.9	7.5
5.9	0.46	3.0	0.00	6.5	3.3	1.27	13.05	3.37	53.9	3.5	15.4	11.5	7.3
7.6	0.41	2.0	-0.05	5.1	92.7	0.96	8.93	2.79	60.7	4.1	24.8	11.3	9.8
8.7	0.55	2.7	-0.01	3.8	5.3	0.76	6.33	2.72	69.9	4.9	18.9	4.1	8.9
6.2	3.47	7.6	-0.01	3.9	1.9	0.82	5.40	2.58	63.4	5.0	44.2	11.2	7.7
5.5	1.30	8.7	0.00	3.3	0.7	0.50	5.48	3.07	78.3	1.8	16.3	20.3	5.3
7.6	0.30	2.1	0.03	6.1	3.0	1.39	12.45	3.06	48.2	2.5	43.0	20.0	7.6
5.8	0.95	6.9	-0.03	3.8	0.2	0.64	6.32	2.40	65.7	3.6	35.6	15.3	4.9
4.2	1.63	12.0	-0.01	3.1	0.9	0.63	7.93	3.18	79.2	2.0	30.4	25.2	4.4
7.6	0.97	5.9	0.09	4.9	44.2	0.89	11.59	2.93	62.9	7.0	43.1	1.2	7.5
7.0	0.00	0.0	-0.02	1.0	-0.1	-0.13	-0.81	2.37	105.3	1.6	31.6	32.9	6.2
5.9	0.15	7.8	0.13	7.9	0.5	2.10	13.59	4.53	48.2	4.1	44.5	15.4	6.8
6.7	0.47	3.3	-0.01	5.6	8.8	1.20	13.88	3.19	52.3	5.3	33.8	9.2	7.8
7.9	1.24	1.8	0.00	7.5	1.2	3.52	25.85	2.39	73.0	5.1	44.2	10.2	4.3
8.1	0.00	0.0	0.00	3.0	1.3	1.32	7.58	3.74	60.9	3.7	20.5	9.6	4.5
8.5	0.48	1.5	-0.05	9.5	39.3	3.59	20.66	2.92	62.6	2.0	22.2	22.5	10.0
9.9	0.55	1.7	0.00	2.2	1.7	0.24	2.56	2.05	86.5	5.7	60.6	12.8	6.6
5.8	0.92	5.4	-0.11	5.3	4.9	1.07	8.16	2.93	58.0	5.3	28.2	2.9	8.2
6.3	1.06	4.4	-0.07	7.4	7.0	1.59	15.37	3.30	53.0	5.5	45.7	8.6	8.6
8.8	0.09	0.5	-0.01	9.1	14.0	2.06	19.56	3.95	54.4	6.1	27.9	1.0	10.0
8.6	0.00	0.0	0.00	8.2	3.4	1.96	18.38	3.43	44.4	4.2	27.7	9.6	9.5
3.7	2.36	8.5	-0.02	5.1	1.6	1.02	9.22	4.16	59.5	2.0	25.7	16.6	6.0
8.6	0.39	1.5	0.00	6.5	1.8	1.64	15.77	2.65	68.7	5.7	50.8	8.8	7.9
5.5	3.68	8.0	0.50	6.2	0.9	1.29	7.94	3.42	40.6	7.0	70.0	5.1	7.5
5.1	0.85	5.4	0.11	5.5	11.5	1.18	11.72	3.51	52.7	1.8	13.8	20.5	8.3
5.4	0.31	5.9	0.06	6.3	1.8	1.83	16.59	4.24	65.5	4.5	32.6	8.0	7.4
4.0	3.58	13.0	0.24	5.5	1.8	1.00	7.13	4.70	66.0	1.7	32.2	31.1	7.3
6.5	0.31	2.8	0.00	6.3	3.8	1.23	14.48	3.59	52.7	4.0	23.6	9.5	6.2
4.9	1.31	5.5	-0.08	8.5	3.8	2.25	20.10	4.04	46.0	4.2	27.7	10.0	9.1
9.0	0.34	1.3	0.16	2.7	0.5	0.77	4.93	3.43	72.7	2.6	35.6	10.9	7.1
6.4	0.00	1.5	0.69	9.5	33.3	2.20	29.82	2.79	36.8	0.5	8.3	6.8	8.9
6.1	1.11	4.6	0.04	6.4	229.7	1.38	13.63	2.89	58.6	5.1	21.7	3.3	8.7

Name	City	State	Rating	2020 Rating	2019 Rating	Total Assets ($Mil)	One Year Asset Growth	Asset Mix (As a % of Total Assets) Comm-ercial Loans	Cons-umer Loans	Mort-gage Loans	Secur-ities	Capital-ization Index	Lever-age Ratio	Risk-Based Capital Ratio
Webster Five Cents Savings Bank	Webster	MA	B-	B-	B	1009.9	4.11	7.3	0.7	16.3	15.3	10.0	12.1	0.0
Welch State Bank of Welch, Okla.	Welch	OK	A-	A-	A-	312.3	0.22	3.4	2.5	15.0	24.0	9.0	10.4	0.0
Welcome State Bank	Welcome	MN	B+	B+	B+	37.6	12.41	11.5	5.8	11.3	4.3	8.6	10.1	17.1
Wellington State Bank	Wellington	TX	C+	C+	B	501.5	8.77	5.3	1.6	4.9	32.5	8.1	9.8	14.5
Wellington Trust Co. N.A.	Boston	MA	U	U	U	113.2	45.62	0.0	0.0	0.0	0.0	10.0	42.1	39.6
Wells Bank	Platte City	MO	A-	A-	A-	327.0	23.02	3.3	0.7	18.0	2.4	6.4	8.4	0.0
Wells Fargo Bank South Central, N.A.	Houston	TX	B-	B	A-	5184.2	-29.89	0.0	0.0	88.3	0.0	10.0	14.2	30.8
▲ Wells Fargo Bank, N.A.	Sioux Falls	SD	B-	C+	B	1776718.0	-1.29	8.5	5.5	13.5	25.0	6.6	8.6	16.1
Wells Fargo Delaware Trust Co., N.A.	Wilmington	DE	U	U	U	234.1	0.12	0.0	0.0	0.0	0.0	10.0	99.6	490.1
▲ Wells Fargo National Bank West	Las Vegas	NV	B+	B	A-	19275.2	12.43	0.0	0.0	60.2	18.2	8.0	9.7	29.7
Wells Fargo Trust Co., N.A.	Salt Lake City	UT	U	U	U	1287.4	-0.56	0.0	0.0	0.0	0.0	10.0	95.0	406.0
Wells River Savings Bank	Wells River	VT	C	C-	C-	213.7	3.29	5.3	5.1	34.9	28.3	9.0	10.4	17.9
▲ WesBanco Bank, Inc.	Wheeling	WV	B+	B	A-	16918.4	1.20	9.5	1.6	11.8	23.0	8.7	10.1	15.7
West Alabama Bank & Trust	Reform	AL	B+	B+	A-	782.9	9.62	7.0	1.3	10.2	40.8	10.0	11.3	0.0
West Bank	West Des Moines	IA	B+	B+	B+	3267.2	19.34	13.4	0.1	2.1	18.4	5.7	8.6	11.5
West Central Bank	Ashland	IL	B	B	B-	224.6	14.73	12.9	6.1	21.5	22.4	7.8	9.5	0.0
West Central Georgia Bank	Thomaston	GA	A-	A-	A	149.7	12.40	3.6	4.6	14.8	41.5	10.0	23.5	0.0
West Gate Bank	Lincoln	NE	A	A	B+	946.1	1.00	9.1	0.2	24.4	6.7	10.0	11.5	0.0
West Iowa Bank	West Bend	IA	A	A-	A-	157.1	12.98	8.6	0.8	6.9	17.7	10.0	13.0	0.0
West Michigan Community Bank	Hudsonville	MI	C+	C+	B-	781.2	11.13	21.4	0.4	7.0	5.9	3.6	9.0	0.0
West Plains Bank	Ainsworth	NE	A-	A-	A-	124.8	-1.61	13.6	1.5	0.8	29.7	10.0	14.6	0.0
▼ West Plains Bank and Trust Co.	West Plains	MO	B+	A-	A-	573.8	20.58	7.2	2.8	7.0	28.5	7.0	9.0	14.8
West Plains S&L Assn.	West Plains	MO	B	B	B-	89.6	3.02	2.2	1.1	58.6	9.9	10.0	21.3	0.0
West Point Bank	Radcliff	KY	B	B	B	375.6	32.22	0.5	1.1	23.4	26.6	6.0	8.0	15.9
▲ West Pointe Bank	Oshkosh	WI	A-	B	C+	307.3	1.39	13.6	0.1	19.0	10.7	10.0	18.0	22.4
West Shore Bank	Ludington	MI	B-	B-	B-	608.2	16.49	15.5	3.2	12.3	18.2	5.6	7.6	12.7
West Suburban Bank	Lombard	IL	B-	C+	B-	2971.6	13.19	18.3	0.3	4.5	41.0	6.1	8.1	13.8
▼ West Texas National Bank	Midland	TX	B	B+	A-	1436.6	3.67	21.6	0.4	14.7	17.5	8.9	10.3	17.1
▼ West Texas State Bank	Snyder	TX	B	B+	B-	182.1	13.30	6.1	1.3	4.5	42.7	8.0	9.7	19.1
West Town Bank & Trust	North Riverside	IL	C-	C	B-	395.9	26.75	35.2	0.0	7.5	4.8	8.6	10.1	14.8
West Union Bank	West Union	WV	B	B	B-	227.2	6.08	4.2	7.8	6.6	55.5	6.8	8.8	17.4
▲ West Valley National Bank	Goodyear	AZ	C+	C-	D-	116.2	-12.13	26.3	0.1	3.9	2.3	5.5	7.5	18.8
West View Savings Bank	Pittsburgh	PA	C+	B-	B-	342.5	-3.53	0.0	0.0	20.2	71.9	8.9	10.2	16.8
WestAmerica Bank	San Rafael	CA	B+	B+	B+	7105.3	10.70	4.1	3.7	0.3	66.6	5.4	7.4	13.1
Westbury Bank	Waukesha	WI	B-	B-	B-	905.6	-0.09	10.3	0.7	12.5	18.0	7.2	9.2	13.4
Western Alliance Bank	Phoenix	AZ	A-	A-	A-	49068.9	53.69	15.3	0.0	18.9	15.5	6.0	8.1	11.8
Western Bank	Lordsburg	NM	A	A	A	266.4	13.40	3.7	1.0	4.4	64.9	7.9	9.6	26.2
Western Bank	Lubbock	TX	B-	B-	B-	394.5	3.32	12.4	0.5	12.9	11.6	5.5	9.0	0.0
Western Bank of Clovis	Clovis	NM	B+	B+	B+	67.4	-10.76	9.5	0.3	2.6	13.7	10.0	14.3	0.0
Western Bank, Artesia, New Mexico	Artesia	NM	B	B	B-	233.2	-10.56	37.1	1.1	1.8	30.8	7.5	9.3	17.1
Western Commerce Bank	Carlsbad	NM	B+	B+	A-	595.5	2.34	15.5	0.4	17.2	21.4	5.1	7.1	25.5
Western Dakota Bank	Timber Lake	SD	C	C	C	50.9	15.32	4.3	2.2	0.0	6.6	5.8	7.8	18.5
Western Heritage Bank	Las Cruces	NM	B-	C+	C+	280.1	-3.14	31.6	0.7	4.4	6.7	7.3	10.0	12.8
Western National Bank	Duluth	MN	C+	C+	C	139.0	18.65	5.8	1.6	13.9	7.5	7.4	9.3	14.8
Western National Bank	Chester	NE	B	B	B	144.6	6.18	10.5	2.8	14.0	0.2	6.6	9.5	0.0
Western National Bank of Cass Lake	Cass Lake	MN	C+	C+	C	40.2	23.84	0.0	1.3	15.6	15.2	6.2	8.2	19.8
▲ Western Nebraska Bank	Curtis	NE	C	C-	C-	149.4	11.52	15.3	1.6	5.0	13.6	3.5	9.3	0.0
Western State Bank	Garden City	KS	A-	A-	A-	580.3	12.39	13.2	0.4	5.3	29.9	10.0	11.1	17.5
Western State Bank	Devils Lake	ND	B	B	B	1591.2	8.94	45.0	0.8	7.3	2.5	8.1	10.7	13.4
Western States Bank	Laramie	WY	B	B	B-	532.3	-0.85	11.6	0.5	8.0	16.9	7.4	9.9	0.0
▲ Westfield Bank	Westfield	MA	B-	C+	B-	2457.6	1.05	12.1	0.2	26.3	13.8	6.7	8.7	13.6
Westfield Bank, FSB	Westfield Center	OH	B	B	B	1956.1	9.00	25.5	10.0	15.2	13.7	7.2	9.4	0.0
▼ Westmoreland Federal S&L Assn. of Latro	Latrobe	PA	D+	C-	C	171.8	-1.42	0.0	0.0	43.6	38.3	10.0	24.5	0.0
Westside State Bank	Westside	IA	B-	B-	B-	146.6	14.49	15.4	4.6	26.9	5.8	6.1	8.1	12.2
WestStar Bank	El Paso	TX	A-	A-	A-	2542.4	14.92	16.4	0.0	2.0	24.1	7.7	9.5	0.0
▼ WEX Bank	Sandy	UT	B+	A-	B+	2982.0	21.54	84.0	0.0	0.0	0.0	5.9	9.9	11.7
Wheatland Bank	Spokane	WA	B+	B+	B+	654.1	22.08	6.2	0.2	3.4	25.5	6.9	8.9	14.1
Wheaton Bank & Trust Co., N.A.	Wheaton	IL	B	B	B	2843.6	10.52	25.6	17.5	3.0	14.5	5.3	8.1	11.2
Wheaton College Trust Co., N.A.	Wheaton	IL	U	U	U	3.7	1.59	0.0	0.0	0.0	81.0	9.8	93.8	0.0
Wheeler County State Bank	Alamo	GA	B+	B+	B+	120.7	11.52	8.5	4.3	12.7	15.4	10.0	14.4	0.0

Asset Quality Index	Adjusted Non-Performing Loans as a % of Total Loans	Adjusted Non-Performing Loans as a % of Capital	Net Charge-Offs Avg Loans	Profitability Index	Net Income ($Mil)	Return on Assets (R.O.A.)	Return on Equity (R.O.E.)	Net Interest Spread	Overhead Efficiency Ratio	Liquidity Index	Liquidity Ratio	Hot Money Ratio	Stability Index
8.1	0.31	1.4	0.12	**3.9**	4.0	0.81	6.48	3.43	73.0	**5.1**	21.0	3.2	**8.5**
7.9	0.38	2.0	0.06	**8.5**	4.0	2.65	24.16	5.50	53.4	**2.5**	19.1	16.7	**8.8**
8.2	0.00	0.0	-0.01	**8.1**	0.4	1.97	19.25	3.78	53.0	**5.2**	34.4	6.3	**7.0**
6.7	0.50	2.2	-0.04	**3.3**	1.5	0.58	5.51	3.48	83.1	**2.4**	26.3	18.7	**6.9**
10.0	na	0.0	na	**9.5**	2.4	4.86	11.43	-67.42	98.6	**4.0**	7.1	0.0	**6.5**
8.4	0.00	0.0	0.00	**9.2**	3.1	1.93	22.79	3.72	51.0	**4.9**	27.2	5.1	**6.9**
5.9	2.59	12.9	-0.09	**4.2**	6.0	0.23	1.61	0.93	32.3	**5.3**	10.9	0.0	**8.3**
5.7	1.52	5.6	0.21	**4.4**	9183.0	1.04	10.72	2.19	70.4	**7.0**	48.8	1.2	**7.8**
10.0	na	0.0	na	**7.3**	1.5	1.31	1.32	0.19	62.4	**4.0**	na	0.0	**6.3**
10.0	0.23	1.5	0.01	**7.2**	103.3	1.00	10.84	1.87	21.1	**5.1**	43.4	0.0	**7.6**
10.0	na	0.0	na	**2.6**	3.2	0.50	0.53	0.35	85.6	**4.0**	na	0.0	**8.2**
6.9	0.60	4.0	0.04	**2.5**	0.5	0.51	4.71	3.73	90.9	**6.0**	43.9	4.7	**5.8**
6.5	0.40	1.6	0.00	**7.0**	147.0	1.75	10.88	3.22	54.7	**4.7**	20.1	5.4	**9.2**
7.3	1.31	3.2	1.18	**4.0**	2.6	0.69	5.58	3.02	63.3	**2.9**	45.2	25.8	**8.2**
5.4	0.63	4.9	-0.01	**7.5**	25.7	1.62	19.70	3.10	39.7	**3.6**	19.1	7.3	**8.2**
5.0	0.30	5.5	0.05	**4.5**	1.4	1.22	12.19	3.46	71.4	**2.8**	38.6	21.6	**5.9**
9.3	0.00	0.0	-0.02	**5.2**	0.8	1.09	4.48	3.38	63.6	**6.8**	77.5	7.8	**8.3**
6.6	0.70	5.0	0.00	**8.6**	7.4	1.58	13.61	4.24	64.9	**3.7**	19.6	11.1	**9.1**
8.5	0.00	0.0	0.00	**7.5**	1.2	1.53	11.14	3.75	47.2	**5.7**	42.3	6.3	**7.9**
8.3	0.24	1.0	-0.01	**6.5**	5.5	1.43	16.16	3.45	55.4	**4.1**	20.5	5.3	**6.4**
8.4	0.58	1.0	-0.28	**6.7**	0.9	1.45	10.00	2.70	51.5	**4.2**	31.8	11.4	**8.7**
6.7	0.57	2.6	0.01	**6.0**	4.0	1.49	15.82	3.39	60.1	**2.3**	31.7	7.1	**7.8**
7.9	1.29	4.7	0.00	**3.8**	0.3	0.77	3.61	3.24	66.5	**2.0**	36.2	31.9	**7.8**
8.4	0.07	0.5	0.01	**5.1**	1.9	1.01	12.71	2.85	52.2	**3.5**	48.3	5.0	**6.2**
6.6	1.33	3.0	-0.01	**7.9**	2.4	1.61	8.83	4.05	47.3	**0.8**	17.4	40.3	**8.5**
4.6	1.44	8.0	-0.01	**4.1**	2.9	0.97	12.09	3.30	74.2	**4.5**	24.2	6.3	**5.3**
5.4	1.74	9.4	-0.02	**4.5**	14.7	1.02	12.35	2.43	57.8	**6.7**	45.9	3.7	**6.3**
6.8	0.85	4.0	0.07	**4.2**	6.0	0.85	7.51	2.93	68.7	**6.2**	38.3	4.6	**7.6**
3.1	4.86	11.0	-0.24	**3.6**	0.5	0.53	4.34	2.50	66.9	**4.7**	46.8	13.4	**5.7**
2.4	2.35	14.5	0.12	**6.9**	3.8	1.92	18.81	3.53	65.6	**1.2**	28.3	27.4	**5.1**
7.7	0.44	1.6	-0.04	**4.6**	1.1	1.01	10.05	3.31	64.9	**5.7**	35.6	3.7	**5.4**
6.2	0.04	0.3	0.00	**4.2**	0.9	1.36	18.72	3.52	72.7	**5.2**	33.7	5.9	**3.6**
10.0	0.00	0.0	0.00	**3.0**	0.5	0.33	3.15	1.52	76.2	**3.9**	35.7	8.6	**5.4**
8.7	0.52	0.7	0.02	**6.7**	42.0	1.24	11.87	2.70	47.1	**7.9**	75.1	1.3	**8.4**
3.6	1.34	9.5	0.00	**5.2**	4.7	1.05	11.30	3.14	60.5	**4.8**	24.7	4.7	**7.0**
6.9	0.36	2.3	0.01	**8.3**	348.5	1.57	18.22	3.38	52.4	**4.6**	19.6	3.7	**9.7**
7.4	1.79	2.8	-0.06	**6.6**	2.0	1.50	14.38	2.91	63.3	**7.0**	67.8	4.9	**8.6**
8.5	0.00	0.0	-0.02	**5.5**	2.7	1.38	14.87	4.22	65.3	**1.6**	17.6	23.7	**6.2**
5.0	3.16	7.1	0.00	**5.1**	0.3	0.83	5.79	4.08	69.7	**2.2**	14.1	17.8	**7.1**
5.1	1.43	6.7	0.01	**8.3**	2.2	1.86	19.07	3.37	45.6	**5.3**	45.3	9.8	**7.4**
8.3	0.07	0.6	0.17	**7.2**	4.2	1.42	19.69	3.69	56.4	**4.8**	31.5	7.7	**7.0**
8.9	0.53	0.3	0.06	**6.9**	0.6	2.20	30.47	6.04	49.7	**6.2**	57.5	6.0	**3.5**
5.4	0.07	0.2	0.00	**4.9**	1.4	0.99	9.26	4.25	69.0	**2.5**	13.6	16.6	**6.3**
7.9	0.00	0.5	0.01	**2.9**	0.3	0.56	4.79	3.48	84.8	**2.3**	32.9	23.7	**5.2**
7.6	0.09	0.6	0.02	**7.2**	1.4	1.95	17.90	3.09	48.0	**0.9**	20.1	31.9	**7.5**
8.6	0.00	1.4	-0.05	**2.7**	0.1	0.44	4.75	3.12	86.1	**4.3**	47.2	14.9	**3.8**
7.1	0.08	0.5	0.27	**4.4**	0.8	1.16	12.04	3.30	62.7	**1.7**	20.4	18.8	**5.4**
6.1	1.29	6.2	-0.01	**9.8**	7.2	2.53	21.71	4.84	44.5	**3.6**	19.4	11.5	**9.1**
4.6	1.39	9.1	0.23	**9.6**	17.4	2.25	22.01	5.15	44.4	**2.8**	12.3	8.8	**9.6**
4.4	3.01	10.9	0.02	**5.5**	3.1	1.16	11.72	4.13	64.3	**4.0**	24.1	10.0	**7.4**
7.0	0.55	3.4	0.02	**4.6**	12.4	1.02	11.69	3.17	62.3	**3.8**	16.9	9.2	**6.9**
6.5	0.51	2.9	-0.06	**5.4**	11.9	1.22	12.03	3.18	56.7	**2.7**	20.1	16.7	**8.9**
9.9	1.08	1.9	0.00	**0.8**	-0.1	-0.16	-0.64	1.32	110.0	**5.5**	72.9	14.1	**6.9**
5.3	1.68	9.4	0.04	**6.8**	1.5	2.14	25.38	5.81	58.8	**2.6**	18.1	15.9	**4.6**
7.5	0.16	0.5	-0.02	**9.7**	27.8	2.29	20.20	3.69	48.1	**5.0**	32.2	10.6	**10.0**
5.6	0.02	5.8	0.76	**10.0**	58.0	4.29	40.26	24.32	82.8	**0.7**	12.0	0.4	**8.0**
8.6	0.01	0.0	0.01	**6.9**	4.8	1.49	17.08	3.53	64.5	**5.8**	34.7	2.3	**6.3**
5.2	0.62	3.7	0.04	**6.1**	17.0	1.28	13.00	2.39	47.4	**3.7**	18.4	5.5	**7.3**
10.0	na	0.0	na	**6.5**	0.1	2.98	3.19	0.18	86.1	**4.0**	na	0.0	**4.9**
8.3	0.47	1.9	-0.25	**4.4**	0.6	1.06	7.31	3.35	69.6	**2.1**	27.6	20.6	**8.0**

Name	City	State	Rating	2020 Rating	2019 Rating	Total Assets ($Mil)	One Year Asset Growth	Asset Mix (As a % of Total Assets) Comm-ercial Loans	Cons-umer Loans	Mort-gage Loans	Secur-ities	Capital-ization Index	Lever-age Ratio	Risk-Based Capital Ratio
Whitaker Bank, Inc	Lexington	KY	**B**	B	B	2050.2	58.98	3.1	2.1	13.4	48.7	**10.0**	11.5	0.0
White State Bank	South English	IA	**B+**	B	B	48.5	9.22	12.5	2.2	6.9	34.6	**10.0**	13.4	0.0
Whitesville State Bank	Whitesville	WV	**C+**	C+	C+	124.0	7.50	1.3	14.7	23.0	39.2	**7.5**	9.3	0.0
Wilcox County State Bank	Abbeville	GA	**B+**	B+	B	141.3	10.52	5.8	4.5	27.8	16.0	**8.6**	10.0	0.0
▼ Wilkinson County Bank	Irwinton	GA	**B-**	B	B	56.5	10.03	3.3	3.6	25.0	40.3	**8.4**	9.9	0.0
Willamette Valley Bank	Salem	OR	**A**	A	A-	376.5	6.68	6.5	0.0	21.4	0.0	**10.0**	18.0	0.0
▼ William Penn Bank	Bristol	PA	**B-**	B+	B+	822.4	11.62	0.6	0.4	37.3	15.0	**10.0**	18.9	0.0
Williamstown Bank, Inc.	Williamstown	WV	**B**	B	B+	189.2	4.59	8.2	11.8	30.1	7.2	**10.0**	11.2	0.0
Williamsville State Bank and Trust	Williamsville	IL	**D+**	C-	C	104.8	4.37	5.0	3.1	27.1	36.1	**10.0**	12.4	31.0
Wilmington Savings Fund Society, FSB	Wilmington	DE	**A-**	B+	A-	15109.7	11.59	8.8	1.8	9.9	22.9	**8.7**	10.1	15.4
Wilmington Trust, N.A.	Wilmington	DE	**C+**	C+	B-	10319.7	81.99	0.0	0.0	0.3	0.1	**5.9**	7.9	30.4
Wilson & Muir Bank & Trust Co.	Bardstown	KY	**B**	B-	B-	644.2	8.46	10.8	1.9	13.7	35.3	**5.6**	7.6	15.2
Wilson Bank & Trust	Lebanon	TN	**A-**	A-	A-	3642.5	15.60	4.3	1.0	16.4	20.6	**8.2**	10.8	0.0
▲ Wilson State Bank	Wilson	KS	**C+**	C	C+	113.9	9.28	17.3	2.7	23.3	26.4	**5.7**	7.7	12.2
Winchester Co-operative Bank	Winchester	MA	**B-**	B-	B	768.8	3.73	1.4	0.4	50.8	9.9	**10.0**	12.3	0.0
Winchester Savings Bank	Winchester	MA	**C+**	C+	C+	605.3	1.40	0.7	0.1	51.5	9.2	**10.0**	12.5	0.0
Windsor Federal S&L Assn.	Windsor	CT	**B-**	B-	B-	707.4	5.09	10.9	0.1	19.9	16.2	**8.2**	9.8	0.0
Winnsboro State Bank & Trust Co.	Winnsboro	LA	**B-**	C+	C	256.7	0.53	7.4	3.3	13.3	18.2	**7.8**	9.5	14.4
Winter Hill Bank, FSB	Somerville	MA	**C**	C	C	346.2	-6.25	0.7	0.5	39.5	16.4	**9.5**	10.6	18.6
▲ Winter Park National Bank	Winter Park	FL	**B+**	B	B	596.7	27.90	11.6	0.1	1.8	40.3	**6.2**	8.2	17.7
Wintrust Bank, N.A.	Chicago	IL	**B**	B	B	8646.8	3.60	40.3	5.6	4.2	3.3	**5.9**	9.1	11.7
▲ Wisconsin Bank & Trust	Madison	WI	**B+**	B	B+	1253.0	4.14	20.4	0.8	3.1	22.4	**7.7**	9.4	14.4
▲ Wisconsin River Bank	Sauk City	WI	**B+**	B	B	167.7	4.55	3.8	0.3	27.9	3.0	**9.0**	10.3	0.0
WNB Financial, N.A.	Winona	MN	**B+**	B+	B+	547.7	11.73	9.2	1.6	13.9	34.0	**7.9**	9.6	0.0
Wolf River Community Bank	Hortonville	WI	**A-**	A-	A-	242.0	7.67	10.3	1.4	19.2	19.0	**10.0**	12.3	0.0
Wood & Huston Bank	Marshall	MO	**A-**	A-	A-	984.3	18.34	18.7	2.0	11.5	13.4	**9.1**	10.5	14.3
Woodford State Bank	Monroe	WI	**B+**	B+	B+	326.6	17.12	10.6	0.8	9.3	25.0	**6.2**	8.2	12.7
Woodforest National Bank	The Woodlands	TX	**B+**	B+	B+	9459.9	13.50	24.8	0.6	4.0	22.5	**5.2**	7.2	11.9
Woodland Bank	Grand Rapids	MN	**B**	B	B	133.4	11.67	13.1	4.2	18.8	13.6	**7.7**	9.5	0.0
Woodlands Bank	Williamsport	PA	**B**	B	B-	539.4	13.54	10.9	0.2	20.9	20.2	**7.2**	9.1	0.0
▼ Woodlands National Bank	Onamia	MN	**B+**	A-	A-	355.0	9.37	22.5	4.1	3.8	28.2	**6.4**	8.4	20.4
Woodruff Federal S&L Assn.	Woodruff	SC	**C**	C	B-	104.6	-1.25	0.0	0.0	40.1	9.3	**10.0**	29.2	66.8
▲ Woodsboro Bank	Woodsboro	MD	**C+**	C	C	367.0	23.70	7.4	0.3	18.9	22.3	**5.3**	7.3	13.3
Woodsfield Savings Bank	Woodsfield	OH	**C**	C	C-	78.1	2.69	2.5	10.5	43.3	16.5	**7.4**	9.3	18.3
Woodsville Guaranty Savings Bank	Woodsville	NH	**C+**	C+	C+	603.9	8.77	8.1	1.5	40.1	18.7	**6.8**	8.8	0.0
WoodTrust Bank	Wisconsin Rapids	WI	**B+**	B	B	576.5	9.93	8.8	1.8	5.6	22.1	**7.8**	9.6	0.0
▲ Woori America Bank	New York	NY	**B**	B-	B+	2515.9	19.81	12.9	0.1	14.3	8.1	**10.0**	11.8	0.0
Worthington FSB, F.S.B.	Worthington	MN	**B**	B	B	97.0	18.07	1.2	3.1	53.3	21.2	**10.0**	14.1	36.7
Worthington National Bank	Arlington	TX	**B+**	B	B	418.9	12.35	11.4	1.3	19.6	0.0	**7.6**	9.4	0.0
Wray State Bank	Wray	CO	**D+**	D+	C-	184.6	10.67	10.8	4.0	9.5	15.5	**8.4**	10.0	14.3
Wrentham Co-operative Bank	Wrentham	MA	**C**	C+	C+	142.7	7.88	0.0	1.5	50.5	7.1	**10.0**	11.8	0.0
WSB Municipal Bank	Watertown	NY	**U**	U	U	164.4	19.21	0.0	0.0	0.0	93.6	**8.4**	9.9	0.0
Wyoming Bank & Trust	Cheyenne	WY	**A**	A	A	257.0	11.26	4.4	0.3	3.9	49.9	**8.9**	10.3	19.8
Wyoming Community Bank	Riverton	WY	**B**	B	B	205.6	19.48	10.8	3.9	7.3	37.6	**7.0**	9.0	0.0
▼ Yakima Federal S&L Assn.	Yakima	WA	**B**	B+	A-	2000.9	5.80	0.0	0.0	28.2	46.5	**10.0**	24.2	0.0
▲ Yampa Valley Bank	Steamboat Springs	CO	**B+**	B	A-	483.2	21.21	8.5	0.9	12.1	17.7	**5.5**	8.4	0.0
Yellowstone Bank	Laurel	MT	**A**	A	A	1022.0	8.44	11.9	0.7	7.9	13.0	**10.0**	15.2	0.0
YNB	Yukon	OK	**B-**	B-	C+	230.9	3.33	5.0	3.4	18.4	33.4	**7.6**	9.4	14.9
York State Bank	York	NE	**B-**	B-	B-	181.6	16.02	12.0	1.4	3.2	11.4	**8.7**	10.2	14.1
Yorktown Bank	Pryor	OK	**B-**	B-	B-	107.1	-6.64	10.1	9.0	20.7	0.0	**6.6**	9.6	12.2
Young Americans Bank	Denver	CO	**D-**	D-	D-	22.5	5.59	0.0	0.3	0.0	0.5	**5.8**	7.8	168.0
Zapata National Bank	Zapata	TX	**B+**	B+	B	91.9	4.40	5.1	5.2	14.7	19.8	**10.0**	12.8	0.0
Zavala County Bank	Crystal City	TX	**B-**	B-	B+	80.9	1.44	2.1	3.9	0.1	64.2	**10.0**	12.0	49.9
Zions BanCorp., N.A.	Salt Lake City	UT	**B+**	B+	A-	87208.4	14.08	17.2	0.6	7.6	21.6	**6.0**	8.0	14.2

Asset Quality Index	Adjusted Non-Performing Loans as a % of Total Loans	Adjusted Non-Performing Loans as a % of Capital	Net Charge-Offs Avg Loans	Profitability Index	Net Income ($Mil)	Return on Assets (R.O.A.)	Return on Equity (R.O.E.)	Net Interest Spread	Overhead Efficiency Ratio	Liquidity Index	Liquidity Ratio	Hot Money Ratio	Stability Index
5.0	3.97	10.2	0.09	**4.5**	9.1	0.92	7.01	3.16	69.4	**6.4**	45.8	5.9	**9.1**
8.1	0.00	0.0	-0.06	**8.3**	0.6	2.33	14.78	2.80	35.4	**4.4**	59.0	16.1	**7.9**
7.0	0.26	1.4	0.12	**2.8**	0.4	0.74	7.69	3.31	89.4	**4.0**	52.1	17.7	**5.0**
5.0	1.78	8.5	0.08	**6.7**	0.9	1.30	13.38	4.33	57.2	**1.8**	19.2	21.6	**7.0**
7.9	0.51	1.6	0.36	**3.2**	0.0	0.12	0.89	3.81	97.6	**4.9**	43.6	11.1	**6.5**
7.7	0.28	1.2	0.00	**9.8**	13.0	7.04	40.93	3.73	64.1	**2.4**	21.5	11.1	**9.5**
7.5	1.34	3.6	0.00	**3.1**	1.8	0.45	2.52	2.86	80.9	**5.1**	43.8	10.5	**7.8**
7.7	0.36	2.3	-0.01	**3.6**	0.6	0.65	5.68	3.63	83.1	**4.4**	28.2	8.7	**6.6**
6.2	3.64	9.0	-0.07	**0.8**	0.0	-0.05	-0.41	2.12	106.0	**6.5**	58.6	6.4	**6.3**
7.1	0.47	1.6	0.19	**7.3**	160.9	2.23	17.34	3.37	59.5	**6.0**	31.3	3.3	**9.1**
10.0	6.32	0.7	0.10	**3.4**	21.6	0.58	6.74	3.43	83.7	**8.7**	104.9	0.0	**5.8**
5.2	1.53	8.2	0.00	**7.8**	6.7	2.07	25.10	3.53	50.7	**6.0**	39.0	3.1	**7.1**
8.7	0.04	0.3	0.01	**6.5**	23.1	1.32	12.09	3.26	58.7	**4.1**	23.9	11.5	**9.8**
3.9	1.43	10.2	0.18	**4.1**	0.5	0.98	11.54	3.40	71.0	**3.0**	32.8	17.5	**4.9**
7.8	0.40	5.1	0.00	**3.1**	1.6	0.42	3.43	1.80	70.0	**2.2**	40.1	31.6	**7.6**
9.1	0.46	2.9	0.00	**2.6**	1.2	0.39	3.42	2.53	83.8	**2.0**	26.3	20.8	**7.3**
5.3	1.52	6.2	0.00	**3.4**	1.9	0.56	5.52	3.03	78.6	**5.0**	30.2	5.8	**6.5**
4.5	0.98	7.7	0.00	**6.1**	2.2	1.64	17.18	4.60	64.5	**1.7**	16.3	22.5	**5.4**
9.3	0.14	0.5	0.00	**2.8**	0.8	0.48	4.50	3.10	83.3	**2.4**	20.9	13.0	**5.7**
9.3	0.00	0.0	0.00	**5.5**	4.0	1.44	16.82	2.60	41.3	**6.9**	51.6	1.0	**7.0**
7.1	0.28	2.1	0.34	**7.0**	58.4	1.39	14.56	2.64	54.6	**3.7**	15.1	7.6	**7.4**
5.3	1.41	5.1	0.13	**6.4**	7.8	1.27	10.67	3.75	60.0	**5.8**	27.2	2.5	**8.4**
7.4	0.00	0.0	0.00	**5.9**	1.1	1.23	11.79	3.40	49.8	**0.8**	19.5	24.4	**7.9**
6.6	0.70	1.9	0.00	**5.3**	3.7	1.43	11.96	3.08	64.6	**5.2**	35.6	6.9	**8.8**
6.5	1.72	5.4	0.00	**7.7**	1.9	1.56	13.08	4.18	56.1	**4.8**	27.0	5.9	**8.0**
7.4	0.39	1.9	0.02	**7.8**	12.8	2.74	26.71	4.46	47.0	**2.9**	9.8	14.0	**8.9**
6.7	0.48	2.7	-0.01	**8.0**	3.9	2.45	28.16	4.07	55.2	**3.7**	36.4	15.1	**6.9**
5.5	1.44	8.2	0.16	**8.3**	100.4	2.20	31.24	2.82	70.7	**7.2**	47.1	0.8	**7.5**
4.8	1.17	8.2	0.06	**5.1**	0.6	0.99	10.41	4.15	70.8	**3.4**	22.8	12.0	**5.4**
5.3	1.02	6.7	-0.07	**5.2**	2.8	1.07	11.26	3.19	64.6	**4.8**	17.7	3.8	**6.7**
7.6	0.34	1.8	-0.10	**6.0**	2.0	1.21	12.70	3.21	54.2	**3.9**	50.8	4.4	**6.3**
9.3	1.40	2.5	0.00	**2.0**	0.1	0.12	0.39	1.87	93.4	**2.5**	52.6	46.2	**7.2**
7.8	0.35	2.5	-0.02	**3.4**	1.0	0.59	7.74	2.95	77.1	**5.6**	41.5	6.8	**3.7**
4.3	1.47	9.9	0.04	**3.1**	0.2	0.60	6.44	3.43	76.8	**4.9**	31.8	7.2	**4.9**
8.9	0.19	1.2	0.01	**3.3**	1.5	0.52	6.11	2.79	80.6	**4.7**	26.8	6.2	**6.1**
5.3	1.41	5.5	0.00	**9.5**	8.4	3.01	31.26	2.42	42.1	**6.5**	44.1	1.7	**8.3**
6.4	0.53	3.2	0.00	**4.1**	8.3	0.67	5.57	2.99	68.3	**3.3**	20.1	12.5	**8.7**
9.6	0.27	1.1	0.00	**3.9**	0.3	0.65	4.54	2.94	66.4	**5.2**	44.8	9.9	**7.5**
8.7	0.09	0.2	-0.01	**5.6**	2.2	1.17	12.64	3.59	66.2	**4.1**	35.0	12.9	**5.6**
1.1	3.92	26.2	-0.11	**6.8**	1.3	1.43	12.92	4.71	55.1	**2.0**	12.8	18.7	**6.2**
10.0	0.40	0.9	0.00	**2.1**	0.1	0.10	0.83	1.99	94.9	**5.0**	46.3	11.4	**7.1**
10.0	na	0.0	na	**3.6**	0.3	0.40	3.70	0.56	9.9	**5.1**	11.5	1.2	**4.6**
9.0	0.01	0.0	0.00	**9.5**	3.2	2.49	21.93	2.84	78.7	**6.2**	55.9	5.1	**8.6**
5.2	1.03	6.1	0.05	**5.0**	1.2	1.20	13.86	3.82	70.2	**4.7**	37.8	10.5	**6.1**
10.0	0.13	0.2	0.00	**3.7**	5.1	0.51	2.11	1.65	65.1	**4.3**	82.5	27.5	**9.7**
8.7	0.17	0.7	-0.01	**9.3**	5.1	2.22	25.88	3.83	51.2	**5.0**	35.9	8.1	**7.2**
8.6	0.02	0.1	0.00	**9.8**	11.7	2.33	14.67	3.78	40.9	**6.1**	35.4	4.6	**10.0**
8.4	0.22	1.0	0.04	**3.7**	1.0	0.85	8.71	3.89	79.1	**4.9**	37.6	9.4	**5.3**
3.9	0.54	2.8	0.05	**5.7**	1.1	1.20	9.41	3.43	55.9	**4.4**	26.9	8.1	**7.7**
6.8	0.00	0.0	0.00	**2.7**	0.1	0.20	1.27	3.67	76.1	**3.1**	10.1	13.0	**7.6**
10.0	0.00	0.0	-16.67	**0.0**	-0.7	-6.66	-88.98	0.89	809.7	**8.1**	106.8	0.5	**0.8**
6.9	3.86	5.3	0.00	**4.2**	0.4	0.90	6.76	2.73	71.1	**2.2**	47.5	38.1	**8.4**
9.7	0.00	0.0	0.10	**3.1**	0.2	0.42	3.56	1.74	84.0	**5.9**	72.8	10.6	**6.4**
5.9	1.23	5.4	0.02	**6.6**	675.6	1.60	17.00	2.78	58.6	**6.6**	37.4	1.4	**7.9**

Section II

Weiss
Recommended Banks by State

A compilation of those

U.S. Commercial Banks and Savings Banks

receiving a Weiss Safety Rating
of A+, A, A-, or B+.

Institutions are ranked by Safety Rating
in each state where they have a branch location.

Section II Contents

This section provides a list of Weiss Recommended Banks by State and contains all financial institutions receiving a Safety Rating of A+, A, A-, or B+. Recommended institutions are listed in each state in which they currently operate one or more branches. If a company is not on this list, it should not be automatically assumed that the firm is weak. Indeed, there are many firms that have not achieved a B+ or better rating but are in good condition with adequate resources to weather an average recession. Not being included in this list should not be construed as a recommendation to immediately withdraw deposits or cancel existing financial arrangements.

Institutions are ranked within each state by their Weiss Safety Rating, and then listed alphabetically by name. Institutions with the same rating should be viewed as having the same relative safety regardless of their ranking in this table.

- **State** The state in which the institution currently operates one or more branches. With the adoption of interstate branching laws, some institutions operating in your area may actually be headquartered in another state. Even so, there are no restrictions on your ability to do business with an out-of-state institution.

- **Institution Name** The name under which the institution was chartered. A bank's name can be very similar to, or the same as, the name of other banks which may not be on our Recommended List, so make sure you note the exact name.

- **Telephone** The telephone number for the institution's headquarters, or main office.

- **Safety Rating** Weiss rating assigned to the institution at the time of publication. Our ratings are designed to distinguish levels of insolvency risk and are measured on a scale from A to F based upon a wide range of factors. Highly rated companies are, in our opinion, less likely to experience financial difficulties than lower rated firms. See *About Weiss Safety Ratings* for more information and a description of what each rating means.

Weiss Safety Ratings are not deemed to be a recommendation concerning the purchase or sale of the securities of any bank that is publicly owned.

Alabama

Name	Telephone
Rating: A+	
First Bank of Boaz	(256) 593-8670
Rating: A	
First Metro Bank	(256) 386-0600
Metro Bank	(205) 884-2265
Metro City Bank	(770) 455-4989
Phenix-Girard Bank	(334) 298-0691
The Citizens Bank of Winfield	(205) 487-4277
Rating: A-	
Brantley Bank & Trust Co.	(334) 527-3206
Centennial Bank	(501) 328-4663
Central State Bank	(205) 668-0711
Community Neighbor Bank	(334) 682-4215
Cullman Savings Bank	(256) 734-1740
Farmers and Merchants Bank	(334) 864-9941
First Citizens Bank	(334) 335-3346
First Jackson Bank	(256) 437-2107
First National Bank of Pulaski	(931) 363-2585
Pinnacle Bank	(205) 221-4111
Robertson Banking Co.	(334) 289-3564
ServisFirst Bank	(205) 949-0302
Southern Independent Bank	(334) 493-2265
The Citizens Bank of Fayette	(205) 932-8911
The HomeTown Bank of Alabama	(205) 625-4434
The Samson Banking Co.	(334) 898-7107
Town-Country National Bank	(334) 682-4155
United Bank	(251) 446-6000
Rating: B+	
Ameris Bank	(404) 814-8114
BancorpSouth Bank	(662) 680-2000
Bank of Frankewing	(931) 363-1796
BankPlus	(662) 247-1811
BankSouth	(334) 677-2265
Cadence Bank, N.A.	(800) 636-7622
Capital City Bank	(850) 402-7700
CCB Community Bank	(334) 222-2561
Citizens Bank and Trust, Inc.	(706) 657-5678
First Bank	(256) 395-2255
First Bank of Alabama	(256) 362-2334
First Community Bank of Central Alabama	(334) 567-0081
First National Bank	(205) 921-7435
First Southern State Bank	(256) 437-2171
First State Bank of the South, Inc.	(205) 698-8116
FirstBank	(615) 313-0080
FirstState Bank	(256) 396-2187
Friend Bank	(334) 886-2367
HNB First Bank	(334) 693-3352
Liberty Bank	(256) 659-2175
Merchants Bank of Alabama	(256) 734-8110
North Alabama Bank	(256) 828-9500
Peoples Bank of Alabama	(256) 737-7000
Peoples Exchange Bank	(251) 575-4555
Peoples Independent Bank	(256) 593-8844
Renasant Bank	(800) 680-1601
River Bank & Trust	(334) 290-1012
SmartBank	(865) 453-2650
South State Bank, N.A.	(863) 551-5500
The Bank of Vernon	(205) 695-7141
The Citizens Bank	(334) 624-8888
The Exchange Bank of Alabama	(205) 589-6334
Traditions Bank	(256) 735-2121
Troy Bank & Trust Co.	(334) 566-4000
Truist Bank	(336) 733-2000
Trustmark National Bank	(601) 208-5111
West Alabama Bank & Trust	(205) 375-6261
Woodforest National Bank	(832) 375-2505

Alaska

Name	Telephone
Rating: A	
First National Bank Alaska	(907) 777-4362
Rating: B+	
KeyBank N.A.	(216) 689-3000
Mt. McKinley Bank	(907) 452-1751
Northrim Bank	(907) 562-0062

Arizona

Name	Telephone
Rating: A	
BNC National Bank	(602) 508-3760
First Savings Bank	(605) 763-2009
Western Bank	(575) 542-3521
Rating: A-	
Academy Bank, N.A.	(877) 712-2265
Alerus Financial, N.A.	(701) 795-3369
Armed Forces Bank, N.A.	(913) 682-9090
Bank of Colorado	(970) 206-1160
Bell Bank	(701) 298-1500
Enterprise Bank & Trust	(314) 725-5500
Glacier Bank	(406) 756-4200
KS StateBank	(785) 587-4000
Meadows Bank	(702) 471-2265
Pacific Premier Bank	(949) 864-8000
Stearns Bank N.A.	(320) 253-6607
Western Alliance Bank	(602) 389-3500
Rating: B+	
1st Bank Yuma	(928) 783-3334
Arizona Bank & Trust	(602) 381-2090
Bank of America, N.A.	(704) 386-5681
BOKF, N.A.	(918) 588-6000
Comerica Bank	(214) 462-4000
First National Bank Texas	(254) 554-4236
FirstBank	(303) 232-2000
First-Citizens Bank & Trust Co.	(919) 716-7050
Gateway Commercial Bank	(480) 358-1000
MidFirst Bank	(405) 767-7000
The Northern Trust Co.	(312) 630-6000
TrustBank	(618) 395-4311
Unison Bank	(701) 253-5600
Washington Federal Bank, N.A.	(206) 204-3446
Zions BanCorp., N.A.	(801) 844-7637

Arkansas

Rating: A+

Name	Telephone
First Security Bank	(501) 279-3400

Rating: A

Name	Telephone
Bank of England	(501) 842-2555
Citizens Bank & Trust Co.	(479) 474-1201
Connect Bank	(870) 628-4286
Eagle Bank and Trust Co.	(501) 223-2000
FSNB, N.A.	(580) 357-9880
Peoples Bank	(870) 942-5707

Rating: A-

Name	Telephone
Bank of Delight	(870) 379-2293
Bank of Lake Village	(870) 265-2241
Bank OZK	(501) 978-2265
Centennial Bank	(501) 328-4663
Fidelity Bank	(870) 735-8700
First National Bank of Izard County	(870) 297-3711
Great Southern Bank	(417) 895-5234
McGehee Bank	(870) 222-3151
Petit Jean State Bank	(501) 354-4988
Premier Bank of Arkansas	(870) 938-6020
Southern Bank	(573) 778-1800
Sterling Bank	(573) 778-3333
The First National Bank of Fort Smith	(479) 788-4600
The Union Bank of Mena	(479) 394-2211

Rating: B+

Name	Telephone
BancorpSouth Bank	(662) 680-2000
Bank of America, N.A.	(704) 386-5681
Bank of Salem	(870) 895-2591
Bodcaw Bank	(870) 533-4486
BOKF, N.A.	(918) 588-6000
Commercial National Bank of Texarkana	(870) 216-3506
Cross County Bank	(870) 238-8171
CS Bank	(479) 253-2265
Farmers Bank	(479) 996-4171
FBT Bank & Mortgage	(870) 352-3107
First Financial Bank	(870) 863-7000
First National Bank	(870) 215-4000
First National Bank Texas	(254) 554-4236
First Service Bank	(501) 679-7200
First State Bank	(479) 498-2400
First Western Bank	(479) 675-3000
Focus Bank	(573) 683-3712
Generations Bank	(479) 986-3990
Grand Savings Bank	(918) 786-2203
Logan County Bank	(479) 938-2511
Relyance Bank, N.A.	(870) 535-7222
Security Bank	(870) 786-5416
Simmons Bank	(870) 541-1000
The First National Bank at Paris	(479) 963-2121
Truist Bank	(336) 733-2000
Union Bank & Trust Co.	(870) 460-6400
United Bank	(479) 756-8811

California

Name	Telephone
Rating: A+	
California First National Bank	(800) 735-2465
Rating: A	
American Plus Bank, N.A.	(626) 821-9188
Bank of Stockton	(209) 929-1600
Citizens Business Bank	(909) 980-4030
First General Bank	(626) 820-1234
Fresno First Bank	(559) 439-0200
Golden Bank, N.A.	(713) 777-3838
Home Bank of California	(858) 270-5881
Pacific City Bank	(213) 210-2000
Royal Business Bank	(213) 627-9888
Santa Cruz County Bank	(831) 457-5000
Savings Bank of Mendocino County	(707) 462-6613
The Bank of Hemet	(951) 248-2000
Rating: A-	
American Continental Bank	(626) 363-8988
American First National Bank	(713) 596-2888
Armed Forces Bank, N.A.	(913) 682-9090
Bank of Marin	(415) 763-4520
Bank of the Sierra	(888) 454-2265
Cathay Bank	(213) 625-4791
Commonwealth Business Bank	(323) 988-3000
CTBC Bank Corp. (USA)	(424) 277-4612
East West Bank	(626) 768-6000
Enterprise Bank & Trust	(314) 725-5500
EverTrust Bank	(626) 993-3800
Exchange Bank (Santa Rosa, CA)	(707) 524-3000
Farmers & Merchants Bank	(209) 367-2300
First Bank	(314) 995-8700
First Commercial Bank (U.S.A)	(626) 300-6000
First IC Bank	(770) 451-7200
Five Star Bank	(916) 851-5440
Heritage Bank of Commerce	(408) 947-6900
Malaga Bank, FSB	(310) 375-9000
Metropolitan Bank	(510) 834-1933
Murphy Bank	(559) 225-0225
New OMNI Bank, N.A.	(626) 284-5555
Open Bank	(213) 892-9999
Pacific Coast Bankers' Bank	(415) 399-1900
Pacific Premier Bank	(949) 864-8000
Plumas Bank	(530) 283-7305
Poppy Bank	(707) 636-9000
Preferred Bank	(213) 891-1188
Summit Bank	(510) 839-8800
Suncrest Bank	(559) 802-1000
Tri Counties Bank	(530) 898-0300
US Metro Bank	(714) 620-8888
Wallis Bank	(979) 478-6151
Western Alliance Bank	(602) 389-3500
Rating: B+	
Avidbank	(408) 200-7390
Axos Bank	(858) 350-6200
Balboa Thrift and Loan Assn.	(619) 397-7700
Bank of America California, N.A.	(925) 988-4801
Bank of America, N.A.	(704) 386-5681
Bank of Santa Clarita	(661) 362-6000
Banner Bank	(509) 527-3636
BOKF, N.A.	(918) 588-6000
C3bank, N.A.	(760) 759-1130
California Pacific Bank	(415) 399-8000
CalPrivate Bank	(858) 875-6900
Central Valley Community Bank	(559) 298-1775
Chino Commercial Bank, N.A.	(909) 393-8880
Comerica Bank	(214) 462-4000
Community Commerce Bank	(909) 450-2050
Community Valley Bank	(760) 352-7777
Farmers & Merchants Bank of Long Beach	(562) 437-0011
First Credit Bank	(310) 273-3120
First Northern Bank of Dixon	(707) 678-3041
FirstBank	(303) 232-2000
First-Citizens Bank & Trust Co.	(919) 716-7050
Flagstar Bank, FSB	(248) 312-5400
Golden Valley Bank	(530) 894-1000
Habib American Bank	(212) 532-4444
Merchants Bank of Commerce	(916) 422-3883
MidFirst Bank	(405) 767-7000
Mission Bank	(661) 859-2500
Mission Valley Bank	(818) 394-2300
Oak Valley Community Bank	(209) 844-7500
Pacific Enterprise Bank	(949) 623-7600
Pacific Western Bank	(310) 887-8500
Pinnacle Bank	(408) 842-8200
Premier Valley Bank	(559) 438-2002
Redwood Capital Bank	(707) 444-9800
Signature Bank	(646) 822-1500
Silicon Valley Bank	(408) 654-7400
Silvergate Bank	(858) 362-6300
State Bank of India (California)	(213) 225-5700
Sterling Bank and Trust, FSB	(248) 355-2400
The Northern Trust Co.	(312) 630-6000

California

Name	Telephone
United Business Bank	(925) 476-1800
United Security Bank	(559) 248-4944
Valley Republic Bank	(661) 371-2000
WestAmerica Bank	(415) 257-8057
Zions BanCorp., N.A.	(801) 844-7637

Colorado

Name	Telephone
Rating: A	
AMG National Trust Bank	(303) 694-2190
Champion Bank	(303) 840-8484
Community State Bank	(719) 336-3272
Farmers & Stockmens Bank	(575) 374-8301
Farmers Bank	(970) 834-2121
First National Bank	(605) 223-2521
First National Bank of Las Animas	(719) 456-1512
Golden Belt Bank, FSA	(785) 726-3157
North Valley Bank	(303) 452-5500
The Dolores State Bank	(970) 882-7600
The Farmers State Bank of Brush	(970) 842-5101
Verus Bank of Commerce	(970) 204-1010
Rating: A-	
5Star Bank	(719) 574-2777
Academy Bank, N.A.	(877) 712-2265
Alamosa State Bank	(719) 589-2564
Alpine Bank	(970) 945-2424
Armed Forces Bank, N.A.	(913) 682-9090
Bank of Burlington	(719) 346-5376
Bank of Colorado	(970) 206-1160
Commerce Bank	(855) 659-1656
First Pioneer National Bank	(970) 332-4824
First State Bank	(308) 632-4158
FirsTier Bank	(308) 235-4633
FirstOak Bank	(620) 331-2265
FNB Bank	(785) 890-2000
Fowler State Bank	(719) 263-4276
Frontier Bank	(719) 336-4351
Glacier Bank	(406) 756-4200
High Country Bank	(719) 539-2516
Independent Bank	(972) 562-9004
Kirkpatrick Bank	(405) 341-8222
NBH Bank	(720) 554-6650
Points West Community Bank	(970) 686-0878
The Colorado B&T Co. of La Junta	(719) 384-8131
The Eastern Colorado Bank	(719) 767-5652
The Gunnison Bank and Trust Co.	(970) 641-0320
The State Bank	(719) 384-5901
Rating: B+	
Adams Bank & Trust	(308) 284-4071
ANB Bank	(303) 394-5143
Bank of America, N.A.	(704) 386-5681
Bank of Estes Park	(970) 586-4485
BOKF, N.A.	(918) 588-6000
Citywide Banks	(303) 365-3800
Farmers State Bank of Calhan	(719) 347-2727
First National Bank of Hugo	(719) 743-2415
FirstBank	(303) 232-2000
First-Citizens Bank & Trust Co.	(919) 716-7050
Grand Valley Bank	(435) 654-7400
High Plains Bank	(719) 765-4000
Integrity Bank & Trust	(719) 484-0077
KeyBank N.A.	(216) 689-3000
Legacy Bank	(719) 829-4811
MidFirst Bank	(405) 767-7000
Pacific Western Bank	(310) 887-8500
Redstone Bank	(720) 880-5000
Solera National Bank	(303) 209-8600
State Bank of Downs	(785) 454-3323
Stockmens Bank	(719) 955-2800
The Central Trust Bank	(573) 634-1302
The Northern Trust Co.	(312) 630-6000
The Pueblo Bank and Trust Co.	(719) 545-1834
United Business Bank	(925) 476-1800
United Fidelity Bank, FSB	(812) 424-0921
Waypoint Bank	(308) 784-2515
Yampa Valley Bank	(970) 879-2993
Zions BanCorp., N.A.	(801) 844-7637

Connecticut

Name	Telephone
Rating: A+	
Stafford Savings Bank	(860) 684-4261
Rating: A	
Bessemer Trust Co., N.A.	(212) 708-9100
Rating: A-	
Chelsea Groton Bank	(860) 823-4800
Rating: B+	
Bank of America, N.A.	(704) 386-5681
KeyBank N.A.	(216) 689-3000
NBT Bank, N.A.	(607) 337-6416
Salisbury Bank and Trust Co.	(860) 435-9801
Signature Bank	(646) 822-1500
The Northern Trust Co.	(312) 630-6000
The Washington Trust Co. of Westerly	(401) 348-1210
Webster Bank, N.A.	(203) 328-8110

Delaware

Name	Telephone
Rating: A	
Calvin B. Taylor Banking Co.	(410) 641-1700
FSNB, N.A.	(580) 357-9880
Rating: A-	
Applied Bank	(888) 839-7952
Bank of Ocean City	(410) 213-0173
Deutsche Bank Trust Co. Delaware	(302) 636-3301
Morgan Stanley Private Bank, N.A.	(212) 762-1803
Wilmington Savings Fund Society, FSB	(302) 571-7080
Rating: B+	
Bank of America, N.A.	(704) 386-5681
County Bank	(302) 226-9800
Fulton Bank, N.A.	(717) 291-2499
Shore United Bank	(410) 822-1400
The Bryn Mawr Trust Co.	(610) 581-4839
The Northern Trust Co.	(312) 630-6000

District of Columbia

Name	Telephone
Rating: A-	
EagleBank	(240) 497-2075
MainStreet Bank	(703) 481-4567
Presidential Bank, FSB	(301) 652-1616
Rating: B+	
Bank of America, N.A.	(704) 386-5681
FVCbank	(703) 436-4740
John Marshall Bank	(703) 584-0840
The Northern Trust Co.	(312) 630-6000
Truist Bank	(336) 733-2000
United Bank	(703) 556-0900

Federated States of Micronesia

Name	Telephone
Rating: B+	
Bank of the Federated States of Micronesia	

Florida

Rating: A+

Name	Telephone
Citizens First Bank	(352) 753-9515
Esquire Bank, N.A.	(516) 535-2002

Rating: A

Name	Telephone
Amerasia Bank	(718) 463-3600
Florida Business Bank	(321) 253-1555
Metro City Bank	(770) 455-4989
Paradise Bank	(561) 392-5444
Republic Bank & Trust Co.	(502) 584-3600
Southeastern Bank	(912) 437-4141

Rating: A-

Name	Telephone
1st Source Bank	(574) 235-2000
American National Bank	(954) 491-7788
Bank OZK	(501) 978-2265
Busey Bank	(217) 351-6500
Centennial Bank	(501) 328-4663
Charlotte State Bank & Trust	(941) 624-5400
Crews Bank & Trust	(863) 494-2220
Drummond Community Bank	(352) 493-2277
Englewood Bank & Trust	(941) 475-6771
First Federal Bank	(386) 755-0600
Flagler Bank	(561) 432-2122
Seacoast National Bank	(772) 221-2760
ServisFirst Bank	(205) 949-0302
Stearns Bank N.A.	(320) 253-6607
The First National Bank of Mount Dora	(352) 383-2111
Thomasville National Bank	(229) 226-3300
United Bank	(251) 446-6000
United Community Bank	(864) 255-7960
Wauchula State Bank	(863) 773-4151

Rating: B+

Name	Telephone
American Commerce Bank, N.A.	(770) 537-2265
Ameris Bank	(404) 814-8114
BancorpSouth Bank	(662) 680-2000
Bank of America, N.A.	(704) 386-5681
Bradesco BAC Florida Bank	(305) 789-8077
Cadence Bank, N.A.	(800) 636-7622
Capital City Bank	(850) 402-7700
CCB Community Bank	(334) 222-2561
Comerica Bank	(214) 462-4000
Commerce National Bank & Trust	(407) 622-8181
Community Bank of the South	(321) 452-0420
First Colony Bank of Florida	(407) 740-0401
First Home Bank	(727) 440-6848
First National Bank of Coffee County	(912) 384-1100
First-Citizens Bank & Trust Co.	(919) 716-7050
FNBT Bank	(850) 796-2000
Hillsboro Bank	(813) 707-6506
Intracoastal Bank	(386) 447-1662
KeyBank N.A.	(216) 689-3000
Lake Forest Bank & Trust Co., N.A.	(847) 234-2882
Peoples Bank of Graceville	(850) 263-3267
Prime Meridian Bank	(850) 907-2300
PrimeSouth Bank	(912) 283-6685
Raymond James Bank	(727) 567-8000
Renasant Bank	(800) 680-1601
SmartBank	(865) 453-2650
South State Bank, N.A.	(863) 551-5500
Surety Bank	(386) 734-1647
The Northern Trust Co.	(312) 630-6000
Truist Bank	(336) 733-2000
TrustCo Bank	(518) 377-3311
Trustmark National Bank	(601) 208-5111
United Fidelity Bank, FSB	(812) 424-0921
Winter Park National Bank	(407) 853-7100
Woodforest National Bank	(832) 375-2505

Georgia

Name	Telephone
Rating: A	
BankSouth	(706) 453-2943
Douglas National Bank	(912) 384-2233
Durden Banking Co., Inc.	(478) 763-2121
Embassy National Bank	(770) 822-9111
Farmers State Bank	(706) 359-3131
First Century Bank, N.A.	(770) 297-8060
First Volunteer Bank	(423) 668-4509
FNB South	(912) 632-7262
FSNB, N.A.	(580) 357-9880
Metro City Bank	(770) 455-4989
South Georgia Bank	(912) 654-1051
Southeastern Bank	(912) 437-4141
The First National Bank of Waynesboro	(706) 554-8100
United Bank	(770) 567-7211
Rating: A-	
Atlantic Capital Bank, N.A.	(404) 995-6050
Bank of Dade	(706) 657-6842
Bank OZK	(501) 978-2265
Century Bank & Trust	(478) 453-3571
Century Bank of Georgia	(770) 387-1922
Commercial Banking Co.	(229) 242-7600
East West Bank	(626) 768-6000
Exchange Bank	(478) 452-4531
Farmers State Bank	(478) 275-3223
First IC Bank	(770) 451-7200
First National Community Bank	(706) 695-9646
First State Bank of Blakely	(229) 723-3711
Glennville Bank	(912) 654-3471
Greater Community Bank	(706) 295-9300
Northeast Georgia Bank	(706) 356-4444
Pinnacle Bank	(615) 744-3705
PromiseOne Bank	(678) 385-0800
Quantum National Bank	(770) 945-8300
ServisFirst Bank	(205) 949-0302
Southern First Bank	(864) 679-9000
SunMark Community Bank	(478) 783-4036
The Citizens Bank of Georgia	(770) 886-9500
The Citizens National Bank of Quitman	(229) 263-7575
The Four County Bank	(478) 962-3221
The Piedmont Bank	(770) 246-0011
The Security State Bank	(229) 868-6431
Thomasville National Bank	(229) 226-3300
United Community Bank	(864) 255-7960
Wallis Bank	(979) 478-6151
West Central Georgia Bank	(706) 647-8951

Name	Telephone
Rating: B+	
American Commerce Bank, N.A.	(770) 537-2265
American Pride Bank	(478) 784-1448
Ameris Bank	(404) 814-8114
BancorpSouth Bank	(662) 680-2000
Bank of America, N.A.	(704) 386-5681
Bank of Camilla	(229) 336-5225
Bank of Dawson	(229) 995-2141
Bank of Dudley	(478) 277-1500
Bank of Madison	(706) 342-1953
Bank of Monticello	(706) 468-6418
Cadence Bank, N.A.	(800) 636-7622
Capital City Bank	(850) 402-7700
Citizens Bank and Trust, Inc.	(706) 657-5678
Citizens Bank of Americus	(229) 924-4011
Citizens Community Bank	(229) 794-2111
Community Banking Co. of Fitzgerald	(229) 423-4321
F&M Bank	(706) 678-2187
Family Bank	(229) 294-2821
Farmers and Merchants Bank	(912) 564-7436
First American Bank and Trust Co.	(706) 354-5000
First National Bank of Coffee County	(912) 384-1100
First State Bank	(706) 547-6502
FirstBank	(615) 313-0080
First-Citizens Bank & Trust Co.	(919) 716-7050
Guardian Bank	(229) 241-9444
Legacy State Bank	(770) 554-2265
Morris Bank	(478) 272-5202
Peoples Bank of East Tennessee	(423) 442-7262
Pinnacle Bank	(706) 283-2854
PrimeSouth Bank	(912) 283-6685
Rabun County Bank	(706) 782-4571
Renasant Bank	(800) 680-1601
South Georgia Banking Co.	(229) 382-4211
South State Bank, N.A.	(863) 551-5500
State Bank of Cochran	(478) 934-4501
The Bank of Soperton	(912) 529-4431
The Citizens Bank of Swainsboro	(478) 237-7001
The Commercial Bank	(706) 743-8184
The Northern Trust Co.	(312) 630-6000
Truist Bank	(336) 733-2000
Waycross Bank & Trust	(912) 283-0001
Wheeler County State Bank	(912) 568-7191
Wilcox County State Bank	(229) 467-2511
Woodforest National Bank	(832) 375-2505

Guam

Name	Telephone
Rating: B+	
First Hawaiian Bank	(808) 525-6340

Hawaii

Name	Telephone
Rating: A-	
Commonwealth Business Bank	(323) 988-3000
Rating: B+	
Central Pacific Bank	(808) 544-0500
Finance Factors, Ltd.	(808) 522-2000
First Hawaiian Bank	(808) 525-6340
Territorial Savings Bank	(808) 946-1400

Idaho

Name	Telephone
Rating: A	
Altabank	(801) 756-7681
Farmers Bank	(208) 543-4351
The Bank of Commerce	(208) 525-9108
Rating: A-	
Bell Bank	(701) 298-1500
Columbia State Bank	(253) 305-1900
D.L. Evans Bank	(208) 678-8615
First FSB of Twin Falls	(208) 733-4222
Glacier Bank	(406) 756-4200
Rating: B+	
Bank of America, N.A.	(704) 386-5681
Bank of Jackson Hole	(307) 733-8064
Banner Bank	(509) 527-3636
First Interstate Bank	(406) 255-5000
Ireland Bank	(208) 766-2211
KeyBank N.A.	(216) 689-3000
Northwest Bank	(208) 332-0700
Twin River Bank	(208) 746-4848
Washington Federal Bank, N.A.	(206) 204-3446
Washington Trust Bank	(509) 353-4204
Zions BanCorp., N.A.	(801) 844-7637

Illinois

Rating: A

Name	Telephone
AMG National Trust Bank	(303) 694-2190
Crossroads Bank	(217) 347-7751
Farmers National Bank	(815) 537-2348
Farmers State Bank	(217) 285-5585
First Eagle Bank	(312) 850-2900
Germantown Trust & Savings Bank	(618) 526-4202
Goodfield State Bank	(309) 965-2221
Heartland Bank and Trust Co.	(309) 662-4444
Lindell Bank & Trust Co.	(314) 645-7700
Municipal Trust and Savings Bank	(815) 935-8000
Park Ridge Community Bank	(847) 384-9200
Royal Business Bank	(213) 627-9888
Teutopolis State Bank	(217) 857-3166
The Bank of Advance	(573) 722-3517
The Federal Savings Bank	(312) 738-6000
The Fisher National Bank	(217) 897-1136
The FNB Community Bank	(618) 283-1141
Town and Country Bank Midwest	(217) 222-0015
Vermilion Valley Bank	(815) 686-2258

Rating: A-

Name	Telephone
Apple River State Bank	(815) 594-2351
Armed Forces Bank, N.A.	(913) 682-9090
Bank of Pontiac	(815) 844-6155
Belmont Bank & Trust Co.	(773) 589-9500
Buena Vista National Bank	(618) 826-2331
Busey Bank	(217) 351-6500
Cathay Bank	(213) 625-4791
Central Bank Illinois	(309) 944-5601
Commerce Bank	(855) 659-1656
Community Bank	(815) 367-5011
Community Bank of Easton	(309) 562-7420
Evergreen Bank Group	(630) 413-9580
First Bank	(314) 995-8700
First Financial Bank, N.A.	(812) 238-6000
First Merchants Bank	(765) 747-1500
First National Bank	(605) 482-8293
First State Bank of Campbell Hill	(618) 426-3396
Illini State Bank	(815) 442-8211
Inland Bank and Trust	(877) 908-6555
Kinmundy Bank	(618) 547-3533
Liberty Bank	(217) 645-3434
Mason City National Bank	(217) 482-3246
Midwest Community Bank	(815) 235-6137
Milledgeville State Bank	(815) 225-7171
Millennium Bank	(847) 296-9500
Northside Community Bank	(847) 244-5100
Old Second National Bank	(630) 892-0202
Petefish, Skiles & Co.	(217) 452-3041
Prairie State Bank & Trust	(217) 993-6260
Providence Bank & Trust	(708) 333-0700
Quad City Bank and Trust Co.	(563) 344-0600
Signature Bank	(847) 268-1001
Southern Bank	(573) 778-1800
Sterling Bank	(573) 778-3333
The Bradford National Bank of Greenville	(618) 664-2200
The First National Bank of Beardstown	(217) 323-4105
The First National Bank of Litchfield	(217) 324-2105
The First National Bank of Sparta	(618) 443-2187
The First Trust and Savings Bank of Watseka	(815) 432-2494
Warren-Boynton State Bank	(217) 488-6091

Rating: B+

Name	Telephone
Albany Bank & Trust Co., N.A.	(773) 267-7300
American Community Bank & Trust	(815) 338-2300
Anna State Bank	(618) 833-2151
Anna-Jonesboro National Bank	(618) 833-8506
Bank of America, N.A.	(704) 386-5681
Bank of Bourbonnais	(815) 933-0570
Bank of O'Fallon	(618) 632-3595
Bank of Rantoul	(217) 892-2143
BankChampaign, N.A.	(217) 351-2870
Bankers' Bank	(608) 833-5550
Blackhawk Bank & Trust	(309) 787-4451
Burling Bank	(312) 408-8400
Catlin Bank	(217) 427-2176
CBI Bank & Trust	(563) 263-3131
Central Bank of St. Louis	(314) 862-8300
CIBM Bank	(217) 355-0900
Citizens Community Bank	(618) 566-8800
Community Bank of Trenton	(618) 224-9258
Community First Bank of the Heartland	(618) 244-3000
Exchange State Bank	(815) 493-2631
Farmers State Bank of Western Illinois	(309) 629-4361
First Federal S&L Assn. of Central Illinois, S.B.	(217) 774-3322
First Financial Bank	(513) 832-6300
First Mid Bank & Trust, N.A.	(217) 234-7454
First National Bank in Olney	(618) 395-8541
First National Bank in Pinckneyville	(618) 357-9393
First National Bank in Taylorville	(217) 824-2241
First National Bank of Brookfield	(708) 485-2770
First National Bank of Pana	(217) 562-3961
First Nations Bank	(773) 594-5900

Illinois

Name	Telephone
First Southern Bank	(618) 997-4341
First State Bank	(815) 538-2265
First State Bank of Beecher City	(618) 487-5161
First State Bank of St. Peter	(618) 349-8343
Glenview State Bank	(847) 729-1900
Gold Coast Bank	(312) 587-3200
Grand Ridge National Bank	(815) 249-6414
Grundy Bank	(815) 942-0130
Illinois Bank & Trust	(815) 489-2114
Ipava State Bank	(309) 753-8202
Lake Forest Bank & Trust Co., N.A.	(847) 234-2882
Lakeside Bank	(312) 435-5100
Lena State Bank	(815) 369-4901
Midland Community Bank	(217) 237-4324
Morton Community Bank	(309) 266-5337
North Central Bank	(815) 925-7373
Peoples State Bank of Colfax	(309) 723-2111
Republic Bank of Chicago	(630) 570-7700
Royal Banks of Missouri	(314) 212-1500
Rushville State Bank	(217) 322-3323
Shelby County State Bank	(217) 774-3911
Solutions Bank	(815) 938-3121
Southern Illinois Bank	(618) 983-8433
Spring Valley City Bank	(815) 663-2211
State Bank of Cherry	(815) 894-2345
State Bank of Davis	(815) 865-5125
State Bank of Industry	(309) 254-3434
State Bank of St. Jacob	(618) 644-5555
State Bank of Texas	(972) 252-6000
Stillman BancCorp, N.A.	(815) 645-2266
The Farmers and Merchants National Bank of Nashvill	(618) 327-4401
The First National Bank of Ava	(618) 426-3303
The Frederick Community Bank	(815) 457-2111
The Northern Trust Co.	(312) 630-6000
The Peoples State Bank of Newton, Illinois	(618) 783-2321
Town and Country Bank	(217) 787-3100
TrustBank	(618) 395-4311
Union National Bank	(847) 888-7500
United Fidelity Bank, FSB	(812) 424-0921
Villa Grove State Bank	(217) 832-2631
Woodforest National Bank	(832) 375-2505

Indiana

Rating: A

Name	Telephone
Alliance Bank	(219) 567-9151
Lake City Bank	(574) 267-6144
Logansport Savings Bank	(574) 722-3855
Republic Bank & Trust Co.	(502) 584-3600
Union Savings Bank	(513) 247-0300

Rating: A-

Name	Telephone
1st Source Bank	(574) 235-2000
Bank of Wolcott	(219) 279-2185
Busey Bank	(217) 351-6500
Centier Bank	(219) 755-6100
CentreBank	(765) 294-2228
Civista Bank	(419) 625-4121
Community State Bank	(260) 897-3361
Farmers and Merchants Bank	(260) 637-5546
Farmers State Bank	(260) 463-7111
First Bank of Berne	(260) 589-2151
First Financial Bank, N.A.	(812) 238-6000
First Merchants Bank	(765) 747-1500
First State Bank of Middlebury	(574) 825-2166
Freedom Bank	(812) 683-8998
German American Bank	(812) 482-1314
Kentland Bank	(219) 474-5155
Providence Bank & Trust	(708) 333-0700
Stock Yards Bank & Trust Co.	(502) 582-2571
The Bippus State Bank	(260) 356-8900
The Farmers Bank, Frankfort, Indiana, Inc.	(765) 654-8731
The Morris Plan Co. of Terre Haute	(812) 238-6063
The Napoleon State Bank	(812) 852-4002
The State Bank and Trust Co.	(419) 783-8950
Wayne Bank and Trust Co.	(765) 478-3561

Rating: B+

Name	Telephone
Bank of America, N.A.	(704) 386-5681
Bankers' Bank	(608) 833-5550
Bedford Federal Savings Bank	(812) 275-5907
CIBM Bank	(217) 355-0900
DeMotte State Bank	(219) 987-4141
FCN Bank, N.A.	(765) 647-4116
First Federal Savings Bank	(260) 356-3311
First Financial Bank	(513) 832-6300
First Harrison Bank	(812) 738-2198
First Savings Bank	(812) 283-0724
First State Bank of Porter	(219) 926-2136
Flagstar Bank, FSB	(248) 312-5400
Fowler State Bank	(765) 884-1200
Greenfield Banking Co.	(317) 462-1431
Greenville National Bank	(937) 548-1114
Horizon Bank	(219) 874-9245
KeyBank N.A.	(216) 689-3000
Springs Valley Bank & Trust Co.	(812) 634-1010
STAR Financial Bank	(260) 467-5500
State Bank	(317) 858-1039
The Farmers & Merchants State Bank	(419) 446-2501
The Fountain Trust Co.	(765) 793-2237
The Friendship State Bank	(812) 667-5101
The Garrett State Bank	(260) 357-3133
The New Washington State Bank	(812) 293-3321
The Peoples State Bank	(812) 876-2228
Truist Bank	(336) 733-2000
United Fidelity Bank, FSB	(812) 424-0921
WesBanco Bank, Inc.	(304) 234-9419
Woodforest National Bank	(832) 375-2505

Iowa

Name	Telephone
Rating: A	
Bank 1st	(563) 422-3883
Bellevue State Bank	(563) 872-4911
Citizens First National Bank	(712) 732-5440
Citizens Savings Bank	(563) 562-3674
Farmers Trust & Savings Bank	(641) 562-2696
Farmers Trust and Savings Bank	(319) 668-2525
First State Bank	(641) 843-4411
First State Bank	(641) 527-2535
Heartland Bank	(515) 467-5561
Hills Bank and Trust Co.	(319) 679-2291
Iowa State Bank	(515) 288-0111
Iowa State Bank	(712) 662-4721
Iowa State Bank	(712) 439-1025
Iowa Trust and Savings Bank	(641) 437-4500
Lee County Bank	(319) 372-2243
Liberty Trust & Savings Bank	(563) 785-4441
Manufacturers Bank & Trust Co.	(641) 585-2825
Midwest Heritage Bank, FSB	(515) 278-6541
Mount Vernon Bank and Trust Co.	(319) 895-8835
Pinnacle Bank	(641) 752-2393
Savings Bank	(712) 957-6815
Solon State Bank	(319) 624-3405
United Bank and Trust Co.	(641) 456-5587
Waukon State Bank	(563) 568-3451
West Iowa Bank	(515) 887-7811
Rating: A-	
American Savings Bank	(319) 882-4279
Audubon State Bank	(712) 563-2644
BANK	(319) 523-5200
Blue Grass Savings Bank	(563) 381-1732
BTC Bank	(660) 425-7285
Cedar Rapids Bank and Trust Co.	(319) 862-2728
Charter Bank	(515) 331-2265
Chelsea Savings Bank	(319) 444-3144
Cherokee State Bank	(712) 225-3000
Citizens Savings Bank	(319) 462-3561
Citizens State Bank	(712) 324-2519
CUSB Bank	(563) 547-2040
Decorah Bank and Trust Co.	(563) 382-9661
Farmers & Merchants Savings Bank	(319) 629-4222
Farmers & Merchants Savings Bank	(563) 927-4475
Farmers & Merchants State Bank	(515) 462-4242
Farmers Bank of Northern Missouri	(660) 947-2474
Farmers Savings Bank	(641) 752-2525
Farmers Savings Bank & Trust	(319) 478-2148
Farmers State Bank	(641) 424-3053
Farmers State Bank	(319) 377-4891
Farmers State Bank	(319) 287-3961
First Bank Hampton	(641) 456-4793
First Central State Bank	(563) 659-3141
First Citizens Bank	(641) 423-1600
First National Bank	(605) 482-8293
First State Bank	(515) 832-2520
First State Bank	(712) 364-3181
First State Bank	(641) 435-4943
FNB Bank	(641) 745-2141
GNB Bank	(319) 824-5431
Great Southern Bank	(417) 895-5234
Hiawatha Bank & Trust Co.	(319) 378-5979
Home Federal Savings Bank	(507) 535-1309
Home State Bank	(712) 933-5511
Houghton State Bank	(712) 623-4823
Iowa Trust & Savings Bank	(712) 852-3451
Liberty National Bank	(712) 224-4425
Maquoketa State Bank	(563) 652-2491
New Albin Savings Bank	(563) 544-4214
NorthStar Bank	(712) 362-3322
Northwestern Bank	(712) 737-4911
NSB Bank	(641) 423-7638
Ohnward Bank & Trust	(563) 852-7696
Primebank	(712) 546-4175
Quad City Bank and Trust Co.	(563) 344-0600
Security State Bank	(515) 295-9501
Shelby County State Bank	(712) 755-5112
St. Ansgar State Bank	(641) 713-4501
Templeton Savings Bank	(712) 669-3322
The Breda Savings Bank	(712) 673-2321
The Readlyn Savings Bank	(319) 279-3321
The Security National Bank of Sioux City, Iowa	(712) 277-6500
United Bank of Iowa	(712) 364-3393
Washington State Bank	(319) 653-2151
Wayland State Bank	(319) 385-8189
Rating: B+	
American National Bank	(402) 399-5000
American State Bank	(641) 342-2175
Ashton State Bank	(712) 724-6326
Atkins Savings Bank & Trust	(319) 446-7700
Bank Midwest	(712) 336-0505
Bank of America, N.A.	(704) 386-5681
Bankers' Bank	(608) 833-5550
Blackhawk Bank & Trust	(309) 787-4451

Iowa

Name	Telephone
Boone Bank & Trust Co.	(515) 432-6200
Bridge Community Bank	(319) 895-8200
CBI Bank & Trust	(563) 263-3131
Citizens State Bank	(319) 465-5921
Citizens State Bank	(563) 488-2211
Clear Lake Bank and Trust Co.	(641) 357-7121
Community Bank of Oelwein	(319) 283-4000
Community State Bank	(515) 331-3100
Community State Bank	(712) 262-3030
Danville State Savings Bank	(319) 392-4261
Dubuque Bank and Trust Co.	(563) 589-2000
Exchange State Bank	(641) 742-3201
F&M Bank	(402) 372-5331
Farmers Savings Bank	(319) 372-5141
Farmers Savings Bank	(563) 856-2525
Farmers State Bank	(515) 295-7221
Farmers State Bank	(712) 376-4154
Farmers Trust & Savings Bank	(712) 747-2000
Fidelity Bank	(515) 221-0022
First Bank	(319) 352-1340
First Iowa State Bank	(641) 932-2144
First National Bank Ames, Iowa	(515) 232-5561
First Security Bank	(712) 881-1131
First Security Bank - Sleepy Eye	(507) 794-3911
First State Bank	(641) 444-3226
First Whitney Bank and Trust	(712) 243-3195
Grinnell State Bank	(641) 236-3174
Guthrie County State Bank	(641) 755-2400
Iowa State Bank	(515) 295-3595
Leighton State Bank	(641) 628-1566
Libertyville Savings Bank	(641) 472-9839
Luana Savings Bank	(563) 539-2166
Maynard Savings Bank	(563) 637-2289
Mediapolis Savings Bank	(319) 394-3191
Northeast Security Bank	(563) 578-3251
Northwest Bank	(712) 580-4100
Peoples Savings Bank	(319) 658-2131
Peoples Savings Bank	(515) 962-1400
Peoples Trust and Savings Bank	(319) 648-2221
Pilot Grove Savings Bank	(319) 469-3951
Pocahontas State Bank	(712) 335-3567
Principal Bank	(800) 672-3343
Security National Bank of Omaha	(402) 344-7300
Security Savings Bank	(515) 352-3333
Security State Bank	(712) 446-3324
Sibley State Bank	(712) 754-2561
Sloan State Bank	(712) 428-3344
South Ottumwa Savings Bank	(641) 682-7541
State Bank & Trust Co.	(515) 382-2191
State Bank of Schaller	(712) 275-4261
State Savings Bank	(515) 457-9533
Success Bank	(641) 664-2006
The Exchange State Bank	(319) 854-6104
The First National Bank in Creston	(641) 782-2195
The First National Bank of Manning	(712) 655-3557
The Home Trust & Savings Bank	(641) 732-3763
The Watkins Savings Bank	(319) 227-7773
Walker State Bank	(319) 448-4317
West Bank	(515) 222-2300
White State Bank	(319) 667-5005

Kansas

Name	Telephone
Rating: A	
Farmers & Merchants Bank of Colby	(785) 460-3321
Farmers Bank & Trust	(620) 792-2411
First State Bank of St. Charles, Missouri	(636) 940-5555
Garden Plain State Bank	(316) 721-1500
Golden Belt Bank, FSA	(785) 726-3157
Kearny County Bank	(620) 355-6222
Midwest Heritage Bank, FSB	(515) 278-6541
Mutual Savings Assn.	(913) 682-3491
NBKC Bank	(913) 905-2100
Security State Bank	(620) 872-7224
State Bank of Bern	(785) 336-6121
The City National B&T Co. of Lawton, Oklahoma	(866) 385-3444
The Denison State Bank	(785) 364-3131
The Farmers State Bank of Oakley, Kansas	(785) 672-3251
The Fidelity State Bank and Trust Co.	(620) 227-8586
Rating: A-	
Academy Bank, N.A.	(877) 712-2265
Armed Forces Bank, N.A.	(913) 682-9090
Bank of Prairie Village	(913) 713-0300
Bankers' Bank of Kansas	(316) 681-2265
CBW Bank	(620) 396-8221
Central National Bank	(785) 238-4114
Commerce Bank	(855) 659-1656
Community State Bank	(620) 251-1313
Enterprise Bank & Trust	(314) 725-5500
Exchange Bank	(308) 237-7711
Exchange Bank & Trust	(913) 367-6000
Farmers National Bank	(785) 543-6541
First Bank	(620) 278-2161
First National Bank and Trust	(785) 543-6511
FirstOak Bank	(620) 331-2265
FNB Bank	(785) 890-2000
Fusion Bank	(620) 285-6931
Grant County Bank	(620) 356-4142
Great Southern Bank	(417) 895-5234
Kansas State Bank	(785) 665-7121
KS StateBank	(785) 587-4000
Mid-America Bank	(785) 594-2100
NBH Bank	(720) 554-6650
Pinnacle Bank	(402) 434-3127
Security Bank of Kansas City	(913) 281-3165
Solomon State Bank	(785) 655-2941
Solutions North Bank	(785) 425-6721
The Bank of Protection	(620) 622-4224
The Eastern Colorado Bank	(719) 767-5652
The Farmers State Bank	(785) 364-4691
The Farmers State Bank	(620) 241-3090
The Farmers State Bank of Aliceville, Kansas	(785) 489-2468
The First National Bank of Scott City	(620) 872-2143
The First State Bank	(785) 798-3347
The Kaw Valley State B&T Co., of Wamego, Kansas	(785) 456-2021
The Stockgrowers State Bank	(785) 256-4241
TriCentury Bank	(913) 583-3222
Western State Bank	(620) 275-4128
Rating: B+	
Adams Bank & Trust	(308) 284-4071
Alliance Bank	(785) 271-1800
ANB Bank	(303) 394-5143
Bank of America, N.A.	(704) 386-5681
Bank of Blue Valley	(913) 234-2334
Bank of Commerce	(620) 431-1400
Bank of Hays	(785) 621-2265
Bank7	(405) 810-8600
BOKF, N.A.	(918) 588-6000
Central Bank of the Midwest	(816) 525-5300
Citizens State Bank and Trust Co.	(785) 742-2101
Community Bank	(785) 440-4400
Community First National Bank	(785) 323-1111
Community National Bank	(785) 336-6143
Country Club Bank	(816) 931-4060
Farmers and Drovers Bank	(620) 767-5138
First Bank Kansas	(785) 825-2211
First Bank of Beloit	(785) 738-2251
First Commerce Bank	(785) 562-5558
First Federal S&L Bank	(913) 782-0026
First Heritage Bank	(785) 857-3341
First Kansas Bank	(620) 653-4921
First National Bank in Fredonia	(620) 378-2151
First National Bank of Spearville	(620) 385-2636
First-Citizens Bank & Trust Co.	(919) 716-7050
Flint Hills Bank	(785) 449-2266
FNB Washington	(785) 325-2221
Great American Bank	(785) 838-9704
Howard State Bank	(620) 374-2127
Kansas State Bank	(785) 242-3600
Landmark National Bank	(785) 565-2000
Lyons Federal Bank	(620) 257-2316
New Century Bank	(785) 527-2772
Peoples Bank	(620) 582-2166
Peoples Bank and Trust Co.	(620) 241-2100
Silver Lake Bank	(785) 232-0102

Kansas

Name	Telephone
Simmons Bank	(870) 541-1000
Southwind Bank	(785) 885-4234
State Bank of Downs	(785) 454-3323
Stockgrowers State Bank	(620) 635-4032
Swedish-American State Bank	(785) 374-4231
The Bank of Tescott	(785) 283-4217
The Bennington State Bank	(785) 827-5522
The Citizens State Bank	(620) 836-2888
The Citizens State Bank	(785) 562-2186
The Citizens State Bank	(620) 345-6317
The Citizens State Bank of Cheney, Kansas	(316) 542-3142
The Farmers State Bank of Blue Mound	(913) 756-2221
The First National Bank of Hutchinson	(620) 663-1521
The First National Bank of Louisburg	(913) 837-5191
The First State Bank of Healy	(620) 398-2215
The First State Bank of Ransom	(785) 731-2261
Union Bank and Trust Co.	(402) 323-1828
United Bank & Trust	(785) 562-2333
Valley State Bank	(620) 488-2211

Kentucky

Rating: A

Name	Telephone
Cumberland Security Bank, Inc.	(606) 679-9361
Edmonton State Bank	(270) 432-3231
Guardian Savings Bank	(513) 942-3500
Jackson County Bank	(606) 287-8484
Kentucky Farmers Bank Corp.	(606) 929-5000
Magnolia Bank, Inc	(270) 324-3226
Planters Bank, Inc.	(270) 886-9030
Republic Bank & Trust Co.	(502) 584-3600
Taylor County Bank	(270) 465-4196
The Paducah Bank and Trust Co.	(270) 575-5700
United Citizens Bank of Southern Kentucky, Inc.	(270) 384-2265
United Community Bank of W Kentucky	(270) 389-3232

Rating: A-

Name	Telephone
Armed Forces Bank, N.A.	(913) 682-9090
Bank of Edmonson County	(270) 597-2175
Citizens Deposit Bank of Arlington, Inc.	(270) 655-6921
City National Bank of West Virginia	(304) 769-1100
Farmers Bank and Trust Co.	(270) 365-5526
First Financial Bank, N.A.	(812) 238-6000
First United Bank and Trust Co., Inc.	(270) 821-5555
Franklin Bank & Trust Co.	(270) 586-7121
German American Bank	(812) 482-1314
PBK Bank, Inc	(606) 365-7098
Peoples Bank Mt Washington	(502) 538-7301
Stock Yards Bank & Trust Co.	(502) 582-2571
The Lincoln National Bank of Hodgenville	(270) 358-4116
The Peoples Bank	(502) 477-2244
The Sacramento Deposit Bank	(270) 736-2212
Town & Country Bank and Trust Co.	(502) 348-3911
Traditional Bank, Inc.	(859) 498-0414
United Cumberland Bank	(606) 376-5031

Rating: B+

Name	Telephone
Bank of America, N.A.	(704) 386-5681
Bank of Clarkson	(270) 242-2111
Bank of Maysville	(606) 564-4001
Bank of The Bluegrass and Trust Co.	(859) 233-4500
Bedford Loan & Deposit Bank	(502) 255-3287
Citizens Bank	(606) 256-2500
Citizens Bank of Cumberland County, Inc.	(270) 864-2323
Citizens Union Bank of Shelbyville	(502) 633-4450
Commercial Bank	(423) 869-5151
Commonwealth Bank and Trust Co.	(502) 259-2200
Elkton Bank & Trust Co.	(270) 265-9841
Farmers Bank & Trust Co.	(270) 965-3106
First Financial Bank	(513) 832-6300
First Harrison Bank	(812) 738-2198
First State Bank	(270) 547-2271
FirstBank	(615) 313-0080
Fredonia Valley Bank	(270) 545-3301
Heartland Bank	(614) 416-4601
Independence Bank of Kentucky	(270) 686-1776
Lewisburg Banking Co.	(270) 755-4818
Limestone Bank, Inc	(502) 499-4800
Meade County Bank, Inc.	(270) 422-4141
Peoples Bank of Kentucky, Inc.	(606) 845-2461
River City Bank, Inc.	(502) 585-4600
Security Bank and Trust Co.	(731) 642-6644
Security Bank and Trust Co.	(606) 564-3304
South Central Bank, Inc.	(270) 651-7466
Springfield State Bank	(859) 336-3939
Summit Community Bank, Inc.	(304) 530-1000
The Cecilian Bank	(270) 862-3294
The Citizens Bank	(270) 236-2525
The Citizens National Bank of Somerset	(606) 679-6341
The Farmers National Bank of Lebanon	(270) 692-3177
The First National Bank of Grayson	(606) 474-2000
Truist Bank	(336) 733-2000
United Citizens Bank & Trust Co.	(502) 532-7392
United Southern Bank	(270) 885-0056
WesBanco Bank, Inc.	(304) 234-9419
Woodforest National Bank	(832) 375-2505

Louisiana

Rating: A

Name	Telephone
First National Bank of Louisiana	(337) 783-4014
FSNB, N.A.	(580) 357-9880
Rayne State Bank & Trust Co.	(337) 334-3191

Rating: A-

Name	Telephone
BOM Bank	(318) 352-3060
First American Bank and Trust	(225) 265-2265
First National Bank USA	(985) 785-8411
Guaranty Bank and Trust Co.	(225) 638-8621
Gulf Coast Bank	(337) 893-7733
Peoples B&T Co. of Pointe Coupee Parish	(225) 638-3713
Red River Bank	(318) 561-4000
Resource Bank	(985) 801-1800
South Louisiana Bank	(985) 851-3434
The Evangeline Bank and Trust Co.	(337) 363-5541

Rating: B+

Name	Telephone
American Bank & Trust Co.	(337) 948-3056
BancorpSouth Bank	(662) 680-2000
Bank of Sunset & Trust Co.	(337) 662-5222
BankPlus	(662) 247-1811
Beauregard Federal Savings Bank	(337) 463-4493
Citizens National Bank, N.A.	(318) 747-6000
Cross Keys Bank	(318) 766-3246
Exchange Bank and Trust Co.	(318) 352-8141
Feliciana Bank & Trust Co.	(225) 683-8565
Fidelity Bank	(504) 569-8640
Franklin State Bank & Trust Co.	(318) 435-3711
Guaranty Bank & Trust Co. of Delhi	(318) 878-3703
Hodge Bank & Trust Co.	(318) 259-7362
Home Bank, N.A.	(337) 237-1960
Home Federal Bank	(318) 841-1170
Jonesboro State Bank	(318) 259-4411
Mississippi River Bank	(504) 392-1111
Sabine State Bank and Trust Co.	(318) 256-7000
Southern Heritage Bank	(318) 339-8505
Synergy Bank	(985) 851-3341
Tensas State Bank	(318) 467-5401
The Bank	(337) 824-0033
The Cottonport Bank	(318) 253-9612
United Community Bank	(985) 537-5283
Woodforest National Bank	(832) 375-2505

Maine

Name	Telephone
Rating: A	
Bath Savings Institution	(207) 442-7711
Kennebec Savings Bank	(207) 622-5801
Norway Savings Bank	(207) 743-7986
Rating: A-	
Camden National Bank	(207) 236-8821
Machias Savings Bank	(207) 255-3347
Partners Bank of New England	(207) 324-2285
Rating: B+	
Bank of America, N.A.	(704) 386-5681
Franklin Savings Bank	(207) 778-3339
KeyBank N.A.	(216) 689-3000
NBT Bank, N.A.	(607) 337-6416

Maryland

Name	Telephone
Rating: A	
Calvin B. Taylor Banking Co.	(410) 641-1700
Rating: A-	
Bank of Ocean City	(410) 213-0173
Cathay Bank	(213) 625-4791
Clear Mountain Bank, Inc.	(304) 379-2265
EagleBank	(240) 497-2075
Essex Bank	(804) 419-4329
Presidential Bank, FSB	(301) 652-1616
Primis Bank	(804) 528-4754
Queenstown Bank of Maryland	(410) 827-8881
Severn Savings Bank, FSB	(410) 260-2000
Rating: B+	
ACNB Bank	(717) 334-3161
Atlantic Union Bank	(804) 327-5720
Bank of America, N.A.	(704) 386-5681
BayVanguard Bank	(410) 477-5000
First-Citizens Bank & Trust Co.	(919) 716-7050
Firstrust Savings Bank	(610) 238-5001
Fulton Bank, N.A.	(717) 291-2499
FVCbank	(703) 436-4740
John Marshall Bank	(703) 584-0840
Shore United Bank	(410) 822-1400
Truist Bank	(336) 733-2000
United Bank	(703) 556-0900
WesBanco Bank, Inc.	(304) 234-9419
Woodforest National Bank	(832) 375-2505

Massachusetts

Rating: A

Name	Telephone
Bank of New England	(603) 894-5700
Cape Ann Savings Bank	(978) 283-0246
Leader Bank, N.A.	(781) 646-3900
MutualOne Bank	(508) 820-4000
Northern Bank & Trust Co.	(781) 937-5400

Rating: A-

Name	Telephone
Boston Trust Walden Co.	(617) 726-7250
Cathay Bank	(213) 625-4791
Dedham Institution for Savings	(781) 329-6700
East West Bank	(626) 768-6000
HarborOne Bank	(508) 895-1000
Hingham Institution for Savings	(781) 749-2200
Mechanics Cooperative Bank	(508) 823-7744
NorthEast Community Bank	(914) 684-2500
Norwood Co-operative Bank	(781) 762-1800
Patriot Community Bank	(781) 935-3318
Rockland Trust Co.	(781) 982-6110
Salem Five Cents Savings Bank	(978) 745-5555

Rating: B+

Name	Telephone
Bank of America, N.A.	(704) 386-5681
Cambridge Trust Co.	(617) 876-5500
Community Bank, N.A.	(315) 445-2282
East Boston Savings Bank	(978) 977-6088
Eastern Bank	(617) 897-1101
Everett Co-operative Bank	(617) 387-1110
KeyBank N.A.	(216) 689-3000
Martha's Vineyard Bank	(774) 310-2001
MountainOne Bank	(855) 444-6861
National Grand Bank of Marblehead	(781) 631-6000
NBT Bank, N.A.	(607) 337-6416
Northmark Bank	(978) 686-9100
Salisbury Bank and Trust Co.	(860) 435-9801
Silicon Valley Bank	(408) 654-7400
The Bank of Canton	(781) 828-1690
The Lowell Five Cent Savings Bank	(978) 452-1300
The Northern Trust Co.	(312) 630-6000
The Provident Bank	(877) 487-2977
TrustCo Bank	(518) 377-3311
Webster Bank, N.A.	(203) 328-8110

Michigan

Rating: A

Name	Telephone
Tri-County Bank	(810) 346-2745
University Bank	(734) 741-5858

Rating: A-

Name	Telephone
1st Source Bank	(574) 235-2000
Alerus Financial, N.A.	(701) 795-3369
Bank of Ann Arbor	(734) 662-1600
Century Bank and Trust	(517) 278-1500
Chelsea State Bank	(734) 475-1355
Farmers State Bank	(260) 463-7111
First Merchants Bank	(765) 747-1500
First National Bank in Howell	(517) 546-3150
Macatawa Bank	(616) 820-1444
Mercantile Bank of Michigan	(616) 242-7760
Northpointe Bank	(616) 940-9400
Peoples State Bank of Munising	(906) 387-2006
Upper Peninsula State Bank	(906) 789-7000

Rating: B+

Name	Telephone
Alden State Bank	(231) 331-4481
Bank of America, N.A.	(704) 386-5681
Charlevoix State Bank	(231) 547-4411
ChoiceOne Bank	(616) 887-7366
Comerica Bank	(214) 462-4000
Exchange State Bank	(810) 657-9333
First Community Bank	(231) 526-2114
First National Bank of America	(517) 351-2660
Flagstar Bank, FSB	(248) 312-5400
Horizon Bank	(219) 874-9245
Independent Bank	(616) 363-1207
KeyBank N.A.	(216) 689-3000
mBank	(906) 341-8401
Nicolet National Bank	(920) 430-1400
Old Mission Bank	(906) 635-9910
Southern Michigan Bank & Trust	(517) 279-5500
Sterling Bank and Trust, FSB	(248) 355-2400
Superior National Bank	(906) 482-0404
The Northern Trust Co.	(312) 630-6000
The Port Austin State Bank	(989) 738-5235
The State Bank	(810) 629-2263

Minnesota

Rating: A+

Name	Telephone
Bank of Alma	(608) 685-4461
Vermillion State Bank	(651) 437-4433

Rating: A

Name	Telephone
Charter Bank	(715) 832-4254
Farmers Trust & Savings Bank	(641) 562-2696
Fidelity Bank	(952) 831-6600
First State Bank Southwest	(507) 376-9747
Lake Central Bank	(320) 274-8216
Liberty Bank Minnesota	(320) 252-2841
Manufacturers Bank & Trust Co.	(641) 585-2825
PrinsBank	(320) 978-6351
State Bank of Wheaton	(320) 563-8142

Rating: A-

Name	Telephone
1st United Bank	(507) 334-2201
21st Century Bank	(763) 479-2178
Alerus Financial, N.A.	(701) 795-3369
American Bank & Trust	(605) 352-9122
American Heritage National Bank	(320) 732-6131
Arcadian Bank	(507) 845-2233
Bell Bank	(701) 298-1500
Bridgewater Bank	(952) 893-6868
Center National Bank	(320) 693-3255
Citizens State Bank of Roseau	(218) 463-2135
Community First Bank	(218) 564-4171
Community Resource Bank	(507) 645-4441
Eagle Bank	(320) 634-4545
ESB Bank	(507) 725-3329
Farmers & Merchants Savings Bank	(563) 927-4475
First Bank Blue Earth	(507) 526-3241
First Citizens Bank	(641) 423-1600
First National Bank	(605) 482-8293
First National Bank Minnesota	(507) 931-4000
First National Bank North	(218) 547-1160
First State Bank of Le Center	(507) 357-2225
First State Bank of Sauk Centre	(320) 352-5771
FM BANK	(320) 564-2111
Great Southern Bank	(417) 895-5234
Home Federal Savings Bank	(507) 535-1309
HomeTown Bank	(507) 637-1000
Janesville State Bank	(507) 234-5108
KodaBank	(701) 454-3317
Minnwest Bank	(507) 637-5731
National Bank of Commerce	(715) 394-5531
North American Banking Co.	(651) 636-9654
North Shore Bank of Commerce	(218) 722-4784
Northeast Bank	(612) 379-8811
Northview Bank	(320) 245-5261
ONB Bank	(507) 280-0621
Premier Bank Minnesota	(651) 463-4440
Red Rock Bank	(507) 648-3871
Saint Clair State Bank (Inc.)	(507) 245-3636
Security State Bank of Marine	(651) 433-2424
State Bank of Danvers	(320) 843-3828
Stearns Bank N.A.	(320) 253-6607
Stearns Bank of Holdingford, N.A.	(320) 746-2261
Stearns Bank of Upsala, N.A.	(320) 573-2111
The Citizens National Bank of Park Rapids	(218) 732-3393
The First National Bank of Bemidji	(218) 751-2430
The First National Bank of Henning	(218) 367-2735
The First National Bank of Moose Lake	(218) 485-4441
United Farmers State Bank	(507) 582-3448
VisionBank	(952) 920-8400

Rating: B+

Name	Telephone
Alliance Bank	(651) 229-0070
American Federal Bank	(701) 461-5900
American National Bank	(402) 399-5000
American National Bank of Minnesota	(218) 824-7900
Bank Forward	(701) 769-2121
Bank Midwest	(712) 336-0505
Bank of America, N.A.	(704) 386-5681
Bank of Maple Plain	(763) 479-1931
Bank of Zumbrota	(507) 732-7555
Bremer Bank, N.A.	(651) 288-3751
Castle Rock Bank	(651) 463-7590
Citizens Bank Minnesota	(507) 354-3165
CornerStone State Bank	(507) 364-2265
F & M Community Bank, N.A.	(507) 765-3823
Farmers & Merchants State Bank	(218) 385-2300
Farmers and Merchants State Bank	(320) 468-6422
Farmers State Bank of Hamel	(763) 478-6611
Farmers State Bank of Trimont	(507) 639-9921
First Bank & Trust	(605) 696-2265
First Farmers & Merchants Bank	(507) 263-3030
First Financial Bank in Winnebago	(507) 893-3155
First Independent Bank	(507) 823-4391
First Minnetonka City Bank	(952) 935-8663
First Security Bank - Canby	(507) 223-7231
First Security Bank - Hendricks	(507) 275-3141
First Security Bank - Sleepy Eye	(507) 794-3911
First State Bank and Trust	(651) 439-5195

Minnesota

Name	Telephone
First State Bank of Wyoming	(651) 462-7611
Frandsen Bank & Trust	(507) 744-2361
Gateway Bank	(651) 209-4800
Highland Bank	(763) 497-2131
Home State Bank	(320) 593-2001
Lake Area Bank	(651) 257-1117
Lake Community Bank	(952) 473-7347
Lake Elmo Bank	(651) 777-8365
Merchants Bank, N.A.	(507) 457-1100
Midwest Bank	(218) 847-4771
Minnesota National Bank	(320) 352-5211
MinnStar Bank N.A.	(507) 726-2137
North Star Bank	(651) 489-8811
Northern State Bank	(715) 682-2772
Northwoods Bank of Minnesota	(218) 732-7221
Park State Bank	(218) 722-3500
Pine Island Bank	(507) 356-8328
Platinum Bank	(651) 332-5200
Premier Bank	(651) 777-7700
Prime Security Bank	(218) 436-2151
Roundbank	(507) 835-4220
Saint Martin National Bank	(320) 548-3555
Security Bank & Trust Co.	(320) 864-3107
Security Bank Minnesota	(507) 373-1481
Security Bank USA	(218) 751-1510
Security State Bank of Aitkin	(218) 927-3765
Security State Bank of Oklee	(218) 796-5157
Security State Bank of Wanamingo, Inc.	(507) 824-2265
Sentry Bank	(320) 363-7721
Sherburne State Bank	(763) 261-4200
The Bank of Elk River	(763) 441-1000
The First National Bank of Fairfax	(507) 426-7242
The First National Bank of Le Center	(507) 357-2273
The First National Bank of Milaca	(320) 983-3101
The First National Bank of Waseca	(507) 835-2740
The Northern Trust Co.	(312) 630-6000
The Wanda State Bank	(507) 550-1678
Think Mutual Bank	(507) 288-3425
Ultima Bank Minnesota	(218) 938-4144
Viking Bank, N.A.	(320) 762-0236
Wadena State Bank	(218) 631-1860
Welcome State Bank	(507) 728-8251
West Bank	(515) 222-2300
WNB Financial, N.A.	(507) 454-8800
Woodlands National Bank	(320) 384-6191

Name	Telephone

Mississippi

Name	Telephone
Rating: A	
FSNB, N.A.	(580) 357-9880
Rating: A-	
Bank of Commerce	(662) 453-4142
BNA Bank	(662) 534-8171
Farmers and Merchants Bank	(662) 365-1200
FNB Picayune Bank	(601) 749-3200
Pike National Bank	(601) 684-7575
RiverHills Bank	(601) 636-1445
The Citizens National Bank of Meridian	(601) 484-5269
The Jefferson Bank	(662) 332-7545
Rating: B+	
BancorpSouth Bank	(662) 680-2000
Bank of Forest	(601) 469-3663
Bank of Franklin	(601) 384-2305
Bank of Kilmichael	(662) 262-7844
BankPlus	(662) 247-1811
Cadence Bank, N.A.	(800) 636-7622
Commerce Bank	(662) 286-5577
First Choice Bank	(662) 489-1631
First Financial Bank	(870) 863-7000
First National Bank of Clarksdale	(662) 627-3261
First Security Bank	(662) 563-9311
First Southern Bank	(601) 736-6378
First State Bank	(601) 735-3124
Grand Bank for Savings, F.S.B.	(601) 264-1467
Home Bank, N.A.	(337) 237-1960
Merchants and Planters Bank	(601) 857-8044
PriorityOne Bank	(601) 849-3311
Renasant Bank	(800) 680-1601
The Bank of Vernon	(205) 695-7141
The Cleveland State Bank	(662) 843-9461
Truist Bank	(336) 733-2000
Trustmark National Bank	(601) 208-5111
Woodforest National Bank	(832) 375-2505

Missouri

Rating: A

Name	Telephone
Adrian Bank	(816) 297-2194
Bank of Saint Elizabeth	(573) 493-2313
Cass Commercial Bank	(314) 506-5544
Central Bank of Kansas City	(816) 483-1210
Citizens' Bank of Charleston	(573) 683-3373
First State Bank of St. Charles, Missouri	(636) 940-5555
HNB National Bank	(573) 221-0050
Home Exchange Bank	(660) 684-6114
Legends Bank	(573) 897-2204
Lindell Bank & Trust Co.	(314) 645-7700
NBKC Bank	(913) 905-2100
North American Savings Bank, FSB	(866) 599-9800
Peoples Community Bank	(573) 224-3267
Senath State Bank	(573) 738-2646
St. Clair County State Bank	(417) 646-8128
The Bank of Advance	(573) 722-3517
The Bank of Grain Valley	(816) 373-1905
The Bank of Old Monroe	(636) 665-5601
The Citizens Bank of Edina	(660) 397-2266
The Nodaway Valley Bank	(660) 562-3232
Town and Country Bank Midwest	(217) 222-0015

Rating: A-

Name	Telephone
Academy Bank, N.A.	(877) 712-2265
Alliant Bank	(660) 291-3041
Armed Forces Bank, N.A.	(913) 682-9090
Bank Northwest	(816) 583-2154
Bank of Monticello	(573) 767-5264
Bank of New Madrid	(573) 748-5551
Bloomsdale Bank	(573) 483-2514
BTC Bank	(660) 425-7285
Busey Bank	(217) 351-6500
Central Bank of Lake of the Ozarks	(573) 348-2761
Citizens Bank of Eldon	(573) 392-3381
Commerce Bank	(855) 659-1656
Community Bank of El Dorado Springs	(417) 876-6811
Community Bank of Missouri	(816) 470-2265
Community First Banking Co.	(417) 255-2265
Concordia Bank	(660) 463-7911
Enterprise Bank & Trust	(314) 725-5500
Exchange Bank & Trust	(913) 367-6000
Exchange Bank of Missouri	(660) 248-3388
Farmers Bank of Northern Missouri	(660) 947-2474
First Bank	(314) 995-8700
First State Bank and Trust Co., Inc.	(573) 333-1700
First State Community Bank	(573) 756-4547
Great Southern Bank	(417) 895-5234
Investors Community Bank	(660) 646-3733
Legacy Bank & Trust Co.	(417) 753-4343
Midwest Independent BankersBank	(573) 636-9555
Montrose Savings Bank	(660) 693-4424
NBH Bank	(720) 554-6650
New Era Bank	(573) 783-3336
Northeast Missouri State Bank	(660) 665-6161
Pinnacle Bank	(402) 434-3127
Putnam County State Bank	(660) 947-2477
Security Bank of Kansas City	(913) 281-3165
Southern Bank	(573) 778-1800
Springfield First Community Bank	(417) 882-8111
Sterling Bank	(573) 778-3333
The Bank of Missouri	(573) 547-6541
The Missouri Bank	(636) 456-3441
Town & Country Bank	(573) 729-3155
Wells Bank	(816) 858-2121
Wood & Huston Bank	(660) 886-6825

Rating: B+

Name	Telephone
Alliance Bank	(573) 334-1010
BancorpSouth Bank	(662) 680-2000
Bank of America, N.A.	(704) 386-5681
Bank of Blue Valley	(913) 234-2334
Bank of Odessa	(816) 230-4512
Bank of Versailles	(573) 378-4626
BOKF, N.A.	(918) 588-6000
Central Bank of Boone County	(573) 874-8100
Central Bank of Branson	(417) 334-4125
Central Bank of Moberly	(660) 263-1234
Central Bank of Oklahoma	(918) 477-7400
Central Bank of Sedalia	(660) 827-3333
Central Bank of St. Louis	(314) 862-8300
Central Bank of the Midwest	(816) 525-5300
Central Bank of the Ozarks	(417) 881-3100
Central Bank of Warrensburg	(660) 429-2101
Citizens Bank of Rogersville	(417) 753-2836
Citizens Community Bank	(660) 834-4725
CNB St. Louis Bank	(314) 645-0666
Commercial Bank of Oak Grove	(816) 690-4416
Commercial Trust Co. of Fayette	(660) 248-2222
Community Bank of Marshall	(660) 886-9621
Community Bank of Pleasant Hill	(816) 540-2525
Community Bank of Raymore	(816) 322-2100
Community Point Bank	(573) 782-3881
Community State Bank of Missouri	(573) 324-2233

Missouri

Name	Telephone
Connections Bank	(660) 665-7703
Country Club Bank	(816) 931-4060
CS Bank	(479) 253-2265
Farmers and Merchants Bank of St. Clair	(636) 629-2225
First Mid Bank & Trust, N.A.	(217) 234-7454
First Midwest Bank of Poplar Bluff	(573) 785-8461
First Missouri State Bank of Cape County	(573) 334-9000
First-Citizens Bank & Trust Co.	(919) 716-7050
Focus Bank	(573) 683-3712
Freedom Bank of Southern Missouri	(417) 846-1719
Great American Bank	(785) 838-9704
Independent Farmers Bank	(816) 449-2182
Jefferson Bank of Missouri	(573) 634-0888
Kearney Trust Co.	(816) 628-6666
La Monte Community Bank	(660) 347-5656
Lamar Bank and Trust Co.	(417) 682-3348
Metz Banking Co.	(417) 667-4550
Mid America Bank	(573) 635-0019
MRV Banks	(573) 883-8222
Parkside Financial Bank and Trust	(314) 290-8600
Peoples Bank	(573) 885-2511
Peoples Bank of Wyaconda	(660) 727-2941
Pony Express Bank	(816) 781-9200
Progressive Ozark Bank	(573) 729-4146
Royal Banks of Missouri	(314) 212-1500
Security Bank of Southwest Missouri	(417) 847-4794
Simmons Bank	(870) 541-1000
Stifel Bank and Trust	(314) 342-2000
Stockmens Bank	(719) 955-2800
Sullivan Bank	(573) 468-3191
The Central Trust Bank	(573) 634-1302
The Citizens-Farmers Bank of Cole Camp	(660) 668-4416
The Maries County Bank	(573) 422-3323
The Mercantile Bank of Louisiana, Missouri	(573) 754-6221
The Northern Trust Co.	(312) 630-6000
The Seymour Bank	(417) 935-2293
The Tipton Latham Bank, N.A.	(660) 433-2004
TPNB Bank	(660) 327-4181
United Security Bank	(573) 386-2233
West Plains Bank and Trust Co.	(417) 256-2147

Montana

Name	Telephone
Rating: A	
Independence Bank	(406) 265-1241
The Bank of Commerce	(208) 525-9108
Yellowstone Bank	(406) 628-7951
Rating: A-	
1st Bank	(406) 436-2611
Bank of Montana	(406) 829-2662
Eagle Bank	(406) 883-2940
First Community Bank	(406) 228-8231
First Federal Bank & Trust	(307) 674-0464
Glacier Bank	(406) 756-4200
Opportunity Bank of Montana	(406) 442-3080
Stockman Bank of Montana	(406) 234-8420
Rating: B+	
American Bank	(406) 587-1234
Belt Valley Bank	(406) 277-3314
Citizens Bank & Trust Co.	(406) 932-5311
Farmers State Bank	(406) 642-3431
First Interstate Bank	(406) 255-5000
First Security Bank of Deer Lodge	(406) 846-2300
First State Bank of Forsyth	(406) 346-2112
Madison Valley Bank	(406) 682-4215
Manhattan Bank	(406) 284-3255
The First State Bank of Shelby	(406) 434-5567
TrailWest Bank	(406) 273-2400
Valley Bank of Kalispell	(406) 752-7123

Nebraska

Name	Telephone
Rating: A	
American Interstate Bank	(402) 289-2551
First Savings Bank	(605) 763-2009
First State Bank	(308) 569-2311
Heritage Bank	(308) 583-2262
Homestead Bank	(308) 784-2000
Madison County Bank	(402) 454-6511
Town & Country Bank	(308) 452-3225
West Gate Bank	(402) 434-3456
Rating: A-	
Adams State Bank	(402) 988-2255
Bank of Dixon County	(402) 755-2224
Bank of Elgin	(402) 843-2228
Bank of Prague	(402) 663-4317
Cattle Bank & Trust	(402) 643-3636
Central National Bank	(785) 238-4114
Charter West Bank	(402) 372-5147
Clarkson Bank	(402) 892-3411
Commercial State Bank	(308) 799-3995
Exchange Bank	(308) 237-7711
Farmers and Merchants State Bank	(402) 373-4321
First State Bank	(308) 632-4158
First State Bank & Trust Co.	(402) 721-2500
First Westroads Bank, Inc.	(402) 330-7200
FirstBank of Nebraska	(402) 443-4117
FirsTier Bank	(308) 235-4633
Five Points Bank	(308) 384-5350
Five Points Bank of Hastings	(402) 462-2228
Great Southern Bank	(417) 895-5234
Horizon Bank	(402) 786-2555
Jones Bank	(402) 643-3602
Minden Exchange Bank & Trust Co.	(308) 832-1600
Nebraska State Bank	(308) 772-3234
Pinnacle Bank	(402) 434-3127
Pinnacle Bank - Wyoming	(402) 697-5990
Platte Valley Bank	(402) 652-3221
Points West Community Bank	(970) 686-0878
Scribner Bank	(402) 664-2561
Security Bank	(402) 256-3247
South Central State Bank	(402) 756-8601
State Nebraska Bank & Trust	(402) 375-1130
Two Rivers Bank	(402) 426-9500
West Plains Bank	(402) 387-2381
Rating: B+	
Access Bank	(402) 763-6008
Adams Bank & Trust	(308) 284-4071
American National Bank	(402) 399-5000
Auburn State Bank	(402) 274-4342
Bank of Hartington	(402) 254-3994
Bruning Bank	(402) 353-2555
Cedar Security Bank	(402) 357-3508
CerescoBank	(402) 665-3431
Chambers State Bank	(402) 482-5222
Commercial Bank of Nelson	(402) 225-3381
Countryside Bank	(402) 828-3210
Elkhorn Valley Bank & Trust	(402) 371-0722
F&M Bank	(402) 372-5331
F&M Bank	(402) 245-2491
First Bank and Trust of Fullerton	(308) 536-2492
First State Bank	(402) 337-0323
First State Bank	(308) 876-2451
Heartland Bank	(402) 759-3114
Lincoln FSB of Nebraska	(402) 474-1400
Midwest Bank	(402) 329-6221
Northwest Bank	(712) 580-4100
Premier Bank	(402) 558-8000
Security National Bank of Omaha	(402) 344-7300
State Bank of Scotia	(308) 245-4201
Stockmens Bank	(719) 955-2800
The First National Bank of Gordon	(308) 282-0050
The Hershey State Bank	(308) 368-5555
Union Bank and Trust Co.	(402) 323-1828
Washington County Bank	(402) 426-2111
Waypoint Bank	(308) 784-2515

Nevada

Rating: A

Name	Telephone
Bank of George	(702) 851-4200
First Savings Bank	(605) 763-2009
First Security Bank of Nevada	(702) 853-0900
Royal Business Bank	(213) 627-9888

Rating: A-

Name	Telephone
American First National Bank	(713) 596-2888
Armed Forces Bank, N.A.	(913) 682-9090
Cathay Bank	(213) 625-4791
Eaglemark Savings Bank	(775) 886-3000
East West Bank	(626) 768-6000
Enterprise Bank & Trust	(314) 725-5500
Glacier Bank	(406) 756-4200
Meadows Bank	(702) 471-2265
Pacific Premier Bank	(949) 864-8000
Plumas Bank	(530) 283-7305
Western Alliance Bank	(602) 389-3500
Wilmington Savings Fund Society, FSB	(302) 571-7080

Rating: B+

Name	Telephone
Bank of America, N.A.	(704) 386-5681
The Northern Trust Co.	(312) 630-6000
Town & Country Bank	(702) 252-8777
Washington Federal Bank, N.A.	(206) 204-3446
Wells Fargo National Bank West	(702) 952-6650
Zions BanCorp., N.A.	(801) 844-7637

New Hampshire

Name	Telephone
Rating: A	
Bank of New England	(603) 894-5700
Rating: A-	
Camden National Bank	(207) 236-8821
Partners Bank of New England	(207) 324-2285
Rating: B+	
Bank of America, N.A.	(704) 386-5681
Cambridge Trust Co.	(617) 876-5500
Eastern Bank	(617) 897-1101
NBT Bank, N.A.	(607) 337-6416
The Lowell Five Cent Savings Bank	(978) 452-1300
The Provident Bank	(877) 487-2977

New Jersey

Rating: A

Name	Telephone
AMG National Trust Bank	(303) 694-2190
Bessemer Trust Co.	(212) 708-9100
Metro City Bank	(770) 455-4989
Pacific City Bank	(213) 210-2000
Parke Bank	(856) 256-2500
Royal Business Bank	(213) 627-9888

Rating: A-

Name	Telephone
Cathay Bank	(213) 625-4791
Cenlar FSB	(609) 883-3900
CTBC Bank Corp. (USA)	(424) 277-4612
First Commerce Bank	(732) 364-0032
First IC Bank	(770) 451-7200
NewBank	(718) 353-9100
Wilmington Savings Fund Society, FSB	(302) 571-7080

Rating: B+

Name	Telephone
Bank of America, N.A.	(704) 386-5681
Cross River Bank	(201) 808-7000
First Bank	(877) 821-2265
Firstrust Savings Bank	(610) 238-5001
Fulton Bank, N.A.	(717) 291-2499
Habib American Bank	(212) 532-4444
Lakeland Bank	(973) 697-2000
Lusitania Savings Bank	(973) 344-5125
Northfield Bank	(732) 499-7200
The Bank of Princeton	(609) 921-1700
The Bryn Mawr Trust Co.	(610) 581-4839
Truist Bank	(336) 733-2000
TrustCo Bank	(518) 377-3311
Unity Bank	(908) 730-7630

New Mexico

Name	Telephone
Rating: A	
Citizens Bank of Las Cruces	(575) 647-4100
Farmers & Stockmens Bank	(575) 374-8301
First American Bank	(575) 746-8000
First New Mexico Bank	(575) 546-2691
First New Mexico Bank of Silver City	(575) 388-3121
First New Mexico Bank, Las Cruces	(575) 556-3000
First Savings Bank	(605) 763-2009
Western Bank	(575) 542-3521
Rating: A-	
Bank of Colorado	(970) 206-1160
Centinel Bank of Taos	(575) 758-6700
Citizens Bank	(806) 350-5600
City Bank	(806) 792-7101
CNB Bank	(575) 234-2500
Enterprise Bank & Trust	(314) 725-5500
First National Bank	(575) 437-4880
Morgan Stanley Bank, N.A.	(801) 236-3600
NBH Bank	(720) 554-6650
The Bank of Clovis	(575) 769-9000
The Citizens Bank	(505) 599-0100
The Citizens Bank of Clovis	(575) 769-1911
Valley Bank of Commerce	(575) 623-2265
WestStar Bank	(915) 532-1000
Rating: B+	
American Heritage Bank	(575) 762-2800
Bank of America, N.A.	(704) 386-5681
BOKF, N.A.	(918) 588-6000
Century Bank	(505) 995-1200
First National Bank Texas	(254) 554-4236
First-Citizens Bank & Trust Co.	(919) 716-7050
James Polk Stone Community Bank	(575) 356-6601
Lea County State Bank	(575) 397-4511
Main Bank	(505) 880-1700
New Mexico Bank & Trust	(505) 830-8100
United Business Bank	(925) 476-1800
Washington Federal Bank, N.A.	(206) 204-3446
Western Bank of Clovis	(575) 769-1975
Western Commerce Bank	(575) 887-6686
Zions BanCorp., N.A.	(801) 844-7637

New York

Name	Telephone
Rating: A+	
Esquire Bank, N.A.	(516) 535-2002
Rating: A	
Amerasia Bank	(718) 463-3600
Bessemer Trust Co., N.A.	(212) 708-9100
Fulton Savings Bank	(315) 592-4201
Genesee Regional Bank	(585) 249-1540
Metro City Bank	(770) 455-4989
Pacific City Bank	(213) 210-2000
Royal Business Bank	(213) 627-9888
Rating: A-	
Armed Forces Bank, N.A.	(913) 682-9090
Bank OZK	(501) 978-2265
Cathay Bank	(213) 625-4791
Centennial Bank	(501) 328-4663
CTBC Bank Corp. (USA)	(424) 277-4612
East West Bank	(626) 768-6000
First IC Bank	(770) 451-7200
Hamlin Bank and Trust Co.	(814) 887-5555
Morgan Stanley Private Bank, N.A.	(212) 762-1803
NewBank	(718) 353-9100
NorthEast Community Bank	(914) 684-2500
Preferred Bank	(213) 891-1188
The First National Bank of Groton	(607) 898-5871
The Westchester Bank	(914) 368-9919
Tioga State Bank, N.A.	(607) 589-7000
Watertown Savings Bank	(315) 788-7100
Rating: B+	
Alpine Capital Bank	(212) 328-2555
American Community Bank	(516) 609-2900
Bank of America, N.A.	(704) 386-5681
Bank of Utica	(315) 797-2700
Citizens & Northern Bank	(570) 724-3411
Community Bank, N.A.	(315) 445-2282
Cross River Bank	(201) 808-7000
Deutsche Bank Trust Co. Americas	(212) 250-2500
Five Star Bank	(585) 786-1100
Glens Falls National Bank and Trust Co.	(518) 793-4121
Habib American Bank	(212) 532-4444
Hanover Community Bank	(516) 248-4868
KeyBank N.A.	(216) 689-3000
Lakeland Bank	(973) 697-2000
Maspeth Federal S&L Assn.	(718) 335-1300
Metropolitan Commercial Bank	(212) 659-0600
NBT Bank, N.A.	(607) 337-6416
Northfield Bank	(732) 499-7200
Peoples Security Bank and Trust Co.	(570) 955-1700
Salisbury Bank and Trust Co.	(860) 435-9801
Saratoga National Bank and Trust Co.	(518) 583-3114
Signature Bank	(646) 822-1500
Sterling Bank and Trust, FSB	(248) 355-2400
The Bank of Greene County	(518) 943-2600
The Northern Trust Co.	(312) 630-6000
Tompkins Trust Co.	(607) 273-3210
TrustCo Bank	(518) 377-3311
Webster Bank, N.A.	(203) 328-8110
Woodforest National Bank	(832) 375-2505

North Carolina

Name	Telephone
Rating: A	
AMG National Trust Bank	(303) 694-2190
FSNB, N.A.	(580) 357-9880
Surrey Bank & Trust	(336) 783-3900
Rating: A-	
Bank OZK	(501) 978-2265
Benchmark Community Bank	(434) 676-9054
BlueHarbor Bank	(704) 662-7700
Farmers and Merchants Bank	(704) 633-1772
First Bank	(910) 692-6222
First Carolina Bank	(252) 937-2152
Pinnacle Bank	(615) 744-3705
Providence Bank	(252) 443-9477
Roxboro Savings Bank, SSB	(336) 599-2137
Southern First Bank	(864) 679-9000
The Fidelity Bank	(919) 552-2242
TowneBank	(757) 638-7500
United Community Bank	(864) 255-7960
Wake Forest Federal S&L Assn.	(919) 556-5146
Rating: B+	
American National Bank and Trust Co.	(434) 792-5111
Ameris Bank	(404) 814-8114
Atlantic Union Bank	(804) 327-5720
Bank of America, N.A.	(704) 386-5681
Bank of Tennessee	(423) 378-9500
Blue Ridge Bank, N.A.	(540) 743-6521
First FSB of Lincolnton	(704) 735-0416
First Reliance Bank	(843) 656-5000
First-Citizens Bank & Trust Co.	(919) 716-7050
Lifestore Bank	(336) 246-4344
Pacific Western Bank	(310) 887-8500
Peoples Bank	(828) 464-5620
Signature Bank	(646) 822-1500
South State Bank, N.A.	(863) 551-5500
Southern Bank and Trust Co.	(919) 658-7000
Truist Bank	(336) 733-2000
United Bank	(703) 556-0900
Woodforest National Bank	(832) 375-2505

North Dakota

Rating: A

Name	Telephone
BNC National Bank	(602) 508-3760
Farmers and Merchants State Bank	(701) 256-5431
First State Bank & Trust	(701) 577-2113
Liberty State Bank	(701) 464-5421
Security First Bank of North Dakota	(701) 794-8758

Rating: A-

Name	Telephone
Alerus Financial, N.A.	(701) 795-3369
American State Bank & Trust Co	(701) 774-4100
Bell Bank	(701) 298-1500
Commercial Bank of Mott	(701) 824-2593
First Security Bank - West	(701) 873-4301
KodaBank	(701) 454-3317
Peoples State Bank	(701) 245-6407
Stock Growers Bank	(701) 724-3216

Rating: B+

Name	Telephone
American Federal Bank	(701) 461-5900
Bank Forward	(701) 769-2121
Bremer Bank, N.A.	(651) 288-3751
Dakota Community Bank & Trust, N.A.	(701) 878-4416
First State Bank of Golva	(701) 872-3656
First United Bank	(701) 284-7244
Frandsen Bank & Trust	(507) 744-2361
Grant County State Bank	(701) 622-3491
Horizon Financial Bank	(701) 682-5331
Starion Bank	(701) 223-6050
The Citizens State Bank of Finley	(701) 524-1921
The Goose River Bank	(701) 788-3110
Unison Bank	(701) 253-5600

Northern Mariana Islands

Name	Telephone
Rating: B+	
First Hawaiian Bank	(808) 525-6340

Ohio

Name	Telephone
Rating: A+	
FDS Bank	(513) 573-2265
Rating: A	
Guardian Savings Bank	(513) 942-3500
Perpetual Federal Savings Bank	(937) 653-1700
Republic Bank & Trust Co.	(502) 584-3600
Spring Valley Bank	(513) 761-6688
The Peoples Bank Co.	(419) 678-2385
The St. Henry Bank	(419) 678-2358
Union Savings Bank	(513) 247-0300
Rating: A-	
CFBank N.A.	(614) 505-5805
City National Bank of West Virginia	(304) 769-1100
Civista Bank	(419) 625-4121
Farmers Savings Bank	(330) 648-2441
First Bank of Berne	(260) 589-2151
First Bank of Ohio	(419) 448-9740
First Merchants Bank	(765) 747-1500
Liberty National Bank	(419) 634-5015
Signature Bank, N.A.	(419) 841-7773
Stock Yards Bank & Trust Co.	(502) 582-2571
Sutton Bank	(419) 426-3641
The Citizens National Bank of Bluffton	(419) 358-8040
The Croghan Colonial Bank	(419) 332-7301
The Home Loan Savings Bank	(740) 622-0444
The Republic Banking Co.	(419) 585-4111
The State Bank and Trust Co.	(419) 783-8950
The Union Bank Co.	(419) 659-2141
Unified Bank	(740) 633-0445
Rating: B+	
Bank of America, N.A.	(704) 386-5681
Buckeye Community Bank	(440) 233-8800
CBank	(513) 651-3000
CenterBank	(513) 965-8505
Eagle.Bank	(513) 574-0700
Farmers & Merchants Bank	(937) 866-2455
FCN Bank, N.A.	(765) 647-4116
First Commonwealth Bank	(724) 463-8555
First Financial Bank	(513) 832-6300
First National Bank in New Bremen	(419) 629-2761
Flagstar Bank, FSB	(248) 312-5400
Greenville National Bank	(937) 548-1114
Heartland Bank	(614) 416-4601
KeyBank N.A.	(216) 689-3000
LCNB National Bank	(513) 932-1414
Minster Bank	(419) 628-2351
Osgood State Bank	(419) 582-2681
Settlers Bank	(740) 373-9200
The Bank of Magnolia Co.	(330) 866-9392
The Cincinnatus S&L Co.	(513) 661-6903
The Citizens Bank Co.	(740) 984-2381
The Commercial & Savings Bank of Millersburg	(330) 674-9015
The Corn City State Bank	(419) 278-0015
The Farmers & Merchants State Bank	(419) 446-2501
The Farmers National Bank of Canfield	(330) 533-3341
The Hamler State Bank	(419) 274-3955
The Killbuck Savings Bank Co.	(330) 276-4881
The Middlefield Banking Co.	(440) 632-8115
The North Side Bank and Trust Co.	(513) 542-7800
The Northern Trust Co.	(312) 630-6000
The Ottoville Bank Co.	(419) 453-3313
The Waterford Commercial and Savings Bank	(740) 984-2357
Truist Bank	(336) 733-2000
United Bank	(703) 556-0900
WesBanco Bank, Inc.	(304) 234-9419
Woodforest National Bank	(832) 375-2505

Oklahoma

Rating: A

Name	Telephone
Community National Bank of Okarche	(405) 263-7491
First Bank	(580) 526-3332
First Bank of Owasso	(918) 272-5301
FSNB, N.A.	(580) 357-9880
Oklahoma Bank and Trust Co.	(580) 323-2345
The Bank of the West	(580) 661-3541
The City National B&T Co. of Lawton, Oklahoma	(866) 385-3444
The Farmers and Merchants National Bank of Fairview	(580) 227-3773
The Payne County Bank	(405) 547-2436

Rating: A-

Name	Telephone
American Bank and Trust Co.	(918) 481-3000
American Exchange Bank	(405) 756-3101
Anchor D Bank	(580) 423-7541
BancFirst	(405) 270-1000
Bank of Hydro	(405) 663-2214
Bank of the Panhandle	(580) 338-2593
Central National Bank of Poteau	(918) 647-2233
Commerce Bank	(855) 659-1656
F&M Bank	(405) 715-1100
First Bank of Okarche	(405) 263-7215
First National B&T, Elk City, Oklahoma	(580) 225-2580
First State Bank	(580) 623-4945
Great Southern Bank	(417) 895-5234
International Bank of Commerce	(405) 841-2100
Kirkpatrick Bank	(405) 341-8222
Liberty National Bank	(580) 351-2265
McClain Bank	(405) 527-6503
McCurtain County National Bank	(580) 584-6262
Prosperity Bank	(979) 543-2200
The First National Bank and Trust Co.	(405) 224-2200
The First National Bank of Fletcher	(580) 549-6106
The First National Bank of Fort Smith	(479) 788-4600
The Idabel National Bank	(580) 286-7656
The Peoples National Bank of Checotah	(918) 473-2237
The State Bank of Wynnewood	(405) 665-2001
The Stock Exchange Bank	(580) 256-3314
Welch State Bank of Welch, Okla.	(918) 788-3373

Rating: B+

Name	Telephone
Bank of America, N.A.	(704) 386-5681
Bank of Commerce	(918) 789-2567
Bank of Cordell	(580) 832-5600
Bank, N.A.	(918) 423-2265
Bank7	(405) 810-8600
BOKF, N.A.	(918) 588-6000
Carson Community Bank	(918) 696-7745
Central Bank of Oklahoma	(918) 477-7400
Community Bank	(918) 367-3343
Community Bank	(580) 327-5500
Fairview S&L Assn.	(580) 227-3735
First Bank & Trust Co.	(580) 255-1810
First Bank of Thomas	(580) 661-3515
First Bethany Bank & Trust	(405) 789-1110
First Enterprise Bank	(405) 681-0771
First Liberty Bank	(405) 608-4500
First National B&T Co. of Weatherford	(580) 772-5574
First National Bank	(918) 653-3200
First State Bank	(405) 247-2471
First-Citizens Bank & Trust Co.	(919) 716-7050
Grand Savings Bank	(918) 786-2203
Great Plains National Bank	(580) 688-3323
MidFirst Bank	(405) 767-7000
Oklahoma State Bank	(918) 256-5585
Security First National Bank of Hugo	(580) 326-9641
Security State Bank	(580) 497-3354
Seiling State Bank	(580) 922-4211
Shamrock Bank, N.A.	(580) 927-2311
Simmons Bank	(870) 541-1000
Sooner State Bank	(405) 381-2326
Southwest Bank of Weatherford	(580) 774-0900
The Exchange Bank	(918) 396-2345
The First Farmers National Bank of Waurika	(580) 228-2326
The First National B&T Co. of Broken Arrow	(918) 251-5371
The First National Bank of Hooker	(580) 652-2448
The First National Bank of Lindsay	(405) 756-4433
The First National Bank of Stigler	(918) 967-4665
The Security National Bank of Enid	(580) 234-5151
Triad Bank, N.A.	(918) 254-1444
Valor Bank	(405) 212-9800
Walters Bank and Trust Co.	(580) 875-3396

Oregon

Name	Telephone
Rating: A+	
Pioneer Trust Bank, N.A.	(503) 363-3136
Rating: A	
Willamette Valley Bank	(503) 485-2222
Rating: A-	
Bank of the Pacific	(360) 537-4052
Clackamas County Bank	(503) 668-5501
Columbia State Bank	(253) 305-1900
Pacific Premier Bank	(949) 864-8000
Riverview Community Bank	(360) 693-6650
Rating: B+	
Bank of America, N.A.	(704) 386-5681
Banner Bank	(509) 527-3636
Citizens Bank	(541) 766-2299
First Interstate Bank	(406) 255-5000
First-Citizens Bank & Trust Co.	(919) 716-7050
KeyBank N.A.	(216) 689-3000
Lewis & Clark Bank	(503) 212-3200
Northwest Bank	(208) 332-0700
Oregon Coast Bank	(541) 265-9000
People's Bank of Commerce	(541) 776-5350
Washington Federal Bank, N.A.	(206) 204-3446
Washington Trust Bank	(509) 353-4204
Zions BanCorp., N.A.	(801) 844-7637

Pennsylvania

Name	Telephone
Rating: A	
Parke Bank	(856) 256-2500
The Haverford Trust Co.	(610) 995-8700
Union Savings Bank	(513) 247-0300
Rating: A-	
Apollo Trust Co.	(724) 478-3151
First Columbia Bank & Trust Co.	(570) 784-1660
Hamlin Bank and Trust Co.	(814) 887-5555
New Tripoli Bank	(610) 298-8811
Port Richmond Savings	(215) 634-7000
PS Bank	(570) 746-1011
Slovenian S&L Assn. of Canonsburg, PA	(724) 745-5000
The Honesdale National Bank	(570) 253-3355
The National Bank of Malvern	(610) 647-0100
The Turbotville National Bank	(570) 649-5118
Wilmington Savings Fund Society, FSB	(302) 571-7080
Rating: B+	
ACNB Bank	(717) 334-3161
American Bank	(610) 366-1800
Asian Bank	(215) 592-1188
Bank of America, N.A.	(704) 386-5681
Citizens & Northern Bank	(570) 724-3411
Commercial Bank & Trust of PA	(724) 539-3501
Community Bank, N.A.	(315) 445-2282
First Bank	(877) 821-2265
First Commonwealth Bank	(724) 463-8555
First Keystone Community Bank	(570) 752-3671
Firstrust Savings Bank	(610) 238-5001
FNCB Bank	(570) 346-7667
Fulton Bank, N.A.	(717) 291-2499
KeyBank N.A.	(216) 689-3000
NBT Bank, N.A.	(607) 337-6416
Peoples Security Bank and Trust Co.	(570) 955-1700
Susquehanna Community Bank	(570) 568-6851
The Bank of Landisburg	(717) 789-3213
The Bank of Princeton	(609) 921-1700
The Bryn Mawr Trust Co.	(610) 581-4839
The Fidelity Deposit and Discount Bank	(570) 802-3081
The Muncy Bank and Trust Co.	(570) 546-2211
The Neffs National Bank	(610) 767-3875
The Northern Trust Co.	(312) 630-6000
The Philadelphia Trust Co.	(215) 979-3434
Truist Bank	(336) 733-2000
United Bank	(703) 556-0900
Unity Bank	(908) 730-7630
VIST Bank	(610) 208-0966
WesBanco Bank, Inc.	(304) 234-9419
Woodforest National Bank	(832) 375-2505

Rhode Island

Name	Telephone
Rating: A-	
HarborOne Bank	(508) 895-1000
Rating: B+	
Bank of America, N.A.	(704) 386-5681
BankNewport	(401) 846-3400
The Washington Trust Co. of Westerly	(401) 348-1210
Webster Bank, N.A.	(203) 328-8110

South Carolina

Name	Telephone
Rating: A	
AMG National Trust Bank	(303) 694-2190
First Century Bank, N.A.	(770) 297-8060
First Piedmont Federal S&L Assn.	(864) 489-6046
Palmetto State Bank	(803) 943-2671
Rating: A-	
Carolina Bank & Trust Co.	(843) 413-9978
First Bank	(910) 692-6222
First Federal Bank	(386) 755-0600
Pinnacle Bank	(615) 744-3705
ServisFirst Bank	(205) 949-0302
Southern First Bank	(864) 679-9000
The Bank of South Carolina	(843) 724-1500
United Community Bank	(864) 255-7960
Rating: B+	
Ameris Bank	(404) 814-8114
Bank of America, N.A.	(704) 386-5681
Bank of Greeleyville	(843) 426-2161
Bank of Travelers Rest	(864) 834-9031
First Palmetto Bank	(803) 432-2265
First Reliance Bank	(843) 656-5000
First-Citizens Bank & Trust Co.	(919) 716-7050
GrandSouth Bank	(864) 770-1000
South State Bank, N.A.	(863) 551-5500
The Bank of Clarendon	(803) 433-4451
The Commercial Bank	(864) 369-7326
The Conway National Bank	(843) 248-5721
Truist Bank	(336) 733-2000
United Bank	(703) 556-0900
Woodforest National Bank	(832) 375-2505

South Dakota

Rating: A

Name	Telephone
First National Bank	(605) 223-2521
First National Bank in Philip	(605) 859-2525
First Premier Bank	(605) 357-3000
First Savings Bank	(605) 763-2009
Pioneer Bank & Trust	(605) 717-2265
Quoin Financial Bank	(605) 853-2473
Security National Bank of South Dakota	(605) 232-6060

Rating: A-

Name	Telephone
American Bank & Trust	(605) 352-9122
Bryant State Bank	(605) 628-2171
Citizens State Bank of Arlington	(605) 983-5594
Dakota Prairie Bank	(605) 223-2337
First National Bank	(605) 482-8293
First Western Federal Savings Bank	(605) 341-1203
Heartland State Bank	(605) 475-5500
Liberty National Bank	(712) 224-4425
Merchants State Bank	(605) 925-4222
Minnwest Bank	(507) 637-5731
Richland State Bank	(605) 627-5671

Rating: B+

Name	Telephone
Bank Midwest	(712) 336-0505
Campbell County Bank	(605) 437-2294
DNB National Bank	(605) 874-2191
Elkhorn Valley Bank & Trust	(402) 371-0722
First Bank & Trust	(605) 696-2265
First Dakota National Bank	(605) 665-7432
First Fidelity Bank	(605) 775-2641
First Interstate Bank	(406) 255-5000
First State Bank of Roscoe	(605) 287-4451
Ipswich State Bank	(605) 426-6031
The Farmers State Bank of Turton	(605) 897-6532
The First National Bank in Sioux Falls	(605) 335-5200

Tennessee

Rating: A

Name	Telephone
Bank of Cleveland	(423) 478-5656
Citizens Bank	(615) 735-1490
Citizens Bank	(423) 543-2265
Citizens Community Bank	(931) 967-3342
Citizens National Bank	(865) 453-9031
First Volunteer Bank	(423) 668-4509
FSNB, N.A.	(580) 357-9880
Planters Bank, Inc.	(270) 886-9030
Republic Bank & Trust Co.	(502) 584-3600
The First Bank and Trust Co.	(276) 889-4622

Rating: A-

Name	Telephone
Andrew Johnson Bank	(423) 783-1000
Bank of Lincoln County	(931) 433-1708
CapStar Bank	(615) 732-7422
CBBC Bank	(865) 977-5900
Citizens Tri-County Bank	(423) 949-2173
Commercial Bank & Trust Co.	(731) 642-3341
Elizabethton Federal Savings Bank	(423) 543-5050
Financial Federal Bank	(901) 756-2848
First Community Bank of Tennessee	(931) 684-5800
First Federal Bank	(615) 446-2822
First Financial Bank, N.A.	(812) 238-6000
First Jackson Bank	(256) 437-2107
First National Bank of Middle Tennessee	(931) 473-4402
First National Bank of Pulaski	(931) 363-2585
Johnson County Bank	(423) 727-7701
McKenzie Banking Co.	(731) 352-2262
Mountain Commerce Bank	(865) 694-5725
Peoples Bank & Trust Co.	(931) 728-3381
Peoples Bank of the South	(423) 562-4921
Pinnacle Bank	(615) 744-3705
Putnam 1st Mercantile Bank	(931) 528-6372
Reliant Bank	(615) 221-2020
ServisFirst Bank	(205) 949-0302
Tennessee State Bank	(865) 453-0873
The Farmers Bank	(615) 325-2265
Truxton Trust Co.	(615) 515-1700
United Community Bank	(864) 255-7960
United Cumberland Bank	(606) 376-5031
Wilson Bank & Trust	(615) 444-2265

Rating: B+

Name	Telephone
BancorpSouth Bank	(662) 680-2000
Bank of America, N.A.	(704) 386-5681
Bank of Crockett	(731) 663-2031
Bank of Frankewing	(931) 363-1796
Bank of Gleason	(731) 648-5506
Bank of Tennessee	(423) 378-9500
Cadence Bank, N.A.	(800) 636-7622
Citizens B&T Co. of Grainger County	(865) 828-5237
Citizens Bank	(615) 666-2195
Citizens Bank	(615) 374-2265
Coffee County Bank	(931) 728-1975
Commercial Bank	(423) 869-5151
Community Bank, Lexington, Tennessee	(731) 968-6624
First Century Bank	(423) 626-7261
First Citizens National Bank	(731) 285-4410
First National Bank	(423) 569-8586
First Vision Bank of Tennessee	(931) 454-0500
FirstBank	(615) 313-0080
First-Citizens Bank & Trust Co.	(919) 716-7050
Independent Bank	(901) 844-5051
Legends Bank	(931) 503-1234
Patriot Bank	(901) 872-2265
Peoples Bank of East Tennessee	(423) 442-7262
Peoples Bank of Middle Tennessee	(931) 684-7222
Renasant Bank	(800) 680-1601
Security Bank and Trust Co.	(731) 642-6644
Security FSB of McMinnville	(931) 473-4483
Simmons Bank	(870) 541-1000
SmartBank	(865) 453-2650
Sumner Bank & Trust	(615) 451-4151
The Bank of Marion	(276) 783-3116
The Citizens Bank	(270) 236-2525
The Peoples Bank	(731) 858-2661
Truist Bank	(336) 733-2000
Trustmark National Bank	(601) 208-5111
Union Bank & Trust Co.	(931) 823-1247

Texas

Rating: A

Name	Telephone
Austin Bank, Texas N.A.	(903) 586-1526
Bessemer Trust Co., N.A.	(212) 708-9100
Citizens 1st Bank	(903) 581-1900
Citizens Bank of Las Cruces	(575) 647-4100
Citizens National Bank at Brownwood	(325) 643-3545
Commerce Bank	(956) 724-1616
Community Bank	(903) 236-4422
Crockett National Bank	(210) 467-5391
Falcon International Bank	(956) 723-2265
First Financial Bank, N.A.	(325) 627-7200
First Savings Bank	(605) 763-2009
First State Bank of Bedias	(936) 395-2141
FSNB, N.A.	(580) 357-9880
Golden Bank, N.A.	(713) 777-3838
International Bank of Commerce	(956) 547-1000
International Bank of Commerce	(956) 765-8361
International Bank of Commerce	(956) 722-7611
Metro City Bank	(770) 455-4989
Muenster State Bank	(940) 759-2257
Security State Bank	(806) 481-3327
Security State Bank & Trust	(830) 997-7575
Southside Bank	(903) 531-7111
Tejas Bank	(432) 943-4230
Texas Bank	(325) 649-9200
Texas Exchange Bank, SSB	(817) 297-4331
The Commercial National Bank of Brady	(325) 597-2961
The Falls City National Bank	(830) 254-3573
The Liberty National Bank in Paris	(903) 785-5555
The Waggoner National Bank of Vernon	(940) 552-2511
Trinity Bank, N.A.	(817) 763-9966

Rating: A-

Name	Telephone
American First National Bank	(713) 596-2888
Amistad Bank	(830) 775-0295
Anchor D Bank	(580) 423-7541
Armed Forces Bank, N.A.	(913) 682-9090
Bank of DeSoto, N.A.	(972) 780-7777
Bank of South Texas	(956) 687-4260
Bank of Texas	(432) 221-6100
Bank OZK	(501) 978-2265
BOC Bank	(806) 779-2461
BOM Bank	(318) 352-3060
Cathay Bank	(213) 625-4791
Central National Bank	(254) 776-3800
Citizens Bank	(806) 350-5600
Citizens State Bank	(979) 885-3571
Citizens State Bank	(325) 468-3311
Citizens State Bank	(936) 398-2566
City Bank	(806) 792-7101
Coleman County State Bank	(325) 625-2172
Commerce Bank	(855) 659-1656
Commercial Bank of Texas, N.A.	(936) 715-4100
Commonwealth Business Bank	(323) 988-3000
Community National B&T of Texas	(903) 654-4500
Crossroads Bank	(361) 293-3572
East West Bank	(626) 768-6000
Ennis State Bank	(972) 875-9676
First IC Bank	(770) 451-7200
First National Bank of Burleson	(817) 295-0461
First State Bank	(325) 732-4386
First State Bank	(806) 832-4525
First State Bank	(806) 396-5521
First State Bank of Ben Wheeler, Texas	(903) 833-5861
First State Bank of Odem	(361) 368-2651
First Texas Bank	(512) 556-3691
First United Bank	(806) 647-4151
Frontier Bank of Texas	(512) 281-1500
Guadalupe Bank	(830) 792-1950
Guaranty Bank & Trust, N.A.	(903) 572-9881
Happy State Bank	(806) 558-2265
HomeBank Texas	(972) 287-2030
Hometown Bank, N.A.	(409) 763-1271
Independent Bank	(972) 562-9004
Industry State Bank	(979) 357-4437
International Bank of Commerce	(405) 841-2100
Inwood National Bank	(214) 358-5281
Liberty Capital Bank	(469) 375-6600
Llano National Bank	(325) 247-5701
Mason Bank	(325) 347-5911
NBH Bank	(720) 554-6650
Open Bank	(213) 892-9999
Peoples State Bank	(830) 683-2119
Pinnacle Bank	(817) 810-9110
PlainsCapital Bank	(214) 525-9000
PromiseOne Bank	(678) 385-0800
Prosperity Bank	(979) 543-2200
Round Top State Bank	(979) 249-3151
Security State Bank	(830) 334-3606
Shelby Savings Bank, SSB	(936) 598-5688
SouthStar Bank, S.S.B.	(361) 596-4611
Spirit of Texas Bank, SSB	(936) 538-1000
T Bank, N.A.	(972) 720-9000
Texas Bank and Trust Co.	(903) 237-5500

Texas

Name	Telephone
Texas Bank Financial	(817) 596-9998
Texas Financial Bank	(325) 869-5511
Texas First Bank	(409) 948-1990
Texas Republic Bank, N.A.	(972) 334-0700
Texas State Bank	(325) 949-3721
The American National Bank of Mount Pleasant	(903) 572-1776
The Buckholts State Bank	(254) 593-3661
The City National Bank of Sulphur Springs	(903) 885-7523
The Cowboy Bank of Texas	(972) 435-2131
The First National Bank of Bastrop	(512) 321-2561
The First National Bank of Eldorado	(325) 853-2561
The First National Bank of Evant	(254) 471-5531
The Perryton National Bank	(806) 435-9641
ValueBank Texas	(361) 888-4451
Wallis Bank	(979) 478-6151
WestStar Bank	(915) 532-1000

Rating: B+

Name	Telephone
Amarillo National Bank	(806) 378-8000
American Bank, N.A.	(214) 358-3111
American National Bank & Trust	(940) 397-2300
Arrowhead Bank	(325) 247-5741
Austin Capital Bank SSB	(512) 693-3600
Austin County State Bank	(979) 865-4200
BancorpSouth Bank	(662) 680-2000
Bank of America, N.A.	(704) 386-5681
Bank of Brenham, N.A.	(979) 836-3332
Bank7	(405) 810-8600
Benchmark Bank	(972) 673-4000
BOKF, N.A.	(918) 588-6000
Brazos National Bank	(979) 265-1911
Burton State Bank	(979) 289-3151
Cadence Bank, N.A.	(800) 636-7622
Capital Bank of Texas	(830) 876-5221
Carmine State Bank	(979) 278-3244
Central Bank	(832) 485-2300
Charter Bank	(361) 241-7681
Ciera Bank	(940) 549-2040
Citizens Bank, N.A.	(325) 695-3000
Citizens National Bank	(254) 697-6653
Citizens National Bank of Texas	(972) 938-4300
Citizens State Bank	(979) 596-1421
City National Bank of Taylor	(512) 671-2265
Classic Bank, N.A.	(254) 697-6461
Comerica Bank	(214) 462-4000
Commercial National Bank of Texarkana	(870) 216-3506
Community Bank & Trust, Waco, Texas	(254) 753-1521
Community First National Bank	(785) 323-1111
Community National Bank	(432) 262-1600
Community National Bank	(830) 426-3066
Communitybank of Texas, N.A.	(409) 861-7200
Farmers State Bank	(254) 729-3272
Fayetteville Bank	(979) 378-4261
First Bank	(940) 569-2221
First Bank & Trust	(806) 788-0800
First Command Bank	(888) 763-7600
First Community Bank	(361) 888-9310
First Community Bank	(956) 399-3331
First Mid Bank & Trust, N.A.	(217) 234-7454
First National Bank in Port Lavaca	(361) 552-6726
First National Bank of Central Texas	(254) 772-9330
First National Bank of Dublin	(254) 445-4400
First National Bank of Fort Stockton	(432) 336-8541
First National Bank of Huntsville	(936) 295-5701
First National Bank Texas	(254) 554-4236
First State Bank	(903) 676-1900
First State Bank	(940) 549-8880
First State Bank	(979) 265-2511
First State Bank	(940) 665-1711
First State Bank and Trust Co.	(903) 693-6606
First State Bank of Burnet	(512) 756-2191
First State Bank of Uvalde	(830) 278-6231
First Texas Bank	(512) 863-2567
First Texas Bank	(254) 634-2132
First-Citizens Bank & Trust Co.	(919) 716-7050
Frost Bank	(210) 220-4011
Gilmer National Bank	(903) 843-5653
Grandview Bank	(817) 866-3316
Great Plains National Bank	(580) 688-3323
Horizon Bank, SSB	(512) 637-5730
Jefferson Bank	(210) 734-4311
Legend Bank, N. A.	(940) 872-2221
Lone Star National Bank	(956) 984-2991
Lone Star State Bank of West Texas	(806) 771-7717
Marion State Bank	(830) 420-2331
MCBank	(325) 648-2216
MidFirst Bank	(405) 767-7000
Moody National Bank	(409) 632-5016
New Mexico Bank & Trust	(505) 830-8100
NewFirst National Bank	(979) 543-3349
NexBank	(972) 934-4700
Pearland State Bank	(281) 485-3211
Pegasus Bank	(214) 353-3000
Peoples Bank	(806) 794-0044

Texas

Name	Telephone
Pointbank	(940) 686-7000
Sabine State Bank and Trust Co.	(318) 256-7000
Sage Capital Bank	(830) 672-8585
Sanger Bank	(940) 458-4600
Schertz Bank & Trust	(210) 945-7400
Security National Bank of Omaha	(402) 344-7300
Simmons Bank	(870) 541-1000
Spring Hill State Bank	(903) 759-0751
State Bank of Texas	(972) 252-6000
Sundown State Bank	(806) 229-2111
Texas Brand Bank	(214) 219-0003
Texas Community Bank	(956) 722-8333
Texas Gulf Bank, N.A.	(713) 595-7400
Texas Security Bank	(469) 398-4800
The American National Bank of Texas	(972) 524-3411
The Bank and Trust, SSB	(830) 774-2555
The Big Bend Banks, N.A.	(432) 729-4344
The Brenham National Bank	(979) 836-4571
The Citizens National Bank of Hillsboro	(254) 582-2531
The First Liberty National Bank	(936) 336-6471
The First National Bank of Aspermont	(940) 989-3505
The First National Bank of Bellville	(979) 865-3181
The First National Bank of East Texas	(903) 843-4100
The First National Bank of Floydada	(806) 983-3717
The First National Bank of Granbury	(817) 573-2655
The First National Bank of Hebbronville	(361) 527-3221
The First National Bank of Hereford	(806) 363-2265
The First National Bank of Livingston	(936) 327-1234
The First National Bank of Shiner	(361) 594-3317
The First National Bank of Stanton	(432) 756-3361
The First National Bank of Winnsboro	(903) 342-5275
The First State Bank	(979) 648-2691
The Jacksboro National Bank	(940) 567-5551
The MINT National Bank	(281) 359-6468
The Northern Trust Co.	(312) 630-6000
The Roscoe State Bank	(325) 766-3311
The Santa Anna National Bank	(325) 348-3108
The State National Bank of Big Spring	(432) 264-2100
The Yoakum National Bank	(361) 293-5225
Titan Bank, N.A.	(940) 325-9821
Tolleson Private Bank	(214) 252-3033
Truist Bank	(336) 733-2000
Trustmark National Bank	(601) 208-5111
VeraBank, N.A.	(903) 657-8521
Washington Federal Bank, N.A.	(206) 204-3446
Woodforest National Bank	(832) 375-2505
Worthington National Bank	(817) 303-5900
Zapata National Bank	(956) 765-4302
Zions BanCorp., N.A.	(801) 844-7637

Utah

Name	Telephone
Rating: A+	
Optum Bank, Inc.	(866) 234-8913
Utah Independent Bank	(435) 529-7459
Rating: A	
Altabank	(801) 756-7681
Bank of Utah	(801) 409-5001
Central Bank	(801) 375-1000
State Bank of Southern Utah	(435) 865-2300
Rating: A-	
BMW Bank of North America	(801) 461-6500
Capital Community Bank	(801) 356-6699
D.L. Evans Bank	(208) 678-8615
Finwise Bank	(801) 545-6000
First Electronic Bank	(801) 572-4004
Glacier Bank	(406) 756-4200
Green Dot Bank	(801) 344-7020
Holladay Bank and Trust	(801) 272-4275
Morgan Stanley Bank, N.A.	(801) 236-3600
NBH Bank	(720) 554-6650
Rock Canyon Bank	(801) 426-0150
The Pitney Bowes Bank Inc.	(801) 832-4440
WebBank	(801) 456-8350
Rating: B+	
Bank of America, N.A.	(704) 386-5681
Continental Bank	(801) 595-7000
EnerBank USA	(801) 832-0700
First Utah Bank	(801) 272-9454
Grand Valley Bank	(435) 654-7400
Home Savings Bank	(801) 523-3878
KeyBank N.A.	(216) 689-3000
LCA Bank Corp.	(435) 658-4824
Marlin Business Bank	(888) 479-9111
Northwest Bank	(208) 332-0700
UBS Bank USA	(801) 741-0310
Washington Federal Bank, N.A.	(206) 204-3446
WEX Bank	(801) 568-4345
Zions BanCorp., N.A.	(801) 844-7637

Vermont

Rating: B+

Name	Telephone
Community Bank, N.A.	(315) 445-2282
KeyBank N.A.	(216) 689-3000
NBT Bank, N.A.	(607) 337-6416
TrustCo Bank	(518) 377-3311

Virgin Islands of the U.S.

Name	Telephone
Rating: B+	
United Fidelity Bank, FSB	(812) 424-0921

Virginia

Name	Telephone
Rating: A	
AMG National Trust Bank	(303) 694-2190
Calvin B. Taylor Banking Co.	(410) 641-1700
Metro City Bank	(770) 455-4989
Surrey Bank & Trust	(336) 783-3900
The First Bank and Trust Co.	(276) 889-4622
Rating: A-	
Armed Forces Bank, N.A.	(913) 682-9090
Benchmark Community Bank	(434) 676-9054
Chesapeake Bank	(804) 435-1181
Citizens and Farmers Bank	(804) 843-2360
Citizens Bank and Trust Co.	(434) 292-8100
City National Bank of West Virginia	(304) 769-1100
EagleBank	(240) 497-2075
Essex Bank	(804) 419-4329
Farmers and Miners Bank	(276) 546-4692
Farmers Bank, Windsor VA	(757) 242-3150
First Carolina Bank	(252) 937-2152
MainStreet Bank	(703) 481-4567
MVB Bank, Inc.	(844) 682-2265
Pinnacle Bank	(615) 744-3705
Presidential Bank, FSB	(301) 652-1616
Primis Bank	(804) 528-4754
The Fidelity Bank	(919) 552-2242
The National Bank of Blacksburg	(540) 951-6205
TowneBank	(757) 638-7500
Virginia National Bank	(434) 817-8621
Rating: B+	
American National Bank and Trust Co.	(434) 792-5111
Atlantic Union Bank	(804) 327-5720
Bank of America, N.A.	(704) 386-5681
Bank of Clarke County	(540) 955-2510
Blue Ridge Bank, N.A.	(540) 743-6521
Farmers & Merchants Bank	(540) 864-5156
First Bank	(540) 465-9121
First-Citizens Bank & Trust Co.	(919) 716-7050
Fulton Bank, N.A.	(717) 291-2499
FVCbank	(703) 436-4740
Highlands Community Bank	(540) 962-2265
John Marshall Bank	(703) 584-0840
Lee Bank and Trust Co.	(276) 546-2211
Shore United Bank	(410) 822-1400
South State Bank, N.A.	(863) 551-5500
Southern Bank and Trust Co.	(919) 658-7000
Summit Community Bank, Inc.	(304) 530-1000
The Bank of Charlotte County	(434) 542-5111
The Bank of Marion	(276) 783-3116
The Bank of Southside Virginia	(434) 246-5211
The Farmers Bank of Appomattox	(434) 352-7171
Truist Bank	(336) 733-2000
United Bank	(703) 556-0900
Woodforest National Bank	(832) 375-2505

Washington

Name	Telephone
Rating: A	
Bessemer Trust Co., N.A.	(212) 708-9100
Timberland Bank	(360) 533-4747
UniBank	(425) 275-9700
Rating: A-	
1st Security Bank of Washington	(800) 683-0973
American Continental Bank	(626) 363-8988
Armed Forces Bank, N.A.	(913) 682-9090
Bank of the Pacific	(360) 537-4052
Cashmere Valley Bank	(509) 782-2624
Cathay Bank	(213) 625-4791
Columbia State Bank	(253) 305-1900
East West Bank	(626) 768-6000
Glacier Bank	(406) 756-4200
Pacific Premier Bank	(949) 864-8000
Riverview Community Bank	(360) 693-6650
Security State Bank	(360) 736-0763
State Bank Northwest	(509) 789-4335
Washington Business Bank	(360) 754-1945
Rating: B+	
Bank of America, N.A.	(704) 386-5681
Banner Bank	(509) 527-3636
Coastal Community Bank	(425) 257-9000
Community First Bank	(509) 783-3435
First Interstate Bank	(406) 255-5000
First-Citizens Bank & Trust Co.	(919) 716-7050
KeyBank N.A.	(216) 689-3000
Kitsap Bank	(360) 876-7834
Lamont Bank of St. John	(509) 648-3636
Northwest Bank	(208) 332-0700
Pacific Crest Savings Bank	(425) 670-9600
Peoples Bank	(360) 715-4200
Sound Community Bank	(206) 436-3150
The Northern Trust Co.	(312) 630-6000
Twin River Bank	(208) 746-4848
United Business Bank	(925) 476-1800
Washington Federal Bank, N.A.	(206) 204-3446
Washington Trust Bank	(509) 353-4204
Wheatland Bank	(509) 458-2265
Zions BanCorp., N.A.	(801) 844-7637

West Virginia

Name	Telephone
Rating: A-	
Bank of Monroe	(304) 772-3034
City National Bank of West Virginia	(304) 769-1100
Clay County Bank, Inc.	(304) 587-4221
Clear Mountain Bank, Inc.	(304) 379-2265
Fayette County National Bank of Fayetteville	(304) 574-1212
MVB Bank, Inc.	(844) 682-2265
Unified Bank	(740) 633-0445
Rating: B+	
Community Bank of Parkersburg	(304) 485-7991
First-Citizens Bank & Trust Co.	(919) 716-7050
Mountain Valley Bank, N.A.	(304) 637-2265
Summit Community Bank, Inc.	(304) 530-1000
The Bank of Romney	(304) 822-3541
The Citizens Bank of Weston, Inc.	(304) 269-2862
Truist Bank	(336) 733-2000
Union Bank, Inc.	(304) 758-2191
United Bank	(703) 556-0900
WesBanco Bank, Inc.	(304) 234-9419
Woodforest National Bank	(832) 375-2505

Wisconsin

Rating: A+

Name	Telephone
Bank of Alma	(608) 685-4461
Bank of Prairie Du Sac	(608) 643-3393

Rating: A

Name	Telephone
Badger Bank	(920) 563-2478
Bank of Lake Mills	(920) 648-8336
Bank of Mauston	(608) 847-6200
Bank of Wisconsin Dells	(608) 253-1111
BLC Community Bank	(920) 788-4141
Bluff View Bank	(608) 582-2233
Charter Bank	(715) 832-4254
Hometown Bank	(920) 907-0788
Intercity State Bank	(715) 359-4231
Johnson Bank	(262) 619-2700
Oostburg State Bank	(920) 564-2336
Richland County Bank	(608) 647-6306
River Falls State Bank	(715) 425-6782
The Bank of Deerfield	(608) 764-5411
The Farmers State Bank of Waupaca	(715) 258-1400
The First National Bank of Bangor	(608) 486-2386
The Northwestern Bank	(715) 723-4461
WaterStone Bank	(414) 761-1000
Waukesha State Bank	(262) 549-8500

Rating: A-

Name	Telephone
American National Bank-Fox Cities	(920) 739-1040
Apple River State Bank	(815) 594-2351
Bank of Cashton	(608) 654-5121
Capitol Bank	(608) 836-1616
Citizens Bank	(262) 363-6500
Collins State Bank	(920) 772-4433
Cumberland Federal Bank, FSB	(715) 822-2249
DMB Community Bank	(608) 846-3711
Farmers & Merchants Union Bank	(920) 623-4000
First Citizens State Bank	(262) 473-2112
First Community Bank	(608) 868-7644
Great Midwest Bank, State Savings Bank	(262) 784-4400
Headwaters State Bank	(715) 547-3383
Home Federal Savings Bank	(507) 535-1309
John Deere Financial, F.S.B.	(608) 821-2000
National Bank of Commerce	(715) 394-5531
National Exchange Bank and Trust	(920) 921-7700
Nekoosa Port Edwards State Bank	(715) 886-3104
Oak Bank	(608) 441-6000
Royal Bank	(608) 462-8401
State Bank of Newburg	(262) 675-2306
The Bank of Brodhead	(608) 897-2121
The International Bank of Amherst	(715) 824-3325
The Peoples Community Bank	(608) 795-2120
West Pointe Bank	(920) 232-2260
Wolf River Community Bank	(920) 779-7000

Rating: B+

Name	Telephone
Alliance Bank	(715) 926-4234
Bank First, N.A.	(920) 652-3100
Bank of Milton	(608) 868-7672
Bankers' Bank	(608) 833-5550
Bay Bank	(920) 490-7600
Black River Country Bank	(715) 284-9448
Bonduel State Bank	(715) 758-2141
Bremer Bank, N.A.	(651) 288-3751
CIBM Bank	(217) 355-0900
Citizens State Bank of Loyal	(715) 255-8526
Clare Bank, N.A.	(608) 348-2727
Community Bank of Cameron	(715) 458-2513
Community First Bank	(608) 375-4117
Community First Bank	(715) 677-4523
Farmers & Merchants State Bank	(920) 478-2181
Farmers Savings Bank	(608) 987-3321
Farmers State Bank-Hillsboro	(608) 489-2621
First National Bank at Darlington	(608) 776-4071
First State Bank and Trust	(651) 439-5195
First-Citizens Bank & Trust Co.	(919) 716-7050
Flagstar Bank, FSB	(248) 312-5400
Forte Bank	(262) 673-5800
Frandsen Bank & Trust	(507) 744-2361
Highland State Bank	(608) 929-4515
Hustisford State Bank	(920) 349-3241
Ixonia Bank	(920) 262-6959
mBank	(906) 341-8401
Merchants Bank, N.A.	(507) 457-1100
Nicolet National Bank	(920) 430-1400
Northern State Bank	(715) 682-2772
One Community Bank	(608) 835-3168
Paper City Savings Assn.	(715) 423-8100
Partners Bank	(715) 659-2430
Peoples State Bank	(715) 842-2191
Shell Lake State Bank	(715) 468-7858
Spring Bank	(262) 754-5555
Starion Bank	(701) 223-6050
State Bank of Cross Plains	(608) 798-3961
Sterling Bank	(715) 537-3141
The First National Bank of River Falls	(715) 425-2401

Wisconsin

Name	Telephone	Name	Telephone
The Northern Trust Co.	(312) 630-6000		
The Park Bank	(608) 283-6821		
The Pineries Bank	(715) 341-5600		
TSB Bank	(920) 269-7777		
Wisconsin Bank & Trust	(608) 203-1200		
Wisconsin River Bank	(608) 643-6300		
WNB Financial, N.A.	(507) 454-8800		
Woodford State Bank	(608) 325-7766		
WoodTrust Bank	(715) 423-7600		

Wyoming

Name	Telephone
Rating: A	
AMG National Trust Bank	(303) 694-2190
RSNB Bank	(307) 362-8801
Wyoming Bank & Trust	(307) 632-7733
Rating: A-	
Bank of Commerce	(307) 324-2265
First Federal Bank & Trust	(307) 674-0464
First State Bank	(308) 632-4158
FirsTier Bank	(308) 235-4633
Glacier Bank	(406) 756-4200
Jonah Bank of Wyoming	(307) 237-4555
Lusk State Bank	(307) 334-2500
Pinnacle Bank - Wyoming	(402) 697-5990
Points West Community Bank	(970) 686-0878
The Bank of Star Valley	(307) 885-0000
Rating: B+	
ANB Bank	(303) 394-5143
Bank of Jackson Hole	(307) 733-8064
Buffalo Federal Bank	(307) 684-5591
Central Bank and Trust	(307) 332-4730
First Interstate Bank	(406) 255-5000
Hilltop National Bank	(307) 265-2740
Platte Valley Bank	(307) 532-2111
Rocky Mountain Bank	(307) 739-9000
The Converse County Bank	(307) 358-5300
Zions BanCorp., N.A.	(801) 844-7637

Section III

Rating Upgrades and Downgrades

A list of all

U.S. Commercial Banks and Savings Banks

receiving a rating upgrade or downgrade
during the current quarter.

Section III Contents

This section identifies those institutions receiving a rating change since the previous edition of this publication, whether it be a rating upgrade, rating downgrade, newly-rated company or the withdrawal of a rating. A rating upgrade or downgrade may entail a change from one letter grade to another, or it may mean the addition or deletion of a plus or minus sign within the same letter grade previously assigned to the company. Ratings are normally updated once each quarter of the year. In some instances, however, an institution's rating may be downgraded outside of the normal updates due to overriding circumstances.

1. **Institution Name** The name under which the institution was chartered. A company's name can be very similar to, or the same as, that of another, so verify the company's exact name, city, and state to make sure you are looking at the correct company.

2. **New Safety Rating** Weiss rating assigned to the institution at the time of publication. Our ratings are designed to distinguish levels of insolvency risk and are measured on a scale from A to F based upon a wide range of factors. Highly rated companies are, in our opinion, less likely to experience financial difficulties than lower rated firms. See *About Weiss Safety Ratings* for more information and a description of what each rating means.

3. **State** The state in which the institution's headquarters or main office is located.

4. **Date of Change** Date that rating was finalized.

New Ratings

Name	State	Date of Change
Rating: B+		
Square Financial Services, Inc.	UT	08/31/21
Rating: C		
Metro Phoenix Bank	AZ	08/31/21
Rating: D+		
The National Capital Bank of Washington	DC	08/31/21
Rating: D		
Climate First Bank	FL	08/31/21
Rating: D-		
Community Bank & Trust-Alabama	AL	08/31/21
First Bank of Central Ohio	OH	08/31/21

Rating Upgrades

Name	State	Date of Change
Rating: A+		
Esquire Bank, N.A.	NY	08/31/21
Stafford Savings Bank	CT	08/31/21
Utah Independent Bank	UT	08/31/21
Rating: A		
Bank of New England	NH	08/31/21
Bank of Wisconsin Dells	WI	08/31/21
BankSouth	GA	08/31/21
Cape Ann Savings Bank	MA	08/31/21
Central Bank of Kansas City	MO	08/31/21
Citizens Savings Bank	IA	08/31/21
Connect Bank	AR	08/31/21
Crossroads Bank	IL	08/31/21
Farmers and Merchants State Bank	ND	08/31/21
Farmers Trust & Savings Bank	IA	08/31/21
Fidelity Bank	MN	08/31/21
First Bank	OK	08/31/21
First National Bank in Philip	SD	08/31/21
First State Bank & Trust	ND	08/31/21
Florida Business Bank	FL	08/31/21
Fulton Savings Bank	NY	08/31/21
Genesee Regional Bank	NY	08/31/21
Golden Bank, N.A.	TX	08/31/21
Golden Belt Bank, FSA	KS	08/31/21
Home Exchange Bank	MO	08/31/21
Kennebec Savings Bank	ME	08/31/21
Mount Vernon Bank and Trust Co.	IA	08/31/21
Norway Savings Bank	ME	08/31/21
Oostburg State Bank	WI	08/31/21
Savings Bank	IA	08/31/21
Southside Bank	TX	08/31/21
State Bank of Bern	KS	08/31/21
State Bank of Wheaton	MN	08/31/21
The Bank of the West	OK	08/31/21
The Dolores State Bank	CO	08/31/21
The Paducah Bank and Trust Co.	KY	08/31/21
UniBank	WA	08/31/21
Rating: A-		
5Star Bank	CO	08/31/21
Adams State Bank	NE	08/31/21
Alliant Bank	MO	08/31/21
American Bank and Trust Co.	OK	08/31/21
Atlantic Capital Bank, N.A.	GA	08/31/21
Bank of South Texas	TX	08/31/21
Bank of the Sierra	CA	08/31/21
Bankers' Bank of Kansas	KS	08/31/21
Blue Grass Savings Bank	IA	08/31/21
BOM Bank	LA	08/31/21
CapStar Bank	TN	08/31/21
Cedar Rapids Bank and Trust Co.	IA	08/31/21
Charter Bank	IA	08/31/21
Citizens Tri-County Bank	TN	08/31/21
Clarkson Bank	NE	08/31/21
CNB Bank	NM	08/31/21
Collins State Bank	WI	08/31/21
Commercial State Bank	NE	08/31/21
Community Bank of Missouri	MO	08/31/21
D.L. Evans Bank	ID	08/31/21
Dakota Prairie Bank	SD	08/31/21
Dedham Institution for Savings	MA	08/31/21
Eagle Bank	MT	08/31/21
Essex Bank	VA	08/31/21
Exchange Bank	NE	08/31/21
Farmers & Merchants Savings Bank	IA	08/31/21
Farmers & Merchants Union Bank	WI	08/31/21
Farmers and Miners Bank	VA	08/31/21
Farmers Bank, Windsor VA	VA	08/31/21
Farmers National Bank	KS	08/31/21
First Carolina Bank	NC	08/31/21
First Commerce Bank	NJ	08/31/21
First IC Bank	GA	08/31/21
First National Bank	SD	08/31/21
First State Bank & Trust Co.	NE	08/31/21
First State Bank of Blakely	GA	08/31/21
First State Bank of Campbell Hill	IL	08/31/21
Five Star Bank	CA	08/31/21
FNB Bank	KS	08/31/21
Franklin Bank & Trust Co.	KY	08/31/21
GNB Bank	IA	08/31/21
Greater Community Bank	GA	08/31/21
HarborOne Bank	MA	08/31/21
Heartland State Bank	SD	08/31/21
Hiawatha Bank & Trust Co.	IA	08/31/21
Holladay Bank and Trust	UT	08/31/21
Houghton State Bank	IA	08/31/21
Illini State Bank	IL	08/31/21
Johnson County Bank	TN	08/31/21
Kansas State Bank	KS	08/31/21
Kinmundy Bank	IL	08/31/21
MainStreet Bank	VA	08/31/21
McKenzie Banking Co.	TN	08/31/21
Merchants State Bank	SD	08/31/21
Mid-America Bank	KS	08/31/21
Montrose Savings Bank	MO	08/31/21
NorthEast Community Bank	NY	08/31/21
NorthStar Bank	IA	08/31/21
Oak Bank	WI	08/31/21

Rating Upgrades

Name	State	Date of Change
Partners Bank of New England	ME	08/31/21
Patriot Community Bank	MA	08/31/21
Peoples Bank & Trust Co.	TN	08/31/21
Peoples Bank of the South	TN	08/31/21
Pike National Bank	MS	08/31/21
Pinnacle Bank	TN	08/31/21
Platte Valley Bank	NE	08/31/21
Premier Bank of Arkansas	AR	08/31/21
PS Bank	PA	08/31/21
Putnam County State Bank	MO	08/31/21
Quad City Bank and Trust Co.	IA	08/31/21
Rock Canyon Bank	UT	08/31/21
Rockland Trust Co.	MA	08/31/21
Saint Clair State Bank (Inc.)	MN	08/31/21
South Central State Bank	NE	08/31/21
Southern Independent Bank	AL	08/31/21
SouthStar Bank, S.S.B.	TX	08/31/21
Spirit of Texas Bank, SSB	TX	08/31/21
Springfield First Community Bank	MO	08/31/21
Suncrest Bank	CA	08/31/21
The Bank of Protection	KS	08/31/21
The Evangeline Bank and Trust Co.	LA	08/31/21
The Farmers State Bank	KS	08/31/21
The First National Bank of Scott City	KS	08/31/21
The Idabel National Bank	OK	08/31/21
The National Bank of Malvern	PA	08/31/21
The Republic Banking Co.	OH	08/31/21
The State Bank	CO	08/31/21
United Bank	AL	08/31/21
United Farmers State Bank	MN	08/31/21
US Metro Bank	CA	08/31/21
West Pointe Bank	WI	08/31/21

Rating: B+

Name	State	Date of Change
Access Bank	NE	08/31/21
American Community Bank	NY	08/31/21
Asian Bank	PA	08/31/21
Atlantic Union Bank	VA	08/31/21
Balboa Thrift and Loan Assn.	CA	08/31/21
Bank of Hays	KS	08/31/21
BankNewport	RI	08/31/21
Bedford Federal Savings Bank	IN	08/31/21
Bedford Loan & Deposit Bank	KY	08/31/21
Blue Ridge Bank, N.A.	VA	08/31/21
BOKF, N.A.	OK	08/31/21
Buffalo Federal Bank	WY	08/31/21
Cadence Bank, N.A.	GA	08/31/21
CalPrivate Bank	CA	08/31/21
CBank	OH	08/31/21
Citizens Bank & Trust Co.	MT	08/31/21
Citizens Bank Minnesota	MN	08/31/21
Citizens National Bank of Texas	TX	08/31/21
CNB St. Louis Bank	MO	08/31/21
Community Bank	KS	08/31/21
Community Bank of Cameron	WI	08/31/21
Community Commerce Bank	CA	08/31/21
Community First Bank of the Heartland	IL	08/31/21
Community Point Bank	MO	08/31/21
DNB National Bank	SD	08/31/21
F & M Community Bank, N.A.	MN	08/31/21
Farmers & Merchants State Bank	MN	08/31/21
Farmers Savings Bank	IA	08/31/21
Farmers State Bank	MT	08/31/21
Farmers State Bank of Trimont	MN	08/31/21
Fayetteville Bank	TX	08/31/21
Finance Factors, Ltd.	HI	08/31/21
First Bank	NJ	08/31/21
First Credit Bank	CA	08/31/21
First Federal Savings Bank	IN	08/31/21
First Home Bank	FL	08/31/21
First Keystone Community Bank	PA	08/31/21
First Liberty Bank	OK	08/31/21
First National B&T Co. of Weatherford	OK	08/31/21
First National Bank of America	MI	08/31/21
First Service Bank	AR	08/31/21
First Texas Bank	TX	08/31/21
First Utah Bank	UT	08/31/21
First Western Bank	AR	08/31/21
Five Star Bank	NY	08/31/21
Fulton Bank, N.A.	PA	08/31/21
Generations Bank	AR	08/31/21
Glenview State Bank	IL	08/31/21
Highland Bank	MN	08/31/21
Home Bank, N.A.	LA	08/31/21
Independent Bank	MI	08/31/21
Integrity Bank & Trust	CO	08/31/21
Ixonia Bank	WI	08/31/21
KeyBank N.A.	OH	08/31/21
Legacy State Bank	GA	08/31/21
Liberty Bank	AL	08/31/21
Libertyville Savings Bank	IA	08/31/21
Limestone Bank, Inc	KY	08/31/21
Lincoln FSB of Nebraska	NE	08/31/21
Lone Star State Bank of West Texas	TX	08/31/21
Marlin Business Bank	UT	08/31/21
mBank	MI	08/31/21
Mediapolis Savings Bank	IA	08/31/21
MidFirst Bank	OK	08/31/21
MinnStar Bank N.A.	MN	08/31/21
MountainOne Bank	MA	08/31/21

Rating Upgrades

Name	State	Date of Change
Northfield Bank	NJ	08/31/21
Pacific Enterprise Bank	CA	08/31/21
Pacific Western Bank	CA	08/31/21
Peoples Bank of Alabama	AL	08/31/21
Peoples Savings Bank	IA	08/31/21
Prime Meridian Bank	FL	08/31/21
Prime Security Bank	MN	08/31/21
Seiling State Bank	OK	08/31/21
Sentry Bank	MN	08/31/21
Sound Community Bank	WA	08/31/21
South State Bank, N.A.	FL	08/31/21
Southern Michigan Bank & Trust	MI	08/31/21
Spring Bank	WI	08/31/21
Springs Valley Bank & Trust Co.	IN	08/31/21
State Bank of Scotia	NE	08/31/21
Sullivan Bank	MO	08/31/21
Swedish-American State Bank	KS	08/31/21
The Bryn Mawr Trust Co.	PA	08/31/21
The Cincinnatus S&L Co.	OH	08/31/21
The Citizens Bank	KY	08/31/21
The Citizens State Bank of Cheney, Kansas	KS	08/31/21
The Farmers National Bank of Lebanon	KY	08/31/21
The Farmers State Bank of Blue Mound	KS	08/31/21
The First Farmers National Bank of Waurika	OK	08/31/21
The First National Bank of Ava	IL	08/31/21
The First National Bank of Hereford	TX	08/31/21
The First State Bank of Healy	KS	08/31/21
The First State Bank of Ransom	KS	08/31/21
The Middlefield Banking Co.	OH	08/31/21
The MINT National Bank	TX	08/31/21
The Park Bank	WI	08/31/21
Town and Country Bank	IL	08/31/21
United Business Bank	CA	08/31/21
Walters Bank and Trust Co.	OK	08/31/21
Webster Bank, N.A.	CT	08/31/21
Wells Fargo National Bank West	NV	08/31/21
WesBanco Bank, Inc.	WV	08/31/21
Winter Park National Bank	FL	08/31/21
Wisconsin Bank & Trust	WI	08/31/21
Wisconsin River Bank	WI	08/31/21
Yampa Valley Bank	CO	08/31/21

Rating: B

Name	State	Date of Change
Abacus Federal Savings Bank	NY	08/31/21
Abbeville Building and Loan, A State Chartered Savings Bank	LA	08/31/21
Abington Bank	MA	08/31/21
Altoona First Savings Bank	PA	08/31/21
Aquesta Bank	NC	08/31/21
Arvest Bank	AR	08/31/21
b1Bank	LA	08/31/21
BANK 34	NM	08/31/21
Bank Iowa	IA	08/31/21
Bank Leumi USA	NY	08/31/21
Bank of Charles Town	WV	08/31/21
Bank of Grandin	MO	08/31/21
Bank of Lewellen	NE	08/31/21
Bank of Little Rock	AR	08/31/21
Bank of Louisiana	MO	08/31/21
Bank of Western Oklahoma	OK	08/31/21
Bank Plus	IA	08/31/21
BankVista	MN	08/31/21
Barrington Bank & Trust Co., N.A.	IL	08/31/21
BMO Harris Bank N.A.	IL	08/31/21
Brentwood Bank	PA	08/31/21
Broadway National Bank	TX	08/31/21
Cambridge Savings Bank	MA	08/31/21
Centera Bank	KS	08/31/21
Choice Financial Group	ND	08/31/21
CIT Bank, N.A.	CA	08/31/21
Citibank, N.A.	SD	08/31/21
Citizens Building and Loan, SSB	SC	08/31/21
Citizens National Bank	KS	08/31/21
Citizens State Bank of Lankin	ND	08/31/21
City National Bank of Florida	FL	08/31/21
Colorado Federal Savings Bank	CO	08/31/21
Columbia Bank	NJ	08/31/21
Commerce State Bank	WI	08/31/21
Community 1st Bank Las Vegas	NM	08/31/21
Cornerstone National Bank & Trust Co.	IL	08/31/21
CorTrust Bank N.A.	SD	08/31/21
Countybank	SC	08/31/21
Crown Bank	NJ	08/31/21
Dacotah Bank	SD	08/31/21
Denmark State Bank	WI	08/31/21
Denver Savings Bank	IA	08/31/21
Dime Bank	CT	08/31/21
Easthampton Savings Bank	MA	08/31/21
Evans Bank, N.A.	NY	08/31/21
Exchange Bank of Northeast Missouri	MO	08/31/21
F&M Bank	TN	08/31/21
Farmers Bank & Trust	KS	08/31/21
Farmers State Bank	TN	08/31/21
Farmers State Bank of Newcastle	TX	08/31/21
First & Peoples Bank and Trust Co.	KY	08/31/21
First American National Bank	MS	08/31/21
First Bank and Trust	LA	08/31/21
First Bank and Trust Co.	NE	08/31/21
First Bank of the Lake	MO	08/31/21
First Bank of Utica	NE	08/31/21
First Federal Bank, A FSB	AL	08/31/21

Rating Upgrades

Name	State	Date of Change
First Fidelity Bank	OK	08/31/21
First Heritage Bank	IA	08/31/21
First Internet Bank of Indiana	IN	08/31/21
First National Bank of North Arkansas	AR	08/31/21
First National Bankers Bank	LA	08/31/21
First State Bank	NE	08/31/21
First State Bank of DeQueen	AR	08/31/21
Flushing Bank	NY	08/31/21
Forward Bank	WI	08/31/21
Freedom Bank	NJ	08/31/21
Frontier Bank	NE	08/31/21
Frontier Bank	SD	08/31/21
GBC International Bank	CA	08/31/21
Global Bank	NY	08/31/21
Goldwater Bank, N.A.	AZ	08/31/21
Grove Bank	MN	08/31/21
Gunnison S&L Assn.	CO	08/31/21
Heritage Bank & Trust	TN	08/31/21
Herring Bank	TX	08/31/21
Hometown Bank	MA	08/31/21
Investar Bank, N.A.	LA	08/31/21
Kearny Bank	NJ	08/31/21
Lake City Federal Bank	MN	08/31/21
Luther Burbank Savings	CA	08/31/21
Marion State Bank	LA	08/31/21
Mechanics Bank	CA	08/31/21
Meridian Bank	PA	08/31/21
Mid Penn Bank	PA	08/31/21
MidWestOne Bank	IA	08/31/21
Mound City Bank	WI	08/31/21
Natbank, N.A.	FL	08/31/21
National Bank of St. Anne	IL	08/31/21
New Frontier Bank	MO	08/31/21
North Shore Bank, a Co-operative Bank	MA	08/31/21
Northeast Bank	ME	08/31/21
Ocean Bank	FL	08/31/21
OceanFirst Bank, N.A.	NJ	08/31/21
Old Plank Trail Community Bank, N.A.	IL	08/31/21
One World Bank	TX	08/31/21
Origin Bank	LA	08/31/21
Partners Bank of California	CA	08/31/21
PCSB Bank	IA	08/31/21
Peapack-Gladstone Bank	NJ	08/31/21
Penn Community Bank	PA	08/31/21
Peoples Bank & Trust Co.	MO	08/31/21
Peoples Bank & Trust Co.	OK	08/31/21
Peoples Bank of Altenburg	MO	08/31/21
Plains Commerce Bank	SD	08/31/21
Quail Creek Bank, N.A.	OK	08/31/21
Regional Missouri Bank	MO	08/31/21
Reliabank Dakota	SD	08/31/21
Reliance Bank	MN	08/31/21
Rhinebeck Bank	NY	08/31/21
River Valley Community Bank	CA	08/31/21
Schaumburg Bank & Trust Co., N.A.	IL	08/31/21
Seattle Bank	WA	08/31/21
Security Federal Bank	SC	08/31/21
Security State Bank	KS	08/31/21
Settlers bank	WI	08/31/21
Signature Bank of Arkansas	AR	08/31/21
Silex Banking Co.	MO	08/31/21
Southwestern National Bank	TX	08/31/21
State Bank & Trust	AL	08/31/21
State Bank of Taunton	MN	08/31/21
State Bank of Toulon	IL	08/31/21
The Adirondack Trust Co.	NY	08/31/21
The Brady National Bank	TX	08/31/21
The Citizens Bank of Cochran	GA	08/31/21
The Citizens State Bank of Ouray	CO	08/31/21
The Commercial Bank	MS	08/31/21
The First National Bank of Ballinger	TX	08/31/21
The Gary State Bank	MN	08/31/21
The Marion National Bank	KS	08/31/21
The Wilmington Savings Bank	OH	08/31/21
Timberline Bank	CO	08/31/21
Traditions Bank	PA	08/31/21
U.S. Century Bank	FL	08/31/21
Umpqua Bank	OR	08/31/21
Union Bank	NC	08/31/21
Union State Bank	IA	08/31/21
United Bank of El Paso del Norte	TX	08/31/21
United Bankers Bank	MN	08/31/21
Vista Bank	TX	08/31/21
Waterford Bank, NA	OH	08/31/21
Wayne County Bank	TN	08/31/21
Woori America Bank	NY	08/31/21

Rating: B-

Name	State	Date of Change
1st Financial Bank USA	SD	08/31/21
Andover State Bank	KS	08/31/21
Arbor Bank	NE	08/31/21
Banc of California, N.A.	CA	08/31/21
Bank of Erath	LA	08/31/21
Bank of Lumber City	GA	08/31/21
Bank of Okolona	MS	08/31/21
Bogota Savings Bank	NJ	08/31/21
Capital One Bank (USA), N.A.	VA	08/31/21
Capital One, N.A.	VA	08/31/21
Carroll County Trust Co.	MO	08/31/21
Cedar Rapids State Bank	NE	08/31/21

Rating Upgrades

Name	State	Date of Change
Central Bank	FL	08/31/21
Commercial Bank of California	CA	08/31/21
Community Bank Mankato	MN	08/31/21
Community Bank of Elmhurst	IL	08/31/21
Community National Bank in Monmouth	IL	08/31/21
Drake Bank	MN	08/31/21
Eagle Bank	MA	08/31/21
Eaton Community Bank	MI	08/31/21
Equity Bank	KS	08/31/21
Fairfax State Savings Bank	IA	08/31/21
Fidelity Co-operative Bank	MA	08/31/21
First National Bank	MN	08/31/21
First National Bank in Ord	NE	08/31/21
First Security Bank and Trust Co.	IA	08/31/21
First State Bank	AR	08/31/21
First State Bank in Temple	OK	08/31/21
FNB Coweta	OK	08/31/21
Freedom Bank, Inc.	WV	08/31/21
Great Western Bank	SD	08/31/21
Heritage Southeast Bank	GA	08/31/21
Idaho Trust Bank	ID	08/31/21
International City Bank	CA	08/31/21
Ion Bank	CT	08/31/21
Lake-Osceola State Bank	MI	08/31/21
Lee Bank	MA	08/31/21
Mainstreet Community Bank of Florida	FL	08/31/21
Malvern Bank	IA	08/31/21
Manasquan Bank	NJ	08/31/21
Midwest BankCentre	MO	08/31/21
Midwest Regional Bank	MO	08/31/21
New Carlisle Federal Savings Bank	OH	08/31/21
New Peoples Bank, Inc.	VA	08/31/21
NobleBank & Trust	AL	08/31/21
One American Bank	SD	08/31/21
Pentucket Bank	MA	08/31/21
Peoples Bank	TN	08/31/21
Peoples Bank	IA	08/31/21
Peoples Bank of Greensboro	AL	08/31/21
Peoples Savings Bank	IA	08/31/21
Peoples State Bank	KS	08/31/21
Ponce Bank	NY	08/31/21
Premier Bank	IA	08/31/21
Professional Bank	FL	08/31/21
Progressive Bank	LA	08/31/21
Provident Savings Bank, F.S.B.	CA	08/31/21
Regent Bank	OK	08/31/21
Republic Bank of Arizona	AZ	08/31/21
Rio Bank	TX	08/31/21
River City Bank	CA	08/31/21
Riverland Bank	MN	08/31/21
Riverstone Bank	NE	08/31/21
Rolling Hills Bank & Trust	IA	08/31/21
Rosedale Federal S&L Assn.	MD	08/31/21
Security Bank of the Ozarks	MO	08/31/21
Seneca Savings	NY	08/31/21
Sewickley Savings Bank	PA	08/31/21
Simmesport State Bank	LA	08/31/21
South Shore Bank	MA	08/31/21
State Bank of New Richland	MN	08/31/21
State Bank of Table Rock	NE	08/31/21
TC Federal Bank	GA	08/31/21
Texas Capital Bank, N.A.	TX	08/31/21
Texas Heritage National Bank	TX	08/31/21
Thayer County Bank	NE	08/31/21
The Bankers Bank	OK	08/31/21
The Bankers' Bank of Kentucky, Inc.	KY	08/31/21
The Elk State Bank	KS	08/31/21
The Farmers State Bank	KS	08/31/21
The Farmers State Bank of Bucklin, Kansas	KS	08/31/21
The First National Bank in Falfurrias	TX	08/31/21
The First National Bank of Bellevue	OH	08/31/21
The First National Bank of Germantown	OH	08/31/21
The First National Bank of Sycamore	OH	08/31/21
The First Security Bank	KS	08/31/21
The First State Bank	TX	08/31/21
The Lyndon State Bank	KS	08/31/21
The National Bank of Coxsackie	NY	08/31/21
The Savings Bank	MA	08/31/21
Thomaston Savings Bank	CT	08/31/21
Today's Bank	AR	08/31/21
Touchstone Bank	VA	08/31/21
Tower Community Bank	TN	08/31/21
Union Bank	ND	08/31/21
Union State Bank	WI	08/31/21
Wells Fargo Bank, N.A.	SD	08/31/21
Westfield Bank	MA	08/31/21

Rating: C+

Name	State	Date of Change
Abbeville First Bank, SSB	SC	08/31/21
AccessBank Texas	TX	08/31/21
Artisans' Bank	DE	08/31/21
Asian Pacific National Bank	CA	08/31/21
Aspire Bank	ND	08/31/21
Bank of Lindsay	NE	08/31/21
Capitol National Bank	MI	08/31/21
Citizens Bank & Trust Co.	NE	08/31/21
Citizens Bank & Trust Co. of Jackson	KY	08/31/21
Citizens Bank and Trust Co.	MO	08/31/21
City Bank & Trust Co.	NE	08/31/21
Clay City Banking Co.	IL	08/31/21

Rating Upgrades

Name	State	Date of Change
Community Bank & Trust Co.	IA	08/31/21
Community Bank of Wichita, Inc.	KS	08/31/21
CornerStone Bank, N.A.	VA	08/31/21
Empire State Bank	NY	08/31/21
Enterprise Bank of South Carolina	SC	08/31/21
Eureka Homestead	LA	08/31/21
Farmers State Bank	OH	08/31/21
Farmers State Bank	TX	08/31/21
Farmers-Merchants Bank & Trust Co.	LA	08/31/21
First Central Savings Bank	NY	08/31/21
First County Bank	CT	08/31/21
First Federal S&L Assn.	KY	08/31/21
First Federal Savings Bank	IL	08/31/21
First Freedom Bank	TN	08/31/21
First National Bank	IL	08/31/21
First State Bank of Forrest	IL	08/31/21
Four Corners Community Bank	NM	08/31/21
Hancock Whitney Bank	MS	08/31/21
Hardin County Bank	TN	08/31/21
Horicon Bank	WI	08/31/21
Howard Bank	MD	08/31/21
Huntingdon Valley Bank	PA	08/31/21
Hyperion Bank	PA	08/31/21
Ladysmith Federal S&L Assn.	WI	08/31/21
LimeBank	MO	08/31/21
Mechanics & Farmers Bank	NC	08/31/21
Merrick Bank Corp.	UT	08/31/21
Modern Bank, N.A.	NY	08/31/21
National Bank of New York City	NY	08/31/21
New Haven Bank	CT	08/31/21
Oklahoma Heritage Bank	OK	08/31/21
Partners Bank	AR	08/31/21
Peoples Bank	KY	08/31/21
Pioneer Bank, SSB	TX	08/31/21
Popular Bank	NY	08/31/21
Prairie Sun Bank	MN	08/31/21
RiverBank	WA	08/31/21
Rondout Savings Bank	NY	08/31/21
SaviBank	WA	08/31/21
Security State Bank of Warroad	MN	08/31/21
Signature Bank of Georgia	GA	08/31/21
Taylorsville Savings Bank, SSB	NC	08/31/21
Texan Bank, N.A.	TX	08/31/21
The Cooperative Bank	MA	08/31/21
The First National Bank of Frederick	SD	08/31/21
The Hill-Dodge Banking Co.	IL	08/31/21
The Leaders Bank	IL	08/31/21
The National Iron Bank	CT	08/31/21
The Southern Bank Co.	AL	08/31/21
The State Bank of Geneva	IL	08/31/21
The Torrington Savings Bank	CT	08/31/21
TNBANK	TN	08/31/21
Toyota Financial Savings Bank	NV	08/31/21
Union County Savings Bank	NJ	08/31/21
Vergas State Bank	MN	08/31/21
Watermark Bank	OK	08/31/21
West Valley National Bank	AZ	08/31/21
Wilson State Bank	KS	08/31/21
Woodsboro Bank	MD	08/31/21

Rating: C

Name	State	Date of Change
Amerant Bank, N.A.	FL	08/31/21
American Equity Bank	MN	08/31/21
Bank of Moundville	AL	08/31/21
Bank of the Rockies	MT	08/31/21
Bank3	TN	08/31/21
Cambridge State Bank	MN	08/31/21
Century Savings Bank	NJ	08/31/21
Citizens Progressive Bank	LA	08/31/21
Citizens State Bank	NE	08/31/21
Citizens State Bank of Milford	IL	08/31/21
Comenity Bank	DE	08/31/21
Community Financial Services Bank	KY	08/31/21
Community Savings	OH	08/31/21
Congressional Bank	MD	08/31/21
COREBANK	OK	08/31/21
Cornerstone Bank	MA	08/31/21
Cowboy State Bank	WY	08/31/21
Crescent Bank & Trust	LA	08/31/21
Dewey Bank	IL	08/31/21
First American Bank	IL	08/31/21
First Bank of Pike	GA	08/31/21
First Federal S&L Assn.	WV	08/31/21
First Federal Savings Bank of Kentucky	KY	08/31/21
First FSB of Washington	IN	08/31/21
First National Bank in Fairfield	IA	08/31/21
First National Bank of Orwell	VT	08/31/21
First Seacoast Bank	NH	08/31/21
Glen Rock Savings Bank	NJ	08/31/21
Golden Pacific Bank, N.A.	CA	08/31/21
Golden State Bank	CA	08/31/21
Greenfield Banking Co.	TN	08/31/21
Greenville Federal	OH	08/31/21
Heritage Bank	IA	08/31/21
Hertford Savings Bank, SSB	NC	08/31/21
Jonestown Bank & Trust Co.	PA	08/31/21
Keystone Bank, SSB	TX	08/31/21
Lakeside State Bank	OK	08/31/21
Medallion Bank	UT	08/31/21
Middlesex Federal Savings, F.A.	MA	08/31/21

Rating Upgrades

Name	State	Date of Change
Movement Bank	VA	08/31/21
MUFG Union Bank, N.A.	CA	08/31/21
New Horizon Bank, N.A.	VA	08/31/21
Oklahoma State Bank	OK	08/31/21
OptimumBank	FL	08/31/21
Pacific Mercantile Bank	CA	08/31/21
Pacific National Bank	FL	08/31/21
Peoples Bank	IA	08/31/21
Peoples Bank of Moniteau County	MO	08/31/21
Riverview Bank	PA	08/31/21
Second Federal S&L Assn. of Philadelphia	PA	08/31/21
South Lafourche Bank & Trust Co.	LA	08/31/21
State Bank	IL	08/31/21
Studio Bank	TN	08/31/21
The Donley County State Bank	TX	08/31/21
The First National Bank of Chisholm	MN	08/31/21
The First State Bank of Fountain	MN	08/31/21
The Milford Bank	CT	08/31/21
TIAA, FSB	FL	08/31/21
TS Bank	IA	08/31/21
United Roosevelt Savings Bank	NJ	08/31/21
Western Nebraska Bank	NE	08/31/21

Rating: C-

Name	State	Date of Change
1st Bank in Hominy	OK	08/31/21
Bank Michigan	MI	08/31/21
Bank of Eastern Oregon	OR	08/31/21
Bank of Labor	KS	08/31/21
Buckeye State Bank	OH	08/31/21
Colonial Savings, FA	TX	08/31/21
Conway Bank	KS	08/31/21
Currie State Bank	MN	08/31/21
Discover Bank	DE	08/31/21
Endeavor Bank	CA	08/31/21
Farmers State Bank	WY	08/31/21
First Bank and Trust Co. of Illinois	IL	08/31/21
First Community National Bank	MO	08/31/21
First Oklahoma Bank	OK	08/31/21
Home Loan Investment Bank, F.S.B.	RI	08/31/21
InBank	NM	08/31/21
Infinity Bank (Santa Ana, CA)	CA	08/31/21
LINKBANK	PA	08/31/21
Metropolitan Capital Bank & Trust	IL	08/31/21
One Florida Bank	FL	08/31/21
Pathway Bank	NE	08/31/21
Rushford State Bank (Inc.)	MN	08/31/21
State Savings Bank	IA	08/31/21
Systematic Savings Bank	MO	08/31/21
The First National Bank of Fleming	CO	08/31/21
The First National Bank of Lipan	TX	08/31/21
The Peoples Bank, Biloxi, Mississippi	MS	08/31/21
Unity National Bank of Houston	TX	08/31/21

Rating: D+

Name	State	Date of Change
Beach Bank	FL	08/31/21
Canyon Community Bank, N.A.	AZ	08/31/21
CapTex Bank	TX	08/31/21
Cornerstone Bank	GA	08/31/21
Dickinson County Bank	KS	08/31/21
Haven Savings Bank	NJ	08/31/21
HomePride Bank	MO	08/31/21
Lexicon Bank	NV	08/31/21
Maple Bank	MN	08/31/21
Oriental Bank	PR	08/31/21
Peoples State Bank	ND	08/31/21
SunSouth Bank	AL	08/31/21
The First National Bank of Hope	KS	08/31/21
The Harbor Bank of Maryland	MD	08/31/21

Rating: D

Name	State	Date of Change
22nd State Bank	AL	08/31/21
Citizens Savings Bank and Trust Co.	TN	08/31/21
DR Bank	CT	08/31/21
Gateway Bank, F.S.B.	CA	08/31/21
HomeBank of Arkansas	AR	08/31/21
Iowa Prairie Bank	IA	08/31/21
Peoples Bank	GA	08/31/21
RockPoint Bank, N.A.	TN	08/31/21
Sevier County Bank	TN	08/31/21
State Bank	WY	08/31/21

Rating: D-

Name	State	Date of Change
Rockhold Bank	OH	08/31/21

Rating: E+

Name	State	Date of Change
Brighton Bank	TN	08/31/21
United Trust Bank	IL	08/31/21

Rating: E

Name	State	Date of Change
Civis Bank	TN	08/31/21

Rating Downgrades

Rating: A-

Name	State	Date of Change
Applied Bank	DE	08/31/21
Clackamas County Bank	OR	08/31/21
Commercial Bank of Mott	ND	08/31/21
Deutsche Bank Trust Co. Delaware	DE	08/31/21
Exchange Bank (Santa Rosa, CA)	CA	08/31/21
Farmers Bank and Trust Co.	KY	08/31/21
Green Dot Bank	UT	08/31/21
Kentland Bank	IN	08/31/21
Macatawa Bank	MI	08/31/21
Millennium Bank	IL	08/31/21
Minden Exchange Bank & Trust Co.	NE	08/31/21
Poppy Bank	CA	08/31/21
Stock Yards Bank & Trust Co.	KY	08/31/21

Rating: B+

Name	State	Date of Change
Alden State Bank	MI	08/31/21
Alpine Capital Bank	NY	08/31/21
American Bank & Trust Co.	LA	08/31/21
Atkins Savings Bank & Trust	IA	08/31/21
Bank of The Bluegrass and Trust Co.	KY	08/31/21
Bay Bank	WI	08/31/21
Citizens State Bank	IA	08/31/21
Community First Bank	KS	08/31/21
Eagle.Bank	OH	08/31/21
First Bank of Alabama	AL	08/31/21
First National Bank	AL	08/31/21
First Security Bank	IA	08/31/21
FirstBank	CO	08/31/21
FNBT Bank	FL	08/31/21
Fowler State Bank	IN	08/31/21
Grandview Bank	TX	08/31/21
Hillsboro Bank	FL	08/31/21
Luana Savings Bank	IA	08/31/21
Metropolitan Commercial Bank	NY	08/31/21
Peoples Bank of East Tennessee	TN	08/31/21
Peoples Bank of Middle Tennessee	TN	08/31/21
Rushville State Bank	IL	08/31/21
The Bank of Clarendon	SC	08/31/21
The Bank of Vernon	AL	08/31/21
The Commercial Bank	GA	08/31/21
The Exchange Bank	OK	08/31/21
The First National Bank of Gordon	NE	08/31/21
The First National Bank of Hebbronville	TX	08/31/21
The First National Bank of Winnsboro	TX	08/31/21
The Frederick Community Bank	IL	08/31/21
The State Bank	MI	08/31/21
The Wanda State Bank	MN	08/31/21
The Yoakum National Bank	TX	08/31/21
Titan Bank, N.A.	TX	08/31/21
West Plains Bank and Trust Co.	MO	08/31/21
WEX Bank	UT	08/31/21
Woodlands National Bank	MN	08/31/21

Rating: B

Name	State	Date of Change
American Exchange Bank	NE	08/31/21
American Momentum Bank	TX	08/31/21
Anahuac National Bank	TX	08/31/21
Bandera Bank	TX	08/31/21
Bankers' Bank of the West	CO	08/31/21
BANKWEST	MN	08/31/21
Brighton Bank	UT	08/31/21
Citizens Bank of The South	GA	08/31/21
Citizens National Bank of Crosbyton	TX	08/31/21
Citizens Savings Bank	IA	08/31/21
Elysian Bank	MN	08/31/21
First Community Bank and Trust	IL	08/31/21
Heartland National Bank	FL	08/31/21
Johnson City Bank	TX	08/31/21
LNB Community Bank	IN	08/31/21
MetaBank, N.A.	SD	08/31/21
Neighborhood National Bank	MN	08/31/21
Oconee Federal S&L Assn.	SC	08/31/21
Pine Country Bank	MN	08/31/21
RBC Bank (Georgia), N.A.	NC	08/31/21
Security State Bank	IA	08/31/21
Sunrise Banks, N.A.	MN	08/31/21
The Casey County Bank, Inc.	KY	08/31/21
The First National Bank of Blanchester	OH	08/31/21
The First National Bank of Dryden	NY	08/31/21
The First National Bank of Lawrence County	AR	08/31/21
West Texas National Bank	TX	08/31/21
West Texas State Bank	TX	08/31/21
Yakima Federal S&L Assn.	WA	08/31/21

Rating: B-

Name	State	Date of Change
Baker Boyer National Bank	WA	08/31/21
Citizens State Bank	IL	08/31/21
Colfax Banking Co.	LA	08/31/21
Community Bank of Oklahoma	OK	08/31/21
Community Bank of Santa Maria	CA	08/31/21
Dollar Bank, A Federal Savings Bank	PA	08/31/21
First Cahawba Bank	AL	08/31/21
First Community Bank of East Tennessee	TN	08/31/21
First National Bank	TX	08/31/21
First National Bank in DeRidder	LA	08/31/21
First National Bank Northwest Florida	FL	08/31/21
First National Bank of Albany/Breckenridge	TX	08/31/21
First National Bank of Nokomis	IL	08/31/21

Rating Downgrades

Name	State	Date of Change
First State Bank	WI	08/31/21
First State Bank of Brownsboro	TX	08/31/21
FNBC Bank and Trust	IL	08/31/21
Gate City Bank	ND	08/31/21
Hawthorn Bank	MO	08/31/21
Junction National Bank	TX	08/31/21
Kress National Bank	TX	08/31/21
Live Oak Banking Co.	NC	08/31/21
Malvern Bank NA	PA	08/31/21
Merchants & Farmers Bank & Trust Co.	LA	08/31/21
Mutual Federal Bank	IL	08/31/21
North Dallas Bank & Trust Co.	TX	08/31/21
Oklahoma State Bank	OK	08/31/21
Philo Exchange Bank	IL	08/31/21
Sanibel Captiva Community Bank	FL	08/31/21
Standard Bank	PA	08/31/21
Sunrise Bank	FL	08/31/21
Sycamore Bank	MS	08/31/21
The Fahey Banking Co.	OH	08/31/21
The First National Bank of Sandoval	IL	08/31/21
The Peoples Bank	MD	08/31/21
The Security State Bank	SD	08/31/21
The State Savings Bank of Manistique	MI	08/31/21
UBank	TN	08/31/21
Union Savings Bank	CT	08/31/21
Wilkinson County Bank	GA	08/31/21
William Penn Bank	PA	08/31/21

Rating: C+

Name	State	Date of Change
Bank of Bearden	AR	08/31/21
Bank of York	SC	08/31/21
Blue Grass Federal S&L Assn.	KY	08/31/21
Campbell & Fetter Bank	IN	08/31/21
Cendera Bank, N.A.	TX	08/31/21
Community Bank	OR	08/31/21
Concorde Bank	MN	08/31/21
Cornerstone Bank	KS	08/31/21
Falcon National Bank	MN	08/31/21
Farmers and Merchants Bank	OK	08/31/21
Farmers State Bank	NE	08/31/21
First Federal S&L Assn. of Lakewood	OH	08/31/21
First Mutual Bank, FSB	OH	08/31/21
First National Bank of South Padre Island	TX	08/31/21
First State Bank of Purdy	MO	08/31/21
First State Bank Shannon-Polo	IL	08/31/21
GENUBANK	NV	08/31/21
Highland Federal S&L Assn.	TN	08/31/21
Jeff Bank	NY	08/31/21
Kahoka State Bank	MO	08/31/21
Merchants & Marine Bank	MS	08/31/21
Mission National Bank	CA	08/31/21
Peoples State Bank	OH	08/31/21
Peoples State Bank	OK	08/31/21
POINTWEST Bank	TX	08/31/21
Portage Community Bank	OH	08/31/21
Putnam County National Bank	NY	08/31/21
Richton Bank & Trust Co.	MS	08/31/21
RiverHills Bank	OH	08/31/21
Saint John's Bank and Trust Co.	MO	08/31/21
Security Trust & Savings Bank	IA	08/31/21
Spencer County Bank	IN	08/31/21
State Bank	IL	08/31/21
State Bank of Bottineau	ND	08/31/21
The First Citizens National Bank of Upper Sandusky	OH	08/31/21
The First National Bank of McGregor	TX	08/31/21
The Gerber State Bank	IL	08/31/21
The Hondo National Bank	TX	08/31/21
The Northern State Bank of Gonvick	MN	08/31/21
Valley Central Bank	OH	08/31/21
Washita State Bank	OK	08/31/21

Rating: C

Name	State	Date of Change
AmeriState Bank	OK	08/31/21
Bank of Crocker	MO	08/31/21
BBVA USA	AL	08/31/21
Citizens State Bank	TX	08/31/21
Commercial State Bank of Wagner	SD	08/31/21
Fieldpoint Private Bank & Trust	CT	08/31/21
First Federal Bank of Louisiana	LA	08/31/21
First Federal S&L Assn.	KY	08/31/21
First National Bank of Absecon	NJ	08/31/21
Freedom Bank	TX	08/31/21
Gibsland Bank & Trust Co.	LA	08/31/21
Haskell National Bank	TX	08/31/21
Home Federal S&L Assn. of Grand Island	NE	08/31/21
Homewood Federal Savings Bank	MD	08/31/21
International Bank of Chicago	IL	08/31/21
Legacy Bank	OK	08/31/21
Maxwell State Bank	IA	08/31/21
Merchants & Farmers Bank	MS	08/31/21
MidSouth Bank	AL	08/31/21
Pioneer Bank	NY	08/31/21
SJN Bank of Kansas	KS	08/31/21
Texana Bank, N.A.	TX	08/31/21
The Bank of Commerce	LA	08/31/21
The Farmers and Merchants State Bank	SD	08/31/21
The First National Bank of Williamson	WV	08/31/21
Vantage Bank	MN	08/31/21

Rating: C-

Rating Downgrades

Name	State	Date of Change
1st Cameron State Bank	MO	08/31/21
1st State Bank of Mason City	IL	08/31/21
Anchor Bank	FL	08/31/21
Armor Bank	AR	08/31/21
Auburn Savings Bank, FSB	ME	08/31/21
Bank of Guam	GU	08/31/21
Bank of Hazlehurst	GA	08/31/21
Cache Valley Bank	UT	08/31/21
Clay County Savings Bank	MO	08/31/21
Community Banks of Shelby County	IL	08/31/21
Eastbank, N.A.	NY	08/31/21
First Federal Bank of Ohio	OH	08/31/21
First National Bank and Trust Co.	OK	08/31/21
First Secure Community Bank	IL	08/31/21
First State Bank	OK	08/31/21
Genesis Bank	MS	08/31/21
Hartsburg State Bank	IL	08/31/21
Hendricks County Bank and Trust Co.	IN	08/31/21
Jackson Federal S&L Assn.	MN	08/31/21
Mariner's Bank	NJ	08/31/21
Miami Savings Bank	OH	08/31/21
Prime Alliance Bank	UT	08/31/21
Southern Bank	GA	08/31/21
Southwest National Bank	KS	08/31/21
State Bank of Burrton	KS	08/31/21
State Bank of Bussey	IA	08/31/21
The Iuka State Bank	IL	08/31/21
The Peoples S&L Co.	OH	08/31/21
UniBank for Savings	MA	08/31/21
Valley Bank of Nevada	NV	08/31/21
Valley Exchange Bank	SD	08/31/21

Rating: D+

Name	State	Date of Change
BancCentral, N.A.	OK	08/31/21
Bank of Newman Grove	NE	08/31/21
Charis Bank	TX	08/31/21
Community State Bank	FL	08/31/21
Farmers and Merchants State Bank	MN	08/31/21
Farmers State Bank	KS	08/31/21
First Progressive Bank	AL	08/31/21
FMB Bank	MO	08/31/21
Freeland State Bank	MI	08/31/21
Kendall Bank	KS	08/31/21
Marion Bank and Trust Co.	AL	08/31/21
Security Bank, s.b.	IL	08/31/21
Shinhan Bank America	NY	08/31/21
The First National Bank of Proctor	MN	08/31/21
Union Bank	MI	08/31/21
United Orient Bank	NY	08/31/21
United Southwest Bank	MN	08/31/21
Westmoreland Federal S&L Assn. of Latrobe	PA	08/31/21

Rating: D

Name	State	Date of Change
Delta National Bank and Trust Co.	NY	08/31/21
First National Bank of Harveyville	KS	08/31/21
Intercredit Bank, N.A.	FL	08/31/21
Mt. Victory State Bank	OH	08/31/21
New Republic Bank	NC	08/31/21
Peoples Bank	MS	08/31/21

Rating: D-

Name	State	Date of Change
AllNations Bank	OK	08/31/21
Bank of Chestnut	IL	08/31/21
BankFlorida	FL	08/31/21
Cache Bank & Trust	CO	08/31/21
Citizens State Bank	TX	08/31/21
Home Federal Bank of Hollywood	FL	08/31/21
Sunnyside Federal S&L Assn. of Irvington	NY	08/31/21
Transact Bank, N.A.	CO	08/31/21
Trustar Bank	VA	08/31/21
Vermont State Bank	IL	08/31/21

Rating: E-

Name	State	Date of Change
Texico State Bank	IL	08/31/21

Appendix

RECENT BANK FAILURES
2021

Institution	Headquarters	Date of Failure	At Date of Failure	
			Total Assets ($Mil)	Safety Rating

2020

Institution	Headquarters	Date of Failure	At Date of Failure	
			Total Assets ($Mil)	Safety Rating
First State Bank	Barboursville, WV	4/06/2020	152.40	E- (Very Weak)
Ericson State Bank	Ericson, NE	2/14/2020	113.02	C- (Fair)
Almena State Bank	Almena, KS	10/23/2020	70.04	D- (Weak)

2019

Institution	Headquarters	Date of Failure	At Date of Failure	
			Total Assets ($Mil)	Safety Rating
City National Bank of NJ	Newark, NJ	11/1/19	142.5	E- (Very Weak)
Resolute Bank	Maumee, OH	10/25/19	27.1	E+ (Very Weak)
Enloe State Bank	Cooper, TX	5/31/19	36.5	C (Fair)

2017

Institution	Headquarters	Date of Failure	At Date of Failure	
			Total Assets ($Mil)	Safety Rating
Washington Federal Banks for Savings	Chicago, IL	12/15/17	166.4	A (Excellent)
Farmers & Merchants State Bk of Argonia	Argonia, KS	10/13/17	34.2	E- (Very Weak)
Fayette County Bank	Saint Elmo, IL	05/26/17	34.8	E- (Very Weak)
Guaranty Bank (MHC)	Milwaukee, WI	05/05/17	1,010.0	E- (Very Weak)
First NBC Bank	New Orleans, LA	04/28/17	4,740.0	E- (Very Weak)
Proficio Bank	Cottonwood Heights, UT	03/03/17	80.3	E- (Very Weak)
Seaway Bank and Trust Co	Chicago, IL	01/27/17	361.2	E- (Very Weak)
Harvest Community Bank	Pennsville, NJ	01/13/17	126.4	E- (Very Weak)

2016

Institution	Headquarters	Date of Failure	At Date of Failure: Total Assets ($Mil)	At Date of Failure: Safety Rating
Allied Bank	Mulberry, AR	09/23/16	66.3	E- (Very Weak)
Woodbury Banking Company	Woodbury, GA	08/19/16	22.5	E- (Very Weak)
First Cornerstone Bank	King of Prussia, PA	05/06/16	107.0	E- (Very Weak)
Trust Co Bank	Memphis, TN	04/29/16	20.7	E- (Very Weak)
North Milwaukee State Bank	Milwaukee, WI	03/11/16	67.1	E- (Very Weak)

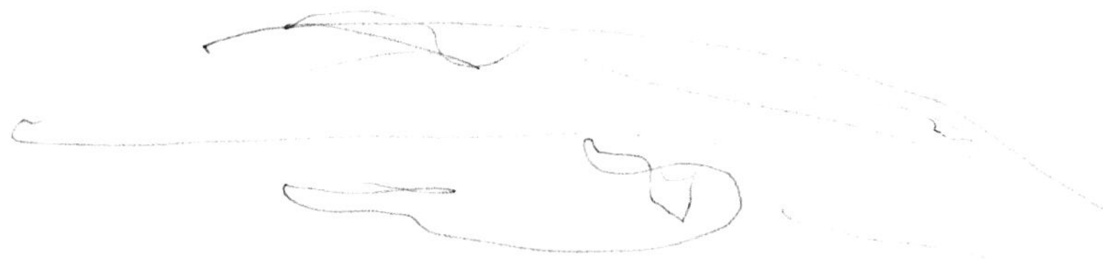

How Do Banks and Credit Unions Differ?

Since credit unions first appeared in 1946, they have been touted as a low-cost, friendly alternative to banks. But with tightening margins, pressure to compete in technology, branch closures, and the introduction of a host of service fees — some even higher than those charged by banks — the distinction between banks and credit unions has been gradually narrowing. Following are the key differences between today's banks and credit unions.

	Banks	Credit Unions
Access	Practically anyone is free to open an account or request a loan from any bank. There are no membership requirements.	Credit unions are set up to serve the needs of a specific group who share a "common bond." In order to open an account or request a loan, you must demonstrate that you meet the credit union's common bond requirements.
Ownership	Banks are owned by one or more investors who determine the bank's policies and procedures. A bank's customers do not have direct input into how the bank is operated.	Although they may be sponsored by a corporation or other entity, credit unions are owned by their members through their funds on deposit. Therefore, each depositor has a voice in how the credit union is operated.
Dividends and Fees	Banks are for-profit organizations where the profits are used to pay dividends to the bank's investors or are reinvested in an effort to increase the bank's value to investors. In an effort to generate more profits, bank services and fees are typically more costly.	Credit unions are not-for-profit organizations. Any profits generated are returned to the credit union's members in the form of higher interest rates on deposits, lower loan rates, and free or low-cost services.
Management and Staffing	A bank's management and other staff are employees of the bank, hired directly or indirectly by its investors.	Credit unions are frequently run using elected members, volunteer staff, and staff provided by the credit union's sponsor. This helps to hold down costs.
Insurance	Banks are insured by the Federal Deposit Insurance Corporation, an agency of the federal government.	Credit unions are insured by the National Credit Union Share Insurance Fund, which is managed by the National Credit Union Administration, an agency of the federal government.

Glossary

This glossary contains the most important terms used in this publication.

ARM	Adjustable-Rate Mortgage. This is a loan whose interest rate is tied to an index and is adjusted at a predetermined frequency. An ARM is subject to credit risk if interest rates rise and the borrower is unable to make the mortgage payment.
Average Recession	A recession involving a decline in real GDP that is approximately equivalent to the average of the postwar recessions of 1957-58, 1960, 1970, 1974-75, 1980, 1981-82, 1990-1991, 2001, and 2007-2009. It is assumed, however, that in today's market, the financial losses suffered from a recession of that magnitude would be greater than those experienced in previous decades. (See also "Severe Recession.")
Bank Holding Company	A company that holds stock in one or more banks and possibly other companies.
Bank Insurance Fund (BIF)	A unit of Federal Deposit Insurance Corporation (FDIC) that provided deposit insurance for banks, other than thrifts. BIF was formed as part of the 1989 savings and loan association bailout bill to keep separate the administration of the bank and thrift insurance programs. There were thus two distinct insurance entities under the FDIC: BIF and savings association insurance fund (SAIF). (See also Federal Deposit Insurance Corporation.")
Brokered Deposits	Deposits that are brought into an institution through a broker. They are relatively costly, volatile funds that are more readily withdrawn from the institution if there is a loss of confidence or intense interest rate competition. Reliance on brokered deposits is usually a sign that the institution is having difficulty attracting deposits from its local geographic markets and could be a warning signal if other institutions in the same areas are not experiencing similar difficulties.
Capital	The cushion an institution has of its own resources to help withstand losses. The basic component of capital is stockholder's equity which consists of common and preferred stock and retained earnings. (See also "Core Capital")
Cash & Equivalents	Cash plus highly liquid assets which can be readily converted to cash.
Core (Tier 1) Capital	A measurement of capital defined by the federal regulatory agencies for evaluating an institution's degree of leverage. Core capital consists of the following: common stockholder's equity, preferred stockholder's equity up to certain limits, and retained earnings net of any intangible assets.
Critical Ranges	Guidelines developed to help you evaluate the levels of each index contributing to a company's Weiss Safety Rating. The sum or average of these grades does not necessarily have a one-to-one correspondence with the final rating for an institution because the rating is derived from a wider range of more complex calculations.

Deposit Insurance Fund (DIF)	In 2005 Congress passed legislation merging the SAIF and BIF into one insurance fund called the deposit insurance fund (DIF). The same law also raised the federal deposit insurance level from $100,000 to $250,000. (See also "Emergency Economic Stabilization Act.")
Emergency Stabilization Act	In 2008 Congress passed the Emergency Economic Stabilization Act that temporarily increased the basic limit on deposit insurance for all ownership categories from $100,000 to $250,000. This increase was set to expire in 2013 but has been extended permanently.
Equity	Total assets minus total liabilities. This is the "capital cushion" the institution has to fall back on in times of trouble. (See also "Capital.")
FDIC	Federal Deposit Insurance Corporation. The provider of insurance on deposits. This agency also plays an active role when banks are found to be insolvent or in need of federal assistance. It is the governing body of the Deposit Insurance Fund (DIF) that now incorporates both the Bank Insurance Fund (BIF) and the Savings Association Insurance Fund (SAIF). (See also "Deposit Insurance Fund.")
Federal Home Loan Bank (FHLB)	A quasi-governmental agency (reporting to the Federal Housing Finance Board) whose chartered purpose is to promote the issuance of mortgage loans by providing increased liquidity to lenders. This agency raises money by issuing notes and bonds and then lends the money to banks and other mortgage lenders.
Federal Reserve	America's central bank, regulating all banks that offer transaction accounts. It works hand-in-hand with the FDIC, providing examination and regulation of its member banks.
Safety Rating	Weiss Safety Ratings, which grade institutions on a scale from A (Excellent) to F (Failed). Ratings are based on many factors, emphasizing capitalization, asset quality, profitability, liquidity, and stability.
FSB	Federal Savings Bank. A thrift institution operating under a federal charter.
Goodwill	The value of an institution as a going concern, meaning the value which exceeds book value on a balance sheet. It generally represents the value of a well-respected business name, good customer relations, high employee morale and other intangible factors which would be expected to translate into greater than normal earning power. In a bank acquisition, goodwill is the value paid by a buyer of the institution in excess of the value of the institution's equity because of these intangible factors.
Hot Money	Individual deposits of $100,000 or more plus those deposits received through a broker. These types of deposits are considered "hot money" because they tend to chase whoever is offering the best interest rates at the time and are thus relatively costly and fairly volatile sources of funds.
Loan Loss Reserves	The amount of capital an institution sets aside to cover any potential losses due to the nonrepayment of loans.
N.A.	National Association. A commercial bank operating under a federal charter.

Net Charge-offs — The amount of foreclosed loans written off the institution's books since the beginning of the year, less any previous write-offs that were recovered during the year.

Net Interest Spread — The difference between the interest income earned on the institution's loans and investments and the interest expense paid on its interest-bearing deposits and borrowings. This "spread" is most commonly analyzed as a percentage of average earning assets to show the institution's net return on income-generating assets.

Since the margin between interest earned and interest paid is generally where the company generates the majority of its income, this figure provides insight into the company's ability to effectively manage interest spreads. A low Net Interest Spread can be the result of poor loan and deposit pricing, high levels of nonaccruing loans, or poor asset/liability management.

Net Profit or Loss — The bottom line income or loss the institution has sustained in its most recent reporting period.

Nonaccruing Loans — Loans for which payments are past due and full repayment is doubtful. Interest income on these loans is no longer recorded on the income statement. (See also "Past Due Loans.")

Nonperforming Loans — The sum of loans past due 90 days or more and nonaccruing loans. These are loans the institution made where full repayment is now doubtful. (See also "Past Due Loans" and "Nonaccruing Loans.")

Past Due Loans — Loans for which payments are at least 90 days in arrears. The institution continues to record income on these loans, even though none is actually being received, because it is expected that the borrower will eventually repay the loan in full. It is likely, however, that at least a portion of these loans will move into nonaccruing status. (See also "Nonaccruing Loans.")

OCC — Office of the Comptroller of the Currency. This agency of the U.S. Treasury Department is the primary regulator of national banks.

Overhead Expense — Expenses of the institution other than interest expense, such as salaries and benefits of employees, rent and utility expenses, and data processing expenses. A certain amount of "fixed" overhead is required to operate a bank, so it is important that the institution leverage that overhead to the fullest extent in supporting its revenue-generating activities.

RBCR — See "Risk-Based Capital Ratio."

Resolution Trust Corp. (RTC) — The now-defunct federal agency that was formed to handle the liquidation of insolvent savings and loans.

Restructured Loans — Loans whose terms have been modified in order to enable the borrower to make payments which he otherwise would be unable to make. Modifications could include a reduction in the interest rate or a lengthening of the time to maturity.

Risk-Based Capital Ratio	A ratio originally developed by the International Committee on Banking as a means of assessing the adequacy of an institution's capital in relation to the amount of credit risk on and off its balance sheet. (See also "Risk-weighted Assets.")
Risk-Weighted Assets	The sum of assets and certain off-balance sheet items after they have been individually adjusted for the level of credit risk they pose to the institution. Assets with close to no risk are weighted 0%; those with minor risk are weighted 20%; those with low risk, 50%; and those with normal or high risk, 100%.
R.O.A	Return on Assets calculated as net profit or loss as a percentage of average assets. This is the most commonly used measure of bank profitability.
R.O.E.	Return on Equity calculated as net profit or loss as a percentage of average equity. This represents the rate of return on the shareholders' investment.
S.A.	Savings Association.
Savings and Loan (S&L)	A financial institution that traditionally offered primarily home mortgages to individuals and served small depositors. However, in 1980, savings and loans were given power to diversify into other areas of lending. Also known as a thrift.
Savings and Loan Holding Company	A company that holds stock in one or more savings and loans and possibly other companies.
Savings Association Insurance Fund (SAIF)	Fund created in 1989 by Congress to replace the FSLIC as the provider of deposit insurance to thrifts. This fund is administered by the Federal Deposit Insurance Corporation (FDIC). (See also "Bank Insurance Fund.")
Savings Bank	A financial institution created to serve primarily the small saver and to lend mortgage money to individuals. Though savings banks have expanded their services, they are still primarily engaged in providing consumer mortgages and accepting consumer deposits. Also known as a thrift.
Severe Recession	A drop in real GDP which is significantly greater than that of an average postwar recession. (See also "Average Recession.")
Stockholder's Equity	See "Equity."
Thrift	Generic term for an institution formed primarily as a depository for consumer savings and a lender for home mortgages, such as a savings and loan or a savings bank.
Total Assets	Total resources of an institution, primarily composed of cash, securities (such as municipal and treasury bonds), loans, and fixed assets (such as real estate, buildings, and equipment).
Total Equity	See "Equity."

Total Liabilities All debts owed by an institution. Normally, the largest liability of a bank is its deposits.

Trust Company A financial institution chartered to provide trust services (legal agreements to act for the benefit of another party), which may also be authorized to provide banking services.